FAMILY NAMES AND FAMILY HISTORY

William Shakespeare (1564–1616).

Shakespeare is a distinctive surname with a single-family origin. It is still largely confined to Warwickshire and the West Midlands. It seems to have been a nickname, but whether it has aggressive or bawdy associations it is not clear.

Family Names
and Family History

David Hey

Hambledon and London

London and New York

Hambledon and London

102 Gloucester Avenue
London, NW1 8HX

838 Broadway
New York
NY 10003-4812

First Published 2000

ISBN 1 85285 255 0

A description of this book is available from the
British Library and from the Library of Congress.

Typeset by Carnegie Publishing,
Lancaster LA1 4SL

Printed on acid-free paper and bound in
Great Britain by Cambridge University Press

Contents

Illustrations

Preface

We have all wondered, from time to time , about how we got our surnames and what they mean. We have no doubt puzzled over why so many of our friends and acquaintances or people that we have read about have such unusual names as Plum or Damson, Pie or Tart, Jelly or Custard. And we have noted that, as in the game of Happy Families, some people seem to have surnames that are singularly appropriate to their jobs. At the University of Sheffield the person in charge of communications is Ms Cable, the man responsible for central heating is Mr Frost and the head of security is a Mr Mole. When I was a child my dentist was Mr Rough. Names can be fascinating as well as amusing. You may also have noticed that when you visit another part of the country the surnames displayed on shop windows are very different from the ones that you are familiar with at home. I am used to seeing Staniforth, Shimwell or Broomhead, but southern names such as Gulliver, Loder or Sturmy catch my eye. Every county still has its distinctive names. My own name places me in the West Riding of Yorkshire, where I was born and bred. Rather to her surprise, my wife's family names – Wilkinson and Wakefield – show that her distant ancestors came from the north of England, not from that part of London where she lived as a child. One of my grandmothers was called Garland, a common name in the south west of England, from where she hailed. One of my wife's grandmothers was a Downer, for her family had originated on the Downs of southern England. Names can tell us a lot about the history of the peoples of our islands, about how they moved around or how they stayed rooted in a particular district. They also have much to teach us about the social structure of medieval and later England, its various ranks and occupations, the languages and dialects that were spoken, the sense of humour in bestowing nicknames, and the strong regional differences that are still apparent today.

Many of our surnames turn out to have had a single-family origin back in the middle ages. In other words, everyone bearing the same rare surname is likely to be distantly, if not closely, related. Some family names that have a single source have spread considerably from their point of origin. A large number of sons who in turn have had a large number of sons could soon make a name common in a locality. One of the chief findings of the study of surnames in recent years is that each of the distinctive names of the various counties of England often sprang from just one medieval person. It is exciting to find that the DNA testing of people bearing the same surname is beginning to prove this assertion. But at the same time, family historians may be alarmed to hear that the tests are also showing that some people with a distinctive surname must be descended from an illegitimate line.

This book is also a manifesto for a multi-disciplinary approach to the study of English surnames. The dictionaries of surnames that are currently on offer were compiled by philologists concerned with establishing the earliest recorded forms of names so that they could interpret the meaning. Their expertise in old languages is clearly an essential aid to an understanding of how surnames arose in the middle ages, but there is now a widespread feeling that this approach has taken us about as far as it will go and that other methods need to be tried.

The attack on the techniques and findings of P. H. Reaney, the distinguished author of *A Dictionary of British Surnames* (1958) and *The Origin of English Surnames* (1967), both of which have gone into later editions as the standard works on the subject, has come from two directions. A new generation of philologists has questioned Reaney's etymologies, particularly his explanations of how pet forms of personal names were derived. For example, Reaney's claims that Pawson is derived from an Old English word for a peacock or that Dawkins comes from a pet form of David have been invalidated by research into local records that point to Paul for Pawson and Ralph (Raw) and other personal names with rhyming forms for Dawkins. Peter McClure has concluded that such names must be studied by looking at all the historical records that deal with the same communities. This wide approach will show which personal names were current in a locality when surnames were formed, and with what frequency, thus allowing us to judge the likelihood of Reaney's suggested sources for pet forms. It will also sometimes highlight variant forms of the personal and pet names that were given to individuals.

The second line of attack has come from local and family historians who have found that Reaney's etymologies, based as they were on a collection of early records from across the country taken from the random sample that was then available in print, often do not fit the local evidence for how a surname came to be adopted. By studying distribution patterns of names over time, and by tracing family names back into the middle ages by genealogical methods, local and family historians have shown that many surnames have a single-family origin; that these names are usually still concentrated near the place where they arose; that local records can suggest more convincing etymologies than those proposed in the dictionaries; and that surnames continued to evolve into different forms long after the period of surname formation in the middle ages.

Philologists and genealogists share the belief that advances in the subject depend on intensive searches of local records. Far more is now available in print or in record offices than when Reaney was collecting his material. Reaney's achievement was outstanding for his time. He was long thought to have said the last word on the subject, but the huge expansion of available information and the growing interest in different approaches to the study of surnames have made us far less certain of his explanations. Not so long ago it looked as if a comprehensive dictionary of surnames could soon be published. Now it appears that we are almost back to square one.

The research that will forward our understanding of how surnames arose and spread will need to be focused on particular parts of the country, looking at how groups of names were formed at different times in particular local communities. This work is best done as a cooperative venture, for it is time-consuming and requires a variety of skills that no one individual possesses. It must combine the detailed investigation of individual names in a local setting with a broader understanding of what was happening in the country at large. The techniques of the philologists must be used alongside those of local and family historians.

For the past twelve years the Names Project Group at the National Centre for English Cultural Tradition and Language at the University of Sheffield has been studying the surnames of south Yorkshire and north Derbyshire under my direction. The current members are Denis Ashurst, Vera Edwards, Anne Giller, Mavis Greaves, Julia Hatfield, Margaret Oversby, June Royston-Tonks, Harold Taylor and Peter Wilkinson. Much of our work is summarised in this book. I am indebted to all of them. I have also benefited enormously from the depth of knowledge of Yorkshire surname history that George Redmonds has so readily passed on to me, particularly during our explorations of the West Riding historical landscape. George is at the forefront of the new approaches to the subject, as will be evident from my many references to his publications. He has encouraged me to write this book and I am grateful for all his help.

I am concerned here with surnames that arose in England or which were brought in by early immigrants, particularly those from Wales, France and the Low Countries. I say a little about surnames that came from Ireland and Scotland in the nineteenth century, but I do not possess the necessary knowledge to comment on the origins and development of Gaelic names.

Nor can I say much that is worthwhile on the surnames of twentieth-century immigrants from more distant lands, for very little work has yet been done in this field.

My views have been shaped by the discipline of preparing and delivering lectures to informed audiences and listening to their subsequent comments. I wish to thank, in particular, those who invited me to give the Phillimore Lecture to the British Association for Local History, the Earl Lecture at the University of Keele and two lectures to the Society for Name Studies in Britain and Ireland. Over the years I have also spoken about surnames at conferences and meetings organised by the Society of Genealogists, the Local Population Studies Society, the Public Record Office, several universities and various family and local history societies. These have helped to provide a wider view than that obtained from a detailed study of my own locality.

Finally, warm thanks are extended to Tony Morris for commissioning this book and to Martin Sheppard for his many editorial suggestions on how the text and shape of the book could be improved. The author and the publishers are grateful to the National Portrait Gallery for permission to reproduce the portraits in the plate section.

PART ONE

The History of Family Names

1

Names and History

Guessing the meaning of a surname is a dangerous game to play. What seems to be an obvious explanation is often completely wrong. One reason for this is that surnames have changed considerably in form over the centuries, and another is that even where the word is the same it may well have had a very different meaning at the time when surnames were being formed back in the middle ages. People with the east midlands surname Daft will tell you that their name originally meant 'meek'; people with the Essex surname Nice are less likely to volunteer the information that their name once meant 'foolish'. We shall no doubt jump to some wrong conclusions when we come across taxpayers recorded in 1377–81 by such delightful names as Roger Dope (Herefordshire) or William Sexy (Bedfordshire), though we may not be far out with Emma Jollybody (Essex). John Harlott and Thomas Horelot who paid the same tax in Dorset took their surname not from a female ancestor of doubtful virtue but from a local word for a 'young man'. Freelove is a rare Bedfordshire name which comes from an Anglo-Saxon personal name; it has none of the connotations of the modern word.

The ways in which some people acquired surnames seem mysterious, almost unbelievable at times. Amongst the taxpayers of Gatcombe in the Isle of Wight in 1379 was a man named William Godbeourhelp. We have to assume that his name was given to him by his neighbours who were amused or exasperated at the frequency with which he used this particular expression. A very different sort of name appears in the Essex poll tax returns of 1381, where three men were recorded with what now seems a comical surname: Walter Inthelane (Gosfield), William Inthelane (Chipping Ongar) and John Inthelane (Stanford Rivers). We shall see that topographical names such as this, which described where a man lived, eventually dropped their preposition. In time, Inthelane became simply Lane. This type of name sounds clumsy to us but it is at least understandable. Others cannot be explained with the same confidence. The name Adam Dragon conjures up a terrifying neighbour for the inhabitants of late fourteenth-century Scarisbrick (Lancashire): perhaps he or an ancestor played the part of a dragon in a mystery play; or was he given the name in jest because he was so meek? The Little John of the Robin Hood legends was the very opposite of his nickname. We shall never know the explanation for many unusual names such as these.

Surnames that are also place-names are amongst the easiest to recognise, but they are not always as straightforward as they seem. Many of these 'locative' names come from tiny places, hard to find on the map, rather than from better-known places with the same name. For example, the geographical distribution of the surname makes it clear that the Rothwells did not come from places of that name in Lincolnshire, Northamptonshire or Yorkshire, but from a small settlement of the same name in Lancashire that is hardly known beyond the county borders. Similarly, most of the Sunderlands originated at a farm near Halifax, not at the Sunderland in County Durham or other places of the same name. Sometimes the settlement which has produced a surname has disappeared from the map entirely. We know of over 3000 deserted medieval villages in England and Wales, many of which are commemorated by family names though little or nothing remains on the ground. The Yorkshire Billams, for instance, came from Bilham, a former village in the parish of Hooton Pagnell whose site is now occupied only by Bilham House Farm. Identifying the home of such names is made more difficult when either the surname or the place-name, sometimes both, have changed over the centuries. During a recent visit to the splendid fourteenth-century church at Patrington, in the flat lands of Holderness beyond Hull, I noticed a tombstone erected to the memory of members of the Escreet family. On checking the national distribution of this unusual name on my database of the indexes of deaths registered in England and Wales in 1842–46, I found only eleven Escreets, all of them clustered between Beverley, Skirlaugh and Hull. I then found that P. H. Reaney had solved the problem before me. He noted that the name had migrated from Escrick, a few miles south of York, and that the pronunciation had changed slightly once the family had settled in their new neighbourhood.[1] The rarity of the name and its concentration in one small district suggests that just one family took the name of their former home when they moved away, so that all present-day Escreets and Escritts are related.

We shall quote many more examples of this sort of puzzle. Some are quite easy to solve. The ancestors of James Edenborow and Jacob Ettenborow, who were taxed on their hearths in Nottinghamshire in Charles II's reign, together with the Lincolnshire Edenboroughs, Edenbrows and Eddingborrows, no doubt hailed from Edinburgh; the last version of the name in my list seems to clinch it. We must keep in mind that place-names and surnames were and are pronounced differently by local people and by outsiders. Mr I. M. Slocombe of Bradford-on-Avon has provided me with the splendid example of the Somerset village of Chedzoy, which educated locals call Chadzee and 'real locals' call Chidgee. The local telephone directory reveals six variations in the resulting surname: Chedzoy, Chidzoy, Chidzey, Chedgey, Chidgey and Chedgy. Likewise, the surname Bristow is the result of the old pronunciation of Bristol; Tickle or Tickell is from Tickhill (Yorkshire); and, less obviously, Sapsford is an old shortening of Sawbridgeworth (Hertfordshire) and Stopford is the former name of Stockport.

We can all see the similarities between the variants once they are pointed out, but in an example such as Stopford the connections are easy to miss. Kneebone is undoubtedly a Cornish surname. The fifty-two Kneebones whose deaths were registered in England and Wales in 1842–46 were mostly from Cornwall, including fifteen from Redruth and ten from Helston. Our first reaction is that this is possibly a nickname, but Patrick Hanks and Flavia Hodges, working from early spellings, make the plausible suggestion that Kneebone is derived from a place called Carnebone in the Cornish parish of Wendron and that it was altered by 'folk etymology'.[2]

So we can be hopelessly wrong in making quick guesses at the meaning of surnames. Some of the Beards came from the small settlement of that name in north-west Derbyshire; Belcher did not imply bad table manners but was a Norman French word meaning 'fine face' or 'cheerful disposition'; the Cowards are descended from cow-keepers; some of the Hampshires moved not from the southern county but from Hallamshire, the ancient name of the district around Sheffield; Rabbitt was a pet form of Robert or of similar-sounding names; Rainbird was an Old French personal name; Raper was a northern form of Roper; Salmon was a shortened form of Solomon; and some, if not all, of the Stringers and Stringfellows were iron workers.

Sometimes a hyphenated name now causes mirth where none was intended at the time. The Pine-Coffins are the result of the amalgamation of the names of two Devonshire gentry families. Pine is thought to come from Le Pin in Calvados, Normandy, but it might have denoted a dweller by a pine tree or have been a nickname for a tall, thin man. Coffin is equally problematical, for the usual explanation that it was an occupational name for a basket maker is unlikely for a medieval gentry family. Sir Elias Coffin held lands at Portledge (Devon) during the reign of King John, 1199–1216. The direct line of descent became extinct when Richard Coffin died in 1766, but his estates were inherited by his nephews and in 1797 their descendants assumed the surname Coffin. Meanwhile, in 1642, a junior member of this family, Tristram Coffyn, had sailed to America to establish the colony of Nantucket. He is probably the ancestor of all the Coffyns or Coffins in the United States.

Association of morbid thoughts brings us from Coffin to the surname Death, a name whose 'correct' pronunciation and etymology continues to cause controversy. Desperate to avoid the unpleasant associations of the name, some Deaths have clung to the straw offered to them by Burke, who derived it from Aeth in Flanders, supposedly giving the forms De'Ath, or D'Aeth. Unfortunately, this claim is not backed up by any evidence. Nor are there any examples to support Weekley's suggestion that it was a pageant name given to someone who played such a part. Reaney offered the most plausible explanation. He observed that the name was and is often pronounced and spelt Deeth, that the early forms were usually Deth or Deeth, and that these references came from Bedfordshire, Cambridgeshire, Suffolk and Essex. (An odd example, however, was recorded in the Lancashire poll tax returns of 1379.) Later distributions of the name, taken from the hearth tax returns of the 1660s and 1670s, support Reaney's belief that the Deaths came from eastern England. His suggestion that the name is an occupational surname derived from a maker of tinder cannot be proved from the geographical distribution of the name, but the regional nature of the surname is clear. In the late seventeenth century numerous Deaths or Deeths lived in south-west Suffolk, in or close to the Stour Valley, and five other households lived over the border in Essex. Much earlier, in 1327, five Deths were taxed in Suffolk; Thomas and Roger Deth lived at Earl Stonham in the central part of the county, John Deth was taxed further east at Blaxhall, Elianor Deth lived close by at Marlesford, and John Deth lived at Cavendish, in the Stour Valley, right on the southern border of the county. Perhaps other Deaths were already living in Essex? An origin from this part of England, not from Flanders, seems more than likely, and Reaney's suggestion that Death is an obsolete occupational name fits the evidence best, though we can never be certain. I once had to call out the name De'Ath at a graduation ceremony. This was a big day for the new graduates and their families, so it was important to get it right. I was relieved to find that, contrary to what I thought from the spelling, she pronounced it Deeth and so I could call it in the 'correct' way without fear of contradiction. Surnames are such a sensitive matter.

The example of the Deaths alerts us to the striking regional distribution of very many English surnames. Even now, at the end of the twentieth century, every county of England has its distinctive surnames. Nottinghamshire has its Boots, Footits and Dafts, Staffordshire has its Rounds, Yapps, Tooths and Fearnihoughs, and Lancashire its Entwistles, Fazackerleys, Rigbys and Singletons, to quote only a few examples. Many Yorkshire people can be identified instantly from their surnames. A photograph taken of my school class in 1953 shows that most of us were undoubtedly from the

West Riding. We included two Hepworths and other boys and girls with the distinctive local surnames of Armitage, Barraclough, Haigh, Hey, Jagger, Micklethwaite and Priestley, names that originated at the heart of the West Riding and which remain characteristic of that part of Yorkshire to this day. We shall have frequent occasion to emphasise the stability of family names.

The persistence of rare names within a recognisable district raises the question of whether all the present bearers of that name share a common descent. This is a matter that we shall return to time and time again. Thus it seems likely that all the Shakespeares are descended from one man whose distinctive nickname became hereditary in the middle ages. The Shakespeares originated a little further north than Warwickshire, but Adam Shakespeare was living at Baddesley Clinton by 1389. The name multiplied in the fifteenth century but was long confined to a few Warwickshire parishes. William's father was born at Snitterfield, just to the north of Stratford-upon-Avon. Whole books have been written in support of the theory that the young William Shakespeare spent some years in Lancashire as a 'player' with the name of William Shakeshafte, but there is no evidence that the two forms of the name were ever connected. A John Shakeshaft was taxed at Aughton in Lancashire in 1381 and many more Shakeshafts, including some named William, have been found thereabouts. The two surnames seem to have been independent of each other.

England's leading literary men often had distinctive surnames. William Wordsworth was descended from a Yorkshire family that took their surname from a West Riding place-name and Samuel Taylor Coleridge's family hailed from one of two minor place-names in Devon which meant 'charcoal ridge'. Anthony Trollope's ancestors came from Troughburn (Northumberland), a place that was once known as Trollope. Appropriately for an imaginative writer, the etymology of the name denotes a remote valley supposedly inhabited by a supernatural being or troll. Anthony's ancestor, John Trolope, lived at Thornlaw (County Durham) in the thirteenth century. William Makepeace Thackeray's surname came from a small place called Thackray in the Yorkshire parish of Great Timble, now under Fewston Reservoir. J. B. Priestley, who was born in Bradford, was descended from a medieval family that lived a few miles away in the 'priest clearing' in Hipperholme and who moved to Bradford about 1600. Rudyard Kipling's ancestors had for several generations been small farmers and craftsmen in and near Kiplin (North Yorkshire). His distinctive first name was taken from a small place near Leek (Staffordshire), close to where he was born.

A good illustration of how we can work backwards in time towards the origin of a rare name is provided by the surname Eardley, which is derived from Eardley Hall or the nearby hamlet of Eardley End in Audley parish, north Staffordshire, not from Eardisley in Herefordshire. The local pronunciation sometimes turned the name into Yeardley, thus occasionally causing confusion with the surname Yardley, which is derived from a place-name in Worcestershire (and possibly from similar places in Northamptonshire and Essex). The deaths of sixty-five Eardleys in England and Wales were registered in 1842–46. Forty-four of these were from registration districts in Staffordshire, particularly those of Wolstanton, Newcastle-under-Lyme and Stoke-on-Trent, which surrounded the place from which the surname was derived five or six hundred years earlier. In the Staffordshire hearth tax returns of 1666 fourteen households of Eardleys were recorded, one from Cheadle and the rest from Pirehill Hundred (which covered north-west Staffordshire), including four from Audley township where the name originated. The lay subsidy returns of 1332–33 recorded a William and two Johns of Erdele in the parish of Audley, but we cannot be certain that the surname had become hereditary by then. It is perfectly clear from this enquiry into past distribution patterns of the name, working backwards in time, that Eardley is a distinctive north Staffordshire surname.

An Eardley 'family get together', organised by Robert Jack Eardley of Lexington, Kentucky, was held at noon on Saturday 15 July in the year 2000, starting with a service at St James Church, Audley, with a special address by the vicar. Three families of Eardleys held pews in the church in 1585. The senior branch were the Eardleys of Eardley Hall, the leading family in the parish in the sixteenth and seventeenth centuries. The Eardleys then began to spread into the neighbouring counties of Shropshire, Cheshire and Derbyshire, so that by 1800 they formed about thirty related families, most of whom lived within fifteen miles radius of Audley. Many of them were farmers but by then some were Burslem potters. Nineteenth-century census returns record the Eardleys in the northern part of the Potteries or nearby at Audley, Silverdale, Newcastle-under-Lyme, Wolstanton, Tunstall and Burslem. The coming of railways and steamships provided opportunities for them to spread further. R. J. Eardley estimates that the Eardleys now consist of some 2000 families, in Britain, Canada, the USA, Australia, South Africa, Switzerland, Hong Kong and Germany. Their story is paralleled by those of many other families.

Another rare surname which is obviously derived from a place-name is Oversby. Names ending in -by are taken from places settled by the Danes over a thousand years ago. In 1995 the British telephone directories listed eighty-four subscribers with this name. Single entries were found in many parts of the country, but fifty-two of the entries were from the six northern counties of England, including twenty-two from Westmorland and north

Lancashire. This pattern is suggestive but not conclusive. Some families had many sons who spread the name. Other surnames have remained rare, so that their distribution on their map is much narrower than those of the families which became prolific. When mapping the surname Oversby it was necessary to extend the search of the indexes of deaths to cover the period between 1 July 1837 and 31 December 1851. Even so, only twenty-five deaths were recorded in England and Wales. All of them were from northern England, including twenty from the four adjacent registration districts of Sedbergh, Lancaster, East Ward and Kendal. The distribution (which was much more concentrated than that based on the modern list of telephone subscribers) suggests that the most likely home for this particular family name is the minor Cumbrian settlement of Overby, a few miles further west of the places where the name was found in 1837–51. Overby is in the parish of Hulme St Cuthbert, overlooking marshland on the north-west Cumbrian coast.

This reasonably clear picture is obscured by genealogical evidence uncovered by a correspondent, Adrian M. Obersby of Australia. In the earliest years of the nineteenth century seven children who were baptised by the surname Oversby were in fact the sons and daughters of a man otherwise described as George Hubbersby or Hubbersty. Now Hubbersty is a lost place-name, near Cockerham (north Lancashire), which has given rise to a family name that was quite separate, at first, from that of the Oversbys. The similarity in sound, however, led to considerable confusion. George Hubbersty's son, John Oversby, had a son who was recorded later as John Hubbersby. The children of this second John were christened Obersby (twice), Hubbersby, Hubbersty, Hubbersby (twice) and Obersby again. John William Obersby's descendants are still called Obersby. Meanwhile, the descendants of Martin Oversby, the younger brother of the first John Oversby, are called Oversby. This is far from being an isolated and unusual example of a subtle change from the original form of a surname.

Names have often had different forms before they settled down to an accepted spelling and pronunciation. Patrick Brontë's name was recorded as Branty, Brunty, Bruntee, Prunty and so on before he made his idiosyncratic choice of spelling after Nelson had been created Duke of Brontë. Some names have been changed deliberately to avoid unpleasant associations; for example, Hogg to Hodd and Daft to Dart. In 1917 anti-German feeling during the First World War caused the royal family itself to change their surname from Wettin to Windsor (which had long been an ordinary English surname). Prince Albert's surname had come from his castle at Wettin in Saxe-Coburg-Gotha. At the same time, Prince Louis of Battenberg changed his name to its English translation, Mountbatten.

Finding the meaning of names is an endless delight, especially if they sound strange or turn out to have a completely different explanation from what might be expected. A Yorkshire gentry family named Anne took their name from Ann (Hampshire), a settlement that was called by an old stream name. Sir William de Anne was constable of Tickhill Castle in 1315, not far from where the family eventually settled at Burghwallis. Lobb is a distinctive west country surname, derived from a Devon place-name. The unusually named Goderie Lobb was the parish priest of Branton Burrows (Devon) in 1136. The Arbuthnots take their name from a Scottish place-name south of Aberdeen, the Bosseys are from one of several places called Bussey in Normandy, and the Clutterbucks are descended from Dutch immigrants of the sixteenth century. Sometimes a person's name resonates over the centuries. Lord Macaulay's judgement on Niccolò Macchiavelli was that: 'Out of his surname they have coined an epithet for a knave, and out of his Christian name a synonym for the devil'.

Writers on Surnames

The first scholar to write about the history of surnames was the eminent Elizabethan antiquary William Camden. In 1605, two decades after the publication of his *Britannia*, he published the rest of the antiquarian material that he had painstakingly gathered over the years, under the title of *Remains concerning Britain*. The most substantial chapter in his new work was concerned with how surnames had been formed and the ways in which they had developed. Writing some two or three centuries after most surnames had become fixed and hereditary, Camden's general explanations are largely correct, though many of his suggested etymologies for individual names have since been disproved. The first major work on the subject can now be seen to have been one of the most significant contributions to our understanding of the meaning of surnames.

Camden rightly insisted that, contrary to common belief at the time that he was writing, English surnames were not formed until after the Norman Conquest. He observed that, 'Perhaps this may seem strange to some English men and Scottish men, who, like the Arcadians, think their surnames as ancient as the Moon, or at least to reach many an age beyond the Conquest'. He went on to explain how additional names, or 'bynames', that distinguished the bearers of similar first names developed into hereditary surnames, starting with those used by the Normans. He concluded that:

> the most surnames in number, the most ancient and of best account, have been local, deduced from places in Normandy, and the Countries confining, being

either patrimonial possessions, or native places of such as served the Conqueror, or came in after out of Normandy; as Mortimer, Warren ... Neither is there any Village in Normandy that gave not denomination to some Family in England.

He quoted surnames that were derived from places in other parts of France, the Netherlands, England and Scotland, and observed that 'every Town, Village, or Hamlet hath afforded names to families'. He also quoted some of the place-name elements that are found in surnames and concluded that 'many names are local which do not seem so, because the places are unknown to most men, and are all known to no one man'. He also realised that many surnames had been altered by 'corruption of speech'.

Camden went on to demonstrate how surnames can be placed in various categories, such as those derived from occupations or professions, from qualities and imperfections, colours, flowers, rivers, trees, fish, birds and fruit, from Christian names and from nicknames. He concluded, correctly, that in 1605 surnames were 'of no great antiquity' and he was scathing about unfounded claims:

> I cannot yet see why men should think that their Ancestors gave names to places, when the places bare those very names before any men did their Surnames ... Neither must all, having their names from places, suppose that their Ancestors were either Lords, or possessors of them; but may assure themselves that they originally came from them, or were born at them.

Nearly four hundred years after Camden wrote these wise words, such mistaken claims are still being made.

Camden was shrewdly observant of the ways that numerous surnames had been formed from personal names that were in use about the time of the Norman Conquest, including those that had arisen from pet forms, e.g. Terry from Theodric. He was also able to show how some surnames had been formed by adding either -s, -son, -kins, -is, -et, or -ot to a personal name, a pet form of a name or a nickname. He was clear that nicknames had been imposed 'in merriment' by others and had not been assumed by persons themselves. On surnames derived from occupations or professions, he observed:

> Neither was there any trade, craft, art, profession, or occupation never so mean, but had a name among us commonly ending in Er, and men accordingly denominated; but some are worn out of use, and therefore the significations are unknown, and others have been mollified ridiculously by the bearers, lest they should seem vilified by them. And yet like names were among the noble Romans.

He noted also that the stock of English surnames was being replenished by 'many new names dayly brought in by Aliens, as French, Scots, Irish, Welsh,

Dutch, etc.', and that many old names had disappeared over time. Camden's book is a remarkable pioneering work that single-handedly laid the foundations of the subject.

Remains concerning Britain long remained the only worthwhile commentary on the subject, but from the middle of the nineteenth century onwards a growing interest in the etymology of surnames led to several publications, notably M. A. Lower, *Patronymica Britannica* (1860), a work that is now hardly known and rarely consulted, and the Revd C. W. Bardsley, *English Surnames: Their Sources and Significations* (1873). Bardsley was one of those Victorian parson-scholars who were deeply interested in antiquarian topics. The posthumous publication of his *A Dictionary of English and Welsh Surnames* (1901) marked a major advance in the subject, acknowledged by all later scholars working in the same field. Ernest Weekley thought that Bardsley 'appears to be the only one who knows that there are such things as chronology and evidence', and P. H. Reaney recognised that he was 'the first to lay down the essential principles on which the study of surnames must be based, the necessity for the collection of numerous early forms of the name, the earlier the better, and from these to deduce an etymology in the light of the known history of the language'. In his preface Bardsley claimed that the dictionary was 'an attempt to trace back our names to their original forms, to clear them from the incrustations of time, and to place each, however misleading its appearance today, in its own particular class'. He regretted that: 'English surnames have been made the subject of endless guessings' and humorously dismissed some of the wilder speculations:

> talk to a very large number of people about their surname and you will find that the family came in with the Conqueror ... William evidently had a very easy time of it. It is clear that he had only a handful of opponents to meet, and that the story of the Battle of Hastings is a gross historical fraud.

Bardsley was the first to divide surnames into the categories that form the basis of modern classifications: 1. Baptismal or Personal Names. 2. Local Surnames. 3. Official Surnames. 4. Occupational Names. 5. Nicknames. He qualified this classification by saying, 'Practically, there are only four classes, for it is often hard to distinguish between occupation and office'. Modern scholars prefer to subdivide the second category (which they label 'toponymic') into 'locative' names derived from settlements and 'topographical' names derived from features of the landscape. Bardsley observed that:

> all the countries of Western Europe seem to have adopted the same means of securing identification, or their neighbours did it for them. Wales is the great

exception. Here, there is scarcely a trade name, only a few nicknames, no official surnames that I know of, just a sprinkling of local surnames, and the rest, quite 95 per cent, are baptismal names.

He correctly identified the major period of the formation of English hereditary surnames as 'say 1250 to 1450', he illustrated the ways in which 'variants of family names are extraordinary in number', and he recognised the regional distribution of many English surnames.

In *The Romance of Names* (1914), Ernest Weekley, Professor of French at the University of Nottingham (now, alas, better remembered as the man whose wife, Frieda, ran off with D. H. Lawrence), thought that Bardsley was the only earlier worker who should be taken seriously but that his dictionary could not be used uncritically, 'for the author does not appear to have been either a linguist, or a philologist, and although he usually refrains from etymological conjecture, he occasionally ventures with disastrous results'. Many of Bardsley's explanations of a name were based merely on the modern form, for he had no early evidence. Weekley was later criticised in his turn by P. H. Reaney for seldom giving the evidence on which his etymologies were based. His book nevertheless remains a readable account, which Reaney acknowledged was based on sound principles. Much less reliable are C. L'Estrange Ewen, *A History of Surnames of the British Isles* (1931) and *Guide to the Origin of British Surnames* (1938). Reaney's criticism of these two works was: 'Generalizations on surnames are valueless if an unimpeachable etymology has not been established. He fails to distinguish between sound and spelling, and postulates impossible forms of Old English names. Worst of all, he rejects sound etymologies which do not fit his preconceived theories'.

By this time, the study of the development of old languages was making enormous strides. Between 1935 and 1950 a group of Swedish scholars at the universities of Lund and Uppsala published several works that advanced the study of the meaning and development of English surnames.[3] Their findings are still of value and are often quoted.

The name that is pre-eminent in the study of surnames in the third quarter of the twentieth century is that of P. H. Reaney, author of *A Dictionary of British Surnames* (1958) and *The Origin of English Surnames* (1967).[4] Reaney was a grammar-school teacher whose enormous output was the result of leisure-time activity. He also wrote at length on place-names, including the county volumes for Essex and Cambridgeshire for the English Place-Name Society and *The Origin of English Place-Names* (1964). Under Reaney, the study of surnames took a great leap forward. When he published his dictionary, Bardsley's volume was out of print and nothing worthwhile had taken its place. Reaney wrote in his preface that since Bardsley's death 'a vast accumulation of printed records has become available to which he had no means of access and our knowledge of the English Language has steadily increased'. A new dictionary was long overdue. Reaney's other book aimed 'to give a general account of the development of English surnames, their classification, changes in pronunciation and spelling, and the gradual growth of hereditary family names'. Both the dictionary and the general account of the origins of surnames remain standard texts and the essential introductions to the subject. The rest of Europe has nothing comparable. Even A. Dauzat, *Dictionnaire étymologique des noms de famille et prénoms de France* (1951), now succeeded by Marie-Thérèse Morlet, *Dictionnaire étymologique des noms de famille* (1991), does not reach the same high standard.

Other philologists have since published dictionaries of surnames which are both scholarly and informative. They include Basil Cottle, *Penguin Dictionary of Surnames* (1978), Patrick Hanks and Flavia Hodges, *The Oxford Dictionary of Surnames* (1989), and works on Scottish, Irish and Welsh surnames, notably G. F. Black, *Surnames of Scotland* (an earlier work of 1946), E. MacLysaght, *Surnames of Ireland* (1969), Robert Bell, *The Book of Ulster Surnames* (1988) and T. J. Morgan and Prys Morgan, *Welsh Surnames* (1985). The philologists have advanced the subject enormously during the second half of the twentieth century.

Yet, as Reaney himself recognised, the study of surname history 'will be a long task demanding patient industry and accuracy [that] cannot be satisfactorily concluded without the cooperation of philologists, genealogists and historians'. Reaney's work is open to the criticism that it takes no account of the past or present distributions of surnames. He performed a necessary task by searching all the available sources in print in order to establish the earliest forms of surnames but he failed to link these thirteenth- and fourteenth-century examples with the surnames of the early modern and modern eras. The Black Death and other diseases in the fourteenth century killed many of the bearers of the surnames which Reaney had recorded in previous centuries, often leaving only a single family to continue the name. Detailed research into the histories of individual families has shown time and time again that the ancestors of present-day bearers of very many surnames never lived in the places recorded by Reaney. A consequence is that the etymologies offered by Reaney are often wrong. We can now see that he came at the end of a long and honourable tradition whereby philologists sought to interpret surnames by the same methods that were applied to the study of place-names. The object of the exercise was to establish the earliest forms of a name and then to interpret its meaning through knowledge of old languages. This took no account of the continuing evolution of surnames, nor of the evidence for single-family origins for many names and their restricted geographical distribution. Although Reaney knew that his own name came from Ranah Stones, a farm in my native parish of Penistone, little more than a dozen miles or so from where he himself was born in Sheffield, and that the local pronunciation Rayney was the 'correct' one, he did not see the implications of this etymology for the wider study of surnames. Thus he explains the surname Bullas as 'one employed at the bull-house', even though all the evidence points to the name being derived from just two places – one in the west midlands and the other from the hamlet of Bullhouse, half a mile away from Ranah Stones.

Reaney's approach to the study of surnames was to collect the earliest examples that he could find in order to arrive at an etymology. He wrote: 'The purpose of a Dictionary of Surnames is to explain the meaning of names, not to treat of genealogy and family history'. Knowledge of old languages enables the philologist to identify ancient personal names that gave rise to certain surnames. Straightforward examples include the surnames Harding, Rimell and Woolrich derived from the Old English names Hearding, Rimhild and Wulfric; the surnames Allgood and Wragg derived from the Old Danish names Algot and Wraghi; and the surnames Trigg and Gammell or Gamble derived from the Old Norse names Tryggr and Gamel. Other surnames are much more difficult to interpret. Some are based on short forms of old personal names and others appear to have been formed from personal names that are not recorded in any surviving sources. It is always tempting, of course, to ascribe a surname to an unrecorded personal name when no obvious explanation is at hand.

Modern scholarship by philologists has challenged many of Reaney's etymologies. Peter McClure has shown that many pet forms of personal names were derived from names that differ from those suggested by Reaney.[5] For example, the principal source for Malkin was Maud, not Mary; the surnames Paw and Pawson were derived from Paul, not from the Old English word for peacock; and, as David was an uncommon name at the period of surname formation, Dawson and Dawkins were probably derived, via rhyming forms, from Ralph. The origins of many other pet forms of names have still to be reliably established.

Reaney's contribution to the study of surnames was outstanding but the time has come to challenge many of his conclusions and to adopt new approaches. Philologists are looking at naming patterns at different times and in different places and at the contexts in which names occur. Local and family historians point out that Reaney was unconcerned with whether or not his early names became hereditary and survived into modern times.

His work takes no account of how surnames continued to evolve in later centuries. The genealogical method of working backwards in time, step by step, often produces evidence of change in the form of a name which invalidates Reaney's etymology. Modern surnames need to be linked to medieval names by the techniques of family historians before we can decide about a name's meaning.

A different approach was outlined more than a century ago by H. B. Guppy, a distinguished scientist whose *Homes of Family Names in Great Britain* was published in 1890. Guppy wished 'to ascertain the homes of family surnames and to ascertain the characteristic surnames of each county'. He decided that, as farmers were 'the most stay-at-home class of the country', he would extract their names from current Kelly's *Post Office Directories* on a county by county basis. Ignoring those surnames with a relative frequency of less than 7 per 10,000 in a county, he classified the rest as follows:

1. General names, occurring in from 30 to 40 counties
2. Common names, occurring in 20–29 counties
3. Regional names, occurring in 10–19 counties
4. District names, occurring in 4–9 counties
5. County names, occurring in 2–3 counties
6. Peculiar names, mostly confined to 1 county

The surnames of each county were arranged into these classes and comments were made on the characteristic ones. Guppy made his study before the appearance of Bardsley and so had to rely on Camden for his etymologies. Like Bardsley, he was an amateur; the study of surnames was his hobby. Perhaps his interest arose from his own surname, which was derived from a small place in the Dorset parish of Wootton Fitzpaine. All the Guppys seem to be descended from William Guppy of Chardstock, who took part in Perkin Warbeck's rebellion in 1497. The surname is still concentrated in Dorset and Devon. (The tropical fish, incidentally, was named in honour of B. M. Guppy, a clergyman in Trinidad who presented the first specimens to the British Museum.)

Reaney was interested in Guppy's approach but was rightly critical of his reliance on the modern form of the names. Restricting the sample of names to farmers was, he thought, a dubious practice, especially as so many farmers had surnames which showed that their ancestors had followed some quite different occupation. Most damagingly of all, 'When we compare Guppy's lists of 1890 with medieval lists of names for the same counties, we find marked differences. To take only one class. In the 1327 Subsidy Roll for

Cambridgeshire, 22 of Guppy's Peculiar Names do not appear; in that for Suffolk 30 out of 56 are missing'. It is possible, however, that some of these names would have appeared if the proportion of people who paid the tax had been higher than it was. Reaney's point is not totally convincing. On the other hand, he found his target when he concluded, 'What Guppy has produced is a valuable mass of material on the distribution of the names of the farmers of the country about 1890, but he gives very little information on the real homes of family names'. Reaney himself is open to a similar charge. What he has provided is not a satisfactory identification of the real homes of family names but a detailed list of medieval bynames, some of which never developed into hereditary surnames.

Guppy's book failed to influence the development of the study of surnames for the next seventy-five years, but he is now regarded as the pioneer (though admittedly an unreliable one) of the approach that has added a huge new dimension to the subject. In 1965 the English Surnames Survey was established by the Marc Fitch Fund in the Department of English Local History at the University of Leicester, with Richard McKinley as Director. The survey is concerned not so much with philology as with the historical origins and distribution of surnames. The first publications in the English Surnames Series were George Redmonds, *Yorkshire: West Riding* (1973) and Richard McKinley, *Norfolk and Suffolk Surnames in the Middle Ages* (1975). These have been followed by McKinley's county volumes on *Oxfordshire* (1977), *Lancashire* (1981) and *Sussex* (1988), and David Postles' volumes on *Devon* (1995) and *Leicestershire and Rutland* (1998). Each of these volumes were based on the study of thousands of names, from the period of surname formation onwards. Richard McKinley, *A History of British Surnames* (1990) draws on this experience in order to provide a history of surnames for readers who have no specialist knowledge of the subject. It also explains 'how to investigate the meaning and etymology of surnames, and the complications involved in the process'. It has become the basic textbook on the new approach to the subject.

McKinley and Redmonds have used the techniques of historical and genealogical research to determine 'the chronology of the rise of stable hereditary surnames, in the different regions of the country, and in the different social classes'. They have shown that each county has its own distinctive surnames which originated there in the middle ages and which have often remained largely confined to the region around the point of origin. They conclude that very many surnames, particularly the locative ones derived from hamlets or individual farmsteads, have a single-family origin, though the limitations of the medieval evidence make this assertion very difficult to prove in any individual case. Their work has shown that although families moved frequently they did not normally travel very far. Locative names prove that some medieval people travelled long distances, particularly to London, but most movement was much more restricted than that. The surname evidence has therefore provided important insights into the nature of geographical mobility and has demonstrated the remarkable stability of very many families. It has equally shed light on social mobility. For instance, McKinley has shown that in Lancashire certain types of surname were originally limited to certain classes of people. The division between bondmen and small free tenants was not clear-cut, despite the legal distinction between them, but the surnames of the larger landowners were markedly different from those of the peasants. In time, however, we find landowners with surnames which arose amongst the peasantry and vice-versa. The study of surnames has thus become a tool for enquiring into wider matters of social and economic history. It is no longer the preserve of the philologists. The genealogical skills of the family historian, coupled with the local historian's familiarity with a place and its records, have become as necessary as a knowledge of old languages in the interpretation of the origins of surnames.

Local and family historians rarely have any expertise in philology. Their starting point must be the dictionaries and other works of scholars who possess these skills. Fortunately, the subject has reached the stage where the philologists have established a body of work on which others may build. The time is opportune for the vast numbers of people who have an interest in a particular surname (usually their own), or in all the names of the families in a chosen locality, to make a contribution, either by proving the diction-aries right or by suggesting other explanations for the 'homes' of family names. Members of the Guild of One-Name Studies, who try to trace every person bearing the distinctive surname that they are interested in, are well placed to make constructive suggestions.

Meanwhile, the study of surname distributions has attracted the attention of geneticists. In *Surnames and Genetic Structure* (1985), G. W. Lasker has argued that a surname is much richer in information content than any biological gene and that as surnames are inherited they can serve as models of the genetic structure of populations. Large quantities of surnames provide easily accessible data, both about the past and the present. Lasker has also analysed the 32,457 surnames of everyone whose marriage was registered in the first quarter of 1975, including 2198 Smiths and 1773 Joneses.[6] He con-cluded that surnames are not bunched in distinct sub-groups but form a 'cline', or slope, with a gradual change in surname frequency over a broad geographical area. Some examples of surname frequency are plotted in G. W. Lasker and C. G. N. Mascie-Taylor, eds, *Atlas of British Surnames*

(1990). This work by the geneticists runs parallel to that of McKinley, Redmonds and the English Surnames Survey.

In 1997 George Redmonds published *Surnames and Genealogy: A New Approach.* This emphasised the need for a fresh multi-disciplinary look at the subject, for each hereditary surname has a unique history. Redmonds has examined hundreds of surnames which originated in Yorkshire, tracing them through medieval manor court rolls, tax lists, wills, parish registers, and civil and ecclesiastical court records, and thereby proving the descent and evolution of names from the middle ages into modern times. In so doing, he has raised the status of genealogy 'by emphasizing its fundamental importance to both the linguist and the historian'. He shows, above all, that 'without some sort of genealogical evidence it can be unwise to link modern surnames with those found in medieval sources'. Time after time, he shows how some surnames changed fundamentally over the generations and how others became identical with similar surnames, or, confusingly, with place-names and personal names with which they had no real connection. The study of surnames has become a minefield for the unwary.

The New Approach

For the past twelve years or so a group of adult students has been meeting under my direction at the National Centre for English Cultural Tradition at the University of Sheffield, researching the history of local surnames. Some of the names that we have studied provide good examples of the results of the new approach pioneered by McKinley and Redmonds, which emphasises the value of studying distribution patterns of names at various points in time and the need to use genealogical methods to trace a name back towards its source. These examples will also highlight the typical problems encountered during research and the variety of directions in which an enquiry may be pursued. The nature of the sources which provide the distribution patterns at various points in time, and the problems of their interpretation, will be considered in later chapters. Here the intention is simply to give a flavour of the approach.

In the 1980s certain tabloid newspapers made great play of the difference between the ordinary ancestors of the Prime Minister of the day, Margaret Thatcher, née Roberts, and the knightly forebears of her adversary, the President of the National Union of Mineworkers, Arthur Scargill. Curiously, Margaret Thatcher and her successor as Prime Minister, John Major, share a descent from John and Elizabeth Crust, Lincolnshire farmers in the eighteenth century. Their family trees are similar to those of most of the English population in showing ancestors who worked the land. It was an amusing paradox that Arthur Scargill, the self-proclaimed champion of the working classes, should apparently have blue blood in his veins. The tabloid press were unconcerned with the burden of proof, however. In fact, the question of whether or not Arthur Scargill was connected with the medieval knights who bore the same name has never been proved one way or the other.

All the Scargills are undoubtedly named after the village of Scargill in the northern Vale of York. No less than 220 of the 310 telephone subscribers nationwide who bore the surname Scargill in the 1980s were still living in Yorkshire. The Leeds and Wakefield directories had 120 subscribers between them. Further back in time the pattern becomes sharper. Between 1842 and 1846 only twenty-eight Scargill deaths were registered nationwide; fourteen of these were in four adjacent districts in the heart of the West Riding, seven were in south Yorkshire, three were in Lancashire or Cheshire, three were from the Lincolnshire coast, and one was from London. The name was therefore very rare outside two separate parts of Yorkshire, and even in that county it was not numerous. Since then, the surname has become much more common in the central parts of the West Riding.

The hearth tax returns of the 1660s and 1670s recorded thirteen Scargill households in south Yorkshire but only one further north. No Scargills were recorded in the returns for Derbyshire or Nottinghamshire. Numerous references to people called Scargill can be found in the sixteenth- and seventeenth-century parish registers of Sheffield, Ecclesfield and Bradfield, where the name was spelt variously as Scargel, Scarghull, Skargell, Skarghull, Skargill and Scargyll. In 1640 Robert Scargell was Master Cutler of the Company of Cutlers in Hallamshire. Further back in time, the Scargills are recorded as having paid their poll tax in 1379 in both Sheffield and Ecclesfield. The same tax returns name other Scargills in scattered places further north in Yorkshire, including some wealthy ones: William of Scargill, knight, at Little Smeaton; William of Schargill, junior, knight, and his wife; John of Schargill and his wife, and Joan of Schargill, all at Thorpe Stapleton; Agnes of Scargill, webster, at Stapleton; John of Scarghyll and his wife at Snaith; and Thomas Scargill and his wife at Clint.

Scargill is a small settlement in north Yorkshire, four miles south of Barnard Castle, well away from later distributions of the surname. A Warin de Scargill lived there in the mid twelfth century. Sir Warin de Scargill entertained King Edward II at Scargill Castle in north Yorkshire in 1323. He also lived at Thorpe Stapleton and his effigy can be seen in a recess in the north wall of the chancel of Darrington church. Other family monuments are found in the nearby church at Whitkirk. Sir William de Skargill was steward of the huge manor of Wakefield in 1332 and held other important positions in Yorkshire in the 1330s and 1340s. The question which cannot be answered with certainty is: are the present-day Scargills in west and south Yorkshire descendants of these medieval knights? The most likely explanation is that they are descended from junior branches of this family but proof is lacking and it is possible that they are descended from a separate (and poorer) family or families that moved south from Scargill at the period of surname formation in the hope of improving their lot. No firm evidence has been discovered to support either case.

Goldthorpe is another surname that has been derived from a Yorkshire settlement which lies some distance from the present concentration of the name, though not as far as Scargill is from Sheffield. Goldthorpe is now a large village between Barnsley and Doncaster that grew quickly at the beginning of the twentieth century when accommodation was provided for colliers at the new Hickleton Main pit. In earlier centuries it was only a hamlet. An early link between the surname and the place-name is provided by the 'William de Goletorp' who held land in the neighbouring hamlet of Thurnscoe in 1219. The telephone directories of the late 1980s listed 664 Goldthorpes or Gouldthorpes in England and Wales. About half of these subscribers were living within thirty-five miles of the village of Goldthorpe, though none lived close to it. London and its environs had, as usual, attracted migrants; otherwise the Goldthorpes were scattered thinly, but far and wide. Only seven telephone districts had no Goldthorpes at all. The evidence is suggestive of a single origin in south Yorkshire, but in view of the large numbers of subscribers it is not conclusive.

When we turn to the national indexes of death registrations in 1842–46, these doubts are removed, for sixty-five of the seventy-seven Goldthorpes whose deaths were registered were from the West Riding of Yorkshire; twenty-seven of them had died in the Huddersfield district. The much wider distribution of the present-day Goldthorpes must be the result of dispersal since the 1840s. We now need to go back in time to the distribution pattern of the name in the hearth tax returns of the 1660s and 1670s and to see how far back we can trace a family tree. Huddersfield lies twenty-two miles west of Goldthorpe. Can the nineteenth-century concentration of the surname in that district be the result of a family or person migrating this short distance from Goldthorpe at, or soon after, the period of surname formation?

The hearth tax returns for the West Riding in 1672 record no Goldthorpes in south Yorkshire (where the settlement is located), but six households near Huddersfield (three in Shepley, two in Flockton, and one in Quarmby), and one further north at Tadcaster. The Derbyshire and Nottinghamshire hearth tax returns make no mention of any Goldthorpes. When we turn to earlier records, Shepley turns out to be the place (eighteen miles west of Goldthorpe) where the family had lived in the late middle ages. The marriage of Robert of Goldthorpe and Isabel, the daughter of William Shepley of Shepley, in 1361 was the occasion when the Goldthorpes settled there. This Robert was the son of another Robert of Goldthorpe. In other records he was named Robertson or Robinson, but his move to Shepley seems to have confirmed Goldthorpe as the surname that the family favoured. The medieval Goldthorpes were of gentry rank and became part owners of the manor of Shepley. Robert and Isabel's son, Thomas Goldthorpe, was described as 'of Goldthorpe and Shepley', and the family retained their property in and around Goldthorpe until late in the reign of Henry VIII. Their pedigree can be traced from Robert and Isabel through three generations to another Thomas Goldthorpe. George Redmonds informs us that 'financial difficulties and disputes with other local families, notably the Beaumonts of Whitley, were responsible for a decline in status after 1542, when Thomas Goldthorpe sold his share of Shepley manor'. It seems to have been these same difficulties that caused Thomas to sell the family's ancient property in and around Goldthorpe. During the sixteenth and seventeenth centuries the Goldthorpes of Shepley were described in the Kirkburton parish register not as gentlemen but further down the social scale as yeomen. In later generations, younger branches spread the family name beyond Shepley, but to this day many of the Goldthorpes remain close to the places where they were rooted in the middle ages.

Scargill and Goldthorpe are surnames which have retained the same forms as the place-names whence they were derived. Other names were more readily corrupted. The name of the Pennine farmstead Bilcliff has been spelt in many different ways over the centuries and is the source of the surnames Bilcliffe and Biltcliff(e). Certain versions of the name have become the preferred pronunciation and spelling in different districts. The 1995 British Telecom CD-ROM of subscribers' addresses has sixty-nine Biltcliff(e)s and forty Bilcliff(e)s, mostly in the West Riding of Yorkshire, Lancashire or Cheshire. The subscriber who lives nearest to the farmstead which is the source of the surname is four miles away at Gunthwaite, within the bounds of the ancient parish of Penistone to which both these settlements belonged. The present Bilcliffes are scattered widely, but the current concentration of the surname is nevertheless sufficiently clear to form a starting point for an enquiry into earlier records in order to test an hypothesis. The surname can be traced back to the district whence it came, to a John of Bilclyf in the poll tax returns of 1379 and to a Thomas of Billecliff who was recorded in an earlier tax return of 1297. The place-name – meaning 'Billa's cliff' – goes back further, to the first decade of the thirteenth century. The present farmstead is called Belle Clive, but it is marked as Bilcliff on earlier maps and this is still the local pronunciation. The first officers of the Ordnance

Survey to venture into these parts either misheard local speech or tried to make the name sound more respectable.

Locative surnames such as those we have just quoted are usually the easiest to identify and the ones that are generally thought of as having striking distribution patterns; but, in fact, many names in other categories lend themselves to the same methods of analysis, with equally spectacular results. Some of the surnames which are derived from personal names or which express the relationship of father and son have patterns which are just as distinctive as those produced by some locative names. The surname Drabble serves as an appropriate example. The 1986 United Kingdom telephone directories listed 456 Drabbles, of whom 234 were living in the four adjacent districts of Sheffield, South Manchester, Chesterfield, and Barnsley and Doncaster. The Drabbles were also well represented in neighbouring parts of Yorkshire, Lancashire and the north midlands. London and the south coast had proved attractive to others but many districts had few or no Drabbles. The pattern is as distinct as that for most locative names in pointing to the place of origin. It strongly suggests the possibility of a single-family origin.

The twentieth-century distribution of the surname can also be discerned from an analysis of the 113 births that were registered in England and Wales between 1934 and 1938. These birthplaces were in much the same areas as those recorded in 1986. (We may also note thirteen Drabwells, most of whom were born in Greater London, and two Drablows in Stepney. Are these names variants of Drabble or are they unconnected?) The ninety-eight Drabbles whose deaths were registered in England and Wales between 1837 and 1842 had also lived in and around the Peak District. The 1841 census for Sheffield recorded 165 people with the surnames Drabble, Drabwell and Dribble. Twenty years later, forty-three Drabbles were recorded in the neighbouring chapelry of Bradfield, which stretched over the moors to the Derbyshire border.

The hearth tax returns two centuries earlier reveal a narrower distribution of the name. No Drabbles were recorded in Nottinghamshire or in west Yorkshire. In south Yorkshire they were to be found at Conisbrough, Doncaster and Hickleton, also on the Pennines in the chapelry of Bradfield, where John Drabble and Francis Drabble were each taxed on one hearth in Stannington, and Jonathan Drabble paid for two smithies in Westnall. In Derbyshire, the Drabbles were living at Hulland and Shottle in the south of the county but were chiefly to be found in the northern hundreds of Scarsdale and High Peak: two in Chelmorton, one in Eyam, one in Brampton, one in Abney and four in Dronfield. The Dronfield Drabbles were better off than the rest, with houses taxed on one, two, three and six hearths. This tight distribution in adjoining parts of north Derbyshire and south-west Yorkshire is spoilt by the discovery that two Drabbles were living in the Bedfordshire townships of Compton and at Yelden in 1671, when they were taxed on one and two hearths. No explanation for the appearance of Drabbles in Bedfordshire can yet be offered.

The Drabbles can be traced back further in south-west Yorkshire through parish registers and manorial court rolls. The sole entry in the Ecclesfield parish register is to the marriage of John Drable in 1621. The surname appears in the Sheffield register from Elizabethan times onwards. The Drabbles who were named on numerous occasions in the Bradfield register between 1560 and 1723 were probably all descended from Thomas and Jennet Drabell, both of whom died in 1596, through their sons, Richard, John and Henry. Further back in time, John Drabble, elder and junior, appear in manorial court rolls at Ecclesfield and Bradfield in 1440–41. In the poll tax returns for the West Riding in 1379 the only person with this surname was Robert Drabill in Thurlstone township, just to the north of the chapelry of Bradfield. In 1331 Matthew Drabel was the executor of the will of Thomas Drabel of the Graveship of Holme, bordering on Thurlstone, and John and Thomas Drabel were living there in the 1330s and 1340s. The Derbyshire poll tax returns of 1381 record William Drabul' at Bakewell. It is possible that all these Drabbles were related.

Reaney and Wilson quote examples of the name from the thirteenth century in Warwickshire, Staffordshire and Cambridgeshire. Their reference to a Ralph Drabelle in Yorkshire in 1302 turns out to be from Appleton-le-Street in the North Riding, a long way away from the Drabbles of the south-west Pennines and therefore not connected. They suggest that the surname is derived from Old English Drabba (evidenced as a personal name in the tenth century and perhaps producing a diminutive form Drabbel) or from drab 'a dirty, untidy woman'. If the surname ever became hereditary in the other counties quoted by Reaney it must have subsequently died out. Its home is undoubtedly in the Peak District. Margaret Drabble, the novelist, was born in Sheffield, close to where her surname originated.

Our second example of a surname in the personal category is Levick. Reaney and Wilson suggest that it was derived from the French évêque, meaning 'bishop', but the distribution in the telephone directories shows that the surname is uncommon except in the Sheffield and Chesterfield districts, which contain 30 per cent of the subscribers. In 1986 Sheffield had sixty-three Levicks, Chesterfield had twenty-four, the rest of the United Kingdom had 196. Beyond Sheffield and Chesterfield, the name was spread widely, but thinly, including sixteen in Scotland. The name may therefore have had multiple origins. However, the forty-seven births registered in

England and Wales between 1837 and 1842 show an even more marked distribution in and around south Yorkshire, north Derbyshire and north Nottinghamshire. The similar surname Levitt was common in many districts but was particularly strong in Yorkshire. Levett was the preferred form of the name in East Anglia and south-eastern England. We shall see that Levick is simply a corruption of this older form of the name.

In 1841 Sheffield had seventy Levicks and eleven Levitts. The south Yorkshire hearth tax returns for 1672 note four Levitts and one Levick (William, of Attercliffe in the parish of Sheffield). Robert Levicke of Newbould was the sole householder with either form of the name in the Derbyshire hearth tax returns of 1670. No Levicks are recorded in the local medieval manorial records, nor in the 1379 poll tax returns, but Robert and Joan Levet were taxed at Eckington in that year. The earliest reference to the surname Levick comes as late as 1599, when Richard Levick married Frances Barker at Norton, the next parish to Eckington. The Norton parish register has many later entries concerning the Levicks. The register of the adjoining parish of Sheffield notes the marriage in 1614 of John Levick and Margaret Revill. When their children were baptised in 1618–19 the surname was given as Levitt, however. Likewise, the Francis Levick who was married at Sheffield in 1615 was named Levitt when his daughter was baptised the following year. It seems that Levick is just a local variant of Levitt. Eventually, Levick became accepted in and around Sheffield and north Derbyshire as the correct pronunciation. Perhaps the same process elsewhere explains how the name has become more widespread since the beginning of Victoria's reign.

A final example from this category is the surname Jeffcock, a pet form of Geoffrey. One might reasonably suppose that this was a common name in the middle ages but it seems that in only one instance did it survive as a hereditary surname. The 1995 British Telecom CD-ROM lists seventy-three Jeffcocks who subscribed to the telephone service; thirty-one of these were in the Sheffield district, with six others in adjoining districts, the other half being scattered thinly elsewhere. The register of births for England and Wales from 1837 to 1842 recorded only nineteen Jeffcocks, of whom eight were born in Sheffield, five in Ecclesall, two in Chesterfield, and one each in Wortley, Rotherham, Manchester and Warrington. This tight distribution of a rare name points to a single-family origin. In 1841 Sheffield had fifty-nine Jeffcocks. One of these was William Jeffcock who was Sheffield's first mayor when the town was incorporated as a borough in 1843. The similar-sounding surname Jeffcott (various spellings), which was registered on fifty-three occasions in the indexes of deaths between 1842 and 1846, was found mostly in north Warwickshire and therefore appears to have been derived from a separate source.

The name Jeffcock was not recorded in south Yorkshire in the middle ages but it was known in Eckington, just across the border in Derbyshire, in the fourteenth century. The Jeffcocks were well established in Sheffield when the parish register commenced in 1560. Lawrence and Robert Jeffcocke were cutlers there in 1614. In the hearth tax returns of the 1670s no Jeffcocks were recorded in Derbyshire or Nottinghamshire and all the eight households in south Yorkshire were living within the boundaries of modern Sheffield. The Handsworth register (which covered what is now a suburb of Sheffield) has over sixty entries for Jeffcocks between 1636 and 1768. This is clearly a local name which is as rare as some of the locative surnames which were derived from Pennine farmsteads.

Some of the surnames which were derived from nicknames have similar local concentrations which suggest a single source for the name. Memmott may have been a Sheffield variant of Mynot, a nickname meaning 'dainty, pleasing', though this suggested etymology is not certain. In 1995 this rare name was listed sixty-three times in the United Kingdom telephone directories; twenty-three of the Memmotts lived in the Sheffield district, the rest had addresses in thirty-six different places. Only twenty-seven births were registered under this name in England and Wales between 1837 and 1842; eighteen of these were in the Sheffield district and eight were in the adjoining district of Ecclesall, the odd one being at Bedminster. Only four householders with this surname were listed in the various hearth tax returns of the 1670s. They were each recorded within the hundred of Scarsdale in north-east Derbyshire. Two Edmund Meymotts were based in Alfreton and John and Robert Mymott were living in Eckington. Perhaps this latter person was the Robert Meymott whose son and namesake was apprenticed to a cutler in Heeley, on the Yorkshire-Derbyshire boundary, and who obtained his freedom of the Cutlers' Company in 1733. Several generations of Memmotts subsequently worked as cutlers in Heeley.

The earliest local references to the surname are to Hugh, John and Lettice Menemot, who were living at Rotherham in 1300; William and Constance Mennock were taxed at the same place in 1379. The Memmots seem to have moved a little further south during the following century and to have put down roots in Eckington parish, where they were living by the 1490s, before migrating north again. By 1841 Sheffield had ninety-nine people with this name.

Occupational names, notably Smith, Turner and Wright, are so common that they must have had numerous origins in many different parts of the country. Even these names, however, are not spread evenly across England. The rarer occupational names have concentrations which are as marked as those outlined above. The Yorkshire surname Flather serves as an example.

No one is quite certain what a flather did. Perhaps he was employed in the leather trade as a flayer of skins? The earliest spellings of the name include Flayer, Flethyr and Fladder. In 1995 the United Kingdom telephone directories listed 106 subscribers with the surname Flather and thirteen named Flathers; seventy-nine of these people lived in Yorkshire, particularly in the central parts of the West Riding and in the Sheffield district.

The Flathers appeared briefly in the Sheffield parish register in 1637 and 1663 but they did not settle there permanently until the eighteenth century. In the Victorian era the Flathers became prominent Sheffield steelmen and in the twentieth century two of them served as Master Cutler. The Sheffield branch appear to be descended from a family that was living further north in Staincross wapentake – at Stainborough, then Thurgoland, then Worsbrough – during the seventeenth century. The Flathers are not found in south Yorkshire before 1614. During the middle ages the name was known only in west Yorkshire. The poll tax returns of 1379 record four men with this surname in Morley wapentake: Robert Flether at Midgley, Roger Flayer at Pudsey, John Flether at Hunslet and John Flether at Clifton. The Hel' Flather who was living at Newland, to the east of Wakefield, in 1338 is the earliest man who is known to have borne this name. Six and a half centuries later most people bearing his surname are still living within the West Riding of Yorkshire.

Sometimes, the distribution patterns of surnames over time help to determine which of the possible etymologies that have been offered for a name are correct. For example, Reaney and Wilson derive the surname Habergham, Habberjam or Habbijam from Habergham Eaves, near Burnley (Lancashire), noting that although the modern pronunciation is Habbergam it was once clearly Habberjam. They derive the surnames Habbeshaw, Habeshaw, Habishaw, Habershon, and some of the Habberjams and Habbijams, from Old French *haubergier*, 'maker of hauberks or coats of mail'. They quote thirteenth-century examples from Northamptonshire and London of the use of this occupational surname.

The 1986 United Kingdom telephone directories list 230 subscribers with one or other of these names: ninety-nine Habberjams and variants, sixty-nine Habbershaws and variants, and sixty-two Habershons. The largest numbers are to be found in Yorkshire and Lancashire, no matter what the form of the name. Thus Yorkshire has seventy-three Habbijams, thirty-two Habbershaws and twenty-two Habershons. In the midlands and the south all forms of the name are rare, except that London has eight Habershons, five Habbijams and three Habbershaws. The distribution pattern suggests that all these names share a common derivation; it casts doubt on the explanation that some forms are derived from the occupation of making coats of mail.

This conclusion is reinforced by tracing the history of a family that settled close to Sheffield. Roger Habergham was at Curbar (Derbyshire) in 1483; the form of his surname suggests that he was one of a number of migrants who had crossed the hills from Lancashire, in his case from Habergham Eaves. Members of this family appear on numerous occasions in parish registers, tax returns, wills and other documents. during the following two or three centuries, in various parts of north Derbyshire and south Yorkshire. The men who recorded them clearly had difficulty in spelling this unusual name. Their attempts include Herbercam (1535), Haberion (1541), Haberjame (1557), Habberiam (1560), Habersham (1658), Habergeon (1666) and Haber-shaw (1713). The boys who were apprenticed to Hallamshire cutlers in the eighteenth century included seven Haberjams, six Habershons, three Haber-shaws and one Habbersham. All these names seem to be variants of the original Habergham. The association between the surname and the place-name is made explicit by the record of the burial of Lawrence Habergham of Habergham at Burnley in 1615.

Finally, it is worth pointing out that the modern distribution of a rare surname does not always point to its original home. In some cases, the original branch has died out, leaving only those who are scattered elsewhere. The rare name Hounsfield had only nineteen entries in the United Kingdom telephone directories in 1995; these subscribers were spread in ones and twos from north Yorkshire to Southampton. None lived in or near Sheffield. Earlier evidence, however, points to an origin only a few miles south west of the city centre. The place-name Holmesfield in north Derbyshire was recorded as Hounsfield at various times in the sixteenth and seventeenth centuries. Hounsfield was the name of this township in the hearth tax returns of 1670. The surname shows a similar change of form at this time. In 1584 William Holmesfield was married at Dronfield (the centre of the parish in which Holmesfield lay), but in 1588 Margaret Hownsfield and her daughter Elizabeth Howensfeld were beneficiaries of a will made in the nearby market town of Chesterfield. In 1644 Francis, the son of Edward Holmesfield, was baptised at Dronfield; in 1670 he was married in the same church, as Francis Hounsfield. His seven children were all baptised between 1671 and 1684 as Hounsfield, but he was buried in 1703 as Francis Holmes-field of Dore (an adjoining township in the same parish). He is not listed in the Derbyshire hearth tax returns of 1670, perhaps because he was too poor to pay. The returns name only Godfrey Hownesfeild and Bartholomew Hounsfeild, at Brimington and Whittington, both in the parish of Chester-field. In 1750, when Bartholomew Hounsfield of Brimington made a loan of £600, a witness to the bond was named George Holmesfield. There can be little doubt that the surname Hounsfield is derived from the place-name

Holmesfield. No Holmesfields are recorded in the current United Kingdom telephone directories.

The Hounsfields remained a small family but one branch became prominent industrialists in nineteenth-century Sheffield. John Hounsfield was Master Cutler in 1819, and Hounsfield Road, near Sheffield University, is named after George Hounsfield of High Hazels, who died in 1870, leaving £20,000 to charity. The name has died out locally.

We have therefore to exercise a degree of caution in placing too much faith in current distributions as indicators of the homes of family names. Nevertheless, enough has been said to show that, on the whole, surnames have persisted in the districts where they originated and that when we go back in time to look at earlier distributions of surnames the patterns become clearer.

Distinctive surnames help to give a district its particular character, Every part of England, except the huge melting-pot of London, has its own peculiar names. The naturalist W. H. Hudson was well aware of this when he was gathering material in Wiltshire for his marvellous and evocative book, *The Shepherd's Life* (1910). In it he records a conversation with an old woman in the churchyard of a downland village about the surname Lampard:

> 'It was a common name in this part of Wiltshire in former days; you find it in dozens of churchyards, but you'll find very few Lampards living in the villages. Why, I could tell you a dozen or twenty surnames, some queer, funny names, that were common in these parts not more than a century ago which seem to have quite died out.'
>
> 'I should like to hear some of them if you'll tell me.'
>
> 'Let me think a moment: there was Thorr, Pizzie, Gee, Every, Pottle, Kiddle, Toomer, Shergold, and -'
>
> Here she interrupted to say that she knew three of the names I had mentioned. Then, pointing to a small, upright gravestone about twenty feet away, she added, 'And there's one'.
>
> 'Very well, I said, but don't keep putting me out – I've got more names in my mind to tell you. There's Maidment, Marchmont, Velvin, Burpitt, Winzur, Rideout, Cullurne.'

Wonderful names, so different in sound and form from the ones that are familiar to Sheffielders.

The Normans

Surnames were introduced into England by the Norman barons. Only a few of these barons possessed hereditary surnames in Normandy before the Conquest and, in most cases, such names went back no more than a generation or two. The Tosny family were exceptional in having taken an hereditary surname from their estate as far back the second half of the tenth century. Two Ralphs, a Roger and then another Ralph de Tosny (who fought at Hastings) bore the family name. They were powerful barons whose chief residence after the Conquest remained in Normandy. Their English lines failed through lack of male heirs, though the Gresleys, a Derbyshire family who owned the Domesday Book manor of Drakelow until 1931, were descended from a Nigel de Stafford, the sheriff of Staffordshire, who may have been a member of the Tosny family. A direct link cannot be proved with certainty.

The mighty Warennes provide an example of the new aristocracy who benefited enormously from the Conquest. Their surname was derived from the hamlet of Varennes, not far from Dieppe. Rudolf de Warenne, a substantial landowner whose property lay mostly near the Seine above Rouen and in the Pays de Caux, was recorded on various occasions from the 1030s to the 1070s. His elder son. Rudolf, inherited the estate in Normandy; the English line descended from his younger son, William, a fierce and distinguished soldier who took a leading part in planning the invasion in 1066 and who fought at Hastings. William was rewarded with the grant of huge estates spread across thirteen counties in England, especially in Sussex, Yorkshire and Norfolk, and with the title of Earl of Surrey. The male line ended with William's grandson, whose son-in-law adopted the surname Warenne and inherited the earldom. This second male line died out in the fourteenth century. It is possible that some of the present-day Warrens are descended through junior lines from the baronial family but it is much more likely that they have acquired their surname from a person who lived near a deer park or a rabbit warren, or perhaps from the warrener himself.

The Mortimers, relations of the Warennes, are another good example of a leading baronial family whose surname was derived from an estate in Normandy before the Conquest; in their case from Mortemer, near Neufchâtel-en-Bray in the département of Seine-Maritime. Roger de Mortimer was the first member of a family who became mighty barons in the Welsh Marches. The family died out in the main line in the fifteenth century. Present-day Mortimers cannot claim descent from the Norman barons simply on the basis of a shared surname, for the name may have been brought across the Channel independently by later migrants. The published poll tax returns of 1381 name Peter Mortemer (Berkshire), Walter and William Mortemer (Dorset), Alban Mortymyr (Essex) and Henry Mortemer (a Gloucestershire farmer), all of whom paid modest amounts of tax. Anyone who claims that these men were descended from junior branches of the powerful family needs to explain how they had ended up in Charlton, Kingston Maurwood, Finchingfield and Shipton, so far away from the baronial family's sphere of influence. It is far more likely that they had separate origins.

A final example of a Norman family with a surname that had become fixed and hereditary before the Conquest and who profited greatly from the spoils of war is that of the Vernons. Far less powerful than the Warennes or the Mortimers, they nevertheless became the leading Derbyshire gentry family in the middle ages, with possessions stretching well beyond the county boundaries. Their main seat was Haddon Hall, a large, rambling manor house perched above the River Wye which has mellowed into one of the most picturesque medieval buildings in the country. The earliest work dates from the twelfth century. The family took their name from Vernon in the province of Eure. Hugh de Verdon was recorded in the 1030s and the family's descent can be traced through records of their donations to religious houses. The senior line of the family continued until the death in 1567 of Sir George Vernon, who built the imposing entrance to the hall and the adjoining ranges and who was known throughout Derbyshire as the 'King of the Peak'. The Vernon estates passed to George's daughter, Dorothy, and her husband, John Manners, who added the splendid long gallery and whose descendants became Dukes of Rutland. Here again, there is no certainty that other present-day Vernons are descended from junior branches of this family rather than from later migrants from Vernon. We may quote Robert and Thomas Vernon, two farmers who paid the lowest rate of poll tax in the Isle of Wight in 1379, as men who were not obviously connected with the Norman landowners of Derbyshire.

Before the Conquest, and for long afterwards, surnames were confined to the baronial families. Even at the top level of society, however, many men did not possess surnames but were distinguished merely by non-hereditary bynames. William FitzOsbern's name meant 'son of Osbern' and was not passed on to his sons. Others were content with occupational names such as Gerold the steward or Baldwin the sheriff. William the Conqueror's sons were distinguished merely by nicknames: Robert Curthose ('short trousers'), William Rufus ('red hair') and Henry Beauclerk ('fine clerk'). Nor were such nicknames confined to the upper class. For example, in 1379–81 poll tax was paid by Richard Schorthose, a Puddletown (Dorset) carpenter, and John Corthose, a fisherman from Thaxted (Essex). A few Norman barons had more than one byname in the eleventh and twelfth centuries. Many of them did not adopt hereditary surnames until well after the Conquest.

The royal family did not take the lead in the new fashion for hereditary surnames. On the contrary, they were amongst the last to acquire such names. The dynasty that ruled England from 1154 to 1399 is known to us in the first three reigns as Angevin, for they were Counts of Anjou, and then as Plantagenet, but this term was not used until the middle of the fifteenth century, long after the reign of Richard II, the last of the line. The name was derived from an emblem of the Counts of Anjou, *Planta Genista* or broom.

When the great Norman landowners did start to acquire surnames, their most common practice was to take the name of the place that was the family's chief residence. This was often still in Normandy. Many Norman barons did not start to call themselves by the name of their original estate until well after 1066. At the upper levels of Anglo-Norman society, surnames derived from place-names, especially French ones, were much more numerous than those that were formed from a father's name or from an occupation. Although surnames that linked a family to their French estate were prestigious, many Normans nevertheless took their names from their newly-acquired English estates, for in the uncertain years after the Conquest the use of hereditary surnames helped to clarify the right of ownership. This may well be the initial reason why surnames developed in this country.

The Norman Barons

By the twelfth century it had become a matter of prestige to claim an ancestor who had fought at Hastings. Much later, to say that 'my ancestor came over with the Conqueror' became a social cachet, on a level with American claims to have an ancestor who came over on the *Mayflower*. Such claimants are apparently undisturbed by the burden of proof. Nor is it clear why anyone should wish to claim descent from such violent men, a foreign army of occupation who for several generations preserved a separate identity from the English. The fact of the matter is that it is impossible to prove descent in a male line from an ancestor who fought at Hastings unless your name is Malet or Mallet(t).

Unfounded claims are perpetuated in what at first sight seem to be official lists of the Normans who took part in the battle. No one, incidentally, seems to want to prove descent from anybody who fought on the losing side. High on the western wall of Our Lady's Church at Dives-sur-Mer, where William's troops assembled before the invasion, is a list of 474 names drawn up in 1862 by Leopold Delisle for the French Society of Archaeology. The list is unsupported by any hint of evidence. Further south, a bronze tablet was placed in 1931 in the chapel of the castle of Falaise, inscribed with the names of 315 persons. The list was soon denounced as spurious by English genealogists. A third list, known as the Battle Abbey Roll, was probably made in the fourteenth century. Scholars have shown that it is absolutely unreliable.

Clearly, a lot of men fought at Hastings, but only the leaders of the expedition can be identified from contemporary or near-contemporary sources. The identities of fifteen men are certain and another four almost certain. A few others have serious claims. Descents in the female line can be proved from several of these names but only William Malet has probable descendants in the male line to the present day. Even in this case, the early links in the family's pedigree have not been proved beyond doubt. William Malet and his son, Robert, were important members of Duke William's court well before the Conquest. The family's castle in Graville-Sainte-Honorine, at the mouth of the Seine, is now buried under the suburbs of Le Havre.

The only complete record we have of the Norman families that were the new rulers of England under William the Conqueror is the Domesday Book of 1086. The small quantity of records from the first two centuries after the Conquest usually prevents the discovery of certain proof of descent from those named in Domesday Book. Most of the proofs are for the baronial families whose names appear in the chronicles or whose gifts are recorded in the chartularies of religious houses. In many other cases, however, we can point to the continuity of a family name, even if the exact relationship between generations is unknown.

The aristocracy of Norman England came mostly from Normandy, as one would expect, but a few baronial families came from neighbouring Brittany, Boulogne and Flanders. Some commanders were men whom Orderic Vitalis described as 'raised from the dust'. Upward social mobility through fighting or a career in royal government enabled men like Geoffrey de Mandeville or Robert D'Oilly to rise to positions of great importance and wealth. At first, the Normans simply took over the estates of conquered

Englishmen. For example, Geoffrey de Mandeville was given the lands of Ansger the Staller, which were spread over several counties. Security demanded radical change in the north and along the Welsh border, where huge lordships, or honours, were created. Several new lordships were formed after the compilation of Domesday Book and both William Rufus and Henry I installed new men from Normandy. Not all medieval barons with Norman surnames fought at Hastings.

The Norman Conquest was a traumatic event for those who had fought on the losing side and had lost their lands. Henry of Huntingdon, writing in the third decade of the twelfth century, noted: 'In the twenty-first year of King William's reign there was hardly a nobleman of English descent left in England, but all were reduced to servitude and mourning, so that it was a disgrace to be called an Englishman'. His observation applied equally to the thegns and sokemen, the lesser native landowners for whom the Norman Conquest was a disaster. Dr Katharine Keats-Rowan's analysis of the genealogies that she has painstakingly constructed from all the surviving eleventh- and twelfth-century sources has shown that very few Normans married into English families. The Norman aristocrats kept themselves a race apart.

The descents of the families of the great Norman landowners have been traced by I. J. Sanders in *English Baronies* (1960). The rate of turnover in the families that held the major lordships is remarkable. Sometimes a family was dispossessed for political reasons after backing an unsuccessful claimant to the throne, but mostly the frequent change of names was the result of a striking failure to produce male heirs. Altogether, fifty-four out of 189 English baronies in existence by 1166 descended in the female line in the hundred years after the Conquest, six of them twice.

Baronial lines tend not to last down to the present day. Where descents from such families can be proved they are usually those of younger branches. Sir Anthony Wagner, *Pedigree and Progress: Essays in the Genealogical Interpretation of History* (1975), traced the successive disappearance of Norman male lines from among the earls. By 1400 such famous names as St-Liz, Ferrers, Bigod, Clare, Warenne, Bohun and other great names had disappeared but Vere, Beauchamp, Courtenay, Fitzalan, Mowbray, Shefford, Mortimer, Percy and Montagu remained. A hundred years later, only Vere, Courtenay, Fitzalan, Stafford and Percy were left but an earldom had come to the Norman, though originally minor, family of Talbot. By 1600 only Vere, Percy and Talbot remained but new earldoms had been created for old Norman families, such as Manners, Clinton, Clifford, Seymour and Devereux. By 1700 only Vere, Talbot, Clinton, Manners and Seymour retained their titles but new men with Norman names such as Sackville,

Villiers and St John had been elevated to earldoms. Wagner commented that by this time, however, the Norman ancestry of all such families was so diluted with English blood that to say a new earl or duke was of Norman male descent might well mean less than to remark that one of English name could prove continuous inheritance through a female line from early Normans. Examples of the latter include the Dukes of Norfolk and Northumberland and Lord Leconfield, though these are respectively by male descent Howard, Smithson and Wyndham.

The Percys were one of the greatest and longest-lasting of the Norman baronial families. The particular settlement that gave rise to the surname has been disputed, for several places in northern France share this name, but it is now accepted that Percy-en-Auge (Eure) is the correct identification. William de Percy (*c.* 1030–96) was the founder of the English dynasty, who were given the responsibility of securing the frontier against the Scots. They became the leading family in the north of England. Sir Henry Percy (1342–1408) was created the first Earl of Northumberland in 1377; his son and namesake was the famous Harry Hotspur. The earldom has continued in the same family to the present day, though it has twice descended through female lines.

The Sackvilles are a good example of a gentry family from Normandy that did not join the ranks of the barons until long after the Conquest; in their case not until the sixteenth century. By about 1070 Herbrand de Sauqueville, who had taken his surname from a manor south west of Dieppe and who served as steward to Walter Giffard, had become the lord of Fawley (Buckinghamshire). An unbroken descent can be traced to Sir Richard Sackville, who died in 1566. His son, Thomas Sackville (1536–1608), rose dramatically in the social scale. He was appointed Lord High Treasurer of England in 1599 and created the first Earl of Dorset in 1604. He acquired a suitable house for a man of such standing when he was given Knole (Kent) in 1603. The family still live in this majestic house, surrounded by its deer park, though it is now owned by the National Trust. In 1720 the seventh Earl was created the first Duke. The title lapsed upon the death of the fourth Duke and the property passed through marriage to George West, fifth Earl de la Warr, who assumed the name of Sackville-West. His son became the first Lord Sackville. Vita Sackville-West, the writer, was the daughter of the third Earl of the new creation.

Although no pedigrees survive from Norman England, aristocratic families must have been well aware of their extensive kindred, for claims that were made in litigation demonstrate a knowledge of family history that went a long way back. Such knowledge was essential for hanging on to property and in making marriages. Primogeniture was the accepted form of inheritance but, as we have seen, male lines often failed and so junior branches took their place. Naming practices gradually came to reflect concerns about inheritance, but for a long time surnames were not fixed and hereditary. Some surnames were abandoned in favour of others after a generation or two, and junior branches of a family sometimes adopted surnames that were different from those of the main line. Occasionally, a son adopted his mother's name when he inherited her land. Thus the son of Eustace FitzJohn by his first marriage to Beatrice de Vesci took the name of William de Vesci; the son of Eustace's second marriage was known as Robert FitzEustace. The family historian is even more confused by William, the son of Robert FitzWalter and Sybil de Chesney, who sometimes used his mother's surname and at other times his father's but who also called himself William the sheriff or William of Norwich. Despite these difficulties, descents can be traced through female lines to the present day from many Norman landowning families. It is very much harder to find male descendants.

Identifying Norman Locative Names

The number of people who followed Duke William to England was small compared with the total English population, probably less than 5 per cent. The better-off Englishmen who were not ruined by the Conquest gradually became bilingual, but the farmers, craftsmen and labourers who formed 85–90 per cent of the English population never learned to speak Norman French. Many of the surnames that the Normans adopted meant nothing to most English people, who found them difficult to pronounce. In later times these names were often twisted into English forms or altered by popular etymology until they were no longer recognisable. So Beaufour became Boffey or Buffey, and Bohun became Boone, Bone and Bown. Names ending in -ville were often Anglicised into – field: Blonville became Blomefield, Sémerville was turned into Somerfield, and Grenville gradually changed to Greenfield and then to Grenfell. In this way, locative surnames of Norman origin have often become indistinguishable from genuine English names. Greenfield, for instance, was formed independently in England, where it meant 'dweller by the green field'.

Such changes alert us to the need to go back to the earliest recorded forms of both surnames and place-names if we are to recognise the homes of family names. P. H. Reaney commented that some of the identifications which early forms prove must be correct may appear at first sight absurd and impossible. Thus the surnames Dabney, Dangerfield, Menzies, Scarfield and Scotney are, respectively, from the French place-names Aubigny,

Aungerville, Mesnières, Scardeville and Etocquiny. It is always unsafe to explain the origin of a surname from present-day forms.

Locative surnames prove that by the time that Domesday Book was compiled in 1086 immigrants had settled in England not just from Normandy, Brittany and Flanders, but from Anjou, Poitou, Paris and the Gâtinais. New settlers, at various social levels, continued to arrive from these districts during the next three centuries. Some are immediately recognisable from their surnames. Fleming and Flanders are obvious; Bremner, Brabner, Brabazon, Brabson, Brabyn and Brabham all came from the duchy of Brabant; Burgoyne, Burgin, Burgon and Burgan came from Burgundy; Chamness and Champney from Champagne; and Wasteneys is a corruption of Gâtinais. In *Old English Bynames* (1938) G. Tengvik used locative names to show that most of the Conqueror's followers came from the départements of Seine-Maritime and Calvados in upper Normandy, and that others came from Manche in west Normandy and from further south in Eure and Orne. His evidence is not always clear-cut but there seems little reason to doubt his general conclusions.

The origins of numerous French families can be pinpointed much more precisely than that. All research into French locative surnames that were introduced into England at or soon after the Norman Conquest must start with Lewis C. Loyd, *The Origins of Some Anglo-Norman Families* (1951).[1] Loyd established some 300 such origins for families (not necessarily now extant) who had migrated from Normandy. Many more families than these were undoubtedly Norman or from other parts of France but their precise origins remain uncertain. The cases where Loyd was satisfied with the evidence form only a small proportion of the total number. His pioneering work has now been largely superseded by Katherine Keats-Rohan, *Domesday People* (1999),[2] a magisterial account which identifies 2477 landowners in 1086, but Loyd's methods remain exemplary. He warned of the danger of assuming that all Normans in England bearing the same name came from the same place in Normandy. He showed that the Balliols had more than one origin and he distinguished three families of Mandevilles, from different places with the same name. Manneville in Seine-Maritime is the most likely home of the family name of Geoffrey de Mandeville, created Earl of Essex in 1141, but we cannot be certain. Other Mandevilles were unrelated to the barons. The poll tax returns of 1379–81 note Richard Manvyle (Berkshire), Nicholas Maundevyll and John Maundevill (Dorset), John Mandevill (Hampshire), Roger Maundevill (Isle of Wight) and Agnes Mandevyle (Leicestershire), all of whom were amongst the poorest taxpayers. John Maundevill was a lowly cottar.

The lack of documentary evidence before the thirteenth century often frustrates attempts to locate the homes of family names. If an Anglo-Norman family kept its lands in the part of Normandy from which it had taken its name until the second half of the twelfth century, the connection between place-name and surname can be made readily. Thus the de Glanvilles can be shown to hail from Glanville in Calvados, which they held until the French kings won control of Normandy in 1204. Loyd showed that even where a place-name is common it is sometimes possible to locate the home of a Norman surname by studying family history and feudal relationships. Although fifty-eight places in France are named Villiers, Loyd was able to identify Villiers-le-Sec (Calvados) as the one from which a Norman land-owning family migrated in the twelfth century. Likewise, despite the frequency of places named Aubigny (17), Beaumont (46), Ferrières (22) and Neuville (58), the original homes of certain families of Daubney, Beaumont, Ferrers and Neville were located with confidence.

Links with religious institutions sometimes provide valuable clues. The Louvetots who became the Norman lords of Hallamshire granted the great tithes of Ecclesfield parish to the Benedictine monastery of St-Wandrille in their native Normandy, an abbey which they had favoured before the Conquest. A great deal of evidence survives in the abbey's archives to suggest that the Louvetot which was the home of the family name is the place that lies less than five miles away from the abbey. Locating the home of the Furnivals, the successors to the Louvetots, presents a different problem, for the place-name has changed from its original form and at first sight other candidates seem more likely. The Furnivals came from Fourneville, a small settlement that lies a few miles south west of Honfleur. At the entrance to the village is a display board which informs us that the place was called Furnvilla in 1070 and Fournevilla by the sixteenth century. This example shows that we must match early forms of a surname with early forms of the relevant place-name.

A few more examples will demonstrate how modern surnames may differ considerably from the present forms of the place-names from which they were derived. Challis comes from Eschalles in Pas-de-Calais; Daltry (with the variants Dawtr(e)y, Daughtr(e)y, Dughtery, Da(u)lytrey, Dealtry, Doughtery, Dowtry and Ha(w)try) from Hauterive in Orne; Dansie (and the variants Dansey, Danc(e)y, Dauncey, Densey, Densie and Denzey) from Anizy in Calvados; Pinkney from Picquigny in Somme; and Samper from various places in northern France called Saint-Pierre. The Savilles probably came from from Sainville (Eure-et-Loire), but other northern French settlements are possible homes for this West Riding family name.

Another trap for the unwary is to assume that a Norman French place-name must always be found across the Channel. Some may have arisen in

England after the Conquest, for Norman French long remained the language of the elite. The surname Cowdray may come from Coudrai (Seine-Maritime) or from Coudray (Eure) but as it is a common Sussex surname it was perhaps derived from the hazel-copse which gave its name to Cowdray Park or to another copse commemorated by Cowdry Farm in Birdham. Beaumont is the name of five places in Normandy and of several others elsewhere in France but it is also a place-name in Cumberland, Essex and Lancashire. The surname is now found in many parts of England but is most common in the West Riding of Yorkshire, especially near Huddersfield, where a gentry family settled at the end of the twelfth century, perhaps from Lancashire. Beaver is another West Riding surname of unknown provenance. Perhaps it was derived from one of several places in France called Beauvoir, or from Belvoir in Leicestershire, but of course it might have started as a nickname from the animal. Flavell is another surname whose etymology is not immediately obvious. This family name is found most commonly in the midlands, a distribution that supports the view that it comes from the Normanised form of Flyford, Worcestershire. Many other examples could be given. P. H. Reaney suggests, for example, that an English origin is likely for the surnames Dellew ('by the water'), Dubois ('by the wood') and Dupont ('by the bridge'). A final complication arises when the place-name from which a Norman surname was derived has not been identified on either side of the Channel. Dammeneys provides a good example. The surname was not borne by any known baronial or knightly family but in 1381 a handful of men with this name were taxed in Berkshire, Derbyshire and Gloucestershire.

As we have noted earlier, some of the most eminent baronial families arrived in England long after the Conquest. The Courtenays of Devon, who take their name from a small town to the south of Paris, did not arrive in England until 1152, when they accompanied Queen Eleanor of Acquitaine, the new wife of Henry II. Reginald de Courtenay's marriage with the heiress of the barony of Okehampton (the largest honour in Devon) established them in south-west England. When they also acquired the honour of Plympton (the second largest in Devon) their pre-eminence was assured. But whether the John Courtenay, a humble farmer in the Isle of Wight in 1379, was descended from these mighty men is not clear. Once again, we cannot make the easy assumption that everyone with the same surname was related, even though in many cases this seems to be the case.

Finally, we ought to note that no medieval examples have been found in England of such names as Dubarry, du Boulay, Dufresnay, Duhamel and Dupuy, all of which are late names brought into England from France by Huguenots or other immigrants.

Nicknames and Patronymics

The surnames favoured by the Norman barons were mostly of the locative type, derived from places, but some of the leading men were content with patronymics (surnames derived from fathers' personal names) or with nicknames, and sometimes with occupational names such as Haimo the Steward (who was sheriff of Kent from 1077 until his death *c.* 1100). Domesday Book names Walter Giffard, the owner of 107 lordships and manors, chiefly in the south midlands, who had inherited his father's nickname, meaning 'chubby cheeks'. Contrary to what is normally claimed, it is unlikely that everyone now bearing that surname shares a common descent from Walter. The published poll tax returns of 1377–81 record several humble people with the surname Giffard: Roger Gyfford in Bedfordshire, Robert Giffard in Essex, two William Gyffards, a Walter Gifford and a Henry Gyfford in three places in Berkshire, three John Gyffards and a Robert Gifford in four settlements in Gloucestershire, and John Giffard, carpenter, and Alice Giffard, who paid the lowest rate of tax in the Isle of Wight.

The family historian needs to be suitably cautious before arriving at the conclusion that all bearers of Norman French nicknames share a common ancestry. In 1377–81 people named Bellamy ('fine friend') were found in Essex and Leicestershire, and three in Gloucestershire, one of whom was a labourer. It is unlikely that all of them were descended from the Norman baronial family. On the other hand, it is possible that the Foljambes ('withered or crippled leg') were all connected to the Derbyshire knights of this name, for in 1377–81 they were taxed only in Derbyshire and neighbouring Leicestershire: John Foliambe, armiger, and Henry Foliambe at Tideswell, and two John Foliambes nearby at Bowden and Ashford; and Roger Foliambe, esquire, and William Foliambe just across the border at Castle Donington. It is not yet clear whether any Foljambes were living at that time in other parts of the country for which we have no comparable records.

Other surnames that are Norman French in origin and which were borne by aristocratic families include Camoys ('snub-nosed'), Crispin (referring to sticking-up hair), Durant ('steadfast, obstinate', and not to be confused with the Yorkshire surname Durrans which is a corruption of the place-name Darwent), Fortescue ('valiant warrior'), Mallory ('unfortunate'), Pauncefoot ('large belly'), Pettifer ('iron foot') and Russell ('red hair'). Corbet ('little crow') was the surname bestowed on a Shropshire family which descended from a Norman baron. After the Conquest, Corbet and his sons, Robert and Roger, came to England and settled in Shropshire. Their descendant, Sir Richard Corbet, was granted land near Shrewsbury in 1223 at the place now called Moreton Corbet, where a ruined manor house may be seen. The

Corbets were still the leading Shropshire gentry family in the seventeenth century. Sir Richard Corbet of Stanwardine Park was the leading justice of the peace in the county and MP in the Protectorate Parliament of 1654–55.

The Continental-Germanic names which the Normans introduced into England quickly became fashionable, to the exclusion of the Anglo-Saxon and Scandinavian names that had previously been favoured. They formed the basis of some of the most common surnames that arose in Norman England. Some less popular surnames that developed from personal names brought in by the Normans included Allard, Beringer, Flewitt (which is found particularly in the midlands), Foulkes, Garbett, Garrett and Waring. Mingay, a surname which is now found chiefly in Norfolk, was originally a Breton personal name. The Continental-Germanic personal name Aunger was used as a surname in Essex (three times) and the Isle of Wight, when a poll tax was levied in 1381. We shall consider the implications of such a restricted geographical range for patronymic surnames in later chapters.

One of the most puzzling of these names is Talbot. Its origins are disputed but it may have come from a Continental-Germanic personal name. The family's original estate was at Sainte-Croix-sur-Buchy, north east of Rouen. Loyd noted that in 1086 Geoffrey Talebot was an under-tenant of Hugh de Gournay in Essex and that Richard Talebot was an under-tenant of Walter Giffard in Bedfordshire. An ancient Irish family of Norman origin, who have held the earldoms of Shrewsbury and Waterford since the fifteenth century, claim to be descended from this Richard but the connection has not been established. Meanwhile, other families acquired the same surname. The poll tax returns of 1377–81 name William Talpot (Berkshire), William Talbaut, farmer (Dorset), John Tolbot (Essex) and John Tabot (Kent), each of whom paid only low levels of tax.

Norman Minor Lords and Knights

The great barons were accompanied to England by retinues of knights from their estates in Normandy, Brittany, other parts of northern France and Flanders; some were their kinsmen. These retainers had to be rewarded with lands in return for the promise of military service upon demand. For example, Roger of Montgomery gave newly-won manors in Sussex and Shropshire to Warin the Bald, William Pantulf, Picot de Sai, Corbet and his sons Roger and Robert, and Gerard of Tournai, all of them men from his continental estates.

We know far less about the descent of such families than we do about the barons. They are first recorded as the smaller tenants-in-chief in Domesday Book. Documentary evidence for the two or three generations of knightly families in the hundred years after Domesday Book is very thin. W. G. Hoskins observed that the Devonshire gentry began to appear in the records during the second half of the twelfth century:

> By 1166 we hear of Ralegh, Cruwys, Kelly, Coffin, Dinham, Champernowne, Speke, Pine, Dennis and Bonville. Within a few years more we hear of Fortescue, Mank and Specott. From other sources we hear of the Aclands, the Fulfords, the Worths, the Giffards, and the Ayshfords; all before the end of the twelfth century. The first Cruwys came into Devon about the middle of the twelfth century, probably from Flanders. Most of those who crossed the Channel at the Conquest and during the succeeding hundred years arrived in Devon from Normandy – such as the Bonvilles, the Pomeroys and the Grenvilles, to name only a few of the greater.[3]

Many families of this rank who appear in late twelfth-century records for the first time may not have been descended from the subtenants of Domesday Book. The difficulty of proving links is increased by the slow way in which hereditary surnames were adopted. Few knights had acquired such names by the time of Domesday Book, though most had them by the middle of the thirteenth century. Grants from lords to retainers were rarely recorded in writing at the time, but if we discover from later records that a family held land by knight service we may reasonably assume that the original grant was made in the first three or four generations after the Conquest. Usually, we cannot be more precise than this.

Feudal links between the barons and their subtenants provide some strong clues that help us to trace knightly pedigrees before the later thirteenth century. The Mounteneys who acquired the sub-manors of Cowley and Shirecliffe, near Sheffield, can be traced back to Arnald de Mounteney, who had married a daughter of the lord of Hallamshire (from which the sub-manors were carved). Arnald's son accompanied his lord, Gerard de Furnival, on crusade and witnessed several of his local charters. The family probably took their surname from Montigni, near Rouen, not far from Louvetot, the home of the previous lords of Hallamshire. They remained an important local family until they died out in the male line in the second half of the seventeenth century. Other people with the same surname may not have been related, however, for Montigni is a common French place-name. The poll tax returns of 1381 for Essex, for example, record John Menteney, a labourer at Stebbing, and a John Mounteneye at Aythorpe Roding.

The Curzons of Kedleston Hall (Derbyshire) have a similar background but their later rise in society was much more spectacular. Loyd used their feudal relationship to the Ferrers family to show that they came from Notre-Dame-de-Courson in Calvados, near Lisieux. In 1086 Hubert held

West Lockinge (Berkshire) of Henry de Ferrers; in 1135 a Hubert de Curcun held three knights' fees of the honour of Ferrers and was succeeded by his son Robert. Richard de Curzon was living at Kedleston (which was also within the Ferrers family's sphere of influence) by the mid twelfth century. The family continued at a modest level for five hundred years then began their spectacular rise under Sir John Curzon (1598–1686), the first baronet, who expanded his estate to nearly 10,000 acres in Derbyshire, the adjoining counties of Staffordshire, Leicestershire and Nottinghamshire, and London. Sir Nathaniel Curzon (1726–1804) built the present magnificent house and surrounded it by a landscaped park. He was created the first Baron Scarsdale in 1761. His great-great-grandson, the first Marquess Curzon, was a major public figure in the late nineteenth and early twentieth centuries as Viceroy of India and later Foreign Secretary. He was also the object of the satirical rhyme:

> My name is George Nathaniel Curzon
> And I am a most superior person.

The family still live in part of the house, now owned by the National Trust.

It is not always possible to use feudal links to point to the likely origins of knightly families, however, and much of their early history remains obscure. The French place-name from which the surname Molineux seems to be derived has not been identified. All the Molineuxs are apparently descended from a knightly family that were settled in south Lancashire by the first half of the twelfth century. Richard McKinley has traced their descent from Robert de Moliness of Down-Litherland. Younger sons made the surname numerous in parts of south Lancashire. By 1379 the Molineuxs were found in Bold, Cuerdale, Liverpool, Rainhill, Samlesbury, Sefton, Sutton, Thornton and Wigan. They ranged from an esquire to men and women who had descended the social scale to the lowest ranks of taxpayers. The Molineuxs of Sefton can trace their descent from Adam, the probable grandson of the first Robert, and have remained one of Lancashire's most important families. The family name ramified in the sixteenth and seventeenth centuries, especially in south-west Lancashire. By then, people named Molineux varied considerably in their status and occupations.

Farmers and Craftsmen

The barons and the knights are of course far better known than the families who are descended from the foot soldiers who fought at Hastings or from the servants in noble households and the skilled workmen, traders and merchants who eventually settled in England. Such men were seldom mentioned in documents before the thirteenth century and then only briefly. Their family histories are unknown. Many of them took surnames from the names of the districts whence they had come. As the Plantagenet kings extended their authority over large parts of France some of these names came from further afield than before: Burgin from Burgundy, Gascoigne from Gascony, and other names from Anjou and Poitou. Sometimes immigrants moved from places that had previously provided surnames for the barons and knights. Reaney gives examples of men in thirteenth-century London who could not have been members of the aristocratic families whose names they bore: William de Furnival, tailor, John de Maundeville, brewer, Thomas de Neville, woodmonger, and Thomas Seyncler, haymonger. Others bore locative surnames that had never been adopted by baronial families: Henry de Arras, vintner, Thomas de Boloyne, merchant, or John de Paris, cook. Many more were simply called French, France or Frenchman.

Lacy provides us with a good example of a French surname that was borne not only by Norman barons but by later immigrants of much more humble status. The surname comes from Lassy in the département of Calvados, about twenty-five miles south of Bayeux. Two brothers came to England at the Norman Conquest. Ilbert (the elder), a follower of Odo, Bishop of Bayeux, was rewarded with lands in the midlands and later was made lord of the new honour of Pontefract. Walter (the younger) attached himself to William FitzOsbern and was based at Weobley (Herefordshire). The two branches of the family were very important barons in the west and the north of England throughout the twelfth century. At the same time, they kept their estates in Normandy. Ilbert's line failed but his neice married Robert FitzEustace; and when their grandson inherited the estates he adopted the Lacy name. This line continued until Henry de Lacy II, Earl of Lincoln, died in 1311, when the estates passed to Henry's daughter, Alice, the wife of Thomas, Earl of Lancaster. Walter de Lacy's descendants are still found in the male line in Ireland. When we consult the published returns of the poll taxes of 1377–81, we find numerous Lacys recorded. It is possible that Joan, Robert and William Lacy, who paid at the lowest rate of 4d. in three separate Herefordshire townships, were descended from cadet lines of Walter de Lacy's family at Weobley; but when we find farmers and labourers called Lacy paying the bottom rate of tax in Berkshire, Essex, Gloucestershire (three), the Isle of Wight, Kent and Leicestershire (three) we are ready to believe that they were more likely to have had separate origins from later immigrants. Hanks and Hodges inform us that the surname Lacy is now most commonly found in Nottinghamshire (which has no printed poll tax returns). Nine households of Lacys were recorded in the Nottinghamshire hearth tax returns of 1674 (six of them with only one hearth and the others with two or three) and seven Lacys (six with only one hearth, the other with three) were recorded in the southern half of the neighbouring county of Derbyshire in similar returns in 1670. It seems likely that most English people who bear the surname Lacy today are not descended from the Norman warriors but from much humbler immigrants.

Montgomery is a similar example but one with a couple of twists to it. A Roger de Montgomery was lord of St-Germain-de-Montgomery in Calvados in the first half of the eleventh century. His son and namesake remained in Normandy as regent during the invasion of 1066 but was summoned to England the following year and given estates in Sussex (with a castle at Arundel) and the earldom of Shrewsbury (with extensive possessions in the Welsh Marches). This younger Roger de Montgomery had at least five sons, two of whom used the name de Montgomery, while the remaining three were known by three different bynames, which were not inherited from their father. The second twist to the tale is that Roger built an enormous castle about a mile to the west of Offa's Dyke and named it and the town that grew alongside it Montgomery, after his estate in Normandy. The result of all this is that some of Roger's male descendants were not called Montgomery, while some of the present-day Montgomerys probably owe their surname to the town on the Welsh border and not to the baronial family.

The French Presence in the Late Fourteenth Century

English villages are often distinguished by the addition of the name of a Norman lord or lady of the manor, names such as Worth Matravers (Dorset), Hooton Pagnell (Yorkshire) or Kibworth Beauchamp (Leicestershire), but on the whole the Norman families which had given their names to their settlements were no longer there by the later fourteenth century. A rare exception in the published poll tax returns of 1377–81 is found in Leicestershire in 1379, where Ralph Turville, esquire, was the lord of Normanton Turville. Of course, many examples could be quoted of Norman landowners who were long resident without ever giving their names to the place where they resided, but the disappearance of families from the manors which they had once owned alerts us to changes of fortune, movement to fresh pastures and the failure to keep producing male heirs that was more characteristic of medieval England that we might have expected.

The publication of the first volume of *The Poll Taxes of 1377, 1379 and 1381* allows us to make some assessment of the numbers and whereabouts of French immigrants in the late fourteenth century.[4] The returns are unsatisfactory in their coverage, because they simply do not survive for many counties or are incomplete, but they are the best source that we have for identifying distribution patterns for surnames close to the period of formation. They help us to locate the homes of numerous family names and to discover the sort of places where immigrants had settled.

The surnames French, France and Frenchman were found in each of the counties for which returns have survived, in some cases in surprising numbers. These names were not adopted by Norman barons and knights but were surnames given to farmers, craftsmen and labourers of French origin by their neighbours in their new settlements. We have no way of knowing how many generations had passed between the bestowal of the surname and the recording of a descendant in 1377–81. Some of those who paid tax in those years may have been the first bearers of the surname but most were probably thoroughly Anglicised by then. Lancashire may have been exceptional, however, for this was a part of England where many surnames were newly formed and some had not yet become fixed. The Lancashire taxpayers included Gylowe le Frencheman and Janyn le Frencheman, two farmers in Rixton-with-Glazebrook, and fourteen others labelled le Frensh, de Fraunce, Franch, de Franse or Alice Frenshewyf.

Nor do we know how people of French descent had come to live in remote villages such as Eyam in the Peak District or in Cheselbourne, Iwerne Courtenay, Osmington, Pulston, Tyneham and Waterston in Dorset. In Berkshire John Fraunch and John, William, Alice and Joan Franch lived in East Challow and ten other places in the county each had a single family named French. In Herefordshire eight households named French paid the lowest rate of tax. In Leicestershire seven householders named Frenchman and seven other people with similar names lived in thirteen scattered places; all but John Fraunch, artificer, who was taxed 6d. at Wymeswold, paid the lowest rate. A few families named French, France, etc. lived in towns – Bakewell, Canterbury, Chelmsford, Colchester, Derby, Luton and Weobley – but most lived deep in the countryside. They were poor farmers and labourers, on the whole, with a couple of tailors and a tanner. No one had sufficient wealth to attract undue attention from the tax collectors.

Some farmers and workers from Brabant had also settled in parts of the English countryside. Thirty taxpayers named Braban, Brabayne or Brabourne were recorded in ones or twos in the surviving returns that have been printed. None appeared in Dorset or the Isle of Wight but five had settled in Lancashire. In 1379 fourteen householders with these distinctive surnames were taxed 4d. each in Leicestershire. Their first names were the common ones of the time and do not betray a Low Countries origin. The Brabans were living in twelve villages and small towns in different parts of Leicestershire. They seem to have been no different from their neighbours except for their distinctive surnames.

The Flemings have a different pattern. The printed poll tax returns for Derbyshire, Dorset, Gloucestershire, Herefordshire and Lancashire have no householders with this surname and Leicestershire had only John Flemyng at Bagworth. Four Flemings lived modestly in the Isle of Wight, one was based in Rochester and another four were taxed in the Berkshire towns of Faringdon, Newbury and Reading. These migrants were outnumbered by the nineteen Flemings who were taxed in Essex alone. Colchester had eight Flemings – including Ermingard and Hammus Flemyng – as well as a John Duch, two John Gaunts and two William Gaunts (from Ghent), Alice and Robert Haus, John van Myre and Reginald van Trude. John Trumpe was a freeholder at Steeple Bumpstead and Christine and Bricard Verbeer were taxed at Willingale. Other Flemings were found at Bocking, Braintree, Broxted, Great Dunmow, Pleshey, Runwell and Stebbing. Significantly, three of the Flemings were recorded as *textor*, textile worker. Many more Flemish textile workers had settled in Norfolk and Suffolk, but no printed poll tax returns are at hand. Only a handful of Flemings or Dutchmen were recorded elsewhere in the country: John de Ipre, the lord of Ufton Robert (Berkshire), Nicholas de Verdon (Derby), William Gaunt of Thruxton (Herefordshire) and John le Duchemon, a labourer of Walton-le-Dale (Lancashire).

The Bretons are not easy to distinguish for it is very likely that in some counties people named Breton took their names from English villages, so-called because of the survival of a Celtic population, rather than from migrants from Brittany. In any case the numbers were not large. Other French regional names were rare indeed: Hugh Burgoyn (Darley, Derbyshire), John Burgoyn (Lonsdale wapentake, Lancashire), two Gascoignes on the Isle of Wight and Geoffrey Gaale [Gaul?] of Colchester. The Champeneys probably came from Champagne, though various villages in France might also have been a source for this name. They were recorded in the Isle of Wight (three), Essex (two) and in Gloucestershire, Canterbury and the Cinque Ports. To these we should add nine people called Paris, who lived in places as far apart as the Isle of Wight and Carlisle or as Gloucestershire from Lancashire.

It is clear from all this that many of the French families that had settled in various parts of England by the late fourteenth century had no connection with the men who had fought at Hastings but were much later arrivals. How they chose their ultimate destinations – sometimes in villages and hamlets far distant from their native land – is a puzzle that can rarely be solved. Some families may have been attracted at first by the special privileges on offer in the new market towns: Doncaster, for instance, still has a central street called French Gate, St Albans has a French Row and Beverley has its Flemingate. Others may have been humble retainers of great Norman lords who were given land to farm, either as freeholders or tenants. Three hundred years after the Conquest, the descendants of the Frenchmen who first settled here were well integrated into English society. Only their surnames preserved the memory of their origins.

Present-day bearers of surnames that are known to have been used by the Norman aristocracy need to be wary of claiming a shared descent, though this may prove to be true in some cases. Many surnames originated with a single individual and downward social mobility was commonplace. Some of the poor farmers and craftsmen who paid a groat (4d.) when taxed by Richard II may perhaps have been descended from a succession of younger sons who had slipped down the social scale, or from those who had fought on the wrong side, or had been unfortunate or just downright stupid. But when we find poor men in places far removed from the sphere of influence of a mighty lord we need to wonder whether or not their surnames reflect a later, independent origin from the same place or indeed from another place with the same name. Genealogical methods are unlikely to solve the problem for us, for the records are thin and unsatisfactory at this early period. Sometimes they may point to a feudal context which makes a family connection possible, but such hints must be treated with the greatest caution.

A few examples will suffice to reinforce this point. The illustrious Simon de Montfort, Earl of Leicester, was born in Normandy in 1205 into the French nobility but inherited his title through his English grandmother. Present-day Mountforts, Mounfords, Mumfords, etc. are unlikely to have any connection with his family, for numerous places across the Channel are known as Montfort, which simply means 'strong hill', and in 1377–81 poor men sharing this surname were taxed in such far-flung places as Frilford and Long Wittenham (Berkshire), Waterston and Clifton Maybank (Dorset), High Laver (Essex), Twyning (Gloucestershire) and Northney (Isle of Wight). Hanks and Hodges inform us that today the surname is chiefly found in the west midlands.

The Beauchamps or Beechams certainly have more than one origin. For a start, the two families prominent in the thirteenth and fourteenth centuries in Somerset and Warwickshire seem to have been unconnected. The possible sources of the surname are numerous, for Beauchamp is a common place-name in France. The poll tax returns name Beauchamps in parts of the country well away from the seats of the great landowners. They were found in Bedfordshire, Carlisle, Derby, Dorset (two), Essex (three) and Herefordshire and they were all taxed at the lowest rates. They seem to have had no connection with the barons in the west of England.

The Colvilles take their name from Colleville in Seine-Maritime. Their descent has been traced from Philip de Colville, who in the twelfth century held land in Roxburghshire. But what are we to make of Richard Colvyle, carpenter, who paid 6*d.* tax in the Isle of Wight in 1379, or of three Colvyles in Lancashire and two in Leicestershire who each paid 4*d.* tax that same year?

A final example is Vescy, a surname which is perhaps derived from a place in La Manche, Normandy. Robert de Veci [sic] was one of the tenant-in-chiefs recorded in Domesday Book. Ivo de Vesci, lord of Alnwick, may have been his descendant. Perhaps the Thomas Vescy who was taxed 4*d.* at Carlisle in 1377 might have been connected with these Norman lords through a cadet line, but it seems unlikely that other Vescys taxed at the lowest rates in Puddletown and Bockhampton (Dorset), Hawling, Rodborough and Farmcote (Gloucestershire), and Great Easton, Great Bowden, Hallaton and Houghton-on-the-Hill were related.

We may end by noting that in a few cases Norman families of modest status sometimes rose spectacularly to the top of the social scale several centuries after the Conquest. The Duke of Westminster is now one of the wealthiest men in Britain, but his surname – Grosvenor – is derived from Norman French words meaning 'chief hunter'. In other words, the ancestor who first bore the family name was in charge of hunting arrangements in a lord's park. The family is seated in Cheshire, near where Robert le Grosvenor of Budworth was granted lands by the Earl of Chester in 1160. Their fortunes arose from the marriage in 1677 of Thomas Grosvenor and Mary Davies. Mary's inheritance included a farm that soon became desirable building land for rich Londoners. Ebury Farm is now known as Grosvenor Square and Belgrave Square.

3

The Origins of English Family Names

The Englishmen who were recorded in Domesday Book as the holders of land before the Conquest did not possess hereditary surnames but were known simply by a personal name, such as Alric, Thorald or Wulfstan. As we have seen, the great Norman landowners introduced hereditary surnames into England, but even amongst this class surnames were used at first only by a minority, for hereditary names were a recent fashion in Normandy. The need to identify themselves and their families with their estates, both in Normandy and England, seems to have motivated the great landowners to assume hereditary surnames. An interesting parallel development can be observed at the same time in the spread of the use of hereditary coats of arms, a fashion which came to England from north-west Europe during the twelfth century. Personal emblems in the form of lance flags had first appeared on the Continent in the late eleventh century and are depicted on the Bayeux Tapestry. The idea spread to shields and then to surcoats. Historians now think that coats of arms were developed for use in tournaments, where ample opportunities were afforded for vain displays, rather than as practical military devices in real battles.

The possession of a hereditary surname was not at first a mark of high status, even amongst the Norman barons. Some junior branches of baronial families are known to have adopted new surnames in the twelfth and thirteenth centuries. Nor did the convention that married women took their husband's surname take hold immediately. During the twelfth and thirteenth centuries some women continued to use the surnames that they had inherited from their fathers and some used other names which they had acquired before or after marriage. Reaney gives the examples of Cecilia de Sanford, a widow who was the daughter of Henry de Sandford, and Katharine Estmare, widow of John de Aulton and daughter of Estmer le Bouler. Occasionally, a woman married twice but continued to use her first husband's surname. Until well into the fourteenth century the rules were not fixed.

The knights who occupied the next rank of landowners usually did not acquire hereditary surnames until long after the Conquest. Many took their names from English rather than Norman estates, so we cannot use their surnames to determine whether they were of French or Low Countries origin rather than Englishmen who had survived by recognising the status quo. We may suspect that the de Ecclesalls who held a sub-manor of Hallamshire were Normans who took their names from their new English estates, rather than survivors from a pre-conquest family, but we have no means of settling the matter one way or the other. The Ralph de Ecclesall who witnessed a grant from Gerard de Furnival to Kirkstead Abbey, which can be dated before 1219, appears to have been the same man as Ralph, the son of Ralph, the son of Gilbert, who witnessed another grant to Kirkstead Abbey. The family therefore did not take an hereditary surname until they acquired the sub-manor of Ecclesall from Gerard de Furnival. Ralph and Gilbert were Norman personal names but then many Englishmen soon learned to call their sons by such names if they wished to advance under the new regime.

The rapid spread of Norman first names hinders our attempts to distinguish English lines before surnames were adopted generally. Only the Ardens and the Berkeleys can trace their descent from pre-conquest Englishmen. The Ardens are descended from Aelfwine, an Anglo-Saxon nobleman who was Sheriff of Warwickshire before the Conquest. His son, Thurkill, who was known both as de Warwick and de Arden, cooperated with the new regime and remained a great landowner. The Berkeleys of Berkeley Castle (Gloucestershire) were descended from Robert, son of Harding, who it seems (though it is not certain) was the son of an English thegn, Eadnoth. Clearly, most of us are descended from people who lived in England before the Norman Conquest, but the meagre records prevent our proving it. This does not stop people from claiming descent from Alfred the Great, Eric Bloodaxe or whoever takes their fancy but we should not believe them. Few English thegns were still in possession of their lands when Domesday Book was compiled in 1086. Alric, who held numerous manors in the south Yorkshire wapentake of Staincross both before the Conquest and in 1086, was a rare exception. His family throve under the Normans. Adam son of Sveinn son of Alric, who died in 1159, held ten knights' fees in the honours of Pontefract and Skipton and the manor of Wakefield. The male line failed with Adam, however, and no continuing descent through a female line can be shown. The inadequacy of the documentary record before the late twelfth century usually renders impossible the task of proving descent from an Anglo-Saxon or Anglo-Scandinavian forebear, even when a personal name that has been converted into a surname suggests it.

Many knightly families in the south of England, the midlands and East Anglia had taken hereditary surnames by the end of the twelfth century. By 1250 the great majority of such families possessed hereditary names. In the north of England the process took longer but the knights who were still without surnames in the fourteenth century formed only a small minority. The adoption of hereditary surnames was a slow and irregular but inexorable process.

Ordinary Families

It is commonplace to find that twelfth- and thirteenth-century deeds refer to, or were witnessed by, people who did not possess surnames. The charters assembled in the Beauchief Abbey chartulary, for example, mention among many others Adam, the son of John of the Cliffe; Adam, the son of Richard the ditcher; Adam the carter of Brincliffe; Adam the cook of Sheffield; Henry, the son of Gunnild (a female name) of Sheffield; Robert, the son of Alice, the nephew of Robert; Robert, the son of Hugh of Little Sheffield; and Wido, the son of Roger of Wadsley. John, the son of Adam at the spring in Greenhill, is recorded elsewhere as John the swane, son of Adam of Greenhill. Even the lord of Alfreton and Norton, the chief benefactor to the abbey, was referred to in a late thirteenth-century charter as Ranulf, the son of William, the son of Robert of Alfreton.

Some rich Londoners possessed hereditary names by the second half of the twelfth century. During the first half of the following century wealthy families with hereditary names were found in the leading provincial towns. Nevertheless, in the late thirteenth century many substantial burgesses were still without hereditary surnames. The first half of the fourteenth century was probably the main period during which urban families came to accept family names. By the time that poll tax was levied in 1377–81 very few townsmen and women had no surname or at least a non-hereditary byname, though of course we do not have information about the numerous people too poor to pay tax.

In the countryside the idea of hereditary surnames took longer to take hold. The fashion began to spread in southern England and East Anglia from about the middle of the thirteenth century so that by 1350 over half the rural families had firm surnames. The servile population adopted surnames at the same time as the small freeholders. Some families were still without surnames in 1377–81, however, so the process was a slow one. The poll tax return for Twycross (Leicestershire) was led by Richard the son of Herberd, esquire, who was taxed at 40*d*., but it was exceptional for a man of his status to be recorded in such a manner as late as that. The process started later in the north of England and took a century longer to complete than in the south and the midlands. The poll tax returns for Lancashire in 1379 show that many men were known simply as the son of someone, while women were frequently recorded as Agnes Spenserdoghter, Alice Flynns-doghter, Eva Jaksonwyf, Agnes Hollinadwyf, and so on. By the early fifteenth century it was rare for an English person not to have a surname, but by then three-and-a-half centuries had passed since the Norman Conquest. As in other European countries, the process had been a long drawn out one.

We do not have satisfactory sources for the long period during which individual bynames were transformed (in unorganised and haphazard ways) into hereditary surnames. A number of English counties have at least one lay subsidy return in print from the period 1290–1334 but these list only the richer inhabitants who were taxed. A lay subsidy was so-called to distinguish it from a tax on the clergy. Another name for the same tax was the tenth and fifteenth because it was levied on one-tenth of movable property in a town and one-fifteenth of similar property in the countryside. This method of taxation fell out of use in 1334 but was revived under Henry VIII. The lay subsidy of 1546 is the last that is of use to local and family historians throughout the land, though occasional assessments were made until 1623.

The poll tax returns of 1377–81 constitute a more comprehensive source and have the advantage of coming at a time when a large proportion of the population possessed hereditary surnames. No returns survive for some counties, however, and only half of the extant returns have so far been published. Collectors for each county arranged their returns by hundred or wapentake and then by vill (township) or borough. The tax was graded according to a person's rank, with 86 per cent paying the basic rate of a groat (4d.). The poor were specifically exempted but we do not know what proportion of the population fell into this category. Medieval records fall very short of being a complete census but they do list an enormous number of names. Treated carefully, they are a rich source of evidence from the period when family names were being formed.

Why Were Surnames Adopted by Everyone?

From about the middle of the twelfth century the number of male first names in general use fell sharply: whereas the Anglo-Saxons and Vikings had used a wide range of personal names, the Normans favoured very few. Just how limited the choice had become by the late fourteenth century is illustrated by the poll tax return of 1379 for Sheffield, Ecclesfield, Bradfield and Handsworth, which provides a list of forenames for 715 men, of all ranks, at a particular point in time. This return is by far the best record that we have of Hallamshire names in any one year during the middle ages. The range of forenames in use was astonishingly narrow. The list is headed by John 236 (33 per cent), William 137 (19 per cent), Thomas 85, Richard 67 and Robert 64. In other words, over half the men in Hallamshire in 1379 were called either John or William and the top five names comprised 82.4 per cent of the total. They were followed by Adam 35, Henry 28, Roger 17, Peter 12, Hugh 7, Nicholas 7, Laurence 4, Ralph 4, Gilbert 3, Stephen 3, Simon 2, Albray 1, Alexander 1, Raynald 1 and Watte 1. The 715 men shared only twenty forenames between them and nine of these occurred only one to four times. No Old English or Scandinavian names were recorded as forenames; the Norman takeover was complete. A similar picture could be drawn from local societies all over England.

The limited range of personal names in use in the middle ages meant that people had to be distinguished by another name. Their neighbours therefore used bynames when speaking of them, names which were taken either from the place where they lived, from their father or mother, from their occupation, or as a nickname. In time some of these bynames became hereditary surnames. The restricted choice of forename explains why bynames were necessary but it does not explain why they became hereditary. This is a puzzle for which we do not have a satisfactory answer.

Fashion no doubt played a large part in the spreading use of surnames but the process may also have been connected with the change from an oral culture to a written one in the manorial courts. From the 1230s onwards, and particularly after 1260, manorial courts throughout the land began to record property transactions on rolls. Local deeds became much more numerous about the same time. Systematic recording was obviously necessary to a well-run estate, but it was also to the advantage of tenants to have surnames which would help to prove a right of inheritance.

At first sight it seems significant that the period of surname formation coincided with the new method of keeping written records. It is not as simple as that. Richard McKinley has concluded that there is little sign that written records influenced the development of surnames. He has shown that many persons appeared in thirteenth- and fourteenth-century documents such as tax assessments without any surnames or bynames at all. This method of recording persisted over a long period and there is no indication that it caused any practical difficulties. Nor is there any evidence that the choice of surname was influenced by manorial clerks. The use of (often scurrilous) nicknames suggests that neighbours rather than clerks were responsible for coining them. Many surnames are derived from diminutives or pet forms of personal names which we rarely come across in medieval administrative and legal documents. It is the same in later centuries when parish registers record a man as Richard, never as Dick; or as James, not as Jim. We are probably correct in thinking that most surnames began as bynames, coined and used in local speech, long before they were written down by clerks.

If a byname was all that was needed to distinguish a person in the records, did the initiative to convert bynames into hereditary surnames come from the families themselves? Peasants were as conscious as lords of the need to secure their property. Perhaps the new fashion for written records was important after all. We cannot put our fingers on a precise reason for the universal adoption of surnames but we need to recognise a tendency for people to follow the lead of influential families and to conform to what others do. The change happened slowly but gradually until everyone came to accept that surnames were a normal feature of everyday life. Many people no doubt did not give much thought to the matter. Some individuals were recorded in medieval documents by more than one name. We cannot always be sure that someone who was known by the name of his farm in the thirteenth century was the ancestor of those who used the same farm name as a surname in later centuries. The exact point in time when a surname became fixed and hereditary usually cannot be identified. Nor shall we ever know why one man was named after his father while others took their occupational name or a nickname, or were known by their place of residence.

The choices that were available at the period of surname formation are made obvious from taxation records, such as the 'fifteenth' that was collected in 1316 and which has been published as D. and R. Cromarty, *The Wealth of Shrewsbury in the Early Fourteenth Century* (1993). This list of taxpayers suggests that in 1316 many Shrewsbury surnames had not then become hereditary but were simply bynames. Hugh, son of Hugh, and Thomas, son of Stephen, may, or may not, have been local sources of the surnames Hewson, Hughes, Stephenson or Stevens. Perhaps (but we cannot be certain) Thomas Willesone, Peter Cox, Peter Gerard, Richard Bernard and Henry Andreu had already acquired surnames that had become fixed and would be passed on to any children that they had. The form in which the name is written sounds more permanent than the form 'son of'. On the other hand, we cannot say that if Roger Moldesonne, butcher, had founded a dynasty his offspring would have been known as Moldson rather than Butcher or indeed by another name. Likewise John le Blak, butcher, may have spawned a family known as Black or Blake rather than Butcher. Some craftsmen recorded in this list may have been the first in a particular line to bear an hereditary surname taken from their trade. John le Sadeler, Thomas le Dissher, Alan le Glovere, William le Colier, John le Reve and William Whelwruyghte are possible examples. Some other craftsmen, however, were also known by the name of their place of origin. What, therefore, became the surnames of John of Lake, dyer, Richard of Upton, smith, or

Hugh of Wygan, apothecary? The records do not allow us to construct genealogies, so we cannot know the answers to these questions.

Some of the other taxpayers in Shrewsbury in 1316 had bynames that we classify as toponymic, sub-divided into either locative or topographical, in other words names from places. They include long-distance migrants, Nicholas of Grymesby and Ralph of London, and people from much nearer or even in Shrewsbury, such as Walter of Mudle (Myddle), and probably Roger Atteyate, Richard atte Wall and Nicholas in le Dich. We can point to these people as early bearers of surnames derived from places, while we cannot know if these names were passed on to their children. It is frustrating to arrive at the period of surname formation and yet not be able, in the great majority of cases, to demonstrate the exact process whereby surnames became fixed and hereditary.

Welsh Immigrants

At first sight, the distinctive Welsh surnames which are found in large numbers in England seem to offer a measure of the extent of migration from Wales over the centuries. The task of plotting the spread of Welsh surnames is, however, fraught with difficulties. It soon becomes clear that it is far from easy to determine which surnames are solely Welsh and which of them have arisen independently on both sides of the border. Even when a surname can be shown to have been formed from the Welsh language the issue is not always straightforward. Fortunately, we have T. J. and Prys Morgan, *Welsh Surnames* (1985) and John and Sheila Rowlands, *The Surnames of Wales* (1996) to act as our guides.

Early Welsh migrants were known to the English as Welshman, Walshman, Welsh, Walsh, Wallace or Wallis. Movement across the border into England was commonplace in Norman times; over a hundred men were described in Domesday Book as Waleis or Walensis. A steady stream of migrants headed for London in the later middle ages, though settlement in other parts of England was on a modest scale compared with later centuries. A rough and ready measure of Welsh settlement in some English counties is provided by the (far from complete) poll tax returns of 1377–81. In Herefordshire, where we might expect considerable Welsh settlement, the 1379 returns survive only for the two hundreds of Stretford and Webtree. They record fifteen people named Walsh (in eleven places), five Walys, one Walshman and Joan de Wales, names which suggest that Welsh migrants were scattered thinly enough to be distinguished by such means. In other parts of Herefordshire the Welsh language was sufficiently familiar to the local English population to allow the creation of surnames from Welsh personal names. In all, seventy-five surnames, including sixteen in the *ap* form used by the Welsh, can be recognised as denoting Welsh origins in these two Herefordshire hundreds.

If Herefordshire and Shropshire offered good opportunities for settlers arriving from mid Wales, other border counties were less attractive to Welsh migrants. The (full) tax return of 1381 for Gloucestershire notes far fewer Welshmen and women. The seven Walshs, two Walshmans, one Welch, one Walleye, two Goughs, two Gittings and one Howell formed an insignificant minority of the local population and were scattered across the county. Nor had many Welsh people migrated north into Lancashire by that time. The poll tax returns of 1379 for that county include only fourteen names that signify a Welsh origin: four called Walshman (including the unmistakable Yorward le Walshman, a farmer in Hindley), three named Walsh, two Waleys, four Madoks and Elizabeth, the daughter of Bronwynd. Here, as in most other counties, the Welsh migrants were taxed at the lowest rate of 4*d*.

A simple model based on distance from Wales is inadequate for explaining the choices made by migrants. It is surprising to find that in 1379 Leicestershire apparently contained far more Welsh settlers than did Gloucestershire or Lancashire. The forty-nine people who can be identified there include thirty-one with the surname Walshman (in twenty-three settlements), ten people called Walsh (in nine settlements), three Walys, one Wales, one Morgan, one Madoc, one Gryffin and one Gauge (Gough?). A much more substantial inhabitant than most of his fellow countrymen was Thomas Walsche, knight, the lord of Wanlip. By this time the surname Walshman was hereditary in the case of Agnes Walscheman (Burton-on-the-Wolds) and was probably so in other families.

Other counties had attracted very few Welsh settlers by the 1370s. Dorset had none, except a man whose name may have been Gough; the Isle of Wight knew only Philip Gryffith, armiger, who was taxed 40*d*., and Robert Waleyss, who paid 4*d*.; High Peak hundred (Derbyshire) contained only two Walchemans, both in Blackwell; and Essex had five Walleys, two Walshs, one Welsche, one Walshman, one Wales, two Gryffins and one Ewen. It also had several people whose name may have been derived from Gough. Had these Welsh people arrived in Essex via London or as seafarers? The patchy evidence from across the country suggests that a steady stream of Welsh people left their native land during the middle ages but that they were an unfamiliar sight in many parts of England. Most modern British families which possess surnames such as Walsh or Welsh have lived in England since the thirteenth or fourteenth centuries, in other words from the time when the English adopted hereditary surnames. The same may be true of many families named Gough, Madox, Griffin, etc.

I must emphasise again that the main period of surname formation lasted a long time and that the dating of the process differed between regions, with the south and the east leading the way. Although the majority of the English population had acquired hereditary surnames by the early fifteenth century, new surnames continued to appear in later centuries. The collection of a third poll tax in 1381 led to such resistance that no government dared to raise money in this way for almost three centuries. A consequence of this hostility is that we do not have comparable records during the fifteenth century and that we cannot study surnames recorded in taxation lists until the lay subsidies of Henry VIII's reign. A number of new surnames appear in sixteenth-century records but it is likely that they had been in existence for some time. They include many patronymic names ending in -son in the northern half of England. Some of these apparently new names may have been used by people who were too poor to pay tax in the fourteenth century. Others may be mutations whose original form can hardly be recognised, if at all, by the time they first appear in documents.

Before we look at each class of surname in turn, it is worth making a final point which at first glance may seem surprising. A larger variety and number of surnames were used in medieval England than at the present day, even though the population was less than one-tenth of what it is now. The decline in the number of surnames (which has been only partly offset by new names brought by immigrants) is the result of loss when male lines failed. The catastrophe of the Black Death and other pestilences in the fourteenth century reduced the English population by at least one-third, probably more. Many of the surnames or bynames recorded by P. H. Reaney were once more widespread than they are now because only one or two families with these names have survived. Some surnames thus become more regional in their distribution than they were before. Other names never had more than one source. Either way, many a surname that has survived to the present day had a single-family origin.

Patronymics

The first large category that we need to deal with here is that of surnames which were derived from a father's personal name. Very often the father's name was used without addition: men came to be called, for example, John Andrew or Thomas Richard. The great Norman landowners tended to use the prefix Fitz- to denote 'son of', hence names such as FitzAlan or Fitz-William. (It was once thought that 'Fitz' denoted bastardy but that is not the case.) Ordinary families added a simple suffix. In the southern half of England, especially in the Welsh border counties, -s was considered sufficient, so people became known as Edwards, Phillips or Williams. The suffix -son was preferred in the northern half of England and across the border in lowland Scotland. On the whole, names such as Robinson or Watkinson originated in the north, but of course exceptions to the rule can be found. Surnames cannot be fitted into watertight compartments.

Germanic personal names had become the choice of nearly everyone in northern and central France by the ninth century. The most common Germanic male names that were brought to England from Normandy were personal names which have remained in general use until today: William, Robert, Richard, Ralph, Roger, Walter, Henry, Hugh, Geoffrey and Gilbert. They were all turned in various ways into numerous surnames. Biblical and saints' names were not common at the time of the Conquest but they too soon became favourites. By the fourteenth century John was the most popular boy's name of all. The same trends are seen with girls' names. Seven names, including their pet forms, accounted for 81 per cent of the 182 female names recorded in Bradfield, Ecclesfield, Handsworth and Sheffield in the poll tax returns of 1379. They were Agnes (31), Alice (25), Joan (24), Margaret and Magot (23), Cecily (20), Isabel and Ibbot or Ebbot (13) and Matilda (12). Emma and Emmot were shared by another seven women, but no other name was recorded more than four times. Seven names appeared only once.

Despite the almost total replacement of the native aristocracy, many Anglo-Saxon or Scandinavian personal names survived long enough to form patronymic surnames. As first names they gradually fell out of favour and were rarely used as such by the time of the poll tax returns of Richard II's reign. Can we therefore conclude that their conversion into surnames happened relatively early in the process of surname formation? The dictionaries of surnames that are available are invaluable in identifying such names, for they have been compiled by people with expertise in old languages, but they rarely note the pronounced regional distribution of many of the surnames which developed from personal names. Patronymic surnames often turn out to have few rather than multiple origins. Indeed the modern bearers of this type of name can sometimes be shown to share descent from a single family. Reaney hardly mentioned this. Instead, he was concerned to tell us that a name such as Algar comes from an Old English personal name composed of elements which meant 'elf-spear'. It is highly unlikely that parents had any inkling of the ancient meanings of such names when they came to bestow them on their children in the eleventh century. Local and family historians are less interested in this sort of information than in identifying the places where such names originated and how they spread over time. Thus it of interest to find that the surname

Algar was recorded in 1377–81 in Berkshire and (on seven occasions) in Essex but not in the other counties for which we have evidence in the form of published poll tax returns. Nearly five centuries later, the deaths of only eighty-one Algars were registered in England and Wales between 1842 and 1846. They were scattered across southern England but were found especially in East Anglia and London. It seems likely that only one or two Algars were responsible for this particular surname and that we should concentrate our enquiries for them in the counties of eastern England.

Of course many personal names, especially the ones that became popular under the Normans, developed into surnames that can be found throughout the country, or at least in large parts of it. It is worth bearing in mind, however, that families with common names might have been just as rooted in a particular district over the centuries as were families with rare names which can be identified easily. For example, some of the present-day Wilsons of Sheffield can trace their ancestry back to the fourteenth-century Wilsons who lived on the edge of the moors a few miles further north at Broomhead.

The common first names were not the only ones that produced surnames which turn up repeatedly. The biblical name Abel, for instance, was recorded as a surname in 1377–81 in Berkshire, Dorset, Hampshire, Lancashire and Leicestershire and was widespread in later times. Likewise, Rolf appeared as a surname in the poll tax returns for Bedfordshire, Berkshire, Dorset, Essex, Gloucestershire, Hampshire and Herefordshire. Many more examples of such popular usage can be given.

Many other surnames which developed from personal names were, however, not spread widely and evenly. They can be judged to have had single or plural rather than multiple origins. When we search for the surname Luff(e), which developed from the Old English personal name Luffa, we find it recorded in Bedfordshire, Dorset and Essex in 1377–81, but not in the other counties for which poll tax returns have been published. Another Old English personal name was the source of a surname which was written variously as Oughtred, Outred, Ughtred, etc. This name is rarely found in our sample of poll tax returns, which record only Alice Oughtred (Isle of Wight), and Henry Outdred and John Hughtred, labourer (Leicestershire). Reaney quotes early examples from Devon, Essex, Kent, Oxfordshire and Suffolk, so the name was once more widespread. Perhaps it fell out of favour because of its unmistakable Anglo-Saxon sound. It remains a a rare surname today.

Another example with a strong regional flavour is the Old Germanic personal name Rumbald, which has given us the surnames Rumball, Rumbell, Rumbold, Rumbolt, Rumbol, Rumboll, Rumble, Rumbles and John Mortimer's fictional character Rumpole of the Bailey. These have sometimes been confused with the separate surname Rumbellow. In 1377–81 the surname was recorded twice in Essex (Bocking and Boreham) and once in Berkshire (Tilehurst). In 1842–46 various forms of the name were found scattered, though not in large numbers, in the counties of south-east England, East Anglia and the south midlands.

Sometimes a surname was derived, in circumstances which are not usually clear to us, from a feminine personal name. Agas or Aggis, for example, is from the feminine name Agace, the Latin form of Agatha. In 1377–81 poll tax was paid by John Agas (Berkshire), William Agas (Gloucestershire), Robert Agas, William Agase and three John Agases (Leicestershire). The surname became very rare in later centuries, no doubt because of the failure of male lines. Only twelve deaths of people named Agus(s), Aggus or Agase were registered in 1842–46: a few were from East London (five in Bethnal Green, one in Lambeth), the rest comprised one in Maldon, two in Depwade, one in Rotherham and two Agusts in the New Forest. Did only one family line survive from the middle ages?

Often a medieval family name has disappeared completely. Giving examples of obsolete surnames is always likely to result in enraged letters from proud survivors in remote parts of the country but I am unaware of anyone still called Raumpayne. They are absent from the indexes of deaths in England and Wales at the beginning of Queen Victoria's reign. In 1377–81 two William Raumpaynes and a Henry Raumpayne paid poll tax in Berkshire, a Robert Rumpayn was taxed in Dorset and William Rampayne paid in Leicestershire. The name does not appear in dictionaries. One that does is the surname Alwin or Alwen, which developed from the Old English personal name Aelfwine. In 1377–81 seven men and women with various spellings of this name were taxed in Berkshire, eight others were taxed in Essex, two more in Gloucestershire, two in Hampshire and two in Leicestershire. All these Alwins favoured first names which had been brought to England by the Normans. Astonishingly, the surname has declined catastrophically since these high numbers were recorded in the late fourteenth century. Just two Alwens (who had died far apart at Bromley and Stourbridge) and none with other spellings of this name were registered in the indexes of deaths in England and Wales in 1842–46.

Viking personal names have also produced numerous surnames, particularly in northern and eastern England. Gunnell, for instance, comes from the Old Norse feminine name Gunnhildr. Hanks and Hodges say that the name was extremely popular in those parts of England that were under Norse influence in the middle ages. The surname was not found in Lancashire in 1379, however, and rather surprisingly the only taxpayers with this name elsewhere were two Williams, a John and a Robert Gunheld, who paid poll tax in Bedfordshire. Reaney quotes examples from Sussex, Surrey, Lincolnshire and Norfolk. Another example is provided by the surname Kettle, which comes from the Old Norse personal name Ketil. In 1377–81 the Kettles were taxed in Cumberland, Essex (3) and Herefordshire, but were absent from many other counties.

The Normans introduced into England many personal names that were Germanic in origin. Baldwin was one that was favoured. Its popularity increased when a Crusader named Baldwin became the first Christian King of Jerusalem in 1100. The personal name became a surname, the most famous bearer being Stanley Baldwin, Prime Minister for three terms in the 1920s and 1930s. Jane Austen also possessed a surname that was derived from a personal name. She was descended from medieval Kent clothiers and her name was a shortened version of Augustine. Members of the Augustinian orders were usually known as Austin canons and friars. The Normans were of course descended from Vikings, hence their name 'the Northmen', so some Old Norse personal names were brought back into favour in post-Conquest England. Dick Turpin was one notorious bearer of such a name. An ancestor of Guy Fawkes acquired his surname from the Norman personal name, Faulques. Samuel Pepys's unusual surname came from an Old French personal name, Pepis. The family were recorded in 1290 in Cambridgeshire, where the diarist still had kinsmen four centuries later.

Some of the personal names brought to England by the Normans are no longer in favour but their popularity lasted long enough to produce widespread surnames. Everard is one such example. In 1377–81 Everards were taxed at Sulhamstead Abbots, Kingston Lisle and West Ginge (Berkshire), Bowden (Derbyshire), Cheselbourne (Dorset), Steeple Bumpstead (Essex), Charlton (Gloucestershire), Canterbury (Kent), and at Ashby-de-la-Zouch and Shangton (Leicestershire). No Everards appeared, however, in the lists for the Isle of Wight, Hampshire, Herefordshire or Lancashire. Nearly five hundred years later, in 1842–46, the deaths of only seventy-nine Everards were registered in England and Wales. They were spread across the eastern and midland counties, and twelve had died in London. The medieval poll tax returns give a reasonable idea of what the later distribution of the surname was going to be.

Other names that were introduced by the Normans never became a prolific source of surnames. A single-family origin can be proposed with some confidence for the present-day Eustaces. In 1377–81 a William Eustace was taxed in Berkshire and John Eustace, senior and junior, were taxed in the Isle of Wight, but the surname was not found in other returns and was obviously a rare one. In 1842–46 the deaths of only forty-nine Eustaces were registered in the country at large, mostly in a group of neighbouring parishes in Oxfordshire, Berkshire, south Buckinghamshire and Bedfordshire, with seven in London and another seven in or near Birmingham. The medieval Berkshire family seem a likely source of the surviving surname. It is perhaps surprising that the surname is so rare, for Eustace was a well-known first name in the middle ages. A pet form of the name gave rise to the surname Stacey.

Enough examples have been given to show that patronymic surnames can have as local or regional a distribution in different parts of England as many a toponymic or rare occupational name. They were often associated with just one small district or neighbourhood for generation after generation. Back in 1946, W. G. Hoskins argued that farming families such as the Randolfs of South Croxton, the Armstons of Cosby, the Lewins of Littlethorpe and many others can be traced back into the fourteenth century and that their surnames can be recognised as coming from Anglo-Saxon or Scandinavian personal names.[1] Family memories of ancestors were much longer in the medieval and early modern periods than they are now. Hoskins quoted a case in the High Court of Chancery in the 1530s, concerning the title of four acres of land, in which the plaintiffs, Edward Palley and his wife Joan, were able to recite Joan's pedigree going back seven generations to the fourteenth century. Joan claimed that she was the daughter of John, son of William, son of John, son of Margaret, daughter of Agnes, daughter of Robert Randolf, husbandman, who had originally been seised of this property. This Robert Randolf of South Croxton was alive in 1377, when he appeared in the poll tax return of that year. The surname survives in Leicestershire in its modern form of Randall.

The stock of patronymic surnames was increased greatly by the use of diminutives and pet names. John Gower's apocalyptic poem, *Vox Clamantis*, written soon after the rising of 1381, names the rioting peasants Watte, Thomme, Symme, Bette, Gibbe, Hykke, Colle, Geffe, Wille, Grigge, Dawe, Hobbe, Lorkyn, Hudde, Judde, Tebbe, Jakke and Hogge. Such pet and shortened forms of first names were not commonly recorded in medieval documents; indeed, first names were usually written in Latin translation. (Surnames were mostly untranslatable and so were left as they were.) Pet and short forms of names can nevertheless be recognised as the source of certain surnames, many of which have remained restricted to one part of the country or another. Mogg (a pet name for Margaret) is a west country surname: William Mogge (Alton Pancras, Dorset, 1379), William and John Mogge (Didbrook, Gloucestershire, 1381) are early examples. Morse (from Maurice) is found in eastern England, where Thomas and Robert Morse were taxed at Sturmer (Essex) in 1381.

The biblical name Absalom is such a rare surname that only sixteen deaths were registered for people with this name between 1842 and 1846. They were scattered, with no obvious cluster. In 1381 two Johns, an Alexander and a Nicholas Absolon paid poll tax in Berkshire, John and Thomas Aspeloun and a John Aspelon were taxed in Essex and Thomas Absolon paid in Hampshire, but in later times this family name fared less well. Pet forms of Absalom produced other surnames, however: Asplen, Aspling and a rare version which was eventually twisted out of recognition into Ashplant, a name which in 1842–46 had only ten registrations in the indexes of deaths, all except one in north-west Devon. The Ashplants almost certainly descended from a single individual.

Pet forms of personal names were often formed by adding -kin to a shortened version. When a surname was created from such a name an extra -s was added. The west country name name Hoskins was formed from a diminutive of various Old English personal names beginning with Os-, such as Osgood or Osborn. Tax was paid in 1377–81 by Matilda Hochekyn at Hanford (Dorset), Isabella Hockyns and John Hodkyns at Aston Subedge (Gloucestershire), and in Herefordshire by William Hoschyns and John Hoschyns at Shobdon, Alice Hochekynes at Dinedor and Roger Hoskyns at Eaton Bishop. The surname Hawkins was formed by the addition of a suffix to the personal name Hawk, usually thought to have been a pet form of Harry, but perhaps a rhyming form of Ralph (Raw). People called Hawkins are found most frequently in the west country and the west midlands. Larkin and Watkin are pet forms of Lawrence and Walter, but other cases need further investigation. Reaney's etymologies for pet names are no longer considered reliable.

Another way of creating a pet name, from the twelfth century onwards, was to add the suffix -cock to a shortened form of one of the personal names that had been brought into England by the Normans. Wilcock is straightforward but some names of this type are not immediately obvious. Battcock comes from Bartholomew, Hancock from Henry or Johan, Hitchcock via a rhyming form from Richard. It is easy to confuse such names with those which end in -cot or -cote or with nicknames from birds, such as Woodcock or Peacock. More pet names came about by the addition of -ot, -mot, -et, -on, -in, -y and other suffixes to shortened names. Hewlett from Hugh is obvious, but Tebbitt or Tebbutt from Theobald or Batty from Bartholomew are not immediately clear, while Gillott could have been derived from Giles, Julian or William (French Guillaume). Marriott and Emmott are two examples of surnames that were derived in this way from feminine names.

As we have seen, patronymic surnames were often formed by the addition of short suffixes and that -s was favoured in the southern half of the country, particularly in the Welsh border counties, whereas northerners generally opted for -son. The surname Phillips, for example, is often considered to be Welsh but it is not exclusively so. Taxpayers in 1377–81 were recorded with this name in five places in Hampshire (four of them in the Isle of Wight), in one Gloucestershire village and in two settlements in Hereford-shire. The Gloucestershire poll tax returns of 1381 record many individuals with this type of name: Adams, Cocks, Collins, Ellis, Gibbs, Harris, Hawkins, Hicks, Hobbs, Hughes, Jennings, Jones, Morris, Phillips, Richards, Robins, Stephens, Thomas, Tomkins, Watts, Wilcocks and Williams. William Tyn-dale, the first translator of the Bible into English, was known as Huchyns when he lived in Gloucestershire.

The poll tax returns for Lancashire in 1379 have a very different appearance from those of the Welsh borders. Names ending in -s are rare and those ending in -son are common. Many men still did not possess surnames but were recorded as *filius de* (son of). Perhaps they eventually acquired patronymic surnames ending in -son. At the same time, a number of females were recorded with names ending in -doghter, -mayden, or -wyf. It is unlikely that these grew into hereditary surnames. If they did, they were soon abandoned.

Nicknames

Two of the boys I was at school with were known as 'Tangy' Plant and 'Slosh' Berry. I cannot remember their real first names and I have no idea how they acquired their nicknames. Those of my contemporaries who remember me know me as Youngus and still greet me by that name. Hardly any of them recall that this nickname arose from our first German lesson when the teacher gave us all German names. Mine was Hans Müller, but that was also the name of the boy in our first text book. On page one we read 'Müller ist ein Junge' (Müller is a boy). This amused the class, I was called Junge, which soon became Junges. Nearly fifty years later I am still known by this nickname. The reason I tell this trivial story is to illustrate how it is usually impossible for outsiders to judge the circumstances under which a nickname was bestowed. Nicknames were and are formed for the most trivial and ephemeral reasons which are often soon forgotten by friends and neighbours. How difficult then it is for us to understand how and why people acquired nicknames in the middle ages. It is even more puzzling to understand how a nickname became a hereditary surname. The bearers of such names probably had no choice in the matter if their neighbours persisted in referring to them by such means.

How did William Goldeneye, who was taxed at East Hendred (Berkshire) in 1381 get his nickname? Presumably one of his eyes had some peculiarity, but beyond that we can say little with certainty. And how did his contemporaries, Henry Wasp and John Wasp of Essex, come to possess such a name? Perhaps they or an ancestor irritated their neighbours or perhaps they were aggressive or a downright nuisance, but we cannot be sure. The obscene and coarse nicknames that were frequently recorded in medieval documents have disappeared or have been changed into something unrecognisable. It is not immediately apparent, for example, that Topliss is a corruption of Toplady or Tiplady, which is thought to have been a name for a philanderer. Some changes were quite subtle, as when the Yorkshire name Smallbehind became Smallbent.

Nicknames were formed at all levels of society, as we have seen with William the Conqueror's sons. Norman French words have given us surnames such as Foljambe ('deformed leg'), Foliot ('to play the fool, to dance') and Papillon ('butterfly, inconstant, imprudent'). In Essex in 1381 John and William Pamphilonn were taxed at High Easter and their namesakes were taxed at Thaxted. At the same time, another John Pampilon, a labourer, lived in the Isle of Wight. These examples alert us to the fact that some nicknames are not immediately recognisable as such. We are dependent upon the expertise in old languages of the compilers of the standard dictionaries. We learn, for instance, that the surname Bligh is derived from an Old English word meaning a cheerful person. This seems singularly inappropriate for William Bligh (1754–1817), the captain of the *Bounty*, but later bearers of a name do not always have the same disposition as their ancestors.

Some nicknames were the result of neighbours' amusement at a man's frequent use of a favourite exclamation. Godbehere is literally 'God be here!'. It has sometimes been confused with the similar surnames, Godber and Godbear, which appear to be variants of the personal name Godbert. None of these names can come from 'good beer', as beer did not replace ale as a common drink until after the period of surname formation. A Robert Godebere was recorded in Sussex in 1296. Hanks and Hodges note that Godber is essentially an east midlands surname, found especially in Derbyshire and Nottinghamshire. In the 1980s the Sheffield telephone directory listed sixty-nine Godbeheres and seventeen Godbers. Nationwide, the 716 subscribers included 116 Godbeheres, fourteen Godbehears and seventy-eight Goodbyers, the rest being Godbers and variants of that name.

Common nicknames such as Fox, Grey, White and Short became surnames in many different parts of the country and so did nicknames like Halliday (born on a holy day) and Christmas (which is found in East Anglia and southern England). It is hard to say exactly why some men were given the nickname Duck but it was coined in several parts of England. Ducks were found in the poll tax returns of 1377–81 in Berkshire, Essex, Gloucestershire, Kent, Lancashire and Leicestershire. Hurlbatt or Hurlbutt was less common, being restricted to certain southern counties. It was a nickname taken from a medieval game, but the precise connotation remains mysterious. Reaney quotes examples from Essex (1327) and Hampshire (1333). Half a century later, Hurlbatts were taxed at Bocking, Braintree, Colchester and Tolleshunt Knights (Essex), Denmead (Hampshire) and Marsh Benham (Berkshire). These counties seem to be the homes of this unusual name.

Hurlbatt is an example of a nickname-turned-surname which originated with only a few families. We may reasonably suspect that some surnames in this category arose from a single individual. Rust, a nickname for someone with red hair or a ruddy complexion, was found only in East Anglia, Essex and London at the beginning of Victoria's reign. Perhaps the Adam Rust who was taxed in Essex in 1381 was a common ancestor. Later distributions of rare names suggest such lines of thought but of course we then have to conduct the detailed genealogical enquiry that might establish or disprove the hypothesis. We are led to wonder whether another Essex taxpayer, John Ramage, was the unique source of his rare name, which in the 1840s was found mostly in or near London (and in Scotland, where it probably has separate origins). Ramage appears to have been a nickname for a savage or unpredictable individual, which came from Middle English and Old French words for a bird of prey. The rarity of the name suggests that it is worth investigating. Another uncommon name is Freebody, which was given to someone who was a freeholder, not a serf. The English population contained thousands of freemen but some local circumstance must have given rise to the surname. John, Richard, Isabella, Agnes and Julian Frebody, apparently all members of the same family, were taxed at Faringdon (Berkshire) in 1381. The name was not recorded in other county lists.

Wildgoose is a name that was perhaps bestowed on a shy, retiring person, but we have no way of telling. The sixty bearers of this name who died between 1842 and 1846 were concentrated in and around Derbyshire, with twenty-six in the Bakewell registration district (Map 20, p. 214). A John Wildegos was recorded across the Staffordshire boundary at Bradnop in 1327. There is a fair chance that he was the only person who acquired his surname from this nickname, so that all the present Wildgooses are descended from him.

We end this section with two surnames that are associated in the popular mind with the Wild West of America. Earp was a nickname for a 'swarthy' man. In Victorian times it was a Birmingham – Black Country – south Staffordshire name, with only seventy-five entries in the indexes of deaths

1. Thomas Cranmer (1489–1556), Archbishop of Canterbury.
Although he was born in Nottinghamshire, the family name probably came from
Cranmore (Somerset). (*National Portrait Gallery*)

ANNA BOLINA VXOR- · · · HENRI· OCTA

2. Anne Boleyn (1507–1536), King Henry VIII's second wife and mother of Queen Elizabeth I. Boleyn is one of several variant spellings of Bullen, a name which is derived from Boulogne. (*National Portrait Gallery*)

3. Nell Gwynn (1650–1687), actress and mistress of King Charles II.
Gwynn is a Welsh word meaning 'light, white, fair', which was given to someone
with fair hair or a pale complexion. Nell came from Hereford, not far from the
Welsh border. (*National Portrait Gallery*)

4. Samuel Pepys (1633–1703). The name is the Old French *Pepis*, which was introduced into England by the Normans. It seems to have been a nickname, meaning 'terrible' or 'awesome', that was given to several Frankish kings, including Charlemagne's father. (*National Portrait Gallery*)

5. Charles Dodgson (1832–1898), better known by his pen name, Lewis Carroll. The name means 'son of Dogge', a pet form of Roger. (*National Portrait Gallery*)

6. Mrs Isabella Beeton (1836–1865), who wrote her famous cookery books
at the surprisingly young age of twenty-two and twenty-three.
Beeton or Beaton is derived from Béthome in Picardy, perhaps also from a
pet form of Beatrice. (*National Portrait Gallery*)

7. Alfred Lord Tennyson, Poet Laureate (1809–1892).
The name means 'son of Dennis'. (*National Portrait Gallery*)

8. Mrs Emmeline Pankhurst (1858–1928), founder of the Suffragettes. The surname was once thought to have been derived from Pentecost, but it has been shown to come from a small place called Pinkhurst in Sussex. (*National Portrait Gallery*)

in 1842–46. Eight households of Earps were taxed in Staffordshire in 1666. In 1532–33 the Earps were living only in Tamworth and Yoxall. A common descent to Wyatt Earp from one swarthy Staffordshire man in the middle ages seems more than likely. Custard is one of those nicknames which send the amateur etymologist down the wrong path. It was originally Costard, which in the middle ages was the name of a popular variety of large apple. The Berkshire taxpayers of 1381 included Ingeram Costard (Barcote), William Costard (Buckland), Agnes Costard (Nunhide) and Matilda Costard (Sul-ham). But having established the original form of the name and its restricted distribution, we are puzzled as to how to classify it. Is it a nickname or an occupational name? In fact, it was known as a personal name before it became a surname. Coster and Custer are variant forms. Did General Custer, whose last stand was on the Little Bighorn in Montana in 1876, have Berkshire ancestors, we wonder? The answer is no, his name was an Anglicised form of the Dutch surname Köster.

Occupational Surnames

Surnames derived from occupations can be found at a very early date. Domesday Book distinguishes some people by occupational names, though they had not then become hereditary but were simply bynames that were not passed on to succeeding generations. This category includes names which came from the holding of an office, names such as Sheriff, Constable, Reeve, Bishop, Abbot, etc., together with those names which denoted rank or status, for example Lord, Burgess, Freeman or Cotter. Most of these ranks are familiar to us but surnames such as Franklin or Vavasour (a Norman French word for a vassal-in-chief or feudal tenant below the rank of a baron) reflect a precise status that no longer has a meaning.

Categories of surnames created by historians have to allow for imprecision and overlap. What at first sight might appear to be status names, such as King, Prince, Bishop, Knight or Squire, were so numerous by the end of the thirteenth century that they must have started as nicknames. We have no evidence that people bearing such names were ever descended from real kings or princes, even in illegitimate lines, nor that they were retainers or servants of such mighty people. Many early examples can be quoted of serfs and other men of humble status who possessed such names. In 1379, for instance, William le Duke, was assessed at the lowest rate of tax at Lowton-with-Kenyon (Lancashire).

Some men with occupational surnames were still practising the trades of their ancestors in the late fourteenth century. Essex taxpayers in 1381 included Robert Carder, cardmaker (Bocking), and John Wryghte, carpenter

(Chelmsford). But many contrary examples can be quoted of men who had turned to other trades by that time. Another John Wryghte of Chelmsford worked as a chandler and in the tax returns for south Yorkshire in 1379 we find a butcher named John Walker, a skinner named William Taylor and a tailor named Richard Smith. Many more such examples could be given. For example, the father and grandfather of Geoffrey Chaucer, the first major poet to write in English, were both vintners, but their surname was derived from a French word for a maker of leggings. Geoffrey was born about 1343 but would have had no memory of the ancestor who earned his living in that way.

The occupational names which are amongst the most common English surnames today – Smith, Taylor, Turner, Wright and so on – were already numerous by the thirteenth century. These trades were practised throughout the country but, as no more than one or two men worked in each village, the occupational name was distinctive and so was readily chosen as a surname. Where a lot of people were involved in the same trade, they could not be distinguished from each other by occupational surnames. Cutler is not a common surname in and around Sheffield; Potter is not very common in Stoke-on-Trent. Few surnames are derived from any of the tasks involved in arable farming because everyone shared the same work, whereas a single shepherd could look after all the sheep. Even so, we do have some problems explaining the distribution of popular occupational names, for they are not spread evenly.

While identifying names in this category is straightforward when dealing with the examples quoted so far, many medieval occupations have become obsolete and so have the terms that were used to describe them. An arblaster, for instance, made cross-bows. Thomas Arblaster (Cropston) and Alice Arblaster (Thurcaston) paid tax in Leicestershire in 1379 and John Arblaster paid in West Hendred (Berkshire) two years later. The decline of the trade may explain why the surname was sometimes changed over time to Alabaster. Making paternosters or rosaries was a medieval trade for which there was little demand after the Reformation. The name comes from the first two words in the Latin version of the Lord's Prayer and is commemorated by Paternoster Row near St Paul's, where the London booksellers had their shops and stalls. In 1379 three John Paternosters and a Robert, William and Alice Paternoster were taxed in the neighbouring Bedfordshire parishes of Dunton and Millow and Nicholas Paternoster was taxed nearby in Biggleswade. Two years later, two Paternosters were taxed in Pusey (Berkshire) and Theydon Bois (Essex) but the name was not found in the other counties for which we have printed returns.

Some occupational surnames mislead us because the meanings of words have altered over the centuries. A collier was not a coal miner but a charcoal burner, which is why Colliers End is a place in Hertfordshire, well away from any coalfield, and why people surnamed Colyer or Collier are found in many different parts of England. In 1377–81 they were recorded as tax-payers in Berkshire, Essex, Gloucestershire, the Isle of Wight, Lancashire and Leicestershire and were no doubt found elsewhere. An engineer was originally a designer of military machines. The surname Jenner is found chiefly in Kent and Sussex, though Edward Jenner, the discoverer of the technique of vaccination, was a doctor in Gloucestershire. A spooner was someone who covered roofs with shingles. During the fourteenth century, however, the word spoon acquired its modern sense, so in some cases the surname may refer to a maker of wooden or horn spoons. Spooner is mainly a northern name, though Robert Spooner was recorded at Sileby (Leicestershire) in 1379. Corker is another north country name, found particularly in Yorkshire and Lancashire. Three Corkers paid poll tax in Lancashire in 1379. The name has nothing to do with corks but was applied to a seller of purple dye. A further example is Crowther, a surname for a player of a particular kind of fiddle. John le Crouther (Chorlton) and William le Crowther (Walton-on-the-Hill) lived in Lancashire in 1379.

Other occupational terms have obvious meanings, even though people no longer perform such tasks. Amongst the taxpayers of 1377–81 were Robert Garlicmonger (Leicestershire), Felicia Pouchemaker and Richard Pouche-maker (Leicestershire), John Mosterdmaker (Gloucestershire) and William Cappemaker, Agnes Arwesmyth, John Dysshwarde, Thomas Dysshewarde, John Dysshward and John Maltgrinder (all from Colchester).

Some common occupations became known by feminine forms of the words that were used to describe them, even though the earliest recorded bearers of such names were often male. Women are presumed to have done these jobs long before records began or surnames were formed. Thus the common surname Webster is derived from the feminine form of weaver, Brewster is the feminine version of brewer, and Baxter comes from the feminine word for a baker. The various forms of these names have different regional distributions. A Kember or Kembster was a comber of wool or flax. Two John Kemberes, Adam and Matilda Kembere, Christine Kembstere and Nicholas Kymbere (Berkshire), two more John Kemberes and Eustace Kemberes (Dorset), Alice and John Kembar, and Emota Kumber (Herefordshire), John Kembestre (Isle of Wight) and Beatrice Kembestere (Kent) were amongst those who paid tax in 1377–81.

Occupational surnames which now sound strange to us were sometimes derived from Norman French words. The Yorkshire surname Frobisher, borne by the Elizabethan seaman, Sir Martin Frobisher, comes from an

Old French term for a 'furbisher' of armour. Hansard was an Old French term for a cutlass or dagger, which became the source of a surname for a maker of such weapons. A family with this name held land in Surrey and Sussex from the late thirteenth century, but Luke Hansard (1752–1818), the originator of the official verbatim report of parliamentary proceedings, was a Norwich man who moved to London. The more widespread name Parmenter comes from the Old French word for a tailor. Three Parmenters were taxed in Essex and four were assessed in Leicestershire in 1377–81. It is not unusual to find Norman French and Old English words for the same occupation each producing surnames. The English Wright is paralleled by the French Carpenter, the English Knifesmith (hence the surname Nasmyth) by the French Cutler. Regional dialect words for the same occupation have produced yet more variety in the development of surnames. A fuller in the cloth trade was known as a walker in parts of the country, especially the north, as a tucker in south-west England, and as a bowker in parts of south-east Lancashire, so we have four surnames instead of one. Devon dialect has given us not only Tucker but other occupational surnames, such as Helier, Webber, Crokker and Clouter.

Surnames derived from the rarer crafts are usually restricted in their distribution to certain districts. Arkwright is a Lancashire name that seems to have a single-family origin (see Map 6, p. 200). Sir Richard Arkwright made his fortune in cotton spinning in Derbyshire but was born in Preston, close to where his surname originated. A few of these rare names have multiplied locally in later centuries. Rimmer, literally a rhymer or poet, ramified in south Lancashire; Trinder, a braider, has spread over a part of Oxfordshire; and Tranter, a carrier or hawker, has proliferated in Shropshire. These rare occupational surnames are as distinctive as the toponymic names which have not spread far from their point of origin.

A jagger was a man in charge of packhorses which carried heavy loads. The surname was recorded in Derbyshire in 1306 and 1318 in places where it is likely that lead ore was the load that was carried. In the West Riding of Yorkshire jaggers transported coal. Jagger's Lane, Emley, is one of the old ridge-routes along which they travelled. The West Riding is the home of the surviving surname. About half of the 1391 Jaggers listed in recent telephone directories live there. The Jaggers are descended from packhorse men, not from the German Jäger (hunter), as has sometimes been claimed.

The Bolers were lead smelters. In the middle ages smelting took place on windy ridges, some of which are still marked as Bole Hill on modern Ordnance Survey maps. All the Bolers who were taxpayers in 1377–81 in the counties for which we have published returns were from the High Peak of Derbyshire: at Ashford, Baslow, Darley, Tideswell and Wormhill. We might expect to find a similar spread of the surname Leadbeater or of the variant names Ledbetter and Leadbitter, but in fact they were not confined to lead mining or smelting areas because the beating of lead into tanks, pipes or other shapes generally took place not where the lead was smelted but at the site to which it was taken, such as an abbey. The only Leadbeaters recorded in the High Peak in 1381 were two William Ledebeters of Ashford and Tideswell. The surname occurs 1552 times in the current telephone directories for England and Wales and is spread widely.

The rarity and limited distribution of some occupational surnames points unerringly to single-family origins. Kellogg is an occupational name, not for a manufacturer of corn flakes but for a pork butcher, literally 'kill hog'. In Essex in 1381 William Kelhog was taxed at Magdalen Laver. Reaney's early examples of the name are from Essex: Geoffrey Kyllehog in 1277 and Walter Kelehoog in 1369. Hanks and Hodges note that Joseph Kellogg of Great Leighs, Essex, emigrated to Connecticut in 1651 and that among his descendants were Albert Kellogg (1813–87), an eminent botanist, son of a prosperous farming family, and William Kellogg (1830–1918), who became Governor of Louisiana. Other Americans include Frank Billings Kellogg (1856–1937), the American Secretary of State who was awarded the Nobel Peace Prize in 1929, and John Harvey Kellogg, who in 1907 started his corn flakes business. No Kellogg deaths were registered in England and Wales in 1842–46. This supports the suggestion that all the Kelloggs were descended from just one Essex pork butcher. Emigration may well explain the disappearance of rare names such as this.

Specialist jobs involving livestock produced other surnames. In 1379 Robert Gyldhog was taxed at Wyboston (Bedfordshire) and the return for Flitwick in the same county included Stephen Hogeman, senior and junior, and Henry Hogeman, so perhaps that surname, though not necessarily the occupation, had become hereditary. The names of those who looked after animals have produced several distinctive surnames. Shepherds are found in most parts of the country; the Cowards who saw to the cows were also numerous. They were men and boys of low status who paid only the basic groat when taxed. In 1377–81 we find Cowards, Cowherdes and Couhirdes in Berkshire, Dorset, Essex, Gloucestershire, Hampshire, and in Lancashire, where John le Cowehird looked after the cows of Pendleton Chase. Leicestershire taxpayers included Richard Couherdman of Burton-on-the-Wolds and six other men named Couherd, Couherde, Couhird, Cowherd or Cowherde. Neither the Derbyshire High Peak nor the Isle of Wight had anyone with these surnames at that time.

Oxenard is the main form of the surname that has come down to us from the keepers of oxen. In 1377–81 Berkshire had nine Oxenherdes in eight villages. No one of this name was taxed in Dorset, Essex or Lancashire, but the Derbyshire return noted Richard le Oxhurde at Wormhill, high in the Peak District. Gloucestershire had a John Oxeman (Shipton) and a John Oxhurde (Lechlade) and the Leicestershire return included Thomas Oxman (Owston), William Oxherd (Great Stretton), John Oxherd of the Park (Belton), John Oxman (Nevill Holt) and Henry Oxherd (Gaddesby). It is noticeable that the Leicestershire ox-keepers were found in villages that were owned by a squire or which had shrunk in size almost to the point of desertion. In contrast, no such men were found in the hundred of Sparkenhoe, which had a different agrarian history.

Neatherd was an alternative name for the keeper of a village's cattle. In the counties for which we have published poll tax returns, this name was found only in Yorkshire and in Leicestershire, where thirty-five men with names spelt Netherd, Netherd, Neetherd, Netard, etc. were recorded in thirty-five villages. Again, few keepers were listed in Sparkenhoe hundred. Neate, which has the same meaning, is a north Wiltshire name, so rare and confined that a single-family origin seems certain.

We have not yet finished with surnames bestowed on the keepers of livestock. Swineherd is a rare surname that was found only in Leicestershire in our 1377–81 tax sample, with one each at Lubenham, Freeley, Burton-on-the-Wolds, Humberstone, Frisby-on-the-Wreake and Ratcliffe-on-the-Wreake. The Hogherds or Hoggarts were much more common, though they may have looked after young sheep rather than pigs. Hogherds, Hoghurds and Hogherdes were recorded in 1377–81 in Berkshire, Dorset, Gloucestershire, Hampshire and Leicestershire and two Hogmans were taxed in Berkshire and Essex. The Wetherherds, who looked after the castrated rams, were found in Berkshire, Derbyshire, Dorset, Gloucestershire and the Isle of Wight. Two Eweherds lived in Berkshire and Gloucestershire and in our sample the Herdmans were confined to Derbyshire, Dorset and Leicestershire.

Toponymic Names

Historians refer to the large category of surnames that are derived from place-names as toponyms. These they divide into *locatives* (from specific places) and *topographical names* (from general features of the landscape). Families acquired surnames from places in two different ways; by owning or renting property there or upon moving away to another settlement.

The great majority of English villages are named in Domesday Book. They were settled long before anyone in this country acquired a surname. The study of place-names is therefore a subject that is largely separate from an investigation of the origins and spread of family names. The Anglo-Saxons or Scandinavians who are commemorated in place-names were not the ancestors of people whose surnames were derived from towns, villages or hamlets. Thus people named Millichop (various spellings) have an ancestor who lived at or moved from the small Shropshire settlement of Millichope, but they are not connected to the Anglo-Saxon landowner whose personal name was attached to this remote valley, probably well over a thousand years ago. The settlement first appears in written records as Melicope in Domesday Book. The surname was not coined until two or three centuries later.

With minor place-names, such as the names of farmsteads, we move into a greyer area. Some of these names are very old and are recorded in Domesday Book. Others do not appear in local records until the twelfth and thirteenth centuries, simply because such records were not made in earlier ages. They include some very old names but also some that had been formed only recently. It is usually impossible to decide which are old and which are new. In the great majority of cases family names are not derived from the people who first settled at a particular farm. However, some farms did not get their present name until late in the middle ages or in more modern times. Quite often an old farm name has changed over time to that of a long-resident family who lived there. For example, to the north of Sheffield Raynaldthorpe became known instead as Hatfield House because three generations of Hatfields lived there during the sixteenth and seventeenth centuries. We therefore need to trace minor place-names back to their origins when we try to unravel their relationships with family names.

As we have seen, great Norman landowners often took their surnames from the estates upon which they resided. At a lower social level, many farming families acquired surnames from their farmsteads. Some families remained on their original farm for several generations but others soon moved elsewhere (though usually not very far) and severed all connection with the place from which they sprang. The Creswicks of Hallamshire, for example, must have taken their name from the hamlet of Creswick near Ecclesfield, but we can find no firm evidence of this association. The first known member of the family, Adam of Creswick, was recorded in a late thirteenth-century charter, at a time which is generally thought to be early in the period of surname formation in this part of England. He was living not at Creswick but at Onesacre, two or three miles to the west.

Other families took their surnames from the places that they had just left when they took up residence in some distant town or village. Why certain settlements produced a crop of names while others spawned very few or no locative surnames remains a mystery. It has nothing to do with size. Some of the former hamlets in what is now Greater Manchester – places such as Butterworth, Clegg, Kershaw or Ogden – have produced far more people with locative surnames than has Manchester itself. The Staffordshire village of Salt and the Derbyshire hamlet of Bagshaw are the sources of more family names than Liverpool and Nottingham. Sometimes a family moved a considerable distance just at the time that surnames were being formed in their new locality but then remained in the same district for centuries. Where this happened, some of the characteristic names of a neighbourhood may have arisen as locative names derived from places far away. Thus north Staffordshire has a large collection of locative surnames that have migrated from Lancashire.

The difficulties faced by the family historian who attempts to identify the home of a locative name can be considerable. Peter McClure estimates that not more than 40 per cent of medieval English towns and villages were uniquely named.[2] More than half the surnames in medieval documents are therefore capable of alternative explanations. Many studies of medieval migration patterns have failed to take sufficient account of this problem. It is not just the numerous Astons, Nortons, Suttons and Westons that cause difficulty, nor is it the several Bradfields, Bramptons, Draytons and Waltons. Some of the Ripons came not from Yorkshire but from a small settlement called Rippon in Norfolk. No one can be expected to know all the alternatives. When identifying the source of the surname Darby we have to consider not only Derby but West Derby (Liverpool) and Darby (Lincolnshire), and when we turn to Wells we have the choice of places in Norfolk and Somerset and of numerous minor wells all over England.

Surnames and the place-names from which they came may have changed their forms over the centuries. We have to trace both sets of names back in time to their earliest spellings in order to show how they are connected. The distinctive Staffordshire surname Huntbach arose at a place, south east of Eccleshall, that was marked as Humpidge Green on Yates's map of Staffordshire (1775) and which is now known as Humbage Green. George Redmonds has explained how the distinctive West Riding surname Atack is not a topographical name meaning 'at the oak', as has usually been assumed, but a locative name derived from the small Lancashire settlement Etough (see Map 11, p. 205). Present forms may mask the true identity of a family name. We must treat every one as a special case and trace it back as far as we can before we can offer a judgement about its origins. Surnames continued to evolve long after their formation in the middle ages, so the obvious etymologies are often proved to be wrong when we look at the individual histories of family names. For instance, it is natural to assume that people in Sheffield called Crookes came from the village of that name which is now a Sheffield suburb. Many of them did, but entries in the parish register show that in the seventeenth century a separate family called Crook gradually changed their name to Crookes to conform to local practice.

We must bear in mind such dangers but not be overwhelmed by them. In the majority of cases we can trace locative surnames back in time towards their origins. One example must suffice. The surname Heathcote is concentrated today in Derbyshire and neighbouring counties. It is derived from a hamlet that stands high on the bleak hills above Hartington and Dovedale near the Staffordshire border. The place-name refers to a cottage on the heath, perhaps a shepherd's cottage, for here was a grange (or outlying farm) of Garendon Abbey, a Cistercian abbey near Loughborough, which was founded in 1133 but which has disappeared completely. References to the grange at Heathcote appear in documents of the late twelfth and thirteenth centuries.

When men moved from Heathcote they took their surname with them. The poll tax returns for Derbyshire in 1381 name William of Hethkote and John Hethekote at Buxton and four other Heathcotes not far away at Tideswell. During the next three centuries they spread a little further. The hearth tax returns of the 1660s and 1670s name thirty Heathcotes in Derbyshire, four in Staffordshire and two in Nottinghamshie. Twenty of these householders still lived in the High Peak, including five who farmed in Hartington parish. The ones who did well for themselves had moved east to Chesterfield. They were already well-established there by 1480 because in that year two of them – a mercer and a brazier – were members of the common council of the town. The Chesterfield Heathcotes became well-to-do bell-founders, butchers and tanners. Others sought their fortunes in distant places and triumphed spectacularly. The family has a unique claim to fame, for in the remarkable year 1711 Gilbert Heathcote became Lord Mayor of London and his brother Caleb became Mayor of New York. Most of the Heathcotes – or Hethketts, as the name is sometimes pronounced – stayed in and around Derbyshire, however. They are still to be found mainly in or close to the Peak District.

The large group of surnames which we label topographical contains numerous obvious examples, such as Bridge, Green, Ford, Hill, Marsh and Wood, derived from landscape features in many different parts of the country. It is usually impossible to show which particular greens, woods or other features gave rise to individual family names, for such features are commonplace. Nevertheless, it is often possible to show that families bearing names of the topographical kind remained in the same neighbourhood for centuries.

Topographical surnames enabled local people to distinguish families by the situation of their homes. In the middle ages names such as Bywater, Townend or Underwood had a precision that is often no longer apparent. Only one family in each village would be known as Green, Hill or Wood, but similar names were given to other families in many other villages. The parallels with common occupational names such as Smith or Taylor are clear.

Not all topographical names, however, are as obvious as these. Some are old words which we no longer use, such as Yate, an obsolete form of gate, or Snape, which came from an Old Norse word for a pasture. Others were Norman French words such as Bois, Malpas or Roche. Medieval topographical terms had precise meanings. It was once important to distinguish different types of woods as hangers, holts, hursts and shaws. In interpreting surnames which are derived from prominent features in the local landscape we need to know that in the twelfth, thirteenth and fourteenth centuries a carr or kerr was marshy ground marked by alder trees or scrub; that a slack was a shallow valley; and that a booth was a shelter where a herdsman lived while he looked after young cows. It is not immediately obvious to most of us that people called Hales and Heles took their name from a nook or corner of land or that the Twitchens once lived at a road junction or cross-roads.

Topographical names have often lost their preposition and so some derivations are not apparent at first sight. The poll tax returns of 1377–81 record many names beginning with atte-, atter- or atten-. The Gloucestershire returns of 1381, for example, list Richard Attewolde, Anthony Attebarre, Joan atte Were [weir], Hugh Attewere, William Attewer, John Attoke, Thomas Attestyle and Richard Atteyate. Some of these sort of names have softened to forms such as Atwell or Atwood. Atten ash became Nash, Atten oak became Noakes, and so on. The final -s in Noakes, and in other topographical names such as Banks, Mills, Styles, etc., was often added long after the surname was formed.

Topographical surnames are found much more commonly in some parts of England than in others. Richard McKinley has demonstrated the popularity of topographical surnames in Sussex, which has far more examples in this category than have neighbouring Kent, Surrey or Hampshire. A sub-group of such names comprises those ending in -er, such as Bridger or Fielder. A man who lived on the Downs was a Downer, in the same sense as when we say that a person is a Londoner. The regional variety in the choice of topographical surnames is enhanced by the use of obsolete terms that were used only in certain neighbourhoods. A knowledge of such words helps us to identify the homes of these family names. A forstal was a peculiar Kentish term for a stock enclosure in front of a farmhouse, so it is unsurprising to find that John, Cecily and Ismania Forstalles lived in Canterbury in 1377. We should look for the Fells (hill) in Cumbria, the Tyes (green or enclosure) in Essex, the Cloughs (ravine) in the Pennines, the Platts (plank bridge) in Lancashire and the Yeos (brook) in Devon and thereabouts.

We are sometimes surprised to find that a common-sounding name is in fact very rare. Fieldsend is a topographical surname which means exactly what we expect, someone whose house was at the end of a field. Surely, we think, thousands of medieval families must have been in a similar situation. But the surname is so rare that it is very likely that it arose from a single place in the West Riding of Yorkshire, probably in one or other of the adjoining parishes of Penistone and Kirkburton, where Fieldsends can still be found.

The distinction between locative and topographical names is sometimes an arbitrary one, for we can point to many examples of surnames which were derived from particular features of the local landscape. Topographical surnames can have as striking a geographical distribution as some of the locative ones. The surname Ackroyd or Akeroyd, for example, is far more concentrated in its distribution than is suggested by its etymology, 'the oak clearing'. Only one such clearing was the source of this family name. George Redmonds has identified it as the Akroyd near Heptonstall, which stands some 800 feet above sea level on the edge of the Pennines, west of Halifax. He notes that John of Aykroide, who in 1381 was constable of Wadsworth (the township in which Akroyd lay), was apparently the first man with that name, and that he may have been the John, son of Richard, who was taxed in the same place two years earlier. The family lived in and around Hepton-stall for centuries. Their continuity is evident from a baptismal entry in the Heptonstall register which refers to Samuel Aykeroyd of Aykeroyd in 1648. By this time, however, other Ackroyds had moved out of the parish. One branch is known to have crossed into Lancashire and to have adopted the spelling of Ecroyd. Although Ackroyd is now the most usual spelling, it was a relatively late development. In 1842–46 the indexes of death registrations for England and Wales name 178 Ackroyds, fifty-seven Akroyds, thirteen Aykroyds and one Akroyed, making 317 in all. The name, in all its variant forms, was concentrated near its point of origin.

Ellam is another of the West Riding's distinctive topographical surnames. The name means 'river-pool' but the family come from a particular spot: Elam, near Morton in the parish of Bingley. The family name was recorded in villages close to Bingley in the fourteenth century and for part of the fifteenth, but then it disappeared, to re-emerge around Huddersfield in the seventeenth century. It has since spread a little further but is still found principally in or near that town. Across the Pennines, Sowerbutts is a distinctive Lancashire surname that was derived from a particular patch of poor farming land. Thomas del Sourebutt and Alice del Sourebutt were each taxed 4*d*. at Thornley with Wheatley in 1379. Older readers may remember the Lancashire accent of Bill Sowerbutts, for many years a stalwart of the BBC radio programme, *Gardeners' Question Time*.

Topographical features are often distinguished by a prefix which sets them apart from the rest, making them in effect locative names. Northern surnames such as Barraclough, Fairclough, Birkenshaw, Longwood or Murgatroyd can be traced back to single-family origins in the neighbour-hoods of the place-names from which they sprung. The Murgatroyds came from a clearing (probably the moor-gate) in Warley, which has since been renamed Hollins. James Murgatroyd, a rich clothier from Warley, bought East Riddlesden Hall (now a National Trust property) in 1638 and built what is now the main range. Some characteristic Lancashire surnames are derived from farmsteads at the bottom of broad Pennine valleys but some of these names have been corrupted over time and so are not recog-nisable at first. Thus the surname Shufflebottom comes from Shipperbottom near Bury while Higginbotham is from Oakenbottom in Bolton-le-Moors.

The famous Staffordshire surname Wedgwood provides a final example. It is derived from a small settlement marked on Yates's county map of 1775 in the parish of Wolstanton. The family name is first recorded in 1327, when William Wegwode was living close by in Tunstall. Only two families with this name were included in a comprehensive list of Staffordshire families in 1532–33: John Wedgwood and his family at Horton; and William Wedgwood and his family at the adjacent settlement of Biddulph, to the north of the district that became known as the Potteries. By 1666 the Wedgwoods had ramified into fifteen branches, four of whom were still living in Tunstall. Josiah Wedgwood (1730–95), England's most famous potter, established the family's fame and fortune. Wedgwood is clearly a north Staffordshire name and very probably has a single-family origin.

4

The Development of Family Names

Estimates of the total population of England during the period of surname formation have been revised considerably by recent historical scholarship. It is clear that numbers grew rapidly during the twelfth and thirteenth centuries but then fell dramatically as a result of the Black Death of 1348–50 and later pestilences. Many historians now believe that the population of England reached five or six million by the year 1300 but that it had fallen back to between 2,200,000 and three million by about 1380. The downward trend continued for a hundred years or so until the population was probably less than two million. Recovery was slow and did not really get going until the 1530s and 1540s, late in the reign of Henry VIII.

A consequence of the dramatic reduction of the population from the mid fourteenth century onwards was that a great many surnames withered almost as soon as they were created. Although the national population was far lower in the middle ages than it is today, England had a much wider range of surnames at the period of their formation than it has had in subsequent centuries. The ending of so many male lines as families succumbed to disease explains why Reaney was able to quote early instances (before the Black Death) of surnames or non-hereditary bynames in counties far removed from the ones where family names have flourished in modern times. The huge fall in the English population during the fourteenth and fifteenth centuries provides the necessary framework for understanding this process.

The whole of western Europe seems to have made a demographic recovery during the sixteenth and early seventeenth centuries. By 1640 England's population is thought to have reached about five million. This recovery did not bring about a corresponding rise in the number of surnames, however, for most families had acquired their hereditary names by the fifteenth century. In the post-medieval period new names evolved from the old but their number did not match those which were lost. Nor did the population rise result in an equal increase in the numbers of people bearing each of the surnames that were then in existence, for at one extreme some families had several sons who in turn had several sons, while at the other extreme families continued to disappear through a failure to produce or raise male heirs to maintain the line.

In his study of *The Surnames of Lancashire* (1981) Richard McKinley drew attention to the spread of local surnames within that county from about 1500 onwards. He observed that many of the surnames which were later to become very common in Lancashire were already present in the late fourteenth century and that many such names appeared in the poll tax returns of 1377–81 as the name of more than one person, but that no individual surname was particularly numerous at that time. When the population grew in the sixteenth and seventeenth centuries, some of these surnames multiplied rapidly and became very common in one part of the county but remained rare or totally lacking in other parts. He noted that a large majority of the names that ramified in this way were locative surnames, nearly all of which were derived from Lancashire place-names. Members of some families with distinctive Lancashire surnames migrated to neighbouring counties during the sixteenth and seventeenth centuries. Emigrants were a small minority of the county's population, however; at least until geographical mobility became far easier in the nineteenth century with the invention of railways and steamships. Even at the close of the twentieth century, a large proportion of Lancashire's native families have remained at or close to their point of origin in the middle ages.

It may be thought that Lancashire is an extreme example of the stability of family names, for until the eighteenth century the county was a remote part of England that attracted relatively few immigrants, but George Redmonds has observed a similar process in the West Riding of Yorkshire and very many families in all parts of England long remained close to their roots. Lancashire offers striking confirmation of the spread of family names within a restricted area because so many of its surnames are derived from distinctive local place-names which are instantly recognisable.

A single example from beyond Lancashire will suffice here to illustrate the way in which family names ramified in the Tudor and Stuart era. Sixty-eight Creswicks formed the largest number of people bearing the same surname baptised in Sheffield between 1560 and 1599, narrowly beating the Staniforths, who had taken their name from a small farm on a site that is now overshadowed by the giant Meadowhall shopping centre. The Creswicks, we may recall, had already moved from the hamlet that gave them their name by the late thirteenth century. They had therefore been around for some time before they began to spread in the sixteenth and seventeenth centuries. Several Creswicks were prominent early members of the Cutlers' Company and six of them served as Master Cutler between 1630 and 1667. Apart from one branch who successfully sought their fortune in London, the Creswicks remained loyal to Hallamshire, the cutlery manufacturing district around Sheffield. All twenty-two households of Creswicks who were taxed on their hearths in south Yorkshire in 1672 lived in this district. They were a family of local origin who had moved to several places within a few miles of their ancestral home, but (with the exception of London) they had gone no further. Their story is entirely typical of the Tudor and Stuart age.

London had long been a powerful magnet for young people from all over the country and from abroad. The population of the capital city rose phenomenally at this time, from about 120,000 in 1550 to nearly half a million in 1700. Half a century later London was the largest city in Europe. About 4 per cent of the population of England and Wales were Londoners in 1550; by 1700 this proportion had grown to 10 per cent. Yet the study of parish registers has shown that more people died in London than were born there. The astonishing growth of the capital city's population can be accounted for only by a continuous inflow of immigrants. This is why distribution maps of surnames that usually show a concentration near the name's point of origin also mark significant numbers in and around London. Some distinctive surnames of foreign origin, brought by traders and crafts-men, were found only in or near London but the city was too densely settled to generate its own characteristic surnames. Nor do the original suburbs seem to have produced locative surnames. William Camden's sur-name is thought to have originated in Gloucestershire, at either Broad Campden or Chipping Campden, not from Camden Town (which took its name from the Marquis of Camden in 1791). The surname London was acquired only by people who moved out of the capital, never to return.

The evidence of parish registers, apprenticeship records, wills, court depositions, poor law settlement disputes, diaries and much incidental material supports the belief that, while people crossed their parish boun-daries regularly, most did not venture beyond their nearest market towns. Thus the men who were recruited as monks by Rievaulx Abbey all hailed from within a twenty-five to thirty mile radius. When Celia Fiennes rode from Redruth to Penzance in the 1690s she remarked, 'The people here are very ill guides, and know but little from home, only to some market town they frequent'. Nearly a hundred years later, on his arrival at an inn in Ringwood, on the south-western edge of the New Forest, John Byng found that he 'could get but blind intelligence of my road, for neither master nor ostler were ever further than twenty miles to the westward'.

The Evolution of Surnames

As family names spread from their base, usually slowly and by stages, they sometimes assumed new forms. Most of these changes are easy to spot, for they involved only slight differences of pronunciation or of accepted spelling;

Couldwell rather than Coldwell, or Gothard instead of Goddard, for example. But sometimes the changes were so drastic that, if we did not have the evidence to prove it, we would hardly believe that a group of names had a common ancestry. It is not at all obvious at first sight that Oldroyd and Olderhead were originally the same name or that Cowgill could become Coldhill. These two examples are taken from George Redmonds, *Surnames and Genealogy: A New Approach* (1997), which has demonstrated beyond doubt that what most of us thought was a minor phenomenon which provided some amusing examples of name changes was in fact of considerable importance in adding to the stock of English surnames in the post-medieval period. His numerous examples are all taken from Yorkshire names, so it is possible that such changes were less common in other parts of the country. It would be unwise to assume that this was so, however. George Redmonds' knowledge of Yorkshire surname history is unrivalled. He has gathered his evidence through many years of painstaking work and has reached his conclusions gradually. Extensive research on the same scale elsewhere might well turn up a similar pile of evidence.

Some of the surnames which were recorded in Yorkshire parish registers changed fundamentally in the course of only two or three generations. Dr Redmonds has shown that family names could 'become identical with other surnames and, more confusingly, with place-names and personal names with which they had no real connection'. The possibility of such change leads us once again to stress the importance of genealogical methods in establishing the original form of a surname before we can offer an opinion about its etymology and its place of origin. Each family name must be treated as a unique case. And as the linguistic changes usually occurred when a family moved away from its native district we need to be cautious in judging what the distribution pattern of a particular name might be. We have to establish the variant forms of a surname before we can draw our maps. This is not a straightforward task when names merge and others become unrecognisable.

George Redmonds' Yorkshire examples show that, although some apparent variations in names were simply misspellings by clerks (or in some cases humorous adaptations by clergymen), many surnames changed permanently. Some alterations were minor ones, involving the dropping of aspirates or of consonants such as a final 'd' or 't', but others were more basic because of the different speech customs of the district into which a family or individual had moved. New neighbours turned an immigrant's name into something that sounded familiar to them, perhaps another surname or a local place-name, or they contracted the name to make it less of a mouthful. Thus when the Cuttforthaighs moved across the Pennines into south Yorkshire they were sometimes called Cutfortha.

A few examples taken from the sixteenth- and seventeenth-century Sheffield parish register illustrate the ways that surnames changed. The Smethursts first appear there in the 1580s. Their surname was derived from a minor place-name near Manchester, a name that Sheffielders found difficult to catch. The 'th' sound in the middle of the name was sometimes pronounced as a 'd' and the end of the name was contracted. The parish register entries read:

Baptism 19 September 1583 Johes Smethehurst fil' Edri Smetheherst
Baptism 5 July 1588 Willus Smedhurst fil' Edri Smedherst
Baptism 22 August 1589 Alicia Smathers fil' Edri Smathers
Marriage 21 January 1590/1 Ric'us Smith & Elizabeth Smadders
Baptism 21 November 1593 Edward Smadders fil' Edwardi Smadd's

Sheffielders were also unsure about the name Pickfork or Pitchford. The entries in the parish register leave us puzzled as to which was the original form of this immigrant name. Did the family name come from Pitchford (Shropshire) or was it, in this case, a nickname? Richard Pickfork was married at Sheffield in 1621 and two or three years later he baptised his daughter Grace. Subsequent entries read:

Marriage 15 October 1639 Phillipp Pitchfork & Hellen Beighton
Baptism 16 August 1640 Samuel fil' Phillippi Pitchforke
Baptism 16 January 1648 Maria fil' Phillippi Pickforke
Baptism 16 March 1651 Jonatha' sonne of Phillip Pitchford

To complicate matters, a Samuel Pickford was taxed in Sheffield in 1672. Was he related to the Pickforks / Pitchfords, or was he one of the Pickfords from the other side of the Peak District who later became famous as national carriers?

The Brownhills and Brownells seem to share a common origin, at least those families who now live in and around Sheffield do. One possible source for these names is Brownhill near Sale (Cheshire), where late thirteenth-century references occur. Another possibility is Brownhill near Holmfirth (Yorkshire), where John del Brounhill was recorded in 1324. The Holmfirth family name can be followed up to about 1550 but it then disappears from local records. Either of these two places is a feasible source for the family that settled in Sheffield, for they are both within reasonable travelling distance. Adam Bronhyll was living at Stannington, just to the north of Sheffield, in 1453. The surname soon assumed a different form. In 1481 William Brownell was said to be the son of Adam Brownehill. A nice example of local speech comes from a record of 1598, when a Brownhill who lived at Greenhill was described as George Brownell of Grennell. In the register of the neighbouring parish of Rotherham the surname was recorded consistently as Brownell in the sixteenth and seventeenth centuries, but in 1705 the name changed to Brownhill for fifty years, after which both forms were recorded inconsistently. In Sheffield, Brownell became the recognised pronunciation. The seven householders who were recorded in the hearth tax returns of 1672 were named Brownell, Brownill and Brownall. By that time, the family had spread into other parts of south Yorkshire and into Derbyshire and Nottinghamshire. Now, however, the Brownhills outnumber the Brownells. People have begun to pronounce their aspirates again.

The Brownells were recorded occasionally as Browneld, Brownswell and even Brownsbyll but these forms seem to have been aberrations, unless the latter one is the separate Lancashire surname Brownbill. Other examples of permanent name changes taken from the Sheffield parish register reinforce what George Redmonds has written. Thus Burnett, a name which first appears in 1611, and which is common locally today, can be shown to have evolved from Bernard and Barnard. Base became Bayes, perhaps to hide the meaning of the name, which denoted illegitimacy. The surname which was derived from the Cheshire place-name Bramhall was clipped to Bramma, Brammas and Brammawe, given an extra consonant as Bramald, and corrupted further to Brabmer and Braman. Several variant forms of the name have survived to this day. The 1991 Sheffield telephone directory lists the following names: Brameld (28), Bramah (5), Bramald (3), Bramall (102), Bramhall (95), Bramhill (13), Brammah (5), Brammall (6), Brammar (2) and Brammer (97). Joseph Bramah (1748–1814), the inventor of Bramah locks and the hydraulic press, came from Stainborough in south Yorkshire, a few miles to the north of Sheffield.

The clerks who compiled the Sheffield parish register often turned the name Brailsford into Brelsforth and sometimes into Brelsworth. Farrand was written as Pharran and Seaton as Sayton. Coombe was occasionally shortened to Coo, which could cause confusion with the entirely separate name Coe, which began as a nickname taken from a common name for a jackdaw. Broxon was altered to Brocksupp, Bolsover to Bowser, Clarborough to Clarber, Gascoigne to Gaskin and Caskin, Newbould to Newbound or Newbowne, and Woolhouse to Woolas. Some of these changes are obvious, others are not. Some were short-lived, others became permanent.

The Lancashire surname Fairclough is derived from an unidentified 'fair ravine'. A family of this name held property in and around Ormskirk from at least 1320 and the name was confined to south-west Lancashire until the sixteenth century. It appears to have had a single-family origin. Variant forms such as Fereclough or Farecloth confuse the distribution pattern, but by the late seventeenth century it had spread into Salford hundred, where it eventually became common. The manner in which one variant form of the name was arrived at is described in John Featley's biography of his uncle, Dr Daniel Featley (1582–1645), which was published in 1660: 'His right name was Faireclough … but this then varied and altered from Faireclough to Faircley, then to Fateley, and at length to Featley'.

George Redmonds has also drawn our attention to the clerks' frequent use of aliases. Several alternative Latin words, which similarly meant 'otherwise', were also used in registers and other documents, e.g. *aliter, sive, vel* and *vulgariter.* Less commonly, the clerks were content with the English phrases 'otherwise called' or 'commonly called'. Thus in 1548 the clerk of the Ecclesfield manor court noted 'Hugh Twell otherwise called Hugh Attwell'.

Aliases arose in different ways. Frequently, they denoted illegitimacy, often they were given to step-children. In a minority of cases, they persisted over several generations. A family in the north Derbyshire parish of Norton, for example, were recorded consistently as Urton *alias* Steven, as if the family themselves insisted on the alternative names. The same form was used for events which took place in neighbouring parishes, such as the marriage in Sheffield on 12 May 1616 of 'Edr' Urton als Stephen & Dionesia Harthorn'. This family were a rare case, however. It was much more common for aliases to last only a generation or two. One such example from the Sheffield parish register is that of a family known alternatively as Roades or Garlick:

Burial 11 August 1588 Johes Roades als Garlick
Baptism 7 August 1590 Anna Roades als Garlicke fil' Robti Roades als Garlick
Baptism 15 April 1599 Maria fil' Robti Roades als Garlicke

Most aliases in the Sheffield parish register refer to illegitimacy. They are written in forms such as:

Baptism 2 August 1573 Anna Fyrthe als Stead fil' Alice Fyrthe
  p're putativo Nicho Steade
Baptism 17 February 1591 Margeria Fyrthe als Hobson fil' Anne Fyrthe
  p're putativo Thoma Hobson

George Redmonds stresses the genealogical value of recorded aliases. He writes, 'A documented alias is valuable because it offers immediate proof of a link between two surnames, links which would otherwise be extremely difficult to establish'. Among the many examples that he quotes are two from an assize case of 1651, when John Mannering said that he was 'sometyme called by the name of John Grosvenor, his mother being of that name', and Nicholas Postgate stated that he was sometimes known as Watson as his grandmother on his father's side had been so called. We have to remember that even as mighty a figure as Oliver Cromwell was once known as Williams and that some people pronounced his name Crummell in the same way as the Nottinghamshire village from which it was derived. Oliver's great-great-grandfather was Morgan Williams, a Welshman who married Katherine, the eldest sister of Thomas Cromwell. Their son, Richard, rose in Cromwell's service and adopted his patron's surname.

It is well known that when a noble or gentry family failed in the male line the heir to the estate might change his surname to that of the family whose property he was to inherit. This was sometimes an explicit condition of inheritance. We may thereby get a false sense of the continuity of the family names of great landowning families. The Sitwells of Renishaw Hall (Derbyshire) provide a good example. The earliest bearer of this name was Simon Sitwell, who was at Ridgeway, in the same parish of Eckington as Renishaw, in 1301, when he was said to be the son and heir of Walter de Boys, or de Bosco ('of the Wood'), who had died on pilgrimage to the Holy Land. In 1310 Roger Cytewelle was one of the founders of the Guild of St Mary of Eckington. A continuous pedigree can be traced from Roger Sitwell of Ridgeway (c. 1411–74). The family's fortunes improved with Robert Sitwell, who left Eckington in the 1540s to settle at Netherthorpe in the neighbouring parish of Staveley, and who made considerable purchases of land there and in Eckington and Chesterfield. Robert's estate passed to his first cousin, Francis, whose grandson, George Sitwell of Renishaw (1601–67), prospered as an ironmaster. George built Renishaw Hall anew about 1625 and received a grant of a coat-of-arms in 1648. His direct line failed after three more generations, however, and in 1777 both the estate and the coat-of-arms passed through marriage to a member of a junior branch, to Jonathan Hurt, whose medieval ancestors were small farmers on the south Yorkshire Pennines. Jonathan Hurt thereupon changed his name to Sitwell. His son, Sitwell Hurt who thus became Sitwell Sitwell, remodelled the hall to its present appearance and in 1808 was created a baronet. The literary trio of Sitwells – Edith, Osbert and Sacheverell – were his descendants.

Naming Patterns in the Choice of First Names

A few comments on the choice of first names in the sixteenth and seventeenth centuries are appropriate here, for these choices may help the genealogist to construct family trees. The personal names brought in by the Normans were still the favourite ones in sixteenth-century England. John, William and Thomas were the three most popular boys' names, at all levels of society, followed by Richard and Robert. A second group of less popular names was formed by Edward, Henry, George, James and

Nicholas. During the seventeenth century Henry and Nicholas, and to a lesser extent Edward, fell out of favour and were partly replaced by the biblical names Samuel and Joseph. Other boys' names that grew in popularity included Charles, Daniel, Ralph and Andrew. The popular girls' names also tended to be the old ones, though Agnes and Joan declined and Mary rose in popularity. Elizabeth and Margaret remained popular throughout the country but were not as dominant as John, William and Thomas. Other popular biblical names included Susan, Hester, Judith, Rebecca and Sarah.

The medieval practice of asking godfathers to name a child was still followed at the close of the sixteenth century. Shakespeare's Richard III asks his brother, the Duke of Clarence, why he has been committed to the Tower. Alluding to an old prophecy, Clarence replies, 'Because my name is George'. Richard's response is: 'Alack, my lord, that fault is none of yours. He should for that commit your godfathers'. We can now see that Shakespeare's play was written just as this practice was beginning to change. In a quantitative analysis which challenges previous accounts that have relied instead on contemporary literary evidence (where writers advocated what they thought ought to happen), Scott Smith-Bannister, *Names and Naming Patterns in England, 1538–1700* (1997) concludes that there is firm evidence that in the sixteenth century a child's name linked him with his baptismal sponsor but that in practice the role played by godparents probably varied greatly. The seventeenth century saw a definite move towards naming the eldest boys and girls after their parents. This trend started in the 1590s for boys and in the second decade of the seventeenth century for girls. The change, however, was not uniform throughout England's different regions. For boys' names the trend began in the south and the south east in the 1590s, spreading to the south west by 1610–19 and the midlands and the north by the 1620s, but not reaching the eastern counties until a decade later. The fashion caught on less in the north than elsewhere.

Dr Smith-Bannister's quantitative analysis has disproved some statements that are still widely accepted as correct. He shows that at no time in the sixteenth or seventeenth centuries was the practice of giving a child the same name as a living elder brother or sister remotely 'common', as Lawrence Stone asserted in *The Family, Sex and Marriage in England, 1500–1800* (1977). The reasons why we find siblings bearing the same first name are that the elder one had died or that the relationship was that of step-brother or -sister. He also shows that the use of non-scriptural saints' names did not decline at the Reformation and that the fashion amongst Puritans for names like Praise-God, Repent or Worship was limited both in scale and time. The heartland for Puritan names was east Sussex and the Kentish border, especially in the period 1587–92. While it is true that

Old Testament names became increasingly popular, and that Puritans searched their Bibles for obscure ones such as Eliasaph or Elkanah, by 1700 about nine out of every ten boys and eight out of every ten girls were still being christened with traditional English names.

Peers often chose names which distinguished them from the rest of the population. The use of distinctive first names by certain gentry families began in the late fifteenth century but the fashion spread very slowly. These names were often taken from medieval romances or classical literature, though sometimes they were names borne by distant ancestors. Sir Mauger Vavasour, the builder of Weston Hall and its delectable banquet house in lower Wharfedale late in Queen Elizabeth's reign, was named after his Norman ancestors who introduced both the first name and the surname into England. The nobility and gentry were the first to use surnames as personal names, but at other levels of society such names were very uncommon before 1700. Scott Smith-Bannister has demonstrated that in the 1690s only 0.67 per cent of the boys baptised in the forty parishes that he has studied in detail were given surnames as first names. The practice of giving children more than one name was even less common at that time. Another of his conclusions, which is of direct interest to the central argument of this book, is that the information that he has amassed on the distribution of first names in different parts of England gives broad support to the notion that migrants generally covered fairly short distances.

In the *Remains concerning Britain* (1605) William Camden commented that it was only 'in late years [that] surnames have been given for Christian names among us'. Such names are a great help to the genealogist. The use of Malin as a male first name seems to have been largely confined to the neighbouring parishes of Handsworth and Sheffield; only two examples have been found in neighbouring parishes. Malin had been a pet form of Matilda (rather than Mary) in the middle ages and had developed into a surname in different parts of the country. The Malyn Stacye who benefited from a Sheffield will in 1566 is the first male who is known to have borne this distinctive forename. A family connection must be assumed, though no one with the surname Malin has been found linked in any way with the Stacys, who were minor gentry at Ballifield in Handsworth parish. The Sheffield Stacys were a junior branch. The Stacys started the fashion for this new first name and, apart from a few isolated examples in later times, continued it long after everyone else. Parish registers and apprenticeship records show that sixteen other south Yorkshire families named a child Malin on at least one occasion, especially during the reign of Charles I, but with a few later cases. It is very likely that members of the Stacy family with the first name Malin acted as godparents. No other surname was used as a first name by so many neighbouring families. The name was taken far beyond the Sheffield district by the last two Stacys of Ballifield who were baptised Malin but who later spelt it in a different way. In 1678 Mahlon Stacy (1638–1704) and his family sailed across the Atlantic with a group of Yorkshire Quakers to West New Jersey, where he named his new home Ballifield. A mill which he erected was the first building in what is now the populous town of Trenton. He and his son and namesake became prominent figures in Burlington County and are well known to local historians in that part of America, who pronounce Mahlon in the way that it was spelt and not in the English manner.

George Redmonds has collected a large number of Yorkshire examples where distinctive Christian names such as Cuthbert or Giles were bestowed on boys who were baptised within the same neighbourhood, in a manner similar to the Malins of the Sheffield district. The influence of godfathers on these naming patterns can sometimes be proved. The incidence of such names in the pre-modern era has little to do with national fashions. Local and family historians need instead to look for the social networks that earlier generations described as 'affinities' or 'kith and kin'. The study of Christian names in the past is still in its infancy. It is a subject that offers local and family historians a chance to make a real contribution.

The Welsh

The gradual way in which Welsh people came to adopt hereditary English-style surnames from the end of the middle ages onwards reminds us of how the English themselves had acquired surnames two or three centuries earlier. The fashion began amongst the wealthier members of society and spread very slowly down the social scale and into the remoter areas. Whereas the English had coined numerous surnames from place-names, nicknames and occupations, the Welsh favoured patronymics. Even within this class the choice was restricted, for pet forms of names were used as surnames much more rarely than they were in England. Lloyd, Vaughan, Bach, Gwyn, Gittins and Beddoes are some of the few surnames that are derived from pet forms, nicknames or terms of endearment. The result was that Wales ended up with a limited range of surnames. As in medieval England, by the sixteenth century many of the personal names that had been favoured in Wales in earlier centuries, such as Cadell or Cynfyn, had been abandoned in favour of a small group of names that had been introduced by the Normans. Only Dafydd, Gruffydd, Hywel, Llywelyn, Madog, Morgan, Orwain and Rhys survived to provide large numbers of surnames. Instead, the English names John, William, Hugh, Thomas, Robert, Richard, Henry,

Edward and Lewis became widely used. Such names were sometimes adopted because they were close to Welsh personal names, or pet forms of them; Edward replaced Iorwerth and in north Wales Hywel often became Hugh. Some of the surnames that are now considered to be typically Welsh, such as Phillips or Williams, were ancient surnames in the counties bordering Wales. Indeed, the prominence of some of these names in the industrial parts of south Wales may be partly due to immigration of English people bearing similar surnames just across the border.

The Tudors took their surname from the Welsh form of the personal name Theodore. One of the Welshmen who had supported Henry Tudor and who accompanied him to the English court was David Cecil, the grandfather of William Cecil, Elizabeth I's great minister who was created Lord Burghley. The Cecils were originally minor Welsh gentry and took their surname from an Old Welsh personal name. Their rise to prominence is demonstrated by their huge residences: Burghley House (Northamptonshire) and Hatfield House (Hertfordshire).

The change from the older system of naming was largely self-defeating, for it did not serve to identify Welshmen from their neighbours. Other naming systems have had to be used to avoid confusion. David Jenkins has noted that in south Cardiganshire people were known by their Christian names or surnames with the names of their farms appended, or simply by the names of their farms.[1] Elsewhere, nicknames distinguish the numerous Joneses and Williamses. Incidentally, the humour in the creation of such a name as Evans Above for the local undertaker alerts us to the ways in which such nicknames as Gotobed or Pennyfather were created in medieval England, even though we cannot recreate the precise situation in which such nicknames were bestowed.

Some of the Welsh gentry began to assume English-style surnames long before the Tudor period, but the Act of Union (1536) signalled the beginning of widespread change. By the seventeenth century the English system of naming was in use in most parts of Wales, though in the remoter areas the old *ap-* or *ab-* form of naming, signifying the relationship of father and son, survived well into the eighteenth century and sometimes into the nineteenth. In the ancient Welsh system, the name Llywelyn ap Gruffydd showed that Llywelyn was the son of Gruffydd. The name could have been extended back a generation to, say, Llywelyn ap Gruffydd ap Morgan, but no hereditary surname was formed. Welsh people had no difficulty in proving their descent in the settling of land disputes, however, for their ability to recite the names of their ancestors over six or seven generations was legendary and led to the popular saying: 'As long as a Welshman's pedigree'. Under the English system, Llywelyn ap Grufydd became Llewellyn

Griffiths, for adding the genitive -s to denote 'son of' was the method that was common in those English counties that border Wales and therefore the one that was copied readily. Many Welsh surnames, such as John or Howell, never acquired the additional -s and in many cases this suffix was not fixed to the patronymic surname until the eighteenth or the nineteenth century. Another complication (which we have already noted) is that Welsh names were often changed to the nearest English one. Thus Llywelyn was softened to Lewis. Families bearing the surname Lewis may be descended either from a long line of English people or from Welsh people who changed their name. The same is true of many other family names that are now common in Wales and the Welsh borders.

A great number of Welsh surnames – Davies, Edwards, Evans, Hughes, Jenkins, Jones, Roberts, Thomas, Williams and so on – were formed in this way. Such names are not exclusive to Wales, for many of them were also used in England from earlier times. Roberts, for instance, has been a West Riding name since the middle ages. Ellis arose separately in England, and so did Edwards, Hughes, Owen, Phillips, Thomas and Williams. People with the surname Jones who were recorded in the poll tax returns of 1377–81 invariably had Norman-English first names, e.g. Henry Jones (Berkshire), John and Thomas Jones (Leicestershire), five John Jones, three William Jones, two Thomas Jones, two Agnes Jones, and an Alice, Edward and Robert Jones (Gloucestershire), John Jones (Hampshire), and Richard, Roger and Thomas Jones (Herefordshire). This type of patronymic name was most popular in the counties that bordered Wales and was the obvious model for the Welsh when they began to follow the English system of naming.

Some distinctive Welsh surnames were formed by the merging of *ap-* or *ab-* with the father's name, particularly if that name began with a vowel, the aspirate or the letter r, which provided grip. Bellis, Bevan, Bowen, Parry, Preece, Pritchard and Pugh are obvious examples. Some of these were formed from Welsh personal names, but many were from English first names or from Welsh names which had been Anglicised. Some of these English names were Norman in origin and had been familiar in Wales for centuries. The Welsh had not found it easy to pronounce certain Norman or English names and had developed their own forms. The 'j' and 'sh' sounds were particularly difficult and had no symbols in the Welsh alphabet, so Roger became Rosser and Jenkin ('young John') became Siencyn. Eventually, Dafydd ap Rosser became David Prosser. The distributions of the surnames Rosser and Prosser are very different from those of their English counterparts, Rogers and Rogerson. Nor is it enough to say that these are Welsh names, for the civil registration records of 1842–46 show that the Rossers and Prossers mostly lived and died in south-east Wales and were largely absent from other parts of the country.

An amusing example of how a Welshman acquired his surname upon moving into Shropshire in the seventeenth century is provided by the *History of Myddle* which Richard Gough wrote in 1701–2. When writing about Martha Dudleston, he observed that she was

> married to a man that they called Welch Franke. Hee could speake neither good Welsh nor good English. When he came first out of Wales, hee lived as a plow-boy with William Geslin, or Goslin, of Myddle, and people called him Franke Goslin; but when hee was marryed hee was called in Court, and when the Steward asked him his name, hee said Franke. And what else? says the Steward. Hee sayd, Francis. Then the Steward asked him his father's name, and hee sayd it was David; soe hee gott the name of Francis Davis.

We shall look at the ways in which Welsh surnames spread in England. The Welsh contribution to the present stock of English names has been considerable.

Immigrants from Continental Europe

During the course of the sixteenth century England experienced foreign immigration on a very significant scale. Between 1540 and 1600 over fifty thousand men, women and children crossed the Channel to settle in England, mostly in London or in smaller towns and villages in Kent and East Anglia.[2] Many of these immigrants were forced to leave their homes because of religious persecution. The English government welcomed them for their craft and business skills. Colonies of privileged foreign workmen settled in Sandwich in 1561, Norwich in 1565, and in Stamford, Southampton, Maidstone and Colchester soon afterwards. By the middle years of Elizabeth's reign Flemings and Walloons from the Spanish Low Countries and groups of French Huguenots formed a substantial and permanent presence in the capital city. In Norwich and Canterbury, and perhaps in a few other eastern and south-eastern towns, foreign immigrants amounted to a third of the total population.

Some of these families can be traced by their distinctive names, though many others soon adopted Anglicised forms. The Tyzacks probably originated from Thisé, near Besançon, where they are recorded from 1431. The du Thisac men were glass makers and Protestants, said to have left France after the Massacre of St Bartholomew's Eve in 1572. In 1576 Jan du Tisac was recorded as having taken communion at Buckholt (Hampshire). Other factors, however, were also at work. The high wages on offer in England may have been tempting. Christophe Thysac fled to England in 1579 after killing his cousin. Before the end of the sixteenth century Tyzacks were found in Sussex and Gloucestershire, and in 1612 one branch of the family moved to Kingswinford, near Stourbridge, where they became established. The hearth tax return of 1666 for Seisdon hundred in Staffordshire names Paul Tyzacke with five hearths at Swinford Regis and Zachery Tizacke with one hearth at Amblecoate. Glass workers were some of the most mobile people at that time. In 1679 William Tizacke took a lease of the western glasshouse, Newcastle-upon-Tyne. The family left Newcastle for Norfolk in the eighteenth century but returned later. Many Tyzack graves stand in the churchyard at Wells on the north Norfolk coast. Another branch from Stourbridge moved east to follow a different trade. By 1702 Benjamin Tyzack, formerly of Hagley, near Stourbridge, was a scythesmith in the Nottingham-shire parish of Cuckney. About 1718 he moved to the north Derbyshire parish of Norton, an ancient centre of the scythe trade. There the Tyzacks put down roots as scythemakers and tool makers until the late twentieth century. Modern telephone directories name 130 Tyzacks, scattered in many parts of England. Others went to South Africa and Australia in the mid nineteenth century.

Glass makers used timber, unlike the iron workers whose fuel came from renewable coppices, so that their activities were destructive of ancient woods. The need to change furnace sites frequently was one reason for their mobility. A second was lucrative offers made by landowners who wished to benefit from the profitable trade in glass. Other glass maker families with foreign surnames include Bisval, Caquerey, Gerrat, Hennezel, Houx, Pero, Petowe, Potier, Thietry and Vaillant, names which are immediately recog-nisable in a variety of spellings. The parish register of Lastingham (North Yorkshire) records a further unusual group of names, many of which were probably borne by Huguenot glass workers at the furnace set up in Rosedale in the late sixteenth century: Agaret, Forva, Langyard, Leder, Merle, Pape, Roulland and Sorow are likely ones, though the temptation to ascribe every unusual name to Huguenots should be resisted. Claiming ancestry from Huguenots has long been fashionable but is often mistaken.

A group of iron workers, mostly from Lorraine, can also be traced by their French surnames, though English clerks often had great difficulty in spelling them. Frenchmen who settled first in the important iron-working district in the Weald have been identified from the lists of 'aliens' in various subsidy rolls from 1524 to 1603 and the 'denization' rolls of 1541–44.[3] Like the glass workers, many of these men and their families moved to other parts of England when invited by great landowners to install charcoal blast furnaces and forges. Their distinctive names can be spotted in parish registers and other local records. For example, the iron workers from the Weald who accepted the invitation of George, sixth Earl of Shrewsbury, to erect furnaces and forges on his estates in and around Sheffield in the 1570s and 1580s included Lawrence Dippray, who was probably the Lawrens Dupre who was recorded in the Weald in 1560. Other surnames that are recorded in both the Sheffield parish register during the 1570s and the earlier lists of iron workers in the Weald include Giles Maryan (1574), who soon returned to the Weald, James Tyler (1574), whose descendants worked at Wadsley Forge until the eighteenth century, John Valliance (1576), who moved further north to another ironworks at Monk Bretton, and Jordan Russell (1577), who worked at Norton Hammer on the River Sheaf.

The Vintins do not appear in the Sheffield parish register until 1611, when William Vintin married Anne Holmes, a Rotherham girl, but their surname suggests a link with two men recorded in the denization rolls of 1541–44. A 'denizen' who worked for Nicolas Eversfield was named as 'Peter Vynten aged forty-four, thirty years in England, from Normandy, with an English wife'. Another, who was employed 'in Master Pelham's Iron Worke' was 'John Vynton aged fifty, twenty-five years in England, also from Normandy and with an English wife'. The Vintins can be traced in Sussex throughout the seventeenth and eighteenth centuries. The descendants of those who came to Sheffield have stayed there. They feature prominently as millwrights in the records of the local iron industry. Eleven Vintins are listed in the 1988 Sheffield telephone directory.

We may suspect that other French families who are not recorded in local records until the seventeenth century had arrived in Sheffield about the same time as their fellow countrymen. The Jelleys of Wadsley Forge (including the splendidly named Dud Jelley) were probably connected with the John Jelet or Jellye, who was living in the Weald in 1552 and 1576. The Husseys, who were described as frying pan makers of Attercliffe Forge in the seventeenth century, may have been descended form Peter Husshe, who was working in the Weald in 1543. William Perigoe of Attercliffe, forgefiner (1657) was in all probability a member of the same family as the 'Perygo' who was recorded without a first name in the Rape of Pevensey in 1543. The family came from Perigueux and are commemorated by a street name, Perigoe Road, in the Sheffield suburb of Woodseats.

Not all the Lorrainers and other Frenchmen, however, possessed such identifiable surnames. Some bore names of French origin that had been introduced into England in earlier centuries and others had names that soon became Anglicised. Some of the Tollys, for example, may be descended from the iron workers in the Weald between 1540 and 1560 who were identified by such names as 'old Tullet', Flyppyng [Phillipe?] Tollett, Antony

Toullet and George Tullye, but others take their surname from a medieval diminutive of Bartholomew. Other examples from the registers of Sheffield and neighbouring parishes where the evidence is uncertain include Barten, Binney, Collyer, Gillott, Harvey, Jordan, Lambert, Lawrence, Longley, Loy, Mallet, Russell and Valeant or Valyance. Some of these names were recorded locally long before they appeared in the Weald in the first half of the sixteenth century.

Immigrants from France and the Low Countries were prepared to move long distances in the first generation or two but, generally speaking, they eventually became as settled in a particular neighbourhood as the native English were wont to be.

Upward Social Mobility

The Tudor and Stuart period provided opportunities for some families to rise considerably, even spectacularly, in the social scale. One of the most successful were the Sidneys, whose surname was derived from a minor place-name in Surrey. About 1280 John de Sydenie held lands in Chidding-fold on the Surrey-Sussex border, where Sidney Farm and Sidney Wood are marked on large-scale maps. The first Sidney who was of more than local importance was William Sidney of Kingsham (Sussex), MP for the county in 1429 and 1433. His grandson, another William, advanced his fortunes at the Tudor Court and was knighted for his services at the battle of Flodden in 1513. His rise was marked by Edward VI's grant of the fine medieval house at Penshurst (Kent) in 1552, two years before his death. Built in the fourteenth century for Sir John Pulteney, former Lord Mayor of London, Penshurst is famous for the impressive roof span of its magnificent open hall. The family held influential positions at Court during the next two generations. William's grandson, the poet Sir Philip Sidney, died in 1586 from wounds received at the battle of Zutphen near the eastern border of the Netherlands and was succeeded by his younger brother, Sir Robert, who brought the house up to date by the addition of a fashionable long gallery. Under James I, Robert was created Viscount de Lisle (1605) and Earl of Leicester (1618). The title expired when the sixth Earl died, but after two generations of descent through female lines Philip Shelley-Sidney was created Lord de L'Isle and Dudley. The present generation are descended from a daughter of the youngest son of the second Lord.

The Hobarts were an East Anglian family who advanced through careers in the law. Their surname is pronounced Hubbert and comes from the old personal name Hubert. Sir Henry Hobart was appointed Lord Chief Justice under James I and in 1616 bought an estate at Blickling (Norfolk), where he was previously the tenant. As a prominent member of Robert Cecil's circle, he was able to secure the services of Robert Lyminge, who had designed Hatfield House. Blickling Hall (now a National Trust property) has several design features copied from Hatfield, especially when viewed from the front. The family prospered and in 1746 Sir Henry's great-grandson was created Earl of Buckinghamshire. Hobart, Tasmania, is named after the fourth Earl.

The Moretons of Little Moreton Hall (Cheshire) rose in a more modest way. The family name is recorded in 1216, when Lettice de Moreton married Sir Gralam de Lostock. Their younger son, Geoffrey de Lostock, inherited the property and from then onwards was known as de Moreton. The earliest part of the present timber-framed house – the hall, parlour and kitchen – was built in the 1440s and 1450s by Sir Richard de Moreton, the ninth in descent, though the surrounding moat is even older. His great-grandson, William Moreton, engaged the carpenter Richard Dale to extend and beautify the house in 1559 by the construction of the elaborate bow windows that greet the visitor across the courtyard from the entrance. William's son, John, inherited the property in 1563 and began to build the delightful range over the entrance, topped of course by a long gallery. Little Moreton Hall is probably the best-known timber-framed building in England. It owes its preservation to the family's decision to move elsewhere in the early eighteenth century. The hall was let to tenant farmers for two hundred years and was never altered to suit changing tastes. It was restored to its original appearance at the end of the nineteenth century. The direct line of the family ended in 1763 after seventeen generations and the estate passed to a female cousin whose son took the name of Moreton. This line ended with two sisters, who left the property to a cousin, the Bishop of Derby. He and his son left the house to the National Trust in 1937.

Another National Trust property that attracts visitors because of the family who lived there is the small manor house known as Washington Old Hall (County Durham). This is the place from which George Washington's family took their name. In 1613 the house was sold by the family and partially demolished, the present house being erected upon its foundations. It had been the home of the Washingtons for five generations, from the time William de Hertburn had moved from Hartburn near Stockton-on-Tees, before 1183, and had assumed his new name upon his arrival at what was to become the family home. The senior branch of the Washingtons lived there until 1399, after which the property passed through a female line down to 1613. William, the great-grandson of the first Washington, moved, on marriage to an heiress, to Westmorland and Warton (north Lancashire). George Washington was descended from his second son. Lawrence Washington (c. 1500–84) went into the wool trade and decided that prospects were better in Northamptonshire. He moved to Sulgrave Manor and prospered as a wool stapler and sheep breeder, becoming Mayor of Northampton in 1532 and rebuilding his manor house. In 1656 his great-great-grandson, Colonel John Washington, emigrated to Virginia, where he settled in Westmoreland County. George Washington, nineteenth in the family line, became the first President of the United States of America.

The Stuarts or Stewarts were upwardly mobile over a long period of time. The surname of the royal family was derived from their hereditary office of steward, which they had held since the eleventh century in Brittany, though the surname did not become fixed until the thirteenth century. They became the royal family of Scotland in the fourteenth century and in 1603 James VI of Scotland became James I of England. The two countries shared a monarch but were not united until the Act of Union of 1707. As James VI was at pains to point out, many people called Stewart acquired their surname independently and had no connection with the royal family.

5

Stability and Change

Reflections on the implications of our findings about the persistent geographical patterns of family names and the histories of individual families over the centuries begin with the obvious points that surnames allow us to trace male lines but not female ones and that the numerous junior branches of a family tend to fade from view. We all share the same genetic pool from far back in time but what are we make of claims that, although we do not have the documents to prove it, we are all descended in some way or other from William the Conqueror? If this assertion is used simply as a metaphor to make the point that ancestry is shared to a much greater extent than most of us imagine, then there can be no objection, but if it is meant literally we ought to be sceptical. Such claims rest on mathematical models that do not take account of the restricted movements of our ancestors and their tendency to marry into families to whom they were already linked. Dr Katherine Keats-Rohan's researches have shown how the Norman aristocracy intermarried and rarely formed alliances with native families for several generations after the Conquest.[1] Family historians regularly come across distinctive local surnames that appear more than once on their family tree. The genetic pool did not expand forever outwards but was dipped into time and time again.

How often we meet people who claim descent from the aristocracy through a junior or an illegitimate line. The claims are rarely substantiated. We cannot make easy assumptions on the basis of a shared surname, though even that evidence is not always offered. Genealogical methods must be used to prove all the links in the chain. The example of the Scargills and the discussion of Norman surnames showed that it is very difficult to prove descent through an ancient junior line from a medieval aristocratic or gentry family, for adequate records are lacking. It is, however, perfectly possible to do this for some families from the seventeenth century onwards and especially in much more recent times. Some gentry families died out in the male line but others ramified astonishingly in the nineteenth century. The Boyses, Dennes and Filmers of Kent, for example, produced successive generations with a dozen children or more. At the present time there could well be several thousand descendants of such families in female lines. The ramification of many old gentry families has led to great social diversity. At first, younger sons were forced off the land to serve as officers in the army and navy, to become lawyers and clergymen, or even to seek their fortune in trade. Their younger sons and grandsons might have had to earn their livings in ways considered unfitting for real gentlemen. Downward social mobility could be rapid, so that surnames that once signified gentry status were borne by members of the working classes. The process through female descents is less obvious to the historian, though it was often quicker.

This point was well understood by Thomas Hardy, who was interested in his own forebears and who once had the romantic notion of changing his name to Thomas le Hardy. At the beginning of his novel, *Tess of the Durbervilles*, 'plain Jack Durbeyfield, the haggler' is greeted by a parson with antiquarian interests with the words, 'Good night, Sir John'. When pressed to explain, the parson reveals that Jack is a lineal descendant of an ancient and knightly family, reputed to come from Normandy with William the Conqueror, whose 'effigies under Purbeck-marble canopies' could be found in a local church. The family consisted of numerous branches but had died out in the main lines. When Jack asked what he had better do about it, the vicar replied:

> Oh – nothing, nothing; except chasten yourself with the thought of 'how are the mighty fallen'. It is a fact of some interest to the local historian and genealogist, nothing more. There are several families among the cottagers of this county of almost equal lustre. Good night.

Jack's new-found knowledge was of course his undoing.

Upward social mobility into the ranks of the gentry and aristocracy was always possible in England but families with such aspirations found it hard going. The English aristocracy were not an open elite; upward social mobility was limited in practice if not in theory. Aristocrats were determined to preserve the purity of blue blood as far as they were able. John Beckett has remarked that, 'Entrance into the aristocracy was far from easy, and penetrating the uppermost reaches took careful planning, considerable good fortune and, above all, patience'.[2] The families that did make it into the upper ranks of society, such as the Cecils or the Cavendishes, achieved their goal through royal office, particularly when the monasteries and other religious houses were dissolved in the middle decades of the sixteenth century and land was transferred to new owners on a scale unparalleled since the Norman Conquest. Many old families seized the opportunity to enrich themselves, but ruthless men who were in the right place at the right time were also presented with a chance to rise from modest backgrounds. The Byrons provide a good example, They seem to have started off as cowmen, for their surname was derived from an Old English word meaning 'at the cattle sheds'. The family's rise dates from the dissolution of the monasteries, when Sir John Byron, the ancestor of the poet, Lord Byron, acquired Newstead Abbey.

The Cavendishes are the most successful example of the new breed. They took their name from their Suffolk estate and were of little importance until Sir William Cavendish (1505–57), the second son of a Suffolk squire, sought his fortune at Court, where he eventually served as Treasurer of the Chamber to Henry VIII and then to Queen Mary. Sir William was one of the hard men who were appointed to act as commissioners for the surrender of the monasteries. Upon moving to the central office as an auditor, he benefited greatly from his share of the spoils and was knighted for his services in 1546. His second wife, the redoubtable Bess of Hardwick, is said to have persuaded him to sell the former monastery lands that he had acquired at bargain prices in different parts of the country and to settle in her native Derbyshire. In 1549 he bought Chatsworth and soon began to build a great house. After Sir William's death, Bess married twice more, the last time to George Talbot, sixth Earl of Shrewsbury. Hardwick Hall is her monument. Sir William and Bess's second son, Sir William Cavendish (1552–1625), was created Baron Cavendish in 1605 and Earl of Devonshire in 1618. The Cavendishes held no land in Devon but the title was vacant and they could not be named after the county where they resided as the Stanleys held the title of earls of Derby, from their estates in West Derby hundred in Lancashire. Four William Cavendishes in turn held the earldom until the fourth earl was elevated to a dukedom in 1694. It is hard to imagine now that the famous Baroque house and magnificent grounds at Chatsworth came about because of chancy, revolutionary activity, the new duke having been instrumental in welcoming William of Orange and in getting rid of James II in the 'Glorious Revolution' of 1688. The line of six William Cavendishes, Dukes of Devonshire, ended with the 'Bachelor Duke' (1790–1858), who was succeeded by another William, the grandson of the fifth Duke's brother. The ninth duke was a nephew, the eleventh duke a younger brother. The surname has continued at Chatsworth over the past 450 years but the line of descent has sometimes been broken.

Alan Everitt makes the point that when one studies the seventeenth-century gentry as a whole, instead of taking selected examples, one finds that families which had risen through trade, law or royal office were not really typical. We tend to notice those families whose fortunes rose dramatically, but most of the greater gentry of the seventeenth century had risen gradually from the ranks of the medieval freeholders or minor armigerous families, while the minor gentry usually had forebears who were yeomen.[3]

The Elizabethan and Jacobean 'prodigy houses', like Wollaton, Burghley, Longleat or the original Chatsworth, provided residences that were very different from the typical houses of the vast majority of the English gentry. Far more characteristic were medieval houses such as Penshurst or Haddon which were extended and adorned at various times during the reigns of the Tudors and Stuarts.

In the seventeenth century gentry families in counties all over England were proud not only of their own descent but of their links through marriage with neighbouring families of similar status. The saying that 'all the Cornish gentlemen are cousins' could have been applied elsewhere. In Kent Mary Honywood provided astonishing personal proof of her family's links with the Kentish gentry. At the time of her death in 1620, aged ninety-three, her living descendants numbered 367 persons. A passionate interest in genealogy led to the production of illuminated pedigrees and, at Gilling Castle in north Yorkshire, a plaster frieze in Sir William Fairfax's Elizabethan great chamber that depicted the coats-of-arms of over four hundred Yorkshire gentry.

Another way of rising in the social scale was the time-honoured one of beneficial marriage. Sir Anthony Wagner notes the famous case of the Howards, who made six marriages with heiresses, great and small, between Sir William Howard, who was made a Justice of the Common Pleas in 1297, and his descendant Sir John Howard, who became Duke of Norfolk in 1483.[4] Between 1555 and 1606 the Howards strengthened their position on four occasions by marrying great heiresses, until they were one of the most powerful families in the land.

The themes of inherited wealth and complicated lines of descent are well illustrated by the case of the Wentworth family. The medieval lords of Wentworth had taken their surname from a south Yorkshire village and had built a house in the wood to the east that came to be known as Wentworth Woodhouse. For several generations the family were of only local importance but William Wentworth (1562–1614) signalled their rise by becoming High Sheriff of Yorkshire and by buying the title of baronet. His son, Sir Thomas Wentworth, became one of the mightiest figures in the land in the reign of Charles I. Upon his execution in 1641, his title of Earl of Strafford (which had been taken from the wapentake in which Wentworth lay) was inherited by his son, William; but when the second Earl died childless in 1695 the earldom became extinct. Thomas Wentworth of Wakefield, the grandson of the first Earl's younger brother, inherited the lesser title of Lord Raby but the estate at Wentworth Woodhouse was bequeathed to his cousin, Thomas Watson, the son of the first Earl's daughter. Watson thereupon adopted the name of Watson-Wentworth. Rivalry between the cousins was intense. Each sought to outdo the other by building first a

Baroque and then a Palladian house within an imposing park and grounds and each sought grand titles to establish their precedence. The new Lord Raby rose rapidly to high positions in the army and diplomatic service during the reign of Queen Anne. In 1708 he bought an estate at Stainborough, a few miles from Wentworth, and built a magnificent new house to the designs of the Berlin architect, Johannes von Bodt. He was winning the race and in 1711 his triumph seemed complete when he was made first Earl of Strafford of the second creation. He erected mock fortifications on an old earthwork in his grounds and renamed his estate Wentworth Castle. Upon his death in 1739 a statute of him in Roman costume was erected at the entrance to the 'castle'.

The battle continued in the second generation, when the fortunes were reversed. In 1723 Thomas Watson-Wentworth, junior, succeeded his father and immediately began to build a Baroque house at Wentworth Woodhouse to match that of his cousins. Sir Robert Walpole rewarded him for his political support in the House of Lords by making him a Knight of the Bath in 1725, Baron Malton in 1728 and Earl of Malton in 1733. Meanwhile, the Baroque style had gone out of fashion, so the new earl set about building the largest Palladian mansion in the country. In 1746 he was rewarded for his support during the invasion of Bonnie Prince Charlie's Highlanders by the grant of the title of Marquis of Rockingham. Unsatisfied by this rapid upward social mobility, he applied for a dukedom ten years later but was disappointed. His son, Charles, the second Marquis, became the leader of the Whig party and briefly Prime Minister. When Charles died in 1782 the Wentworth Woodhouse estate passed to the fourth Earl Fitzwilliam, his sister's son.

Back at Wentworth Castle, the second Earl added a Palladian range to his house and adorned his park with monuments and follies in the best taste of the age. When he died childless in 1791 he was succeeded by his cousin's son, Frederick. Upon Frederick's death without issue in 1799, the title of Earl of Strafford became extinct (though it was subsequently created for a third time for the great-grandson of the first Earl of the second creation). Frederick's estate passed to his sister and, after her death in 1802, to Frederick Thomas William Vernon, the grandson of the sister of William Wentworth, the second Earl of Strafford of the second creation and a member of a junior branch of the family which was Norman in origin and which had once owned Haddon Hall and Sudbury Hall in Derbyshire. The new owner, who was still a child, assumed the surname of Vernon-Wentworth. He was succeeded by a son Thomas, and a grandson Bruce, a bachelor who sold the house in 1948. The confusion between the two places deepened when both Wentworth Castle and Wentworth Woodhouse became teacher training colleges.

Many more examples could be given to show that the timeless appearance of England's great country houses can mislead us into thinking that the descent of the owners' families was equally certain. In fact, the surnames of numerous aristocratic and gentry families have been prolonged beyond their natural life to give a false sense of continuity. This rarely happened at lower levels of society.

Ruritarian titles and costumes, and institutions like the House of Lords, help to foster an image of antiquity but in fact the titles of the majority of the present peerage do not go back very far. In 1956, for example, little more than a quarter of the 550 baronies then in existence had been created before 1832. In the seventeenth century successive monarchs rewarded faithful friends with a dukedom or earldom, and lesser men with knighthoods or with a baronetcy if they were prepared to pay for the privilege. Office holders and lawyers were always more generally acceptable to the old county aristocracy and gentry than men with a background in trade, though a few became so spectacularly prosperous that they forced their way into the ranks of county society. Richard Arkwright was knighted, purchased the lordship of a manor, and became High Sheriff of Derbyshire, but he was exceptional. It is only in the late twentieth century that it has become quite common for millionaires to rise from working-class backgrounds. Most families have remained at pretty much the same level over the centuries. Most still live in the same part of England as their ancestors did, often close to the place where the family name was coined back in the middle ages.

Stable Families in Stuart England

In 1963 Peter Laslett and John Harrison published a classic paper which showed that, contrary to received wisdom at the time, the composition of pre-industrial rural communities was constantly changing.[5] They demonstrated that no less than 61.8 per cent of the inhabitants of the north Nottinghamshire parish of Clayworth who were recorded in a list drawn up by their clergyman in 1676 were not there when a similar list was compiled twelve years later. The article inspired much research into parish registers and other sources of demographic information and it soon became clear that Clayworth and Cogenhoe (Northamptonshire), the other parish that Laslett and Harrison studied, were not exceptional. Historical demographers have shown beyond doubt that people in the past were not confined in their movements by their parish boundaries. The crossing of such boundaries was commonplace.

The new orthodoxy is that our ancestors did not remain in the place where they were born. On the contrary, they were frequently on the move. But now we are beginning to see that the undoubted evidence for movement in and out of a parish obscures the underlying stability of what we might label 'core families', the ones who gave a particular community its sense of uniqueness. Peter Laslett urged caution in reading too much into the figures from Clayworth when he wrote that 'it might be easy to exaggerate the importance of the rate of *structural* change which these figures imply'. Most of the movement turns out to have been that of young people, who as servants and apprentices moved away in search of employment, but who often returned in later life to inherit the family farm or cottage. Nor did they move very far. Studies of the mobility of the population in many different parts of the country have concluded that most people travelled only short distances and that they stayed within the neighbourhood, or 'country', with which they were familiar. These neighbourhoods were usually no more than ten or twenty miles in radius and were bounded by the nearest market towns. Within them, people spoke with the same accents and shared the same distinctive surnames. Families were not contained within the boundaries of a parish but they were slow to spread beyond their 'country'. Unless of course, as was so often the case, young members of families were attracted to London. The capital city is the only place in England that does not have its distinctive surnames, for immigrants poured in continually from near and far.

If we analyse the two lists for Clayworth by households rather than by individuals a different picture emerges. The underlying stability of the Clayworth families is then made clear. If we compare the lists of 1676 and 1688 with a hearth tax return of 1664 and a protestation return of 1642 we find that the ninety householders of 1688 included thirty-seven who possessed surnames that had belonged to families in the parish forty-six years earlier. Two out of every five surnames in seventeenth-century Clayworth had been present for almost half a century. When we look at the figures in this way, the community of Clayworth seems far more settled than the lists of individuals in 1676 and 1688 would have us believe. Moreover, those who left the parish never to return during these years probably did not travel far down the road.

Wherever the rural communities of Stuart England have been studied in detail the continuity of 'core families', even within parish boundaries, has been remarked upon. The very different communities of the open-field village of Wigston Magna (Leicestershire), the scattered settlement of the wood-pasture parish of Myddle (Shropshire) and the scythe-making parish of Norton (Derbyshire) each demonstrate the ways in which families persisted over the generations, often in the same farmstead. Richard Gough, who wrote a history of his native parish of Myddle in 1701–2, spoke admiringly of the ancient families who formed the backbone of his community. Gough could trace his own ancestors back almost two hundred years. The fact that so many of his neighbours' families had stayed not just in Myddle but often on the same farm for five, six or seven generations made it natural for him to combine the approaches of the local and family historian when writing his history and to think of his community as a collection of families that had long been established in the parish or just beyond.

Some industrial rural parishes, notably Whickham in County Durham, saw a rapid turnover of population in the Tudor and Stuart period as men came to work in the new coal mines. But where employment depended on a tradition of craftsmanship the families were as stable as those in agricultural parishes. The township of Attercliffe, which covered the eastern part of the huge parish of Sheffield, had fifty-one smithies attached to its twenty-three houses when hearth tax was levied in 1672. The economy of the township was dependent on the manufacture of knives and scissors. Many of the families that were recorded in the tax return had lived in Attercliffe since the parish register began in 1560. Indeed, some had been there since the fourteenth century. The Beightons, Brewells, Bullases, Dungworths and Staniforths had taken their surnames from nearby place-names and some of the families with common names such as Allen, Carr, Green or Hibbert can be traced back several generations in Attercliffe. These were the families which provided the officers of the township: overseers, constables and churchwardens. The stability of the Attercliffe families during the sixteenth and seventeenth centuries was even more marked than that of the 'core families' of many contemporary agricultural parishes.

Although the turnover of urban populations was quicker than in the villages and hamlets, the underlying structural continuity was similar, particularly when the local economy was dominated by a distinctive craft and sons succeeded fathers in the same occupation. The sense of community that came from the residential persistence of 'core families' was enhanced by the links that can be traced over the generations through various masters and their apprentices. When Lewis Nawl of Sheffield Park died in 1695 he left seven gross of pen- and pocket-knives, or 'spring knives' as they were called locally. A direct line of learning can be traced through the apprenticeship records of the Cutlers' Company to the spring knife makers who were listed in a trade directory of 1787. By the last quarter of the eighteenth century thirty-eight apprentices, journeymen and freemen formed the fifth generation of training descent from Lewis Nawl. This example could be multiplied many times in all the various branches of the cutlery trades.

The apparent conflict between the findings of historical demographers who have worked on parish lists and the evidence of distinctive family names that were so often restricted in their distribution to recognisable neighbourhoods has turned out to be unreal. People moved but on the whole they travelled only short distances. In Tudor and Stuart England family names were borne mostly by people who lived within a few miles of the homes of their ancestors.

Migration within England

London was the great exception to this rule, as it attracted migrants from all over the land. The capital city grew at an astonishing rate during the sixteenth and seventeenth centuries, from about 120,000 in 1550 to 200,000 in 1600, 375,000 by 1650 and 490,000 in 1700. A hundred years later it had reached 900,000. Yet the number of recorded burials in London's hundred or so parishes was consistently greater than the number of recorded baptisms. The city's growth was fuelled by immigration. It has been estimated that the huge rise in London's population between 1650 and 1750 can be accounted for only if the annual number of migrants numbered at least 8000. London's rate of growth in the sixteenth and seventeenth centuries was far higher than that of the rest of England. In 1550 only about 4 per cent of the national population lived in the capital city; by 1700 nearly 10 per cent were Londoners. As their surnames showed, Londoners were an rich mixture of people from all parts of England and from many parts of Wales, Scotland and continental Europe. At any one time, only a minority of the inhabitants had been born there. Population levels in the towns of provincial England were modest in comparison. In the late seventeenth century Norwich was the next largest place, with 30,000 inhabitants. The cathedral cities and county towns attracted immigrants only from a restricted area that was often no larger than the 'countries' that surrounded the market towns. The pull of London was truly exceptional.

The hearth tax returns of the 1660s and 1670s are our best source for the study of surnames half way between the period of surname formation and the present day. Most of the counties for which we have printed returns had large numbers of distinctive surnames and relatively few names which can be shown to have arisen in other parts of England. As we have repeatedly emphasised, the great majority of families were mobile only within the neighbourhoods with which they were familiar, unless some members took the plunge and went to seek their fortune in London.

Staffordshire was exceptional in having absorbed a significant group from beyond its borders, but even there the immigrants formed only a small proportion of the total number of families. The contrast between the small numbers of people who migrated to Staffordshire from the west and the south of the county and the number of immigrants who entered from the north is striking. Forty-two householders in the Staffordshire hearth tax returns of 1666 bore surnames derived from Yorkshire place-names and a handful, including two Kendalls, came from even further north.[6] These numbers pale into insignificance when they are compared with the 339 Staffordshire householders whose surnames were derived from forty-two settlements in Cheshire and the 210 householders with locative surnames which can be identified with forty-eight different places in Lancashire. When we add those householders whose surnames arose in north-west Derbyshire, near the Lancashire and Cheshire borders, the total rises to well over 600 Staffordshire families who possessed distinctive locative surnames which were coined in or from places north of the county boundary. This is a large number, though we have to bear in mind that a total of 20,648 householders were taxed in Staffordshire in 1666. We have no way of judging how many other surnames, in different categories, came from the same direction. Nor can we say when they came. This drift of the population in a southerly direction occurred over a long period of time. It fits into a larger national pattern of movement, with London acting as the ultimate attraction.

If we disregard locative surnames that may have had multiple origins and if we ignore distinctive Cheshire surnames of the non-locative type, such as Strongitharm, we are still left with 339 Staffordshire householders whose surnames were derived from Cheshire place-names. We cannot always be sure that we have found the real home of some of these names. Wardle, for example, may have been derived from places in either Lancashire or Cheshire. All the eighteen households of Wardles who paid the hearth tax in Staffordshire in 1666 were living in Totmanslow hundred, which covered the Staffordshire Moorlands, bordering on Cheshire. Whatever their origin, they illustrate my general point about migration from the north.

Naturally, the bearers of locative surnames which were derived from places in Cheshire lived mostly in the northern half of Staffordshire. They included forty Asburys, thirty-four Bradburys, nineteen Davenports, seventeen Clewlows, fourteen Mottrams, and several Budworths, Malpases, Millingtons, Minshalls, Shallcrosses, Tattons and Wincles. Brindley is a good example of a surname that was derived from a Cheshire place-name but which became more common in Staffordshire than in its home county. Fifty-six of the 132 Brindleys whose deaths were registered in 1842–46 in England and Wales came from Staffordshire, compared with twenty from Cheshire. Apart from nine who died in Wolverhampton, the Staffordshire

Brindleys were scattered throughout the northern half of the county. James Brindley, the great civil engineer who was responsible for the Bridgewater and the Grand Trunk canals, was born not far away at Thornsett in the parish of Chapel-en-le-Frith.

The proportion of surnames in medieval Lancashire that can be classified as locatives amounts to about 50 per cent. Such names are relatively easy to spot when they occur beyond the county's boundaries. Even if we exclude names such as Mellor, Wardle or Eccles, which have more than one origin, and if we stick tightly to surnames in the locative category, we have a minimum of 210 Staffordshire householders who in 1666 bore surnames that were derived from Lancashire settlements. They included people called Higginbotham and Shipplebotham, together with numerous others whose names came from minor settlements such as Belfield, Clegg, Fairclough, Hassall, Latham, Lummas, Naden, Ogden, Tarbox and Tunnicliff, as well as surnames that were derived from villages and towns. Three-quarters of the householders who bore these Lancashire names were living in the two northern hundreds of Staffordshire, as we should expect. Surnames from Cheshire or Lancashire help to distinguish the pool of north Staffordshire names from those in the south of the county.

The drift of the population into north Staffordshire from Cheshire and Lancashire began long before these names were recorded in 1666. Thirty-eight locative surnames from Lancashire, shared by ninety-nine families, appeared in a long list of Staffordshire families in 1532–33. Some of these surnames had gone by 1666 but they had been replaced by twenty-six new locative surnames from Lancashire. Twenty-two surnames from Lancashire were recorded both in the hearth tax returns and in the list that had been drawn up 134 years earlier. We are left wondering just how long some of these Lancashire migrants had been settled in Staffordshire before 1532–33.

Welsh Migrants

Surnames recorded in hearth tax returns and other lists provide some evidence, though not an accurate measure, of the movement of Welsh people into English counties by the second half of the seventeenth century. The counties that were the most attractive to the Welsh were Shropshire and Herefordshire, just across the border. Some migrants went as small farmers or labourers, others were involved in the woollen cloth trade organised by the Shrewsbury drapers. The Shropshire hearth tax return of 1672[7] lists 202 Welshmen who were still using the *ap-* form of surname, which was presumably familiar enough to their English neighbours. Large numbers of householders were recorded with surnames of Welsh origin:

Evans (219), Pryce or Preece (160), Lloyd (146), Griffiths (110), Powell (107), Gough (70), Gittins (62), Howell(s) (55), Bowen (51), Vaughan (47), Maddox (45), Beddowes (42), Meredith (39), Pritchard (39) and Pugh (39), etc., with many others such as Jones (377), Davies (368), Edwards (153) and Morris (143), which could have arisen on either side of the border.

The likeliest explanation for this strong Welsh presence seems to be the trading links provided by the woollen cloth trade. The other border counties did not attract Welsh migrants in quite such large numbers, nor did the *ap-* form of surname remain in common use there. Herefordshire was the next most popular destination for the Welsh. The Herefordshire militia assessment of 1663 contains 985 surnames which were derived from the Welsh language (listed according to their most common spelling): Bedowes (7), Bevan (16), Benyon (1), Bowen (10), Cadwallader (2), Evans (23), Gittins (1), Gittoes (11), Gough (16), Gower (4), Griffiths (34), Gwatkin(s) (12), Gwillim (49), Howells (26), Ap Howell (1), Ap John or John (7), Lloyd (17), Meredith (14), Morgan (35), Onions (1), Parry (41), Penrice (1), Powell (139), Preece (24), Price (74), Pritchard (46), Probert (15), Prosser (28), Pugh (7), Rees (12), Rice (1), Tudor (4) and Vaughan (56). Names which could have arisen either side of the border included David (20), Davis or Davies (102), Edwards (37), Hopkins (25), Hughes (9), Jenkins (42), Jones or Johns (103), Lewis (61), Morris (35), Owen(s) (7), Phillips (71), Robert(s) (20), Thomas (42), Watkins (62) and Williams (72).

The evidence from Gloucestershire comes from much earlier in the seventeenth century, and so is not directly comparable. A muster roll of 1608 names 19,402 men, arranged on a parish basis by name, approximate age, and occupation.[8] Only ten men were recorded with the *ap-* form of surname. The most common names that were derived from the Welsh language were Powell (75), Price (59), Evans (51), Morgan (44), Griffin (37), Howell (33), Guilliam(s) 25, Gough (24), Pritchard (22), Vaughan (18), Griffyth (10), Rice (10) and Gethin (9); the rest were recorded in only ones, twos or threes. Welsh-language surnames amounted to only 2.2 per cent of all the names in the muster roll. Popular surnames which had arisen on either side of the border included Jones (176), Davies (138), Phillips (80), Watkins (67), Roberts (64), Lewis (59), Edwards (51), Hopkins (50), Jenkins (26), Richards (25), Morris (22) and Davis (18). If these are included with the ones of undoubted Welsh-language origin, the total is raised to 1196 or 6.2 per cent of the whole, a significant presence.

Welsh-language surnames were rarer in counties that lay a little further east. A listing for the whole of Worcestershire is not available in print, but a return for the city of Worcester records 117 Welsh names, together with Jones (75), Davis (40) and another 162 which could have arisen on either side of the border.[9] The hearth tax returns of 1666 for Staffordshire recorded only three men with the *ap-* form of surname, a marked contrast with neighbouring Shropshire. Even if we include the forty Joneses, only 253 of the 20,648 Staffordshire householders had surnames which originated in Wales. On the whole, the Welsh people who had settled in the county were poor; nearly half of them were exempt from payment of the tax and only 16 per cent were taxed on more than one hearth. Hearth tax returns have been printed for only parts of Warwickshire and Cheshire. Sixty Welsh names were recorded in the Tamworth and Atherstone divisions of Hemlingford hundred. In Cheshire the Northwich hundred contained seventy-two surnames with a Welsh or Welsh borders origin.

A few Welsh-language names were recorded in the hearth tax returns of some other English counties. Hampshire had 139 undoubted Welsh names and more than two hundred that were either Welsh or English. Suffolk had twenty Evanses, seven Rices, and an Onyon, as well as fifteen Joneses. These counties are distant from Wales but could be reached by sea. In other parts of seventeenth-century England Welsh names were so rare as to be almost non-existent. Thus the 7933 names recorded in the 1672 hearth tax returns for south Yorkshire included only one Gwlland, one Jones and one Unyon. The people of Welsh descent who live in this area today are mostly first- or second-generation immigrants. The Pennines long remained an effective barrier; in earlier times the Welsh had more obvious and easier places to move to.

Movement was not of course all one way. Michael A. Williams's analysis of the hearth tax returns of 1663 for Monmouthshire has shown that in Usk Hundred about 9 per cent of local taxpayers had English descriptive or locative names and that in the borough of Newport the figure was higher at 16 per cent.[10] These are small percentages compared with the later period of massive industrialisation, when English migrants sought work in the valleys, but they demonstrate that the border between England and Wales had long ceased to be an effective barrier.

Emigration

During the seventeenth century the slow trickle of emigrants to foreign lands swelled into a steady stream. Ireland was their first destination. James I tried to solve the political upheavals in west Ulster, that Elizabeth I's government had been unable to solve, by encouraging settlement on 'plantations' there. By 1659 settlers from Scotland and England accounted for 37 per cent of the 70,800 householders in Ulster. The consequences of this policy still make front-page news, for the new settlers were Protestants and the natives were Catholics. Scottish and English surnames which were recorded in the poll tax and hearth tax returns of the 1660s reveal a high rate of turnover of individual families in the early years. The new settlers outnumbered the Irish in the newly established towns and villages but were a scattered minority in the countryside. The English settlers came mostly from the western counties, particularly from Devon, Warwickshire and Staffordshire, less so from Cheshire and Lancashire. The Scots (who seem to have outnumbered the English by five to one) came from Galloway, Ayrshire, Renfrew and Lanark, and from the Borders and near Edinburgh, but not from the Highlands.

The Scots settled principally in Fermanagh, where by the mid seventeenth century the clan names Johnson, Armstrong, Elliott, Irvine, Nixon and Crozier had become dominant. It is not easy now to distinguish the descendants of settlers from the native families, for Irish surnames were Anglicised to English forms that approximated to the Gaelic sound and the prefixes Mac- and O' disappeared until many families resumed them in the late nineteenth and twentieth centuries. For example, O'Dubhthaigh became O'Duffy, then Duffy. Robert Bell has shown how very many Irish families acquired or were given an English or Scottish name that was often only vaguely similar in sound.[11] Thus Mac Cuinneagain was turned into Cunningham, while Mac Cathmhaoil, which was once one of the most common names in Tyrone, has now become lost in a variety of Anglicised forms. Others names were translated or half-translated; for instance, some of the O'Gowans, MacGowans and Gows became Smiths. As a result, very many people in Ulster who have English names may not be of English descent. Moreover, some families now living in England with English surnames are descended from irish immigrants whose ancestors once possessed very different names.

From the 1630s onwards the new colonies in North America and the West Indies replaced northern Ireland as the popular destinations for emigrants. Of the 540,000 or so people who left England between 1630 and 1700 roughly 380,000 went to the New World. These figures sound impressive, but in fact the emigrants amounted to less than half of 1 per cent of the English population. About 20 per cent of present-day Americans trace their ancestry to England and 16 per cent to Ireland, but the bulk of these ancestors crossed the Atlantic much later than the seventeenth century. American surnames often point to the particular part of England from which a family's original settler emigrated. Surnames derived from, say, remote Pennine farmsteads or from west country hamlets are common in New England. Some families, like the Tankersleys, are numerous in their adopted land but are now hard to find in England. Others have acquired variant forms of names that are sometimes difficult to link to the originals. A further complication is that emigrants from other countries have sometimes changed their names to an Anglicised form. Present-day forms of American surnames often mask their real origins.

Migration in the Nineteenth Century

The huge rise of the population of England and Wales from about 9,000,000 in 1801 to over 36 million in 1911 increased the likelihood of more people travelling beyond the ancient limits of the neighbourhood that they still knew as their 'country'. The new railways and steamships offered cheap and quick travel to distant destinations and the hope of a better life. During the nineteenth century about 10,000,000 people left the British Isles to set up home in America, Canada, Australia, New Zealand or South Africa. Some poor families in the depressed agricultural counties took the opportunity to travel unprecedented distances in search for work in coal mines, iron and steel works and textile factories. One of my great-grandfathers, a farm labourer in Somerset, brought his family to south Yorkshire, where he found employment at the coke ovens attached to a mine. His brothers emigrated to America and South Africa. Their story is typical of very many others.

It might be thought that this new mobility of quite ordinary families would alter the distribution patterns of surnames dramatically. It does when we consider emigration to distant lands. Very often a surname of English origin is now far more common in another part of the world than it is in the locality where it originated or even within the British Isles. But the modern distribution patterns of surnames within England have not changed in a fundamental way from the patterns in the past. Although we can all find examples from the history of our own extended families of people moving long distances from one place to another during the reign of Victoria, together they formed only a small proportion of the national population. Most people stayed within a day's journey of the neighbourhood in which they were born and to which they felt they belonged.

Immigration into Sheffield during the Victorian period was on a massive scale. The new giant steel works offered higher wages than farmers were prepared to give to their labourers. Some immigrants came from much greater distances than in earlier times. Thus, although Sheffield's Irish community was small compared to those in Lancashire towns, the Irish formed a significant element in some streets by the time of the 1851 and 1861 census returns. The new borough's population also included a number of Germans, a few Poles, families that had returned from America and one or two from a great variety of other foreign countries. Sheffield was also beginning to attract immigrants from the southern counties of England for the first time. Nevertheless, birth places recorded in the nineteenth-century census returns make it clear that the majority of immigrants into Sheffield's industrial east end came from much shorter distances, mainly from south Yorkshire, north Derbyshire and adjacent parts of Nottinghamshire and Lincolnshire. The net was cast wider than before, and the numbers involved were much greater, but the bulk of the immigrants travelled no further than had the boys who had been apprenticed to cutlers in earlier centuries. While it is true that very many Sheffielders are only first or second generation 'incomers', it is also evident that many other families have been there for a very long time. They often bear surnames that have been peculiar to the district since the middle ages.

This local picture reflects the experience of the country at large. A recent study by Colin Pooley and Jean Turnbull based on the family histories of 1388 respondents has analysed the 73,864 recorded residential moves made during the lifetimes of 16,091 individuals born between 1750 and 1930.[12] The huge amount of data that has been studied makes the authors' conclusions authoritative. They emphasise the significance of frequent short-distance mobility and play down the importance of long-distance moves. They have found that most movement undertaken in all time periods was short-distance and was contained within regional migration systems. The Sheffield experience was typical of the major towns, whose immigrants were drawn mainly from surrounding areas. As in earlier periods, only London had a truly national migration field. This pattern was not greatly altered by the opportunities offered by improved communications but was fairly stable over time. Pooley and Turnbull have calculated that mean migration distances were quite small until about 1880, when they were around twenty-two miles, but that they increased in the twentieth century to around thirty-five miles. Growing affluence and improved communications have not altered the ancient patterns of movement in significant ways. All parts of Britain experienced essentially similar trends. Long-distance moves, in all periods of time, were of minor importance when we consider the population at large.

Writing about the sixteenth and seventeenth centuries, Peter Spufford has noted how the common patterns of movement in much of rural England were strongly related to the life-cycle.[13] Pooley and Turnbull, too, stress the importance of studying later migration within the context of a person's whole life course. They demonstrate that for almost all categories of migration the most common experience was movement as a family grouping, though younger single migrants (both male and female) were more likely to move over longer distances and to the larger towns. The migration experiences of men and women were very similar. The level or nature of mobility did not change dramatically in the two centuries after 1750. On the contrary, patterns of mobility show a high degree of stability over time and space.

These findings encourage us to use late nineteenth- and twentieth-century sources to see how surnames are distributed in the modern period, so that we can compare these findings with earlier patterns. Alan Everitt's analysis of the nineteenth-century farming dynasties of Kent has shown how families continued to reside within the same district over the generations long after the coming of railways.[14] Taking the 220 most common surnames, borne by over 4000 families in Kent, he showed that, with few exceptions, each surname was predominantly restricted to a small group of nearby parishes. These Kentish families remained intensely localised in their outlook and connections. A century later, their distinctive surnames remain ones that are particularly associated with that county; often with east Kent rather than west Kent and vice-versa. They offer further proof that even today, when examples of individual long-distance movements have become more common, the distribution patterns of English surnames demonstrate the remarkable attachment of families to their native districts.

We shall see in Part Two how the civil registration records of the early years of Victoria's reign can be used to plot the distribution patterns of all types of family names and how these patterns demonstrate the continuing loyalty of families to their neighbourhood or 'country'. But first we should note how the indexes of death registrations in England and Wales in 1842–46 allow us to witness the spread of Welsh names and the arrival of Gaelic names in nineteenth-century England.

Welsh Surnames

We may start with a Welsh name that was known in England by the late thirteenth century. *Goch*, or *coch*, is the Welsh word for 'red' and probably indicated someone with this colour hair. It has given rise to the surname Gough. Lists of taxpayers in medieval Shrewsbury include Agnes Goch and Madoc Waleus (1297), William Vaghan (1309) and Thomas Vaghan (1316).[15] These surnames came from the Welsh language, so the original bearers were obviously Welsh, but they were formed long before surnames became hereditary in Wales. In what sense then can Gough be said to be a Welsh surname? In the poll tax returns of 1377–81 which have survived for various English counties a William Goff was recorded in Bedfordshire, a John Gof in Berkshire, a John Gouyegh (?) in Dorset, a Thomas Gauge in Leicestershire, a Thomas and a Henry Goffe in Gloucestershire and eleven Goughs (various spellings) in Herefordshire. The presence of Rose Goffe in Colchester supports the belief that the Essex surname Gooch or Goodge is a version of Gough; the seven other examples of the name in Essex in 1381 are recorded as Gogge, Gauge, Guch and Gugge. Richard Gough (1635–1723), the historian of the parish of Myddle, was descended from several generations of Goughs who had lived in north Shropshire since at least the early sixteenth century. When we look at the distribution of the surname Gough in the civil registration death indexes for England and Wales in 1842 we find that the surname was rare in Wales but common in the border counties (particularly Gloucestershire and Shropshire). By then, other Goughs had headed for Liverpool, Birmingham and London, in preference to searching for work in the industrial valleys of south Wales. Gough can therefore be judged to be a surname that became hereditary on the English side of the Welsh border, even though it is derived from the Welsh language.

Gittins is a similar case. The 190 registrations of deaths in England and Wales between 1842 and 1846 show that the surname was found in mid Wales, the adjoining English counties of Shropshire, Herefordshire and Worcestershire, and in the Black Country and south Lancashire. The pattern may be explained as migration eastwards from a heartland in mid Wales. The poll tax returns for Gloucestershire in 1381 record, however, a John Guytyngs in Chipping Campden and a Walter Kytinge in Quenington, and a Gittins family was resident in Shrewsbury (and from the 1520s in the parish of Myddle, a few miles further north) before the Act of Union had encouraged the Welsh to adopt the English style of surnames. Families named Gittins may have acquired their hereditary surnames when the son of a Welshman settled in England. The name was either a pet form of Gruffydd or was derived from the Welsh word *gethin*, a nickname for a swarthy person. Other forms of the surname include Gething, Gettens, Gettings, Gitting and Gittings.

Lloyd, which is derived from the Welsh *llwyd*, meaning 'grey or brown', is a much more common name than Gough or Gittins. The death indexes for 1842 record 532 people named Lloyd, 210 of whom were from Wales. Unlike some Welsh names, which have a marked regional distribution, the surname Lloyd was found in every part of Wales. The name was also strongly represented in all the counties bordering Wales and in Birmingham and the Black Country, Liverpool and the Manchester conurbation. Another sixty-five of the Lloyds in this sample had settled in London. Away from Merseyside, the name was rare in the north of England; the industrial West Riding had attracted very few Lloyds. They were found only occasionally in southern and eastern England and were absent from large parts of the midlands. This was the classic pattern of Welsh migration before the railways and the steamships took them further afield. Like the Goughs and Gittinses, some of these Lloyds may well have had a Welsh ancestor who was living in the English border counties several centuries earlier at the period of surname formation, though none has been found in the extant poll tax returns. (Other early migrants became known as Floyd(e), for the English could not imitate the Welsh pronunciation.)

A few other personal names which became surnames can be shown to have originated in certain parts of Wales. The rare name Anwyl or Anwell was derived from a personal name that arose in north-east Wales from a term of endearment. In 1842–46 only twenty-five deaths were recorded in Wales and England: eight in Holywell, two in Festiniog and one each in St Asaph, Conway, Dolgelly, Bala and Abergavenny; with four in Liverpool, one in Salford and five in London. The limited scale of this distribution is similar to that of a rare English locative name. The surname Meredith is from the Welsh personal name Maredudd. The 112 Merediths who died in 1842 included forty-four who were registered in Wales, especially in the industrial valleys of the south east and in mid Wales. The Merediths were also to be found in the border counties, particularly Herefordshire, but also in Shropshire, Worcestershire and Gloucestershire. Others had reached the Black Country or Merseyside and ten had set up home in London. The migration pattern was similar to that of the Lloyds, though the numbers were much smaller. Neither Meredith nor Anwyl features in the surviving poll tax returns, even in the two hundreds of Herefordshire.

John was overwhelmingly a south Wales name. No less than 161 of the 177 Johns whose deaths were registered in 1842–46 came from that part of the country. The rest were mostly in London or Cornwall; none were registered in the northern half of Wales. By contrast, 140 of the 327 Parrys who died in 1842 were found in Anglesey, Holywell, Bangor, Caernarvon, Ruthin, St Asaph and other parts of north Wales, and twenty more had died in Liverpool. The Parrys were scattered much more widely than the Johns and some had moved to south Wales, though not in large numbers.

T. J. and Prys Morgan have commented on how the counties on the English side of the border have retained Welsh personal names and numerous pet forms of these names as surnames, often in corrupted or misspelt forms.[16] Some of these pet forms, such as Bedo and Bedyn from Maredudd (Meredith), are far from obvious. Nor do they conform to the broad patterns of Welsh dialect. The Morgans conclude that usage varied greatly from name to name and from place to place. It seems likely that these surnames were formed in England (though from Welsh names) before the Welsh adopted English naming practices.

The civil registration records of the 1840s give a good idea of the geographical distribution of Welsh surnames before steam trains and steam ships allowed people to move far away from their places of birth. The deaths of seventy-five people with the surname Howel(l)s, which is derived from the Welsh personal name Hywel, were registered in 1842. They were spread across south and mid Wales but were rarely found in the north of the country, for, as we have noted, here the name had been largely replaced by the English name, Hugh. For this reason, the Howellses had not migrated towards Merseyside but had settled in the counties across the Severn and in the Black Country. None in this sample had died in London; the only one to travel far had died in Doncaster. There is no doubting that Howells is a Welsh surname. Rather surprisingly, however, the surname Howell (a direct rendering of the personal name Hywel, without the addition of -s) had a much wider distribution pattern in the 1840s. In Wales, the surname was found in all the counties along the southern coast. It was also present in the northerly parts of mid Wales, but was absent in between these areas and in the north of the country. Quite large numbers had crossed the Bristol Channel to settle in Gloucestershire and neighbouring counties. London had also proved a magnet. Others had moved to Birmingham, Merseyside and even Yorkshire. A thin scattering can also be observed in south-eastern and eastern England. Reaney and Wilson suggest that these eastern families were descended from Breton settlers rather than from Welshmen. (Their other suggestion that the Lincolnshire place-name Howell may also have given rise to this surname is not supported by the evidence of the death registers.) The poll tax returns of 1377–81 point unambiguously to the Welsh origin of the name. Ten of the eleven Howells lived in Herefordshire and the other one came from Gloucestershire. Two of these had the *ap* form of surname and two bore the name of the legendary leader, Hywel Dda. No returns survive in print for Norfolk and Suffolk, unfortunately.

The surname Powell is derived from ap Hywel, 'the son of Howell', and is far more numerous than either Howell or Howells. In the first quarter of 1842 alone 170 Powell deaths were recorded. In Wales, the forty-six registrations were overwhelmingly from southern districts. A few Powells had lived in north-east Wales, but the name was absent from the west and much of the middle of the country. The neighbouring English counties – Herefordshire, Gloucestershire and Shropshire – had considerable numbers of Powells, though Cheshire had very few. Birmingham and the Black Country, London, and to a lesser extent Merseyside, and even the industrial West Riding, had attracted some immigrants who bore this name. More puzzling are the numbers scattered in ones and twos elsewhere in midland

and eastern England. Reaney and Wilson note the alternative etymology from 'pool', which may account for some instances of this name. Nevertheless, the distribution pattern of the surname Powell in 1842 clearly points to a Welsh origin for the great majority of people bearing this surname.

The Pritchards (ap Richard) fit into the broad patterns outlined above. Thirty-seven of the 160 deaths registered in 1842 were from two separate parts of Wales: the northern coast and the south east. The English border counties had been the homes of a further forty-four Pritchards and Merseyside, Birmingham and the Black Country and London had proved attractive venues. A few others were scattered elsewhere, including far away Tynemouth.

Another example of an *ap-* or *ab-* form of Welsh surname is Bevan (ab Evan). The registrations of ninety-seven deaths for people with this surname in 1842 show that Bevan is a south Wales name (see Map 14, p. 208). Aneurin Bevan, the prominent Labour politician in the 1940s and 1950s, was born at Tredegar in 1897. The surname was largely absent from mid and north Wales. Gloucestershire was the favoured destination amongst the border counties and, as usual, London had proved attractive. Only six of this sample had moved to Merseyside, and, surprisingly, none had settled in and around Birmingham. Another small group had moved to west Kent, perhaps through a maritime connection.

Our two final examples in this group – Hopkins and Watkins – are surnames that are often identified with Wales but which in fact have English forms. Do the distribution patterns shed any light on their origins? Are these patterns substantially different from those outlined above or are they basically similar? Hopkins is an English name derived from a diminutive of Hobb, which was a pet form of Robert, but Hopcyn was used as a personal name in Wales from the thirteenth century. In 1842 the registrations of deaths name 221 people with the surname Hopkins. Only twenty-eight of these people died in Wales, nearly all of them in the south of the country. The Hopkinses were not present in Cheshire or Shropshire but large numbers occupied the lower Severn Valley (particularly Gloucestershire) and significant groups lived in Warwickshire and Staffordshire. The name was also recorded in ones, twos and threes throughout much of the south midlands, also in Kent and in other southern counties. London had been the home of twenty-seven, with others living nearby. The surname was also known in the Fens and eighteen of the Hopkinses had lived in various parts of northern England. The surname is therefore widespread and appears to be overwhelmingly English. Moreover, at least some of the people bearing this surname in south Wales probably had English ancestors who migrated into the southern valleys in search of work in the coal mines and foundries.

The other name ending in -kins that is worth examining in this way is Watkins, a diminutive of Walter. This name has a much stronger Welsh presence than does Hopkins. A total of 301 deaths were registered in 1842. The stronghold of the name was clearly south-east Wales (Glamorganshire, Monmouthshire and Breconshire) and the adjoining English counties of Herefordshire, Worcestershire and Gloucestershire. Very few Watkinses had ventured further north than Birmingham. London had thirty Watkinses, and a few others lived close by, but otherwise the name was rarely found south of the Thames and was largely absent in eastern England. Watkins is an English name that was characteristic of the counties that bordered south-east Wales. For reasons that are unclear, the name appears to have been adopted in neighbouring parts of Wales when the English practice of naming was adopted in the sixteenth century.

The geographical distributions of Welsh surnames revealed by an analysis of the civil registration records fit those that John and Sheila Rowlands have discovered from their survey of surnames in Welsh marriage registers, from 1813 to 1837.[17] They have shown how marked regional preferences in the choice of personal names at the time of surname formation have produced distinctive patterns of surnames: Foulkes in Denbighshire, Gittins in Montgomeryshire, Edmunds in Monmouthshire, Hopkins in Glamorgan and Eynon in Pembrokeshire. Thomas is strongly represented in south Wales, except Monmouthshire, Davies is prominent in many parts of south Wales, particularly Cardiganshire, and Jenkins, James and Rees are other names that are well known in the south but which are seldom found in the north. Conversely, Ellis and Roberts are northern names that are uncommon in the south. Even the Joneses are not spread evenly across the country.

A final point that is worth making about Welsh surnames is that in the nineteenth and twentieth centuries some families have adopted doubled or hyphenated forms such as Lloyd George or Williams-Ellis in order to distinguish themselves from the vast numbers of Welsh people with common names. This practice has not usually had the same snobbish impulse that drove many Victorian English families to adopt hyphenated names or to insist on variant spellings such as Smythe for Smith.

Gaelic Surnames

The civil registration records of the 1840s give a clear picture of migration from Ireland and the Highlands of Scotland into certain parts of England by that date. Gaelic surnames have often been Anglicised into forms that are far removed from the originals. They are nonetheless usually so distinctive that their distributions can be plotted with confidence. Rourke, for example, is a common name in Ireland, particularly in Leinster, where it seems to have originated as a surname formed from a personal name. Twenty-six of the fifty-four Rourkes who died in England and Wales between 1842 and 1846 were registered in Merseyside and another ten had settled in London. These districts are well known to have been the favourite Irish destinations. The great emigration during the Famine was just beginning to be reflected in the numbers recorded in the 1842–46 indexes and, of course, for most Irish people, Liverpool and Manchester were the nearest urban centres where jobs could be found. But some Irish families had emigrated much earlier than the 1840s and Irish men had long searched for seasonal employment, gathering in the harvest. This is probably why some of the Rourkes died in what, at first sight, appear to be unlikely registration districts such as Cheltenham.

Keegan is an Anglicised form of another Irish personal name. It was also spelt Kegan, Kiggan, Kiggen, Keggyn and Kegeen in the forty-three occurrences of the name in the death indexes of 1842–46. Lancashire was the favoured destination of the Keegans, though six had died in London and nine elsewhere. Similar patterns can be observed with other Irish names. Eleven of the thirty-seven Kavanaghs whose deaths were registered in England and Wales between 1842 and 1846 had died in ten London districts, ten others had died in Liverpool, four in other parts of south Lancashire and twelve in places as far apart as Newcastle-upon-Tyne and Portsea Island. The forty-four Keoghs, Keoughs, Keows or Keohs (this was a difficult name for the English to catch) included twenty from Lancashire (mostly Merseyside) and eleven from London. Nearly half of the seventy-three Kearneys were from Lancashire and another eleven had died in London, but the rest were scattered in ones and twos throughout the land. The thirty-one Agnews were less dispersed, with ten in Liverpool, seven in Manchester, four in London and ten in eight other places.

The Keefs or Keefes had headed for London in greater numbers than the rest of their countrymen. No less than sixty of the 108 whose deaths were registered between 1842 and 1846 had died in the capital city. Nine of these had died in Marylebone but the others were registered in twenty-two different districts across London. Lancashire had been a less favoured destination, twenty-six people dying there. Bristol and the neighbouring district of Clifton each had three registrations, and three deaths were registered in south Wales. The distribution pattern suggests that most of the Keefes came from parts of Ireland that were distant from the usual crossing to Liverpool. Their ancient home was, in fact, in south Munster, particularly in County Cork. Irish surnames, too, have their regional concentrations.

It is often impossible to separate Irish names from the Gaelic names of Scotland, especially as there has been so much ancient migration between the two countries. Kennedy, a Gaelic name meaning 'ugly head', was a surname in both Ireland and Scotland long before any Kennedys migrated to England. It is therefore impossible to assign the 248 Kennedys whose deaths were registered in England and Wales between 1842 and 1846 to their families' places of origin. We may reasonably conclude that most, if not all, the ninety-two Kennedys who died in south Lancashire or north Cheshire (37 per cent of the whole) were members of Irish families and that most of the thirty-six Kennedys in the four northernmost counties of England were of Scottish descent; but the origins of the fifty-four who were scattered throughout midland and southern England and of the seventy-four who were registered in London are uncertain.

Names beginning with Mac- or Mc- are derived from the Gaelic word meaning 'son of'.[18] It is often popularly supposed that the choice of the particular form, Mac- or Mc-, determines whether a family came from Scotland or Ireland but this is not so. Such names were very rare in England before the later eighteenth century but by the 1840s they were found in many parts of the land, particularly in the largest towns. The deaths registered in England and Wales between 1842 and 1846 include those of 9382 men, women and children whose names began with Mc-. (I have chosen these for study because they provide a large sample and because the even larger number of names beginning with Mac- include English names, such as Machon or Macey, which would be troublesome to elimi-nate.) The distribution of names in this sample gives a broad indication (though obviously not a precise measure) of the places in England and Wales which were attractive to early migrants from Ireland and the Highlands and Islands of Scotland.

The map of their whereabouts in the 1840s contains few surprises. The single registration district of Liverpool recorded 1791 Mc- names, 19 per cent of the whole. Another 1898 deaths (21.5 per cent) were registered in all the registration districts of London except Hampstead. Next came Manchester (850, or 9 per cent), West Derby (338), Newcastle-upon-Tyne (270), Carlisle (186), Ashton-under-Lyne (183), Chorlton (179), Berwick (178), Whitehaven (169), Salford (135), Greenwich (118), Medway (107), Stockport (103) and Birmingham (100). These districts were either close to the Scottish border, next to London or not far from Liverpool. By contrast, no Mc- deaths were registered in the rural Welsh counties of Cardiganshire, Montgomeryshire or Merionethshire, and only one each was recorded in Brecknockshire and Radnorshire. The whole of Wales accounted for only ninety-two registrations, mostly in the industrial valleys of the south.

Relatively few Mc-s had settled in the Welsh borders. Herefordshire, Shropshire and Worcestershire had not proved attractive, for they had no industrial centres. Gloucestershire had drawn a few more, mainly because of Bristol, which had presumably been the port of entry. Likewise, because of its proximity to Liverpool, Cheshire had 243 registrations, including 103 in Stockport and sixty in Wirral The rural counties of eastern England offered few opportunities for employment for migrants and therefore they too had attracted only small numbers. Some Mc-s had entered south-western England via another port, for in 1842–46 the death registrations included forty-three in Stoke Damerel and eighteen in Plymouth. They had not ventured far inland, however, for only another eighty-three were registered in the rest of Cornwall, Devon, Somerset, Dorset and Wiltshire. Portsmouth and the Thames estuary were other points of entry; 118 Irish people had died in Gravesend and 107 in Medway during these five years.

The midland counties present a similar picture of low numbers except where employment was available in industrial districts. Given the larger populations of those districts, the Mc-s were probably distributed in similar proportions to the rest wherever they chose to settle outside London and the six northern counties of England. Birmingham and the Black Country was the only other district that had attracted large numbers.

The north of England had provided jobs and homes for both the Scottish and the Irish Mc-s, for it was accessible and its industrial districts offered plenty of opportunities for unskilled workers. Northumberland's 598 registrations included 178 in Berwick on the Scottish border, 270 in Newcastle-upon-Tyne and seventy-three in Tynemouth. The industrial districts of Cumberland and County Durham had also proved attractive to migrants but Westmorland had little to offer. No doubt, many of these Mc-s were Irish people who had crossed the sea to find industrial employment. By this time, Yorkshire was one of the country's major industrial districts but it was not the first choice for Scottish migrants and the Pennines acted as a difficult hurdle (both physically and psychologically) for the Irish. Leeds had attracted a similar-sized group to that in Birmingham but the numbers in the other Yorkshire towns were much smaller than those in the Lancashire registration districts. As yet, neither the West Riding nor the west midlands had acquired sizable Irish communities.

Lancashire was the principal destination of these migrants. Altogether, the county accounted for 3988, or 42.5 per cent, of those Mc-s whose deaths were registered in 1842–46. The overwhelming majority had settled in Merseyside and other parts of south Lancashire. The northern half of the county was like most other English counties in having only a sprinkling of people with Mc- names.

The migration of Welsh, Irish and Scottish people into England became much more pronounced as the population of the British Isles soared from the late eighteenth century onwards. The census of 1801 counted 8.9 million people in England and Wales. By 1851 the population of the two countries had risen to 17.9 million and by 1911 to 36.1 million. The industrial regions grew at an astonishing rate. Lancashire's population was 673,486 in 1801; by 1851 it had grown to 2,026,462; and by 1901 it had reached 4,286,666. Much of this growth was due to the natural increase of the native population (around two-thirds of it from earlier marriages and more children, the other third from lower death rates). The majority of Lancashire people therefore continued to bear surnames that had long been familiar in the county. But immigrants were far more numerous than in earlier times. The 1851 census revealed that 1,928,579 people in Lancashire and Cheshire had been born in one or other of these counties, 242,500 people had been born in other parts of England, 214,000 in Ireland, 76,000 in Wales, 31,000 in Scotland and 10,900 abroad. Of course, the size of the immigrant population is understated by these figures, for some of those who had been born in Lancashire or Cheshire were children with Irish, Welsh or Scottish parents. Nevertheless, the local origins of most families is clear. The people whose families had been born within the county boundaries far outnumbered the immigrants from the rest of the United Kingdom.

Family Names and Local History

It has been the argument of this book that past and present distributions of surnames show that families have tended to remain settled within a district bounded by their nearest market towns, which in the past they thought of as their 'country'. Richard Gough, the Shropshire freeholder who wrote a *History of Myddle* (1701–2), used the term naturally in phrases such as 'He was a person well reputed in his country' or 'Shee did much good in the country'. He wrote about the disreputable Richard Clayton, who left his wife and 'went out of the country' with another woman, and about Habbakuk Heylin, who upon his marriage took his wife back 'to her owne country agen'. Travel writers and novelists used the term freely, sometimes in the vague sense of 'a corn country' or an industrial district such as the Black Country, but often they applied it more precisely in the sense of one of the definitions of the *Oxford English Dictionary*: 'A tract or district having more or less definite limits in relation to human occupation, e.g. owned by the same lord or proprietor, or inhabited by people of the same race, dialect, occupation, etc.'. George Eliot and Thomas Hardy were very conscious of this usage and Anthony Trollope supplied a map of 'The

Barchester Country' to accompany his set of ecclesiastical novels. In the preface to *The Mayor of Casterbridge*, which he set in Dorchester, Hardy referred to 'the real history of the town called Casterbridge and the neighbouring country'; and one of his characters says, 'We will leave Casterbridge as quietly as we have come, and go back to our own country'. The term is a useful one for local historians, for it indicates a sense of belonging not just to a particular town or rural parish but also to a wider district in which families had friends and relations and people with whom they did business.

While we can still observe the sudden changes of scenery that so impressed travellers as they journeyed at a leisurely pace through England's many 'countries' before the coming of the railways and the motor car, it is much more difficult for us to appreciate the equally marked sudden changes of society, even within a single county, that were glaringly obvious in earlier times. Provincial life was more diverse, even in the nineteenth century, than it is today, for communications with other parts of the land were so much slower. Alan Everitt has remarked on how two seventeenth-century towns as similar in size and function as Leicester and Northampton could be so different in their social structure, political temper and economic fortunes. Farming on the Lincolnshire Wolds was a very different business to what it was in the nearby Fens, the potters of north Staffordshire had little in common with the metal workers and coal miners in the south of the county, and in Warwickshire the River Avon divided the wood-pastures of the Forest of Arden from the open-field, corn-growing 'felden' country to the south. Even within a 'country', neat, trim estate villages such as Coxwold in north Yorkshire could be very different in appearance and in the attitudes of their inhabitants to owner-occupier villages such as Husthwaite, a mile or two down the road. The contrasting fortunes of neighbouring communities in Leicestershire are nowhere more apparent than when looking across the huge sheep pastures that surround the mounds and depressions of the site of the deserted medieval village of Foston towards Wigston Magna, which was always the most populous village in the county.

In his *Natural History of Wiltshire*, unfinished at his death in 1697, John Aubrey famously divided his county into 'cheese' and 'chalk' countries. The 'chalk country' lay on the downs, 'where 'tis all upon tillage, and where the shepherds labour hard, their flesh is hard, their bodies strong, being weary after hard labour, they have not leisure to read or contemplate of religion'. In the 'dirty, clayey country' to the north, by contrast, the people 'speak drawling; they are phlegmatic, skins pale and livid, slow and dull, heavy of spirit; hereabout is but little tillage or hard labour, they only milk the cows and make cheese; they feed chiefly on milk meats, which cools their brains too much, and hurts their inventions'. Aubrey's explanations sound extravagant to modern ears but historians have concluded that he was right to identify the major cultural differences between the two districts.

Unravelling family networks is just one of the ways of identifying the numerous 'countries' of England. The physical setting, building materials that reflected the nature of the surface geology, the administrative framework, the nature of the predominant form of work, characteristic speech patterns, religious and political affiliations all play their part. They can be mentioned only in passing here.

Most of us share a sense of belonging to both a particular place – a town or a village – and to a wider district. We no longer call this a 'country' but it often corresponds to the neighbourhood that was familiar to our ancestors. By the sixteenth and seventeenth centuries gentry families were linked at the level of the shire, but ordinary families did not share this attachment to counties until much later, probably not until the late eighteenth or nineteenth centuries. In earlier times the tie of loyalty was to town or parish, then to one's 'country' and finally to England. London provided the vital link that gave provincial people a sense of belonging to the whole of England. By the early seventeenth century, if not before, it was connected by carrying services to all parts of the provinces. Young migrants were attracted to the capital city in droves, so much so that in 1680 Sir John Reresby remarked that London 'drained all England of its people'. Many English men and women who did not settle there permanently spent some time in London before returning to their own 'country'. Those who made their fortunes in the capital city regularly left a bequest in their wills to the inhabitants of the distant places they had left in their youth. Sometimes this was in the form of a personal memorial, such as the village school at Burnsall in the Yorkshire Dales, which was founded in 1602 by Sir William Craven, a native of the parish who had been Lord Mayor of London; or an almshouse like that in Newland (Gloucestershire), founded in 1615 by William Jones, 'Citizen and Haberdasher of London' for sixteen poor parishioners. If Londoners were attached to their birthplaces so many miles away, how much stronger that feeling of loyalty must have been amongst those who stayed behind.

While people were prepared to travel considerable distances to get to London, once they arrived they tended to be as restricted in their movements as the families they had left and as attached to their new neighbourhood as their rural cousins were to their 'countries'. My wife's ancestors, the Wilkinsons, have a northern name, but they were amongst those who migrated to the capital city so long ago that we cannot trace their origins. A James Henry Wilkinson, whose son, James John Wilkinson, was baptised at St Andrew's church, Holborn, in 1754, seems a likely ancestor but this cannot be proved with certainty. Can we identify the son with the James Wilkinson, hatter, whose own son was baptised James John Wilkinson at the same church in 1816? The chances seem high. This younger James John Wilkinson followed his father's occupation but moved a short distance to the north of Holborn. In 1842 he married Sarah Gostick at St John's church, Islington. In the 1841 census (the year before his marriage) he was a lodger at the home of his future bride in Albany Place, Holloway. Upon his marriage he moved to nearby Hope Street, where his son, James Joseph Wilkinson, was born in 1848. When the son married in 1870, he and his bride were both living in her parents' home in Dorset Street, just off Liverpool Street, Islington. The family were still resident in the same district in 1915 when Edward Horace Wilkinson (1889–1962) was married at St James's church, Holloway, but the younger generation then moved a little further north, to Kingsbury, Wembley, Tottenham, Wood Green, Muswell Hill and neighbouring places, all of which were nevertheless within a well-defined area of north London. For at least two centuries, the family's movements had been as limited in scale as those of people who lived in provincial England.

The core groups of families who remained rooted in their 'country' were the ones who shaped local culture and passed on their traditions. In *Anna of the Five Towns* (1902), Arnold Bennett wrote, 'Mynors belonged to a family now otherwise extinct in the Five Towns – one of those families which by virtue of numbers, variety, and personal force seem to permeate a whole district, to be a calculable item of it, an essential part of its identity'. Networks of long-resident families were formed and repeatedly strengthened by intermarriage. Many of these old urban dynasties continued to run provincial towns over several generations, while in the countryside networks of farming clans set the standards for local society. Whenever a dispute arose over local customs or practices the contending parties turned to old people who had lived locally all their lives. Newcomers learned to conform to the accepted ways of the natives.

Two examples of the deep influence of core families on the character of their 'countries' must suffice here: religious dissent and speech. The crucial role of core groups of families in establishing and preserving patterns of religious behaviour is well documented in a group of studies of various parishes in the south midlands, which show, for example, that in the sixteenth and seventeenth centuries families with Lollard ancestry were much less mobile than other families in the Chilterns. Similar surnames had suggested family links between the old Lollards and the new Dissenters of the later seventeenth century; genealogical methods proved them. The extraordinary immobility of such groups over long periods of time aided efforts to trace the descent of many Nonconformist families within the same small geographical area and led to the conclusion that 'radical dissent was a family affair'.[19]

Speech is the most distinctive characteristic that separates one local society from another and the one that is immediately apparent. Nowadays accents and rhythms of speech rather than the use of dialect words provide the clues, though the unconscious use of dialect may betray a speaker's origins. The use of the word frit, for frightened, by a former Prime Minister in the House of Commons, placed her firmly in the east midlands, despite the considerable changes to her accent that she had made over the years. In the days when crafts such as the making of pots, knives or hosiery were the major occupations of well-defined districts, the terminology of the workplace helped to set people apart from each other. The decline of traditional industries has meant that distinctive vocabularies have been lost. Accents continue to flourish, however, despite the spread of received pronunciation in modern times. Most people can immediately recognise a Geordie or a Brummie accent or quickly sense that a speaker is from somewhere in the north of England but the identification can be much more precise than that. An informed listener can place a speaker within a restricted area that corresponds to the old idea of a 'country'. Sheffielders are puzzled by my accent, for I come from a place that lies thirteen miles to the north, in a different 'country' where my surname is common. The persistence of local patterns of speech can be explained only by the immobility of the core families who set the standards to which newcomers, or their children, eventually conformed. It is very noticeable that the children of Commonwealth immigrants into English cities in recent years have learned that the best way to become accepted is to speak as the natives do.

The evidence from surnames and family histories for the stability of populations within well-defined areas is supported by the work of medical researchers who have used blood-groups, and, more recently, DNA samples, to demonstrate genetic differences between various groups of people. We can well believe that the inhabitants of the Orkneys or of central Lakeland are different from other people but it was more surprising to read a report of the summer meeting of the British Association for the Advancement of Science in 1992 which said that the genetic composition of people in Norfolk was different from that of people living in Suffolk. There is no physical barrier of any importance to prevent movement between the two counties, yet the invisible barrier of the county boundary has apparently been an effective deterrent to large-scale migration for well over a thousand years. The descendants of the Saxon immigrants are still broadly divided into the north folk and the south folk.

The conclusions of the geneticists are supported by the researches of local historians. Charles Phythian-Adams has observed that in 1841 over 91 per cent of the inhabitants of Norfolk and Suffolk had been born in the county where they resided on census night.[20] He noted also 'the manifest lack of demographic integration' between Devon and Cornwall, or between Dorset and Somerset, and he showed that in 1841–61 an overwhelming majority of adults in England and Wales were living in the county in which they were born. The invisible line of the county boundary acted as a real barrier to geographical mobility. Even a south midland county like Bedfordshire shared this general characteristic. Bedfordshire, like other counties, had its own distinctive surnames. These barriers were less effective where burgeoning industrial conurbations straddled county boundaries, as in the Birmingham district, or in Manchester and Merseyside, but they continued to function where the old agrarian economy was largely untouched by industrialisation.

The study of the origins, spread and distribution patterns of family names helps us to determine the nature and boundaries of local societies. In years to come, we shall be able to use far more sophisticated quantitative methods than are available at present. The regional nature of mobility patterns will become clearer but I doubt whether the broad outlines of the picture will be much different. We can already see that the 'core families' which have often remained in the same district since surnames began formed the backbone of the numerous local societies in England and largely determined what sort of places they were. Some of these families bore common surnames such as Taylor or Wright but they can nevertheless be traced back in the same locality over the centuries. Some persistent local families, like the Twiggs who have lived in Sheffield since at least 1440, possessed names which were less common but which had separate origins elsewhere. Most distinctive of all, however, were the many other families, in every part of England, whose surnames are peculiar to the 'countries' where they were formed six or seven centuries ago. At the end of the twentieth century a person's surname can still be a badge of identity, as clear an indication of the family's place of origin as his or her way of speaking.

PART TWO

Tracing Surnames Back in Time

6

The Nineteenth and Twentieth Centuries

Identifying the home of a family name depends on determining the geographical distribution of the name at various points in time and on genealogical research to prove a descent. Some surprising results can be obtained from the analysis of information that is readily available for the present day. Telephone directories are the most easily accessible source for plotting the current distribution of surnames. They are not comprehensive but, according to the 1995 edition of *Social Trends*, in 1991 as many as 90 per cent of all households in Britain had a telephone, including the unknown (but growing) number who prefer to be ex-directory. This is a large sample of the population. Directories include the names of subscribers who choose other organisations such as Mercury instead of British Telecom. They nevertheless need to be handled with care. Counts of surnames should not include businesses but must concentrate on domestic lines. This is not difficult, as businesses are usually picked out in bold type or arranged separately. A more serious problem is caused by the growing practice of overlapping entries in neighbouring directories. British Telecom also reorganise their catchment areas from time to time; the London area has been completely reorganised. Ideally, one should use a set of earlier directories which were in use before reorganisation and the practice of overlapping began and before large numbers of people chose to go ex-directory. Directories from the 1980s are the best, but these are hard to come by. An almost complete set of telephone directories from 1879 to the present day is available at British Telecom's Archives and Historical Information Centre, 24 Temple Avenue, London, EC4Y 0HL, which is open to the public, but public reference libraries do not keep past copies of directories.

A simple count of the number of phone book entries for a surname can produce some striking results. For common names a rough estimate can be arrived at by counting the number of pages containing individual entries, allowing for about 350 entries per page. Problems arise immediately when one is confronted by variant spellings of a name: it is often hard to decide which names are variants and which are derived from another source. There is no simple solution and each case must be taken on its merits. The total number of surname entries per directory can be plotted on a map of the

United Kingdom divided into the telephone districts. Such a map can be drawn from the maps provided in each directory. A set of blank maps based on the master copies which name the districts will allow information to be plotted for each surname. Unfortunately, the boundaries of telephone districts do not correspond to those of any other administrative unit, such as a civil registration district or parish, so comparisons with data derived from earlier records are not direct. Such comparisons will nevertheless allows us to see whether the name was concentrated in the same geographical area at different points in time.

The 1986 Sheffield telephone directory may be regarded as fairly typical of the larger urban areas. It lists 238,556 subscribers with 19,510 different surnames (if each variant spelling is counted as a different name). Of these names, 8318 appear only once, 2723 twice, 1500 three times, and 1028 four times. Most of these rare names are not medieval survivals but are later variants; many belong to a transient part of the population whose names are more common elsewhere. A name has been judged to be rare if it had less than twenty-five entries, i.e. 1:10,000 of the subscribers. The rarest names, which appeared only one to four times, amounted to 13,569 of the 19,510 different surnames. They were held by only 21,376 of the 238,556 subscribers. The remaining 5941 surnames were shared by 217,180 subscribers. It is these names that are of particular interest to the local and family historian concerned with the common stock of surnames in his or her locality, though one must always bear in mind that some of the rare names may be local ones that have never multiplied or which are declining in numbers.

Patrick Hanks, whose Survey of Contemporary Surnames began in 1980, using 1980–81 telephone directories, has found that, despite all the vicissitudes of migration and social upheaval, the patterns of distribution of many surnames were still almost as marked in 1980 as they were in 1890, when H. B. Guppy was publishing his pioneering study.[1] It is clear from work such as this that a name which today is clustered in a particular locality either originated there or arrived there early in the period of hereditary surname formation; or else it is a very rare name borne by a single family who have moved out of their original district.

The raw data from simple counts of entries in telephone directories can be skewed by the concentrations of people living in the major urban areas. The largest population covered by a telephone district is fifty times the size of the smallest. Hanks's survey uses a threshold of fifteen to twenty listings per directory in choosing which surnames to count. Many distributions are obvious from the raw figures. He remarks that 'it does not take sophisticated statistics to notice that the name Calladine has seventy-three entries in the

Nottinghamshire directory and fewer than twenty anywhere else'. Nevertheless, he concludes that 'since the different telephone areas are of different sizes, it is desirable to express the figures in a way that makes instant comparison possible'. His raw data counts are therefore normalised by expressing them as a frequency per 100,000.

The Guild of One-Name Studies (founded 1979) encourages its members to make a count of their surnames in the current telephone directories. They have acquired considerable expertise in dealing with the problems of interpreting this source. One of the problems that they have addressed is how to convert the total number of subscribers with a particular surname into an approximate total number of holders of that name. Correspondence in their journal has suggested a multiplier ranging from 3.7 to 4.3. These figures have been arrived at through a comparison of birth, marriage and death registrations since 1837, with some allowance made for emigration. They can only be approximations, but the general agreement is that a multiplier of four will give a figure which is reasonably accurate.

The problems of overlapping entries and business addresses are eliminated if one has access to British Telecom's CD-ROM of current subscribers, which enables the searcher to call up a complete list of residential subscribers by surname, arranged alphabetically by first name. This information cannot readily be mapped according to telephone districts but, as precise locations are given, a firm geographical pattern can be noted. The CD-ROM is constantly being updated. Thus it is possible to enter Toynton and to read sixty-four entries for this rare surname. Half of these names are scattered thinly nationwide but the other half are found in Lincolnshire (especially the southern part) or just across the county boundary. This is a clear indication of the surname's present distribution and is the starting point for an enquiry into the origin of the name, which is complicated by the discovery that between Horncastle and Skegness are no less than five settlements called High Toynton, Low Toynton, Toynton All Saints, Toynton St Peter and Toynton Fen Side.

Sometimes the telephone directories confirm a belief that a rare surname was derived from a minor local place-name. The modern directories list only seventy Gilberthorpes. Forty-two of them live in Yorkshire, and twenty-three, or 33 per cent, are listed in the Sheffield and Rotherham directory. No Gilberthorpes are recorded in the London directories. The modern distribution supports the local historian's guess that the surname is derived from a minor place-name on a hill top just inside the parish of Rotherham. The place-name is unrecorded before 1554 but the surname appears much earlier, in 1379, when Robert of Gilberthorp paid 4d. poll tax in Tinsley on the opposite side of the River Don. No document provides a definite link

between the surname and the place-name but the identity of the Gilberthorpes' original home can hardly be doubted. We find them from time to
time in the manorial and parish records of Sheffield and Rotherham from
1440 onwards but the family name never ramified. The Gilberthorpes just
managed to keep going in the male line. The hearth tax returns of the 1670s
name Edward and John at Wickersley, not far from Gilberthorpe, and
Thomas a few miles to the south in the Derbyshire parish of Whittington,
where a branch of the family had lived since at least 1600. The Gilberthorpes
were only slightly more numerous in later centuries. The 1898–99 Sheffield
and Rotherham directory lists five of them: a shop keeper, a drug store
owner, a boot maker, a cow keeper and William Gilberthorpe of Heeley,
who was described as a muffin and pikelet baker. The modern telephone
directories have prompted a fruitful line of enquiry for detailed genealogical
research.

Although the Kinders are spread more widely than the Gilberthorpes,
there seems little doubt that they came from a bleak spot high in the Peak
District, where Kinderscout forms a formidable initial barrier to walkers
attempting the Pennine Way. Modern telephone directories list 463 Kinders,
of whom 20 per cent are found in the four Manchester directories. The
distribution pattern of the name is a typical one, radiating out from the
Peak District into Lancashire, the West Riding of Yorkshire and other
neighbouring counties, thinning out beyond until another significant group
are found in London. When we go back in time to 1842–46 we find that
the civil registration indexes of deaths record 124 Kinders. The name had
ramified in Ashton-under-Lyne (32) and Huddersfield (18), but no other
registration district had more than four entries. This earlier pattern rein-
forces the information derived from telephone directories. Further back in
time, the Derbyshire hearth tax returns of 1670 record seven householders
name Kinder, including Ralph Kinder at Kinder Hamlet and three nearby
at Edale and Lose Hill. A few more were found in neighbouring counties.
The early parish register entries transcribed in the International Genealogical
Index confirm the later picture, for the Kinders were baptising their children
in Derbyshire, nearby moorland parts of Cheshire, Staffordshire, the West
Riding and Lancashire (especially Ashton-under-Lyne and Manchester).
Back in the middle ages, we find the Kinders paying poll tax in the Peak
District, close to the hamlet that provided their name. William of Kinder
was taxed at Tideswell and William, Hugh and Thomas Kinder paid at
Bowden, near Chapel-en-le-Frith. The earliest reference to the surname
which has been found is to Philota de Kender in 1274.

Place-names sometimes gave rise to surnames with different forms.
Wigfield Farm, which originated as a medieval clearing near Worsbrough,

south of Barnsley, is the most likely origin of the surnames Wigfield, Wigfall
and Wigfull. The British Telecom CD-ROM (1995) listed 132 Wigfields, of
whom fifty-one lived in the West Riding of Yorkshire and eleven in north
Derbyshire. The only other concentration of people bearing this form of
the surname consists of sixteen subscribers in Birkenhead and the Wirral;
a separate Merseyside origin for the surname therefore seems possible,
though the concentration might be explained by later migration. The matter
can be determined only by detailed genealogical research. In 1995 the national
telephone directories also named thirty-seven Wigfalls and fifteen Wigfulls
nationwide; seven of these Wigfalls and five Wigfulls were listed in the
Sheffield directory but nobody with either forms of these surnames appeared
in the adjoining Barnsley directory (which includes Worsbrough).

Research into the earlier history of the name confirms the usefulness of
modern telephone directories in pointing to the likely source of origin. The
ancient shape of the *assart*, or clearing, that was known as Wigfall by the first
half of the thirteenth century, survives in the Worsbrough landscape. A tithe
commutation map of 1838 marks twenty closes on either side of a lane,
within a well-defined, curving boundary which can still be observed. The
first reference to the inherited surname is from 1330, when Jordan of Wiggefall
granted the farmstead which he had inherited from his father Simon to his
son Richard. In 1379 John and Agnes Wigfall, Alice of Wigfall, Ibot of Wigfall,
and Henry and Matilda of Wigfall paid poll tax in Worsbrough township.
Two centuries later, some of the Wigfalls had settled a little further south
in the parishes of Sheffield and Ecclesfield. William Wigfall was granted a
cutler's mark by the manorial court at Sheffield in 1567. In the hearth tax
returns of the 1670s Derbyshire had one Wigfall, Nottinghamshire had one
Wigfield and south Yorkshire had six Wigfields, all within walking distance
of Wigfield Farm. The name of the farmstead had changed from Wigfall to
the modern Wigfield during the seventeenth century. The surname began
to change about the same time. A twist in the pursuit of the Wigfalls and
Wigfields occurs in the Worsbrough parish register where, from 1692,
numerous incoming Wigfields are recorded as farmers and nailers, including
a family from neighbouring Hoyland, but a genealogical connection between
the earlier Wigfalls and the modern Wigfields has proved elusive. Henry,
the last local male Wigfall of the original medieval family in Worsbrough,
left the district in the early eighteenth century to become a prosperous 'soap
boiler' in London.

Telephone directories and indexes of the modern civil registration records
of births, marriages and deaths also provide information about the geographical distribution of the surnames of immigrants who have arrived since
the late nineteenth century. The number of Jewish immigrants rose steadily

in Victorian times, especially during the 1880s and 1890s, when thousands
of families sought refuge from persecution in Russia, Poland, Lithuania and
other parts of the Russian empire, and again in the 1930s to escape the
Nazis. The East End of London, particularly Stepney, was the favourite
destination but the Leylands district of Leeds and parts of Manchester
attracted others. Some Jewish surnames are easy to spot but others were
changed to similar-sounding English names or altered altogether. Prominent
members of recent Conservative governments have included Sir Leon Brit-
tan, Michael Howard, Sir Keith Joseph and Nigel Lawson, whose immediate
ancestors were Jewish immigrants with very different names. The eminent
economic historian Sidney Pollard began life as Siegfried Pollack in Vienna.
Commonwealth immigrants who have arrived since the 1950s can be even
more difficult to identify in this way, for many came with English surnames.
Some of the bearers of distinctive surnames derived from English villages
and hamlets turn out to be descendants of African slaves who were shipped
to the West Indies and given the name of a slave-owner whose family
originated in England. For example, Comberbatch, a surname which is
derived from a village in Cheshire, is a very common name in Barbados
and has been reintroduced into England by West Indian immigrants. In
Leicester, Bradford, parts of London and certain other populous districts,
however, Asian names are amongst the most common in the local telephone
directories. In such places, Patel has begun to rival Smith and Jones. Many
surnames from the Indian sub-continent have as localised an origin and
present distribution as do English names. As immigrants tend to cluster
together, some of their distinctive surnames are now confined to particular
localities in Britain.

Electoral Rolls and Census Returns

Telephone directories, despite their inadequacies, remain the most useful
starting point when plotting the distributions of surnames. Colin Rogers
notes that for small areas it is also practical to use the electoral register,
which is now computerised and so can be presented in alphabetical order
of surname.[2] Many local authorities, however, have refused to make this
information available to the public. The annual electoral register gives all
the names on one day, 'the qualifying date', but it is estimated that, even
before the introduction of the poll tax, or 'community charge', by the
Thatcher government, up to 14 per cent of the electorate were not registered.
This source is therefore far from complete. Nevertheless, Dr Kevin Schürer
has used national data to great effect in plotting the modern distribution
of surnames for a public display at the Science Museum, London. His maps

show that the geographical distributions of surnames in England and Wales at the end of the twentieth century are not markedly different from the patterns revealed by the census returns of 1881.

Census returns are more comprehensive but they are not available for consultation until a hundred years have passed since their compilation. The development of the software package *GenMap UK* has recently enabled us to make computer-based analyses of surname distributions in 1881, now that the census returns in that year have been indexed for the whole of England, Scotland, Wales, Channel Islands, Isle of Man and Royal Navy in a joint project of the Mormon Church, the Public Record Office and family history societies throughout the land. In 1999 this index was made available in a set of CD-ROMs available from the Church of Latter Day Saints (the Mormons). Unlike the documents that we have used for earlier periods, these returns provide almost complete coverage of the population at a particular moment in time. Here is a wonderful opportunity to map all the surnames in every part of the country on a much more systematic basis than before. The Science Museum display includes thousands of maps that Kevin Schürer has drawn from this source. The 1881 census returns will undoubtedly become a major source for the study of surname distributions in the next few years.

Civil Registration Records

The civil registration of births, marriages and deaths in England and Wales, which began on 1 July 1837 and continues to this day, has provided an enormous set of records which can be used to determine the distribution patterns of surnames throughout the two countries. The records are kept at the Family Records Centre, Myddelton Street, London EC1R 1UW, where indexes of names may be consulted in large volumes arranged chrono-logically on open shelves. Microfiche copies of the indexes may be purchased by individuals and are available at record offices and some public libraries, at the record centres of the Mormon Church (where they are made freely available to all-comers) and at the meeting places of the larger family history societies. The earliest records capture patterns of family names at the very beginning of the reign of Victoria, just before the railways provided quick and cheap travel to all parts of the kingdom and steamships facilitated emigration overseas.

The original system of registration districts was based on the unions of parishes which had been created by the Poor Law Amendment Act of 1834. Some of these districts were changed on 1 January 1852 to take account of recent population changes. Fortunately for the majority of surnames, the period 1 July 1837 to 31 December 1851, that is from the start of civil registration to the formation of some new districts, provides a large enough sample for distributions of names to be assessed with confidence. Indeed, for most surnames a much shorter period is sufficient. The maps of the 1834 poor law unions which were published for each county in the 1849 edition of Samuel Lewis, *Atlas to the Topographical Dictionaries of England and Wales*, enable us to reconstruct the registration districts that were in use until 31 December 1851. A number of minor problems need to be resolved about the boundaries of some of the districts, especially the smaller ones, and some inconsistencies appear in the original civil registration data, but these are small difficulties that do not detract from the great value of having a map of all the original registration districts in England and Wales on which to plot the information contained in the indexes.

The fourteen years and six months between 1 July 1837 and 31 December 1851 is a period that is long enough for family names (other than the exceedingly rare ones) to be recorded in statistically significant numbers. In practice, the distribution of most surnames can be assessed with confidence from a five-year block within this period and that of some common names can be judged from a single year, for the entries are so numerous. I began by analysing the registers of births but found that in the early decades of registration, births – particularly in certain counties, such as Surrey, Sussex, Middlesex, Essex and Shropshire, together with parts of Wales – were seriously under-recorded. It also became clear that, as many women gave birth to two or three children during a five-year period, the distribution of surnames was skewed by this duplicating or triplicating. I decided therefore to extract information from the registers of deaths rather than births. As I was concerned merely with identifying the distribution of surnames at a particular point in time, the objections that people had commonly moved from their place of birth and that women had changed their maiden name upon marriage were irrelevant. The number of people who died away from home in another registration district was unlikely to have been significant, for registration districts were much larger than parishes. In any case my purpose would be served if I could show clusterings over neighbouring registration districts. The populous conurbations naturally had more registered deaths than did rural districts, but this did not prevent the recognition of regional distributions of surnames. Nor did attempts to correlate the data with population totals derived from the 1841 and 1851 census returns reveal anything that could not be seen from the crude figures. The patterns were striking enough.

As the microfiche copies of the handwritten indexes for the earliest years are difficult to read, the easiest starting date for the extraction of data is

1 January 1842, from when the indexes are typed. The Registrar-General's *Sixteenth Annual Report*, published in 1856, noted that surnames beginning with the letter R accounted for 5.0 per cent of all surnames recorded in the civil registration indexes in the early 1850s. The letter A accounted for a further 3.1 per cent, the letter E for 2.4 per cent and the letter K for another 2.0 per cent, making 12.5 per cent or one-eighth of the whole set of names. I have chosen these four letters to create a computer database of over 220,000 individual names from the civil registration indexes of deaths for each quarter between 1 January 1842 and 31 December 1846. Many of these names, together with some beginning with other letters and others with slightly different registration dates, will be used in this chapter to illustrate how numerous family names were still remarkably restricted in their geographical distribution in the middle years of the nineteenth century. We shall see that many family names had not moved far from their point of origin by the 1840s. Indeed a high number have remained very local in their distribution to this day.

Telephone directories, electoral registers, census returns and civil registration records are our major sources for plotting the geographical distributions of surnames in the nineteenth and twentieth centuries. The maps that we produce, particularly for the rarer names, usually show that a surname is still surprisingly concentrated close to its point of origin in the middle ages. They demonstrate that, although a minority were very mobile, most people had stayed within a few miles of their birthplaces. The civil registration records of the early years of Victoria's reign demonstrate that this is true of each of the types of surname that we have discussed earlier: the classes that we call locative, topographical, personal, nicknames and occupational. These are simply categories devised by historians to make the study of surnames more manageable. The beginner does not need to decide which category his or her name belongs to when collecting data and drawing maps. All types of surname can be mapped from these records, and all but the very common ones will have interesting concentrations in different parts of the country.

Locative Names

Surnames derived from place-names are naturally the easiest to place in a particular part of England. In most cases, they are still concentrated near the place from which they were derived. Thus the fifty-nine Attenboroughs or Attenborrows who died between 1842 and 1846 had lived mostly in the Trent Valley (Nottinghamshire, Derbyshire and Leicestershire), close to the village of Attenborough, which was only a small settlement in the middle ages. Likewise, twenty-six of the thirty-eight Ramshaws were from County Durham, near the Pennine village of that name, the forty-three people named Antrobus were nearly all from Merseyside (fifteen in north Cheshire and nineteen in south Lancashire), not far from Antrobus, a settlement in north Cheshire, and eight of the twelve people with the rare name Aldwinkle had lived close to the Northamptonshire settlement from which the name was derived. Cases such as these are absolutely straightforward and surprisingly common.

Lancashire is particularly rich in names of this sort. The 166 Kershaws who died in the single year 1842 were nearly all from Lancashire or neighbouring parts of the West Riding of Yorkshire; ninety of them were registered in Manchester and Oldham, close to the hamlet of Kershaw in Middleton parish. Another example from the same parish is Ainsworth, a surname which is derived from a small settlement half way between Bolton and Bury. Twenty-eight of the seventy-seven Ainsworths whose deaths were recorded between 1842 and 1846 were from the Blackburn registration district and thirty-two from the rest of Lancashire. Richard McKinley has shown that the surname was recorded in Middleton parish in the thirteenth century, as the name of landowners, and in the fourteenth and fifteenth centuries in a number of places in Salford hundred, in which Middleton lay.[3] William Harrison Ainsworth, the Victorian writer of historical novels, was born and bred in Manchester, close to where his surname originated.

An example from Yorkshire of a surname whose home can be spotted from its distribution at the beginning of Victoria's reign is provided by the 134 Asquiths or Askwiths who were concentrated in the heart of the West Riding in 1842–46, though others were found in north Yorkshire, with a few in Durham and Cumberland. Herbert Asquith, Prime Minister from 1908 to 1916, came from Morley, a few miles from where his surname originated. The place-name Askwith was recorded in Domesday Book, in the parish of Weston, in the wapentake of Upper Claro. The name means 'ash wood' and is unusual in that district in being of Scandinavian origin. Although the place-name is a minor one, there is no difficulty in identifying it.

An example of a marked concentration of a locative surname in a different part of the country is provided by Ackland or Acland, which is derived from Acland Barton in Landkey (Devon), a property which remained in the the possession of the Aclands until 1945 (see Map 1, p. 195). Junior branches of the family ventured over the county boundary into Somerset, but in the period 1842–46 the eighty Aclands whose deaths were registered were overwhelmingly from south-western England, including twenty-eight from Devon. Nine Aclands achieved sufficient fame to be included in *The Dictionary of National Biography*. The rare surname Raddon is also derived from a Devon place-name, near Marystow; twelve of the fourteen Raddons who died in 1842–46 were from Devon, the other two from London. Luscombe is another Devon name that was still mostly confined to the county at the beginning of Victoria's reign. The surname Kessel(l), Kestle or Kestell is even more localised in the south west, near the village of Kestle in east Cornwall. Sixteen of the thirty deaths that were registered in 1842–46 were from Truro or Penzance districts and all (but one in Westminster) were from south-western England.

Alsop (and its variant spellings of Allsop, Allsopp, Allsup and Allsoop) is derived from Alsop-en-le-Dale, on the Derbyshire-Staffordshire border. The 391 people bearing that name in the 1842–46 indexes of deaths were registered in 115 places. The Alsops had migrated in all directions; westwards into Staffordshire, Warwickshire and other parts of the west midlands, and down the Severn Valley, northwards into Lancashire and eastwards into other parts of Derbyshire, Nottinghamshire and Leicestershire; twenty-seven had died in London. But some parts of England had not been reached by the Alsops. They were prolific but the distribution pattern still points to their original home.

In many other cases, surnames of the locative type have a narrow distribution but the place which has given rise to the name cannot readily be found. Reaney and Wilson identify the surname Ardern from Arden (Cheshire), which was spelt Arderne in a document of 1260. The distribution of the surname in the 1840s supports this identification, for it is highly concentrated in north Cheshire, adjoining parts of north-west Derbyshire, and just across the Mersey in south Lancashire. The local and family historian's task of identifying a place-name is not always as straightforward as this, however, for many settlements were minor ones, some of which have disappeared.

Another problem in locating the home of a family name is caused by local pronunciations of place-names, which may differ markedly from the pronunciation suggested by the spelling. The surname Rothwell comes from a small place with that name in Lancashire, not from places with the same name in Yorkshire, Lincolnshire or Northamptonshire. The reason why the Northamptonshire settlement did not produce a family called Rothwell is that the local pronunciation of the place is Rowlett. This form has given rise to a local surname. In 1842–46 eleven of the thirty-three Rowletts or Rowlatts were registered as having died in Oundle and the rest were from Kettering, Peterborough, Thrapstone and elsewhere in the midlands.

The link between a surname and a place-name is usually firm when the place-name is distinctive, less so when more than one candidate for the home of a family name is available. Sometimes the distribution pattern of the surname solves the problem but on many other occasions doubts remain. Reaney and Wilson suggest that the surname Alderton could have arisen from various place-names in Essex, Gloucestershire, Northamptonshire, Suffolk and Wiltshire, from Allerton in either Lancashire or the West Riding of Yorkshire, or from Ollerton in either Cheshire or Nottinghamshire. The choice of derivations is narrowed by the evidence of the death registers of 1842–46, which record seventy-five Aldertons in thirty-five different places. They were concentrated in East Anglia, especially in north Suffolk and central Norfolk. We can therefore discount most of the places mentioned by Reaney and Wilson, probably even Essex. The Suffolk Alderton is the most likely point of origin; but we cannot be certain, for it is situated on the coast north of Felixstowe, away from the district where the surname is concentrated. The evidence from the 1840s provides a starting point for enquiries but genealogical methods are necessary to test the hypothesis.

These problems of identification can sometimes be solved by looking at earlier distributions of the name. For example, between 1842 and 1846 the surname Axford was registered on sixty-seven occasions, in thirty-seven different places, including eleven deaths in ten London districts. A significant concentration of the name is found in west Wiltshire (with twelve in Warminster) and in neighbouring counties. Two Axfords are possible sources for the surname; one in Wiltshire, just east of Marlborough, and the other (less likely) a mile south of Basingstoke (Hampshire). As no Axfords are recorded in the hearth tax returns of the 1660s and 1670s for Hampshire and Dorset, the case for the Wiltshire place-name is strength-ened. It appears to be clinched by the appearance of an Adam of Axforde in a Wiltshire taxation return of 1332.

The source of the surname Ashdown cannot be pinpointed so precisely but the options can be narrowed. Reaney and Wilson suggest either Ashdown, which was the name of the Berkshire Downs until the eighteenth century, Ashdon (Essex) or Ashdown Forest (Sussex); they quote thirteenth- and fourteenth-century examples of the surname from Oxfordshire, Essex and Sussex. These are very reasonable suggestions but the evidence of the 1842–46 death registers throws up another possibility and indicates that the surnames or bynames recorded in Essex and Oxfordshire in the middle ages did not survive into the nineteenth century. In those five years, ninety-five Ashdowns were recorded in forty-two places (see map 8, p. 202). They were found particularly in the Maidstone and Sevenoaks registration districts in west Kent and in Sussex; twenty-three had died in fourteen London parishes. The surname was not otherwise found north of the Thames. We can therefore probably rule out Berkshire and Essex as the places of origin for the families which still bear this surname. Sussex remains a strong possibility but another

Ashdown, which is sited thirteen miles east of Maidstone, in Lenham (Kent), has emerged from this exercise as a very strong candidate for the home of this family name (see Map 8, p. 202). The distribution pattern in the 1840s narrows the choice to two likely sources and leaves open the question of whether the surname is of single-family origin or not.

The derivation of some other names is less clear, even after we have examined the pattern established by the 1840s. Thus Ashfield is noted by Reaney and Wilson as a Suffolk or Shropshire name, with early examples from Suffolk and Essex, but other places called Ashfield are found in Herefordshire, Hampshire and Nottinghamshire. Between 1842 and 1846 only forty-seven Ashfield deaths were registered; none of these was in Shropshire and only three were in Suffolk. A group of twenty-one in the west midlands, Worcestershire and Gloucestershire supports the claims of the Herefordshire Ashfield to be at least one of the homes of this name, but the pattern suggests other sources as well, for seven people with the surname Ashfield died in Oxfordshire, eight in London and eight in eastern England, including the three in Suffolk. In the case of the Ashfields, the conclusions to be drawn from the distribution of the name are unclear. Earlier records need to be searched in the districts which have been identified as possible homes of this name.

Ainsley or Aynsley is another name where the distribution does not support Reaney and Wilson's suggested derivation – Annesley (Nottingham-shire) or Ansley (Warwickshire). Of the 100 registered deaths for this name, sixty-two were in Northumberland or Durham and twenty-two were scat-tered thinly throughout other parts of northern England. No Ainsleys were recorded in either Nottinghamshire or Warwickshire. They were found mostly on the banks of the Tyne, which is where a search for a likely place-name should be concentrated.

These examples demonstrate that Reaney and Wilson's dictionary, valu-able as it is, should be treated with caution when trying to locate the homes of family names. Local and family historians are often able to propose more convincing origins for certain surnames, particularly those that are locative in origin. The explanations offered by philologists are useful starting points but should not be accepted uncritically.

One of the biggest problems faced by those who try to locate the homes of family names is that presented by alternate versions of a surname. This is not simply a matter of variant spellings, which can be quickly recognised as such, for it involves transformations that are not at all obvious. It is not until one traces a name back in time that it becomes clear that, for example, the surname Brummitt is a variant of Broomhead. One name which has undergone considerable changes as it migrated from its point of origin in west Lancashire is Aspinall, which is derived from Aspinwall, a small place in Ormskirk. Richard McKinley has shown that it remained uncommon, though not extremely rare, during the middle ages, when it was confined to the district around its original home; the surname increased after 1500 and became very numerous in and around Ormskirk. McKinley has shown that another, very similar but apparently distinct surname, Aspinhalgh, which was recorded in Salford hundred in east Lancashire in 1380–81, moved north in the sixteenth century to Blackburn and Clitheroe but was not found after 1600 in Lancashire; it may well have been assimilated into the more common surname Aspinall. Meanwhile, the Aspinalls had migrated east from the Ormskirk area. From the sixteenth century onwards they appear in Yorkshire. As they moved, their name took on a variety of forms. In Lancashire variants such as Asmall, Asmold and Asmah are recorded in the sixteenth and seventeenth centuries. The place-name Aspinwall also changed form and is now often spelt Asmall. By the 1840s, although the surname remained common in Ormskirk, far more Aspinalls were found in east Lancashire than in the west and a lot had crossed the Pennines into the West Riding of Yorkshire. Another thirty-nine people who died between 1842 and 1846 favoured the old spelling Aspinwall, including eighteen in Ormskirk (where only three Aspinal(l)s were recorded); all but two of the Aspinwalls were from Lancashire.

The variants of the name in the 1840s included Aspenwall, Aspindale, Asmale and Ashmall. As was usual, the number of variations increased with the distance from the source. They become so different from the original name that it is far from clear where one should draw the line. Aspinshaw (registered in Ashby de la Zouch and Shardlow) is a tempting possibility but this surname turns out to be derived from a place-name in Derbyshire and thus has to be discounted. Aspall (two from Cheshire) and Aspald (West Ham) were probably derived from Aspul, a small place near Wigan, recorded in 1212. But what is one to make of the Lancashire surname Aspden, and its variants Aspdin, Aspin and Aspen, all of which were concentrated in central and east Lancashire? They do not appear in the dictionaries or studies of surnames and one is left wondering whether they are shortened forms of Aspinall or whether they have an entirely different derivation. All but seven of the sixty Aspins were registered in Lancashire, including thirty-nine in Blackburn; the three Aspens had all lived in Lancashire; the one Aspdin came from Rochdale; and the 118 Aspdens were all Lancashire people, except for one who lived just across the border; sixty-nine of the Aspdens were registered in Blackburn. Aspden or Aspen, however, turns out to be another minor Lancashire place-name – 'the aspen valley' – in the parish of Whalley, at the heart of the district where the surname was still concentrated at the beginning of Victoria's reign. The Aspdens are quite distinct from the Aspinalls.

All these examples are reasonably straightforward but the modern distribution of a surname does not always point to its origin. Anslow appears to be a case where the surname has migrated a short distance from its home. The family name seems to have been derived from a Staffordshire place-name, near Burton-on-Trent, just beyond the eastern edge of the distribution of the name in 1842–46, when sixty-five Anslows were recorded, mostly in the west midlands and the Welsh borders. Another reason why a surname might not be found near its original home by the 1840s is that sometimes a junior branch had moved away and the elder branch that had remained close to their origins had died out.

Other cases where the modern pattern might obscure the place of origin arise where emigrants had several sons, who in turn had several sons to spread the name. Nearly one-third of the households of people named Glossop who possess a telephone reside within the Sheffield telephone district. Between 1842 and 1846 the Glossops were concentrated in the same area and in adjacent districts to the south; sixty of the eighty-four registrations were from south Yorkshire or Derbyshire. Yet no Glossops were living in south Yorkshire at the time of the hearth tax returns of Ladyday in 1672. Six householders with this name paid tax on their hearths in Derbyshire but none of them lived very close to the village of Glossop in the north west of the county, which is clearly the source of the surname. The first male Glossop to appear in the Sheffield parish register was recorded in 1679. More immigrants came in during the following century, many of them as apprentices to local cutlers. By the time of the 1841 census Sheffield had 224 Glossops living within its boundaries. The Glossops had gradually moved east from their point of origin but most of them were nevertheless still found within thirty miles or so of the place-name.

As we noted earlier, another problem that arises in locating the homes of family names is that the places from which some names are derived are so minor that they are difficult to find. The civil registration records suggest which districts should be searched but only the local historians of those districts will have the detailed knowledge to make a confident identification. Many of these minor names do not appear on Ordnance Survey maps, while others have been changed almost out of recognition. A typical tricky problem is posed by the surname Arkinstall; the twenty-one deaths registered under that name in 1842–46 were mostly in Staffordshire but they were physically separate from the twenty-five Artingstalls in south Lancashire and north Cheshire. The two names are probably derived from a common source but it is not obvious which county should be searched first or which form of the name should be favoured. The civil registration records establish the pattern and narrow the choice but much more research still needs to be done before we can be certain of the origin of this particular name.

Another example from the same part of the country is Ackerley. If we include variant spellings, the deaths of fifty people with this name were recorded in 1842–46, including sixteen in Cheshire, twenty-two in south Lancashire, but also five in Falmouth and six in other places. North Cheshire and south Lancashire are the obvious starting points for a search for the place-name which has given rise to this surname. Many surnames contain elements such as -ley, -stall, or -den, which point to a place-name origin. Ashenden is one such example. Reaney and Wilson suggest the Berkshire place-name, Ashendon, but the distribution of the surname in 1842–46 shows that this is incorrect. Only eighteen Ashendens were registered, of whom seventeen died in Kent and the other in London. Ashenden turns out to be a minor Kentish place-name. This is where the surname came from.

A few more examples will show just how concentrated were the distributions of surnames derived from minor place-names. The eleven Addenbrookes were all registered in the Black Country, the twenty-five Addicoats or Addicotts were nearly all from the south west, especially Devon, and the thirteen Keenleysides were all from north-eastern England. Reaney and Wilson's derivation of Arscott from one or other of two minor place-names in Ashwater or Holsworthy (Devon) is correct. In 1842–46 the forty-one Arscott deaths were registered mostly in Devon, in adjoining districts. W. G. Hoskins noted that the family were an example of freeholders who rose to gentry status, partly on a fortune made in law. He located the home of the family name in the Arscott which is now called South Arscott.[4] The Arscotts were there in Henry III's time and a junior branch settled at Tetcott about 1550.

Beyond Devon, some distinctive Cornish surnames were derived from minor place-names. Argall, meaning a 'retreat, shelter', is a settlement in Budock parish that was recorded in 1327. Only ten Argall deaths were registered in 1842–46; three in Truro, two in St Columb, two in Tavistock, one in Redruth and two in London. Hanks and Hodges derive the surname Knuckey from one of three Cornish settlements: Kenneggy in the parish of Breage, Kenegie in the parish of Gulval or Kenneggy in the parish of Kenwyn, all of which place-names come from the Cornish word *keunegy*, which is the plural form of *keunok*, meaning 'reed-bed' or 'marsh'. The thirty-three Knuckeys registered in 1842–46 were mostly from Cornwall, including nineteen from Redruth.

Not all locative surnames remained as close to their place of origin as these examples. Families from Kendal (Westmorland), Pickering (Yorkshire) and Bickerstaffe (Lancashire) spread far and wide. Occasionally, locative names from beyond the borders of the country became established in England. Thus the twenty-five Afflecks registered in 1842–46 were spread thinly and widely, especially in coastal areas in Lancashire and the north east and in London. This surname, Hanks and Hodges tell us, is from the Scottish place-name Auchinleck, found both in Ayrshire and in Angus.

Topographical Names

Topographical names are those derived from common features of the landscape: a bridge, ford, green, hill, wood, etc. The common ones are found in many different parts of the country for they clearly had numerous separate origins. But some striking patterns in the distribution of the less common topographical surnames are revealed by an analysis of the civil registration records. Indeed in some cases the distinction between the categories of locative and topographical can be shown to be a false one, for some of the so-called topographical surnames are in fact derived from a single feature in the English landscape, a place that can be identified as precisely as one derived from a farm or hamlet.

A 'hurst' was a small wood, so at first sight a surname such as Broadhurst seems likely to have had multiple origins. The 1842–46 indexes of deaths note 234 Broadhursts, who were spread so widely as to suggest that the surname might indeed have arisen independently in a few places. The surname nevertheless has a strong regional distribution, with seventy-eight in Cheshire, fifty-eight in Lancashire, seventy-five in neighbouring counties and the rest scattered elsewhere. If we look more closely at the pattern we will find that the Cheshire registrations were mainly from the three adjacent districts of Macclesfield, Stockport and Congleton, and that the Lancashire ones were mostly from the south of the county, bordering on to Cheshire. The number of 'broad hursts' from which the surname is derived is unlikely to have been as large as was first thought. Broadhurst appears as a field name on the tithe-award maps for Yeardsley-cum-Whaley (1844) and Rainow (1848), both within Macclesfield hundred. The name was also recorded in New Mills parish, just across the Derbyshire boundary, in Elizabeth I's time. Each of these minor place-names are possible sources of origin for the surname. With the wide distribution pattern of the surname Alsop in mind, we cannot (at this stage of the enquiry) rule out the possibility of a single point of origin for the Broadhursts.

The Brocklehursts were neighbours of the Broadhursts. In 1842–46 the name was indexed 109 times in the death registers, with forty-five in Cheshire, twenty-seven in Lancashire and twenty-four in Derbyshire. No less than thirty-one of the Cheshire registrations were from the Macclesfield district and nine of the twenty-four Derbyshire examples were from just across the county boundary in Hayfield. The Brocklehurst which is recorded as a minor place-name on several occasions between 1287 and 1380 in the parish of Yeardsley-cum-Whaley is a strong candidate for the source of the surname in and around Macclesfield. A single-family origin for this name is a real possibility. However, a Ralph of Brocklehurst who was recorded in Lancashire in 1246 may have come from the place with the same name in that county. It remains to be seen whether the Macclesfield Brocklehursts arose independently or whether they were descended from a Lancashire migrant who had moved south.

Akehurst means a small oak wood. Numerous such woods adorn the English countryside but only one of them has given rise to a family name that has continued to this day. Reaney and Wilson's derivation of the surname from Akehurst Farm, Hellingly (Sussex), appears to be correct, for fifty-three of the sixty-seven Akehursts whose deaths were registered in 1842–46 were from Sussex or central Kent (including seventeen in Brighton), with eleven others from nine London districts (see Map 2, p. 196). The narrow distribution of this rare name leads us to believe that all the Akehursts share a common descent.

Atwater is another topographical surname from the south of England which is uncommon enough and sufficiently concentrated in its distribution to suggest a single family origin. Only twenty-five At(t)water(s) were registered in 1842–46, ten of them in the two adjacent Kentish districts of Milton and Medway, five in Horsham (Sussex), at the other side of the Weald, one in Alton (Hampshire) and nine in four London districts. Atwell, on the other hand, must have had more than one point of origin, for the sixty-three Atwells and Attwells were spread across south-western England and eighteen had died in London. Eleven of the fourteen Atwills were from Devon. The twenty-three Attewells, however, were scattered across the south midlands, well away from the homes of the At(t)wells and Atwills.

Other topographical surnames had a definite northern distribution. According to Reaney and Wilson, Airey may come from an Old Norse word meaning 'dweller by the gravel bank', or it may be derived from Aira Force (Ullswater) or some similar named place in Cumbria. The civil registration records of deaths in 1842–46 provide 143 names, including thirty-nine from Cumbria, fifty-one from north and central Lancashire and twenty from Yorkshire. The concentration of the name in north-west England is evident, even though small numbers of Aireys had moved far from home. Thirteen of them had died in London.

The problems of identification are similar to those which we encountered in the search for the homes of those locative names which are derived from minor (and sometimes lost) place-names. The indexes of deaths in 1842–46 record twenty Aldcrofts, sixteen Allcrofts and three Alcrofts, chiefly in south Lancashire and north Cheshire. The minor place-name, meaning 'the old croft', from which the surname sprung is not readily identifiable, however. Only an historian with detailed local knowledge can perhaps solve the problem.

The surname Amphlett was concentrated in the Welsh Borders in the 1840s, particularly in Worcestershire. Hanks and Hodges note that this is a Worcestershire name, a variant of the habitation name Fleet, which is found elsewhere. They quote the will of Agnes Anfleete of Ombersley (Worcestershire), who died in 1373, and inform us that property in this area remained with the family until the nineteenth century. A single-family origin for the surname seems likely.

The etymology of Aked and its variants Akid and Akitt, as provided by Reaney and Wilson, is 'dweller by the oak-covered headland'. One might reasonably assume that many such places existed but the 1842–46 distribution of the surname points firmly to the West Riding. Of the twenty-seven registered names, eleven were from Halifax and eight from neighbouring districts. George Redmonds, the foremost authority on Yorkshire surnames, has found no medieval references to the name in the West Riding, the earliest being those found in such places as Tadcaster and Cottingham in the 1540s. The family is recorded in the Bradford parish register in 1596. During the seventeenth century they moved to Shelf in the parish of Halifax. Dr Redmonds thinks that the most likely explanation of the origin of the name, and one that is borne out by the varied spellings in Bradford around 1600, is that it is derived from Akehead in Cumberland.[5] The surname has migrated from its original home in north-western England as the result of the movement of a single family.

It is more difficult to come to firm conclusions about the surname Appleyard. A family of this name lived in Thurlstone township in south-west Yorkshire from the thirteenth to the nineteenth century but then disappeared, probably failing in the male line. Appleyard is commonly found further north in the West Riding, where it had a separate origin in the township of Allerton. The orchard, or apple yard, which gave rise to the surname has been identified by Stephen Moorhouse as a site which was known by 1664 as the Oaks, a name that was abandoned when the area was developed during the 1960s. In 1842–46 the civil registration indexes note 181 Appleyards, of whom 138 were from Yorkshire, mainly in heart of the West Riding, close to Allerton. However, another cluster lived by or near the Lincolnshire coast and eleven lived in London. The Lincolnshire Appleyards seem to have had a separate origin from the West Riding family.

It is hardly surprising to find that a surname derived from an orchard had more than one point of origin; it is far more surprising to find that apparently no more than three families derived their name in this way and that only two have survived.

The surname Applegate is said by Reaney and Wilson to come from Applegarth; they quote appropriate place-names in the North and East Ridings of Yorkshire and in Cambridgeshire. In 1842–46, however, no Applegates were found in Yorkshire. They were concentrated in two separate areas: fifteen of the forty-seven registered names were from four adjacent districts on the north Norfolk coast; and twenty-one were from a group of districts in Wiltshire and neighbouring counties. Another ten lived in London and one stray was registered in Nottingham. The name seems to have two separate points of origin.

Other topographical surnames have marked regional distributions even where they undoubtedly have multiple origins. This is what might be expected when we consider that many features of the landscape were named in local speech. It is no surprise to find that the surname Raw is largely confined to northern England, for Reaney and Wilson tell us that in northeast Yorkshire 'raw' is a name for a hill. (It is possible, however, that the surname is also derived from a variant of the surname Ralph.) The distribution of the surname in 1842–46 is emphatically northern, but the Raws were natives of the Yorkshire Dales in the north west of the county as well as hailing from the Whitby-Pickering-Guisborough area in the north east.

Enough has been said to show that topographical names can have distribution patterns as striking as the locative ones. It is again clear that the etymologies offered in the dictionaries are merely starting points for further enquiries. This conclusion is also true for other surnames, whether they were derived from personal names, nicknames or occupations.

Personal Names

Reaney and Wilson's dictionary is of particular use when it provides etymologies for names which are derived from Old English, Old Danish, Old Norse, Old French or Old German. Expertise in these ancient languages is obviously necessary to show how surnames developed. Yet the local and family historian still has much to offer, even in the interpretation of the large category of surnames known as patronymics. Distribution patterns of surnames derived from personal names are often marked as clearly as those which have arisen from place-names. Patronymic surnames are very often confined to particular regions of England and in many cases their distribution is so restricted as to suggest a single-family origin.

The Avisons, for example, lived in the heart of the West Riding of Yorkshire. The surname means 'son of Avice', a feminine Christian name in use in the thirteenth and fourteenth centuries. George Redmonds has identified a John Avisson in the poll tax return for Methley in 1379 as the likely ancestor of this West Riding family. By the middle of the sixteenth century they had spread in the Wakefield area, not far from their original home, but three hundred years later they had not spread much further. The forty-seven Avisons whose deaths were registered in 1842–46 included thirty-one from the West Riding; all but three in London were from the northern counties (see Map 13, p. 207).

Examples of such concentrations of surnames derived from personal names can be given from many different parts of the country. The seventy-five registered deaths in 1842–46 of people named Allaway, Alloway or Alway were from forty different districts, mostly in the south west but also running across the south of England below a line drawn from Gloucestershire to London; no one with this name was registered north of Birmingham. Anning is another south-western surname, which appears to have descended from a single bearer of a personal name. In 1842–46 thirteen of the Annings were registered in Axminster, another twenty-one were from neighbouring parts of the south Devon coast and only seven others had died elsewhere.

The surname Algood, which is derived from the Viking personal name Algot, was recorded in Colchester, the Cinque Ports and two other parts of Essex in 1377–81 but not in the other counties for which we have printed poll tax returns. The surname was always a rare one. In 1842–46 the deaths of only fifteen Allgoods were registered, scattered thinly in Norfolk and the midlands. Gummer was an Old English personal name which was not recorded as a surname in any of the published poll tax returns. The deaths of fifty-one Gummers were registered In 1842–46, some in and around London, some in Cornwall, and others dispersed in different parts of southern England. It seems that the surname had no more than two or three origins and that it remained a regional name. No Gummers were registered in the northern half of the country.

Aldous or Aldis is a very distinctive East Anglian name of plural origins. Reaney and Wilson suggest that it is a pet form of some woman's name beginning with Ald- and meaning old. The 1842–46 distribution shows that the sixty-seven people bearing the name Aldis and the forty-eight people named Aldous were nearly all from Norfolk and Suffolk (see Map 3, p. 197). Further back in time, the Suffolk hearth tax returns of 1674 recorded forty-six householders named Aldous, Aldis or Aldus, ranging from exempted poor to a Mr Aldus with ten hearths in Ipswich. The majority of the Aldouses were solid, middling householders; five of them paid tax on six hearths, another six had five hearths, a further four had twelve hearths. The surname was concentrated in the north-eastern hundreds of Hoxne and Blything. Another five householders were taxed on one or two hearths in Norfolk in 1664, two of them in townships on the Suffolk border. The only person with this name in the Essex return was Thomas Aldust of Colchester.

In some cases, pet forms of surnames varied from one part of the country to another. The eighteen Ashwins were found in Worcestershire and adjacent parts, the thirty-one Asletts were mainly in Hampshire or London, and the thirty-two people with the surname Ayles were mostly found on the Hampshire or Dorset coast or in London; the only one who had ventured north of the Thames had got as far as Stratford-upon-Avon. By contrast, the twenty-eight Aldens were found mostly in eastern England and although the fifteen Alkins were registered in fourteen different districts they were associated particularly with Staffordshire. Other pet forms were exceedingly common. however. Elliot(t), a pet form of Ellis which has also absorbed one or two Old English personal names with a similar sound, was recorded 1678 times across the country in the death registers of 1842–46. The Ellises were even more common, with 2700 registrations evenly spread.

We have seen earlier that alternate forms of names become accepted as the norm in certain districts. These forms were not usually the result of variations in phonetic spellings, which changed back and forth, but of slightly different pronunciations. Sometimes, however, a particular spelling of the surname did become the preferred one, for example Taylor rather than Tailor or Smythson instead of Smithson. In some cases, surnames derived from personal names were eventually changed out of immediate recognition.

But it is not just the rare names that have striking geographical patterns. Some surnames that are very familiar to us because so many people bear them are nevertheless widespread in certain counties but absent in others. Most Robsons are from Northumberland or County Durham, most Dysons are from the West Riding of Yorkshire. Rawson, 'son of Ralph', is a familiar name in many parts of the north and the north midlands but is absent from much of the country. The 226 deaths registered in 1842–46 comprise eighty-one from Yorkshire (nearly all from the West Riding), thirty-nine from Lancashire, thirty-six from Nottinghamshire, forty-nine from other midland counties, fifteen from London and a few scattered elsewhere. The name clearly has multiple origins but is confined to a broad swathe of the country.

Reaney and Wilson regularly quote early examples of bearers of surnames in parts of England where the name was not found in later times. In some cases these names may never have become hereditary, but death caused by the great pestilences of the fourteenth century is probably the explanation for many of these surnames failing to develop.

Nicknames

Nicknames such as Fox, Grey, Swallow or White are found in most parts of the country but some other nicknames are surprisingly local or regional in their distribution. They have as concentrated a pattern as do surnames in other categories which are derived from a single family.

Yapp is a nickname from an Old English word denoting 'bent'. Although the earliest known examples are from Nottinghamshire and Yorkshire in the thirteenth century, six hundred years later Yapp was a Welsh borders name, particularly from Herefordshire and to a lesser extent from Shropshire and other parts of the west midlands. The distribution of the forty-four names registered in 1842–46 suggests a single-family origin. By contrast, Nice, meaning 'foolish', is an Essex and south Suffolk name that has spread into other parts of eastern England and into London. As only fifty-two names were registered in 1842–46, the concentration again suggests the possibility that a single ancestor acquired this nickname.

Footit (with its variant spellings Foottit and Footett) appears thirty-six times in the death registrations indexes of 1842–46. The name is said by Reaney and Wilson to be from Middle English 'fot-hot', meaning 'quickly, suddenly', and thus was most likely a nickname. It is recorded as a surname in London in the 1290s. The 1840s distribution, however, suggests an east midlands origin, with nineteen examples from Lincolnshire and Nottinghamshire, for the surviving family name. Kibble, a nickname for a clumsy or thick set person, was recorded in Worcestershire in 1185 and in Staffordshire in 1327; the fifty-two Kibbles whose deaths were registered in 1842–46 were spread thinly across the west and south midlands, with twelve in London. In this case, a single-family origin for the surname seems unlikely.

Many more Amblers – 170 in all – were registered in 1842–46. The name may have been derived from the occupation of enamelling but perhaps it was a nickname, for in the middle ages an ambler was a horse with an easy-going disposition. Chaucer uses the word in this sense and we still refer to an ambling gait. William and Henry Ambler were taxed at Stretford (Herefordshire) in 1379 but the name disappeared subsequently from the Welsh borders. In 1842–46 the Amblers were nearly all found in the districts at the heart of the West Riding. George Redmonds has traced the history of the surname back to the Halifax area, where a Nicholas le Aumbleour was recorded in 1307; by 1545 several Amblers were taxed at Ambler Thorn in the area now called Queensbury.[6] The Amblers had more sons than some of the families quoted above and had thus ramified much more successfully, but the present bearers of the name nevertheless seem to be descended from a common ancestor who had acquired his distinctive name during the period when surnames became hereditary.

Verity is another distinctive West Riding surname which has arisen from a nickname, in this case one meaning 'truth' (though the attractive suggestion has been made that Verity was one of the surnames that were derived from a part played – perhaps on a regular annual basis – in a Corpus Christi mystery play). The eighty-six Veritys whose deaths were registered in 1842–46 comprised seventy-one from the West Riding, with seven others in and around Manchester, five in south Wales and three in London.

It is perhaps more surprising that a name like Senior should have such a pronounced Yorkshire distribution, especially as Reaney and Wilson quote early examples, from 1164 onwards, from Norfolk, Suffolk, Staffordshire, Oxfordshire, Somerset and Cumberland. The name is derived either from Old French *seignour*, meaning 'lord', or from the Latin *senior*, meaning 'older', and seems most likely to have been a nickname. In the two years, 1842 and 1843, the deaths of 199 Seniors were registered, 156 of them in the West Riding and most of the rest in adjacent counties (see Map 19, p. 213). The name was concentrated in central and southern parts of the West Riding. Senior may have several Yorkshire origins, for it occurs in different parts of the West Riding in early records. The name was well-established in both Bradfield and Kirkburton in the middle ages.

Finally, it is worth observing that some surnames which appear to be nicknames in origin were in fact derived differently. Broadhead is not a nickname, as might be thought, but a surname which has arisen from a topographical feature, 'the broad headland'. Moreover, it is one of those topographical names which really fit into the locative category, for it is derived from a single place in the Holme Valley, in the West Riding of Yorkshire, where the Broadheads were living in the early fourteenth century. In 1333 Thomas del Brodhede held a messuage and twelve acres in the township of Austonley which can be identified with the present farm known as Broadhead Edge. A total of 168 deaths of people bearing this surname were registered between 1842 and 1846, of whom 120 came from the West Riding. The name was still concentrated not far from its original home.

Occupational Names

Although the Smiths, Taylors, Turners and Wrights are found in all parts of England, some of the rarer occupational names, such as the Yorkshire names Crapper and Flather, have a pronounced regional character. Even the Smiths are not evenly distributed across the country. The distribution patterns of surnames derived from occupations are as interesting as those of any other category of name.

Ashburner, 'a burner of ashes' or 'maker of potash', is a surname that is largely confined to north-western England. Three Lancashire men – two Adam Askbrenners and a Thomas Askbrenner – were taxed at the lowest rate of 4*d.* in 1379 and Matilda Askebrenner was taxed at Eyam (Derbyshire) two years later. Reaney and Wilson quote early examples from Lancashire, Cumberland, Yorkshire and Sussex, but we may discount the last two counties as sources of the surviving surname. In 1842–46 the deaths of only forty-one Ashburners were registered, twenty-one of them in the Ulverstone district and all but seven of the rest in other parts of Lancashire (see Map 7, p. 201).

Ashburnham is a very rare locative surname derived from a place in Sussex and should not be confused with Ashburner. Ashman is more complicated. The name is said to come from an Old Norse byname for a shipman, sailor or pirate, but its distribution is neither near the coast nor in areas where Old Norse was spoken. The 114 registrations of deaths in 1842–46 were spread amongst forty places. The largest numbers were registered in six adjacent districts in the south west but others were clustered in eastern England and in east Kent. Many parts of the country, e.g. Devon, Cornwall, Hampshire, Sussex, Surrey and several midlands counties, had no Ashmans at all and only two were registered in the north. The name must have had multiple origins, in well-defined parts of the country, but it seems unlikely that it had anything to do with sailors or pirates. Perhaps the name meant 'servant of Ash'?

Another surname ending in -man is Acreman, Ackerman or Akerman. Reaney and Wilson quote early examples from Huntingdonshire and Essex and offer the meaning of 'farmer'. The fifty-six registered deaths in 1842–46 were mostly in south-western England, with twelve in Bridport. Even though so few names were recorded, the gaps between the clusters in Dorset, Somerset, Wiltshire, Oxfordshire and London indicate a multiple origin for the Acremans. No one with this name was registered in either Huntingdonshire or Essex, so the surname either died out or never became hereditary there.

Angove is the Cornish version of smith. All but one of the twenty-four Angoves registered in 1842–46 were from Cornwall. So were all five of the Angroves. However, Angrave is a midlands name of unknown derivation. Only eleven Angraves were registered in 1842–46, eight in Leicestershire and three nearby. It is possible that they were all descended from a Cornish migrant but Leicestershire and neighbouring counties were not the usual destinations of such travellers. Earlier records from these midland counties need to be searched before we can come to firmer conclusions about the origin of this name. No Angraves, however, paid the poll tax in Leicestershire in 1379.

It is often unclear whether a surname was a nickname or an occupational name in origin. For instance, Ram or Ramm may have been a nickname for a lusty or forceful man, it may have been an occupational name for a shepherd, or it may have been applied to the landlord of a hostelry with the sign of the Ram. Reaney and Wilson quote William atte Ramme (Cambridgeshire, 1307) in support of the latter explanation. Matilda and John Ram paid poll tax in Essex in 1381 but the name was not common. The fifty-nine Ram(m)s whose deaths were registered in 1842–46 were mostly from Norfolk; the distribution pattern of the surname is consistent with a single-family origin.

Two Puzzles

Finally, surnames which the etymologists have not yet placed in any of their categories are made more intriguing by their distribution patterns. Two examples will suffice. The surname Arch was registered on forty-one occasions in 1842–46. An isolated pocket of ten Arches were registered at Linton (Cambridgeshire). Others were scattered in various parts of eastern England. The rest were either from the lower Severn valley or in and around Coventry and Birmingham, not far from Barford, the home of Joseph Arch, the farm labourers' champion in Victorian times. Although the name is a rare one, it seems to have had more than one origin.

Hanks and Hodges suspect that the literal explanation for Rid(e)out – 'a rider' – is 'no more than folk etymology'. The distribution pattern in 1842–46 shows that this is a Dorset name; fifty-eight of the eighty-eight deaths were registered in that county, and the rest were mainly in other southern parts of England. This concentration of the name is confirmed by the Dorset hearth tax returns of the 1660s, which record twenty-seven Rid(e)outs, most of whom were living in the Sherborne and Shaftesbury divisions. None appear in the Dorset poll tax returns of 1379, however.

These two puzzles remind us that we cannot be certain about the origins of some surnames. A great amount of detailed research needs to be done and even then many problems will remain unsolved. Nevertheless, it is clear from the examples quoted above that very many surnames had restricted distributions in early Victorian England and that a surprising number of all categories of names probably had a single-family origin. We now need to trace such names further back in time.

7

The Seventeenth Century and Earlier

We have seen that even in the modern era surnames have distinctive geographical patterns which serve as pointers to the places where names originated in earlier centuries. We now need to see whether we can bring into focus the geography of surnames half way between the period of their formation and the present day. The records which are available to us are not as comprehensive as we would like, nor are they always readily accessible. Nevertheless, we still have an enormous amount of data at our disposal. Our principal source is the collection of hearth tax returns of the reign of Charles II, arranged county by county for most parts of England and Wales.

Hearth Tax Returns

A tax on hearths or chimneys was levied by the central government twice a year between 1662 and 1688. Each head of household was charged according to the number of fireplaces in the house, unless he or she were exempted from payment on the grounds of poverty. Lists of taxpayers (and sometimes of the exempted poor) were drawn up for each township and arranged by hundred or wapentake. A township was the smallest unit of local government, the equivalent of the vill in medieval taxation records. In some parts of England it corresponded to the ecclesiastical parish but in other parts of the country large parishes were divided up into several townships. The arrangement of the returns into townships allows us to record the distribution of family names accurately and to make comparisons with both later and earlier records. We must bear in mind that the returns did not always list the exempted poor, who often accounted for a third or more of the local population, so some family names will escape our net. Nevertheless, we are provided with an enormous sample of names across the country.[1]

Most of the original returns are kept at the Public Record Office, under class E 179, but an increasing number of counties now have at least one return in print. While it will be many years before returns covering all, or most, parts of England and Wales are available in a suitable form for comparative purposes, Professor Margaret Spufford and her colleagues at the Roehampton Institute, London, are hoping to produce a computerised base map on which to plot the data. Once that is available, it will be much easier to identify distributions of surnames across county boundaries. In the meantime, we have to proceed county by county, rather laboriously.

East Anglia

We start with the Suffolk hearth tax return of 1674,[2] which provides us with the names of 29,125 householders throughout the county. Some comparisons will be made with the list of names in the Norfolk hearth tax assessment of 1664,[3] and with the Essex hearth tax return of 1662.[4]

One way of proceeding is to consider surnames that can be identified in the civil registration records of the nineteenth century as being peculiar to Suffolk or at least to East Anglia. How does the geographical pattern of the name in 1842–46 compare with that revealed by the hearth tax returns 170 years earlier? Do these two sources of information point us in the same direction in our search for the place where the name originated?

One name that stands out as a rare one that is found only in this part of England is Cobbold, a surname which was derived from an Old English personal name and which is best known today as part of the name of a Suffolk brewery. It was recorded only twenty-two times in the indexes of deaths in 1842–46, when all these Cobbolds (except two in London) were clustered in south Suffolk. The hearth tax returns for Suffolk for 1674 recorded six householders with this distinctive surname: Henry Cobboult (eight hearths) in Raydon, on the Essex border, and others with one or two hearths, namely Henry Cobbolt, John Cobbold and Martin Cobbolt in the neighbouring township of Layham, John Cobbold in Ipswich and another John Cobbold in Fakenham, further north beyond Bury St Edmunds. The distribution of the name is markedly similar to the pattern of 170 years later. No Cobbolds were recorded in the hearth tax returns of Norfolk or Essex. We can therefore confine our genealogical enquiries to a few parishes when we try to trace the name back in time. And what are we to make of the similar surname Cobble or Cobbell? Reaney and Wilson derive it from Middle English *cobel*, a rowboat, therefore giving a nickname for a sailor. But the surname Cobble is very rare and in 1842–46 was found only in Bury St Edmunds, Swaffham and West Ham. In Suffolk in 1674 Henry Cobble was taxed in Shelley, the township next to Layham and Raydon, and Robert Coble and Widow Cobble were taxed in Tostock, east of Bury St Edmunds. Another five Cobbles, Cobles or Cobells were taxed in the Norfolk townships of Weston Longville, King's Lynn and Ridlington. It seems possible, indeed likely, that Cobble is simply a variant of Cobbold. We shall need to keep an eye open for this variant form when we search parish registers, wills, manorial records and other sources of genealogical information.

We conclude from our analysis of the civil registration records and the hearth tax returns that it is not enough to say that Cobbold is derived from an Old English personal name. It appears that the surname originated in, and remained within, Suffolk. So few families bore this name at various points in time that it seems reasonable to suppose that it began with a single person called Cobbold. This, of course, is only a working hypothesis at the present stage of the enquiry; detailed genealogical research is needed to link the names recorded in 1842–46 with those of 1674 and earlier times. It is rarely possible to trace family lines all the way back to the period of surname formation, but we can often show that names such as Cobbold have remained in the same county, and often in the same district, from the time that records begin right through to the present day.

A list of 11,721 taxpayers in Suffolk in 1327 enables us to take our enquiry right back to the period of surname formation.[5] Like the other records that we have used, this return is not comprehensive, for we do not know how many people were exempt from the tax, nor how many evaded paying. It nonetheless provides a large sample of names which make interesting comparisons with those of three and a half centuries later. In 1674 the Cobbolds were clustered in south Suffolk, except for one household who lived further north at Fakenham, beyond Bury St Edmunds. In 1327, however, the five Cobbolds who were listed were all living in Wangford and Hoxne hundreds, near the Norfolk border at South Elham, Mettingham, Syleham and Weybread. The Cobbolds have always been a Suffolk family but between 1327 and 1674 they appear to have migrated from the north to the south of the county.

The same conclusion about a single-family origin is suggested by the distribution pattern of the surname Abb(e)s, which Peter McClure has shown to be a shortened form of the female name Albrei or Aubrey, rather than of Abel or Abraham, as was once thought.[6] The rarity of the surname in 1842–46 points to Norfolk as the home of this family name. Only twenty-eight deaths were registered during those five years. Ten of these were in the Erpingham district on the north coast of Norfolk and only three were from beyond the county boundary. In the Suffolk hearth tax returns of 1674 only four people with this surname were listed; in Gorleston and in Bungay, right on the Norfolk border, in Cookle, south of Bungay, and in Sotterly, a few miles south east. These Abbeses were moderately well-off with seven, four, four and two hearths. Nine more households of Abbeses were living in Norfolk at the time of the hearth tax assessment of 1664. They were found at Aylmerton, Cley, Hanworth and Salthouse (all within the later Erpingham registration district), with just one at Acle on the edge of the Norfolk Broads. No Abbeses were recorded in Essex. The absence of people named Abbes in the Suffolk tax return of 1327 confirms this as a Norfolk rather than a Suffolk name in origin. It appears to have belonged to a single family in the north of the county.

So far, we have worked backwards in time from surnames which we have extracted from the civil registration records to the hearth tax returns, but it is just as likely that a study of earlier records will produce surnames that appear to have a distinctive character. In such cases, we need to work the other way, checking the civil registration records to see whether or not the seventeenth-century names that have attracted our attention are indeed regional in their distributions. We also need to consult the hearth tax returns of the other counties which have appeared in print, to see how widespread these surnames were in the seventeenth century.

Surnames derived from local place-names are not as common in East Anglia as they are in some other parts of England, especially Lancashire, the West Riding of Yorkshire and Devon, where settlements commonly consisted of scattered farms and hamlets. They include surnames that have come from the Suffolk settlement of Brundish, the Essex village of Stebbing and occasionally from places overseas. The twelve householders named Brundish in 1674 undoubtedly came from a family which had taken its name from a Suffolk village. In 1327 William of Brondich who was taxed at Wickham Market, about eight miles south of Brundish, was the only person in the return with that surname. Although Suffolk had thirty-five taxpayers named Stebbing in 1674, in 1327 it had none, so migration from the Essex village of that name appears to be the correct explanation. The common Suffolk name Blomfield is said by Reaney and Wilson to come from Blonville-sur-Mer in Calvados. They quote a William de Blunvill in Suffolk in 1207 and other early examples from Norfolk. Eleven Bloom(e)fields were recorded in the Norfolk hearth tax return of 1664. The Blomfields appear to have migrated south from Norfolk and to have ramified considerably between 1327 (when Suffolk had no taxpayers with this name) and 1674 (when it had fifty-two Blomfields).

A topographical name that has strong associations with East Anglia is Ling. Members of the Ling family feature prominently in George Ewart Evans's book, *Ask the Fellows Who Cut the Hay*, which deals with the Suffolk village of Blaxhall. In 1327 John del Lyng was living at Brome and Richard del Lyng was taxed two miles further south at Eye, close to the Norfolk border; a Bernard del Ling was recorded in Suffolk in 1207. The possibility of a single-family origin for the forty-three Lings who were taxed in Suffolk in 1674 and the nine who were taxed in Norfolk ten years earlier is a strong one, despite the large number of families who bore this name by the late seventeenth century. Successive families with several boys would explain how the name ramified within the same district. Another surname of this type is Sallowes. The twenty-one people in the Suffolk return of 1674 who were named Sallowes or Sally had surnames which meant 'dweller by the willows'. The Norfolk hearth tax assessment of 1674 included a Sale, a Sallie, a Saul and ten Salls. They may well have all been descended from the William Sallowes who lived in Suffolk in 1524 and the Edmund del Sale who was taxed at Thrandeston, the next village to Brome, in 1327. On the evidence so far available, however, we cannot be certain about the original homes of the Lings and the Sales, nor how many families they sprang from.

Surnames derived from Old English and Old Danish personal names appear in the 1674 list of Suffolk householders. As we extend our searches to other counties, some of these names will turn out to be more widespread but others will be confirmed as names that are found only in eastern England. Baldry is one of the names that appear elsewhere; five examples are found in the Norfolk hearth tax assessment of 1664, for example, and five in the Hampshire hearth tax return of 1665. Nevertheless, it is striking that as many as fifty-five Suffolk households shared this name in 1674 and that no Baldrys were recorded in the hearth tax returns for Derbyshire, Essex, Nottinghamshire, Oxfordshire, Bedfordshire or Dorset. Twelve Baldrys were taxed in Suffolk in 1327, so even within this one county the surname had plural, if not multiple, origins.

Many more personal names that appear to have a strong connection with eastern England can be spotted in the Suffolk hearth tax returns. Chittocke was recorded as a surname in Huntingdonshire in 1279. The eleven Chittocke households in Suffolk in 1674 were perhaps descended from either Henry Chittok at Westleton, near Dunwich, or Richard Chittok at Stradbroke, fourteen miles further west, both of whom were taxpayers in 1327. Early examples of Cuttinge, a surname well represented in Norfolk and Suffolk in the seventeenth century, have been noted in Norfolk and Essex. The name meant 'the son of Cutt', which in turn was a pet form of Cuthbert. Fourteen Cuttinges were taxed on their hearths in Norfolk in 1664; the Suffolk taxpayers included twenty-two Cuttinges in 1674, six in 1327. The surname Dowsing, which seems to have been derived from an Old Danish name, was popular in Norfolk and Suffolk back in the thirteenth and fourteenth centuries and remains common in East Anglia, particularly in Suffolk, to this day. None of these three surnames was recorded in the Essex hearth tax assessment of 1662. The Suffolk Dowsings numbered six in 1327, thirty-two in 1674, so they appear to have had multiple origins. The notorious William Dowsing, the iconoclast who destroyed stained glass windows, images and woodwork in numerous Suffolk churches during the Civil War, was a local man. The thirty-five Woolnoes or Woolnoughs, by contrast, were probably all descended from Robert Wolthnoth, who in 1327 lived at Rattlesden in the centre of the county. Today the surname is usually spelt Woolner.

We are not surprised to find that Old English personal names gave rise to numerous surnames in the part of England that was most intensively settled by the Anglo-Saxons, nor that many patronymic surnames there clearly had multiple origins. A few more examples will suffice. The name Folkard or Fokard was recorded in both Norfolk and Suffolk in the twelfth century and Suffolk had three taxpayers with that surname in 1327. The hearth tax returns name twenty Folkards or Fokards in Suffolk, seven Fo(a)kers and one Folkard in Norfolk, but no one of this distinctive name in Essex. Stannard had long been a popular name in Suffolk. Twelve Stannards paid tax in Suffolk in 1327 and fifty-four paid on their hearths in 1674, so the name must have had multiple origins. Only six Stannards were taxed in Norfolk in 1664 and only one householder with this rare name had ventured south into Essex. In the early nineteenth century Joseph Stannard was a member of the famous Norwich school of artists. The Stannards ramified more strongly than our final example, the Wyards, whose eight households in 1327 had grown only to fourteen by 1674.

Some other East Anglian names, not found in Reaney and Wilson's dictionary, might also have been Old English personal names in origin. Goymer, Scotchmer and Wiffin are perhaps examples. Kerridge is a surname that has been thought to come from a place-name in Cheshire, or from a similar one in Devon, but as it is not recorded in the hearth tax returns for Northwich hundred, Cheshire, nor in any of the other counties in our sample, including Norfolk and Essex, but is noted twenty-five times in the Suffolk hearth tax return a derivation from an Old English personal name in that county is the more likely explanation. The sixty-nine Kerridges whose deaths were registered in 1842–46 were overwhelmingly from eastern England. The John Kerrich who was living at Leiston in 1327 may well have been the ancestor of all the bearers of this name. Likewise, Lilly is more probably derived from a pet form of Elizabeth than from place-names in Hertfordshire and Berkshire. Suffolk had thirty-eight Lillys in 1674, Norfolk had five Lillies ten years earlier, but only one Lilly was taxed in Hampshire and none appear in the returns for other counties. The five Lylies who were taxed in Suffolk in 1327 were living in three places that were situated wide apart from each other. Finally, although the surname Kemball or Kimball could have been derived from the Buckinghamshire place-name Kimble, its distribution well beyond that county suggests that an origin as an Old English personal name is more likely. The Kemballs or Kimballs comprised seventeen households in Suffolk in 1674; in 1327 Suffolk taxpayers included four Kymbels, three Kembolds, two Kenebelles and a Kemel.

The occupational names recorded in Suffolk in 1674, but not in Norfolk or Essex, include Botwright, a maker of boats, Catchpole, a tax gatherer, literally 'chase fowl', a collector of poultry in default of money, and Thrower, a name which was probably derived from silk thrower. Two very common names in Suffolk in the seventeenth century were Last, a surname which was recorded in the county in 1385 and which seems to denote a maker of wooden foot moulds for shoemakers, and Ke(e)ble, which is thought to have been applied to a maker or seller of cudgels, or perhaps to have been a nickname. A Keble was recorded in Bury St Edmunds in 1095.

This list of possible distinctive surnames is far from exhaustive. Some will prove not to be confined to Suffolk, but they catch the eye of one who comes from a different part of the country. This group of names appear worthy of further investigation. The outsider can also spot the surnames of some of the families which had migrated to Suffolk at some point between the period of surname formation and the later seventeenth century. They include a few Welsh names, the northern names Kendal, Lancaster, Pickering, Pomfret and Wakefield, and a few from the south west: Bristowe, Cornish, Cornwall and Cornwell. These immigrant names, however, form only a tiny proportion of the complete list of householders. The great majority of Suffolk families had deep roots in East Anglia. Many of them were still confined to the neighbourhoods that had been familiar to their ancestors centuries earlier.

Hampshire and Bedfordshire

A few examples from the hearth tax returns for Hampshire (1665)[7] and Bedfordshire (1671)[8] provide further illustrations of the usefulness of this source for the study of surnames. Many of the surnames in the Hampshire hearth tax return sound strange to someone who comes from other parts of England, especially those that arose from small settlements in the southern counties. They can be spotted immediately. A few other locative surnames that stand out in the returns of 1665 were derived from places in France or the Low Countries. Bulbeck is from Bolbec in Seine-Maritime, Diaper or Dyaper is from Ypres, Pewsey from a place in Eure-et-Loire. Another group of surnames sound as if they came from local place-names that the outsider cannot place immediately. Local and family historians in and around Hampshire may have little difficulty in identifying them. Some minor place-names can be identified in the invaluable *The Ordnance Survey*

Gazetteer of Great Britain (second edition, London, 1989), which lists all the names that appear on the 1:50,000 Landranger Map Series. Harfeild, Harfell, etc. can thus be seen to have been derived from the Hampshire place-name Harfield, and Winckworth to have arisen from either of two farms of that name in Wiltshire or Surrey. A few puzzles remind us how difficult it is to identify the homes of locative surnames unless we have detailed local knowledge. Which of the numerous places called Hockley gave rise to the Hampshire surname? Hockley is recorded as a place-name in six counties but not in Hampshire or its neighbouring counties. And did the Puckeridges really hail from the Hertfordshire place of that name or was there once a local place-name that explains the derivation?

A number of Hampshire surnames that were derived from Old English personal names and from one or two Old Norse ones seem worthy of further investigation. Some may turn out to have been spread widely throughout the south of England but others may have been very local in their distributions. They include Budd, Drew, Eedes, Eades or Edes, Gass, Godwin or Goodwin, Godden, Gooding, Noyes, Osgood, Osmond, the Old Norse name Skeate, another Old Norse name Tolefrey, Tombs, the Norman name Warner, and Woolgar. Curiously, a Welsh personal name which had developed into the surname Craddock was recorded thirteen times in Hampshire and once in Dorset. We need also to consider Eames or Eambs, which is derived from the Middle English word for 'uncle'; May, which perhaps means 'young lad, girl', or which could have come from Matthew, via Mayhew; and Sone, Soane, Soone or Sowne, a surname which was derived from 'son' or 'the younger, junior'. They all add to the collection of distinctive names in these southern counties.

Hampshire nicknames included Bastard, Faithfull, Moth and Wisdom. Less obvious to modern ears are Beane, perhaps meaning 'pleasant, genial, kindly', though it could also have been an occupational name; Blanchard, meaning 'white hair'; Chubb, for someone who was lazy or a simpleton, or possibly short and thick like the fish; Purdue or Purd(e)y, a nickname for one who repeatedly swore the oath, *par dieu*; Stepto(e), for someone who was lightfooted; and Keepen, Keeping, Kippen, etc., for a fat person. In 1842–46 the fifty-six deaths which were registered under various forms of this name were all except one from the southern half of England; twenty-six were from Hampshire or Dorset, and twelve were from London.

Hampshire's distinctive occupational names include Dicker or Dicher, Goater or Goter, Hooker and Twine. Less straightforward are Bargent, Bargen or Bargin, from bargain, hence 'merchant, trader'; Booker, meaning either a scribe or the very different trade of bleacher; Bushell, for a maker of measures; Hellier and its variants and the possibly connected names of Hillar and Hillard, for a slater or tiler; Hoggsflesh, possibly a nickname for a pork butcher; Pescod, for a seller of peas; Talmage, from an Old French word for a knapsack; Tredgold, from Threadgold, 'embroiderer'; and Wassell, for a maker or seller of wastels, a cake or bread made of the finest flour. Waterman probably came from 'water carrier' or 'boatman' but it could also have referred to the servant of Walter. Some of these names may turn out to have been more widely based, but for the present we may assume (as a working hypothesis) that in the seventeenth century they were particularly associated with Hampshire.

The value of the dictionaries of surnames becomes all too apparent when we are left floundering for explanations of names that do not appear in their pages. Most of us are reliant on the dictionaries as starting points, even if we come to disagree with some of the explanations on offer. The Hampshire hearth tax returns contain some rare surnames that are not in Reaney and Wilson's dictionary. They include Bagin(e), Bye, Caute, Cawt, Clungeon, Glasspoole or Glaspell, Holdipp, Kinchen or Kenchen, Mowd(a)y, Quallett, Scullard, Sherryer and its variants, Strugnell, Taplin, Tribb, Tribbick, Trebeck, Truddle, Trusler and Weekes. They pose an even greater challenge than normal to local and family historians, most of whom do not have the necessary linguistic knowledge to suggest etymologies but who can nevertheless trace these delightful names back in time and point to their likely places of origin. Kinchin or Kinchen is a particular puzzle. Only twenty-five deaths were registered under this name in 1842–46, with just three in Hampshire. Another small group were registered in Worcestershire and Warwickshire and nine were recorded in London. The ten households in the Hampshire hearth tax returns seem to have dwindled in number by the beginning of Victoria's reign.

The Bedfordshire hearth tax return of 1671 lists 9382 householders with 2134 different surnames for this south midlands county. Surnames such as Bunyan (see Map 15, p. 209), Mouse and Empey, that appear to be largely or totally confined to Bedfordshire and which are localised in their distribution within the county, are likely to have single-family origins. So has Freelove, a name which is now very rare, and which was derived from an Old English name that was recorded in the tenth century. Most of the nine Bedfordshire families that shared this surname in 1671 lived just south of Ampthill, which is where we must concentrate our genealogical enquiries. Four centuries earlier, Nicholas Frelove was recorded at Biddenham, just to the west of Bedford, in the Bedfordshire Hundred Rolls of 1279. Perhaps he was an ancestor of all the Freeloves? Other rare Bedfordshire names include Samms, Hebbs and Abbis. Several other Bedfordshire surnames are so rare that they do not merit a mention in the dictionaries: Thody, Bithwray, Branklin, Deamer, Negus and Yarrell.

Comparisons between the surnames listed in the hearth tax return of 1671 and those recorded in fourteenth-century taxation rolls are made possible for Bedfordshire by the publication of two subsidy lists for 1309 and 1332.[9] Thus Adam Frelove of Toddington was taxed in 1332. Some of the other rare names which we identified in the return of 1671 were absent from both of these fourteenth-century lists. In 1309 and 1332 Bedfordshire had no taxpayers called Sam(m)s, Thody, Bithwray, Branklin, Deamer or Yarrell. The only Hebbs was Simon Hebbe at Marston, the sole Abbis was Elena Abbesse at Kempston and the only Berringer was Nicholas Beringer of Felmersham. We have to recall that many people were exempt from these taxes and that others may have managed to evade payment but it is likely that some of the surnames which were confined to Bedfordshire three and a half centuries later had not yet been formed.

Militia Assessments: Herefordshire

A much rarer source of information for this period is provided by a Herefordshire militia assessment of 1663.[10] This assessment is almost as useful as a hearth tax return, except that it does not include those families which at the time had no men of serviceable age. As Herefordshire does not have a hearth tax return in print, this contemporary militia assessment is particularly valuable. Although it is not comprehensive, it offers a very large sample, a record of the names of 7291 men. Relatively few of the county's surnames will have gone unrecorded. The assessment gives us a very good picture of the geographical distribution of Herefordshire surnames three hundred years or more after their formation. It suggests which parish records are likely to help us in our genealogical research.

Herefordshire names are strikingly different from those in Suffolk, Hampshire and Bedfordshire. For a start, many are unmistakably Welsh in origin, while others were common either side of the border. Some distinctive names were derived from Welsh border place-names: Bodenham, Lingen, Maund and Wigmore (Herefordshire), Kinnersley (Herefordshire or Worcestershire), Mutlow (Cheshire or Worcestershire), Berrington and Crowles (Worcestershire), Brace and Millichap (Shropshire) and Apperley (Gloucestershire or Somerset). Locative surnames which I have not identified include Colcombe, Dubberley, Eckley, Greenly, Ketherow, Kidley, Kirwood, Mon(n)ingham and Venmore. Reaney and Wilson suggest that Scudamore is derived from an unidentified Skidmore, probably somewhere in the west or south west of England, but as fifty-three people were recorded with this name in the Herefordshire militia assessment a more local source is likely. The ancestor of the fourteen households of Coningsbys had travelled unusually far, for they seem to have taken their name from the place of that name in Lincolnshire; -by is a Danish place-name suffix that would not have arisen in the Welsh Borders beyond the Danelaw. There must be a special reason, such as service on an important manor or marriage with an heiress, to account for this move. The Cornish name Treherne had also migrated a long distance. These two families were exceptional, however. Nearly every other family with locative surnames had moved only within their own neighbourhood or from neighbouring counties.

Topographical names in the Herefordshire militia assessment include Badland, Boswood and Clee (from the Clee Hills, Shropshire). Amongst the personal names that stand out are Addis or Addice, a form of Addy, Gunter, Mayo and Stallard. The most distinctive nicknames in the list were Careless, Chinn, Crump(e) (from 'crooked, bent'), Deeme ('judge'), Munn ('monk') and Yapp ('bent'). Yapp was predominantly a Herefordshire sur-name in 1842–46 and Shropshire had the next largest numbers. Occupational names range from the uncommon Traunter ('carrier, hawker') to the very common Smith, the name of 119 people in the assessment. Finally, as usual, a number of surnames which do not appear in the dictionaries strike an outsider as being distinctive to the region. They include Hannis or Hennis, Jauncey, Kyrle, Passey, Pember, Scandret(t) and Vobe. Not a single Kyrle or Kirle was named in the death registers of 1842–46 but perhaps they were entered under Curl? Most of the twelve Kerl(e)s whose deaths were registered at that time came from Somerset.

Protestation Return: Westmorland and Lincolnshire

In 1642 men aged eighteen and over were expected to sign an oath of loyalty to 'the true Reformed Protestant Religion expressed in the doctrine of the Church of England'. Where lists of subscribers survive, they appear to be remarkably comprehensive. A list of the parishes or chapelries for which returns are preserved will be found in the appendix to the *Fifth Report of the Historical Manuscripts Commission* (1876), pp. 120–34. The original documents are housed in the House of Lords Record Office but some have appeared in print. A good example is the Westmorland returns for East and West Wards (known alternatively as the Barony of Appleby), which comprise more than half of the county.[11] They provide a list of 3432 names.

Surnames derived from local place-names stand out in this list. The 173 people named Adamthwaite, Birkbeck, Blenkarn, Bousfield, Branthwaite, Cliburn, Copeland, Douthwaite, Gaskill, Kendall, Lowther, Martindale,

Murthwaite, Salkeld, Threlkeld, Ubank and Warcop were descended from families which had taken their names from localities in Westmorland or Cumberland two or three centuries earlier. These surnames have a pronounced regional character, often being derived from minor place-names with the Old Norse elements -thwaite, -beck or -gill. The Blenkinsops had crossed the Pennines from their original home in Northumberland; the Teasdells had come from Teesdale; the Lancasters, Owthwaites and Furnesses had migrated a short distance from north Lancashire; and the Fawcetts, Dents, Blands and Pickerings had come from north Yorkshire. Some other locative surnames have more than one possible point of origin. They include Birkett, Crosby, Sowerby, Fallowfield, Fothergill, Morland, Orton, Raisebeck, Thornborow and its variants, Thwaites and Wharton. Some of these surnames are very likely to have had local origins; for example, Crosby, Wharton, Orton and Morland are names of parishes and chapelries listed in this return.

As in other parts of the country, some of the minor place-names which have produced surnames are known only to those who are familiar with the history of the region. Amongst the surnames included in the Westmorland Protestation return are Aiskill, Brunskill, Cloudsdayle, Crakenthorp, Garthwaite, Gowthorp, Hastwhittle, Hayton, Howgill, Lickbarrow, Railton and Yarre. They have an unmistakable north-western ring.

The other categories of surname in this list are nowhere near as distinctive. A large number of Westmorland names end in -son, in a manner that is characteristic of the whole of northern England and lowland Scotland, e.g. Dennison, Harrison, Hewitson, Nicholson, Richardson, Robinson, Robertson and Sanderson. However, the return includes only two Robsons, in sharp contrast to the large numbers found on the other side of the Pennines. The range of old personal names which had led to hereditary surnames was narrower in Westmorland than in the south and east of England. Only Lowes, Lowis, etc. and the Old English name Ellwood stand out in the list.

Occupational names included Bowman, Farar or Fairer, Hoggert, Steadman and Twentyman, but these are not confined to Westmorland. Nicknames ranged from Noble and Rudd to Todd (which is chiefly northern in its distribution) and Raickstray, a nickname for a scavenger. Remaining puzzles include Spedding, Measand or Meason, Laidman or Leadman, Langhorne and Knewstubb. The deaths of only four Knewstubbs were registered in 1842–46 in England and Wales; three of them in East Ward, Westmorland, and the other in Sheppey, Kent.

A comparison between the rugged north west and a lowland county in eastern England is made possible by the publication of the Lincolnshire return, which records about 33,000 names.[12] Some Lincolnshire place-names can be quickly identified as the source of some common surnames: Barkwith, Brumby, Bucknall, Cawkwell, Elsham, Keal, Luddington, Lusby, Mumby and Pinchbeck. The surname Toynton was recorded at Market Rasen, Louth and Grainthorpe, three settlements that lie a few miles to the north of the various Toyntons from which the name is derived. A few other surnames have their points of origin in place-names in nearby counties: Markham (Nottinghamshire), Padley (Derbyshire), Kelke and Pickering (Yorkshire) and Seagrave (Leicestershire). The Chattertons had presumably migrated even further, from Lancashire. Other surnames which sound as if they have come from minor place-names include Ackreland, Beck(e) and Inderwell.

Old personal names which developed into hereditary surnames in Lincolnshire include Christian, Frow(e), Gamble, Otter, Pell, Sewell and Uttinge. Gutterson, the son of Gutter, is derived ultimately from a topographical name. Jeckell or Jeckill is said by Reaney and Wilson to have been especially popular in Yorkshire and Lincolnshire. Apart from one man who lived further south, on the coast at Anderby, all the Lincolnshire Jeckells who were recorded in 1642 were living in a group of villages close to Grimsby. This tight distribution suggests a single-family origin for the Lincolnshire Jeckells but not of course for others who lived elsewhere. The twenty men whose surname was spelt variously as Odlin, Odline, Odlinn, Odling or Odlinge were scattered more widely but they too were confined to Lindsey, the northern part of Lincolnshire. Their distribution in 1642 suggests that they shared a common ancestor.

Lincolnshire nicknames include Codd, Coy, Crust, Good, Petch ('sin') and Winter ('sad, miserable'). Some of these names were also found in other counties. Surnames derived from occupations include Farmery ('worker at the infirmary'), Farrow (a worker in iron), Garner, Gelder, Hoode, Horne, Hurd, Plummer and Tunnard. But what are we to make of Snart or Snarke, a name which was clustered in Kesteven, particularly in the south west, near the border with Leicestershire and Rutland? Amongst the 2901 names listed in the Rutland hearth tax return of 1665 is that of Thomas Snart, one of the exempted poor, who lived at Barleythorpe, just north of Oakham, not far from these Lincolnshire men.[13] The Rutland hearth tax returns provides a check on the distinctive nature of other Lincolnshire surnames mentioned above. They note Christian, Coy, Elsome, Farey, Gamble, Garner, Good(e), Seagrave, Sewell and Winter.

We have seen that there is plenty of evidence from the various corners of England to enable us to plot the distribution of surnames in the seventeenth century. The patterns which we can establish help to focus enquiries as to where a distinctive surname may have originated. Thus when a hearth tax was levied in 1664, Nottinghamshire had many surnames that it could call its own. Some Nottinghamshire place-names, including Cottam, Elston, Gunthorpe, Hawkesmoor and Keyworth, gave rise to surnames that were still confined to the county in Charles II's reign. Topographical names such as Caunt, occupational names such as Boot, personal names such as Alvey, delightful nicknames such as Bee and Blonk, and names whose meanings are unknown to me, such as Gabbitas or Nettleship, were found in Not-ting-hamshire but rarely elsewhere.

The International Genealogical Index

No earlier sets of records provide a sample of names to allow us to plot their distribution across the country, though occasionally we are able to do this at county level. Staffordshire has a comprehensive list of about 51,000 names in 1532–33 but this is a unique and indeed astonishing source. The lay subsidies and the poll tax returns of the fourteenth century are invaluable sources close to the period of surname formation but they are far from complete in their coverage. We have to proceed backwards in time by genealogical methods as far as we can and then use whatever taxation and manorial records that are available in our search for the homes of family names. The evidence is more defective the further back in time that we go.

The development of computer software, however, has opened up a new avenue that takes us back another century from the period of the hearth tax returns. The Mormon International Genealogical Index (known to family historians as the IGI) is now available on CD-ROM as British Vital Records and the information that it provides can be downloaded and mapped on Stephen Archer's program, *GenMap UK*.

The IGI has been compiled by members of the Church of Jesus Christ of Latter Day Saints (the Mormons), who seek out their ancestors in order to baptise them by proxy. Members of the Mormon Church are required to undertake genealogical research and construct family trees. A huge pro-gramme of microfilming historical records has facilitated this research and special family history centres have been opened at Mormon churches all over the country and abroad. The combined results of this research have been indexed and made available to anyone who is interested in genealogy, whether they are members of the Mormon Church or not, first of all on microfilm and now on the Internet. The index is arranged in an alphabetical order of surnames, with entries placed chronologically by surname, county by county. These entries are transcripts of the records of baptisms and marriages (though not burials) in the parish registers of the Church of England and the registers of Nonconformist churches, many of which have been microfilmed for this purpose. As the data has been collected by amateurs, individual entries need checking, especially in the earliest period when the handwriting is difficult to decipher. Fortunately, a few errors are not critical for the purpose of plotting the distributions of surnames. We should, however, delete all the entries which estimate the date of birth from other information, for example by subtracting twenty-five years from the date of a marriage. These deletions can be done quickly and easily on a computer.

GenMap UK enables us to map this information and thus to demonstrate the distribution patterns of surnames during various periods of time. The data does not allow us to pinpoint certain years but it can be used to cover broad periods, for instance from the start of parish registration in 1538 to the end of the sixteenth century. The coverage of the IGI is far from comprehensive, however, and certain counties, particularly Cambridgeshire, Huntingdonshire and Somerset, are badly under-represented. We also need to be aware that few parish registers survive for Northumberland and County Durham until well into the seventeenth century. Some of the blank spaces on our distribution maps may reflect this lack of data.

Despite these deficiencies, maps based on the IGI entries usually point us in the right direction in our search for the homes of family names. For instance, all the sixteenth-century references to the surname Staniforth are from within a small circle centred on Sheffield, where a farm situated by a stony ford gave rise to the surname in the thirteenth century. We may therefore dismiss fears that the name might have had a separate origin at Stainforth, in the low-lying lands beyond Doncaster, or that later references to Staniforths in Lancashire might point to another home across the Pennines. The Lancashire entries can be explained satisfactorily by recorded movement to Manchester and Liverpool. But we have to be constantly aware that the IGI data is imperfect and that the distribution of a rare name can be distorted by migration. If a family were the sole bearers of a particular name in the sixteenth century, their movement away from their native heath and the subsequent ramification of the name at and near their new home would change the surname's distribution pattern fundamentally. Fortunately, this does not seem to have happened very often.

Local and family historians sometimes do not realise just how local some of the surnames of their particular neighbourhood are until they map them in this way. An article in a local paper about the early retirement of a Sheffield man named Simmonite prompted an enquiry into this name, which I had also seen written as Simmonet. I had assumed that occasional references in local parish registers were to a name that had strayed into the Sheffield district and that the home of the name was elsewhere.

Dictionaries of English and French surnames said that Simmonet was a pet form of Simon. Occasional examples of the name occur in the fourteenth century in Yorkshire, Staffordshire and London. A John Symonet was taxed in the Isle of Wight in 1379. A map of the baptismal data in the IGI from the sixteenth to the nineteenth century surprised me, therefore, when it showed that Simmonite or Simmonet is definitely a Sheffield and south Yorkshire name, rare enough to have a single-family origin. The name was recorded in this district in 1345, when a grant of land in the chapelry of Bradfield was confirmed to Reginald, son of John Symonet, but no other references to the surname appear locally until 1561, when Elizabeth Semenat was living at Aston, a few miles to the south east. The first mention of the name in the Sheffield parish register is the entry recording the marriage of George Simminet and Elizabeth Carre on 28 January 1616. Their daughter Anne was baptised on 10 April 1616; other children followed. This George Simmonett was named in a list of Hallamshire cutlers a couple of years earlier, so perhaps he had arrived to serve an apprenticeship in the previous decade. The records of the Cutlers' Company note that in 1637 John, son of William Simonett, of Woodall, husbandman, was apprenticed to the trade. Woodall lies close to Aston, where the surname was recorded in 1561. During the following century other apprentices named Symonett, Simmonite, Siminet or Simonet(t) came from Woodall, Tickhill, Whiston and neighbouring places. The hearth tax returns of 1672 recorded two Symonetts in Aston and one each in Sheffield and Hickleton. The name was also found further north in the parish of Mirfield, where the clerks had a great deal of trouble in deciding how to spell the name. Between 1649 and 1682 they tried Simonet, Simolet, Surmolit and Synamond. As the surname was known in France, and as the spelling caused so much difficulty, we are led to wonder whether the Simmonets were immigrants from the Continent. We have no evidence to support such a hypothesis, however. It is just as likely that the family were resident in south Yorkshire well before 1561 and that we have not found them because of the scarcity of records before the beginnings of parish registration. They do not, however, appear in the poll tax return for the West Riding in 1379. The map of the IGI data has thrown up an intriguing problem that has not yet been solved.

Another name that occurs in the early Sheffield parish register is Belk. Turning to the IGI, we find that this is not a rare name like Simmonite but nor is it common. The IGI records 373 baptisms from the sixteenth to the nineteenth century, of which 65 per cent were in Yorkshire. The 243 entries from Yorkshire are followed by ninety-three for Nottinghamshire, Lincolnshire, Derbyshire and Lancashire; 90 per cent of all the entries are

from these five neighbouring counties. Another thirty-two are from south-
eastern England, however, including twenty-one from Kent. The earliest
recording of the name was in London (1592), followed by one in Chilham
(Kent) in 1600. Are we to assume a separate origin for these southern Belks,
or does early migration from the north to London and then to Kent seem
a better hypothesis? And do the northern Belks have more than one origin?
Reaney quotes a Henry del Belk in Nottinghamshire in 1252 and says that
this is a topographical name meaning 'dweller by the bank or ridge'. The
IGI data has at least suggested the directions in which further enquiries
might go and has narrowed the options in a search for the home or homes
of this distinctive name.

These three examples, in their different ways, have shown how useful the
IGI can be in demonstrating the local or regional nature of many surnames
in the Tudor and Stuart period and even later. The data is far from perfect
but can still be used to good effect in plotting surname distributions. It
can also help us to identify immigrant names and to see how they spread
across the country.

The Origin of the Heys

My own surname comes from the name of a farm on the edge of the
Pennine moors near Halifax, close to where the M62 now passes Scammonden Reservoir. It provides a final illustration of how the approach of
the local and family historian differs from that of the compilers of dictionaries who are concerned principally with etymologies. My own interest was
not just with the name's meaning. I wished to trace the family name as far
back as possible, hopefully to the exact spot where it was formed. The
journey was a long one but I was not disappointed.

The place-name is derived from two Old English words and a similar
Scandinavian word, all of which meant a hedge but which came to mean
the land enclosed by a hedge. Heys often seem to lie on old manorial or
forest boundaries, at the limit of cultivation. Similar surnames derived from
the same group of words are Hay, Haye, Hayes, Hays, Heyes, Heighes,
Haigh, Hague, Haugh and Hough.

As a minor place-name Hey was once common in the southern Pennines.
It can be spotted readily enough on the Yorkshire side of the River Derwent
and further north in the West Riding. Newly-cleared moorland or sections
of a forest fenced off for hunting were often named Ox Hey, Cow Hey,
Calf Hey, Wood Hey, New Hey, etc. In other parts of England, for example
Devon, the place-name evolved as Hay. The variations were products of
local speech. West Riding dialect speakers still pronounce my surname with

a harder, rougher sound than Hay, so it is easy to see why the local spelling persisted. Hey is also a French word with the same meaning and so is found as a surname in France, especially northern France, Belgium and Alsace-Lorraine. I once came across a Pierre Hey, a Swiss architect, at a campsite in the Loire valley.

The poll tax returns of 1377–81 show that the farm name Hey or Hay gave rise to surnames in several parts of England. The Derby taxpayers of 1379 included John de Heye, John and Peter del Heye and Richard del Haye, labourers and craftsmen. Those in Leicestershire included Richard de Hey, Robert Hay and Nicholas de Hey. In Essex in 1381 Thomas atte Hey was taxed at East Hanningfield and William le Hey at Tolleshunt Knights, together with five people named Oxenhey at Felsted and Rayne. In the same year, John Hey was taxed in Gloucestershire, John Hay in Hampshire and Alice Hay in Herefordshire. Despite the widespread use of the word both as a place-name and a surname, however, none of these taxpayers seems to be an ancestor of the present-day Heys. The surname is concentrated in the West Riding of Yorkshire and neighbouring parts of Lancashire and appears to have a single-family origin. The Lancashire list of taxpayers in 1379 does create problems for this assertion, however, for it includes five people named Hey or Hay. It is possible that one or more of these lines did not die out, like those in the other counties quoted above, and that the surname evolved independently on that side of the Pennines. Heys appear in some early Lancashire parish registers two hundred years later. Only genealogical research will establish whether or not these people were native Lancastrians in origin or whether their ancestors migrated from just across the border. The distribution of people named Hey or Hay in Lancashire in 1379 – one in Lonsdale wapentake, two in Ashton-in-Makerfield, one in Newton-le-Willows and one in Culcheth – does not match the later concentration of the Heys in the east of the county, however. Migration from Scammonden seems the more plausible hypothesis

The same process by which most families bearing the surname Hey withered is paralleled by Hay, which is a Scottish surname. The Haighs and Hagues are as West Riding as the Heys, but they do not have a single-family origin. Genealogical research is needed to disentangle the various family names which are derived from farm names in Elland, Longwood, South Kirkby, West Ardsley and Haigh near West Bretton. In south Yorkshire Hague became the normal spelling. William Hague, the leader of the Conservative Party, was born there and is no doubt descended from a long line of local people.

The geographical distribution of the surname Hey can be plotted from the 1842–46 indexes of deaths in England and Wales. A total of 204 deaths were recorded during these five years, of which 161 were in the West Riding. The distribution is strikingly emphatic. The search for the original home of the surname must concentrate on the Pennine parishes of west Yorkshire and just over the hills in parts of east Lancashire.

The hearth tax returns of 1672 and the earlier evidence of parish registers, wills and manorial court rolls confirm that our search is in the right area. It would be tedious to note the detailed evidence by which a genealogist traces a family back towards its roots. Suffice it to say that in this case the trail takes us to Scammonden township, where a group of Hey place-names are marked on the Ordnance Survey map on the north side of the M62. Scammonden was first recorded in 1275 but is probably a much older settlement. Its name is derived from Old Norse and means 'Skammbein's valley'.

The poll tax returns for the West Riding in 1379 record Richard del Haye and Alice, his wife, in Quarmby township (which included Scammonden), followed immediately by Thomas del Haye. In the adjacent township of Barkisland Robert del Heye was taxed at the same basic rate of 4d. Thomas and Robert were perhaps Richard and Alice's sons. Elsewhere in the West Riding, William de Hey and Agnes, his wife, were taxed 4d. at Tickhill and Peter del Hay, sergeant, and Johanna, his wife, were taxed at the much higher rate of 3s. 4d. at Skelbrooke, but these are lines that failed.

The huge manor of Wakefield extended up on to the moors around Scammonden and Barkisland. The court rolls of this manor form one of the finest collections in England, surviving in a fragmentary series from 1274 to 1326 and then in an almost uninterrupted run to 1925. They are of enormous value to family and local historians in the West Riding. To ease administration, the manor was sub-divided into twelve graveships; Scammonden graveship was created in 1343, long after the others. Each graveship was served by a greave who was selected annually on rotation from the tenants. The Richard del Heye of the poll tax returns was greave of Scammonden on five occasions between 1374 and 1397.[14] This Richard was followed by thirteen generations of Heys who served as greave from time to time. This list does not provide firm proof of direct ancestry but it does demonstrate family succession in the same township and, almost certainly, the same farm. It reads as follows:

1401 and 1406	Thomas del Heye
1412	Richard del Hey
1417, 1426 and 1427	Thomas de Hey or Thomas Hey
1432	John del Hey
1436 and 1437	Thomas Heye

1448	John Hey
1463	John Heye
1466 and 1467	Richard Hey
1472	John Hey
1476 and 1477	Richard Hey
1483	John Hey
1486, 1487, 1493, 1496, 1497,1513, 1526, 1528, 1531 and 1532	Richard Hey
1537, 1543, 1546 and 1547	Edward Hey
1553	Margaret Hey, widow
1564 and 1565	Edward Hey
1566	Edward and Richard Hey and John Smith
1577	Edward Hey

Significantly, in 1592 George Firth of Firthhous served as greave 'for le hey', i.e. the farm that had given rise to the surname. George Redmonds informs me that the commonplace book of John Kaye of Woodsome Hall refers to the purchase of this farm in 1580: 'I bought the moytie of hei Land wch I lett for £4.10s. Yt coost me above iii^{xxli} '. Three years later, Kaye's rental included land at Scammonden, some of which was rented by John Hey. In 1592 Kaye 'sold my moytie of Hey landes wch I late purchasyd, to James Dison and Edmund my tenents for tow Hundrith pounes and dyd gyve unto my sone Robert all the said some'.

The Heys had left the farm where they had lived for well over 200 years, though they remained elsewhere in the township of Scammonden until Victorian times. Junior branches had left in previous generations and had established themselves in several places that radiated out from Scammonden but which never lay very far away. My own branch settled in Kirkburton parish, a few miles to the south east. A John Heye was involved in an affray in Thurstonland, in that parish, in 1467 and he or another John Hey served as the constable of Thurstonland in 1491. The Thomas Hey who was recorded in the manor court rolls of 1505–8 at Cumberworth, Kirkburton and Holme, and as the constable of Shelley in 1514, was probably my ancestor, for in 1524 he was taxed at Birk House, Shelley, where proven ancestors were living in the seventeenth century. In 1568 John Hey of Byrke Hows was buried in Kirkburton churchyard but gaps in the parish register prevent firm proof of ancestry until the John Hey of Birk House who died in 1633. I am ten generations down the line from this John.

It is a common experience for a family historian to fail to find firm evidence of ancestry in the early parish registers but to discover tantalising clues about earlier generations. These clues often point to the original home of the family name. The Wakefield manorial court rolls allow me to go back even further than the poll tax returns of 1379. In 1323 Alan del Haye appeared before the court to answer a charge of digging a ditch across a path in Scammonden and two years later he was asked to explain why he had cut greenwood belonging to the lord. Other Heys appear in earlier manorial court rolls but he is the first whom we can link to later members of the family. In 1333 the rolls record that twelve and a quarter acres of land in Scammonden were let to to Alan del Heye and Thomas, his son, upon the payment of a ten shillings entry fine. Seven years later Alan enlarged his farm to just over eighteen acres. It is clear from the rolls that a great deal of communal assarting or taking in of new land from the woods and the moors was occurring in Scammonden at this time.

On 18 May 1350 Richard, son of Alan del Hey, inherited a messuage and twenty acres of land in Scammonden after the death of Thomas del Hey his brother, 'whose heir he is, to hold according to the custom of the manor'. The date is probably significant. The rolls of 1349–50 seem to indicate the passage of the Black Death, for in those years land was frequently inherited by uncles, brothers, sisters and other relations, instead of by sons and daughters, and manorial business came almost to a standstill. The Richard who inherited the farm at Scammonden was probably the one who heads our list of greaves and who paid poll tax in 1379.

The site of the original farm that has produced the surname Hey can be identified with a fair degree of confidence. Two maps enable us to recreate the ancient landscape, which in fact has been little altered to this day. A map of 1607 in the Public Record Office, entitled 'A true Plott of all ye Coppihold Land w[ith]in the Towneshipp or Graveshipp of Scamonden', can be compared with the 1908 edition of the six–inch Ordnance Survey map. The seventeenth-century map marks 'The Haies', a long, narrow, wooded enclosure of eighteen acres by the streams that form the northern boundary of the graveship. This is undoubtedly the hey that we are looking for. It was the same size in 1607 as it had been in 1340. On the ground, a stream flows along a deep ravine that was a natural choice for the north-eastern boundary. The western boundary is marked by a well-defined ditch and bank now surmounted by a stone wall but once no doubt topped by the hedge that gave its name to this particular hey. The two properties marked within 'The Haies' on the 1607 map correspond, on the 1908 map, to Hey Laith and The Shoulder of Mutton (now three properties known as Glen Hey, one of which is inscribed 'Hey Farm 1855') on Hey Lane. We cannot be certain where the original farm stood within the eighteen-acre, hedged enclosure, but as Hey Laith stands on a spur of land in the classic manner of a medieval Pennine farm it is the most likely choice. The woods shown within the enclosure on the 1607 map had shrunk to the Hey Wood of the 1908 map, which also marks all the other farms that are named in 1607: Hey Croft, Ley Field, Han Head, Turner House, Broad Lee, Dean Head and Croft House. And just across the boundary to the west stood (and still stand) Upper and Lower Hey House, named after the branch of the family that was taxed in Barkisland in 1379. A few more buildings had been erected in the three centuries that elapsed between the making of the two maps and some fields had been subdivided, but the landscape of 1607 could easily have been recognised in 1908 and is still obvious on a visit today.

PART THREE

Tracing Your Own Name

Steps in Tracing Your Own Name

Consulting a dictionary of surnames is the obvious first step. Despite my criticisms of their approach and findings, they often provide a ready answer to the meaning of a name. P. H. Reaney and R. M. Wilson, *A Dictionary of English Surnames* (revised edition, 1997) and P. Hanks and F. Hodges, *A Dictionary of Surnames* (1988), both published by Oxford University Press, are the best. However, no dictionary can include all the thousands of surnames that are still in use, so many of the rarer names are missing.

The next step is to discover whether your name is a common one that is found all over the country or whether it is one of the many names that are found in certain areas but are unknown elsewhere. The collection of current telephone directories in a general reference library can often be a great help in determining the present spread of a name. An overwhelming concentration in one county or another points to the possibility of a single-family origin. A *UK Telephone Directory CD* is available for use on computers with a CD-ROM drive.

The geographical distribution of the name then needs to be plotted further back in time. The 1881 British census returns are the easiest starting point as they have been indexed by surname. They are available on microfiche at record offices and major libraries. If you have a computer with a CD-ROM drive and Windows 95 (or higher) the task is made much easier. The *1881 British Census and National Index* set of CDs is available from the Church of Jesus Christ, 399 Garretts Green, Birmingham, B33 0UH at a moderate price. The census information can be converted by the *RTF Wizard for the British Census on CD-ROM* into formats appropriate for surname studies. Stephen Archer's *GenMap UK* and *LDS Companion* enable us to make location maps, using the census information. All these CDs (apart from the census returns) are available from S & N Genealogy Supplies, Greenacres, Salisbury Road, Chilmark, Salisbury, SP3 5AH. It is, of course, perfectly possible, though more laborious, to construct your own maps without the aid of a computer.

The indexes of the birth, marriage and death certificates for England and Wales from 1837 to the present day, and those for Scotland and Ireland from later periods, can also be used to map distributions of surnames. In this book I have used the indexes of deaths from 1842 to 1846, but other periods could be sampled. The indexes are usually available on microfiche at the Family Records Centre, 1 Myddelton Street, London, EC1, which is most easily reached via the Angel underground station on the Northern Line.

Further back in time, it is more difficult to plot surname distributions with accuracy. An increasing number of counties now have one or more hearth tax returns from the 1660s or 1670s in print. Where they are available, they are an invaluable source halfway between the period of surname formation in the middle ages and the present day. They record the names of householders, arranged by township (or 'constabulary'), a unit of local government that was often smaller than a parish, so they give a precise indication of the whereabouts of family names before the great rise of the population in the eighteenth and nineteenth centuries.

Having discovered where a name is likely to be found, we need to use genealogical methods to trace families back in time. In practice, most people will have done much of this before they start on the wider search for the origin of the family name. Several good handbooks explain how to trace a family tree step by step. The most comprehensive is Mark D. Herber, *Ancestral Trails* (Sutton, in association with the Society of Genealogists, 1997), which includes the addresses of record offices. My own book, *The Oxford Guide to Family History* (Oxford University Press, 1993), provides the national background. Parish registers are the principal source of information before civil registration began in 1837. The Mormon Church has assembled a huge number of baptismal and marriage entries for parish registers in their International Genealogical Index (IGI), which is widely available for consultation. Most record offices and county libraries hold microfiche copies. The IGI is also available on CD-ROM and surname distributions based on this source can be mapped using *GenMap UK*. The IGI is far from being a complete index, however, so the distribution maps must be used with caution. Nonetheless, they often provide striking evidence of where a name was located.

Tracing a family back in time alerts us to variant spellings and to the ways in which some names have changed their form. We cannot always explain the meaning of a name from the way it is written and pronounced today. We need to get back to the earliest records that are available. Unfortunately, most of us will not be able to prove a direct line before the sixteenth or seventeenth centuries, when parish registers began and the making of wills became more common. But if we have got that far back we have probably got a fair idea of where the name came from. Even if we cannot prove the links between the generations, earlier references to a family name in manorial court rolls or tax returns in the same district usually point to its place of origin. Only then can we confirm or deny the explanation of the name offered in the dictionaries.

9

The Most Common Surnames

A list of the fifty most common surnames in England and Wales in the mid nineteenth century was compiled by the Registrar General in 1853. They are given here with explanations of their meanings. Later, some of these names were adopted by Gaelic and Jewish immigrants whose names the English could not pronounce.

1. SMITH. Most places required the services of a smith, but as only one would be needed the craft name distinguished him from his neighbours.

2. JONES. 'Son of John'. The most popular Welsh name, but Jones was a common surname in the English counties bordering Wales long before the Welsh adopted English-style surnames.

3. WILLIAMS. 'Son of William'. Found in many English counties in the west, all the way down to Cornwall, before it became a popular Welsh name.

4. TAYLOR. Another craft that was widespread but which had just one man to each village or district.

5. DAVIES. 'Son of David'. Found throughout Wales, especially the south-west.

6. BROWN. A nickname referring to the colour of hair or complexion. It may occasionally have been derived from an Old English or Old Norse personal name.

7. THOMAS. The biblical name which became popular with the cult of St Thomas Becket and then with the Welsh.

8. EVANS. A Welsh name meaning 'son of John'.

9. ROBERTS. 'Son of Robert'. Found particularly in north Wales, but known earlier in the West Riding of Yorkshire and other parts of England.

10. JOHNSON. 'Son of John'. The northern English equivalent of Jones.

11. ROBINSON. 'Son of Robin', a pet form of Robert. A northern English name.

12. WILSON. 'Son of Will', the short form of William. A northern English name.

13. WRIGHT. A craft name. Others were distinguished as Cartwright, Wainwright, etc.

14. WOOD. A name for someone who lived by a wood. In each case the position of the house by a wood would have distinguished a family from their neighbours.

15. HALL. Usually a servant at a hall, though perhaps sometimes a name for someone who lived near a large house.

16. WALKER. A craft name for a fuller of cloth, found particularly in northern England.

17. HUGHES. 'Son of Hugh'. Widely used in western medieval England, it became a popular Welsh name.

18. GREEN. Either a topographical name for someone who lived by a green or sometimes a nickname for someone who dressed in green clothes.

19. LEWIS. From an Old Germanic personal name introduced by the Normans and from an Anglicisation of the Welsh name Llywelyn.

20. EDWARDS. 'Son of Edward', an Old English personal name. It became popular with the Welsh, sometimes as the equivalent of the Welsh name Iorwerth.

21. THOMPSON. The northern English version of 'son of Thomas'.

22. WHITE. A nickname for someone with white hair or a pale complexion.

23. JACKSON. A northern English and Lowland Scottish name from a pet form of John.

24. TURNER. A widespread craft name for a maker of wooden, metal or bone objects turned on a lathe.

25. HILL. A topographical name for someone whose house on or by a hill distinguished him from his neighbours.

26. HARRIS. 'Son of Harry', a pet form of Henry.

27. CLARK. An occupational name for a scribe or professional secretary or a member of a minor religious order who were permitted to marry.

28. COOPER. A maker of barrels and other wooden vessels.

29. HARRISON. The northern English version of 'son of Harry'.

30. DAVIS. 'Son of David'. In England this form was preferred, whereas the Welsh favoured Davies.

31. WARD. A watchman or guard.

32. BAKER. An occupational name for the owner of a communal oven or for someone employed in the kitchen of a great house.

33. MARTIN. An old personal name popularised by Martin of Tours, the fourth-century saint.

34. MORRIS. From the Old French personal name Maurice, introduced by the Normans.

35. JAMES. Ultimately from the biblical name Jacob, James was a popular saint's name in the middle ages.

36. MORGAN. A Celtic name that was popular for centuries. The surname is found particularly in south and mid Wales.

37. KING. A nickname applied jokingly or given to someone who played a part in a pageant or who won a contest.

38. ALLEN. A Celtic name introduced into England by Bretons at or after the Norman Conquest.

39. CLARKE. An alternative spelling of Clark. The two names combined would be placed ninth in this list.

40. COOK. An occupational name, especially for a keeper of an eating house.

41. MOORE. Usually someone who lived by a moor, but sometimes a nickname for a man with a swarthy complexion.

42. PARKER. The keeper of a lord's park.

43. PRICE. A Welsh surname from ap Rhys, 'son of Rees'.

44. PHILLIPS. 'Son of Philip'. A widespread English surname before it was adopted by the Welsh.

45. WATSON. 'Son of Wat', a pet form of Walter.

46. SHAW. Someone who lived by a small wood.

47. LEE. Someone who lived in or near a woodland clearing.

48. BENNETT. A pet form of Benedict.

49. CARTER. An occupational name.

50. GRIFFITHS. 'Son of Gruffydd', from an Old Welsh personal name.

Kevin Schürer of the University of Essex has analysed the 1881 British census returns for a display in the Wellcome Wing at the Science Museum, Kensington. He shows that 40 per cent of the population at that time shared just 500 different surnames, and 60 per cent 1000 surnames. At the other end of the scale, 10 per cent of the population shared 30,000 rare surnames.

Maps

Registered Deaths in England and Wales, 1842–46

In Chapter 6 we saw how maps of the civil registration units from 1837 to 1851 could be drawn by adjusting the maps of the original poor law unions depicted in the 1849 edition of Samuel Lewis, *Atlas to the Topographical Dictionaries of England and Wales*. The registered deaths for a five year period from 1 January 1842 to 31 December 1846 regularly show remarkable concentrations of surnames in various parts of the country, as these examples demonstrate.

1. Acland: 80. A locative name from Acland Barton in Landkey (Devon).

2. Akehurst: 67. A locative name from Akehurst Farm, Hellingly (Sussex).

3. Aldous/Aldis: 115. From a pet form of one or more feminine personal names beginning with Ald-.

4. Annear: 19. A Cornish name, 'an hyr', meaning 'the long or tall man'.

5. Apps: 46. A topographical name for one who lived by a prominent aspen tree.

6. Arkwright: 46. An occupational name for a maker of arks or chests.

7. Ashburner: 41. An occupational name for a maker of potash.

8. Ashdown: 95. The distribution suggests that the name comes from Ashdown (Kent).

9. Ashurst: 83. The concentration of 59 in the Wigan registration district points to Ashurst Beacon as the source of the name.

10. Aslin(g): 23. A diminutive of the Old German personal name Azilin.

11. Atack: 49. A Yorkshire variant of a name derived from Etough (Lancashire).

12. Auty/Alty: 93. From the Old Norse personal name Auti.

13. Avison: 47. From the Old French feminine personal name Avice.

14. Bevan: 97. A south Wales name from ap or ab Evan, the son of Evan.

15. Bunyan: 55. A nickname from Bedfordshire.

16. Dymond: 37. A Devon name for a dairyman.
17. Ramsbottom: 222. A Lancashire locative name.
18. Rigden: 28. A diminutive of Richard.
19. Senior: 199. A nickname, meaning either 'lord' or 'elder'.
20. Wildgoose: 60. A nickname from the bird.

1. Acland registered deaths 1842–46
80 (2 in north Wales)

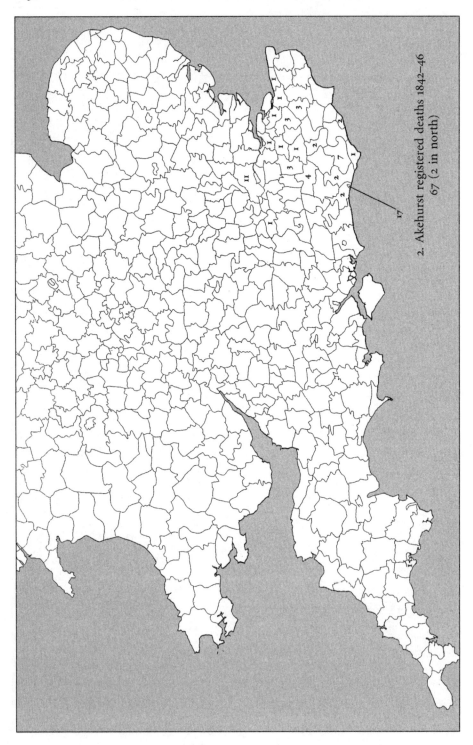

2. Akehurst registered deaths 1842–46
67 (2 in north)

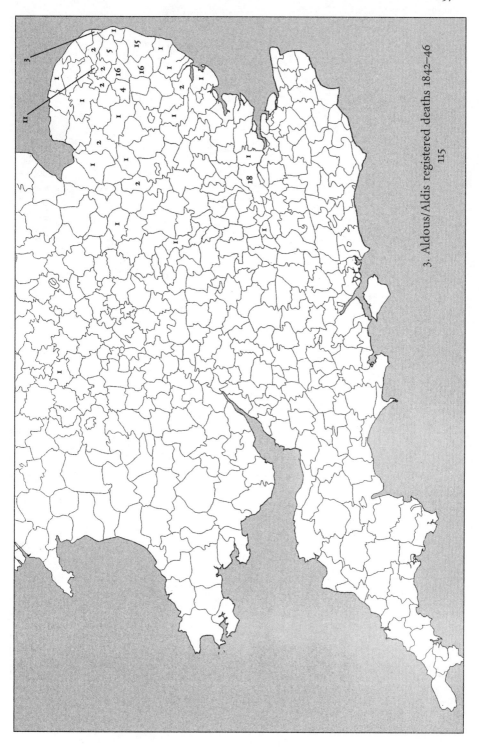

3. Aldous/Aldis registered deaths 1842–46

115

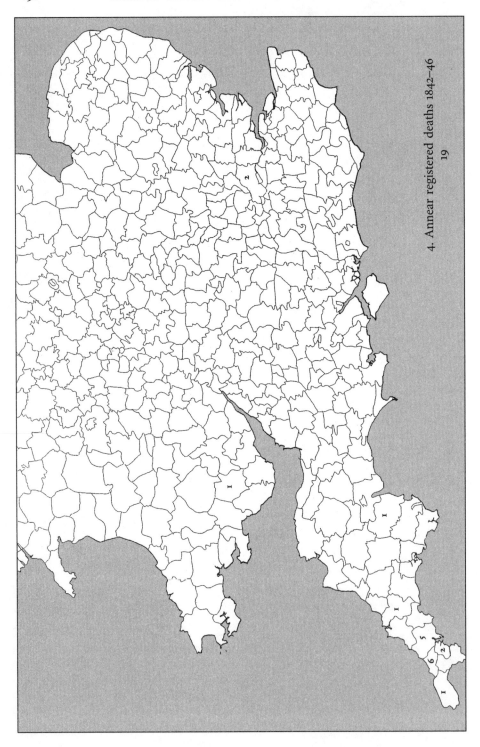

4. Annear registered deaths 1842–46
19

5. Apps registered deaths 1842–46
65 (1 in Liverpool)

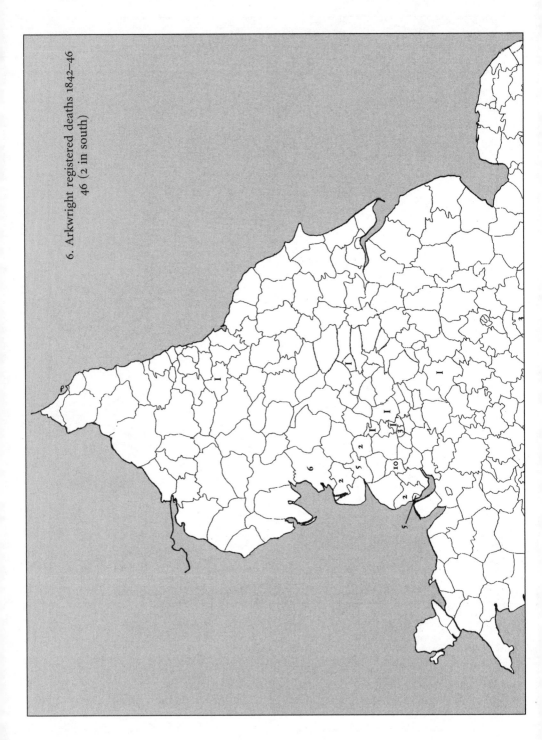

6. Arkwright registered deaths 1842–46 (2 in south)

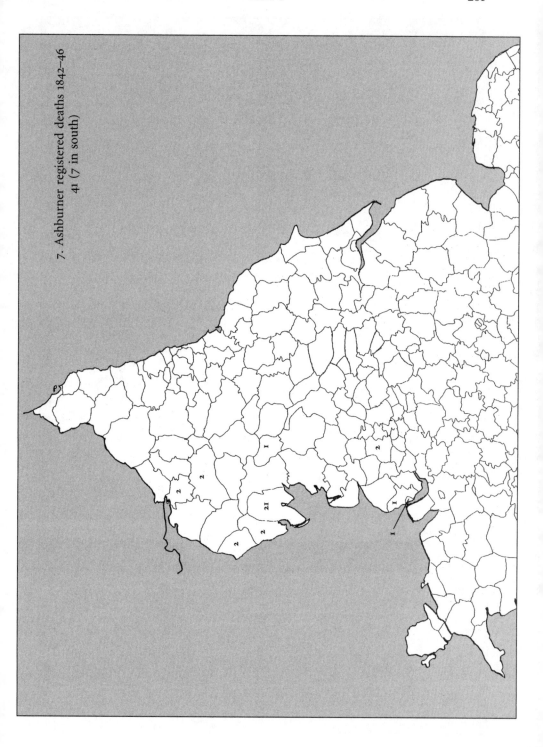

7. Ashburner registered deaths 1842–46
41 (7 in south)

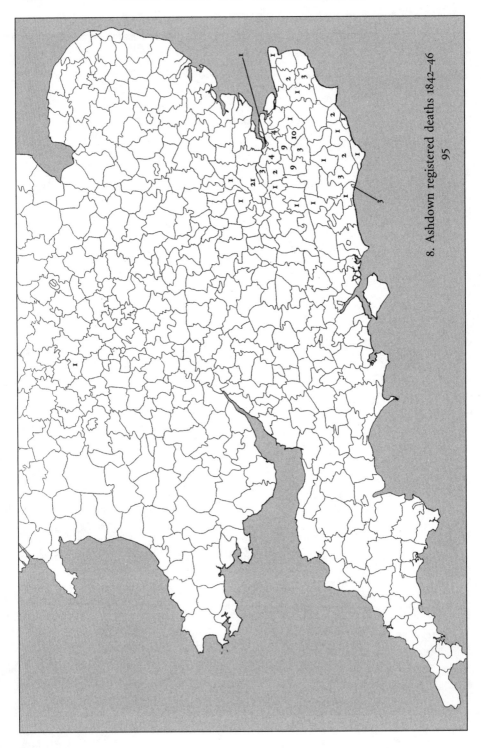

8. Ashdown registered deaths 1842–46

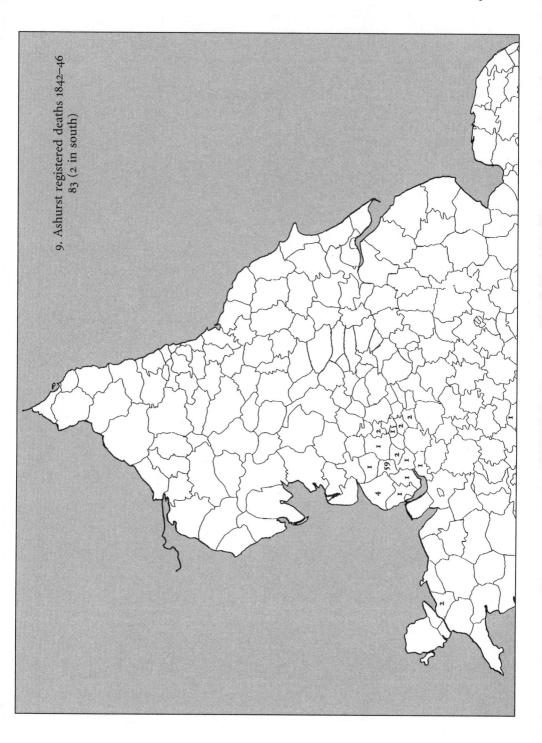

9. Ashurst registered deaths 1842–46
83 (2 in south)

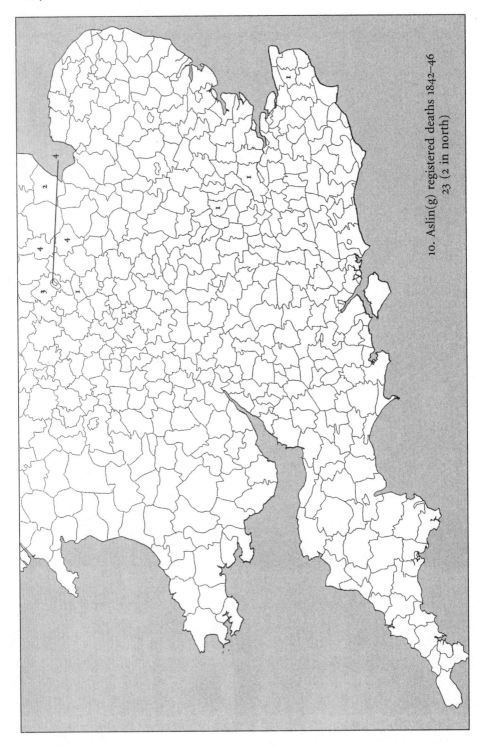

10. Aslin(g) registered deaths 1842–46
23 (2 in north)

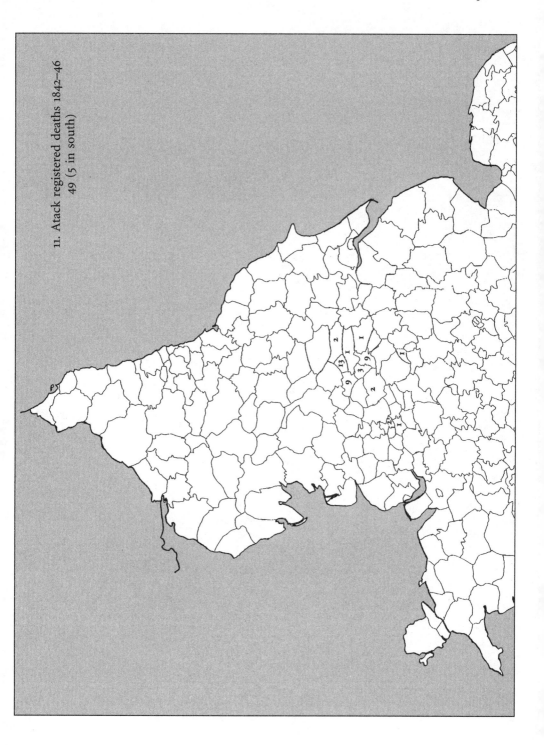

11. Atack registered deaths 1842–46 49 (5 in south)

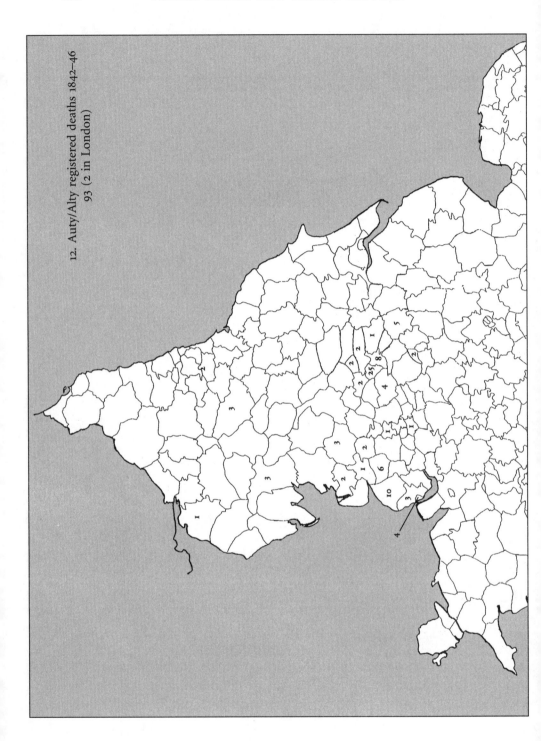

12. Auty/Alty registered deaths 1842–46
93 (2 in London)

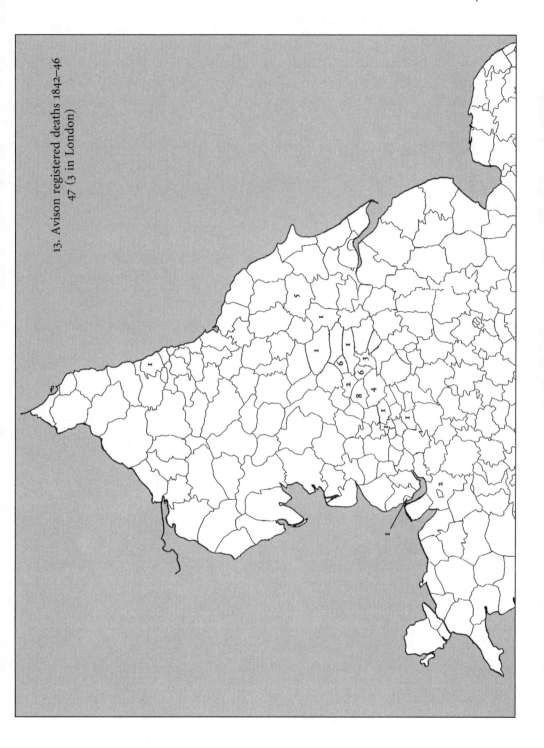

13. Avison registered deaths 1842–46
47 (3 in London)

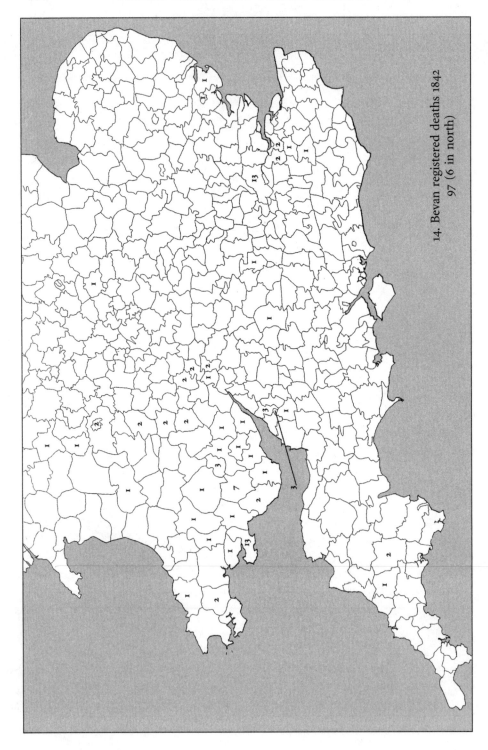

14. Bevan registered deaths 1842
97 (6 in north)

15. Bunyan registered deaths 1842–46
55 (4 in north)

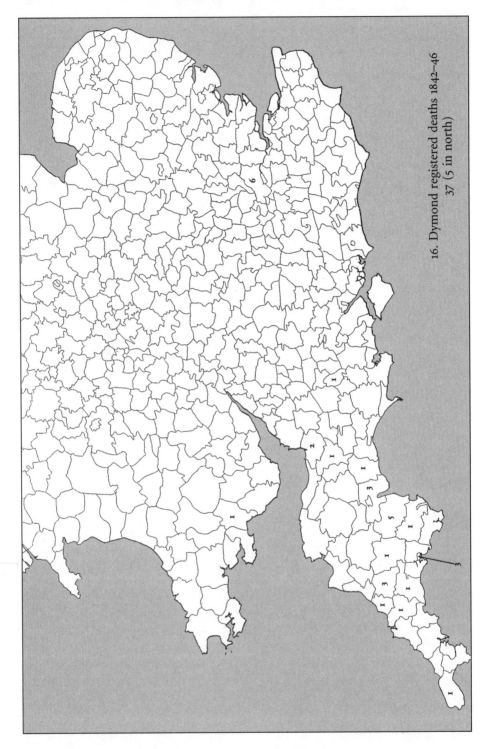

16. Dymond registered deaths 1842–46
37 (5 in north)

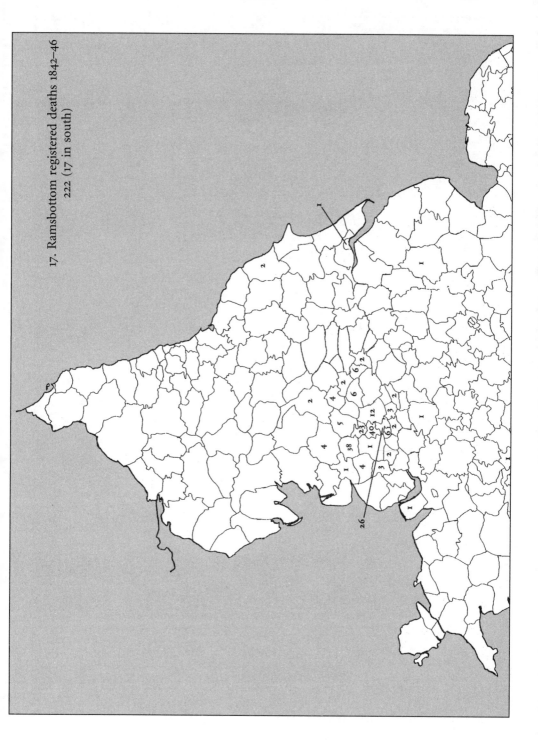

17. Ramsbottom registered deaths 1842–46
222 (17 in south)

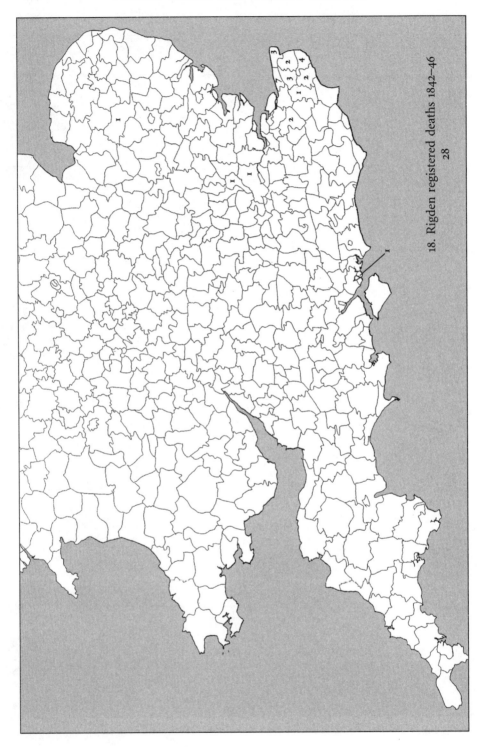

18. Rigden registered deaths 1842–46

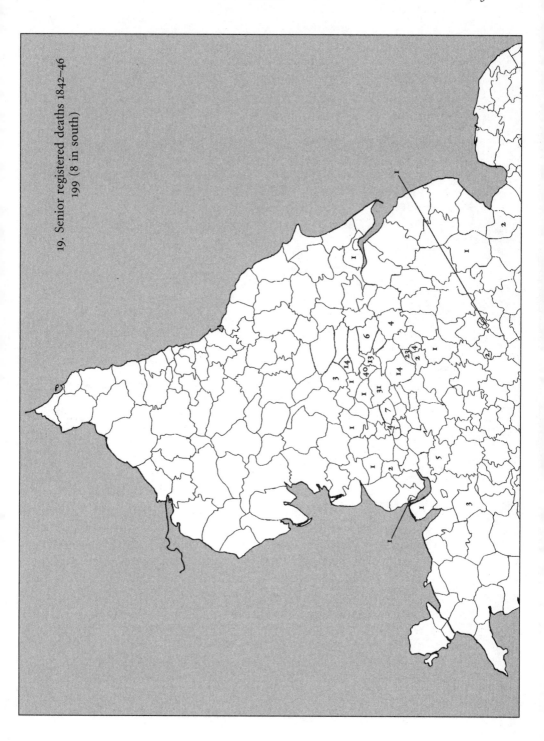

19. Senior registered deaths 1842–46
199 (8 in south)

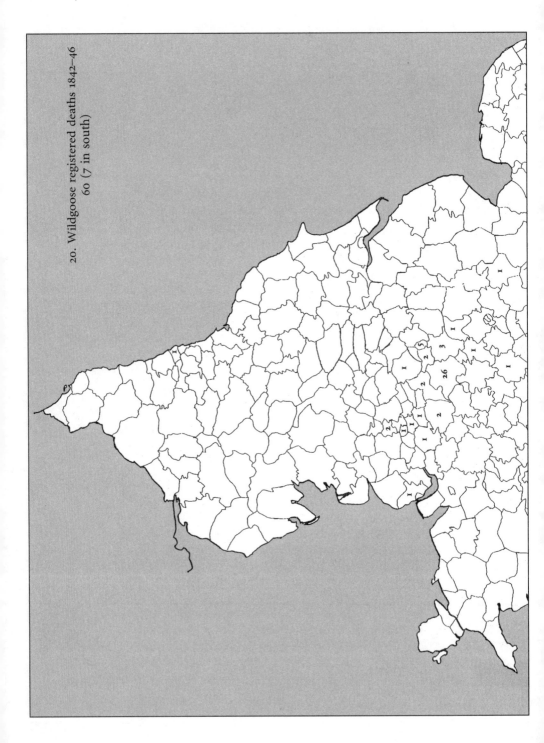

20. Wildgoose registered deaths 1842–46
60 (7 in south)

Notes

Notes to Chapter 1: Names and History

1. P. H. Reaney and R. M. Wilson, *A Dictionary of English Surnames* (revised edition, Oxford, 1997).
2. P. Hanks and F. Hodges, *A Dictionary of Surnames* (Oxford, 1988).
3. G. Franson, *Middle English Surnames of Occupation, 1100–1350* (Lund, 1935); O. Von Feilitzen, *The Pre-Conquest Personal Names of Domesday Book* (Uppsala, 1937); G. Tenvik, *Old English Bynames* (Uppsala, 1938); M. Lofvenberg, *Middle English Local Surnames* (Lund, 1942); and B. Thuresson, *Middle English Occupational Terms* (Lund, 1950).
4. The current editions are as in note 1 and P. H. Reaney, *The Origins of English Surnames* (London, 1987).
5. P. McClure, 'The Interpretation of Hypocoristic Forms of Middle English Baptismal Names', *Nomina*, 21 (1998).
6. G. W. Lasker, 'The Frequency of Surnames in England and Wales', *Human Biology*, 55 (1983).

Notes to Chapter 2: The Normans

1. L. C. Loyd, *The Origins of Some Anglo-Norman Families*, ed. C. T. Clay and D. C. Douglas, Harleian Society, 103 (1951).
2. K. S. B. Keats-Rohan, *Domesday People: A Prosopography of Persons Occurring in English Documents, 1066–1166*, i, *Domesday Book* (1999).
3. W. G. Hoskins, *Devon* (1972).
4. Carolyn C. Fenwick, ed., *The Poll Taxes of 1377, 1379 and 1381: Bedfordshire -Leicestershire* (Oxford, 1998).

Notes to Chapter 3: The Origins of English Family Names

1. W. G. Hoskins, 'Leicestershire Yeoman Families and their Pedigrees', *Transactions of the Leicestershire Archaeological Society*, 23 (1946).
2. P. McClure, 'Patterns of Migration in the Late Middle Ages: The Evidence of English Place-Name Surnames', *Economic History Review*, second series, 32 (1979).

Notes to Chapter 4; The Development of Family Names.

1. D. Jenkins, *The Agricultural Community in South-West Wales at the Turn of the Twentieth Century* (Cardiff, 1971).
2. A. Pettigree, *Foreign Protestant Communities in Sixteenth-Century London* (Oxford, 1986).
3. B. Awty, 'Aliens in the Ironworking Areas of the Weald: The Subsidy Rolls, 1524–1603', *Bulletin of the Wealden Iron Research Group*, second series, 4 (1984).

Notes to Chapter 5; Stability and Change

1. K. S. B. Keats-Rohan, *Domesday People: A Prosopography of Persons Occurring in English Documents, 1066–1166*, i, *Domesday Book* (1999).
2. J. V. Beckett, *The Aristocracy in England, 1660–1914* (Oxford, 1986).
3. A. Everitt, *Change in the Provinces: The Seventeenth Century* (Leicester, 1969).
4. A. Wagner, *Pedigree and Progress: Essays in the Genealogical Interpretation of History* (Chichester, 1975).
5. P. Laslett and J. Harrison, 'Clayworth and Cogenhoe', in H. E. Bell and R. L. Ollard, eds, *Historical Essays Presented to David Ogg* (London, 1963).
6. These are printed in *Collections for a History of Staffordshire* (Staffordshire Record Society) for the years 1921, 1923, 1925, 1927 and 1936. See D. Hey, 'The Distinctive Surnames of Staffordshire', *Staffordshire Studies*, 10 (1998).
7. W. Watkins-Pritchard, ed., *The Shropshire Hearth Tax Roll of 1672*, Shropshire Archaeological and Parish Register Society (1949).
8. J. Smith, *Men and Armour for Gloucestershire in 1608* (Stroud, 1980).
9. C. A. F. Meekings, S. Porter and I. Roy, eds, *The Hearth Tax Collector's Book for Worcester, 1678–1680*, Worcestershire Historical Society, new series, 2 (1983).
10. M. A. Williams, *Researching Local History: The Human Journey* (London, 1996).
11. R. Bell, *The Book of Ulster Surnames* (Belfast, 1988).
12. C. Pooley and J. Turnbull, *Migration and Mobility in Britain since the Eighteenth Century* (London, 1998).
13. P. Spufford, 'The Comparative Mobility and Immobility of Lollard Descendants in Early Modern England', in M. Spufford, ed., *The World of Rural Dissenters, 1520–1725* (Cambridge, 1995).
14. A. Everitt, 'Dynasty and Community since the Seventeenth Century', in *Landscape and Community in England* (London, 1985).
15. D. and R. Cromarty, *The Wealth of Shrewsbury in the Early Fourteenth Century* (Shrewsbury, 1993).
16. T. J. and P. Morgan, *Welsh Surnames* (Cardiff, 1985).
17. J. and S. Rowlands, *The Surnames of Wales* (Birmingham, 1996).
18. D. P. Dorward, 'Scottish *Mac* Names', in W. F. H. Nicolaisen, ed., *Proceedings of the XIXth International Congress of Onomastic Sciences*, iii (Aberdeen, 1998).

19. N. Evans, 'The Descent of Dissenters in the Chiltern Hundreds', in Spufford, ed., *The World of Rural Dissenters*.
20. C. V. Phythian-Adams, *Re-Thinking English Local History* (Leicester, 1987).

Notes to Chapter 6: The Nineteenth and Twentieth Centuries

1. P. Hanks, 'The Present-Day Distribution of Surnames in the British Isles', *Nomina*, 16 (1993).
2. C. D. Rogers, *The Surname Detective* (Manchester, 1995).
3. R. McKinley, *The Surnames of Lancashire* (London, 1981).
4. W. G. Hoskins, *Devon* (Newton Abbott, 1972).
5. G. Redmonds, *Yorkshire Surnames Series*, i, *Bradford and District* (Lepton, 1990).
6. Ibid.

Notes to Chapter 7: Family Names in the Seventeenth Century and Earlier

1. In *The Oxford Guide to Family History* (Oxford, 1993) I looked at a sample of 56,408 taxpayers in very different parts of the country by using the printed hearth tax returns for Bedfordshire (1671), Dorset (1664), Nottinghamshire (1674), Oxfordshire (1665) and Surrey (1664). I also made some use of the 16,380 names in the hearth tax returns of 1672 for Shropshire. These lists provided numerous examples of families that were living close to the place where their surname had originated three or four centuries earlier.
2. *The Suffolk Green Book*, ix, pt 1 (Woodbridge, 1905).
3. *Norfolk Genealogy*, 15 (1983).
4. Available on microfilm from the Society of Genealogists.
5. *The Suffolk Green Book*, ix, pt 2 (Woodbridge, 1906).
6. P. McClure, 'The Interpretation of Hypocoristic Forms of Middle English Baptismal Names', *Nomina*, 21 (1998).
7. Elizabeth Hughes and Philippa White, eds, *The Hampshire Hearth Tax Assessment, 1665, with the Southampton Assessments for 1662 and 1670*, Hampshire Record Series, 11 (1992). The Isle of Wight returns have been published separately as P. D. Russell, ed., *The Hearth Tax Returns for the Isle of Wight, 1664 to 1674*, Isle of Wight Record Series, 1 (1981). The 22,500 or so names recorded here may be compared with those in the returns for the neighbouring counties of Dorset and Surrey, which have been published as C. A. F. Meekings, ed., *Dorset Hearth Tax Assessments, 1662–1664*, Dorset Natural History and Archaeological Society (1951) and C. A. F. Meekings, ed., *Surrey Hearth Tax, 1664*, Surrey Record Society, 17 (1940). The returns for the other counties on Hampshire's borders, namely Sussex, Berkshire and Wiltshire, are not available in print.
8. Lydia M. Marshall, *The Bedfordshire Hearth Tax Return for 1671*, Bedfordshire Historical Record Society, 16 (reprinted 1990).
9. *Suffolk Green Books*, 18 (1925).

10. M. A. Faraday, ed., *Herefordshire Militia Assessments of 1663*, Camden Fourth Series, 10 (Royal Historical Society, 1972).

11. M. A. Faraday, ed., *The Westmorland Protestation Returns, 1641/2*, Cumberland and Westmorland Antiquarian and Archaeological Society Tract Series, 17 (1971).

12. W. F. Webster, ed., *Protestation Returns, 1641/2: Lincolnshire* (privately printed, Nottingham, 1984).

13. Jill Bourne and Amanda Goode, eds, *Rutland Hearth Tax, 1665*, Rutland Record Society, 1 (1991).

14. J. Horsfall Turner, *The Yorkshire Genealogist*, i (Bingley, 1888).

Bibliography

Anon., ed., *Suffolk in the 1327 Subsidy Return* (Woodbridge, 1906).

Awty, B., 'Aliens in the Ironworking Areas of the Weald: The Subsidy Rolls, 1524–1603', *Bulletin of the Wealden Iron Research Group*, second series, 4 (1984).

Bardsley, C. W., *English Surnames: Their Sources and Significations* (London, 1873).

Bardsley, C. W., *A Dictionary of English and Welsh Surnames* (London, 1901).

Beckett, J. V., *The Aristocracy in England, 1660–1914* (Oxford, 1986).

Bell, R., *The Book of Ulster Surnames* (Belfast, 1988).

Black, G. F., *Surnames of Scotland* (New York, 1946).

Bourne, Jill and Goode, Amanda, eds, *Rutland Hearth Tax, 1665*, Rutland Record Society (1991).

Brett, D., 'The Use of Telephone Directories in Surname Studies', *Local Historian*, 16 (1985).

Camden, W., *Remains concerning Britain* (London, 1605).

Collections for a History of Staffordshire, volumes for 1921, 1923, 1925, 1927 and 1936 (Stafford).

Cromarty, D. and R., *The Wealth of Shrewsbury in the Early Fourteenth Century*, Shropshire Archaeological and Historical Society (1993).

Everitt, A., *Change in the Provinces: The Seventeenth Century* (Leicester, 1969).

Everitt, A., *Landscape and Community in England* (London, 1985).

Faraday, M. A., ed., *Herefordshire Militia Assessments of 1663*, Camden fourth series, 10 (1972).

Faraday, M. A., ed., *The Westmorland Protestation Returns, 1641/2*, Cumberland and Westmorland Antiquarian and Archaeological Society, tract series, 17 (1971).

Fenwick, Carolyn C., *The Poll Taxes of 1377, 1379 and 1381, i, Bedfordshire–Leicestershire* (Oxford, 1998).

Gough, R., ed. D. Hey, *The History of Myddle* (Harmondsworth, 1981).

Green, Judith A., *The Aristocracy of Norman England* (Cambridge, 1997).

Guppy, H. B., *Homes of Family Names in Great Britain* (London, 1890).

Hanks, P. and Hodges, Flavia, *A Dictionary of Surnames* (Oxford, 1988).

P. Hanks, 'The Present-Day Distribution of Surnames in the British Isles', *Nomina*, 16 (1993).

Hey, D., 'The Distinctive Surnames of Staffordshire', Keele University, Earl Lecture, *Staffordshire Studies*, 10 (1998).

Hey, D., *The Local History of Family Names*, British Association for Local History, Phillimore Lecture (Chichester, 1997).

Hey, D., *The Oxford Guide to Family History* (Oxford, 1993).

Hoskins, W. G., *Devon* (David & Charles, Newton Abbot, 1972).

Hoskins, W. G., 'Leicestershire Yeoman Families and their Pedigrees', *Transactions of the Leicestershire Archaeological Society*, 23, part 1 (1946).

Hudson, W. H., *The Shepherd's Life* (London, 1910).

Hughes, Elizabeth and White, Philippa, eds, *The Hampshire Hearth Tax Assessment, 1665, with the Southampton Assessments for 1662 and 1670*, Hampshire Record Series, 40 (Winchester, 1992).

Jenkins, D., *The Agricultural Community in South-West Wales at the Turn of the Twentieth Century* (Cardiff, 1971).

Keats-Rohan, K. S. B., *Domesday People: A Prosopography of Persons Occurring in English Documents, 1066–1166*, i, *Domesday Book* (Woodbridge, 1999).

Lasker, G. W., *Surnames and Genetic Structure* (Cambridge, 1985).

Lasker, G. W., 'The Frequency of Surnames in England and Wales', *Human Biology*, 55 (1983).

Lasker, G. W. and Mascie-Taylor, C. G. N., eds, *Atlas of British Surnames* (Cambridge, 1990).

Laslett, P. and Harrison, J., 'Clayworth and Cogenhoe', in H. E. Bell and R. L. Ollard, eds, *Historical Essays Presented to David Ogg* (London, 1963).

Lawton, G. O., ed., *Northwich Hundred: Poll Tax 1660 and Hearth Tax 1664*, Record Society of Lancashire and Cheshire, 119 (1979).

Lewis, S., *Topographical Dictionaries of England and Wales* (5 vols, London, 1849).

Loyd, L. C., *The Origins of Some Anglo-Norman Families*, ed. C. T. Clay and D. C. Douglas, Harleian Society, 103 (1951).

MacLysaght, E., *Surnames of Ireland* (3rd edition, Dublin, 1978).

McClure, P., 'Patterns of Migration in the Late Middle Ages: The Evidence of English Place-Name Surnames', *Economic History Review*, second series, 32 (1979).

McClure, P., 'Nicknames and Petnames: Linguistic Forms and Social Contexts', *Nomina*, 5 (1981).

McClure, P., 'The Interpretation of Hypocoristic Forms of Middle English Baptismal Names', *Nomina*, 21 (1998).

McKinley, R., *A History of British Surnames* (London, 1990).

McKinley, R., *Norfolk and Suffolk Surnames in the Middle Ages* (Chichester, 1975).

McKinley, R., *The Surnames of Lancashire* (London, 1981).

McKinley, R., *The Surnames of Oxfordshire* (London, 1977).

McKinley, R., *The Surnames of Sussex* (London, 1988).

Marshall, Lydia M., *The Bedfordshire Hearth Tax Return for 1671*, Bedfordshire Historical Record Society, 16 (reprinted 1990).

Meekings, C. A. F., ed., *Dorset Hearth Tax Assessments, 1662–1664*, Dorset Natural History and Archaeology Society (1951).

Meekings, C. A. F., *Surrey Hearth Tax, 1664*, Surrey Record Society, 17 (1940).

Meekings, C. A. F., Porter, S. and Roy, I., eds, *The Hearth Tax Collector's Book for Worcester, 1678–1680*, Worcestershire Historical Society, new series, 2 (1983).

Morgan, T. J. and Morgan, P., *Welsh Surnames* (Cardiff, 1985).

Morlet, Marie-Thérèse, *Dictionnaire étymologique des noms de famille* (Paris, 1991).

Pettigree, A., *Foreign Protestant Communities in Seventeenth-Century London* (Oxford, 1986).

Phythian-Adams, C. V., *Re-Thinking English Local History* (Leicester, 1987).

Pooley, C. and Turnbull, Jean, *Migration and Mobility in Britain since the Eighteenth Century* (London, 1998).

Postles, D., *The Surnames of Devon* (London, 1995).

Postles, D., *The Surnames of Leicestershire and Rutland* (London, 1998).

Reaney, P. H. and Wilson, R. M., *A Dictionary of English Surnames* (Oxford, 1997).

Reaney, P. H., *The Origin of English Surnames* (London, 1967).

Redmonds, G., *Yorkshire: West Riding* (Chichester, 1973).

Redmonds, G., *Surnames and Genealogy: A New Approach* (Genealogical Society, Boston, Massachusetts, 1997).

Registrar-General, *Sixteenth Annual Report* (London, 1856).

Rodgers, C. D., *The Surname Detective* (Manchester, 1995).

Rowlands, J. and S., *The Surnames of Wales*, Federation of Family History Societies (Birmingham, 1996).

Russell, P. D. D., *The Hearth Tax Returns for the Isle of Wight, 1664 to 1674*, Isle of Wight Record Series, 1 (1981).

Sanders, I. J., *English Baronies* (Oxford, 1960).

Smith, J., *Men and Armour for Gloucestershire in 1608* (Stroud, 1980).

Smith-Bannister, S., *Names and Naming Patterns in England, 1538–1700* (Oxford, 1997).

Spufford, Margaret, ed., *The World of Rural Dissenters, 1520–1725* (Cambridge, 1995).

The Ordnance Survey Gazetteer of Great Britain (2nd edition, London, 1989).

Wagner, Sir Anthony, *Pedigree and Progress: Essays in the Genealogical Interpretation of History* (Phillimore, Chichester, 1975).

Walker, Margaret, ed., *Warwick County Records: Hearth Tax Returns, 1, Hemingford Hundred: Tamworth and Atherstone Divisions*, Warwickshire County Records (1957).

Webster, W. F., *Protestation Returns, 1641/2: Lincolnshire* (privately printed, Nottingham, 1984).

Williams, M. A., *Researching Local History: The Human Journey* (London, 1996).

Wrigley, E. A., Davies, R. S., Oeppen, J. E. and Schofield, R. S., *English Population History from Family Reconstitution, 1580–1837* (Cambridge, 1997).

Index of Family Names

General Index

Zane's gaze met hers.

A bolt of sexual awareness flooded through her and she looked away, shaken to the core of her being by the sharp stab of desire that whipped through her.

Zane's expression was unreadable and Carly was unnerved by the taut silence between them.

Then Zane swung out of his saddle and stepped between the rails. Carly felt dwarfed by his presence as he stood, tall and lean, towering over her, smelling like a man on a well-thought-out mission.

His gaze moved over her, settling on her face, her mouth. Her breath caught in her throat, and the world stopped turning as she waited. It seemed to take forever while he made up his mind, and then he pulled her into his arms and kissed her like she'd never been kissed before.

That's when Carly knew this cowboy had lassoed her heart....

Dear Reader,

Egad! This month we're up to our eyeballs in royal romances!

In *Fill-In Fiancée* (#1694) by DeAnna Talcott, a British lord pretends marriage to satisfy his parents. But will the hasty union last? Only time will tell, but matchmaker Emily Winters has her fingers crossed and so do we! This is the third title of Silhouette Romance's exclusive six-book series, MARRYING THE BOSS'S DAUGHTER.

In *The Princess & the Masked Man* (#1695), the second book of Valerie Parv's THE CARRAMER TRUST miniseries, a clever princess snares the affections of a mysterious single father. Look out for the final episode in this enchanting royal saga next month.

Be sure to make room on your reading list for at least one more royal. *To Wed a Sheik* (#1696) is the last title in Teresa Southwick's exciting DESERT BRIDES series. A jaded desert prince is no match for a beautiful American nurse in this tender and exotic romance.

But if all these royal romances have put you in the mood for a good old-fashioned American love story, look no further than *West Texas Bride* (#1697) by bestselling author Madeline Baker. It's the story of a city girl who turns a little bit country to win the heart of her brooding cowboy hero.

Enjoy!

Mavis C. Allen
Associate Senior Editor

Please address questions and book requests to:
Silhouette Reader Service
U.S.: 3010 Walden Ave., P.O. Box 1325, Buffalo, NY 14269
Canadian: P.O. Box 609, Fort Erie, Ont. L2A 5X3

West Texas Bride

MADELINE BAKER

SILHOUETTE *Romance*®

Published by Silhouette Books

America's Publisher of Contemporary Romance

To my agent, Ethan Ellenberg,
for making one of my dreams come true.

To Kim Abner,
for her help and encouragement.

To Glen H. Welker,
for allowing me to use the story
"The Origin of the Prairie Rose" in
Dude Ranch Bride.

SILHOUETTE BOOKS

ISBN 0-373-19697-0

WEST TEXAS BRIDE

Copyright © 2003 by Madeline Baker

Visit Silhouette at www.eHarlequin.com

Printed in U.S.A.

Books by Madeline Baker

Silhouette Romance

Dude Ranch Bride #1642
West Texas Bride #1697

MADELINE BAKER

has written over twenty historical novels, half a dozen short stories under her own name and over seventeen paranormal novels under the name Amanda Ashley as well as Madeline Baker. Born and raised in California, she admits balancing her love for historical romance and vampires isn't easy—but she wouldn't like to choose between them. The award-winning author has now found another outlet for her writing—Silhouette Romance! Readers can send an SASE to P.O. Box 1703, Whittier, CA 90609-1703 or visit her at her Web site http://madelinebaker.net.

This Is All I Ask

to walk by his side
to be warmed by his light
to bask in his love
all thorough the night

to savor his touch
to know his embrace
to see that he cares
by the smile on his face

to hear his sweet voice
filled with love and desire
to lie in his arms
by the glow of a fire

to hear his heart beating
in rhythm with mine
to know that I'm his
for now and all time

this is all I ask
this is all I need
just one man by my side
for all eternity

—Carly Kirkwood
August 25, 2003

Chapter One

"What on earth did I get myself into?"

The words echoed in Carly Kirkwood's mind as she hurried out of the smelly rest room at the Twisted River Fairgrounds and made her way across a dusty stretch of ground toward the grandstand. The air was filled with the smell of dust, hot dogs, cotton candy, popcorn, beer and a thoroughly disgusting odor that was the result of a lot of sweaty men, cows and horses all crammed together in a small area.

Everywhere she looked she saw men, women, children and even babies dressed in jeans, colorful cowboy shirts and boots. Well, what had she expected? Armani suits and Gucci loafers? She was in the middle of Texas, after all. *Come up to the ranch for your vacation,* her best friend, Brenda Clark had begged. *You'll love it. And you'll love Texas.*

Carly had been looking forward to having some time off work. Not that her job as a web designer was particularly difficult or stressful, but hey, she was entitled to a vacation and she intended to take it. Originally, she had planned to go to Yosemite or maybe Sequoia but had jumped at the

chance to spend some time with Brenda. Three weeks of
wide-open spaces had sounded like a wonderful break from
web layouts and html codes.

The Circle C Ranch *was* nice; Carly had to admit that.
The main part of the house had been built in the late 1800s.
The original structure had been added to and modernized
through the years, but the Clarks had managed to keep the
Old West feel to the place. Brenda's family raised and
trained quarter horses and also ran a few thousand head of
beef cattle.

But, as nice as the ranch was, she didn't love it. Her idea
of a vacation was a four-star hotel with room service, a
heated pool and a mall within walking distance.

Even though the ranch house was comfortable and the
surrounding countryside pretty, the weather was hot and
sticky and there were horses, cows and chickens everywhere and, even worse, the droppings, large and small, that
they left behind. A rooster that sounded as if it had a bad
case of bronchitis woke her every morning long before she
was ready to get up, and Brenda and her husband, Jerry,
kept the same hours as the sun. Carly wasn't used to going
to bed so early. She had tried to adjust her hours to
Brenda's the first two days she had been at the ranch, but
all she had done was lie awake looking up at the ceiling
and listening to the clock downstairs chime the hours.

They had driven into Twisted River and gone to lunch
and a movie last weekend. Twisted River was a small town.
It reminded Carly of a Western movie set, complete with
cowboys in hats and chaps. She had seen a couple of Native
American girls with long black braids walking down the
street. There had even been a horse tied up in front of one
of the stores.

After the movie, Brenda had taken her to the local ice-
cream parlor and they had spent an hour getting caught up
on what had happened since Brenda moved to Twisted
River three years ago. Brenda hadn't wanted to leave Los
Angeles; she had been as much a city girl as Carly, but

Brenda's father-in-law had died suddenly and her mother-in-law had needed help in running the ranch. Jerry had insisted on going back home. He had reminded Brenda that he had been in L.A. on business when they met and that he hadn't intended to stay three weeks, let alone three years. Brenda's leaving had been a blow to Carly. Brenda was her best friend; they had been practically inseparable since kindergarten. People had often assumed they were sisters, they spent so much time together. They had bought their first bras together, discovered boys together, consoled each other over broken hearts. Carly had been at Brenda's side, offering comfort, when Brenda's brother was killed in a car accident four years earlier. Brenda had been there to help Carly when she dumped her longtime boyfriend the year after that.

Carly let out a sigh of exasperation as she barely missed stepping in a large pile of manure that was still steaming. Honestly, she thought, these people needed a law about picking up after horses like the one they had in L.A. about picking up after your dog!

She had almost reached the grandstand when she barreled into what felt like a stone wall. Looking up, she found herself staring into a pair of deep black eyes set beneath a pair of equally black brows that were drawn together in a frown.

"Whoa, there, gal, you'd best watch where you're going." His voice was as deep and dark as his eyes and evoked a shiver from somewhere deep inside her.

"I was watching," she muttered.

If she hadn't been watching where she put her feet, she never would have run into him. She took a step back, intimidated by his height and the breadth of his shoulders. His skin was the color of old copper; there were fine lines around his eyes, a faint white scar just above his left eyebrow. He wore a pair of black jeans, a pale blue shirt and a black cowboy hat with a snakeskin band. A red kerchief was loosely knotted at his throat.

"Yeah?" he asked skeptically. "Just what were you watching?"

"The ground."

She felt a warm flush spread through her as his gaze met hers. If she had been in the market for a new man, this one would have been at the top of her list. She cut the thought off before it was fully formed. After Richard, the last thing she wanted right now was another man in her life.

"You lose something?" he asked.

"No. I was trying not to step in any more, ah…horse manure."

His lips twitched in a way that made her think he was trying not to laugh.

"Well, good luck." He touched a finger to the brim of his hat, stepped around her and walked briskly away.

Carly glanced over her shoulder. His jeans fit like a second skin, outlining long, long legs and a taut behind. A pair of well-worn leather gloves were jammed into one of his back pockets. She didn't mean to stare, but the view was just too good to miss. He moved with a lithe grace that was beautiful to see. Unable to drag her gaze away, she watched him until he was out of sight.

With a shake of her head, she rounded the corner of the grandstand and made her way up to where Brenda was sitting.

"Hey, girl, what took you so long?" Brenda asked, wiping a bit of mustard from the corner of her mouth. "Did you get lost?"

"No, I ran into a brick wall."

"What?"

"Never mind."

Brenda frowned at her a minute, then shrugged. "Here, I bought you a corn dog and a Coke."

"Thanks."

"You got back just in time. Bronc riding is the next event. Several of our hands are entered."

Carly nodded, then took a bite of her corn dog. That

morning, they had watched barrel racing and team roping. Barrel racing had looked like fun. Brenda had explained that the barrels had to be at least twenty yards apart and set in a triangle. The winner was the rider who got around the barrels in the fastest time without knocking one down.

Early in the afternoon, they had watched steer wrestling and calf roping. Steer wrestling was a contest of speed, timing and strength as a cowboy launched himself from the back of his horse, caught the steer and wrestled it to the ground.

Calf roping had been fun to watch. Once the cowboy caught the calf, he stepped off his horse, went hand over hand down the rope and tossed the calf on its side. The cowboy then tied three of the calf's legs with a rope—a "piggin' string," Brenda had called it—by throwing a loop over one of the calf's front legs and then pushing the hind legs up and tying all three together with "two wraps and a hooey." Again, the cowboy with the fastest time won.

Taking another bite of her corn dog, Carly glanced around. Just about everyone wore blue jeans or denim skirts and cowboy shirts. And of course everyone wore a cowboy hat. She'd had no idea that they came in such a wide variety of sizes, shapes and colors.

Cowboys also came in a wide variety of shapes and sizes and colors. They hung on the fences or stood around in small groups. She laughed at the antics of a couple of rodeo clowns who were fooling around down in the arena while they waited for the next event to begin. Brenda had explained that the clowns were indispensable in bull riding. Barrel clowns hid out in a barrel until they were needed. It was their job to distract dangerous bulls from injuring a thrown rider. They also led bulls away from the cowboys and out of the arena. A really good clown could coax a better performance out of a bucking bull.

The last event they had watched had been bull riding. After watching the bull riders, Carly was certain the cowboys had to be crazy. No one in their right mind would climb on the back of a bull that might weigh as much as two thousand pounds.

"It isn't really a question of *if* a bull rider will get hurt," Brenda told her. "It's more a question of when and how bad. Nowadays, a lot of bull riders wear a Kevlar vest to protect their chests and internal organs. Of course, the most common injury is concussion, either from a cowboy hitting his head against the bull's or against the horns, or from hitting his head when he's thrown."

Compared to bull riding, bronc riding didn't seem quite so dangerous, but in Carly's opinion, it was still foolhardy. Was it really worth a few hundred dollars or a ribbon to try and sit on some wild horse for eight seconds? She knew there were professional rodeo riders who made a lot more than a couple of hundred dollars. Of course, she thought they were all a brick short of a load, too, but at least the money made the risk seem a little more worthwhile.

"Bronc riding's next," Brenda said. "I hope none of our men draw Windy. He's a bad one. Likes to swap ends and turn back right out of the chute. Tosses a lot of riders that way."

Carly nodded even though she didn't have the slightest idea what Brenda was talking about. Swap ends? Turn back?

She shook her head as the announcer's voice crackled to life over the PA system, introducing the first rider in the next event.

Several people in the stands cheered as a cowboy mounted on a stocky brown horse burst out of the gate. The horse bucked several times and the cowboy went flying. A moment later, the whistle blew.

The next rider was disqualified for grabbing hold of the saddle with his free hand.

"It's called pulling leather," Brenda remarked. "A definite no-no."

In spite of herself, Carly was soon caught up in the excitement of it all. She clapped and cheered loudly for the riders. After all, any man who was crazy enough to compete deserved his share of applause.

As soon as the next rider mounted, the horse threw itself over backward before he even left the chute. Carly gasped as she imagined the cowboy being crushed beneath the saddle, but somehow the rider managed to roll free and scramble under the fence with no more than a few scrapes and scratches. The audience applauded wildly as the announcer declared that the unlucky cowboy would be allowed a re-ride.

Carly sat back, one hand pressed over her heart.

"Next up, our own Zane Roan Eagle," the commentator announced, a touch of pride in his voice. "Roan Eagle has drawn Hazard Ranch's devil horse, Blue Dynamite. No one's managed to grab eight seconds on this salty stallion in the past three years."

"Zane works for us," Brenda said. "He's one of the best horse trainers in the country. We were darn lucky to get him. He's one of the best bronc riders, too. He used to ride the circuit, but now he just competes at our local events."

"The circuit?" Carly asked, only half listening as she watched the cowboy settle himself on the back of the biggest, meanest-looking horse she had ever seen.

"The rodeo circuit."

"Oh, of course."

"Those cowboys are always on the road, driving from Reno to Greeley to Cody, up to Canada for the Stampede. It's a rough life." Brenda leaned forward as Zane Roan Eagle approached the chute. "Blue Dynamite's a hard ride but he's a good honest horse. I'll bet Zane wins on him today."

Carly nodded. Blue Dynamite was aptly named, she thought. Sitting on top of that horse would be like sitting on a pile of explosives.

Brenda glanced at Carly. "Remember, he has to last eight seconds to qualify. The judges score both the horse and the rider from zero to twenty-five points. Watch now. When the bronc leaves the chute, Zane's spurs have to be over Blue Dynamite's shoulders before the horse's front feet hit the ground. It's called marking out. He has to spur the horse from the shoulders to the rigging and back. Riders aren't allowed to touch the horse or themselves with their free hand during the course of the ride.''

Carly nodded again, her eyes narrowing as she watched the cowboy. Was it possible? Leaning forward, she studied him intently as he tugged his hat down on his head, then raised his free hand. It was him, she thought, the handsome brick wall with the tight buns she had bumped into earlier. She started to say as much to Brenda, then quickly changed her mind. Brenda wasn't going to be happy until there was a new man in Carly's life and Carly wasn't ready for that. But that didn't mean she couldn't appreciate a good-looking cowboy when she saw one.

Grabbing her camera, she snapped several quick pictures before the gate opened and the horse shot into the arena.

Head down, back humped, Blue Dynamite bucked for all he was worth. Zane Roan Eagle clung to the saddle like dry paint to a wall.

Time seemed to slow as Carly watched the ride. Zane Roan Eagle seemed to anticipate Blue Dynamite's every move. There was a kind of fierce beauty in the way man and horse moved. It was almost like a ballet, she thought, a furiously fast and dangerous ballet. The rider's hat flew off and his long black hair whipped around his face as the horse dropped his head and bucked from one end of the arena to the other.

She let out a sigh of relief when the shrill blast of the whistle signaled time was up. A pickup man rode up alongside Zane. Zane caught the man's outstretched arm and vaulted from the back of Blue Dynamite onto the pickup man's horse, then slid over the horse's rump, landing on his feet. Crossing the arena to the sound of wild applause, he picked up his hat and waved it at the crowd. Carly applauded, too. And then Zane turned. Shading his face with his hat, he looked up into the stands, right in her direction. She felt a funny little tickle in her stomach. Even though it was impossible to tell at this distance, she would have sworn he was looking right at her. She was tempted to stand up and wave but she didn't, of course. It was ridiculous to think he was looking for her. They'd hardly spoken ten words to each other.

Nevertheless, the thought made her smile the rest of the day.

Chapter Two

To Carly's chagrin, the tall cowboy's image followed her home from the rodeo and crept into her dreams that night. Even worse, he was the first thing she thought of when she woke on Sunday morning. She had never been one to go gaga over a man's good looks, but Zane Roan Eagle was more than just good-looking. He was tall, dark and gorgeous.

Brenda was in the kitchen when Carly went downstairs.

"Hi, sleepyhead," Brenda said, slathering mayonnaise on a piece of homemade wheat bread. "You're just in time for lunch."

Carly made a face at her friend as she reached for the coffeepot and poured herself a cup. "It's Sunday," she said, taking a seat at the table. "You know, day of rest."

"Not around here. We've already done the morning chores and been to church."

"Church?" Carly felt a twinge of guilt. She hadn't been to church in years.

"Jerry's mother never misses a Sunday," Brenda said. "I sort of got in the habit of going with her."

"What's it like, living with your mother-in-law?"

"Not bad. Edna's pretty easy to get along with, and the house is big enough that we don't get in each other's way. Plus, she goes to visit her sister in Boston a couple times a year. That's where she is now."

Carly nodded and sipped her coffee. Glancing out the window, she wondered what the hands did on Sundays, and how one particular cowboy spent the day. Brenda had told her that he worked on the ranch.

With a shake of her head, Carly thrust the man from her mind. She would probably never see him again and even if she did, it wouldn't matter. She was certain they had little, if anything, in common.

"Hey, girlfriend, you remember I promised you riding lessons?" Brenda asked. "Well, you start tomorrow morning."

"Come on, Bren, don't you think I'm a little too old for riding lessons?"

"Of course not. I want to take you out and show you the ranch, but not until you've had a few lessons."

"Why can't we just go in your truck?"

"Horses can get to a lot of places where the truck can't. We can pack a lunch and ride out to the lake. You'll love it."

Carly grimaced. "I doubt it."

Brenda fixed her with "that" look and Carly raised her hands in a gesture of surrender. "All right, all right, I'll learn to ride. But if I break a leg, I'll never speak to you again."

Zane sighed with resignation as he rolled out of bed Monday morning. Word had come down from the main house that the Clarks' houseguest wanted to learn to ride, along with a request that Zane do the teaching.

After breakfast, he went into the barn and looked over the stock, finally deciding that Sam was probably the best horse for a beginner. Leading the horse out of the barn, he tied it to the hitching post and, after giving the gelding a good brushing, he pulled a hoof pick from his jeans and began cleaning the horse's hooves.

He was just about finished when he heard someone come up behind him, and then a female voice that was faintly familiar said, "Hello."

Zane glanced over his shoulder, felt a jolt of recognition when he saw the woman standing there. "Hello yourself," he said with a grin.

Carly felt her heart skip a beat when she found herself staring at the man she had literally run into at the rodeo. Earlier, she had done everything she could to put off this lesson. She had helped Brenda make breakfast, complimented her on her homemade strawberry jam, lingered over a second cup of coffee. Stalling for time, she had offered to clear the table, but Brenda had waved off her help and finally there was nothing to do but show up for her first lesson. She was glad now that she hadn't changed her mind.

A slow smile spread over his face and turned her insides to mush.

Zane put the horse's foot down. "Are you Miss Kirkwood?"

"Yes, but please, call me Carly."

"Zane Roan Eagle."

He offered her his hand. It was large and callused and completely dwarfed her own.

"Zane. That's a name you don't hear very often."

"My dad was a big fan of Zane Grey."

"Who?"

"Zane Grey. He was a popular writer back in the early 1900s. Wrote a lot of westerns. *Riders of the Purple Sage* is the only one I recall."

"Ah. Cowboys and Indians."

"Ms. Clark said you wanted to learn to ride." His gaze moved over her. "Are you ready?"

"Not really, but I promised Brenda I'd give riding a try."

He made a broad gesture, covering the area around the barn. "Be careful where you walk," he cautioned with a grin. "You never know what you'll run into."

She felt her cheeks grow warm as she recalled how she had run into him.

"Did you enjoy the rodeo?" he asked.

"Yes, it was very exciting. You were wonder... I mean, congratulations. It was a great ride."

"Thanks."

A long moment passed between them. Carly felt a little thrill of excitement as his gaze held hers, and even though he didn't say anything, she felt connected to him somehow.

"So," he said at last, "have you ever been on a horse before?"

She shook her head.

He blew out an exaggerated sigh. "Okay. We'll start at the beginning. This is a horse."

"Very funny."

He grinned at her. "Actually, it's a gelding. His name is Sam, he's a quarter Morgan cross, and he's thirteen years old."

Carly eyed Sam warily. "He's awfully big, isn't he?"

"He's about fifteen hands, give or take a little."

"What does that come to, in inches?"

"Well, a hand is roughly four inches. You measure from the ground to the point of the horse's shoulder."

Carly did some quick arithmetic in her head. "So, about five feet?"

"Right. Come on over and get acquainted."

Carly walked up to Sam's head. The horse looked at her through big brown eyes, its foxlike ears twitching back and forth.

"All right," Zane said. "Take hold of the saddle horn, put your left foot in the stirrup, push off with your right foot and then throw your right leg over the saddle."

Carly eyed the stirrup, wondering if she could even lift her foot that high. She knew physical fitness and exercise were all the rage but, to tell the truth, her idea of exercise was playing Free Cell on the computer.

Taking a deep breath, she grabbed for the saddle horn, lifted her foot and managed to get it into the stirrup, but she couldn't seem to pull herself up.

After a moment, Zane Roan Eagle put his hands around her waist and lifted her onto the horse's back.

When she was settled in the saddle, he adjusted the stirrups, then snapped a lead rope onto the hackamore. That done, he handed her the reins, which were made from a single strip of leather unlike the double ones she always saw in the movies.

"I thought reins came in two pieces," she said.

"Some do, but I prefer these for beginners. If you drop them, you can easily pick them up again, and you don't have to worry about the horse stepping on one, the way you do with split reins."

"Oh."

"Sam's the most easygoing horse on the place. Mrs. Clark lets her nieces and nephews ride him, so you should be perfectly safe. Just relax and let him do all the work. Ready?"

She nodded grimly.

"Okay, here we go."

Clucking to the horse, Zane moved out at a brisk walk and Sam followed at his heels like an overgrown puppy. Carly grabbed hold of the saddle horn with one hand.

"Loosen up," Zane said, looking back at her. "Try to relax. No, not that much. Keep your back straight and your elbows close to your sides. That's better. Keep your heels down. And hold the reins with both hands," he said, leading the gelding into a large corral.

Reluctantly she let go of her death grip on the saddle horn.

He led Sam around the corral three times, then turned the horse and went the other way.

Carly tried to relax but the ground seemed a long way down and her position in the saddle felt precarious at best.

Zane led her around the corral several more times, then stopped. "Okay, time to try it on your own," he said, unsnapping the lead line. "You're using a hackamore, which means there's no bit in the horse's mouth. Sam's a trailwise old guy and used to beginners, so don't worry. If you want him to go left, you can either pull back on the left rein, or you can lay the right rein against his neck. To go right, pull on the right rein, or lay the left rein against his neck. To stop, pull back on both reins, gently. Got it?"

Carly swallowed hard, then nodded. Pull left to go left, pull right to go right, back to stop.

"All right. To make him move out, you can either cluck to him and lift the reins, or you can press your heels against his sides."

Carly took a deep, calming breath and clucked to the horse. He moved forward at a walk, pretty as you please, making her feel as though she had been riding for years instead of about twenty minutes.

"That's good," Zane called. "Now turn him around."

She pulled on the left rein and Sam obediently turned to the left and they walked around the corral in the opposite direction.

"Keep your heels down," Zane admonished, "and ease up on the reins a little."

Carly did as she was told and Sam continued to walk around the corral at a nice slow, steady walk. It certainly wasn't what she would call fun, she mused, but it wasn't as bad as she'd expected, either.

Until he decided she was ready to go a little faster.

"Try to move *with* the horse," Zane said as she bounced up and down.

She definitely didn't like trotting. Try as she might, she couldn't seem to get the hang of it. She bounced around like a kernel of popcorn in a hot-air popper. She was relieved when Zane took pity on her and called it a day.

"Well," she said as she reined the gelding to a stop. "Thanks for trying. I guess I'm just not cowgirl material."

"I've seen worse."

He grinned up at her as he lifted her from the saddle. Shivers of awareness sizzled through her at the feel of his hands at her waist. Her legs felt weak, though she wasn't sure if it was from his touch or having spent the past hour on the back of a horse.

"It's only your first lesson," he said. "You'll do better tomorrow."

Tomorrow! "But..."

"You're not giving up, are you?" he asked.

She looked up at him, felt herself drowning in the midnight depths of his eyes. At that moment, she would have agreed to ride Blue Dynamite naked and bareback. "Of course not."

He smiled at her. "Good. See you tomorrow, then. Same time."

She nodded. Dear Lord, the man's smile could light up a city.

Brenda was canning tomatoes when Carly got back to the house. "Hey, girl, how'd it go?"

"All right, I guess."

"How'd you get along with Zane?"

"Fine. I'm sure he's a good teacher when he has something to work with." Carly's eyes narrowed. "You're not matchmaking, are you, Bren?"

"Me? Of course not."

"Uh-huh."

"For goodness' sakes, Carly, it's been months since you've been out with a man."

"Brenda!"

"Oh, for heaven's sake, calm down. What would it hurt if you went out with him while you're here? He's a nice guy."

"I'm sure he is, but the last thing I want is a summer

fling with some cowboy I'll never see again after I get back
to L.A.''

Brenda held up her hands. "Okay, okay, I'm sorry."

"I'm going up to change my clothes. I smell like a
horse."

Carly was at the barn the following morning a few
minutes sooner than the appointed hour, even though she
wasn't sure she was up to riding at all. Muscles she had
never known she possessed had made themselves known to
her last night and hurt only a little less this afternoon.

But something drew her toward the barn, and it wasn't
Sam.

She found Zane brushing the gelding. She couldn't help
but notice the way Zane's muscles flexed beneath his shirt
or the way the sun glinted on his long black hair. Or the
way his jeans clung to his backside. There was something
terribly sexy about those gloves dangling from his back
pocket.

She felt her face flush when he glanced over his shoulder
and found her staring at him. That sizzle of awareness that
had passed between them yesterday sparked to life as his
gaze met hers.

"You're early," he remarked.

She nodded.

"Well, come on over here. You might as well learn to
do this part, too."

He spent the next twenty minutes or so showing her how
to groom a horse and how to clean its feet with a hoof pick,
which, to her chagrin, involved using a little hook-shaped
pick to dig dirt and manure out of the horse's hooves.

He nodded his approval as she finished cleaning Sam's
feet. "Ready to learn how to saddle him?"

"Why not?" she asked.

He cocked one eyebrow at the aggrieved tone in her
voice. "It's not that bad."

"I thought learning how to ride just meant learning how to ride."

He shrugged. "If that's all you want to learn, that's all I'll teach you."

She didn't want him to think she was a wimp or, worse yet, some snooty city girl afraid to get her hands dirty, so she smiled sweetly and said, "No, I want to learn everything."

It wasn't true, but it won her another heart-stopping smile.

Saddling the horse wasn't as difficult as she thought it would be, though the saddle seemed to weigh a ton and even after she had cinched it up as tight as she could, he told her it wasn't tight enough.

"Nothing more embarrassing than taking a header because your saddle wasn't cinched tight enough," he remarked.

She nodded, took a deep breath and pulled on the leather strap for all she was worth.

"That'll do it," Zane said, handing her the reins. "Let's take him into the corral and see how much you remember from yesterday."

Carly followed Zane toward the workout corral. She wasn't sure she liked having a thousand pounds of horse trailing at her heels.

"Walk beside his shoulder," Zane said, glancing back to see how she was doing. "He won't be able to kick you from there, and you won't have to worry about him stepping on your feet."

"Kick me!" she exclaimed. "I thought you said he was gentle."

"He is. It's just a safety precaution. Horses can't kick sideways."

Carly moved back a little until she was walking beside Sam's shoulder.

When they reached the corral, Zane unlatched the gate and held it open while she led Sam inside. She dropped the reins over the gelding's head, grabbed hold of the saddle horn and put her foot in the stirrup.

And felt Zane's hands at her waist. Big hands. Strong hands that lifted her easily into the saddle. Hands that lingered at her waist a few moments longer than necessary.

Carly murmured her thanks, acutely aware of his nearness.

"Ready?" His voice was low and husky.

She nodded, not trusting herself to speak.

He handed her the reins, his long brown fingers brushing hers, sending little frissons of excitement running through her.

For the next forty-five minutes, she walked and trotted, walked and trotted. Gradually she got the hang of the trot, though, given her druthers, she was sure she would never ask Sam to trot.

"Ready to try a canter?" Zane asked.

"Am I ready for that?" she asked dubiously.

"I think so. And it's a lot more comfortable than a trot." Well, that sounded promising.

"Start at a walk, then go into a trot, and then a canter."

"How do I make him canter?"

"Reach back with your right heel and give him a nudge. You'll need to hold on with your legs, the way you do at the trot. Ready?"

Carly nodded, her heart pounding with anticipation and anxiety as Sam moved out. Conscious of Zane's gaze watching her every move, she nudged Sam with her heel and he broke into a canter. She reached instinctively for the saddle horn, but after a moment, she let it go, caught up in the joy of the ride, the wind blowing in her hair, the sense of being in control of a horse that outweighed her by almost nine hundred pounds.

Feeling daring, she pulled on the left rein. The next thing she knew, she was spitting dirt out of her mouth.

"You all right?" Zane knelt beside her, his brow furrowed with worry.

"What happened?"

"Sam turned and you didn't. He used to be a cutting horse, which means he can turn on a dime and give you a nickel change."

She blinked up at him. It had happened so fast she didn't remember falling at all.

"You sure you're all right?"

She nodded, suddenly embarrassed. He rode bucking broncs and she couldn't even stay on a horse!

"Come on." Rising, he offered her his hand. His long brown fingers folded over hers and he pulled her to her feet. "Do you want to call it a day?"

"No."

His smile of approval went straight to her heart.

Picking up the reins, he led Sam over to her, then lifted her into the saddle.

"Ready?" he asked.

At her nod, he handed her the reins. She watched him walk toward the corral fence and hop up on the top rail.

Taking a deep breath, she clucked to Sam and the gelding moved out. Walk. Trot. Canter. This time, when she pulled on the left rein, she was ready for the sudden change in direction. Exhilaration rose up within her. She'd done it!

Zane applauded when she drew Sam to a halt a few minutes later. Hopping down from the rail, he walked toward her. "You're a quick study."

"You're a good teacher."

"Thanks. I'll see you tomorrow."

"I guess so."

She smiled at him, her brown eyes sparkling. Dismounting, she handed him the reins, then left the corral.

Zane stared after her, admiring the way her jeans outlined her long legs, the sway of her hips, the way the sunlight turned her blond hair to gold. She was trouble with a capital *T,* he thought. Big trouble, because he wasn't looking for a woman, especially a forever kind of woman, and that's what Miss Carly Kirkwood was. And even though she looked mighty fine walking away, he wasn't falling into that trap again. No sir. He'd gone head over heels for a long-legged woman once before and look how that had turned out. Once burned, twice shy, he reminded himself, and Elaine had burned him for life.

Tomorrow, he would get Poteet to take over Carly's riding lessons for him and that would be the end of it. But that didn't stop him from watching the tantalizing sway of her hips until she was out of sight.

Chapter Three

"So," Carly said, picking up another potato to peel. "Tell me about Zane."

"What do you want to know?"

"He's Native American, isn't he?"

"Duh! With a name like Roan Eagle, what else could he be?"

"I've never met a Native American before."

"Well, there are lots of them around here." Brenda dropped a potato in the pan and started peeling another one. "How are the riding lessons coming along?"

"All right, I guess. He's a good teacher."

Brenda wiggled her eyebrows suggestively. "Uh-huh."

"All right, he's handsome, too," Carly said, though handsome seemed a woefully inadequate description. With his dark eyes and warm sexy smile, he was…

"Gorgeous," Brenda said. "He's simply gorgeous. All that long black hair and—"

"Brenda, shame on you. You're a married woman."

"Married, not blind." Brenda placed one hand over her heart. "Oh, my, if I was single…"

"Is he…?"

"Married? No."

"How'd you know that was what I was going to ask?"

Brenda rolled her eyes. "How long have we been friends?"

"All right, so you know me better than my own mother. Why isn't he married?"

"That's something you'll have to ask him yourself."

"It doesn't matter. I'll be going home in a couple weeks, anyway."

"I wish you'd think about moving here," Brenda said. "I've sure missed you."

"I know, I miss you, too, but what on earth would I do here?"

"Hey, we have computers in Texas, you know? You can do what you do anywhere they have phone lines and a modem."

"Forget it, Bren. I'm a city girl through and through."

"So was I, once."

Carly shook her head. Looking at Brenda now, clad in a pair of faded blue jeans and a plaid cowboy shirt, her long brown hair pulled back in a ponytail, it was hard to remember that Brenda had once been something of a fashion plate, or that she had gone to the beauty shop every week and the spa every month, and that she had changed the color of her hair almost as often as she changed her nail polish.

"Do you really like living out here?" Carly asked. "Don't you miss the excitement of the city? Going to the theater? Shopping at the Galleria?"

"Are you kidding? Dallas has more shopping centers and restaurants per capita than New York City. It has a ton of malls and, oh, you name it, Dallas has it. Bigger and better than anything in L.A." Brenda cocked her hip against the counter, a half-peeled potato in one hand, the peeler in the other. "Sometimes I wish we lived a little closer to the city, but life on the ranch seems more real, you know?"

Carly shook her head. "What do you mean?"

"Oh, I don't know how to explain it. The ranch provides beef and jobs for lots of people. I feel like what we're doing here is important, like we're contributing something. It's a great place to raise kids. When J.J. gets older, he'll have lots of space to run and play, and he'll be able to have all the animals he wants, and…"

Carly held up her hand. Brenda had always been an animal lover. As far back as Carly could remember, Brenda had asked for a horse for her birthday and for Christmas. Now she could have as many as she wanted.

"Slow down, girl. I know you love it here, and I'm glad you're happy. But I just can't see myself buried in the country."

"Okay, okay." Brenda held up her hands in a gesture of defeat and their conversation turned to whether to have corn or peas for dinner and whether they should broil or barbecue the steaks. But lying in bed later that night, Carly tried to imagine herself living on a ranch. Try as she might, she just couldn't picture herself as a ranch wife. But she had no trouble at all picturing Zane Roan Eagle as her husband.

Carly Roan Eagle. Turning on her side, she grinned into the darkness. "I don't think so," she murmured. But she dreamed of him again that night.

Carly's steps slowed as she neared the barn the following morning. Sam was saddled and waiting. A tall, lanky, bow-legged cowboy wearing jeans and an orange-and-brown-plaid shirt stood at the gelding's head. Carly looked around, but there was no sign of Zane.

"Miss Kirkwood? I'm Jim Poteet. I'll be taking over for Roan Eagle."

"Oh." Disappointment sat on her chest like a lead weight, but she pasted a smile on her face.

Poteet didn't offer to help her mount. She managed to

get her foot in the stirrup and then pulled herself into the saddle.

Poteet opened the corral gate for her and she rode around the corral—walk, trot, canter—but for some reason, she found no joy in it. She told herself the fact that Zane Roan Eagle wasn't there had nothing to do with her lack of interest, but she knew it was a lie.

She was about to call it quits for the day when she heard a familiar voice.

"Woman, how many times do I have to tell you to keep your heels down?"

At the sound of his voice, she sat up straighter, squared her shoulders and put her heels down. Riding was fun again.

"That's better."

She basked in his praise, in the knowledge that he was there.

"Come on in." Zane glanced at Poteet. "I'll take it from here," he said, dismissing the other man.

Carly slowed Sam to a walk and rode toward Zane. He wore faded Levi's, a dark green shirt with the sleeves rolled up past his elbows and a pair of well-worn boots. His hat was shoved back on his head. Just looking at him made her stomach flutter with excitement.

"So," he said, "you tired of riding around in circles yet?"

"Well, maybe a little."

"How would you feel about going out on a short trail ride?"

"Do you think I'm ready?"

"I wouldn't suggest it if I didn't."

"When?"

"How about now?"

"I'm game if you are."

"All right. Give me a few minutes to saddle up and we'll go."

Zane shook his head as he walked toward the barn. He

had meant to busy himself elsewhere today but for some reason he didn't care to examine too closely, he had hung around the barn. He had watched Poteet with Carly, surprised by the sharp sting of jealousy he'd felt when he saw the two of them together.

The fact that it made him jealous to see her with another man annoyed the hell out of him. Hadn't he learned anything the last time? He hardly knew Carly Kirkwood and he had intended to keep it that way and yet, in spite of all his good intentions, here he was, as eager as some randy teenager at the thought of being with her again. And it wasn't just that she was prettier than she had a right to be, or that he wanted to do things to her and with her that he had no business thinking about. There was no denying the attraction between them, he thought, but, more than that, he genuinely liked being with her.

Leading a flashy bay mare out of one of the stalls, Zane gave the mare a quick brushing, checked her feet and had her saddled and ready to go in less than ten minutes.

Carly was circling in the corral when he rode up. The first time he'd seen her, he had been certain trying to teach her to ride would be a waste of time, but she had surprised him. She was a quick study and seemed to have a natural seat.

"Ready?" he called.

"Ready." She headed toward the gate and he opened it for her. Side by side, they rode away from the house, following a wide path that ran parallel to a shallow stream.

As they left the house behind, trees and shrubs grew thicker, completely blocking the view of the stream in some places. Birds called to one another. The hum of insects filled the air.

"It's really pretty here," Carly remarked.

"It is that."

"Have you lived in Texas all your life?"

"No. I was born on the rez in South Dakota."

"Oh."

"What about you?"

"I was born in Los Angeles. We moved around a lot when I was a little girl but when my folks finally decided to settle down, we came back to L.A. They stayed until my dad was transferred to Arizona last year. Have you ever been to L.A.?"

"Yeah, once."

"You didn't like it?"

He shook his head. "Too noisy. Too crowded. Too many cars. Not enough horses."

"I don't know about that. I seem to recall reading somewhere that there are just about more horses in California than anywhere else. Anyway, I love it there."

He grunted softly. "How long will you be staying with the Clarks?"

"Another week and a half, I guess. I haven't decided."

"I take it you're on vacation?"

"Yes."

"What is it you do?"

"I'm a web designer."

"I figured you worked inside."

"Oh? Why?"

"Just a hunch."

They rode in silence for a few moments. Carly couldn't remember a time when she had felt so peaceful or so content. The countryside was lush and green and beautiful. She glanced over her shoulder as they rode through a stand of tall timber. The ranch house was out of sight now and there was nothing to be seen for miles around except trees and grass and a bold blue sky.

"Have you always wanted to be a cowboy?" she asked after a while.

"Pretty much."

"How long have you worked for the Clarks?"

"About four years, I reckon."

"What is it, exactly, that you do?"

"A little bit of everything. Mostly, I train their horses.

Sometimes I work horses from other ranches.'' He smiled at her. "I guess I can add giving riding lessons to my résumé.''

"What did you do before you started working here?"

"I did a hitch in the navy. My old man was hoping I'd make a career of it like he did, but that wasn't for me. I followed the rodeo circuit until I got stomped by a bull."

"How awful!"

He shrugged. "After I got out of the hospital, I hired on here." He reined his horse to a halt. "Do you want to rest a while?"

Carly nodded. The stream gurgled nearby, and several cottonwood trees provided shade. She started to dismount but Zane was there beside her horse, lifting her from the saddle as if she weighed no more than a child.

He lowered her slowly to her feet. Her breasts brushed against his shirtfront. His hands lingered at her waist and she stared up at him, hardly daring to breathe.

Her gaze lingered on his lips. They were full and finely shaped, sensual. What would it be like, she wondered, to feel his mouth on hers?

As if reading her mind, he lowered his head and kissed her.

His lips were warm and firm but not demanding. He held her close, but not so close she felt trapped in his embrace.

She tilted her head a little, her arms sliding up around his neck, surprised by the rush of desire that streaked through her as his tongue slid over her lower lip. She leaned into him, aroused by the feel of his hard muscular length pressing against her, by the sudden urge to draw him down on the ground and let him ease the growing ache inside her.

Stunned by her quick response to his kiss, she drew back, embarrassed. She had never responded to a man's kiss like that before, never experienced such a wild desire to forget who and where she was and succumb to the lustful urgings of her own body.

She took a deep breath and blew it out in a long sigh.

He was far too handsome, his kisses far too potent. The man should have a warning label tattooed on his forehead, *Caution—may be dangerous to your libido.*

"What are you grinning at?" he asked.

Heat fired her cheeks. "Oh, nothing."

He scowled at her. "Uh-huh."

Had she somehow hurt his feelings by grinning after he kissed her?

Taking up the reins, he led both horses down to the stream, stood between them while they drank.

Carly took the time to admire the view. His long black hair glistened in the sunlight. His shoulders were broad, his back tapered to a trim waist. Blue denim hugged his backside and his long, well-muscled legs. Just looking at him did funny things in the pit of her stomach. She had never really been attracted to the outdoor type, to men with rippling muscles and long hair. She preferred slender men with short hair who wore Armani suits and carried briefcases, men who worked in offices and who were as computer oriented as she was.

Zane turned around and she was taken again by his rugged good looks, his rough masculinity.

"Ready to go back?" he asked.

"Do we have to?"

"It's up to you. I just thought you might be getting a little saddle sore."

She was, but she refused to admit it.

He offered her a leg up, then handed her the reins and swung agilely onto the back of his own horse. He rode as if he had been born in the saddle, his body moving in perfect rhythm with that of his mount. Man and horse made a beautiful picture. She was going to have to snap a couple of photos before she went home.

Watching him, she noticed that he seemed to be aware of everything around him, from the eagle soaring effortlessly overhead to the increasing bunches of cattle scattered across the grassland. She had never seen a cow up close before she came to Texas, never realized how really big they were. The only cattle she had ever seen were in Western movies or on television advertising California cheese. She smiled, remembering Norman, the cute little calf in *City Slickers*. She had always wondered if they had put false eyelashes on the calf.

"Can we let the horses run?" she asked when they reached a stretch of flat ground.

"Sure, if you want."

She did. She drummed her heels into Sam's flanks and the gelding broke into a gallop. For the first time, she understood why people were so crazy for horseback riding. It was a thrill beyond belief to be riding through the tall grass, with the wind in her hair and the sun shining down on her. It gave her a sense of power, a sense of freedom she had never known before.

Then Sam tripped or stepped in a hole.

For a moment, she was sure he was going to fall. Her heart plunged to her toes as she contemplated being crushed beneath a thousand pounds of horseflesh, but, miraculously, it didn't happen. Sam regained his balance and raced onward. Carly pulled back on the reins, aware of the danger for the first time. She must have been crazy, racing across the prairie like that! If Sam had fallen, she could have been seriously injured, even killed.

Zane pulled up beside her. "You okay?"

She nodded, but she was shaken right down to the soles of her designer boots.

"You look a little green around the gills."

"All right, it scared me. He could have fallen...I could have been killed, or worse."

"You can get killed on the freeways in L.A."

She couldn't argue with that.

"Do you want to go back?"

Would he think she was a coward if she said yes? Did she really care what he thought? Once she left the ranch, she would never see him again. "No."

He smiled at her, as though pleased by her decision. He clucked to his horse and Sam fell into step beside the mare.

A short time later, Zane came to a halt atop a flower-strewn hill that overlooked a small valley. Cows grazed on the lush grass. The stream was wider and deeper here, flanked by stands of timber.

"Oh, look!" Carly exclaimed, pointing at the trees. "Is that a deer?"

Zane nodded. "She's got a fawn by her side."

"She does? Where? I don't see it."

"It's there, to her left, just behind that low-hanging branch."

Carly leaned forward, her eyes narrowed. She would never have seen it if the fawn hadn't taken a step forward. "Oh, it's adorable."

She clucked to Sam, but Zane held her back. "If you ride down there, you'll spook 'em."

"Oh, right."

The doe stepped out of the cover of the trees, her head lifted to sniff the air. The fawn trailed at her heels.

"They're so beautiful," Carly murmured. "I wish I had my camera."

"Next time," Zane remarked.

Next time, Carly mused, pleased by the thought.

They sat there for several minutes, watching the doe and her fawn pick their way between the cattle toward the stream to drink. The doe's ears twitched back and forth.

Carly blew out a breath when the deer retreated into the trees again. She had to admit, she had never seen anything like that in L.A.

"Do you come out here often?" she asked.

He leaned forward in the saddle, his arms crossed on the horn. "As often as I can."

"To watch the deer?"

"No," he said, grinning. "Because it's mine."

"Yours? But I thought...doesn't it belong to Jerry and Brenda?"

"Nope. This little corner of the world belongs to me."

"Are the cows yours, too?"

"No, they belong to the Clarks. I lease them the grazing rights. In another month or so, I'll have enough money to start building a place of my own."

"Oh. Well, that's wonderful."

"Yep." Pointing, he said, "I thought I'd put the house over there, near that clump of mesquite, and the barn over there." He pointed to another patch of land.

Carly nodded. "It's a lovely setting. What kind of house are you going to build?"

"I'm not sure. Something long and low with a wide verandah and a big brick fireplace in the living room. Maybe a fireplace in the master bedroom, too." Eyes narrowed, he glanced up at the sky. "It's getting late. We'd better be heading back. Mrs. Clark will be wondering what happened to you."

"Yes, I guess so," Carly agreed.

She took a last long look at the verdant valley, somehow reluctant to leave. She imagined a ranch-style house nestled in the valley, white with dark green trim. Smoke curling from the chimney. A swing big enough for two on the front porch. Herself, with a dark-haired baby in her arms.

Startled by the unexpected turn of her thoughts, she followed Zane back the way they had come.

Chapter Four

"So, did you have a nice ride this afternoon?" Brenda asked.

Carly nodded. They were sitting on the sofa in front of a cozy fire. She gazed down at the baby in her arms. Jerald Jason Clark, affectionately known as J.J., was one of the prettiest babies she had ever seen. Carly had never been one to get all gooey inside when she saw a baby. Sure, she thought they were cute, but she'd never really wanted the home, family, white picket fence package. She liked being independent, loved her job and her condo and being part of the singles scene in L.A. Part of the reason she had split up with Richard had been because he wanted her to quit her job, stay home and have babies. He had come from a large family and wanted about a dozen kids. Carly's mother had been a stay-at-home mom and perfectly happy to look after her husband and daughter, but Carly didn't want to be just a housewife.

Now, looking down at the pink-cheeked infant sleeping in her arms, she found herself wondering what it would be like to have a baby of her own. A baby with Zane's thick black hair and dark eyes...

She glanced up, aware that Brenda had asked her a question. "What?"

"Where were you?" Brenda asked.

"Just daydreaming, I guess. Why isn't Zane married?"

"Ah," Brenda said, a knowing look in her eyes.

"Don't 'ah' me. I was just curious. After all, he's not bad-looking."

Brenda snorted softly. "I thought we'd agreed he's gorgeous."

"All right, he's gorgeous. So why isn't he married?"

"I don't know. He's pretty closemouthed about his private life. I asked him about it once, but he changed the subject. All I know is that the buckle bunnies were all hot for him when he was on the circuit."

"Buckle bunnies?"

"Rodeo groupies."

"Oh."

"Anyway, I guess he fell hard for one of them. That's all I know. How far it went or why they broke up—" Brenda shrugged "—I couldn't say."

Carly nodded. It didn't really matter. She would be leaving in ten days or so and she wasn't ready to settle down, anyway.

She looked up as Jerry came into the room and sank down on the arm of the sofa beside Brenda, his arm falling naturally around his wife's shoulders. Brenda smiled up at her husband and they exchanged a look of such affection it made Carly feel as though she were intruding on an intimate moment.

Rising, she placed the sleeping baby on the sofa. "I'm going upstairs to relax in a nice hot bubble bath before dinner."

Carly went out to the barn looking for Zane after dinner that night, intending to ask him if she could curry Sam before their lesson the next day. He had shown her how it was done, and she had found it to be far more enjoyable than she would have thought, though why brushing a horse should make her feel good was beyond her. In any case, it was something she wanted to do again.

She heard a lot of voices raised in excitement as she neared the barn. When she drew closer, she saw about a dozen cowboys perched on the corral fence. They all seemed to be shouting at once, their attention fixed on whatever was happening inside the pen.

Two of the men scooted aside a little at her approach so that she could see what was going on. Peering between the fence rails, she saw Zane perched on the back of a big wildly bucking gray horse.

"Holy cow, he's gonna do it!" one of the men exclaimed. "He's gonna ride that outlaw into the ground."

"Five on the gray."

"Ten on Roan Eagle."

Carly stared at Zane. He stuck to the saddle like a burr to a blanket. His hat was off, there was a sheen of perspiration on his brow, his dark eyes were alight with exhilaration as the horse bucked from one end of the corral to the other and back again.

He looked as wild as the horse he rode. She wished fleetingly that she had her camera with her.

The noise around her faded into the distance as she watched him, her heart in her throat as the gray suddenly reared, came down hard on all fours, and then dropped to the ground and started to roll in an effort to crush the man on its back.

Zane quickly rolled free, dodging the horse's flailing hooves. It was a frightening thing to watch. When the horse regained its feet, Zane was in the saddle again.

She had never seen anything like it, not even in the rodeo. This was not an event to be won in eight seconds, but a contest of wills between man and beast to see who would be the boss.

The stallion plunged and kicked and screamed its rage, but the man would not be unseated and finally, its coat streaked with foamy lather, its sides heaving mightily, the gray stood in the center of the corral, its ears twitching, its head hanging in defeat.

"By damn, he did it!" one of the cowhands crowed. "I never would have believed that outlaw horse could be broke, but he did it! Red, you owe me twenty dollars. Pay up!"

Zane rode the horse around the corral once and when he came to a stop, his gaze met hers. She looked away, shaken to the core of her being by the sharp stab of desire that whipped through her like a desert wind, a wild yearning that was mirrored in the depths of his eyes.

She was only vaguely aware of the men climbing down from the corral fence, of money changing hands as they walked away, talking and laughing, until she was the only one left standing there.

Slowly she looked up at Zane to find him watching her, his expression suddenly unreadable.

"That was quite a ride," she remarked, unnerved by the taut silence between them.

He shrugged.

"You could have been killed."

"It goes with the job."

"And you love it, don't you?"

"Yes, ma'am, I surely do."

He swung out of the saddle, tall and lean, his shirt and jeans coated with a layer of dust. He stripped the rigging from the gray and dropped the saddle over the top rail of the corral. Removing the hackamore, he draped it over the saddle horn.

Ducking his head, he stepped between the rails. Carly felt dwarfed by his presence as he stood towering over her smelling of dust and sweat and victory.

His gaze moved over her, settling on her face, her mouth. Her breath caught in her throat, and the world stopped turning as she waited. It seemed to take forever while he made up his mind and then, muttering an oath, he pulled her into his arms and kissed her, hard and fast.

She was breathless when he let her go.

His eyes were filled with an emotion she could not fathom, and then he turned on his heel and stalked away.

Feeling suddenly bereft, she stared after him, her lips still tingling from the force of his kiss.

She didn't know how long she stood there before she turned and went back to the house.

Brenda was waiting for her at the back door. "I hear there was quite a show down at the corral this evening."

Carly looked at her friend, her cheeks on fire. Had Jerry seen Zane kissing her at the corral and told Brenda?

"A show?" she asked, her voice little more than a squeak.

Brenda nodded. "Jerry told me Zane rode that big gray stud they brought in off the range last week."

"Oh." Carly forced a smile. "Yes. It was exciting to watch."

"I told you Zane was the best."

"He is that," Carly said, remembering his quick kiss. She could still feel the heat of his mouth on hers.

"How are the lessons coming along?"

"Just fine. You were right. I love riding."

Brenda beamed at her. "I knew you would. One day next week we'll take that trail ride up to the lake."

"All right."

"I told Jerry I wanted to spend some time with you, so tomorrow you and I are going in to the city for lunch and shopping, and Friday night the three of us are going out to dinner, and then dancing at The Cowboy."

"Sounds like fun, Bren."

"I really expected us to have more time together," Brenda said. "I didn't realize Jerry's mother was going to be gone while you were here. If she hadn't gone back to

Boston to see her new grandchild, I'd have more time to spend with you."

"Don't worry about it. I'm a big girl. When I get bored, I'll let you know."

Brenda grinned at her. "I'll turn you into a country girl yet."

"I wouldn't count on it. Three weeks of this is fun. Three months, and I'd be a raving lunatic."

"We'll see," Brenda replied with a sly smile. "A lot can happen in the time you've got left."

With a shake of her head, Carly stood and headed for the stairs. "Night, matchmaker."

"Sweet dreams," Brenda said.

Carly fixed her friend with a pointed stare. Given a choice, they both knew who Carly would be dreaming about.

Brenda's laughter followed her to bed.

Dallas was a whole lot bigger than Twisted River. And as Brenda had said, it had malls galore with all the same big brand stores as any other major city.

Shopping with Brenda was always fun and Carly enjoyed having a chance to spend a few hours alone with her friend. But, all the while, in the back of her mind, she was thinking about Zane. She really had it bad, she mused. She had only known the man a short time and yet thoughts of him filled her every waking moment, and a good part of her dreams at night.

Knowing they were going dancing the next evening, Carly bought a calico skirt, a blue off-the-shoulder blouse, and a poofy petticoat. She also bought a pair of boots more suitable for riding than the ones she had brought with her.

"You should buy a hat," Brenda suggested. She held up a pretty cream-colored one with a plain leather band. "This is pretty."

"I've never liked hats," Carly said, trying on.

"Well, that one looks good on you."

Carly looked at herself in the mirror. What would Zane think? "All right, I'll take it."

Leaving the department store, they headed for the ice-cream shop across the street. Brenda ordered a strawberry parfait; Carly asked for a hot-fudge sundae.

"We're having a party for Jerry next Thursday," Brenda remarked. She took a bite of her ice cream. "It's his thirtieth birthday. We're gonna have cake and ice cream, and then a hayride."

"Sounds like fun," Carly said. "I've never been on a hayride."

"You'll love it. We don't usually have parties during the week, but I wanted a surprise party, and he won't expect it on a Thursday night."

"Who's coming?"

"Just some friends and neighbors."

Carly nodded. Apparently the hired help wasn't invited.

"Do you think you could help me decorate for the party? Jerry will be away from the ranch on business all day Thursday. I thought I'd string some paper lanterns and, oh, I don't know, put up some balloons and streamers, stuff like that."

"Sure, I'd love to help. What about a cake? Do you want me to make one?"

"Would you? That would be terrific."

Before heading back to the ranch, they made one more stop at a men's shop so Carly could buy Jerry a present.

It was dark when they got back to the ranch. Carly looked for Zane when they drove up, but the barn was dark and there was no sign of him.

Maybe tomorrow, she thought as she followed Brenda into the house.

Carly woke late the following morning. Dressing quickly, she pulled on her new boots and hurried downstairs.

"Morning," Brenda said. She held J.J. on her hip while

she stirred some milk into a bowl of rice cereal. "There's some pancake batter in the fridge if you're hungry."

"No, thanks, just coffee." Carly poured herself a cup, then sat down at the table. "Anything I can help you with today?"

"No, silly. I didn't ask you here to help with the housework."

"I know, but I feel guilty, out riding every day while you're slaving over a hot stove."

Brenda laughed. "Hardly that."

"Well, don't say I didn't offer."

"Go on," Brenda said. "Get out of here."

Carly finished her coffee and stood up. "See ya later."

Leaving the house, Carly went to the barn searching for Zane, but he was nowhere to be found and there wasn't anyone around to ask where he might be, so she went back to the house, determined to help Brenda with the housework whether she wanted help or not. What else did she have to do?

The Cowboy was a country bar located in the heart of the city. Even before they reached the front door, Carly could hear Brooks and Dunn belting out their latest hit. She followed Brenda and Jerry inside, paused to watch the couples dancing in the middle of the room. Small tables surrounded the dance area; there were booths along one wall, a bar along another. Sawdust covered the floor. Old spurs, bits and bridles, branding irons, and pieces of barbed wire of various lengths decorated the walls, while antique handguns and badges were displayed in a glass-fronted shelf behind the bar.

"Over here," Jerry said, and Brenda and Carly followed him to a booth in the corner.

A barmaid wearing tight black jeans, a white midriff top and white boots appeared a few minutes later to take their order.

"I'll have a whiskey sour," Jerry said. "You want a martini, Bren?"

"No, just orange juice."

"What'll you have, Carly?" Jerry asked.

"I'd like a 7UP."

"You girls on the wagon tonight?" Jerry asked.

"You know I won't drink while I'm nursing," Brenda reminded her husband.

Jerry turned to Carly. "What's your excuse?"

Carly shrugged. "I just don't drink. Never have."

Grunting softly, he dropped some money on the table to cover their order and a tip, then reached for Brenda's hand. "Come on, honey, let's dance."

Brenda smiled at Carly, then followed her husband out onto the dance floor.

Carly leaned back in the booth, watching the two of them. She smiled her thanks when the waitress brought their order a short time later. Picking up her drink, she sipped it slowly, her gaze moving around the room. The place was crowded, filled with couples dancing cheek to cheek and singles on the prowl.

Her stomach fluttered nervously when a tall man with sandy-blond hair stopped in front of her table. He wore jeans, a dark blue cowboy shirt and a black string tie.

"Care to dance, little lady?" he asked, holding out his hand.

She was about to refuse and then gave herself a mental shake. She was here to have a good time. She liked to dance.

With a smile, she placed her hand in his and let him lead her onto the floor.

"I've never seen you here before," he said.

"I've never been here before."

He grinned. "I guess that explains it. I'm Russ Stafford."

"Carly Kirkwood."

"Pleased to meet you, Carly."

"Likewise."

They made small talk as they danced. He was thirty-two years old, a corporate lawyer, divorced, with two kids—a girl, age eleven, and a boy, nine.

She was telling him about herself when she saw a familiar figure crossing the room toward her. He wore black jeans and a cowboy shirt open at the collar. The shirt was white, a sharp contrast to his dark skin and black hair.

Her heart began to pound as Zane Roan Eagle tapped her partner on the shoulder.

"Thanks for the dance," Russ said, releasing her.

She nodded and then Zane was twirling her away. "I didn't expect to see you here tonight," she said.

"Why not?"

"I don't know."

He smiled down at her. "A man can't spend all his time with horses and cows, you know."

Russ had smiled at her, too, and she had felt nothing. But when Zane smiled, her heart seemed to turn over in her chest, and it was suddenly hard to breathe.

"Besides," Zane went on, "Jerry told me you would be here."

Her pulse rate accelerated at his words. He wasn't here by chance, but to see her.

His arm tightened around her, not much, just enough to draw her up against him, to let her feel the hard, masculine lines of his body. "You look mighty pretty tonight," he said.

"Thank you." She wasn't wearing anything special, just the calico skirt and ruffled off-the-shoulder blouse she had bought the day before, but the look in his eyes made her feel she was wearing a Dior gown.

She was sorry when the music ended, relieved when it started again and he swept her into his arms once more.

They danced every dance after that until Jerry decided it was time to leave.

Carly looked up into Zane's eyes. "Thank you. I had a wonderful time."

"Let me take you home."

"I don't know…."

"Go ahead," Brenda said, giving her a little push. "We don't mind, do we, Jerry?"

Jerry shrugged. "Makes no never mind to me." He wrapped his arm around Brenda's waist and winked at her. "Give us a chance to neck a little on the way home."

Brenda slapped him playfully on the shoulder. "Last time we necked on the way home, I got pregnant with J.J.!"

"Time he had a little brother," Jerry said.

"A brother!" Brenda exclaimed. "He's not even six months old yet."

"So, we'll practice a little. G'night, you two."

Carly felt suddenly nervous and more than a little shy as Zane helped her into his truck. It was one thing to spend time with him on the ranch, another to share the dark cozy cave in the front seat of his truck. She had only known the man for a few days, after all.

He pulled out of the parking lot and on to the highway.

Carly searched her brain for something to say, but nothing came to mind. Heart pounding, stomach churning, she stared at the dark road that stretched before them, every nerve and cell in her body aware of the man sitting beside her. He smelled faintly of horses and leather and hay, of perspiration and a faint trace of aftershave. She studied his profile, all sharp planes and angles that combined into an arrestingly handsome face.

He was far too handsome. Far too appealing. And she was starting to care for him far too much.

He pulled the truck off the road, killed the engine and the headlights, leaving them in thick darkness broken only by the faint glow of the moon.

Before she could speak, he drew her into his arms and kissed her. "I've been wanting to do that ever since the last one," he said with a rueful grin. "I just couldn't put it off any longer."

Carly stared up at him, shaken right down to her toes. Where had the man learned to kiss like that?

She placed her hands on his shoulders, her gaze melding with his. "And I've been wanting to do this," she said, and kissed him back.

"Damn." The word whispered past Zane's lips, leaving him to wonder if his voice sounded as shaken as he felt. Where had she learned to kiss like that? She was watching him, looking as dazed as he felt. He had kissed a lot of women in his time. Hell, during his rodeo days, he'd practically had to fight the buckle bunnies off with a stick. He'd had his pick of women—young, old, married, divorced and in-between, pretty and plain—but not a one of them had ever kissed him like this.

He was tempted to kiss her again, just to make sure he hadn't imagined it, and he might have, too, if a pair of headlights hadn't lit up the night.

Zane glanced out the window as a horn honked and then a truck drew up beside them. Feeling as awkward and embarrassed as a high school kid caught necking in the parking lot, he rolled down the window.

"Hey, you two." The grin on Brenda's face was as high and wide as a Texas sky. "What'cha all doing in there?"

Carly felt a rush of heat climb into her cheeks as she heard Brenda's voice. She was never going to hear the end of this!

"Why don't you mind your own business?" Carly said, leaning forward so she could see her friend's face.

Brenda's eyes widened in mock innocence. "Why, Carly Kirkwood, whatever would your mother say?"

"Why don't you go home and call her?" Carly retorted with a sugary smile.

"Oh?" Brenda pressed a hand to her heart. "Did you two want to be alone?"

Jerry leaned around his wife. "Sorry, Zane, she made me stop."

Zane lifted his hand in a gesture of understanding.

Jerry gunned the engine. "Say good night, Brenda."

"Good night, you two," Brenda called with a smug smile. "Don't hurry home."

Carly stared after the truck as it disappeared into the darkness. Darn that Brenda! How was she ever going to face Zane or Jerry again?

"I haven't been caught necking since I was fourteen," Zane remarked, a grin twitching his lips.

"Is that what we were doing? Necking?"

"Weren't we?"

"I suppose so."

"I reckon, now that we've been caught, we'd best go on home."

"Yes," Carly agreed dryly, affecting her best Clint Eastwood impression. "I reckon so."

Zane pulled up in front of the porch and put the truck in park. "Here we are."

"Thank you. I had a good time tonight. Dancing," she added quickly.

He nodded. "I had a good time dancing, too," he said, though he knew neither of them was talking about dancing.

"Will I see you tomorrow?"

"I don't know. I'm supposed to ride out first thing in the morning and take a look at the river up on the south range. I think something might be blocking the flow of the water."

"Oh." She couldn't keep the disappointment from her voice. "That's all right. I think Brenda wanted to go shopping anyway."

Her heart skipped a beat when he said, "You could go with me."

"I'd like that."

"It's a long ride."

"How long?"

He shrugged. "A couple of hours one way."

She nodded, wondering if he had changed his mind and was trying to discourage her from going.

"Brenda told me once that a person should never ride farther than they wanted to walk home, in case they found themselves afoot, you know?"

Zane winked at her. "True enough, but there's little chance of both of us getting bucked off. So, are you game?"

"I'll have to talk to Brenda, see what she wants to do."

"Sure," he said, "I understand." Getting out of the truck, he walked around to her side and opened the door for her, then helped her out of her seat.

"Well," she murmured, "good night."

"Good night."

She didn't move and neither did he. The silence stretched between them.

"Well, good night," she said again, and started to move past him.

His hand on her shoulder stayed her. "Dammit," he muttered, and dragging her into his arms, he kissed her, hard and long, then let her go.

He was in the truck and driving away before she could think, before she could move.

Zane slammed one hand against the steering wheel. He never should have kissed her again. It was like playing with a burning stick of dynamite. Sooner or later there was going to be a hell of an explosion. And why the devil had he invited her to ride out with him tomorrow? And what would he do if she showed up at the barn, all ready to go? He didn't need another female complicating his life. He had enough problems with the ones he had.

He parked the truck in front of the bunkhouse and got out. She'd be going home in a week and a half or so, he thought, and his troubles would be over.

* * *

Carly stared at the truck's taillights as Zane drove away, then slowly turned and walked up the steps to the front porch. She opened the door as quietly as she could, hoping that Brenda and Jerry had already gone to bed. She wasn't looking forward to facing either one of them again.

As luck would have it, Brenda was sitting on the sofa, nursing J.J. A small lamp burned on a side table, filling the room with shadows.

Carly held up her hand. "Don't say anything."

Brenda laughed. "Hey, girl, I'm sorry. It was a mean thing to do, but I just couldn't resist. Forgive me?"

"No." Carly dropped down into the chair across from the sofa. "Where's Jerry?"

"Taking the babysitter home. Don't try to change the subject."

"Brenda."

"It sure looks like the two of you are getting to know each other better."

"Brenda! For heaven's sake, it was just a kiss." Just a kiss? It had been far, far more than that.

"Just a kiss, huh?"

Carly blew out a sigh. "Oh, Bren, I've never been kissed like that in my whole life."

Brenda's eyes twinkled merrily. "Am I a great match-maker, or what?"

"Is he the reason you asked me here?"

"Well, not the only reason."

"Oh, Brenda!" She lifted her hands to her burning cheeks. "Does he know that's why I'm here?" She would never, never be able to face him again if he thought she had come here solely to meet him.

"Of course not."

"Pinky swear?"

"Pinky swear. Zane is such a great guy. I just thought you two might hit it off, even if it's only for a couple of weeks. And if you didn't, well, at least it would give us a chance to spend some time together." She lifted the baby to her shoulder and began to pat his back. "So, he's a good kisser?"

"Better than good. He must have had a lot of practice."

"Not since he's been here; at least not that I know of. I've heard the men talk. He doesn't go into town with them much. As far as I know, he hasn't had a relationship since he's been here. In fact, I was surprised to see him at The Cowboy tonight."

Carly felt a faint warmth in her cheeks. Zane had been there because he knew she was going to be there.

"You really like him, don't you?"

Carly nodded. "Way too much, I'm afraid."

"Why do you say that?"

"What's the point? His life is here, mine's in L.A."

"You might get to like it here, if you gave it a chance."

"Are you nuts?" She held up her hand, staying Brenda's next words. "Don't try to change my mind. I'm happy where I am and I don't intend to uproot myself and move to the country, not even for Mr. Roan Eagle."

"Are you sure about that?" Brenda asked.

"Of course I am. I'm going to bed. See you tomorrow."

Tomorrow, she thought as she climbed the stairs to her bedroom. Zane had invited her to ride out with him tomorrow. Should she go? Brenda would understand if she skipped shopping to go riding with Zane. Carly shook her head. Maybe it would be best to ignore him from now on. After all, the more she saw him, the harder it would be to leave. Why ask for heartache?

She took a quick shower and climbed into bed. Tomorrow, she would stay at the house and spend the day with Brenda.

Chapter Five

Carly cracked an eye open as the rooster's insistent crowing invaded her dreams and brought her awake in the real world. It had been such a lovely dream, too. She lifted her fingertips to her lips. In her dreams, Zane had been kissing her again....

Zane! He was leaving first thing this morning! Was she too late? Had he left already?

She bounded out of bed, her decision not to see him again disappearing like dewdrops on a sunny day. He was like chocolate, she mused. He wasn't good for her, she knew she shouldn't eat it, but how could she refuse something so handsomely packaged?

She couldn't. Grabbing her jeans and a cotton shirt, she dressed quickly, pulled on her socks and her boots, tied her hair back in a ponytail and flew down the stairs.

Hurrying into the kitchen, she said a quick good-morning to Brenda, then poured herself a cup of coffee.

"Well, you seem to be in a bit of a rush," Brenda remarked. "Is the house on fire?"

"No, I'm going riding with Zane, I think."

"You think?"

"If he hasn't left without me."

"Don't you want some breakfast first?"

"No, no time." She swallowed the coffee, burning her tongue in the process. "He said we might be home late. I don't know how late. Don't wait dinner for me."

"Have fun," Brenda said, laughing. "Don't forget to wear your new hat."

"I left it upstairs. I've got to go."

Brenda grabbed her own hat off the hook near the back door. "Here, wear this one then."

"Thanks, Bren. See ya later!"

Jamming Brenda's hat on her head, Carly hurried out of the house and down the narrow path that led to the barn. Several cowhands were gathered there, saddling up, but there was no sign of Zane.

"Mornin', miss, can I help you?"

Carly smiled at the tall, gangly cowboy. "I was looking for Zane. Is he here?"

The cowboy glanced over his shoulder. "Hey, Tomas, you seen the chief?"

"He rode out with Gallagher early this morning." Tomas looked at Carly and smiled. "He said to tell you he was sorry and that he'd see you later."

"Thank you."

Disappointed she wouldn't be spending the day with Zane, she watched the men ride out of the yard. They all tipped their hats to her as they went by.

She stood there for several minutes, then, with a sigh, she went into the barn.

Inside, she walked down the aisle, stopping now and then to pet the horses that looked at her over their stall doors. Some rubbed their noses against her chest, snuffling softly.

She found Sam at the end of the row. She stroked his forehead for a few minutes and then, impulsively, opened the stall door and led him out. She was dressed to go riding, so why not ride? She wouldn't go far.

It took her a good twenty minutes to get saddle and bridle
in place. Leading Sam outside, she climbed into the saddle
and rode out of the yard.

It was a beautiful day for a ride. The sky was as blue as
J.J.'s eyes, and the tall grass swayed to the rhythm of a
gentle breeze. She smiled inwardly, surprised at how much
she enjoyed riding. Leaning forward, she stroked Sam's
neck. There was something infinitely peaceful about riding
across the land all alone.

She glanced over her shoulder now and then to make
sure the house was still within sight. Just a little farther and
then she'd head back.

But every time she started to turn around, there was
something new to see—a doe drinking at a watering hole,
a spotted cow nursing a calf, a hawk soaring high overhead,
its wings spread wide. Riding on, she spied a patch of
bright yellow wildflowers and later, a skunk moving
through the tall grass. Topping a hill blanketed with wildflowers, she saw a small herd of wild horses grazing below,
their coats like a colorful patchwork quilt against the green
of the meadow.

Sam's head went up when he scented the mustangs.
Carly grabbed the saddle horn as her horse tugged on the
reins and quickened his pace.

"Easy, boy," she murmured.

She watched the wild horses, thinking how beautiful they
were, until the herd's stallion pranced toward them, neck
arched, ears back. She didn't know much about horses, but
there was something ominous in the stallion's posture. Apparently Sam thought so, too. With a toss of his head, the
gelding turned tail and began to run.

Carly clung to the saddle horn, her heart pounding. Gradually Sam slowed to a trot and then a walk. Carly risked a
glance over her shoulder, relieved to see that there was no
sign of the wild horses or the stallion.

It took her a moment to realize there was no sign of the
ranch, either.

*   *   *

Zane took off his Stetson. Using his kerchief, he wiped the sweat from his brow, then wiped the inside band of his hat before settling it back on his head. Stringing fence was hard work and he quietly cursed the cattle that had decided to try and go through this stretch of fence line. Cows had to be some of the stupidest critters ever made. They wandered into bogs and got stuck. They got tangled in barbed wire. They went crazy on loco weed. He didn't usually do this kind of work, but Gallagher had needed help and Zane had been the only hand available.

"I'm about done here," Gallagher hollered. "How about you?"

"Yeah, let's go home."

Zane glanced at the sun. It was right around five o'clock. By the time they got back to the ranch, it would be near dark.

Pulling off his gloves, he walked over to where his horse was grazing in a patch of shade. He tightened the cinch and slipped the bridle over the horse's head. After untying the lead line from the tree, he coiled the rope and dropped it over the pommel, then stepped into the saddle. He wondered, not for the first time, how Carly had spent the day. Had she shown up at the barn? With a shake of his head, he rode over to where Gallagher was waiting.

"Wish I had a beer," the cowboy muttered.

Zane nodded. A cold beer would hit the spot, but if he'd had a wish, he sure as hell wouldn't have wasted it on a beer!

The area around the barn was in an uproar when Zane and Gallagher rode into the ranch yard a little over two hours later.

Dismounting, Zane tossed his horse's reins over the hitching post.

"Hey, T.J., what's going on?"

"That gal visitin' the Clarks has gone missing."

"What do you mean, missing?"

T.J. shrugged. "Near as we can figure, she took Sam out this morning and she ain't come back yet." He frowned. "The boss lady said she was supposed to be with you."

Zane swore softly, then turned at the sound of Brenda Clark's voice calling his name.

"Zane! Thank goodness!" Mrs. Clark said, hurrying toward him. "Where is she? Is she all right?"

"I don't know. I've been gone all day. Just got back."

"But she told me she was riding out with you this morning."

"Yeah. I was gonna go check the river in the south pasture. I asked her last night if she wanted to go along, but Nolan came in early this morning and said some of the fences were down over near Cougar Canyon. He told Gallagher to take care of it, and I went along with him to check it out."

Brenda nodded. Grant Nolan was the Clarks' foreman. "Where can she be?"

"Don't worry," Jerry said, coming up behind her. "We'll find her. Charlie, you and Gallagher go north. I'll take Tomas and head east. T.J., Poteet, you two go check Craggy Point. Zane..."

"I'll ride out toward Cross Creek." He didn't ask for permission, and he didn't ask anyone to go with him. The last thing he wanted was someone to slow him down.

"All right," Jerry said, "let's go. Bren, if she shows up, fire three quick shots."

Brenda nodded. "Hurry!"

Zane saddled a fresh mount and rode out of the yard. Damn, if anything had happened to her...he didn't finish the thought. Where the devil was she?

Carly reined Sam to a halt near a stand of slender pines. She was hopelessly lost. Tamping down a growing sense of panic, she glanced around, wondering if she should stay where she was, or keep trying to find her way back. She seemed to remember reading somewhere that waiting for someone to find you was the smart thing to do.

With that in mind, she dismounted near a shallow stream and, after letting the horse drink, she looped the reins over a low branch. Dropping down on her hands and knees, she took a few swallows of water, wondering if it was safe to drink.

Rising, she dusted off the knees of her jeans. She stood there a moment, then began to walk back and forth along the edge of the stream to stretch her legs. She had been gone for hours. Surely Brenda would be missing her after all this time. No doubt some of the cowhands were searching for her, even now. All she had to do was wait.

It wasn't as easy to do as it sounded.

Her stomach growled loudly, reminding her that she hadn't eaten since the night before.

A cool breeze made her wish she'd thought to bring a jacket.

Moving next to Sam, she stroked his neck, grateful for the horse's company.

Gradually the sky went from blue to navy to indigo. A few stars twinkled overhead. Alone in the quiet night, she felt small and very, very alone. Noises that wouldn't have bothered her had someone been with her suddenly sounded ominous. Drifting shadows took on frightening shapes.

"Someone will come." She whispered the words over and over again. "Someone will come."

Zane's gaze cut back and forth as he rode toward Cross Creek. It had been next to impossible to pick Sam's tracks out of all the others around the barn. He'd gotten lucky once he got away from the yard in that he had found a couple of fresh prints in a patch of dirt, but as soon as he got out into the grassland, the tracks grew harder to follow. With full dark, it had become impossible.

What the devil was she doing out here, anyway? She'd only had a few lessons. What insanity had sent her riding away from the ranch on her own? It was all too easy to get lost in the endless sea of grass that surrounded the ranch house. If she had been hurt, he would never forgive himself.

He pulled up on the reins, sat listening for several minutes, yet heard nothing but the sighing of the wind and the call of a night bird.

Damn. Where was she?

Taking a deep breath, he sought for the calm deep within himself. Years ago, his grandfather had taught him to read the signs of earth and sky, to listen to the inner voice that resided in his heart and soul, that spiritual power that connected him to all living creatures, both the two-leggeds and the four-leggeds. Early in his life, Zane had learned that the hawk was his totem. The shaman had told him that the hawk totem denoted perception, focus and protection. One who had the hawk for his guide was strong and observant. To have the hawk as a totem also gave one visionary power. It was that power that Zane sought now. Lifting his head, he offered a prayer to Wakan Tanka and then, closing his eyes, he put everything from his mind but finding Carly.

It came to him then, a strong impression that he should head toward the watering hole where the mustangs came to drink.

Lifting the reins, he turned his horse toward the northeast.

Sitting down on the grass, Carly rested her head on her bent knees. "Someone will come," she murmured, but there was no longer any conviction in her voice. She would stay here tonight and tomorrow she would try and find her way back to the ranch.

A low whinny roused her from the edge of sleep. She lurched to her feet, her gaze anxiously sweeping the darkness. Had she imagined it? But no, there it was again.

Sam's head went up and he whinnied in reply.

A moment later, a dark shape moved out of the shadows

of the night. Fear shot through her, to be quickly replaced by relief when she saw that it was a horse and rider.

"Zane? Oh, Zane!"

His name had no sooner escaped her lips than she was in his arms.

"Are you all right?" His hands slid over her back, up and down her arms.

"I'm fine."

"You're sure?"

She nodded. Now that she was safe in his arms, she felt utterly foolish.

Now that he knew she was all right, his relief turned to anger. "What the hell are you doing out here anyway?"

She glared at him, even though she knew he couldn't see her expression in the darkness, then collapsed against his broad chest. "I only meant to go for a ride around the ranch, but…" She shrugged. "We just kept going farther and farther and then we saw some mustangs, and the stallion came toward us and…"

"And spooked Sam," Zane finished for her.

"Yeah."

"Well, you're all right now."

"I feel so stupid."

"I guess maybe I'd better teach you how to navigate by the location of the sun and the moon and the stars."

"I guess so."

He looked down at her, his expression hidden in the shadow of his hat. She felt his need in the sudden trembling of his hands on her shoulders. His lips brushed hers, warm and all too fleeting.

"Zane…" His name whispered past her lips.

"I'm here," he murmured, and kissed her again.

With his lips on hers, it was easy to forget everything else. She pressed herself against him. His body was hard and strong; she knew nothing could hurt her now, not with his arms around her.

She moaned a soft protest when he let her go.

"I know," he said wryly, "but we'd best get back. Mrs. Clark is worried sick."

All the lights were on in the house and in the yard when they rode up.

Dismounting, Zane lifted her from the back of her horse. "I still need to check the river in the south pasture." He ran his hands up and down her arms, as if to assure himself she was there. "Are you game to go out with me Monday morning, or has today soured you on riding forever?"

"I don't know. Are you going to show up this time?"

"Yeah. I'm sorry about today. The foreman came in early this morning and said some fences were down. He sent Gallagher out to check on it, but it was a two-man job, so I went along with him. So, are you game to try again?"

"I'm game, cowboy."

"Good." His hands dropped to his sides and he took a step back as Brenda came running out the back door.

"Carly!" Brenda threw her arms around her. "Good heavens, girl, I've been worried to death!"

"I know, I'm sorry. I…"

"You can explain later. Come on in the house. You must be starved."

Carly glanced over her shoulder. She smiled at Zane as Brenda hurried her up the back steps and into the kitchen.

"Sit down," Brenda said. "I'll fix you something to eat. Do you want some coffee?"

"Yes, thanks."

Brenda bustled around the kitchen, reheating the spaghetti they'd had for dinner. She filled a cup with coffee and placed it on the table, pulled silverware from the drawer, a plate from the cupboard.

"So," she said, dropping into the chair across from Carly's. "What happened?"

Carly blew out a breath. "I just wanted to go for a little ride around the ranch. I didn't mean to go so far." She shrugged, embarrassed. "I got lost."

"You've got to be careful," Brenda admonished.

"Yes, I found that out."

"Jeez, I was scared out of my mind trying to figure out what I'd tell your mom and dad if they found you at the bottom of a canyon or something."

Carly laughed in spite of herself.

"It's not funny!"

"I know," Carly said, sobering instantly. "I'm sorry. I guess I just didn't think…"

"This is still the Wild West in a lot of ways," Brenda said. "There are still snakes and wolves and coyotes running around out there."

"And Native Americans," Carly murmured, remembering the overwhelming relief that had engulfed her when she saw Zane riding toward her.

"What?"

"Nothing. Is that spaghetti ready yet? I'm starved."

Carly went to church with Brenda and Jerry Sunday morning. After church, they went out to lunch at the local café.

When they got back to the ranch, Carly went upstairs to change clothes while Brenda put J.J. down for a nap.

When she went downstairs, she found Brenda and Jerry sprawled on the sofa watching *Dances With Wolves*.

"This is a great movie," Carly exclaimed. Grabbing a throw pillow from one of the chairs, she plopped down on her stomach on the floor, her arms folded on the pillow. "I read the book years ago, before the movie came out. If I'm not mistaken, they were Comanches in the book."

"Really?" Brenda said. "I wonder why they changed it."

"I don't know."

"I love this part," Brenda said.

Carly nodded. She stared at the screen as hundreds of buffalo burst into view. In her mind's eye, she pictured Zane as one of the warriors. She wondered where he was and what he was doing, wished that he was there, watching the movie with her. It would be interesting to get a different point of view regarding Kevin Costner's take on the Lakota, to know how accurate the story really was. Funny how quickly the time passed when she was with Zane, and how slowly it passed without him.

Tomorrow, she thought, smiling inwardly, she would see him tomorrow.

Chapter Six

Monday morning, after a quick breakfast of toast, orange juice and coffee, Carly grabbed her camera and her new hat and hurried down to the barn. She hated to admit it but, after what happened Saturday, she was a little apprehensive about leaving the ranch even though she knew there was nothing to worry about as long as she was with Zane.

Several cowboys were milling around in front of the barn while the foreman issued the day's orders.

Zane was easy to spot. He stood head and shoulders above most of the others.

She slowed her steps as she drew closer. She didn't want to appear too anxious, but she could hardly contain her excitement at the thought of spending the day in his company.

He glanced her way just then and her heartbeat sped up. Lord, but that man was far too handsome for his own good and for her peace of mind. He said something to the foreman, then left the group.

A slow smile spread over his face as he walked toward her. "Mornin'."

"Hi."

Heat flowed between them, reminding her of the kisses they had shared. His gaze lingered on her mouth. Was he remembering, too?

"Come on." His voice moved over her like velvet. "I'll saddle a horse for you."

She followed him toward the corral, acutely aware that some of the cowboys loitering in the area had been out searching for her on Saturday night. She still felt foolish for causing so much trouble.

Zane roped a pretty little buckskin mare and led it out of the corral. He gave the horse a quick brushing, cleaned its hooves and had it saddled and ready to go in practically no time at all.

She eyed the buckskin warily. "Where's Sam?"

"He's all right for lessons, but you don't want to take him out on a long ride."

"I don't?" She was used to riding the tranquil gelding.

"Nah. He's too old and slow for a long ride."

"Oh." She looped the strap of her camera's carrying case over the pommel.

He looked at her, one brow raised. "A camera?"

"I thought I might take some pictures. I might even take one of you, if you wouldn't mind."

He grunted softly. "In the old days, my people were superstitious about having their pictures taken. Even in this day and age, visitors at powwows are asked to get permission before they take photographs."

"Really? I didn't know that. Do I need to ask your permission?"

"No. Just don't ask me to smile." Grimacing, he held the buckskin's reins while she climbed into the saddle, then handed her the reins while he adjusted the stirrups for her. "How's that?"

"Perfect," she said.

His gaze met hers again and a smile sizzled between them.

Her heart was doing somersaults when he turned away to get his own horse. She watched him mount the bay, admiring the fluid way he moved, his effortless strength.

"Ready?" he asked.

She nodded, butterflies fluttering in her stomach as the buckskin moved out after the bay. The buckskin's walk was faster than Sam's, but just as smooth.

Zane looked over at her. "You okay?"

She was nervous about riding a new horse, but she didn't want him to know that. "Fine, don't worry about me. What's her name?"

"Queenie."

Leaning forward, Carly patted the mare's neck. "Hiya, Queenie."

The barn and the corrals fell behind and soon there was nothing but rolling grassland and the blue vault of the sky as far as the eye could see, save for a few fluffy white clouds off in the distance. Now and then they passed a stand of timber. A jet flew high overhead, seeming out of place in this quiet part of the country. It must have been like this when the Indians roamed the land, she thought.

She glanced at Zane. He had a strong profile, his Lakota blood evident in his high cheekbones and the dusky color of his skin. She wondered if his ancestors had roamed the wilds of South Dakota two hundred years ago, if he had any relatives living in Texas, why he wasn't married.

"Pretty country," she remarked as they crossed a shallow stream.

"Yeah."

"What kind of Indian are you?"

He looked at her, one brow raised.

"Sorry, I…I didn't mean to offend you."

"You didn't. I'm just surprised it took you so long to ask."

"Oh?"

"Most people ask sooner, that's all. I'm Lakota."

"I thought the Sioux were in South Dakota or Montana, somewhere up there. How did you wind up in Texas?"

He grunted softly. "I'm not sure."

"Do you have family there, in South Dakota?"

"Yeah. Mother, father, aunts, uncles, cousins, nephews, you name it."

"No brothers or sisters?"

"I had a brother, but he was killed in a car accident last year. His wife and kids live on the rez with my folks."

"Oh, I'm sorry."

"What about you?" he asked.

"My mom and dad live in Tucson. My sister's married to an airline pilot. They live in D.C."

"And you live in Los Angeles. You like it there?"

"Very much. And you don't," she said, remembering their earlier conversation.

She felt a keen sense of disappointment. She had been born in a town about thirty miles from Los Angeles and couldn't imagine settling down anywhere else. The beach and the mountains were within easy driving distance. You could go to Sea World one day and Disneyland the next, hit the roller coasters at Magic Mountain, pan for gold at Knott's Berry Farm. She'd seen *The Phantom of the Opera* and *The Lion King* at the Ahmanson Theater, and *Beauty and the Beast* at the Pantages. As far as she was concerned, L.A. had it all.

Zane made a broad gesture that encompassed the land around them. "I didn't see anything like this in Los Angeles."

She couldn't argue with that. Back home, it seemed that every time she turned around, another hill was being flattened and covered with look-alike tract houses that were packed so close together you could practically reach out the window and shake hands with your neighbor. There were also the dizzying number of new freeways and malls that were springing up like mushrooms.

Zane pulled up in the shade of a tall tree.

"Why are we stopping?"

"I thought you might need a break."

"No, I'm fine." She patted Queenie on the neck.

Leaning forward, Zane crossed his forearms on the pommel. "You said you designed Web sites back home. Do you enjoy it?"

"Yes. very much. It's not only profitable, it's fun."

He shook his head. "Doesn't sound like much fun to me, sitting inside all day."

"I don't guess you've got a computer?"

"Who, me?" He glanced at the river and the hills beyond. "Not much use out here."

"Good way to stay in touch."

"Yeah? With who?"

She shrugged. "Your family." Me, when I go back home.

Dismounting, he lifted her from her horse. "I like staying in touch like this," he drawled as he let her slide slowly down the front of him until her feet touched the ground.

She swallowed hard, her body tingling where it touched his. "Your way is good, too."

His hands lingered at her waist; his gaze burned into hers. "You can't beat the personal touch."

She looked up into his eyes, those deep black eyes that held secrets she yearned to uncover. "No, you can't…"

He drew her closer. "A computer can't deliver a message like this," he said, and claimed her lips with his.

It was like drowning in dark chocolate, she thought, warm and sweet and irresistible, a combination no female could resist, though resistance was the farthest thing from her mind. She melted against him, vaguely aware of his arms going around her, one hand sweeping up and down her back, wanting and restless.

His mouth moved over hers, slow and deliberate, as if he wanted to brand her lips with his, or memorize the touch and the taste and the texture of them.

She kissed him back, her lips parting a little in invitation, a thrill of pleasure rising up within her as his tongue teased hers. Heat spread through her, stealing the strength from her legs as it moved downward, pooling in the deepest part of her.

A soft moan of regret rose in her throat when he drew away.

"Damn, woman," he murmured. "Do you know what you're doing to me?"

She smiled a knowing smile.

He blew out a sigh that seemed to come from the depths of his soul. "Come on, pretty lady," he said, releasing her. "As much as I'd like to continue this, I've got work to do."

Tempting as it was to put his hands on her and lift her into the saddle, he wisely let her mount the horse on her own. He didn't want to be responsible for what might happen if he touched her again.

Once she was settled in the saddle, he swung onto the back of the bay, acutely conscious of the woman riding beside him. He was playing with fire, he thought bleakly. He had no business getting involved with her or with any other woman. No right to even think about it until he got his own life straightened out.

Carly noticed more and more cattle as the day went on. It made her nervous, riding among them. They were so *big*. Some lay in the shade, quietly chewing their cud. Others grazed on the lush grass. They looked up at her through liquid brown eyes as she followed Zane across the river again. Now and then she saw a horse in among the cows.

"Mustangs," Zane said. "We round them up from time to time and cut out the best of the young ones."

Carly nodded. She had seen her fill of mustangs Saturday night, thank you very much.

Taking her camera from the case, she snapped several pictures of the cows and the countryside. She even managed to take a couple of Zane when he wasn't looking.

As they rode on, she couldn't help thinking that while times had changed in the past hundred and fifty years or so, the land was probably pretty much the way it had been in the 1800s. She tried to imagine how it must have been back then, when horses were the primary mode of transportation and Zane's ancestors roamed the Great Plains. She slid a glance at him, trying to imagine him clad in little more than a breechclout and feathers.

He looked over at her just then, one brow raising inquisitively. "Something wrong?"

"What? Oh, no, I was just…" Her voice trailed off. Suddenly embarrassed at the turn of her thoughts, she drew her gaze away from his.

"Come on, what's wrong?"

"Nothing, really."

"Uh-uh. So, why were you looking at me like my face just turned blue?"

She shook her head. "How long until we get where we're going?"

"Another two hours or so. Come on, girl, spit it out."

She blew out a sigh of resignation. "If you must know, I was trying to picture you…I mean…I was…can't we just forget it?" she asked desperately.

"Not now we can't."

He wasn't going to let her off the hook. "I was just wondering what you'd look like wearing buckskins and, you know, feathers."

A slow grin spread across his face, and then he laughed out loud. "I could show you, if you like."

"Never mind."

"Hey, I was just trying to help."

"You have stuff like that?"

"Sure. Over at the rez. My mom insists I attend a powwow now and then." He grinned at her. "I might be a cowboy on the ranch, but I'm all Lakota on the rez."

"I've never been to a powwow, although I saw one on

TV. Lot of Native Americans dancing in fancy costumes, right?''

Zane nodded. ''You just missed one.''

''Bummer. I would have liked to see you dance.''

''Would you?''

She nodded, her heart pounding like a trip-hammer. She had a feeling he wasn't talking about dancing anymore. His next words convinced her.

''I'll dance for you,'' he said, his voice sinfully seductive, ''if you'll dance for me.''

It was a good thing she was sitting on a horse, she thought. Had she been standing, she wasn't certain her legs would have held her up. Clad in a dark red shirt, faded jeans, scuffed boots and a black Stetson, he looked good enough to eat.

Her mouth went dry as he reined his horse closer, and now they were practically thigh to thigh. If he leaned toward her, and she leaned toward him… She licked her lips as the whole world narrowed down to the two of them.

Carly wasn't sure afterward how it happened. One minute she was leaning toward Zane, her heart pounding in anticipation, and the next her horse was running flat out over the prairie and she was hanging on for dear life.

She sawed on the reins, trying to slow the mare down, but to no avail. The countryside went by in a blur. Her hat flew off her head. Wind stung her eyes. Oh, Lord, if her horse fell now…

And then Zane was riding up alongside her. Like a hero out of a Western movie, he pulled his horse up beside hers. His arm snaked out. He grabbed her around the waist, lifted her from her horse and plopped her down in front of him. She clung to his arm around her waist, relief washing through her as his horse slowed to a trot, a walk, then came to a halt.

''You all right?'' he asked.

She nodded, then collapsed against the hard wall of his chest. ''What…what happened?''

"I'm not sure. I think maybe Queenie got stung by a wasp. There was one flying around."

She closed her eyes. She might have been killed, and all because a wasp stung her horse.

Zane wheeled his horse around and rode back the way they had come.

"Where are we going?" Carly asked, clutching at his arm.

"To get your hat. It's new, isn't it?"

"Yes."

"Looks good on you." After retrieving her hat and settling it firmly on her head, he turned the horse around. "Now to get your horse."

"How will you find her?"

"She won't have gone far. As soon as she realizes she's okay, she'll stop and graze."

Sure enough. They found Queenie calmly munching on a patch of clover a few minutes later.

Dismounting, Zane caught the mare's reins and ran his hand over her rump.

"Is she all right?" Carly asked dubiously.

"She'll be fine. Just scared her, is all." He glanced at her over his shoulder. "You game to get back on?"

"I guess so."

With a nod, he transferred her from his horse to Queenie's back. He spent a lot of time lifting her, she mused, but she wasn't complaining.

The rest of the ride passed without incident. When they reached the river, she saw what was causing the problem. A large branch had broken off a nearby tree and fallen across the river. Two large boulders held it in place. Other smaller branches and debris had piled up behind it, slowing the flow of water.

Zane dismounted and ground-tied his horse. Carly did the same. Grabbing her camera, she followed him to the edge of the river.

"I'll have to drag that large branch out of there." He

pulled his gloves from out of his back pocket and slipped them on, then removed the rope coiled around his saddle horn.

She quickly snapped several pictures as he shook out a loop and swung it over his head.

With a flick of his wrist, he sent the rope sailing through the air. It landed around the end of the branch and he gave a sharp tug, pulling the loop tight.

"Stay back," he warned. Stepping up and into the saddle, he urged his horse away from the river. The rope grew taut and he urged the horse onward.

The branch, which was about as big around as she was, started to move, then caught on one of the boulders.

Muttering an oath, Zane swung out of the saddle and walked back to where Carly was standing.

"I'm going to have to wade in and see if I can dislodge it," he said. "Think you can handle my horse?"

"Are you sure you want me to? I don't seem to have much luck with them."

He chuckled. "You're not going to let a couple of little setbacks slow you down, are you?"

"I don't know." She eyed the big bay warily, then shrugged. "Promise she won't run away with me?"

"I promise."

"All right."

"Good girl."

She set the camera on a rock, then walked over to the bay. The bay mare was a couple of hands taller than the buckskin mare and it took her several tries to pull herself into the saddle.

When she was settled, she looked over her shoulder. Zane was already in the water, which was about hip deep. He removed the smaller branches and tossed them on the shore, then backed away from the branch.

Standing with his legs spread wide for balance, he hollered, "Okay, go!"

She touched her heels to the bay's flanks and the big

horse moved forward, straining against the drag on the rope.

"Keep going," Zane hollered. "Go on, a little more... good."

Zane was walking toward the shore when there was a sharp crack, and the branch broke in half.

Carly stared in horror as part of the branch flew into the air.

And part of it struck Zane alongside his head. The water, which had been held back by the limb, rushed forward, sweeping Zane along with it.

Carly stared at the spot where Zane had been standing. With a cry of dismay, she wheeled the horse around and slammed her heels into the bay's flanks. With a snort, the horse took off running, half of the branch bouncing along behind them at the end of the rope.

Carly gave a sharp tug on the reins when she saw Zane sprawled on the riverbank. The bay came to an abrupt halt and only the fact that she was clinging to the saddle horn for dear life kept her from being tossed over the horse's head.

Leaping out of the saddle, she ran toward Zane, afraid of what she might find. Grabbing him by the arm, she rolled him over. There was a purplish bruise on the side of his head, but very little swelling.

"Zane. Zane!"

He moaned softly as he opened his eyes. "Do I know how to show a girl a good time, or what?"

"Are you all right?" she asked anxiously.

"Honey, I've been stomped by bulls bigger than that."

"This is no time for jokes. Are you all right?"

He lifted a hand to his head, winced as his fingers found the bruise. "I'm fine," he said. "That damn branch knocked me off balance and I just sort of drifted away on the tide."

She hovered nearby as he gained his feet, afraid he was

hurt worse than he wanted her to know, but he did, indeed, seem to be fine.

He ran a hand through his hair, slicking it back. "Damn, I lost my hat."

Untying the rope from the branch, he coiled it and looped it over the saddle horn.

He shook the excess water off his jeans, removed his shirt and his wet gloves and laid them out on a rock to dry.

Carly tried not to stare at him, but it was impossible. He had a great physique, like that of a bodybuilder, only he didn't get it by lifting weights. Those muscles were the result of hard physical labor. It was all she could do to keep from reaching out to touch that hard muscled chest, to keep from running her hands over his biceps.

"Are you hungry?" he asked. "Cookie packed me a couple of sandwiches and a thermos of coffee, and who knows what else."

"A sandwich sounds good," she replied.

He pulled a sack and a thermos out of one of his saddlebags and thrust them into her hands, then loosened the cinch on his mare and her mare, which, to Carly's surprise, had followed her. Zane tied both horses to a nearby shrub.

They found a shady place to sit. Carly opened the sack and pulled out three sandwiches, a bag of chips, a couple of apples, a knife and some brownies. She handed one of the sandwiches to Zane, then uncapped the thermos and poured some coffee into the cup.

She unwrapped her sandwich—roast beef, cheese, onions, lettuce, tomato, and avocado. "This sandwich is thick enough to feed both of us."

"Not a chance," Zane replied. "You're lucky I'm letting you have that one."

"Big eater, are you?" she asked, cutting the sandwich in half.

"You bet." He cocked his head to one side, wincing at the movement. "I bet you're one of those women who're always on a diet."

"You lose. I eat everything in sight."

His gaze moved over her, long and slow. She had a trim figure, slender but not skinny, with nicely rounded hips, a narrow waist and breasts that were just right. "You'd never know it by looking at you."

"Thank you, kind sir." She looked him over much the same way he had looked at her. "You're not so bad yourself."

"Why, thank you, ma'am." How long had it been since he'd let himself have fun, since he'd bantered words with a pretty woman? With any woman?

"You're welcome."

"I like a girl with a healthy appetite."

"Then you came to the right place."

She bit into her sandwich, warmed by the glow in his eyes, the easy repartee they shared. She liked that he smiled so often, that he had a sense of humor. That was one thing her old boyfriend had lacked in spades, along with honesty. Richard had told her he was divorced when, in fact, he was still living with the woman who was not only still his wife, but was pregnant with his child! She couldn't believe she had wasted three years of her life on the creep. Even worse, she couldn't believe she had never even suspected he was lying to her. How could she have been so naive? All the clues had been there, but she had refused to see them. Just thinking about him made her blood boil.

Taking a deep, calming breath, she booted Richard out of her mind once and for all, which was remarkably easy with Zane sitting there. The sun caressed his skin. She wished she could do the same.

Zane finished his first sandwich and reached for another. He unwrapped it and lifted it to his mouth, then looked at her over the top of it. "Do you want half of this?"

"I haven't even finished this one yet." Who could think of food when he was sitting there half-naked, his wet jeans molded to every line of his lower body, his long black hair framing a rugged face and gorgeous eyes? How could she think of food when all she wanted to do was gobble *him* up?

"Well, get busy, woman. I'm one up on you."

"Maybe I should give you the other half of mine."

"I can think of things I'd rather have."

She looked at him, the sandwich in her hand forgotten. She wanted to say "me, too" but she seemed to have lost the power of speech.

Zane started to reach for her and then shook his head. What the hell was he doing? He had been a fool to bring her out here with him. The more time he spent with her, the more he would miss her when she went back home. As much as he yearned to make love to her, he knew if he did, he would never be able to let her go. In spite of the strong physical attraction between them, they had nothing else in common. She was probably just looking for a summer fling anyway, amusing herself with the hired help, entertained by the novelty of spending time with a Native American. No doubt the time she spent with him would make for some entertaining stories when she went back to Los Angeles. He grunted softly. He couldn't understand why anyone would want to live in a city, any city.

His appetite gone, he dropped his untouched sandwich on the blanket, gained his feet and walked away from her. What the hell was he doing here? The last time he had played this game, it had turned his whole life upside down and left him with responsibilities he hadn't been ready for.

Frowning, Carly stared after him. What had just happened? Her appetite gone, she shoved the rest of her sandwich into the plastic bag, then gathered up the remains of their lunch and dumped it in the sack. She wanted to go after him, to ask him what was wrong. Instead, she sat there and watched him stroke his horse's neck. She wished she could see his face. Perhaps it would give her a clue as to what he was thinking, feeling.

After a few minutes, Zane shrugged into his still damp shirt, then picked up his gloves and jammed them into his back pocket. He tightened the cinch on his horse, then hers. Taking up the reins, he led the horses to where Carly was sitting.

"You ready to go?"

With a nod, she rose and brushed off the seat of her jeans.

Zane shoved the sack into his saddlebags, then swung into the saddle.

With a sigh, Carly pulled herself onto Queenie's back. After retrieving her camera, they started for home.

The ride back to the ranch seemed a lot longer than the ride out.

"Hey, girl," Brenda said, "how did it go?"

Carly plopped down on the chair across from Brenda and blew out a sigh of exasperation. "It went."

"Didn't you have a good time?"

"Yes and no. It started out okay, but then, all of a sudden, he just…I don't know."

Brenda lifted little J.J. to her shoulder and began patting his back. "I'm sorry."

"Well, it doesn't matter. How was your day?"

"Busy. Seems I never catch up." She brushed a kiss across the top of the baby's head. "He takes up a lot of time, for such a little thing."

Carly nodded. She knew next to nothing about caring for a baby.

"He's been fussy all day. Jerry thinks I should just let him cry a little, but I can't stand it. I remember my mom saying we all grew up way too fast. I had such a hard time getting pregnant, who knows, maybe I won't have any more kids, and if that's the case, well, I want to spend as much time as I can with this one."

"Well, I can't blame you. He's adorable." Leaning forward, she stroked the baby's cheek, marveling at how soft his skin was, wondering if she would ever have a baby of her own, a little boy with dusky skin and thick black hair….

She shook the thought from her mind. "I think I'll go up and soak in a hot bath. I've got aches and pains in places I didn't know existed."

Brenda laughed. "Long hours in the saddle will do that."

Carly forced a grin. "Now you tell me." No need to mention that the worst hurt of all was in the region of her heart.

"Are you hungry? We've already had dinner, but..."

"Don't worry about it. I'll get something later."

Up in her room, Carly sat on the edge of the bed and tugged off her boots and socks, then wiggled her toes.

Rising, she undressed and went into the bathroom. Standing there, watching the tub fill with water, she wondered what Zane was doing and if she would see him tomorrow, and what had happened between them today. One minute she'd been sure he was going to kiss her and the next he was a million miles away.

She poured some bubble bath into the water. She told herself it didn't really matter. She was going home next week and she would never see Zane Roan Eagle again.

Somehow, the thought of going back to L.A. only made her feel worse.

"Stop meddling, Brenda, it's none of your business."

Brenda pulled the covers up over the baby, then lightly stroked his hair. "But they seem so right for each other."

Jerry shook his head. "Right for each other? She's white, he's Lakota. She's a city girl, he's a cowboy. She reads *Cosmopolitan,* he reads the *Western Livestock Journal.* I can't think of two people more wrong for each other."

Turning away from the crib, Brenda jabbed her forefinger in her husband's chest. "Do I need to remind you that *you're* a cowboy, and *I'm* a city girl?"

"That's different," Jerry retorted, taking her in his arms.

"Oh? And just how is it different?"

"It just is."

"Because he's Lakota?"

"That's part of it. I don't think Carly would be happy living out here, and I know for a fact that Zane will never leave."

"He might."

"He has ties and responsibilities here you don't know about."

"What ties?" Brenda leaned back a little to get a better look at his face. "Tell me."

"I can't."

"Can't, or won't?"

"I promised him I wouldn't tell anyone, and that includes you."

"I thought we weren't going to have any secrets between us."

"This one isn't between us, sweetie. It's between me and Zane."

"Fine," she said, pouting. "Don't tell me."

"Stop worrying about Carly," he growled, nuzzling her neck. "You've got a man right here that needs some attention."

"Oh, I do, do I? And just what kind of attention do you need, cowboy?"

"Come with me, city girl," he said, backing her out of the nursery toward their bedroom, "and I'll show you."

The glow in his eyes made her forget about everything else.

Chapter Seven

"**I** need to run into town this morning," Brenda said. "J.J.'s wearing his last diaper. Do you want to come with me?"

Carly shook her head. She didn't feel like doing anything. She had tossed and turned all night, upset at the way she and Zane had parted the day before. Had she said or done something to make him mad? And if so, what?

"Carly, is something wrong?"

"No."

"Are you sure?"

"I'm fine, really. Do you want to leave J.J. here? I'll be glad to watch him."

"That's okay, but thanks for offering. Can I bring you anything?"

"A Milky Way?"

"Right. I won't be gone long." Grabbing the diaper bag and J.J., Brenda gave Carly a last worried look and then left the house.

Carly blew out a sigh. She probably should have gone with Brenda. They really hadn't spent a lot of time together, but she didn't think she would be very good company just now.

Rising, she went to the kitchen window and looked out, her gaze drawn to the barn.

She saw several cowboys milling around, some grooming their horses, some shoveling manure into a couple of wheelbarrows.

Her heart turned over in her chest when she saw Zane lead the big gray stallion out of the barn and into the workout corral. She recognized the horse. It was the one that had bucked so wildly only days before.

She watched as Zane saddled the horse then swung agilely into the saddle. He was easy on the eyes, she mused, thinking she would be content to stand there watching him all day.

If she went out there, would he be happy to see her? There was no denying the sparks that sizzled between them whenever they were together. Maybe she had read more into his sudden mood shift than was there.

And maybe not.

Chewing on her thumbnail, she watched him for another five minutes; then, turning away from the window, she went out the back door, determined to find out exactly where she stood with Mr. Zane Roan Eagle.

Zane knew Carly was there even before he caught a glimpse of her out of the corner of his eye. A change in the atmosphere. He grinned. A disturbance in the force. Whatever it was, he knew she was there, standing near the old oak to the left of the corral.

He sat up a little straighter in the saddle as he put the gray stud through its paces. With an effort, he put Carly out of his mind. The stallion demanded all his attention. The horse was still green broke and more than a little skittish.

One of the cowhands dropped something heavy inside

the barn. It made a resounding crash that sent the stud crow hopping to the far side of the corral.

Zane brought the stallion under control once again. "Easy, fella," he murmured soothingly. "Easy, now."

He rode the horse around the corral at a slow trot, then brought him down to a walk to cool him out, always aware that Carly was nearby, watching his every move. He hadn't expected to see her again after the way he had treated her the day before. He'd thought of sending her a note of apology, even considered going up to the house and telling her he was sorry, but staying away had seemed like the smart thing to do. Why pursue a relationship that didn't have a chance in hell of being more than a summer fling?

But then she moved away from the tree and approached the corral. His gaze met hers. Electricity flowed between them, hot and strong, and he knew that he couldn't let her go, that no matter what the consequences were, he wanted to spend as much time with her as possible.

Clucking to the horse, he rode over to where she was standing. She looked up at him, her expression guarded. He cursed softly, hating himself for putting that look in her eyes.

"I'm sorry, Carly."

She smiled, and it was like seeing the sun after a cold and bitter winter.

Dismounting, Zane led the gray out of the corral. He tossed the gray's reins to Poteet and then, heedless of the cowboys who stood nearby, gawking, he pulled Carly into his arms and kissed her.

"Can you forgive me?" he asked.

"Always."

Grinning, Zane looked over her head to where Poteet was standing. "If anyone wants me, you don't know where I am."

"Right," Poteet said, grinning back.

They spent the rest of the day out at the lake. Carly felt a little guilty for being there; it was the one place Brenda had wanted to take her. But the feeling didn't last long, not when Zane was there beside her.

Happiness welled up inside her. She had never felt like this before. She didn't know if it was possible to fall in love so fast, but she loved everything about Zane Roan Eagle, from the color of his skin to the way his eyes crinkled when he smiled. She loved his laugh and the sound of his voice. She loved his sense of humor. Loved the way he looked at her, as if she was the most beautiful woman in the world. Loved the sense of belonging she felt when she was in his arms.

She didn't know how Zane managed it, but he got the next day off, too. They packed a picnic lunch and spent the afternoon on his land.

"Don't you have to work?" she asked. They were lying side by side, watching a handful of fluffy white clouds drift across the sky.

"It doesn't matter when I work the horses," he replied. "As long as it gets done." He rolled over on his side, lowered his head and kissed the tip of her nose. "Since you've been here, the horses have been sleeping days and working nights."

She smiled up at him. "It really is pretty out here."

"Almost as pretty as you."

That deserved a kiss. Carly put her arms around him and they spent the next few minutes doing some hot and heavy making out before Carly pulled away.

"Wow," she said, her voice shaky.

He grinned at her. "Thank you, ma'am. Come on," he said, pulling her to her feet. "We'd better go cool off."

Hand in hand, they walked down to the lake. Sitting down on the grass, Carly pulled off her boots and socks, put her feet in the water and wiggled her toes.

Zane watched her a moment, then sat down beside her, pulled off his boots and socks and plopped his feet in the water. A few drops splashed up on Carly's face.

"You did that on purpose!" she accused.

"No way!" Leaning forward, he put his hand in the water and then flicked the drops in her face. "I did *that* on purpose."

"Oh!" Bending down, she splashed him back. "And I did *that* on purpose."

"You're in trouble now," he warned, a mischievous glint in his eye, and the next thing she knew, they were engaged in a lively water fight.

Her shirt was soaked when she cried, "All right, all right, I give!" She looked up at Zane, who was straddling her hips. "Uncle! Uncle!"

"Me mighty chief." His voice mimicked the way the Native Americans talked in old cowboy movies as he thumped his chest with his thumb.

"You're mighty heavy." She shook her head as water from his hair dripped onto her cheeks. "And mighty wet."

"You give 'um big chief heap big kiss," he said. "Me no take 'um scalp."

Laughing, she clasped her hands around his neck and drew his head down.

One kiss led to another and then another. By the time they came up for air, her shirt was nearly dry.

Later, Carly noted the way Zane's eyes lit up when he talked about his plans for the future, about the house he hoped to build, the horses he wanted to raise. She felt a dull ache in her heart as she listened to him, knowing some other woman would share the dream with him.

Carly spent Thursday afternoon helping Brenda get ready for Jerry's party.

"I wish you could stay longer," Brenda said. "It's been such fun having you here."

"I might be able to get another week," Carly replied. "I haven't taken a vacation since I started working for the company."

"That would be great," Brenda said enthusiastically.

"Jerry's mom will be home early Saturday night. She can keep an eye on J.J. for me and that will give us some time to spend together."

Carly nodded. It would give her another week with Zane, too.

The party was a big success. Jerry was suitably surprised and after the presents were opened and everyone had their fill of cake and ice cream, the guests went outside for the hayride. Carly couldn't help feeling a twinge of loneliness as she shrugged into her jacket. It seemed everyone had a partner except her. Even Jerry's maiden aunt had a date.

Carly was about to climb into the back of the last wagon when Brenda called, "Over here, Carly."

Climbing into the back of the lead wagon, she made her way forward to where Brenda and Jerry were sitting.

"We saved you a seat," Brenda said, scooting closer to Jerry.

"Thanks."

"You about ready to go, Mrs. Clark?"

A thrill of excitement rippled through Carly at the sound of his voice. Glancing over her shoulder, she saw Zane smiling down at her from the spring seat of the wagon.

"Any time you are," Brenda said.

With a wink, Zane faced front again. He clucked to the team and the wagon lurched forward.

Brenda leaned over to Carly. "You could ride up front with him, if you want," she whispered.

"Still matchmaking?"

"Yes, and aren't you glad?"

Carly gave Brenda a quick hug, and then climbed over the low back of the seat to sit beside Zane.

"This is my first hayride," she said, looking over at him. "Hope you don't mind if I sit up here, with you."

"Not at all, pretty lady," he said with a smile. "I'm glad for your company."

It was pleasant, riding through the night. A full moon

shone down on them, dappling trees and shrubs in silver. More stars than she had ever seen back home twinkled brightly overhead. Crickets serenaded them along their way, together with the clip-clop of the horses' hooves, the creak of wagon wheels, and the jangle of the harness.

But it was Zane who filled her senses. She was acutely aware of his nearness, his heat, his masculinity. His arm brushed hers when the wagon hit a bump in the road. His thigh pressed intimately against her own. The scent of his aftershave tickled her nostrils, his nearness teased and tempted her. She clenched her hands to keep from touching him, all too aware that Brenda and Jerry were sitting right behind her.

One of the guests had brought a guitar. Another had brought a banjo and the soft strains of a country song filled the air. When the musicians broke into "Take Me Home, Country Roads" people began to sing along.

Zane glanced over at Carly. "Don't you sing?"

"Not me. I couldn't carry a tune in a bucket. How about you?"

He shrugged. "I sing in the shower from time to time."

"How about pretending you're in the shower?"

"You askin' me to sing, Miz Kirkwood?" he drawled.

"I reckon I am."

The strains of "Country Roads" faded away. There was a moment of silence, then the guitarist began to play "Annie's Song."

After a moment, Zane began to sing quietly. As she'd suspected, he had a beautiful voice, deep and rich.

She had never had a man sing to her before and she suddenly realized why so many women were enamored with country crooners. There was something wonderfully intimate and romantic about looking into a man's eyes while he sang a love song, just for you.

All too soon, the song was over and they were back at the ranch.

Zane parked the wagon near the barn and set the brake.

Dropping to the ground, he lifted Carly from the seat, his hands lingering at her waist. She looked up at him, wishing he would take her in his arms. She felt a sharp stab of regret when he let her go. She had been so sure he was going to kiss her. And then she heard Brenda's voice. Only then did reality return, and with it the realization that they were not alone.

"There's a powwow tomorrow," Zane said. "I asked the boss for the day off. Do you wanna go with me?

"Oh, I'd love to!"

"Pick you up at eight."

Someone called Zane's name. Glancing over his shoulder, he called, "Hang on, I'm coming." Turning back to Carly, he gave her hand a squeeze. "I've gotta go."

She watched him until he was out of sight, then made her way back to the house where Brenda was serving coffee and doughnuts to her guests.

"Anything I can do to help?" she asked.

"No, we're just about done here. Did you have a good time?"

"Oh, yes."

Brenda smiled a knowing smile. "Jerry told me Zane's taking the day off tomorrow."

"He asked me to go to a powwow with him. Do you mind if I go?"

"Of course not. Have a good time."

"I feel guilty, spending so much time with him. I came here to see you."

Brenda waved her hand in a gesture of dismissal. "Forget it. I invited you here to have a good time, and it seems like you are. Besides, we've got all next week."

"Right. And maybe you and J.J. can come and visit me in L.A. when he's a little older."

"I'd like that," Brenda said. "Oh, we're planning to go out to dinner Saturday night after we pick up Jerry's mom from the airport. Sort of a combination welcome home for his mom and a birthday dinner for Jerry, since Saturday is his actual birthday. You'll come with us, won't you?''

"Sure. Sounds like fun," Carly said, but she was already thinking about tomorrow and spending the day with Zane.

Carly woke early Friday morning, butterflies of excitement fluttering in her stomach. She was going to a powwow with Zane. Would he be dancing? She certainly hoped so. She was dying to see him in feathers and paint.

Brenda, that sweet girl, had breakfast waiting for her when she went downstairs.

Carly was too excited to eat, but she didn't want to hurt Brenda's feelings, so she ate every bite. Hurrying back upstairs, she brushed her teeth, checked her makeup, grabbed her handbag and a lightweight jacket, and went back downstairs.

It was two minutes after eight when she reached the barn. Zane was standing beside his truck, waiting for her. A smile lit his face at her approach.

"Mornin'."

"Hi."

"You ready?"

"Yes."

He opened the door for her. She climbed into the cab, then slid across the seat and opened his door for him.

"What did Mrs. Clark say about your leaving?" he asked, slipping the key into the ignition.

"She told me to have a good time. Where are we going?"

"Over to the community college. There'll be drums and dancers there from a number of different tribes from around the country, including a drum from the rez. My mom came down with them."

"Are you going to dance?"

He looked at her and winked. "I might."

The parking lot was full when they arrived. There were Native Americans of all ages everywhere Carly looked, many of them in elaborate costumes. She could hear the sound of drumming even before Zane switched off the engine.

Hand in hand, they walked around the school toward the field. Flags flapped in the breeze. She heard a voice over the PA system announcing that the next event, the Men's Grass Dance, was about to begin. A man wearing Levi's, a blue shirt, a beaded vest, and a cowboy hat handed Carly a pamphlet and wished them a good day.

Zane and Carly were almost at the grandstand when a tall woman wearing a calico skirt, a vibrant green blouse and a turquoise necklace hurried toward them. There were silver bracelets on her wrists, silver hoops in her ears.

"*Cinks,*" she said, thrusting a bundle at him, "hurry, you're on next."

"Thanks. *Ina,* this is Carly Kirkwood. Carly, this is my mother, Irene Roan Eagle."

Carly stared at the other woman. She was lovely, with smooth, dusky-colored skin, hair the color of ebony and deep brown eyes beneath delicately curved brows.

"I'm pleased to meet you, Mrs. Roan Eagle."

Irene Roan Eagle looked up at her son, then back at Carly.

"Yes, it's nice to meet you, too, Miss Kirkwood," she said, though her tone indicated otherwise. "Zane…"

"Where's *neyho?*"

"He had to make a run to Georgia."

Zane looked over at Carly. "My dad works part-time driving a truck for one of the lumber companies," he explained.

"Oh."

"Zane." There was no mistaking the impatience in his mother's voice.

"Okay, okay. Carly, why don't you go with my mother? I've got to change."

Carly glanced at Irene Roan Eagle, certain the older woman wasn't any happier with the idea than she was.

Zane's mother led the way to the football field where the dancing was taking place. They passed several booths along the way. Most held Native American crafts—dolls, key chains, dream catchers, fans, flutes, kachinas, even knives and hatchets.

The grandstands were filled with spectators. Benches ringed the field. Irene Roan Eagle lifted a blanket from one of the benches and sat down. Sitting beside her, Carly took in the scene. Three men sat around a large drum. Carly glanced at the pamphlet the man had given her. On the front page there was an article on powwow etiquette, which said, in part, that while visitors might consider a powwow to be a form of entertainment, it was a celebration of fellowship and a sharing of cultures.

Reading on, she learned that the center of a powwow is the circle, which was to be treated with respect and honor. Outsiders were not to enter the circle unless invited to do so. Photos were to be taken only after asking permission; during some ceremonies, visitors might be asked to turn off video cameras and tape recorders and to refrain from taking still photographs.

She thought it interesting that visitors were cautioned not to pick up a feather if they saw one fall from a costume, but to let the dancer know immediately as feathers were considered to be symbolic and, in the case of an eagle feather, sacred.

The last paragraph informed her that the people singing and beating the drum were called "The Drum." It came as no surprise for her to realize that outsiders were not to touch the drum.

A few minutes later, the dancers for the Men's Traditional Dance were called on to the field. Carly stared at the costumes, which were breathtaking. It took her a few minutes to pick Zane out from the others. He wore some sort of long fuzzy thing on his head, a breastplate over a long-sleeved white shirt, a breechcloth, which fell past his knees, a feather bustle, and leggings. There were bells tied to a leather strap around his knees. A choker circled his neck. Yellow paint zigzagged across his cheeks. He carried a feather fan in one hand.

She glanced at the pamphlet in her hand, which described some of the dances and also described the kind of clothing the dancers wore. Carly learned that the thing on Zane's head was called a roach, and that porcupine hair was preferred because it was longer and added to the dancer's movements. In the old days, warriors had worn a breastplate for protection against arrows, a neck choker for protection against knives. Traditional dancers often wore a single bustle containing eagle feathers, which, as had been mentioned earlier, were considered sacred to Native Americans since they believed that eagles carried the prayers of the people to their creator.

A short time later, the drumming started and the men began to dance.

Carly forgot everything else as she watched Zane. She had never seen anything more fascinating in her life. He looked foreign and frightening and sexy as all get-out.

The article had mentioned that the Traditional Dance was the oldest form of dance in the Indian culture, and that the costumes were often thought to represent animals that the creator had put on the earth.

It went on to say that the steps were sometimes characterized as being similar to the movements of a prairie chicken. Carly had no idea if this was true, since she had never seen a prairie chicken. The article mentioned that the movements could also be interpreted as those of a warrior stalking game or doing battle with an enemy.

Watching Zane, she could easily imagine him creeping up on some enemy warrior. His footsteps were light, accompanied by the tinkling of the bells that sounded with every footstep. The movements told of warrior actions—hunting, stalking the game, battling an enemy. There was applause when the dancing ended and the dancers left the field. Carly smiled when she saw Zane walking toward her.

"You were wonderful," she said, rising.

"Thanks." He looked down at his mother. "How'd I do?"

"Lila waste."

Leaning down, he kissed his mother on the cheek. "Thanks, *Ina.* I need to go change."

"Aren't you dancing anymore?" Carly asked, disappointed.

"No. I just came to support the school. They're earning money for new football uniforms. Come on, let's go get something to eat. *Ina,* are you coming?"

"No. Linda Three Feathers is dancing in the next event and I told her I would be there."

"All right. Maybe we'll see you later."

Irene Roan Eagle's gaze drifted over Carly, and then she nodded. "Maybe."

Zane squeezed Carly's hand. "I'll go change and be right back."

"Okay."

"I don't think your mother likes me," Carly remarked when Zane returned from changing out of his dance costume. "Is it because I'm not Lakota?"

"I'm sure she likes you fine. She's just a little shy around strangers."

Carly doubted that, but didn't argue the point. "What's fry bread?" she asked, pointing to a sign a short distance away.

"Just what it sounds like. Bread that's deep fried." He led her to a stand beneath a sign that read "Indian Tacos" and ordered two tacos and two Cokes.

Indian tacos turned out to be made with fry bread and stuffed with beef, pinto beans, shredded lettuce, shredded American cheese, diced tomatoes and onions.

"So," he said, jerking his chin toward the field, "what did you think?"

"It's wonderful. I'd love to watch some more, if you don't mind."

"I don't mind, come on."

They found a seat in the grandstand. Carly was enthralled by it all. She watched the Hoop Dance and the Men's Fancy Dance, and then watched the women do the Cloth Dance, the Fancy Dance, the Buckskin Dance, and the Jingle Dance. There was also a Gourd Dance. They were all beautiful to watch.

And always, she was aware of Zane beside her, of the beat of the drum, which seemed to echo the beat of her heart whenever she looked at him, whenever his hand brushed hers.

Later they wandered through the booths and Zane bought her a necklace that held a tiny turquoise eagle.

It was late afternoon when they bid his mother goodbye and left the field.

"I'm sorry she doesn't like me," Carly said as they walked toward the parking lot. "I have a feeling she'd be happier if you were dating Linda what's-her-name."

"But I don't like Linda what's-her-name," he said with a wry grin. "I like you."

She smiled at him. "And I like you."

The look that passed between them warmed her clear down to her toes.

When they reached Zane's truck, he plucked a flyer off the front window. He read it quickly, then looked over at Carly. "Are you in a hurry to get back?"

"No, why?"

He waved the paper in the air. "There's an auction not far from here. Bob Murphy is offering some of his stock. Do you wanna go?"

"Sure."

They reached the stockyards about forty minutes later. Carly looked around with interest as they made their way around corrals filled with horses and a few donkeys.

"Doesn't look like we missed much," Zane remarked. "The corrals are still full."

Entering the weathered wooden building, they found a

seat in the stands. There was an arena in the middle of the floor. An auctioneer stood on a platform at one end.

"All right, ladies and gents," the auctioneer said, "this next string is from the Hampton ranch not far from Amarillo."

Carly leaned forward as a cowhand led a high-stepping bay horse into the arena. He led the horse around the corral so that everyone could get a good look at it.

"This here mare's six years old, gentle as a lamb."

"She's pretty," Carly said.

"Bowed tendons," Zane said. "A bad buy."

The PA crackled to life. "I need a hundred-dollar bid," the auctioneer said. "A hundred dollars, who'll give me a hundred dollars...got a hundred, got a hundred, who'll make it two...got two, got two, lemme hear three, three, got three...who'll make it four?"

The mare went for twelve hundred and fifty dollars.

Carly got an education on horses as the evening wore on. This one had popped knees, that one was too high in the withers, another was sickle-hocked, a fourth was sway-backed.

"This next string comes from Bob Murphy," the auctioneer said. "If you know anything about horses, you know old Murphy breeds some of the best."

"Take a look at this one," Zane said as the handler led a pretty sorrel into the corral. "Her conformation is near perfect. See that? She carries her head just right, ears alert, deep chest, good slope to her shoulders." He nodded to himself. "Good croup, well-muscled hindquarters, nice back..."

He broke off as the auctioneer said, "First up is a two-year-old filly. She's prime, gents. Pretty as a pup in a field of clover. Check that conformation. She's the best we've seen all day. We're gonna start the bidding at five hundred dollars. Five, I need five, who'll give me five? Five, five, got five, who'll make it six...six, got six, need seven."

Zane raised his hand.

"Seven, I've got seven, who'll make it eight...eight, eight...I've got eight...going for nine, nine..."

Zane raised his hand again.

"Got nine, nine, who'll make it a thousand...one thousand...do I hear a thousand? Yessir, a thousand, got me a thousand, who'll make it eleven? Eleven, eleven..."

Zane's hand went up again.

"Eleven, I've got eleven, do I hear twelve? Twelve, twelve....ladies and gentleman, this mare's a steal at eleven hundred dollars. There's twelve, thank you, sir, do I hear thirteen? Thirteen, thirteen, looking for thirteen."

Again Zane raised his hand.

The bidding went on for another twenty minutes and when it ended, Zane had the high bid at twenty-three hundred dollars.

"A steal," he told her as they went to settle his bid.

"If you say so."

"This is a memorable moment." He jerked his head in the mare's direction. "She's gonna be the start of my herd."

Warmth filled her heart, as much from his smile as from the fact that she was there to share the moment with him. "Are you going to bid on any others?"

"Can't afford it." He shook his head. "I can't really afford this one, either, but it was too good a deal to pass up. Why don't you wait here? I'll be back as soon as I settle up at the desk."

"All right."

She watched him walk away, noticing, as she did so, that she wasn't the only female watching.

They left as soon as he returned.

"I had a great time today," she said.

"Me, too. I wish you didn't have to go home so soon."

"Oh! Didn't I tell you? I e-mailed my boss last night and asked if I could stay for another week, and he said yes."

He looked over at her, his dark eyes alight. "That's terrific."

"I think so. Will I see you tomorrow?"

"I don't know. I'm supposed to take one of our mares over to the Double Z. The boss wants to breed her to one of Zimmerman's studs."

"Will it take all day?"

Zane shrugged. "She's in season, so we might try breeding her tomorrow, although it'd probably be better if we let her settle in for a day or so. She's never been bred before. Either way, I need to hang around a while, make sure she's all right, you know? And I've got to go pick up that mare I bought at the auction, too."

She nodded, disappointed that he hadn't asked her to go with him.

"How about dinner tomorrow night?"

"I can't. I told Brenda I'd go to the airport with them to pick up Jerry's mother. We're going out to dinner afterward." She sighed. "Maybe Sunday?"

Zane shifted from one foot to the other. "Yeah, maybe," he murmured, knowing, even as he did so, that it was impossible. His Sundays belonged to Katy.

Taking Carly by the hand, he changed the subject.

Chapter Eight

Carly couldn't help feeling a little blue when she got up on Saturday morning. She tried to tell herself she was being silly. Just because she wasn't going to see Zane was no reason to be depressed. She had spent all day with him yesterday, and she would see him again on Monday. Besides, she had come here to see Brenda, not fall in love with some cowboy....

Love! Where had that come from? Even as she tried to tell herself it was impossible to fall in love so quickly, she knew it was true. She loved Zane Roan Eagle. The thought made her as giddy as a schoolgirl with her first crush.

Brenda was in the living room nursing J.J. when Carly went downstairs.

Brenda lifted one brow when Carly entered the room. "Well, you look almighty happy this morning," she remarked. "Did you win the lottery or something?"

"No, nothing like that." Carly ran her fingertips over the necklace Zane had bought her at the powwow. She tried to stop smiling but couldn't.

"You gonna let me know what's got you grinning like the cat who ate the canary?"

"Nothing, really. I'm just..." Carly shrugged. "Just happy. So, what are we going to do today?"

"Whatever you want, but we have to be back by six to pick up Edna from the airport." Brenda looked thoughtful for a moment. "I was thinking of driving over to the Double Z sometime today. They've got a mare for sale that I'd kind of like to buy."

"Sounds like fun." Carly sat down on the other end of the sofa. "I'd love to go."

Brenda studied her a moment, and then grunted softly. "Your enthusiasm wouldn't have anything to do with the fact that a certain cowboy is going over to the Double Z this morning, would it?"

"Of course not," Carly said, trying to sound nonchalant. "Why would you think that?"

"Gee, no reason, except that the two of you have been practically inseparable. If Jerry didn't like Zane so much, he probably would have fired him for goofing off the past two weeks."

Carly's smile disappeared in an instant. "Zane's not in trouble, is he? Jerry wouldn't really fire him?"

"No, no, of course not. I was kidding. In spite of all the time Zane has spent with you, he's still doing his job, though where he finds the time, I don't know."

Relief washed through Carly. She was pretty sure Zane would never forgive her if he lost his job because of her.

"All right," Brenda said, rising. "Let me go change the baby's diaper and put on some lipstick and I'll be ready to go."

The Double Z was even bigger than Brenda's ranch. A long winding driveway lined by tall trees led up to the ranch house. Another road veered off to the right and led to the barns.

Carly was quick to notice that Brenda parked her truck

next to Zane's. A horse trailer with the Clark logo was hooked to the back of his truck. Brenda got J.J. out of his car seat and they walked toward the barn.

"I wonder what's going on over there?" Carly said, pointing toward a corral surrounded by people.

"I don't know," Brenda said. "Let's go see."

Carly slid in between two tall, lean cowboys, peered between the rails of the corral and smiled. She should have known. The man seemed to be the center of attention wherever he went.

Zane was on the back of a big black horse that was bucking for all it was worth.

"Oh, my," murmured Brenda, who had managed to get in beside her. "Can that man ride, or what?"

"I thought he came here to see about breeding one of your horses," Carly said.

"Yeah, that's what I thought, too," Brenda replied, but Carly wasn't paying any attention. Her whole being was focused on Zane. She noted the width of his shoulders, the way his muscles bunched and flexed, the narrow patch of sweat along the vee in his back. He had lost his hat and his long black hair whipped back and forth. He looked as wild and rugged as the horse, and just as beautiful.

The men gathered around the fence cheered loudly as the horse bucked one last time and then, surrendering the fight to the man in the saddle, trotted docilely around the corral.

Carly cheered, too, felt her cheeks grow hot when Zane looked in her direction.

He winked at her, and then swung agilely out of the saddle.

A rather rotund man in Levi's and a Western-style jacket ducked into the corral. "Well done!" he said, clapping Zane on the shoulder. "Well done! I didn't think anyone could break that outlaw."

Another man followed the first one into the corral. "Didn't I tell you Zane could break anything on four legs!

Come on up to the house, Mac, and let's sign those papers before you change your mind about selling that stud.''

The man called Mac smiled jovially. "Zane, you come, too. There wouldn't be any sale if you hadn't proved that stud could be ridden. I reckon that's worth something.''

Zane nodded and followed the two men out of the corral. As he passed Carly, he lifted one shoulder and let it fall, as if to say *What can I do?*

As the crowd around the corral thinned, a short stocky man tipped his hat at Brenda. "Hello, Mrs. Clark, I didn't see you.''

"Hi, Frank. I came to have another look at that mare.''

"Sure, come on, she's in the barn.''

Carly followed Brenda and Frank into the barn, stood back while the man opened a stall door and led out a pretty chestnut mare.

"She's got great conformation,'' Frank said, leading the mare up and down in front of Brenda. "Good bloodlines.''

"She's five years old, right?''

"Right.''

"Do you mind if I try her out?''

"Help yourself. I'll saddle her up for you.''

"Thanks.''

Frank saddled the mare and they went out to the corral. Brenda turned to Carly. "Will you hold J.J. for me?''

"Sure.'' Carly took the baby, then stood outside the corral, watching as Brenda put the mare through its paces.

Brenda rode as if she had been doing it all her life. Carly watched enviously, wondering if she would ever ride as well. Maybe it was something you were born with, like curly hair or green eyes.

At the sound of footsteps, Carly turned to see Zane walking toward her.

At the sight of him, her heart seemed to beat a little faster, the sun seemed a little brighter, the world a little better.

"Hi.''

He smiled at her. "Hi."

He hadn't expected to see her today, couldn't help noticing how good she looked with a baby in her arms. He had a sudden mental image of her holding a baby with tawny skin and black eyes. His baby.

He cursed under his breath, wondering where that thought had come from, and then he shook his head. Who was he trying to kid? She hadn't been out of his thoughts for more than a minute since he had bumped into her at the fairgrounds.

"That was some ride," Carly said.

He grinned at her. "Yeah, well…" He shrugged. "Zimmerman wanted to buy the stud for breeding, but the stud had been running wild and hadn't been ridden for a couple of years. He asked me if I thought I could ride him."

"And you had to give it a try."

"Yeah." His grin widened. "You know what they say, ain't a horse that can't be rode…"

"Or a cowboy who can't be throwed," Brenda said, reining up alongside them.

"That's what they say," Zane agreed.

"Where's our mare?" Brenda asked.

"She's over in the other barn, settling in. Zimmerman wants to have a go at breeding her later this afternoon, so I thought I'd hang around."

"Good."

Zane jerked his chin at the mare Brenda was riding. "How do you like her?"

"I love her. She rides like a dream. I'm gonna take her. Bring her home with you, will you?"

"Sure."

Dismounting, Brenda exited the corral and handed the reins to Frank. "Zane's going to bring her home for me. Tell Zimm I'll bring him a check first thing in the morning."

"Yes, ma'am." Tipping his hat, Frank led the mare back to the barn.

"I think we'll breed her to Jerry's stallion," Brenda said to Zane. "What do you think?"

Zane nodded. "Should make for a great foal."

"I think so, too. Carly, are you ready to go?"

"What? Oh, sure."

"See you at home, Zane," Brenda said.

He touched his forefinger to the brim of his hat. "Yes, ma'am."

"Bye," Carly said.

His gaze caressed her, soft as a sigh, warm as the sun shining down on her. "See ya."

Carly smiled, then hurried after Brenda.

Carly woke early Sunday morning. She went downstairs, expecting to see Brenda and Jerry. Surprisingly, the kitchen was empty. Or maybe it wasn't so surprising, she thought as she put the coffee on. Edna's plane had been delayed last night. By the time her flight landed and they picked up her luggage, it was after ten. They had stopped on the way home to grab a quick bite to eat. When they got back to the ranch, no one felt like going to bed and they had stayed up and watched a late movie.

After drinking a cup of coffee and eating a slice of buttered toast, Carly left the house. She wandered around the yard for a few minutes, pretending she wanted some fresh air when all she really wanted was to go down to the barn and see Zane. She was only going to be here one more week and she wanted to spend every minute she could with him.

Summoning her nerve, she headed for the barn. A grizzled old cowhand was sitting outside, mending a piece of harness, when she arrived.

"Howdy, miss," he said, smiling. "Kin I help you?"

"I was looking for Zane."

"He ain't here."

"Oh." She didn't have the nerve to ask where he was. "Well, thank you."

She tried not to be hurt that he hadn't wanted to spend what must be his day off with her.

Brenda was in the kitchen when Carly returned to the house.

"Hi," Brenda said. "I thought you were still sleeping."

"No, I...I went for a walk."

"Any place in particular?"

"All right, if you must know, I went down to the barn looking for Zane, but he wasn't there."

"It's his day off. I forgot to tell you."

"I thought the cowboys had Saturday nights off?"

"They do, all except Zane. He always takes Sundays. Do you want to come to church with us?"

"No, I don't think so, but I'd like to go along for the ride. Maybe do some shopping."

"Most everything's closed on Sundays," Brenda said. "The only stores open are the gift shops that cater to the tourists."

"That's all right."

"Okay," Brenda said. "We'll be leaving right after breakfast."

Brenda and Jerry dropped her off on the corner near the ice-cream parlor.

"We'll pick you up here in an hour or so and go out to lunch, okay?"

"Sounds good to me."

She watched them drive away, then wandered down the sidewalk, pausing now and then to peer into one window or another. Twisted River didn't offer much in the way of shopping. There was a small department store, a drugstore with souvenirs in the window, a barbershop, the movie theater, a motel and a couple of restaurants. The post office and the bank shared a building. There was a used car lot and a Ford dealership.

She was about to cross the street when she saw Zane at the far end of the block. He hadn't seen her and she spent a pleasant few moments watching him. Several women who passed him on the street also sent appreciative glances in his direction, and who could blame them. He was stunningly handsome, with his dark skin and long black hair. He wore a pair of black Levi's, a black and white shirt, and a gray Stetson.

She was thinking how surprised he would be to see her when a pretty little girl with long black hair emerged from a battered old Chevy truck and ran toward him.

"Daddy!" she cried, and hurled herself into his arms.

He lifted the girl high in the air, laughed at her squeal of delight, then gave her a bear hug.

Carly ducked back into the shelter of a doorway as a woman with long red hair stepped out of the car and walked toward Zane. He smiled and kissed her on the cheek and then the three of them disappeared into the movie theater.

Feeling suddenly sick to her stomach, Carly stared after them.

Zane Roan Eagle was a married man. And a father.

She walked blindly down the street to where she was supposed to meet Brenda. Married. He was married. Why hadn't Brenda told her?

She stared into the distance, her thoughts in turmoil. He had kissed her. He was married. She had kissed him back, hadn't wanted to stop….he was married, married, married…

She didn't know how many times Brenda called her name before she heard it. Opening the car door, she slid into the back seat next to Edna and closed the door.

"You okay?" Brenda asked, glancing over her shoulder. "You looked like you were in a trance."

"I'm fine."

Brenda looked at her dubiously for a moment but apparently decided not to pursue the matter, at least for the time being. "We thought we'd drive into the city for lunch. Is that all right with you?"

"Yes, sure. Whatever you want."

Brenda frowned but didn't say anything else.

Carly stared out the window, only half listening to the conversation in the front seat. Brenda turned up the volume on the radio. It was a country station, naturally. Carly had never been a big country fan. Most of the songs were the sad, somebody-leaving-somebody kind of songs and the one playing on the radio was no different. Zane had sung to her the other night. She had listened to the lyrics, imagining they had been written just for her, that he had meant every word. What a fool she had been!

She forced all thought of Zane Roan Eagle out of her mind while they were at the restaurant, determined not to let him spoil the time she had left with Brenda and Jerry.

They walked around the town after lunch. Brenda bought a new dress; Carly bought a Texas T-shirt for herself, sent a postcard to her mom and dad, and one to her sister. Edna picked out a cowboy outfit for J.J. and when Brenda admired a silver bracelet, Edna insisted on buying that, as well.

It was near dark when they returned to the ranch.

As they pulled into the driveway, Carly saw Zane getting out of his truck down near the barn. Pain twisted in her heart at the sight of him.

His gaze met hers when she got out of the car. He started toward her but she turned on her heel and went into the house without a backward glance.

Zane stared after Carly, puzzled by the look of accusation he had seen in her eyes.

He tried to think of what he might have done or said yesterday that could have upset her, but nothing came to mind. She couldn't be mad because he hadn't kissed her goodbye, could she? He shook his head. That couldn't be it.

He was tempted to go after her, but he couldn't. The Clarks were good people and treated him right, but no matter how friendly they were, he was acutely aware of the

line between the boss and the hired help. He would see
Carly tomorrow afternoon. Time enough then to find out
what was bothering her and make it right.

He blew out a deep breath. They had a lot to talk about.

"Leaving?" Brenda exclaimed. "But you're supposed
to stay another week!"

"I know, but…I need to go."

Brenda sat down on the edge of Carly's bed. "All right,
spill it. You moped around all day, looking like you'd lost
your best friend. But I'm your best friend," she said with
a wry grin, "so that can't be it. What's wrong?"

"Nothing. I'm just…just homesick, that's all."

Brenda cocked her head to one side, her eyes narrowed
thoughtfully. "I know you better than that, Carly Marie
Kirkwood. It's Zane, isn't it? What happened?"

"Nothing."

Brenda crossed her arms over her chest. "You might as
well tell me, 'cause I'm gonna hound you until you do."

"Brenda…"

"Did he do something? Say something?"

"He didn't do anything. For heaven's sake, I hardly
know the man. I just want to go home and spend a few
days at the beach before I get back to work, that's all."

Looking hurt, Brenda stood and moved toward the door.
"All right, girlfriend, if that's the way you want it."

"I'm sorry, Bren." She smiled to take the sting out of
her words. "Ranch life just isn't for me."

"When are you leaving?"

"Tomorrow afternoon. My flight leaves at noon. Do you
think you could drive me to the airport? If you can't, I'll
call a cab."

"Of course I'll drive you."

"Thanks."

Later, alone in her room, Carly fought the urge to cry as
she packed her clothes. She wouldn't cry for him. She
wouldn't! He didn't deserve a single tear, but they slipped

down her cheeks anyway. How could she have been so wrong about him?

She tossed and turned for hours and when she finally fell asleep, her dreams were filled with images of a dark-haired man with eyes as black as a midnight sky and smooth coppery skin. When she tried to run away from him, he ran after her. And tagging at his heels were dozens of black-eyed boys and girls, all screaming, "Daddy! Daddy!"

She woke feeling irritable after a restless night. Dressing quickly, she packed the last of her things, then carried her bags downstairs.

Brenda and Jerry were sitting at the table.

"Are you sure you won't change your mind?" Brenda asked.

"I'm sure." Carly set her bags down by the back door, then poured herself a cup of coffee. She sipped it slowly, her heart aching. She would have loved to spend another week with Brenda, but she couldn't, not now. She had let Richard make a fool out of her. She wasn't going to make the same mistake twice.

Jerry glanced at his watch. "We'd better go."

"All right." Carly rinsed her cup and placed it in the sink.

"Call me when you get home," Brenda said.

"I will."

Carly hugged her friend. "Thanks for having me."

"Anytime, you know that."

Feeling dangerously close to tears, Carly nodded. She gave Brenda one last hug, then picked up her bags and left the house. She kept her gaze straight ahead, refusing to look back at the barn to see if he was there.

Home. She was going home, back to the bright lights and big city where she belonged.

Chapter Nine

Where was she? Zane slipped a halter over the head of the gray stud and led the horse out of the barn. Tying the stud to the hitching post, he plucked a brush out of the bucket and ran it over the gray's back, his gaze constantly turning toward the house, hoping to see Carly. She never missed her riding lessons.

He finished grooming the stud, checked its feet, gave it a carrot, then led it back into the barn, and brought out the little buckskin mare Carly had ridden. He patted the mare's neck, remembering the day he and Carly had spent together out by the lake, the way she had felt in his arms, the touch of her, the taste of her. Lord, he had kissed a lot of women in his day, but none of them had stirred him the way Carly did.

He hadn't meant to let her get under his skin, but she had. He knew only too well that she wasn't cut out for ranch life any more than he was cut for living nine-to-five in the city. But no matter how many times he told himself they weren't right for each other, he couldn't stop thinking of her, couldn't stop wanting her. Couldn't stop imagining the two of them together. Nights, when he lay in his cot thinking about the house he hoped to build next year, it was Carly he imagined sharing it with him.

He looked up at the ranch house again. She should have been here by now. Had something happened to her? Was she sick?

He ran the brush over the mare's neck one last time, then tossed the brush into the bucket.

He had never gone up to the main house on anything but ranch business, but he couldn't wait any longer. He had to know if Carly was all right.

Brenda Clark opened the back door at his knock. "Hi, Zane. Is something wrong?"

"No, ma'am, I was just wondering…that is…" He cleared his throat. "Miss Kirkwood didn't show up for her lesson today and…"

Mrs. Clark sighed. "I'm sorry, I should have told you. Carly went home. She left this morning."

"I see. Thank you, ma'am."

Turning, he strode back toward the barn, his gut churning. She'd gone home. Just like that. Packed her bags and left without a word of goodbye. He swore a vile oath, then laughed bitterly. Why was he so surprised? Hadn't he known all along that she was just amusing herself with him? That he was no more than a diversion to pass the time? He could just hear her now, telling all her friends about the big dumb Lakota who had taught her how to ride a horse and amused her by singing to her on a hayride one summer night.

He slammed his fist against the barn door. What a fool he'd been, to think she was any different from the others. Maybe she didn't follow the rodeo circuit, but she was cut from the same cloth—just another white woman looking for a thrill.

Well, to hell with her! He didn't need her. He'd never needed anyone and he wasn't about to start now. But he couldn't forget the merry sound of her laughter, or the way she had looked at him, as if he was some kind of hero after he'd plucked her off the back of that runaway mare. He loved the way she said his name, the way she looked up at him, her deep brown eyes warm and soft with affection....

Damn!

He didn't know where she lived. He didn't even have her phone number in Los Angeles. But Brenda Clark knew. He glanced up at the house, then swore under his breath. He wasn't going up there again. If Carly had wanted to stay in touch with him, she would have left him a way to get in touch with her. It was up to her now. She knew where he was.

Striding into the barn, he threw a saddle on the gray stud. The horse needed a workout, and he needed to let off some steam before he exploded. A long ride would do them both some good.

Once clear of the ranch, he urged the gray into a lope, but no matter how far or how fast the gray went, Zane couldn't outrun the empty feeling that Carly's unexpected departure had left in his life.

Carly stared out the window of the taxi. Had the city always been this noisy, the streets this crowded, the air this thick with smog? She had always loved it here. Why did it suddenly seem so ugly, so alien?

When they reached her apartment, she paid the cab driver, grabbed her bags and hurried up the stairs.

Unlocking the door, she dropped her luggage on the floor, then opened the curtains in the living room and the kitchen. The apartment seemed smaller than she remembered.

Standing in the middle of the living room, she kicked off her sandals, then glanced around, wondering what Zane would think. The furniture was white wicker with cushions covered in a blue-gray print, the carpet was French-blue, the walls were off-white. A vase of dried blue flowers stood on the end table, along with a lamp and a silver frame that held a picture of her parents on their twentieth anniversary. A bookshelf held books and videos, her TV was in the corner, her desk and her computer were against the wall across from the door.

Zane. Lord, how could she miss him so much so soon? What she had felt for Richard was nothing compared to the love she felt for her Texas cowboy. As much as she loved her life in L.A., she would have given up her apartment, her job, her whole lifestyle, to be with him. Why couldn't he have just been honest with her?

Picking up her bags, she shook thoughts of Zane from her mind. Intent on a hot bath, a quick dinner and an early bed, she went into the bedroom and began to unpack. She stopped when she lifted her camera from the suitcase. Forgetting everything else, she removed the film, grabbed her car keys and drove to the drugstore. She dropped the film off at the one-hour photo booth, then drove to the market.

She did her shopping, stopped at the video store and picked up a couple of movies, then went to the drugstore to pick up her film.

Back at home, she carried her groceries inside and set them on the counter.

Grabbing the envelope with the pictures, she sat down and looked through them. And there he was. Zane, riding a bucking bronc at the rodeo; Zane, shaking out a loop, roping the deadfall in the river. Her favorite was a snapshot of Zane sitting on his horse. She had taken it without his knowing. Candid and unposed, the photo seemed to capture the very essence of the man. Next time she went to the drugstore, she would have it enlarged.

There were pictures of J.J., Brenda and Jerry, one of Queenie and one of Sam, as well as a couple of pictures of the ranch house and the land around it.

With a sigh, she put them all back in the envelope, all except the one of Zane on his horse. Looking at it made her ache inside. If she was smart, she would put this picture away with the others and never look at it again. But sometimes she just wasn't smart.

Propping the photo on her desk beside her computer, she went into the kitchen to put her groceries away.

"There has to be a way to get the two of them back together," Brenda said.

Jerry shook his head. "Forget it. They're like oil and water, honey. They just don't mix."

"Baloney."

Jerry blew out a sigh. "You're determined, aren't you?"

"Yes, I am," she said, smiling. "You know, I think I need to write to Carly."

Jerry looked at her, his brows drawing together in a frown. "Just what are you cooking up?"

"Me?" She batted her eyelashes at him with mock innocence. "Little ol' me?"

"Yeah, little ol' you."

"Well, I want to write to Carly, but you know, I'm all out of stamps...."

"Yeah?"

"So, I think I'll just give the letter to Zane and ask him to mail it for me when he goes to town on Sunday."

"The post office is closed on Sunday."

"But the market's open. He can buy stamps there, and then mail my letter."

Jerry shook his head. "I still don't get it," he muttered, and then his eyes widened with understanding. "Oh. I get it now."

"Took you long enough. Here, hold J.J. for a minute. I have to write a letter."

Zane stared at the envelope in his hand. It was addressed to Carly Kirkwood in big bold strokes. He read the address once and knew he would never forget it.

"You don't mind mailing that for me, do you?" Brenda asked sweetly.

"No, ma'am."

"Thank you, Zane."

He touched a forefinger to his hat brim, then turned away from the door. All the way to town, he told himself it didn't matter one little bit that he now knew where Miss Kirkwood lived. He wouldn't go to her even if she lived right next door to the Clarks. She had left him; he hadn't left her.

He bought some stamps and a six-pack at the market, dropped the letter in the mailbox out front, and then forced all thoughts of Carly Kirkwood from his mind. Sunday was his day to spend with his daughter and he wasn't going let anything spoil what little time they had together. Sliding behind the wheel of his truck, he drove to his ex-wife, Elaine's, house.

Katy burst out the front door and ran to meet him as she always did, her eyes lighting up as she flung herself into his arms.

"Daddy! I missed you!"

"I missed you, too, darlin'! How's my best girl?"

"She's growing like a weed. She's outgrown three pairs of jeans and two pairs of shoes in the last week."

Zane looked over his daughter's head to the woman standing on the porch. "Hello, Elaine."

She was as pretty as ever with her long red hair and vibrant green eyes. Eyes that had once glowed softly when she looked at him but were now as cold as emerald ice. Hard to believe he had once thought himself in love with her. Harder still to believe she had ever loved him. Clad in skintight red jeans and a low-cut tank top, she looked as sexy as hell as she descended the porch steps, her hips undulating provocatively, and he cursed his body's instant response to her feminine allure.

Reaching into the pocket of his jeans, he withdrew a

hundred dollars and thrust the bills into Elaine's hand. "Buy whatever she needs."

He smiled at Katy. "We're going over to the malt shop and then to the movies. I'll have her back by six."

Elaine kissed Katy on the cheek. "Have fun, sweetie. I'll see you later."

"Bye, Mom."

"So," Zane said, taking Katy by the hand as they walked toward the truck, "what'll it be today? A root beer float, or a hot-fudge sundae?"

"Can't I have both?"

He grinned at her. "Only if you promise not to tell your mom."

"I promise!"

"All right, how about a hot-fudge sundae now, and a root beer float with dinner after the movie?"

Katy looked up at him, her dark brown eyes twinkling. "Can we have spaghetti for dinner?"

"Whatever you want, honey."

It was during dinner that Katy asked the inevitable question. "When are you going to come and live with me and Mom?"

It was the same question she asked every week. He had explained to her once that divorced people didn't live together. He supposed he couldn't blame Katy for wanting her parents to live together, even though he knew she had no memory of the three of them living together as a family. She'd been a baby during the few months he'd lived with Elaine.

"Dad?"

Since she refused to accept "Never" for an answer, he replied the same way he did every time. "I don't know."

"We're having a father-daughter picnic next week at school. Can you come?"

"I'll be there."

"Promise?"

"I promise."

"Will you wear your black cowboy hat?"

He laughed. "Sure, if you want me to."

"Can you bring your horse?"

"I don't know if your teacher would like that."

"If she says it's okay, will you?"

"Sure."

Katy beamed at him.

When she looked at him like that, he was powerless to refuse her anything. It was a look that went straight to his heart and threatened to cost him a small fortune when she got a little older and learned how to take advantage of it.

After dinner, he dropped Katy off at home, once again promising her that he would be at the father-daughter picnic with hat and horse.

He was smiling when he pulled onto the highway.

It wasn't until he reached the turnoff that led to the ranch that Carly Kirkwood crept back into his thoughts.

Chapter Ten

Carly spent her first two days home at the beach working on her tan.

She drove up to Big Bear the next day and wandered through the shops. She had intended to buy a new sundress; instead, she bought a painting of an eagle soaring over a snowcapped mountain.

She called a friend and went to Disneyland, wondering all the while what Zane would think of the Haunted Mansion and Star Tours. He'd told her he had come to California. Had he brought his wife and daughter to the Magic Kingdom? She imagined Zane taking his little girl on the rides, smiling at his wife as they watched their daughter's face light up when she saw Mickey Mouse and Winnie the Pooh. The thought twisted through her like a knife.

Saturday night, she went to see Brad Pitt's new movie, but it was Zane's face she saw on the screen.

At home that night, she stared at his photo. What was he doing? Did he think of her at all?

Her emotions were in turmoil. One minute she missed him like crazy, missed him so much she told herself it didn't matter if he was married, didn't matter if he had lied to her, if only she could see him again, hold him again. Hear his voice. Taste his kisses. The next minute she hated him and wanted nothing more than to slap him silly for lying to her, for making her fall in love with him when he had no right to.

She stared at the phone, willing it to ring. Why hadn't he at least called and given her a chance to unleash the anger and frustration that was churning inside her?

She slapped her hand on the arm of the sofa. How could he call when she hadn't even given him her phone number? But that was no excuse. If he had wanted to call, he could easily have gotten her number from Brenda. And why would he want to call her anyway, when he was married to a gorgeous long-legged redhead with a flawless complexion and a cover model's figure?

"Damn you, Zane Roan Eagle," she muttered, and burst into tears.

She was glad when Monday morning came, glad to step back into the daily routine of work. It was good to be at her desk again, surrounded by things that were familiar, things that didn't remind her of him.

She waved and nodded to her friends, got caught up on all the latest office gossip, poured herself a cup of coffee and made her way to her desk.

She booted up her computer and for the next eight hours, she lost herself in her work. She didn't understand men, and probably never would, but she could understand html and applets just fine. Designing web pages was something she truly enjoyed, whether she was making a home page for a popular author, a health guru, or an actor whose star was on the rise.

At five o'clock, she shut down her computer and headed home.

One week followed another. She acquired five new clients. She got a raise and her own office. At work, life was good. She got through the days fine. As long as she kept busy, she was able to keep him out of her thoughts. But he crept into her thoughts every night. As soon as dinner was over and the TV was off and she was lying in bed, Zane Roan Eagle stalked the corridors of her mind. She relived every day they had spent together, every look and every touch, every smile. Every kiss.

She tried to escape him in sleep, but he was there, too, haunting her dreams—dreams that started with a kiss and ended with the two of them tangled in each other's arms.

Dreams she knew would never come true.

Zane looked at his watch for the fifth time in as many minutes. Where the heck was she? It was after seven o'clock. She couldn't still be at work.

He paced the sidewalk in front of her condo, wondering how anyone could be happy living in a city. The apartment houses were so close together, the occupants probably had to whisper to keep the people in the next complex from hearing their conversations. The sky was hazy with thick gray smog that burned his eyes and stung his nostrils. The freeways were clogged with cars.

He looked at his watch again—7:17 p.m.

He swore softly. Maybe she wasn't coming home after work.

Maybe she had a date. The thought made him swear again. He was going to feel like a first-class fool if he'd made the trip all the way out here only to find out that she was dating someone else.

He should have stayed home where he belonged. For three weeks he had resisted asking Mr. Clark for some time off. And with the passing of each day, Zane had grown more surly, more withdrawn. He hadn't really been aware of it until Katy asked him why he was so unhappy. He had started to tell her he wasn't unhappy but the words had died in his throat. Looking at the concern in his daughter's face, he realized she was right. He was unhappy. He had assured Katy that she wasn't to blame and that night, when he returned to the ranch, he took his courage in hand and went up to the main house to ask Mr. Clark for a week off. Zane had been certain Clark was about to refuse when Mrs. Clark jabbed her elbow into her husband's side.

To Zane's surprise, after Mr. Clark went back into the house, Brenda Clark had given him Carly's phone number, as well as her work number, pager number and cell phone number.

Now, pacing the sidewalk, he wondered if he shouldn't have called first. It might have spared them both a lot of embarrassment. With every passing moment, he became more convinced that he had been right all along. Carly hadn't been looking for anything but a summer fling. She probably had a steady boyfriend, and she was probably out with him now. Damn, damn, damn, he should have called her before he left the ranch. It would probably have saved him the cost of a flight to Los Angeles, not to mention the cost of a rental car and a motel room.

He was suddenly glad she wasn't home. He'd just get back in his ugly little rental car and get out of here while the getting was good.

He was striding toward the curb where he had left his car when he saw her. She was carrying a bag of groceries in one arm, and fumbling in her purse with her free hand.

He drank in the sight of her like a man dying of thirst, felt the pain in his heart ease for the first time in weeks.

"Carly." Her name whispered past his lips like a sigh.

And then she was there, standing in front of him, her eyes wide with surprise.

"What are you doing here?" Her voice was sharp enough to cut through solid oak.

"I came to see you."

She lifted her chin and narrowed her eyes. "Really? Why?"

Damn. This was going a lot worse than he had imagined. He wondered again what he had done or said to make her so angry. Try as he might, he couldn't think of any reason for her to be so hostile. When they had parted the Saturday before she left for home, she had looked at him as if she thought he could single-handedly hang the moon and the stars. Now she looked at him as if he had just crawled out from under a rock.

"Carly…"

She stared at him, then swept past him and headed for the steps that led up to her condo.

Instinctively he grabbed her by the arm. "Carly, dammit, wait a minute."

"Take your hands off me."

"Not until you tell me what put that burr under your saddle."

"If you think about it a minute, I'm sure it'll come to you."

He shook his head. "I don't know what you're talking about. Dammit, woman, make sense!"

She glanced past him, took a deep breath, and let it out in a huff. "We can't talk out here," she muttered, and jerking her arm from his grasp, she went up the stairs and unlocked the door to her apartment.

He followed her inside, his gaze quickly taking in the room and its furnishings, settling for a long moment on the photograph located on the desk beside the computer. He frowned, then grunted softly as he recognized the river in the background. She must have taken it when he wasn't looking.

"Mind if I sit down?" he asked.

She put the grocery bag on the kitchen counter. "Yes, I do. You won't be here that long."

He turned to face her, his arms crossed over his chest to keep from grabbing her again, whether to kiss her or shake her until her teeth rattled, he wasn't sure.

"I missed you." He hadn't meant to say the words out loud, but they spilled out, unbidden.

"Really?" She shrugged. "I hardly thought of you at all."

"Really?" He tossed the word back at her, then glanced pointedly at the eight-by-ten photo beside the computer.

She went to the desk and knocked the frame over so that it was facedown. "That doesn't mean anything."

"All right," he said, his own anger rising. "Spit it out. What's bothering you?"

"Nothing much," she said coolly, hoping he couldn't see the hurt beneath her attempts at a calm exterior. "Just the fact that you're a married man."

His arms dropped to his sides and he stared at her. "Married? Who told you I was married?"

"No one told me. I saw you with her."

He frowned. "You saw me? With her? When?"

"What difference does that make? I saw you together." She took a deep breath, blinking back her tears. She would not let him see her cry. "I saw you with...with your wife. And your daughter."

Zane shook his head. "We're divorced."

Carly stared at him. "Divorced?"

"Yeah."

"Why didn't you tell me?"

"I was going to, but..." He shrugged. "I never thought there was a chance that you and I..." He blew out a deep breath. "I never thought things would go this far between us."

She sat down on the sofa, hard. Divorced. Why hadn't he told her sooner? If he truly cared for her, how could he have kept from telling her something so important?

"How long have you been divorced?"

"Six years."

She frowned. "How long were you married?" His little girl couldn't be more than six or seven. He must have gotten divorced before the ink was dry on the license.

"I divorced Elaine when Katy was three months old. We were married a little less than a year."

"Why did you split up?"

He sat down in the chair across from her, his expression

bleak. "I met Elaine when I was on the circuit. She was young and cute and I was young and stupid." He shook his head ruefully. "She followed me from city to city and…" He spread his hands wide. "I finally took what she was offering."

Carly said nothing, just continued to look at him.

"She came to me a few weeks later and told me she was pregnant. Said she wanted money for an abortion. I told her to forget it, she's wasn't getting rid of my kid like that. She said I couldn't stop her, that she'd get the money somewhere else. I finally persuaded her to marry me and give me the baby. She said okay…" He blew out a sigh.

"After she had the baby, she fell in love with Katy and changed her mind. But she didn't like being married, so we got divorced. It made no difference to me. By then, all I wanted was my daughter. Elaine got herself a good lawyer. As things worked out, I pay her child support and I'm allowed to see Katy on Sundays and every other Thanksgiving and Christmas."

"She's a lovely child."

"I think so."

"Does Brenda know about all this?"

"No one on the ranch knows, except the boss. Elaine knows I love the ranch and riding so she won't let me take Katy there. I've never mentioned being divorced or being a father because I didn't want to answer a lot of questions that are nobody else's business."

"I can't believe you could keep a secret like that, that no one on the ranch ever saw you with Katy."

"We've been seen once or twice."

"And no one ever said anything?"

"No. Back in the old days, no one ever asked a man his name or where he hailed from or pried into his past. That hasn't changed much in these parts." He shrugged. "Anyway, the men never go into the city on Sundays, and most of the time Katy and I go someplace where we can be alone. She likes to fish and hike, things like that. It's easy to avoid being seen if you've a mind to. When she was younger, Elaine went out on Sundays and I spent the day at the house. It's only been the last couple of years that I've been taking Katy away for the day.''

"Oh." She couldn't think of anything to say. She loved him. He had lied to her, just like Richard. Not outright, not in what he'd said, but in what he hadn't said, and once again, she felt betrayed by the man she loved. He should have told her the truth right up-front, before she started to care, before he kissed her the first time.

"I can't believe you never mentioned her to me."

"I guess I wasn't ready to have this conversation. So,'' he asked quietly, "where do we go from here?''

"I don't know.''

"I thought about you every day,'' he said. "And every night.''

"You could have called and told me so.''

"You could have given me your number,'' he retorted. "You could have stayed and told me what was bothering you. It would have saved a lot of trouble.''

"I'm sorry,'' she murmured contritely.

"Do you want me to leave?''

She shook her head. It was the last thing she wanted. "No. Would you like to stay for dinner?''

He nodded. "Thanks.''

"Make yourself at home. Is spaghetti all right?''

"Sure.''

"It won't take long. The sauce is already made.'' Rising, she headed for the kitchen. "If you want to watch TV, the remote is on the coffee table.''

Zane stared after her. She hadn't thrown him out. He figured that was a good sign.

Picking up the remote, he switched on the TV, then sat back, his legs stretched out before him. He could almost pretend that this was his home, that Carly was his wife. He felt very domestic, sitting there, watching some foolish situation comedy while she fixed dinner in the kitchen. Lean-

ing his head against the back of the chair, he closed his
eyes. He hadn't had a real home since he left the rez. On
the circuit, he had stayed in cheap motels. On the ranch,
he bunked with the other hands. He had bought the house
Elaine lived in. Originally, he had planned for her to live
there until she had the baby. Once the baby was born,
Elaine was supposed to move out and he'd intended to live
there with his daughter. But then Elaine decided to keep
Katy, and Zane let her keep the house.

"Zane? Zane, wake up. Dinner's ready."

He opened his eyes to find Carly gazing down at him.
"Sorry," he muttered.

"Nothing to be sorry for. What would you like to
drink?"

With a shrug, he stood up. "Whatever you're having is
fine with me."

He followed her into the kitchen, sat down where she
indicated. Somehow, he hadn't expected her to be a good
cook, but she was. She served spaghetti (with homemade
sauce), French bread, a green salad and a slice of water-
melon. It was one of the best meals he'd had in a long
time, and he wasn't sure if it was the food or the fact that
he was eating it with Carly, or a combination of the two.

Their conversation was sporadic. She asked about
Brenda and the baby, about Sam and Queenie, and then fell
silent, but she couldn't keep her eyes off him any more
than he could stop looking at her.

When the meal was over, she began to clear the table.
"Would you like a cup of coffee?"

"Yeah, thanks."

She quickly put the dishes into the dishwater, then
poured two cups of coffee.

"Let's go into the living room, okay?"

"Sure."

He sat down in the same chair he had occupied before.
She handed him a cup of coffee, then sat down on the sofa.

"Carly, I asked you before. Now I'm asking you again. Where do we go from here?"

"I told you, I don't know. You lied to me."

"I didn't lie to you."

"All right, maybe it wasn't a lie, but you should have told me."

"You're right, I should have told you. I said I was sorry. What else do you want from me?"

She stared at him over the rim of her cup. What *did* she want? She was being unreasonable and she knew it, but she couldn't help how she felt, wasn't even sure how she felt. She had known him for such a short time, fallen so hard so fast. "How long can you stay?"

"I asked the boss for a week off."

"I'm no longer on vacation, you know."

"I know."

"Where are you staying?"

"A little motel not far from here. I thought maybe we could spend some time together when you get off work." He shrugged. "If you want to?"

"I'd like that."

"What time do you get off work?"

"Five."

"All right, I'll pick you up tomorrow night and we'll go out to dinner and maybe a movie, okay?"

"Okay."

Carly felt as nervous as a teenager going out on her first date as she got ready the next night. She changed clothes three times, then shook her head in exasperation. For goodness' sakes, this was Zane, not a stranger. But something had shifted in their relationship. He hadn't said he loved her, though his coming to see her proved that he cared.

She put on her lipstick, checked her hair. She was stepping into her shoes when the doorbell rang. With one shoe on and the other in her hand, she ran toward the door and opened it.

"Hello," she said, breathless.

His gaze moved over her. She wore a blue sundress with skinny little straps and one white sandal. "Hi, Cinderella."

She frowned at him a moment, then looked at the shoe in her hand. "Very funny. Come on in. I'm almost ready."

Sitting down on the arm of the sofa, she put her shoe on, then plucked a sweater from the back of the couch. "Let's go."

Downstairs, he opened the car door for her, held it while she climbed in, closed it softly. Rounding the car, he slid behind the wheel and put the key in the ignition, careful to look both ways before pulling away from the curb. If there was one thing he really hated, it was city traffic.

"Where would you like to eat?" he asked.

"Oh, I don't care. What are you in the mood for? Italian? Mexican? Sushi?"

"Sushi?" He grimaced. "Mexican sounds good to me."

"Great, I know just the place. It's just a few blocks from here."

"So, how was your day?"

"Same as always. What did you do?"

"Not much. Slept late. Had breakfast. Drove over to the Southwest Museum and looked around."

Carly nodded. The museum was one of her favorite places. It was the oldest museum in L.A. and had a number of exhibits, including collections of Meso-American and South American Pre-Columbian pottery and textiles, as well as Hispanic folk and decorative arts. The museum had four main exhibit halls featuring the native peoples of California, the Great Plains, the Southwest and the Northwest Coast.

"Turn left at the next corner," Carly said. "What did you think of the Museum?"

"Pretty impressive, especially that Cheyenne tepee and the samples of Indian clothing."

"There's the restaurant, over on the right."

Zane nodded. He pulled into the right lane, made a turn, and parked in the lot.

It was a small, family restaurant. Carly ordered a quesadilla and a Coke, Zane ordered a couple of tacos, two beef enchiladas and a beer.

He glanced around. "Nice place."

"Yes, I come here quite often."

He grunted softly, wondering if she brought all her dates here. The thought left a bad taste in his mouth.

The waitress brought them a basket of chips and a bowl of salsa. They talked of mundane things while waiting for their meal. Carly told him about her latest client, a young rock and roll star; Zane told her that Queenie missed her.

Carly laughed softly. "Don't be silly."

"I'm serious. She's been off her feed ever since you left. So have I."

"Is that right?"

"Yep. I've been wasting away."

The waitress brought their food just then. Carly lifted a brow as the waitress placed Zane's plate in front of him. Tacos, enchiladas, beans and rice.

"I take it you're making up for all the food you missed," Carly remarked with a wry grin.

"Yes, ma'am."

His smile wrapped around her heart.

After dinner, they decided against a movie; instead, they drove down to the beach and walked along the shore.

"Forgive me, Carly," Zane murmured, taking her hand in his. "I never meant to hurt you."

"I know." She moved into his arms, her hands stroking his back. "I know."

His kiss came as no surprise. She had been waiting for it, yearning for it all evening. He tasted of salsa and coffee and warm, wet desire and she leaned into him, wanting more, wanting all of him, his heart and his mind, his very soul.

"Carly…"

His hands skimmed over her back, her buttocks, slid between their bodies to lightly caress her breast.

She moaned softly. "I wish..."

"What do you wish?"

"Nothing." She drew back, aware that they weren't alone on the beach. She saw another couple walking hand in hand toward them, heard the sound of laughter as several teenagers ran past.

Zane looked down at her, thinking he had never seen anything more lovely than Carly Kirkwood in the moonlight, her eyes glowing with passion, her lips swollen from his kisses.

They walked on until they found a secluded place behind a pile of rocks. Out of sight of passersby, Zane drew Carly into his arms and kissed her again. Coming to L.A. had been the right thing to do, he thought as he drew her down on the sand. Somehow, they would work things out.

She made a soft, hungry sound in her throat as she pressed against him and for a time he forgot everything but the woman in his arms. Just holding her fired his desire, made his blood run hot and heavy in his veins. His hand stroked her back, slid lightly over her bottom to rest on her thigh. She quivered at his touch and he knew if they were anywhere except a public beach, they'd be out of their clothes and in a bed in a heartbeat.

As much as he wanted her, this wasn't the time, or the place. He kissed her again, hard and quick, then stood and reached for her hand.

"Come on, Cinderella," he muttered. "I'd better get you home so you can get some sleep."

She nodded, though sleep was the last thing on her mind.

Chapter Eleven

They went to a movie Tuesday night and to Medieval Times on Wednesday. It was one of Carly's favorite places. A feast without benefit of silverware, knights jousting, beautiful horses, ladies in long gowns, a wizard and a bit of magic. What more could anyone ask? Zane thought the dinner was a little on the skimpy side, but he had only praise for the horses and their riders.

On Thursday, they went to Disneyland. It was a weeknight, so the lines were short.

"I'll have to bring Katy here someday," Zane remarked as they left the Pirates of the Caribbean ride. "She'd love it."

"Maybe the two of you could come during Christmas vacation. I might be able to get a few days off then."

"Yeah, maybe. I'm not sure Elaine would let me take her out of the state."

"Oh. I didn't think of that."

They went on Star Tours, and Thunder Mountain, got dizzy on the teacups, played hide-and-seek on Tom Sawyer Island, laughed at the really bad jokes told by the guide on the Jungle Cruise, climbed the stairs of Tarzan's tree house, kissed on all the dark rides. She knew she would never be able to go through the Haunted Mansion again without remembering Zane's mouth on hers, his tongue teasing her lips, his hand caressing the inside of her thigh.

"Let's go on the merry-go-round next," Carly said. "It's one of my favorite rides."

They walked down Main Street and across the bridge to Sleeping Beauty's castle.

Zane lifted her onto the back of one of the horses, then swung his leg over the saddle of the one beside her. Leaning forward, he tapped his finger on her horse's neck.

"Don't reckon you'll have any trouble staying on this one," he said with a grin.

"Ha-ha," she said. "Very funny!"

It was near midnight when they walked down Main Street toward the exit. "I've been to Disneyland about a hundred times," Carly remarked, squeezing his hand as they waited in line for the tram to take them to their car. "But it was never this much fun."

The next day, at work, she was sitting in front of her computer, thinking about Zane and what a good time they'd had the night before when a delivery man approached her desk carrying a dozen of the most beautiful long-stemmed red roses she had ever seen.

He glanced down at his clipboard. "Carly Kirkwood?"

"Yes."

"Sign here." He handed her the clipboard and, after she had signed her name in the place indicated, he handed her the flowers. "Must be love," he muttered, and turned away.

She withdrew the card from the bouquet, smiled as she read Zane's note. *"You're more fun than Alice in Wonderland and prettier than Snow White and Cinderella put together. See you tonight. Love, Z."*

She buried her face in the flowers, inhaling the lovely fragrance. Tonight. She could hardly wait.

She left work early. Hurrying home, she put the roses in

two vases and placed them on either end of the mantel. She took a quick shower, brushed her hair and applied fresh makeup, then dressed with care in a pair of slinky black pants and a pale blue off-the-shoulder sweater.

She put a clean tablecloth on the table, fluffed the pillows on the sofa, turned on one of the lamps.

Going into the kitchen, she put the lasagna she had made the night before into the oven to heat, then put the glasses and silverware on the table, as well as a pair of candles.

Moments later, she heard his knock at the door. She took a deep, calming breath before she opened it. And there he was. Just looking at him made her heart skip a beat. Her cowboy. Clad in a Western shirt and jeans, his hat tilted low, he was, quite simply, gorgeous. His broad shoulders filled the doorway.

"Hi," she said, her voice a little breathy. "Come in."

Stepping inside, he closed the door, tossed his hat on a chair and then swept her into his arms for a quick kiss that left her knees weak.

"Hi."

"I hope you're hungry," she said.

"Starved."

"Good. I've been slaving over a hot stove all day."

He lifted one brow. "All day?"

"Okay, for an hour. Anyway, dinner's almost ready. Think you could help me with the salad?"

"Sure," he said, his voice gruff. "But it's not food I'm hungry for."

Wiggling her eyebrows, she said, "Later, big boy."

"So, what's for dinner?"

"Lasagna."

"Italian again, huh?"

"Hope you don't mind."

"Nope, it's my favorite."

"Mine too."

He followed her into the kitchen, watching the sway of her hips. She opened the fridge and he admired the way her slacks hugged her buttocks when she bent over to pull a head of lettuce out of the crisper.

She handed him a knife and while he cut up the lettuce, she pulled the other ingredients out and, in no time at all, the salad was ready.

Carly opened the refrigerator again. "What kind of dressing do you like?"

"Ranch, of course."

She glanced over her shoulder to find him grinning at her. "Of course," she muttered. She handed him a bottle of dressing. "Think you could put the salad and the dressing on the table for me?"

"Sure thing."

The lasagna was ready a few moments later. Carly picked up a couple of pot holders and pulled the pan out of the oven.

"Smells good," Zane remarked.

"Thanks. Think you could light the candles on the table while I dish this up?"

"Yes, ma'am, whatever you want."

Zane thought this was the best meal he'd ever eaten. Lasagna—homemade, she told him with a touch of pride—garlic bread, salad and cantaloupe.

"I didn't get any work done today," she remarked.

"Why not?"

A faint blush crept into her cheeks. "I spent the whole day thinking about you."

His grin was one of pure masculine pleasure. "I didn't get any work done either."

She made a face at him. "That's very funny."

"I was just trying to make you feel better."

"So, what did you do all day?"

"I drove down to the beach and walked around the pier. And thought about you." He reached into his pocket and withdrew a narrow white box. "Here," he said, handing it to her across the table.

"For me?"

"I don't see anyone else in the room. Open it."

She lifted the lid, revealing a silver charm bracelet. The single charm was of a horse, running. "Oh, Zane, it's lovely." She looked up at him and smiled. "So, which is it, Sam or Queenie?"

"Look at the horse," he said.

"Must be Queenie," she guessed, "since it's running."

"Right the first time."

She fastened the bracelet on her wrist. "Thank you. And thank you for the flowers. They're beautiful."

Putting her napkin on the table, she stood. Zane also rose. As if by a prearranged signal, they moved to the couch and into each other's arms. His lips teased hers, sending a rush of pleasure through every fiber of her being.

"More," she whispered. "More, more, more."

"My pleasure," he murmured. His arm tightened around her waist, crushing her breasts against his chest. His tongue swept over her lower lip, boldly dipped inside.

She moaned softly and pressed herself more fully against him.

"You're a good cook and a good kisser," he said. "What else are you good at?"

"You'll have to wait and see," she said. "I don't want to spoil the surprise."

He laughed softly and kissed her again. "I wish I could stay longer."

"Me, too. Why don't you move here?"

"I have a job in Texas," he reminded her. "And a daughter."

How could she have forgotten that? Even if he wanted to move here, he couldn't.

"How soon do you have to leave?"

"Tomorrow morning."

"Tomorrow? Can't you stay until Sunday?"

"I can't. I promised Katy I'd take her riding on my next day off."

"Oh. It must be hard, only seeing her once a week."

"Yeah, it is. I've been trying to talk Elaine into letting Katy spend her summers with me. I don't know why she's against it. She's always complaining about how hard it is to find a sitter. I think the only reason she says no is because she knows how much I'd love having Katy with me."

"That's awful."

"That's Elaine."

"I wish you didn't have to go."

He ran his knuckles over her cheek, brushed a kiss across her brow, then took a deep breath and blew it out in a long sigh. "I love you."

"You do?" She stared at him, unable to believe he'd said the words she had been longing to hear.

He nodded. "I think I loved you the first minute I saw you. I didn't want to. I tried not to, but…"

Happiness welled up inside her, as effervescent as champagne bubbles. "Oh, Zane, I love you, too!"

"Carly!" He crushed her close. "If I was to ask you to marry me, what do you think you'd say?"

She blinked at him. "Marry you? Me? Are you serious?"

"I seem to be. So, what would you say?"

She threw her arms around him and kissed him soundly. "I'd say yes!"

"What about your job? I have to tell you straight-out, I'm not in favor of long-distance romances."

"Oh, I can do what I do anywhere," she said, smiling. "All I need is a desk and a computer."

He nuzzled her neck. "How long do you need to plan the wedding?"

"I don't know. Are you in a hurry?"

"You'd better believe it."

"Well, I suppose at least a month…what will your daughter say?"

"I'm sure she'll love you as much as I do," he said, and hoped it was the truth. "So, a month from Saturday?"

"All right, but you'll have to help."

"Sure, what do you want me to do?"

"Find out if the church is available."

"That's all?"

"For now. If I stay with my current employer, we won't be able to have any kind of honeymoon, since I've already used my vacation time for the year…"

"So have I, but I'm not willing to wait any longer, so let's get married now. We can have a weekend honeymoon and then go on a real honeymoon sometime next summer."

"That sounds good to me. And if my boss doesn't want a long distance employee, then I'll just quit and start my own business and… Oh!" she exclaimed. "Wait until I tell Brenda. She was matchmaking the whole time I was there."

"She did a damn fine job."

Carly grinned. "Didn't she though? But, oh, she'll be impossible to live with. I'll never hear the end of it."

"What kind of ring do you want?"

"I don't know. Surprise me."

"Guess I'd better start building that house, unless you want to bed down in the bunkhouse with me and the men."

She made a face. "Start building, cowboy."

"Carly, I'll do whatever I can to make you happy."

"Then kiss me," she whispered. "Just kiss me."

He drew her close, feathering kisses on her brow, her cheeks, teasing her lips. Her arms crept around his neck. His hand roamed the length of her back, stroked her buttocks, lightly caressed her breasts.

"A month seems like a long time to wait," he said, his voice husky with longing.

"I know, but it'll go fast…" She closed her eyes, her body on fire for him. "I'll call Brenda…" She moaned softly as he trailed kisses along her neck. "And ask her to see about flowers and a cake…and…oh."

He looked down at her, his eyes smoky with desire. "I think I'd better go."

"Go?" She blinked up at him. "Now?"

"I won't be responsible for what happens next if I stay."

She loved him all the more for his honesty, and for his willingness to let her make the decision. Regretfully she moved out of his arms. Call her old-fashioned, she wanted to have something to look forward to on their wedding night.

"Will you call me when you get home?"

"What do you think?" Rising, he pulled her to her feet and into his arms once more. "Miss me a little, okay?"

"I already do." She locked her arms around his waist, wishing she didn't have to let him go.

"It's only for two weeks."

"Only?"

"It seems like a long time to me, too." He kissed the top of her head. "Behave yourself."

"Tell me," she whispered.

"I love you."

"I love you more."

He kissed her and kissed her again, then reached for his hat. "I'll be counting the days, darlin'."

"Me, too." She walked him to the door, stood on her tiptoes for one last kiss.

"Don't forget, call me as soon as you get home."

"I will." He smiled at her, and then he was gone.

Hurrying to the window, she stared down at the street. Moments later, he emerged from the building. She watched him open the door to the truck, his face momentarily lit by the dome light.

When he pulled away from the curb, she felt as though he was taking her heart with her.

Chapter Twelve

Zane got up early the following morning. After a quick breakfast, he dropped his car off at the rental agency, then waited in line to board his flight. After what seemed like an eternity, he was deemed safe and allowed to board.

He removed his hat, then settled down in his seat, smiling as he thought of Carly, who was probably just getting to work. He still couldn't believe he had proposed to her, or that she had said yes. He'd been gun-shy ever since his fiasco with Elaine. Of course, it hadn't been a complete disaster. She had given him Katy.

Just thinking of his daughter made him smile. He remembered the first time he had held her, the way her tiny hand had curled around his finger. Her skin had been incredibly soft and smooth, her hair as fine as dandelion down. She had looked up at him through deep blue eyes and stolen his heart. For Katy's sake, he had tried to make a go of it with Elaine, but Elaine hadn't been interested in settling down. He had thought of trying to prove that she was an unfit mother, but Katy thrived under her care. Elaine wasn't cruel. She wasn't abusive. And there was no law against leaving a child with a baby-sitter. To her credit, Elaine cut back on her drinking and didn't bring her lovers home. Katy had nice clothes, she was rarely sick, her attendance at school was almost perfect and so were her grades. It was obvious Elaine cared for their daughter.

Looking out the window, he stared at the clouds below. What would Katy think about his getting married? She wanted very much for him to live with her and Elaine and Katy was certain that if she was very good, her wish would come true. He should have told her a long time ago that no matter how hard she wished, it was never going to happen. But he hadn't wanted to hurt her.

He shook off his dreary thoughts. Maybe he was worrying for nothing. Katy was sure to love Carly once they got acquainted. After all Carly was young and pretty and fun to be with.

Holding to that positive thought, he closed his eyes and drifted off to sleep.

"Married?" Katy reined her little mare to a halt and looked up at her father. "That's great! When? What did Mom say when you asked her?"

"Whoa, girl," Zane said. "Slow down."

Katy nodded, her dark brown eyes shining as she obviously envisioned her wish coming true. "Can I be the flower girl? Will we live on the ranch with you?"

"Katy, will you please be quiet and listen to me?"

"Sorry, Daddy."

"I met someone a few weeks ago. Her name's Carly..."

Katy's eyes narrowed. "Is she going to be the flower girl?"

"Katy!" Zane exclaimed in exasperation. "Just listen!"

"All right!"

He leaned forward, his arms folded across the saddle horn. "Like I was saying, I met this woman and we fell in love...."

Katy stared at him in disbelief. "But you love Mom."

"No, I don't."

"Yes, you do! You told me that you did."

"I love your mother, Katy, because she gave me you. But I'm not *in* love with her. There's a big difference. Do you understand?"

"No."

Zane drew in a deep calming breath. He'd known this wouldn't be easy. He knew how much Katy wanted her parents to be together; he hated being the one to put an end to those hopes, but it couldn't be helped. "Carly will be here in a couple of weeks."

"Here? She's coming here?"

"Of course."

"I don't want her here."

"Katy…"

She shook her head. "I don't want her here!" she cried, and giving her mare a kick, she raced away.

Zane stared after her, his anger and frustration melting away as he admired his daughter's horsemanship. She rode like a true Lakota, her little body moving in perfect rhythm with her horse. Her long black hair flowed behind her like a battle flag.

Lifting the reins, he put his own horse into a lope. He had two weeks to change Katy's mind. Knowing her as he did, he didn't think it would be long enough.

Carly glanced at the calendar. Tomorrow she would be on her way back to Texas. Two weeks ago, it had seemed her last day at work would never get here and now, suddenly, it was here. She had mixed emotions about leaving. She loved her job, got along well with her co-workers. She was fond of her boss, who had agreed to a three-month trial period to see if it was feasible for her to continue working for the company from Twisted River.

The girls in the office had taken her out for a farewell lunch and given her a beautiful white nightgown and peignoir for her honeymoon, as well as a bottle of perfume and a pair of slippers.

Gathering up the last of her personal items, she thanked them again, promising to keep in touch via e-mail.

At home, she packed a few last-minute things in her suitcase, then took a long, leisurely bath. She had sold her condo, furniture and all, save for her computer, her portable TV, and a few other odds and ends that she had already shipped. She had notified the post office of her new address, notified the phone company she was moving, stopped the newspaper, closed her account at the bank. The day after Zane proposed, she had called her parents and her sister and given them the good news.

Of course, her first call had been to Brenda. Carly grinned, remembering how excited Brenda had been, and her shock at learning that Zane had been married before and had a daughter.

She glanced at the time. Zane would be calling soon. He had called her at least once a day every day since he left. Smiling, she washed quickly, slipped into her nightgown, made a cup of tea, then curled up on the sofa, the phone in her lap, to wait for his call.

She answered it on the first ring. "Hello?"

"Hey, darlin'."

Her insides seemed to melt at the sound of his voice. "Hi."

"So, you ready for the big move?"

"Yes." She was ready but, every now and then, she had doubts about moving to the country. She had no doubts about marrying Zane, though. "I can't believe we're getting married in two weeks! Married! Isn't that a beautiful word?"

He laughed softly. "I guess so. I never gave it any thought."

"Two weeks. I haven't even found a dress yet. And where are we going to live until our own place is built?"

"The Clarks said we could use the guest house out back."

"I didn't know they had one."

"It's fairly new. The Clarks built it for the boss's grand-mother. No one's lived in it since she passed away."

"She didn't die in the house, did she?"

"No. Anyway, it's furnished, more or less. I'll move my TV in there, and get a phone installed. They poured the foundation for our house today."

"Our own place," she said dreamily. "I can't wait. How's Katy?"

"Being as ornery as ever."

"What'll we do if she doesn't like me?"

"Let's cross that bridge when we come to it."

Carly twisted the phone cord around her finger. "She's gonna hate me, isn't she?"

"I hope not."

"Me, too. I wish you were here."

"Yeah? What would you do if I was?"

"Oh, I'm sure I could think of something," she said, smiling inwardly.

"Tell me."

"Well, I might kiss you."

"That's a good start. What else?"

"Kiss you again."

He chuckled. "You turning shy on me?"

"What would you do if you were here?"

"A lot more than kiss you."

"Soon," she said."

"Not soon enough," he said, his voice suddenly gruff. "I love you."

"I love you, too. What time's your flight due in?"

"Three."

"All right, I'll see you then. Sweet dreams, darlin'."

"You, too. Night."

"Night."

With a sigh, she hung up the receiver. Not for the first

time, she wondered what her family would think of Zane, what his father would think of her. She already had a pretty good idea what his mother thought. And what about Katy? Carly chewed on a fingernail. She didn't have a lot of experience with children, but she'd heard lots of horror stories from her girlfriends who had remarried and how difficult it could be to win the affection of the first wife's children. It had never occurred to her that she might one day find herself in a similar position.

Maybe she was worrying for nothing. After all, Katy didn't live with Zane. He only saw his daughter once a week. How much trouble could the girl cause?

With a shake of her head, Carly put thoughts of Katy out of her mind and went to bed, courting dreams of Zane and their upcoming wedding.

He was waiting for her when she got off the plane. With a glad cry, she ran into his arms. "I'm so glad to see you!"

"I missed you, too, darlin'."

"Show me."

He lifted one brow. "Here?"

"Here."

Lowering his head, he kissed her quickly.

She looked up at him. "You call that a kiss?"

"You're something else," he muttered, and drawing her up against him, he kissed her again, hard enough and deep enough so that there could be no doubt in her mind that he had missed her.

She stared up at him when he drew away. "Wow."

"Believe me now?" he asked with a wry grin.

"Oh, yeah."

"Good. Come on, let's find your luggage and get out of here."

She sat as close to him as she could get in the truck on the way home. She couldn't stop looking at him, couldn't believe that she was here.

He glanced over at her and frowned. "Something wrong?"

"No, why?"

"You're staring."

"Sorry." She shrugged one shoulder. "You're just so darn cute."

He shook his head. "Right. Do you want to stop and get something to eat?"

"Not really. I ate on the plane. Are you hungry?"

"No, I just thought you might be."

"Is Katy any happier about our getting married?"

"No." He looked at her and smiled. "Don't worry about it. She'll come around."

"I hope so."

She forgot about Katy when the ranch came into view. Zane had no sooner turned off the ignition than the back door opened and Brenda came hurrying toward them.

"Carly!"

"Hi, Bren. I sure didn't expect to be back here so soon."

Brenda beamed at her. "I never doubted you'd be back, not for a minute."

Carly looked at Zane and shook her head. "Didn't I tell you she'd be impossible?"

"Yeah." He kissed Carly on the cheek. "I'll carry your bags into the house."

"Thanks."

She was watching him walk away when Carly tugged on her arm. "Come on."

"I'm coming."

Brenda laughed. "I've got to admit, he looks good walkin' away."

"Doesn't he though? Brenda, I've got so much to do and so little time to do it in."

"Relax. Edna's going to watch J.J. for me on Monday so we can go into the city and look for a dress. I've got some pictures of cakes for you to look at. We can look at flowers on Monday, if there's time. You said Zane's already booked the church. What else do you need?''

"Nothing, I guess.''

By nightfall, it was as if she had never left. Her belongings were back in the guest room, she was wearing jeans and boots—real cowboy boots, this time.

She met Zane at the barn after dinner.

"I thought you'd like to see where we'll be living until our house is finished," he said.

"I would."

Hand in hand, they followed the path that led to the guest house. Zane opened the door and flipped the switch inside, flooding the room with light.

"Oh," Carly sighed. "It's lovely. Not at all what I expected."

"What were you expecting?"

"Well, I'm not sure. Nothing as nice as this."

It was a lovely house. The floor was oak, the walls were painted off-white, there was a bear rug in front of the hearth. The furniture was covered in a muted blue-and-burgundy print. There were several Western paintings on the wall.

She followed Zane through the rest of the house. There was a large kitchen with pale yellow walls and a window with an eastern exposure, two bedrooms with a shared bathroom between.

"Think you'll be happy here?" Zane asked, taking her into his arms.

She wound her arms around his neck. "I think I'd be happy anywhere with you."

"I'm glad you're here."

"Me, too."

"I think it was easier when you were half a country away."

"Why?"

His arms tightened around her waist. "We're here, all alone. There's a bed in the next room, and I want you so bad I can taste it."

The heat in his eyes stirred something hot and liquid deep within her. "I know, cowboy. I want you, too."

"Two weeks." Resting his forehead against hers, he groaned softly. "I'm not sure I can wait that long, Carly." He blew out a sigh and moved away from her. "Come on, we'd better go for a walk. That bed is far too tempting."

Grinning, she went outside to wait while he turned off the lights.

Chapter Thirteen

The next two weeks seemed to fly by. Carly found the perfect wedding dress, picked out a veil and shoes, lacy white underwear and a shimmery silk slip. She bought a garter with little blue flowers on it. They picked out flowers—white daisies for Carly, yellow ones for her attendants. Her sister, Diana, was going to be her maid of honor. Brenda was going to be a bridesmaid, of course. Carly had asked Mary, her best friend in L.A., to be her other bridesmaid, but Mary had had to back out at the last minute due to an illness in her family. Carly had asked Zane's cousin, Vanessa, to take Mary's place. Though she had only met Vanessa a couple of times, they had immediately hit it off.

Carly had ordered the cake. At Brenda's urging, they had decided to have the reception at the ranch. They rented several large canopies to provide shade. Carly's father sent her a check to cover the cost of the caterer, and told her they would be arriving the Friday before the big day. Carly was amazed that a wedding could be planned in such a short time.

She had met Zane's father and some of his cousins. Carly

had to admit, she had been nervous at meeting Zane's father, but Mr. Roan Eagle had quickly put her at ease, declaring he was glad that his son was finally settling down, then added that he thought they might be rushing things a bit. Zane told her later that his mother had asked him if they *had* to get married. She knew Zane's mother would have been a lot happier if he was marrying Linda what's-her-name, or some other Indian woman, but that was just too bad. Her own parents had also expressed some concern at her marrying a man she'd known such a short time, but in her heart, Carly knew she was doing the right thing and she refused to let anything Zane's mother or her own parents said make her think differently.

Carly had spent one Sunday with Zane and Katy. The atmosphere had been tense, to say the least. Katy refused to speak to Carly unless spoken to, answered in a dull monotone and asked to go home early.

And suddenly the big day was upon her.

She woke early after a restless night. She lingered in the shower, skipped breakfast. Brenda helped her with her hair, then they packed everything in the truck and drove to the church to dress.

Her mother and sister were already there, waiting. After exchanging hugs, they trooped into the bride's room to change.

Carly looked in the mirror while her mother pinned her veil in place. Helen Kirkwood was tall and slender with dark brown hair, pale blue eyes, and a sprinkling of freckles on her cheeks. On a sigh, she said, "Carly, you're lovely."

"Thanks, Mom."

"I always knew you'd make a beautiful bride."

Carly glanced at her sister. "What do you think?"

"You're gorgeous," Diana said with a wave of her hand. "You always were."

"Oh, stop. You were always the pretty one. None of the boys ever noticed me once they got a look at my older sister."

Helen Kirkwood looked at Brenda and shook her head. "They haven't changed a bit since third grade."

"Well, I don't know about that," Diana said, looking at herself and Carly in the mirror. "We've got breasts now."

Brenda laughed. Helen let out an aggrieved sigh.

Carly turned away from the mirror and began to pace the floor. "What if he doesn't show up?"

"What are you talking about?" Brenda exclaimed. "Of course he'll show up. He's crazy about you, anyone can see that."

"Katy hates me."

"She'll get over it."

"What if she doesn't?"

"Here, now," her mother said. "Stop fretting."

"Of course he'll show up," Diana said. "I saw the way he looked at you last night at dinner."

"How did he look?" Carly asked.

"Like he wanted to throw you over a horse and carry you off," Brenda replied with a leer.

Carly and Brenda looked at each other and laughed, only to fall silent as Katy and her mother entered the room.

Katy wore a long pink dress tied with a wide white sash. Her hair was pulled away from her face and tied at her nape with a white bow. Her expression was mutinous.

Carly took a step forward and extended her hand to Katy's mother. "You must be Elaine. It's…it's nice to meet you."

Elaine took her hand, briefly.

"This is my friend, Brenda Clark. This is my mother, Helen, and my sister, Diana Malone."

Elaine nodded at the three women, then turned to her daughter. "Behave yourself, Kate. I'll see you tonight."

"I want to spend the night with daddy."

"Not tonight."

"Why can't I? Tomorrow's my day with him. Why can't I spend the night?"

"Daddy will be going away for the weekend. You can stay with him next Sunday."

"But I want to go tonight!"

"Well, you can't. Now, behave yourself. I'll see you at home later."

"Aren't you staying?"

"No, I don't think so."

Katy glared at Carly, as though it were Carly's fault that her mother was leaving.

"Well," Elaine said, speaking to Carly, "good luck."

"Thank you."

Elaine left the room. A moment later, there was a knock at the door and Katy's father called, "They're ready when you are."

"See," Brenda said with a smirk, "he did show up."

Carly's father was waiting for her in the foyer. She thought he looked quite handsome in his tux. He had blond hair that was just going gray at the temples. His eyes were the same shade of brown as Carly's.

"You look wonderful, princess," he said, a touch of pride evident in his tone.

"Thanks, Dad."

"You all right? No second thoughts?"

"I'm fine." She glanced around. "Where's Vanessa?"

Brenda shrugged. "I don't know, maybe…"

Just then the doors opened and Zane's cousin rushed in. "Sorry I'm late. I had a flat tire!"

"You're not quite late," Carly said, smiling.

Vanessa smoothed a hand over her skirt, patting her hair. "Do I look all right?"

"Yes, fine. Vanessa, this is my sister, Diana. Diana, this is Zane's cousin, Vanessa."

The two women nodded at each other and smiled.

Vanessa expelled a deep breath, then bent down to hug Katy. "*Ishna*, how pretty you look!"

Katy muttered a sullen thank-you.

"Here we go," Brenda said as the music began to play. "You go first, Katy. Remember, walk slowly."

Placing her hand on her father's arm, Carly took a deep breath. This was it.

The doors opened.

Katy walked down the aisle, scattering white rose petals.

Vanessa went next, followed by Brenda and Diana.

Moving up to the doorway, Carly got her first look at the guests. Zane's family had turned out in force. They filled one whole side of the church, dozens of men, women and children with glossy black hair and coppery skin.

Her gaze moved to the altar. Zane stood there, flanked by three of his cousins. Just looking at him fairly took her breath away. Everything else—the people, the music, the flowers—all faded into the background as she walked down the aisle toward him.

She had never seen anyone who did more for a tux than her future husband. The black coat emphasized his tawny skin and black hair, made his shoulders seem broader, his legs longer. He would have done credit to the cover of *GQ*.

A slow smile curved his lips as his gaze met hers.

The minister spoke. Her father placed her hand in Zane's. The minister began to speak on the solemnity and sanctity of marriage.

Her stomach growled.

Zane looked at her, one brow raised.

"I didn't have any breakfast," she whispered.

He squeezed her hand. "You look beautiful."

"So do you."

"I love you."

"Then feed me."

Stifling a laugh, Zane looked up at the minister.

"Zane Roan Eagle, do you take this woman…"

Carly's heart swelled with love as Zane spoke the words that made her his wife.

She repeated her vows and then Zane was lifting her veil, claiming his first kiss as her husband.

He was smiling when he drew back. "Hello, wife."

"Hello, husband."

When they turned to face their guests, the minister said, "Ladies and gentlemen, may I present Mr. and Mrs. Zane Roan Eagle."

Carly glanced from side to side, pleased to see that everyone was smiling at them.

Everyone but Katy, who looked like she had just lost her best friend.

Outside, there were hugs and kisses from family and friends and then they posed for pictures while everyone who wasn't in the wedding party went to the ranch.

Carly felt as though thousands of hummingbirds were whizzing around in her stomach as she stood next to Zane, smiling for the camera. The photographer took pictures of her with Zane, her with her parents, her and Zane with his parents, and every other combination imaginable. Her stomach growled throughout until Brenda fished a dark chocolate Milky Way out of her handbag.

"Bless you!" Unwrapping the candy bar, Carly turned her back and wolfed it down while the photographer set up another shot.

Finally they climbed into the limo and drove to the ranch, where the party was in full swing. Carly sat beside Zane, who had his arm around her. Diana sat across from Carly. Katy sat beside Diana, sullen and silent.

Zane tried to get her to smile but to no avail. The girl didn't approve of her father getting married and it seemed she intended for everyone to know it.

The band was playing "Moon River" when they arrived. As soon as they caught sight of Carly and Zane, they broke into "Here Comes the Bride" and applause rippled through the crowd.

Carly had opted not to have a reception line. Instead, she

and Zane went from table to table, smiling and shaking hands, accepting the good wishes of friends and family.

When they found a moment alone, Carly tugged on Zane's hand. "I've got to have something to eat."

"Okay, wife," he said with a grin.

"Wife," she repeated, slipping her arm through his. "I sure like the sound of that."

"Me, too."

The servers beamed at them when they approached the refreshment tables.

Carly piled her plate high with potato salad, macaroni salad, green salad and a variety of fresh fruits.

Zane looked at her, one brow arched in a gesture she was growing familiar with. "Do you think you can eat all that?" he asked dubiously.

She grinned at him. "Just watch me,"

With a shake of his head, he followed her to the table reserved for the bridal party.

Katy wasn't eating, of course.

Zane looked at his cousin.

"I tried," Vanessa said with a shake of her head. "She says she's not hungry, that she'll eat at home, later."

Zane started to say something, then blew out a sigh. It wouldn't hurt Katy to miss a meal, and this was hardly the time or the place to make a scene. Instead, he stood up and offered his daughter his hand. "Come and dance with your old man."

For a moment, Carly thought Katy would refuse, but then she took Zane's hand and let him lead her to the dance area. Watching them, she hoped the time Katy spent with her father would relieve some of the tension.

"They look cute together, don't they?" Brenda asked. "I can't believe he's had a daughter all this time and I didn't even know it. That Jerry…" She shook her head. "Boy, did I tell him off."

"I can't believe how much she dislikes me."

"Well, you can't blame her, I guess…"

"What?"

"How would you feel if you were a little girl who only saw your daddy once a week and all of a sudden someone else moved in on your territory?"

"I never thought of it like that. I guess I can't blame her for feeling threatened. He's a good father." Something for which she should be grateful, she mused.

The song ended and Zane and Katy returned to the table. Katy sat down, her expression turning sullen when Zane asked Carly to dance.

Zane drew her into his arms. "How soon before we can sneak out of here and be alone?"

"Well, we should stick around long enough to cut the cake and do the garter thing."

He drew her closer. "And then we can go?"

"Well, you should probably dance with your mother, and I should dance with my dad..."

Leaning down, he nuzzled her neck. "And then can we go?"

She laughed softly. "Anxious, are you?"

"You could say that. I was never any good at waiting."

"All right, let's give it another hour and then we'll go."

He groaned. "Another hour."

"What about Katy?"

"My folks will take her home."

"And then we'll be all alone, just the two of us."

Carly rested her head on Zane's shoulder. "Just the two of us, at last," she murmured as he pulled onto the highway.

"About time," he growled.

"It was a nice wedding, don't you think?"

He grunted softly. "Only because you were there."

"Thank you. I think."

He slid his arm around her. "Sorry, honey. It's just that my first experience with marriage left me feeling pretty sour about the whole thing."

"Where did you get married last time?"

"Justice of the peace. Should have been the secretary of war."

"I hope this one lasts longer."

He gave her shoulders a squeeze. "I'm in it for the long haul this time, babe."

"You'd better be, 'cause I don't intend to ever let you go."

The thought made her smile.

She was still smiling when they pulled into the parking lot. The valet smiled at them. "Congratulations," he said.

Zane nodded. "Thanks."

People turned to stare at them as they entered the lobby and walked toward the desk. Carly had decided to wear her wedding gown to the hotel. It was a beautiful dress and she felt beautiful in it and since she probably wouldn't have an occasion to wear it again, she figured she might as well wear it as long as she could.

She stood beside Zane while he signed the register—Mr. and Mrs. Zane Roan Eagle.

The clerk grinned at them as he handed Zane the key. "Good luck."

A bellboy brought their luggage in from the limo and they followed him toward the elevators.

Carly knew she was blushing as the boy opened the door to the bridal suite.

He put the luggage down, Zane tipped him, and then they were truly alone.

Carly glanced around. "Nice room."

Coming up behind her, Zane slid his arms around her waist. Carly leaned back against him, reveling in his nearness, then slowly turned in his arms.

"So, Mr. Roan Eagle, what would you like to do?"

"Is that a trick question?" he asked, his dark eyes alight with mischief.

She laughed softly as she slid his jacket off his shoulders

and down his arms. "I know what I want to do." She tossed his jacket on the chair.

"Oh? What do you want to do?"

"I'd like a closer look at the man I married." She grinned impishly. "I want to make sure he's all there."

Zane pulled her hips up against his. "Trust me, darlin', it's all there."

"Do you just want me to take your word for it?" She began to unfasten his shirt. In moments, it joined his jacket on the chair.

"No." He sucked in a breath as she pulled his T-shirt over his head, then leaned forward to kiss his chest. "I think you should see everything for yourself."

"I was pretty sure you'd see things my way." She unfastened his belt and tossed it aside, began to unzip his trousers.

"Careful there," he warned, a husky tremor in his voice.

"Oh, I'll be careful."

He removed his shoes and socks and stepped out of his trousers. "My turn now?" he asked.

Carly nodded, her gaze fixed on his as he removed her veil and placed it on the foot of the bed. Unpinning her hair, he ran his fingers through it, loving the silky feel of it in his hands.

"You have beautiful hair," he murmured. Reaching behind her, he began to unfasten the long row of cloth-covered buttons.

Carly shivered with anticipation as his fingers moved down her back. She stepped out of her dress and petticoat and tossed them onto the chair.

Zane whistled softly. She looked vulnerable and beautiful clad in a lacy white bra and panties, hose and heels.

Drawing her into his arms, he kissed her until she was breathless, and then they fell back on the bed and finished undressing each other.

"You're beautiful," he murmured, his gaze caressing

her. "Remind me to send a dozen roses to Brenda in the morning."

"Brenda?"

"For introducing us," he explained.

Wrapping her arms around his neck, she drew him down beside her. "Better make it two dozen," she murmured, and then she forgot all about Brenda and everything else except the man beside her.

She let her fingers move over him, exploring every inch of his rugged masculine frame, loving the feel of his skin beneath her hands, the soft groan that escaped his lips when she caressed him, a groan that she echoed when he turned the tables on her and began an exploration of his own.

She was ready for him when he rose over her. She was glad now that she had waited for this moment, this man, glad she had not surrendered her virtue to anyone else, not even to Zane before they were married. This was right. This was the way it was meant to be, the way she had always dreamed of it.

She was startled when, abruptly, he drew back.

"What's wrong?" she asked, feeling bereft.

"Carly...you're still...you've never...?"

She smiled up at him, a slow, seductive smile. "No. Never."

"Sweetheart!"

The love in his eyes made the moment all the more wonderful, all the more beautiful.

He made love to her ever so tenderly, every touch, every kiss, an affirmation of his love for her, his delight in knowing that she was his, and only his.

She was drifting on a warm sweet cloud, happier and more content than she had ever been in her life, when she became aware of a heavy weight resting on her stomach.

Opening her eyes, she saw Zane sleeping beside her. He was lying on his stomach, one arm flung across her stomach. She noted the bristles that shadowed his jaw, the thick stubby length of his lashes, the fullness of his lower lip. A slow warmth crept through her as she thought of the previous night, of the joy she had found in his arms. His skin looked very brown against the white sheets. Unable to resist, she ran her fingertips along the line of his spine, past his narrow waist, over his taut buttocks.

"I'll give you an hour to stop that."

She gave a little start, then grinned down at him. "I thought you were asleep."

He rolled onto his side and drew her up against him. "Were you planning to ravish me while I slept?"

"Maybe." Her tongue skimmed his lower lip.

"Careful, now, pretty lady."

"Oh, I'll be careful." She dropped feathery kisses on his cheeks, his brow, the tip of his nose, the cleft in his chin. "Is that careful enough?"

"Too careful." With a growl, he rolled her onto her back and rose over her.

"And just what do you want?" She looked up at him through the veil of her lashes.

"I don't know. What have you got?"

"Did you forget already?" she asked with a pout.

His lips twitched in a grin. "I've got a terrible memory. Maybe you'd better show me again."

"Maybe you'd better take notes this time." Putting her hands behind his head, she drew him down toward her until their lips were only a kiss apart. "We start here…"

It was much later when they went downstairs to check out. Once that was done, they went into the hotel dining room for breakfast.

"It's almost time for lunch," Carly remarked, glancing at the menu. "What are you going to have?"

"I'm so hungry, I think I could eat everything on the menu."

A waitress filled their coffee cups and took their order.

"What do you want to do today?" Zane asked.

"I don't care. Anything you want is fine with me." She glanced at the pretty silver horse charm on her bracelet and smiled, remembering how pleased she had been the day Zane had given it to her. "Do you think I could have a horse of my own?"

"I don't see why not."

"I wonder if Brenda would consider selling Queenie. It would be nice to have a horse I'm already familiar with. Zane?"

"Sorry, darlin', did you say something?"

"Nothing important. Where were you just now?"

"Oh, I was thinking about Katy. She looked so unhappy last night and…I'm sorry. What were you saying before?"

"It doesn't matter. Do you want to go see Katy?"

He shrugged. "Of course, but we've only got a one-day honeymoon—"

"I don't mind sharing you with your daughter. She needs you, too. Maybe more now than ever."

"Are you sure you don't mind?"

"I'm sure."

Lifting her hand, he kissed her palm. "Have I told you lately that I love you?"

"Not in the last ten minutes."

"Remind me later, when we're alone."

"I'll do that."

Elaine lived in a single-story house on a quiet street. A couple of young children were playing outside. An elderly woman was watering her yard. A teenage boy was changing a tire in his driveway.

Zane parked the car in front of the house, then turned to Carly. "Do you want to come in?"

"No, I'll wait here."

"Okay, I won't be long."

He'd no sooner gotten out of the truck when the front door opened and Katy came running toward him. "Daddy!"

She jumped into his arms and gave him a big hug. "I knew you'd come. Mama said you wouldn't, but I didn't believe her."

"How are you, princess?"

"Fine. Where are we going today? Can we go to the movies?"

"Sure, if you want. Just let me tell your mother we're leaving."

Still holding Katy, he climbed the porch steps. He was about to open the door when Elaine stepped outside. "Aren't you supposed to be on your honeymoon?"

"Yeah, well…" He shrugged. "Okay if I take Katy for a while?"

"It's your day to have her."

"I'll have her back by six."

"I don't suppose there's any chance you could keep her overnight?"

Katy's eyes lit up. "Please, Daddy? I've never stayed overnight at the ranch." She cupped his face in her hands and planted a big kiss on his cheek. "Please?"

How could he say no? "All right, princess. Go get your duds."

"Can we go to the movies?"

"Sure."

She beamed at him, then ran into the house.

Zane looked at Elaine. "Got some big plans for tonight?"

She shrugged. "Maybe."

"I guess having a kid in the house cramps your style."

"Don't start."

"You could let me have her on weekends instead of just on Sunday, you know. It would give you more time to do…whatever it is you do."

"What would your new wife think about that?"

"What do you care? Dammit, Elaine, I deserve to have Katy more than one day a week, and you know it."

"I think you're right."

Zane frowned, suspicious of her sudden about-face. And then he nodded. "I take it you've found somebody new."

"What if I have?"

"Kind of sudden, isn't it?"

Elaine stared pointedly at the truck. "Who are you to talk about sudden? Anyway, I've known Ken for quite some time. It's just that lately, well, lately, we've gotten serious."

"I take it he doesn't want Katy around?"

"Do you want her weekends or not?"

"Of course I do."

Before he could say anything else, Katy burst out of the door, a backpack slung over her shoulder. She grabbed Zane's hand and smiled up at him. "I'm ready."

"All right, princess, let's go." He nodded at Elaine and started down the stairs.

"We can start next weekend, if that's okay with you," Elaine called after him.

He lifted a hand to acknowledge that he had heard her.

Katy came to a dead stop when she saw Carly sitting by the window. "What's *she* doing here?"

"Katy, mind your manners."

"I thought it would be just the two of us."

"We just got married yesterday," Zane said. "You can't expect me to leave Carly home alone."

"But..."

Zane hunkered down on his heels so he and Katy were at eye level. "Listen, princess, I love Carly. She's my wife now, and you'll treat her with the respect she deserves. Understand?"

Katy nodded, her expression mutinous. "You love her more than me."

"No, not more. Just different. You'll understand when you get older."

Katy's lower lip was quivering when Zane opened the door and lifted her onto the seat.

"Hi, Katy," Carly said brightly.

"Hullo."

"Katy wants to go to a movie," Zane said. Closing the door, he walked around the truck and slid behind the wheel.

"Sounds like fun," Carly said. "I love movies."

Katy stared straight ahead.

Zane looked at Carly. With an apologetic shake of his head, he turned the key in the ignition and pulled away from the curb.

Carly would not have called the day a success by any means. Zane sat between the two of them at the movies. They went out to dinner after the show and then drove to the ranch.

"Big day tomorrow," Zane told Katy. "Better get to bed early."

She looked at him through wide brown eyes. "Is it time to brand the calves?"

"Yep. Come on, I'll run some water for your bath, and then you'd better turn in."

For once, she didn't argue.

Leaving Zane to look after his daughter, Carly went into the larger of the two bedrooms and began to unpack her suitcase. Her belongings had arrived at the ranch before she had and had been waiting for her in the garage next to the house. She had planned on setting up her office in the second bedroom, but she realized that probably wouldn't work. Katy would be coming to stay with Zane from time to time; she would need a place of her own.

Carly hung her dresses in the closet. Perhaps she could set up her computer in a corner of the kitchen. After all, it wouldn't be for long, only until their own house was built. As always, the thought of finally having a house of her own brought a smile to her lips. It was a topic she and Zane had discussed at length by phone. They had decided on a two-story house, with living room, separate dining room, kitchen and bath downstairs, and four bedrooms and a bath and a half upstairs. She would use one of the bedrooms for her office.

She turned, smiling, as Zane entered the bedroom.

"We need to talk."

Carly paused in the act of putting her underwear in a drawer. "That sounds serious."

"I wouldn't call it serious, but Elaine's decided to let Katy spend her weekends with me. That means she'll be here Saturdays and Sundays."

"I see." Carly's heart sank at the thought of having Katy there on the weekends, not because she didn't like the child, but because the child so obviously didn't like her.

Zane slid his arms around her waist. "How do you feel about that?"

"Well, knowing how she feels about me, I can't say I'm crazy about the idea, but..." Carly shrugged. "She's your daughter, and that makes her my daughter."

"I knew there was a reason I loved you."

"Well, you couldn't prove it by me," she said with a pout. "You haven't kissed me in at least an hour."

"This should hold you for a little while," he said, giving her a quick but thorough kiss. "I've got to get Katy out of the tub and tuck her into bed and tell her a story."

"All right. Do you want me to unpack for you?"

"Yeah, if you don't mind."

"I don't. Any chance you could make it a short story?"

He grinned at her. "I'll do my best."

Chapter Fourteen

Carly stood in the shower, her forehead braced against the wall. When Zane had said they were getting up early, she hadn't realized he meant the crack of dawn! It wasn't even really light outside yet. Why did cattle have to be branded so early?

Staggering out of the shower, she dried off and reached for her underwear. She could hear Zane and Katy talking in the next room.

When she was dressed, they went to the bunkhouse to have breakfast with the cowboys. The table was practically groaning beneath the weight of pancakes, sausage, bacon, fried potatoes and eggs.

The men all smiled at her and tipped their hats, then went back to their breakfast. In practically no time at all, every plate, pan and pot was empty and the men were trooping out of the bunkhouse.

Carly felt suddenly wide-awake as she followed Zane and Katy out the door. She had always enjoyed new and unusual experiences and this one was definitely unusual! Rounding the barn, they headed for the big corral behind it. She waved to Brenda and Jerry, who were standing near the gate. There were perhaps another dozen men and women, not counting kids, clustered around. When asked, Zane told her they were nearby neighbors come to help with the branding.

They had no sooner reached the corral than she heard a distant rumble. Looking toward the sound, she saw what looked like a million cattle surging over the hill. Cowboys whooped and hollered "Yep, yep, yep!" as they swung their lariats over their heads, urging the cattle down the hill toward the corral.

Zane ruffled Katy's hair. "Stay close to me, princess."

Jerry opened the gate and the bawling cattle barreled into the corral, bellowing in protest.

Sitting on the rail, Carly watched Zane lasso a calf and drag it out of the corral. He wrestled the frightened critter onto its back, where it was vaccinated and, if it was a male, castrated, and then branded on its left hip with the Clarks' brand. The air was filled with the bawling of calves and the smell of singed hair.

Numerous kids wearing jeans and leather chaps hovered around, the younger ones watching, the older ones pitching in. She saw a boy who was probably eleven or twelve wrestle one of the calves to the ground while his father looked on, beaming with pride. She couldn't help smiling at a little girl all duded up in red cowboy boots and a too-big hat.

Here and there, boys were throwing dried manure at each other.

She figured everyone but the calves were having a good time.

"So," Brenda said, coming up to stand beside Carly, "what do you think?"

"I think if I never see another castration, it'll be just fine with me." Carly made a broad gesture that included the cattle and the men. "Except for the baseball caps, it looks like a scene from an old western movie."

"Some things haven't changed much," Brenda said.

"This is one of them. In spite of the hard work, the men love it. It reminds them of the old days, of what being a cowboy is really all about." She grinned. "They think this is fun. I need to get back to the house and help the women. These guys are going to be mighty hungry when they get done."

"I'll come with you."

"No, you stay here and watch. You can help next year."

"Are you sure?"

"I'm sure. You ought to get to enjoy your first roundup."

"Thanks, Bren."

With a wave, Brenda headed up to the house and Carly again turned her attention to Zane.

There were sweat stains on his shirt. He had rolled the sleeves up and she could see the powerful muscles in his arms bunch and relax as he wrestled yet another calf to the ground.

Hopping down off the fence, Carly joined him. "Doesn't it hurt the calf?"

Zane looked up at her and grinned. "I reckon so, but only for a few minutes. Look over yonder." He jerked his chin to where one of the cowboys had just released a calf. The calf shook its head then trotted to its mother's side; a moment later, it was poking its nose in the grass, as placid as ever.

"Doesn't seem to bother them for long, does it?" she said.

"Nope. There's some who call it cruel, but I don't see it that way."

"I've heard hot-body branding is getting popular for people," Carly remarked. "I read in the paper some time ago that people are paying over a hundred dollars an hour to sear away the skin of their arms or chests with the same technique used to brand cattle. They described the process as euphoric, addictive, even a wonderful experience." She grimaced. "I can't imagine it being wonderful. It sounds awful to me."

"Well, a lot of states require that all cattle grazing on open land be branded, so until the law's changed…" Zane shrugged. "Anyway, it's still the most effective way of telling which cow belongs where. Wanna try?"

She started to refuse, but then she saw the look on Katy's face, a look that said Carly was nothing but a city girl and wouldn't have the nerve to stick a hot brand to a calf's hide.

Carly held out her hand. "Sure."

"Okay, stick it in the fire while I get another calf."

Carly did as she was told, then looked over at Katy. "Are you having a good time?"

"Maybe."

"I'd really like for us to be friends," Carly said. "I'm not trying to take your mother's place…."

"Well, you couldn't, even if you were."

"I know that. And I'm not trying to steal your daddy away from you, either."

Katy stared at her, her lower lip jutting out.

"I love your daddy, too. And he loves me, but that doesn't mean he can't love you, too, just as much as before."

Katy started to reply, but Zane appeared dragging another bawling calf.

"Now," Zane said.

Taking a deep breath, Carly lifted the iron from the fire and placed it where Zane indicated. Smoke curled upward. The calf bawled louder. Swallowing a deep breath, she grinned at both of them.

They broke for lunch. Endless pots of chili and beans were brought out of the house and placed on tables in the shade. There were baskets of homemade bread, pitchers of lemonade and ice water, coolers filled with soft drinks, and dozens of strawberry pies for dessert.

Sitting between Zane and Brenda, Carly listened to the

talk up and down the table, talk about cattle prices and the price of hay and feed, the weather, the fact that some fast-food chains were considering a ban on buying beef from branded cattle. There was talk of ear tags, and a big discussion about microchips that could be clipped to an ear tag or injected into the first chamber of the animal's stomach, which Carly thought sounded revolting. Such microchips were capable of carrying an animal's complete health record, which could be updated by a handheld computer at the end of every treatment.

"Probably won't be long until branding goes the way of the spinning wheel and the horse and buggy," opined one old-timer. "Hope I ain't around to see it happen. Branding was good enough for my old man and his old man and his old man before him, and I don't need no idiot from the gov'ment telling me how to mark my cows."

The cowboy sitting across from the old-timer nodded. "Far as I'm concerned, branding is the only way to keep track of my herd. It's quick. It's easy. It's affordable."

Nods of agreement could be seen up and down the length of the table.

"I have to agree," Jerry said. "It makes me feel proud to see my brand on so many new calves. Not only that, it gives me a chance to spend some time with my neighbors."

"Hear, hear," replied a man at the far end of the table. "And don't forget, we expect to see you over at our place next week."

"We'll be there." Jerry promised.

Carly felt a sense of contentment, of belonging, as she sat there listening to the conversation around her. Zane's thigh was pressed intimately against hers and when she looked up at him, he winked at her. She smiled at him, remembering the night they had spent in the hotel, thinking of the night to come when she would be in his arms again. Making love to Zane had been everything, and more, than she had dreamed of. Just looking at him made her feel good all over. He was perfect, she thought. Kind, considerate, a wonderful lover, a good father. She placed her hand on her stomach. She could be pregnant, even now. A baby, she thought, with Zane's dusky skin and black hair.

"What are you grinning about?" Zane asked, his voice pitched low so only she could hear.

"How happy I am. And how much I love you."

"All right, you lovebirds," Jerry said, slapping his hands down on the table. "It's time to get back to work."

Good-natured laughter greeted Jerry's words. Moments later, the men went back to work while the women cleared the tables and did the dishes.

Four hours later, the last calf had been branded, the fires were out, and the cattle had been turned out. Jerry and Brenda had thanked each of their neighbors for their help, promised their own in return, and said their good-byes.

Carly had done her share of branding and found it to be hot and tiring. Now, walking with Zane and Katy toward the house, all she wanted was a hot bath to soothe her aching back.

She could hear the phone ringing as they approached the house. Katy ran past Carly, opened the door and dashed into the house.

"It's probably Elaine wanting to know what time I'm bringing Katy home," Zane said. He held the door open for her, then followed her inside.

"It's Mom," Katy said, holding out the receiver. "She wants to talk to you."

"Thanks, princess."

Carly looked at Katy. "Do you want to go take a bath while I fix dinner?"

"I guess so."

"What would you like to eat?"

Katy shrugged. "I don't care."

"Maybe we could stop and have pizza before we take you home."

Katy shrugged again, then headed for the bathroom. A moment later, Carly heard the water running in the bathtub.

Zane swore, then slammed the receiver back into the cradle.

Carly lifted one brow. "What's wrong?"

"She got married."

"Elaine?"

"Who else? Not only that, but she wants me to tell Katy." He looked at Carly a moment, his expression thoughtful.

"There's more?"

"Oh, yeah. She's pregnant."

Carly stared at Zane, waiting for the other shoe to fall.

"Now that she's married and expecting a baby, Elaine's decided that Katy should live with me and spend her weekends with Elaine."

Carly felt suddenly numb. She had never been around kids much, never given much thought to having any of her own. Now, in the course of a couple of days, she not only had a husband but a six-year-old child who would be living with them five days a week instead of one.

"Carly?"

"Why don't you get Katy out of the tub? I'm going to make some coffee."

He studied her for a moment, then turned and went into the bathroom, unable to shake the feeling that part of the reason Elaine had decided to give him custody of Katy was because she knew it would put a strain on his new marriage, which it surely would. If there was anything Elaine loved, it was causing him trouble whenever she could.

Katy smiled at him over the rim of the tub. "Guess what? Mom says I can spend the night again!"

Zane smiled at his daughter. "Yeah, she told me."

Lifting Katy from the tub, he wrapped her in a towel and hugged her tight. How could he tell Katy that her mother had gotten married and no longer wanted her around? As much as Katy loved him, as much as she liked being with him, he knew it would come as a shock, knew she would be hurt. No doubt she would feel as though her mother had

abandoned her. Damn Elaine. Her marriage couldn't have
come at a worse time. She could have at least given Katy
time to get used to the idea of her father having a new wife
before she had to accept the fact that her mother had a new
husband.

He kissed the top of Katy's head. It would have been
nice to be able to spend some time alone with Carly, but
he couldn't be sorry Katy was going to live with him. He
had always felt his daughter would be better off with him
than with Elaine. He only hoped Carly would feel the same
way.

Zane carried Katy into her bedroom, turned his back
while she put on her pajamas.

"I'm sleepy," she said, yawning.

"Don't you want some dinner? I thought I heard Carly
say something about pizza."

Katy yawned again. "I'm not hungry."

"All right."

Sitting down on the edge of the bed, Zane lifted Katy
onto his lap. "Did you have a good time today?"

She snuggled against him. "Uh-huh."

"How would you like to go to Ranch Camp over at the
Double Z for the rest of the summer?"

Katy sat up straight, the weariness gone from her eyes.
"Really? You mean it?"

Zane nodded. "Your friend Jennifer goes there, doesn't
she?"

Katy nodded exuberantly. "Did Mom say it was okay?"

"Listen, princess, about your mother…"

Katy sobered suddenly, her eyes wide. "Did you and
Mom have another fight?"

"No, nothing like that." Zane stroked Katy's hair. It was
as thick and black as his own. "Your mother got married
today."

Katy stared at him for several seconds, then shook her
head. "No. She wouldn't do that. Not without telling me.
She would have wanted me to be there."

"I'm sorry, princess…"

"No!" She scrambled out of his lap and flung herself facedown on the bed.

"Katy, listen…"

She shook her head and he heard the muffled sound of her tears.

Zane stroked her back. "Remember how I've always wanted you to stay with me? Well, your mother's decided to let you stay here with me, for a while."

"That woman won't want me."

"What woman? You mean Carly? Of course she does." He wiped the tears from her cheeks. "You'll have two families to love you now, princess."

She sniffed loudly, then pulled the covers over her head, effectively shutting him out.

Zane sat there for a moment, his brow furrowed. Rarely had he felt so helpless or so inadequate or so angry at his ex. What could he possibly say to make Katy feel better? Would she even listen to anything he had to say? Dammit, Elaine's timing couldn't have been worse. Why hadn't she told him she was planing to marry? He would have put off his own wedding, if necessary.

"Katy?"

She didn't answer, but he could tell by the way her small shoulders were shaking that she was still crying. He wanted to hold her, to comfort her. Instead, he got up and left the room, quietly closing the door behind him. Perhaps she just needed some time alone.

He found Carly sitting at the table in the kitchen, a cup of coffee cradled in her hands. She looked up as he entered the room.

"Is she all right?"

Zane pulled out a chair and dropped into it. "I don't know. She won't talk to me."

"Do you want something to eat?"

"No." He draped one arm over the back of the chair

and blew out a sigh. "I don't know what to do. What can I say to her…"

"What did you say?"

He shrugged. "I told her the truth, that her mother got married today and that she would be staying with us for a while. I thought she'd be happy about it. I mean, she's always asking to stay overnight…"

"But her security is with her mother."

"Yeah, I guess it is." Muttering an oath, Zane stood and began to pace the floor. "I don't know what Elaine was thinking." He laughed derisively. "Hell, if I know Elaine, she wasn't thinking about anybody but herself. I've wanted Katy to stay with me ever since she was born, but Elaine refused just because she knew it was what I wanted. Now she's got a new man in her life and she doesn't care that she's hurting Katy. All she's thinking about is herself. Again."

Rising, Carly poured a cup of coffee for Zane and refilled her own mug. "Calm down," she said, handing him a cup. "And sit down. What's done is done, and you can't change it. I'm sure Katy will be fine once she gets used to the idea of living here."

"I don't know…"

"Well, I don't know, either, but I do know Katy loves you."

"What if that's not enough?"

Katy was quiet at breakfast the following morning. She smiled and looked more like her old self when Zane told her he was taking her over to the Double Z for the day. Zane and Carly had discussed it the night before and decided it might be better for Katy to go to camp and be with her friends rather than spend the day with Carly. Carly had agreed that it might be easier on both Katy and herself if they got to know each other a little at a time rather than forcing them to be together when they were still virtually strangers, and each more than a little uncomfortable with the other.

Katy bid Carly a barely audible goodbye when she left the house.

"Remember what you said," Zane murmured, taking Carly in his arms. "It'll work out."

"I hope I don't have to eat those words."

He dropped a kiss on the tip of her nose. "What are you going to do today?"

"Set up my computer. Get in touch with my boss." She traced the outline of his jaw with her forefinger. "Any chance you'll be home for lunch?"

"Count on it."

"What do want to eat?"

His grin was delightfully wicked. "Just you, honey."

In spite of herself, Carly felt herself blush.

Zane kissed her goodbye, a long, slow kiss that left her hoping the hours until lunchtime would pass quickly.

The phone rang.

Zane answered it on the second ring. Still lost in the hazy afterglow of lovemaking, Carly listened to his side of the conversation, only to sit up, wide-awake, when he said, "How long has she been missing?"

Carly tapped him on the arm, a sudden coldness in the pit of her stomach. "What's wrong? Who's missing?"

He looked at her over his shoulder. "Katy."

"Oh, no!"

"We'll be there in thirty minutes or so," he said, and hung up the receiver.

"What happened?" Carly asked.

"I don't know. Jennifer said she was with a group of kids who were headed for the barn. Apparently Katy said she had to go to the bathroom. When the kids came back to the house for lunch, they noticed Katy was missing."

"You don't suppose…" Carly bit down on her lower lip, reluctant to say what she was thinking.

"What?"

"You don't think she was kidnapped, do you?"

"No. It's a possibility, I guess, but I think she's just run away."

"Well, she can't have been gone very long. We'll find her."

Ten minutes later, they were on their way to the Double Z.

Carly stared out the window. "Where do you think she'd go?"

"I don't know." He slammed his fist on the steering wheel. "Dammit, I should have seen this coming."

"It's not your fault."

"Of course it is. I handled everything badly. I knew she was upset because we were getting married, but I thought she'd get over it. I should have given her more time to get used to the idea, but I wanted you so damn bad, I didn't want to wait."

Carly put her hand on his arm. "You can't blame yourself."

"Can't I?"

Carly pulled her hand away. Last night, he had been blaming Elaine for Katy's misery. Now he was blaming himself. And if he blamed himself, then he must surely blame her, as well.

Oh, Lord, what if they never found Katy? Zane would never forgive her. Every time he looked at her, he would remember that marrying her had been the reason he lost his daughter.

She shook the horrible thought from her mind. Of course they would find Katy. She was only six years old. How far could she go?

The Double Z ranch house was in something of an uproar when they arrived.

Martha Zimmerman hurried over to greet Zane when he exited the truck. She quickly brought them up-to-date on what was going on. The three women who ran the summer camp program had corralled the kids by the pool. All the ranch hands that weren't out on the range had been sent to look for Katy. Zimm had gone with them.

"As far as we can tell, she's been missing for about an hour and a half," Martha said. "I was just about to call the police."

"Do you have any idea which way she was headed?"

"No, I'm afraid not." Martha ran her hand through her hair. "I just can't believe this happened."

"It wasn't your fault, Mrs. Zimmerman," Zane assured her. "I'm afraid Katy's life has turned upside down in the past couple of days."

"I'm sorry to hear that," Martha said. "But that doesn't excuse the fact that a child in our care is missing. We can't discount the possibility that she's been kidnapped, although way out here, that seems unlikely."

"Is it all right if I borrow one of your horses?"

"Of course. Take any one you want."

Zane touched a forefinger to his hat. "Obliged."

Carly followed Zane as he headed for the barn. "I want to help, too."

"Thanks, but I think you'd best stay here. You're liable to get lost out there on the range."

She didn't argue. She just waited until he rode out of the yard, then she saddled a docile-looking gelding and rode out after him. She felt partly responsible for Katy's need to run away. She couldn't just sit around and not do anything. She needed to look for Katy, needed to feel like she was helping.

Knowing Zane was right about the possibility of her getting lost, she was careful to pay attention to the landmarks around her. Figuring most of the searchers would be searching well away from the ranch house, she decided to just stay close. After all, Katy was only six years old. It wasn't likely that she'd struck out for the big city. She was probably just hiding nearby, hoping to get a little attention, or maybe just put a good scare into her father.

Carly had intended to ride a circle around the ranch house only to find that fences here and there made that impossible. She reined her horse to a halt, thinking she would just turn back, when she saw a narrow path that seemed to wind through the trees that flanked the yard on this side. The path seemed to parallel the outskirts of the ranch yard and she clucked to her horse, deciding she would explore it for a short distance to see if it would take her back to the barn.

Her horse snorted and shook its head as they entered the grove of trees. Overhead, the branches grew close together, shutting out the sunlight.

Leaning forward, Carly stroked her horse's neck. "It's all right, nothing to be afraid of," she murmured, wondering who she was hoping to convince, herself or her horse.

The path widened out a little as she rode deeper in the trees. The sound of birds chirping high in the branches, the muffled clop of her horse's hooves and the creak of saddle leather were the only sounds she heard.

When she finally emerged from the tree-lined tunnel, she found herself in an open meadow. Reining her horse to a stop, she stood up in the stirrups and glanced around. The house was nowhere to be seen.

So much for a shortcut, she thought with a rueful shake of her head. Now she'd have to turn around and go back the way she had come.

And then she heard a faint cry.

Frowning, Carly urged her horse toward the sound, only to stop when the cry faded away. From which direction had it come?

She sat there for a moment, listening, and then it came again, a faint cry for help.

Setting her sights on the direction it had come from, she urged her horse into a lope. A fairly steep hill rose ahead of her and she leaned forward in the saddle, the way Zane had taught her, to make it easier for the horse to climb. When she reached the top, she saw a splash of blue against the green grass. It was the same shade of blue as the shirt Katy had been wearing when she left the house this morning. A horse grazed a few feet away.

Filled with relief and dread, Carly drummed her heels into her mount's sides and the gelding streaked down the hill. Too late, she realized her mistake. The horse lost its footing on the slick grass, scrambled to regain its balance and didn't make it.

Carly had no time to be afraid, no time to cry out. One minute she was clinging to the saddle horn and the next she was flat on her back while stars danced in front of her eyes.

It took her several moments to get her breath back. When she sat up, she realized two things at the same time. Her horse had apparently headed for home, and her right wrist was either broken or badly sprained.

"That's the last time I get on a horse," she muttered, cradling her wounded arm. "They're all out to get me!"

"Carly?"

Carly glanced over her shoulder to find that Katy was sitting up and staring back at her. The girl's shirt was torn, her eyes were red and wet with tears.

"Katy! Are you all right?"

She shook her head. "N...no. I think my leg's broke."

Gaining her feet, Carly walked over to Katy and knelt beside her. "Where does it hurt?"

"Here." Katy pointed to her left leg. Through the ragged hole in the denim, Carly could see the girl's leg was badly swollen.

"I want my dad."

"I know, honey." Carly glanced at Katy's horse. Should she leave Katy here and ride back to the ranch for help? Or try to lift Katy onto the horse? The way her arm was throbbing, trying to lift the child didn't seem like a good idea for either one of them.

"I'm thirsty."

"Katy, I think I should ride back to the ranch for help."

"No! I don't want to stay here alone."

"I won't be gone long."

Tears flowed down Katy's cheeks. "No."

Carly looked over at the horse again, only then noticing that the bridle was missing and that the animal seemed to be favoring its left foreleg.

"Well," she muttered, "it looks like we've all got breaks and sprains, doesn't it?"

Katy sniffed, and then laughed. "You're not supposed to lean forward when you run your horse down a hill."

"Especially a slippery hill," Carly acknowledged with a rueful grin. Moving gingerly, she sat down beside Katy. "I guess we'll just wait here for someone to find us. It shouldn't take long."

Katy eyed her warily for a moment. "Why did you marry my dad?"

"Because I love him." She smiled. "And because he asked me."

"Now my mom's married to someone else, too."

"That's true, Katy, but they both still love you," Carly said. "Nothing will change that. You can love more than one person at a time. You know that, don't you?"

Katy frowned at her.

"You love your mother, don't you?"

"Uh-huh."

"Does that mean you can't love your father, too? Or that you don't love him just as much?"

Katy frowned again.

"Love's a funny thing. It never runs out. You can love one person, or you can love a hundred people. Think about your friends who have brothers and sisters. Their parents love all their kids, don't they?"

Katy nodded, her eyes narrowed thoughtfully.

"Maybe someday you'll even love me," Carly said, and realized at that moment that she very much wanted Katy to like and accept her.

"I don't have to call you Mom, do I?"

"Not unless you want to."

A sob rose in Katy's throat. "I want to go home. My leg really hurts."

Carly put her right arm around Katy's shoulders and gave her a comforting squeeze. "I'm sure someone will find us soon. Do you want to put your head in my lap and take a nap?"

Katy hesitated a moment, and then nodded.

Once Katy was settled, Carly lightly stroked the girl's brow. Gradually, exhaustion overcame Katy's pain and she fell into a restless sleep.

Carly licked her lips, hoping that someone would find them soon. It was hot. Her wrist throbbed with every breath. If a sprain hurt this bad, how much worse was the pain in Katy's leg?

She was dozing when she felt a tremor in the earth beneath her. Looking up, she saw Zane riding toward her. For a moment, she forgot everything else. He had lost his hat somewhere along the way and his long black hair streamed behind him as his horse plunged down the hill and streaked across the grassy flat below at a full gallop.

Sitting tall and easy in the saddle, he raced toward her, the epitome of every hero in every cowboy movie she had ever seen.

He pulled back on the reins and was out of the saddle before his horse came to a stop. Dropping down on one knee, his gaze moved over Katy and then over Carly.

"Are you all right?"

"I think I sprained my wrist. And I think Katy's got a broken leg."

Zane looked at Katy's leg, then grunted softly. "I hate to move her, but there's no way to get a car back here." He glanced around, his eyes narrowed.

"How'd you find us?"

"I rode back to the yard to see if anyone had found her yet. I saw a horse come in with an empty saddle, and tracked it back here. Sit a spell while I fix up a travois."

"Can't I help?"

"No. You're hurt. You just sit there and take it easy."

A short time later, Zane had constructed a travois out of branches and strips of rope cut from the coil that had been looped around the saddle horn. He had padded the contraption with grass and covered it with the saddle blanket from Katy's horse.

Carly watched Zane with his daughter, moved by his gentleness, by the way he held Katy and comforted her, promising her that she would be all right, that he would stay with her every minute at the hospital. He assured her several times that he wasn't angry, just relieved that she hadn't been hurt worse.

After Zane got Katy settled on the travois, he lifted Carly onto the back of his horse, then took up the reins.

Katy glanced over her shoulder. "What about my horse?"

"Don't worry about him. I reckon he'll follow us home. If not, I'll send someone back for him."

Zane went to stand beside Carly. "You all right?"

"I'm fine."

"Didn't I tell you to stay at the house?"

Her gaze slid away from his. "I know, but I couldn't just sit there while everyone else was out looking for her. I had to feel like I was doing my share."

His fingertips caressed her cheek. "That's my girl."

Warmth flowed through Carly and she knew she could endure any pain, any hardship life might hold in store for them, so long as she could see Zane's dark eyes filled with love at the end of the day, so long as she could hear that husky note of longing in his voice.

Carly glanced back at Katy, felt her heart swell even more when Katy managed a weak smile.

It would be all right now, Carly thought. It had to be.

Later that night, lying in Zane's arms, Carly thought about the events of the day. The police search had been called off. Zane had driven her and Katy to the hospital. X-rays had proved that Katy did, indeed, have a broken leg. Carly's sprain was minor and quickly treated. They had stayed at the hospital with Katy until visiting hours were over. Even though Katy had been sound asleep by then, Zane had been reluctant to leave her.

"I think we're over the worst of it now," Zane remarked, lightly stroking her back.

"What do you mean?"

"Katy's running away, even though she got hurt, I think maybe it was good for the two of you."

Carly nodded. "I think you're right." Being alone with Katy under difficult circumstances had created a bond—however tenuous it might be—between them. It was something to build on.

"It was a brave thing you did," Zane said, nuzzling her neck.

Sighing, she closed her eyes and snuggled against him, utterly at peace. Deep in her heart she knew that, with love and patience, the three of them would live happily ever after, after all.

Epilogue

Carly sat on the front porch of their new house, one hand resting on her stomach. She smiled as she felt the baby move beneath her fingertips. They had finished the house just in time, she thought. The baby, a boy, was due any day now.

She had quit her job and started her own business. Being her own boss allowed her to set her own hours and decide how many accounts she wanted to handle.

She grinned as she watched Katy romping with the puppy Zane had bought her.

Elaine's baby had been born five months ago. Yesterday, Brenda had announced that she was pregnant again.

She glanced over her shoulder when she heard the screen door open.

"How you feeling, honey?" Zane asked.

"Fine. A little anxious."

Zane dropped down on his haunches beside the chair and placed his hand over hers. "How's our son doing?"

"I think he's trying to kick his way out."

"Probably can't wait to see his mother," he said, kissing her cheek. "I hope he looks like you."

"I hope he looks like you."

"I hope he looks like me!"

Carly and Zane looked at each other and laughed as Katy ran up the stairs, the puppy clutched to her chest.

"Maybe he'll look like Chipper," Zane said, scratching the dog's ears.

Katy made a face. "Oh, Daddy, that's silly."

Carly smiled at father and daughter. It hadn't been easy at first, but Carly had won Katy's love and trust and the three of them were a family now.

Even Zane's mother was slowly coming around. The last time she had come to visit, she had given Carly a hug and called her *cunksi,* which meant "My daughter" in Lakota. Yes, sir, life was good.

Sighing with contentment, Carly gazed out over the land. Brenda had been right. Carly loved Texas. She loved being a ranch wife. She loved the wide-open spaces and vast blue vault of the sky. But most of all, she loved the rugged cowboy who had stolen her heart and given her his in return.

She had once heard someone say that everything was bigger and better in Texas.

And they were right.

*   *   *   *   *

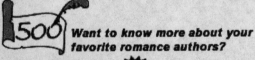

Your opinion is important to us! Please take a few moments to share your thoughts with us about your experiences with Harlequin and Silhouette books. Your comments will be very useful in ensuring that we deliver books you love to read. *Please take a few minutes to complete the questionnaire, then send it to us at the address below.*

Send your completed questionnaires to:
Harlequin/Silhouette Reader Survey, P.O. Box 9046, Buffalo, NY 14269-9046

1. As you may know, there are many different lines under the Harlequin and Silhouette brands. Each of the lines is listed below. Please check the box that most represents your reading habit for each line.

Line	Currently read this line	Do not read this line	Not sure if I read this line
Harlequin American Romance	❏	❏	❏
Harlequin Duets	❏	❏	❏
Harlequin Romance	❏	❏	❏
Harlequin Historicals	❏	❏	❏
Harlequin Superromance	❏	❏	❏
Harlequin Intrigue	❏	❏	❏
Harlequin Presents	❏	❏	❏
Harlequin Temptation	❏	❏	❏
Harlequin Blaze	❏	❏	❏
Silhouette Special Edition	❏	❏	❏
Silhouette Romance	❏	❏	❏
Silhouette Intimate Moments	❏	❏	❏
Silhouette Desire	❏	❏	❏

2. Which of the following best describes why you bought *this book?* One answer only, please.

the picture on the cover	❏	the title	❏
the author	❏	the line is one I read often	❏
part of a miniseries	❏	saw an ad in another book	❏
saw an ad in a magazine/newsletter	❏	a friend told me about it	❏
I borrowed/was given this book	❏	other: _____	❏

3. Where did you buy *this book?* One answer only, please.

at Barnes & Noble	❏	at a grocery store	❏
at Waldenbooks	❏	at a drugstore	❏
at Borders	❏	on eHarlequin.com Web site	❏
at another bookstore	❏	from another Web site	❏
at Wal-Mart	❏	Harlequin/Silhouette Reader	❏
at Target	❏	Service/through the mail	
at Kmart	❏	used books from anywhere	❏
at another department store or mass merchandiser	❏	I borrowed/was given this book	❏

4. On average, how many Harlequin and Silhouette books do you buy at one time?

I buy _____ books at one time	❏
I rarely buy a book	❏

MRQ403SR-1A

5. How many times per month do you shop for any *Harlequin and/or Silhouette* books? One answer only, please.

1 or more times a week	❑	a few times per year	❑
1 to 3 times per month	❑	less often than once a year	❑
1 to 2 times every 3 months	❑	never	❑

6. When you think of your ideal heroine, which *one* statement describes her the best? One answer only, please.

She's a woman who is strong-willed	❑	She's a desirable woman	❑
She's a woman who is needed by others	❑	She's a powerful woman	❑
She's a woman who is taken care of	❑	She's a passionate woman	❑
She's an adventurous woman	❑	She's a sensitive woman	❑

7. The following statements describe types or genres of books that you may be interested in reading. Pick *up to 2 types* of books that you are most interested in.

I like to read about truly romantic relationships	❑
I like to read stories that are sexy romances	❑
I like to read romantic comedies	❑
I like to read a romantic mystery/suspense	❑
I like to read about romantic adventures	❑
I like to read romance stories that involve family	❑
I like to read about a romance in times or places that I have never seen	❑
Other: _____	❑

The following questions help us to group your answers with those readers who are similar to you. Your answers will remain confidential.

8. Please record your year of birth below.

19 _____

9. What is your marital status?

single ❑   married ❑   common-law ❑   widowed ❑
divorced/separated ❑

10. Do you have children 18 years of age or younger currently living at home?

yes ❑   no ❑

11. Which of the following best describes your employment status?

employed full-time or part-time ❑   homemaker ❑   student ❑
retired ❑   unemployed ❑

12. Do you have access to the Internet from either home or work?

yes ❑   no ❑

13. Have you ever visited eHarlequin.com?

yes ❑   no ❑

14. What state do you live in?

_____

15. Are you a member of Harlequin/Silhouette Reader Service?

yes ❑   Account # _____   no ❑   MRQ403SR-1B

PENGUIN BOOKS

THE ADVENTURES OF SALLY

P. G. Wodehouse was born in Guildford in 1881 and educated at Dulwich College. After working for the Hong Kong and Shanghai Bank for two years he left to earn his living as a journalist and storywriter, writing the 'By the Way' column in the old *Globe*. He also contributed a series of school stories to a magazine for boys, the *Captain*, in one of which Psmith made his first appearance. Going to America before the First World War, he sold a serial to the *Saturday Evening Post*; for the next twenty-five years almost all his books appeared in it. He was part-author and writer of the lyrics of eighteen musical comedies including *Kissing Time*; he married in 1914 and in 1955 took American citizenship. He wrote over ninety books and his work won world-wide acclaim, being translated into many languages. *The Times* hailed him as a 'comic genius' recognized in his lifetime as a classic and an old master of farce!

P. G. Wodehouse said, 'I believe there are two ways of writing novels. One is mine, making a sort of musical comedy without music and ignoring real life altogether; the other is going right deep down into life and not caring a damn . . .' He was created a Knight of the British Empire in the New Year's Honours List in 1975. In a B.B.C. interview he said that he had no ambitions left, now that he had been knighted and there was a waxwork of him in Madame Tussaud's. He died on St Valentine's Day in 1975 at the age of ninety-three.

D0650869

THE
ADVENTURES
OF SALLY

P. G. WODEHOUSE

PENGUIN BOOKS

Penguin Books Ltd, Harmondsworth, Middlesex, England
Viking Penguin Inc., 40 West 23rd Street, New York, New York 10010, U.S.A.
Penguin Books Australia Ltd, Ringwood, Victoria, Australia
Penguin Books Canada Limited, 2801 John Street, Markham, Ontario, Canada L3R 1B4
Penguin Books (N.Z.) Ltd, 182–190 Wairau Road, Auckland 10, New Zealand

First published by Herbert Jenkins Ltd 1922
Published in Penguin Books 1986
Reprinted 1987

Reproduced, printed and bound in Great Britain by
Hazell Watson & Viney Limited,
Member of the BPCC Group,
Aylesbury, Bucks
Typeset in Baskerville

DEDICATION
TO
GEORGE GROSSMITH

Dear George,—

The production of our mutual effort, *The Cabaret Girl*, is a week distant as I write this; and who shall say what the harvest will be? But, whether a week from now we are slapping each other on the back or shivering in the frost, nothing can alter the fact that we had a lot of fun writing the thing together. Not a reproach or a nasty look from start to finish. Because of this, and because you and I were side by side through the Adventure of the Ship's Bore, the Episode of the Concert In Aid of the Seamen's Orphans and Widows, and the Sinister Affair of The Rose of Stamboul, I dedicate this book to you.

P. G. Wodehouse.

Garrick Club.

CONTENTS

CHAPTER I

SALLY GIVES A PARTY

I

SALLY looked contentedly down the long table. She felt happy at last. Everybody was talking and laughing now, and her party, rallying after an uncertain start, was plainly the success she had hoped it would be. The first atmosphere of uncomfortable restraint, caused, she was only too well aware, by her brother Fillmore's white evening waistcoat, had worn off; and the male and female patrons of Mrs. Meecher's select boarding-house (transient and residential) were themselves again.

At her end of the table the conversation had turned once more to the great vital topic of Sally's legacy and what she ought to do with it. The next best thing to having money of one's own, is to dictate the spending of somebody else's, and Sally's guests were finding a good deal of satisfaction in arranging a Budget for her. Rumour having put the sum at their disposal at a high figure, their suggestions had a certain spaciousness.

"Let me tell you," said Augustus Bartlett, briskly, "what I'd do, if I were you." Augustus Bartlett, who occupied an intensely subordinate position in the firm of Kahn, Morris and Brown, the Wall Street brokers, always affected a brisk, incisive style of speech, as befitted a man in close touch with the great ones of Finance. "I'd sink a couple of hundred thousand in some good, safe bond-issue—we've just put one out which you would do well to consider—and play about with the rest. When I say play about, I mean have a flutter in anything good that crops up. Multiple Steel's worth looking at. They tell me it'll be up to a hundred and fifty before next Saturday."

Elsa Doland, the pretty girl with the big eyes who sat on Mr. Bartlett's left, had other views.

"Buy a theatre, Sally, and put on good stuff."

"And lose every bean you've got," said a mild young man, with a deep voice across the table. "If I had a few hundred

9

thousand," said the mild young man, "I'd put every cent of it on Benny Whistler for the heavyweight championship. I've private information that Battling Tuke has been got at and means to lie down in the seventh . . ."

"Say, listen," interrupted another voice, "lemme tell you what I'd do with four hundred thousand . . ."

"If I had four hundred thousand," said Elsa Doland, "I know what would be the first thing I'd do."

"What's that?" asked Sally.

"Pay my bill for last week, due this morning."

Sally got up quickly, and flitting down the table, put her arm round her friend's shoulder and whispered in her ear:

"Elsa darling, are you really broke? If you are, you know, I'll . . ."

Elsa Doland laughed.

"You're an angel, Sally. There's no one like you. You'd give your last cent to anyone. Of course I'm not broke. I've just come back from the road, and I've saved a fortune. I only said that to draw you."

Sally returned to her seat, relieved, and found that the company had now divided itself into two schools of thought. The conservative and prudent element, led by Augustus Bartlett, had definitely decided on three hundred thousand in Liberty Bonds and the rest in some safe real estate; while the smaller, more sporting section, impressed by the mild young man's inside information, had already placed Sally's money on Benny Whistler, doling it out cautiously in small sums so as not to spoil the market. And so solid, it seemed, was Mr. Tuke's reputation with those in the inner circle of knowledge that the mild young man was confident that, if you went about the matter cannily and without precipitation, three to one might be obtained. It seemed to Sally that the time had come to correct certain misapprehensions.

"I don't know where you get your figures," she said, "but I'm afraid they're wrong. I've just twenty-five thousand dollars."

The statement had a chilling effect. To these jugglers with half-millions the amount mentioned seemed for the moment almost too small to bother about. It was the sort of sum which they had been mentally setting aside for the heiress's car fare. Then they managed to adjust their minds to it. After all, one could do something even with a pittance like twenty-five thousand.

"If I'd twenty-five thousand," said Augustus Bartlett, the first to rally from the shock, "I'd buy Amalgamated . . ."

"If I had twenty-five thousand . . ." began Elsa Doland.

"If I'd had twenty-five thousand in the year nineteen hundred," observed a gloomy-looking man with spectacles, "I could have started a revolution in Paraguay."

He brooded sombrely on what might have been.

"Well, I'll tell you exactly what I'm going to do," said Sally. "I'm going to start with a trip to Europe . . . France, specially. I've heard France well spoken of—as soon as I can get my passport; and after I've loafed there for a few weeks, I'm coming back to look about and find some nice cosy little business which will let me put money into it and keep me in luxury. Are there any complaints?"

"Even a couple of thousand on Benny Whistler . . ." said the mild young man.

"I don't want your Benny Whistler," said Sally. "I wouldn't have him if you gave him to me. If I want to lose money, I'll go to Monte Carlo and do it properly."

"Monte Carlo," said the gloomy man, brightening up at the magic name. "I was in Monte Carlo in the year '97, and if I'd had another fifty dollars . . . just fifty . . . I'd have . . ."

At the far end of the table there was a stir, a cough, and the grating of a chair on the floor; and slowly, with that easy grace which actors of the old school learned in the days when acting was acting, Mr. Maxwell Faucitt, the boarding-house's oldest inhabitant, rose to his feet.

"Ladies," said Mr. Faucitt, bowing courteously, "and . . ." ceasing to bow and casting from beneath his white and venerable eyebrows a quelling glance at certain male members of the boarding-house's younger set who were showing a disposition towards restiveness, " . . . gentlemen. I feel that I cannot allow this occasion to pass without saying a few words."

His audience did not seem surprised. It was possible that life, always prolific of incident in a great city like New York, might some day produce an occasion which Mr. Faucitt would feel that he could allow to pass without saying a few words; but nothing of the sort had happened as yet, and they had given up hope. Right from the start of the meal they had felt that it would be optimism run mad to expect the old gentleman to abstain from speech on the night of Sally

Nicholas' farewell dinner party; and partly because they had braced themselves to it, but principally because Miss Nicholas' hospitality had left them with a genial feeling of repletion, they settled themselves to listen with something resembling equanimity. A movement on the part of the Marvellous Murphys—new arrivals, who had been playing the Bushwick with their equilibristic act during the preceding week—to form a party of the extreme left and heckle the speaker, broke down under a cold look from their hostess. Brief though their acquaintance had been, both of these lissom young gentlemen admired Sally immensely.

And it should be set on record that this admiration of theirs was not misplaced. He would have been hard to please who had not been attracted by Sally. She was a small, trim, wisp of a girl with the tiniest hands and feet, the friendliest of smiles, and a dimple that came and went in the curve of her rounded chin. Her eyes, which disappeared when she laughed, which was often, were a bright hazel; her hair a soft mass of brown. She had, moreover, a manner, an air of distinction lacking in the majority of Mrs. Meecher's guests. And she carried youth like a banner. In approving of Sally, the Marvellous Murphys had been guilty of no lapse from their high critical standard.

"I have been asked," proceeded Mr. Faucitt, "though I am aware that there are others here far worthier of such a task—Brutuses compared with whom I, like Marc Antony, am no orator—I have been asked to propose the health . . ."

"Who asked you?" It was the smaller of the Marvellous Murphys who spoke. He was an unpleasant youth, snubnosed and spotty. Still, he could balance himself with one hand on an inverted ginger-ale bottle while revolving a barrel on the soles of his feet. There is good in all of us.

"I have been asked," repeated Mr. Faucitt, ignoring the unmannerly interruption, which, indeed, he would have found it hard to answer, "to propose the health of our charming hostess (applause), coupled with the name of her brother, our old friend Fillmore Nicholas."

The gentleman referred to, who sat at the speaker's end of the table, acknowledged the tribute with a brief nod of the head. It was a nod of condescension; the nod of one who, conscious of being hedged about by social inferiors, nevertheless does his best to be not unkindly. And Sally, seeing it, debated in her mind for an instant the advisability of throwing an orange at her brother. There was one lying ready to her hand, and his glistening shirt-front offered an admirable mark; but she restrained herself. After all, if a hostess yields to her primitive impulses, what happens? Chaos. She had just frowned down the exuberance of the rebellious Murphys, and she felt that if, even with the highest motives, she began throwing fruit, her influence for good in that quarter would be weakened.

She leaned back with a sigh. The temptation had been hard to resist. A democratic girl, pomposity was a quality which she thoroughly disliked; and though she loved him, she could not disguise from herself that, ever since affluence had descended upon him some months ago, her brother Fillmore had become insufferably pompous. If there are any young men whom inherited wealth improves, Fillmore Nicholas was not one of them. He seemed to regard himself nowadays as a sort of Man of Destiny. To converse with him was for the ordinary human being like being received in audience by some more than stand-offish monarch. It had taken Sally over an hour to persuade him to leave his apartment on Riverside Drive and revisit the boarding-house for this special occasion; and, when he had come, he had entered wearing such faultless evening dress that he had made the rest of the party look like a gathering of tramp-cyclists. His white waistcoat alone was a silent reproach to honest poverty, and had caused an awkward constraint right through the soup and fish courses. Most of those present had known Fillmore Nicholas as an impecunious young man who could make a tweed suit last longer than one would have believed possible; they had called him "Fill" and helped him in more than usually lean times with small loans: but to-night they had eyed the waistcoat dumbly and shrank back abashed.

"Speaking," said Mr. Faucitt, "as an Englishman—for though I have long since taken out what are technically known as my 'papers' it was as a subject of the island kingdom that I first visited this great country—I may say that the two factors in American life which have always made the pro-foundest impression upon me have been the lavishness of American hospitality and the charm of the American girl. To-night we have been privileged to witness the American girl in the capacity of hostess, and I think I am right in saying, in asseverating, in committing myself to the statement that

13

his has been a night which none of us present here will ever ·rget. Miss Nicholas has given us, ladies and gentlemen, a anquet. I repeat, a banquet. There has been alcoholic refreshment. I do not know where it came from: I do not ask how it was procured, but we have had it. Miss Nicholas . . ."

Mr. Faucitt paused to puff at his cigar. Sally's brother Fillmore suppressed a yawn and glanced at his watch. Sally continued to lean forward raptly. She knew how happy it made the old gentleman to deliver a formal speech; and though she wished the subject had been different, she was prepared to listen indefinitely.

"Miss Nicholas," resumed Mr. Faucitt, lowering his cigar, " . . . But why," he demanded abruptly, do I call her Miss Nicholas?"

"Because it's her name," hazarded the taller Murphy.

Mr. Faucitt eyed him with disfavour. He disapproved of the marvellous brethren on general grounds because, himself a resident of years standing, he considered that these transients from the vaudeville stage lowered the tone of the boarding-house; but particularly because the one who had just spoken had, on his first evening in the place, addressed him as "grandpa."

"Yes, sir," he said severely, "it is her name. But she has another name, sweeter to those who love her, those who worship her, those who have watched her with the eye of sedulous affection through the three years she has spent beneath this roof, though that name," said Mr. Faucitt, lowering the tone of his address and descending to what might almost be termed personalities, "may not be familiar to a couple of dud acrobats who have only been in the place a week-end, thank heaven, and are off to-morrow to infest some other city. That name," said Mr. Faucitt, soaring once more to a loftier plane, "is Sally. Our Sally. For three years our Sally has flitted about this establishment like— I choose the simile advisedly—like a ray of sunshine. For three years she has made life for us a brighter, sweeter thing. And now a sudden access of worldly wealth, happily synchronizing with her twenty-first birthday, is to remove her from our midst. From our midst, ladies and gentlemen, but not from our hearts. And I think I may venture to hope, to prognosticate, that, whatever lofty sphere she may adorn in the future, to whatever heights in the social world she may soar, she will still continue to hold a corner in her own golden heart for the comrades of her Bohemian days. Ladies and gentlemen, I give you our hostess, Miss Sally Nicholas, coupled with the name of our old friend, her brother Fillmore."

Sally, watching her brother heave himself to his feet as the cheers died away, felt her heart beat a little faster with anticipation. Fillmore was a fluent young man, once a power in his college debating society, and it was for that reason that she had insisted on his coming here to-night. She had guessed that Mr. Faucitt, the old dear, would say all sorts of delightful things about her, and she had mistrusted her ability to make a fitting reply. And it was imperative that a fitting reply should proceed from someone. She knew Mr. Faucitt so well. He looked on these occasions rather in the light of scenes from some play; and, sustaining his own part in them with such polished grace, was certain to be pained by anything in the nature of an anti-climax after he should have ceased to take the stage. Eloquent himself, he must be answered with eloquence, or his whole evening would be spoiled.

Fillmore Nicholas smoothed a wrinkle out of his white waistcoat; and having rested one podgy hand on the table-cloth and the thumb of the other in his pocket, glanced down the table with eyes so haughtily drooping that Sally's fingers closed automatically about her orange, as she wondered whether even now it might not be a good thing . . .

It seems to be one of Nature's laws that the most attractive girls should have the least attractive brothers. Fillmore Nicholas had not worn well. At the age of seven he had been an extraordinarily beautiful child, but after that he had gone all to pieces; and now, at the age of twenty-five, it would be idle to deny that he was something of a mess. For the three years preceding his twenty-fifth birthday, restricted means and hard work had kept his figure in check; but with money there had come an ever-increasing sleekness. He looked as if he fed too often and too well.

All this, however, Sally was prepared to forgive him, if he would only make a good speech. She could see Mr. Faucitt leaning back in his chair, all courteous attention. Rolling periods were meat and drink to the old gentleman.

Fillmore spoke.

"I'm sure," said Fillmore, "you don't want a speech.

15

Very good of you to drink our health. Thank you."

He sat down.

The effect of these few simple words on the company was marked, but not in every case identical. To the majority the emotion which they brought was one of unmixed relief. There had been something so menacing, so easy and practised, in Fillmore's attitude as he had stood there that the gloomier-minded had given him at least twenty minutes, and even the optimists had reckoned that they would be lucky if they got off with ten. As far as the bulk of the guests were concerned, there was no grumbling. Fillmore's, to their thinking, had been the ideal after-dinner speech.

Far different was it with Mr. Maxwell Faucitt. The poor old man was wearing such an expression of surprise and dismay as he might have worn had somebody unexpectedly pulled the chair from under him. He was feeling the sick shock which comes to those who tread on a non-existent last stair. And Sally, catching sight of his face, uttered a sharp wordless exclamation as if she had seen a child fall down and hurt itself in the street. The next moment she had run round the table and was standing behind him with her arms round his neck. She spoke across him with a sob in her voice.

"My brother," she stammered, directing a malevolent look at the immaculate Fillmore, who, avoiding her gaze, glanced down his nose and smoothed another wrinkle out of his waistcoat, "has not said quite—quite all I hoped he was going to say. I can't make a speech, but . . ." Sally gulped, " . . . but, I love you all and of course I shall never forget you, and . . . and . . ."

Here Sally kissed Mr. Faucitt and burst into tears.

"There, there," said Mr. Faucitt, soothingly.

The kindest critic could not have claimed that Sally had been eloquent: nevertheless Mr. Maxwell Faucitt was conscious of no sense of anti-climax.

2

Sally had just finished telling her brother Fillmore what a pig he was. The lecture had taken place in the street outside the boarding-house immediately on the conclusion of the festivities, when Fillmore, who had furtively collected his hat and overcoat, had stolen forth into the night, had been over-taken and brought to bay by his justly indignant sister. Her remarks, punctuated at intervals by bleating sounds from the accused, had lasted some ten minutes.

As she paused for breath, Fillmore seemed to expand, like an indiarubber ball which has been sat on. Dignified as he was to the world, he had never been able to prevent himself being intimidated by Sally when in one of these moods of hers. He regretted this, for it hurt his self-esteem, but he did not see how the fact could be altered. Sally had always been like that. Even the uncle, who after the death of their parents had become their guardian, had never, though a grim man, been able to cope successfully with Sally. In that last hectic scene three years ago, which had ended in their going out into the world together like a second Adam and Eve, the verbal victory had been hers. And it had been Sally who had achieved triumph in the one battle which Mrs. Meecher, apparently as a matter of duty, always brought about with each of her patrons in the first week of their stay. A sweet-tempered girl, Sally, like most women of a generous spirit, had cyclonic potentialities.

As she seemed to have said her say, Fillmore kept on expanding till he had reached the normal, when he ventured upon a speech for the defence.

"What have *I* done?" demanded Fillmore plaintively.

"Do you want to hear all over again?"

"No, no," said Fillmore hastily. "But, listen, Sally, you don't understand my position. You don't seem to realize that all that sort of thing, all that boarding-house stuff, is a thing of the past. One's got beyond it. One wants to drop it. One wants to forget it, darn it! Be fair. Look at it from my viewpoint. I'm going to be a big man . . ."

"You're going to be a fat man," said Sally, coldly.

Fillmore refrained from discussing the point. He was sensitive.

"I'm going to do big things," he substituted. "I've got a deal on at this very moment which . . . well, I can't tell you about it, but it's going to be big. Well, what I'm driving at, is about all this sort of thing"—he indicated the lighted front of Mrs. Meecher's home-from-home with a wide gesture—"is that it's over. Finished and done with. These people were all very well when . . ."

" . . . when you'd lost your week's salary at poker and wanted to borrow a few dollars for the rent."

"I always paid them back," protested Fillmore, defensively.

"I did."

"Well, *we* did," said Fillmore, accepting the amendment with the air of a man who has no time for chopping straws. "Anyway, what I mean is, I don't see why, just because one has known people at a certain period in one's life when one was practically down and out, one should have them round one's neck for ever. One can't prevent people forming an I-knew-him-when club, but, darn it, one needn't attend the meetings."

"One's friends . . ."

"Oh, *friends*," said Fillmore. "That's just where all this makes me so tired. One's in a position where all these people are entitled to call themselves one's friends, simply because father put it in his will that I wasn't to get the money till I was twenty-five, instead of letting me have it at twenty-one like anybody else. I wonder where I should have been by now if I could have got that money when I was twenty-one."

"In the poor-house, probably," said Sally.

Fillmore was wounded.

"Ah! you don't believe in me," he sighed.

"Oh, you would be all right if you had one thing," said Sally.

Fillmore passed his qualities in swift review before his mental eye. Brains? Dash? Spaciousness? Initiative? All present and correct. He wondered where Sally imagined the hiatus to exist.

"One thing?" he said. "What's that?"

"A nurse."

Fillmore's sense of injury deepened. He supposed that this was always the way, that those nearest to a man never believed in his ability till he had proved it so masterfully that it no longer required the assistance of faith. Still, it was trying; and there was not much consolation to be derived from the thought that Napoleon had had to go through this sort of thing in his day.

"I shall find my place in the world," he said sulkily.

"Oh, you'll find your place all right," said Sally. "And I'll come round and bring you jelly and read to you on the days when visitors are allowed . . . Oh, hullo."

The last remark was addressed to a young man who had been swinging briskly along the sidewalk from the direction of Broadway and who now, coming abreast of them, stopped.

"Good evening, Mr. Foster."

"Good evening, Miss Nicholas."

"You don't know my brother, do you?"

"I don't believe I do."

"He left the underworld before you came to it," said Sally. "You wouldn't think it to look at him, but he was once a prune-eater among the proletariat, even as you and I. Mrs. Meecher looks on him as a son."

The two men shook hands. Fillmore was not short, but Gerald Foster with his lean, well-built figure seemed to tower over him. He was an Englishman, a man in the middle twenties, clean-shaven, keen-eyed, and very good to look at. Fillmore, who had recently been going in for one of those sum-up-your-fellow-man-at-a-glance courses, the better to fit himself for his career of greatness, was rather impressed. It seemed to him that this Mr. Foster, like himself, was one of those who Get There. If you are that kind yourself, you get into the knack of recognizing the others. It is a sort of gift.

There was a few moments of desultory conversation, of the kind that usually follows an introduction, and then Fillmore, by no means sorry to get the chance, took advantage of the coming of this new arrival to remove himself. He had not enjoyed his chat with Sally, and it seemed probable that he would enjoy a continuation of it even less. He was glad that Mr. Foster had happened along at this particular juncture. Excusing himself briefly, he hurried off down the street.

Sally stood for a minute, watching him till he had disappeared round the corner. She had a slightly regretful feeling that, now it was too late, she would think of a whole lot more good things which it would have been agreeable to say to him. And it had become obvious to her that Fillmore was not getting nearly enough of that kind of thing said to him nowadays. Then she dismissed him from her mind; and turning to Gerald Foster, slipped her arm through his.

"Well, Jerry, darling," she said. "What a shame you couldn't come to the party. Tell me all about everything."

3

It was exactly two months since Sally had become engaged to Gerald Foster; but so rigorously had they kept the secret that nobody at Mrs. Meecher's so much as suspected it.

To Sally, who all her life had hated concealing things, secrecy of any kind was objectionable: but in this matter Gerald had shown an odd streak almost of furtiveness in his character. An announced engagement complicated life. People fussed about you and bothered you. People either watched you or avoided you. Such were his arguments, and Sally, who would have glossed over and found excuses for a disposition on his part towards homicide or arson, put them down to artistic sensitiveness. There is nobody so sensitive as your artist, particularly if he be unsuccessful: and when an artist has so little success that he cannot afford to make a home for the woman he loves, his sensitiveness presumably becomes great indeed. Putting herself in his place, Sally could see that a protracted engagement, known by everybody, would be a standing advertisement of Gerald's failure to make good: and she acquiesced in the policy of secrecy, hoping that it would not last long. It seemed absurd to think of Gerald as an unsuccessful man. He had in him, as the recent Fillmore had perceived, something dynamic. He was one of those men of whom one could predict that they would succeed very suddenly and rapidly—overnight, as it were.

"The party," said Sally, "went off splendidly." They had passed the boarding-house door, and were walking slowly down the street. "Everybody enjoyed themselves, I think, even though Fillmore did his best to spoil things by coming looking like an advertisement of What The Smart Men Will Wear This Season. You didn't see his waistcoat just now. He had covered it up. Conscience, I suppose. It was white and bulgy and gleaming and full up of pearl buttons and everything. I saw Augustus Bartlett curl up like a burnt feather when he caught sight of it. Still, time seemed to heal the wound, and everybody relaxed after a bit. Mr. Faucitt made a speech and I made a speech and cried, and . . . oh, it was all very festive. It only needed you."

"I wish I could have come. I had to go to that dinner, though. Sally . . ." Gerald paused, and Sally saw that he was electric with suppressed excitement. "Sally, the play's going to be put on!"

Sally gave a little gasp. She had lived this moment in anticipation for weeks. She had always known that sooner or later this would happen. She had read his plays over and over again, and was convinced that they were wonderful. Of course, hers was a biased view; but then Elsa Doland also admired them; and Elsa's opinion was one that carried weight. Elsa was another of those people who were bound to succeed suddenly. Even old Mr. Faucitt, who was a stern judge of acting and rather inclined to consider that nowadays there was no such thing, believed that she was a girl with a future who would do something big directly she got her chance.

"Jerry!" She gave his arm a hug. "How simply terrific! Then Goble and Kohn have changed their minds after all and want it? I knew they would."

A slight cloud seemed to dim the sunniness of the author's mood.

"No, not that one," he said reluctantly. "No hope there, I'm afraid. I saw Goble this morning about that, and he said it didn't add up right. The one that's going to be put on is 'The Primrose Way.' You remember? It's got a big part for a girl in it."

"Of course! The one Elsa liked so much. Well, that's just as good. Who's going to do it? I thought you hadn't sent it out again."

"Well, it happens . . ." Gerald hesitated once more. "It seems that this man I was dining with to-night—a man named Cracknell . . ."

"Cracknell? Not *the* Cracknell?"

"The Cracknell?"

"The one people are always talking about. The man they call the Millionaire Kid."

"Yes. Why, do you know him?"

"He was at Harvard with Fillmore. I never saw him, but he must be rather a painful person."

"Oh, he's all right. Not much brains, of course, but—well, he's all right. And, anyway, he wants to put the play on."

"Well, that's splendid," said Sally: but she could not get the right ring of enthusiasm into her voice. She had had ideals for Gerald. She had dreamed of him invading Broadway triumphantly under the banner of one of the big managers whose name carried a prestige, and there seemed something unworthy in this association with a man whose chief claim to eminence lay in the fact that he was credited by metropolitan gossip with possessing the largest private stock of alcohol in existence.

"I thought you would be pleased," said Gerald.

21

"Oh, I am," said Sally.

With the buoyant optimism which never deserted her for long, she had already begun to cast off her momentary depression. After all, did it matter who financed a play so long as it obtained a production? A manager was simply a piece of machinery for paying the bills; and if he had money for that purpose, why demand asceticism and the finer sensibilities from him? The real thing that mattered was the question of who was going to play the leading part, that deftly drawn character which had so excited the admiration of Elsa Doland. She sought information on this point.

"Who will play Ruth?" she asked. "You must have somebody wonderful. It needs a tremendously clever woman. Did Mr. Cracknell say anything about that?"

"Oh, yes, we discussed that, of course."

"Well?"

"Well, it seems . . ." Again Sally noticed that odd, almost stealthy embarrassment. Gerald appeared unable to begin a sentence to-night without feeling his way into it like a man creeping cautiously down a dark alley. She noticed it the more because it was so different from his usual direct method. Gerald, as a rule, was not one of those who apologize for themselves. He was forthright and masterful and inclined to talk to her from a height. To-night he seemed different.

He broke off, was silent for a moment, and began again with a question.

"Do you know Mabel Hobson?"

"Mabel Hobson? I've seen her in the 'Follies,' of course."

Sally started. A suspicion had stung her, so monstrous that its absurdity became manifest the moment it had formed. And yet was it absurd? Most Broadway gossip filtered eventually into the boarding-house, chiefly through the medium of that seasoned sport, the mild young man who thought so highly of the redoubtable Benny Whistler, and she was aware that the name of Reginald Cracknell, which was always getting itself linked with somebody, had been coupled with that of Miss Hobson. It seemed likely that in this instance rumour spoke truth, for the lady was of that compellingly blonde beauty which attracts the Cracknells of this world. But even so . . .

"It seems that Cracknell . . ." said Gerald. "Apparently this man Cracknell . . ." He was finding Sally's bright, horrified gaze somewhat trying. "Well, the fact is Cracknell

22

believes in Mabel Hobson . . . and . . . well, he thinks this part would suit her."

"Oh, Jerry!"

Could infatuation go to such a length? Could even the spacious heart of a Reginald Cracknell so dominate that gentleman's small size in heads as to make him entrust a part like Ruth in "The Primrose Way" to one who, when desired by the producer of her last revue to carry a bowl of roses across the stage and place it on a table, had rebelled on the plea that she had not been engaged as a dancer? Surely even lovelorn Reginald could perceive that this was not the stuff of which great emotional actresses are made.

"Oh, Jerry!" she said again.

There was an uncomfortable silence. They turned and walked back in the direction of the boarding-house. Somehow Gerald's arm had managed to get itself detached from Sally's. She was conscious of a curious dull ache that was almost like a physical pain.

"Jerry! Is it worth it?" she burst out vehemently.

The question seemed to sting the young man into something like his usual decisive speech.

"Worth it? Of course it's worth it. It's a Broadway production. That's all that matters. Good heavens! I've been trying long enough to get a play on Broadway, and it isn't likely that I'm going to chuck away my chance when it comes along just because one might do better in the way of casting."

"But, Jerry! Mabel Hobson! It's . . . it's murder! Murder in the first degree."

"Nonsense. She'll be all right. The part will play itself. Besides, she has a personality and a following, and Cracknell will spend all the money in the world to make the thing a success. And it will be a start, whatever happens. Of course, it's worth it."

Fillmore would have been impressed by this speech. He would have recognized and respected in it the unmistakable ring which characterizes even the lightest utterances of those who get there. On Sally it had not immediately that effect. Nevertheless, her habit of making the best of things, working together with that primary article of her creed that the man she loved could do no wrong, succeeded finally in raising her spirits. Of course Jerry was right. It would have been foolish to refuse a contract because all its clauses were not ideal.

"You old darling," she said affectionately attaching herself to the vacant arm once more and giving it a penitent squeeze, "you're quite right. Of course you are. I can see it now. I was only a little startled at first. Everything's going to be wonderful. Let's get all our chickens out and count 'em. How are you going to spend the money?"

"I know how I'm going to spend a dollar of it," said Gerald completely restored.

"I mean the big money. What's a dollar?"

"It pays for a marriage-licence."

Sally gave his arm another squeeze.

"Ladies and gentlemen," she said. "Look at this man. Observe him. *My* partner!"

CHAPTER II

ENTER GINGER

I

SALLY was sitting with her back against a hillock of golden sand, watching with half-closed eyes the denizens of Roville-sur-Mer at their familiar morning occupations. At Roville, as at most French seashore resorts, the morning is the time when the visiting population assembles in force on the beach. Whiskered fathers of families made cheerful patches of colour in the foreground. Their female friends and relatives clustered in groups under gay parasols. Dogs roamed to and fro, and children dug industriously with spades, ever and anon suspending their labours in order to smite one another with these handy implements. One of the dogs, a poodle of military aspect, wandered up to Sally: and discovering that she was in possession of a box of sweets, decided to remain and await developments.

Few things are so pleasant as the anticipation of them, but Sally's vacation had proved an exception to this rule. It had been a magic month of lazy happiness. She had drifted luxuriously from one French town to another, till the charm of Roville, with its blue sky, its Casino, its snow-white hotels along the Promenade, and its general glitter and gaiety, had brought her to a halt. Here she could have stayed indefinitely, but the voice of America was calling her back. Gerald had written to say that "The Primrose Way" was to be produced in Detroit, preliminary to its New York run, so soon that, if she wished to see the opening, she must return at once. A scrappy, hurried, unsatisfactory letter, the letter of a busy man: but one that Sally could not ignore. She was leaving Roville to-morrow.

To-day, however, was to-day: and she sat and watched the bathers with a familiar feeling of peace, revelling as usual in the still novel sensation of having nothing to do but bask in the warm sunshine and listen to the faint murmur of the little waves.

But, if there was one drawback, she had discovered, to a

morning on the Roville *plage*, it was that you had a tendency to fall asleep: and this is a degrading thing to do so soon after breakfast, even if you are on a holiday. Usually, Sally fought stoutly against the temptation, but to-day the sun was so warm and the whisper of the waves so insinuating that she had almost dozed off, when she was aroused by voices close at hand. There were many voices on the beach, both near and distant, but these were talking English, a novelty in Roville, and the sound of the familiar tongue jerked Sally back from the borders of sleep. A few feet away, two men had seated themselves on the sand.

From the first moment she had set out on her travels, it had been one of Sally's principal amusements to examine the strangers whom chance threw in her way and to try by the light of her intuition to fit them out with characters and occupations: nor had she been discouraged by an almost consistent failure to guess right. Out of the corner of her eye she inspected these two men.

The first of the pair did not attract her. He was a tall, dark man whose tight, precise mouth and rather high cheeks bones gave him an appearance vaguely sinister. He had the dusky look of the clean-shaven man whose life is a perpetual struggle with a determined beard. He certainly shaved twice a day, and just as certainly had the self-control not to swear when he cut himself. She could picture him smiling nastily when this happened.

"Hard," diagnosed Sally. "I shouldn't like him. A lawyer or something, I think."

She turned to the other and found herself looking into his eyes. This was because he had been staring at Sally with the utmost intentness ever since his arrival. His mouth had opened slightly. He had the air of a man who, after many disappointments, has at last found something worth looking at.

"Rather a dear," decided Sally.

He was a sturdy, thick-set young man with an amiable, freckled face and the reddest hair Sally had ever seen. He had a square chin, and at one angle of the chin a slight cut. And Sally was convinced that, however he had behaved on receipt of that wound, it had not been with superior self-control.

"A temper, I should think," she meditated. "Very quick, but soon over. Not very clever, I should say, but nice."

She looked away, finding his fascinated gaze a little embarrassing.

The dark man, who in the objectionably competent fashion which, one felt, characterized all his actions, had just succeeded in lighting a cigarette in the teeth of a strong breeze, threw away the match and resumed the conversation, which had presumably been interrupted by the process of sitting down.

"And how *is* Scrymgeour?" he inquired.

"Oh, all right," replied the young man with red hair absently. Sally was looking straight in front of her, but she felt that his eyes were still busy.

"I was surprised at his being here. He told me he meant to stay in Paris."

There was a slight pause. Sally gave the attentive poodle a piece of nougat.

"I say," observed the red-haired young man in clear, penetrating tones that vibrated with intense feeling, "that's the prettiest girl I've seen in my life!"

2

At this frank revelation of the red-haired young man's personal opinions, Sally, though considerably startled, was not displeased. A broad-minded girl, the outburst seemed to her a legitimate comment on a matter of public interest. The young man's companion, on the other hand, was unmixedly shocked.

"My dear fellow!" he ejaculated.

"Oh, it's all right," said the red-haired young man, unmoved. "She can't understand. There isn't a bally soul in this dashed place that can speak a word of English. If I didn't happen to remember a few odd bits of French, I should have starved by this time. That girl," he went on, returning to the subject most imperatively occupying his mind, "is an absolute topper! I give you my solemn word I've never seen anybody to touch her. Look at those hands and feet. You don't get them outside France. Of course, her mouth is a bit wide," he said reluctantly.

Sally's immobility, added to the other's assurance concerning the linguistic deficiencies of the inhabitants of Roville, seemed to reassure the dark man. He breathed again. At no period of his life had he ever behaved with anything but the most scrupulous correctness himself, but he had quailed at the idea of being associated even remotely with incorrectness in another. It had been a black moment for him when the red-haired young man had uttered those few kind words.

"Still you ought to be careful," he said austerely.

He looked at Sally, who was now dividing her attention between the poodle and a raffish-looking mongrel, who had joined the party, and returned to the topic of the mysterious Scrymgeour.

"How is Scrymgeour's dyspepsia?"

The red-haired young man seemed but faintly interested in the vicissitudes of Scrymgeour's interior.

"Do you notice the way her hair sort of curls over her ears?" he said. "Eh? Oh, pretty much the same, I think."

"What hotel are you staying at?"

"The Normandie."

Sally, dipping into the box for another chocolate cream, gave an imperceptible start. She, too, was staying at the Normandie. She presumed that her admirer was a recent arrival, for she had seen nothing of him at the hotel.

"The Normandie?" The dark man looked puzzled. "I know Roville pretty well by report, but I've never heard of any Hotel Normandie. Where is it?"

"It's a little shanty down near the station. Not much of a place. Still, it's cheap, and the cooking's all right."

His companion's bewilderment increased.

"What on earth is a man like Scrymgeour doing there?" he said. Sally was conscious of an urgent desire to know more and more about the absent Scrymgeour. Constant repetition of his name had made him seem almost like an old friend. "If there's one thing he's fussy about . . ."

"There are at least eleven thousand things he's fussy about," interrupted the red-haired young man disapprovingly. "Jumpy old blighter!"

"If there's one thing he's particular about, it's the sort of hotel he goes to. Ever since I've known him he has always wanted the best. I should have thought he would have gone to the Splendide." He mused on this problem in a dissatisfied sort of way for a moment, then seemed to reconcile himself to the fact that a rich man's eccentricities must be humoured. "I'd like to see him again. Ask him if he will dine with me at the Splendide to-night. Say eight sharp."

Sally, occupied with her dogs, whose numbers had now been augmented by a white terrier with a black patch over its left eye, could not see the young man's face: but his voice, when he replied, told her that something was wrong. There was a false airiness in it.

"Oh, Scrymgeour isn't in Roville."

"No? Where is he?"

"Paris, I believe."

"What!" The dark man's voice sharpened. He sounded as though he were cross-examining a reluctant witness. "Then why aren't you there? What are you doing here? Did he give you a holiday?"

"Yes, he did."

"When do you rejoin him?"

"I don't."

"What!"

The red-haired young man's manner was not unmistakably dogged.

"Well, if you want to know," he said, "the old blighter fired me the day before yesterday."

3

There was a shuffling of sand as the dark man sprang up. Sally, intent on the drama which was unfolding itself beside her, absent-mindedly gave the poodle a piece of nougat which should by rights have gone to the terrier. She shot a swift glance sideways, and saw the dark man standing in an attitude rather reminiscent of the stern father of melodrama about to drive his erring daughter out into the snow. The red-haired young man, outwardly stolid, was gazing before him down the beach at a fat bather in an orange suit who, after six false starts, was now actually in the water, floating with the dignity of a wrecked balloon.

"Do you mean to tell me," demanded the dark man, "that, after all the trouble the family took to get you what was practically a sinecure with endless possibilities if you only behaved yourself, you have deliberately thrown away . . ." A despairing gesture completed the sentence. "Good God, you're hopeless!"

The red-haired young man made no reply. He continued to gaze down the beach. Of all outdoor sports, few are more stimulating than watching middle-aged Frenchmen bathe. Drama, action, suspense, all are here. From the first stealthy testing of the water with an apprehensive toe to the final seal-like plunge, there is never a dull moment. And apart from the excitement of the thing, judging it from a purely aesthetic standpoint, his must be a dull soul who can fail to be uplifted by the spectacle of a series of very stout men with whiskers, seen in tight bathing suits against a background of brightest blue. Yet the young man with red hair, recently in the employment of Mr. Scrymgeour, eyed this free circus without any enjoyment whatever.

"It's maddening! What are you going to do? What do you expect us to do? Are we to spend our whole lives getting you positions which you won't keep? I can tell you we're . . . it's monstrous! it's sickening! Good God!"

And with these words the dark man, apparently feeling, as Sally had sometimes felt in the society of her brother Fillmore, the futility of mere language, turned sharply and stalked away up the beach, the dignity of his exit somewhat marred a moment later by the fact of his straw hat blowing off and being trodden on by a passing child.

He left behind him the sort of electric calm which follows the falling of a thunderbolt; that stunned calm through which the air seems still to quiver protestingly. How long this would have lasted one cannot say: for towards the end of the first minute it was shattered by a purely terrestrial uproar. With an abruptness heralded only by one short, low gurgling snarl, there sprang into being the prettiest dog fight that Roville had seen that season.

It was the terrier with the black patch who began it. That was Sally's opinion: and such, one feels, will be the verdict of history. His best friend, anxious to make out a case for him, could not have denied that he fired the first gun of the campaign. But we must be just. The fault was really Sally's. Absorbed in the scene which had just concluded and acutely inquisitive as to why the shadowy Scrymgeour had seen fit to dispense with the red-haired young man's services, she had thrice in succession helped the poodle out of his turn. The third occasion was too much for the terrier.

There is about any dog fight a wild, gusty fury which affects the average mortal with something of the helplessness induced by some vast clashing of the elements. It seems so outside one's jurisdiction. One is oppressed with a sense of the futility of interference. And this was no ordinary dog fight. It was a stunning mêlée, which would have excited

favourable comment even among the blasé residents of a
negro quarter or the not easily-pleased critics of a Lancashire
mining-village. From all over the beach dogs of every size,
breed, and colour were racing to the scene: and while some
of these merely remained in the ringside seats and barked, a
considerable proportion immediately started fighting one
another on general principles, well content to be in action
without bothering about first causes. The terrier had got the
poodle by the left hind-leg and was restating his war-aims.
The raffish mongrel was apparently endeavouring to fletch-
erize a complete stranger of the Sealyham family.

Sally was frankly unequal to the situation, as were the
entire crowd of spectators who had come galloping up from
the water's edge. She had been paralysed from the start.
Snarling bundles bumped against her legs and bounced away
again, but she made no move. Advice in fluent French rent
the air. Arms waved, and well-filled bathing suits leaped up
and down. But nobody did anything practical until in the
centre of the theatre of war there suddenly appeared the red-
haired young man.

The only reason why dog fights do not go on for ever is
that Providence has decided that on each such occasion
there shall always be among those present one Master Mind;
one wizard who, whatever his shortcomings in other battles
of life, is in this single particular sphere competent and
dominating. At Roville-sur-Mer it was the red-haired young
man. His dark companion might have turned from him in
disgust: his services might not have seemed worth retaining by
the haughty Scrymgeour: he might be a pain in the neck to
"the family"; but he did know how to stop a dog fight. From
the first moment of his intervention calm began to steal over
the scene. He had the same effect on the almost inextricably
entwined belligerents as, in mediaeval legend, the Holy
Grail, sliding down the sunbeam, used to have on battling
knights. He did not look like a dove of peace, but the most
captious could not have denied that he brought home the
goods. There was a magic in his soothing hands, a spell in
his voice: and in a shorter time than one would have believed
possible dog after dog had been sorted out and calmed down;
until presently all that was left of Armageddon was one
solitary small Scotch terrier, thoughtfully licking a chewed
leg. The rest of the combatants, once more in their right
mind and wondering what all the fuss was about, had been

31

captured and haled away in a whirl of recrimination by voluble owners.

Having achieved this miracle, the young man turned to Sally. Gallant, one might say reckless, as he had been a moment before, he now gave indications of a rather pleasing shyness. He braced himself with that painful air of effort which announces to the world that an Englishman is about to speak a language other than his own.

"*J'espère*," he said, having swallowed once or twice to brace himself up for the journey through the jungle of a foreign tongue, "*J'espère que vous n'êtes pas*—oh, dammit, what's the word—*j'espère que vous n'êtes pas blessée?*"

"*Blessée?*"

"Yes, *blessée.* Wounded. Hurt, don't you know. Bitten. Oh, dash it. *J'espère* . . ."

"Oh, bitten!" said Sally, dimpling. "Oh, no, thanks very much. I wasn't bitten. And I think it was awfully brave of you to save all our lives."

The compliment seemed to pass over the young man's head. He stared at Sally with horrified eyes. Over his amiable face there swept a vivid blush. His jaw dropped.

"Oh, my sainted aunt!" he ejaculated.

Then, as if the situation was too much for him and flight the only possible solution, he spun round and disappeared at a walk so rapid that it was almost a run. Sally watched him go and was sorry that he had torn himself away. She still wanted to know why Scrymgeour had fired him.

4

Bedtime at Roville is an hour that seems to vary according to one's proximity to the sea. The gilded palaces along the front keep deplorable hours, polluting the night air till dawn with indefatigable jazz: but at the *pensions* of the economical like the Normandie, early to bed is the rule. True, Jules, the stout young native who combined the offices of night-clerk and lift attendant at that establishment, was on duty in the hall throughout the night, but few of the Normandie's patrons made use of his services.

Sally, entering shortly before twelve o'clock on the night of the day on which the dark man, the red-haired young man, and their friend Scrymgeour had come into her life, found the little hall dim and silent. Through the iron cage of the lift a single faint bulb glowed: another, over the desk in the far corner, illuminated the upper half of Jules, slumbering in a chair. Jules seemed to Sally to be on duty in some capacity or other all the time. His work, like women's, was never done. He was now restoring his tissues with a few winks of much-needed beauty sleep. Sally, who had been to the Casino to hear the band and afterwards had strolled on the moonlit promenade, had a guilty sense of intrusion.

As she stood there, reluctant to break in on Jules' rest—for her sympathetic heart, always at the disposal of the oppressed, had long ached for this overworked peon—she was relieved to hear footsteps in the street outside, followed by the opening of the front door. If Jules would have had to wake up anyway, she felt her sense of responsibility lessened. The door, having opened, closed again with a bang. Jules stirred, gurgled, blinked, and sat up, and Sally, turning, perceived that the new arrival was the red-haired young man.

"Oh, good evening," said Sally welcomingly.

The young man stopped, and shuffled uncomfortably. The morning's happenings were obviously still green in his memory. He had either not ceased blushing since their last meeting or he was celebrating their reunion by beginning to blush again: for his face was a familiar scarlet.

"Er—good evening," he said, disentangling his feet, which, in the embarrassment of the moment, had somehow got coiled up together.

"Or *bon soir*, I suppose *you* would say," murmured Sally.

The young man acknowledged receipt of this thrust by dropping his hat and tripping over it as he stooped to pick it up.

Jules, meanwhile, who had been navigating in a sort of somnambulistic trance in the neighbourhood of the lift, now threw back the cage with a rattle.

"It's a shame to have woken you up," said Sally, commiseratingly, stepping in.

Jules did not reply, for the excellent reason that he had not been woken up. Constant practice enabled him to do this sort of work without breaking his slumber. His brain, if you could call it that, was working automatically. He had shut up the gate with a clang and was tugging sluggishly at the correct rope, so that the lift was going slowly up instead of retiring down into the basement, but he was not awake.

Sally and the red-haired young man sat side by side on the small seat, watching their conductor's efforts. After the first spurt, conversation had languished. Sally had nothing of immediate interest to say, and her companion seemed to be one of these strong, silent men you read about. Only a slight snore from Jules broke the silence.

At the third floor Sally leaned forward and prodded Jules in the lower ribs. All through her stay at Roville, she had found in dealing with the native population that actions spoke louder than words. If she wanted anything in a restaurant or at a shop, she pointed; and, when she wished the lift to stop, she prodded the man in charge. It was a system worth a dozen French conversation books.

Jules brought the machine to a halt: and it was at this point that he should have done the one thing connected with his professional activities which he did really well—the opening, to wit, of the iron cage. There are ways of doing this. Jules' was the right way. He was accustomed to do it with a flourish, and generally remarked "V'la!" in a modest but self-congratulatory voice as though he would have liked to see another man who could have put through a job like that. Jules' opinion was that he might not be much to look at, but that he could open a lift door.

To-night, however, it seemed as if even this not very exacting feat was beyond his powers. Instead of inserting his key in the lock, he stood staring in an attitude of frozen horror. He was a man who took most things in life pretty seriously, and whatever was the little difficulty just now seemed to have broken him all up.

"There appears," said Sally, turning to her companion, "to be a hitch. Would you mind asking what's the matter? I don't know any French myself except 'oo la la!'"

The young man, thus appealed to, nerved himself to the task. He eyed the melancholy Jules doubtfully, and coughed in a strangled sort of way.

"Oh, *esker . . . esker vous . . .*"

"Don't weaken," said Sally. "I think you've got him going."

"*Esker vous . . . Pourquoi vous ne . . .* I mean *ne vous . . .* that's to say, *quel est le raison . . .*"

He broke off here, because at this point Jules began to explain. He explained very rapidly and at considerable length. The fact that neither of his hearers understood a

34

word of what he was saying appeared not to have impressed itself upon him. Or, if he gave a thought to it, he dismissed the objection as trifling. He wanted to explain, and he explained. Words rushed from him like water from a geyser. Sounds which you felt you would have been able to put a meaning to if he had detached them from the main body and repeated them slowly, went swirling down the stream and were lost for ever.

"Stop him!" said Sally firmly.

The red-haired young man looked as a native of Johnstown might have looked on being requested to stop that city's celebrated flood.

"Stop him?"

"Yes. Blow a whistle or something."

Out of the depths of the young man's memory there swam to the surface a single word—a word which he must have heard somewhere or read somewhere: a legacy, perhaps, from long-vanished school-days.

"*Zut!*" he barked, and instantaneously Jules turned himself off at the main. There was a moment of dazed silence, such as might occur in a boiler-factory if the works suddenly shut down.

"Quick! Now you've got him!" cried Sally. "Ask him what he's talking about—if he knows, which I doubt—and tell him to speak slowly. Then we shall get somewhere."

The young man nodded intelligently. The advice was good.

"*Lentement,*" he said. "*Parlez lentement. Pas si*—you know what I mean—*pas si* dashed *vite!*"

"Ah-a-ah!" cried Jules, catching the idea on the fly. "*Lentement. Ah, oui, lentement.*"

There followed a lengthy conversation which, while conveying nothing to Sally, seemed intelligible to the red-haired linguist.

"The silly ass," he was able to announce some few minutes later, "has made a bloomer. Apparently he was half asleep when we came in, and he shoved us into the lift and slammed the door, forgetting that he had left the keys on the desk."

"I see," said Sally. "So we're shut in?"

"I'm afraid so. I wish to goodness," said the young man, "I knew French well. I'd curse him with some vim and not a little animation, the chump! I wonder what 'blighter' is in French," he said, meditating.

"It's the merest suggestion," said Sally, "but oughtn't we to *do* something?"

"What could we do?"

"Well, for one thing, we might all utter a loud yell. It would scare most of the people in the hotel to death, but there might be a survivor or two who would come and investigate and let us out."

"What a ripping idea!" said the young man, impressed.

"I'm glad you like it. Now tell him the main out-line, or he'll think we've gone mad."

The young man searched for words, and eventually found some which expressed his meaning lamely but well enough to cause Jules to nod in a depressed sort of way.

"Fine!" said Sally. "Now, all together at the word 'three.' One—two—Oh, poor darling!" she broke off. "Look at him!"

In the far corner of the lift, the emotional Jules was sobbing silently into the bunch of cotton-waste which served him in the office of a pocket-handkerchief. His broken-hearted gulps echoed hollowly down the shaft.

5

In these days of cheap books of instruction on every subject under the sun, we most of us know how to behave in the majority of life's little crises. We have only ourselves to blame if we are ignorant of what to do before the doctor comes, of how to make a dainty winter coat for baby out of father's last year's under-vest and of the best method of coping with the cold mutton. But nobody yet has come forward with practical advice as to the correct method of behaviour to be adopted when a lift-attendant starts crying. And Sally and her companion, as a consequence, for a few moments merely stared at each other helplessly.

"Poor darling!" said Sally, finding speech. "Ask him what's the matter."

The young man looked at her doubtfully.

"You know," he said, "I don't enjoy chatting with this blighter. I mean to say, it's a bit of an effort. I don't know why it is, but talking French always makes me feel as if my nose were coming off. Couldn't we just leave him to have his cry out by himself?"

"The idea!" said Sally. "Have you no heart? Are you one of those fiends in human shape?"

He turned reluctantly to Jules, and paused to overhaul his vocabulary.

"You ought to be thankful for this chance," said Sally. "It's the only real way of learning French, and you're getting a lesson for nothing. What did he say then?"

"Something about losing something, it seemed to me. I thought I caught the word *perdu*."

"But that means a partridge, doesn't it? I'm sure I've seen it on the menus."

"Would he talk about partridges at a time like this?"

"He might. The French are extraordinary people."

"Well, I'll have another go at him. But he's a difficult chap to chat with. If you give him the least encouragement, he sort of goes off like a rocket." He addressed another question to the sufferer, and listened attentively to the voluble reply.

"Oh!" he said with sudden enlightenment. "Your *job?*" He turned to Sally. "I got it that time," he said. "The trouble is, he says, that if we yell and rouse the house, we'll get out all right, but he will lose his job, because this is the second time this sort of thing has happened, and they warned him last time that once more would mean the push."

"Then we mustn't dream of yelling," said Sally, decidedly.

"It means a pretty long wait, you know. As far as I can gather, there's just a chance of somebody else coming in later, in which case he could let us out. But it's doubtful. He rather thinks that everybody has gone to roost."

"Well, we must try it. I wouldn't think of losing the poor man his job. Tell him to take the car down to the ground-floor, and then we'll just sit and amuse ourselves till something happens. We've lots to talk about. We can tell each other the story of our lives."

Jules, cheered by his victims' kindly forbearance, lowered the car to the ground floor, where, after a glance of infinite longing at the keys on the distant desk, the sort of glance which Moses must have cast at the Promised Land from the summit of Mount Pisgah, he sagged down in a heap and resumed his slumbers. Sally settled herself as comfortably as possible in her corner.

"You'd better smoke," she said. "It will be something to do."

"Thanks awfully."

"And now," said Sally, "tell me why Scrymgeour fired you."

Little by little, under the stimulating influence of this nocturnal adventure, the red-haired young man had lost that shy confusion which had rendered him so ill at ease when he had encountered Sally in the hall of the hotel; but at this question embarrassment gripped him once more. Another of those comprehensive blushes of his raced over his face, and he stammered.

"I say, I'm glad . . . I'm fearfully sorry about that, you know!"

"About Scrymgeour?"

"You know what I mean. I mean, about making such a most ghastly ass of myself this morning. I . . . I never dreamed you understood English."

"Why, I didn't object. I thought you were very nice and complimentary. Of course, I don't know how many girls you've seen in your life, but . . ."

"No, I say, don't! It makes me feel such a chump."

"And I'm sorry about my mouth. It *is* wide. But I know you're a fair-minded man and realize that it isn't my fault."

"Don't rub it in," pleaded the young man. "As a matter of fact, if you want to know, I think your mouth is absolutely perfect. I think," he proceeded, a little feverishly, "that you are the most indescribable topper that ever . . ."

"You were going to tell me about Scrymgeour," said Sally.

The young man blinked as if he had collided with some hard object while sleep-walking. Eloquence had carried him away.

"Scrymgeour?" he said. "Oh, that would bore you."

"Don't be silly," said Sally reprovingly. "Can't you realize that we're practically castaways on a desert island? There's nothing to do till to-morrow but talk about ourselves. I want to hear all about you, and then I'll tell you all about myself. If you feel diffident about starting the revelations, I'll begin. Better start with names. Mine is Sally Nicholas. What's yours?"

"Mine? Oh, ah, yes, I see what you mean."

"I thought you would. I put it as clearly as I could. Well, what is it?"

"Kemp."

"And the first name?"

"Well, as a matter of fact," said the young man, "I've always rather hushed up my first name, because when I was christened they worked a low-down trick on me!"

"You can't shock *me*," said Sally, encouragingly. "My father's name was Ezekiel, and I've a brother who was christened Fillmore."

Mr. Kemp brightened. "Well, mine isn't as bad as that . . . No, I don't mean that," he broke off apologetically. "Both awfully jolly names, of course . . ."

"Get on," said Sally.

"Well, they called me Lancelot. And, of course, the thing is that I don't look like a Lancelot and never shall. My pals," he added in a more cheerful strain, "call me Ginger."

"I don't blame them," said Sally.

"Perhaps you wouldn't mind thinking of me as Ginger?" suggested the young man diffidently.

"Certainly."

"That's awfully good of you."

"Not at all."

Jules stirred in his sleep and grunted. No other sound came to disturb the stillness of the night.

"You were going to tell me about yourself?" said Mr. Lancelot (Ginger) Kemp.

"I'm going to tell you *all* about myself," said Sally, "not because I think it will interest you . . ."

"Oh, it will!"

"Not, I say, because I think it will interest you . . ."

"It will, really."

Sally looked at him coldly.

"Is this a duet?" she inquired, "or have I the floor?"

"I'm awfully sorry."

"Not, I repeat for the third time, because I think it will interest you, but because if I do you won't have any excuse for not telling me your life-history, and you wouldn't believe how inquisitive I am. Well, in the first place, I live in America. I'm over here on a holiday. And it's the first real holiday I've had in three years—since I left home, in fact." Sally paused. "I ran away from home," she said.

"Good egg!" said Ginger Kemp.

"I beg your pardon?"

"I mean, quite right. I bet you were quite right."

"When I say home," Sally went on, "it was only a sort of imitation home, you know. One of those just-as-good homes which are never as satisfactory as the real kind. My father and mother both died a good many years ago. My brother and I were dumped down on the reluctant doorstep of an uncle."

"Uncles," said Ginger Kemp, feelingly, "are the devil. I've got an . . . but I'm interrupting you."

"My uncle was our trustee. He had control of all my brother's money and mine till I was twenty-one. My brother was to get his when he was twenty-five. My poor father trusted him blindly, and what do you think happened?"

"Good Lord! The blighter embezzled the lot?"

"No, not a cent. Wasn't it extraordinary! Have you ever heard of a blindly trusted uncle who was perfectly honest? Well, mine was. But the trouble was that, while an excellent man to have looking after one's money, he wasn't a very lovable character. He was very hard. Hard! He was as hard as—well, nearly as hard as this seat. He hated poor Fill . . ."

"Phil?"

"I broke it to you just now that my brother's name was Fillmore."

"Oh, your brother. Oh, ah, yes."

"He was always picking on poor Fill. And I'm bound to say that Fill rather laid himself out as what you might call a pickee. He was always getting into trouble. One day, about three years ago, he was expelled from Harvard, and my uncle vowed he would have nothing more to do with him. So I said, if Fill left, I would leave. And, as this seemed to be my uncle's idea of a large evening, no objection was raised, and Fill and I departed. We went to New York, and there we've been ever since. About six months' ago Fill passed the twenty-five mark and collected his money, and last month I marched past the given point and got mine. So it all ends happily, you see. Now tell me about yourself."

"But, I say, you know, dash it, you've skipped a lot. I mean to say, you must have had an awful time in New York, didn't you? How on earth did you get along?"

"Oh, we found work. My brother tried one or two things, and finally became an assistant stage-manager with some theatre people. The only thing I could do, having been raised in enervating luxury, was ballroom dancing, so I ball-room danced. I got a job at a place in Broadway called 'The Flower Garden' as what is humorously called an 'instructress,' as if anybody could 'instruct' the men who came there. One was lucky if one saved one's life and wasn't quashed to death."

"How perfectly foul!"

"Oh, I don't know. It was rather fun for a while. Still," said Sally, meditatively, "I'm not saying I could have held out much longer: I was beginning to give. I suppose I've been trampled underfoot by more fat men than any other girl of my age in America. I don't know why it was, but every man who came in who was a bit overweight seemed to make for me by instinct. That's why I like to sit on the sands here and watch these Frenchmen bathing. It's just heavenly to lie back and watch a two hundred and fifty pound man coming along and feel that he isn't going to dance with me."

"But, I say! How absolutely rotten it must have been for you!"

"Well, I'll tell you one thing. It's going to make me a very domesticated wife one of these days. You won't find *me* gadding about in gilded jazz-palaces! For me, a little place in the country somewhere, with my knitting and an Elsie book, and bed at half-past nine! And now tell me the story of *your* life. And make it long because I'm perfectly certain there's going to be no relief-expedition. I'm sure the last dweller under this roof came in years ago. We shall be here till morning."

"I really think we had better shout, you know."

"And lose Jules his job? Never!"

"Well, of course, I'm sorry for poor old Jules' troubles, but I hate to think of you having to . . ."

"Now get on with the story," said Sally.

6

Ginger Kemp exhibited some of the symptoms of a young bridegroom called upon at a wedding-breakfast to respond to the toast. He moved his feet restlessly and twisted his fingers.

"I hate talking about myself, you know," he said.

"So I supposed," said Sally. "That's why I gave you my autobiography first, to give you no chance of backing out. Don't be such a shrinking violet. We're all shipwrecked mariners here. I am intensely interested in your narrative.

And, even if I wasn't, I'd much rather listen to it than to Jules' snoring."

"He *is* snoring a bit, what? Does it annoy you? Shall I stir him?"

"You seem to have an extraordinary brutal streak in your nature," said Sally. "You appear to think of nothing else but schemes for harassing poor Jules. Leave him alone for a second, and start telling me about yourself."

"Where shall I start?"

"Well, not with your childhood, I think. We'll skip that."

"Well . . ." Ginger Kemp knitted his brow, searching for a dramatic opening. "Well, I'm more or less what you might call an orphan, like you. I mean to say, both my people are dead and all that sort of thing."

"Thanks for explaining. That has made it quite clear."

"I can't remember my mother. My father died when I was in my last year at Cambridge. I'd been having a most awfully good time at the 'varsity,' " said Ginger, warming to his theme. "Not thick, you know, but good. I'd got my rugger and boxing blues and I'd just been picked for scrum-half for England against the North in the first trial match, and between ourselves it really did look as if I was more or less of a snip for my international."

Sally gazed at him wide eyed.

"Is that good or bad?" she asked.

"Eh?"

"Are you reciting a catalogue of your crimes, or do you expect me to get up and cheer? What is a rugger blue, to start with?"

"Well, it's . . . it's a rugger blue, you know."

"Oh, I see," said Sally. "You mean a rugger blue."

"I mean to say, I played rugger—footer—that's to say, football—Rugby football—for Cambridge, against Oxford. I was scrum-half."

"And what is a scrum-half?" asked Sally, patiently. "Yes, I know you're going to say it's a scrum-half, but can't you make it easier?"

"The scrum-half," said Ginger, "is the half who works the scrum. He slings the pill out to the fly-half, who starts the three-quarters going. I don't know if you understand?"

"I don't."

"It's dashed hard to explain," said Ginger Kemp, unhappily. "I mean, I don't think I've ever met anyone before who didn't know what a scrum-half was."

"Well, I can see that it has something to do with football, so we'll leave it at that. I suppose it's something like our quarter-back. And what's an international?"

"It's called getting your international when you play for England, you know. England plays Wales, France, Ireland, and Scotland. If it hadn't been for the smash, I think I should have played for England against Wales."

"I see at last. What you're trying to tell me is that you were very good at football."

Ginger Kemp blushed warmly.

"Oh, I don't say that. England was pretty short of scrum-halves that year."

"What a horrible thing to happen to a country! Still, you were likely to be picked on the All-England team when the smash came? What was the smash?"

"Well, it turned out that the poor old pater hadn't left a penny. I never understood the process exactly, but I'd always supposed that we were pretty well off; and then it turned out that I hadn't anything at all. I'm bound to say it was a bit of a jar. I had to come down from Cambridge and go to work in my uncle's office. Of course, I made an absolute hash of it."

"Why, of course?"

"Well, I'm not a very clever sort of chap, you see. I somehow didn't seem able to grasp the workings. After about a year, my uncle, getting a bit fed-up, hoofed me out and got me a mastership at a school, and I made a hash of that. He got me one or two other jobs, and I made a hash of those."

"You certainly do seem to be one of our most prominent young hashers!" gasped Sally.

"I am," said Ginger, modestly.

There was a silence.

"And what about Scrymgeour?" Sally asked.

"That was the last of the jobs," said Ginger. "Scrymgeour is a pompous old ass who think's he's going to be Prime Minister some day. He's a big bug at the Bar and has just got into Parliament. My cousin used to devil for him. That's how I got mixed up with the blighter."

"Your cousin used . . .? I wish you would talk English."

"That was my cousin who was with me on the beach this morning."

"And what did you say he used to do for Mr. Scrymgeour?"

"Oh, it's called devilling. My cousin's at the Bar, too—one of our rising nibs, as a matter of fact . . ."

"I thought he was a lawyer of some kind."

"He's got a long way beyond it now, but when he started he used to devil for Scrymgeour—assist him, don't you know. His name's Carmyle, you know. Perhaps you've heard of him? He's rather a prominent johnny in his way. Bruce Carmyle, you know."

"I haven't."

"Well, he got me this job of secretary to Scrymgeour."

"And why did Mr. Scrymgeour fire you?"

Ginger Kemp's face darkened. He frowned. Sally, watching him, felt that she had been right when she had guessed that he had a temper. She liked him none the worse for it. Mild men did not appeal to her.

"I don't know if you're fond of dogs?" said Ginger.

"I used to be before this morning," said Sally. "And I suppose I shall be again in time. For the moment I've had what you might call rather a surfeit of dogs. But aren't you straying from the point? I asked you why Mr. Scrymgeour dismissed you."

"I'm telling you."

"I'm glad of that. I didn't know."

"The old brute," said Ginger, frowning again, "has a dog. A very jolly little spaniel. Great pal of mine. And Scrymgeour is the sort of fool who oughtn't to be allowed to own a dog. He's one of those asses who isn't fit to own a dog. As a matter of fact, of all the blighted, pompous, bullying, shrivelled-souled old devils . . ."

"One moment," said Sally. "I'm getting an impression that you don't like Mr. Scrymgeour. Am I right?"

"Yes!"

"I thought so. Womanly intuition! Go on."

"He used to insist on the poor animal doing tricks. I hate seeing a dog do tricks. Dogs loathe it, you know. They're frightfully sensitive. Well, Scrymgeour used to make this spaniel of his do tricks—fool-things that no self-respecting dogs would do: and eventually poor old Billy got fed up and jibbed. He was too polite to bite, but he sort of shook his head and crawled under a chair. You'd have thought anyone would have let it go at that, but would old Scrymgeour? Not a bit of it! Of all the poisonous . . ."

"Yes, I know. Go on."

"Well, the thing ended in the blighter hauling him out from under the chair and getting more and more shirty, until finally he laid into him with a stick. That is to say," said Ginger, coldly accurate, "he *started* laying into him with a stick." He brooded for a moment with knit brows. "A spaniel, mind you! Can you imagine anyone beating a spaniel? It's like hitting a little girl. Well, he's a fairly oldish man, you know, and that hampered me a bit: but I got hold of the stick and broke it into about eleven pieces, and by great good luck it was a stick he happened to value rather highly. It had a gold knob and had been presented to him by his constituents or something. I minced it up a goodish bit, and then I told him a fair amount about himself. And then— well, after that he shot me out, and I came here."

Sally did not speak for a moment.

"You were quite right," she said at last, in a sober voice that had nothing in it of her customary flippancy. She paused again. "And what are you going to do now?" she said.

"I don't know."

"You'll get something?"

"Oh, yes, I shall get something, I suppose. The family will be pretty sick, of course."

"For goodness' sake! Why do you bother about the family?" Sally burst out. She could not reconcile this young man's flabby dependence on his family with the enterprise and vigour which he had shown in his dealings with the unspeakable Scrymgeour. Of course, he had been brought up to look on himself as a rich man's son and appeared to have drifted as such young men are wont to do; but even so . . . "The whole trouble with you," she said, embarking on a subject on which she held strong views, "is that . . ."

Her harangue was interrupted by what—at the Normandie, at one o'clock in the morning—practically amounted to a miracle. The front door of the hotel opened, and there entered a young man in evening dress. Such persons were sufficiently rare at the Normandie, which catered principally for the staid and middle-aged, and this youth's presence was due, if one must pause to explain it, to the fact that, in the middle of his stay at Roville, a disastrous evening at the Casino had so diminished his funds that he had been obliged to make a hurried shift from the Hotel Splendide to the

45

humbler Normandie. His late appearance to-night was caused by the fact that he had been attending a dance at the Splendide, principally in the hope of finding there some kind-hearted friend of his prosperity from whom he might borrow.

A rapid-fire dialogue having taken place between Jules and the newcomer, the keys were handed through the cage, the door opened and the lift was set once more in motion. And a few minutes later, Sally, suddenly aware of an over-powering sleepiness, had switched off her light and jumped into bed. Her last waking thought was a regret that she had not been able to speak at length to Mr. Ginger Kemp on the subject of enterprise, and resolve that the address should be delivered at the earliest opportunity.

CHAPTER III

THE DIGNIFIED MR. CARMYLE

I

BY six o'clock on the following evening, however, Sally had been forced to the conclusion that Ginger would have to struggle through life as best he could without the assistance of her contemplated remarks: for she had seen nothing of him all day and in another hour she would have left Roville on the seven-fifteen express which was to take her to Paris, *en route* for Cherbourg and the liner whereon she had booked her passage for New York.

It was in the faint hope of finding him even now that, at half-past six, having conveyed her baggage to the station and left it in charge of an amiable porter, she paid a last visit to the Casino Municipale. She disliked the thought of leaving Ginger without having uplifted him. Like so many alert and active-minded girls, she possessed in a great degree the quality of interesting herself in—or, as her brother Fillmore preferred to put it, messing about with—the private affairs of others. Ginger had impressed her as a man to whom it was worth while to give a friendly shove on the right path; and it was with much gratification, therefore, that, having entered the Casino, she perceived a flaming head shining through the crowd which had gathered at one of the roulette-tables.

There are two Casinos at Roville-sur-Mer. The one on the Promenade goes in mostly for sea-air and a mild game called *boule*. It is the big Casino Municipale down in the Palace Massena near the railway station which is the haunt of the earnest gambler who means business; and it was plain to Sally directly she arrived that Ginger Kemp not only meant business but was getting results. Ginger was going extremely strong. He was entrenched behind an opulent-looking mound of square counters: and, even as Sally looked, a wooden-faced croupier shoved a further instalment across the table to him at the end of his long rake.

"*Epatant!*" murmured a wistful man at Sally's side, remov-

47

ing an elbow from her ribs in order the better to gesticulate Sally, though no French scholar, gathered that he was startled and gratified. The entire crowd seemed to be startled and gratified. There is undoubtedly a certain altruism in the make-up of the spectators at a Continental roulette-table. They seem to derive a spiritual pleasure from seeing somebody else win.

The croupier gave his moustache a twist with his left hand and the wheel a twist with his right, and silence fell again. Sally, who had shifted to a spot where the pressure of the crowd was less acute, was now able to see Ginger's face, and as she saw it she gave an involuntary laugh. He looked exactly like a dog at a rat-hole. His hair seemed to bristle with excitement. One could almost fancy that his ears were pricked up.

In the tense hush which had fallen on the crowd at the restarting of the wheel, Sally's laugh rang out with an embarrassing clearness. It had a marked effect on all those within hearing. There is something almost of religious ecstasy in the deportment of the spectators at a table where anyone is having a run of luck at roulette, and if she had guffawed in a cathedral she could not have caused a more pained consternation. The earnest worshippers gazed at her with shocked eyes, and Ginger, turning with a start, saw her and jumped up. As he did so, the ball fell with a rattling click into a red compartment of the wheel; and, as it ceased to revolve and it was seen that at last the big winner had picked the wrong colour, a shuddering groan ran through the congregation like that which convulses the penitents' bench at a negro revival meeting. More glances of reproach were cast at Sally. It was generally felt that her injudicious behaviour had changed Ginger's luck.

The only person who did not appear to be concerned was Ginger himself. He gathered up his loot, thrust it into his pocket, and elbowed his way to where Sally stood, now definitely established in the eyes of the crowd as a pariah. There was universal regret that he had decided to call it a day. It was to the spectators as though a star had suddenly walked off the stage in the middle of his big scene; and not even a loud and violent quarrel which sprang up at this moment between two excitable gamblers over a disputed five-franc counter could wholly console them.

"I say," said Ginger, dexterously plucking Sally out of the

crowd, "this is topping, meeting you like this. I've been looking for you everywhere."

"It's funny you didn't find me, then, for that's where I've been. I was looking for you."

"No, really?" Ginger seemed pleased. He led the way to the quiet ante-room outside the gambling-hall, and they sat down in a corner. It was pleasant here, with nobody near except the gorgeously uniformed attendant over by the door. "That was awfully good of you."

"I felt I must have a talk with you before my train went." Ginger started violently.

"Your train? What do you mean?"

"The puff-puff," explained Sally. "I'm leaving to-night, you know."

"Leaving?" Ginger looked as horrified as the devoutest of the congregation of which Sally had just ceased to be a member. "You don't mean *leaving?* You're not going away from Roville?"

"I'm afraid so."

"But why? Where are you going?"

"Back to America. My boat sails from Cherbourg to-morrow."

"Oh, my aunt!"

"I'm sorry," said Sally, touched by his concern. She was a warm-hearted girl and liked being appreciated. "But . . ."

"I say . . ." Ginger Kemp turned bright scarlet and glared before him at the uniformed official, who was regarding their *tête-à-tête* with the indulgent eye of one who has been through this sort of thing himself. "I say, look here, will you marry me?"

2

Sally stared at his vermilion profile in frank amazement. Ginger, she had realized by this time, was in many ways a surprising young man, but she had not expected him to be as surprising as this.

"Marry you!"

"You know what I mean."

"Well, yes, I suppose I do. You allude to the holy state. Yes, I know what you mean."

"Then how about it?"

Sally began to regain her composure. Her sense of humour was tickled. She looked at Ginger gravely. He did not meet her eye, but continued to drink in the uniformed official, who was by now so carried away by the romance of it all that he had begun to hum a love-ballad under his breath. The official could not hear what they were saying, and would not have been able to understand it even if he could have heard; but he was an expert in the language of the eyes.

"But isn't this—don't think I am trying to make difficulties —isn't this a little sudden?"

"It's got to be sudden," said Ginger Kemp, complainingly. "I thought you were going to be here for weeks."

"But, my infant, my babe, has it occurred to you that we are practically strangers?" She patted his hand tolerantly, causing the uniformed official to heave a tender sigh. "I see what has happened," she said. "You're mistaking me for some other girl, some girl you know really well, and were properly introduced to. Take a good look at me, and you'll see."

"If I take a good look at you," said Ginger, feverishly, "I'm dashed if I'll answer for the consequences."

"And this is the man I was going to lecture on 'Enterprise.'"

"You're the most wonderful girl I've ever met, dash it!" said Ginger, his gaze still riveted on the official by the door "I dare say it *is* sudden. I can't help that. I fell in love with you the moment I saw you, and there you are!"

"But . . ."

"Now, look here, I know I'm not much of a chap and all that, but . . . well, I've just won the deuce of a lot of money in there . . ."

"Would you buy me with your gold?"

"I mean to say, we should have enough to start on, and . . . of course I've made an infernal hash of everything I've tried up till now, but there must be something I can do, and you can jolly well bet I'd have a goodish stab at it. I mean to say, with you to buck me up and so forth, don't you know. Well, I mean . . ."

"Has it struck you that I may already be engaged to someone else?"

"Oh, golly! Are you?"

For the first time he turned and faced her, and there was a look in his eyes which touched Sally and drove all sense of the ludicrous out of her. Absurd as it was, this man was really serious.

"Well, yes, as a matter of fact I am," she said soberly.

Ginger Kemp bit his lip and for a moment was silent.

"Oh, well, that's torn it!" he said at last.

Sally was aware of an emotion too complex to analyse. There was pity in it, but amusement too. The emotion, though she did not recognize it, was maternal. Mothers, listening to their children pleading with engaging absurdity for something wholly out of their power to bestow, feel that same wavering between tears and laughter. Sally wanted to pick Ginger up and kiss him. The one thing she could not do was to look on him, sorry as she was for him, as a reasonable, grown-up man.

"You don't really mean it, you know."

"Don't I!" said Ginger, hollowly. "Oh, don't I!"

"You can't! There isn't such a thing in real life as love at first sight. Love's a thing that comes when you know a person well and . . ." She paused. It had just occurred to her that she was hardly the girl to lecture in this strain. Her love for Gerald Foster had been sufficiently sudden, even instantaneous. What did she know of Gerald except that she loved him? They had become engaged within two weeks of their first meeting. She found this recollection damping to her eloquence, and ended by saying tamely: "It's ridiculous."

Ginger had simmered down to a mood of melancholy resignation.

"I couldn't have expected you to care for me, I suppose, anyway," he said, sombrely. "I'm not much of a chap."

It was just the diversion from the theme under discussion which Sally had been longing to find. She welcomed the chance of continuing the conversation on a less intimate and sentimental note.

"That's exactly what I wanted to talk to you about," she said, seizing the opportunity offered by this display of humility. "I've been looking for you all day to go on with what I was starting to say in the lift last night when we were interrupted. Do you mind if I talk to you like an aunt—or a sister, suppose we say? Really, the best plan would be for you to adopt me as an honorary sister. What do you think?"

Ginger did not appear noticeably elated at the suggested relationship.

"Because I really do take a tremendous interest in you."

Ginger brightened. "That's awfully good of you."

51

"I'm going to speak words of wisdom. Ginger, why don't you brace up?"

"Brace up?"

"Yes, stiffen your backbone and stick out your chin, and square your elbows, and really amount to something. Why do you simply flop about and do nothing and leave everything to what you call 'the family'? Why do you have to be helped all the time? Why don't you help yourself? Why do you have to have jobs found for you? Why don't you rush out and get one? Why do you have to worry about what 'the family' thinks of you? Why don't you make yourself independent of them? I know you had hard luck, suddenly finding yourself without money and all that, but, good heavens, everybody else in the world who has ever done anything has been broke at one time or another. It's part of the fun. You'll never get anywhere by letting yourself be picked up by the family like . . . like a floppy Newfoundland puppy and dumped down in any old place that happens to suit them. A job's a thing you've got to choose for yourself and get for yourself. Think what you can do—there must be something—and then go at it with a snort and grab it and hold it down and teach it to take a joke. You've managed to collect some money. It will give you time to look round. And, when you've had a look round, *do* something! Try to realize you're alive, and try to imagine the family isn't!"

Sally stopped and drew a deep breath. Ginger Kemp did not reply for a moment. He seemed greatly impressed.

"When you talk quick," he said at length, in a serious meditative voice, "your nose sort of goes all squiggly. Ripping, it looks!"

Sally uttered an indignant cry.

"Do you mean to say you haven't been listening to a word I've been saying," she demanded.

"Oh, rather! Oh, by Jove, yes."

"Well, what did I say?"

"You . . . er . . . And your eyes sort of shine, too."

"Never mind my eyes. What did I say?"

"You told me," said Ginger, on reflection, "to get a job."

"Well, yes. I put it much better than that, but that's what it amounted to, I suppose. All right, then. I'm glad you . . ."

Ginger was eyeing her with mournful devotion.

"I say," he interrupted, "I wish you'd let me write to you.

Letters, I mean, and all that. I have an idea it would kind of buck me up."

"You won't have time for writing letters."

"I'll have time to write them to you. You haven't an address or anything of that sort in America, have you, by any chance? I mean, so that I'd know where to write to."

"I can give you an address which will always find me." She told him the number and street of Mrs. Meecher's boarding-house, and he wrote them down reverently on his shirt-cuff. "Yes, on second thoughts, do write," she said. "Of course, I shall want to know how you've got on. I . . . oh, my goodness! That clock's not right?"

"Just about. What time does your train go?"

"Go! It's gone! Or, at least, it goes in about two seconds." She made a rush for the swing-door, to the confusion of the uniformed official who had not been expecting this sudden activity. "Good-bye, Ginger. Write to me, and remember what I said."

Ginger, alert after his unexpected fashion when it became a question of physical action, had followed her through the swing-door, and they emerged together and started running down the square.

"Stick it!" said Ginger, encouragingly. He was running easily and well, as becomes a man who, in his day, had been a snip for his international at scrum-half.

Sally saved her breath. The train was beginning to move slowly out of the station as they sprinted abreast on to the platform. Ginger dived for the nearest door, wrenched it open, gathered Sally neatly in his arms, and flung her in. She landed squarely on the toes of a man who occupied the corner seat, and, bounding off again, made for the window. Ginger, faithful to the last, was trotting beside the train as it gathered speed.

"Ginger! My poor porter! Tip him. I forgot."

"Right ho!"

"And don't forget what I've been saying."

"Right ho!"

"Look after yourself and 'Death to the Family!' "

"Right ho!"

The train passed smoothly out of the station. Sally cast one last look back at her red-haired friend, who had now halted and was waving a handkerchief. Then she turned to apologize to the other occupant of the carriage.

"I'm so sorry," she said, breathlessly. "I hope I didn't hurt you."

She found herself facing Ginger's cousin, the dark man of yesterday's episode on the beach, Bruce Carmyle.

3

Mr. Carmyle was not a man who readily allowed himself to be disturbed by life's little surprises, but at the present moment he could not help feeling slightly dazed. He recognized Sally now as the French girl who had attracted his cousin Lancelot's notice on the beach. At least he had assumed that she was French, and it was startling to be addressed by her now in fluent English. How had she suddenly acquired this gift of tongues? And how on earth had she had time since yesterday, when he had been a total stranger to her, to become sufficiently intimate with Cousin Lancelot to be sprinting with him down station platforms and addressing him out of railway-carriage windows as Ginger? Bruce Carmyle was aware that most members of that sub-species of humanity, his cousin's personal friends, called him by that familiar—and, so Carmyle held, vulgar—nickname: but how had this girl got hold of it?

If Sally had been less pretty, Mr. Carmyle would undoubtedly have looked disapprovingly at her, for she had given his rather rigid sense of the proprieties a nasty jar. But as, panting and flushed from her run, she was prettier than any girl he had yet met, he contrived to smile.

"Not at all," he said in answer to her question, though it was far from the truth. His left big toe was aching confoundedly. Even a girl with a foot as small as Sally's can make her presence felt on a man's toe if the scrum-half who is handling her aims well and uses plenty of vigour.

"If you don't mind," said Sally, sitting down, "I think I'll breathe a little."

She breathed. The train sped on.

"Quite a close thing," said Bruce Carmyle, affably. The pain in his toe was diminishing. "You nearly missed it."

"Yes. It was lucky Mr. Kemp was with me. He throws very straight, doesn't he."

"Tell me," said Carmyle, "how do you come to know my cousin? On the beach yesterday morning . . ."

"Oh, we didn't know each other then. But we were staying

at the same hotel, and we spent an hour or so shut up in an elevator together. That was when we really got acquainted."

A waiter entered the compartment, announcing in unexpected English that dinner was served in the restaurant car.

"Would you care for dinner?"

"I'm starving," said Sally.

She reproved herself, as they made their way down the corridor, for being so foolish as to judge anyone by his appearance. This man was perfectly pleasant in spite of his grim exterior. She had decided by the time they had seated themselves at the table she liked him.

At the table, however, Mr. Carmyle's manner changed for the worse. He lost his amiability. He was evidently a man who took his meals seriously and believed in treating waiters with severity. He shuddered austerely at a stain on the table-cloth, and then concentrated himself frowningly on the bill of fare. Sally, meanwhile, was establishing cosy relations with the much too friendly waiter, a cheerful old man who from the start seemed to have made up his mind to regard her as a favourite daughter. The waiter talked no English and Sally no French, but they were getting along capitally, when Mr. Carmyle, who had been irritably waving aside the servitor's light-hearted advice—at the Hotel Splendide the waiters never bent over you and breathed cordial suggestions down the side of your face—gave his order crisply in the Anglo-Gallic dialect of the travelling Briton. The waiter remarked, "*Boum!*" in a pleased sort of way, and vanished.

"Nice old man!" said Sally.

"Infernally familiar!" said Mr. Carmyle.

Sally perceived that on the topic of the waiter she and her host did not see eye to eye and that little pleasure or profit could be derived from any discussion centring about him. She changed the subject. She was not liking Mr. Carmyle quite so much as she had done a few minutes ago, but it was courteous of him to give her dinner, and she tried to like him as much as she could.

"By the way," she said, "my name is Nicholas. I always think it's a good thing to start with names, don't you?"

"Mine . . ."

"Oh, I know yours. Ginger—Mr. Kemp told me."

Mr. Carmyle, who since the waiter's departure, had been thawing, stiffened again at the mention of Ginger.

"Indeed?" he said, coldly. "Apparently you got intimate."

Sally did not like his tone. He seemed to be criticizing her, and she resented criticism from a stranger. Her eyes opened wide and she looked dangerously across the table.

"Why 'apparently'? I told you that we had got intimate, and I explained how. You can't stay shut up in an elevator half the night with anybody without getting to know him. I found Mr. Kemp very pleasant."

"Really?"

"And very interesting."

Mr. Carmyle raised his eyebrows.

"Would you call him interesting?"

"I *did* call him interesting." Sally was beginning to feel the exhilaration of battle. Men usually made themselves extremely agreeable to her, and she reacted belligerently under the stiff unfriendliness which had come over her companion in the last few minutes.

"He told me all about himself."

"And you found that interesting?"

"Why not?"

"Well . . ." A frigid half-smile came and went on Bruce Carmyle's dark face. "My cousin has many excellent qualities, no doubt—he used to play football well, and I understand that he is a capable amateur pugilist—but I should not have supposed him entertaining. We find him a little dull."

"I thought it was only royalty that called themselves 'we.' "

"I meant myself—and the rest of the family."

The mention of the family was too much for Sally. She had to stop talking in order to allow her mind to clear itself of rude thoughts.

"Mr. Kemp was telling me about Mr. Scrymgeour," she went on at length.

Bruce Carmyle stared for a moment at the yard or so of French bread which the waiter had placed on the table.

"Indeed?" he said. "He has an engaging lack of reticence."

The waiter returned bearing soup and dumped it down.

"*V'la!*" he observed, with the satisfied air of a man who has successfully performed a difficult conjuring trick. He smiled at Sally expectantly, as though confident of applause from this section of his audience at least. But Sally's face was set and rigid. She had been snubbed, and the sensation was as pleasant as it was novel.

"I think Mr. Kemp had hard luck," she said.

56

"If you will excuse me, I would prefer not to discuss the matter."

Mr. Carmyle's attitude was that Sally might be a pretty girl, but she was a stranger, and the intimate affairs of the Family were not to be discussed with strangers, however prepossessing.

"He was quite in the right. Mr. Scrymgeour was beating a dog . . ."

"I've heard the details."

"Oh, I didn't know that. Well, don't you agree with me, then?"

"I do not. A man who would throw away an excellent position simply because . . ."

"Oh, well, if that's your view, I suppose it *is* useless to talk about it."

"Quite."

"Still, there's no harm in asking what you propose to do about Gin—about Mr. Kemp."

Mr. Carmyle became more glacial.

"I'm afraid I cannot discuss . . ."

Sally's quick impatience, nobly restrained till now, finally got the better of her.

"Oh, for goodness' sake," she snapped, "do try to be human, and don't always be snubbing people. You remind me of one of those portraits of men in the eighteenth century, with wooden faces, who look out of heavy gold frames at you with fishy eyes as if you were a regrettable incident."

"Rosbif," said the waiter genially, manifesting himself suddenly beside them as if he had popped up out of a trap.

Bruce Carmyle attacked his roast beef morosely. Sally who was in the mood when she knew that she would be ashamed of herself later on, but was full of battle at the moment, sat in silence.

"I am sorry," said Mr. Carmyle ponderously, "if my eyes are fishy. The fact has not been called to my attention before."

"I suppose you never had any sisters," said Sally. "They would have told you."

Mr. Carmyle relapsed into an offended dumbness, which lasted till the waiter had brought the coffee.

"I think," said Sally, getting up, "I'll be going now. I don't seem to want any coffee, and, if I stay on, I may say something rude. I thought I might be able to put in a good word for Mr. Kemp and save him from being massacred,

57

but apparently it's no use. Good-bye, Mr. Carmyle, and thank you for giving me dinner.

She made her way down the car, followed by Bruce Carmyle's indignant, yet fascinated, gaze. Strange emotions were stirring in Mr. Carmyle's bosom.

CHAPTER IV

GINGER IN DANGEROUS MOOD

SOME few days later, owing to the fact that the latter, being preoccupied, did not see him first, Bruce Carmyle met his cousin Lancelot in Piccadilly. They had returned by different routes from Roville, and Ginger would have preferred the separation to continue. He was hurrying on with a nod, when Carmyle stopped him.

"Just the man I wanted to see," he observed.

"Oh, hullo!" said Ginger, without joy.

"I was thinking of calling at your club."

"Yes?"

"Yes. Cigarette?"

Ginger peered at the proffered case with the vague suspicion of the man who has allowed himself to be lured on to the platform and is accepting a card from the conjurer. He felt bewildered. In all the years of their acquaintance he could not recall another such exhibition of geniality on his cousin's part. He was surprised, indeed, at Mr. Carmyle's speaking to him at all, for the *affaire* Scrymgeour remained an unhealed wound, and the Family, Ginger knew, were even now in session upon it.

"Been back in London long?"

"Day or two."

"I heard quite by accident that you had returned and that you were staying at the club. By the way, thank you for introducing me to Miss Nicholas."

Ginger started violently.

"What!"

"I was in that compartment, you know, at Roville Station. You threw her right on top of me. We agreed to consider that an introduction. An attractive girl."

Bruce Carmyle had not entirely made up his mind regarding Sally, but on one point he was clear, that she should not, if he could help it, pass out of his life. Her abrupt departure had left him with that baffled and dissatisfied feeling which, though it has little in common with love at first sight, frequently produces the same effects. She had had, he could not disguise it from himself, the better of their late encounter; and he was conscious of a desire to meet her again and show her that there was more in him than she apparently supposed. Bruce Carmyle, in a word, was piqued: and, though he could not quite decide whether he liked or disliked Sally, he was very sure that a future without her would have an element of flatness.

"A very attractive girl. We had a very pleasant talk."

"I bet you did," said Ginger enviously.

"By the way, she did not give you her address by any chance?"

"Why?" said Ginger suspiciously. His attitude towards Sally's address resembled somewhat that of a connoisseur who has acquired a unique work of art. He wanted to keep it to himself and gloat over it.

"Well, I—er—I promised to send her some books she was anxious to read . . ."

"I shouldn't think she gets much time for reading."

"Books which are not published in America."

"Oh, pretty nearly everything is published in America, what? Bound to be, I mean."

"Well, these particular books are not," said Mr. Carmyle shortly. He was finding Ginger's reserve a little trying, and wished that he had been more inventive.

"Give them to me and I'll send them to her," suggested Ginger.

"Good Lord, man!" snapped Mr. Carmyle. "I'm capable of sending a few books to America. Where does she live?"

Ginger revealed the sacred number of the holy street which had the luck to be Sally's headquarters. He did it because with a persistent devil like his cousin there seemed no way of getting out of it: but he did it grudgingly.

"Thanks." Bruce Carmyle wrote the information down with a gold pencil in a dapper little morocco-bound notebook. He was the sort of man who always has a pencil, and the backs of old envelopes never enter into his life.

There was a pause. Bruce Carmyle coughed.

"I saw Uncle Donald this morning," he said.

His manner had lost its geniality. There was no need for it now, and he was a man who objected to waste. He spoke coldly, and in his voice there was a familiar sub-tingle of reproof.

"Yes?" said Ginger moodily. This was the uncle in whose office he had made his debut as a hasher: a worthy man, highly respected in the National Liberal Club, but never a favourite of Ginger's. There were other minor uncles and a few subsidiary aunts who went to make up the Family, but Uncle Donald was unquestionably the managing director of that body and it was Ginger's considered opinion that in this capacity he approximated to a human blister.

"He wants you to dine with him to-night at Bleke's."

Ginger's depression deepened. A dinner with Uncle Donald would hardly have been a cheerful function, even in the surroundings of a banquet in the Arabian Nights. There was that about Uncle Donald's personality which would have cast a sobering influence over the orgies of the Emperor Tiberius at Capri. To dine with him at a morgue like that relic of Old London, Bleke's Coffee House, which confined its custom principally to regular patrons who had not missed an evening there for half a century, was to touch something very near bed-rock. Ginger was extremely doubtful whether flesh and blood were equal to it.

"To-night?" he said. "Oh, you mean to-night? Well . . ."

"Don't be a fool. You know as well as I do that you've got to go." Uncle Donald's invitations were royal commands in the Family. "If you've another engagement you must put it off."

"Oh, all right."

"Seven-thirty sharp."

"All right," said Ginger gloomily.

The two men went their ways, Bruce Carmyle eastwards because he had clients to see in his chambers at the Temple; Ginger westwards because Mr. Carmyle had gone east. There was little sympathy between these cousins: yet, oddly enough, their thoughts as they walked centred on the same object. Bruce Carmyle, threading his way briskly through the crowds of Piccadilly Circus, was thinking of Sally: and so was Ginger as he loafed aimlessly towards Hyde Park Corner, bumping in a sort of coma from pedestrian to pedestrian.

Since his return to London Ginger had been in bad shape. He mooned through the days and slept poorly at night. If there is one thing rottener than another in a pretty blighted world, one thing which gives a fellow the pip and reduces him to the condition of an absolute onion, it is hopeless love. Hopeless love had got Ginger all stirred up. His had been hitherto a placid soul. Even the financial crash which had so altered his life had not bruised him very deeply. His temperament had enabled him to bear the slings and arrows of outrageous fortune with a philosophic "Right ho!" But now everything seemed different. Things irritated him acutely, which before he had accepted as inevitable—his Uncle Donald's moustache, for instance, and its owner's habit of employing it during meals as a sort of zareba or earthwork against the assaults of soup.

"By gad!" thought Ginger, stopping suddenly opposite Devonshire House. "If he uses that damned shrubbery as soup-strainer to-night, I'll slosh him with a fork!"

Hard thoughts . . . hard thoughts! And getting harder all the time, for nothing grows more quickly than a mood of rebellion. Rebellion is a forest fire that flames across the soul. The spark had been lighted in Ginger, and long before he reached Hyde Park Corner he was ablaze and crackling. By the time he returned to his club he was practically a menace to society—to that section of it, at any rate, which embraced his Uncle Donald, his minor uncles George and William, and his aunts Mary, Geraldine, and Louise.

Nor had the mood passed when he began to dress for the dismal festivities of Bleke's Coffee House. He scowled as he struggled morosely with an obstinate tie. One cannot disguise the fact—Ginger was warming up. And it was just at this moment that Fate, as though it had been waiting for the psychological instant, applied the finishing touch. There was a knock at the door, and a waiter came in with a telegram.

Ginger looked at the envelope. It had been readdressed and forwarded on from the Hotel Normandie. It was a wireless, handed in on board the White Star liner *Olympic*, and it ran as follows:

Remember. Death to the Family. S.

Ginger sat down heavily on the bed.

The driver of the taxi-cab which at twenty-five minutes past seven drew up at the dingy door of Bleke's Coffee House in the Strand was rather struck by his fare's manner and appearance. A determined-looking sort of young bloke, was the taxi-driver's verdict.

CHAPTER V

SALLY HEARS NEWS

IT had been Sally's intention, on arriving in New York, to take a room at the St. Regis and revel in the gilded luxury to which her wealth entitled her before moving into the small but comfortable apartment which, as soon as she had the time, she intended to find and make her permanent abode. But when the moment came and she was giving directions to the taxi-driver at the dock, there seemed to her something revoltingly Fillmorian about the scheme. It would be time enough to sever herself from the boarding-house which had been her home for three years when she had found the apartment. Meanwhile, the decent thing to do, if she did not want to brand herself in the sight of her conscience as a female Fillmore, was to go back temporarily to Mrs. Meecher's admirable establishment and foregather with her old friends. After all, home is where the heart is, even if there are more prunes there than the gourmet would consider judicious.

Perhaps it was the unavoidable complacency induced by the thought that she was doing the right thing, or possibly it was the tingling expectation of meeting Gerald Foster again after all these weeks of separation, that made the familiar streets seem wonderfully bright as she drove through them. It was a perfect, crisp New York morning, all blue sky and amber sunshine, and even the ash-cans had a stimulating look about them. The street cars were full of happy people rollicking off to work: policemen directed the traffic with jaunty affability: and the white-clad street-cleaners went about their poetic tasks with a quiet but none the less noticeable relish. It was improbable that any of these people knew that she was back, but somehow they all seemed to be behaving as though this were a special day.

The first discordant note in this overture of happiness was struck by Mrs. Meecher, who informed Sally, after expressing her gratification at the news that she required her old room, that Gerald Foster had left town that morning.

"Gone to Detroit, he has," said Mrs. Meecher. "Miss Doland, too." She broke off to speak a caustic word to the boarding-house handyman, who, with Sally's trunk as a weapon, was depreciating the value of the wall-paper in the hall. "There's that play of his being tried out there, you know, Monday," resumed Mrs. Meecher, after the handyman had bumped his way up the staircase. "They been rehearsing ever since you left."

Sally was disappointed, but it was such a beautiful morning, and New York was so wonderful after the dull voyage in the liner that she was not going to allow herself to be depressed without good reason. After all, she could go on to Detroit to-morrow. It was nice to have something to which she could look forward.

"Oh, is Elsa in the company?" she said.

"Sure. And very good too, I hear." Mrs. Meecher kept abreast of theatrical gossip. She was an ex-member of the profession herself, having been in the first production of "Florodora," though, unlike everybody else, not one of the original Sextette. "Mr. Faucitt was down to see a rehearsal, and he said Miss Doland was fine. And he's not easy to please, as you know."

"How is Mr. Faucitt?"

Mrs. Meecher, not unwillingly, for she was a woman who enjoyed the tragedies of life, made her second essay in the direction of lowering Sally's uplifted mood.

"Poor old gentleman, he ain't over and above well. Went to bed early last night with a headache, and this morning I been to see him and he *don't* look well. There's a lot of this Spanish influenza about. It might be that. Lots o' people have been dying of it, if you believe what you see in the papers," said Mrs. Meecher buoyantly.

"Good gracious! You don't think . . .?"

"Well, he ain't turned black," admitted Mrs. Meecher with regret. "They say they turn black. If you believe what you see in the papers, that is. Of course, that may come later," she added with the air of one confident that all will come right in the future. "The doctor'll be in to see him pretty soon. He's quite happy. Toto's sitting with him."

Sally's concern increased. Like everyone who had ever spent any length of time in the house, she had strong views on Toto. This quadruped, who stained the fame of the entire canine race by posing as a dog, was a small woolly animal with a persistent and penetrating yap, hard to bear with equanimity in health and certainly quite outside the range of a sick man. Her heart bled for Mr. Faucitt. Mrs. Meecher, on the other hand, who held a faith in her little pet's amiability and power to soothe which seven years' close association had been unable to shake, seemed to feel that, with Toto on the spot, all that could be done had been done as far as pampering the invalid was concerned.

"I must go up and see him," cried Sally. "Poor old dear."

"Sure. You know his room. You can hear Toto talking to him now," said Mrs. Meecher complacently. "He wants a cracker, that's what he wants. Toto likes a cracker after breakfast."

The invalid's eyes, as Sally entered the room, turned wearily to the door. At the sight of Sally they lit up with an incredulous rapture. Almost any intervention would have pleased Mr. Faucitt at that moment, for his little playmate had long outstayed any welcome that might originally have been his: but that the caller should be his beloved Sally seemed to the old man something in the nature of a return of the age of miracles.

"Sally!"

"One moment. Here, Toto!"

Toto, struck momentarily dumb by the sight of food, had jumped off the bed and was standing with his head on one side, peering questioningly at the cracker. He was a suspicious dog, but he allowed himself to be lured into the passage, upon which Sally threw the cracker down and slipped in and shut the door. Toto, after a couple of yaps, which may have been gratitude or baffled fury, trotted off downstairs, and Mr. Faucitt drew a deep breath.

"Sally, you come, as ever, as an angel of mercy. Our worthy Mrs. Meecher means well, and I yield to no man in my respect for her innate kindness of heart: but she errs in supposing that that thrice-damned whelp of hers is a combination of sick-nurse, soothing medicine, and a week at the seaside. She insisted on bringing him here. He was yapping then, as he was yapping when, with womanly resource which I cannot sufficiently praise, you decoyed him hence. And each yap went through me like hammer-strokes on sheeted tin. Sally, you stand alone among womankind. You shine

65

like a good deed in a naughty world. When did you get back?"

"I've only just arrived in my hired barouche from the pier."

"And you came to see your old friend without delay? I am grateful and flattered, Sally, my dear."

"Of course I came to see you. Do you suppose that, when Mrs. Meecher told me you were sick, I just said 'Is that so?' and went on talking about the weather? Well, what do you mean by it? Frightening everybody. Poor old darling, do you feel very bad?"

"One thousand individual mice are nibbling the base of my spine, and I am conscious of a constant need of cooling refreshment. But what of that? Your presence is a tonic. Tell me, how did our Sally enjoy foreign travel?"

"Our Sally had the time of her life."

"Did you visit England?"

"Only passing through."

"How did it look?" asked Mr. Faucitt eagerly.

"Moist. Very moist."

"It would," said Mr. Faucitt indulgently. "I confess that, happy as I have been in this country, there are times when I miss those wonderful London days, when a sort of cosy brown mist hangs over the streets and the pavements ooze with a perspiration of mud and water, and you see through the haze the yellow glow of the Bodega lamps shining in the distance like harbour-lights. Not," said Mr. Faucitt, "that I specify the Bodega to the exclusion of other and equally worthy hostelries. I have passed just as pleasant hours in Rule's and Short's. You missed something by not lingering in England, Sally."

"I know I did—pneumonia."

Mr. Faucitt shook his head reproachfully.

"You are prejudiced, my dear. You would have enjoyed London if you had had the courage to brave its superficial gloom. Where did you spend your holiday? Paris?"

"Part of the time. And the rest of the while I was down by the sea. It was glorious. I don't think I would ever have come back if I hadn't had to. But, of course, I wanted to see you all again. And I wanted to be at the opening of Mr. Foster's play. Mrs. Meecher tells me you went to one of the rehearsals."

66

"I attended a dog-fight which I was informed was a rehearsal," said Mr. Faucitt severely. "There is no rehearsing nowadays."

"Oh dear! Was it as bad as all that?"

"The play is good. The play—I will go further—is excellent. It has fat. But the acting . . ."

"Mrs. Meecher said you told her that Elsa was good."

"Our worthy hostess did not misreport me. Miss Doland has great possibilities. She reminds me somewhat of Matilda Devine, under whose banner I played a season at the Old Royalty in London many years ago. She has the seeds of greatness in her, but she is wasted in the present case on an insignificant part. There is only one part in the play. I allude to the one murdered by Miss Mabel Hobson."

"Murdered!" Sally's heart sank. She had been afraid of this, and it was no satisfaction to feel that she had warned Gerald. "Is she very terrible?"

"She has the face of an angel and the histrionic ability of that curious suet pudding which our estimable Mrs. Meecher is apt to give us on Fridays. In my professional career I have seen many cases of what I may term the Lady Friend in the rôle of star, but Miss Hobson eclipses them all. I remember in the year '94 a certain scion of the plutocracy took it into his head to present a female for whom he had conceived an admiration in a part which would have taxed the resources of the ablest. I was engaged in her support, and at the first rehearsal I recollect saying to my dear old friend, Arthur Moseby—dead, alas, these many years. An excellent juvenile, but, like so many good fellows, cursed with a tendency to lift the elbow—I recollect saying to him 'Arthur, dear boy, I give it two weeks.' 'Max,' was his reply, 'you are an incurable optimist. One consecutive night, laddie, one consecutive night.' We had, I recall, an even half-crown upon it. He won. We opened at Wigan, our leading lady got the bird, and the show closed next day. I was forcibly reminded of this incident as I watched Miss Hobson rehearsing."

"Oh, poor Ger—poor Mr. Foster!"

"I do not share your commiseration for that young man," said Mr. Faucitt austerely. "You probably are almost a stranger to him, but he and I have been thrown together a good deal of late. A young man upon whom, mark my words, success, if it ever comes, will have the worst effects.

I dislike him, Sally. He is, I think, without exception, the most selfish and self-centred young man of my acquaintance. He reminds me very much of old Billy Fothergill, with whom I toured a good deal in the later eighties. Did I ever tell you the story of Billy and the amateur who . . . ?"

Sally was in no mood to listen to the adventures of Mr. Fothergill. The old man's innocent criticism of Gerald had stabbed her deeply. A momentary impulse to speak hotly in his defence died away as she saw Mr. Faucitt's pale, worn old face. He had meant no harm, after all. How could he know what Gerald was to her?

She changed the conversation abruptly.

"Have you seen anything of Fillmore while I've been away?"

"Fillmore? Why yes, my dear, curiously enough I happened to run into him on Broadway only a few days ago. He seemed changed—less stiff and aloof than he had been for some time past. I may be wronging him, but there have been times of late when one might almost have fancied him a trifle up-stage. All that was gone at our last encounter. He appeared glad to see me and was most cordial."

Sally found her composure restored. Her lecture on the night of the party had evidently, she thought, not been wasted. Mr. Faucitt, however, advanced another theory to account for the change in the Man of Destiny.

"I rather fancy," he said, "that the softening influence has been the young man's fiancée."

"What? Fillmore's not engaged?"

"Did he not write and tell you? I suppose he was waiting to inform you when you returned. Yes, Fillmore is betrothed. The lady was with him when we met. A Miss Winch. In the profession, I understand. He introduced me. A very charming and sensible young lady, I thought."

Sally shook her head.

"She can't be. Fillmore would never have got engaged to anyone like that. Was her hair crimson?"

"Brown, if I recollect rightly."

"Very loud, I suppose, and overdressed?"

"On the contrary, neat and quiet."

"You've made a mistake," said Sally decidedly. "She can't have been like that. I shall have to look into this. It does seem hard that I can't go away for a few weeks without

68

all my friends taking to beds of sickness and all my brothers getting ensnared by vampires."

A knock at the door interrupted her complaint. Mrs. Meecher entered, ushering in a pleasant little man with spectacles and black bag.

"The doctor to see you, Mr. Faucitt." Mrs. Meecher cast an appraising eye at the invalid, as if to detect symptoms of approaching discoloration. "I've been telling him that what *I* think you've gotten is this here new Spanish influenza. Two more deaths there were in the paper this morning, if you can believe what you see . . ."

"I wonder," said the doctor, "if you would mind going and bringing me a small glass of water?"

"Why, sure."

"Not a large glass—a small glass. Just let the tap run for a few moments and take care not to spill any as you come up the stairs. I always ask ladies, like our friend who has just gone," he added as the door closed, "to bring me a glass of water. It keeps them amused and interested and gets them out of the way, and they think I am going to do a conjuring trick with it. As a matter of fact, I'm going to drink it. Now let's have a look at you."

The examination did not take long. At the end of it the doctor seemed somewhat chagrined.

"Our good friend's diagnosis was correct. I'd give a leg to say it wasn't, but it was. It *is* this here new Spanish influenza. Not a bad attack. You want to stay in bed and keep warm, and I'll write you out a prescription. You ought to be nursed. Is this young lady a nurse?"

"No, no, merely . . ."

"Of course I'm a nurse," said Sally decidedly. "It isn't difficult, is it, doctor? I know nurses smooth pillows. I can do that. Is there anything else?"

"Their principal duty is to sit here and prevent the excellent and garrulous lady who has just left us from getting in. They must also be able to aim straight with a book or an old shoe, if that small woolly dog I met downstairs tries to force an entrance. If you are equal to these tasks, I can leave the case in your hands with every confidence."

"But, Sally, my dear," said Mr. Faucitt, concerned, "you must not waste your time looking after me. You have a thousand things to occupy you."

"There's nothing I want to do more than help you to get better. I'll just go out and send a wire, and then I'll be right back."

Five minutes later, Sally was in a Western Union office, telegraphing to Gerald that she would be unable to reach Detroit in time for the opening.

CHAPTER VI

FIRST AID FOR FILLMORE

I

IT was not till the following Friday that Sally was able to start for Detroit. She arrived on the Saturday morning and drove to the Hotel Statler. Having ascertained that Gerald was stopping in the hotel and having 'phoned up to his room to tell him to join her, she went·into the dining-room and ordered breakfast.

She felt low-spirited as she waited for the food to arrive. The nursing of Mr. Faucitt had left her tired, and she had not slept well on the train. But the real cause of her depression was the fact that there had been a lack of enthusiasm in Gerald's greeting over the telephone just now. He had spoken listlessly, as though the fact of her returning after all these weeks was a matter of no account, and she felt hurt and perplexed.

A cup of coffee had a stimulating effect. Men, of course, were always like this in the early morning. It would, no doubt, be a very different Gerald who would presently bound into the dining-room, quickened and restored by a cold shower-bath. In the meantime, here was food, and she needed it.

She was pouring out her second cup of coffee when a stout young man, of whom she had caught a glimpse as he moved about that section of the hotel lobby which was visible through the open door of the dining-room, came in and stood peering about as though in search of someone. The momentary sight she had had of this young man had interested Sally. She had thought how extraordinarily like he was to her brother Fillmore. Now she perceived that it was Fillmore himself.

Sally was puzzled. What could Fillmore be doing so far west? She had supposed him to be a permanent resident of New York. But, of course, your man of affairs and vast interests flits about all over the place. At any rate, here he was, and she called him. And, after he had stood in the doorway looking in every direction except the right one for another minute, he saw her and came over to her table.

"Why, Sally?" His manner, she thought, was nervous—one might almost have said embarrassed. She attributed this to a guilty conscience. Presently he would have to break to her the news that he had become engaged to be married without her sisterly sanction, and no doubt he was wondering how to begin. "What are you doing here? I thought you were in Europe."

"I got back a week ago, but I've been nursing poor old Mr. Faucitt ever since then. He's been ill, poor old dear. I've come here to see Mr. Foster's play, 'The Primrose Way,' you know. Is it a success?"

"It hasn't opened yet."

"Don't be silly, Fill. Do pull yourself together. It opened last Monday."

"No, it didn't. Haven't you heard? They've closed all the theatres because of this infernal Spanish influenza. Nothing has been playing this week. You must have seen it in the papers."

"I haven't had time to read the papers. Oh, Fill, what an awful shame!"

"Yes, it's pretty tough. Makes the company all on edge. I've had the darndest time, I can tell you."

"Why, what have you got to do with it?"

Fillmore coughed.

"I—er—oh, I didn't tell you that. I'm sort of—er—mixed up in the show. Cracknell—you remember he was at college with me—suggested that I should come down and look at it. Shouldn't wonder if he wants me to put money into it and so on."

"I thought he had all the money in the world."

"Yes, he has a lot, but these fellows like to let a pal in on a good thing."

"Is it a good thing?"

"The play's fine."

"That's what Mr. Faucitt said. But Mabel Hobson . . ."

Fillmore's ample face registered emotion.

"She's an awful woman, Sally! She can't act, and she throws her weight about all the time. The other day there was a fuss about a paper-knife . . ."

"How do you mean, a fuss about a paper-knife?"

"One of the props, you know. It got mislaid. I'm certain it wasn't my fault . . ."

"How could it have been your fault?" asked Sally wonderingly. Love seemed to have the worst effects on Fillmore's mentality.

"Well—er—you know how it is. Angry woman . . . blames the first person she sees . . . This paper-knife . . ."

Fillmore's voice trailed off into pained silence.

"Mr. Faucitt said Elsa Doland was good."

"Oh, she's all right," said Fillmore indifferently. "But—" His face brightened and animation crept into his voice. "But the girl you want to watch is Miss Winch. Gladys Winch. She plays the maid. She's only in the first act, and hasn't much to say, except 'Did you ring, madam?' and things like that. But it's the way she says 'em! Sally, that girl's a genius! The greatest character actress in a dozen years! You mark my words, in a darned little while you'll see her name up on Broadway in electric light. Personality? Ask me! Charm? She wrote the words and music! Looks? . . ."

"All right! All right! I know all about it, Fill. And will you kindly inform me how you dared to get engaged without consulting me?"

Fillmore blushed richly.

"Oh, do you know?"

"Yes. Mr. Faucitt told me."

"Well . . ."

"Well?"

"Well, I'm only human," argued Fillmore.

"I call that a very handsome admission. You've got quite modest, Fill."

He had certainly changed for the better since their last meeting.

It was as if someone had punctured him and let out all the pomposity. If this was due, as Mr. Faucitt had suggested, to the influence of Miss Winch, Sally felt that she could not but approve of the romance.

"I'll introduce you sometime," said Fillmore.

"I want to meet her very much."

"I'll have to be going now. I've got to see Bunbury. I thought he might be in here."

"Who's Bunbury?"

"The producer. I suppose he is breakfasting in his room. I'd better go up."

"You *are* busy, aren't you. Little marvel! It's lucky they've got you to look after them."

Fillmore retired and Sally settled down to wait for Gerald, no longer hurt by his manner over the telephone. Poor Gerald! No wonder he had seemed upset.

A few minutes later he came in.

"Oh, Jerry darling," said Sally, as he reached the table, "I'm so sorry. I've just been hearing about it."

Gerald sat down. His appearance fulfilled the promise of his voice over the telephone. A sort of nervous dullness wrapped him about like a garment.

"It's just my luck," he said gloomily. "It's the kind of thing that couldn't happen to anyone but me. Damned fools! Where's the sense in shutting the theatres, even if there is influenza about? They let people jam against one another all day in the stores. If that doesn't hurt them why should it hurt them to go to theatres? Besides, it's all infernal nonsense about this thing. I don't believe there is such a thing as Spanish influenza. People get colds in their heads and think they're dying. It's all a fake scare."

"I don't think it's that," said Sally. "Poor Mr. Faucitt had it quite badly. That's why I couldn't come earlier."

Gerald did not seem interested either by the news of Mr. Faucitt's illness or by the fact that Sally, after delay, had at last arrived. He dug a spoon sombrely into his grape-fruit.

"We've been hanging about here day after day, getting bored to death all the time . . . The company's going all to pieces. They're sick of rehearsing and rehearsing when nobody knows if we'll ever open. They were all keyed up a week ago, and they've been sagging ever since. It will ruin the play, of course. My first chance! Just chucked away."

Sally was listening with a growing feeling of desolation. She tried to be fair, to remember that he had had a terrible disappointment and was under a great strain. And yet . . . it was unfortunate that self-pity was a thing she particularly disliked in a man. Her vanity, too, was hurt. It was obvious that her arrival, so far from acting as a magic restorative, had effected nothing. She could not help remembering, though it made her feel disloyal, what Mr. Faucitt had said about Gerald. She had never noticed before that he was remarkably self-centred, but he was thrusting the fact upon her attention now.

"That Hobson woman is beginning to make trouble,"

went on Gerald, prodding in a despairing sort of way at scrambled eggs. "She ought never to have had the part, never. She can't handle it. Elsa Doland could play it a thousand times better. I wrote Elsa in a few lines the other day, and the Hobson woman went right up in the air. You don't know what a star is till you've seen one of these promoted clothes-props from the Follies trying to be one. It took me an hour to talk her round and keep her from throwing up her part."

"Why not let her throw up her part?"

"For heaven's sake talk sense," said Gerald querulously. "Do you suppose that man Cracknell would keep the play on if she wasn't in it? He would close the show in a second, and where would I be then? You don't seem to realize that this is a big chance for me. I'd look a fool throwing it away."

"I see," said Sally, shortly. She had never felt so wretched in her life. Foreign travel, she decided, was a mistake. It might be pleasant and broadening to the mind, but it seemed to put you so out of touch with people when you got back. She analysed her sensations, and arrived at the conclusion that what she was resenting was the fact that Gerald was trying to get the advantages of two attitudes simultaneously. A man in trouble may either be the captain of his soul and superior to pity, or he may be a broken thing for a woman to pet and comfort. Gerald, it seemed to her, was advertising himself as an object for her commiseration, and at the same time raising a barrier against it. He appeared to demand her sympathy while holding himself aloof from it. She had the uncomfortable sensation of feeling herself shut out and useless.

"By the way," said Gerald, "there's one thing. I have to keep her jollying along all the time, so for goodness' sake don't go letting it out that we're engaged."

Sally's chin went up with a jerk. This was too much.

"If you find it a handicap being engaged to me . . ."

"Don't be silly." Gerald took refuge in pathos. "Good God! It's tough! Here am I, worried to death, and you . . ."

Before he could finish the sentence, Sally's mood had undergone one of those swift changes which sometimes made her feel that she must be lacking in character. A simple, comforting thought had come to her, altering her entire outlook. She had come off the train tired and gritty, and what seemed the general out-of-jointness of the world was entirely due, she decided, to the fact that she had not had a bath and that

75

her hair was all anyhow. She felt suddenly tranquil. If it was merely her grubby and dishevelled condition that made Gerald seem to her so different, all was well. She put her hand on his with a quick gesture of penitence.

"I'm so sorry," she said. "I've been a brute, but I do sympathize, really."

"I've had an awful time," mumbled Gerald.

"I know, I know. But you never told me you were glad to see me."

"Of course I'm glad to see you."

"Why didn't you say so, then, you poor fish? And why didn't you ask me if I had enjoyed myself in Europe?"

"Did you enjoy yourself?"

"Yes, except that I missed you so much. There! Now we can consider my lecture on foreign travel finished, and you can go on telling me your troubles."

Gerald accepted the invitation. He spoke at considerable length, though with little variety. It appeared definitely established in his mind that Providence had invented Spanish influenza purely with a view to wrecking his future. But now he seemed less aloof, more open to sympathy. The brief thunderstorm had cleared the air. Sally lost that sense of detachment and exclusion which had weighed upon her.

"Well," said Gerald, at length, looking at his watch, "I suppose I had better be off."

"Rehearsal?"

"Yes, confound it. It's the only way of getting through the day. Are you coming along?"

"I'll come directly I've unpacked and tidied myself up."

"See you at the theatre, then."

Sally went out and rang for the lift to take her up to her room.

2

The rehearsal had started when she reached the theatre. As she entered the dark auditorium, voices came to her with that thin and reedy effect which is produced by people talking in an empty building. She sat down at the back of the house, and, as her eyes grew accustomed to the gloom, was able to see Gerald sitting in the front row beside a man with a bald head fringed with orange hair whom she took correctly to be Mr. Bunbury, the producer. Dotted about the house in ones and twos were members of the company whose presence was not required in the first act. On the stage, Elsa Doland, looking very attractive, was playing a scene with a man in a bowler hat. She was speaking a line, as Sally came in.

"Why, what do you mean, father?"

"Tiddly-omty-om," was the bowler-hatted one's surprising reply. "Tiddly-omty-om . . . long speech ending in 'find me in the library.' *And exit*," said the man in the bowler hat, starting to do so.

For the first time Sally became aware of the atmosphere of nerves. Mr. Bunbury, who seemed to be a man of temperament, picked up his walking-stick, which was leaning against the next seat, and flung it with some violence across the house.

"For God's sake!" said Mr. Bunbury.

"Now what?" inquired the bowler hat, interested, pausing halfway across the stage.

"Do speak the lines, Teddy," exclaimed Gerald. "Don't skip them in that sloppy fashion."

"You don't want me to go over the whole thing?" asked the bowler hat, amazed.

"Yes!"

"Not the whole damn thing?" queried the bowler hat, fighting with incredulity.

"This is a rehearsal," snapped Mr. Bunbury. "If we are not going to do it properly, what's the use of doing it at all?"

This seemed to strike the erring Teddy, if not as reasonable, at any rate as one way of looking at it. He delivered the speech in an injured tone and shuffled off. The atmosphere of tenseness was unmistakable now. Sally could feel it. The world of the theatre is simply a large nursery and its inhabitants children who readily become fretful if anything goes wrong. The waiting and the uncertainty, the loafing about in strange hotels in a strange city, the dreary rehearsing of lines which had been polished to the last syllable more than a week ago—these things had sapped the nerve of the Primrose Way company and demoralization had set in. It would require only a trifle to produce an explosion.

Elsa Doland now moved to the door, pressed a bell, and, taking a magazine from the table, sat down in a chair near the footlights. A moment later, in answer to the ring, a young woman entered, to be greeted instantly by an impassioned bellow from Mr. Bunbury.

"Miss Winch!"

The new arrival stopped and looked out over the foot-lights, not in the pained manner of the man in the bowler hat, but with the sort of genial indulgence of one who has come to a juvenile party to amuse the children. She was a square, wholesome, good-humoured looking girl with a serious face, the gravity of which was contradicted by the faint smile that seemed to lurk about the corner of her mouth. She was certainly not pretty, and Sally, watching her with keen interest, was surprised that Fillmore had had the sense to disregard surface homeliness and recognize her charm. Deep down in Fillmore, Sally decided, there must lurk an unsuspected vein of intelligence.

"Hello?" said Miss Winch, amiably.

Mr. Bunbury seemed profoundly moved.

"Miss Winch, did I or did I not ask you to refrain from chewing gum during rehearsal?"

"That's right, so you did," admitted Miss Winch, chummily.

"Then why are you doing it?"

Fillmore's fiancée revolved the critized refreshment about her tongue for a moment before replying.

"Bit o' business," she announced, at length.

"What do you mean, a bit of business?"

"Character stuff," explained Miss Winch in her pleasant, drawling voice. "Thought it out myself. Maids chew gum, you know."

Mr. Bunbury ruffled his orange hair in an over-wrought manner with the palm of his right hand.

"Have you ever seen a maid?" he asked, despairingly.

"Yes, *sir*. And they chew gum."

"I mean a parlour-maid in a smart house," moaned Mr. Bunbury. "Do you imagine for a moment that in a house such as this is supposed to be the parlour-maid would be allowed to come into the drawing-room champing that disgusting, beastly stuff?"

Miss Winch considered the point.

"Maybe you're right." She brightened. "Listen! Great idea! Mr. Foster can write in a line for Elsa, calling me down, and another giving me a good come-back, and then another for Elsa saying something else, and then something really funny for me, and so on. We can work it up into a big comic scene. Five or six minutes, all laughs."

This ingenious suggestion had the effect of depriving the

producer momentarily of speech, and while he was struggling for utterance, there dashed out from the wings a gorgeous being in blue velvet and a hat of such unimpeachable smartness that Sally ached at the sight of it with a spasm of pure envy.

"Say!"

Miss Mabel Hobson had practically every personal advantage which nature can bestow with the exception of a musical voice. Her figure was perfect, her face beautiful, and her hair a mass of spun gold; but her voice in moments of emotion was the voice of a peacock.

"Say, listen to me for just one moment!"

Mr. Bunbury recovered from his trance.

"Miss Hobson! Please!"

"Yes, that's all very well . . ."

"You are interrupting the rehearsal."

"You bet your sorrowful existence I'm interrupting the rehearsal," agreed Miss Hobson, with emphasis. "And, if you want to make a little easy money, you go and bet somebody ten seeds that I'm going to interrupt it again every time there's any talk of writing up any darned part in the show except mine. Write up other people's parts? Not while I have my strength!"

A young man with butter-coloured hair, who had entered from the wings in close attendance on the injured lady, attempted to calm the storm.

"Now, sweetie!"

"Oh, can it, Reggie!" said Miss Hobson, curtly.

Mr. Cracknell obediently canned it. He was not one of your brutal cave-men. He subsided into the recesses of a high collar and began to chew the knob of his stick.

"I'm the star," resumed Miss Hobson, vehemently, "and, if you think anybody else's part's going to be written up . . . well, pardon me while I choke with laughter! If so much as a syllable is written into anybody's part, I walk straight out on my two feet. You won't see me go, I'll be so quick."

Mr. Bunbury sprang to his feet and waved his hands.

"For heaven's sake! Are we rehearsing, or is this a debating society? Miss Hobson, nothing is going to be written into anybody's part. Now are you satisfied?"

"She said . . ."

"Oh, never mind," observed Miss Winch, equably. "It

was only a random thought. Working for the good of the show all the time. That's me."

"Now, sweetie!" pleaded Mr. Cracknell, emerging from the collar like a tortoise.

Miss Hobson reluctantly allowed herself to be reassured.

"Oh, well, that's all right, then. But don't forget I know how to look after myself," she said, stating a fact which was abundantly obvious to all who had had the privilege of listening to her. "Any raw work, and out I walk so quick it'll make you giddy."

She retired, followed by Mr. Cracknell, and the wings swallowed her up.

"Shall I say my big speech now?" inquired Miss Winch, over the footlights.

"Yes, yes! Get on with the rehearsal. We've wasted half the morning."

"Did you ring, madam?" said Miss Winch to Elsa, who had been reading her magazine placidly through the late scene.

The rehearsal proceeded, and Sally watched it with a sinking heart. It was all wrong. Novice as she was in things theatrical, she could see that. There was no doubt that Miss Hobson was superbly beautiful and would have shed lustre on any part which involved the minimum of words and the maximum of clothes: but in the pivotal rôle of a serious play, her very physical attributes only served to emphasize and point her hopeless incapacity. Sally remembered Mr. Faucitt's story of the lady who got the bird at Wigan. She did not see how history could fail to repeat itself. The theatrical public of America will endure much from youth and beauty, but there is a limit.

A shrill, passionate cry from the front row, and Mr. Bunbury was on his feet again. Sally could not help wondering whether things were going particularly wrong to-day, or whether this was one of Mr. Bunbury's ordinary mornings.

"Miss Hobson!"

The action of the drama had just brought that emotional lady on left centre and had taken her across to the desk which stood on the other side of the stage. The desk was an important feature of the play, for it symbolized the absorption in business which, exhibited by her husband, was rapidly breaking Miss Hobson's heart. He loved his desk better than his young wife, that was what it amounted to, and no wife can stand that sort of thing.

"Oh, gee!" said Miss Hobson, ceasing to be the distressed wife and becoming the offended star. "What's it this time?"

"I suggested at the last rehearsal and at the rehearsal before and the rehearsal before that, that, on that line, you should pick up the paper-knife and toy negligently with it. You did it yesterday, and to-day you've forgotten it again."

"My God!" cried Miss Hobson, wounded to the quick. "If this don't beat everything! How the heck can I toy negligently with a paper-knife when there's no paper-knife for me to toy negligently with?"

"The paper-knife is on the desk."

"It's not on the desk."

"No paper-knife?"

"No paper-knife. And it's no good picking on me. I'm the star, not the assistant stage manager. If you're going to pick on anybody, pick on him."

The advice appeared to strike Mr. Bunbury as good. He threw back his head and bayed like a bloodhound.

There was a momentary pause, and then from the wings on the prompt side there shambled out a stout and shrinking figure, in whose hand was a script of the play and on whose face, lit up by the footlights, there shone a look of apprehension. It was Fillmore, the Man of Destiny.

3

Alas, poor Fillmore! He stood in the middle of the stage with the lightning of Mr. Bunbury's wrath playing about his defenceless head, and Sally, recovering from her first astonishment, sent a wave of sisterly commiseration floating across the theatre to him. She did not often pity Fillmore. His was a nature which in the sunshine of prosperity had a tendency to grow a trifle lush; and such of the minor ills of life as had afflicted him during the past three years, had, she considered, been wholesome and educative and a matter not for concern but for congratulation. Unmoved, she had watched him through that lean period lunching on coffee and buckwheat cakes, and curbing from motives of economy a somewhat florid taste in dress. But this was different. This was tragedy. Somehow or other, blasting disaster must have smitten the Fillmore bank-roll, and he was back where he had started. His presence here this morning could mean nothing else.

She recalled his words at the breakfast-table about financing the play. How like Fillmore to try to save his face for the moment with an outrageous bluff, though well aware that he would have to reveal the truth sooner or later. She realized how he must have felt when he had seen her at the hotel. Yes, she was sorry for Fillmore.

And, as she listened to the fervent eloquence of Mr. Bunbury, she perceived that she had every reason to be. Fillmore was having a bad time. One of the chief articles of faith in the creed of all theatrical producers is that if anything goes wrong it must be the fault of the assistant stage manager: and Mr. Bunbury was evidently orthodox in his views. He was showing oratorical gifts of no mean order. The paper-knife seemed to inspire him. Gradually, Sally began to get the feeling that this harmless, necessary stage-property was the source from which sprang most, if not all, of the trouble in the world. It had disappeared before. Now it had disappeared again. Could Mr. Bunbury go on struggling in a universe where this sort of thing happened? He seemed to doubt it. Being a red-blooded, one-hundred-per-cent American man, he would try hard, but it was a hundred to one shot that he would get through. He had asked for a paper-knife. There was no paper-knife. Why was there no paper-knife? Where *was* the paper-knife anyway?

"I assure you, Mr. Bunbury," bleated the unhappy Fillmore, obsequiously. "I placed it with the rest of the properties after the last rehearsal."

"You couldn't have done."

"I assure you I did."

"And it walked away, I suppose," said Miss Hobson with cold scorn, pausing in the operation of brightening up her lower lip with a lip-stick.

A calm, clear voice spoke.

"It was taken away," said the calm, clear voice.

Miss Winch had added herself to the symposium. She stood beside Fillmore, chewing placidly. It took more than raised voices and gesticulating hands to disturb Miss Winch.

"Miss Hobson took it," she went on in her cosy, drawling voice. "I saw her."

Sensation in court. The prisoner, who seemed to feel his position deeply, cast a pop-eyed glance full of gratitude at his advocate. Mr. Bunbury, in his capacity of prosecuting attorney, ran his fingers through his hair in some embarrassment, for he was regretting now that he had made such a fuss. Miss Hobson thus assailed by an underling, spun round and dropped the lip-stick, which was neatly retrieved by the assiduous Mr. Cracknell. Mr. Cracknell had his limitations, but he was rather good at picking up lip-sticks.

"What's that? *I* took it? I never did anything of the sort."

"Miss Hobson took it after the rehearsal yesterday," drawled Gladys Winch, addressing the world in general, "and threw it negligently at the theatre cat."

Miss Hobson seemed taken aback. Her composure was not restored by Mr. Bunbury's next remark. The producer, like his company, had been feeling the strain of the past few days, and, though as a rule he avoided anything in the nature of a clash with the temperamental star, this matter of the missing paper-knife had bitten so deeply into his soul that he felt compelled to speak his mind.

"In future, Miss Hobson, I should be glad if, when you wish to throw anything at the cat, you would not select a missile from the property box. Good heavens!" he cried, stung by the way fate was maltreating him, "I have never experienced anything like this before. I have been producing plays all my life, and this is the first time this has happened. I have produced Nazimova. Nazimova never threw paper-knives at cats."

"Well, I hate cats," said Miss Hobson, as though that settled it.

"I," murmured Miss Winch, "love little pussy, her fur is so .warm, and if I don't hurt her she'll do me no . . ."

"Oh, my heavens!" shouted Gerald Foster, bounding from his seat and for the first time taking a share in the debate. "Are we going to spend the whole day arguing about cats and paper-knives? For goodness' sake, clear the stage and stop wasting time."

Miss Hobson chose to regard this intervention as an affront.

"Don't shout at me, Mr. Foster!"

"I wasn't shouting at you."

"If you have anything to say to me, lower your voice."

"He can't," observed Miss Winch. "He's a tenor."

"Nazimova never . . ." began Mr. Bunbury.

Miss Hobson was not to be diverted from her theme by reminiscences of Nazimova. She had not finished dealing with Gerald.

"In the shows I've been in," she said, mordantly, "the author wasn't allowed to go about the place getting fresh with the leading lady. In the shows I've been in the author sat at the back and spoke when he was spoken to. In the shows I've been in . . ."

Sally was tingling all over. This reminded her of the dog-fight on the Roville sands. She wanted to be in it, and only the recognition that it was a private fight and that she would be intruding kept her silent. The lure of the fray, however, was too strong for her wholly to resist it. Almost unconsciously, she had risen from her place and drifted down the aisle so as to be nearer the white-hot centre of things. She was now standing in the lighted space by the orchestra-pit, and her presence attracted the roving attention of Miss Hobson, who, having concluded her remarks on authors and their legitimate sphere of activity, was looking about for some other object of attack.

"Who the devil," inquired Miss Hobson, "is *that?*"

Sally found herself an object of universal scrutiny and wished that she had remained in the obscurity of the back rows.

"I am Mr. Nicholas' sister," was the best method of identification that she could find.

"Who's Mr. Nicholas?"

Fillmore timidly admitted that he was Mr. Nicholas. He did it in the manner of one in the dock pleading guilty to a major charge, and at least half of those present seemed surprised. To them, till now, Fillmore had been a nameless thing, answering to the shout of "Hi!"

Miss Hobson received the information with a laugh of such exceeding bitterness that strong men blanched and Mr. Cracknell started so convulsively that he nearly jerked his collar off its stud.

"Now, sweetie!" urged Mr. Cracknell.

Miss Hobson said that Mr. Cracknell gave her a pain in the gizzard. She recommended his fading away, and he did so—into his collar. He seemed to feel that once well inside his collar he was "home" and safe from attack.

"I'm through!" announced Miss Hobson. It appeared that Sally's presence had in some mysterious fashion fulfilled the function of the last straw. "This is the by-Goddest show I was ever in! I can stand for a whole lot, but when it comes to the assistant stage manager being allowed to fill the theatre with his sisters and his cousins and his aunts it's time to quit."

"But, sweetie!" pleaded Mr. Cracknell, coming to the surface.

"Oh, go and choke yourself!" said Miss Hobson, crisply. And, swinging round like a blue panther, she strode off. A door banged, and the sound of it seemed to restore Mr. Cracknell's power of movement. He, too, shot up stage and disappeared.

"Hello, Sally," said Elsa Doland, looking up from her magazine. The battle, raging all round her, had failed to disturb her detachment. "When did you get back?"

Sally trotted up the steps which had been propped against the stage to form a bridge over the orchestra pit.

"Hello, Elsa."

The late debaters had split into groups. Mr. Bunbury and Gerald were pacing up and down the central aisle, talking earnestly. Fillmore had subsided into a chair.

"Do you know Gladys Winch?" asked Elsa.

Sally shook hands with the placid lodestar of her brother's affections. Miss Winch, on closer inspection, proved to have deep grey eyes and freckles. Sally's liking for her increased.

"Thank you for saving Fillmore from the wolves," she said. "They would have torn him in pieces but for you."

"Oh, I don't know," said Miss Winch.

"It was noble."

"Oh, well!"

"I think," said Sally, "I'll go and have a talk with Fill-·more. He looks as though he wanted consoling.

She made her way to that picturesque ruin.

4

Fillmore had the air of a man who thought it wasn't loaded. A wild, startled expression had settled itself upon his face and he was breathing heavily.

"Cheer up!" said Sally. Fillmore jumped like a stricken jelly. "Tell me all," said Sally, sitting down beside him. "I leave you a gentleman of large and independent means, and I come back and find you one of the wage-slaves again. How did it all happen?"

"Sally," said Fillmore, "I will be frank with you. Can you lend me ten dollars?"

"I don't see how you make that out an answer to my question, but here you are."

"Thanks." Fillmore pocketed the bill. "I'll let you have it back next week. I want to take Miss Winch out to lunch."

"If that's what you want it for, don't look on it as a loan, take it as a gift with my blessing thrown in." She looked over her shoulder at Miss Winch, who, the cares of rehearsal being temporarily suspended, was practising golf-shots with an umbrella at the other side of the stage. "However did you have the sense to fall in love with her, Fill?"

"Do you like her?" asked Fillmore, brightening.

"I love her."

"I knew you would. She's just the right girl for me, isn't she?"

"She certainly is."

"So sympathetic."

"Yes."

"So kind."

"Yes." And she's got brains enough for two, which is the exact quantity the girl who marries you will need.

Fillmore drew himself up with as much hauteur as a stout man sitting in a low chair can achieve.

"Some day I will make you believe in me, Sally."

"Less of the Merchant Prince, my lad," said Sally, firmly. "You just confine yourself to explaining how you got this way, instead of taking up my valuable time telling me what you mean to do in the future. You've lost all your money?"

"I have suffered certain reverses," said Fillmore, with dignity, "which have left me temporarily . . . Yes, every bean," he concluded simply.

"How?"

"Well . . ." Fillmore hesitated. "I've had bad luck, you know. First I bought Consolidated Rails for the rise, and they fell. So that went wrong."

"Yes?"

"And then I bought Russian Roubles for the fall, and they rose. So that went wrong."

"Good gracious! Why, I've heard all this before."

"Who told you?"

"No, I remember now. It's just that you remind me of a man I met at Roville. He was telling me the story of his life,

86

and how he had made a hash of everything. Well, that took all you had, I suppose?"

"Not quite. I had a few thousand left, and I went into a deal that really did look cast-iron."

"And that went wrong!"

"It wasn't my fault," said Fillmore querulously. "It was just my poisonous luck. A man I knew got me to join a syndicate which had bought up a lot of whisky. The idea was to ship it into Chicago in herring-barrels. We should have cleaned up big, only a mutt of a detective took it into his darned head to go fooling about with a crowbar. Officious ass! It wasn't as if the barrels weren't labelled 'Herrings' as plainly as they could be," said Fillmore with honest indignation. He shuddered. "I nearly got arrested."

"But that went wrong? Well, that's something to be thankful for. Stripes wouldn't suit your figure." Sally gave his arm a squeeze. She was very fond of Fillmore, though for the good of his soul she generally concealed her affection beneath a manner which he had once compared, not without some reason, to that of a governess who had afflicted their mutual childhood. "Never mind, you poor ill-used martyr. Things are sure to come right. We shall see you a millionaire some day. And, oh heavens, brother Fillmore, what a bore you'll be when you are! I can just see you being interviewed and giving hints to young men on how to make good. 'Mr. Nicholas attributes his success to sheer hard work. He can lay his hand on his bulging waistcoat and say that he has never once indulged in those rash get-rich-quick speculations, where you buy for the rise and watch things fall and then rush out and buy for the fall and watch 'em rise.' Fill . . . .I'll tell you what I'll do. They all say it's the first bit of money that counts in building a vast fortune. I'll lend you some of mine."

"You will? Sally, I always said you were an ace."

"I never heard you. You oughtn't to mumble so."

"Will you lend me twenty thousand dollars?"

Sally patted his hand soothingly.

"Come slowly down to earth," she said. "Two hundred was the sum I had in mind."

."I want twenty thousand."

"You'd better rob a bank. Any policeman will direct you to a good bank."

"I'll tell you *why* I want twenty thousand."

"You might just mention it."

"If I had twenty thousand, I'd buy this production from Cracknell. He'll be back in a few minutes to tell us that the Hobson woman has quit: and, if she really has, you take it from me that he will close the show. And, even if he manages to jolly her along this time and she comes back, it's going to happen sooner or later. It's a shame to let a show like this close. I believe in it, Sally. It's a darn good play. With Elsa Doland in the big part, it couldn't fail."

Sally started. Her money was too recent for her to have grown fully accustomed to it, and she had never realized that she was in a position to wave a wand and make things happen on any big scale. The financing of a theatrical production had always been to her something mysterious and out of the reach of ordinary persons like herself. Fillmore, that spacious thinker, had brought it into the sphere of the possible.

"He'd sell for less than that, of course, but one would need a bit in hand. You have to face a loss on the road before coming into New York. I'd give you ten per cent on your money, Sally."

Sally found herself wavering. The prudent side of her nature, which hitherto had steered her safely through most of life's rapids, seemed oddly dormant. Sub-consciously she was aware that on past performances Fillmore was decidedly not the man to be allowed control of anybody's little fortune, but somehow the thought did not seem to grip her. He had touched her imagination.

"It's a gold-mine!"

Sally's prudent side stirred in its sleep. Fillmore had chosen an unfortunate expression. To the novice in finance the word gold-mine had repellent associations. If there was one thing in which Sally had proposed not to invest her legacy, it was a gold-mine; what she had had in view, as a matter of fact, had been one of those little fancy shops which are called Ye Blue Bird or Ye Corner Shoppe, or something like that, where you sell exotic bric-à-brac to the wealthy at extortionate prices. She knew two girls who were doing splendidly in that line. As Fillmore spoke those words, Ye Corner Shoppe suddenly looked very good to her.

At this moment, however, two things happened. Gerald and Mr. Bunbury, in the course of their perambulations, came into the glow of the footlights; and she was able to see

88

Gerald's face: and at the same time Mr. Reginald Cracknell hurried on to the stage, his whole demeanour that of the bearer of evil tidings.

The sight of Gerald's face annihilated Sally's prudence at a single stroke. Ye Corner Shoppe, which a moment before had been shining brightly before her mental eye, flickered and melted out. The whole issue became clear and simple. Gerald was miserable and she had it in her power to make him happy. He was sullenly awaiting disaster and she with a word could avert it. She wondered that she had ever hesitated.

"All right," she said simply.

Fillmore quivered from head to foot. A powerful electric shock could not have produced a stronger convulsion. He knew Sally of old as cautious and clear-headed, by no means to be stampeded by a brother's eloquence; and he had never looked on this thing as anything better than a hundred to one shot.

"You'll do it?" he whispered, and held his breath. After all he might not have heard correctly.

"Yes."

All the complex emotion in Fillmore's soul found expression in one vast whoop. It rang through the empty theatre like the last trump, beating against the back wall and rising in hollow echoes to the very gallery. Mr. Bunbury, conversing in low undertones with Mr. Cracknell across the footlights, shied like a startled mule. There was reproach and menace in the look he cast at Fillmore, and a minute earlier it would have reduced that financial magnate to apologetic pulp. But Fillmore was not to be intimidated now by a look. He strode down to the group at the footlights.

"Cracknell," he said importantly, "one moment, I should like a word with you."

CHAPTER VII

SOME MEDITATIONS ON SUCCESS

IF actors and actresses are like children in that they are readily depressed by disaster, they have the child's compensating gift of being easily uplifted by good fortune. It amazed Sally that any one mortal should have been able to spread such universal happiness as she had done by the simple act of lending her brother Fillmore twenty thousand dollars. If the Millennium had arrived, the members of the Primrose Way Company could not have been on better terms with themselves. The lethargy and dispiritedness, caused by their week of inaction, fell from them like a cloak. The sudden elevation of that creature of the abyss, the assistant stage manager, to the dizzy height of proprietor of the show appealed to their sense of drama. Most of them had played in pieces where much the same thing had happened to the persecuted heroine round about eleven o'clock, and the situation struck them as theatrically sound. Also, now that she had gone, the extent to which Miss Hobson had acted as a blight was universally recognized.

A spirit of optimism reigned, and cheerful rumours became current. The bowler-hatted Teddy had it straight from the lift-boy at his hotel that the ban on the theatres was to be lifted on Tuesday at the latest; while no less an authority than the cigar-stand girl at the Pontchatrain had informed the man who played the butler that Toledo and Cleveland were opening to-morrow. It was generally felt that the sun was bursting through the clouds and that Fate would soon despair of the hopeless task of trying to keep good men down.

Fillmore was himself again. We all have our particular mode of self-expression in moments of elation. Fillmore's took the shape of buying a new waistcoat and a hundred half-dollar cigars and being very fussy about what he had for lunch. It may have been an optical illusion, but he appeared to Sally to put on at least six pounds in weight on the first day of the new regime. As a serf looking after paper-knives and other properties, he had been—for him—almost slim. As a manager he blossomed out into soft billowy curves, and when he stood on the sidewalk in front of the theatre, gloating over the new posters which bore the legend,

FILLMORE NICHOLAS
PRESENTS

the populace had to make a detour to get round him.

In this era of bubbling joy, it was hard that Sally, the fairy godmother responsible for it all, should not have been completely happy too; and it puzzled her why she was not. But whatever it was that cast the faint shadow refused obstinately to come out from the back of her mind and show itself and be challenged. It was not till she was out driving in a hired car with Gerald one afternoon on Belle Isle that enlightenment came.

Gerald, since the departure of Miss Hobson, had been at his best. Like Fillmore, he was a man who responded to the sunshine of prosperity. His moodiness had vanished, and all his old charm had returned. And yet . . . it seemed to Sally, as the car slid smoothly through the pleasant woods and fields by the river, that there was something that jarred.

Gerald was cheerful and talkative. He, at any rate, found nothing wrong with life. He held forth spaciously on the big things he intended to do.

"If this play get over—and it's going to—I'll show 'em!" His jaw was squared, and his eyes glowed as they stared into the inviting future. "One success—that's all I need—then watch me! I haven't had a chance yet, but . . ."

His voice rolled on, but Sally had ceased to listen. It was the time of year when the chill of evening follows swiftly on the mellow warmth of afternoon. The sun had gone behind the trees, and a cold wind was blowing up from the river. And quite suddenly, as though it was the wind that had cleared her mind, she understood what it was that had been lurking at the back of her thoughts. For an instant it stood out nakedly without concealment, and the world became a forlorn place. She had realized the fundamental difference between man's outlook on life and woman's.

Success! How men worshipped it, and how little of themselves they had to spare for anything else. Ironically, it was the theme of this very play of Gerald's which she had saved from destruction. Of all the men she knew, how many had any view of life except as a race which they must strain every nerve to win, regardless of what they missed by the wayside in their haste? Fillmore—Gerald—all of them. There might be a woman in each of their lives, but she came second —an afterthought—a thing for their spare time. Gerald was everything to her. His success would never be more than a side-issue as far as she was concerned. He himself, without any of the trappings of success, was enough for her. But she was not enough for him. A spasm of futile jealousy shook her. She shivered.

"Cold?" said Gerald. "I'll tell the man to drive back . . . I don't see any reason why this play shouldn't run a year in New York. Everybody says it's good . . . if it does get over, they'll all be after me. I . . ."

Sally stared out into a bleak world. The sky was a leaden grey, and the wind from the river blew with a dismal chill.

CHAPTER VIII

REAPPEARANCE OF MR. CARMYLE—AND GINGER

I

WHEN Sally left Detroit on the following Saturday, accompanied by Fillmore, who was returning to the metropolis for a few days in order to secure offices and generally make his presence felt along Broadway, her spirits had completely recovered. She felt guiltily that she had been fanciful, even morbid. Naturally men wanted to get on in the world. It was their job. She told herself that she was bound up with Gerald's success, and that the last thing of which she ought to complain was the energy he put into efforts of which she as well as he would reap the reward.

To this happier frame of mind the excitement of the last few days had contributed. Detroit, that city of amiable audiences, had liked "The Primrose Way." The theatre, in fulfilment of Teddy's prophecy, had been allowed to open on the Tuesday, and a full house, hungry for entertainment after its enforced abstinence, had welcomed the play wholeheartedly. The papers, not always in agreement with the applause of a first-night audience, had on this occasion endorsed the verdict, with agreeable unanimity hailing Gerald as the coming author and Elsa Doland as the coming star. There had even been a brief mention of Fillmore as the coming manager. But there is always some trifle that jars in our greatest moments, and Fillmore's triumph had been almost spoilt by the fact that the only notice taken of Gladys Winch was by the critic who printed her name—spelt Wunch—in the list of those whom the cast "also included."

"One of the greatest character actresses on the stage," said Fillmore bitterly, talking over this outrage with Sally on the morning after the production.

From this blow, however, his buoyant nature had soon enabled him to rally. Life contained so much that was bright that it would have been churlish to concentrate the attention on the one dark spot. Business had been excellent all through the week. Elsa Doland had got better at every performance. The receipt of a long and agitated telegram from Mr. Cracknell, pleading to be allowed to buy the piece back, the passage of time having apparently softened Miss Hobson, was a pleasant incident. And, best of all, the great Ike Schumann, who owned half the theatres in New York and had been in Detroit superintending one of his musical productions, had looked in one evening and stamped "The Primrose Way" with the seal of his approval. As Fillmore sat opposite Sally on the train, he radiated contentment and importance.

"Yes, do," said Sally, breaking a long silence.

Fillmore awoke from happy dreams.

"Eh?"

"I said 'Yes, do.' I think you owe it to your position."

"Do what?"

"Buy a fur coat. Wasn't that what you were meditating about?"

"Don't be a chump," said Fillmore, blushing nevertheless. It was true that once or twice during the past week he had toyed negligently, as Mr. Bunbury would have said, with the notion, and why not? A fellow must keep warm.

"With an astrakhan collar," insisted Sally.

"As a matter of fact," said Fillmore loftily, his great soul ill-attuned to this badinage, "what I was really thinking about at the moment was something Ike said."

"Ike?"

"Ike Schumann. He's on the train. I met him just now."

"We call him Ike!"

"Of course I call him Ike," said Fillmore heatedly. "Everyone calls him Ike."

"*He* wears a fur coat," Sally murmured.

Fillmore registered annoyance.

"I wish you wouldn't keep on harping on that damned coat. And, anyway, why shouldn't I have a fur coat?"

"Fill . . . ! How can you be so brutal as to suggest that I ever said you shouldn't? Why, I'm one of the strongest supporters of the fur coat. With big cuffs. And you must roll up Fifth Avenue in your car, and I'll point and say 'That's my brother!' 'Your brother? No!' 'He is, really.' 'You're joking. Why, that's the great Fillmore Nicholas.' 'I know. But he really is my brother. And I was with him when he bought that coat.'"

"Do leave off about the coat!"

" 'And it isn't only the coat,' I shall say. 'It's what's underneath. Tucked away inside that mass of fur, dodging about behind that dollar cigar, is one to whom we point with pride . . .' "

Fillmore looked coldly at his watch.

"I've got to go and see Ike Schumann."

"We are in hourly consultation with Ike."

"He wants to see me about the show. He suggests putting it into Chicago before opening in New York."

"Oh no," cried Sally, dismayed.

"Why not?"

Sally recovered herself. Identifying Gerald so closely with his play, she had supposed for a moment that if the piece opened in Chicago it would mean a further prolonged separation from him. But of course there would be no need, she realized, for him to stay with the company after the first day or two.

"You're thinking that we ought to have a New York reputation before tackling Chicago. There's a lot to be said for that. Still, it works both ways. A Chicago run would help us in New York. Well, I'll have to think it over," said Fillmore, importantly, "I'll have to think it over."

He mused with drawn brows.

"All wrong," said Sally.

"Eh?"

"Not a bit like it. The lips should be compressed and the forefinger of the right hand laid in a careworn way against the right temple. You've a lot to learn, Fill."

"Oh, stop it!"

"Fillmore Nicholas," said Sally, "if you knew what pain it gives me to josh my only brother, you'd be sorry for me. But you know it's for your good. Now run along and put Ike out of his misery. I know he's waiting for you with his watch out. 'You *do* think he'll come, Miss Nicholas?' were his last words to me as he stepped on the train; and oh, Fill, the yearning in his voice. 'Why, of *course* he will, Mr. Schumann,' I said. 'For all his exalted position, my brother is kindliness itself. Of course he'll come.' 'If I could only think so!' he said with a gulp. 'If I could only think so. But you know what these managers are. A thousand calls on their time. They get brooding on their fur coats and forget everything else.' 'Have no fear, Mr. Schumann,' I said. 'Fillmore Nicholas is a man of his word.' "

She would have been willing, for she was a girl who never believed in sparing herself where it was a question of entertaining her nearest and dearest, to continue the dialogue, but Fillmore was already moving down the car, his rigid back a silent protest against sisterly levity. Sally watched him disappear, then picked up a magazine and began to read.

She had just finished tracking a story of gripping interest through a jungle of advertisements, only to find that it was in two parts, of which the one she was reading was the first, when a voice spoke.

"How do you do, Miss Nicholas?"

Into the seat before her, recently released from the weight of the coming manager, Bruce Carmyle of all people in the world insinuated himself with that well-bred air of deferential restraint which never left him.

2

Sally was considerably startled. Everybody travels nowadays, of course, and there is nothing really remarkable in finding a man in America whom you had supposed to be in Europe: but nevertheless she was conscious of a dream-like sensation, as though the clock had been turned back and a chapter of her life reopened which she had thought closed for ever.

"Mr. Carmyle!" she cried.

If Sally had been constantly in Bruce Carmyle's thoughts since they had parted on the Paris express, Mr. Carmyle had been very little in Sally's—so little, indeed, that she had had to search her memory for a moment before she identified him.

"We're always meeting on trains, aren't we?" she went on, her composure returning. "I never expected to see you in America."

"I came over."

Sally was tempted to reply that she gathered that, but a sudden embarrassment curbed her tongue. She had just remembered that at their last meeting she had been abominably rude to this man. She was never rude to anyone without subsequent remorse. She contented herself with a tame "Yes."

"Yes," said Mr. Carmyle, "it is a good many years since I have taken a real holiday. My doctor seemed to think I was a trifle run down. It seemed a good opportunity to visit America. Everybody," said Mr. Carmyle oracularly, endeavouring, as he had often done since his ship had left England, to persuade himself that his object in making the trip had not been merely to renew his acquaintance with Sally, "everybody ought to visit America at least once. It is part of one's education."

"And what are your impressions of our glorious country?" said Sally rallying.

Mr. Carmyle seemed glad of the opportunity of lecturing on an impersonal subject. He, too, though his face had shown no trace of it, had been embarrassed in the opening stages of the conversation. The sound of his voice restored him.

"I have been visiting Chicago," he said after a brief travelogue.

"Oh!"

"A wonderful city."

"I've never seen it. I've come from Detroit."

"Yes, I heard you were in Detroit."

Sally's eyes opened.

"You heard I was in Detroit? Good gracious! How?"

"I—ah—called at your New York address and made inquiries," said Mr. Carmyle a little awkwardly.

"But how did you know where I lived?"

"My ccusin—er—Lancelot told me."

Sally was silent for a moment. She had much the same feeling that comes to the man in the detective story who realizes that he is being shadowed. Even if this almost complete stranger had not actually come to America in direct pursuit of her, there was no disguising the fact that he evidently found her an object of considerable interest. It was a compliment, but Sally was not at all sure that she liked it. Bruce Carmyle meant nothing to her, and it was rather disturbing to find that she was apparently of great importance to him. She seized on the mention of Ginger as a lever for diverting the conversation from its present too intimate course.

"How is Mr. Kemp?" she asked.

Mr. Carmyle's dark face seemed to become a trifle darker.

"We have had no news of him," he said shortly.

"No news? How do you mean? You speak as though he had disappeared."

"He has disappeared!"

"Good heavens! When?"

"Shortly after I saw you last."

"Disappeared!"

Mr. Carmyle frowned. Sally, watching him, found her antipathy stirring again. There was something about this man which she had disliked instinctively from the first, a sort of hardness.

"But where has he gone to?"

"I don't know." Mr. Carmyle frowned again. The subject of Ginger was plainly a sore one. "And I don't want to know," he went on heatedly, a dull flush rising in the cheeks which Sally was sure he had to shave twice a day. "I don't care to know. The Family have washed their hands of him. For the future he may look after himself as best he can. I believe he is off his head."

Sally's rebellious temper was well ablaze now, but she fought it down. She would dearly have loved to give battle to Mr. Carmyle—it was odd, she felt, how she seemed to have constituted herself Ginger's champion and protector—but she perceived that, if she wished, as she did, to hear more of her red-headed friend, he must be humoured and conciliated.

"But what happened? What was all the trouble about?"

Mr. Carmyle's eyebrows met.

"He—insulted his uncle. His uncle Donald. He insulted him—grossly. The one man in the world he should have made a point of—er—"

"Keeping in with?"

"Yes. His future depended upon him."

"But what did he do?" cried Sally, trying hard to keep a thoroughly reprehensible joy out of her voice.

"I have heard no details. My uncle is reticent as to what actually took place. He invited Lancelot to dinner to discuss his plans, and it appears that Lancelot—defied him. Defied him! He was rude and insulting. My uncle refuses to have anything more to do with him. Apparently the young fool managed to win some money at the tables at Roville, and this seems to have turned his head completely. My uncle insists that he is mad. I agree with him. Since the night of that dinner nothing has been heard of Lancelot."

Mr. Carmyle broke off to brood once more, and before Sally could speak the impressive bulk of Fillmore loomed up in the aisle beside them. Explanations seemed to Fillmore to be in order. He cast a questioning glance at the mysterious stranger, who, in addition to being in conversation with his sister, had collared his seat.

"Oh, hullo, Fill," said Sally. "Fillmore, this is Mr. Carmyle. We met abroad. My brother Fillmore, Mr. Carmyle."

Proper introduction having been thus effected, Fillmore approved of Mr. Carmyle. His air of being someone in particular appealed to him.

"Strange you meeting again like this," he said affably.

The porter, who had been making up berths along the car, was now hovering expectantly in the offing.

"You two had better go into the smoking room," suggested Sally. "I'm going to bed."

She wanted to be alone, to think. Mr. Carmyle's tale of a roused and revolting Ginger had stirred her.

The two men went off to the smoking-room, and Sally found an empty seat and sat down to wait for her berth to be made up. She was aglow with a curious exhilaration. So Ginger had taken her advice! Excellent Ginger! She felt proud of him. She also had that feeling of complacency, amounting almost to sinful pride, which comes to those who give advice and find it acted upon. She had the emotions of a creator. After all, had she not created this new Ginger? It was she who had stirred him up. It was she who had unleashed him. She had changed him from a meek dependent of the Family to a ravening creature, who went about the place insulting uncles.

It was a feat, there was no denying it. It was something attempted, something done: and by all the rules laid down by the poet it should, therefore, have earned a night's repose. Yet, Sally, jolted by the train, which towards the small hours seemed to be trying out some new buck-and-wing steps of its own invention, slept ill, and presently, as she lay awake, there came to her bedside the Spectre of Doubt, gaunt and questioning. Had she, after all, wrought so well? Had she been wise in tampering with this young man's life?

"What about it?" said the Spectre of Doubt.

3

Daylight brought no comforting answer to the question. Breakfast failed to manufacture an easy mind. Sally got off the train, at the Grand Central station in a state of remorseful concern. She declined the offer of Mr. Carmyle to drive her to the boarding-house, and started to walk there, hoping that the crisp morning air would effect a cure.

She wondered now how she could ever have looked with approval on her rash act. She wondered what demon of interference and meddling had possessed her, to make her blunder into people's lives, upsetting them. She wondered that she was allowed to go around loose. She was nothing more nor less than a menace to society. Here was an estimable young man, obviously the sort of young man who would always have to be assisted through life by his relatives, and she had deliberately egged him on to wreck his prospects. She blushed hotly as she remembered that mad wireless she had sent him from the boat.

Miserable Ginger! She pictured him, his little stock of money gone, wandering foot-sore about London, seeking in vain for work; forcing himself to call on Uncle Donald; being thrown down the front steps by haughty footmen; sleeping on the Embankment; gazing into the darkwaters of the Thames with the stare of hopelessness; climbing to the parapet and . . .

"Ugh!" said Sally.

She had arrived at the door of the boarding-house, and Mrs. Meecher was regarding her with welcoming eyes, little knowing that to all practical intents and purposes she had slain in his prime a red-headed young man of amiable manners and—when not ill-advised by meddling, muddling females—of excellent behaviour.

Mrs. Meecher was friendly and garrulous. *Variety*, the journal which, next to the dog Toto, was the thing she loved best in the world, had informed her on the Friday morning that Mr. Foster's play had got over big in Detroit, and that Miss Doland had made every kind of hit. It was not often that the old *alumni* of the boarding-house forced their way after this fashion into the Hall of Fame, and, according to Mrs. Meecher, the establishment was ringing with the news. That blue ribbon round Toto's neck was worn in honour of the triumph. There was also, though you could not see it, a chicken dinner in Toto's interior, by way of further celebration.

And was it true that Mr. Fillmore had bought the piece? A great man, was Mrs. Meecher's verdict. Mr. Faucitt had always said so . . .

"Oh, how is Mr. Faucitt?" Sally asked, reproaching herself for having allowed the pressure of other matters to drive all thoughts of her late patient from her mind.

"He's gone," said Mrs. Meecher with such relish that to Sally, in her morbid condition, the words had only one meaning. She turned white and clutched at the banisters.

"Gone!"

"To England," added Mrs. Meecher.

Sally was vastly relieved.

"Oh, I thought you meant . . ."

"Oh no, not that." Mrs. Meecher sighed, for she had been a little disappointed in the old gentleman, who started out as such a promising invalid, only to fall away into the dullness of robust health once more. "He's *well* enough. I never seen anybody better. You'd think," said Mrs. Meecher, bearing bearing up with difficulty under her grievance, "you'd think this here new Spanish influenza was a sort of a tonic or somep'n, the way he looks now. Of course," she added, trying to find justification for a respected lodger, "he's had good news. His brother's dead."

"What!"

"Not, I don't mean, that that was good news, far from it, though, come to think of it, all flesh is as grass and we all got to be prepared for somep'n of the sort breaking loose . . . but it seems this here new brother of his—I didn't know he'd a brother, and I don't suppose *you* knew he had a brother. Men are secretive, ain't they!—this brother of his has left him a parcel of money, and Mr. Faucitt he had to get on the Wednesday boat quick as he could and go right over to the other side to look after things. Wind up the estate, I believe they call it. Left in a awful hurry, he did. Sent his love to you and said he'd write. Funny him having a brother, now, wasn't it? Not," said Mrs. Meecher, at heart a reasonable woman, "that folks *don't* have brothers. I got two myself, one in Portland, Oregon, and the other goodness knows where he is. But what I'm trying to say . . ."

Sally disengaged herself, and went up to her room. For a brief while the excitement which comes of hearing good news about those of whom we are fond acted as a stimulant, and she felt almost cheerful. Dear old Mr. Faucitt. She was sorry for his brother, of course, though she had never had the pleasure of his acquaintance and had only just heard that he had ever existed; but it was nice to think that her old friend's remaining years would be years of affluence.

Presently, however, she found her thoughts wandering back into their melancholy groove. She threw herself wearily on the bed. She was tired after her bad night.

But she could not sleep. Remorse kept her awake. Besides, she could hear Mrs. Meecher prowling disturbingly about the house, apparently in search of someone, her progress indicated by creaking boards and the strenuous yapping of Toto.

Sally turned restlessly, and, having turned remained for a long instant transfixed and rigid. She had seen something, and what she had seen was enough to surprise any girl in the privacy of her bedroom. From underneath the bed there peeped coyly forth an undeniably masculine shoe and six inches of a grey trouser-leg.

Sally bounded to the floor. She was a girl of courage, and she meant to probe this matter thoroughly.

"What are you doing under my bed?"

The question was a reasonable one, and evidently seemed to the intruder to deserve an answer. There was a muffled sneeze, and he began to crawl out.

The shoe came first. Then the legs. Then a sturdy body in a dusty coat. And finally there flashed on Sally's fascinated gaze a head of so nearly the maximum redness that it could only belong to one person in the world.

"Ginger!"

Mr. Lancelot Kemp, on all fours, blinked up at her.

"Oh, hullo!" he said.

CHAPTER IX

GINGER BECOMES A RIGHT-HAND MAN

IT was not till she saw him actually standing there before her with his hair rumpled and a large smut on the tip of his nose, that Sally really understood how profoundly troubled she had been about this young man, and how vivid had been that vision of him bobbing about on the waters of the Thames, a cold and unappreciated corpse. She was a girl of keen imagination, and she had allowed her imagination to riot unchecked. Astonishment, therefore, at the extraordinary fact of his being there was for the moment thrust aside by relief. Never before in her life had she experienced such an overwhelming rush of exhilaration. She flung herself into a chair and burst into a screech of laughter which even to her own ears sounded strange. It struck Ginger as hysterical.

"I say, you know!" said Ginger, as the merriment showed no signs of abating. Ginger was concerned. Nasty shock for a girl, finding blighters under her bed.

Sally sat up, gurgling, and wiped her eyes.

"Oh, I *am* glad to see you," she gasped.

"No, really?" said Ginger, gratified. "That's fine." It occurred to him that some sort of apology would be a graceful act. "I say, you know, awfully sorry. About barging in here, I mean. Never dreamed it was your room. Unoccupied, I thought."

"Don't mention it. I ought not to have disturbed you. You were having a nice sleep, of course. Do you always sleep on the floor?"

"It was like this . . . ."

"Of course, if you're wearing it for ornament, as a sort of beauty-spot," said Sally, "all right. But in case you don't know, you've a smut on your nose."

"Oh, my aunt! Not really?"

"Now would I deceive you on an important point like that?"

"Do you mind if I have a look in the glass?"

"Certainly, if you can stand it."

Ginger moved hurriedly to the dressing-table.

"You're perfectly right," he announced, applying his handkerchief.

"I thought I was. I'm very quick at noticing things."

"My hair's a bit rumpled, too."

"Very much so."

"You take my tis," said Ginger, earnestly, "and never lie about under beds. There's nothing in it."

"That reminds me. You won't be offended if I asked you something?"

"No, no. Go ahead."

"It's rather an impertinent question. You may resent it."

"No, no."

"Well, then, what *were* you doing under my bed?"

"Oh, under your bed?"

"Yes. Under my bed. This. It's a bed, you know. Mine. My bed. You were under it. Why? Or putting it another way, why were you under my bed?"

"I was hiding."

"Playing hide-and-seek? That explains it."

"Mrs. What's-her-name—Beecher—Meecher—was after me."

Sally shook her head disapprovingly.

"You mustn't encourage Mrs. Meecher in these childish pastimes. It unsettles her."

Ginger passed an agitated hand over his forehead.

"It's like this . . ."

"I hate to keep criticizing your appearance," said Sally, "and personally I like it; but, when you clutched your brow just then, you put about a pound of dust on it. Your hands are probably grubby."

Ginger inspected them.

"They are!"

"Why not make a really good job of it and have a wash?"

"Do you mind?"

"I'd prefer it."

"Thanks awfully. I mean to say it's your basin, you know, and all that. What I mean is, I seem to be making myself pretty well at home."

"Oh, no."

"Touching the matter of soap . . ."

"Use mine. We Americans are famous for our hospitality."

"Thanks awfully."

"The towel is on your right."

"Thanks awfully."

"And I've a clothes brush in my bag."

"Thanks awfully."

Splashing followed like a sea-lion taking a dip.

"Now, then," said Sally, "why were you hiding from Mrs. Meecher?"

A careworn, almost hunted look came into Ginger's face.

"I say, you know, that woman is rather by way of being one of the lads, what! Scares me! Word was brought that she was on the prowl, so it seemed to me a judicious move to take cover till she sort of blew over. If she'd found me, she'd have made me take that dog of hers for a walk."

"Toto?"

"Toto. You know," said Ginger, with a strong sense of injury, "no dog's got a right to be a dog like that. I don't suppose there's anyone keener on dogs than I am, but a thing like a woolly rat." He shuddered slightly. "Well, one hates to be seen about with it in the public streets."

"Why couldn't you have refused in a firm but gentlemanly manner to take Toto out?"

"Ah! There you rather touch the spot. You see, the fact of the matter is, I'm a bit behind with the rent, and that makes it rather hard to take what you might call a firm stand."

"But how can you be behind with the rent? I only left here the Saturday before last and you weren't in the place then. You can't have been here more than a week."

"I've been here just a week. That's the week I'm behind with."

"But why? You were a millionaire when I left you at Roville."

"Well, the fact of the matter is, I went back to the tables that night and lost a goodish bit of what I'd won. And, somehow or another, when I got to America, the stuff seemed to slip away."

"What made you come to America at all?" said Sally, asking the question which, she felt, any sensible person would have asked at the opening of the conversation.

One of his familiar blushes raced over Ginger's face.

"Oh, I thought I would. Land of opportunity, you know."

"Have you managed to find any of the opportunities yet?"

"Well, I have got a job of sorts, I'm a waiter at a rummy

little place on Second Avenue. The salary isn't big, but I'd have wangled enough out of it to pay last week's rent, only they docked me a goodish bit for breaking plates and what not. The fact is, I'm making rather a hash of it."

"Oh, Ginger! You oughtn't to be a waiter!"

"That's what the boss seems to think."

"I mean, you ought to be doing something ever so much better."

"But what? You've no notion how well all these blighters here seem to be able to get along without my help. I've tramped all over the place, offering my services, but they all say they'll try to carry on as they are."

Sally reflected.

"I know!"

"What?"

"I'll make Fillmore give you a job. I wonder I didn't think of it before."

"Fillmore?"

"My brother. Yes, he'll be able to use you."

"What as?"

Sally considered.

"As a—as a—oh, as his right-hand man."

"Does he want a right-hand man?"

"Sure to. He's a young fellow trying to get along. Sure to want a right-hand man."

"'M yes," said Ginger reflectively. "Of course, I've never been a right-hand man, you know."

"Oh, you'd pick it up. I'll take you round to him now. He's staying at the Astor."

"There's just one thing," said Ginger.

"What's that?"

"I might make a hash of it."

"Heavens, Ginger! There must be something in this world that you wouldn't make a hash of. Don't stand arguing any longer. Are you dry? and clean? Very well, then. Let's be off."

"Right ho."

Ginger took a step towards the door, then paused, rigid, with one leg in the air, as though some spell had been cast upon him. From the passage outside there had sounded a shrill yapping. Ginger looked at Sally. Then he looked—longingly—at the bed.

"Don't be such a coward," said Sally, severely.

"Yes, but . . ."

"How much do you owe Mrs. Meecher?"

"Round about twelve dollars, I think it is."

"I'll pay her."

Ginger flushed awkwardly.

"No, I'm hanged if you will! I mean," he stammered, "it's frightfully good of you and all that, and I can't tell you how grateful I am, but honestly, I couldn't . . ."

Sally did not press the point. She liked him the better for a rugged independence, which in the days of his impecuniousness her brother Fillmore had never dreamed of exhibiting.

"Very well," she said. "Have it your own way. Proud. That's me all over, Mabel. Ginger!" She broke off sharply. "Pull yourself together. Where is your manly spirit? I'd be ashamed to be such a coward."

"Awfully sorry, but, honestly, that woolly dog . . ."

"Never mind the dog. I'll see you through."

They came out into the passage almost on top of Toto, who was stalking phantom rats. Mrs. Meecher was man-oeuvring in the background. Her face lit up grimly at the sight of Ginger.

"*Mister Kemp!* I been looking for you."

Sally intervened brightly.

"Oh, Mrs. Meecher," she said, shepherding her young charge through the danger zone, "I was so surprised to meet Mr. Kemp here. He is a great friend of mine. We met in France. We're going off now to have a long talk about old times, and then I'm taking him to see my brother . . ."

"Toto . . ."

"Dear little thing! You ought to take him for a walk," said Sally. "It's a lovely day. Mr. Kemp was saying just now that he would have liked to take him, but we're rather in a hurry and shall probably have to get into a taxi. You've no idea how busy my brother is just now. If we're late, he'll never forgive us."

She passed on down the stairs, leaving Mrs. Meecher dissatisfied but irresolute. There was something about Sally which even in her pre-wealthy days had always baffled Mrs. Meecher and cramped her style, and now that she was rich and independent she inspired in the châtelaine of the boarding-house an emotion which was almost awe. The front door had closed before Mrs. Meecher had collected her faculties; and Ginger, pausing on the sidewalk, drew a long breath.

"You know, you're wonderful!" he said, regarding Sally with unconcealed admiration.

She accepted the compliment composedly.

"Now we'll go and hunt up Fillmore," she said. "But there's no need to hurry, of course, really. We'll go for a walk first, and then call at the Astor and make him give us lunch. I want to hear all about you. I've heard something already. I met your cousin, Mr. Carmyle. He was on the train coming from Detroit. Did you know that he was in America?"

"No, I've—er—rather lost touch with the Family."

"So I gathered from Mr. Carmyle. And I feel hideously responsible. It was all through me that all this happened."

"Oh, no."

"Of course it was. I made you what you are to-day—I hope I'm satisfied—I dragged and dragged you down until the soul within you died, so to speak. I know perfectly well that you wouldn't have dreamed of savaging the Family as you seem to have done if it hadn't been for what I said to you at Roville. Ginger, tell me, what *did* happen? I'm dying to know. Mr. Carmyle said you insulted your uncle!"

"Donald. Yes, we did have a bit of a scrap, as a matter of fact. He made me go out to dinner with him and we—er—sort of disagreed. To start with, he wanted me to apologize to old Scrymgeour, and I rather gave it a miss."

"Noble fellow!"

"Scrymgeour?"

"No, silly! You."

"Oh, ah!" Ginger blushed. "And then there was all that about the soup, you know."

"How do you mean, 'all that about the soup'? What about the soup? What soup?"

"Well, things sort of hotted up a bit when the soup arrived."

"I don't understand."

"I mean, the trouble seemed to start, as it were, when the waiter had finished ladling out the mulligatawny. Thick soup, you know."

"I know mulligatawny is a thick soup. Yes?"

"Well, my old uncle—I'm not blaming him, don't you know—more his misfortune than his fault—I can see that now—but he's got a heavy moustache. Like a walrus, rather, and he's a bit apt to inhale the stuff through it. And I—well, I asked him not to. It was just a suggestion, you know.

108

He cut up fairly rough, and by the time the fish came round we were more or less down on the mat chewing holes in one another. My fault, probably. I wasn't feeling particularly well-disposed towards the Family that night. I'd just had a talk with Bruce—my cousin, you know—in Piccadilly, and that had rather got the wind up me. Bruce always seems to get on my nerves a bit somehow and—Uncle Donald asking me to dinner and all that. By the way, did you get the books?"

"What books?"

"Bruce said he wanted to send you some books. That was why I gave him your address."

Sally stared.

"He never sent me any books."

"Well, he said he was going to, and I had to tell him where to send them."

Sally walked on, a little thoughtfully. She was not a vain girl, but it was impossible not to perceive in the light of this fresh evidence that Mr. Carmyle had made a journey of three thousand miles with the sole object of renewing his acquaintance with her. It did not matter, of course, but it was vaguely disturbing. No girl cares to be dogged by a man she rather dislikes.

"Go on telling me about your uncle," she said.

"Well, there's not much more to tell. I'd happened to get that wireless of yours just before I started out to dinner with him, and I was more or less feeling that I wasn't going to stand any rot from the Family. I'd got to the fish course, hadn't I? Well, we managed to get through that somehow, but we didn't survive the fillet steak. One thing seemed to lead to another, and the show sort of bust up. He called me a good many things, and I got a bit fed-up, and finally I told him I hadn't any more use for the Family and was going to start out on my own. And—well, I did, don't you know. And here I am."

Sally listened to this saga breathlessly. More than ever did she feel responsible for her young protégé, and any faint qualms which she had entertained as to the wisdom of trans-ferring practically the whole of her patrimony to the care of so erratic a financier as her brother vanished. It was her plain duty to see that Ginger was started well in the race of life, and Fillmore was going to come in uncommonly handy.

"We'll go to the Astor now," she said, "and I'll introduce you to Fillmore? He's a theatrical manager and he's sure to have something for you."

"It's awfully good of you to bother about me."

"Ginger," said Sally, "I regard you as a grandson. Hail that cab, will you?"

CHAPTER X

SALLY IN THE SHADOWS

I

IT seemed to Sally in the weeks that followed her reunion with Ginger Kemp that a sort of golden age had set in. On all the frontiers of her little kingdom there was peace and prosperity, and she woke each morning in a world so neatly smoothed and ironed out that the most captious pessimist could hardly have found anything in it to criticize.

True, Gerald was still a thousand miles away. Going to Chicago to superintend the opening of "The Primrose Way"; for Fillmore had acceded to his friend Ike's suggestion in the matter of producing it first in Chicago, and he had been called in by a distracted manager to revise the work of a brother dramatist, whose comedy was in difficulties at one of the theatres in that city; and this meant he would have to remain on the spot for some time to come. It was disappointing, for Sally had been looking forward to having him back in New York in a few days; but she refused to allow herself to be depressed. Life as a whole was much too satisfactory for that. Life indeed, in every other respect, seemed perfect. Fillmore was going strong; Ginger was off her conscience; she had found an apartment; her new hat suited her; and "The Primrose Way" was a tremendous success. Chicago, it appeared from Fillmore's account, was paying little attention to anything except "The Primrose Way." National problems had ceased to interest the citizens. Local problems left them cold. Their minds were riveted to the exclusion of all else on the problem of how to secure seats. The production of the piece, according to Fillmore, had been the most terrific experience that had come to stir Chicago since the great fire.

Of all these satisfactory happenings, the most satisfactory, to Sally's thinking, was the fact that the problem of Ginger's future had been solved. Ginger had entered the service of the Fillmore Nicholas Theatrical Enterprises Ltd. (Managing Director, Fillmore Nicholas)—Fillmore would have made the title longer, only that was all that would go on the brass plate—and was to be found daily in the outer office, his duties consisting mainly, it seemed, in reading the evening papers. What exactly he was, even Ginger hardly knew. Sometimes he felt like the man at the wheel, sometimes like a glorified office boy, and not so very glorified at that. For the most part he had to prevent the mob rushing and getting at Fillmore, who sat in semi-regal state in the inner office pondering great schemes.

But, though there might be an occasional passing uncertainty in Ginger's mind as to just what he was supposed to be doing in exchange for the fifty dollars he drew every Friday, there was nothing uncertain about his gratitude to Sally for having pulled the strings and enabled him to do it. He tried to thank her every time they met, and nowadays they were meeting frequently; for Ginger was helping her to furnish her new apartment. In this task, he spared no efforts. He said that it kept him in condition.

"And what I mean to say is," said Ginger, pausing in the act of carrying a massive easy chair to the third spot which Sally had selected in the last ten minutes, "if I didn't sweat about a bit and help you after the way you got me that job . . ."

"Ginger, desist," said Sally.

"Yes, but honestly . . ."

"If you don't stop it, I'll make you move that chair into the next room."

"Shall I?" Ginger rubbed his blistered hands and took a new grip. "Anything you say."

"Silly! Of course not. The only other rooms are my bedroom, the bathroom and the kitchen. What on earth would I want a great lumbering chair in them for? All the same, I believe the first we chose was the best."

"Back she goes, then, what?"

Sally reflected frowningly. This business of setting up house was causing her much thought.

"No," she decided. "By the window is better." She looked at him remorsefully. "I'm giving you a lot of trouble."

"Trouble!" Ginger, accompanied by a chair, staggered across the room. "The way I look at it is this." He wiped a bead of perspiration from his freckled forehead. "You got me that job, and . . ."

"Stop!"

"Right ho . . . Still, you did, you know."

Sally sat down in the armchair and stretched herself. Watching Ginger work had given her a vicarious fatigue. She surveyed the room proudly. It was certainly beginning to look cosy. The pictures were up, the carpet down, the furniture very neatly in order. For almost the first time in her life she had the restful sensation of being at home. She had always longed, during the past three years of boarding-house existence, for a settled abode, a place where she could lock the door on herself and be alone. The apartment was small, but it was undeniably a haven. She looked about her and could see no flaw in it . . . except . . . She had a sudden sense of something missing.

"Hullo!" she said. "Where's that photograph of me? I'm sure I put it on the mantelpiece yesterday."

His exertions seemed to have brought the blood to Ginger's face. He was a rich red. He inspected the mantelpiece narrowly.

"No. No photograph here."

"I know there isn't. But it was there yesterday. Or was it? I know I meant to put it there. Perhaps I forgot. It's the most beautiful thing you ever saw. Not a bit like me; but what of that? They touch 'em up in the dark-room, you know. I value it because it looks the way I should like to look if I could."

"I've never had a beautiful photograph taken of myself," said Ginger, solemnly, with gentle regret.

"Cheer up!"

"Oh, I don't *mind*. I only mentioned . . ."

"Ginger," said Sally, "pardon my interrupting your remarks, which I know are valuable, but this chair is—not—right! It ought to be where it was at the beginning. Could you give your imitation of a pack-mule just once more? And after that I'll make you some tea. *If* there's any tea—or milk—or cups."

"There are cups all right. I know, because I smashed two the day before yesterday. I'll nip round the corner for some milk, shall I?"

"Yes, please nip. All this hard work has taken it out of me terribly."

Over the tea-table Sally became inquisitive.

"What I can't understand about this job of yours, Ginger—which as you are just about to observe, I was noble enough to secure for you—is the amount of leisure that seems to go with it. How is it that you are able to spend your valuable time—Fillmore's valuable time, rather—juggling with my furniture every day?"

"Oh, I can usually get off."

"But oughtn't you to be at your post doing—whatever it is you do? What *do* you do?"

Ginger stirred his tea thoughtfully and gave his mind to the question.

"Well, I sort of mess about, you know." He pondered. "I interview divers blighters and tell 'em your brother is out and take their names and addresses and . . . oh, all that sort of thing."

"Does Fillmore consult you much?"

"He lets me read some of the plays that are sent in. Awful tosh most of them. Sometimes he sends me off to a vaudeville house of an evening."

"As a treat?"

"To see some special act, you know. To report on it. In case he might want to use it for this revue of his."

"Which revue?"

"Didn't you know he was going to put on a revue? Oh, rather. A whacking big affair. Going to cut out the Follies and all that sort of thing."

"But—my goodness!" Sally was alarmed. It was just like Fillmore, she felt, to go branching out into these expensive schemes when he ought to be moving warily and trying to consolidate the small success he had had. All his life he had thought in millions where the prudent man would have been content with hundreds. An inexhaustible fount of optimism bubbled eternally within him. "That's rather ambitious," she said.

"Yes. Ambitious sort of cove, your brother. Quite the Napoleon."

"I shall have to talk to him," said Sally decidedly. She was annoyed with Fillmore. Everything had been going so beautifully, with everybody peaceful and happy and prosperous and no anxiety anywhere, till he had spoiled things. Now she would have to start worrying again.

"Of course," argued Ginger, "there's money in revues. Over in London fellows make pots out of them.

Sally shook her head.

"It won't do," she said. "And I'll tell you another thing

that won't do. This armchair. Of *course* it ought to be over by the window. You can see that yourself, can't you."

"Absolutely!" said Ginger, patiently preparing for action once more.

2

Sally's anxiety with regard to her ebullient brother was not lessened by the receipt shortly afterwards of a telegram from Miss Winch in Chicago.

Have you been feeding Fillmore meat?

the telegram ran: and, while Sally could not have claimed that she completely understood it, there was a sinister suggestion about the message which decided her to wait no longer before making investigations. She tore herself away from the joys of furnishing and went round to the headquarters of the Fillmore Nicholas Theatrical Enterprises Ltd. (Managing Director, Fillmore Nicholas) without delay.

Ginger, she discovered on arrival, was absent from his customary post, his place in the outer office being taken by a lad of tender years and pimply exterior, who thawed and cast off a proud reserve on hearing Sally's name, and told her to walk right in. Sally walked right in, and found Fillmore with his feet on an untidy desk, studying what appeared to be costume-designs.

"Ah, Sally!" he said in the distrait, tired voice which speaks of vast preoccupations. Prosperity was still putting in its silent, deadly work on the Hope of the American Theatre. What, even at as late an epoch as the return from Detroit, had been merely a smooth fullness around the angle of the jaw was now frankly and without disguise a double chin. He was wearing a new waistcoat and it was unbuttoned. "I am rather busy," he went on. "Always glad to see you, but I *am* rather busy. I have a hundred things to attend to."

"Well, attend to me. That'll only make a hundred and one. Fill, what's all this I hear about a revue?"

Fillmore looked as like a small boy caught in the act of stealing jam as it is possible for a great theatrical manager to look. He had been wondering in his darker moments what Sally would say about that project when she heard of it, and he had hoped that she would not hear of it until all the preparations were so complete that interference would be impossible. He was extremely fond of Sally, but there was, he knew, a lamentable vein of caution in her make-up which might lead her to criticize. And how can your man of affairs carry on if women are buzzing round criticizing all the time? He picked up a pen and put it down; buttoned his waistcoat and unbuttoned it; and scratched his ear with one of the costume-designs.

"Oh yes, the revue!"

"It's no good saying 'Oh yes'! You know perfectly well it's a crazy idea."

"Really . . . these business matters . . . this interference . . ."

"I don't want to run your affairs for you, Fill, but that money of mine does make me a sort of partner, I suppose, and I think I have a right to raise a loud yell of agony when I see you risking it on a . . ."

"Pardon me," said Fillmore loftily, looking happier. "Let me explain. Women never understand business matters. Your money is tied up exclusively in 'The Primrose Way,' which, as you know, is a tremendous success. You have nothing whatever to worry about as regards any new production I may make."

"I'm not worrying about the money. I'm worrying about you."

A tolerant smile played about the lower slopes of Fillmore's face.

"Don't be alarmed about *me*. I'm all right."

"You aren't all right. You've no business, when you've only just got started as a manager, to be rushing into an enormous production like this. You can't afford it."

"My dear child, as I said before, women cannot understand these things. A man in my position can always command money for a new venture."

"Do you mean to say you have found somebody silly enough to put up money?"

"Certainly. I don't know that there is any secret about it. Your friend, Mr. Carmyle, has taken an interest in some of my forthcoming productions."

"What!"

Sally had been disturbed before, but she was aghast now. This was something she had never anticipated. Bruce Carmyle seemed to be creeping into her life like an advancing tide. There appeared to be no eluding him. Wherever she turned, there he was, and she could do nothing but rage impotently. The situation was becoming impossible.

Fillmore·misinterpreted the note of dismay in her voice.

"It's quite all right," he assured her. "He's a very rich man. Large private means, besides his big income. Even if anything goes wrong . . ."

"It isn't that. It's . . ."

The hopelessness of explaining to Fillmore stopped Sally. And while she was chafing at this new complication which had come to upset the orderly routine of her life there was an outburst of voices in the other office. Ginger's understudy seemed to be endeavouring to convince somebody that the Big Chief was engaged and not to be intruded upon. In this he was unsuccessful, for the door opened tempestuously and Miss Winch sailed in.

"Fillmore, you poor nut," said Miss Winch, for though she might wrap up her meaning somewhat obscurely in her telegraphic communications, when it came to the spoken word she was directness itself, "stop picking straws in your hair and listen to me, You're dippy!"

The last time Sally had seen Fillmore's fiancée, she had been impressed by her imperturbable calm. Miss Winch, in Detroit, had seemed a girl whom nothing could ruffle. That she had lapsed now from this serene placidity, struck Sally as ominous. Slightly though she knew her, she felt that it could be no ordinary happening that had so animated her sister-in-law-to-be.

"Ah! Here you are!" said Fillmore. He had started to his feet indignantly at the opening of the door, like a lion bearded in its den, but calm had returned when he saw who the intruder was.

"Yes, here I am!" Miss Winch dropped despairingly into a swivel-chair, and endeavoured to restore herself with a stick of chewing-gum. "Fillmore, darling, you're the sweetest thing on earth, and I love you, but on present form you could just walk straight into Bloomingdale and they'd give you the royal suite."

"My dear girl . . ."

"What do *you* think?" demanded Miss Winch, turning to Sally.

"I've just been telling him," said Sally, welcoming this ally, "I think it's absurd at this stage of things for him to put on an enormous revue . . ."

"Revue?" Miss Winch stopped in the act of gnawing her gum. "What revue?" She flung up her arms. "I shall have to swallow this gum," she said. "You can't chew with your head going round. Are you putting on a revue *too*?"

Fillmore was buttoning and unbuttoning his waistcoat. He had a hounded look.

"Certainly, certainly," he replied in a tone of some feverishness. "I wish you girls would leave me to manage . . ."

"Dippy!" said Miss Winch once more. "Telegraphic address: Tea-Pot, Matteawan." She swivelled round to Sally again. "Say, listen! This boy must be stopped. We must form a gang in his best interests and get him put away. What do you think he proposes doing? I'll give you three guesses. Oh, what's the use? You'd never hit it. This poor wandering lad has got it all fixed up to star me—*me*—in a new show!"

Fillmore removed a hand from his waistcoat buttons and waved it protestingly.

"I have used my own judgment . . ."

"Yes, *sir!*" proceeded Miss Winch, riding over the interruption. "That's what he's planning to spring on an unsuspicious public. I'm sitting peacefully in my room at the hotel in Chicago, pronging a few cents' worth of scrambled eggs and reading the morning paper, when the telephone rings. Gentleman below would like to see me. Oh, ask him to wait. Business of flinging on a few clothes. Down in elevator. Bright sunrise effects in lobby."

"What on earth do you mean?"

"The gentleman had a head of red hair which had to be seen to be believed," explained Miss Winch. "Lit up the lobby. Management had switched off all the electrics for sake of economy. An Englishman he was. Nice fellow. Named Kemp."

"Oh, is Ginger in Chicago?" said Sally. "I wondered why he wasn't on his little chair in the outer office."

"I sent Kemp to Chicago," said Fillmore, "to have a look at the show. It is my policy, if I am unable to pay periodical visits myself, to send a representative . . ."

"Save it up for the long winter evenings," advised Miss Winch, cutting in on this statement of managerial tactics. "Mr. Kemp may have been there to look at the show, but his chief reason for coming was to tell me to beat it back to New York to enter into my kingdom. Fillmore wanted me on the spot, he told me, so that I could sit around in this office here, interviewing my supporting company. Me! Can you or can you not," inquired Miss Winch frankly, "tie it?"

"Well . . ." Sally hesitated.

"Don't say it! I know it just as well as you do. It's too sad for words."

"You persist in underestimating your abilities, Gladys," said Fillmore reproachfully. "I have had a certain amount of experience in theatrical matters—I have seen a good deal of acting—and I assure you that as a character-actress you . . ."

Miss Winch rose swiftly from her seat, kissed Fillmore energetically, and sat down again. She produced another stick of chewing-gum, then shook her head and replaced it in her bag.

"You're a darling old thing to talk like that," she said, "and I hate to wake you out of your daydreams, but, honestly, Fillmore, dear, do just step out of the padded cell for one moment and listen to reason. I know exactly what has been passing in your poor disordered bean. You took Elsa Doland out of a minor part and made her a star overnight. She goes to Chicago, and the critics and everybody else rave about her. As a matter of fact," she said to Sally with enthusiasm, for hers was an honest and generous nature, "you can't realize, not having seen her play there, what an amazing hit she has made. She really is a sensation. Everybody says she's going to be the biggest thing on record. Very well, then, what does Fillmore do? The poor fish claps his hand to his forehead and cries 'Gadzooks! An idea! I've done it before, I'll do it again. I'm the fellow who can make a star out of anything.' And he picks on *me!*"

"My dear girl . . ."

"Now, the flaw in the scheme is this. Elsa is a genius, and if he hadn't made her a star somebody else would have done. But little Gladys? That's something else again." She turned to Sally. "You've seen me in action, and let me tell you you've seen me at my best. Give me a maid's part, with a tray to carry on in act one and a couple of 'Yes, madam's' in act two, and I'm *there!* Ellen Terry hasn't anything on me when it comes to saying 'Yes, madam,' and I'm willing to back myself for gold, notes, or lima beans against Sarah Bernhardt as a tray-carrier. But there I finish. That lets me out. And anybody who thinks otherwise is going to lose a lot of money. Between ourselves the only thing I can do really well is to cook . . ."

"My dear Gladys!" cried Fillmore revolted.

"I'm a heaven-born cook, and I don't mind notifying the world to that effect. I can cook a chicken casserole so that you would leave home and mother for it. Also my English pork-pies! One of these days I'll take an afternoon off and assemble one for you. You'd be surprised! But acting—no. I can't do it, and I don't want to do it. I only went on the stage for fun, and my idea of fun isn't to plough through a star part with all the critics waving their axes in the front row, and me knowing all the time that it's taking money out of Fillmore's bankroll that ought to be going towards buying the little home with stationary wash-tubs . . . Well, that's that, Fillmore, old darling. I thought I'd just mention it."

Sally could not help being sorry for Fillmore. He was sitting with his chin on his hands, staring moodily before him—Napoleon at Elba. It was plain that this project of taking Miss Winch by the scruff of the neck and hurling her to the heights had been very near his heart.

"If that's how you feel," he said in a stricken voice, "there is nothing more to say."

"Oh, yes there is. We will now talk about this revue of yours. It's off!"

Fillmore bounded to his feet: He thumped the desk with a well-nourished fist. A man can stand just so much.

"It is not off! Great heavens! It's too much! I will not put up with this interference with my business concerns. I will not be tied and hampered. Here am I, a man of broad vision and . . . and . . . broad vision . . . I form my plans . . . my plans . . . I form them . . . I shape my schemes . . . and what happens? A horde of girls flock into my private office while I am endeavouring to concentrate . . . and concentrate . . . I won't stand it. Advice, yes. Interference, no. I . . . I . . . I . . . and kindly remember that!"

The door closed with a bang. A fainter detonation announced the whirlwind passage through the outer office. Footsteps died away down the corridor.

Sally looked at Miss Winch, stunned. A roused and militant Fillmore was new to her.

Miss Winch took out the stick of chewing-gum again and unwrapped it.

"Isn't he cute!" she said. "I hope he doesn't get the soft kind," she murmured, chewing reflectively.

"The soft kind."

"He'll be back soon with a box of candy," explained Miss Winch, "and he will get that sloshy, creamy sort, though I keep telling him I like the other. Well, one thing's certain. Fillmore's got it up his nose. He's beginning to hop about and sing in the sunlight. It's going to be hard work to get that boy down to earth again." Miss Winch heaved a gentle sigh. "I *should* like him to have enough left in the old stocking to pay the first year's rent when the wedding bells ring out." She bit meditatively on her chewing-gum. "Not," she said, "that it matters. I'd be just as happy in two rooms and a kitchenette, so long as Fillmore was there. You've no notion how dippy I am about him." Her freckled face glowed. "He grows on me like a darned drug. And the funny thing is that I keep right on admiring him though I can see all the while that he's the most perfect chump. He *is* a chump, you know. That's what I love about him. That and the way his ears wiggle when he gets excited. Chumps always make the best husbands. When you marry, Sally, grab a chump. Tap his forehead first, and if it rings solid, don't hesitate. All the unhappy marriages come from the husband having brains. What good are brains to a man? They only unsettle him." She broke off and scrutinized Sally closely. "Say, what do you do with your skin?"

She spoke with solemn earnestness which made Sally laugh.

"What do I do with my skin? I just carry it around with me."

"Well," said Miss Winch enviously, "I wish I could train my darned fool of a complexion to get that way. Freckles are the devil. When I was eight I had the finest collection in the Middle West, and I've been adding to it right along. Some folks say lemon-juice'll cure 'em. Mine lap up all I give 'em and ask for more. There's only one way of getting rid of freckles, and that is to saw the head off at the neck."

"But why do you want to get rid of them?"

"Why? Because a sensitive girl, anxious to retain her future husband's love, doesn't enjoy going about looking like something out of a dime museum."

"How absurd! Fillmore worships freckles."

"Did he tell you so?" asked Miss Winch eagerly.

'Not in so many words, but you can see it in his eye."

"Well, he certainly asked me to marry him, knowing all about them, I will say that. And, what's more, I don't think

121

feminine loveliness means much to Fillmore, or he'd never have picked on me. Still, it is calculated to give a girl a jar, you must admit, when she picks up a magazine and reads an advertisement of a face-cream beginning, 'Your husband is growing cold to you. Can you blame him? Have you really *tried* to cure those unsightly blemishes?' —meaning what I've got. Still, I haven't noticed Fillmore growing cold to me, so maybe it's all right."

It was a subdued Sally who received Ginger when he called at her apartment a few days later on his return from Chicago. It seemed to her, thinking over the recent scene, that matters were even worse than she had feared. This absurd revue, which she had looked on as a mere isolated outbreak of foolishness, was, it would appear, only a specimen of the sort of thing her misguided brother proposed to do, a sample selected at random from a wholesale lot of frantic schemes. Fillmore, there was no longer any room for doubt, was preparing to express his great soul on a vast scale. And she could not dissuade him. A humiliating thought. She had grown so accustomed through the years to being the dominating mind that this revolt from her authority made her feel helpless and inadequate. Her self-confidence was shaken.

And Bruce Carmyle was financing him . . . It was illogical, but Sally could not help feeling that when—she had not the optimism to say "if"—he lost his money, she would somehow be under an obligation to him, as if the disaster had been her fault. She disliked, with a whole-hearted intensity, the thought of being under an obligation to Mr. Carmyle.

Ginger said he had looked in to inspect the furniture, on the chance that Sally might want it shifted again: but Sally had no criticisms to make on that subject. Weightier matters occupied her mind. She sat Ginger down in the arm-chair and started to pour out her troubles. It soothed her to talk to him. In a world which had somehow become chaotic again after an all too brief period of peace, he was solid and consoling.

"I shouldn't worry," observed Ginger with Winch-like calm, when she had finished drawing for him the picture of a Fillmore rampant against a background of expensive revues. Sally nearly shook him.

"It's all very well to tell me not to worry," she cried. "How can I help worrying? Fillmore's simply a baby, and he's just playing the fool. He has lost his head completely. And

I can't stop him! That is the awful part of it. I used to be able to look him in the eye, and he would wag his tail and crawl back into his basket, but now I seem to have no influence at all over him. He just snorts and goes on running round in circles, breathing fire."

Ginger did not abandon his attempts to indicate the silver lining.

"I think you are making too much of all this, you know. I mean to say, it's quite likely he's found some mug . . . what I mean is, it's just possible that your brother isn't standing the entire racket himself. Perhaps some rich Johnnie has breezed along with a pot of money. It often happens like that, you know. You read in the paper that some manager or other is putting on some show or other, when really the chap who's actually supplying the pieces of eight is some anonymous lad in the background."

"That is just what has happened, and it makes it worse than ever. Fillmore tells me that your cousin, Mr. Carmyle, is providing the money."

This did interest Ginger. He sat up with a jerk.

"Oh, I say!" he exclaimed.

"Yes," said Sally, still agitated but pleased that she had at last shaken him out of his trying attitude of detachment.

Ginger was scowling.

"That's a bit off," he observed.

"I think so, too."

"I don't like that."

"Nor do I."

"Do you know what I think?" said Ginger, ever a man of plain speech and a reckless plunger into delicate subjects. "The blighter's in love with you."

Sally flushed. After examining the evidence before her, she had reached the same conclusion in the privacy of her thoughts, but it embarrassed her to hear the thing put into bald words.

"I know Bruce," continued Ginger, "and, believe me, he isn't the sort of cove to take any kind of flutter without a jolly good motive. Of course, he's got tons of money. His old guvnor was the Carmyle of Carmyle, Brent & Co.—coal mines up in Wales, and all that sort of thing—and I suppose he must have left Bruce something like half a million. No need for the fellow to have worked at all, if he hadn't wanted to. As far as having the stuff goes, he's in a position to back all the shows he wants to. But the point is, it's right out of his line. He doesn't do that sort of thing. Not a drop of sporting blood in the chap. Why I've known him stick the whole family on to me just because it got noised about that I'd dropped a couple of quid on the Grand National. If he's really brought himself to the point of shelling out on a risky proposition like a show, it means something, take my word for it. And I don't see what else it can mean except . . . well, I mean to say, *is* it likely that he's doing it simply to make your brother look on him as a good egg and a pal, and all that sort of thing?"

"No, it's not," agreed Sally. "But don't let's talk about it any more. Tell me all about your trip to Chicago."

"All right. But, returning to this binge for a moment, I don't see how it matters to you one way or the other. You're engaged to another fellow, and when Bruce rolls up and says: 'What about it?' you've simply to tell him that the shot isn't on the board and will he kindly melt away. Then you hand him his hat and out he goes."

Sally gave a troubled laugh.

"You think that's simple, do you? I suppose you imagine that a girl enjoys that sort of thing? Oh, what's the use of talking about it? It's horrible, and no amount of arguing will make it anything else. Do let's change the subject. How did you like Chicago?"

"Oh, all right. Rather a grubby sort of place."

"So I've always heard. But you ought not to mind that, being a Londoner."

"Oh, I didn't mind it. As a matter of fact, I had rather a good time. Saw one or two shows, you know. Got in on my face as your brother's representative, which was all to the good. By the way, it's rummy how you run into people when you move about, isn't it?"

"You talk as if you had been dashing about the streets with your eyes shut. Did you meet somebody you knew?"

"Chap I hadn't seen for years. Was at school with him, as a matter of fact. Fellow named Foster. But I expect you know him, too, don't you? By name, at any rate. He wrote your brother's show."

Sally's heart jumped.

"Oh! Did you meet Gerald—Foster?"

"Ran into him one night at the theatre."

"And you were really at school with him?"

"Yes. He was in the footer team with me my last year."

"Was he a scrum-half, too?" asked Sally, dimpling.

Ginger looked shocked.

"You don't have two scrum-halves in a team," he said, pained at this ignorance on a vital matter. "The scrum-half is the half who works the scrum and . . ."

"Yes, you told me that at Roville. What was Gerald— Mr. Foster then? A six and seven-eighths, or something?"

"He was a wing-three," said Ginger with a gravity befitting his theme. "Rather fast, with a fairly decent swerve. But he would *not* learn to give the reverse pass inside to the centre."

"Ghastly!" said Sally.

"If," said Ginger earnestly, "a wing's bottled up by his wing and the back, the only thing he *can* do, if he doesn't want to be bundled into touch, is to give the reverse pass."

"I know," said Sally. "If I've thought that once, I've thought it a hundred times. How nice it must have been for you meeting again. I suppose you had all sorts of things to talk about?"

Ginger shook his head.

"Not such a frightful lot. We were never very thick. You see, this chap Foster was by way of being a bit of a worm."

"What!"

"A tick," explained Ginger. "A rotter. He was pretty generally barred at school. Personally, I never had any use for him at all."

Sally stiffened. She had liked Ginger up to that moment, and later on, no doubt, she would resume her liking for him: but in the immediate moment which followed these words she found herself regarding him with stormy hostility. How dare he sit there saying things like that about Gerald?

Ginger, who was lighting a cigarette without a care in the world, proceeded to develop his theme.

"It's a rummy thing about school. Generally, if a fellow's good at games—in the cricket team or the footer team and so forth—he can hardly help being fairly popular. But this blighter Foster somehow—nobody seemed very keen on him. Of course, he had a few of his own pals, but most of the chaps rather gave him a miss. It may have been because he was a bit sidey . . . had rather an edge on him, you know . . . Personally, the reason I barred him was because he wasn't straight. You didn't notice it if you weren't thrown a goodish bit with him, of course, but he and I were in the same house, and . . ."

Sally managed to control her voice, though it shook a little.

"I ought to tell you," she said, and her tone would have warned him had he been less occupied, "that Mr. Foster is a great friend of mine."

But Ginger was intent on the lighting of his cigarette, a delicate operation with the breeze blowing in through the open window. His head was bent, and he had formed his hands into a protective framework which half hid his face.

"If you take my tip," he mumbled, "you'll drop him. He's a wrong 'un."

He spoke with the absent-minded drawl of preoccupation, and Sally could keep the conflagration under no longer. She was aflame from head to foot.

"It may interest you to know," she said, shooting the words out like bullets from between clenched teeth, "that Gerald Foster is the man I am engaged to marry."

Ginger's head came slowly up from his cupped hands. Amazement was in his eyes, and a sort of horror. The cigarette hung limply from his mouth. He did not speak, but sat looking at her, dazed. Then the match burnt his fingers, and he dropped it with a start. The sharp sting of it seemed to wake him. He blinked.

"You're joking," he said, feebly. There was a note of wistfulness in his voice. "It isn't true?"

Sally kicked the leg of her chair irritably. She read insolent disapproval into the words. He was daring to criticize . . .

"Of course it's true . . ."

"But . . ." A look of hopeless misery came into Ginger's pleasant face. He hesitated. Then, with the air of a man bracing himself to a dreadful, but unavoidable, ordeal, he went on. He spoke gruffly, and his eyes, which had been fixed on Sally's, wandered down to the match on the carpet. It was still glowing, and mechanically he put a foot on it.

"Foster's married," he said shortly. "He was married the day before I left Chicago."

3

It seemed to Ginger that in the silence which followed, brooding over the room like a living presence, even the noises in the street had ceased, as though what he had said had been a spell cutting Sally and himself off from the outer world. Only the little clock on the mantelpiece ticked—ticked—ticked, like a heart beating fast.

He stared straight before him, conscious of a strange rigidity. He felt incapable of movement, as he had sometimes felt in nightmares; and not for all the wealth of America could he have raised his eyes just then to Sally's face. He could see her hands. They had tightened on the arm of the chair. The knuckles were white.

He was blaming himself bitterly now for his oafish clumsiness in blurting out the news so abruptly. And yet, curiously, in his remorse there was something of elation. Never before had he felt so near to her. It was as though a barrier that had been between them had fallen.

Something moved . . . It was Sally's hand, slowly relaxing. The fingers loosened their grip, tightened again, then, as if reluctantly relaxed once more. The blood flowed back.

"Your cigarette's out."

Ginger started violently. Her voice, coming suddenly out of the silence, had struck him like a blow.

"Oh, thanks!"

He forced himself to light another match. It sputtered noisily in the stillness. He blew it out, and the uncanny quiet fell again.

Ginger drew at his cigarette mechanically. For an instant he had seen Sally's face, white-cheeked and bright-eyed, the chin tilted like a flag flying over a stricken field. His mood changed. All his emotions had crystallized into a dull, futile rage, a helpless fury directed at a man a thousand miles away.

Sally spoke again. Her voice sounded small and far off, an odd flatness in it.

"Married?"

Ginger threw his cigarette out of the window. He was shocked to find that he was smoking. Nothing could have been farther from his intention than to smoke. He nodded.

"Whom has he married?"

Ginger coughed. Something was sticking in his throat, and speech was difficult.

"A girl called Doland."

"Oh, Elsa Doland?"

"Yes."

"Elsa Doland." Sally drummed with her fingers on the arm of the chair. "Oh, Elsa Doland?"

There was silence again. The little clock ticked fussily on the mantelpiece. Out in the street automobile horns were blowing. From somewhere in the distance came faintly the rumble of an elevated train. Familiar sounds, but they came to Sally now with a curious, unreal sense of novelty. She felt as though she had been projected into another world where everything was new and strange and horrible—every thing except Ginger. About him, in the mere sight of him, there was something known and heartening.

Suddenly, she became aware that she was feeling that Ginger was behaving extremely well. She seemed to have been taken out of herself and to be regarding the scene from outside, regarding it coolly and critically; and it was plain to her that Ginger, in this upheaval of all things, was bearing himself perfectly. He had attempted no banal words of sympathy. He had said nothing and he was not looking at her. And Sally felt that sympathy just now would be torture, and that she could not have borne to be looked at.

Ginger was wonderful. In that curious, detached spirit that had come upon her, she examined him impartially, and gratitude welled up from the very depths of her. There he sat, saying nothing and doing nothing, as if he knew that all she needed, the only thing that could keep her sane in this world of nightmare, was the sight of that dear, flaming head of his that made her feel that the world had not slipped away from her altogether.

Ginger did not move. The room had grown almost dark now. A spear of light from a street lamp shone in through the window.

Sally got up abruptly. Slowly, gradually, inch by inch, the great suffocating cloud which had been crushing her had lifted. She felt alive again. Her black hour had gone, and she was back in the world of living things once more. She was afire with a fierce, tearing pain that tormented her almost beyond endurance, but dimly she sensed the fact that she had passed through something that was worse than pain, and, with Ginger's stolid presence to aid her, had passed triumphantly.

"Go and have dinner, Ginger," she said. "You must be starving."

Ginger came to life like a courtier in the palace of the

Sleeping Beauty. He shook himself, and rose stiffly from his chair.

"Oh, no," he said. "Not a bit, really."

Sally switched on the light and set him blinking. She could bear to be looked at now.

"Go and dine," she said. "Dine lavishly and luxuriously. You've certainly earned . . ." Her voice faltered for a moment. She held out her hand. "Ginger," she said shakily, "I . . . Ginger, you're a pal."

When he had gone, Sally sat down and began to cry. Then she dried her eyes in a business-like manner.

"There, Miss Nicholas!" she said. "You couldn't have done that an hour ago . . . We will now boil you an egg for your dinner and see how that suits you!"

CHAPTER XI

SALLY RUNS AWAY

IF Ginger Kemp had been asked to enumerate his good
qualities, it is not probable that he would have drawn
up a very lengthy list. He might have started by claiming
for himself the virtue of meaning well, but after that he would
have had to chew the pencil in prolonged meditation. And,
even if he could eventually have added one or two further
items to the catalogue, tact and delicacy of feeling would not
have been among them.

Yet, by staying away from Sally during the next few days
he showed considerable delicacy. It was not easy to stay
away from her, but he forced himself to do so. He argued
from his own tastes, and was strongly of opinion that in times
of travail, solitude was what the sufferer most desired. In his
time he, too, had had what he would have described as nasty
jars, and on these occasions all he had asked was to be allowed
to sit and think things over and fight his battle out by himself.

By Saturday, however, he had come to the conclusion that
some form of action might now be taken. Saturday was
rather a good day for picking up the threads again. He had
not to go to the office, and, what was still more to the point,
he had just drawn his week's salary. Mrs. Meecher had
deftly taken a certain amount of this off him, but enough
remained to enable him to attempt consolation on a fairly
princely scale. There presented itself to him as a judicious
move the idea of hiring a car and taking Sally out to dinner
at one of the road-houses he had heard about up the Boston
Post Road. He examined the scheme. The more he looked
at it, the better it seemed.

He was helped to this decision by the extraordinary perfection of the weather. The weather of late had been a
revelation to Ginger. It was his first experience of America's
Indian Summer, and it had quite overcome him. As he stood
on the roof of Mrs. Meecher's establishment on the Saturday

morning, thrilled by the velvet wonder of the sunshine, it seemed to him that the only possible way of passing such a day was to take Sally for a ride in an open car.

The Maison Meecher was a lofty building on one of the side-streets at the lower end of the avenue. From its roof, after you had worked your way through the groves of washing which hung limply from the clothes-line, you could see many things of interest. To the left lay Washington Square, full of somnolent Italians and roller-skating children; to the right was a spectacle which never failed to intrigue Ginger, the high smoke-stacks of a Cunard liner moving slowly down the river, sticking up over the house-tops as if the boat was travelling down Ninth Avenue.

To-day there were four of these funnels, causing Ginger to deduce the *Mauretania*. As the boat on which he had come over from England, the *Mauretania* had a sentimental interest for him. He stood watching her stately progress till the higher buildings farther down the town shut her from his sight; then picked his way through the washing and went down to his room to get his hat. A quarter of an hour later he was in the hall-way of Sally's apartment house, gazing with ill-concealed disgust at the serge-clad back of his cousin Mr. Carmyle, who was engaged in conversation with a gentleman in overalls.

No care-free prospector, singing his way through the Mojave Desert and suddenly finding himself confronted by a rattlesnake, could have experienced so abrupt a change of mood as did Ginger at this revolting spectacle. Even in their native Piccadilly it had been unpleasant to run into Mr. Carmyle. To find him here now was nothing short of nauseating. Only one thing could have brought him to this place. Obviously, he must have come to see Sally; and with a sudden sinking of the heart Ginger remembered the shiny, expensive automobile which he had seen waiting at the door. He, it was clear, was not the only person to whom the idea had occurred of taking Sally for a drive on this golden day.

He was still standing there when Mr. Carmyle swung round with a frown on his dark face which seemed to say that he had not found the janitor's conversation entertaining. The sight of Ginger plainly did nothing to lighten his gloom.

"Hullo!" he said.

"Hullo!" said Ginger.

Uncomfortable silence followed these civilities.

"Have you come to see Miss Nicholas?"

"Why, yes."

"She isn't here," said Mr. Carmyle, and the fact that he had found someone to share the bad news, seemed to cheer him a little.

"Not here?"

"No. Apparently . . ." Bruce Carmyle's scowl betrayed that resentment which a well-balanced man cannot but feel at the unreasonableness of others. " . . . Apparently, for some extraordinary reason, she has taken it into her head to dash over to England."

Ginger tottered. The unexpectedness of the blow was crushing. He followed his cousin out into the sunshine in a sort of dream. Bruce Carmyle was addressing the driver of the expensive automobile.

"I find I shall not want the car. You can take it back to the garage."

The chauffeur, a moody man, opened one half-closed eye and spat cautiously. It was the way Rockefeller would have spat when approaching the crisis of some delicate financial negotiation.

"You'll have to pay just the same," he observed, opening his other eye to lend emphasis to the words.

"Of course I shall pay," snapped Mr. Carmyle, irritably. "How much is it?"

Money passed. The car rolled off.

"Gone to England?" said Ginger, dizzily.

"Yes, gone to England."

"But why?"

"How the devil do I know why?" Bruce Carmyle would have found his best friend trying at this moment. Gaping Ginger gave him almost a physical pain. "All I know is what the janitor told me, that she sailed on the *Mauretania* this morning."

The tragic irony of this overcame Ginger. That he should have stood on the roof, calmly watching the boat down the river . . .

He nodded absently to Mr. Carmyle and walked off. He had no further remarks to make. The warmth had gone out of the sunshine and all interest had departed from his life. He felt dull, listless, at a loose end. Not even the thought that his cousin, a careful man with his money, had had to pay a day's hire for a car which he could not use brought him any balm. He loafed aimlessly about the streets. He wandered in the Park and out again. The Park bored him. The streets bored him. The whole city bored him. A city without Sally in it was a drab, futile city, and nothing that the sun could do to brighten it could make it otherwise.

Night came at last, and with it a letter. It was the first even passably pleasant thing that had happened to Ginger in the whole of this dreary and unprofitable day: for the envelope bore the crest of the good ship *Mauretania*. He snatched it covetously from the letter-rack, and carried it upstairs to his room.

Very few of the rooms at Mrs. Meecher's boarding-house struck any note of luxury. Mrs. Meecher was not one of your fashionable interior decorators. She considered that when she had added a Morris chair to the essentials which make up a bedroom, she had gone as far in the direction of pomp as any guest at seven-and-a-half per could expect her to go. As a rule, the severity of his surroundings afflicted Ginger with a touch of gloom when he went to bed; but to-night—such is the magic of a letter from the right person—he was uplifted and almost gay. There are moments when even illuminated texts over the wash-stand cannot wholly quell us.

There was nothing of haste and much of ceremony in Ginger's method of approaching the perusal of his correspondence. He bore himself after the manner of a small boy in the presence of unexpected ice-cream, gloating for awhile before embarking on the treat, anxious to make it last out. His first move was to feel in the breast-pocket of his coat and produce the photograph of Sally which he had feloniously removed from her apartment. At this he looked long and earnestly before propping it up within easy reach against his basin, to be handy, if required, for purposes of reference. He then took off his coat, collar, and shoes, filled and lit a pipe, placed pouch and matches on the arm of the Morris chair, and drew that chair up so that he could sit with his feet on the bed. Having manoeuvred himself into a position of ease, he lit his pipe again and took up the letter. He looked at the crest, the handwriting of the address, and the post-mark. He weighed it in his hand. It was a bulky letter.

He took Sally's photograph from the wash-stand and

scrutinized it once more. Then he lit his pipe again, and, finally, wriggling himself into the depths of the chair, opened the envelope.

"*Ginger, dear.*"

Having read so far, Ginger found it necessary to take up the photograph and study it with an even greater intentness than before. He gazed at it for many minutes, then laid it down and lit his pipe again. Then he went on with the letter.

"Ginger, dear—I'm afraid this address is going to give you rather a shock, and I'm feeling very guilty. I'm running away, and I haven't even stopped to say good-bye. I can't help it. I know it's weak and cowardly, but I simply can't help it. I stood it for a day or two, and then I saw that it was no good. (Thank you for leaving me alone and not coming round to see me. Nobody else but you would have done that. But then, nobody ever has been or ever could be so understanding as you.)"

Ginger found himself compelled at this point to look at the photograph again.

"There was too much in New York to remind me. That's the worst of being happy in a place. When things go wrong you find there are too many ghosts about. I just couldn't stand it. I tried, but I couldn't. I'm going away to get cured—if I can. Mr. Faucitt is over in England, and when I went down to Mrs. Meecher for my letters, I found one from him. His brother is dead, you know, and he has inherited, of all things, a fashionable dress-making place in Regent Street. His brother was Laurette et Cie. I suppose he will sell the business later on, but, just at present, the poor old dear is apparently quite bewildered and that doesn't seem to have occurred to him. He kept saying in his letter how much he wished I was with him, to help him, and I was tempted and ran. Anything to get away from the ghosts and have something to do. I don't suppose I shall feel much better in England, but, at least, every street corner won't have associations. Don't ever be happy anywhere, Ginger. It's too big a risk, much too big a risk.

"There was a letter from Elsa Doland, too. Bubbling over with affection. We had always been tremendous friends. Of course, she never knew anything about my being engaged to Gerald. I lent Fillmore the money to buy that piece, which gave Elsa her first big chance, and so she's very grateful.

She says, if ever she gets the opportunity of doing me a good turn . . . Aren't things muddled?

"And there was a letter from Gerald. I was expecting one, of course, but . . . what would you have done, Ginger? Would you have read it? I sat with it in front of me for an hour, I should think, just looking at the envelope, and then . . . You see, what was the use? I could guess exactly the sort of thing that would be in it, and reading it would only have hurt a lot more. The thing was done, so why bother about explanations? What good are explanations, anyway? They don't help. They don't do anything . . . I burned it, Ginger. The last letter I shall ever get from him. I made a bonfire on the bathroom floor, and it smouldered and went brown, and then flared a little, and every now and then I lit another match and kept it burning, and at last it was just black ashes and a stain on the tiles. Just a mess!

"Ginger, burn this letter, too. I'm pouring out all the poison to you, hoping it will make me feel better. You don't mind, do you? But I know you don't. If ever anybody had a real pal . . .

"It's a dreadful thing, fascination, Ginger. It grips you and you are helpless. One can be so sensible and reasonable about other people's love affairs. When I was working at the dance place I told you about there was a girl who fell in love with the most awful little beast. He had a mean mouth and shiny black hair brushed straight back, and anybody would have seen what he was. But this girl wouldn't listen to a word. I talked to her by the hour. It makes me smile now when I think how sensible and level-headed I was. But she wouldn't listen. In some mysterious way this was the man she wanted, and, of course, everything happened that one knew would happen.

"If one could manage one's own life as well as one can manage other people's! If all this wretched thing of mine had happened to some other girl, how beautifully I could have proved that it was the best thing that could have happened, and that a man who could behave as Gerald has done wasn't worth worrying about. I can just hear myself. But, you see, whatever he has done, Gerald is still Gerald and Sally is still Sally and, however much I argue, I can't get away from that. All I can do is to come howling to my red-headed pal, when I know just as well as he does that a girl of any spirit would be dignified and keep her troubles to herself and be much too proud to let anyone know that she was hurt.

"Proud! That's the real trouble, Ginger. My pride has been battered and chopped up and broken into as many pieces as you broke Mr. Scrymgeour's stick! What pitiful creatures we are. Girls, I mean. At least, I suppose a good many girls are like me. If Gerald had died and I had lost him that way, I know quite well I shouldn't be feeling as I do now. I should have been broken-hearted, but it wouldn't have been the same. It's my pride that is hurt. I have always been a bossy, cocksure little creature, swaggering about the world like an English sparrow; and now I'm paying for it! Oh, Ginger, I'm paying for it! I wonder if running away is going to do me any good at all. Perhaps, if Mr. Faucitt has some real hard work for me to do . . .

"Of course, I know exactly how all this has come about. Elsa's pretty and attractive. But the point is that she is a success, and as a success she appeals to Gerald's weakest side. He worships success. She is going to have a marvellous career, and she can help Gerald on in his. He can write plays for her to star in. What have I to offer against that? Yes, I know it's grovelling and contemptible of me to say that, Ginger. I ought to be above it, oughtn't I—talking as if I were competing for some prize . . . But I haven't any pride left. Oh, well!

"There! I've poured it all out and I really do feel a little better just for the moment. It won't last, of course, but even a minute is something. Ginger, dear, I shan't see you for ever so long, even if we ever do meet again, but you'll try to remember that I'm thinking of you a whole lot, won't you? I feel responsible for you. You're my baby. You've got started now and you've only to stick to it. Please, please, *please* don't 'make a hash of it'! Good-bye. I never did find that photograph of me that we were looking for that afternoon in the apartment, or I would send it to you. Then you could have kept it on your mantelpiece, and whenever you felt inclined to make a hash of anything I would have caught your eye sternly and you would have pulled up.

"Good-bye, Ginger. I shall have to stop now. The mail is just closing.

"Always your pal, wherever I am.—SALLY."

136

Ginger laid the letter down, and a little sound escaped him that was half a sigh, half an oath. He was wondering whether even now some desirable end might not be achieved by going to Chicago and breaking Gerald Foster's neck. Abandoning this scheme as impracticable, and not being able to think of anything else to do he re-lit his pipe and started to read the letter again.

CHAPTER XII

SOME LETTERS FOR GINGER

Laurette et Cie.,
Regent Street,
London, W.,
England.

January 21st.

DEAR GINGER,—I'm feeling better. As it's three
months since I last wrote to you, no doubt you will
say to yourself that I would be a poor, weak-minded creature
if I wasn't. I suppose one ought to be able to get over anything in three months. Unfortunately, I'm afraid I haven't
quite succeeded in doing that, but at least I have managed
to get my troubles stowed away in the cellar, and I'm not
dragging them out and looking at them all the time. That's
something, isn't it?

I ought to give you all my impressions of London, I suppose;
but I've grown so used to the place that I don't think I have
any now. I seem to have been here years and years.

You will see by the address that Mr. Faucitt has not yet
sold his inheritance. He expects to do so very soon, he tells
me—there is a rich-looking man with whiskers and a keen
eye whom he is always lunching with, and I think big deals
are in progress. Poor dear! he is crazy to get away into the
country and settle down and grow ducks and things. London
has disappointed him. It is not the place it used to be. Until
quite lately, when he grew resigned, he used to wander about
in a disconsolate sort of way, trying to locate the landmarks
of his youth. (He has not been in England for nearly thirty
years!) The trouble is, it seems, that about once in every
thirty years a sort of craze for change comes over London,
and they paint a shop-front red instead of blue, and that
upsets the returned exile dreadfully. Mr. Faucitt feels like
Rip Van Winkle. His first shock was when he found that the
Empire was a theatre now instead of a music-hall. Then he
was told that another music-hall, the Tivoli, had been
pulled down altogether. And when on top of that he went

to look at the baker's shop in Rupert Street, over which he he had lodgings in the eighties, and discovered that it had been turned into a dressmaker's, he grew very melancholy, and only cheered up a little when a lovely magenta fog came on and showed him that some things were still going along as in the good old days.

I am kept quite busy at Laurette et Cie., thank goodness. (Not being a French scholar like you—do you remember Jules?—I thought at first that Cie was the name of the junior partner, and looked forward to meeting him. "Miss Nicholas, shake hands with Mr. Cie, one of your greatest admirers.") I hold down the female equivalent of your job at the Fillmore Nicholas Theatrical Enterprises Ltd.— that is to say, I'm a sort of right-hand woman. I hang around and sidle up to the customers when they come in, and say, "Chawming weather, moddom!" (which is usually a black lie) and pass them on to the staff, who do the actual work. I shouldn't mind going on like this for the next few years, but Mr. Faucitt is determined to sell. I don't know if you are like that, but every other Englishman I've ever met seems to have an ambition to own a house and lot in Loamshire or Hants or Salop or somewhere. Their one object in life is to make some money and "buy back the old place"— which was sold, of course, at the end of act one to pay the heir's gambling debts.

Mr. Faucitt, when he was a small boy, used to live in a little village in Gloucestershire, near a place called Cirencester—at least, it isn't: it's called Cissister, which I bet you didn't know—and after forgetting about it for fifty years, he has suddenly been bitten by the desire to end his days there, surrounded by pigs and chickens. He took me down to see the place the other day. Oh, Ginger, this English country! Why any of you ever live in towns I can't think. Old, old grey stone houses with yellow haystacks and lovely squelchy muddy lanes and great fat trees and blue hills in the distance. The peace of it! If ever I sell my soul, I shall insist on the devil giving me at least forty years in some English country place in exchange.

Perhaps you will think from all this that I am too much occupied to remember your existence. Just to show how interested I am in you, let me tell you that, when I was reading the paper a week ago, I happened to see the headline, "International Match." It didn't seem to mean anything at first, and then I suddenly recollected. This was the thing you had once been a snip for! So I went down to a place called Twickenham, where this football game was to be, to see the sort of thing you used to do before I took charge of you and made you a respectable right-hand man. There was an enormous crowd there, and I was nearly squeezed to death, but I bore it for your sake. I found out that the English team were the ones wearing white shirts, and that the ones in red were the Welsh. I said to the man next to me, after he had finished yelling himself black in the face, "Could you kindly inform me which is the English scrum-half?" And just at that moment the players came quite near where I was, and about a dozen assassins in red hurled themselves violently on top of a meek-looking little fellow who had just fallen on the ball. Ginger, you are well out of it! *That* was the scrum-half, and I gathered that that sort of thing was a mere commonplace in his existence. Stopping a rush, it is called, and he is expected to do it all the time. The idea of you ever going in for such brutal sports! You thank your stars that you are safe on your little stool in Fillmore's outer office, and that, if anybody jumps on top of you now, you can call a cop. Do you mean to say you really used to do these dare-devil feats? You must have hidden depths in you which I have never suspected.

As I was taking a ride down Piccadilly the other day on top of a bus, I saw somebody walking along who seemed familiar. It was Mr. Carmyle. So he's back in England again. He didn't see me, thank goodness. I don't want to meet anybody just at present who reminds me of New York.

Thanks for telling me all the news, but please don't do it again. It makes me remember, and I don't want to. It's this way, Ginger. Let me write to you, because it really does relieve me, but don't answer my letters. Do you mind? I'm sure you'll understand.

So Fillmore and Gladys Winch are married! From what I have seen of her, it's the best thing that has ever happened to Brother F. She is a splendid girl. I must write to him . . .

Laurette et Cie.,
March 12th.   London.

DEAR GINGER,—I saw in a Sunday paper last week that "The Primrose Way" had been produced in New York, and was a great success. Well, I'm very glad. But I don't think the papers ought to print things like that. It's unsettling.

Next day, I did one of those funny things you do when you're feeling blue and lonely and a long way away from everybody. I called at your club and asked for you! Such a nice old man in uniform at the desk said in a fatherly way that you hadn't been in lately, and he rather fancied you were out of town, but would I take a seat while he inquired. He then summoned a tiny boy, also in uniform, and the child skipped off chanting, "Mister Kemp! Mister Kemp!" in a shrill treble. It gave me such an odd feeling to hear your name echoing in the distance. I felt so ashamed for giving them all that trouble; and when the boy came back I slipped twopence into his palm, which I suppose was against all the rules, though he seemed to like it.

Mr. Faucitt has sold the business and retired to the country, and I am rather at a loose end . . .

Monk's Crofton,
(*whatever that means*)
Much Middleford,
Salop,
(*slang for Shropshire*)
England.

April 18*th*.

DEAR GINGER,—What's the use? What *is* the use? I do all I can to get right away from New York, and New York comes after me and tracks me down in my hiding-place. A week or so ago, as I was walking down the Strand in an aimless sort of way, out there came right on top of me—who do you think? Fillmore, arm in arm with Mr. Carmyle! I couldn't dodge. In the first place, Mr. Carmyle had seen me; in the second place, it is a day's journey to dodge poor dear Fillmore now. I blushed for him, Ginger! Right there in the Strand I blushed for him. In my worst dreams I had never pictured him so enormous. Upon what meat doth this our Fillmore feed that he is grown so great? Poor Gladys! When she looks at him she must feel like a bigamist.

Apparently Fillmore is still full of big schemes, for he talked airily about buying all sorts of English plays. He has come over, as I suppose you know, to arrange about putting on "The Primrose Way" over here. He is staying at the

Savoy, and they took me off there to lunch, whooping joyfully as over a strayed lamb. It was the worst thing that could possibly have happened to me. Fillmore talked Broadway without a pause, till by the time he had worked his way past the French pastry and was lolling back, breathing a little stertorously, waiting for the coffee and liqueurs, he had got me so homesick that, if it hadn't been that I didn't want to make a public exhibition of myself, I should have broken down and howled. It was crazy of me ever to go near the Savoy. Of course, it's simply an annex to Broadway. There were Americans at every table as far as the eye could reach. I might just as well have been at the Astor.

Well, if Fate insists in bringing New York to England for my special discomfiture, I suppose I have got to put up with it. I just let events take their course, and I have been drifting ever since. Two days ago I drifted here. Mr. Carmyle invited Fillmore—he seems to love Fillmore—and me to Monk's Crofton, and I hadn't even the shadow of an excuse for refusing. So I came, and I am now sitting writing to you in an enormous bedroom with an open fire and armchairs and every other sort of luxury. Fillmore is out golfing. He sails for New York on Saturday on the *Mauretania*. I am horrified to hear from him that, in addition to all his other big schemes, he is now promoting a fight for the light-weight championship in Jersey City, and guaranteeing enormous sums to both boxers. It's no good arguing with him. If you do, he simply quotes figures to show the fortunes other people have made out of these things. Besides, it's too late now, anyway. As far as I can make out, the fight is going to take place in another week or two. All the same, it makes my flesh creep.

Well, it's no use worrying, I suppose. Let's change the subject. Do you know Monk's Crofton? Probably you don't, as I seem to remember hearing something said about it being a recent purchase. Mr. Carmyle bought it from some lord or other who had been losing money on the Stock Exchange. I hope you haven't seen it, anyway, because I want to describe it at great length. I want to pour out my soul about it. Ginger, what has England ever done to deserve such paradises? I thought, in my ignorance, that Mr. Faucitt's Cissister place was pretty good, but it doesn't even begin. It can't compete. Of course, his is just an ordinary country house, and this is a Seat. Monk's Crofton is the sort of place they used to write about in the English novels. *You* know. "The sunset was falling on the walls of G—— Castle, in B——shire, hard by the picturesque village of H——, and not a stone's throw from the hamlet of J——." I can imagine Tennyson's Maud living here. It is one of the stately homes of England; how beautiful they stand, and I'm crazy about it.

You motor up from the station, and after you have gone about three miles, you turn in at a big iron gate with stone posts on each side with stone beasts on them. Close by the gate is the cutest little house with an old man inside it who pops out and touches his hat. This is only the lodge, really, but you think you have arrived; so you get all ready to jump out, and then the car goes rolling on for another fifty miles or so through beech woods full of rabbits and open meadows with deer in them. Finally, just as you think you are going on for ever, you whizz round a corner, and there's the house. You don't get a glimpse of it till then, because the trees are too thick.

It's very large, and sort of low and square, with a kind of tower at one side and the most fascinating upper porch sort of thing with battlements. I suppose in the old days you used to stand on this and drop molten lead on visitors' heads. Wonderful lawns all round, and shrubberies and a lake that you can just see where the ground dips beyond the fields. Of course it's too early yet for them to be out, but to the left of the house there's a place where there will be about a million roses when June comes round, and all along the side of the rose-garden is a high wall of old red brick which shuts off the kitchen garden. I went exploring there this morning. It's an enormous place, with hot-houses and things, and there's the cunningest farm at one end with a stable yard full of puppies that just tear the heart out of you, they're so sweet. And a big, sleepy cat, which sits and blinks in the sun and lets the puppies run all over her. And there's a lovely stillness, and you can hear everything growing. And thrushes and blackbirds . . . Oh, Ginger, it's heavenly!

But there's a catch. It's a case of "Where every prospect pleases and only man is vile." At least, not exactly vile, I suppose, but terribly stodgy. I can see now why you couldn't hit it off with the Family. Because I've seen 'em all! They're here! Yes, Uncle Donald and all of them. Is it a habit of your family to collect in gangs, or have I just happened to stumble into an accidental Old Home Week? When I came down to dinner the first evening, the drawing-room was full to bursting point—not simply because Fillmore was there, but because there were uncles and aunts all over the place. I felt like a small lion in a den of Daniels. I know exactly now what you mean about the Family. They *look* at you! Of course, it's all right for me, because I am snowy white clear through, but I can just imagine what it must have been like for you with your permanently guilty conscience. You must have had an awful time.

By the way, it's going to be a delicate business getting this letter through to you—rather like carrying the despatches through the enemy's lines in a Civil War play. You're supposed to leave letters on the table in the hall, and some-one collects them in the afternoon and takes them down to the village on a bicycle. But, if I do that some aunt or uncle is bound to see it, and I shall be an object of loathing, for it is no light matter, my lad, to be caught having correspondence with a human Jimpson weed like you. It would blast me socially. At least, so I gather from the way they behaved when your name came up at dinner last night. Somebody mentioned you, and the most awful roasting party broke loose, Uncle Donald acting as cheer-leader. I said feebly that I had met you and had found you part human, and there was an awful silence till they all started at the same time to show me where I was wrong, and how cruelly my girlish inexperience had deceived me. A young and innocent half-portion like me, it appears, is absolutely incapable of suspecting the true infamy of the dregs of society. You aren't fit to speak to the likes of me, being at the kindest estimate little more than a blot on the human race. I tell you this in case you may imagine you're popular with the Family. You're not.

So I shall have to exercise a good deal of snaky craft in smuggling this letter through. I'll take it down to the village myself if I can sneak away. But it's going to be pretty difficult, because for some reason I seem to be a centre of attraction. Except when I take refuge in my room, hardly a moment passes without an aunt or an uncle popping out and having a cosy talk with me. It sometimes seems as though they were weighing me in the balance. Well, let 'em weigh!

Time to dress for dinner now. Good-bye.

Yours in the balance,

SALLY.

P.S.—You were perfectly right about your Uncle Donald's

moustache, but I don't agree with you that it is more his misfortune than his fault. I think he does it on purpose.

(*Just for the moment*)
Monk's Crofton,
Much Middleford,
Salop,

April 20th.   England.

DEAR GINGER,—Leaving here to-day. In disgrace. Hard, cold looks from the family. Strained silences. Uncle Donald far from chummy. You can guess what has happened. I might have seen it coming. I can see now that it was in the air all along.

Fillmore knows nothing about it. He left just before it happened. I shall see him very soon, for I have decided to come back and stop running away from things any longer. It's cowardly to skulk about over here. Besides, I'm feeling so much better that I believe I can face the ghosts. Anyway, I'm going to try. See you almost as soon as you get this.

I shall mail this in London, and I suppose it will come over by the same boat as me. It's hardly worth writing, really, of course, but I have sneaked up to my room to wait till the motor arrives to take me to the station, and it's something to do. I can hear muffled voices. The Family talking me over, probably. Saying they never really liked me all along. Oh, well!

Yours moving in an orderly manner to the exit,

SALLY.

CHAPTER XIII

STRANGE BEHAVIOUR OF A SPARRING-PARTNER

I

SALLY'S emotions, as she sat in her apartment on the morning of her return to New York, resembled somewhat those of a swimmer who, after wavering on a raw morning at the brink of a chill pool, nerves himself to the plunge. She was aching, but she knew that she had done well. If she wanted happiness, she must fight for it, and for all these months she had been shirking the fight. She had done with wavering on the brink, and here she was, in mid-stream, ready for whatever might befall. It hurt, this coming to grips. She had expected it to hurt. But it was a pain that stimulated, not a dull melancholy that smothered. She felt alive and defiant.

She had finished unpacking and tidying up. The next move was certainly to go and see Ginger. She had suddenly become aware that she wanted very badly to see Ginger. His stolid friendliness would be a support and a prop. She wished now that she had sent him a cable, so that he could have met her at the dock. It had been rather terrible at the dock. The echoing customs sheds had sapped her valour and she felt alone and forlorn.

She looked at her watch, and was surprised to find how early it was. She could catch him at the office and make him take her out to lunch. She put on her hat and went out.

The restless hand of change, always active in New York, had not spared the outer office of the Fillmore Nicholas Theatrical Enterprises Ltd. in the months of her absence. She was greeted on her arrival by an entirely new and original stripling in the place of the one with whom at her last visit she had established such cordial relations. Like his predecessor he was generously pimpled, but there the resemblance stopped. He was a grim boy, and his manner was stern and suspicious. He peered narrowly at Sally for a moment as if he had caught her in the act of purloining the office blotting-paper, then, with no little acerbity, desired her to state her business.

"I want Mr. Kemp," said Sally.

The office-boy scratched his cheek dourly with a ruler. No one would have guessed, so austere was his aspect, that a moment before her entrance he had been trying to balance it on his chin, juggling the while with a pair of paper-weights. For, impervious as he seemed to human weaknesses, it was this lad's ambition one day to go into vaudeville.

"What name?" he said, coldly.

"Nicholas," said Sally. "I am Mr. Nicholas' sister."

On a previous occasion when she had made this announcement, disastrous results had ensued; but to-day it went well. It seemed to hit the office-boy like a bullet. He started convulsively, opened his mouth, and dropped the ruler. In the interval of stooping and recovering it he was able to pull himself together. He had not been curious about Sally's name. What he had wished was to have the name of the person for whom she was asking repeated. He now perceived that he had had a bit of luck. A wearying period of disappointment in the matter of keeping the paper-weights circulating while balancing the ruler, had left him peevish, and it had been his intention to work off his ill-humour on the young visitor. The discovery that it was the boss's sister who was taking up his time, suggested the advisability of a radical change of tactics. He had stooped with a frown: he returned to the perpendicular with a smile that was positively winning. It was like the sun suddenly bursting through a London fog.

"Will you take a seat, lady?" he said, with polished courtesy .even unbending so far as to reach out and dust one with the sleeve of his coat. He added that the morning was a fine one.

"Thank you," said Sally. "Will you tell him I'm here."

"Mr. Nicholas is out, miss," said the office-boy, with gentlemanly regret. "He's back in New York, but he's gone out."

"I don't want Mr. Nicholas. I want Mr. Kemp.". .

"Mr. Kemp?"

"Yes, Mr. Kemp."

Sorrow at his inability to oblige shone from every hill-top on the boy's face.

"Don't know of anyone of that name around here," he said, apologetically.

"But surely . . ." Sally broke off suddenly. A grim foreboding had come to her. "How long have you been here?" she asked.

"All day, ma'am," said the office-boy, with the manner of a Casabianca.

"I mean, how long have you been employed here?"

"Just over a month, miss."

"Hasn't Mr. Kemp been in the office all that time?"

"Name's new to *me*, lady. Does he look like anything? I meanter say, what's he look like?"

"He has very red hair."

"Never seen him in here," said the office-boy.

The truth shone coldly on Sally. She blamed herself for ever having gone away, and told herself that she might have known what would happen. Left to his own resources, the unhappy Ginger had once more made a hash of it. And this hash must have been a more notable and outstanding hash than any of his previous efforts, for, surely, Fillmore would not lightly have dismissed one who had come to him under her special protection.

"Where is Mr. Nicholas?" she asked. It seemed to her that Fillmore was the only possible source of information. "Did you say he was out?"

"Really out, miss," said the office-boy, with engaging candour. "He went off to White Plains in his automobile half-an-hour ago."

"White Plains? What for?"

The pimpled stripling had now given himself up whole-heartedly to social chit-chat. Usually he liked his time to himself and resented the intrusion of the outer world, for he who had chosen jugglery for his walk in life must neglect no opportunity of practising: but so favourable was the impression which Sally had made on his plastic mind that he was delighted to converse with her as long as she wished.

"I guess what's happened is, he's gone up to take a look at Bugs Butler," he said.

"*Whose* butler?" said Sally mystified.

The office-boy smiled a tolerant smile. Though an admirer of the sex, he was aware that women were seldom hep to the really important things in life. He did not blame them. That was the way they were constructed, and one simply had to accept it.

"Bugs Butler is training up at White Plains, miss."

"Who is Bugs Butler?"

Something of his former bleakness of aspect returned to the office-boy. Sally's question had opened up a subject on which he felt deeply.

"Ah!" he replied, losing his air of respectful deference as he approached the topic. "Who *is* he! That's what they're all saying, all the wise guys. Who has Bugs Butler ever licked?"

"I don't know," said Sally, for he had fixed her with a penetrating gaze and seemed to be pausing for a reply.

"Nor nobody else," said the stripling vehemently. "A lot of stiffs out on the coast, that's all. Ginks nobody has ever heard of, except Cyclone Mullins, and it took that false alarm fifteen rounds to get a referee's decision over *him*. The boss would go and give him a chance against the champ, but I could have told him that the legitimate contender was K-leg Binns. K-leg put Cyclone Mullins out in the fifth. Well," said the office-boy in the overwrought tone of one chafing at human folly, "if anybody thinks Bugs Butler can last six rounds with Lew Lucas, I've two bucks right here in my vest pocket that says it ain't so."

Sally began to see daylight.

"Oh, Bugs—Mr. Butler is one of the boxers in this fight that my brother is interested in?"

"That's right. He's going up against the lightweight champ. Lew Lucas is the lightweight champ. He's a bird!"

"Yes?" said Sally. This youth had a way of looking at her with his head cocked on one side as though he expected her to say something.

"Yes, *sir!*" said the stripling with emphasis. "Lew Lucas is a hot sketch. He used to live on the next street to me," he added as clinching evidence of his hero's prowess. "I've seen his old mother as close as I am to you. Say, I seen her a hundred times. Is any stiff of a Bugs Butler going to lick a fellow like that?"

"It doesn't seem likely."

"You spoke it!" said the lad crisply, striking unsuccessfully at a fly which had settled on the blotting-paper.

There was a pause. Sally started to rise.

"And there's another thing," said the office-boy, loath to close the subject. "Can Bugs Butler make a hundred and thirty-five ringside without being weak?"

"It sounds awfully difficult."

"They say he's clever." The expert laughed satirically.

"Well, what's that going to get him? The poor fish can't punch a hole in a nut-sundae."

"You don't seem to like Mr. Butler."

"Oh, I've nothing against him," said the office-boy magnanimously. "I'm only saying he's no licence to be mixing it with Lew Lucas."

Sally got up. Absorbing as this chat on current form was, more important matters claimed her attention.

"How shall I find my brother when I get to White Plains?" she asked.

"Oh, anybody'll show you the way to the training-camp. If you hurry, there's a train you can make now."

"Thank you very much."

"You're welcome."

He opened the door for her with an old-world politeness which disuse had rendered a little rusty: then, with an air of getting back to business after a pleasant but frivolous interlude, he took up the paper-weights once more and placed the ruler with nice care on his upturned chin.

2

Fillmore heaved a sigh of relief and began to sidle from the room. It was a large room, half barn, half gymnasium. Athletic appliances of various kinds hung on the walls and in the middle there was a wide roped-off space, around which a small crowd had distributed itself with an air of expectancy. This is a commercial age, and the days when a prominent pugilist's training activities used to be hidden from the public gaze are over. To-day, if the public can lay its hands on fifty cents, it may come and gaze its fill. This afternoon, plutocrats to the number of about forty had assembled, though not all of these, to the regret of Mr. Lester Burrowes, the manager of the eminent Bugs Butler, had parted with solid coin. Many of those present were newspaper representatives and on the free list—writers who would polish up Mr. Butler's somewhat crude prognostications as to what he proposed to do to Mr. Lew Lucas, and would report him as saying, "I am in really superb condition and feel little apprehension of the issue," and artists who would depict him in a state of semi-nudity with feet several sizes too large for any man.

The reason for Fillmore's relief was that Mr. Burrowes,

who was a great talker and had buttonholed him a quarter of an hour ago, had at last had his attention distracted elsewhere, and had gone off to investigate some matter that called for his personal handling, leaving Fillmore free to slide away to the hotel and get a bite to eat, which he sorely needed. The zeal which had brought him to the training-camp to inspect the final day of Mr. Butler's preparation—for the fight was to take place on the morrow—had been so great that he had omitted to lunch before leaving New York.

So Fillmore made thankfully for the door. And it was at the door that he encountered Sally. He was looking over his shoulder at the moment, and was not aware of her presence till she spoke.

"Hallo, Fillmore!"

Sally had spoken softly, but a dynamite explosion could not have shattered her brother's composure with more completeness. In the leaping twist which brought him facing her, he rose a clear three inches from the floor. He had a confused sensation, as though his nervous system had been stirred up with a pole. He struggled for breath and moistened his lips with the tip of his tongue, staring at her continuously during the process.

Great men, in their moments of weakness, are to be pitied rather than scorned. If ever a man had an excuse for leaping like a young ram, Fillmore had it. He had left Sally not much more than a week ago in England, in Shropshire, at Monk's Crofton. She had said nothing of any intention on her part of leaving the country, the county, or the house. Yet here she was, in Bugs Butler's training-camp at White Plains, in the State of New York, speaking softly in his ear without even going through the preliminary of tapping him on the shoulder to advertise her presence. No wonder that Fillmore was startled. And no wonder that, as he adjusted his faculties to the situation, there crept upon him a chill apprehension.

For Fillmore had not been blind to the significance of that invitation to Monk's Crofton. Nowadays your wooer does not formally approach a girl's nearest relative and ask permission to pay his addresses; but, when he invites her and that nearest relative to his country home and collects all the rest of the family to meet her, the thing may be said to have advanced beyond the realms of mere speculation. Shrewdly Fillmore had deduced that Bruce Carmyle was in love with Sally, and mentally he had joined their hands and given them a brother's blessing. And now it was only too plain that disaster must have occurred. If the invitation could mean only one thing, so also could Sally's presence at White Plains mean only one thing.

"Sally!" A croaking whisper was the best he could achieve. "What . . . what . . .?"

"Did I startle you? I'm sorry."

"What are you doing here? Why aren't you at Monk's Crofton?"

Sally glanced past him at the ring and the crowd around it.

"I decided I wanted to get back to America. Circumstances arose which made it pleasanter to leave Monk's Crofton."

"Do you mean to say . . .?"

"Yes. Don't let's talk about it."

"Do you mean to say," persisted Fillmore, "that Carmyle proposed to you and you turned him down?"

Sally flushed.

"I don't think it's particularly nice to talk about that sort of thing, but—yes."

A feeling of desolation overcame Fillmore. That conviction, which saddens us at all times, of the wilful boneheadedness of our fellows swept coldly upon him. Everything had been so perfect, the whole arrangement so ideal, that it had never occurred to him as a possibility that Sally might take it into her head to spoil it by declining to play the part allotted to her. The match was so obviously the best thing that could happen. It was not merely the suitor's impressive wealth that made him hold this opinion, though it would be idle to deny that the prospect of having a brother-in-lawful claim on the Carmyle bank-balance had cast a rosy glamour over the future as he had envisaged it. He honestly liked and respected the man. He appreciated his quiet and aristocratic reserve. A well-bred fellow, sensible withal, just the sort of husband a girl like Sally needed. And now she had ruined everything. With the capricious perversity which so characterizes her otherwise delightful sex, she had spilled the beans.

"But why?"

"Oh, Fill!" Sally had expected that realization of the facts would produce these symptoms in him, but now that they had presented themselves she was finding them rasping to the nerves. "I should have thought the reason was obvious."

"You mean you don't like him?"

"I don't know whether I do or not. I certainly don't like him enough to marry him."

"He's a darned good fellow."

"Is he? You say so. I don't know."

The imperious desire for bodily sustenance began to compete successfully for Fillmore's notice with his spiritual anguish.

"Let's go to the hotel and talk it over. We'll go to the hotel and I'll give you something to eat."

"I don't want anything to eat, thanks."

"You don't want anything to eat?" said Fillmore incredulously. He supposed in a vague sort of way that there were eccentric people of this sort, but it was hard to realize that he had met one of them. "I'm starving."

"Well, run along then."

"Yes, but I want to talk . . ."

He was not the only person who wanted to talk. At the moment a small man of sporting exterior hurried up. He wore what his tailor's advertisements would have called a "nobbly" suit of checked tweed and—in defiance of popular prejudice—a brown bowler hat. Mr. Lester Burrowes, having dealt with the business which had interrupted their conversation a few minutes before, was anxious to resume his remarks on the subject of the supreme excellence in every respect of his young charge.

"Say, Mr. Nicholas, you ain't going'? Bugs is just getting ready to spar."

He glanced inquiringly at Sally.

"My sister—Mr. Burrowes," said Fillmore faintly. "Mr. Burrowes is Bugs Butler's manager."

"How do you do?" said Sally.

"Pleased to meecher," said Mr. Burrowes. "Say . . ."

"I was just going to the hotel to get something to eat," said Fillmore.

Mr. Burrowes clutched at his coat-button with a swoop, and held him with a glittering eye.

"Yes, but, say, before-you-golemme-tell-ya-somef'n. You've never seen this boy of mine, not when he was feeling *right*. Believe me, he's there! He's a wizard. Say, he's a Hindoo! Say, he's been practising up a left shift that . . ."

Fillmore's eye met Sally's wanly, and she pitied him. Presently she would require him to explain to her how he had dared to dismiss Ginger from his employment—and make that explanation a good one: but in the meantime she remembered that he was her brother and was suffering.

"He's the cleverest lightweight," proceeded Mr. Burrowes fervently, "since Joe Gans. I'm telling you and I *know!* He . . ."

"Can he make a hundred and thirty-five ringside without being weak?" asked Sally.

The effect of this simple question on Mr. Burrowes was stupendous. He dropped away from Fillmore's coat-button like an exhausted bivalve, and his small mouth opened feebly. It was as if a child had suddenly propounded to an eminent mathematician some abstruse problem in the higher algebra. Females who took an interest in boxing had come into Mr. Burrowes' life before—in his younger days, when he was a famous featherweight, the first of his three wives had been accustomed to sit at the ringside during his contests and urge him in language of the severest technicality to knock opponents' blocks off—but somehow he had not supposed from her appearance and manner that Sally was one of the elect. He gaped at her, and the relieved Fillmore sidled off like a bird hopping from the compelling gaze of a snake. He was not quite sure that he was acting correctly in allowing his sister to roam at large among the somewhat Bohemian surroundings of a training-camp, but the instinct of self-preservation turned the scale. He had breakfasted early, and if he did not eat right speedily it seemed to him that dissolution would set in.

"Whazzat?" said Mr. Burrowes feebly.

"It took him fifteen rounds to get a referee's decision over Cyclone Mullins," said Sally severely, "and K-leg Binns . . ."

Mr. Burrowes rallies.

"You ain't got it *right*," he protested. "Say, you mustn't believe what you see in the papers. The referee was dead against us, and Cyclone was down once for all of half a minute and they wouldn't count him out. Gee! You got to *kill* a guy in some towns before they'll give you a decision. At that, they couldn't do nothing so raw as make it anything but a win for my boy, after him leading by a mile all the way. Have you ever *seen* Bugs, ma'am?"

Sally had to admit that she had not had that privilege. Mr. Burrowes with growing excitement felt in his breast-pocket and produced a picture-postcard, which he thrust into her hand.

"That's Bugs," he said. "Take a slant at that and then tell me if he don't look the goods."

The photograph represented a young man in the irreducible minimum of clothing who crouched painfully, as though stricken with one of the acuter forms of gastritis.

"I'll call him over and have him sign it for you," said Mr. Burrowes, before Sally had had time to grasp the fact that this work of art was a gift and no mere loan. "Here, Bugs—wantcher."

A youth enveloped in a bath-robe, who had been talking to a group of admirers near the ring, turned, started languidly towards them, then, seeing Sally, quickened his pace. He was an admirer of the sex.

Mr. Burrowes did the honours.

"Bugs, this is Miss Nicholas, come to see you work out. I have been telling her she's going to have a treat." And to Sally. "Shake hands with Bugs Butler, ma'am, the coming lightweight champion of the world."

Mr. Butler's photograph, Sally considered, had flattered him. He was, in the flesh, a singularly repellent young man. There was a mean and cruel curve to his lips and a cold arrogance in his eye; a something dangerous and sinister in the atmosphere he radiated. Moreover, she did not like the way he smirked at her.

However, she exerted herself to be amiable.

"I hope you are going to win, Mr. Butler," she said.

The smile which she forced as she spoke the words removed the coming champion's doubts, though they had never been serious. He was convinced now that he had made a hit. He always did, he reflected, with the girls. It was something about him. His chest swelled complacently beneath the bath-robe.

"You betcher," he asserted briefly.

Mr. Burrows looked at his watch.

"Time you were starting, Bugs."

The coming champion removed his gaze from Sally's face, into which he had been peering in a conquering manner, and cast a disparaging glance at the audience. It was far from being as large as he could have wished, and at least a third of it was composed of non-payers from the newspapers.

"All right," he said, bored.

His languor left him, as his gaze fell on Sally again, and his spirits revived somewhat. After all, small though the numbers of spectators might be, bright eyes would watch and admire him.

"I'll go a couple of rounds with Reddy for a starter," he said. "Seen him anywheres? He's never around when he's wanted."

"I'll fetch him," said Mr. Burrowes. "He's back there somewheres."

"I'm going to show that guy up this afternoon," said Mr. Butler coldly. "He's been getting too fresh."

The manager bustled off, and Bugs Butler, with a final smirk, left Sally and dived under the ropes. There was a stir of interest in the audience, though the newspaper men, blasé through familiarity, exhibited no emotion. Presently Mr. Burrowes reappeared, shepherding a young man whose face was hidden by the sweater which he was pulling over his head. He was a sturdily built young man. The sweater, moving from his body, revealed a good pair of shoulders.

A last tug, and the sweater was off. Red hair flashed into view, tousled and disordered: and, as she saw it, Sally uttered an involuntary gasp of astonishment which caused many eyes to turn towards her. And the red-headed young man, who had been stooping to pick up his gloves, straightened himself with a jerk and stood staring at her blankly and incredulously, his face slowly crimsoning.

3

It was the energetic Mr. Burrowes who broke the spell.

"Come on, come on," he said impatiently. "Li'l speed there, Reddy."

Ginger Kemp started like a sleep-walker awakened; then recovering himself, slowly began to pull on the gloves. Embarrassment was stamped on his agreeable features. His face matched his hair.

Sally plucked at the little manager's elbow. He turned irritably, but beamed in a distrait sort of manner when he perceived the source of the interruption.

"Who—him?" he said in answer to Sally's whispered question. "He's just one of Bugs' sparring-partners."

"But . . ."

Mr. Burrowes, fussy now that the time had come for action, interrupted her.

"You'll excuse me, miss, but I have to hold the watch. We mustn't waste any time."

Sally drew back. She felt like an infidel who intrudes upon the celebration of strange rites. This was Man's hour, and women must keep in the background. She had the sensation of being very small and yet very much in the way, like a puppy who has wandered into a church. The novelty and solemnity of the scene awed her.

She looked at Ginger, who with averted gaze was fiddling with his clothes in the opposite corner of the ring. He was as removed from communication as if he had been in another world. She continued to stare, wide-eyed, and Ginger, shuffling his feet self-consciously, plucked at his gloves.

Mr. Butler, meanwhile, having doffed his bath-robe, stretched himself, and with leisurely nonchalance put on a second pair of gloves, was filling in the time with a little shadow boxing. He moved rhythmically to and fro, now ducking his head, now striking out with his muffled hands, and a sickening realization of the man's animal power swept over Sally and turned her cold. Swathed in his bath-robe, Bugs Butler had conveyed an atmosphere of dangerousness: in the boxing-tights which showed up every rippling muscle, he was horrible and sinister, a machine built for destruction, a human panther.

So he appeared to Sally, but a stout and bulbous eyed man standing at her side was not equally impressed. Obviously one of the Wise Guys of whom her friend the sporting office-boy had spoken, he was frankly dissatisfied with the exhibition.

"Shadow-boxing," he observed in a cavilling spirit to his companion. "Yes, he can do that all right, just like I can fox-trot if I ain't got a partner to get in the way. But one good wallop, and then watch him."

His friend, also plainly a guy of established wisdom, assented with a curt nod.

"Ah!" he agreed.

"Lew Lucas," said the first wise guy, "is just as shifty, and he can punch."

"Ah!" said the second wise guy.

"Just because he beats up a few poor mutts of sparring-partners," said the first wise guy disparagingly, "he thinks he's someone."

"Ah!" said the second wise guy.

As far as Sally could interpret these remarks, the full meaning of which was shrouded from her, they seemed to be reassuring. For a comforting moment she ceased to regard Ginger as a martyr waiting to be devoured by a lion. Mr. Butler, she gathered, was not so formidable as he appeared. But her relief was not to be long-lived.

"Of course he'll eat this red-headed gink," went on the first wise guy. "That's the thing he does best, killing his sparring-partners. But Lew Lucas . . ."

Sally was not interested in Lew Lucas. That numbing fear had come back to her. Even these cognoscenti, little as they esteemed Mr. Butler, had plainly no doubts as to what he would do to Ginger. She tried to tear herself away, but something stronger than her own will kept her there standing where she was, holding on to the rope and staring forlornly into the ring.

"Ready, Bugs?" asked Mr. Burrowes.

The coming champion nodded carelessly.

"Go to it," said Mr. Burrowes.

Ginger ceased to pluck at his gloves and advanced into the ring.

4

Of all the learned professions, pugilism is the one in which the trained expert is most sharply divided from the mere dabbler. In other fields the amateur may occasionally hope to compete successfully with the man who has made a business of what is to him but a sport, but at boxing never: and the whole demeanour of Bugs Butler showed that he had laid this truth to heart. It would be too little to say that his bearing was confident: he comported himself with the care-free jauntiness of an infant about to demolish a Noah's Ark with a tack-hammer. Cyclone Mullinses might withstand him for fifteen rounds where they yielded to a K-leg Binns in the fifth, but, when it came to beating up a sparring-partner and an amateur at that, Bugs Butler knew his potentialities. He was there forty ways and he did not attempt to conceal it. Crouching as was his wont, he uncoiled himself like a striking rattlesnake and flicked Ginger lightly over his guard. Then he returned to his crouch and circled sinuously about the ring with the amiable intention of showing the crowd, payers and deadheads alike, what real footwork was. If there was one thing on which Bugs Butler prided himself, it was foot-work.

The adverb "lightly" is a relative term, and the blow which had just planted a dull patch on Ginger's cheekbone affected those present in different degrees. Ginger himself appeared stolidly callous. Sally shuddered to the core of her being and had to hold more tightly to the rope to support herself. The two wise guys mocked openly. To the wise guys, expert connoisseurs of swat, the thing had appeared richly farcical. They seemed to consider the blow, adminis-tered to a third party and not to themselves, hardly worth calling a blow at all. Two more, landing as quickly and neatly as the first, left them equally cold.

"Call that punching?" said the first wise guy.

"Ah!" said the second wise guy.

But Mr. Butler, if he heard this criticism—and it is probable that he did—for the wise ones had been restrained by no delicacy of feeling from raising their voices, was in no way discommoded by it. Bugs Butler knew what he was about. Bright eyes were watching him, and he meant to give them a treat. The girls like smooth work. Any roughneck could sail into a guy and knock the daylights out of him, but how few could be clever and flashy and scientific? Few, few, indeed, thought Mr. Butler as he slid in and led once more.

Something solid smote Mr. Butler's nose, rocking him on to his heels and inducing an unpleasant smarting sensation about his eyes. He backed away and regarded Ginger with astonishment, almost with pain. Until this moment he had scarcely considered him as an active participant in the scene at all, and he felt strongly that this sort of thing was bad form. It was not being done by sparring-partners.

A juster man might have reflected that he himself was to blame. He had undeniably been careless. In the very act of leading he had allowed his eyes to flicker sideways to see how Sally was taking this exhibition of science, and he had paid the penalty. Nevertheless, he was piqued. He shimmered about the ring, thinking it over. And the more he thought it over, the less did he approve of his young assistant's conduct. Hard thoughts towards Ginger began to float in his mind.

Ginger, too, was thinking hard thoughts. He had not had an easy time since he had come to the training camp, but never till to-day had he experienced any resentment towards his employer. Until this afternoon Bugs Butler had pounded him honestly and without malice, and he had gone through it, as the other sparring-partners did, phlegmatically, taking it as part of the day's work. But this afternoon there had been a difference. Those careless flicks had been an insult, a deliberate offence. The man was trying to make a fool of him, playing to the gallery: and the thought of who was in that gallery inflamed Ginger past thought of consequences. No one, not even Mr. Butler, was more keenly alive than he to the fact that in a serious conflict with a man who to-morrow night might be light-weight champion of the world he stood no chance whatever: but he did not intend to be made an exhibition of in front of Sally without doing something to hold his end up. He proposed to go down with his flag flying, and in pursuance of this object he dug Mr. Butler heavily in the lower ribs with his right, causing that expert to clinch and the two wise guys to utter sharp barking sounds expressive of derision.

"Say, what the hell d'ya think you're getting at?" demanded the aggrieved pugilist in a heated whisper in Ginger's ear as they fell into the embrace. "What's the idea, you jelly bean?"

Ginger maintained a pink silence. His jaw was set, and the temper which Nature had bestowed upon him to go with his hair had reached white heat. He dodged a vicious right which whizzed up at his chin out of the breaking clinch, and rushed. A left hook shook him, but was too high to do more. There was rough work in the far corner, and suddenly with startling abruptness Bugs Butler, bothered by the ropes at his back and trying to side-step, ran into a swing and fell.

"Time!" shouted the scandalized Mr. Burrowes, utterly aghast at this frightful misadventure. In the whole course of his professional experience he could recall no such devastating occurrence.

The audience was no less startled. There was audible gasping. The newspaper men looked at each other with a wild surmise and conjured up pleasant pictures of their sporting editors receiving this sensational item of news later on over the telephone. The two wise guys, continuing to pursue Mr. Butler with their dislike, emitted loud and raucous laughs, and one of them, forming his hands into a megaphone, urged the fallen warrior to go away and get a rep. As for Sally, she was conscious of a sudden, fierce, cave-womanly rush of happiness which swept away completely the sickening qualms of the last few minutes. Her teeth were clenched and her eyes blazed with joyous excitement. She looked at Ginger yearningly, longing to forget a gentle up-bringing and shout congratulation to him. She was proud of him. And mingled with the pride was a curious feeling that was almost fear. This was not the mild and amiable young man whom she was wont to mother through the difficulties of a world in which he was unfitted to struggle for himself. This was a new Ginger, a stranger to her.

On the rare occasions on which he had been knocked down in the past, it had been Bugs Butler's canny practice to pause for a while and rest before rising and continuing the argu-ment, but now he was up almost before he had touched the boards, and the satire of the second wise guy, who had begun to saw the air with his hand and count loudly, lost its point. It was only too plain that Mr. Butler's motto was that a man may be down, but he is never out. And, indeed, the knock-down had been largely a stumble. Bugs Butler's edu-cated feet, which had carried him unscathed through so many contests, had for this single occasion managed to get themselves crossed just as Ginger's blow landed, and it was to his lack of balance rather than the force of the swing that his downfall had been due.

"Time!" he snarled, casting a malevolent side-glance at his manager. "Like hell it's time!"

And in a whirlwind of flying gloves he flung himself upon Ginger, driving him across the ring, while Mr. Burrowes, watch in hand, stared with dropping jaw. If Ginger had seemed a new Ginger to Sally, still more did this seem a new Bugs Butler to Mr. Burrowes, and the manager groaned in spirit. Coolness, skill and science—these had been the qualities in his protégé which had always so endeared him to Mr. Lester Burrowes and had so enriched their respective bank accounts: and now, on the eve of the most important fight in his life, before an audience of newspaper men, he had thrown them all aside and was making an exhibition of himself with a common sparring-partner.

That was the bitter blow to Mr. Burrowes. Had this lapse into the unscientific primitive happened in a regular fight, he might have mourned and poured reproof into Bug's ear when he got him back in his corner at the end of the round; but he would not have experienced this feeling of helpless horror—the sort of horror an elder of the church might feel if he saw his favourite bishop yielding in public to the fascination of jazz. It was the fact that Bugs Butler was lowering himself to extend his powers against a sparring-partner that shocked Mr. Burrowes. There is an etiquette in these things. A champion may batter his sparring-partners into insensibility if he pleases, but he must do it with nonchalance. He must not appear to be really trying.

And nothing could be more manifest than that Bugs Butler was trying. His whole fighting soul was in his efforts to corner Ginger and destroy him. The battle was raging across the ring and down the ring, and up the ring and back again; yet always Ginger, like a storm-driven ship, contrived somehow to weather the tempest. Out of the flurry of swinging arms he emerged time after time bruised, bleeding, but fighting hard.

For Bugs Butler's fury was defeating its object. Had he remained his cool and scientific self, he could have demolished Ginger and cut through his defence in a matter of seconds. But he had lapsed back into the methods of his unskilled novitiate. He swung and missed, swung and missed again, struck but found no vital spot. And now there was blood on his face, too. In some wild mêlée the sacred fount had been tapped, and his teeth gleamed through a crimson mist.

The Wise Guys were beyond speech. They were leaning against one another, punching each other feebly in the back. One was crying.

And then suddenly the end came, as swiftly and unexpectedly as the thing had begun. His wild swings had tired Bugs Butler, and with fatigue prudence returned to him. His feet began once more their subtle weaving in and out. Twice his left hand flickered home. A quick feint, a short, jolting stab, and Ginger's guard was down and he was swaying in the middle of the ring, his hands hanging and his knees a-quiver.

Bugs Butler measured his distance, and Sally shut her eyes.

CHAPTER XIV

MR. ABRAHAMS RE-ENGAGES AN OLD EMPLOYEE

I

THE only real happiness, we are told, is to be obtained by bringing happiness to others. Bugs Butler's mood, accordingly, when some thirty hours after the painful episode recorded in the last chapter he awoke from a state of coma in the ring at Jersey City to discover that Mr. Lew Lucas had knocked him out in the middle of the third round, should have been one of quiet contentment. His inability to block a short left-hook followed by a right to the point of the jaw had ameliorated quite a number of existences.

Mr. Lew Lucas, for one, was noticeably pleased. So were Mr. Lucas's seconds, one of whom went so far as to kiss him. And most of the crowd, who had betted heavily on the champion, were delighted. Yet Bugs Butler did not rejoice. It is not too much to say that his peevish bearing struck a jarring note in the general gaiety. A heavy frown disfigured his face as he slouched from the ring.

But the happiness which he had spread went on spreading. The two Wise Guys, who had been unable to attend the fight in person, received the result on the ticker and exuberantly proclaimed themselves the richer by five hundred dollars. The pimpled office-boy at the Fillmore Nicholas Theatrical Enterprises Ltd. caused remark in the Subway by whooping gleefully when he read the news in his morning paper, for he, too, had been rendered wealthier by the brittleness of Mr. Butler's chin. And it was with fierce satisfaction that Sally, breakfasting in her little apartment, informed herself through the sporting page of the details of the contender's downfall. She was not a girl who disliked many people, but she had acquired a lively distaste for Bugs Butler.

Lew Lucas seemed a man after her own heart. If he had been a personal friend of Ginger's he could not, considering the brief time at his disposal, have avenged him with more thoroughness. In round one he had done all sorts of diverting things to Mr. Butler's left eye: in round two he had continued the good work on that gentleman's body; and in round three he had knocked him out. Could anyone have done more? Sally thought not, and she drank Lew Lucas's health in a cup of coffee and hoped his old mother was proud of him.

The telephone bell rang at her elbow. She unhooked the receiver.

"Hullo?"

"Oh, hullo," said a voice.

"Ginger!" cried Sally delightedly.

"I say, I'm awfully glad you're back. I only got your letter this morning. Found it at the boarding-house. I happened to look in there and . . ."

"Ginger," interrupted Sally, "your voice is music, but I want to *see* you. Where are you?"

"I'm at a chemist's shop across the street. I was wondering if . . ."

"Come here at once!"

"I say, may I? I was just going to ask."

"You miserable creature, why haven't you been round to see me before?"

"Well, as a matter of fact, I haven't been going about much for the last day. You see . . ."

"I know. Of course." Quick sympathy came into Sally's voice. She gave a sidelong glance of approval and gratitude at the large picture of Lew Lucas which beamed up at her from the morning paper. "You poor thing! How are you?"

"Oh, all right, thanks."

"Well, hurry."

There was a slight pause at the other end of the wire.

"I say."

"Well?"

"I'm not much to look at, you know."

"You never were. Stop talking and hurry over."

"I mean to say . . ."

Sally hung up the receiver firmly. She waited eagerly for some minutes, and then footsteps came along the passage. They stopped at her door and the bell rang. Sally ran to the door, flung it open, and recoiled in consternation.

"Oh, Ginger!"

He had stated the facts accurately when he had said that he was not much to look at. He gazed at her devotedly out of an unblemished right eye, but the other was hidden altogether by a puffy swelling of dull purple. A great bruise marred his left cheek-bone, and he spoke with some difficulty through swollen lips.

"It's all *right*, you know," he assured her.

"It isn't. It's awful! Oh, you poor darling!" She clenched her teeth viciously. "I wish he had killed him!"

"Eh?"

"I wish Lew Lucas or whatever his name is had murdered him. Brute!"

"Oh, I don't know, you know." Ginger's sense of fairness compelled him to defend his late employer against these harsh sentiments. "He isn't a bad sort of chap, really. Bugs Butler, I mean."

"Do you seriously mean to stand there and tell me you don't loathe the creature?"

"Oh, he's all right. See his point of view and all that. Can't blame him, if you come to think of it, for getting the wind up a bit in the circs. Bit thick, I mean to say, a sparring-partner going at him like that. Naturally he didn't think it much of a wheeze. It was my fault right along. Oughtn't to have done it, of course, but somehow, when he started making an ass of me and I knew you were looking on . . . well, it seemed a good idea to have a dash at doing something on my own. No right to, of course. A sparring-partner isn't supposed . . ."

"Sit down," said Sally.

Ginger sat down.

"Ginger," said Sally, "you're too good to live."

"Oh, I say!"

"I believe if someone sandbagged you and stole your watch and chain you'd say there were faults on both sides or something. I'm just a cat, and I say I wish your beast of a Bugs Butler had perished miserably. I'd have gone and danced on his grave . . . But whatever made you go in for that sort of thing?"

"Well, it seemed the only job that was going at the moment. I've always done a goodish bit of boxing and I was very fit and so on, and it looked to me rather an opening. Gave me something to get along with. You get paid quite fairly decently, you know, and it's rather a jolly life . . ."

"Jolly? Being hammered about like that?"

"Oh, you don't notice it much. I've always enjoyed scrapping rather. And, you see, when your brother gave me the push . . ."

Sally uttered an exclamation.

"What an extraordinary thing it is—I went all the way out to White Plains that afternoon to find Fillmore and tackle him about that and I didn't say a word about it. And I haven't seen or been able to get hold of him since."

"No? Busy sort of cove, your brother."

"Why did Fillmore let you go?"

"Let me go? Oh, you mean . . . well, there was a sort of mix-up. A kind of misunderstanding."

"What happened?"

"Oh, it was nothing. Just a . . ."

"What happened?"

Ginger's disfigured countenance betrayed embarrassment. He looked awkwardly about the room.

"It's not worth talking about."

"It *is* worth talking about. I've a right to know. It was I who sent you to Fillmore . . ."

"Now *that*," said Ginger, "was jolly decent of you."

"Don't interrupt! I sent you to Fillmore, and he had no business to let you go without saying a word to me. What happened?"

Ginger twiddled his fingers unhappily.

"Well, it was rather unfortunate. You see, his wife— I don't know if you know her? . . ."

"Of course I know her."

"Why, yes, you would, wouldn't you? Your brother's wife, I mean," said Ginger acutely. "Though, as a matter of fact, you often find sisters-in-law who won't have anything to do with one another. I know a fellow . . ."

"Ginger," said Sally, "it's no good your thinking you can get out of telling me by rambling off on other subjects. I'm grim and resolute and relentless, and I mean to get this story out of you if I have to use a corkscrew. Fillmore's wife, you were saying . . ."

Ginger came back reluctantly to the main theme.

"Well, she came into the office one morning, and we started fooling about . . ."

"Fooling about?"

"Well, kind of chivvying each other."

"Chivvying?"

"At least *I* was."

"You were what?"

"Sort of chasing her a bit, you know."

Sally regarded this apostle of frivolity with amazement.

"What *do* you mean?"

Ginger's embarrassment increased.

"The thing was, you see, she happened to trickle in rather quietly when I happened to be looking at something, and I didn't know she was there till she suddenly grabbed it . . ."

"Grabbed what?"

"The thing. The thing I happened to be looking at. She bagged it . . . collared it . . . took it away from me, you know, and wouldn't give it back and generally started to rot about a bit, so I rather began to chivvy her to some extent, and I'd just caught her when your brother happened to roll in. I suppose," said Ginger, putting two and two together, "he had really come with her to the office and had happened to hang back for a minute or two, to talk to somebody or something . . . well, of course, he was considerably fed to see me apparently doing jiu-jitsu with his wife. Enough to rattle any man, if you come to think of it," said Ginger, ever fair-minded. "Well, he didn't say anything at the time, but a bit later in the day he called me in and administered the push."

Sally shook her head.

"It sounds the craziest story to me. What was it that Mrs. Fillmore took from you?"

"Oh, just something."

Sally rapped the table imperiously.

"Ginger!"

"Well, as a matter of fact," said her goaded visitor, "it was a photograph."

"Who of? Or, if you're particular, of whom?"

"Well . . . you, to be absolutely accurate."

"Me?" Sally stared. "But I've never given you a photograph of myself."

Ginger's face was a study in scarlet and purple.

"You didn't exactly *give* it to me," he mumbled. "When I say give, I mean . . ."

"Good gracious!" Sudden enlightenment came upon Sally. "That photograph we were hunting for when I first came here! Had you stolen it all the time?"

"Why, yes, I did sort of pinch it . . ."

"You fraud! You humbug! And you pretended to help me look for it." She gazed at him almost with respect. "I never knew you were so deep and snaky. I'm discovering all sorts of new things about you."

There was a brief silence. Ginger, confession over, seemed a trifle happier.

"I hope you're not frightfully sick about it?" he said at length. "It was lying about, you know, and I rather felt I must have it. Hadn't the cheek to ask you for it, so . . ."

"Don't apologize," said Sally cordially. "Great compliment. So I have caused your downfall again, have I? I'm certainly your evil genius, Ginger. I'm beginning to feel like a regular rag and a bone and a hank of hair. First I egged you on to insult your family—oh, by the way, I want to thank you about that. Now that I've met your Uncle Donald I can see how public-spirited you were. I ruined your prospects there, and now my fatal beauty— cabinet size—has led to your destruction once more. It's certainly up to me to find you another job, I can see that."

"No, really, I say, you mustn't bother. I shall be all right."

"It's my duty. Now what is there that you really *can* do? Burglary, of course, but it's not respectable. You've tried being a waiter and a prize-fighter and a right-hand man, and none of those seems to be just right. Can't you suggest anything?"

Ginger shook his head.

"I shall wangle something, I expect."

"Yes, but what? It must be something good this time. I don't want to be walking along Broadway and come on you suddenly as a street-cleaner. I don't want to send for an express-man and find you popping up. My idea would be to go to my bank to arrange an overdraft and be told the president could give me two minutes and crawl in humbly and find you prezzing away to beat the band in a big chair. Isn't there anything in the world that you can do that's solid and substantial and will keep you out of the poor-house in your old age? Think!"

"Of course, if I had a bit of capital . . ."

"Ah! The business man! And what," inquired Sally, "would you do, Mr. Morgan, if you had a bit of capital?"

"Run a dog-thingummy," said Ginger promptly.

"What's a dog-thingummy?"

"Why, a thingamajig. For dogs, you know."

Sally nodded.

"Oh, a thingamajig for dogs? Now I understand. You

will put things so obscurely at first. Ginger, you poor fish, what are you raving about? What on earth is a thingamajig for dogs?"

"I mean a sort of place like fellows have. Breeding dogs, you know, and selling them and winning prizes and all that. There are lots of them about."

"Oh, a *kennels?*"

"Yes, a kennels."

"What a weird mind you have, Ginger. You couldn't say kennels at first, could you? That wouldn't have made it difficult enough. I suppose, if anyone asked you where you had your lunch, you would say, 'Oh, at a thingamajig for mutton chops' . . . Ginger, my lad, there is something in this. I believe for the first time in our acquaintance you have spoken something very nearly resembling a mouthful. You're wonderful with dogs, aren't you?"

"I'm dashed keen on them, and I've studied them a bit. As a matter of fact, though it seems rather like swanking, there isn't much about dogs that I don't know."

"Of course. I believe you're a sort of honorary dog yourself. I could tell it by the way you stopped that fight at Roville. You plunged into a howling mass of about a million hounds of all species and just whispered in their ears and they stopped at once. Why, the more one examines this, the better it looks. I do believe it's the one thing you couldn't help making a success of. It's very paying, isn't it?"

"Works out at about a hundred per cent on the original outlay, I've been told."

"A hundred per cent? That sounds too much like something of Fillmore's for comfort. Let's say ninety-nine and be conservative. Ginger, you have hit it. Say no more. You shall be the Dog King, the biggest thingamajigger for dogs in the country. But how do you start?"

"Well, as a matter of fact, while I was up at White Plains, I ran into a cove who had a place of the sort and wanted to sell out. That was what made me think of it."

"You must start to-day. Or early to-morrow."

"Yes," said Ginger doubtfully. "Of course, there's the catch, you know."

"What catch?"

"The capital. You've got to have that. This fellow wouldn't sell out under five thousand dollars."

"I'll lend you five thousand dollars."

"No!" said Ginger.

Sally looked at him with exasperation. "Ginger, I'd like to slap you," she said. It was maddening, this intrusion of sentiment into business affairs. Why, simply because he was a man and she was a woman, should she be restrained from investing money in a sound commercial undertaking? If Columbus had taken up this bone-headed stand towards Queen Isabella, America would never have been discovered.

"I can't take five thousand dollars off you," said Ginger firmly.

"Who's talking of taking it off me, as you call it?" stormed Sally. "Can't you forget your burglarious career for a second? This isn't the same thing as going about stealing defenceless girls' photographs. This is business. I think you would make an enormous success of a dog-place, and you admit you're good, so why make frivolous objections? Why shouldn't I put money into a good thing? Don't you want me to get rich, or what is it?"

Ginger was becoming confused. Argument had never been his strong point.

"But it's such a lot of money."

"To you, perhaps. Not to me. I'm a plutocrat. Five thousand dollars! What's five thousand dollars? I feed it to the birds."

Ginger pondered woodenly for a while. His was a literal mind, and he knew nothing of Sally's finances beyond the fact that when he had first met her she had come into a legacy of some kind. Moreover, he had been hugely impressed by Fillmore's magnificence. It seemed plain enough that the Nicholases were a wealthy family.

"I don't like it, you know," he said.

"You don't have to like it," said Sally. "You just do it."

A consoling thought flashed upon Ginger.

"You'd have to let me pay you interest."

"Let you? My lad, you'll *have* to pay me interest. What do you think this is—a round game? It's a cold business deal."

"Topping!" said Ginger relieved. "How about twenty-five per cent."

"Don't be silly," said Sally quickly. "I want three."

"No, that's all rot," protested Ginger. "I mean to say— three. I don't," he went on, making a concession, "mind saying twenty."

"If you insist, I'll make it five. Not more."

"Well, ten, then?"

"Five!"

"Suppose," said Ginger insinuatingly, "I said seven?"

"I never saw anyone like you for haggling," said Sally with disapproval. "Listen! Six. And that's my last word."

"Six?"

"Six."

Ginger did sums in his head.

"But that would only work out at three hundred dollars a year. It isn't enough."

"What do you know about it? As if I hadn't been handling this sort of deal in my life. Six! Do you agree?"

"I suppose so."

"Then that's settled. Is this man you talk about in New York?"

"No, he's down on Long Island at a place on the south shore."

"I mean, can you get him on the 'phone and clinch the thing?"

"Oh, yes. I know his address, and I suppose his number's in the book."

"Then go off at once and settle with him before somebody else snaps him up. Don't waste a minute."

Ginger paused at the door.

"I say, you're absolutely sure about this?"

"Of course."

"I mean to say . . ."

"Get on," said Sally.

2

The window of Sally's sitting-room looked out on to a street which, while not one of the city's important arteries, was capable, nevertheless, of affording a certain amount of entertainment to the observer: and after Ginger had left, she carried the morning paper to the window-sill and proceeded to divide her attention between a third reading of the fight-report and a lazy survey of the outer world. It was a beautiful day, and the outer world was looking its best.

She had not been at her post for many minutes when a taxi-cab stopped at the apartment-house, and she was surprised and interested to see her brother Fillmore heave himself out of the interior. He paid the driver, and the cab moved off, leaving him on the sidewalk casting a large shadow in the sunshine. Sally was on the point of calling to him, when his behaviour became so odd that astonishment checked her.

From where she sat Fillmore had all the appearance of a man practising the steps of a new dance, and sheer curiosity as to what he would do next kept Sally watching in silence. First, he moved in a resolute sort of way towards the front door; then, suddenly stopping, scuttled back. This movement he repeated twice, after which he stood in deep thought before making another dash for the door, which, like the others, came to an abrupt end as though he had run into some invisible obstacle. And, finally, wheeling sharply, he bustled off down the street and was lost to view.

Sally could make nothing of it. If Fillmore had taken the trouble to come in a taxi-cab, obviously to call upon her, why had he abandoned the idea at her very threshold? She was still speculating on this mystery when the telephone-bell rang, and her brother's voice spoke huskily in her ear.

"Sally?"

"Hullo, Fill. What are you going to call it?"

"What am I . . . Call what?"

"The dance you were doing outside here just now. It's your own invention, isn't it?"

"Did you see me?" said Fillmore, upset.

"Of course I saw you. I was fascinated."

"I—er—I was coming to have a talk with you, Sally . . ." Fillmore's voice trailed off.

"Well, why didn't you?"

There was a pause—on Fillmore's part, if the timbre of of his voice correctly indicated his feelings, a pause of discomfort. Something was plainly vexing Fillmore's great mind.

"Sally," he said at last, and coughed hollowly into the receiver.

"Yes."

"I—that is to say, I have asked Gladys . . . Gladys will be coming to see you very shortly. Will you be in?"

"I'll stay in. How is Gladys? I'm longing to see her again."

"She is very well. A trifle—a little upset."

"Upset? What about?"

"She will tell you when she arrives. I have just been

'phoning to her. She is coming at once." There was another pause. "I'm afraid she has bad news."

"What news?"

There was silence at the other end of the wire.

"What news?" repeated Sally, a little sharply. She hated mysteries.

But Fillmore had rung off. Sally hung up the receiver thoughtfully. She was puzzled and anxious. However, there being nothing to be gained by worrying, she carried the breakfast things into the kitchen and tried to divert herself by washing up. Presently a ring at the door-bell brought her out, to find her sister-in-law.

Marriage, even though it had brought with it the lofty position of partnership with the Hope of the American Stage, had effected no noticeable alteration in the former Miss Winch. As Mrs. Fillmore she was the same square, friendly creature. She hugged Sally in a muscular manner and went on in the sitting-room.

"Well, it's great seeing you again," she said. "I began to think you were never coming back. What was the big idea, springing over to England like that?"

Sally had been expecting the question, and answered it with composure.

"I wanted to help Mr. Faucitt."

"Who's Mr. Faucitt?"

"Hasn't Fillmore ever mentioned him? He was a dear old man at the boarding-house, and his brother died and left him a dressmaking establishment in London. He screamed to me to come and tell him what to do about it. He has sold it now and is quite happy in the country."

"Well, the trip's done you good," said Mrs. Fillmore. "You're prettier than ever."

There was a pause. Already, in these trivial opening exchanges, Sally had sensed a suggestion of unwonted gravity in her companion. She missed that careless whimsicality which had been the chief characteristic of Miss Gladys Winch and seemed to have been cast off by Mrs. Fillmore Nicholas. At their meeting, before she had spoken, Sally had not noticed this, but now it was apparent that something was weighing on her companion. Mrs. Fillmore's honest eyes were troubled.

"What's the bad news?" asked Sally abruptly. She wanted

to end the suspense. "Fillmore was telling me over the 'phone that you had some bad news for me."

Mrs. Fillmore scratched at the carpet for a moment with the end of her parasol without replying. When she spoke it was not in answer to the question.

"Sally, who's this man Carmyle over in England?"

"Oh, did Fillmore tell you about him?"

"He told me there was a rich fellow over in England who was crazy about you and had asked you to marry him, and that you had turned him down."

Sally's momentary annoyance faded. She could hardly, she felt, have expected Fillmore to refrain from mentioning the matter to his wife.

"Yes," she said. "That's true."

"You couldn't write and say you've changed your mind?"

Sally's annoyance returned. All her life she had been intensely independent, resentful of interference with her private concerns.

"I suppose I could if I had—but I haven't. Did Fillmore tell you to try to talk me round?"

"Oh, I'm not trying to talk you round," said Mrs. Fillmore quickly. "Goodness knows, I'm the last person to try and jolly anyone into marrying anybody if they didn't feel like it. I've seen too many marriages go wrong to do that. Look at Elsa Doland."

Sally's heart jumped as if an exposed nerve had been touched.

"Elsa?" she stammered, and hated herself because her voice shook. "Has—has her marriage gone wrong?"

"Gone all to bits," said Mrs. Fillmore shortly. "You remember she married Gerald Foster, the man who wrote 'The Primrose Way'?"

Sally with an effort repressed an hysterical laugh.

"Yes, I remember," she said.

"Well, it's all gone bloo-ey. I'll tell you about that in a minute. Coming back to this man in England, if you're in any doubt about it . . . I mean, you can't always tell right away whether you're fond of a man or not . . . When first I met Fillmore, I couldn't see him with a spy-glass, and now he's just the whole shooting-match . . . But that's not what I wanted to talk about. I was saying one doesn't always know one's own mind at first, and if this fellow really is a good fellow . . . and Fillmore tells me he's got all the money in the world . . ."

Sally stopped her.

"No, it's no good. I don't want to marry Mr. Carmyle."

"That's that, then," said Mrs. Fillmore. "It's a pity, though."

"Why are you taking it so much to heart?" said Sally with a nervous laugh.

"Well . . ." Mrs. Fillmore paused. Sally's anxiety was growing. It must, she realized, be something very serious indeed that had happened if it had the power to make her forthright sister-in-law disjointed in her talk. "You see . . ." went on Mrs. Fillmore, and stopped again. "Gee! I'm hating this!" she murmured.

"What is it? I don't understand."

"You'll find it's all too darned clear by the time I'm through," said Mrs. Fillmore mournfully. "If I'm going to explain this thing, I guess I'd best start at the beginning. You remember that revue of Fillmore's—the one we both begged him not to put on. It flopped!"

"Oh!"

"Yes. It flopped on the road and died there. Never got to New York at all. Ike Schumann wouldn't let Fillmore have a theatre. The book wanted fixing and the numbers wanted fixing and the scenery wasn't right: and while they were tinkering with all that there was trouble about the cast and the Actors Equity closed the show. Best thing that could have happened, really, and I was glad at the time, because going on with it would only have meant wasting more money, and it had cost a fortune already. After that Fillmore put on a play of Gerald Foster's and that was a frost, too. It ran a week at the Booth. I hear the new piece he's got in rehearsal now is no good either. It's called 'The Wild Rose,' or something. But Fillmore's got nothing to do with that."

"But . . ." Sally tried to speak, but Mrs. Fillmore went on.

"Don't talk just yet, or I shall never get this thing straight. Well, you know Fillmore, poor darling. Anyone else would have pulled in his horns and gone slow for a spell, but he's one of those fellows whose horse is always going to win the next race. The big killing is always just round the corner with him. Funny how you can see what a chump a man is and yet love him to death . . . I remember saying something like that to you before . . . He thought he could get it all back

175

by staging this fight of his that came off in Jersey City last night. And if everything had gone right he might have got afloat again. But it seems as if he can't touch anything without it turning to mud. On the very day before the fight was to come off, the poor mutt who was going against the champion goes and lets a sparring-partner of his own knock him down and fool around with him. With all the newspaper men there too! You probably saw about it in the papers. It made a great story for them. Well, that killed the whole thing. The public had never been any too sure that this fellow Bugs Butler had a chance of putting up a scrap with the champion that would be worth paying to see; and, when they read that he couldn't even stop his sparring-partners slamming him all around the place they simply decided to stay away. Poor old Fill! It was a finisher for him. The house wasn't a quarter full, and after he'd paid these two pluguglies their guarantees, which they insisted on having before they'd so much as go into the ring, he was just about cleaned out. So there you are!"

Sally had listened with dismay to this catalogue of misfortunes.

"Oh, poor Fill!" she cried. "How dreadful!"

"Pretty tough."

"But 'The Primrose Way' is a big success, isn't it?" said Sally, anxious to discover something of brightness in the situation.

"It was." Mrs. Fillmore flushed again. "This is the part I hate having to tell you."

"It was? Do you mean it isn't still? I thought Elsa had made such a tremendous hit. I read about it when I was over in London. It was even in one of the English papers."

"Yes, she made a hit all right," said Mrs. Fillmore drily. "She made such a hit that all the other managements in New York were after her right away, and Fillmore had hardly sailed when she handed in her notice and signed up with Goble and Cohn for a new piece they are starring her in."

"Ah, she couldn't!" cried Sally.

"My dear, she did! She's out on the road with it now. I had to break the news to poor old Fillmore at the dock when he landed. It was rather a blow. I must say it wasn't what I would call playing the game. I know there isn't supposed to be any sentiment in business, but after all we had given Elsa her big chance. But Fillmore wouldn't put her name up over the theatre in electrics, and Goble and Cohn made it a clause in her contract that they would, so nothing else mattered. People are like that."

"But Elsa . . . She used not to be like that."

"They all get that way. They must grab success if it's to be grabbed. I suppose you can't blame them. You might just as well expect a cat to keep off catnip. Still, she might have waited to the end of the New York run." Mrs. Fillmore put out her hand and touched Sally's. "Well, I've got it out now," she said, "and, believe me, it was one rotten job. You don't know how sorry I am, Sally. I wouldn't have had it happen for a million dollars. Nor would Fillmore. I'm not sure that I blame him for getting cold feet and backing out of telling you himself. He just hadn't the nerve to come and confess that he had fooled away your money. He was hoping all along that this fight would pan out big and that he'd be able to pay you back what you had loaned him, but things didn't happen right."

Sally was silent. She was thinking how strange it was that this room in which she had hoped to be so happy had been from the first moment of her occupancy a storm centre of bad news and miserable disillusionment. In this first shock of the tidings, it was the disillusionment that hurt most. She had always been so fond of Elsa, and Elsa had always seemed so fond of her. She remembered that letter of Elsa's with all its protestations of gratitude . . . It wasn't straight. It was horrible. Callous, selfish, altogether horrible . . .

"It's . . ." She choked, as a rush of indignation brought the tears to her eyes. "It's . . . beastly! I'm . . . I'm not thinking about my money. That's just bad luck. But Elsa . . ."

Mrs. Fillmore shrugged her square shoulders.

"Well, it's happening all the time in the show business," she said. "And in every other business, too, I guess, if one only knew enough about them to be able to say. Of course, it hits you hard because Elsa was a pal of yours, and you're thinking she might have considered you after all you've done for her. I can't say I'm much surprised myself." Mrs. Fillmore was talking rapidly, and dimly Sally understood that she was talking so that talk would carry her over this bad moment. Silence now would have been unendurable. "I was in the company with her, and it sometimes seems to me as if you can't get to know a person right through till you've been in the same company with them. Elsa's all right, but she's two people really, like these dual identity cases you read about. She's awfully fond of you. I know she is. She was always saying so, and it was quite genuine. If it didn't interfere with business there's nothing she wouldn't do for you. But when it's a case of her career you don't count. Nobody counts. Not even her husband. Now that's funny. If you think that sort of thing funny. Personally, it gives me the willies."

"What's funny?" asked Sally, dully.

"Well, you weren't there, so you didn't see it, but I was on the spot all the time, and I know as well as I know anything that he simply married her because he thought she could get him on in the game. He hardly paid any attention to her at all till she was such a riot in Chicago, and then he was all over her. And now he's got stung. She throws down his show and goes off to another fellow's. It's like marrying for money and finding the girl hasn't any. And she's got stung, too, in a way, because I'm pretty sure she married him mostly because she thought he was going to be the next big man in the play-writing business and could boost her up the ladder. And now it doesn't look as though he had another success in him. The result is they're at outs. I hear he's drinking. Somebody who'd seen him told me he had gone all to pieces. You haven't seen him, I suppose?"

"No."

"I thought maybe you might have run into him. He lives right opposite."

Sally clutched at the arm of her chair.

"Lives right opposite? Gerald Foster? What do you mean?"

"Across the passage there," said Mrs. Fillmore, jerking her thumb at the door. "Didn't you know? That's right, I suppose you didn't. They moved in after you had beaten it for England. Elsa wanted to be near you, and she was tickled to death when she found there was an apartment to be had right across from you. Now, that just proves what I was saying a while ago about Elsa. If she wasn't fond of you, would she go out of her way to camp next door? And yet, though she's so fond of you, she doesn't hesitate about wrecking your property by quitting the show when she sees a chance of doing herself a bit of good. It's funny, isn't it?"

The telephone-bell, tinkling sharply, rescued Sally from the necessity of a reply. She forced herself across the room to answer it.

"Hullo?"

Ginger's voice spoke jubilantly.

"Hullo. Are you there? I say, it's all right, about that binge, you know."

"Oh, yes?"

"That dog fellow, you know," said Ginger, with a slight diminution of exuberance. His sensitive ear had seemed to detect a lack of animation in her voice. "I've just been talking to him over the 'phone, and it's all settled. If," he added, with a touch of doubt, "you still feel like going into it, I mean."

There was an instant in which Sally hesitated, but it was only an instant.

"Why, of course," she said, steadily. "Why should you think I had changed my mind?"

"Well, I thought . . . that is to say, you seemed . . . oh, I don't know."

"You imagine things. I was a little worried about something when you called me up, and my mind wasn't working properly. Of course, go ahead with it, Ginger. I'm delighted."

"I say, I'm awfully sorry you're worried."

"Oh, it's all right."

"Something bad?"

"Nothing that'll kill me. I'm young and strong."

Ginger was silent for a moment.

"I say, I don't want to butt in, but can I do anything?"

"No, really, Ginger, I know you would do anything you could, but this is just something I must worry through by myself. When do you go down to this place?"

"I was thinking of popping down this afternoon, just to take a look round."

"Let me know what train you're making and I'll come and see you off."

"That's ripping of you. Right ho. Well, so long."

"So long," said Sally.

Mrs. Fillmore, who had been sitting in that state of suspended animation which comes upon people who are present at a telephone conversation which has nothing to do with themselves, came to life as Sally replaced the receiver.

"Sally," she said, "I think we ought to have a talk now about what you're going to do."

Sally was not feeling equal to any discussion of the future.

All she asked of the world at the moment was to be left alone.

"Oh, that's all right. I shall manage. You ought to be worrying about Fillmore."

"Fillmore's got me to look after him," said Gladys, with quiet determination. "You're the one that's on my mind. I lay awake all last night thinking about you. As far as I can make out from Fillmore, you've still a few thousand dollars left. Well, as it happens, I can put you on to a really good thing. I know a girl . . ."

"I'm afraid," interrupted Sally, "all the rest of my money, what there is of it, is tied up."

"You can't get hold of it?"

"No."

"But listen," said Mrs. Fillmore, urgently. "This is a really good thing. This girl I know started an interior decorating business some time ago and is pulling in the money in handfuls. But she wants more capital, and she's willing to let go of a third of the business to anyone who'll put in a few thousand. She won't have any difficulty getting it, but I 'phoned her this morning to hold off till I'd heard from you. Honestly, Sally, it's the chance of a lifetime. It would put you right on easy street. Isn't there really any way you could get your money out of this other thing and take on this deal?"

"There really isn't. I'm awfully obliged to you, Gladys dear, but it's impossible."

"Well," said Mrs. Fillmore, prodding the carpet energetically with her parasol, "I don't know what you've gone into, but, unless they've given you a share in the Mint or something, you'll be losing by not making the switch. You're sure you can't do it?"

"I really can't."

Mrs. Fillmore rose, plainly disappointed.

"Well, you know best, of course. Gosh! What a muddle everything is. Sally," she said, suddenly stopping at the door, "you're not going to hate poor old Fillmore over this, are you?"

"Why, of course not. The whole thing was just bad luck."

"He's worried stiff about it."

"Well, give him my love, and tell him not to be so silly."

Mrs. Fillmore crossed the room and kissed Sally impulsively.

"You're an angel," she said. "I wish there were more like

you. But I guess they've lost the pattern. Well, I'll go back and tell Fillmore that. It'll relieve him."

The door closed, and Sally sat down with her chin in her hands to think.

3

Mr. Isadore Abrahams, the founder and proprietor of that deservedly popular dancing resort poetically named "The Flower Garden," leaned back in his chair with a contented sigh and laid down the knife and fork with which he had been assailing a plateful of succulent goulash. He was dining, as was his admirable custom, in the bosom of his family at his residence at Far Rockaway. Across the table, his wife, Rebecca, beamed at him over her comfortable plinth of chins, and round the table his children, David, Jacob, Morris and Saide, would have beamed at him if they had not been too busy at the moment ingurgitating goulash. A genial, honest, domestic man was Mr. Abrahams, a credit to the community.

"Mother," he said.

"Pa?" said Mrs. Abrahams.

"Knew there was something I'd meant to tell you," said Mr. Abrahams, absently chasing a piece of bread round his plate with a stout finger. "You remember that girl I told you about some time back—girl working at the Garden—girl called Nicholas, who came into a bit of money and threw up her job . . ."

"I remember. You liked her. Jakie, dear, don't gobble."

"Ain't gobbling," said Master Abrahams.

"Everybody liked her," said Mr. Abrahams. "The nicest girl I ever hired, and I don't hire none but nice girls, because the Garden's a nice place, and I like to run it nice. I wouldn't give you a nickel for any of your tough joints where you get nothing but low-lifes and scare away all the real folks. Everybody liked Sally Nicholas. Always pleasant and always smiling, and never anything but the lady. It was a treat to have her around. Well, what do you think?"

"Dead?" inquired Mrs. Abrahams, apprehensively. The story had sounded to her as though it were heading that way. "Wipe your mouth, Jakie dear."

"No, not dead," said Mr. Abrahams, conscious for the first time that the remainder of his narrative might be con-

181

sidered by a critic something of an anti-climax and lacking in drama. "But she was in to see me this afternoon and wants her job back."

"Ah!" said Mrs. Abrahams, rather tonelessly. An ardent supporter of the local motion-picture palace, she had hoped for a slightly more gingery *dénouement*, something with a bit more punch.

"Yes, but don't it show you?" continued Mr. Abrahams, gallantly trying to work up the interest. "There's this girl, goes out of my place not more'n a year ago, with a good bank-roll in her pocket, and here she is, back again, all of it spent. Don't it show you what a tragedy life is, if you see what I mean, and how careful one ought to be about money? It's what I call a human document. Goodness knows how she's been and gone and spent it all. I'd never have thought she was the sort of girl to go gadding around. Always seemed to me to be kind of sensible."

"What's gadding, Pop?" asked Master Jakie, the goulash having ceased to chain his interest.

"Well, she wanted her job back and I gave it to her, and glad to get her back again. There's class to that girl. She's the sort of girl I want in the place. Don't seem quite to have so much get-up in her as she used to . . . seems kind of quieted down . . . but she's got class, and I'm glad she's back. I hope she'll stay. But don't it show you?"

"Ah!" said Mrs. Abrahams, with more enthusiasm than before. It had not worked out such a bad story after all. In its essentials it was not unlike the film she had seen the previous evening—Gloria Gooch in "A Girl against the World."

"Pop!" said Master Abrahams.

"Yes, Jakie?"

"When I'm grown up, I won't never lose no money. I'll put it in the bank and save it."

The slight depression caused by the contemplation of Sally's troubles left Mr. Abrahams as mist melts beneath a sunbeam.

"That's a good boy, Jakie," he said.

He felt in his waistcoat pocket, found a dime, put it back again, and bent forward and patted Master Abrahams on the head.

CHAPTER XV

THERE is in certain men—and Bruce Carmyle was one of them—a quality of resilience, a sturdy refusal to acknowledge defeat, which aids them as effectively in affairs of the heart as in encounters of a sterner and more practical kind. As a wooer, Bruce Carmyle resembled that durable type of pugilist who can only give of his best after he has received at least one substantial wallop on some tender spot. Although Sally had refused his offer of marriage quite definitely at Monk's Crofton, it had never occurred to him to consider the episode closed. All his life he had been accustomed to getting what he wanted, and he meant to get it now.

He was quite sure that he wanted Sally. There had been moments when he had been conscious of certain doubts, but in the smart of temporary defeat these had vanished. That streak of Bohemianism in her which from time to time since their first meeting had jarred upon his orderly mind was forgotten; and all that Mr. Carmyle could remember was the brightness of her eyes, the jaunty lift of her chin, and the gallant trimness of her. Her gay prettiness seemed to flick at him like a whip in the darkness of wakeful nights, lashing him to pursuit. And quietly and methodically, like a respectable wolf settling on the trail of a Red Riding Hood, he prepared to pursue. Delicacy and imagination might have kept him back, but in these qualities he had never been strong. One cannot have everything.

His preparations for departure, though he did his best to make them swiftly and secretly, did not escape the notice of the Family. In many English families there seems to exist a system of inter-communication and news-distribution like that of those savage tribes in Africa who pass the latest item of news and interest from point to point over miles of intervening jungle by some telepathic method never properly explained. On his last night in London, there entered to

Bruce Carmyle at his apartment in South Audley Street, the Family's chosen representative, the man to whom the Family pointed with pride—Uncle Donald, in the flesh.

There were two hundred and forty pounds of the flesh Uncle Donald was in, and the chair in which he deposited it creaked beneath its burden. Once, at Monk's Crofton, Sally had spoiled a whole morning for her brother Fillmore, by indicating Uncle Donald as the exact image of what he would be when he grew up. A superstition, cherished from early schooldays, that he had a weak heart had caused the Family's managing director to abstain from every form of exercise for nearly fifty years; and, as he combined with a distaste for exercise one of the three heartiest appetites in the south-western postal division of London, Uncle Donald, at sixty-two, was not a man one would willingly have lounging in one's armchairs. Bruce Carmyle's customary respectfulness was tinged with something approaching dislike as he looked at him.

Uncle Donald's walrus moustache heaved gently upon his laboured breath, like seaweed on a ground-swell. There had been stairs to climb.

"What's this? What's this?" he contrived to ejaculate at last. "You packing?"

"Yes," said Mr. Carmyle, shortly. For the first time in his life he was conscious of that sensation of furtive guilt which was habitual with his cousin Ginger when in the presence of this large, mackerel-eyed man.

"You going away?"

"Yes."

"Where you going?"

"America."

"When you going?"

"To-morrow morning."

"Why you going?"

This dialogue has been set down as though it had been as brisk and snappy as any cross-talk between vaudeville comedians, but in reality Uncle Donald's peculiar methods of conversation had stretched it over a period of nearly three minutes: for after each reply and before each question he had puffed and sighed and inhaled his moustache with such painful deliberation that his companion's nerves were finding it difficult to bear up under the strain.

"You're going after that girl," said Uncle Donald, accusingly.

Bruce Carmyle flushed darkly. And it is interesting to record that at this moment there flitted through his mind the thought that Ginger's behaviour at Bleke's Coffee House, on a certain notable occasion, had not been so utterly inexcusable as he had supposed. There was no doubt that the Family's Chosen One could be trying.

"Will you have a whisky and soda, Uncle Donald?" he said, by way of changing the conversation.

"Yes," said his relative, in pursuance of a vow he had made in the early eighties never to refuse an offer of this kind. "Gimme!"

You would have thought that that would have put matters on a pleasanter footing. But no. Having lapped up the restorative, Uncle Donald returned to the attack quite unsoftened.

"Never thought you were a fool before," he said severely.

Bruce Carmyle's proud spirit chafed. This sort of interview, which had become a commonplace with his cousin Ginger, was new to him. Hitherto, his actions had received neither criticism nor been subjected to it.

"I'm not a fool."

"You *are* a fool. A damn fool," continued Uncle Donald, specifying more exactly. "Don't like the girl. Never did. Not a nice girl. Didn't like her. Right from the first."

"Need we discuss this?" said Bruce Carmyle, dropping, as he was apt to do, into the grand manner.

The Head of the Family drank in a layer of moustache and blew it out again.

"Need we discuss it?" he said with asperity. "We're *going* to discuss it! Whatch think I climbed all these blasted stairs for with my weak heart? Gimme another!"

Mr. Carmyle gave him another.

"'S a bad business," moaned Uncle Donald. having gone through the movements once more. "Shocking bad business. If your poor father were alive, whatch think he'd say to your tearing across the world after this girl? I'll tell you what he'd say. He'd say . . . What kind of whisky's this?"

"O'Rafferty Special."

"New to me. Not bad. Quite good. Sound. Mellow. Wherej get it?"

"Bilby's in Oxford Street."

"Must order some. Mellow. He'd say . . . well, God knows *what* he'd say. Whatch doing it for? Whatch doing it *for?* That's what I can't see. None of us can see. Puzzles your uncle George. Baffles your aunt Geraldine. Nobody can understand it. Girl's simply after your money. Anyone can see that."

"Pardon me, Uncle Donald," said Mr. Carmyle, stiffly, "but that is surely rather absurd. If that were the case, why should she have refused me at Monk's Crofton?"

"Drawing you on," said Uncle Donald, promptly. "Luring you on. Well-known trick. Girl in 1881, when I was at Oxford, tried to lure *me* on. If I hadn't had some sense and a weak heart . . . Whatch know of this girl? Whatch *know* of her? That's the point. Who *is* she? Wherej meet her?"

"I met her at Roville, in France."

"Travelling with her family?"

"Travelling alone," said Bruce Carmyle, reluctantly.

"Not even with that brother of hers? Bad!" said Uncle Donald. "Bad, bad!"

"American girls are accustomed to more independence than English girls."

"That young man," said Uncle Donald, pursuing a train of thought, "is going to be *fat* one of these days, if he doesn't look out. Travelling alone, was she? What did you do? Catch her eye on the pier?"

"Really, Uncle Donald!"

"Well, must have got to know her somehow."

"I was introduced to her by Lancelot. She was a friend of his."

"Lancelot!" exploded Uncle Donald, quivering all over like a smitten jelly at the loathed name. "Well, that shows you what sort of a girl she is. Any girl that would be a friend of . . . Unpack!"

"I beg your pardon?"

"Unpack! Mustn't go on with this foolery. Out of the question. Find some girl make you a good wife. Your aunt Mary's been meeting some people name of Bassington-Bassington, related Kent Bassington-Bassingtons . . . eldest daughter charming girl, just do for you."

Outside the pages of the more old-fashioned type of fiction nobody ever really ground his teeth, but Bruce Carmyle came nearer to it at that moment than anyone had ever come before. He scowled blackly, and the last trace of suavity left him.

"I shall do nothing of the kind," he said briefly. "I sail to-morrow."

Uncle Donald had had a previous experience of being defied by a nephew, but it had not accustomed him to the sensation. He was aware of an unpleasant feeling of impotence. Nothing is harder than to know what to do next when defied.

"Eh?" he said.

Mr. Carmyle having started to defy, evidently decided to make a good job of it.

"I am over twenty-one," said he. "I am financially independent. I shall do as I please."

"But, consider!" pleaded Uncle Donald, painfully conscious of the weakness of his words. "Reflect!"

"I have reflected."

"Your position in the county . . ."

"I've thought of that."

"You could marry anyone you pleased."

"I'm going to."

"You are determined to go running off to God-knows-where after this Miss I-can't-even-remember-her-dam-name?"

"Yes."

"Have you considered," said Uncle Donald, portentously, "that you owe a duty to the Family."

Bruce Carmyle's patience snapped and he sank like a stone to absolutely Gingerian depths of plain-spokenness.

"Oh, damn the Family!" he cried.

There was a painful silence, broken only by the relieved sigh of the armchair as Uncle Donald heaved himself out of it.

"After that," said Uncle Donald, "I have nothing more to say."

"Good!" said Mr. Carmyle rudely, lost to all shame.

"'Cept this. If you come back married to that girl, I'll cut you in Piccadilly. By George, I will!"

He moved to the door. Bruce Carmyle looked down his nose without speaking. A tense moment.

"What," asked Uncle Donald, his fingers on the handle, "did you say it was called?"

"What was what called?"

"That whisky."

"O'Rafferty Special."

"And wherj get it?"

"Bilby's, in Oxford Street."

"I'll make a note of it," said Uncle Donald.

CHAPTER XVI

AT THE FLOWER GARDEN

I

"AND after all I've done for her," said Mr. Reginald Cracknell, his voice tremulous with self-pity and his eyes moist with the combined effects of anguish and over-indulgence in his celebrated private stock, "after all I've done for her she throws me down."

Sally did not reply. The orchestra of the Flower Garden was of a calibre that discouraged vocal competition; and she was having, moreover, too much difficulty in adjusting her feet to Mr. Cracknell's erratic dance-steps to employ her attention elsewhere. They manoeuvred jerkily past the table where Miss Mabel Hobson, the Flower Garden's newest "hostess," sat watching the revels with a distant hauteur. Miss Hobson was looking her most regal in old gold and black, and a sorrowful gulp escaped the stricken Mr. Cracknell as he shambled beneath her eye.

"If I told you," he moaned in Sally's ear, "what . . . was that your ankle? Sorry! Don't know what I'm doing to-night . . . If I told you what I had spent on that woman, you wouldn't believe it. And then she throws me down. And all because I said I didn't like her in that hat. She hasn't spoken to me for a week, and won't answer when I call up on the 'phone. And I was right, too. It was a rotten hat. Didn't suit her a bit. But that," said Mr. Cracknell, morosely, "is a woman all over!"

Sally uttered a stifled exclamation as his wandering foot descended on hers before she could get it out of the way. Mr. Cracknell interpreted the ejaculation as a protest against the sweeping harshness of his last remark, and gallantly tried to make amends.

"I don't mean you're like that," he said. "You're different. I could see that directly I saw you. You have a sympathetic nature. That's why I'm telling you all this. You're a sensible and broad-minded girl and can understand. I've done everything for that woman. I got her this job as hostess here—you wouldn't believe what they pay her. I starred her in a show once. Did you see those pearls she was wearing? I gave her those. And she won't speak to me. Just because I didn't like her hat. I wish you could have seen that hat. You would agree with me, I know, because you're a sensible, broad-minded girl and understand hats. I don't know what to do. I come here every night." Sally was aware of this. She had seen him often, but this was the first time that Lee Schoenstein, the gentlemanly master of ceremonies, had inflicted him on her. "I come here every night and dance past her table, but she won't look at me. What," asked Mr. Cracknell, tears welling in his pale eyes, "would you do about it?"

"I don't know," said Sally, frankly.

"Nor do I. I thought you wouldn't, because you're a sensible, broad-minded . . . I mean, nor do I. I'm having one last try to-night, if you can keep a secret. You won't tell anyone, will you?" pleaded Mr. Cracknell, urgently. "But I know you won't because you're a sensible . . . I'm giving her a little present. Having it brought here to-night. Little present. That ought to soften her, don't you think?"

"A big one would do it better."

Mr. Cracknell kicked her on the shin in a dismayed sort of way.

"I never thought of that. Perhaps you're right. But it's too late now. Still, it might. Or wouldn't it? Which do you think?"

"Yes," said Sally.

"I thought as much," said Mr. Cracknell.

The orchestra stopped with a thump and a bang, leaving Mr. Cracknell clapping feebly in the middle of the floor. Sally slipped back to her table. Her late partner, after an uncertain glance about him, as if he had mislaid something but could not remember what, zigzagged off in search of his own seat. The noise of many conversations, drowned by the music, broke out with renewed vigour. The hot, close air was full of voices; and Sally, pressing her hands on her closed eyes, was reminded once more that she had a headache.

Nearly a month had passed since her return to Mr. Abrahams' employment. It had been a dull, leaden month, a monotonous succession of lifeless days during which life had become a bad dream. In some strange nightmare fashion, she seemed nowadays to be cut off from her kind. It was weeks since she had seen a familiar face. None of the companions of her old boarding-house days had crossed her path. Fillmore, no doubt from uneasiness of conscience, had not sought her out, and Ginger was working out his destiny on the south shore of Long Island.

She lowered her hands and opened her eyes and looked at the room. It was crowded, as always. The Flower Garden was one of the many establishments of the same kind which had swum to popularity on the rising flood of New York's dancing craze; and doubtless because, as its proprietor had claimed, it was a nice place and run nice, it had continued, unlike many of its rivals, to enjoy unvarying prosperity. In its advertisement, it described itself as "a supper-club for after-theatre dining and dancing," adding that "large and spacious, and sumptuously appointed," it was "one of the town's wonder-places, with its incomparable dance-floor, enchanting music, cuisine, and service de luxe." From which it may be gathered, even without his personal statements to that effect, that Isadore Abrahams thought well of the place.

There had been a time when Sally had liked it, too. In her first period of employment there she had found it diverting, stimulating and full of entertainment. But in those days she had never had headaches or, what was worse, this dreadful listless depression which weighed her down and made her nightly work a burden.

"Miss Nicholas."

The orchestra, never silent for long at the Flower Garden, had started again, and Lee Schoenstein, the master of ceremonies, was presenting a new partner. She got up mechanically.

"This is the first time I have been in this place," said the man, as they bumped over the crowded floor. He was big and clumsy, of course. To-night it seemed to Sally that the whole world was big and clumsy. "It's a swell place. I come from up-state myself. We got nothing like this where I come from." He cleared a space before him, using Sally as a battering-ram, and Sally, though she had not enjoyed her recent excursion with Mr. Cracknell, now began to look back to it almost with wistfulness. This man was undoubtedly the worst dancer in America.

"Give me li'l old New York," said the man from up-state, unpatriotically. "It's good enough for me. I been to some swell shows since I got to town. You seen this year's 'Follies'?"

"No."

"You go," said the man earnestly. "You *go!* Take it from me, it's a swell show. You seen 'Myrtle takes a Turkish Bath'?"

"I don't go to many theatres."

"You go! It's a scream. I been to a show every night since I got here. Every night regular. Swell shows all of 'em, except this last one. I cert'nly picked a lemon to-night all right. I was taking a chance, y'see, because it was an opening. Thought it would be something to say, when I got home, that I'd been to a New York opening. Set me back two-seventy-five, including tax, and I wish I'd got it in my kick right now. 'The Wild Rose,' they called it," he said satirically, as if exposing a low subterfuge on the part of the management. " 'The Wild Rose!' It sure made me wild all right. Two dollars seventy-five tossed away, just like that."

Something stirred in Sally's memory. Why did that title seem so familiar? Then, with a shock, she remembered. It was Gerald's new play. For some time after her return to New York, she had been haunted by the fear lest, coming out of her apartment, she might meet him coming out of his; and then she had seen a paragraph in her morning paper which had relieved her of this apprehension. Gerald was out on the road with a new play, and "The Wild Rose," she was almost sure, was the name of it.

"Is that Gerald Foster's play?" she asked quickly.

"I don't know who wrote it," said her partner, "but let me tell you he's one lucky guy to get away alive. There's fellows breaking stones on the Ossining Road that's done a lot less to deserve a sentence. Wild Rose! I'll tell the world it made me go good and wild," said the man from up-state, an economical soul who disliked waste and was accustomed to spread out his humorous efforts so as to give them every chance. "Why, before the second act was over, the people were beating it for the exits, and if it hadn't been for someone shouting 'Women and children first' there'd have been a panic."

Sally found herself back at her table without knowing clearly how she had got there.

"Miss Nicholas."

She started to rise, and was aware suddenly that this was not the voice of duty calling her once more through the gold teeth of Mr. Schoenstein. The man who had spoken her name had seated himself beside her, and was talking in precise, clipped accents, oddly familiar. The mist cleared from her eyes and she recognized Bruce Carmyle.

2

"I called at your place," Mr. Carmyle was saying, "and the hall porter told me that you were here, so I ventured to follow you. I hope you do not mind? May I smoke?"

He lit a cigarette with something of an air. His fingers trembled as he raised the match, but he flattered himself that there was nothing else in his demeanour to indicate that he was violently excited. Bruce Carmyle's ideal was the strong man who can rise superior to his emotions. He was alive to the fact that this was an embarrassing moment, but he was determined not to show that he appreciated it. He cast a sideways glance at Sally, and thought that never, not even in the garden at Monk's Crofton on a certain momentous occasion, had he seen her looking prettier. Her face was flushed and her eyes aflame. The stout wraith of Uncle Donald, which had accompanied Mr. Carmyle on this expedition of his, faded into nothingness as he gazed.

There was a pause. Mr. Carmyle, having lighted his cigarette, puffed vigorously.

"When did you land?" asked Sally, feeling the need of saying something. Her mind was confused. She could not have said whether she was glad or sorry that he was there. Glad, she thought, on the whole. There was something in his dark, cool, stiff English aspect that gave her a curious feeling of relief. He was so unlike Mr. Cracknell and the man from up-state and so calmly remote from the feverish atmosphere in which she lived her nights that it was restful to look at him.

"I landed to-night," said Bruce Carmyle, turning and faced her squarely.

"To-night!"

"We docked at ten."

He turned away again. He had made his effect, and was content to leave her to think it over.

Sally was silent. The significance of his words had not escaped her. She realized that his presence there was a challenge which she must answer. And yet it hardly stirred

193

her. She had been fighting so long, and she felt utterly inert. She was like a swimmer who can battle no longer and prepares to yield to the numbness of exhaustion. The heat of the room pressed down on her like a smothering blanket. Her tired nerves cried out under the blare of music and the clatter of voices.

"Shall we dance this?" he asked.

The orchestra had started to play again, a sensuous, creamy melody which was making the most of its brief reign as Broadway's leading song-hit, overfamiliar to her from a hundred repetitions.

"If you like."

Efficiency was Bruce Carmyle's gospel. He was one of those men who do not attempt anything which they cannot accomplish to perfection. Dancing, he had decided early in his life, was a part of a gentleman's education, and he had seen to it that he was educated thoroughly. Sally, who, as they swept out on to the floor, had braced herself automatically for a repetition of the usual bumping struggle which dancing at the Flower Garden had come to mean for her, found herself in the arms of a masterful expert, a man who danced better than she did, and suddenly there came to her a feeling that was almost gratitude, a miraculous slackening of her taut nerves, a delicious peace. Soothed and contented, she yielded herself with eyes half closed to the rhythm of the melody, finding it now robbed in some mysterious manner of all its stale cheapness, and in that moment her whole attitude towards Bruce Carmyle underwent a complete change.

She had never troubled to examine with any minuteness her feelings towards him: but one thing she had known clearly since their first meeting—that he was physically distasteful to her. For all his good looks, and in his rather sinister way he was a handsome man, she had shrunk from him. Now, spirited away by the magic of the dance, that repugnance had left her. It was as if some barrier had been broken down between them.

"Sally!"

She felt his arm tighten about her, the muscles quivering. She caught sight of his face. His dark eyes suddenly blazed into hers and she stumbled with an odd feeling of helplessness; realizing with a shock that brought her with a jerk out of the half-dream into which she had been lulled that this dance had not postponed the moment of decision, as she had looked to it to do. In a hot whisper, the words swept away on the flood of the music which had suddenly become raucous and blaring once more, he was repeating what he had said under the trees at Monk's Crofton on that far-off morning in the English springtime. Dizzily she knew that she was resenting the unfairness of the attack at such a moment, but her mind seemed numbed.

The music stopped abruptly. Insistent clapping started it again, but Sally moved away to her table, and he followed her like a shadow. Neither spoke. Bruce Carmyle had said his say, and Sally was sitting staring before her, trying to think. She was tired, tired. Her eyes were burning. She tried to force herself to face the situation squarely. Was it worth struggling? Was anything in the world worth a struggle? She only knew that she was tired, desperately tired, tired to the very depths of her soul.

The music stopped. There was more clapping, but this time the orchestra did not respond. Gradually the floor emptied. The shuffling of feet ceased. The Flower Garden was as quiet as it was ever able to be. Even the voices of the babblers seemed strangely hushed. Sally closed her eyes, and as she did so from somewhere up near the roof there came the song of a bird.

Isadore Abrahams was a man of his word. He advertised a Flower Garden, and he had tried to give the public something as closely resembling a flower-garden as it was possible for an overcrowded, overheated, overnoisy Broadway dancing-resort to achieve. Paper roses festooned the walls; genuine tulips bloomed in tubs by every pillar; and from the roof hung cages with birds in them. One of these, stirred by the sudden cessation of the tumult below, had began to sing.

Sally had often pitied these birds, and more than once had pleaded in vain with Abrahams for a remission of their sentence, but somehow at this moment it did not occur to her that this one was merely praying in its own language, as she often had prayed in her thoughts, to be taken out of this place. To her, sitting there wrestling with Fate, the song seemed cheerful. It soothed her. It healed her to listen to it. And suddenly before her eyes there rose a vision of Monk's Crofton, cool, green, and peaceful under the mild English sun, luring her as an oasis seen in the distance lures the desert traveller . . .

She became aware that the master of Monk's Crofton had placed his hand on hers and was holding it in a tightening grip. She looked down and gave a little shiver. She had always disliked Bruce Carmyle's hands. They were strong and bony and black hair grew on the back of them. One of the earliest feelings regarding him had been that she would hate to have those hands touching her. But she did not move. Again that vision of the old garden had flickered across her mind . . . a haven where she could rest . . .

He was leaning towards her, whispering in her ear. The room was hotter than it had ever been, noisier than it had ever been, fuller than it had ever been. The bird on the roof was singing again and now she understood what it said. "Take me out of this!" Did anything matter except that? What did it matter how one was taken, or where, or by whom, so that one was taken.

Monk's Crofton was looking cool and green and peaceful . . .

"Very well," said Sally.

3

Bruce Carmyle, in the capacity of accepted suitor, found himself at something of a loss. He had a dissatisfied feeling. It was not the manner of Sally's acceptance that caused this. It would, of course, have pleased him better if she had shown more warmth, but he was prepared to wait for warmth. What did trouble him was the fact that his correct mind perceived now for the first time that he had chosen an unsuitable moment and place for his outburst of emotion. He belonged to the orthodox school of thought which looks on moonlight and solitude as the proper setting for a proposal of marriage; and the surroundings of the Flower Garden, for all its niceness and the nice manner in which it was conducted, jarred upon him profoundly.

Music had begun again, but it was not the soft music such as a lover demands if he is to give of his best. It was a brassy, clashy rendering of a ribald one-step, enough to choke the eloquence of the most ardent. Couples were dipping and swaying and bumping into one another as far as the eye could reach; while just behind him two waiters had halted in order to thrash out one of those voluble arguments in which waiters love to indulge. To continue the scene at the proper emotional level was impossible, and Bruce Carmyle began his career as an engaged man by dropping into small-talk.

"Deuce of a lot of noise," he said querulously.

"Yes," agreed Sally.

"Is it always like this?"

"Oh, yes."

"Infernal racket!"

"Yes."

The romantic side of Mr. Carmyle's nature could have cried aloud at the hideous unworthiness of these banalities. In the visions which he had had of himself as a successful wooer, it had always been in the moments immediately succeeding the all-important question and its whispered reply that he had come out particularly strong. He had been accustomed to picture himself bending with a proud tenderness over his partner in the scene and murmuring some notably good things to her bowed head. How could any man murmur in a pandemonium like this. From tenderness Bruce Carmyle descended with a sharp swoop to irritability.

"Do you often come here?"

"Yes."

"What for?"

"To dance."

Mr. Carmyle chafed helplessly. The scene, which should be so romantic, had suddenly reminded him of the occasion when, at the age of twenty, he had attended his first ball and had sat in a corner behind a potted palm perspiring shyly and endeavouring to make conversation to a formidable nymph in pink. It was one of the few occasions in his life at which he had ever been at a complete disadvantage. He could still remember the clammy discomfort of his too high collar as it melted on him. Most certainly it was not a scene which he enjoyed recalling; and that he should be forced to recall it now, at what ought to have been the supreme moment of his life, annoyed him intensely. Almost angrily he endeavoured to jerk the conversation to a higher level.

"Darling," he murmured, for by moving his chair two feet to the right and bending sideways he found that he was in a position to murmur, "you have made me so . . ."

"*Batti, batti! I presto ravioli hollandaise,*" cried one of the disputing waiters at his back—or to Bruce Carmyle's prejudiced hearing it sounded like that.

"*La Donna e mobile spaghetti napoli Tettrazina,*" rejoined the second waiter with spirit.

" . . . you have made me so . . ."

"*Infanta Isabella lope de Vegas mulligatawny Toronto,*" said the first waiter, weak but coming back pluckily.

" . . . so happy . . ."

"*Funiculi funicula Vincente y Blasco Ibanez vermicelli sul campo della gloria risotto!*" said the second waiter clinchingly, and scored a technical knockout.

Bruce Carmyle gave it up, and lit a moody cigarette. He was oppressed by that feeling which so many of us have felt in our time, that it was all wrong.

The music stopped. The two leading citizens of Little Italy vanished and went their way, probably to start a vendetta. There followed comparative calm. But Bruce Carmyle's emotions, like sweet bells jangled, were out of tune, and he could not recapture the first fine careless rapture. He found nothing within him but small-talk.

"What has become of your party?" he asked.

"My party?"

"The people you are with," said Mr. Carmyle. Even in the stress of his emotion this problem had been exercising him. In his correctly ordered world girls did not go to restaurants alone.

"I'm not with anybody."

"You came here by yourself?" exclaimed Bruce Carmyle, frankly aghast. And, as he spoke, the wraith of Uncle Donald, banished till now, returned as large as ever, puffing disapproval through a walrus moustache.

"I am employed here," said Sally.

Mr. Carmyle started violently.

"Employed here?"

"As a dancer, you know. I . . ."

Sally broke off, her attention abruptly diverted to something which had just caught her eye at a table on the other side of the room. That something was a red-headed young man of sturdy build who had just appeared beside the chair in which Mr. Reginald Cracknell was sitting in huddled gloom. In one hand he carried a basket, and from this basket, rising above the din of conversation, there came a sudden sharp yapping. Mr. Cracknell roused himself from his stupor, took the basket, raised the lid. The yapping increased in volume.

Mr. Cracknell rose, the basket in his arms. With uncertain steps and a look on his face like that of those who lead forlorn hopes he crossed the floor to where Miss Mabel Hobson sat, proud and aloof. The next moment that haughty lady, the centre of an admiring and curious crowd, was hugging to her bosom a protesting Pekingese puppy, and Mr. Cracknell, seizing his opportunity like a good general, had deposited himself in a chair at her side. The course of true love was running smooth again.

The red-headed young man was gazing fixedly at Sally.

"As a dancer!" ejaculated Mr. Carmyle. Of all those within sight of the moving drama which had just taken place, he alone had paid no attention to it. Replete as it was with human interest, sex-appeal, the punch, and all the other qualities which a drama should possess, it had failed to grip him. His thoughts had been elsewhere. The accusing figure of Uncle Donald refused to vanish from his mental eye. The stern voice of Uncle Donald seemed still to ring in his ear.

A dancer! A professional dancer at a Broadway restaurant! Hideous doubts began to creep like snakes into Bruce Carmyle's mind. What, he asked himself, did he really know of this girl on whom he had bestowed the priceless boon of his society for life? How did he know what she was—he could not find the exact adjective to express his meaning, but he knew what he meant. Was she worthy of the boon? That was what it amounted to. All his life he had had a prim shrinking from the section of the feminine world which is connected with the light-life of large cities. Club acquaintances of his in London had from time to time married into the Gaiety Chorus, and Mr. Carmyle, though he had no objection to the Gaiety Chorus in its proper place—on the other side of the footlights—had always looked on these young men after as social outcasts. The fine dashing frenzy which had brought him all the way from South Audley Street to win Sally was ebbing fast.

Sally, hearing him speak, had turned. And there was a candid honesty in her gaze which for a moment sent all those creeping doubts scuttling away into the darkness whence they had come. He had not made a fool of himself, he protested to the lowering phantom of Uncle Donald. Who, he demanded, could look at Sally and think for an instant that she was not all that was perfect and lovable? A warm revulsion of feeling swept over Bruce Carmyle like a returning tide.

"You see, I lost my money and had to do something," said Sally.

"I see, I see," murmured Mr. Carmyle; and if only Fate had left him alone who knows to what heights of tenderness he might not have soared? But at this moment Fate, being no respecter of persons, sent into his life the disturbing personality of George Washington Williams.

George Washington Williams was the talented coloured gentleman who had been extracted from small-time vaudeville by Mr. Abrahams to do a nightly speciality at the Flower Garden. He was, in fact, a trap-drummer: and it was his amiable practice, after he had done a few minutes trap-drumming, to rise from his seat and make a circular tour of the tables on the edge of the dancing-floor, whimsically pretending to clip the locks of the male patrons with a pair of drumsticks held scissor-wise. And so it came about that, just as Mr. Carmyle was bending towards Sally in an access of manly sentiment, and was on the very verge of pouring out his soul in a series of well-phrased remarks, he was surprised and annoyed to find an Ethiopian to whom he had never been introduced leaning over him and taking quite unpardonable liberties with his back hair.

One says that Mr. Carmyle was annoyed. The word is weak. The interruption coming at such a moment jarred every ganglion in his body. The clicking noise of the drumsticks maddened him. And the gleaming whiteness of Mr. Williams' friendly and benignant smile was the last straw. His dignity writhed beneath this abominable infliction. People at other tables were laughing. At him. A loathing for the Flower Garden flowed over Bruce Carmyle, and with it a feeling of suspicion and disapproval of everyone connected with the establishment. He sprang to his feet.

"I think I will be going," he said.

Sally did not reply. She was watching Ginger, who still stood beside the table recently vacated by Reginald Cracknell.

"Good night," said Mr. Carmyle between his teeth.

"Oh, are you going?" said Sally with a start. She felt embarrassed. Try as she would, she was unable to find words of any intimacy. She tried to realize that she had promised to marry this man, but never before had he seemed so much a stranger to her, so little a part of her life. It came to her with a sensation of the incredible that she had done this thing, taken this irrevocable step.

The sudden sight of Ginger had shaken her. It was as though in the last half-hour she had forgotten him and only now realized what marriage with Bruce Carmyle would mean to their comradeship. From now on he was dead to her. If anything in this world was certain that was. Sally Nicholas was Ginger's pal, but Mrs. Carmyle, she realized, would never be allowed to see him again. A devastating feeling of loss smote her like a blow.

"Yes, I've had enough of this place," Bruce Carmyle was saying.

"Good night," said Sally. She hesitated. "When shall I see you?" she asked awkwardly.

It occurred to Bruce Carmyle that he was not showing himself at his best. He had, he perceived, allowed his nerves to run away with him.

"You don't mind if I go?" he said more amiably. "The fact is, I can't stand this place any longer. I'll tell you one thing, I'm going to take you out of here quick."

"I'm afraid I can't leave at a moment's notice," said Sally, loyal to her obligations.

"We'll talk over that to-morrow. I'll call for you in the morning and take you for a drive somewhere in a car. You want some fresh air after this." Mr. Carmyle looked about him in stiff disgust, and expressed his unalterable sentiments concerning the Flower Garden, that apple of Isadore Abrahams' eye, in a snort of loathing. "My God! What a place!"

He walked quickly away and disappeared. And Ginger, beaming happily, swooped on Sally's table like a homing pigeon.

4

"Good Lord, I say, what ho!" cried Ginger. "Fancy meeting you here. What a bit of luck!" He glanced over his shoulder warily. "Has that blighter pipped?"

"Pipped?"

"Popped," explained Ginger. "I mean to say, he isn't coming back or any rot like that, is he?"

"Mr. Carmyle? No, he has gone."

"Sound egg!" said Ginger with satisfaction. "For a

moment, when I saw you yarning away together, I thought he might be with your party. What on earth is he doing over here at all, confound him? He's got all Europe to play about in, why should he come infesting New York? I say, it really is ripping, seeing you again. It seems years ... Of course, one get's a certain amount of satisfaction writing letters, but it's not the same. Besides, I write such rotten letters. I say, this really is rather priceless. Can't I get you something? A cup of coffee, I mean, or an egg or something? By jove! this really is top-hole."

His homely, honest face glowed with pleasure, and it seemed to Sally as though she had come out of a winter's night into a warm friendly room. Her mercurial spirits soared.

"Oh, Ginger! If you knew what it's like seeing you!"

"No, really? Do you mean, honestly, you're braced?"

"I should say I am braced."

"Well, isn't that fine! I was afraid you might have forgotten me."

"Forgotten you!"

With something of the effect of a revelation it suddenly struck Sally how far she had been from forgetting him, how large was the place he had occupied in her thoughts.

"I've missed you dreadfully," she said, and felt the words inadequate as she uttered them.

"What ho!" said Ginger, also internally condemning the poverty of speech as a vehicle for conveying thought.

There was a brief silence. The first exhilaration of the reunion over, Sally deep down in her heart was aware of a troubled feeling as though the world were out of joint. She forced herself to ignore it, but it would not be ignored. It grew. Dimly she was beginning to realize what Ginger meant to her, and she fought to keep herself from realizing it. Strange things were happening to her to-night, strange emotions stirring her. Ginger seemed somehow different, as if she were really seeing him for the first time.

"You're looking wonderfully well," she said trying to keep the conversation on a pedestrian level.

"I *am* well," said Ginger. "Never felt fitter in my life. Been out in the open all day long ... simple life and all that ... working like blazes. I say, business is booming. Did you see me just now, handing over Percy the Pup to what's-his-name? Five hundred dollars on that one deal. Got the cheque in my pocket. But what an extraordinarily rummy thing that I should have come to this place to deliver the goods just when you happened to be here. I couldn't believe my eyes at first. I say, I hope the people you're with won't think I'm butting in. You'll have to explain that we're old pals and that you started me in business and all that sort of thing. Look here," he said lowering his voice, "I know how you hate being thanked, but I simply must say how terrifically decent . . ."

"Miss Nicholas."

Lee Schoenstein was standing at the table, and by his side an expectant youth with a small moustache and pince-nez. Sally got up, and the next moment Ginger was alone, gaping perplexedly after her as she vanished and reappeared in the jogging throng on the dancing floor. It was the nearest thing Ginger had seen to a conjuring trick, and at that moment he was ill-attuned to conjuring tricks. He brooded, fuming, at what seemed to him the supremest exhibition of pure cheek, of monumental nerve, and of undiluted crust that had ever come within his notice. To come and charge into a private conversation like that and whisk her away without a word . . .

"Who *was* that blighter?" he demanded with heat, when the music ceased and Sally limped back.

"That was Mr. Schoenstein."

"And who was the other?"

"The one I danced with? I don't know."

"You don't *know?*"

Sally perceived that the conversation had arrived at an embarrassing point. There was nothing for it but candour.

"Ginger," she said, "you remember my telling you when we first met that I used to dance in a Broadway place? This is the place. I'm working again."

Complete unintelligence showed itself on Ginger's every feature.

"I don't understand," he said—unnecessarily, for his face revealed the fact.

"I've got my old job back."

"But why?"

"Well, I had to do something." She went on rapidly. Already a light dimly resembling the light of understanding was beginning to appear in Ginger's eyes. "Fillmore went smash, you know—it wasn't his fault, poor dear. He had the worst kind of luck—and most of my money was tied up in his business, so you see . . ."

She broke off confused by the look in his eyes, conscious of an absurd feeling of guilt. There was amazement in that look and a sort of incredulous horror.

"Do you mean to say . . ." Ginger gulped and started again. "Do you mean to tell me that you let me have . . . all that money . . . for the dog-business . . . when you were broke? Do you mean to say . . ."

Sally stole a glance at his crimson face and looked away again quickly. There was an electric silence.

"Look here," exploded Ginger with sudden violence, "you've got to marry me. You've jolly well got to marry me! I don't mean that," he added quickly. "I mean to say I know you're going to marry whoever you please . . . but *won't* you marry me? Sally, for God's sake have a dash at it! I've been keeping it in all this time because it seemed rather rotten to bother you about it, but now . . . Oh, dammit, I wish I could put it into words. I always was rotten at talking. But . . . well, look here, what I mean is, I know I'm not much of a chap, but it seems to me you must care for me a bit to do a thing like that for a fellow . . . and . . . I've loved you like the dickens ever since I met you . . . I do wish you'd have a stab at it, Sally. At least I could look after you, you know, and all that . . . I mean to say, work like the deuce and try to give you a good time . . . I'm not such an ass as to think a girl like you could ever really . . . er . . . *love* a blighter like me, but . . ."

Sally laid her hand on his.

"Ginger, dear," she said, "I do love you. I ought to have known it all along, but I seem to be understanding myself to-night for the first time." She got up and bent over him for a swift moment, whispering in his ear, "I shall never love anyone but you, Ginger. Will you try to remember that."

She was moving away, but he caught at her arm and stopped her.

"Sally . . ."

She pulled her arm away, her face working as she fought against the tears that would not keep back.

"I've made a fool of myself," she said. "Ginger, your cousin . . . Mr. Carmyle . . . just now he asked me to marry him, and I said I would."

She was gone, flitting among the tables like some wild

creature running to its home: and Ginger, motionless, watched her go.

<h1 style="text-align:center">5</h1>

The telephone-bell in Sally's little sitting-room was ringing jerkily as she let herself in at the front door. She guessed who it was at the other end of the wire, and the noise of the bell sounded to her like the voice of a friend in distress crying for help. Without stopping to close the door, she ran to the table and unhooked the receiver. Muffled, plaintive sounds were coming over the wire.

"Hullo . . . Hullo . . . I say . . . Hullo . . ."

"Hullo, Ginger," said Sally quietly.

An ejaculation that was half a shout and half gurgle answered her.

"Sally! Is that you?"

"Yes, here I am, Ginger."

"I've been trying to get you for ages."

"I've only just come in. I walked home."

There was a pause.

"Hullo."

"Yes?"

"Well, I mean . . ." Ginger seemed to be finding his usual difficulty in expressing himself. "About that, you know. What you said."

"Yes?" said Sally, trying to keep her voice from shaking.

"You said . . ." Again Ginger's vocabulary failed him. "You said you loved me."

"Yes," said Sally simply.

Another odd sound floated over the wire, and there was a moment of silence before Ginger found himself able to resume.

"I . . . I . . . Well, we can talk about that when we meet. I mean, it's no good trying to say what I think over the 'phone, I'm sort of knocked out. 'I never dreamed . . . But, I say, what did you mean about Bruce?"

"I told you, I told you." Sally's face was twisted and the receiver shook in her hand. "I've made a fool of myself. I never realized . . . And now it's too late."

"Good God!" Ginger's voice rose in a sharp wail. "You can't mean you really . . . You don't seriously intend to marry the man?"

"I must. I've promised."

"But, good heavens . . ."

"It's no good. I must."

"But the man's a blighter!"

"I can't break my word."

"I never heard such rot," said Ginger vehemently. "Of course you can. A girl isn't expected . . ."

"I can't, Ginger dear, I really can't."

"But look here . . ."

"It's really no good talking about it any more, really it isn't . . . Where are you staying to-night?"

"Staying? Me? At the Plaza. But look here . . ."

Sally found herself laughing weakly.

"At the Plaza! Oh, Ginger, you really do want somebody to look after you. Squandering your pennies like that . . . Well, don't talk any more now. It's so late and I'm so tired. I'll come and see you to-morrow. Good night."

She hung up the receiver quickly, to cut short a fresh out-burst of protest. And as she turned away a voice spoke behind her.

"Sally!"

Gerald Foster was standing in the doorway.

CHAPTER XVII

SALLY LAYS A GHOST

I

THE blood flowed slowly back into Sally's face, and her heart, which had leaped madly for an instant at the sound of his voice, resumed its normal beat. The suddenness of the shock over, she was surprised to find herself perfectly calm. Always when she had imagined this meeting, knowing that it would have to take place sooner or later, she had felt something akin to panic: but now that it had actually occurred it hardly seemed to stir her. The events of the night had left her incapable of any violent emotion.

"Hullo, Sally!" said Gerald.

He spoke thickly, and there was a foolish smile on his face as he stood swaying with one hand on the door. He was in his shirt-sleeves, collarless: and it was plain that he had been drinking heavily. His face was white and puffy, and about him there hung like a nimbus a sodden disreputableness.

Sally did not speak. Weighed down before by a numbing exhaustion, she seemed now to have passed into that second phase in which over-tired nerves enter upon a sort of Indian summer of abnormal alertness. She looked at him quietly, coolly and altogether dispassionately, as if he had been a stranger.

"Hullo!" said Gerald again.

"What do you want?" said Sally.

"Heard your voice. Saw the door open. Thought I'd come in."

"What do you want?"

The weak smile which had seemed pinned on Gerald's face vanished. A tear rolled down his cheek. His intoxication had reached the maudlin stage.

"Sally . . . S-Sally . . . I'm very miserable." He slurred awkwardly over the difficult syllables. "Heard your voice. Saw the door open. Thought I'd come in."

Something flicked at the back of Sally's mind. She seemed to have been through all this before. Then she remembered.

This was simply Mr. Reginald Cracknell over again.

"I think you had better go to bed, Gerald," she said steadily. Nothing about him seemed to touch her now, neither the sight of him nor his shameless misery.

"What's the use? Can't sleep. No good. Couldn't sleep. Sally, you don't know how worried I am. I see what a fool I've been."

Sally made a quick gesture, to check what she supposed was about to develop into a belated expression of regret for his treatment of herself. She did not want to stand there listening to Gerald apologizing with tears for having done his best to wreck her life. But it seemed that it was not this that was weighing upon his soul.

"I was a fool ever to try writing plays," he went on. "Got a winner first time, but can't repeat. It's no good. Ought to have stuck to newspaper work. I'm good at that. Shall have to go back to it. Had another frost to-night. No good trying any more. Shall have to go back to the old grind, damn it."

He wept softly, full of pity for his hard case.

"Very miserable," he murmured.

He came forward a step into the room, lurched, and retreated to the safe support of the door. For an instant Sally's artificial calm was shot through by a swift stab of contempt. It passed, and she was back again in her armour of indifference.

"Go to bed, Gerald," she said. "You'll feel better in the morning."

Perhaps some inkling of how he was going to feel in the morning worked through to Gerald's muddled intelligence, for he winced, and his manner took on a deeper melancholy.

"May not be alive in the morning," he said solemnly. "Good mind to end it all. End it all!" he repeated with the beginning of a sweeping gesture which was cut off abruptly as he clutched at the friendly door.

Sally was not in the mood for melodrama.

"Oh, go to bed," she said impatiently. The strange frozen indifference which had gripped her was beginning to pass, leaving in its place a growing feeling of resentment—resentment against Gerald for degrading himself like this, against herself for ever having found glamour in the man. It humiliated her to remember how utterly she had once allowed his personality to master hers. And under the sting of this humiliation she felt hard and pitiless. Dimly she was aware that a curious change had come over her to-night. Normally, the sight of any living thing in distress was enough to stir her quick sympathy: but Gerald mourning over the prospect of having to go back to regular work made no appeal to her—a fact which the sufferer noted and commented upon.

"You're very unsymp . . . unsympathetic," he complained.

"I'm sorry," said Sally. She walked briskly to the door and gave it a push. Gerald, still clinging to his chosen support, moved out into the passage, attached to the handle, with the air of a man the foundations of whose world have suddenly lost their stability. He released the handle and moved uncertainly across the passage. Finding his own door open before him, he staggered over the threshold; and Sally, having watched him safely to his journey's end, went into her bedroom with the intention of terminating this disturbing night by going to sleep.

Almost immediately she changed her mind. Sleep was out of the question. A fever of restlessness had come upon her. She put on a kimono, and went into the kitchen to ascertain whether her commissariat arrangements would permit of a glass of hot milk.

She had just remembered that she had that morning presented the last of the milk to a sandy cat with a purposeful eye which had dropped in through the window to take breakfast with her, when her regrets for this thriftless hospitality were interrupted by a muffled crash.

She listened intently. The sound had seemed to come from across the passage. She hurried to the door and opened it. As she did so, from behind the door of the apartment opposite there came a perfect fusillade of crashes, each seeming to her strained hearing louder and more appalling than the last.

There is something about sudden, loud noises in the stillness of the night which shatters the most rigid detachment. A short while before, Gerald, toying with the idea of ending his sorrows by violence, had left Sally unmoved: but now her mind leapt back to what he had said, and apprehension succeeded indifference. There was no disputing the fact that Gerald was in an irresponsible mood, under the influence of which he was capable of doing almost anything. Sally, listening in the doorway, felt a momentary panic.

A brief silence had succeeded the fusillade, but, as she stood there hesitating, the noise broke out again; and this time it was so loud and compelling that Sally hesitated no longer. She ran across the passage and beat on the door.

2

Whatever devastating happenings had been going on in his home, it was plain a moment later that Gerald had managed to survive them: for there came the sound of a dragging footstep, and the door opened. Gerald stood on the threshold, the weak smile back on his face.

"Hullo, Sally!"

At the sight of him, disreputable and obviously unscathed, Sally's brief alarm died away, leaving in its place the old feeling of impatient resentment. In addition to her other grievances against him, he had apparently frightened her unnecessarily.

"Whatever was all that noise?" she demanded.

"Noise?" said Gerald, considering the point open-mouthed.

"Yes, noise," snapped Sally.

"I've been cleaning house," said Gerald with the owl-like gravity of a man just conscious that he is not wholly himself.

Sally pushed her way past him. The apartment in which she found herself was almost an exact replica of her own, and it was evident that Elsa Doland had taken pains to make it pretty and comfortable in a niggly feminine way. Amateur interior decoration had always been a hobby of hers. Even in the unpromising surroundings of her bedroom at Mrs. Meecher's boarding-house she had contrived to create a certain daintiness which Sally, who had no ability in that direction herself, had always rather envied. As a decorator Elsa's mind ran in the direction of small, fragile ornaments, and she was not afraid of over-furnishing. Pictures jostled one another on the walls: china of all description stood about on little tables: there was a profusion of lamps with shades of parti-coloured glass: and plates were ranged along a series of shelves.

One says that the plates were ranged and the pictures jostled one another, but it would be more correct to put it they had jostled and had been ranged, for it was only by guess-work that Sally was able to reconstruct the scene as it must have appeared before Gerald had started, as he put it, to clean house. She had walked into the flat briskly enough, but she pulled up short as she crossed the threshold, appalled by the majestic ruin that met her gaze. A shell bursting in the little sitting-room could hardly have created more havoc.

The psychology of a man of weak character under the influence of alcohol and disappointed ambition is not easy to plumb, for his moods follow one another with a rapidity which baffles the observer. Ten minutes before, Gerald Foster had been in the grip of a clammy self-pity, and it seemed from his aspect at the present moment that this phase had returned. But in the interval there had manifestly occurred a brief but adequate spasm of what would appear to have been an almost Berserk fury. What had caused it and why it should have expended itself so abruptly, Sally was not psychologist enough to explain; but that it had existed there was ocular evidence of the most convincing kind. A heavy niblick, flung petulantly—or remorsefully—into a corner, showed by what medium the destruction had been accomplished.

Bleak chaos appeared on every side. The floor was littered with every imaginable shape and size of broken glass and china. Fragments of pictures, looking as if they had been chewed by some prehistoric animal, lay amid heaps of shattered statuettes and vases. As Sally moved slowly into the room after her involuntary pause, china crackled beneath her feet. She surveyed the stripped walls with a wondering eye, and turned to Gerald for an explanation.

Gerald had subsided on to an occasional table, and was weeping softly again. It had come over him once more that he had been very, very badly treated.

"Well!" said Sally with a gasp. "You've certainly made a good job of it!"

There was a sharp crack as the occasional table, never designed by its maker to bear heavy weights, gave way in a splintering flurry of broken legs under the pressure of the master of the house: and Sally's mood underwent an abrupt change. There are few situations in life which do not hold equal potentialities for both tragedy and farce, and it was the ludicrous side of this drama that chanced to appeal to Sally at this moment. Her sense of humour was tickled. It was, if she could have analysed her feelings, at herself that she was mocking—at the feeble sentimental Sally who had once conceived the absurd idea of taking this preposterous man seriously. She felt light-hearted and light-headed, and she sank into a chair with a gurgling laugh.

The shock of his fall appeared to have had the desirable effect of restoring Gerald to something approaching intelligence. He picked himself up from the remains of a set of water-colours, gazing at Sally with growing disapproval.

"No sympathy," he said austerely.

"I can't help it," cried Sally. "It's too funny."

"Not funny," corrected Gerald, his brain beginning to cloud once more.

"What did you do it for?"

Gerald returned for a moment to that mood of honest indignation, which had so strengthened his arm when wielding the niblick. He bethought him once again of his grievance.

"Wasn't going to stand for it any longer," he said heatedly. "A fellow's wife goes and lets him down . . . ruins his show by going off and playing in another show . . . why *shouldn't* I smash her things? Why should I stand for that sort of treatment? Why should I?"

"Well, you haven't," said Sally, "so there's no need to discuss it. You seem to have acted in a thoroughly manly and independent way."

"That's it. Manly independent." He waggled his finger impressively. "Don't care what she says," he continued. "Don't care if she never comes back. That woman . . ."

Sally was not prepared to embark with him upon a discussion of the absent Elsa. Already the amusing aspect of the affair had begun to fade, and her hilarity was giving way to a tired distaste for the sordidness of the whole business. She had become aware that she could not endure the society of Gerald Foster much longer. She got up and spoke decidedly.

"And now," she said, "I'm going to tidy up."

Gerald had other views.

"No," he said with sudden solemnity. "No! Nothing of the kind. Leave it for her to find. Leave it as it is."

"Don't be silly. All this has got to be cleaned up. I'll do it. You go and sit in my apartment. I'll come and tell you when you can come back."

"No!" said Gerald, wagging his head.

Sally stamped her foot among the crackling ruins. Quite suddenly the sight of him had become intolerable.

"Do as I tell you," she cried.

Gerald wavered for a moment, but his brief militant mood

was ebbing fast. After a faint protest he shuffled off, and Sally heard him go into her room. She breathed a deep breath of relief and turned to her task.

A visit to the kitchen revealed a long-handled broom, and, armed with this, Sally was soon busy. She was an efficient little person, and presently out of chaos there began to emerge a certain order. Nothing short of complete re-decoration would ever make the place look habitable again, but at the end of half an hour she had cleared the floor, and the fragments of vases, plates, lamp-shades, pictures and glasses were stacked in tiny heaps against the walls. She returned the broom to the kitchen, and, going back into the sitting-room, flung open the window and stood looking out.

With a sense of unreality she perceived that the night had gone. Over the quiet street below there brooded that strange, metallic light which ushers in the dawn of a fine day. A cold breeze whispered to and fro. Above the house-tops the sky was a faint, level blue.

She left the window and started to cross the room. And suddenly there came over her a feeling of utter weakness. She stumbled to a chair, conscious only of being tired beyond the possibility of a further effort. Her eyes closed, and almost before her head had touched the cushions she was asleep.

3

Sally woke. Sunshine was streaming through the open window, and with it the myriad noises of a city awake and about its business. Footsteps clattered on the sidewalk, automobile horns were sounding, and she could hear the clank of street cars as they passed over the points. She could only guess at the hour, but it was evident that the morning was well advanced. She got up stiffly. Her head was aching.

She went into the bathroom, bathed her face, and felt better. The dull oppression which comes of a bad night was leaving her. She leaned out of the window, revelling in the fresh air, then crossed the passage and entered her own apartment. Stertorous breathing greeted her, and she perceived that Gerald Foster had also passed the night in a chair. He was sprawling by the window with his legs stretched out and his head resting on one of the arms, an unlovely spectacle.

Sally stood regarding him for a moment with a return of the distaste which she had felt on the previous night. And yet, mingled with the distaste, there was a certain elation. A black chapter of her life was closed for ever. Whatever the years to come might bring to her, they would be free from any wistful yearnings for the man who had once been woven so inextricably into the fabric of her life. She had thought that his personality had gripped her too strongly ever to be dislodged, but now she could look at him calmly and feel only a faint half-pity, half-contempt. The glamour had departed.

She shook him gently, and he sat up with a start, blinking in the strong light. His mouth was still open. He stared at Sally foolishly, then scrambled awkwardly out of the chair.

"Oh, my God!" said Gerald, pressing both his hands to his forehead and sitting down again. He licked his lips with a dry tongue and moaned. "Oh, I've got a headache!"

Sally might have pointed out to him that he had certainly earned one, but she refrained.

"You'd better go and have a wash," she suggested.

"Yes," said Gerald, heaving himself up again.

"Would you like some breakfast?"

"Don't!" said Gerald faintly, and tottered off to the bathroom.

Sally sat down in the chair he had vacated. She had never felt quite like this before in her life. Everything seemed dreamlike. The splashing of water in the bathroom came faintly to her, and she realized that she had been on the point of falling asleep again. She got up and opened the window, and once more the air acted as a restorative. She watched the activities of the street with a distant interest. They, too, seemed dreamlike and unreal. People were hurrying up and down on mysterious errands. An inscrutable cat picked its way daintily across the road. At the door of the apartment house an open car purred sleepily.

She was roused by a ring at the bell. She went to the door and opened it, and found Bruce Carmyle standing on the threshold. He wore a light motor-coat, and he was plainly endeavouring to soften the severity of his saturnine face with a smile of beaming kindliness.

"Well, here I am!" said Bruce Carmyle cheerily. "Are you ready?"

With the coming of daylight a certain penitence had descended on Mr. Carmyle. Thinking things over while shaving and subsequently in his bath, he had come to the conclusion that his behaviour overnight had not been all that could have been desired. He had not actually been brutal, perhaps, but he had undoubtedly not been winning. There had been an abruptness in the manner of his leaving Sally at the Flower Garden which a perfect lover ought not to have shown He had allowed his nerves to get the better of him, and now he desired to make amends. Hence a cheerfulness which he did not usually exhibit so early in the morning.

Sally was staring at him blankly. She had completely forgotten that he had said that he would come and take her for a drive this morning. She searched in her mind for words, and found none. And, as Mr. Carmyle was debating within himself whether to kiss her now or wait for a more suitable moment, embarrassment came upon them both like a fog, and the genial smile faded from his face as if the motive-power behind it had suddenly failed.

"I've—er—got the car outside, and . . ."

At this point speech failed Mr. Carmyle, for, even as he began the sentence, the door that led to the bathroom opened and Gerald Foster came out. Mr. Carmyle gaped at Gerald: Gerald gaped at Mr. Carmyle.

The application of cold water to the face and head is an excellent thing on the morning after an imprudent night, but as a tonic it only goes part of the way. In the case of Gerald Foster, which was an extremely serious and aggravated case, it had gone hardly any way at all. The person unknown who had been driving red-hot rivets into the base of Gerald Foster's skull ever since the moment of his awakening was still busily engaged on that task. He gazed at Mr. Carmyle wanly.

Bruce Carmyle drew in his breath with a sharp hiss, and stood rigid. His eyes, burning now with a grim light, flickered over Gerald's person and found nothing in it to entertain them. He saw a slouching figure in shirt-sleeves and the foundations of evening dress, a disgusting, degraded figure with pink eyes and a white face that needed a shave. And all the doubts that had ever come to vex Mr. Carmyle's mind since his first meeting with Sally became on the instant certainties. So Uncle Donald had been right after all! This was the sort of girl she was!

At his elbow the stout phantom of Uncle Donald puffed with satisfaction.

"I told you so!" it said.

Sally had not moved. The situation was beyond her. Just as if this had really been the dream it seemed, she felt incapable of speech or action.

"So . . ." said Mr. Carmyle, becoming articulate, and allowed an impressive aposiopesis to take the place of the rest of the speech. A cold fury had gripped him. He pointed at Gerald, began to speak, found that he was stuttering, and gulped back the words. In this supreme moment he was not going to have his dignity impaired by a stutter. He gulped and found a sentence which, while brief enough to insure against this disaster, was sufficiently long to express his meaning.

"Get out!" he said.

Gerald Foster had his dignity, too, and it seemed to him that the time had come to assert it. But he also had a most excruciating headache, and when he drew himself up haughtily to ask Mr. Carmyle what the devil he meant by it, a severe access of pain sent him huddling back immediately to a safer attitude. He clasped his forehead and groaned.

"Get out!"

For a moment Gerald hesitated. Then another sudden shooting spasm convinced him that no profit or pleasure was to be derived from a continuance of the argument, and he began to shamble slowly across to the door.

Bruce Carmyle watched him go with twitching hands. There was a moment when the human man in him, somewhat atrophied from long disuse, stirred him almost to the point of assault; then dignity whispered more prudent counsel in his ear, and Gerald was past the danger-zone and out in the passage. Mr. Carmyle turned to face Sally, as King Arthur on a similar but less impressive occasion must have turned to deal with Guinevere.

"So . . ." he said again.

Sally was eyeing him steadily—considering the circumstances, Mr. Carmyle thought with not a little indignation, much too steadily.

"This," he said ponderously, "is very amusing."

He waited for her to speak, but she said nothing.

"I might have expected it," said Mr. Carmyle with a bitter laugh.

Sally forced herself from the lethargy which was gripping her.

"Would you like me to explain?" she said.

"There can be no explanation," said Mr. Carmyle coldly.

"Very well," said Sally.

There was a pause.

"Good-bye," said Bruce Carmyle.

"Good-bye," said Sally.

Mr. Carmyle walked to the door. There he stopped for an instant and glanced back at her. Sally had walked to the window and was looking out. For one swift instant something about her trim little figure and the gleam of her hair where the sunlight shone on it seemed to catch at Bruce Carmyle's heart, and he wavered. But the next moment he was strong again, and the door had closed behind him with a resolute bang.

Out in the street, climbing into his car, he looked up involuntarily to see if she was still there, but she had gone. As the car, gathering speed, hummed down the street, Sally was at the telephone listening to the sleepy voice of Ginger Kemp, which, as he became aware who it was that had woken him from his rest and what she had to say to him, magically lost its sleepiness and took on a note of riotous ecstasy.

Five minutes later, Ginger was splashing in his bath, singing discordantly.

CHAPTER XVIII

JOURNEY'S END

DARKNESS was beginning to gather slowly and with almost an apologetic air, as if it regretted the painful duty of putting an end to the perfect summer day. Over to the west beyond the trees there still lingered a faint afterglow, and a new moon shone like a silver sickle above the big barn. Sally came out of the house and bowed gravely three times for luck. She stood on the gravel, outside the porch, drinking in the sweet evening scents, and found life good.

The darkness, having shown a certain reluctance at the start, was now buckling down to make a quick and thorough job of it. The sky turned to a uniform dark blue, picked out with quiet stars. The cement of the state road which led to Patchogue, Babylon, and other important centres ceased to be a pale blur and became invisible. Lights appeared in the windows of the houses across the meadows. From the direction of the kennels there came a single sleepy bark, and the small white woolly dog which had scampered out at Sally's heels stopped short and uttered a challenging squeak.

The evening was so still that Ginger's footsteps, as he pounded along the road on his way back from the village, whither he had gone to buy provisions, evening papers, and wool for the sweater which Sally was knitting, were audible long before he turned in at the gate. Sally could not see him, but she looked in the direction of the sound and once again felt that pleasant, cosy thrill of happiness which had come to her every evening for the last year.

"Ginger," she called.

"What ho!"

The woolly dog, with another important squeak, scuttled down the drive to look into the matter, and was coldly greeted. Ginger, for all his love of dogs, had never been able to bring himself to regard Toto with affection. He had protested when Sally, a month before, finding Mrs. Meecher distraught on account of a dreadful lethargy which had seized her pet, had begged him to offer hospitality and country air to the invalid.

"It's wonderful what you've done for Toto, angel," said Sally, as he came up frigidly eluding that curious animal's leaps of welcome. "He's a different dog."

"Bit of luck for him," said Ginger.

"In all the years I was at Mrs. Meecher's I never knew him move at anything more rapid than a stately walk. Now he runs about all the time."

"The blighter had been overeating from birth," said Ginger. "That was all that was wrong with him. A little judicious dieting put him right. We'll be able," said Ginger brightening, "to ship him back next week."

"I shall quite miss him."

"*I* nearly missed him—this morning—with a shoe," said Ginger. "He was up on the kitchen table wolfing the bacon, and I took steps."

"My cave-man!" murmured Sally. "I always said you had a frightfully brutal streak in you. Ginger, what an evening!"

"Good Lord!" said Ginger suddenly, as they walked into the light of the open kitchen door.

"Now what?"

He stopped and eyed her intently.

"Do you know you're looking prettier than you were when I started down to the village!"

Sally gave his arm a little hug.

"Beloved!" she said. "Did you get the chops?"

Ginger froze in his tracks, horrified.

"Oh, my aunt! I clean forgot them!"

"Oh, Ginger, you are an old chump. Well, you'll have to go in for a little judicious dieting, like Toto."

"I say, I'm most awfully sorry. I got the wool."

"If you think I'm going to eat wool . . ."

"Isn't there anything in the house?"

"Vegetables and fruit."

"Fine! But, of course, if you want chops . . ."

"Not at all. I'm spiritual. Besides, people say that vegetables are good for the blood-pressure or something. Of course you forgot to get the mail, too?"

"Absolutely not! I was on to it like a knife. Two letters from fellows wanting Airedale puppies."

"No! Ginger, we *are* getting on!"

"Pretty bloated," agreed Ginger complacently. "Pretty bloated. We'll be able to get that two-seater if things go buzzing on like this. There was a letter for you. Here it is."

"It's from Fillmore," said Sally, examining the envelope as they went into the kitchen. "And about time, too. I haven't had a word from him for months."

She sat down and opened the letter. Ginger, heaving himself on to the table, wriggled into a position of comfort and started to read his evening paper. But after he had skimmed over the sporting page he lowered it and allowed his gaze to rest on Sally's bent head with a feeling of utter contentment.

Although a married man of nearly a year's standing, Ginger was still moving about a magic world in a state of dazed incredulity, unable fully to realize that such bliss could be. Ginger in his time had seen many things that looked good from a distance, but not one that had borne the test of a closer acquaintance—except this business of marriage.

Marriage, with Sally for a partner, seemed to be one of the very few things in the world in which there was no catch. His honest eyes glowed as he watched her.

Sally broke into a little splutter of laughter.

"Ginger, look at this!"

He reached down and took the slip of paper which she held out to him. The following legend met his eye, printed in bold letters:

POPP'S

OUTSTANDING

SUCCULENT—APPETIZING—NUTRITIOUS.

(JUST SAY "POP!" A CHILD
CAN DO IT.)

Ginger regarded this cipher with a puzzled frown.

"What is it?" he asked.

"It's Fillmore."

"How do you mean?"

Sally gurgled.

"Fillmore and Gladys have started a little restaurant in Pittsburg."

"A restaurant!" There was a shocked note in Ginger's voice. Although he knew that the managerial career of that modern Napoleon, his brother-in-law, had terminated in something of a smash, he had never quite lost his reverence for one whom he considered a bit of a master-mind. That Fillmore Nicholas, the Man of Destiny, should have descended to conducting a restaurant—and a little restaurant at that—struck him as almost indecent.

Sally, on the other hand—for sisters always seem to fail in proper reverence for the greatness of their brothers—was delighted.

"It's the most splendid idea," she said with enthusiasm. "It really does look as if Fillmore was going to amount to something at last. Apparently they started on quite a small scale, just making pork-pies . . ."

"Why Popp?" interrupted Ginger, ventilating a question which was perplexing him deeply.

"Just a trade name, silly. Gladys is a wonderful cook, you know, and she made the pies and Fillmore toddled round selling them. And they did so well that now they've started a regular restaurant, and that's a success, too. Listen to this." Sally gurgled again and turned over the letter. "Where is it? Oh yes! ' . . . sound financial footing. In fact, our success has been so instantaneous that I have decided to launch out on a really big scale. It is Big Ideas that lead to Big Business. I am contemplating a vast extension of this venture of ours, and in a very short time I shall organize branches in New York, Chicago, Detroit, and all the big cities, each in charge of a manager and each offering as a special feature, in addition to the usual restaurant cuisine, these Popp's Outstanding Pork-pies of ours. That done, and having established all these branches as going concerns, I shall sail for England and introduce Popp's Pork-pies there . . . ' Isn't he a little wonder!"

"Dashed brainy chap. Always said so."

"I must say I was rather uneasy when I read that. I've seen so many of Fillmore's Big Ideas. That's always the way with him. He gets something good and then goes and overdoes it and bursts. However, it's all right now that he's got Gladys to look after him. She has added a postscript. Just four words, but oh! how comforting to a sister's heart. 'Yes, I don't think!' is what she says, and I don't know when I've read anything more cheering. Thank heaven, she's got poor dear Fillmore well in hand."

"Pork-pies!" said Ginger, musingly, as the pangs of a healthy hunger began to assail his interior. "I wish he'd *sent* us one of the outstanding little chaps. I could do with it."

Sally got up and ruffled his red hair.

"Poor old Ginger! I knew you'd never be able to stick it. Come on, it's a lovely night, let's walk to the village and revel at the inn. We're going to be millionaires before we know where we are, so we can afford it."

THE END

MORE ABOUT PENGUINS, PELICANS, PEREGRINES AND PUFFINS

For further information about books available from Penguins please write to Dept EP, Penguin Books Ltd, Harmondsworth, Middlesex UB7 0DA.

In the U.S.A.: For a complete list of books available from Penguins in the United States write to Dept DG, Penguin Books, 299 Murray Hill Parkway, East Rutherford, New Jersey 07073.

In Canada: For a complete list of books available from Penguins in Canada write to Penguin Books Canada Ltd, 2801 John Street, Markham, Ontario L3R 1B4.

In Australia: For a complete list of books available from Penguins in Australia write to the Marketing Department, Penguin Books Australia Ltd, P.O. Box 257, Ringwood, Victoria 3134.

In New Zealand: For a complete list of books available from Penguins in New Zealand write to the Marketing Department, Penguin Books (N.Z.) Ltd, Private Bag, Takapuna, Auckland 9.

In India: For a complete list of books available from Penguins in India write to Penguin Overseas Ltd, 706 Eros Apartments, 56 Nehru Place, New Delhi 110019.

P. G. Wodehouse in Penguins

Aunts Aren't Gentlemen   Bachelors Anonymous
Big Money   Blandings Castle
Carry on, Jeeves   The Code of the Woosters
Company for Henry   Do Butlers Burgle Banks?
Full Moon   Galahad at Blandings
The Heart of a Goof   Heavy Weather
Hot Water   The Indiscretions of Archie
The Inimitable Jeeves   Jeeves in the Offing
Laughing Gas   Leave it to Psmith
The Little Nugget   Lord Emsworth and Others
The Luck of the Bodkins
The Man Upstairs and Other Stories
The Man with Two Left Feet and Other Stories
The Mating Season   Meet Mr Mulliner
Money in the Bank   Much Obliged, Jeeves
Mulliner Nights   Pearls, Girls and Monty Bodkin
A Pelican at Blandings   Piccadilly Jim
Pigs Have Wings   Psmith in the City
Psmith, Journalist   Quick Service
Right Ho, Jeeves   Sam the Sudden
Service with a Smile   Something Fresh
Spring Fever   Stiff Upper Lip, Jeeves!

and two handsome Wodehosue omnibuses

LIFE AT BLANDINGS
containing:
Something Fresh
Summer Lightning
Heavy Weather

LIFE WITH JEEVES
containing:
Right Ho, Jeeves
The Inimitable Jeeves
Very Good, Jeeves!

THE HUNCHBACK OF NOTRE-DAME

VICTOR-MARIE HUGO
1802–1885

THE HUNCHBACK OF NOTRE-DAME

VICTOR HUGO

Translated by
J. CARROLL BECKWITH

With an Introduction by
M. L. M. YOUNG

Rupa & Co

This reprint in Rupa Paperback 2000

Published by
Rupa & Co.
7/16, Ansari Road, Daryaganj
New Delhi 110 002

ISBN 81-7167-449-6

Printed in India by
Rekha Printers Pvt. Ltd.
A-102/1 Okhla Industrial Area
New Delhi 110 020

Rs. 50

VICTOR HUGO

VICTOR HUGO's life and work are closely bound up with the history of France during the nineteenth century. He was the mirror and echo, sometimes also the voice of his age. Indeed some have spoken of the nineteenth century as 'The Century of Victor Hugo.' His childhood coincided with the rise and fall of the Napoleonic Empire; his old age with the birth of the Third Republic. In between lay the restoration of the Bourbon dynasty under Louis XVIII and Charles X, the July Revolution of 1830, the reign of Louis Philippe, the revolution of 1848, the short-lived Second Republic, the Second Empire and the defeat of France in her war with Prussia. Every one of those phases marked a definite period in Victor Hugo's life and work.

Victor-Marie Hugo was born on February 26th 1802 at Besançon, capital of the Franche-Comté, the third son of Commandant (later General and Count) Léopold-Sigisbert Hugo an ardent Bonapartist, and of his wife Sophie, née Trébuchet, who came from a royalist family in Nantes, Brittany. His parents were ill-matched and separated later. For very many years Hugo's sympathies were divided between his father and mother and the respective causes they represented.

His early years were marked by a series of peregrinations which took him to Marseilles, Corsica, Elba, Naples, Paris, Madrid (where he attended for one year the College of Nobles), and finally back to Paris in 1813. From 1813–1818 he attended school at the Pension Cordier, the only systematic education he ever received. At that time he began to try his hand at every possible form of verse: odes, satires, tragedies, elegies, idylls, translations of Latin Poets—even a comic opera. At fifteen he was awarded an Honourable Mention by the French Academy in a poetry contest, and at seventeen two literary prizes by the Academy of Toulouse. In 1819 he founded, together with his elder brother, a fortnightly review *Le Conservateur Littéraire*. In 1821 his mother died.

Lean months followed for the young poet trying to make his own living. However, in 1822 King Louis XVIII, in recognition of Hugo's royalist sentiments, expressed in the ode *Vision*, granted him an annuity of 1200 Frs. which enabled him to marry Adèle Foucher to whom he had been secretly engaged for some time.

The years that followed saw the advance of the Romantic Movement of which Hugo and his friends—among them the poet Alfred de Vigny and the critic Sainte-Beuve—became the leaders.

The plays *Cromwell, Marion de Lorme, Hernani*; the collection of poems *Les Orientales*, and the historical novel *Notre-Dame de Paris* (The Hunchback of Notre-Dame), the latter published in 1831, are the most important works of Hugo's romantic period.

Five children—one of whom died in infancy—were born to Hugo in the first eight years of his married life which remained happy until 1830 when Sainte-Beuve, his best friend, fell in love with his wife. In the period of estrangement between husband and wife which followed this episode, Hugo formed a liaison with the actress Juliette Drouet. The liaison was to last over fifty years, in the course of which it acquired almost legitimate status in the eyes of the world.

In the period 1830–1845 which was marked by his growing intimacy with the Royal House and by his growing interest in social conditions and politics, into which he actively entered after having been made a peer of France by Louis Philippe (1845), Hugo established himself as the leading lyrical poet of France. From these years date some of his most famous collections of poems, among them *Les Feuilles d'Automne* and *Les Chants du Crépuscule*; also the plays '*Le Roi s'amuse*' (on which Verdi's opera '*Rigoletto*' is based), *Ruy Blas, Marie Tudor*. In 1841 he was elected a Member of the French Academy.

In 1848, after the revolution which ended with the abdication of Louis Philippe, Hugo was elected Deputy to the National Assembly. Later, for a short while he supported Louis Napoleon as President of the Republic, but after the *coup d'état* of 1851 he turned against him and went to the barricades on the side of the people. In danger of arrest, he fled to Brussels and the following year began his exile, first in Jersey and later in Guernsey (where he settled with his wife, family and Juliette Drouet)—an exile which was to last until 1870. During those years he wrote some of his most famous works: *Les Châtiments* (1853) a satirical and prophetic denunciation of Napoleon III, *Les Contemplations* (1856), the first part of *Légende des Siècles, Les Misérables* (1862), the great historical novel which contains the essence of his moral philosophy, *Les Travailleurs de la Mer* (1866) and *L'Homme qui rit* (1869).

Madame Hugo died in 1868 and two years later Hugo returned to his native country. He lived through the siege and capitulation of Paris (1871) and in the years to follow took an active part in the political life of the new republic. In 1879 he published his last great novel *Quatre-vingt-treize*.

During the last few years of his life—the final apotheosis—he lived as the singer and prophet of democratic France, venerated by his countrymen as no living Frenchman had ever been venerated.

He died on May 22nd 1885 and was laid to rest in circumstances of unparalleled pomp and ceremony in the Panthéon.   H. d. R.

CONTENTS

CONTENTS

CONTENTS

BOOK ELEVEN

INTRODUCTION

VICTOR HUGO described his soul as a 'resounding echo' and in this he was not merely using a fine metaphor, he was expressing a deep truth. His voice is a magnificent one; he says what he has to say in language of unrivalled richness and matchless imagery, but what he says is not new. It is the echo of other voices, the reverberation of other minds. Because he is a poet and artist of the first order his words remain in our memories and strike our fancy; humbler, less eloquent predecessors have failed to express the same ideas in such unforgettable fashion. Thus it is that when we come to read *Notre-Dame de Paris* we find little that is new in the inspiration but much that is novel in the form, and therein lie the strength and originality of the work. It is the arrangement of the material that counts, as Pascal reminds us: 'with the same stones one can build a Roman temple or a Gothic cathedral.'

In 1830 when Hugo was engaged in writing *Notre-Dame de Paris*, the historical novel was greatly in vogue. Sir Walter Scott began to be read and loved from the eighteen-twenties onwards (Defauconpret's translations date from 1822) and a flood of imitations deluged a public avid for romantic tales set against a vaguely historical background. That Scott was primarily an antiquarian and mainly interested in an accurate reconstruction of certain periods of history was not always fully appreciated, and considerable licence was taken by the authors as regards the local colour and the characters presented in such novels. Vigny in *Cinq-Mars* (1826) allows himself great liberty in the invention of romanesque details against a background of history while Prosper Mérimée in his *Chronique du Règne de Charles IX* (1829) achieves historical accuracy in a slightly ironic imitation of Scott's work. Hugo was, then, following a tradition rather than breaking new ground in choosing a bygone age as the framework of his novel. His enthusiasm for Scott was already manifest in a laudatory article on *Ivanhoe*, nor can one fail to note the similarities in period and setting, if not in tone, between *Quentin Durward* and *Notre-Dame de Paris*.

That Hugo should choose as his setting a Gothic cathedral and the fifteenth century is only another proof of his extraordinary sensitivity to the spirit of his age. It was Chateaubriand—the acknowledged fount of inspiration to the Romantic writers—who popularized in his *Génie du Christianisme* (1802) the feeling for history and the love of the picturesque, especially in Gothic architecture. For long the classical or neo-classic style reigned supreme in Western Europe and it is only towards the end of the eighteenth century that a renewed interest was shown in the magnificent heritage of the Middle Ages. The public was only beginning, after centuries of neglect, to appreciate medieval architecture, and it is no small part of the merit of *Notre-Dame de Paris* to have described in language accessible to the many some of the features of the Gothic style, and to have castigated those modern vandals who in the name of progress destroy or alter what has taken centuries to build. Already Charles Nodier in his *Voyage Pittoresque et Romantique dans L'Ancienne France* (1820) had defended French architecture in spirited fashion against the demolishers. Hugo, in his constant zeal to instruct, brought his heavy guns to bear on the same positions.

With this reaction against classicism went a contempt for order, proportion and regularity; what was made according to the rules (whether in art or literature) was instantly condemned. The Romantic writers discovered a new beauty in the irregular, a strange charm even in ugliness. Citing Shakespeare and his poetic monsters, Hugo, in the Preface to his drama of Cromwell (1827), proclaimed the love of the grotesque to be the hall-mark of Romantic literature. Side by side in one work Caliban and Ariel complete each other, for the sublime and the ridiculous are two facets of the same reality. Notre-Dame and Quasimodo are alike worthy of our interest. With a romantic zest for exaggeration, Hugo pushes the ugliness of Quasimodo to the last limit of belief; he is not merely ugly—he is perfectly so—a gem as it were of unloveliness, and by that perfection he reaches sublimity.

Such, then, were some of the tendencies of the age which influenced Hugo in the composition of *Notre-Dame de Paris*. Let us see now what was his aim. He himself supplies the answer: 'It is a picture of Paris and the fifteenth century and of the fifteenth century in relation to Paris. The book has no historical pretensions save perhaps that of depicting with some degree of knowledge and conscientiousness—but only in glimpses and peeps—the state of the customs, the beliefs, the laws, the arts, in a word, the civilisation of the fifteenth century.' In this Hugo is successful. Lacking the historical sense of a Scott or the accuracy of a Mérimée, he yet, by dint of careful study of certain chroniclers of the period, contrives to fashion for us a vast tableau of the tumultuous life of the late medieval period. His descriptions of the cathedral itself, of the bird's eye view of Paris, of the crowded streets, the houses on the bridges, the squalid picturesqueness of it all, are models of vivid delineation in which the general impression is one of forceful imaginative insight. He is careful to give an authentic ring to the speech of his characters. The names—Claude Frollo, Robin Poussepain, Jacques Charmolue—are those of the period. The frequent introduction of Latin tags (one of Hugo's weaknesses) has for once a *raison d'être* in the description of an age whose acquaintance with the humanities was so profound and an occasional archaism gives an air of antiquity to thoughts which often strike the reader by their modernity. Undoubtedly the triumph of the book is the sense of the crowd which it conveys—these mobs of vagrants, beggars, gypsies with their strange customs, their rough justice, their camaraderie, assembled in the 'Cour des Miracles' or assailing the doors of Notre-Dame in a vain and heroic attempt to save La Esmeralda. The crowds in fact come to life more than do the individuals; here the general is more interesting than the particular. La Esmeralda—charming and pathetic as she is—pales to insignificance before the mob; Gringoire serves as a useful organ for philosophic speculation and as a link between the gypsy world and the great powers of Church and State. Claude Frollo himself, who promises to be a fascinating character study, develops into a melodramatic villain in whom sensual passion destroys all possibility of fruitful psychological struggle. Phoebus is a type rather than a personality—the blustering blasphemous soldier ready with the sword and the oath, as fickle in his favours as La Esmeralda is faithful to him. If the characters are intended simply to represent different aspects of the medieval mind, it is unfair to reproach them for their banality, but we may justifiably ask why a period, in which Christian devotion was the rule rather than the exception, contains no example of the churchman save that of Claude Frollo. This monk—half-atheist, half-scientist—smacks more of modern times and the horrific novel of the early nineteenth century than of 1482. True, it is not impossible that he could have existed then, but he is by no means a typical representative of the church of that period.

The character which comes most to life is that of Quasimodo on whom Hugo expends more loving care and insight than on all the others. The poet whose love of creation extended to the insects and the very stones of the field, shows a peculiar sympathy for this wretched outcast of humanity, this misshapen reject in whom all proportion and grace are lacking, whose sole perfection is that of ugliness. To him is given the task of saving La Esmeralda a first time from the gallows, and of making a dramatic defence of the Cathedral against the attack of the vagrants—a defence the purpose of which is destroyed by its complete uselessness, for the aim of both sides was the preservation of the same person.

In a historical novel the plot is of little importance. It suffices that it should provide the author with scope for a series of tableaux in which he can bring to life some of the features of the period dealt with, that it should allow for great liberty in the action of the characters, an intermingling of all classes and conditions of men, a variety of scene with some common core to give unity to the whole. The plot of *Notre-Dame de Paris*, banal as it is, answers to these needs. A lovely girl of mysterious origin is adored by a priest, a hunchback, and (spasmodically) by a roisterer. She meets with a series of misadventures including abduction, trial, torture, attempted hanging, the finding of a long-lost mother only to be snatched from her for the gallows, this time with no chance of escape. This is the stuff of melodrama, of cloak and sword tragedy, and Hugo does not confine himself to probabilities. Quasimodo tears La Esmeralda from the executioner's hands in a way little short of miraculous and Gringoire keeps meeting Claude Frollo at most unlikely moments. The spectacle is however so vast, the times so distant, that imagination accepts what reason tends to reject. We are carried away by the writer's enthusiasm, his enjoyment of the teeming life of fifteenth century Paris, his appreciation of its beauty and variety, his poet's delight in its colour and harmony, his love of movement, his feeling for grandeur. How Hugo revels in enumeration, accumulation, antithesis! Concision indeed is not his strong-point; often he uses two epithets when one would suffice. He has a surprising wealth of vocabulary of which he is anxious to make full use. There is a wordiness which weighs heavily on some of the chapters, but almost in spite of ourselves we are carried on, dazzled by the imagery, swept along by the flow of rhetoric. He himself may have gone further than he intended. In a letter dated 17th September 1830 he writes . . . . 'I am plunged up to the eyes in Notre-Dame, I pile page upon page and the material spreads and enlarges before me to such an extent as I proceed that I shall probably end by describing the very height of its Towers.'

Finally we come back to Notre-Dame itself. The great cathedral, mighty edifice of stone and glass, stands at the centre of the novel, as it stands at the centre of the Cité. It alone gives unity to the book, binds up the odd threads, brings together the disparate ends, and never fails to rouse our interest and touch our hearts. The cathedral is more real, more living than the little pantomime figures which run to and fro before it, with their useless gestures and vain agitation, their petty quarrels, their strident cries. Silent, unmoved, yet alive, Notre-Dame towers above it all, reminding man both of his littleness and of his strength—for what is the cathedral but a creation made by hands, a reminder of the skill of which these pantomime figures are capable, a memorial to the artists of a bygone age, a monument to human as well as to divine glory? Indeed it is as well, in this tale of devilry, torture and violent death, that some element of joy and pride is left to the reader else he would close the book in a spirit of unrelieved gloom.   M. L. M. YOUNG

NOTE BY TRANSLATOR

VICTOR HUGO is one of the masters of literature whose themes are especially difficult to render in a foreign tongue. If translated too literally, the English becomes harsh, disconnected; if rendered into modern, well-rounded phrases, the virility, the peculiar historical accent, disappear. In *Notre-Dame of Paris*, the medieval Latin flavour, the intimate knowledge of the times, the manners and customs, the old Paris,—the distinguishing characteristics of this effort of genius which have revived for us, like a phantasmagoria, the life of the fifteenth century,—difficult enough for a master of modern French, are still more difficult to render in modern English. In the necessary fidelity to this supreme characteristic a single word, an accent, is of value,—it behooves the translator to consider his quantities even more carefully, if possible, than did the author himself,—working as he does in an alien tongue as well as an alien time. It is with this conception of his task that the present translator has endeavoured to accomplish it.

Quotations in Latin, Spanish and other languages are translated. The notes added by the translator, it is hoped, will aid the reader in setting before himself still more clearly this presentation of medieval life,—so veracious, though clothed in the garb of fiction.

J. CARROLL BECKWITH

PREFACE TO THE FIRST EDITION

A few years ago while visiting or, to speak more properly, exploring Notre-Dame, the author of this book discovered in a dark recess of one of the towers the following word carved on the wall:

ΑΝΑΓΚΗ

Those Greek capitals, black with age and cut pretty deep into the stone—a certain Gothic peculiarity of form and attitude, showing them to have been the work of some hand of the Middle Ages—and, above all, their grim and fatal meaning (DOOM)—impressed the author profoundly.

Whose, he questioned himself, whose, he strove to conjecture, could be the soul in pain that was unwilling to quit this world without leaving behind such a vivid record of crime or of misfortune stamped on the walls of the old church?

Since that time, these walls have been whitewashed or rubbed smooth—I forget which—and the inscription has disappeared. This is in fact how the wonderful churches of the Middle Ages have been treated for the last two hundred years. Mutilation attacks them from all quarters—from within as well as from without: they are whitewashed by the priest, curry-combed by the architect, and demolished by the mob.

Hence, save the perishing memoir here devoted to it by the author of this book, nothing remains to-day of the mysterious word cut in the gloomy tower of Notre-Dame, nothing of the unknown destiny that it summarized so mournfully. The man that wrote the word upon the wall vanished centuries ago from the midst of the generations; the word in its turn vanished from the walls of the church; and the church itself, perhaps soon, will vanish forever from the face of the earth.

That word was the text upon which this book has been written.

Note added to the Edition of 1832

Through some misunderstanding the announcement has been made that this edition was to be enlarged by several 'new' chapters. 'Unpublished' is the proper word. For, if 'new' means 'lately written,' the chapters added to this edition are anything but 'new.' They were written when the rest of the work was written; they date from the same epoch, have sprung from the same thought, and have at all times formed portion of the manuscript of *Notre-Dame of Paris*.

Besides, the author fails to understand how new developments *can* be added to a work of this kind. Such a work is not to be manufactured to order. A romance is *born* into the world, so to speak, complete with all its chapters, a drama complete in all its scenes. You must not suppose that it is a mere question of convenience to decide what number of parts shall combine to make this *whole*, this mysterious microcosm that you call a drama or a romance. Grafting, mortising, soldering, patching of any kind, is here totally out of place. Such works should spring forth at one bound, and then stay as they are for good and all. Once it is made, the thing admits of no revising, no retouching. The book once published, the sex, virile or not, once recognized and proclaimed, the babe's cry once heard, it is born—there it is—such as it is—father or mother can no longer better it—it is in the world—in the sun and air—let it take its chances to live or die!

Has your book missed? Don't add chapters then to a miscarriage. Is it incomplete? You should have completed it while you were at it. Has your tree grown up crooked? Never more will come the time to straighten it. Is your novel consumptive, droopy, unable to live? The vital air that it needs it is now too late to supply. Does your drama limp? It won't move the better for a wooden leg.

The author is therefore particularly desirous to have the public aware of the fact that the chapters now added have not been written expressly for this edition. It is for a very simple reason that they have not appeared before. Just as the printers were busy at the first edition of *Notre-Dame*, a small package containing three chapters of the story was mislaid and could not be found. What was to be done? Write them over again, or let them go? The author began to reflect that the only two of these chapters long enough to be of any importance treated exclusively of art and history, and therefore in no way whatever affected the march of the drama; that the public could never notice any omission; and that he himself, the author, was the only one that would ever know the secret of the missing links. Therefore he concluded to let the chapters go. Besides, since all must be known, his laziness shrank from the task of rewriting three lost chapters. To write a new work would be far easier.

These chapters—the last one of Book Fourth, and the whole of Book Fifth—are, however, now recovered, and he takes the first opportunity to insert them in their proper place.

The reader has therefore the whole work now before him, such as the author dreamed it, such as he wrote it, good or bad, lasting or short-lived, such in fact as he wished it to be.

It is not to be doubted that these recovered chapters will find little value in the eyes of such readers as—with no imputation on their taste or judgment—will never look for more in *Notre-Dame* than the run of the action and the development of the plot. But there are possibly other readers who will not deem it useless to study the hidden æstheticism and philosophy of the book, who, while reading *Notre-Dame*, will take pleasure in detecting under the guise of romance something very different from romance, and will be delighted to pursue through the fanciful vision of the poet —pardon such conceited expressions—the ever-present system of the historian and the constant aim of the artist.

It is for this second class of readers especially that the chapters added to this edition will complete *Notre-Dame*, admitting that it is worth completing.

In one of these chapters—that treating on the present decline of architecture and the impending death of this prince of arts—the author expresses and develops an opinion which he has carefully reflected over, so that unfortunately it has now become a fixed one—though of course he earnestly hopes that the future will prove him to be wrong. He does not deny that art, in each and every one of its various forms, has everything to hope for from the rising generations, whose budding genius we can already witness in our studios and workshops. The grain is indeed in the furrow, and the harvest should be a plentiful one. Only—here is his opinion, examine the second volume of this edition for his reason —he is afraid that the sap has altogether left the old architectural soil that had been for many centuries art's best nursery.

Still, our young artists of to-day are so full of life, power, of predestination, so to speak, that, especially in the present schools of architecture, the professors, who are the worst possible, sometimes send forth, not only unknown to themselves but even in spite of themselves, most excellent pupils—precisely the contrary to Horace's potter who wished to make vases, but could never get beyond a saucepan—*Currit rota, urceus exit* (the wheel turns and turns, all that comes out is a pipkin).

But whatever the future of architecture may be, in whatever way our young artists may solve the question finally, it is the duty of us outsiders while waiting for new monuments to be careful to preserve the old. If at all possible, let us inspire the nation with a love for the architecture of the nation. This the author candidly declares to be the principal object of his book, one of the principal aims of his life.

Notre-Dame of Paris has already given perhaps some correct notions regarding art in the Middle Ages, that wonderful art so little known by some and, worst still, so misknown by others. But the author by no means considers his self-imposed task as finished. Far from it. Often as he has pleaded the cause of our old architecture, loudly as he has denounced the profanations, the demolitions, the impieties to which it has been subjected, he will do so again. He has pledged himself to return often to the question, and often he will return. He will be just as unflinching in defending our historic buildings as the iconoclasts of our schools and academies have been rabid in attacking them. It is extremely painful to see into what hands the architecture of the Middle Ages has fallen and to watch how the 'plaster-slashers' of the present day are treating the wrecks of this majestic art. It is even worse than painful. It is disgraceful for us intelligent men to look on calmly while this is done, or at most to show our dissatisfaction by merely hooting at the transgressors. For I speak not only of what is going on in the provinces, but of what takes place every day at our doors, before our windows, in Paris, in the 'great' city, the literary city, the city of the press, of language, of thought!

To conclude this note, I must record in black and white a few of the acts of vandalism that are every day projected, debated, started, continued, and carried out to the bitter end, under our very eyes, under the eyes of all lovers of art, under the eyes of our critics, apparently paralyzed and struck dumb at the audacity. When we pulled down the archbishop's palace, we perhaps did no great harm, the building being one of rather poor taste. But the mischief was that the very same blow destroyed the bishop's palace also, a rare and precious waif of the fourteenth century. The vandal architect never saw the difference. He pulled up good grain, tares and all. As to which was which he neither knew nor cared.

They are talking of demolishing the admirable chapel of Vincennes and using its stones for some fortification—without Daumesnil even asking for such a thing. That wreck, the Bourbon Palace, we are repairing and restoring at immense expense, and at the same time we allow the magnificent stained glass windows of the Sainte Chapelle to be ruined by continued exposure to the equinoctial gales. For some days past we have seen scaffolding on the tower of Saint Jacques de la Boucherie, and one of these mornings we shall find the pickax there busy at its work. One mason has built a white cottage between the venerable towers of the Palace of Justice; another has mutilated Saint Germain des Prés, the feudal abbey of three belfries; a third is ready and willing to tear down Saint Germain l'Auxerrois, and all these masons— they call themselves architects—are paid by the State, or by the royal purse, and they wear green coats. Every injury that false taste can inflict on correct taste these 'architects' are guilty of. Even while I am writing, one of them is omnipotent in the Tuileries, where he has left an ugly scar on the face of Philibert Delorme by striking him right between the two eyes. It is certainly one of the most intolerable grievances of our day to witness the effrontery with which this gentleman's 'architecture' has presumed to waddle over one of the most delicate façades of the Renaissance!

BOOK ONE

I

The Great Hall

ONE morning, three hundred and forty-eight years, six months and nineteen days ago, the Parisians were awakened by a grand peal from all the bells, within the triple enclosure of the City, the University and the Town.

Yet the 6th of January, 1482, was not a day of which history has preserved any record. There was nothing remarkable in the event that so early in the morning set in commotion the bells and the bourgeois of Paris. It was neither a sudden attack made by Picards or by Burgundians; nor a shrine carried in procession; nor a student fight in the city of Laas; nor the entry of 'our most dread lord the King;' nor even a goodly stringing up of thieves, male and female, on the Place de la Justice. Nor was it a sudden arrival, so common in the fifteenth century, of some ambassador and his train, all belaced and beplumed. Only about two days ago, indeed, the last cavalcade of this kind, Flemish envoys commissioned to conclude the marriage treaty between the young dauphin and Margaret of Flanders, had made entry into Paris, to the great annoyance of Cardinal Bourbon. To please the king, his Eminence had undertaken to give gracious reception to the rough crowd of Flemish burgomasters, and to entertain them at his Hôtel de Bourbon with a 'very fine morality, burletta and farce,' whilst a beating rain was all the time drenching his magnificent tapestries at his portals.

But on this 6th of January, what 'set in motion the whole *populaire* of Paris,' as Jehan of Troyes, the old chronicler, phrases it, was the fact of its being a double holiday, united since time immemorial—the Epiphany, or Feast of the Kings, and the *Fête des Fous*, or Feast of the Fools. To celebrate such a day there was to be a bonfire kindled on the Place de Grève, a maypole raised at the Chapelle de Braque, and a mystery performed in the Palace of Justice. Proclamation had been made the evening before, to the sound of the trumpet, in all the public squares by the provost's men in fine coats of purple camlet, with great white crosses on the breast.

Crowds of people had accordingly been flocking all the morning, their houses and shops shut up, from all quarters of the town towards one of the three places appointed. Everyone had made his selection—the bonfire, the maypole, or the mystery. Thanks to the good common sense so characteristic of the Parisian sight-seers, the greater part of the multitude directed their steps either towards the bonfire, which was quite in season, or towards the mystery, which was to be performed in the Grande Salle, or great hall of the Palace of Justice, well roofed and well sheltered—wisely leaving the poor, ill-garlanded maypole to shiver all alone under a January sky in the cemetery of the Chapelle de Braque.

The greatest crowds, however, were to be found on the approaches to the Palace of Justice, because it was known that the Flemish ambassadors, who had arrived two days previously, intended to be present, not only at the performance of the mystery, but also at the election of the Fool's Pope, which was likewise to take place in the Great Hall.

On that day it was no easy matter to make one's way into the Great Hall, then and long afterwards considered to be the largest covered apartment in the world (Sauval, the Paris historian, it is hardly necessary to state, had not yet measured the great hall in the château of Montargis). The open square in front of the Palace, thronged with people, presented to the gazers from the windows the aspect of a sea into which five or six streets, like the mouths of so many rivers, every moment discharged fresh floods of human heads. The waves of this deluge, constantly increasing, broke against the angles of the houses that projected here and there, like so many promontories, into the irregularly shaped basin of the square. In the centre of the high Gothic façade of the Palace, the great triple-faced staircase, continually ascended and descended by the restless multitudes, with currents breaking on the intermediate landing or streaming over the two lateral slopes, flowed like a waterfall tumbling into a lake. In the square itself, the noise made by the shouting, laughing, tramping of these thousands of feet, great as it was, was redoubled every now and then, as something occurred to check, disturb or eddy the stream that surged towards the great staircase. At one time it was an archer clubbing somebody; at another it was the prancing horse of a provost's sergeant kicking right and left—the regular good old way to establish order, handed down from the *provostry* to the *constablery*, from the *constablery* to the *marshalry*, and from the *marshalry* to the *gendarmerie* of our Paris of to-day.

At the doors, at the windows, at the skylights, and on the roofs, swarmed thousands of good-natured *bourgeois* faces, looking calmly and quietly at the Palace, at the crowd, and asking nothing more to look at; for many honest Paris folks are quite content with gazing at the gazers, and can even regard a wall with intense interest when they think there is something going on behind it.

If we, men of 1830, could possibly mingle in imagination with those Parisians of the fifteenth century, and enter with them, pulled, elbowed, crushed, into the Great Hall, that proved so small on this 6th of January, 1482, we should witness a spectacle at once interesting and charming, where everything would be so very old as to appear perfectly new.

If the reader consent, we shall cross the threshold of the Great Hall together. Let me endeavour to reproduce the impression made on his senses as we struggle through the surging crowd in frock, smock, jerkin, doublet, and every conceivable dress of the period.

At first our ears are stunned with the buzzing, our eyes are dazzled with the glare. Over our heads is the roof, consisting of a double vault of pointed arches, lined with carved wood, painted light blue, and sprinkled with golden *fleurs-de-lis*. Under our feet the marble floor, like a checkerboard, is alternated with black and white squares. A few paces from us stands an enormous pillar, then another, then a third, seven altogether, extending the whole length of the Hall, and supporting the central line that separates the double vaults of the roof. Around the first four are dealers' stands glittering with glass and tinsel ware; around the other three are oaken benches, worn and polished by the gowns of the lawyers and the breeches of those that employ them. Everywhere around the building, along the lofty walls, between the doors, between the windows, between the pillars, appears an interminable line of the statues of the kings of France, from Pharamond down —the sluggards, with arms pendent and eyes downcast, the warriors, with arms and heads boldly raised on high. In the long Gothic windows, the stained glass shines with a thousand colours. In the wide entrances the doors are richly and delicately carved. Everywhere all around—on vaults, pillars, walls, lintels, panels, doors, and statues—glows a rich tint of blue and gold, already a little faded, but even seventy years later, in spite of dust and cobwebs, Du Breul, the historian, will see enough to admire it from tradition.

If the reader now represents to himself this vast hall, visible in the pale light of a January day, filled with a motley and noisy mob drifting along the walls and eddying around the seven pillars, he will have some faint idea of the picture in general, whose curious details we shall now try to indicate more precisely.

It is certain, that if Ravaillac had not assassinated Henry IV, no documents of his trial would have been deposited in the Palace registry, no accomplices would have been interested in causing the said documents to disappear, no incendiaries would have been obliged, lacking a better method, to burn the registry in order to burn the documents, and to burn the Palace in order to burn the registry. Therefore there would have been no fire of 1618. The old Palace would be still standing, with its Grand Hall, and I could say to my reader, 'Go and look at it'—which would be a great convenience for us both; saving me from writing, him from reading, my imperfect description. Which goes to prove the novel truth: the results of great events are beyond calculation.

It is true that it is very possible that Ravaillac did not have any accomplices; secondly, that his accomplices, if by chance he had any, had nothing to do with the conflagration of 1618. There are two other explanations, both very plausible. According to the first it was set on fire and consumed by a shooting star, a foot wide and a cubit high, that fell on the Palace, as everyone knows, on the 7th of March after midnight. For the second is quoted the quatrain of Théophile:

> *Certes, ce fut un triste jeu*
> *Quand à Paris Dame Justice,*
> *Pour avoir mangé trop d'épice,*
> *Se mit tout le palais en feu.* *

But whatever we may think of this triple explanation, political, physical and poetical, one fact is unfortunately but too true—the burning itself. Thanks to this catastrophe, thanks especially to the various successive restorations which effectually finished up whatever little the conflagration had spared, we have hardly any remains to-day of this first abode of the kings of France, of this palace, the elder sister of the Louvre, already so old in the times of Philip the Fair that traces could then be found of the magnificent buildings erected by King Robert and described by Helgaldus. Almost every portion of it has disappeared. What has become of the chamber of the chancellery, where Saint Louis 'consummated his marriage?' The garden where he administered justice 'clad in a cotte of camlet, a surcoat of tiretaine without sleeves, and over all a mantle of black sendal, reclining upon carpets by the side of Joinville?' Where is the chamber of the Emperor Sigismond? that of Charles IV? that of John Lackland? Where is the staircase whence Charles VI proclaimed his gracious amnesty? Where are the flagstones on which Marcel murdered, before the young dauphin's eyes, the Marshals of Normandy and of Champagne? Where is the gate at which Anti-pope Benedict's bull was torn to pieces, and from which those who had brought it started on its procession through Paris, coped and mitred in derision, to make *amende honorable?* Where is the Great Hall itself with its gildings, its azure, its pointed arches, its statues, its pillars, its vast vaulted roofs all checkered and variegated with carvings? and the golden

---

* It was certainly poor fun when Lady Justice set fire to her palace in Paris just because she had eaten too many *sugar-plums* (*bribes*).

chamber? Where is the marble lion, kneeling at the gate, like the lions before Solomon's throne, head down, tail between legs, in the attitude of humility that force should present when before Justice? Where are the beautiful doors, the splendid windows? Where the chiselled ironwork that threw Biscornette into despair? Where is Du Hancy's delicate cabinet-work? What has time, what have men done with these wonders? What has been given to us in exchange for all this Gallic history, for all this Gothic art? For art, we have the heavy flat arches of De Brosse, the tasteless architect of the portal of St. Gervais; and for history, we have the twaddling Souvenirs of the Big Pillar, still resounding with the Patrus' small gossip. Neither being much to speak of, let us return to the story taking place in the real Great Hall of the real old Palace.

The two ends of this gigantic parallelogram were occupied differently. At the west end could be seen the famous Marble Table, said to be of one single block, and so long, wide and high that 'no other such slice of marble was ever seen in the world,' as is recorded by the old chroniclers in a style that would have given an appetite to Gargantua. The east end contained the little chapel lately built by Louis XI, in which he had himself sculptured in stone kneeling before the Virgin, and to which he had also brought, without concerning himself with their two niches thus left vacant in the file of royal statues, the statues of Charlemagne and Saint Louis—two saints whom he supposed to be very much in favour in Heaven as kings of France. The little chapel itself, in all the charms of newness—it had hardly been built six years—was characterized all through by the exquisite taste in delicate architecture, wonderful sculpture and fine, deep carving, which, ending our Gothic era, is perpetuated to the middle of the sixteenth century in the fairy-like fancies of the Renaissance. The little *rosace à jour*, in particular, a wheel-shaped window over the portal, was a masterpiece of such lightness and elegance that it could be called a star of lace.

Towards the middle of the Hall, opposite the main entrance, a balcony, covered with gold brocade, backed by the wall, and accessible by a private entrance from a corridor opening into the Gilded Chamber, had been erected for the special honour of the Flemish envoys and the other grand personages invited to the representation of the mystery.

This entertainment was to be given, according to ancient customs, on the Marble Table, where all the preparations had been made since the morning. The thick marble slab, scratched by the heels of the Basochians—a famous guild of lawyers' clerks —supported a solid construction of wood, sufficiently elevated, whose upper surface, high enough to be visible from the farthest parts of the Hall, was to serve as the stage, while the interior, masked with curtains, was to be the actors' dressing-room. A ladder, standing artlessly outside, was to connect dressing-room and stage, and help exits and entrances by its solid rungs. By this ladder and this only, actor the most unexpected, scene the most entrancing, effect the most telling, was to gain access to the stage. Innocent yet venerable infancy of the mechanical resources of theatrical art!

At each of the four corners of the Marble Table stood a sergeant of the bailiff of the Palace to preserve order. The regular guardians of the people's amusements, whether on holidays or days of execution, there they now stood, stiff and motionless as statues.

The play was not to begin until the great clock of the Palace had struck the last stroke announcing noon. This was, no doubt, rather late for a mystery, but as ambassadors were to be present their convenience was to be regarded.

The most of the crowd had been waiting all the morning. A good many of these honest sight-seers had shivered on the grand staircase at daybreak; some even insisted that they had passed the night close to the great doorway so as to make sure of being the first to enter. The crowd, continually increasing, became by degrees too great for the room and, like a river overflowing its banks, began to rise along the walls, to swell around the pillars, and even inundate the window-sills, the tops of the columns, the cornices and every projection of the sculptures. As a matter of course, impatience, discomfort, weariness, the unrestraint of the occasion, the quarrels continually springing up from unavoidable causes—a sharp elbow,—a heavy heel,—the long delay,—all these sources of discontent at last began to tell. The noise made by a crowd so squeezed, packed, crushed, trodden on, smothered, began to assume a tone of decided acrimony. Complaints and imprecations began to be plainly heard, against the Flemings, the Provost of the Merchants, Cardinal Bourbon, the Governor of the Palace, Margaret of Austria, the sergeants with their rods, the cold, the heat, the bad weather, the Bishop of Paris, the Fools' Pope, the pillars, the statues, this closed door, that open window,—the whole to the great amusement of the bands of students and lackeys scattered through the crowd, who mingled with all this discontentment their teasing remarks and their malicious suggestions, and pricked the general ill humour with a pin, so to speak.

There was, amongst others, a group of these joyous rascals who, after breaking the glass of a window, had established themselves boldly upon the entablature, and from there cast their looks and their railleries alternately within and without, upon the crowd in the Hall and the crowd out of doors. From their mimicry of well-known personages, their flippant remarks exchanged with their comrades from one end of the Hall to the other, and their uproarious laughter, it was easy to see that these young clerks, far from participating in the general languor or vexation, were enjoying themselves heartily by making so much out of one spectacle that they never minded waiting for another.

'Upon my soul, it's you, Joannes Frollo de Molendino!' cried a friend in the crowd to a little blond with a pretty and malicious face straddled on an acanthus of the capital of one of the lofty columns. 'Hello! Jack of the windmill! You are well named to-day, anyway, for your two legs and your two arms keep moving like the four sails that go in the wind. How long have you been perched up there?'

'Four hours at least, by the devil's mercy,' answered Joannes. 'I hope they will be put to my credit in purgatory. I heard the beginning of the high mass sung in the Sainte Chapelle by the King of Sicily's eight chanters.'

'Sweet chanters they are too!' cried one of the students, 'with voices sharper than their pointed caps. Before founding a mass for Monsieur Saint John, the king would have done well to have found out whether Monsieur Saint John liked Latin psalmody with a Provençal accent.'

'It was all for the sake of employing those cursed chanters of the King of Sicily that he did it,' screamed bitterly an old woman in the crowd beneath the window. 'What think you of a thousand livres parisis for a mass, and charged, too, upon the farm of the saltwater fish of the fish-market of Paris!'

'Peace, old woman!' replied a grave and portly personage, who was stopping his nose at the side of the fish-seller; 'it was quite necessary to found a mass. Would you have had the king fall sick again?'

'Bravely spoken, Sir Gilles Lecornu, master furrier to the king's wardrobe!' cried the little scholar clinging to the capital.

A burst of laughter from the whole tribe of the scholars greeted the unlucky name of the poor furrier to the king's wardrobe.

'Lecornu! Gilles Lecornu!' said some.

'*Cornutus et hirsutus*,' (horned and hirsute), answered another.

'Oh, to be sure,' continued the little imp at the top of the pillar; 'what have they to laugh at? Is not worthy Gilles Lecornu brother to Maître Jehan Lecornu, provost of the king's household, son of Maître Mahiet Lecornu, first gatekeeper of the Bois de Vincennes —all citizens of Paris—all married, from father to son?'

The gaiety redoubled. The stout furrier, without answering a word, strove to escape the looks fixed upon him from all sides; but he exerted himself in vain, for all his efforts served only to wedge more solidly between the shoulders of his neighbours his great apoplectic face, purple with anger and vexation.

At last one of these neighbours, fat, short, and reverend-looking, like himself, raised his voice in his behalf.

'Abominable!' he exclaimed, 'that scholars should talk thus to a townsman. In my time they would have been first beaten with a fagot and then burned with it.'

At this the whole tribe burst out afresh.

'Hello! who sings that stave? who's that ill-boding screech-owl?'

'Oh! I know him,' said one; 'it's Maître Andry Musnier.'

'Because he's one of the four sworn booksellers to the University,' said the other.

'All goes by fours in that shop,' cried a third; 'there are four nations, the four faculties, the four fêtes, the four attorneys, the four electors, and the four booksellers.'

'Well, then,' resumed Jehan Frollo, 'we must play four devils with them.'

'Musnier, we'll burn thy books.'

'Musnier, we'll beat thy lackey.'

'Musnier, we'll kiss thy wife—'

'The good fat Mademoiselle Oudarde—'

'Who's as fresh and buxom as if she were a widow.'

'The devil take you!' growled Maître Andry Musnier.

'Maître Andry,' said Jehan, still hanging by the capital, 'hold your tongue, or I'll drop on your head.'

Maître Andry looked up, seemed to calculate for a moment the height of the pillar and the weight of the little rogue, multiplied in his mind that height by the square of the velocity, and was silent.

Jehan, master of the field, continued triumphantly—

'Yes, I would do it, though I am brother to an archdeacon.'

'Fine fellows, in truth, are our gentlemen of the University, not even to have taken care that our privileges were respected on a day like this: for here are a maypole and a bonfire in the Town; a mystery, a fools' pope, and Flemish ambassadors, in the City; and in the University, nothing at all!'

'And yet the Place Maubert is large enough,' observed one of the young clerks posted on the window seat.

'Down with the rector, the electors, and the attorneys!' cried Joannes.

'We must build a bonfire to-night in the Champ-Gaillard,' continued the other, 'with Maître Andry's books.'

'And the desks of the scribes,' said his neighbour.

'And the wands of the beadles.'

'And the spitting-boxes of the deans.'

'And the buffets of the attorneys.'

'And the hutches of the electors.'

'And the rector's stools.'

'Down, then,' said little Jehan, as counterpoint, 'down with Maître Andry, the beadles, and the scribes—the theologians, the physicians, and the decretists—the attorneys, the electors, and the rector!'

'This is then the end of the world,' muttered Maître Andry, stopping his ears.

'Apropos! the rector himself! here he comes through the Place!' cried one of those in the window seat.

Every one now strove to turn towards the Place.

'Is it really our venerable rector, Maître Thibaut?' asked Jehan Frollo du Moulin, who, as he was clinging to one of the internal pillars, could not see what was passing outside.

'Yes, yes,' answered all the rest, 'it is he—he himself—Maître Thibaut, the rector.'

It was, in fact, the rector and all the dignitaries of the University going in procession to meet the ambassadors, and crossing at that moment the Place of the Palace. The scholars all crowded together at the window, greeted them as they passed by with sarcasms and ironical plaudits. The rector, marching at the head of his band, received the first broadside, and it was a rough one.

'Good-day, monsieur le recteur! Hello! good-day to you!'

'How has the old gambler contrived to be here? has he really quitted his dice?'

'How he goes trotting along on his mule—its ears are not so long as his.'

'Hello! good-day to you, monsieur le recteur Thibaut! *Tybalde aleator!* (Tybald the gamester)—Ah! you old imbecile! you old gambler!'

'God preserve you! did you often throw double-six last night?'

'Oh! what a scarecrow countenance; leaden, wrinkled and battered through his love of dice and gaming.'

'Where are you going to now, Thibaut, *Tybalde ad dados* (Tybald of the dice)—turning your back on the University and trotting toward the town?'

'No doubt he's going to seek a lodging in the Rue Thibautodé (*Thibaut aux dés*),' cried Jehan du Moulin.

The whole gang repeated the pun with a voice of thunder and a furious clapping of hands.

'You are going to seek lodgings in the Rue Thibautodé, aren't you, monsieur le recteur, the devil's own gamester?'

Then came the turn of the other dignitaries.

'Down with the beadles! down with the mace-bearers!'

'Tell me, Robin Poussepain, who's that man there?'

'It's Gilbert de Suilly, *Gilbertus de Soliaco*, chancellor of the college of Autun.'

'Here, take my shoe—you're better placed than I am—throw it in his face.'

'*Saturnalitias mittimus ecce nuces.*' (We send Saturnalian nuts).

'Down with the six theologians with their white surplices!'

'Are those the theologians? I thought they were the six white geese that Saint Geneviève gave to the Town for the fief of Roogny.'

'Down with the physicians!'

'Down with the disputations, cardinal, and quadlibetary!'

'Here goes my cap at yon chancellor of Saint Geneviève—I owe him a grudge.'

'True—and he gave my place in the nation of Normandy to little Ascanio Falzaspada, belonging to the province of Bourges, because he's an Italian.'

'It's an injustice!' exclaimed all the scholars. 'Down with the chancellor of Saint Geneviève!'

'Ho, there! Maître Joachim de Ladehors! Ho! Louis Dahuille! Ho! Lambert Hoctement!'

'The devil smother the attorney of the nation of Germany!'

'And the chaplains of the Sainte Chapelle, with their gray amices, *cum tunicis grisis!*' (with gray tunics).

'*Seu de pellibus grisis furratis*' (or gray furred skins).

'Hello! the masters of arts! All the fine black copes; all the fine red copes!'

'That makes the rector a fine tail!'

'One would say a doge of Venice going to marry the sea.'

'Now, again, Jehan! the canons of Saint Geneviève!'

'The devil take the canons!'

'Abbé Claude Choart! Doctor Claude Choart, are you seeking Marie-la-Giffarde?'

'She's in the Rue de Glatigny.'

'She's making the bed for the king of the ribalds.'

'She's paying her four deniers, *quattuor denarios.*'

'*Aut unum bombum.*'

'Would you have her pay you in the nose?'

'Comrades, there goes Maître Simon Sanguin, elector of Picardy, with his wife on the pillion.'

'*Post equitem sedet atra cura.*' (Black Care sits behind the horseman.)

'Stoutly, Maître Simon!'

'Good-day, monsieur l'électeur.'

'Good-night, madame l'électrice.'

'Now, aren't they happy, to be seeing all that?' sighed Joannes de Molendino, still from his perch on the capital.

Meanwhile the sworn bookseller to the University, Maître Andry Musnier, whispered in the ear of the king's furrier, Maître Gilles Lecornu:

'I tell you, monsieur, the world's at an end. Never were there seen such breakings-out of the students! It's the accursed inventions of the age that are ruining everything—the artillery—the serpentines—the bombards—and, above all, the printing-press, that other German pest! No more manuscripts—no more books! Printing puts an end to bookselling—the end of the world is at hand!'

'I can see it by velvets coming so much into fashion,' sighed the furrier.

At that moment it struck twelve.

'Ha!' exclaimed the whole crowd, with one voice of satisfaction. The scholars became quiet.

Then there was a great shuffling about, a great movement of feet and heads, a general detonation of coughing and blowing of noses; each one arranged himself, posted himself to the best advantage, raised himself on his toes. Then there was a deep silence, every neck remaining outstretched, every mouth open, every eye turned toward the marble table—but nothing appeared. The bailiff's four sergeants still kept their posts, as stiff and motionless as if they had been four painted statues. All eyes then turned toward the gallery reserved for the Flemish envoys. The door remained shut, and the gallery empty. The multitude had been waiting since the early morning for three things, that is to say, for the hour of noon, for the Flemish embassy, and for the mystery; but only the first of the three had arrived on time.

This was really too bad.

They waited one—two—three—five minutes, a quarter of an hour—but nothing came. The gallery remained empty; the stage, mute. Meanwhile impatience was succeeded by displeasure. Angry words began to circulate, though as yet only in whispers. 'The mystery! the mystery!' was uttered in an undertone. The heads of the multitude began to ferment. A storm, which as yet only growled, was agitating the surface of that human sea. It was our friend Jehan du Moulin that elicited the first explosion.

'The mystery! and the devil take the Flemings!' cried he, with the whole force of his lungs, twisting himself, like a serpent, about his pillar.

The multitude clapped their hands. 'The mystery!' they all shouted, 'and let Flanders go to all the devils!'

'We must have the mystery immediately!' resumed the scholar; 'or my advice is that we hang the bailiff of the Palace in the way of comedy and morality.'

'Well said!' exclaimed the people, 'and let us begin the hanging with his sergeants!'

A great acclamation followed. The four poor devils of sergeants began to turn pale and look anxiously at each other. The multitude pressed toward them, and they already saw the slight wooden balustrade which separated them from the crowd bending inwards under the pressure.

The moment was critical.

'Bag them! bag them!' was shouted from all sides.

At that instant the hangings of the dressing-room which we have described above were lifted, giving passage to a personage, the mere sight of whom sufficed to stop the eager multitude, and changed their anger into curiosity as if by enchantment.

'Silence! silence!' was the cry from all sides.

The personage, but little reassured, and trembling in every limb, advanced to the edge of the marble table, making a profusion of bows, which, the nearer he approached approximated more and more to genuflexions.

Calm, however, was gradually restored. Only that slight murmur was heard which is always exhaled from the silence of a great crowd.

'Messieurs les bourgeois,' said he, 'and mesdemoiselles les bourgeoises, we shall have the honour of declaiming and performing before his eminence monsieur le cardinal, a very fine morality, entitled *The Good Judgment of Madame the Virgin Mary*. I play Jupiter. His eminence is at this moment accompanying the most honourable embassy from monsieur the Duke of Austria, which is at this moment detained by hearing the harangue of monsieur the rector of the University, at the Baudets gate. As soon as the most eminent cardinal is arrived, we shall begin.'

It is certain that nothing less than the intervention of Jupiter was necessary to save the four unhappy sergeants of the bailiff of the Palace. If we had had the happiness of inventing this very true and veritable history, and had consequently been responsible for it before Our Lady of Criticism, it is not in this place, at all events, that we should have incurred any citation against us of the classical precept, *nec Deus intersit* (Ever let a god intervene), etc. Furthermore, the costume of Seigneur Jupiter was very fine, and had contributed not a little to quiet the irritated assemblage by attracting all their attention. Jupiter was clad in a brigandine covered with black velvet and gilded nails; his head-dress was a bicoquet ornamented with silver-gilt buttons; and but for the rouge and the great beard which covered each one-half of his face—but for the scroll of gilt pasteboard sprinkled with spangles and stuck all over with shreds of tinsel, which he carried in his hand, and in which experienced eyes easily recognized his thunderbolts—and but for his flesh-coloured feet, sandal-bound with ribbons *à la Grecque*—he might have borne a comparison, for the severity of his aspect, with a Breton archer of the corps of Monsieur de Berry.

2

Pierre Gringoire

WHILE, however, Jupiter was delivering his harangue, the satisfaction, the admiration unanimously excited by his costume, were dissipated by his words; and when he arrived at that unhappy conclusion, 'as soon as the most eminent cardinal is arrived, we shall begin,' his voice was lost in a thunder of hooting.

'Begin immediately! The mystery! the mystery at once!' cried the people. And above all the other voices was heard that of Joannes de Molendino, piercing through the general uproar, like the sound of the fife in a charivari at Nimes. 'Begin directly!' squeaked the scholar.

'Down with Jupiter and the Cardinal de Bourbon!' vociferated Robin Poussepain and the other young clerks perched in the window.

'The morality directly!' repeated the crowd immediately; 'go on! go on! The sack and the rope for the actors and the cardinal!'

Poor Jupiter, haggard, frightened, pale under his rouge, let fall his thunderbolts, took his bicoquet in his hand; then, bowing and trembling, he stammered: 'His eminence—the ambassadors—Madame Margaret of Flanders'—he knew not what to say.

The fact was, he was afraid he should be hanged—hanged by the populace for waiting, or hanged by the cardinal for not having waited—on either hand he beheld an abyss, that is to say, a gallows.

Happily, some one came forward to extricate him and assume the responsibility.

An individual who stood within the railing, in the space which it left clear around the marble table, and whom no one had yet perceived, so completely was his long and slender person sheltered from every visual ray by the diameter of the pillar against which he had set his back—this individual, we say, tall, thin, pale, light complexioned—still young, though wrinkles were already visible in his forehead and his cheeks—with sparkling eyes and a smiling mouth—clad in a garment of black serge, threadbare and shining with age—approached the marble table, and made a sign to the poor sufferer. But the other, in his perturbation, did not observe it.

The new-comer advanced another step forward.

'Jupiter,' said he, 'my dear Jupiter!'

The other did not hear him.

At last, the tall, fair man, losing all patience, shouted almost under his nose, 'Michel Giborne!'

'Who calls me?' said Jupiter, as if starting from a trance.

'I do,' answered the personage clad in black.

'Ah!' exclaimed Jupiter.

'Begin directly,' returned the other; 'satisfy the people, and I take upon myself to appease monsieur the bailiff, who will appease monsieur the cardinal.'

Jupiter now took breath. 'Messeigneurs les bourgeois,' cried he, at the utmost stretch of his lungs, to the multitude who continued to hoot him, 'we are going to begin directly.'

'*Evoe! Jupiter! plaudite, cives!*' (Well done, Jupiter! applaud, citizens!) cried the scholars.

'Noël! Noël!' cried the people. (That cry being the burden of a canticle sung in the churches at Christmas, in honour of the Nativity, whence, apparently, it was adopted by the populace as a general mark of approbation and jubilation as long as the season lasted.)

Then followed a deafening clapping of hands, and the hall still shook with acclamations when Jupiter had withdrawn behind his tapestry.

Meanwhile, the unknown, who had so magically changed the 'tempest into calm,' as says our old and dear Corneille, had modestly retired into the penumbra of his pillar, and would no doubt have remained there, invisible, and motionless, and mute as before, if he had not been drawn from it by two young women, who, being in the first line of the spectators, had remarked his colloquy with Michel Giborne-Jupiter.

'Maître,' said one of them, beckoning to him to approach.

'Hush! my dear Liénarde,' said her fair neighbour, pretty, blooming, and quite courageous by virtue of her holiday attire—'it is not a clerk, it is a layman. You should not say *Maître*, but—*Messire*.'

'Messire!' then said Liénarde.

The unknown approached the balustrade.

'What is your pleasure with me, mesdemoiselles?' asked he impressively.

'Oh, nothing,' said Liénarde, all confused. 'It's my neighbour here, Gisquette la Gencienne, that wants to speak to you.'

'No, no,' rejoined Gisquette, blushing; 'it was Liénarde that said *Maître* to you—I only told her that she should say *Messire*.'

The two girls cast down their eyes. The gentleman who asked

nothing better than to enter into conversation, looked at them, smiling:

'You have nothing to say to me, then, mesdemoiselles?'

'Oh, no, nothing at all,' answered Gisquette.

'Nothing,' said Liénarde.

The tall, fair young man made a step to retire; but the two curious damsels were not inclined to let him go so soon.

'Messire,' said Gisquette, with the impetuosity of water escaping through a sluice, or a woman taking a resolution, 'you then know this soldier who is going to play Madame the Virgin in the mystery?'

'You mean the role of Jupiter,' returned the unknown.

'Oh, dear, yes,' said Liénarde; 'is she not stupid! You are acquainted with Jupiter, then?'

'With Michel Giborne!' answered the unknown, 'yes, madam.'

'He has a grand beard!' answered Liénarde.

'Will it be very fine, what they are all going to say?' asked Gisquette, timidly.

'Very fine, indeed, mademoiselle,' answered the informant without the least hesitation.

'What will it be?' asked Liénarde.

'*The Good Award of Madame the Virgin*—a morality, if it please you, mademoiselle.'

'Ah! that's different,' returned Liénarde.

A short silence followed, which was broken by the stranger. 'It is a morality entirely new,' said he, 'which has never yet been played.'

'Then is it not the same,' said Gisquette, 'as was played two years ago on the day of the entry of monsieur the legate, and in which three beautiful girls performed—'

'As sirens,' interrupted Liénarde.

'And quite naked,' added the young man.

Liénarde modestly cast down her eyes. Gisquette looked at her, and did likewise. The other continued, smiling, 'It was a very pretty thing to see. But to-day it is a morality made on purpose for the Lady of Flanders.'

'Will they sing pastorals?' asked Gisquette.

'Oh, fie!' said the unknown. 'What! in a morality! We must not confound one kind of pieces with another. In a shepherd's song, indeed, it would be quite right.'

'That's a pity,' rejoined Gisquette. 'That day there were, at the fountain of Ponceau, savage men and women scrambling and making gestures, singing catches, couplets and pastorals.'

'That which is suitable for a legate,' said the stranger, very dryly, 'is not suitable for a princess.'

'And near them,' continued Liénarde, 'played a number of bass instruments, that gave out wonderful melodies.'

'And to refresh the passengers,' resumed Gisquette, 'the fountain threw out, by three mouths, wine, milk, and hyppocrass, and everybody drank that liked.'

'And a little below the Ponceau fountain,' continued Liénarde, 'at the Trinity, there was a Passion performed without speech.'

'Oh, yes, how I remember!' exclaimed Gisquette; 'Our Lord on the cross, and the two thieves on each side of Him!'

Here the young gossips, warming in the recollection of the legate's entry, talked both at once.

'And further on, at the Artists' gate, there were other characters very richly habited'—

'And do you remember, at St. Innocent's fountain, that huntsman following a hind, with a great noise of dogs and hunting horns?'—

'And then at the meat-market, those scaffolds that represented the Bastile of Dieppe'—

'And when the legate was going by, you know, Gisquette, they gave the assault, and the English all had their throats cut'—

'And what fine characters there were over by the Châtelet gate!'

'And on the Pont-au-Change, which was all hung with cloth from one end to the other.'

'And when the legate crossed over, they let fly from the bridge above two hundred dozen of all kinds of birds. Was that not a fine sight, Liénarde?'

'There will be a finer to-day,' at length interrupted their interlocutor, who seemed to listen to them with impatience.

'You promise us that this shall be a fine mystery,' said Gisquette.

'Without doubt,' returned he. And then he added, with peculiar emphasis, 'Mesdemoiselles, *I* it is who am the author of it.'

'Say you so!' cried the young women, open-mouthed.

'Yes, in truth,' answered the poet, bridling a little—'that is to say, there are two of us—Jehan Marchand, who has sawn the planks and put together the framework of the theatre; and I, who have written the piece. My name is Pierre Gringoire.'

The author of the Cid himself could not have more proudly said, 'My name is Pierre Corneille.'

The reader may have observed that some time must already have elapsed since the moment at which Jupiter retired behind the drapery and that at which the author of the new morality revealed himself thus abruptly to the simple admiration of Gisquette and Liénarde. It is worthy of remark that all that assemblage, who a few minutes before had been so tumultuous, now waited quietly on the faith of the player's promise—an evidence of this everlasting truth, still daily noted in our theatres—that the best means of making the audience wait patiently is, to assure them that the performance is about to begin.

However, the schoolboy Joannes was not asleep. 'Hello!' shouted he suddenly, amidst the peaceful expectation which had succeeded the disturbance. 'Jupiter! Madame the Virgin! you devil's boatmen! are you joking with one another? The piece! the piece! Begin! or it is we who will begin again!'

This was enough. A music of high and low-keyed instruments now struck up underneath the stage; the hangings were lifted, and four characters in motley attire, with painted faces, issued forth, clambered up the steep ladder already mentioned, and reaching the upper platform, drew up in line before the audience, whom they saluted with a profound obeisance, whereupon the musical sounds ceased and the mystery began.

The four characters, after receiving abundant payment for their salutations in the plaudits of the multitude, commenced, amidst a profound silence, the delivery of a prologue, which we gladly spare the reader. However, as is still the case in our own time, the audience paid more attention to the gowns they wore than to the parts they were enacting—and in truth they did right. They were all four clad in robes half yellow and half white, differing only in the nature of the material; the first being of gold and silver brocade, the second of silk, and the third of wool, and the fourth of coarse linen. The first character carried in the right hand a sword; the second, two golden keys; the third, a pair of scales; and the fourth, a spade: and in order to assist such indolent minds as might not have seen clearly through the transparency of these attributes, there might be read in large black letters worked at the bottom of the brocade gown, MY NAME IS NOBILITY; at the bottom of the silken one, MY NAME IS CLERGY; at the bottom of the woollen, MY NAME IS TRADE; and at the bottom of the linen garment, MY NAME IS LABOUR. The sex of the two male characters was clearly indicated to every judicious spectator by the comparative shortness of their garments and the *cramignole* (flat cap) which they wore upon their heads; while the two female characters, besides that their robes were of ampler length, were distinguishable by their hoods.

One would also have been very dull not to have discovered through the poetic drapery of the prologue, that Labour was married to Trade, and Clergy to Nobility, and that these two happy couples possessed in common a magnificent golden dolphin which they intended to adjudge only to the most beautiful damsel. Accordingly, they were going over the world in search of this beauty; and after successively rejecting the Queen of Golconda, the Princess of Trebizond, the daughter of the Cham of Tartary, etc., etc.; Labour and Clergy, Nobility and Trade, were come to rest themselves upon the marble table of the Palace of Justice, and deliver at the same time to the worthy auditory as many moral sentences and maxims as might in that day be expended upon the members of the faculty of arts, at the examinations, sophisms, determinances, figures and acts, at which the masters took their degrees.

All this was truly very fine.

Meanwhile, in all that assemblage upon which the four allegorical personages seemed to be striving which could pour out the most copious floods of metaphor, no ear was so attentive, no heart so palpitating, no eye so eager, no neck so outstretched, as were the eye, ear, neck and heart of the author, the poet, the brave Pierre Gringoire, who a moment before had been unable to forego the joy of telling his name to two fair damsels.

He had retired a few paces from them, behind his pillar; and there it was that he listened, looked and enjoyed. The benevolent plaudits which had greeted the opening of his prologue still resounded in his breast; and he was completely absorbed in that species of ecstatic contemplation with which a dramatic author marks his ideas falling one by one from the lips of the actor, amid the silence of a crowded auditory. Happy Pierre Gringoire!

It pains us to relate, this first ecstasy was very soon disturbed. Scarcely had Gringoire's lips approached this intoxicating cup of joy and triumph before a drop of bitterness was cruelly mingled in it.

A tattered mendicant who, lost as he was among the crowd, could receive no contributions, and who, we may suppose, had not found sufficient indemnity in the pockets of his neighbours, had bethought himself of roosting on some conspicuous perch from which to attract the attention and the alms of the good people. Accordingly, during the first lines of the prologue, he had hoisted himself up by means of the pillars that supported the reserved gallery, to the cornice which ran along the bottom of its balustrade; and there he had seated himself, soliciting the attention and the pity of the multitude by the display of his rags, and of a hideous sore that covered his right arm. He did not, however, utter a word.

His silence allowed the prologue to proceed without any distraction; and no noticeable disorder would have occurred had not, as ill luck would have it, the boy Joannes espied, from his perch at the top of one of the great pillars, the beggar and his grimaces. The young wag burst into an immoderate fit of laughter; and, regardless of the interruption to the performance, and the disturbance of the general attention, cried out in a tone of gaiety, 'See now! the mangy beggar there asking alms!'

Any one that has ever thrown a stone into a pond full of frogs, or fired a gun among a flock of birds, may form an idea of the effect produced by these unseasonable words dropped in the midst of the universal attention. Gringoire started as if he had felt an electric shock. The prologue stopped short; and all heads were turned tumultuously toward the mendicant, who, far from being disconcerted, found in this incident a good opportunity of reaping a harvest, and began to cry out with a doleful whine, half shutting his eyes, 'Charity! if you please.'

'I say, on my soul,' cried Joannes, 'it's Clopin Troillefou. Hello! friend—so thy sore wasn't comfortable on thy leg, that thou'st changed it to thine arm?'

So saying he threw, with the dexterity of a monkey, a small white coin into the old greasy hat which the beggar held out with his diseased arm. The beggar received without change of expression both the alms and the sarcasm, and continued in a piteous tone, 'Charity! if you please.'

This episode had considerably distracted the audience; and a goodly number of the spectators, with Robin Poussepain and all the clerks leading, merrily applauded this whimsical duet which had been struck up thus unexpectedly in the middle of the prologue, between the urchin with his shrill voice, and the beggar with his imperturbable drone.

Gringoire was grievously displeased. Having recovered from his first stupefaction, he shouted earnestly to the four characters on the stage, 'Go on!—what the devil!—go on;' without even deigning to cast a look of disdain at the two interrupters.

At that moment he felt some one pulling at the skirt of his coat; he turned round, not without some little annoyance, and forced with some difficulty a smile. Nevertheless he found it necessary to do so, for it was the pretty arm of Gisquette la Gencienne, which, extended through the balustrade, thus solicited his attention.

'Monsieur,' said the girl, 'will they go on?'

'Surely,' answered Gringoire, shocked at the question.

'Oh, then, messire,' she resumed, 'would you have the courtesy to explain to me—'

'What they are going to say?' interrupted Gringoire. 'Well—listen.'

'No,' said Gisquette, 'but what they have said already.'

Gringoire started as if touched to the quick.

'A plague on the little stupid, witless wench!' said he between his teeth.

From that moment Gisquette ceased to exist in his mind.

Meanwhile the actors had obeyed his injunction; and the audience, observing that they were once again trying to make themselves heard, had set themselves to listen—not, however, without having lost certain points of beauty in the soldering together of the two parts of the piece which had been so abruptly cut short. Gringoire reflected bitterly. However, tranquillity had been gradually restored; the schoolboy held his tongue, the beggar counted some coin in his hat, and the piece had resumed its sway.

It was really a very fine composition, and we think it might be turned to some account, even now, by means of a few changes. The performance, rather long indeed, and rather dry, was simple; and Gringoire, in the candid sanctuary of his own judgment, admired its clearness. As may well be supposed, the four allegorical personages were a little fatigued with travelling over the three known quarters of the world without finding an opportunity of suitably disposing of their golden dolphin. Thereupon a long eulogy upon the marvellous fish with numberless delicate allusions to the young prince betrothed to Margaret of Flanders—which young prince was at that time in very dismal seclusion at Amboise, without the slightest suspicion that Labour and Clergy, Nobility and Trade, had just been making the tour of the world on his account. The dolphin aforesaid, then, was young, was handsome, was vigorous, and above all (magnificent origin of all the royal virtues!) was son of the lion of France. I declare that this bold metaphor is admirable, and that dramatic natural history, on a day of allegory and of a royal epithalamium, finds nothing at all shocking in a dolphin the son of a lion. On the contrary, it is precisely those rare and pindaric mixtures that prove the popular enthusiasm. However, to have disarmed criticism altogether, the poet might have developed this fine idea in less than two hundred verses. It is true that the mystery was to last, according to the order of monsieur the provost, from noon till four o'clock, and that it was necessary to say something. Moreover, it was patiently listened to.

All at once, in the midst of a fine quarrel between Mademoiselle Trade and Madame Nobility, at the moment when Master Labour was pronouncing this predictive line:

Beast more triumphant ne'er in woods was seen

the door of the reserved gallery, which had until then been so inopportunely shut, opened still more inopportunely, and the stentorian voice of the usher, abruptly announced, 'His Eminence Monsieur, the Cardinal of Bourbon!'

3

The Cardinal

POOR Gringoire! The noise of all the great double petards let off
on Saint John's day—the discharge of a score of crooked arque-
busses—the report of that famous serpentine of the Tour de Billy,
which, during the siege of Paris, on Sunday, the 29th of September,
1465, killed seven Burgundians at a shot—the explosion of all the
gunpowder stored at the Temple gate—would have split his ears
less violently at that solemn and dramatic moment, than those
few words from the lips of an usher, 'His Eminence Monsieur, the
Cardinal of Bourbon.'

It is not that Pierre Gringoire either feared the cardinal or
despised him. He was neither weak enough to do the one, nor
presumptuous enough to do the other. A true eclectic, as one would
say now-a-days, Gringoire was one of those firm and elevated
spirits, calm and temperate, who can preserve their composure
under all circumstances—*stare in dimidio rerum*—and who are full of
reason and of a liberal philosophy even while making some account of cardinals. Invaluable and uninterrupted line of philosophers—to whom wisdom, like another Ariadne, seems to have
given a skein which they have gone on unwinding from the beginning of the world through the labyrinth of human affairs. They
are to be found in all times, and ever the same—that is to say, ever
in accord with the times. And not to mention our Pierre Gringoire,
who would be their representative of the fifteenth century if we
could succeed in obtaining for him the distinction which he deserves, it was certainly their spirit which animated Father du Breul
in the sixteenth, when writing these words of sublime simplicity,
worthy of any age: 'I am a Parisian by birth, and a *parrhisian* by
my speech; for *parrhisia* in Greek signifies liberty of speech, which
liberty I have used even to messeigneurs the cardinals, uncle and
brother to monseigneur the Prince of Conti, albeit with respect
for their greatness, and without giving offence to any of their train,
and that is a great deal to say.'

So there was neither hatred for the cardinal, nor contempt of
his presence, in the disagreeable impression which he made upon
Pierre Gringoire. On the contrary, our poet had too much good
sense and too threadbare a coat not to attach a particular value
to the circumstance, that several allusions in his prologue, and in
particular the glorification of the dolphin, son of the lion of France,
would fall upon the ear of so eminent a personage. But personal

interest is not the ruling motive in the noble nature of poets. Supposing the entity of a poet to be represented by the number ten, it is certain that a chemist, on analyzing and pharmaco-pœizing, as Rabelais says, would find it to be composed of one part of self-interest with nine parts of self-esteem. Now, at the moment when the door was opened to admit the cardinal, Gringoire's nine parts of self-esteem, inflated and expanded by the breath of popular admiration, were in a state of prodigious enlargement, quite overwhelming and smothering that imperceptible molecule of self-interest which we just now distinguished in the constitution of poets—a precious ingredient, by-the-way, a ballast of reality and humanity, without which they would never touch the earth. It was a delight to Gringoire to see and feel that an entire assemblage (of poor varlets, it is true, but what then?) were stupefied, petrified, and breathless by the immeasurable tirades which burst from every part of his epithalamium. I affirm that he himself shared the general beatitude; and that, quite the reverse of La Fontaine, who, at the performance of his play of *The Florentine*, asked, 'What poor wretch has written that rhapsody?' Gringoire would willingly have asked of his neighbour, 'By whom is this masterpiece?' It may, therefore, be supposed what sort of effect was produced upon him by the brusque and tempestuous arrival of the cardinal.

His fears were but too fully realized. The entrance of his Eminence disorganized the audience completely. All eyes were turned toward the gallery, and there was a general buzz: 'The cardinal! the cardinal!' repeated every tongue. The unfortunate prologue was cut short a second time.

The cardinal stopped a moment upon the threshold of the gallery; and while casting his eyes with great indifference over the assemblage the tumult redoubled. Each one wished to obtain a better view of him. Each one stretching his neck over his neighbour's shoulder.

He was in truth an exalted personage, the sight of whom was worth almost any other spectacle. Charles, Cardinal de Bourbon, Archbishop and Count of Lyons, and Primate of Gaul, was allied both to Louis XI, through his brother Pierre, Seigneur de Beaujeu, who had espoused the king's eldest daughter, and at the same time to Charles the Bold, through his mother, Agnes of Burgundy. Now, the ruling, the characteristic, the distinctive feature in the character of the Primate of Gaul, was his courtier-like spirit and his devotion to power. Hence, it may well be supposed in what numberless perplexities this double relationship had involved him, and among how many temporal shoals his spiritual bark must have tacked, to have escaped foundering either upon Louis or upon Charles, the Charybdis and the Scylla which had swallowed up the Duke of Nemours and the Constable of Saint-Pol. Heaven be praised, however, he had got happily through his voyage, and reached Rome without accident. But although he was now in port—and indeed, precisely because he was in port—he never recollected, without a feeling of uneasiness, the various chances of his political life, which had so long been both perilous and laborious. So, also, he used to say, that the year 1476 had been to him both a black and white year, meaning thereby that he had lost in that one year his mother, the Duchess of Bourbonnais, and his cousin, the Duke of Burgundy, and that mourning the one had consoled him for the other.

However, he was a very worthy man; he led a joyous cardinal's life; was wont to make merry with wine of the royal vintage of Challuau; did not detest Richarde-la-Gamoise and Thomasse-la-Saillarde; gave alms to pretty girls rather than old women; and for all these reasons was in great favour with the populace of Paris. He always went surrounded by a little court of bishops and abbots of high degree, gallant, jovial, and fond of good eating; and more than once had the good devotees of Saint Germain d'Auxerre, in passing at night under the windows of the Hôtel de Bourbon, all blazing with light, been scandalized by hearing the same voices which had sung vespers to them in the day-time, chanting to the sound of glasses, the bacchanalian proverb of Benedict XII, the pope who had added a third crown to the tiara—*Bibamus papaliter*. (Let us drink like the popes.)

No doubt it was this popularity, so justly acquired, which, upon his entrance, prevented any unpleasant reception on the part of the mob, who a few minutes before had been so dissatisfied, and so little disposed to pay respect to a cardinal, even on the day when they were going to elect a pope. (The Lord of Misrule was called the Fools' Pope.) But the Parisians bear little malice; and besides, by ordering the performance to begin by their own authority, the good citizens had had the better of the cardinal, and this triumph satisfied them. Moreover, Monsieur le Cardinal de Bourbon was a handsome man—he had on a vastly fine scarlet robe, which he wore in excellent style—which is to say, that he had in his favour all the women, and, consequently, the better part of the audience. Certainly it would be both injustice and bad taste to hoot a cardinal for being too late at the play when he is a handsome man, and wears well his scarlet robe.

He entered, then, saluted the company with that hereditary smile which the great have always in readiness for the people, and moved slowly towards his armchair of crimson velvet placed for his reception, looking as if some other matter occupied his mind.

His escort—or what we should now call his staff—of bishops and priests, issued after him upon the gallery, not without exciting redoubled tumult and curiosity among the spectators below. All were busied in pointing them out, or in telling their names, each one striving to show that he knew at least some one of them; one pointing to the Bishop of Marseilles (Alaudet, if we remember right); some to the Dean of Saint Denis; others to Robert de Lespinasse, Abbot of the great neighbouring monastery of Saint-Germain-des-Prés, the libertine brother of a mistress of Louis XI —all their names being repeated with a thousand mistakes and mispronunciations. As for the students, they swore. It was their own day—their Feast of Fools—their saturnalia—the annual orgies of the *basoche* (Lawyers' clerks of the Parliament of Paris) and the schools. No liberty but was permissible that day. And then there were numberless wanton hussies among the crowd—Simone Quatre-livres, Agnès-la-Gadine, Robine Pièdebou. Was it not the least that could be expected, that they should swear at their ease, and profane God's name a little, on such a day as that, in such a goodly company of churchmen and courtezans? And accordingly, they did not mince matters; but amidst the uproarious applause a frightful din of blasphemies and obscenities proceeded from all those tongues let loose, those tongues of clerks and scholars, tied up all the rest of the year by the fear of Saint Louis's brandingiron. Poor Saint Louis! how they set him at defiance in his own Palace of Justice! Each one of them had singled out among the newly-arrived company in the gallery some one of the cassocks, black, gray, white, or violet. As for Joannes Frollo de Molendino, and his being brother to an archdeacon, it was the red robe that he audaciously assailed, singing out as loud as he could bawl, and fixing his shameless eyes upon the cardinal, '*Cappa repleta mero!*' (Head, or hood, full of wine.)

All these particulars, which are thus clearly detailed for the reader's edification, were so completely covered by the general hum of the multitude that they were lost before they could reach the reserved gallery; though, indeed, the cardinal would have been little moved by them; so completely did the license of the day belong to the customs of the age. He had something else to think of, which preoccupation appeared in his manner—another cause of solicitude, which followed closely behind him, and made its appearance in the gallery almost at the same time as himself. This was the Flemish embassy.

Not that he was a profound politician, or concerned himself about the possible consequences of the marriage of madame, his cousin, Margaret of Burgundy, with monsieur, his cousin, Charles, Dauphin of Vienne—nor how long the patched-up reconciliation

between the Duke of Austria and the French king might endure—
nor how the King of England would take this slight toward his
daughter. All this gave him little anxiety; and he did honour each
night to the wine of the royal vineyard of Chaillot without ever
suspecting that a few flasks of that same wine (revised and corrected
a little by the physician Coictier), cordially presented to Edward
IV by Louis XI, might possibly, some fine morning, rid Louis XI
of Edward IV. The most honourable embassy of the Duke of
Austria brought none of these cares to the cardinal's mind, but
annoyed him in another respect. It was, in truth, somewhat hard,
and we have already said a word or two about it in the first pages
of this book, that he should be obliged to give welcome and
entertainment—he, Charles de Bourbon—to obscure burghers;
he, a cardinal, to a pack of scurvy sheriffs—he, a Frenchman and
a connoisseur in good living, to Flemish beerdrinkers—and in
public, too! Certes, it was one of the most irksome parts he had
ever gone through for the *bon plaisir* of the king.

However, he had so perfectly studied his role, that he turned
toward the door with the best grace in the world, when the usher
announced in a sonorous voice, 'Messieurs the Envoys of the Duke
of Austria!' It is needless to say that the entire hall did likewise.

Then appeared, two by two, with a gravity which strongly
contrasted with the flippant air of the cardinal's ecclesiastical
train, the forty-eight ambassadors from Maximilian of Austria,
having at their head the reverend father in God, Jehan, Abbot of
Saint-Bertin, chancellor of the Golden Fleece, and Jacques de
Goy, Lord of Dauby, high bailiff of Ghent. A deep silence now
took place in the assemblage, occasionally interrupted by
smothered laughter at all the uncouth names which each of these
personages transmitted with imperturbable gravity to the usher,
who then gave out their names and callings, pell-mell and with
all sorts of mutilations, to the crowd below. There were Maître
Loys Roelof, Sheriff of the town of Louvain; Messire Clays
d'Etuelde, Sheriff of Brussels; Messire Paul de Baeust, Lord of
Voirmizelle, president of Flanders; Maître Jehan Coleghens,
burgomaster of the city of Antwerp; Maître George de la Moere,
principal sheriff of the *kuere* of the city of Ghent; Maître Gheldolf
van der Hage, principal sheriff of the *parchons* of the said city; and
the Sieur de Bierbecque, and Jehan Pinnock, and Jehan
Dimaerzelle, etc., etc., etc., bailiffs, sheriffs and burgomasters
—burgomasters, sheriffs and bailiffs—all stiff, sturdy, starched
figures, dressed out in Sunday clothes of velvet and damask, and
hooded with black velvet *cramignoles* decorated with great tufts of
gold thread of Cyprus—good Flemish heads after all, with severe
and respectable countenances, akin to those which Rembrandt has

made stand out with such force and gravity from the dark background of his picture of *The Night Watch*—personages on every one of whose foreheads it was written, that Maximilian of Austria was right in 'confiding to the full,' as his manifesto expressed it, 'in their sense, valour, experience, loyalty and good prudence.'

There was one exception, however; it was a face, subtle, intelligent, crafty-looking—a mixture of the monkey and the diplomatist —toward whom the cardinal made three steps in advance and a low bow, but who, nevertheless, was called simply Guillaume Rym, counsellor and pensionary of the town of Ghent.

Few persons at that time knew aught of Guillaume Rym—a rare genius, who, in a time of revolution, would have appeared with *éclat* on the surface of events; but who, in the fifteenth century, was confined to the practice of covert intrigue and to 'live in the mines,' as the Duke de Saint-Simon expresses it. However, he was appreciated by the first 'miner' in Europe—he frequently lent a helping hand in the secret operations of Louis XI—all which was perfectly unknown to this multitude, who were amazed at the cardinal's politeness to that sorry-looking Flemish bailiff.

4

Master Jacques Coppenole

AT the moment when the pensioner of Ghent and his Eminence were exchanging a very low bow, and a few words in a tone still lower, a man of lofty stature, large-featured, and broad-shouldered, presented himself to enter abreast with Guillaume Rym, looking something like a mastiff dog by the side of a fox. His felt hat and his leathern jerkin were oddly conspicuous amidst the velvet and silk that surrounded him. Presuming it to be some groom who knew not whither he was going, the usher stopped him.

'Hold, friend! you cannot pass.'

The man of the leathern jerkin shouldered him aside. 'What would this fellow with me?' said he, in a thundering voice, which drew the attention of the entire hall to this strange colloquy. 'Seest thou not that I am of the party?'

'Your name?' demanded the usher.

'Jacques Coppenole.'

'Your titles?'

'A hosier, at the sign of the Three Chains at Ghent.'

The usher shrank back. To announce sheriffs and burgomasters might indeed be endured—but a hosier!—it was too bad. The cardinal was upon thorns. The people were looking and listening.

For two days his Eminence had been doing his utmost to smooth these Flemish bears into presentable shape, and this freak was too much for him. Meanwhile Guillaume Rym, with his cunning smile, went up to the usher. 'Announce Maître Jacques Coppenole, clerk to the sheriffs of the city of Ghent,' said he to the officer in a very low whisper.

'Usher,' then said the cardinal aloud, 'announce Maître Jacques Coppenole, clerk to the sheriffs of the illustrious city of Ghent.'

This was an error. Guillaume Rym, by himself, would have evaded the difficulty; but Coppenole had heard the cardinal's direction.

'No! by the Holy Rood!' he cried, with his voice of thunder: 'Jacques Coppenole, hosier. Dost thou hear, usher? Neither more nor less. By the Holy Rood! a hosier—that's fine enough. Monsieur the archduke has more than once sought his gloves among my hose.'

A witticism is quickly appreciated in Paris and this occasioned a burst of laughter and applause from the people below.

We must add that Coppenole was one of the people, and that the audience around him were of the people also; so that the communication between them and him had been quick, electric, and, as it were, on equal footing. The lofty airs which the Flemish hosier gave himself, while humbling the courtiers, had stirred in the plebeian breasts a certain latent feeling of dignity, of independence, which, in the fifteenth century, was as yet vague and undefined. They beheld one of their equals in this hosier, who had just borne himself so sturdily before the cardinal—a comforting reflection to poor devils accustomed to pay respect and obedience even to the servants of the sergeants of the bailiff of the Abbot of Sainte Geneviève, the cardinal's train-bearer.

Coppenole bowed haughtily to his Eminence, who returned the salute of the all-powerful burgher, formidable to Louis XI. Then, while Guillaume Rym, *sage homme et malicieux* (wise and malicious), as Philippe de Comines expresses it, followed them both with a smile of raillery and superiority, they moved each to his place— the cardinal thoughtful and out of countenance—Coppenole quite at his ease, thinking, no doubt, that, after all, his title of hosier was as good as another, and that Mary of Burgundy, mother of that Margaret for whose marriage he was to-day treating, would have feared less the cardinal than the hosier; for no cardinal would have aroused the people of Ghent against the favourites of the daughter of Charles the Bold; nor could any cardinal, by a single word, have hardened the multitude against her tears and prayers, when the Lady of Flanders came and supplicated her people on their behalf, even to the foot of the scaffold, while the hosier had only to raise his leathern elbow to cause both your heads to be struck off, most illustrious seigneurs, Guy d'Hymbercourt and Chancellor Guillaume Hugonet.

However, the poor cardinal had not yet finished penance; he was doomed to drain to the dregs the chalice of being in such bad company.

The reader has doubtless not forgotten the audacious mendicant, who at the time of the commencement of the prologue, had climbed up to the fringes of the dais reserved for the cardinal. The arrival of the illustrious guests had in no way disturbed him; and while the prelates and the ambassadors were packing themselves away like real Flemish herrings within the narrow compass of the tribune, he had made himself quite comfortable, with his legs bravely crossed upon the architrave. This insolence was extraordinary; yet nobody had remarked it at the first moment, all attention being fixed elsewhere. He, for his part, took notice of nothing in the hall; he was wagging his head backward and forward with the unconcern of a Neapolitan beggar, repeating from time to time, amidst the general hum, and as if by a mechanical habit, 'Charity, if you please!' and indeed, among all present, he was probably the only one who would not have deigned to turn his head on hearing the altercation between Coppenole and the usher. Now it so chanced that his hosiership of Ghent, with whom the people already were warmly in sympathy, and upon whom all eyes were fixed, went and seated himself in the front line of the gallery, just over the place where the beggar was sitting; and it excited no small amazement to see the Flemish ambassador, after scrutinizing the fellow beneath him, give him a friendly slap upon his ragged shoulder. The beggar turned. Surprise, recognition and kindly gratulation were visible in both faces; then, without giving themselves the slightest concern about the spectators, the hosier and the leper fell into conversation in a low voice, clasping each other by the hand; while the tattered arm of Clopin Trouillefou, displayed at length upon the cloth of gold that decorated the dais, had somewhat the appearance of a caterpillar upon an orange.

The novelty of this singular scene excited such wild gaiety among the crowd that the cardinal soon remarked it: he leaned forward; and as, from the point where he was situated, he caught only an imperfect glimpse of Trouillefou's ignominious garment, he figured to himself that the beggar was soliciting alms, and, shocked at his audacity, he exclaimed, 'Monsieur the bailiff of the Palace, throw me that fellow into the river.'

'By God's Cross! monseigneur le cardinal,' said Coppenole, without leaving hold of Clopin's hand, 'this is one of my friends.'

'Noël! Noël!' cried the mob. And from that moment Maître Coppenole had in Paris, as in Ghent, 'great credit with the people;

as men of great stature have,' said Philippe de Comines, 'when they are thus presuming.'

The cardinal bit his lip. He leaned toward the Abbot of Sainte Geneviève, who sat next him, and said in a half-whisper:

'Pleasant ambassadors, truly, monsieur the archduke sends us to announce the Lady Margaret.'

'Your Eminence's politeness,' returned the abbot, 'is wasted upon these Flemish grunters—*Margaritas ante porcus.*' (Pearls before swine.)

'Say rather,' rejoined the cardinal, smiling, '*porcus ante Margaritam.*' (Swine before pearls.)

The whole of the little clerical court were in ecstasy at this play of words. The cardinal felt a little relieved. He was now even with Coppenole, for he too had had his pun applauded.

And now, such of our readers as have the power of generalizing an image or an idea, as we say in the style of to-day, will permit us to ask them whether they figure to themselves quite clearly the spectacle presented, at this moment when we pause to call their attention to the vast parallelogram of the great hall of the Palace.

In the middle of the western wall is a spacious and magnificent gallery hung with drapery of gold brocade, while there enters, in procession, through a small Gothic doorway, a series of grave-looking personages, announced successively by the clamorous voice of the usher; on the first benches are already seated a number of reverend figures enveloped in velvet, ermine and scarlet cloth. About this gallery, which remains silent and stately—below, in front and around—is the multitude and the noise. A thousand looks are cast from the crowd upon every face in the gallery—a thousand murmured repetitions of every name. The spectacle is indeed curious and deserves the attention of the spectators. But what is that down there, quite at the extremity of the hall—that sort of scaffolding, with four motley-attired puppets upon it, and four others below? And at one side of the staging, who is that pale-faced man in a long black sacque? Alas! dear reader, it is Pierre Gringoire and his prologue.

We had all utterly forgotten him.

That is precisely what he had feared.

From the moment at which the cardinal entered, Gringoire had been incessantly exerting himself for the salvation of his prologue. He had first enjoined the actors, who were waiting in suspense, to proceed, and elevate their voices; then, finding that no one listened, he had stopped them; and for nearly a quarter of an hour, during which the interruption had continued, he had been constantly beating with his foot and gesticulating, calling upon Gisquette and Liénarde, and urging those near him to have the prologue proceeded with—but all in vain. No one could be turned aside from the cardinal, the embassy and the gallery—the sole centre of that vast circle of visual rays. It is to be feared also, we regret to say it, that the prologue was beginning to be a little tiresome to the audience at the moment his Eminence's arrival had made so terrible a distraction. And after all, in the gallery, as on the marble table, it was still in fact the same spectacle - the conflict of Labour with Clergy, of Nobility with Trade; and most people liked better to see them in downright reality, living, breathing, elbowing and pushing one another in plain flesh and blood, in that Flemish embassy, in that episcopal court, under the cardinal's robe, under Coppenole's jerkin, than tricked out, painted, talking in verse, and stuffed, as it were, with straw, wearing the yellow and white gowns in which Gringoire had disguised them.

Nevertheless, when our poet saw tranquillity a little restored, he bethought himself of a stratagem which might have saved the performance.

'Monsieur,' said he, turning to one of his neighbours, of fair round figure, with a patient-looking countenance, 'suppose they were to begin again?'

'Begin what?' said the man.

'Why, the mystery,' said Gringoire.

'Just as you please,' returned the other.

This demi-approbation was enough for Gringoire, and taking the affair into his own hands, he began to call out, confounding himself at the same time as much as possible with the crowd. 'Begin the mystery again!—begin again!'

'The devil!' said Joannes de Molendino. 'What is it they're singing out at yon end?' for Gringoire was making the noise of four people. 'Tell me, comrades, is not that mystery finished? They want to begin it again; 'tis not fair.'

'No! no!' cried the students, 'down with the mystery!—down with it!'

But Gringoire only multiplied himself the more, and he bawled the louder—'Begin again!—begin again!'

These clamours attracted the attention of the cardinal. 'Monsieur the bailiff of the Palace,' quoth he to a tall, dark man who stood but a few paces from him, 'are those knaves in a font of holy water that they make so much noise?'

The bailiff of the Palace was a kind of amphibious magistrate, a sort of bat of the judicial order, a compound of the rat and the bird, of the judge and the soldier.

He approached his Eminence, and with no small apprehension of his displeasure, he stammered forth an explanation of the people's refractoriness—that noon had arrived before his Eminence, and that the players had been forced to begin without waiting for his Eminence.

The cardinal laughed aloud. 'I' faith,' said he, 'monsieur the rector of the University should e'en have done as much. What say you, Maître Guillaume Rym?'

'Monseigneur,' answered Rym, 'let us be content with having escaped one-half the play. 'Tis so much gained.'

'May those rogues go on with their farce?' asked the bailiff.

'Go on—go on,' said the cardinal, ''tis all the same to me; I shall read my breviary the while.'

The bailiff advanced to the edge of the gallery, and shouted, after procuring silence by a motion of his hand—'Townsmen! householders! and inhabitants!—to satisfy those who will that the play should begin again, and those who will that it should finish, his Eminence orders that it shall go on.'

Thus both parties were obliged to yield, although both the author and the auditors long bore a grudge on this score against the cardinal.

The characters on the stage accordingly took up their text where they had left off; and Gringoire hoped that at least the remainder of his composition would be listened to. This hope, however, was soon dispelled, like the rest of his illusions. Silence had indeed been somehow or other restored among the audience; but Gringoire had not observed that, at the moment when the cardinal had given his order for the continuance of the play, the gallery was far from being full, and that subsequently to the arrival of the Flemish envoys there were come other persons forming part of the escort, whose names and titles, thrown out in the midst of his dialogue by the intermitted cries of the usher, made considerable ravage in it. Only imagine, in the midst of a theatrical piece, the yelp of a doorkeeper, throwing in, between the two lines of a couplet, and often between the first half of a line and the last, such parentheses as these:

'Maître Jacques Charmolue, king's attorney in the ecclesiastical court!'

'Jehan de Harlay, esquire, keeper of the office of the night-watch of the town of Paris!'

'Messire Galiot de Genoilhac, knight, seigneur of Brussac, master of the king's artillery!'

'Maître Dreux-Raguier, commissioner of our lord the king's waters and forests in the domains of France, Champagne and Brie!'

'Messire Louis de Graville, knight, councillor and chamberlain to the king, admiral of France, guardian of the Bois de Vincennes!'

'Maître Denis le Mercier, governor of the house of the blind at Paris!' etc., etc.

It was becoming insupportable.

All this strange accompaniment, which made it difficult to follow the tenor of the piece, was the more provoking to Gringoire, as it was obvious to him that the interest was increasing, and that nothing was needed for his composition but to be listened to. It was, indeed, difficult to imagine a plot more ingeniously or dramatically woven. While the four personages of the prologue were bewailing their hopeless perplexity, Venus in person—*vera incessu patuit dea* (her step revealed the real goddess)—had presented herself before them, clad in a fine coat of mail, having blazoned fair upon its front the ship displayed on the escutcheon of Paris. She was come to claim for herself the dolphin promised to the most beautiful. She was supported by Jupiter, whose thunder was heard to rumble in the dressing-room; and the goddess was about to bear away the prize—that is to say, frankly, to espouse monsieur the dauphin—when a little girl dressed in white damask, and carrying a marguerite or daisy in her hand, (lucid personification of the Lady of Flanders,) had come to contend with Venus. Here were at once theatrical effect and sudden transformation. After a proper dispute, Venus, Margaret, and those behind the scenes, had agreed to refer the matter to the wise judgment of the Holy Virgin. There was another fine part, that of Don Pedro, King of Mesopotamia; but amid so many interruptions it was difficult to discover his exact utility. All these personages climbed up the ladder to the stage.

But it was of no use; not one of these beauties was felt or understood. It seemed as if, at the cardinal's entrance, some invisible and magical thread had suddenly drawn away every look from the marble table to the gallery, from the southern extremity of the hall to its western side. Nothing could disenchant the audience; all eyes remained fixed in that direction; and the persons who successively arrived, and their cursed names, and their faces, and their dresses, made a continual diversion. The case was desperate. Save Gisquette and Liénarde, who turned aside from time to time when Gringoire pulled them by the sleeve—save the patient fat man who stood near him—no one listened to, no one looked at, the poor abandoned morality. Gringoire, in looking back upon his audience, sould see nothing but profiles.

With what bitterness did he see all his fabric of poetry and of glory thus falling to pieces! Only to think that this multitude had been on the point of rebelling against monsieur the bailiff through their impatience to hear his composition: and now that they had had it, they were indifferent about it—that same performance which had begun amid such unanimous acclamation! Everlasting ebb and flow of the popular favour! Only to think, that they had been on the point of hanging the bailiff's sergeants!—what would he not have given to have returned to that blissful hour!

The usher's brutal monologue ceased at last; everybody had arrived: so that Gringoire took breath; and the actors were going on bravely, when Maître Coppenole, the hosier, rose suddenly, and Gringoire heard him deliver, in the midst of the universal attention to his piece, this abominable harangue:

'Messieurs the citizens and squires of Paris—by the Holy Rood! I know not what we be doing here. I do indeed see, down in that corner, upon that stage, some people who look as if they wanted to fight. I know not whether that be what ye call a mystery; but I do know that 'tis not amusing. They belabour one another with their tongues, but nothing more. For this quarter of an hour I've been waiting the first blow—but nothing comes—they're cowards, and maul one another but with foul words. You should have had boxers from London or Rotterdam. Aye! then indeed we should have had hard knocks, which ye might have heard even out upon the square—but those creatures there are pitiful. They should at least give us a Morris-dance or some other piece of mummery. This is not what I was told it was to be—I'd been promised a feast of fools with an election of the Lord of Misrule. We at Ghent, too, have our Fools' Pope; and in that, by the Rood! we're behind nobody. But we do thus:—a mob comes together, as here for instance; then each in his turn goes and puts his head through a hole and makes faces at the others; he who makes the ugliest face according to general acclamation, is chosen pope. That's our way, and it's very diverting. Shall we make your pope after the fashion of my country? At any rate it will be less tiresome than listening to those babblers. If they've a mind to come and try their hands at face-making, they shall be in the game. What say ye, my masters? Here's a droll sample enough of both sexes to give us a right hearty Flemish laugh, and we can show ugly mugs enow to give us hopes of a fine grinning-match.'

Gringoire would fain have replied, but amazement, resentment, and indignation deprived him of utterance. Besides, the motion made by the popular hosier was received with such enthusiasm by those townsfolk, flattered at being called squires, that all resistance would have been unavailing. All he could now do was to go with the stream. Gringoire hid his face with both his hands, not being so fortunate as to possess a mantle wherewith to veil his countenance like the Agamemnon of Timanthes.

5

Quasimodo

In the twinkling of an eye, everything was ready for putting Coppenole's idea into execution. Townspeople, students and clerks had all set themselves to work. The small chapel, situated opposite to the marble table, was fixed upon to be the scene of the grimaces. The glass being broken out of one of the divisions of the pretty rose-shaped window over the doorway, left free a circle of stone through which it was agreed that the candidates should pass their heads. To reach it they had to climb upon two casks which had been laid hold of somewhere and placed one upon another. It was settled that each candidate, whether man or woman (for they might make a popess), in order to leave fresh and entire the impression of their grimace, should cover their faces and keep themselves unseen in the chapel until the moment of making their appearance. In less than an instant the chapel was filled with competitors, and the door was closed upon them.

Coppenole, from his place in the gallery, ordered everything, directed everything, arranged everything. During the confusion, the cardinal, no less out of countenance than Gringoire himself, had, on pretext of business and of the hour of vespers, retired with all his suite; while the crowd, among whom his arrival had caused so great a sensation, seemed not to be in the slightest degree interested in his departure. Guillaume Rym was the only one who remarked the retreat of his Eminence. The popular attention, like the sun, pursued its revolution; after beginning at one end of the hall it had stayed for awhile at the middle, and was now at the other end. The marble table, the brocaded gallery, had each had its season of interest; and it was now the turn of Louis XI's chapel. The field was henceforward clear for every sort of extravagance; no one remained but the Flemings and the mob.

The grimaces commenced. The first face that appeared at the hole, with eyelids turned up to show the red, cavernous mouth, and a forehead wrinkled in like our hussar boots in the time of the Empire, excited such an inextinguishable burst of laughter that Homer would have taken all those boors for gods. Nevertheless, the Grande Salle was anything but an Olympus, as no one could better testify than Gringoire's own poor Jupiter. A second face, and a third, succeeded—then another—then another,—the spectators each time laughing and stamping their feet with delight. There was in this spectacle a certain delirious joy—a certain intoxication and fascination—of which it is difficult to give an idea to the reader of the present day and polite society. Let him imagine a series of visages, presenting in succession every geometrical figure, from the triangle to the trapezium, from the cone to the polyhedron—every human expression, from that of anger to that of lust—every age, from the wrinkles of the new-born infant to those of extreme old age—every religious phantasm, from Faunus to Beelzebub—every animal profile, from the jowl to the beak, from the snout to the muzzle. Picture to yourself all the grotesque heads carved on the Pont-Neuf, those nightmares petrified by the hand of Germain Pilon, taking life and breath, and coming one after another to look you in the face with flaming eyes—all the masks of a Venetian carnival passing successively before your eye-glass—in short, a sort of human kaleidoscope.

The orgie became more and more Flemish. Teniers himself would have given but a very imperfect idea of it. Imagine the 'battle' of Salvator Rosa turned to a bacchanal. There was no longer any distinction of scholars, ambassadors, townspeople, men, or women. There was now neither Clopin Trouillefou, nor Gilles Lecornu, nor Marie Quartre-Livres, nor Robin Poussepain. All were confounded in the common license. The Grande Salle had become, as it were, one vast furnace of audacity and joviality, in which every mouth was a shout, every face a grimace, every figure a posture—the sum total howling and roaring. The strange visages that came one after another to grind their teeth at the broken window were like so many fresh brands cast upon the fire; and from all that effervescent multitude there escaped, as the exhalation of the furnace, a noise, shar p, penetrating like the buzzing of the wings of gnats.

'Curse me,' cries one, 'if ever I saw the like of that.'

'Only look at that face.'

'It's nothing.'

'Let's have another.'

'Guillemette Maugerepuis, just look at that bull's muzzle—it wants nothing but horns. It can't be thy husband.'

'Here comes another.'

'By the pope! what sort of a grin's that?'

'Hello! that's not fair. You must show but thy face.'

'That devil, Perette Calebotte! She is capable of such a trick.'

'Nöel! Nöel!'

'Oh! I smother!'

'There's one that can't get his ears through'—etc., etc.

We must, however, do justice to our friend Jehan. In the midst of this infernal revel, he was still to be seen at the top of his pillar like a middy on a top-sail. He was exerting himself with incredible fury. His mouth was wide open, and there issued from it a shriek which, however, no one heard—not that it was drowned by the general clamour, all intense as that was—but because, no doubt, it attained the utmost limit of perceptible sharp notes, of the twelve thousand vibrations of Sauveur, or the eight thousand of Biot.

As for Gringoire—as soon as the first moment of depression was over, he had regained his self-possession. He had hardened himself against adversity. 'Go on,' he had said for the third time to his players—who, after all, were mere talking machines—then he strode up and down before the marble table; he felt tempted to go and take his turn at the hole in the chapel-window, if only to have the pleasure of making faces at the ungrateful people. 'But no—that would be unworthy of us—no revenge—let us struggle to the last,' muttered he to himself—'the power of poetry over the people is great—I will bring them back. We will see which of the two shall prevail—grimaces or belles-lettres.'

Alas! he was left the sole spectator of his piece.

This was worse than before; for instead of profiles, he now saw only backs.

We mistake. The big, patient man whom he had already consulted at a critical moment had remained with his face toward the stage; as for Gisquette and Liénarde, they had deserted long ago.

Gringoire was touched to the heart by the fidelity of his only remaining spectator; he went up to and accosted him, at the same time slightly shaking him by the arm, for the good man had leaned himself against the balustrade, and was taking a gentle nap.

'Monsieur,' said Gringoire, 'I thank you.'

'Monsieur,' answered the big man with a yawn, 'what for?'

'I see what annoys you,' returned the poet; 'all that noise prevents you from hearing comfortably; but make yourself easy —your name shall go down to posterity. Your name, if you please?'

'Renauld Château, Keeper of the Seals of the Châtelet of Paris, at your service.'

'Monsieur,' said Gringoire, 'you are here the sole representative of the Muses.'

'You are too polite, monsieur,' answered the Keeper of the Seals of the Châtelet.

'You are the only one,' continued Gringoire, 'who has given suitable attention to the piece. What do you think of it?'

'Why—why,' returned the portly magistrate, but half awake —'in effect, it was very diverting.'

Gringoire was obliged to content himself with this eulogy, for a thunder of applause, mingled with a prodigious exclamation, cut short their conversation. The Lord of Misrule was at last elected.

'Noël! Noël! Noël!' cried the people from all sides.

It was indeed a miraculous grin that now beamed through the Gothic aperture. After all the figures, pentagonal, hexagonal and heteroclite, which had succeeded each other at the window, without realizing that idea of the grotesque which had formed itself in the imagination of the people heated by the orgie, it required nothing less to gain their suffrages than the sublime grimace which now dazzled the assemblage. Maître Coppenole himself applauded; and Clopin Trouillefou, who had been a candidate, (and God knows his visage could attain an intensity of ugliness), acknowledged himself to be outdone. We shall do likewise. We shall not attempt to give the reader an idea of that tetrahedron nose—that horse-shoe mouth—that small left eye overshadowed by a red bushy brow, while the right eye disappeared entirely under a monstrous wart—of those straggling teeth with breaches here and there like the battlements of a fortress—of that horny lip, over which one of those teeth projected like the tusk of an elephant—of that forked chin—and, above all, of the expression diffused over the whole—that mixture of malice, astonishment and melancholy. Imagination alone can picture this combination.

The acclamation was unanimous; the crowd precipitated itself toward the chapel, and the happy Lord of Misrule was led out in triumph. And now the surprise and admiration of the people redoubled. They found the wondrous grin to be but his ordinary face.

Or rather, his whole person was a grimace. His large head, bristling with red hair—between his shoulders an enormous hump, to which he had a corresponding projection in front—a framework of thighs and legs, so strangely gone astray that they touched only at the knees, and when viewed in front, looked like two sickles joined together by the handles—sprawling feet—monstrous hands —and yet, with all that deformity, a certain awe-inspiring vigour, agility and courage—strange exception to the everlasting rule which prescribes that strength, like beauty, shall result from harmony. Such was the pope whom the fools had just chosen.

One would have said a giant that had been broken and awkwardly mended.

When this sort of cyclop appeared on the threshold of the chapel, motionless, squat, almost as broad as he was high—'squared by the base,' as a great man has expressed it—the populace recognized him at once by his coat half red and half violet, figured over with little silver bells, and still more by the perfection of his ugliness —and exclaimed with one voice: 'It's Quasimodo the bell-ringer! It's Quasimodo the hunchback of Notre-Dame! Quasimodo the one-eyed! Quasimodo the bandy-legged! Noël! Noël!'

The poor devil, it seems, had a choice of surnames.

'All ye pregnant women, get out of the way!' cried the scholars.

'And all that want to be,' added Joannes.

The women, in fact, hid their faces.

'Oh, the horrid baboon!' said one.

'As wicked as he is ugly,' added another.

'It's the devil!' added a third.

'I have the misfortune to live near Notre-Dame, and at night I hear him scrambling in the gutter on the roof.'

'With the cats.'

'He always is on our roofs.'

'He casts spells at us down our chimneys.'

'The other night he came and grinned at me through my attic window. I thought it was a man. I was in such a fright!'

'I'm sure he goes to meet the witches—he once left a broomstick on my leads.'

'Oh, the shocking face of the hunchback!'

'Oh, the horrid creature!'

'Ugh!'

The men, on the contrary, were delighted, applauding loudly.

Quasimodo, the object of the tumult, stood in the doorway of the chapel, gloomy and grave, letting himself be admired.

One of the students (Robin Poussepain, we believe,) laughed in his face, rather too near. Quasimodo quietly took him by the belt and threw him half-a-score yards among the crowd, without uttering a word.

Maître Coppenole, wondering, went up to him. 'By the Rood! Holy Father! why, thou hast the prettiest ugliness I did ever see in my life! Thou wouldst deserve to be pope at Rome as well as at Paris.'

So saying, he clapped his hand merrily upon the other's shoulder. Quasimodo never moved. Coppenole continued: 'Thou art a fellow with whom I long to feast, though it should cost me a new douzain of twelve livres tournois. What say'st thou to it?'

Quasimodo made no answer.

'By the Holy Rood!' cried the hosier, 'art thou deaf?'

He was indeed deaf.

However, he began to be impatient at Coppenole's manners, and he all at once turned toward him with so formidable a grinding of his teeth that the Flemish giant recoiled like a bull-dog before a cat.

A circle of terror and respect was instantly made round this strange personage, the radius of which was at least fifteen geometrical paces. And an old woman explained to Maître Coppenole that Quasimodo was deaf.

'Deaf?' cried the hosier, with his boisterous Flemish laugh. 'Holy Rood! then he's a pope indeed!'

'Ho! I know him,' cried Jehan, who was at last come down from his capital to have a nearer look at Quasimodo; 'it's my brother the archdeacon's bell-ringer. Good-day to you, Quasimodo.'

'What a devil of a man,' said Robin Poussepain, who was bruised from his fall. 'He shows himself—and you see he's a hunchback. He walks—and you see he's bow-legged. He looks at you—and you see he's short an eye. You talk to him—and you find he's deaf. Why, what does this Polyphemus with his tongue?'

'He talks when he lists,' said the old woman. 'He's lost his hearing with ringing of the bells. He's not dumb.'

'No—he's that perfection short,' observed Jehan.

'And has an eye too many,' added Robin Poussepain.

'No, no,' said Jehan, judiciously ; 'a one-eyed man is much more incomplete than a blind man, for he knows what it is that's wanting.'

Meanwhile, all the beggars, all the lackeys, all the cutpurses, together with the students, had gone in procession to fetch from the wardrobe of the clerks the pasteboard tiara and the mock robe appropriated to the Fools' Pope or Lord of Misrule. Quasimodo allowed himself to be arrayed in them without a frown, and with a sort of proud docility. They then seated him upon a parti-coloured litter. Twelve officers of the brotherhood of Fools, laying hold of the poles that were attached to it, hoisted him upon their shoulders; and a sort of bitter and disdainful joy seemed to overspread the sullen face of the cyclop when he beheld under his deformed feet all those heads of handsome and well-shaped men. Then the whole bawling and tattered procession set forth to make, according to custom, the inner circuit of the galleries of the Palace, before parading through the streets and squares.

6

Esmeralda

WE are delighted to inform our readers that during all this scene Gringoire and his piece had held out. His actors, goaded on by himself, had not ceased spouting their parts, nor had he ceased to listen. He had resigned himself to the uproar, and was determined to go on to the end, not despairing of a return of public attention. This gleam of hope revived when he saw Quasimodo, Coppenole, and the noisy train of the Fool's Pope march with great clamour out of the hall. The rest of the crowd rushing eagerly after them. 'Good!' said he to himself—'there go all the marplots at last!' But, unfortunately, all the hare-brained people composed the audience. In a twinkling the great hall was empty.

It is true there still remained a few spectators, some scattered about, and others grouped around the pillars—women, old men and children—exhausted with the crush and the tumult. A few students still remained astride the window seats looking out into the Place.

'Well,' thought Gringoire, 'here are still enough to hear the end of my mystery. They are few, but they are a select, a literary audience.'

But a moment later a symphony, which was to have produced the greatest impression at the arrival of the Holy Virgin, was missing. Gringoire discovered that his music had been carried off by the procession of the Fools' Pope. 'Do without,' said he stoically.

He approached a group of townspeople who seemed to him to be talking about his piece. Here is the fragment of their conversation which he heard:

'Maître Cheneteau, you know the Hôtel de Navarre, which belonged to Monsieur de Nemours?'

'Oh, yes—opposite to the Chapelle de Braque.'

'Well—the Treasury has just let it to Guillaume Alixandre, heraldry painter, for six livres eight Paris pence a year.'

'How rents are rising!'

'Well, well!' said Gringoire, with a sigh—'but the others are listening.'

'Comrades!' suddenly cried one of the young fellows in the windows, 'Esmeralda! Esmeralda is in the Square!'

This word produced a magical effect. All who remained in the hall rushed toward the windows, climbing up the walls to see, and repeating, 'Esmeralda! Esmeralda!'

At the same time was heard a great noise of applause without.

'What do they mean by Esmeralda?' said Gringoire, clasping his hands in despair. 'Heavens! it seems to be the turn of the windows now!'

He turned toward the marble table, and saw that the performance was interrupted. It was precisely the moment when Jupiter was to enter with his thunder. But Jupiter remained motionless at the foot of the stage.

'Michel Giborne!' cried the irritated poet, 'what art thou doing there? is that thy part?—go up, I tell thee.'

'Alas!' exclaimed Jupiter, 'one of the students has taken away the ladder.'

Gringoire looked. It was but too true. All communication between his plot and its solution was cut off.

'The rascal!' he muttered; 'and why did he take that ladder?'

'To go and see Esmeralda,' cried Jupiter in a piteous tone. 'He said: "Hello! here's a ladder nobody's using;" and away he went with it.'

This was the finishing blow. Gringoire received it with resignation.

'The devil take you all!' said he to the players; 'and if they pay me I'll pay you.'

Then he made his retreat, hanging his head, but the last in the field, like a general who has fought well.

And as he descended the winding staircase of the Palace, 'A fine drove of asses and dolts are these Parisians!' he muttered between his teeth. 'They come to hear a mystery, and pay no attention to it. They were occupied with everybody else—with Clopin Trouillefou—with the cardinal—with Coppenole—with Quasimodo—with the devil!—but with our Lady, the Virgin, not at all. Had I but known it, I'd have given you Virgin Marys, you wretched gapers! And I! for me to come here to see faces, and see nothing but backs!—to be a poet, and have the success of an apothecary! True it is that Homer begged his bread through the villages of Greece, and that Naso died in exile among the Muscovites. But the devil flay me if I understand what they mean by their Esmeralda. Of what language can that word be?—it must be Egyptian!'

BOOK TWO

I

From Charybdis into Scylla

THE night comes on early in January. The streets were already growing dark when Gringoire quitted the Palace. This nightfall pleased him; he longed to reach some obscure and solitary alley, that he might there meditate at his ease, and that the philosopher might lay the first healing balm to the wounds of the poet. Philosophy was, indeed, his only refuge, for he knew not where to find a lodging place. After the signal failure of his first dramatic attempt, he dared not return to that which he occupied in the Rue Grenier sur l'Eau, opposite to the Port au Foin; having reckoned upon what the provost was to give him for his epithalamium to enable him to pay to Maître Guillaume Doulx-Sire, collector of the taxes upon cloven-footed beasts brought into Paris, the six months' rent which he owed him, that is to say, twelve pence of Paris, twelve times the value of all he possessed in the world, including his breeches, his shirt and his hat. After a moment's reflection, while sheltered under the wicket-gate of the prison belonging to the treasurer of the Sainte Chapelle, as to what place of refuge he should select for the night, all the pavements of Paris being at his service, he recollected having espied, the week before, in the Rue de la Savaterie, at the door of a parliamentary counsellor, a footstone for mounting on mule-back, and having remarked to himself that this stone might serve upon occasion as an excellent pillow for a beggar or a poet. He thanked Providence for having sent him this happy idea; but as he was preparing to cross the Square of the Palace in order to reach the tortuous labyrinth of the City, formed by the windings of all those sister streets, the Rue de la Barillerie, Rue de la Vieille-Draperie, Rue de la Savaterie, Rue de la Juiverie, etc., which are still standing, with their houses of nine stories, he saw the procession of the Fools' Pope, which was also issuing from the Palace, and rushing across the courtyard with loud shouts, with great glare of torches, and with Gringoire's own band of music. This sight revived the blow to his pride, and he fled. In the bitterness of his dramatic misadventure, everything which recalled to his mind the festival of the day irritated his wound, and made it bleed afresh.

He turned to cross the Bridge of Saint Michel, where he found boys running up and down with squibs and crackers.

'A plague on the fireworks!' said Gringoire; and he turned back upon the Exchange Bridge. Attached to the front of the houses at the entrance of the bridge were three banners, representing the king, the dauphin and Margaret of Flanders; and six bannerets, on which were portrayed the Duke of Austria, the Cardinal de Bourbon, and Monsieur de Beaujeu, Madame Jeanne of France, and Monsieur the bastard of Bourbon, and I know not who else, all illuminated by torches—and a crowd admiring.

'Happy painter, Jehan Fourbault!' said Gringoire, with a heavy sigh, as he turned his back upon the banners. A street lay before him; and it seemed so dark and forsaken that he hoped there to escape his mental sufferings as well as the illuminations; he plunged into it accordingly. A few moments later his foot struck against some obstacle; he stumbled and fell. It was the bundle of hawthorn which the clerks had placed in the morning at the door of a president of the Parliament in honour of the day. Gringoire bore this new accident heroically; he arose, and reached the waterside. After leaving behind him the Civil Tower and the Criminal Tower, and passing along by the high wall of the king's gardens, on that unpaved shore in which he sank to the ankles in mud, he arrived at the western end of the City, and stood gazing for some time at the small island of the Passeur aux Vaches (cow ferry-man), which has since disappeared under the bronze horse and esplanade of the Pont-Neuf. The islet appeared to his eyes in the darkness as a black mass beyond the narrow stream of whitish water which separated him from it. He could discern by the rays of a small glimmering light a sort of hut in the form of a beehive, in which the ferryman sheltered himself during the night.

'Happy ferryman!' thought Gringoire, 'thou dreamest not of glory! thou writest not wedding songs—what are the marriages of kings and Burgundian duchesses to thee! Thou knowest no Marguerites but the daisies which thy April greensward gives thy cows to crop!—while I, a poet, am hooted—and shiver—and owe twelve pence—and my shoe-sole is so transparent that thou mightest use it to glaze thy lantern! Thanks, ferryman! thy cabin gives rest to my eyes, and makes me forget Paris!'

He was awakened from his almost lyric ecstasy by a great double Saint John's rocket, which suddenly arose from the peaceful cabin. It was the ferryman also taking his share in the festivities of the day, and letting off his fireworks.

This rocket sent a shiver through Gringoire.

'Oh, cursed holiday!' cried he, 'wilt thou follow me everywhere —good God! even to the ferryman's hut!'

Then he looked into the Seine at his feet, and felt a horrible temptation.

'Oh!' said he, 'how willingly would I drown myself—if the water were not so cold!'

Then he took a desperate resolution. It was—since he could not escape the Fools' Pope, Jehan Fourbaults' paintings, the bundles of hawthorn, the squibs and the rockets—to plunge boldly into the very heart of the illumination, and go to the Place de Grève.

'At least,' thought he, 'I shall perhaps get a brand to warm my fingers at the bonfire; and I shall manage to sup on some morsel from the three great shields of royal sugar that were to be set out on the public refectory.'

2

The Place de Grève

THERE remains to-day but a small and scarcely perceptible vestige of the Place de Grève (one of the places for public executions in the old city of Paris), such as it existed formerly; all that is left is the charming turret which occupies the northern angle of the Square, and which, already buried under the ignoble white-washing which obstructs the delicate lines of its carving, will soon, perhaps, have totally disappeared, under that increase of new houses which is so rapidly consuming all the old *façades* in Paris.

Those who, like ourselves, never pass over the Place de Grève without casting a look of pity and sympathy on this poor little tower, squeezed between two ruins of the time of Louis XV, can easily reconstruct in their mind's eye the assemblage of edifices to which it belonged, and thus imagine themselves in the old Gothic Square of the fifteenth century.

It was then, as now, an irregular place, bounded on one side by the quay, and on the three others by a series of lofty houses, narrow and sombre. In the daytime you might admire the variety of these buildings, carved in stone or in wood, and already presenting complete examples of the various kinds of domestic architecture of the Middle Ages, going back from the fifteenth to the eleventh century—from the perpendicular window which was beginning to supersede the Gothic to the circular Roman arch which the Gothic had in turn supplanted, and which still occupied underneath the first story of that ancient house of the Tour-Rolland, forming the angle of the Place with the Seine, on the side of the Rue de la Tannerie. By night, nothing was distinguishable of that mass of buildings but the black indentation of their gables, extending its range of acute angles round three sides of the Place. For it is one of the essential differences between the towns of that day and those of the present, that now it is the fronts of the houses that look to the squares and streets, but then it was the gable ends. During the two centuries past they have turned fairly around.

In the centre of the eastern side of the Square rose a heavy and hybrid construction formed by three dwellings juxtaposed. The whole was called by three several names, describing its history, its purpose and its architecture; the Maison au Dauphin, or Dauphin's House, because Charles V, when dauphin, had lived there—the Trades House, because it was used as the Hôtel de Ville, or Town Hall—and the Maison aux Piliers (*domus ad piloria*) or Pillar House, on account of a series of heavy pillars which supported its three stories. The City had there all that a goodly town like Paris needs; a chapel to pray in; a court-room for holding magisterial sittings, and, when needed, reprimanding the king's officers; and in the garrets an arsenal stored with artillery and ammunition. For the good people of Paris, well knowing that it was not sufficient, in every emergency, to plead and to pray for the franchises of their city, had always in reserve, in the attics of the Town Hall, some few good though rusty arquebusses.

The Square of La Grève had then that sinister aspect which it still derives from the execrable ideas which it awakens, and from the gloomy-looking Town Hall built by Dominique Bocador, which has taken the place of the Maison aux Piliers. It must be observed that a permanent gibbet and pillory, *a justice* and *a ladder*, as they were then called, erected side by side in the centre of the Square, contributed not a little to make the passer-by avert his eyes from this fatal spot, where so many beings in full life and health had suffered their last agony; and which was to give birth, fifty years later, to that Saint Vallier's fever, as it was called, that disease which was but the terror of the scaffold, the most monstrous of all maladies, inflicted as it was, not by the hand of God, but by that of man.

It is consolatory, we may remark, to reflect that the punishment of death, which, three centuries ago, with its iron wheels, with its stone gibbets, with all its apparatus for torture permanently fixed in the ground, encumbered the Square of the Grève, the Market Place, the Place Dauphine, the Croix du Trahoir, the Pig Market, the hideous Montfaucon, the Barrière des Sergens, the Place aux Chats, the Gate of Saint Denis, Champeaux, the Baudets Gate, the Porte Saint Jacques—not to mention the innumerable pilleries of the provosts, of the bishop, of the chapters, of the abbots, of the priors who dealt justice—not to mention judicial drownings in the river Seine—it is consolatory to reflect that now, after losing, one after another every fragment of her panoply, her profusion of executions, her refined and fanciful penal laws, her torture, for applying which she made anew every five years a bed of leather in the Grand Châtelet—this ancient queen of feudal society, nearly thrust from our laws and our towns, tracked from code to code, driven from place to place, now possesses, in our vast metropolis of Paris, but one dishonoured corner of the Grève—but one miserable guillotine—stealthy—timid—ashamed—which seems always afraid of being taken in the act, so quickly does it disappear after giving its blow.

3

Kisses for Blows

WHEN Pierre Gringoire arrived at the Place de Grève he was benumbed with cold. He had gone over the Miller's Bridge to avoid the crowd on the Pont au Change and Jehan Fourbault's banners; but the wheels of all the bishop's mills had splashed him as he crossed, so that his coat was wet through; and it seemed to him that the fate of his piece had rendered him even colder. Accordingly, he hurried toward the bonfire which burned magnificently in the middle of the Place; a considerable crowd, however, encircled it.

'You villainous Parisians!' said he to himself (for Gringoire, like a true dramatic poet, was addicted to monologues), 'so, now you keep me from the fire! And yet I've good need of a chimney-corner. My shoes are sponges in the water—and then, all those execrable mills have been raining upon me. The devil take the Bishop of Paris with his mills! I wonder what a bishop can do with a mill! Does he think, from being a bishop, to turn miller? If he only wants my malediction to do so, I heartily give it him, and his cathedral, and his mills! Let us see, now, if any of those lazy rascals will disturb themselves. What are they doing there the while? Warming themselves—a fine pleasure, truly! Looking at a hundred bunches of fagots burning—a fine sight, to be sure!'

On looking nearer, however, he perceived that the circle of people was much wider than was requisite to warm themselves at the bonfire, and that this concourse was not attracted alone by the beauty of a hundred blazing bundles.

In a wide space left clear between the fire and the crowd, a young girl was dancing.

Whether she was a human being, a fairy, or an angel, was what Gringoire, sceptical philosopher and ironical poet as he was, could not at the first moment decide, so much was he fascinated by this dazzling vision.

She was not tall, but the elasticity of her slender shape made her appear so. She was a brunette, but it was obvious that in the daylight her complexion would have that golden gleam seen upon the women of Spain and of Rome. Her tiny foot, as well, was Andalusian, for it was at once tight and at ease in its light and graceful sandal. She was dancing, turning, whirling upon an antique Persian carpet spread negligently under her feet; and each time as she turned and her radiant countenance passed before you, her large black eyes seemed to flash upon you.

Every look was fixed upon her, every mouth was open in the circle about her; and, indeed, while she danced to the sound of the tambourine which her two round and delicate arms lifted above her head—slender, fragile, active, as a wasp—with her golden girdle without a fold—her skirt of varied colours swelling out below her slender waist, giving momentary glimpses of her fine-formed legs—her round bared shoulders—her black hair and her sparkling eyes—she looked like something more than human.

'Truly,' thought Gringoire, ''tis a salamander—a nymph—a goddess—a bacchante of Mount Mænalus!'

At that moment one of the braids of the salamander's hair became detached, and a small piece of brass that had been attached to it rolled upon the ground.

'Ah! no,' said he, ''tis a gypsy.'

All illusion disappeared.

She resumed her dance. She took up from the ground two swords, the points of which she supported upon her forehead, making them whirl in one direction, while she turned in the other. She was indeed no other than a gypsy. Yet, disenchanted as was Gringoire, the scene, taken altogether, was not without its charm, not without its magic. The bonfire cast upon her a red flaring light, which flickered brightly upon the circle of faces of the crowd and the brown forehead of the young girl and, at the extremities of the Square threw a wan reflection, mingled with the wavering shadows—on one side, upon the old dark wrinkled front of the Maison aux Piliers—on the other, upon the stone arms of the gibbet.

Among the thousand faces tinged by the scarlet light, there was one which seemed to be more than all the rest absorbed in the contemplation of the dancer. It was the face of a man, austere, calm and sombre. This man, whose costume was hidden by the crowd that surrounded him, seemed to be not more than thirty-five years of age; yet he was bald, having only a few thin tufts of hair about his temples, which were already gray; his broad and high forehead was beginning to be furrowed with wrinkles; but in his deep-set eyes there shone an extraordinary youth, an intense animation, a depth of passion. He kept them constantly fixed upon the gypsy;

and while the giddy young girl of sixteen danced and swung to the delight of all, his reverie seemed to grow more and more gloomy. From time to time a smile and a sigh met each other on his lips; but the smile was far more sad than the sigh.

The girl, breathless, stopped at last, while the crowd lovingly applauded.

'Djali!' cried the gypsy.

Gringoire then saw come up to her a little white goat, alert, brisk and glossy, with gilt horns, gilt hoofs and a gilt collar, which he had not before observed, because until that moment it had been lying crouched upon one corner of the carpet, looking at her mistress dance.

'Djali,' said the dancer, 'it's your turn now;' and sitting down, she gracefully held out her tambourine to the goat.

'Djali,' she continued, 'what month of the year is this?'

The animal lifted its fore-foot and struck one stroke upon the tambourine. It was, in fact, the first month of the year. The crowd applauded.

'Djali!' resumed the girl, turning her tambourine another way, 'what day of the month is it?'

Djali lifted her little golden foot, and struck six times upon the tambourine.

'Djali!' said the gypsy, with a new turn of the tambourine, 'what hour of the day is it?'

Djali struck seven strokes, and at that very moment the clock of the Maison aux Piliers rang seven.

The people were wonderstruck.

'There is witchcraft in all that,' said a sinister voice in the crowd. It was that of the bald man who had his eyes constantly upon the gypsy.

She shuddered and turned around. But the applause burst forth again and smothered the sinister exclamation.

Indeed, they so completely effaced it from her mind, that she continued to interrogate her goat.

'Djali!' said she, 'how does Maître Guichard Grand-Remy, captain of the town pistoliers, go in the procession at Candlemas?'

Djali reared on her hind legs and began to bleat, marching at the same time with so seemly a gravity that the whole circle of spectators burst into a laugh at this parody of the hypocritical devotion of the captain of pistoliers.

'Djali!' resumed the girl, emboldened by this increased success, 'how does Maître Jacques Charmolue, the king's attorney in the ecclesiastical court—how does he preach?'

The goat sat down on her haunches and began to bleat, shaking its fore-feet after so strange a fashion, that, with the exception of the bad French and the bad Latin, it was Jacques Charmolue to the life, gesture, accent and attitude.

The crowd applauded with all their might.

'Sacrilege! profanation!' cried the voice of the bald-headed man.

The gypsy turned round again.

'Ah!' said she, 'it's that ugly man!'

Then putting out her lower lip beyond the upper one she made a little pouting grimace which seemed familiar to her, turned upon her heel, and began to collect in her tambourine the contributions of the multitude.

Big pieces of silver, little pieces of silver, pennies and farthings were now showered upon her. In taking her round, she all at once came in front of Gringoire; and as he, in perfect absence of mind, thrust his hand into his pocket, she stopped, expecting something. 'Diable!' exclaimed the poet, finding at the bottom of his pocket the reality, that is to say, nothing at all; the pretty girl standing before him all the while, looking at him with her large eyes, holding out her tambourine, and waiting. Gringoire perspired from every pore.

Had he all the riches of Peru in his pocket, he would assuredly have given it to the dancer; but Gringoire had not the wealth of Peru—nor, indeed, was America yet discovered.

Fortunately an unexpected incident came to his relief.

'Wilt thou begone, thou Egyptian locust?' cried a harsh voice from the darkest corner of the Place.

The girl turned affrighted. This was not the voice of the bald-headed man; it was the voice of a woman—bigoted and malicious.

This cry, which frightened the gypsy, highly delighted a troop of children that were rambling about.

'It's the recluse of the Tour-Rolland,' cried they with uproarious bursts of laughter—'it's the nun that's scolding. Hasn't she had her supper? Let's carry her something from the town buffet.'

And they all ran toward the Maison aux Piliers.

Gringoire had availed himself of this agitation of the dancer to disappear among the crowd. The shouts of the children reminded him that he too had not supped. He therefore hastened to the public buffet. But the little rogues had better legs than he, and when he arrived they had cleared the table. They had not even left one wretched cake at five sous the pound. There remained nothing but the bare decorations against the wall—the light fleurs-de-lis intermingled with rose-trees painted there in 1434 by Mathieu Biterne; and they offered but a meagre supper.

'Tis an unpleasant thing to go without one's dinner. 'Tis less gratifying still to go without one's supper, and not know where to sleep. Gringoire was at that point. Without food, without lodging, he found himself pressed by necessity on every hand, and he thought necessity very ungracious. He had long discovered this truth—that Jupiter created man in a fit of misanthropy, and that throughout the life of the wisest man his destiny keeps his philosophy in a state of siege. For his own part, he had never found the blockade so complete. He heard his stomach sound a truce, and he thought it very unkind that his evil destiny should reduce his philosophy by simple starvation.

He was sinking more and more deeply into this melancholy reverie, when he was suddenly startled from it by the sound of a strange but very sweet song. It was the young gypsy singing.

Her voice had the same character as her dance and her beauty. It had an undefinable charm—something clear, sonorous, aerial—winged, as it were. There was a continued succession of harmonious notes, of swells, of unexpected cadences—then simple strains, interspersed with sharp and shrill notes—then trills that would have bewildered a nightingale—then soft undulations, which rose and fell like the bosom of the youthful songstress. The expression of her sweet face followed with singular flexibility every capricious variation of her song, from the wildest inspiration to the most chastened dignity. She seemed now all frenzy, and now all majesty.

The words that she sang were in a language unintelligible to Gringoire, and which seemed to be unknown to herself, so little did the expression which she gave in singing correspond with the sense of the words. For instance, she gave these four lines with the most sportive gaiety:

> *Un cofre de gran riqueza*
> *Hallaron dentro un pilar,*
> *Dentro del, nuevas banderas*
> *Con figuras de espantar.* *

And a moment after, at the tone which she gave to this stanza—

> *Alarabes de cavallo*
> *Sin poderse menear,*
> *Con espadas, y los cuellos,*
> *Ballestas de buen echar . . .* †

Gringoire felt the tears come to his eyes. Yet above all her song breathed gaiety, and she seemed to warble, like a bird, from pure lightness of heart.

---

* A coffer of great richness
   In a pillar's heart was found,
   Within it lay new banners,
   With figures to astound.

† The Moorish horsemen
   Without being able to move,
   With swords, and at their necks
   Ready cross-bows . . .

The gypsy's song had disturbed Gringoire's reverie, but it was as the swan disturbs the water. He listened to it with a sort of ecstasy, and oblivion of all else. It was the first moment, for several hours, in which he felt no suffering.

The moment was short.

The same female voice which had interrupted the gypsy's dance, now interrupted her song.

'Wilt thou be silent, thou infernal cricket?' it cried, still from the same dark corner of the Place.

The poor 'cricket' stopped short, and Gringoire clapped his hands over his ears.

'Oh!' he cried, 'thou cursed, broken-toothed saw, that comest to break the lyre!'

The rest of the bystanders murmured with him. 'The devil take the nun!' cried some of them. And the invisible disturber might have found cause to repent of her attacks upon the gypsy had not their attention been diverted at that moment by the procession of the Fools' Pope, which, after traversing many a street and square, was now pouring into the Place de Grève, with all its torches and all its clamour.

This procession, which our readers have seen take its departure from the Palace, had increased on the way, having enlisted all the ragamuffins, the unemployed thieves and idle scamps in Paris, so that when it reached the Grève it presented quite a respectable aspect.

First of all marched the Egyptians. The Duke of Egypt was at their head, with his counts on foot, holding his bridle and stirrup; behind them came the Egyptians, men and women, pell-mell, with their infants squalling upon their shoulders; all of them, duke, counts and people, covered with rags and tinsel. Then followed the kingdom of Argot, that is, all the thieves of France, arranged in bands according to the order of their dignities, the least important walking first. Thus marched on, four abreast, with the different insignia of their degrees in that strange faculty, most of them crippled in some way or other—some limping, some with only one hand—the shoplifters, the false pilgrims, the card sharps, the pickpockets, the tramps, the rogues, the lepers and those who wore false sores, and those of hidden lives—denominations enough to have wearied Homer himself to enumerate, and some explanation of which will occur as we proceed. It was with some difficulty that you could discern, in the centre of the band of wharf rats, archisuppôts, arch thieves, the King of Argot himself, the 'Grand-Coësre,' as he was called, sitting squat in a little waggon drawn by two large dogs. After the kingdom of the Argotiers came the empire of Galilee (gamblers). Guillaume Rousseau, Emperor of the empire of Galilee, walking majestically in his robe of purple stained with wine, preceded by mummers dancing Pyrrhic dances, and surrounded by his mace-bearers, his under-strappers and the clerks of the chambre des comptes. Lastly came the members of the *basoche* (lawyers' clerks), with their garlanded staffs, their black gowns, their music, worthy of witches' Sabbath, and their great candles of yellow wax. In the centre of this latter crowd, the great officers of the brotherhood of Fools bore upon their shoulders a stretcher, more loaded with wax-tapers than the shrine of Sainte Geneviève in time of pestilence; and seated upon this stretcher shone, crosiered and mitred, the new Fools' Pope, the ringer of Notre-Dame, Quasimodo the hunchback.

Each division of this grotesque procession had its particular music. The Egyptians sounded their balafos and their African tabours. The Argotiers, a very unmusical race, had advanced no further than the viol, the buglehorn and the Gothic rubebbe of the twelfth century. The empire of Galilee had made little more progress. You could but just distinguish in its music the sounds of the ancient rebeck of the infancy of the art still limited to the do, re, mi. But it was around the Fools' Pope that were congregated, in magnificent discordance, all the musical riches of the age; there was nothing visible but ends of rebecks of all sizes and shapes; not to mention the flutes and the cuivres. Alas! our readers will recollect that it was poor Gringoire's orchestra.

It is not easy to give an idea of the expression of proud and beatific joy which the melancholy and hideous visage of Quasimodo had attained in the journey from the Palace to the Grève. It was the first thrill of vanity that he had ever experienced. He had hitherto experienced nothing but humiliation, disdain at his condition, and disgust for his person. So, deaf as he was, he nevertheless relished, like a true pope, the acclamations of that crowd whom he had hated because he felt himself hated by them. What though his people were a gathering of fools, of cripples, thieves and beggars—still they were a people, and he was a sovereign. And he took in earnest all the ironical applause and mock reverence which they gave him; with which, at the same time, we must not forget to observe there was mingled, in the minds of the crowd, a degree of fear quite real; for the hunchback was strong; though bow-legged, he was active; though deaf, he was malicious —three qualities which have the effect of tempering the ridicule.

Moreover, that the new Pope of the Fools analyzed the feelings which he experienced, or those which he inspired, we can by no means presume. The mind that was lodged in that misshapen body, was necessarily itself incomplete and dull of hearing; so that what he felt at that moment was both vague and confused to him. Only, joy beamed through all, and pride predominated. Around that dismal and unhappy countenance there was a perfect radiance.

It was, therefore, not without surprise and alarm that all at once, at the moment when Quasimodo, in that state of semi-intoxication, passed triumphantly before the Maison aux Piliers, a man was seen to dart from the crowd, and, with an angry gesture, snatch from his hands the crosier of gilt wood, ensign of his mock papacy.

The person who had this temerity was the man with the bald head, who, the moment before, standing in the crowd that encircled the gypsy, had chilled the poor girl's blood with his words of menace and hatred. He was in ecclesiastical dress. The moment he rushed forth from the crowd he was recognized by Gringoire, who had not before observed him. 'What!' said he, with a cry of astonishment. 'Why, 'tis my master in Hermes, Don Claude Frollo, the archdeacon! What the devil can he want with that one-eyed brute? He will be devoured!'

A cry of terror proceeded from the multitude. The formidable Quasimodo had leaped down from his seat; and the women turned away their eyes, that they might not see him tear the archdeacon to pieces.

He made one bound toward the priest, looked in his face, and then fell on his knees, before him.

The priest snatched his tiara from his head, broke his crosier, and rent his tinsel cope.

Quasimodo remained upon his knees, bowed down his head, and clasped his hands.

They then entered into a strange dialogue of signs and gestures, for neither of them uttered a word. The priest, erect, angry, threatening, imperious; Quasimodo prostrate, humble, suppliant. And yet it is certain that Quasimodo could have crushed the priest with his thumb.

At last the priest, roughly shaking Quasimodo's powerful shoulder, made him a sign to rise and follow.

Quasimodo rose accordingly.

Then the brotherhood of Fools, their first amazement having passed, offered to defend their pope, thus abruptly dethroned. The Egyptians, the Argotiers, and all the Basoche, came yelping round the priest.

Quasimodo, placing himself before the priest, gave full play the muscles of his athletic fists, and regarded the assailants, gnashing his teeth like an angry tiger.

The priest resumed his sombre gravity, and making a sign to Quasimodo, withdrew in silence.

Quasimodo walked before him, scattering the crowd in his passage.

When they had made their way through the populace and across the Place, the crowd of the curious and idle wished to follow them. Quasimodo then placed himself in the rear, and followed the archdeacon backwards, looking squat, snarling, monstrous, shaggy, gathering up his limbs, licking his tusks, growling like a wild beast, and swaying backward the crowd by a mere glance or gesture.

At length they both disappeared down a gloomy narrow street, into which no one dared to follow them; so effectually was its entrance barred by the mere image of Quasimodo gnashing his teeth.

'All this is astonishing,' said Gringoire to himself; 'but where the devil shall I find a supper?'

4

*The Danger of Following a Pretty Woman
in the Streets by Night*

GRINGOIRE had set himself to follow the gypsy girl at all hazards He had seen her, with her goat, turn down the Rue de la Contellerie; and, accordingly, he turned into the Rue de la Contellerie likewise.

'Why not?' said he to himself.

As a practical philosopher of the streets of Paris, Gringoire had remarked that nothing is more favourable to a state of reverie than to follow a pretty woman without knowing whither she is going. In this voluntary surrender of one's free-will—in this fancy subjecting itself to the fancy of another, while that other is totally unconscious of it—there is a mixture of fantastic independence with blind obedience, a something intermediate between slavery and freedom, which was pleasing to Gringoire, whose mind, essentially mixed, undecided and complex, held the medium between all extremes in constant suspense amongst all human propensities, and neutralizing one of them by another. He compared himself willingly to the tomb of Mahomet, attracted by two lodestones in opposite directions, and hesitating eternally between the top and the bottom, between the roof and the pavement, between fall and ascension, between the zenith and the nadir.

Had Gringoire been living in our time, what a happy medium he would have maintained between the classic and the romantic!

But he was not primitive enough to live three hundred years; and 'tis a pity. His absence leaves a void which, in these days of ours, is but too sensibly felt.

However, nothing better disposes a man for following people in the street (especially when they happen to be women), a thing Gringoire was always ready to do, than not knowing where to sleep.

He walked along, therefore, thoughtfully, behind the young girl, who quickened her step, making her pretty little four-footed companion trot beside her, as she saw the townsfolk reaching their homes and the taverns (the only shops allowed opened on this festival) closing for the night.

'After all,' he half thought to himself, 'she must have a lodging somewhere—the gypsy women have good hearts—who knows?'

And there were some points of suspension around which he wove certain very charming and flattering ideas.

At intervals, meanwhile, as he passed before the last groups of people busy closing their doors, he caught certain fragments of their conversation which broke the chain of his pleasing hypotheses.

Now it was two old men accosting each other.

'Maître Thibaut Fernicle, do you know, it's very cold?'

(Gringoire had known it ever since the winter had set in).

'Yes, indeed, Maître Boniface Disome. Are we going to have such a winter as we had three years ago, in the year '80, when wood rose to eight sols the measure, think you?'

'Bah! that's nothing at all, Maître Thibaut, to the winter of 1407, when it froze from Martinmas to Candlemas—and so sharp that the ink in the pen of the parliament's registrar froze, in the Grand Chamber, at every three words, which interrupted the registering of the judgments!'

Then farther on, two good female neighbours, gossiping to each other from their windows with candles in their hands that glimmered through the fog.

'Has your husband told you of the mishap, Mademoiselle la Boudraque?'

'No, Mademoiselle Turquant, what is it?'

'The horse of Monsieur Gilles Godin, notary at the Châtelet, took fright at the Flemish and their procession, and knocked over Maître Philipot Avrillot, lay-brother of the Celestines.'

'Really?'

'Assuredly.'

'A paltry hack-horse, too! It seems impossible—had it been a cavalry horse, now!'

And the windows were shut again. But Gringoire had none the less lost the thread of his ideas.

Luckily, he soon found it again, and easily tied it together, at the sight of the gypsy girl and of Djali, who were still trotting on before him, two slender, delicate and charming creatures, whose small feet, pretty figures, and graceful motions he gazed at with

admiration, almost confounding them together in his contemplation; fancying them both young girls from their intelligence
and mutual affection; while from their light, quick and graceful
step, they might have been both young hinds.

Meanwhile, the streets were every moment becoming darker
and more solitary. The curfew had long ceased to ring, and it was
only at long intervals that a person passed along the pavement,
or a light was seen at a window. Gringoire, in following the gypsy,
had involved himself in that inextricable labyrinth of alleys, courts
and crossings which surrounds the ancient sepulchre of the Holy
Innocents, and may be compared to a skein of thread tangled by
the playing of a kitten. 'Very illogical streets, in truth!' muttered
Gringoire, quite lost in the thousand windings which seemed to be
everlastingly turning back upon themselves, but through which the
girl followed a track that seemed to be well known to her, and
with a step of increasing rapidity. For his own part he would have
been perfectly ignorant as to his whereabout, had he not observed,
at the bend of a street, the octagonal mass of the pillory of the
Halles (Principal Market), the perforated top of which traced its
dark outline against a solitary light yet visible in a window of the
Rue Verdelet.

For some moments past his step had attracted the girl's attention;
she had several times turned her head towards him with uneasiness:
once, indeed, she had stopped short, had availed herself of a ray
of light that escaped from a half-open bakehouse, to survey him
steadily from head to foot; then, after this scrutiny, Gringoire had
observed on her face the little grimace which he had already
remarked, and she had gone on without more ado.

This same little pout furnished Gringoire with a subject of
reflection. There certainly was both disdain and mockery in that
pretty grimace. And he was beginning to hang his head, to count
the paving-stones, and to follow the girl at a rather greater
distance; when, at the turn of a street which for a moment hid her
from view, he heard her utter a piercing shriek.

He quickened his step.

The street was filled with deep shadows. Yet, a wick soaked in
oil, which was burning in a sort of iron cage, at the foot of a statue
of the Holy Virgin at the corner of the street, enabled Gringoire
to discern the gypsy struggling in the arms of two men, who were
endeavouring to stifle her cries, while the poor little goat, in great
alarm, put down her horns, bleating.

'Hither! hither! gentlemen of the watch!' cried Gringoire; and
he advanced bravely.

One of the men who had laid hold of the girl, turned toward
him. It was the formidable visage of Quasimodo.

Gringoire did not fly—but he did not advance another step.

Quasimodo came up to him, and hurling him some four paces off upon the pavement with a backstroke of his hand, plunged rapidly into the darkness, bearing the girl, whose figure drooping over his arm was like a silken scarf. His companion followed him, and the poor goat ran behind with its plaintive bleat.

'Murder! murder!' cried the unfortunate gypsy.

'Stand, there! you scoundrels! and let go the wench!' was all at once heard in a voice of thunder, from a horseman, who suddenly made his appearance from the neighbouring crossway.

It was a captain of the king's archers, armed from head to foot with broadsword in hand.

He snatched the gypsy from the grasp of the amazed Quasimodo, laid her across his saddle, and, at the moment when the redoubtable hunchback, having recovered from his surprise, was rushing upon him to regain possession of his prey, fifteen or sixteen archers, who followed close upon their captain, made their appearance, each brandishing his two-edged blade. They were a detachment of the royal troop on extra duty, by order of Messire Robert d'Estouteville, Warden of the Provost of Paris.

Quasimodo was surrounded, seized and garroted. He roared, he foamed, he bit; and had it been daylight, no doubt his visage alone, rendered yet more hideous by rage, would have put the whole detachment to flight. But the darkness had disarmed him of his most formidable weapon, his ugliness.

His companion had disappeared during the struggle.

The gypsy gracefully gained her seat upon the officer's saddle, rested both her hands upon the young man's shoulders, and looked fixedly at him for a few seconds, as if delighted with his fine countenance and the effectual succour he had rendered her. Then speaking first, and making her sweet voice still sweeter, she said to him:

'Monsieur le gendarme, what is your name?'

'Captain Phœbus de Chateaupers, at your service, my fair one,' said the officer, drawing himself up.

'Thank you,' said she.

And while Captain Phœbus was curling his moustache *à la Bourguignonne*, she glided down from the horse like an arrow falling to the ground, and fled.

A flash of lightning could not have vanished more quickly.

'By the Pope's head!' exclaimed the captain, while he tightened the bands upon Quasimodo, 'I'd rather have kept the wench.'

'What would you have, captain?' said one of the archers. 'The linnet is flown—the bat remains.'

5

Continuation of the Danger

GRINGOIRE, quite stunned with his fall, lay stretched upon the pavement before the good Virgin at the corner of the street. By degrees, however, he recovered his senses. At first, he was for some minutes in a sort of half-somnolent reverie, which was not altogether disagreeable, and in which the airy figures of the gypsy and the goat were confounded in his imagination with the weight of Quasimodo's fist. This state of his feelings was of short duration. A very lively sense of cold upon that part of his body which was in contact with the pavement, suddenly awoke him, and brought his mind to the surface.

'Whence is this chill that I feel?' said he hastily to himself. He then perceived that he lay somewhat in the middle of the gutter.

'The devil take the humpbacked cyclop!' grumbled he between his teeth, as he strove to get up. But he was too much stunned, and too much bruised; he was forced to remain where he was. Having, however, the free use of his hand, he stopped his nose, and resigned himself to his situation.

'The mud of Paris,' thought he, for he now believed it to be decided that the gutter was to be his lodging:

And what do in a refuge but to dream?

'the mud of Paris is particularly foul. It must contain a large proportion of volatile and nitrous salts. Such too is the opinion of Maître Nicolas Flamel and the hermetics. . . .'

This word *hermetics* reminded him of the Archdeacon Claude Frollo. He reflected on the scene of violence of which he had just had a glimpse; that he had seen the gypsy struggling between two men; that Quasimodo had a companion; and the sullen and haughty countenance of the archdeacon floated confusedly in his memory. 'That would be strange,' thought he; and then, with this data and upon this basis, he began to erect the fantastic framework of hypothesis, that house of cards of the philosophers; then suddenly returning once more to reality, 'Oh, I freeze!' he cried.

The position was in fact becoming less and less tenable. Each particle of water in the channel carried off a particle of caloric from the loins of Gringoire; and an equilibrium of temperature between his body and the water was beginning to establish itself in the most cruel manner.

All at once he was assailed by an annoyance of quite a different nature.

A troop of children, of those little barefooted savages that have in all times run wild in the streets of Paris, with the everlasting name of *gamins*, and who, when we were children also, used to throw stones at us as we were leaving school in the evening, because our trousers were not torn,—a swarm of these urchins ran to the crossing where Gringoire lay, laughing and shouting in a manner that showed very little concern for the sleep of the neighbours. They were dragging after them some sort of a shapeless sack; and the noise of their wooden shoes alone was enough to waken the dead. Gringoire, who was not yet quite dead, half raised himself.

'Hello! Hennequin Dandèche! Hello! Jehan Pincebourde!' cried they at the top of their voices; 'old Eustache Moubon, the old junkseller of the corner, is just dead. We've got his straw mattress, and we're going to make a bonfire with it. This is the Flemings' day!'

Whereupon they threw the mattress precisely on top of Gringoire, whom they had come up to without seeing. At the same time one of them took a handful of straw, and went to light it at the lamp of the Blessed Virgin.

'S'death!' muttered Gringoire, 'am I going to be too hot now?'

The moment was critical. He was about to be caught between fire and water. He made a supernatural effort, such as a counterfeiter might have made in trying to escape when they were going to boil him to death. He rose up, threw back the mattress upon the gamins, and took to his heels.

'Holy Virgin!' cried the boys, 'it's the old junkman's ghost!' And they too ran in the opposite direction.

The mattress remained master of the field of battle. Those judicious historians, Belle-forêt, Father Le Juge and Corrozet, assure us that the next morning it was gathered up with great pomp by the clergy of that quarter of the town and placed among the treasures of Sainte Opportune's church, where, until the year 1789, the sacristan made a very handsome income from the great miracle worked by the statue of the Virgin at the corner of the Rue Mauconseil, which, by its presence alone, in the memorable night between the 6th and the 7th of January, 1482, had exorcised the deceased Eustache Moubon, who, to cheat the devil, had, when dying, slyly hidden his soul within his mattress.

6

The Broken Jug

AFTER running for some time as fast as his legs would carry him, without knowing whither, headlong round many a corner, striding over many a gutter, traversing many a court and alley, seeking escape and passage through all the windings of the old pavement of the Halles, exploring in his panic what are called in the elegant Latin of the charters, *tota via, cheminum, et viaria* (every way, highway and by-way), our poet all at once halted, first because he was out of breath, and then because he was collared, as it were, by a dilemma which had suddenly arisen in his mind. 'It seems to me, Maître Pierre Gringoire,' said he to himself, applying his finger to his forehead, 'that you are running all this while like a brainless fellow. The little rogues were no less afraid of you than you were of them—it seems to me, I say, that you heard the clatter of their wooden shoes running away southward while you were running away northward. Now, one of two things must have taken place; either they have run away, and then the mattress which they must have forgotten in their fright is precisely that hospitable couch for which you have been hunting since the morning, and which Madame the Virgin miraculously sends you as a reward for having composed, in honour of her, a morality, accompanied with triumphs and mummeries—or, the boys have not run away; in that case they will have put a light to the mattress, and there you have precisely the excellent fire of which you are in need, to comfort, warm and dry you. In either case—good bed or good fire—the mattress is a gift from heaven. The sanctified Virgin Mary that stands at the corner of the Rue Mauconseil perhaps caused the death of Eustache Moubon for the very purpose; and 'tis folly in you to thus hasten away, like a Picard running from a Frenchman, leaving behind what you are running forward to seek—and you are a blockhead!'

He then began to retrace his steps, and ferreting about to discover where he was—snuffing the wind, and with his ears to the ground—he strove to find his way back to the blessed mattress —but in vain. All was intersections of streets, courts and blind alleys, amongst which he incessantly doubted and hesitated, more entangled in that strange network of dark lanes than he would have been in the labyrinth of the Hôtel des Tournelles itself. At length he lost patience, and vehemently exclaimed, 'A curse upon these crossroads! the devil himself has made them after the image of his pitchfork!'

This exclamation relieved him a little; and a sort of reddish reflection, which he at that moment perceived at the end of a long and narrow street, completed the restoration of his courage.

'God be praised,' said he, 'there it is! There is my blazing mattress!' And, likening himself to the boatman foundering in the night-time, '*Salve,*' added he, piously, '*salve, maris stella!*' (Hail, Star of the Sea.)

Did he address this fragment of a litany to the Holy Virgin, or to the straw mattress? We really are unable to say.

He had no sooner advanced a few paces down the long street or lane, which was on a declivity, unpaved, descending more abruptly and becoming more miry the farther he proceeded, than he observed something very singular. The street was not deserted; here and there were to be seen crawling certain vague shapeless masses, all moving toward the light which was flickering at the end of the street, like those heavy insects which drag themselves along at night, from one blade of grass to another, toward a shepherd's fire.

Nothing makes a man so adventurous as an empty pocket. Gringoire went forward, and soon came up with that one of the larvæ which seemed to be dragging itself along indolently after the others. On approaching it, he found that it was nothing other than a miserable cripple fixed in a bowl, without legs or thighs, jumping along with the aid of his two hands, like a mutilated spider, with only two of its feet remaining. The moment he came up to this sort of human insect it lifted up to him a lamentable voice: '*La buona mancia, signor! la buona mancia!*' (Charity, sir! charity!)

'The devil take thee!' said Gringoire, 'and me along with thee, if I know what you mean.'

And he passed on.

He came up to another of these ambulatory masses, and examined it. It was a cripple, both in arms and legs, after such a manner that the complicated system of crutches and wooden legs that supported him made him look like a perambulating mason's scaffolding.

Gringoire, being fond of noble and classical similes, compared him, in fancy, to the living tripod of Vulcan.

This living tripod saluted him as he went by; but staying his hat just at the height of Gringoire's chin, after the manner of a shaving dish, and shouting in his ears, '*Señor Cabarellero, para comprar un pedaso de pan!*' (Sir, Cavalier, something with which to buy a piece of bread!)

'It appears,' said Gringoire, 'that this one talks too; but it's a barbarous language, and he's more lucky than I if he understands it.' Then striking his forehead through a sudden transition of idea:

'Apropos! what the devil did they mean this morning with their Esmeralda?'

He resolved to double his pace; but for the third time something blocked up the way. This something, or rather this some one, was a blind man, a little man, with a bearded Jewish face, who, rowing in the space about him with a stick, and towed along by a great dog, whined out to him with a Hungarian accent, *'Facitote caritatem!'* (Give alms.)

'Well enough!' said Pierre Gringoire, 'here is one at last that talks a Christian language. Truly, I must have a most alms-giving mien, that they should ask charity of me when my purse is so lean. My friend,' said he, turning to the blind man, 'a week since I sold my last shirt; that is to say, since you understand no language but that of Cicero, *Vendidi hebdomade nuper transita meam ultimam chemisam.*'

This said, he turned his back upon the blind man and pursued his way. But the blind man lengthened his pace at the same time; and behold, also, the cripple and the stump came up in great haste, with much noise of the platter that carried the one, and the crutches that sustained the other. All three, tumbling over each other at the heels of poor Gringoire, and singing their several staves:

'*Caritatem!*' sang the blind man.

'*La buona mancia!*' sang the stump.

And the man of the wooden legs took up the strain with, '*Un pedaso de pan!*'

Gringoire stopped his ears. 'Oh, tower of Babel!' he cried.

He began to run. The blind man ran. The wooden legs ran. The stump ran.

And then, as he hurried still farther down the street, stump men, wooden-legged men, and blind men came swarming around him —men with but a single hand, men with but one eye, lepers with their sores—issued from out houses, adjacent alleys, cellar-holes —howling, bellowing, yelping—all hobbling and clattering along, making their way toward the light, and wallowing in the mire like so many slugs after the rain.

Gringoire, still followed by his three persecutors, and not knowing what was to come of it all, walked on affrighted among the others, turning aside the limpers, striding over the stumpies, his feet entangled in that ant-hill of deformities, like the English captain who found himself beset by a legion of crabs.

The idea occurred to him of trying to retrace his steps. But it was too late; all this army had closed upon his rear, and his three beggars held him. He went on, therefore, urged forward at once by that irresistible flood, by fear, and by a dizziness which made it all seem to him like a sort of horrible dream.

At last he reached the extremity of the street. It opened into an immense square, where a thousand scattered lights were wavering in the thick gloom of the night. Gringoire threw himself into it, hoping to escape by the speed of his legs from the three deformed spectres that had fixed themselves upon him.

'*Onde vas, hombre?*' (Whither goest, man?) cried the wooden legs, throwing aside his scaffolding, and running after him with as good a pair of legs as ever measured a geometrical pace upon the pavement of Paris.

Meanwhile the stumpy, erect upon his feet, clapped his heavy iron-sheathed platter over Gringoire's head, while the blind man stared him in the face with great flaming eyes.

'Where am I?' said the terrified poet.

'In the Court of Miracles,' answered a fourth spectre who had accosted them.

'On my soul,' returned Gringoire, 'I do indeed find here that the blind see and the lame walk—but where is the Saviour?'

They answered with a burst of laughter of a sinister kind.

The poor poet cast his eyes around him. He was in fact in that same terrible Cour des Miracles, or Court of Miracles, where no honest man had ever penetrated at such an hour—a magic circle, in which the officers of the Châtelet and the sergeants of the provostry, when they ventured thither, disappeared in morsels—the city of the thieves—a hideous wart on the face of Paris—a sink from whence escaped every morning, and to which returned to stagnate every night, that stream of vice, mendicity and vagrancy which ever flows through the streets of a capital—a monstrous hive, into which all the hornets of society returned each evening with their booty—a lying hospital, in which the gypsy, the unfrocked monk, the abandoned scholar—the worthless of every nation, Spaniards, Italians, Germans—of every religion, Jews, Christians, Mahometans, idolaters—covered with painted sores, beggars in the daytime, transformed themselves at night into robbers—in short, an immense cloak-room, in which dressed and undressed at that period all the actors in that everlasting drama which robbery, prostitution and murder enacted upon the pavements of Paris.

It was a large open space, irregular and ill-paved, as was at that time every square in Paris. Fires, around which swarmed strange groups, were gleaming here and there. All was motion and clamour. There were shrieks of laughter, squalling of children and shrill voices of women. The arms and heads of this crowd cast a thousand fantastic gestures in dark outline upon the luminous background. Now and then, upon the ground, over which the light of the fires was wavering, intermingled with great undefined shadows, was seen to pass a dog resembling a man, or a man resembling a dog.

The limits of race and species seemed to be effaced in this commonwealth as in a pandemonium. Men, women, beasts; age, sex; health, sickness; all seemed to be in common among this people; all went together mingled, confounded, superimposed, each participating in all.

The weak and wavering rays that streamed from the fires enabled Gringoire, amid his perturbation, to distinguish, all round the extensive enclosure, a hideous framing of old houses, the decayed, shrivelled, and stooping fronts of which, pierced by one or two circular attic windows with lights behind them, seemed to him, in the dark, like enormous old women's heads, ranged in a circle, looking monstrous and crabbed, and winking upon the diabolical revels.

It was like a new world, unknown, unimagined, deformed, creeping, swarming, fantastic.

Gringoire, more and more affrighted, held by the three mendicants as by three pairs of pincers and deafened by the crowd of vagrants that flocked barking round him—the unlucky Gringoire strove to muster sufficient presence of mind to recollect whether it was Saturday (witches' day) or not; but his efforts were vain; the thread of his memory and his thoughts was broken; and, doubting of everything—floating between what he saw and what he felt—he put the insoluble question to himself—'If I am I, are these things then real? If these things be real, am I really I?'

At that moment a distinct shout was raised from the buzzing mob that surrounded him. 'Take him to the king! take him to the king!'

'Holy Virgin!' muttered Gringoire, 'the king of this place must surely be a goat!'

'To the king! to the king!' repeated every voice.

They dragged him along, each striving to fix his talons upon him. But the three beggars kept their hold, and tore him away from the others, vociferating, 'He is ours!'

The poet's frail doublet gave up the ghost in this struggle.

In crossing the horrible place his dizziness left him. After proceeding a few paces the feeling of reality returned. He began to adapt himself to the atmosphere of the place. During the first moments from his poet's head, or perhaps, indeed, quite simply and prosaically, from his empty stomach, there had risen a fume, a vapour, as it were, which, spreading itself between him and surrounding objects, had allowed him a glimpse of them only in the incoherent mist of a nightmare in those shadowy dreams that distort every outline, and cluster the objects together in disproportioned groups, enlarging things into chimeras, and human beings into phantoms. By degrees this hallucination gave way to a less bewildered and less magnifying state of vision. The reality made

its way to his senses—struck upon his eyes—struck against his feet
—and bit by bit destroyed the frightful poetry with which he had
at first fancied himself surrounded. He could not but perceive at
last that he was walking, not in the Styx, but in the mud; that he
was elbowed, not by demons, but by thieves; that not his soul,
but, in simple sooth, his life was in danger—seeing that he lacked
that invaluable conciliator which places itself so effectually between
the robber and the honest man—the purse. In short, on examining
the orgie more closely and with greater calmness, he dropped from
the witches' sabbath to the pot-house.

The Court of Miracles was, in truth, no other than a pot-house
of thieves, but as red with blood as with wine.

The spectacle which presented itself to him when his tattered
escort at length deposited him at his journey's end was little
adapted to bring back his mind to poetry, though it were the
poetry of hell. It was more than ever the prosaic and brutal reality
of the tavern. Were we not in the fifteenth century, we should say
that Gringoire had fallen from Michael Angelo to Callot.

Round a large fire burning upon a great round flagstone, and
the blaze of which had heated red-hot the legs of an iron trivet,
empty for the moment, some worm-eaten tables were set out here
and there in confusion, no lackey of any geometrical pretensions
having condescended to adjust their parallelism, or see that, at
least, they should not meet at too unaccustomed angles. Upon
these tables shone a few pots dripping with wine and beer, around
which were grouped a number of bacchanalian visages, reddened
by the fire and the wine. There would be a man with a fair round
belly and a jovial face, noisily throwing his arms round a girl of
the town, thick-set and brawny. Then a sort of false soldier, a
narquois, as they called him in their language, who whistled away
while he was undoing the bandages of his false wound, and
unstiffening his sound and vigorous knee, which had been bound
up since the morning in ample ligatures. Beyond him there was a
mumper preparing, with suet and ox-blood, his *Visitation from God*,
or sore leg, for the morrow. Two tables farther on a sham pilgrim
with complete garb was spelling out the lament of Sainte Reine,
the psalmody and the nasal drone included. In another place a
young scamp was taking a lesson in epilepsy from an old *sabouleux*,
or hustler, who was teaching him the art of foaming at the mouth
by chewing a piece of soap; while four or five women thieves, just
by them, were contending, at the same table, for the possession of
a child stolen in the course of the evening. All which circumstances,
two centuries later, 'seemed so laughable at court,' says Sauval,
'that they furnished pastime to the king, and an opening to the
royal ballet entitled "Night," which was divided into four parts,

and danced upon the stage of the Petit Bourbon.' And 'never,'
adds an eye-witness, in the year 1653, 'were sudden metamorphoses
of the Court of Miracles more happily represented. Benserade prepared us for them by some very genteel verses.'

Coarse laughter, with obscene songs, burst forth on all sides.
Each one held forth in his own way, carping and swearing, without
heeding his neighbour. Pots rattled, and quarrels arose out of their
collision, the smashing of pots thus leading to the tearing of rags.

A large dog, sitting on his haunches, looked into the fire. There
were some children mingled in this orgie. The stolen child was
crying. Another, a bouncing boy four years old, was seated with
his legs dangling upon a bench too high for him, with his chin just
above the table, saying not a word. A third was gravely smearing
the table with his finger in the melted tallow running from the
candle. A fourth, a little one, squatting in the mud, was almost
lost in a great iron pot which he was scraping with a tile, drawing
from it a sound which would have made Stradivarius faint.

Near the fire was a barrel, and upon the barrel was seated one
of the beggars. This was the king upon his throne.

The three who held Gringoire brought him before this cask, and
the whole bacchanalia were silent for a moment, excepting the
caldron tenanted by the child.

Gringoire dared not breathe nor raise his eyes.

'*Hombre, quita tu sombrero!*' (Man, take off thy hat) said one of
the three fellows who had hold of him; and before he could understand what that meant, another of them had taken his hat—a
wretched covering, it is true, but still of use on a day of sunshine
or a day of rain. Gringoire heaved a sigh.

But the king, from the top of his barrel, put the interrogatory,
'What is this knave?'

Gringoire started. This voice, though menacing in tone, reminded him of another voice which that very morning had struck
the first blow at his mystery, by droning out in the midst of the
audience, 'Charity, if you please!' He raised his eyes—it was indeed Clopin Trouillefou.

Clopin Trouillefou, arrayed in his regal ensigns, had not one
rag more or less upon him. His sore on the arm had disappeared.
In his hand he held one of those whips with lashes of whitleather,
which were, at that time, used by the sergeants of the wand to
drive back the crowd, and were called boullayes. He had upon
his head a circular coif closed at the top; but it was difficult to
distinguish whether it was a child's cushion or a king's crown, so
similar are the two things.

However, Gringoire, without knowing why, had felt some
revival of hope on recognizing in the king of the Court of Miracles

his cursed beggar of the Grande Salle. 'Maître,' stammered he, '—Monseigneur—Sire— How must I call you?' said he at last, having mounted to his utmost stretch of ascent, and neither knowing how to mount higher nor how to come down again.

'Monseigneur—Your Majesty—or Comrade—call me what you like, only despatch. What hast thou to say in thy defence?'

'In my defence!' thought Gringoire. 'That is unpleasant.' He replied, hesitating, 'I am he—he who this morning—'

'By the devil's claws!' interrupted Clopin, 'thy name, rascal! and nothing more. Hark ye—thou art before three mighty sovereigns: me, Clopin Trouillefou, King of Tunis, successor to the Grand Coësre, supreme sovereign of the kingdom of Argot; Mathais Hungadi Spicali, Duke of Egypt and Bohemia, that yellow old fellow that thou seest there with a clout round his head; and Guillaume Rousseau, Emperor of Galilee, that fat fellow, that's not attending to us, but to that wench. We are thy judges. Thou hast entered into the kingdom of Argot without being an Argotier—thou hast violated the privileges of our stronghold. Thou must be punished, unless thou art either a capon, a franc-mitou, or a rifodé, that is to say, in the language of the honest men, either a thief, a beggar, or a vagrant. Art thou anything of that sort? Justify thyself—tell over thy qualifications.'

'Alas!' said Gringoire, 'I have not that honour. I am the author—'

'That's enough,' interrupted Trouillefou; 'thou shalt be hanged. It's a matter of course, messieurs the honest townsfolk. As you treat our people amongst you, so we treat yours amongst us. Such law as you mete to the Truands (vagabonds and outlaws) the Truands mete to you. It is but your fault if it be evil. 'Tis quite necessary that an honest man or two should now and then grin through the hempen collar—that makes the thing honourable. Come, friend, merrily share thy tatters among these young ladies. I'll have thee hanged for the amusement of the Truands, and thou shalt give them thy purse to drink thy health. If thou hast any mumming to do, there is yonder, in that mortar, a capital God the Father in stone that we stole from Saint Pierre aux Bœufs. Thou hast four minutes' time to throw thy soul at his head.'

This was a formidable harangue.

'Well said! upon my soul. Clopin Trouillefou preaches as well as any pope!' cried the Emperor of Galilee, smashing his pot at the same time to prop his table-leg.

'Messeigneurs the emperors and kings!' said Gringoire coolly (for I do not know how his resolution had returned to him, and he spoke quite firmly), 'you do not consider. My name is Pierre Gringoire—I am the poet whose morality was performed this morning in the Grande Salle of the Palace.'

'Ah! it is thee, master, is it? I was there, by God's head! Well, comrade, is it any reason, because thou tiredst us to death this morning, that thou shouldst not be hanged to-night?'

'I shall have trouble to get off,' thought Gringoire. However, he made another effort. 'I don't very well see,' said he, 'why the poets are not classed among the Truands. A vagrant!—why Æsopus was a vagrant. A beggar—Homerus was a beggar. A thief—was not Mercurius a thief?'

Clopin interrupted him. 'Methinks,' said he, 'thou'st a mind to matagrabolize us with thy gibberish. *Pardieu!* Be hanged quietly, man; and don't make so much ado.'

'Pardon me, monseigneur the king of Tunis,' replied Gringoire, disputing the ground inch by inch; 'it's really worth your while —Only one moment—Hear me—You'll not condemn me without hearing me?'

His unfortunate voice was in fact drowned by the uproar that was made around him; the little boy was scraping his kettle with more energy than ever; and, as a climax, an old woman had just come and set upon the redhot trivet a frying-pan full of fat, which shrieked over the fire with a noise like the shouts of a flock of children running after a masquerade.

Meanwhile, Clopin Trouillefou seemed to confer a moment with the duke of Egypt, and with the emperor of Galilee, who was completely drunk. Then he called out sharply, 'Silence!' and as the pot and the frying-pan paid no attention to him, but continued their duet, he jumped down from his barrel, gave the caldron a kick which rolled it and the child half a score yards off; gave the frying-pan another, upsetting all the fat into the fire; and then gravely reascended his throne, regardless of the smothered cries of the child, and of the grumbling of the old woman, whose supper was evaporating in a beautiful white flame.

Trouillefou made a sign; whereupon the duke, and the emperor, and the *archisuppôts* (receiver of stolen goods), and the *cagoux* (those living in hiding), came and ranged themselves about him in the form of a horseshoe, of which Gringoire, still roughly held, occupied the centre. It was a semi-circle of rags, tatters and tinsel—of pitchforks and hatchets—of staggering legs and brawny arms—of sordid, dull and sottish faces. In the midst of this round table of beggary, Clopin Trouillefou, as the doge of this senate, the king of this peerage, the pope of this conclave, dominated—in the first place, by the height of his cask—and then, by a certain haughty, savage and formidable air, which made his eyes flash, and corrected in his fierce profile the bestial type of the Truand race. One would have said a wild boar among swine.

'Hark ye,' said he to Gringoire, while he caressed his shapeless chin with his horny hand, 'I don't see why thou shouldst not be hanged. To be sure, thou dost not seem to like it, and that's but natural—you burghers aren't used to it. You have exaggerated its importance. After all, we don't wish thee any harm. There's one way of getting off for the moment. Wilt thou be one of us?'

One can imagine the effect this proposal produced upon Gringoire, who saw life about to escape him, and felt his grasp beginning to fail. He caught at it energetically.

'That I will—certainly, assuredly,' said he.

'Thou dost consent,' said Clopin, 'to enlist thyself among the men of the *petite flambe?*' (small banner)

'Of the *petite flambe*—exactly so,' responded Gringoire.

'Thou dost acknowledge thyself a member of the free *bourgeoisie?*' added the king of Tunis.

'Of the free *bourgeoisie*.'

'A subject of the kingdom of Argot?'

'Of the kingdom of Argot.'

'A Truand?'

'A Truand.'

'In thy soul?'

'In my soul.'

'I will just observe to thee,' resumed the king, 'that thou wilt be none the less hanged for all that.'

'The devil!' exclaimed the poet.

'Only,' continued Clopin, quite imperturbably, 'thou wilt be hanged later, with more ceremony, at the expense of the good city of Paris, upon a fine stone gibbet, and by honest men. That's some consolation.'

'Just so,' answered Gringoire.

'There are other advantages. As being a free burgher, thou wilt have to pay neither tax on the pavements, the lamps, nor for the poor; to which the burghers of Paris are subject.'

'Be it so,' said the poet; 'I consent. I am a Truand, an Argotier, a free burgher, a *petite flambe*, whatever you please—and indeed I was all that beforehand, monsieur the king of Tunis; for I am a philosopher; and, as thou knowest, *Omnia in philosophia, omnes in philosopho continentur—*' (all things are included in philosophy—all men in the philosopher).

The king of Tunis knit his brows.

'What dost thou take me for, friend? What cant of a Hungarian Jew art thou singing us now? I don't understand Hebrew. Because a man is a bandit, he is not obliged to be a Jew. Nay, I don't even rob now—I'm above that—a cut-throat, if you like, but no cut-purse.'

Gringoire strove to slip in an excuse between these brief and angry ejaculations. 'I ask your pardon, monseigneur—it's not Hebrew, it's Latin.'

'I tell thee,' rejoined Clopin, in a rage, 'that I'm no Jew, and that I'll have thee hanged, *ventre de synagogue!* (by the stomach of the synagogue) as well as that little shopkeeper of Judea that stands by thee, and whom I hope to see, one of these days, nailed to a counter like a piece of bad coin as he is!'

So saying, he pointed with his finger to the little bearded Hungarian Jew, who had accosted Gringoire with his *Facitote caritatem!* and who, understanding no other language, was surprised to see the ill-humour of the king of Tunis vent itself upon him.

At length Monseigneur Clopin became calm. 'Varlet,' said he to our poet, 'then thou'rt willing to be a Truand?'

'Undoubtedly,' answered the poet.

'It is not alone enough to be willing,' said Clopin, surlily. 'Goodwill doesn't put one onion more into the soup, and is of no use but for going to heaven—and there's a difference between heaven and Argot. To be received in Argot thou must prove that thou art good for something; and to do that thou must rummage the mannikin.'

'I will rummage anything you like,' said Gringoire.

Clopin made a sign; whereupon several Argotiers detached themselves from the circle, and returned a moment later. They brought two posts, terminated at the lower extremity by two wooden feet, which made them stand firmly on the ground. To the upper extremities of these posts they applied a cross-beam; the whole forming a very pretty portable gallows, which Gringoire had the satisfaction of seeing erected before him in the twinkling of an eye. Everything was there, including the rope, which gracefully depended from the transverse beam.

'What will be the end of all this?' thought Gringoire, with some uneasiness. But a noise of little bells which he heard at that moment put an end to his anxiety; it proceeded from a stuffed figure of a man which the Truands were suspending by the neck to the rope, a sort of scarecrow, clothed in red, and so completely covered with little bells and hollow jingling brasses, that there were enough to have harnessed thirty Castilian mules. These thousand miniature bells jingled for a time under the vibrations of the cord; their sound dying away gradually into a profound silence, which resulted from the state of perfect rest into which the body of the mannikin was speedily brought by that law of the pendulum which has superseded the use of the water clock and the hour-glass.

Then Clopin, pointing to an old tottering stool beneath the mannikin, said to Gringoire, 'Get upon that.'

'*Mort-diable!*' objected Gringoire, 'I shall break by neck. Your stool halts like one of Martial's couplets—it has one hexameter leg and one pentameter.'

'Get up,' repeated Clopin.

Gringoire mounted upon the stool, and succeeded, not without some oscillations of his head and his arms, in recovering his centre of gravity.

'Now,' proceeded the king of Tunis, 'turn thy right foot round thy left leg, and rise on the toe of thy left foot.'

'Monseigneur,' said Gringoire, 'you are then absolutely determined that I shall break a limb!'

Clopin shook his head. 'Hark ye, friend,' said he, 'thou dost talk too much. It all amounts to this : thou must stand on tip-toe, then thou canst reach the mannikin's pocket, thrust in thy hand and pull out the purse concealed therein, and if thou dost all this without the sounding of a bell, well and good—thou shalt be a Truand. We shall then have nothing more to do but belabour thee soundly for a week.'

'*Ventre-Dieu!* I shall take good care,' said Gringoire. 'And if I make the bells jingle?'

'Then thou shalt be hanged. Dost thou understand?'

'Nay, I understand it not at all,' answered Gringoire.

'Hark ye once more. You're to put your hand in the mannikin's pocket and take out his purse. If one single bell stirs in the doing of it, you shall be hanged. Now dost understand?'

'Well,' said Gringoire, 'I understand that. What next?'

'If you manage to draw out the purse without making a jingle, you're a Truand, and will be soundly belaboured for eight days together. You understand now, I dare say.'

'No, monseigneur, I do not yet understand. Where is my advantage? To be hanged in one case, or beaten in the other!'

'And to be a Truand,' rejoined Clopin—'to be a Truand! Is that nothing? 'Tis for thine own advantage we shall beat thee, to harden thee against stripes.'

'I am greatly beholden to you,' answered the poet.

'Come, hasten!' said the king, striking his barrel with his foot, which resounded like a big drum. 'Rifle the mannikin's pocket, and let's have done with it. I tell thee, once for all, that if I hear the smallest tinkle, thou shalt take the mannikin's place.'

The whole company of Argotiers applauded the words of Clopin, and ranged themselves in a circle round the gallows with so pitiless a laugh that Gringoire saw plainly enough that he gave them too much amusement not to have everything to fear. He had, therefore, no hope left but in the faint chance of succeeding in the terrible operation which was imposed upon him. He resolved to risk it;

but he first addressed a fervent prayer to the stuffed figure whom he was about to rob, and whose heart was even more likely to be softened than those of the Truands. The myriad bells, with their little brazen tongues, appeared to him like so many asps open mouthed, ready to hiss and to sting.

'Oh!' said he, in a low voice, 'and can it be that my life depends upon the smallest vibration of the smallest of those bits of metal? Oh!' he added, clasping his hands, 'ye bells, tinkle not—ye balls, jingle not!'

He made one more effort with Trouillefou.

'And if there come a breath of wind,' demanded he.

'Thou shalt be hanged,' replied the other, without hesitation.

Finding that there was no respite, delay, or subterfuge whatsoever, he bravely set about the feat. He turned his right foot about his left leg, lifted himself on the toe of his left foot, and stretched out his arm; but the moment that he touched the mannikin, his body, which was supported only by one foot, tottered upon the stool, which had only three, he mechanically caught at the mannikin, lost his balance and fell heavily to the ground, quite deafened by the fatal vibration of the scarecrow's thousand bells; while the figure, yielding to the impulse which his hand had given it, first revolved on his own axis, and then swung majestically backwards and forwards between the two posts.

'*Malédiction!*' he exclaimed as he fell; and he lay with his face to the ground as if he were dead.

However, he heard the awful chime above him, and the diabolical laughter of the Truands and the voice of Trouillefou, saying, 'Lift the fellow up, and hang him promptly.'

He rose by himself. They had already unhooked the mannikin to make room for him.

The Argotiers made him get upon the stool again. Clopin came up to him, passed the rope round his neck, and, slapping him on the shoulder, 'Good-bye, friend,' said he; 'thou'lt not escape now, though thou shouldst have the digestion of the pope himself.'

The word 'Mercy!' expired on Gringoire's lips—he cast his eyes round, but saw no gleam of hope—all were grinning.

'Bellevigne de l'Etoile,' said the king of Tunis to an enormous Truand, who stepped out of the ranks, 'do you get upon the crossbeam.'

Bellevigne de l'Etoile climbed nimbly up to the transverse bar; and an instant after, Gringoire, looking up, saw him with terror squatted just above his head.

'Now,' continued Clopin Trouillefou, 'as soon as I clap my hands do thou, Andry le Rouge, knock down the stool with thy knee; thou, François Chante-Prune, hang on the rascal's feet; and thou, Bellevigne, drop upon his shoulders; and all three at the same time—do you hear?'

Gringoire shuddered.

'Are you ready?' said Clopin Trouillefou to the three Argotiers, about to throw themselves upon the poet. The poor sufferer had a moment of horrible expectation, while Clopin was quietly pushing into the fire with the point of his shoe some twigs which the flame had not reached. 'Are you ready?' he repeated, and he opened his hands to give the signal. A second more, and all would have been over.

But he stopped as if struck by a sudden idea. 'Wait a moment,' said he; 'I am forgetful. It is our custom not to hang a man without first asking if there be a woman who will have him. Comrade, it's thy last chance! thou must marry either a Truand or the halter.'

(This gypsy law, strange as it may seem to the reader, is to-day written out in full in the old English code. See Burington's Observations.)

Gringoire took breath. This was the second time he had come to life within half an hour; so that he dared not be too confident.

'Hello!' shouted Clopin, who had reascended his cask: 'hello, there! women! females! is there among you all, from the witch to her cat, ever a jade that will have this rogue? Hello! Collette la Charonne! Elizabeth Trouvain! Simone Jodouyne! Marie Piédebou! Thonne la Longue! Bérarde Fanouel! Michelle Genaille! Claude Rougeorielle! Mathurine Girorou!—Hello! Isabeau la Thierrye! Come and see! A man for nothing! Who will have him?'

Gringoire, in this miserable plight, was, it may be supposed, not over-inviting. The women displayed no great enthusiasm at the proposal. The unhappy fellow heard them answer: 'No, no —hang him! it will amuse us all!'

Three of them, however, stepped out of the crowd to examine him. The first was a large, square-faced young woman. She carefully inspected the philosopher's deplorable doublet. The coat was threadbare, and had more holes in it than a chestnut-roaster. The woman made a wry face at it. 'An old rag!' muttered she; and then, addressing Gringoire, 'Let's see thy cloak.'

'I have lost it,' said Gringoire.

'Thy hat?'

'They've taken it from me.'

'Thy shoes?'

'They've hardly a bit of sole left.'

'Thy purse?'

'Alas!' stammered Gringoire, 'I've not a single penny.'

'Let them hang thee—and be thankful,' replied the Truandess, turning her back upon him.

The second woman, old, dark, wrinkled, of an ugliness conspicuous even in the Court of Miracles, now made the circuit of Gringoire. He trembled least she should want to have him. But she only muttered, 'He's too lean,' and went her way.

The third that came was a young girl, fresh-complexioned, and not ill-looking. 'Save me!' whispered the poor devil. She looked at him for a moment with an air of pity, then cast down her eyes, made a plait in her skirt, and remained undecided. He watched her every motion—it was his last gleam of hope. 'No,' said the girl at last; 'no—Guillaume Longue-joue would beat me.' And she returned into the crowd.

'Comrade,' said Clopin, 'thou'rt unlucky.'

Then rising on his barrel, 'So nobody bids?' cried he, mimicking the tone of an auctioneer, to the great diversion of all—'so nobody bids? Going—going—going—' then turning toward the gallows with a motion of his head, 'gone.'

Bellevigne de l'Etoile, Andry le Rouge, and François Chante-Prune again approached Gringoire.

At that moment a cry was raised among the Argotiers, of 'La Esmeralda! La Esmeralda!'

Gringoire started, and turned toward the side from which the shout proceeded. The crowd opened and made way for a clear and dazzling figure.

It was the gypsy girl.

'La Esmeralda!' said Gringoire, stupefied, in the midst of his emotions, by the suddenness with which that magic word linked together all his recollections of the day.

This fascinating creature seemed to exercise, even over the Court of Miracles, her sway of grace and beauty. Argotiers, male and female, drew up gently to let her pass by; and their brutal countenances softened at her look.

She approached the victim with her elastic step, her pretty Djali following her. Gringoire was more dead than alive. She gazed at him for a moment in silence.

'Are you going to hang this man?' said she gravely to Clopin.

'Yes, sister,' answered the king of Tunis, 'unless thou wilt take him for thy husband.'

She made her pretty little grimace with her under lip.

'I will take him,' she said.

Gringoire was firmly persuaded that he must have been in a dream ever since the morning, and that this was but a continuation of it.

In fact, this sudden turn of fortune, though agreeable, was abrupt.

They undid the noose, and let the poet descend from the stool. His agitation obliged him to sit down.

The duke of Egypt, without uttering a word, brought forth a clay pitcher. The gypsy girl presented it to Gringoire. 'Throw it on the ground,' said she.

The pitcher broke in four pieces.

'Brother,' said the duke of Egypt, laying his hands upon their foreheads, 'she is thy wife—sister, he is thy husband—for four years. Go your ways.'

7

A Wedding Night

In a few minutes our poet found himself in a little chamber with a Gothic-vaulted ceiling, very snug, very warm, seated before a table which seemed to ask nothing better than to borrow a few articles from a hanging cupboard near by; having a good bed in prospect, and alone with a pretty girl. The adventure partook of enchantment. He began seriously to take himself for the hero of a fairy tale; now and then he cast his eyes around him, as if to see whether the fiery chariot drawn by two winged steeds, which alone could have transported him so swiftly from Tartarus to Paradise, were still there. At intervals, too, he fixed his eyes steadfastly upon the holes in his coat, by way of clinging to reality, so as not to let the earth altogether slip from under him. His reason, tossed to and fro in imaginative space, had only that thread left to cling to.

The girl seemed to pay no attention to him. She was going back and forth, shifting first one article and then another, chatted with her goat, repeating her little grimace every now and then. At length she came and sat down near the table, and Gringoire could contemplate her at leisure.

You have been a child, reader, and perhaps you have the happiness to be so still. It is quite certain, then, that you have more than once followed from brier to brier (and for my own part, I can say that I have passed whole days in that manner, the best spent days of my life), on the brink of a rivulet, on a sunshiny day, some lovely green or azure dragon-fly, checking its flight at sharp angles, and kissing the tip of every twig. You recollect with what loving curiosity your thoughts and your looks were fixed upon that little whirl of whiz and hum, of blue and purple wings, in the midst of which floated an intangible form, veiled as it was by the very rapidity of its motion. The aërial creature confusedly perceptible amid the quivering of wings, appeared chimerical, imaginary, impossible to touch, impossible to see. But when, at last, the dragon-fly settled on the tip end of a reed, and you could examine, holding your breath the while, the long gauze pinions, the long enamel robe, the two globes of crystal, what amazement did you not feel, and what fear lest it should again fade to a shadow, and the creature to a chimera! Recall these impressions, and you will easily understand the feelings of Gringoire on contemplating, under her visible and palpable form, that Esmeralda of whom, until then, he had only caught a glimpse amid a whirl of dance, song, and the noise of the populace.

Sinking deeper and deeper into his reverie—

'This, then,' said he to himself, as his eyes vaguely followed her, 'is the Esmeralda—a heavenly creature!—a dancer in the streets —so much, and yet so little! She it was who gave the finishing blow to my mystery this morning—she it is who saves my life to-night. My evil genius!—my good angel! A pretty woman, upon my word!—and who must love me to distraction, to take me in this fashion. Now I think on't,' said he, suddenly rising up from his seat, with that feeling of the real which formed the substance of his character and of his philosophy, 'I know not quite how it is —but I am her husband!'

With this idea in his head, and in his eyes, he approached the young girl in so military and lover-like a manner that she drew back. 'What do you want?' she said.

'Can you ask, adorable Esmeralda?' replied Gringoire, in such impassioned tones that he himself was astonished at his own accents.

The gypsy opened her large eyes. 'I know not your meaning.'

'What!' rejoined Gringoire, growing more and more excited, and thinking that, after all, he was only dealing with the ready-made virtue of the Court of Miracles, 'am I not thine, sweet friend? —art thou not mine?'

And quite guilelessly he clasped her waist.

The girl's bodice slipped through his hands like the skin of an eel. She sprang from one end of the little cell to the other, stooped, and rose again with a small poniard in her hand, before Gringoire had time to see whence the poniard came—irritated and indignant, with swelling lips, dilated nostrils, cheeks red as crab apples, and her eyes flashing lightning. At the same time the little white goat placed itself before her, and presented a battle-front to Gringoire, bristling with two pretty gilded and very sharp horns. This was all done in the twinkling of an eye.

The damsel had turned wasp, with every disposition to sting.

Our philosopher stood crestfallen, looking confusedly, first at the goat and then at its mistress. 'Holy Virgin!' he exclaimed at last, as soon as his surprise permitted him to speak, 'here are two tricksters!'

The gypsy now broke silence. 'Thou must be a very bold rascal!' she said.

'Forgive me, mademoiselle,' said Gringoire, with a smile; 'but why did you marry me then?'

'Was I to let them hang thee?'

'So,' rejoined the poet, somewhat disappointed in his amorous expectations, 'you had no other intention in marrying me but to save me from the gibbet?'

'And what other intention dost think I could have had?'

Gringoire bit his lip. 'Humph!' said he, 'I am not yet quite so successful a Lothario as I thought. But then what was the use of breaking that poor jug?'

But Esmeralda's poniard and the horns of the goat were still on the defensive.

'Mademoiselle Esmeralda,' said the poet, 'let us compromise. I am not registering clerk at the Châtelet, and will not quibble with you about your thus carrying a dagger in Paris in the teeth of monsieur the provost's ordinances and prohibitions. You must know, however, that Noël Lescrivain was condemned, only a week ago, to pay a fine of ten Paris pence for wearing a broad sword. Now that is not my business—and so, to the point. I swear to you, by my chance of salvation, that I will not approach you without your leave and permission. But pray, give me supper.'

The truth is, that Gringoire, like Despréaux, was 'very little of a voluptuary.' He was not of that cavalier and mousquetaire species who carry girls by assault. In a love affair, as in every other affair, he willingly resigned himself to temporizing and to middle terms; and a good supper, in comfortable tête-à-tête, appeared to him, especially when he was hungry, to be a very good interlude between the prologue and the issue of an intrigue.

The gypsy made no answer. She gave her little disdainful pout; drew up her head like a bird; then burst out laughing; and the dainty dagger disappeared, as it came, without Gringoire's being able to discover where the bee hid its sting.

A moment later a rye loaf, a slice of bacon, some withered apples and a jug of beer were on the table. Gringoire set to with avidity. To hear the furious clatter of his iron fork upon his earthen-ware plate, it seemed as if all his love had turned to hunger.

The young girl, seated near him, looked on in silence, evidently preoccupied by some other thought, at which she smiled from time to time, while her delicate hand caressed the intelligent head of the goat, pressed softly against her knee.

A candle of yellow wax lighted this scene of voracity and reverie.

However, the first cravings of his stomach being appeased, Gringoire felt a twinge of shame at seeing that there was only an apple left.

'Mademoiselle Esmeralda,' said he, 'you do not eat.'

She answered by a negative motion of the head; and her pensive gaze seemed to fix itself upon the vaulted ceiling of the chamber.

'What the deuce is she thinking about?' thought Gringoire; 'it can not be that grinning dwarf's face carved upon that keystone, that attracts her so mightily. The devil's in it if I can not at least bear that comparison.'

He raised his voice—'Mademoiselle.'

She seemed not to hear him.

He repeated, louder still, 'Mademoiselle Esmeralda!' It was in vain. The girl's mind was elsewhere, and Gringoire's voice had not the power to bring it back. Luckily, the goat interfered. She began to pull her mistress gently by the sleeve. 'What do you want, Djali?' said the gypsy, briskly, with a sudden start.

'She is hungry,' said Gringoire, delighted at an opportunity of entering into conversation.

La Esmeralda began to crumble some bread, which Djali nibbled daintily from the hollow of her hand.

Gringoire, however, allowed her no time to resume her reverie. He ventured a delicate question: 'You will not have me for your husband, then?'

The girl looked fixedly at him, and answered, 'No.'

'For your lover?' proceeded Gringoire.

She pouted, and again answered, 'No.'

'For your friend?' then demanded the poet.

Again she looked at him fixedly; and, after a moment's reflection, said, 'Perhaps.'

This 'perhaps,' so dear to philosophers, encouraged Gringoire. 'Do you know what friendship is?' he asked.

'Yes,' answered the gypsy, 'it is to be like brother and sister— two souls meeting without mingling—two fingers on the same hand.'

'And love?' proceeded Gringoire.

'Oh! love!' said she—and her voice trembled and her eye beamed—'that is to be two and yet but one—a man and woman blended into an angel—it is heaven!'

The street dancer, while saying this, was beautified in a way that struck Gringoire singularly and seemed to him in perfect harmony with the almost Oriental exaltation of her words. Her pure, roseate lips were half smiling. Her clear, calm brow was momentarily ruffled by her thoughts, as a mirror dimmed by a passing breath. And from her long, dark, drooping lashes there emanated an ineffable light, giving her profile that ideal sweetness which Raphael has since found at the mystic point of intersection of virginity, maternity and divinity.

Gringoire, nevertheless, continued.

'What must one be then to please you?'

'He must be a man.'

'And I,' said he, 'what am I then?'

'A man has a helmet on his head, a sword in his hand and gilt spurs at his heels.'

'Good!' said Gringoire; 'the horse makes the man. Do you love anybody?'

'As a lover?'

'Yes—as a lover.'

She remained pensive a moment. Then she said, with a peculiar expression, 'I shall know soon.'

'Why not to-night?' rejoined the poet, in a tender tone. 'Why not me?'

She gave him a grave look, and said: 'I can not love a man who can not protect me.'

Gringoire coloured and took the reflection to himself. The girl evidently alluded to the feeble assistance he had lent her in the critical situation in which she had found herself two hours before. This recollection, effaced by his other adventures of the evening, now returned to him. He struck his forehead. 'Apropos, mademoiselle,' said he, 'I ought to have begun with that—pardon my foolish distractions—how did you contrive to escape from the clutches of Quasimodo?'

At this question the gypsy started. 'Oh! the horrible hunchback!' said she, hiding her face in her hands, and she shivered as if icy cold.

'Horrible, indeed!' said Gringoire, still pursuing his idea. 'But how did you manage to escape him?'

La Esmeralda smiled, sighed and was silent.

'Do you know why he followed you?' asked Gringoire, striving to come round again to the object of his inquiry.

'I don't know,' said the girl. Then she added quickly, 'But you were following me also. Why did you follow me?'

'In good faith,' replied Gringoire, 'I do not know.'

There was a pause. Gringoire was marking the table with his knife. The girl smiled, and seemed to be looking at something through the wall. All at once she began to sing in a voice scarcely audible:

'Quando las pintadas aves
Mudas estan, y la tierra . . .' *

She suddenly stopped short, and fell to caressing Djali.

'You have a pretty creature there,' said Gringoire.

'It is my sister,' answered she.

'Why do they call you La Esmeralda?' asked the poet.

'I don't know at all.'

'But why do they?'

She drew from her bosom a small oblong bag, suspended from her neck by a chain of grains of adrez arach (sweet-scented gum). A strong smell of camphor exhaled from the bag; it was covered with green silk, and had in the centre a large piece of green glass in imitation of an emerald.

'Perhaps it's on account of that,' said she.

Gringoire offered to take the bag, but she drew back. 'Touch it not,' she said, ''tis an amulet. Thou wouldst do mischief to the charm, or the charm to thee.'

The poet's curiosity was more and more awakened. 'Who gave it you?' said he.

She placed her finger on her lip, and hid the amulet again in her bosom. He tried a few more questions but could hardly obtain an answer.

'What's the meaning of that word, La Esmeralda?'

'I do not know,' she replied.

'What language does it belong to?'

'I think it is a gypsy word.'

'So I suspected,' said Gringoire; 'you are not a native of France?'

'I know nothing about it.'

'Are your parents living?'

She began to sing, to an old tune:

> *'A bird was my mother;*
> *My father, another;*
> *Over the water I pass without ferry,*
> *Over the water I pass without wherry;*
> *A bird was my mother;*
> *My father, another.'*

'Very good,' said Gringoire. 'At what age did you come to France?'

'When very little.'

'And when to Paris?'

'Last year. At the moment we were coming in by the Porte

---

* When the gay-plumaged birds
   Grow weary, and the earth . . .

Papale I saw the reed linnet fly through the air—it was at the end of August—I said it will be a hard winter.'

'It has been so,' said Gringoire, delighted at this beginning of conversation—'I've done naught but blow upon my fingers. You have the gift of prophecy?'

She fell again into her laconism.

'No.'

'That man whom you call the duke of Egypt is the chief of your tribe?'

'Yes.'

'But was it he who married us?' timidly remarked the poet.

She made her usual pretty grimace—'I don't even know thy name.'

'My name?—You shall have it if you wish: Pierre Gringoire.'

'I know a finer one,' said she.

'Cruel girl!' rejoined the poet. 'No matter—you shall not provoke me. Nay, you will perhaps love me when you know me better—and then, you have told me your history so confidingly that I owe you somewhat of mine. You must know, then, that my name is Pierre Gringoire, and that I am the son of a notary of Gonesse. My father was hanged by the Burgundians, and my mother ripped open by the Picards, at the time of the siege of Paris twenty years ago. At six years of age, then, I was an orphan, without any other sole to my foot than the pavement of Paris. How I managed to exist from six to sixteen, I do not know. A fruit woman would give me a plum, a baker would throw me a crust. At night I used to get myself picked up by the Onze-vingts (night watch), who put me in prison, and there I found a bundle of straw. All this did not prevent my growing tall and thin, as you see. In winter I warmed myself in the sun, under the porch of the Hôtel de Sens; and I thought it very ridiculous that the great bonfires on the feast of Saint John should be reserved for the dog-days. At sixteen, I wished to choose a calling. I tried everything in succession. I turned soldier, but was not brave enough. I then turned monk, but was not devout enough—and besides, I'm a poor drinker. In despair, I apprenticed myself to carpenters, but was not strong enough. I had more inclination to be a schoolmaster; true, I could not read; but that need not have hindered me. I perceived, at the end of a certain time, that I was in want of some requisite for everything—and so, finding that I was good for nothing, I, of my own free will and pleasure, turned poet and composer of rhymes. 'Tis a calling that a man can always embrace when he's a vagabond; and is better than stealing, as I was advised to do by some young light-fingered fellows of my acquaintance. Fortunately, I met, one fine day, with Dom Claude Frollo, the reverend archdeacon of Notre-Dame. He took an interest in me; and to him I owe it that I am now a true man of letters, acquainted with Latin, from Cicero's Offices to the Mortuology of the Celestine fathers, and not absolutely barbarous either in scholastics, in poetics, or in rhythmics, nor yet in hermetics, that science of sciences. I am the author of the miracle play that was performed to-day, with great triumph and concourse of people, in the Grande Salle of the Palace. I've also written a book that will make six hundred pages, upon the prodigious comet of 1465, about which one man went mad. I have also had other successes; being something of an artillery carver, I worked upon that great bomb of Jean Maugue, which you know burst at the bridge of Charenton the first time it was tried, and killed four-and-twenty of the spectators. You see that I'm not so indifferent a match. I know many sorts of very clever tricks, which I will teach your goat—for instance, to mimic the Bishop of Paris, that accursed Pharisee whose mill-wheels splash the passengers the whole length of the Pont aux Meuniers. And then, my mystery will bring me in plenty of ready money if they pay me. In short, I am at your service—I, and my wit, and my science, and my learning—ready to live with you, damsel, as it shall please you—soberly or merrily—as husband and wife, if you see fit—as brother and sister, if you like it better.'

Here Gringoire was silent, awaiting the effect of his speech upon the young girl. Her eyes were fixed upon the ground.

'Phœbus,' said she, in an undertone; then, turning to the poet, 'Phœbus,' said she, 'what does that mean?'

Gringoire, though not at all understanding what relation there could be between his address and this question, was not sorry to show his erudition. He answered, bridling with dignity, ''Tis a Latin word, that signifies the sun.'

'The sun!' repeated she.

''Tis the name of a certain handsome archer, who was a god,' added Gringoire.

'A god!' repeated the gypsy; and there was something pensive and impassioned in her tone.

At that moment, one of the bracelets came unfastened and fell. Gringoire eagerly stooped to pick it up; and when he rose again, the girl and the goat had both disappeared. He heard the sound of a bolt. It was a small door, communicating no doubt with an adjoining chamber, which was fastened on the other side.

'Has she, at least, left me a bed?' said our philosopher.

He made the tour of the chamber. There was no piece of furniture at all adapted to repose, except a very long wooden chest; and the lid of that was carved; so that it gave Gringoire, when he stretched himself upon it, a sensation much like that which Micromegas, of Voltaire's story, would experience, lying at full length upon the Alps.

'Come!' said he, making the best of it, 'there's nothing for it but resignation. And yet this is a strange wedding night. 'Tis pity, too. That broken-pitcher marriage had something simple and antediluvian about it that quite pleased me.'

BOOK THREE

I

The Cathedral of Notre-Dame

THE church of Notre-Dame at Paris is doubtless still a majestic and sublime edifice. But, however beautiful it has remained, in growing old, it is difficult to suppress a sigh, to restrain a feeling of indignation at the numberless degradations and mutilations which the hand of Time and that of man have inflicted upon this venerable monument, regardless alike of Charlemagne, who laid the first stone, and of Philip Augustus, who laid the last.

Upon the face of this ancient queen of French cathedrals, beside each wrinkle we constantly find a scar. *Tempus edax, homo edacior* (Time is destructive, man more destructive)—which we would willingly render thus—Time is blind, but man is stupid.

If we had leisure to examine one by one, with the reader, the traces of destruction imprinted on this ancient church, those due to Time would be found to form the lesser portion—the worst destruction has been perpetrated by men—especially by 'men of art.' Since there are individuals who have styled themselves architects during the last two centuries.

And first of all—to cite only a few leading examples—there are, assuredly, few finer architectural pages than that front of that cathedral, in which, successively and at once, the three receding portals with their pointed arches, the decorated and indented band of the twenty-eight royal niches, the immense central rose-window, flanked by the two lateral windows, like the priest by the deacon and sub-deacon; the lofty and slender gallery of trifoliated arcades, supporting a heavy platform upon its light and delicate columns; and lastly the two dark and massive towers, with their eaves of slate—harmonious parts of one magnificent whole—rising one above another in five gigantic stories—unfold themselves to the eye, collectively and simply—with their innumerable details of statuary, sculpture and carving, powerfully contributing to the calm grandeur of the whole; a vast symphony in stone, if we may so express it; the colossal work of a man and of a nation; combining unity with complexity, like the Iliads and the old Romance epics to which it is a sister-production; the prodigious result of a draught upon the whole resources of an era—in which, upon every stone, is seen displayed, in a hundred varieties, the fancy of the workman disciplined by the genius of the artist—a sort of human Creation, in short, mighty and prolific like the Divine Creation, of which it seems to have caught the double character—variety and eternity.

And what we say of the front must be said of the whole church —and what we say of the cathedral church of Paris must be said of all the churches of Christendom in the Middle Ages. Everything is in its place in that art, self-created, logical and well-proportioned. To measure the toe is to measure the giant.

Let us return to the front of Notre-Dame, as it still appears to us when we gaze in pious admiration upon the solemn and mighty cathedral, inspiring terror, as its chroniclers express it—*quae mole sua terrorem incutit spectantibus* (which by its massiveness strikes terror into the beholders).

This front is now lacking in three things of importance: first, the flight of eleven steps which formerly raised it above the level of the ground; then, the lower range of statues, which occupied the niches of the three portals; and lastly, the upper series, of the twenty-eight most ancient kings of France, which filled the gallery on the first story, beginning with Childebert and ending with Philip Augustus, each holding in his hand the imperial ball.

As for the flight of steps, it is Time that has caused it to disappear, by raising, with slow but resistless progress, the level of the ground in the City. But while this flood-tide of the pavements of Paris devoured, one after another, the eleven steps which added to the majestic elevation of the structure, Time has given to the church, perhaps, yet more than it has taken away; for it is Time who has spread over its face that dark gray tint of centuries which makes of the old age of architectural monuments their season of beauty.

But who has thrown down the two ranges of statues? who has left the niches empty? who has cut, in the middle of the central portal, that new and bastard pointed arch? and who has dared to frame in that doorway the heavy, unmeaning wooden door, carved in the style of Louis XV, beside the arabesques of Biscornette? The men, the architects, the artists of our times.

And—if we enter the interior of the edifice—who has overturned the colossal Saint Christopher, proverbial for his magnitude among statues as the Grand Hall of the Palace was among halls—as the spire of Strasburg among steeples? And those myriads of statues which thronged the spaces between the columns of the nave and the choir—kneeling—standing—and on horseback, men, women, children, kings, bishops, warriors, in stone, in marble, in gold, in silver, in brass, and even in wax—who has brutally swept them out? It is not Time.

And who has substituted for the ancient Gothic altar, splendidly loaded with shrines and reliquaries, that heavy sarcophagus of marble, with angels' heads and clouds, looking like an unmatched fragment from the Val de Grâce or the Invalides? Who has stupidly fixed that heavy anachronism of stone into the Carlovingian pavement of Hercandus? Was it not Louis XIV fulfilling the vow of Louis XIII?

And who has put cold white glass in place of those deep-stained panes which made the wondering eyes of our forefathers hesitate between the round window over the grand doorway and the lancet windows of the chancel? And what would a precentor of the sixteenth century say could he see that fine yellow stain with which the Vandal archbishops have besmeared their cathedral? He would remember that it was the colour with which the hangman painted such buildings as were adjudged infamous—he would recollect the hotel of the Petit-Bourbon, which had thus been besmeared with yellow for the treason of the constable—'yellow, after all, so well mixed,' says Sauval, 'and so well applied, that the lapse of a century and more has not yet taken its colour.' He would believe that the holy place had become accursed, and would flee from it.

And, then, if we climb higher in the cathedral—without stopping at a thousand barbarities of every kind—what have they done with that charming little spire which rose from the intersection of the cross, and which, no less bold and light than its neighbour, the spire of the Sainte Chapelle (destroyed also), pierced into the sky yet farther than the towers—perforated, sharp, sonorous, airy? An architect 'of good taste' amputated it in 1787, and thought it was sufficient to hide the wound with that great plaster of lead which resembles the lid of a porridge-pot.

Thus it is that the wondrous art of the Middle Ages has been treated in almost every country, and especially in France. In its ruin three sorts of inroads are distinguishable, having marred it to different depths; first, Time, which has insensibly made breaches here and there, and rusted its whole surface; then, religious and political revolutions, which, blind and furious in their nature, have tumultuously wreaked their wrath upon it, torn its rich garment of sculpture and carving, shivered its rose-shaped windows, broken its necklace of arabesques and miniature figures, torn down its statues, here for their mitre, there for their crown; and lastly, changing fashion, growing ever more grotesque and absurd, commencing with the anarchical yet splendid deviations of the Renaissance, have succeeded one another in the unavoidable decline of architecture. Fashion has done more mischief than revolutions. It has cut to the quick—it has attacked the very bone and framework of the art. It has mangled, dislocated, killed the edifice—in its form as well as in its meaning—in its logic as well as in its beauty. And then it has restored—which at least neither

Time nor revolutions have pretended to do. It has audaciously fitted into the wounds of Gothic architecture its wretched gewgaws of a day—its marble ribands—its metal plumes—a very leprosy of egg-shaped mouldings, volutes and wreaths—of draperies, garlands and fringes—of stone flames, brazen clouds, fleshy Cupids, and lastly, cherubim—which we find beginning to ravage the face of art in the oratory of Catherine de Médicis, and destroying it two centuries after, tortured and convulsed, in the Dubarry's boudoir.

Thus, to sum up the points which we have here laid down, three kinds of ravages which to-day disfigure Gothic architecture: wrinkles and warts upon the surface—these are the work of Time; violences, brutalities, contusions, fractures—these are the work of revolutions, from Luther down to Mirabeau; amputations, dislocation of members, *restorations*—these are the labours, Grecian, Roman and barbaric, of the professors according to Vitruvius and Vignola. That magnificent art which the Vandals had produced, the academies have murdered. To the work of centuries and of revolutions, which, at least, devastate with impartiality and grandeur, has been added that cloud of school-trained architects, licensed, privileged and patented, degrading with all the discernment and selection of bad taste—substituting the gingerbread-work of Louis XV for the Gothic tracery, to the greater glory of the Parthenon. This is the kick of the ass at the dying lion. 'Tis the old oak, in the last stage of decay, stung and gnawed by caterpillars.

How remote is all this from the time when Robert Cenalis, comparing Notre-Dame at Paris to the famous temple of Diana at Ephesus, 'so much vaunted by the ancient pagans,' which immortalized Erostratus, thought the Gaulish cathedral 'more excellent in length, breadth, height and structure.' *

Notre-Dame, however, as an architectural monument, is not one of those which can be called complete, definite, belonging to a class. It is no longer a Roman, nor is it yet Gothic. This edifice is not a typical one. It has not, like the abbey of Tournus, the solemn and massive squareness, the round broad vault, the icy bareness, the majestic simplicity, of the edifices which have the circular arch for their base. Nor is it, like the cathedral of Bourges, the magnificent, airy, multiform, tufted, pinnacled, florid production of the pointed arch. Impossible to rank Notre-Dame among that antique family of churches, gloomy, mysterious, lowering, crushed, as it were, by the weight of the circular arch—almost Egyptian, even to their ceilings—all hieroglyphical, all sacerdotal, all symbolical—more abounding, in their ornaments, in lozenges

* The quotations in this paragraph are made by M. Hugo from Cenalis, *Gallican History,* Book II, Period III, fo. 130, p. 1.—J. C. B.

and zigzags than in flowers—more in flowers than animals—more in animals than human figures—the work not so much of the architect as of the bishop—the first transformation of the art—all stamped with theocratical and military discipline—having its root in the Lower Empire, and stopping at the time of William the Conqueror. Nor can our cathedral be ranked in that other family of lofty, airy churches, rich in sculpture and stained glass, of pointed forms and daring attitudes—belonging to commoners and plain citizens, as political symbols—as works of art, free, capricious, lawless—the second transformation of architecture—no longer hieroglyphical, immutable and sacerdotal, but artistic, progressive and popular—beginning at the return from the crusades and ending with Louis XI. Notre-Dame of Paris, then, is not of purely Roman race like the former, nor of purely Arabic race like the latter.

It is an edifice of the transition period. The Saxon architect was just finishing the first pillars of the nave, when the pointed arch, arriving from the crusade, came and placed itself as a conqueror upon the broad Roman capitals which had been designed to support only circular arches. The Gothic arch, thenceforward master of the field, constituted the remainder of the church. However, inexperienced and timid at its commencement, we find it widening its compass, and, as it were, self-restraining, not yet daring to spring into arrows and lancets, as it did later in so many wonderful cathedrals. One would have said it was conscious of the neighbourhood of the heavy Roman pillars.

Indeed, these edifices of the transition from the Roman to the Gothic are not less valuable studies than the pure models. They express a blending in art which would be lost without them. It is the grafting of the Gothic upon the circular arch.

Notre-Dame, in particular, is a curious example of this variety. Every face, every stone, of this venerable monument, is a page not only of the history of the country, but of the history of science and art. Thus, to point out here only some of the principal details; while the small Porte Rouge attains almost to the limits of the Gothic delicacy of the fifteenth century, the pillars of the nave, in their amplitude and solemnity, go back almost as far as the Carlovingian abbey of Saint Germain des Prés. One would think there was an interval of six centuries between that door and those pillars. Even the hermetics find, in the emblematical devices of the great portal, a satisfactory compendium of their science, of which the church of Saint Jacques de la Boucherie was so complete a hieroglyphic. Thus the Roman abbey—the philosophers' church —Gothic art—Saxon art—the heavy round pillar, which recalls Gregory VII—the hermetical symbolism by which Nicolas Flamel anticipated Luther—papal unity and schism—Saint Germain des Prés and Saint Jacques de la Boucherie, all are mingled, combined and amalgamated in Notre-Dame. This central and maternal church is, among the other old churches of Paris, a sort of chimera; she has the head of one, the limbs of another, the back of a third —something of all.

We repeat it, these hybrid constructions are not the least interesting to the artist, the antiquary and the historian. They show us in how great a degree architecture is a primitive thing—demonstrating (as the Cyclopean vestiges, the Egyptian pyramids and the gigantic Hindoo pagodas demonstrate) that the greatest productions of architecture are not so much the work of individuals as of society—the offspring rather of national efforts than the conceptions of men of genius, a deposit left by a whole people—the piled up works of centuries—the residue of successive evaporations of human society—in short, a species of formation. Each wave of time leaves its alluvium—each race deposits its strata upon the monument—each individual contributes his stone. So do the beavers—so do the bees—so does man. The great symbol of architecture, Babel, is a beehive.

Great edifices, like great mountains, are the work of ages. Art often undergoes a transformation while they are still pending— *pendent opera interrupta* (the interrupted work is discontinued); they go on again quietly, in accordance with the change in the art. The altered art takes up the monument where it was left off, incrusts itself upon it, assimilates it to itself, develops it after its own fashion, and finishes it if it can. The thing is done without disturbance, without effort, without reaction, according to a law natural and tranquil. It is like a budding graft—a sap that circulates—a vegetation that goes forward. Certainly there is matter for very large volumes, and often for the universal history of humanity, in those successive weldings of several species of art at different elevations upon the same monument. The man, the artist, the individual, disappear upon those great masses, leaving no name of an author behind. Human intelligence is there to be traced only in its aggregate. Time is the architect—the nation is the builder.

To consider in this place only the architecture of Christian Europe, the younger sister of the great masonries of the East; it presents to us an immense formation, divided into three superincumbent zones, clearly defined; the Roman zone, the Gothic zone, and the zone of the Renaissance, which we would willingly entitle the Græco-Roman. The Roman stratum, the most ancient and the deepest, is occupied by the circular arch, which reappears rising from the Grecian column, in the modern and upper stratum of the Revival. The pointed arch is found between the two. The buildings which belong exclusively to one or other of these three strata are perfectly distinct, uniform and complete. Such is the abbey of Jumièges; such is the cathedral of Rheims; such is the church of Sainte Croix at Orleans. But the three zones mingle and combine at their borders, like the colours of the prism. And hence the complex monuments—the edifices of gradation and transition. One is Roman at the base, Gothic in the middle and Græco-Roman at the top. This is caused by the fact that it has taken six hundred years to build it. This variety is rare; the donjon tower of Etampes is a specimen. But monuments of two formations are more frequent. Such is Notre-Dame at Paris, a structure of the pointed arch, which, in its earliest columns, dips into that Roman zone in which the portal of Saint Denis and the nave of Saint Germain des Prés are entirely immersed. Such is the charming semi-Gothic chapter-house of Bocherville, which the Roman layer mounts half-way. Such is the cathedral of Rouen, which would have been entirely Gothic had not the extremity of its central spire pierced into the zone of the Renaissance.

However, all these gradations, all these differences, only affect the surface of an edifice. Art has but changed its skin—the conformation of the Christian temple itself has remained untouched. It is ever the same internal framework, the same logical disposition of parts. Whatever be the sculptured and decorated exterior of a cathedral, we always find beneath it at least the germ and rudiment of the Roman basilica. It unfolds itself upon the ground forever according to the same law. There are invariably two naves intersecting each other in the form of a cross, the upper extremity of which cross is rounded into a chancel forming the choir; there are always two side aisles for processions and chapels—a sort of lateral gallery communicating with the principal nave by the spaces between the columns. This settled, the number of chapels, doorways, steeples, spires, may be modified indefinitely, following the fancy of the age, the people, of the art. The performance of the worship being provided for, architecture is at liberty to do what she pleases. Statues, painted glass, rose-shaped windows, arabesques, indentations, capitals, bas-reliefs—all these objects of imagination she combines in such arrangement as best suits her. Hence the prodigious external variety of these edifices, in the main structure of which dwells so much order and unity. The trunk of the tree is unchanging—the foliage is variable.

A Bird's-Eye View of Paris

WE have endeavoured to restore for the reader the admirable church of Notre-Dame de Paris. We have briefly indicated the greater part of the beauties which it possessed in the fifteenth century, and which are now wanting; but we have omitted the principal—the view of Paris as it then appeared from the summit of the towers.

Indeed, when, after feeling your way for a long time up the dark spiral staircase that perpendicularly perforates the thick walls of the steeples, you at last emerged suddenly upon one of the two elevated platforms inundated with light and air, it was a fine picture that opened upon you on every side, a spectacle *sui generis*, some idea of which may easily be formed by such of our readers as have had the good fortune to see a Gothic town, entire, complete, homogeneous—of which there are still a few remaining, such as Nuremberg in Bavaria and Vittoria in Spain—or even smaller specimens, provided they be in good preservation, as Vitré in Brittany and Nordhausen in Prussia.

The Paris of three hundred and fifty years ago, the Paris of the fifteenth century, was already a giant city. We modern Parisians are mistaken as to the ground which we think we have gained. Since the time of Louis XI, Paris has not increased much more than a third. She certainly has lost much more in beauty than she has gained in size.

Paris was born, as every one knows, in that ancient island of the Cité, or City, which is shaped like a cradle. The shores of this island were its first enclosure; the Seine its first moat. For several centuries Paris remained in its island state; with two bridges, one on the north, the other on the south; and two *tête-de-ponts* (bridge towers), which were at once its gates and its fortresses—the Grand Châtelet on the right bank of the northern channel of the river, and the Petit Châtelet on the left bank of the southern channel. When, however, under the first line of French kings, Paris found herself too much confined within the limits of her island, and unable to turn about, she crossed the water. Then on each side, beyond either Châtelet, a first line of walls and towers began to cut into the country on both sides of the Seine. Of this ancient boundary wall some vestiges still remained as late as the last century; now nothing but the memory of it survives, with here and there a local tradition, as the Baudets or Baudoyer gate— *porta Bagauda*. By degrees, the flood of houses, perpetually driven from the heart of the town outward, overflowed and wore away this enclosure. Philip Augustus made a new embankment. He imprisoned Paris within a circular chain of great towers, lofty and massive. For upwards of a century the houses pressed upon one another, accumulated and rose higher in this basin, like water in a reservoir. They began to deepen—to pile story on story—to climb, as it were, one upon another. They shot out in height, like growth that is compressed laterally; and strove each to lift its head above its neighbours, in order to get a breath of air. The streets became deeper and narrower, and every open space was overrun by buildings and disappeared. The houses at last leaped the wall of Philip Augustus, and scattered themselves merrily over the plain, irregularly and all awry, like children escaped from school. There they strutted proudly about, cut themselves gardens from the fields and took their ease. In 1367, the suburbs already extended so far that a new boundary wall became necessary, particularly on the right bank of the river; Charles V built it. But a city like Paris is perpetually on the increase—and it is only such cities that become capitals. They are a sort of funnel, through which flow all that is geographical, political, moral and intellectual in a country—all the natural tendencies of a people—wells of civilization, as it were, and also sinks—where commerce, manufactures, intelligence, population—all the vigour, all the life, all the soul of a nation— filter and collect incessantly, drop by drop, and century after century. So the boundary of Charles V suffered the same fate as that of Philip Augustus. At the end of the fifteenth century, the Faubourg strides across it, passes beyond it, and runs farther. In the sixteenth we find it rapidly receding, and becoming buried deeper and deeper in the old town, so dense was the new town becoming outside it. Thus, in the fifteenth century—to stop there —Paris had already worn away the three concentric circles of walls which, in the time of Julian the Apostate, existed, so to speak, in germ in the Grand Châtelet and the Petit Châtelet. The growing city had successively burst its four girdles of walls, like a child grown too large for its garments of last year. In the reign of Louis XI were to be seen rising here and there, amid that sea of houses, some groups of ruinous towers belonging to the ancient bulwarks, like hill-tops in a flood—like archipelagoes of the old Paris submerged under the inundation of the new.

Since then, unhappily for us, Paris has undergone another transformation; but it has overleaped only one boundary more— that of Louis XV—the wretched wall of mud and spittle, worthy of the king who built it, worthy of the poet who sang it—

Le mur murant Paris rend Paris murmurant. *

* Play upon words, literally: The wall walling Paris makes Paris murmur.

In the fifteenth century, Paris was still divided into three wholly distinct and separate towns, having each its peculiar features, manners, customs, privileges and history—the City, the University and the Ville or Town properly so called. The City, which occupied the island, was the most ancient, the smallest, and the mother of the other two—sqeezed between them (if we may be allowed the comparison) like a little old woman between two tall handsome daughters. The University covered the left bank of the Seine, from the Tournelle to the Tour de Nesle, points which correspond to-day in modern Paris, the one to the Halle aux Vins or Wine Mart, and the other to the Monnaie or Mint. Its circuit embraced a large portion of that tract where Julian had constructed his baths, and comprised the hill of Sainte Geneviève. The culminating point of this curve of walls was the Porte Papale or Papal Gate, that is to say, very nearly, the present site of the Panthéon. The Town, which was the largest of the three portions of Paris, occupied the right bank. Its quay, in which there were several breaks and interruptions, ran along the Seine from the Tour de Billy to the Tour du Bois, that is, from the spot where the Granary of Abundance now stands, to that occupied by the Tuileries. These four points where the Seine intersected the wall of the capital—on the left, the Tournelle and the Tour de Nesle, and on the right, the Tour de Billy and the Tour du Bois—were called, pre-eminently, the four towers of Paris. The Town encroached still more deeply into the country bordering on the Seine than the University. The most salient points of its enclosure (the wall constructed by Charles V) were at the Portes Saint Denis and Saint Martin, the sites of which are unchanged.

As we have just said, each of these three great divisions of Paris was a city in itself—but a city too individual to be complete—a city which could not dispense with the other two. Hence, each had its characteristic aspect. Churches abounded in the City; palaces in the Town, and colleges in the University. Leaving apart the minor eccentricities of old Paris, and the caprices of those who held the *droit de voirie*, or right of road, we make the general statement —and speaking only of the great masses in the chaos of the communal jurisdictions—that the island belonged to the bishop; the right bank, to the *prévôt des marchands* or provost of the shop-keepers; and the left bank to the rector of the University. The provost of Paris, a royal and not a municipal officer, had authority over all. The City contained Notre-Dame; the Town, the Louvre and the Hôtel de Ville; and the University, the Sorbonne. Again, the Town had the Great Market; the City, the Hospital; and the University, the Pré aux Clercs (common). Offences committed by the students on the left bank, in their Pré aux Clercs, were tried in the Palace of Justice, on the island, and punished on the right bank at Montfaucon; unless the rector, feeling the University to be strong at that particular time, and the king weak, thought proper to interfere—for it was a privilege of the scholars to be hanged at home, that is to say, within the University precincts. Most of these privileges, it may be noted in passing, and there were some of greater value than the above, had been extorted from the kings by revolts and mutinies. Such has been the course of events from time immemorial. As the French proverb saith, *Le roi ne lache que quand le peuple arrache* (the king only grants what the people wrest from him). There is an old French charter which states the fact with great simplicity: speaking of loyalty, it says, *Civibus fidelitas in reges, quae tamen aliquoties seditionibus interrupta, multa peperit privilegia* (the fidelity toward kings, which was nevertheless interrupted at different times—interrupted by seditious uprisings—preserved many privileges to the people).

In the fifteenth century, the Seine bathed the shores of five islands within the circuit of Paris; the Ile Louviers, on which there were then trees, though now there are only piles of wood; the Ile aux Vaches and the Ile Notre-Dame, both deserted, or nearly so, both fiefs of the bishop (which two islands, in the seventeenth century, were made into one, since built upon, and now called the Ile Saint Louis); finally, the City, having at its western extremity, the islet of the Passeur aux Vaches, since lost under the esplanade of the Pont-Neuf. The City had, at that time, five bridges; three on the right—the Pont Notre-Dame, and the Pont au Change, of stone, and the Pont aux Meuniers, of wood—and two on the left —the Petit Pont, of stone, and the Pont Saint Michel, of wood; all of them laden with houses. The University had six gates, built by Philip Augustus, which, starting from the Tournelle, came in the following order: the Porte Saint Victor, the Porte Bordelle, the Porte Papale, the Porte Saint Jacques, the Porte Saint Michel and the Porte Saint Germain. The Town had also six gates, built by Charles V, viz., beginning with the Tour de Billy, they were the Porte Saint Antoine, the Porte du Temple, the Porte Saint Martin, the Porte Saint Denis, the Porte Montmartre and the Porte Saint Honoré. All these gates were strong, and handsome withal—which latter attribute is by no means incompatible with strength. A wide and deep moat, with a swift current during the winter floods, washed the base of the wall around Paris; the Seine furnishing the water. At night the gates were shut, the river was barred at the two extremities of the town with massive iron chains, and Paris slept tranquilly.

A bird's-eye view of these three burghs, the City, the University and the Ville, presented each an inextricable network of strangely tangled streets. Yet a glance was sufficient to show the spectator that these three portions of a city formed but one complete whole. One immediately perceived two long parallel streets, unbroken, undisturbed, traversing, almost in a straight line, the three towns, from one extremity to the other, from north to south, at right angles with the Seine, connecting and mingling them, and incessantly pouring the people of each into the precincts of the other, making the three but one. The first of these two streets ran from the Porte Saint Jacques to the Porte Saint Martin; and was called in the University, Rue Saint Jacques; in the City, Rue de la Juiverie (Jewery or Jewry); and in the Town, Rue Saint Martin. It crossed the water twice, under the names of Petit Pont and Pont Notre-Dame. The second, called, on the left bank, Rue de la Harpe; in the island, the Rue de la Barillerie; on the right bank, Rue Saint Denis; over one arm of the Seine, Pont Saint Michel, and over the other Pont au Change; ran from the Porte Saint Michel in the University to the Porte Saint Denis in the Town. However, under all these names, they were still but two streets; but they were the parent streets—the two arteries of Paris, by which all the other veins of the triple city were fed, or into which they emptied themselves.

Independently of these two principal, diametrical streets, running quite across Paris, common to the whole capital, the Town and the University had each its own special street, traversing its length, parallel to the Seine, and intersecting the two *arterial* streets at right angles. Thus, in the Town, one went down in a straight line from the Porte Saint Antoine to the Porte Saint Honoré; in the University, from the Porte Saint Victor to the Porte Saint Germain. These two great ways, crossing the two first mentioned, formed with them the canvas upon which was wrought, knotted up and crowded together on every hand, the tangled Dædalian web of the streets of Paris. In the unintelligible designs of this network one distinguished likewise, on looking attentively, two clusters of great streets, like magnified sheaves, one in the University, the other in the Town, spreading out from the bridges to the gates.

Somewhat of this geometric plan still exists.

Now, what aspect did all this present viewed from the top of the towers of Notre-Dame in 1482? This is what we will endeavour to describe.

For the spectator, who arrived panting upon this summit, it was at first a dazzling confusion of roofs, chimneys, streets, bridges, squares, spires, steeples. All burst upon the eye at once—the formally-cut gable, the acute-angled roof, the hanging turret at the angles of the walls, the stone pyramid of the eleventh century, the slate obelisk of the fifteenth; the donjon tower, round and bare; the church tower, square and decorated; the large and the small, the massive and the airy. The gaze was for some time lost in the bewilderment of this labyrinth; in which there was nothing without its originality, its purpose, its genius—nothing but proceeded from art—from the smallest house, with its carved and painted front, with external beams, elliptical doorway, with projecting stories, to the royal Louvre itself, which then had a colonnade of towers. But these are the principal masses that were distinguishable when the eye became accustomed to this medley of edifices.

First, the City. The island of the City, as Sauval says, who, amidst all his rubbish, has occasional happy turns of expression— *The isle of the City is shaped like a great ship, stuck in the mud, and stranded in the current near the middle of the Seine.* We have already shown that, in the fifteenth century, this ship was moored to the two banks of the river by five bridges. This likeness to a vessel had also struck the heraldic scribes; for, it is thence, and not from the Norman siege, according to Favyn and Pasquier, that the ship emblazoned upon the old escutcheon of Paris comes. To him who can decipher it, heraldry is an algebra—heraldry is a tongue. The whole history of the second half of the Middle Ages is written in heraldry, as that of the former half is in the symbolism of the Roman churches. They are the hieroglyphics of feudalism succeeding those of theocracy.

The City, then, first presented itself to the view, with its stern to the east and its prow to the west. Looking toward the prow, there was before one an innumerable collection of old roofs, with the lead-covered top of Sainte Chapelle rising above them broad and round, like an elephant's back laden with its tower. Only in this case the tower was the most daring, most open, most daintily wrought, most delicately carved spire that ever showed the sky through its lacework cone. In front of Notre-Dame, close at hand, three streets opened into the Cathedral Square, which was a fine square of old houses. The southern side of this Place was overhung by the furrowed and wrinkled front of the Hôtel Dieu, and its roof, which looks as if covered with pustules and warts. Then, right and left, east and west, within that narrow circuit of the City, were ranged the steeples of its twenty-one churches, of all dates, forms and sizes; from the low and worm-eaten Roman campanile of Saint Denis du Pas, *carcer Glaucini* (Prison of Glaucinus), to the slender spires of Saint Pierre aux Bœufs and Saint Laundry. Behind Notre-Dame were revealed northward, the cloister, with its Gothic galleries; southward, the semi-Roman palace of the bishop; and eastward, the uninhabited point of the Terrain, or waste ground. Amid that accumulation of houses the eye could also distinguish, by the high perforated mitres of stone, which at that period were placed aloft upon the roof itself, surmounting the highest range of palace windows, the mansion presented by the Parisians, in the reign of Charles VI, to Juvénal des Ursins; a little farther on, the tarred booths of the Palus Market; and in another direction, the new apse of Saint Germain le Vieux, lengthened, in 1458, by a bit of the Rue aux Febves; and then, at intervals, a square crowded with people—a pillory set up at some street corner—a fine piece of the pavement of Philip Augustus—magnificent flagging, furrowed for the horses' feet in the middle of the roadway, and so badly replaced in the sixteenth century by the wretched pebbling called *pavé de la Ligue* (pavements of the League)—some solitary backyard, with one of those open turret staircases, which were built in the fifteenth century, one of which is still to be seen in the Rue des Bourdonnais. Finally, on the right of the Sainte Chapelle, to the westward, the Palace of Justice rested its group of towers upon the water's brink. The groves of the royal gardens which occupied the western point of the City hid from view the islet of the Paseur. As for the water itself, it was hardly visible from the towers of Notre-Dame, on either side of the City; the Seine disappearing under the bridges, and the bridges under the houses.

And when the glance passed these bridges, the roofs of which were visibly turning green from mould, before their time, from the vapours of the water; if it turned to the left, toward the University, the first edifice that struck it was a large low cluster of towers, the Petit Châtelet, whose yawning porch seemed to devour the extremity of the Petit Pont. Then, if your view ran along the bank from east to west, from the Tournelle to the Tour de Nesle, there were to be seen a long line of houses exhibiting sculptured beams, coloured window-glass, each story overhanging that beneath it—an interminable zigzag of homely gables, cut at frequent intervals by the intersection of some street, and now and then also by the front or the corner of some great stone-built mansion, which seemed to stand at its ease, with its courtyards and gardens, its wings and its compartments, amid that rabble of houses crowding and pinching one another, like a grand seigneur amidst a mob of rustics. There were five or six of these mansions upon the quay, from the Logis de Lorraine, which shared with the house of the Bernardines the great neighbouring enclosure of the Tournelle, to the Hôtel de Nesle, the principal tower of which bounded Paris on that side, and the pointed roofs of which were so situated as to cut with their dark triangles, during three months of the year, the scarlet disc of the setting sun.

This side of the Seine, however, was the least mercantile of the two; students were noisier and more numerous than artisans; and there was not, properly speaking, any quay, except from the Pont

Saint Michel to the Tour de Nesle. The rest of the bank of the
Seine was either a bare strand, as was the case beyond the
Bernardine monastery, or a close range of houses with the water
at their base, as between the two bridges.

There was a great clamour of washerwomen along the waterside,
talking, shouting, singing, from morning till night along the shore,
and beating away at their linen—as they do in our day. This is
not the least of the gaieties of Paris.

The University presented a huge mass to the eye. From one end
to the other it was a compact and homogeneous whole. The myriad
roofs, dense, angular, adherent, nearly all composed of the same
geometrical element, when seen from above, looked like a crystalli-
zation of one substance. The capricious hollows of the streets
divided this pasty of houses into slices not too disproportioned. The
forty-two colleges were distributed among them very evenly, and
were to be seen in every quarter. The amusingly varied pinnacles
of those fine buildings were the product of the same art as the
simple roofs which they overtopped, being really but a multipli-
cation of the square or cube, of the same geometrical figure. Thus
they made the whole more intricate without confusing it, complete
without overloading it. Geometry is harmony. Several fine mansions also made here and there magnificent outlines against the
picturesque attics of the left bank; the Nevers house, the house of
Rome, the Reims house, which have disappeared; and the Hôtel
de Cluny, which still exists for the consolation of the artist, but
the tower of which was so stupidly shortened a few years ago.
Near by Cluny, that Roman palace, with fine semicircular arches,
was formerly the Baths of Julian. There were also a number of
abbeys of a more ecclesiastical beauty, of a more solemn grandeur
than the mansions, but not less beautiful nor less grand. Those
which first attracted the eye were the monastery of the Bernardines,
with its three bell-towers; Sainte Geneviève, whose square tower,
still standing, makes us regret the rest so much; the Sorbonne,
half-college, half-monastery, of which so admirable a nave still
remains; the fine quadrangular cloister of the Mathurins; its
neighbour, the cloister of Saint Benedict, within whose walls they
have had time to knock up a theatre between the seventh and
eighth editions of this book; the Cordeliers, with their three
enormous gables; side by side the Augustins, whose graceful spire
was, after the Tour de Nesle, the second lofty projection on that
side of Paris, from the westward. The colleges—which are in fact
the intermediate link between the cloister and the world—held the
central point in the architectural series between the fine private
residences and the abbeys, exhibiting a severe elegance, a sculpture
less airy than that of the palaces, an architecture less severe than

that of the convents. Unfortunately, scarcely anything remains of these structures, in which Gothic art held so just a balance between richness and economy. The churches (and they were numerous and splendid in the University, and there displayed every period of architecture, from the round arches of Saint Julian to the Gothic ones of Saint Severin)—the churches rose above the whole; and, like one harmony the more in that mass of harmonies, they pierced, one after another, the varied outline of gables, of sharply-defined spires, of perforated steeples and slender pinnacles, whose outline was but a magnificent exaggeration of the acute angle of the roofs.

The ground of the University was hilly. The mountain of Sainte Geneviève, on the southeast, formed an enormous swell; and it was a sight well worth seeing, from the top of Notre-Dame, that crowd of narrow, tortuous streets (to-day the Latin quarter), those clusters of houses which, scattered in every direction from the top of that eminence, spread themselves in disorder, and almost precipitously down its sides, to the water's edge; looking, some as if they were falling, others as if they were climbing up, and all as if holding on to one another. The continual motion of a myriad black dots crossing and recrossing each other on the pavement, gave a shimmering look to everything. These were the people in the streets, seen from a height and a distance.

Finally in the spaces between these roofs, these spires, these innumerable and irregular structures, which so fantastically bent, twisted and indented the extreme outline of the University, one caught a glimpse here and there of some great patch of moss-covered wall, some thick round tower, or some crenellated town gate, resembling a fortress—this was the wall of Philip Augustus. Beyond extended the green meadows; beyond these ran the high-ways, along which were scattered a few more suburban houses which became more infrequent as they became more distant. Some of these suburbs were of considerable importance. There were first (starting from the Tournelle) the burgh Saint Victor, with its bridge of one arch over the Bievre; its abbey, in which was to be read the epitaph of King Louis the Fat—*epitaphium Ludovici Grossi;* and its church with an octagonal spire flanked by four small bell-towers, of the eleventh century (a similar one can be seen at Etampes; it is not yet destroyed). Next, the burgh Saint Marceau, which had already three churches and a convent. Then, leaving the mill of the Gobelins and its four white walls on the left, there was the Faubourg Saint Jacques, with the beautiful carved cross in its square; the church of Saint Jacques du Haut Pas, which was then Gothic, pointed and delightful; Saint Magloire, with a fine fourteenth century nave, which Napoleon turned into a hay-loft; Notre-Dame des Champs, where there were Byzantine mosaics.

Lastly, after leaving in the open country the Carthusian monastery, a rich structure of the same period as the Palace of Justice, with its little gardens in sections and the ill-famed ruins of Vauvert, the eye fell to westward, upon the three Roman spires of Saint Germain des Prés. The borough Saint Germain, already a large community, had fifteen or twenty streets in the rear; the sharp steeple of Saint Sulpice indicating one of its corners. Close by it might be seen the square enclosure of the Saint Germain fair ground where the market now stands; then the abbot's pillory, a pretty little round tower, neatly capped with a cone of lead; the tilekiln was farther on as well as the Rue du Four, which led to the common bakehouse, with the mill on its knoll—and the lazaretto, a small, detached, and half-seen building. But that which especially attracted the eye, and long held the attention, was the abbey itself. It is certain that this monastery, which had an aspect of grandeur both as a church and as a seigniory, this abbatial palace, in which the bishops of Paris deemed themselves happy to sleep a single night —this refectory, upon which the architect had bestowed the air, the beauty, and the splendid rose-shaped window of a cathedral —this elegant chapel of the Virgin—this monumental dormitory —those spacious gardens—the portcullis and drawbridge—the circuit of battlements which marked its indented outline against the verdure of the surrounding meadows—those courtyards where gleamed men-at-arms intermingled with golden copes—the whole grouped and clustered about three tall spires with their semi-circular arches solidly planted upon a Gothic apse—made a magnificent outline upon the horizon.

When at length, after long contemplating the University, you turned toward the right bank towards the Town, the character of the scene was suddenly changed. The Town was not only much larger than the University, but also less uniform. At first sight it appeared to be divided into several portions, singularly distinct from each other. First, to the East, in that part of the Town which still takes its name from the marsh in which Camulogenes mired Cæsar, there was a collection of palaces, which extended to the waterside. Four great mansions almost contiguous—the Hôtels de Jouy, de Sens, and de Barbeau and the Logis de la Reine— mirrored their slated roofs broken by slender turrets in the Seine. These four edifices filled the space from the Rue des Nonaindières to the abbey of the Celestines, whose spire formed a graceful relief to their line of gables and battlements. Some sorry, moss-grown structures overhanging the water in front of these sumptuous mansions did not conceal from view the fine lines of their fronts, their great square stone-framed windows, their Gothic porches loaded with statues, the boldly-cut borderings about their walls, and all those charming accidents of architecture which make Gothic art seem to begin again its series of combinations at every fresh building. Behind these palaces ran in every direction, in some places cloven, palisaded and embattled, like a citadel, in others concealed by large trees like a Carthusian monastery, the vast and multiform circuit of that wonderful Hôtel de Saint Pol, in which the French king had room to lodge superbly twenty-two princes of the rank of the dauphin and the Duke of Burgundy, with their trains and their domestics, without counting the grands seigneurs and the emperor when he came to visit Paris, and the lions that had a separate residence within the royal establishment. And we must here observe that a prince's lodgings then consisted of not less than eleven principal apartments, from the audience-chamber to the oratory; besides all the galleries, baths, stove-rooms and other 'superfluous places,' with which each suite of apartments was provided; not to mention the private gardens for each of the king's guests; besides the kitchens, cellars, pantries and general refectories of the household; the servants' quarters, in which there were two-and-twenty general offices, from the bake-house to the wine cellars; games of different kinds, as mall, tennis, riding at the ring, etc.; aviaries, fish-ponds, menageries, stables, cattle-stalls, libraries, armouries and foundries. Such was, at that day, a royal palace—a Louvre—a Hôtel Saint Pol; a city within a city.

From the tower upon which we have placed ourselves, the Hôtel Saint Pol, though almost half hidden by the four great dwelling-houses of which we have just spoken, was, nevertheless, very vast and very wonderful to behold. One could clearly distinguish in it, although they had been skilfully joined to the main building by means of long windowed and pillared galleries, the three residences which Charles V had thrown into one, together with his former palace; the Hôtel du Petit-Muce, with the open-work balustrade so gracefully bordering its roof; the hôtel of the abbot of Saint Maur, having the aspect of a stronghold, a massive tower, bastions, loop-holes, iron cornice, and over the wide Saxon gateway, the abbot's escutcheon between the two grooves for the drawbridge; the residence of the Count d'Etampes, whose donjon-keep in ruins at the top, looked rounded and indented, like the crest of a cock; here and there three or four ancient oaks, forming a tuft together like enormous cauliflowers; swans disporting themselves amid the clear waters of the fish-ponds, all rippling with light and shade; numerous courtyards afforded picturesque glimpses; the Hôtel des Lions, with its low-pointed arches upon short Saxon pillars, its iron portcullises and its perpetual roaring; through all this the scaly spire of the Ave Maria; on the left, the house of the provost of Paris, flanked by four turrets delicately moulded and perforated; and, in the centre in the background, the Hôtel Saint Pol, properly speaking, with its multiple fronts, its successive embellishments since the time of Charles V, the hybrid excrescences with which the fancy of the artists had loaded it in the course of two centuries; with all the apses of its chapels, all the gables of its galleries, its endless weathercocks, turned to the four winds, and its two contiguous towers, the conical roof of which, surrounded by battlements at its base, looked like cocked hats.

Continuing to mount the steps of this amphitheatre of palaces spread out afar upon the ground, after crossing a deep fissure in the roofs of the Town, which marked the passage of the Rue Saint Antoine, the eye travelled on to the Logis d'Angoulême, a vast structure of several different periods, in which there were some parts quite new and almost white, that did not harmonize with the rest any better than a red patch on a blue doublet. However, the singularly sharp and elevated roof of the modern palace, bristling with carved gutters, and covered with sheets of lead, over which ran sparkling incrustations of gilt copper in a thousand fantastic arabesques—that roof so curiously damaskeened, darted upwards gracefully from amid the brown ruins of the ancient edifice, the old massive towers of which were bellying with age into the shape of casks, their height shrunk with decrepitude, and breaking asunder from top to bottom. Behind rose the forest of spires of the Palais des Tournelles. No view in the world, not even at Chambord nor at the Alhambra, could be more magical, more aërial, more enchanting, than that grove of spires, turrets, chimneys, weathercocks, spiral staircases, perforated lanterns, which looked as if struck out with a die, pavilions, spindle-shaped turrets, or tournelles, as they were then called—all differing in form, height and position. It might well have been compared to a gigantic stone checkerboard.

To the right of the Tournelles, that group of enormous inky black towers, growing, as it were, one into another, and looking as if bound together by their circular moat; that donjon tower, more thickly pierced with loop-holes than with windows; that drawbridge always raised; that portcullis always lowered; that is the Bastille. Those black muzzles, peering from the battlements, and which, at this distance, you would take for gutter spouts, are cannon.

Within gunshot below the terrible edifice is the Porte Saint Antoine, almost buried between its two towers.

Beyond the Tournelles, as far as the wall of Charles V, spread out in rich compartments of verdure and of flowers, a tufted carpet of garden-grounds and royal parks, in the midst of which one recognized, by its labyrinth of trees and alleys, the famous Dædalus garden that Louis XI gave to Coictier. The doctor's observatory rose above the labyrinth, like a great isolated column with a small house for its capital. In that small study terrible astrological predictions were made.

Upon that spot now stands the Place Royale.

As we have already observed, the region of the Palace, of which we have endeavoured to give the reader some idea, though by specifying only its most salient points, filled up the angle which Charles V's wall made with the Seine on the east. The centre of the Town was occupied by a pile of houses for the populace. It was there, in fact, that the three bridges of the City disgorged upon the right bank; and bridges lead to the building of houses rather than palaces. This collection of common dwelling-houses, pressed against one another like cells in a hive, had a beauty of its own. The roofs of a great city have a certain grandeur, like the waves of the sea. In the first place, the streets, crossed and intertwined, diversified the mass with a hundred amusing figures; around the Halles, it was like a star with a thousand rays.

The Rues Saint Denis and Saint Martin, with their innumerable ramifications, rose one after the other, like two great trees with intermingling branches; and then crooked lines, the Rues de la Plâtrerie, de la Verrerie, de la Tixeranderie, etc., wound in and out among the whole. There were also fine edifices lifting their heads above the fixed swell of this sea of gables. There, at the entrance of the Pont aux Changeurs, behind which the Seine was seen foaming under the mill-wheels at the Pont aux Meuniers, there was the Châtelet; no longer a Roman tower as under Julian, the Apostate, but a feudal tower of the thirteenth century, of a stone so hard that, in three hours' work, the pick would not remove a piece the size of a man's fist. Then there was the rich square steeple of Saint Jacques de la Boucherie, its sides all encrusted with sculptures, and already worthy of admiration, although it was not finished in the fifteenth century. (It lacked particularly those four monsters which, still perched on the four corners of its roof, look like four sphinxes giving modern Paris the riddle of ancient Paris to solve. Rault, the sculptor, only placed them in position in 1526; and received twenty francs for his trouble.) There was the Maison aux Piliers, overlooking that Place de Grève of which we have already given the reader some idea. There was the church of Saint Gervais, which a large portal *in good taste* has since spoiled; that of Saint Méry, whose ancient pointed arches were still almost rounded; and that of Saint Jean, whose magnificent spire was proverbial; besides twenty other structures which disdained not to bury their wonders in this wilderness of deep, dark and narrow streets. Add to these the carved stone crosses, even more abundant at cross-roads than gibbets; the cemetery of the Innocents, whose architectural wall was to be seen in the distance, over the house-tops; the market pillory, the top of which was visible between two chimneys of the Rue de la Cossonnerie; the 'ladder' of the Croix du Trahoir, with its cross-roads always black with people; the circular buildings of the wheat-mart; the broken fragments of the old wall of Philip Augustus, distinguishable here and there, buried among the houses—towers over-run with ivy, ruined gateways—crumbling and shapeless pieces of wall; the quay with its countless shops, and its bloody knackers' yards; the Seine covered with boats, from the Port au Foin to the For-l'Evéque; and you will have a dim idea of the appearance, in 1482, of the central trapezium, or irregular quadrangle, of the Town.

Together with these two quarters, the one of princely mansions, the other of ordinary houses, the third great feature then observable in the Town, was a long belt of abbeys bordering it almost in its entire circumference, from east to west, and, behind the line of fortification by which Paris was shut in, formed a second inner circle, consisting of convents and chapels. Thus, close to the park of the Tournelles, between the Rue Saint Antoine and the old Rue du Temple, there was Saint Catherine's, with its immense grounds, bounded only by the wall of Paris. Between the old and the new Rue du Temple there was the Temple itself, a sinister group of towers, lofty, erect and isolated in the midst of a vast, battlemented enclosure. Between the Rue Neuve du Temple and the Rue Saint Martin, in the midst of its gardens, stood Saint Martin's, a superb fortified church, whose girdle of towers, whose tiara of steeples, were second in strength and splendour only to Saint Germain des Prés. Between the two streets of Saint Martin and Saint Denis were the precincts of the convent of the Trinity. And between the Rue Saint Denis and the Rue Montorgueil was that of the Filles Dieu. Close by might be seen the decayed roofs and unpaved enclosures of the Court of Miracles. This was the only profane link in this pious chain of convents.

Lastly, the fourth division, clearly outlined in the conglomeration of roofs upon the right bank, formed by the western angle of the great enclosure, and the banks of the river down stream, was a fresh knot of palaces and great mansions crowding at the foot of the Louvre. The old Louvre of Philip Augustus, that immense structure—the great tower of which mustered around it twenty-three principal towers, besides all the smaller ones—seemed, at a distance, to be set within the Gothic summits of the Hôtel d'Alençon and the Petit Bourbon. This hydra of towers, the

giant keeper of Paris, with its four-and-twenty heads ever erect
—with its monstrous cruppers covered with lead or scaly with
slates, and all rippling with glittering metallic reflections—terminated with wonderful effect the configuration of the Town on
the west.

An immense mass, therefore—what the Romans called an
insula or island—of ordinary dwelling-houses, flanked on either
side by two great clusters of palaces, crowned, the one by the
Louvre, the other by the Tournelles, bounded on the north by a
long belt of abbeys and cultivated enclosures—blending and mingling together as one gazed at them—above these thousand
buildings, whose tiled and slated roofs stood out in such strange
outlines, the crimped, twisted and ornamented steeples of the forty-
four churches on the right bank—myriads of cross-streets—the
boundary, on one side, a line of lofty walls with square towers
(those of the University wall being round), and on the other, the
Seine, intersected by bridges and crowded with numberless boats
—such was the Town in the fifteenth century.

Beyond the walls some few suburbs crowded to the gates, but
less numerous and more scattered than those on the University
side. Thus, behind the Bastille, a score of mean houses clustered
around the curious carvings of the cross of Faubin, and the
buttresses of the abbey of Saint Antoine des Champs; then there
was Popincourt, lost amid the corn-fields; then, La Courtille, a
jolly village of taverns; the borough of Saint Laurent, with its
church, whose steeple seemed, at a distance, to belong to the
pointed towers of the Porte Saint Martin; the Faubourg Saint
Denis, with the vast enclosure of Saint Ladre; beyond the Montmartre gate, the Grange Batelière, encircled with white walls;
behind it, with its chalky declivities—Montmartre, which had then
almost as many churches as windmills, but which has kept only
the mills, for society no longer demands anything but bread for
the body. Then, beyond the Louvre, could be seen, stretching
away into the meadows, the Faubourg Saint Honoré, even then
of considerable extent; La Petite Bretagne, looking green; and
the Pig Market, spreading itself out, in the centre of which rose the
horrible cauldron used for boiling alive coiners of counterfeit
money. Between La Courtille and Saint Laurent, the eye noted
on the summit of a hill that crouched amid a desert plain, a sort of
structure, which looked at a distance like a ruined colonnade
standing upon foundations laid bare. It was neither a Parthenon
nor a temple of the Jupiter Olympus; it was Montfaucon.

Now, if the enumeration of so many edifices, brief as we have
sought to make it, has not destroyed, as fast as we constructed it,
in the reader's mind, the general image of old Paris, we will reca-

pitulate it in a few words. In the centre the island of the City, shaped like a huge turtle, extending on either side its bridges all scaly with tiles, like so many legs, from under its gray shell of roofs. On the left, the close, dense, bristling, monolithic trapezium of the University; on the right, the vast semicircle of the Town, where houses and gardens were much more mingled. The three divisions—City, University and Town—veined with countless streets. Through the whole runs the Seine, 'the nourishing Seine,' as Father du Breul calls it, obstructed with islands, bridges and boats. All around an immense plain, checkered with a thousand different crops, strewn with beautiful villages; on the left, Issy, Vanvres, Vaugirard, Montrouge, Gentilly, with its round tower and its square tower, etc.; and on the right, twenty others, from Conflans to Ville l'Evêque. In the horizon a border of hills arranged in a circle, like the rim of the basin. Finally, in the distance, to eastward, was Vincennes, with its seven quadrangular towers; to southward, Bicêtre, and its pointed turrets; to northward, Saint Denis and its spire; to westward, Saint Cloud and its donjon. Such was the Paris seen from the top of the towers of Notre-Dame by the crows who lived in 1482.

And yet it is of this city that Voltaire has said, that *before the time of Louis XIV it possessed only four fine pieces of architecture :*—that is to say, the dome of the Sorbonne, the Val de Grâce, the modern Louvre, and I know not what the fourth was, perhaps the Luxembourg. Fortunately, Voltaire was none the less the author of *Candide ;* nor is he the less, among all the men who have succeeded one another in the long series of humanity, the one who has best possessed the *rire diabolique,* the sardonic smile. This proves, moreover, that a man may be a fine genius, and yet understand nothing of an art which he has not studied. Did not Molière think he was doing great honour to Raphael and Michael Angelo when he called them 'those Mignards of their age?'

Let us return to Paris and to the fifteenth century.

It was not then merely a handsome city—it was a homogeneous city—an architectural and historical production of the Middle Ages—a chronicle in stone. It was a city composed of two architectural strata only, the bastard Roman and the Gothic layer—for the pure Roman stratum had long disappeared, except in the Baths of Julian, where it still pierced through the thick crust of the Middle Ages. As for the Celtic, no specimen of that was now to be found, even when digging wells.

Fifty years later, when the Renaissance came breaking into that unity so severe and yet so varied, with the dazzling profuseness of its fantasies and its systems, rioting among Roman arches, Grecian columns and Gothic windows—its sculpture tender and imagina-

tive—its fondness for arabesques and acanthus leaves—its architectural paganism contemporary with Luther—Paris was perhaps
more beautiful, though less harmonious to the eye and to the mind.
But that splendid period was of short duration. The Renaissance
was not impartial. Not content with building up, it thought proper to pull down—it is true it needed space. Thus Gothic Paris
was complete but for a moment. Scarcely was Saint Jacques de
la Boucherie finished before the demolition of the old Louvre
began.

Since then this great city has been daily sinking into deformity.
The Gothic Paris, under which the Roman Paris was disappearing,
has disappeared in its turn; but what name shall we give to the
Paris that has taken its place?

There is the Paris of Catherine de Medicis at the Tuileries;*
the Paris of Henry II at the Hôtel de Ville—two buildings which
are still in the best taste;—the Paris of Henry IV at the Place
Royale—brick fronts with corners of stone and slated roofs—tri-
coloured houses;—the Paris of Louis XIII at the Val de Grâce—
of architecture crushed and squat—with basket-handle vaults, big-
bellied columns and a hump-backed dome;—the Paris of Louis
XIV at the Invalides—grand, rich, gilded and cold;—the Paris
of Louis XV at Saint Sulpice—with volutes, knots of ribbons,
clouds, vermicelli and chiccory, all in stone;—the Paris of Louis
XVI at the Pantheon—Saint Peter's at Rome ill-copied (the
building stands awkwardly, which has not bettered its lines);—the
Paris of the Republic at the School of Medicine—a bit of poor
Greek and Roman taste, as much to be compared to the Coliseum
or the Parthenon as the constitution of the year III to the laws
of Minos; it is called in architecture, *le gout messidor* (the tenth
month of the French republican calendar, from the 19th of June
to the 18th of July);—the Paris of Napoleon at the Place Vendôme
—this is sublime—a bronze column made of cannon;—the Paris
of the Restoration, at the Bourse or Exchange—a very white
colonnade, supporting a very smooth frieze; the whole is square,
and cost twenty million francs.

To each of these characteristic structures is allied, by similarity

* It is with grief mingled with indignation that we learn of a proposition to enlarge,
reconstruct and make over, that is, destroy this admirable palace. The architects
of our day do not possess the lightness of hand necessary to touch the works of the
Renaissance. We continue to hope they will not dare to undertake the task. Furthermore, the present destruction of the Tuileries is not only a brutal proceeding of which
a drunken Vandal would blush, but it is an act of treason. The Tuileries is not only
a masterpiece of sixteenth century art, but a page from the history of the nineteenth
century. This palace is no longer the property of the king, but of the people. Leave
it as it is. Twice has our Revolution branded it upon the forehead. On one of its two
facades are the bullets of the 10th of August; on the other those of the 29th of July.
It is sacred.—Paris, 7th April, 1831.—(*Note to the Fifth Edition*).

of style, manner and disposition, a certain number of houses scattered over the different quarters, which the eye of the connoisseur easily distinguishes and assigns to their respective dates. When one knows how to look, one finds the spirit of a century and the physiognomy of a king even in the knocker on a door.

The Paris of to-day has therefore no general physiognomy. It is a collection of specimens of several different ages, and the finest have disappeared. The capital is increasing in houses only—and what houses! At the rate at which Paris moves it will be renewed every fifty years. Thus, also, the historical meaning of its architecture is daily becoming effaced. Its great structures are becoming fewer and fewer, seeming to be swallowed up one after another by the flood of houses. Our fathers had a Paris of stone—our sons will have a Paris of plaster.

As for the modern structures of the new Paris, we would gladly be excused from enlarging upon them. Not, indeed, that we do not grant them the admiration they merit. The Sainte Geneviève of M. Soufflot is certainly the finest Savoy cake that was ever made of stone. The Palace of the Legion of Honour is also a very distinguished piece of confectionery. The dome of the Corn Market is an English jockey-cap on a magnificent scale. The towers of Saint Sulpice are two great clarinets; a good enough shape in its way; and then, the telegraph, crooked and grinning, makes a charming ornamentation upon the roof. The church of Saint Roch has a doorway with whose magnificence only that of Saint Thomas d'Aquin can compare; it has also a crucifix in relief in a vault, and an ostensary of gilded wood. These things are fairly marvellous. The lantern of the labyrinth at the Jardin des Plantes, too, is vastly ingenious. As for the Palais de la Bourse, which is Grecian in its colonnade, Roman by the circular arches of its doors and windows, and Renaissance by its great elliptic arch, it is undoubtedly a very correct and pure structure; the proof being that it is crowned by an attic such as was never seen at Athens, a fine straight line, gracefully intersected here and there by chimney-pots. Let us add, that if it be a rule that the architecture of a building should be so adapted to the purpose of the building itself, that the aspect of the edifice should at once declare that purpose, we can not too much admire a structure which, from its appearance, might be either a royal palace, a chamber of deputies, a town-hall, a college, a riding-school, an academy, a warehouse, a courthouse, a museum, a barrack, a mausoleum, a temple, or a theatre—and which, all the while, is an exchange. It has been thought, too, that an edifice should be made appropriate to the climate—and so this one has evidently been built on purpose for a cold and rainy sky. It has a roof almost flat, as they are in the East; and, consequently, in winter, when it snows, the roof has to be swept—and it is sure roofs are made to be swept. As for that purpose of which we were just speaking, the building fulfils it admirably. It is an exchange in France, as it would have been a temple in Greece. True it is that the architect has had much ado to conceal the clock-face, which would have destroyed the purity of the noble lines of the façade; but to make amends, there is that colonnade running round the whole structure, under which, on days of high religious ceremony, the schemes of money-brokers and stock-jobbers may be magnificently developed.

These, doubtless, are very superb structures. Add to these many a pretty street, amusing and diversified, like the Rue de Rivoli; and I am not without hope that Paris, as seen from a balloon, may yet present that richness of outline and opulence of detail—that diversity of aspect—that something grandiose in its simplicity—unexpected in its beauty—that characterizes a checker-board.

However, admirable as you may think the present Paris, recall the Paris of the fifteenth century; reconstruct it in thought; look at the sky through that surprising forest of spires, towers and steeples; spread out amid the vast city, tear asunder at the points of the islands, and fold round the piers of the bridges, the Seine, with its large green and yellow slimy pools, more variegated than the skin of a serpent; project clearly upon a blue horizon the Gothic profile of that old Paris. Make its outline float in a wintry mist clinging to its innumerable chimneys; plunge it in deep night, and observe the fantastic play of the darkness and the lights in that gloomy labyrinth of buildings; cast upon it a ray of moonlight, which shall reveal it dimly, with its towers lifting their great heads from that foggy sea—or recall that black silhouette; enliven with shadows the thousand sharp angles of its spires and gables, and make it stand out more indented than a shark's jaw upon the glowing western sky at sunset—and then, compare the two.

And if you would receive an impression from the old city which the modern one can never give you, climb on the morning of some great holiday, at sunrise, on Easter, or Whitsunday—climb to some elevated point whence you overlook the whole capital—and assist at the wakening of the chimes. Behold, at a signal from heaven—for it is the sun that gives it—those thousand churches starting from their sleep. At first you hear but scattered tinklings, going from church to church, as when musicians are giving one another notice to begin. Then, of a sudden, behold—for there are moments when the ear itself seems to see—behold, ascending at the same moment, from every steeple, a column of sound, as it were, a cloud of harmony. At first the vibration of each bell mounts up direct, clear, and, so to speak, isolated from the rest, into the splendid morning sky; then, by degrees, as they expand, they mingle, unite, are lost in each other, and confounded in one magnificent concert. It is no longer anything but a mass of sonorous vibrations, incessantly sent forth from the innumerable belfries—floating, undulating, bounding and eddying, over the town, and prolonging far beyond the horizon the deafening circle of its oscillations. Yet that sea of harmony is not a chaos. Wide and deep as it is, it has not lost its transparency; you perceive the windings of each group of notes that escapes from the chimes. You can follow the dialogue, by turns solemn and shrill, of the treble and the bass; you perceive the octaves leaping from one steeple to another; you observe them springing aloft, winged, light and whirring, from the bell of silver; falling broken and limping from the bell of wood. You admire among them the rich gamut incessantly descending and reascending the seven bells of Saint Eustache; and you see clear and rapid notes, running criss-cross, in three or four luminous zigzags, and vanishing like flashes of lightning. Yonder is the abbey Saint Martin's, a shrill and broken-voiced songstress; here is the sinister and sullen voice of the Bastille; at the other end is the great tower of the Louvre, with its counter-tenor. The royal peal of the Palais unceasingly flings on every side resplendent trills, and upon them fall, at regular intervals, heavy strokes from the belfry of Notre-Dame, which strike sparks from them like the hammer from the anvil. At intervals, you see passing tones, of every form, coming from the triple peal of Saint Germain des Prés. Then, again, from time to time, this mass of sublime sounds half opens, and makes way to the stretto of the Ave-Maria, which flashes and sparkles like a cluster of stars. Below, in the heart of the harmony, you vaguely catch the chanting inside the churches, exhaled through the vibrating pores of their vaulted roofs. This is, certainly, an opera worth hearing. Usually, the murmur that rises up from Paris by day is the city talking; in the night it is the city breathing; but here it is the city singing. Listen, then, to this chorus of bell-towers—diffuse over the whole the murmur of half a million of people—the eternal lament of the river—the endless sighing of the wind—the grave and distant quartet of the four forests placed upon the hills, in the distance, like immense organ-pipes—extinguish to a half light all in the central chime that would otherwise be too harsh or too shrill; and then say whether you know of anything in the world more rich, more joyous, more golden, more dazzling, than this tumult of bells and chimes—this furnace of music—these thousands of brazen voices, all singing together in flutes of stone three hundred feet high, than this city, which is but one orchestra—this symphony which roars like a tempest.

BOOK FOUR

I

Good, Honest Souls

SIXTEEN years previous to the period of this story, on a fine morning of the first Sunday after Easter—called in France, Quasimodo Sunday—a living creature had been laid, after mass, in the church of Notre-Dame, upon the wooden bed fastened into the pavement on the left hand, opposite to that great image of Saint Christopher, which the carved stone figure of Messire Antoine des Essarts, knight, had been contemplating on his knees since the year 1413, when it was thought proper to throw down both the saint and his faithful adorer. Upon this bed it was customary to expose foundlings to public charity; whoever cared to, took them. In front of the bed was a copper basin for alms.

The sort of living creature which lay upon that board on Quasimodo Sunday morning, in the year of our Lord 1467, appeared to excite, in a high degree, the curiosity of a very considerable group of persons which had gathered around the bed. It consisted, in great measure, of individuals of the fair sex. They were nearly all old women.

In the first row, and bending the farthest over the bed, were four, who by their gray *cagoule* (a sort of cassock), appeared to be attached to some religious community. I know not why history should not have handed down to posterity the names of these discreet and venerable damsels. They were Agnès la Herme, Jehanne de la Tarme, Henriette la Gaultière and Gauchère la Violette—all four widows, all four dames of the Etienne Haudry chapel, who had come thus far from their house, with their mistress's leave, and in conformity with the statutes of Pierre d'Ailly, to hear the sermon.

However, if these good Haudriettes were for the time being obeying the statutes of Pierre d'Ailly, they certainly were violating, to their heart's content, those of Michel de Brache and the Cardinal of Pisa, which so inhumanly enjoined silence upon them.

'What ever can that be, sister?' said Agnès to Gauchère, as she looked at the little exposed creature, which lay yelping and wriggling upon the wooden bed, frightened at being looked at by so many people.

'What is to become of us,' said Jehanne, 'if that is the way children are made now?'

'I am not learned in the matter of children,' resumed Agnès, 'but it must surely be a sin to look at such a one as this!'

''Tis no child at all, Agnès.'

''Tis a misshapen baboon,' observed Gauchère.

'It is a miracle,' said Henriette la Gaultière.

'Then,' remarked Agnès, 'this is the third since Lætare Sunday; for a week has not passed since we had the miracle of the mocker of pilgrims divinely punished by Our Lady of Aubervilliers; and that was the second miracle of the month.'

'This pretended foundling is a very monster of abomination,' resumed Jehanne.

'He brawls loud enough to deafen a chanter,' added Gauchère; 'hold thy tongue, thou little bellower.'

'To think that Monsieur of Rheims sends this monstrosity to Monsieur of Paris!' exclaimed La Gaultière, clasping her hands.

'I believe,' said Agnès la Herme, 'that it's some beast, or animal —the fruit of a Jew and a sow—something not Christian, in short, and which ought to be thrown into the water or into the fire.'

'I truly hope,' resumed La Gaultière, 'that nobody will offer to take him!'

'Oh, heavens!' exclaimed Agnès, 'those poor nurses yonder in the foundling asylum at the bottom of the alley, going down to the river, close by the lord bishop's; what if this little monster were carried to them to suckle! I'd rather give suck to a vampire.'

'Is she not a simpleton, that poor La Herme?' rejoined Jehanne. 'Do you not see, my dear sister, that this little monster is at least four years old, and would have less appetite for your breast than for a roast.'

In fact, the 'little monster' (for we ourselves would find it hard to describe him otherwise) was no new-born infant. It was a little, angular, restless mass, imprisoned in a canvas bag marked with the cipher of Messire Guillaume Chartier, then bishop of Paris— with a head coming out at one end. This head was a misshapen enough thing; there was nothing of it to be seen but a shock of red hair, one eye, a mouth and some teeth. The eye wept; the mouth bawled; and the teeth seemed only waiting a chance to bite. The whole lump was struggling violently in the bag, to the great wonderment of the increasing and incessantly renewing crowd around it.

Dame Aloïse de Gondelaurier, a wealthy and noble lady, holding by the hand a pretty little girl about six years of age, and trailing after her a long veil attached to the golden horn of her head-dress, halted as she passed the wooden bed, and looked for a moment at the unfortunate creature; while her charming little daughter,

Fleur-de-Lys de Gondelaurier, clad in silk and velvet, spelled out with her pretty little finger, the inscription hanging on the wooden framework: For Foundlings.

'Really,' said the dame, turning away with disgust, 'I thought they exhibited here nothing but children.'

She turned her back; at the same time throwing into the basin a silver florin, which rang among the liards, and made the poor good women of the Etienne Haudry chapel stare.

A moment afterward the grave and learned Robert Mistricolle, king's prothonotary, passed by, with an enormous missal under one arm, and his wife under the other (Damoiselle Guillemette la Mairesse), having thus on either side his two regulators, spiritual and temporal.

'Foundling!' said he, after examining the object; 'yes—found, apparently, upon the banks of the river Phlegethon!'

'It has but one eye to be seen,' observed Damoiselle Guillemette; 'there is a wart upon the other.'

'That is no wart,' replied Maître Robert Mistricolle; 'it is an egg, which contains just such another demon, who bears upon its eye another little egg containing another devil—and so on.'

'How do you know that?' asked Guillemette la Mairesse.

'I know it for very sufficient reasons,' answered the prothonotary.

'Monsieur the prothonotary,' asked Gauchère, 'what do you prognosticate from this pretended foundling?'

'The greatest calamities,' answered Mistricolle.

'Heaven save us!' said an old woman among the bystanders; 'withal that there was quite a pestilence last year, and that they say the English are going to land in great company at Harfleur!'

''Twill perhaps prevent the queen from coming to Paris in September,' observed another; 'and trade so bad already!'

'In my opinion,' cried Jehanne de la Tarme, 'it would be better for the commoners of Paris if the little sorcerer there were lying upon a fagot rather than a board.'

'A fine flaming fagot!' added the old woman.

'It would be more prudent,' said Mistricolle.

For some moments a young priest had been listening to the arguments of the Haudriettes and the oracular decrees of the prothonotary. His was a severe countenance, with a broad forehead and a penetrating eye. He silently put aside the crowd, scrutinized the *little sorcerer* and stretched out his hand over him. It was high time; for all the devout old women were already regaling themselves with the anticipation of the 'fine flaming fagot.'

'I adopt this child,' said the priest.

He wrapped it in his cassock, and bore it away; the bystanders looked after him with frightened glances. A moment later he disappeared through the Red Door, which then led from the church to the cloister.

When the first surprise was over, Jehanne de la Tarme whispered in the ear of La Gaultière:

'I always said to you, sister, that that young clerk, Monsieur Claude Frollo, was a sorcerer.'

2

Claude Frollo

CLAUDE FROLLO was in fact no common person. He belonged to one of those families of middle rank called indifferently, in the impertinent language of the last century, high commoners or petty nobility. This family had inherited from the brothers Paclet the fief of Tirechappe, which was held of the Bishop of Paris, and the twenty-one houses of which had been, in the thirteenth century, the object of so many suits before the judges. As possessor of this fief, Claude Frollo was one of the one hundred and forty-one seigneurs, claiming manorial dues, in Paris and its suburbs; and in that capacity his name was long to be seen inscribed between that of the Hôtel de Tancarville, belonging to Master François Le Rez, and that of the college of Tours, in the records deposited at Saint Martin des Champs.

Claude Frollo had, from infancy, been destined by his parents for the ecclesiastical state. He had been taught to read in Latin; he had been trained to cast down his eyes and to speak low. While yet a child, his father had cloistered him in the college of Torchi, in the University. There it was that he had grown up, on the missal and the lexicon.

He was, moreover, a melancholy, grave and serious boy, who studied ardently and learned quickly; he was never boisterous at play; he mixed little in the bacchanalia of the Rue du Fouarre; knew not what it was to *dare alapas et capillos laniare* (to give blows and to pull out hair); nor had he figured in that insurrection of 1463, which the annalists gravely record under the title of 'Sixième Trouble de l'Université.' (Sixth trouble of the University.) It did not often occur to him to annoy the poor scholars of Montaigu upon their *cappettes* (little hoods), from which they derived their nickname; nor the fellows of the college of Dormans, upon their smooth tonsure and their parti-coloured frock, made of cloth, gray, blue and violet—*azurini coloris et bruni* (of a blue and prune colour), as the charter of the Cardinal des Quatre Couronnes expresses it.

But, on the other hand, he was assiduous at both the great and the small schools of the Rue Saint Jean de Beauvais. The first scholar whom the abbot of Saint Pierre de Val, at the moment of beginning his reading on canon law, always perceived, glued to a pillar of the school Saint Vendregesile, opposite his rostrum, was Claude Frollo, armed with his inkhorn, chewing his pen, scribbling upon his thread-bare knee, and, in winter, blowing on his fingers. The first auditor whom Messire Miles d'Isliers, doctor of decretals, saw arrive every Monday morning, quite out of breath, at the opening of the doors of the Chef Saint Denis schools, was Claude Frollo. Thus, at the age of sixteen, the young clerk was a match, in mystical theology, for a father of the Church; in canonical theology, for a father of the Council; and in scholastic theology, for a doctor of the Sorbonne.

Theology passed, he plunged into the décret, or study of decretals. After the 'Master of Sentences,' he had fallen upon the 'Capitularies of Charlemagne;' and had successively devoured, in his appetite for knowledge, decretals upon decretals; those of Theodore, Bishop of Hispala ; those of Bouchard, Bishop of Worms ; those of Yves, Bishop of Chartres ; then the decretal of Gratian, which succeeded the Capitularies of Charlemagne; then the collection by Gregory IX; then the epistle, *Super specula* (on Imitations), of Honorius III. He gained a clear idea of and made himself familiar with that vast and tumultuous period when the civil law and the canon law were struggling and labouring in the chaos of the Middle Ages—a period which opens with Bishop Theodore, in 618, and closes, in 1227, with Pope Gregory.

Having digested the decretals, he rushed into medicine and the liberal arts. He studied the science of herbs, the science of unguents. He became expert in the treatment of fevers and contusions, of wounds and sores. Jacques d'Espars would have admitted him as doctor of medicine; Richard Hellain, as a surgeon. In like manner he ran through all the degrees of licentiate, master, and doctor of arts. He studied the languages, Latin, Greek, Hebrew; a triple shrine, then but little worshipped. He was possessed by an absolute fever for the acquiring and storing of knowledge. At eighteen, he had made his way through the four faculties; it seemed to the young man that life had but one sole aim : knowledge.

It was about this period that the excessive heat of the summer of 1466 gave birth to the great plague which carried off more than forty thousand souls within the viscounty of Paris, and among others, says John of Troyes, 'Maître Arnoul, the king's astrologer, a man full honest, wise and pleasant.' The rumour spread through the University that the Rue Tirechappe was especially devastated by the pestilence. It was there, in the midst of their fief, that the parents of Claude resided. The young scholar hastened in great

alarm to his paternal mansion. On entering, he found that his
father and mother had both died the preceding day. A baby
brother, in swaddling clothes, was yet living, and lay crying abandoned in its cradle. It was all that remained to Claude of his
family. The young man took the child under his arm, and went
away thoughtfully. Hitherto, he had lived only in science; he was
now beginning to live in the world.

This catastrophe was a crisis in Claude's existence. An orphan,
the eldest head of the family at nineteen, he felt himself rudely
aroused from scholastic reveries to the realities of this world. Then,
moved with pity, he was seized with love and devotion for
this infant, his brother; and strange at once and sweet was this
human affection to him who had never yet loved anything
but books.

This affection developed itself to a singular degree; in a soul so
new to passion it was like a first love. Separated since childhood
from his parents, whom he had scarcely known—cloistered and
immured, as it were, in his books—eager above all things to study
and to learn—exclusively attentive, until then, to his understanding, which broadened in science—to his imagination, which
expanded in literature—the poor scholar had not yet had time to
feel that he had a heart. This little brother, without father or
mother—this little child which had fallen suddenly from heaven
into his arms—made a new man of him. He discovered that there
was something else in the world besides the speculations of the
Sorbonne and the verses of Homerus—that man has need of
affections; that life without tenderness and without love was but
dry machinery, noisy and wearing. Only he fancied—for he was
still at that age when illusions are replaced by illusions—that the
affections of blood and kindred were the only ones necessary; and
that a little brother to love sufficed to fill a whole existence.

He threw himself, then, into the love of his little Jehan, with
all the intensity of a character already deep, ardent, concentrated.
This poor, helpless creature, pretty, fairhaired, rosy and curly—
this orphan with none to look to for support but another orphan
—moved him to the inmost soul; and, serious thinker as he was,
he began to reflect upon Jehan with a feeling of the tenderest pity.
He cared for him and watched over him as over something very
fragile and very precious; he was more than a brother to the
infant—he became a mother to it.

Little Jehan having lost his mother before he was weaned,
Claude put him out to nurse. Besides the fief of Tirechappe, he
inherited from his father that of Moulin, which was a dependency
of the square tower of Gentilly; it was a mill upon a hill, near the
Château de Winchestre, since corrupted into Bicêtre. The miller's

wife was suckling a fine boy, not far from the University, and Claude himself carried his little Jehan to her in his arms.

Thenceforward, feeling that he had a burden to bear, he took life very seriously. The thought of his little brother became not only his recreation, but the object of his studies. He resolved to consecrate himself entirely to a future for which he made himself answerable before God, and never to have any other wife, nor any other child, than the happiness and prosperity of his brother. He accordingly became more than ever attached to his clerical vocation. His merit, his learning, his quality as an immediate vassal of the Bishop of Paris, threw the doors of the Church wide open to him. At twenty years of age, by special dispensation from the Holy See, he was ordained priest; and served, as the youngest of the chaplains of Notre-Dame, at the altar called, on account of the late mass that was said at it, *altare pigrorum*, the altar of the lazy.

There, more than ever buried in his dear books, which he only left to hasten for an hour to the fief Du Moulin, this mixture of learning and austerity, so rare at his age, had speedily gained him the admiration and respect of the cloister. From the cloister his reputation for learning had spread to the people, among whom it had been in some degree changed, as not unfrequently happened in those days, into reputation for sorcery.

It was when he was returning, on the Quasimodo Sunday, from saying his mass of the slothful at their altar, which was at the side of that gate of the choir which opened into the nave, on the right hand, near the image of the Virgin, that his attention had been aroused by the group of old women chattering around the bed for foundlings.

Then it was that he had approached the unfortunate little creature, the object of so much hatred and menace. Its distress, its deformity, its abandonment, the thought of his little brother—the idea which suddenly crossed his mind that, were he to die, his dear little Jehan might also be cast miserably upon the board for foundlings—all this rushed into his heart at once—a deep feeling of pity had taken possession of him, and he had borne away the child.

When he took the child from the bag, he found it to be very deformed indeed. The poor little imp had a great wart covering its left eye—the head compressed between the shoulders—the spine crooked—the breastbone prominent—and the legs bowed. Yet it seemed to be full of life; and although it was impossible to discover what language it babbled, its cry proclaimed a certain degree of health and strength. Claude's compassion was increased by this ugliness; and he vowed in his heart to bring up this child for the love of his brother; in order that, whatever might be the future faults of little Jehan, there might be placed to his credit this piece of charity performed on his account. It was a sort of investment of good works in his little brother's name—a stock of good deeds which he wished to lay up for him beforehand—in case the little rascal should one day find himself short of that coin, the only kind taken at the toll-gate of Paradise.

He baptized his adopted child by the name of Quasimodo; whether it was that he chose thereby to mark the day upon which he had found him, or that he meant to characterize by that name how incomplete and imperfect the poor little creature was. Indeed, Quasimodo, one-eyed, hump-backed and knock-kneed, could hardly be considered anything more than a sketch.

3

Immanis Pecoris Custos, Immanior Ipse *

Now, in 1482, Quasimodo had grown up, and for several years had been ringer of the bells of Notre-Dame, thanks to his foster-father, Claude Frollo; who had become Archdeacon of Josas, by the grace of his suzerain, Messire Louis de Beaumont; who had become Bishop of Paris in 1472, on the death of Guillaume Chartier, by the grace of his patron, Olivier le Daim, barber to Louis XI, king by the grace of God.

Quasimodo was, therefore, ringer of the chimes of Notre-Dame.

With time, a certain bond of intimacy had been established, uniting the bell-ringer to the church. Separated forever from the world by the double fatality of his unknown birth and his deformity —imprisoned from his infancy within that double and impassable circle—the poor wretch had been accustomed to see nothing of the world beyond the religious walls which had received him under their shadow. Notre-Dame had been to him, by turns, as he grew and developed, egg—nest—home—country—universe.

And it is certain that there was a mysterious and pre-existing harmony between this creature and the edifice. When, while yet quite little, he used to drag himself along, twisting and jerking, in the gloom of its arches, he seemed, with his human face and his bestial members, the native reptile of that damp, dark pavement, upon which the shadows of the Roman capitals projected so many fantastic forms.

And, later, the first time that he grasped mechanically the bell-rope in the towers, hung himself upon it and set the bell in motion,

Huge the guardian of the flock, more huge he.

the effect upon Claude, his adoptive father, was that of a child whose tongue is loosed and who begins to talk.

Thus it was that his being, gradually unfolding, took its mould from the cathedral—living there—sleeping there—scarcely ever going out of it—receiving every hour its mysterious impress—he came at length to resemble it, to be fashioned like it, to make an integral part of it. His salient angles fitted themselves (if we may be allowed the expression) into the retreating angles of the edifice, and he seemed to be not only its inhabitant, but even the natural tenant of it. He might almost be said to have taken its form, as the snail takes that of its shell. It was his dwelling-place—his hole—his envelope. There existed between the old church and himself an instinctive sympathy so profound—so many affinities, magnetic and material—that he in some sort adhered to it, like the tortoise to its shell.

It is needless to inform the reader that he is not to accept literally the figures of speech that we are here obliged to employ in order to express that singular assimilation, symmetrical—immediate—consubstantial, almost—of a man to an edifice. It is likewise needless to allude to the degree of familiarity he must have attained with the whole cathedral during so long and so intimate a cohabitation. It was his own particular dwelling-place. It had no depths which Quasimodo had not penetrated, no heights which he had not scaled. Many a time had he clambered up its front, one story after another, with no other aid than the projecting bits of carving; the towers, over the exterior of which he was frequently seen crawling like a lizard gliding upon an upright wall—those twin giants—so lofty, so threatening, so formidable—had for him neither vertigo, fright, nor sudden giddiness. So gentle did they appear under his hand, so easy to scale, one would have said that he had tamed them. By dint of leaping, climbing, sporting amid the abysses of the gigantic cathedral, he had become something of both monkey and chamois—like the Calabrian child, which swims before it can walk, and plays with the sea while still a babe.

Moreover, not only his body, but also his mind, seemed to be moulded by the cathedral. In what state was that soul? what folds had it contracted, what form had it taken, under that knotty covering, in that wild and savage life? It would be difficult to determine. Quasimodo was born one-eyed, hump-backed, limping. It was with great difficulty and great patience that Claude Frollo had taught him to speak. But a fatality pursued the poor foundling. Bell-ringer of Notre-Dame at fourteen years of age, a fresh infirmity had come to complete his desolation—the sound of the bells had broken the drum of the ear; he had become deaf. The only door that nature had left wide open between him and the external world, had been suddenly closed forever.

In closing, it intercepted the sole ray of joy and light that still penetrated to the soul of Quasimodo. That soul was now wrapped in profound darkness. The poor creature's melancholy became as incurable and as complete as his deformity; add to which, his deafness rendered him in some sort dumb. For, that he might not be laughed at by others, from the moment that he realized his deafness, he determined resolutely to observe a silence which he scarcely ever broke, except when alone. He voluntarily tied up that tongue which Claude Frollo had worked so hard to set free. And hence it was that, when necessity compelled him to speak, his tongue was heavy and awkward, like a door the hinges of which have grown rusty.

If now we were to endeavour to penetrate through this thick and obdurate bark to the soul of Quasimodo—could we sound the depths of that ill-formed organization—were it possible for us to look, with a torch, behind these untransparent organs—to explore the darksome interior of that opaque being—to illumine its obscure corners and absurd blind-alleys—to throw all at once a strong light upon the Psyche chained in the depths of that drear cavern —doubtless we should find the poor creature in some posture of decrepitude, stunted and rickety—like those prisoners who grow old under the Leads of Venice, bent double in a stone chest too low and too short for them either to stand or to lie at full length.

It is certain that the spirit becomes crippled in a misshapen body. Quasimodo barely felt, stirring blindly within him, a soul made after his own image. The impressions of objects underwent a considerable refraction before they reached his apprehension. His brain was a peculiar medium; the ideas which passed through it issued completely distorted. The reflection which proceeded from that refraction was necessarily divergent and astray.

Hence, he was subject to a thousand optical illusions, a thousand aberrations of judgment, a thousand wanderings of thought, sometimes foolish, sometimes idiotic.

The first effect of this fatal organization was to disturb the view which he took of external objects. He received from them scarcely any immediate perception. The external world seemed to him much farther off than it does to us.

The second effect of his misfortune was to render him mischievous.

He was mischievous, indeed, because he was savage; and he was savage because he was deformed. There was a logic in his nature as in ours.

His strength, so extraordinarily developed, was another cause of mischievousness, *malus puer robustus* (the wicked boy is strong), says Hobbes.

We must, nevertheless, do him justice; malice was probably not innate in him. From his very first intercourse with men he had felt, and then had seen, himself repulsed, branded, despised. Human speech had never been to him aught but mockery and curses. As he grew up, he had found around him nothing but hatred. What wonder that he should have caught it! He had contracted it—he had but picked up the weapon that had wounded him.

After all, he turned towards mankind reluctantly—his cathedral was sufficient for him. It was peopled with figures in marble—with kings, saints, bishops—who, at all events, did not burst out laughing in his face, but looked upon him with calmness and benevolence. The other statues, those of monsters and demons, had no hatred for him, Quasimodo. He was too much like them for that. Their raillery seemed rather to be directed toward the rest of mankind. The saints were his friends, and blessed him; the monsters were his friends, and guarded him. Accordingly, he used to have long communings with them; he would sometimes pass whole hours crouched before one of these statues, holding solitary converse with it; if any one happened to approach, he would fly like some lover surprised in a serenade.

And the cathedral was not only his society, but his world—it was all nature to him. He dreamed of no other hedgerows than the stained windows always in bloom—no other shade than that of the stone foliage which spreads out, loaded with birds, in the bushy Saxon capitals—no mountains but the colossal towers of the church—no ocean but Paris, murmuring at their feet.

That which he loved above all in the maternal edifice—that which awakened his soul, and made it stretch forth its poor pinions, that otherwise remained so miserably folded up in its cavern—that which even sometimes made him happy—was, the bells. He loved them, caressed them, talked to them, understood them. From the chimes in the central steeple to the great bell over the doorway, they all shared his affections. The belfry of the transept and the two towers were to him three great cages, in which the birds taught by himself sang for him alone. It was, however, those same bells that had deafened him. But a mother is often fondest of that child which has cost her the most suffering.

It is true that their voices were the only ones he was still capable of hearing. On this account, the great bell was his best beloved. She it was whom he preferred among this family of noisy sisters that fluttered about him on festival days. This great bell was named Marie. She hung in the southern tower, where she had no companion but her sister Jacqueline, a bell of smaller dimensions, shut up in a smaller cage by the side of her own. This Jacqueline was so named after the wife of Jean Montagu, who had given her to the church—a donation which, however, had not prevented him from figuring without his head at Montfaucon. In the second tower were six other bells; and finally the six smallest inhabited the central steeple, over the transept, together with the wooden bell, which was rung only from the afternoon of Holy Thursday until the morning of Holy Saturday, or Easter eve. Thus Quasimodo had fifteen bells in his seraglio; but the big Marie was his favourite.

It is impossible to form a conception of his joy on the days of the great peals. The instant the archdeacon let him off with the word 'go,' he ascended the spiral staircase quicker than any other person could have gone down. He rushed, breathless, into the aërial chamber of the great bell; gazed at her for a moment attentively and lovingly; then began to talk to her softly; patted her with his hand, like a good horse setting out on a long journey. He pitied her for the labour she was about to undergo. After these first caresses, he called out to his assistants, placed in the lower story of the tower, to begin. The latter then hung their weight upon the ropes, the windlass creaked and the enormous cone of metal moved slowly. Quasimodo, with heaving breast, followed it with his eye. The first stroke of the tongue against the brazen wall that encircled it shook the scaffolding upon which he stood. Quasimodo vibrated with the bell. 'Vah!' he would cry, with a mad burst of laughter. Meanwhile, the motion of the bell was accelerated; and as it went on, taking an ever-increasing sweep, Quasimodo's eye, in like manner, opened more and more widely, phosphorescent and flaming. At length the grand peal began—the whole tower trembled—rafters, leads, stones—all shook together—from the piles of the foundation to the trefoils of the parapet. Then Quasimodo boiled and frothed; he ran to and fro, trembling, with the tower, from head to foot. The bell, let loose, and in a frenzy, turned first to one side and then to the other side of the tower its brazen throat, from whence issued a roar that was audible at four leagues' distance. Quasimodo placed himself before this gaping throat—he crouched down and rose with the oscillations of the bell—inhaled that furious breath—looked by turns down upon the Place which was swarming with people two hundred feet below him, and upon the enormous brazen tongue which came, second after second, to bellow in his ear. This was the only speech that he could hear, the only sound that broke for him the universal silence. He expanded in it, like a bird in the sunshine. All at once the frenzy of the bell would seize him; his look became wild—he lay in wait for the great bell as a spider for a fly, and then flung himself head-long upon it. Now, suspended over the abyss, borne to and fro by the formidable swinging of the bell, he seized the brazen monster by the ears—gripped it with his knees—spurred it with his heels—and redoubled, with the shock and weight of his body, the fury of the peal. Meanwhile, the tower trembled; he shouted and gnashed his teeth—his red hair bristled—his breast heaved and puffed like the bellows of a forge—his eye flashed fire—the monstrous bell neighed panting beneath him. Then it was no longer either the great bell of Notre-Dame, nor Quasimodo—it was a dream—a whirl—a tempest—dizziness astride upon clamour—a strange centaur, half man, half bell—a spirit clinging to a winged monster—a sort of horrible Astolpho, borne away upon a prodigious hippogriff of living bronze.

The presence of this extraordinary being seemed to infuse the breath of life into the whole cathedral. There seemed to issue from him—at least according to the growing superstitions of the crowd—a mysterious emanation, which animated all the stones of Notre-Dame, and to make the very entrails of the old church heave and palpitate. To know that he was there was enough to make one think the thousand statues in the galleries and doorways moved and breathed. The old cathedral seemed to be a docile and obedient creature in his hands; waiting his will to lift up her mighty voice; being filled and possessed with Quasimodo as with a familiar spirit. One would have said that he made the immense building breathe. He was everywhere; he multiplied himself upon every point of the structure. Sometimes one beheld with dread, at the very top of one of the towers, a fantastic dwarfish-looking figure—climbing—twisting—crawling on all fours—descending outside over the abyss—leaping from projection to projection—and diving to ransack the belly of some sculptured gorgon; it was Quasimodo dislodging the crows. Again, in some obscure corner of the church, one would stumble against a sort of living chimera, crouching and scowling—it was Quasimodo musing. Sometimes one caught sight, under a belfry, of an enormous head and a bundle of ill-adjusted limbs, swinging furiously at the end of a rope—it was Quasimodo ringing the vespers, or the angelus. Often, at night, a hideous form was seen wandering upon the frail open-work balustrade which crowns the towers and runs around the top of the apse—it was still the hunchback of Notre-Dame. Then, so said the good women of the neighbourhood, the whole church assumed a fantastic, supernatural, horrible aspect—eyes and mouths opened in it here and there—the dogs, and the dragons and the griffins of stone, that watch day and night, with outstretched necks and open jaws, around the monstrous cathedral, were heard to bark. And if it was a Christmas eve—while the big bell, that seemed to rattle in its throat, called the faithful to the blazing midnight mass, the gloomy façade assumed such an aspect that the great doorway seemed to swallow the multitude, while the rose-window above it looked on—and all this came from Quasimodo. Egypt would have taken him for the god of this temple—the Middle Ages believed him to be its demon —he was its soul.

So much so that, to those who know that Quasimodo once existed, Notre-Dame is now deserted, inanimate, dead. They feel that something has disappeared. That vast body is empty—it is a skeleton—the spirit has quitted it—they see its place and that is all. It is like a skull, which still has holes for the eyes, but no longer sight.

4

The Dog and his Master

THERE was, however, one human creature whom Quasimodo excepted from his malice and hatred for others, and whom he loved as much, perhaps more, than his cathedral : this was Claude Frollo.

The case was simple enough. Claude Frollo had taken him, adopted him, fed him, brought him up. While yet quite little, it was between Claude Frollo's knees that he had been accustomed to take refuge when the dogs and the children ran yelping after him. Claude Frollo had taught him to speak, to read, to write. Claude Frollo, in fine, had made him ringer of the bells—and to give the great bell in marriage to Quasimodo, was giving Juliet to Romeo.

Accordingly, Quasimodo's gratitude was deep, ardent, boundless ; and although the countenance of his adoptive father was often clouded and severe—although his mode of speaking was habitually brief, harsh, imperious—never had that gratitude wavered for a single instant. The archdeacon had in Quasimodo the most submissive of slaves, the most tractable of servants, the most vigilant of watch-dogs. When the poor bell-ringer became deaf, between him and Claude Frollo was established a language of signs, mysterious and intelligible only to themselves. Thus the archdeacon was the only human being with whom Quasimodo had preserved a communication. He had intercourse with only two things in this world—Notre-Dame and Claude Frollo.

Unexampled were the sway of the archdeacon over the bell-ringer, and the bell-ringer's devotion to the archdeacon. One sign from Claude, and the idea of pleasing him would have sufficed to make Quasimodo throw himself from the top of the towers of Notre-Dame. There was something remarkable in all that physical strength, so extraordinarily developed in Quasimodo, and blindly placed by him at the disposal of another. In this there was undoubtedly filial devotion and domestic attachment; but there was also fascination of one mind by another mind. There was a poor, awkward, clumsy organization, which stood with lowered head and supplicating eyes before a lofty and profound, a powerful and commanding intellect. Lastly, and above all, it was gratitude— gratitude pushed to its extremest limit, that we know not to what to compare it. This virtue is not one of those of which the finest examples are to be met with among men. We will say, then, that Quasimodo loved the archdeacon as no dog, no horse, no elephant ever loved his master.

5

Claude Frollo, Continued

IN 1482, Quasimodo was about twenty years old, and Claude Frollo about thirty-six. The one had grown up; the other had grown old.

Claude Frollo was no longer the simple student of the Torchi college—the tender protector of a little boy—the young dreaming philosopher, who knew many things and was ignorant of many. He was a priest, austere, grave, morose—charged with the care of souls—Monsieur the Archdeacon of Josas—the second acolyte of the bishop—having charge of the two deaneries of Montlhéry, and Châteaufort and one hundred and seventy-four of the rural clergy. He was a sombre and awe-inspiring personage, before whom the choir-boys in albs and jaquette, the precentors, the brothers of Saint Augustine, and the matutinal clerks of Notre-Dame trembled, when he passed slowly beneath the lofty arches of the choir, majestic, thoughtful, with arms folded and head so bent upon his breast that nothing could be seen of his face but the high bald forehead.

Dom Claude Frollo, however, had abandoned neither science nor the education of his young brother, those two occupations of his life. But in the course of time, some bitterness had been mingled with these things once so sweet. In the long run, says Paul Diacre, the best bacon turns rancid. Little Jehan Frollo, surnamed Du Moulin (of the mill) from the place where he had been nursed, had not grown up in the direction which Claude had been desirous of leading him. The elder brother, had reckoned upon a pious, docile, studious, creditable pupil. But the younger brother like those young plants which baffle the endeavours of the gardener, and turn obstinately toward the quarter whence they receive air and sunshine—the younger brother grew up, and shot forth full and luxuriant branches, only on the side of idleness, ignorance and debauchery. He was a very devil—very unruly—which made Dom Claude knit his brows—but very droll and very shrewd—which made the big brother smile.

Claude had consigned him to the same college de Torchi where he had passed his early years in study and meditation; and it grieved him that this sanctuary, once edified by the name of Frollo, should now be scandalized by it. He sometimes read Jehan very long and very severe lectures upon the subject, which the latter bore undaunted. After all the young scapegrace had a good heart —as is always the case in all comedies. But the lecture over, he nevertheless quietly resumed his dissolute and turbulent ways. At one time it was a yellow-beak (as a new-comer at the University was called), whom he had plucked for his entrance-money—a precious tradition, which has been carefully handed down to the present day. At another he had instigated a band of students, *quasi classico excitati* (to make a classic attack) upon some tavern—then had beaten the tavern-keeper 'with offensive cudgels,' and merrily pillaged the tavern, even to staving in the casks of wine in the cellar. And then there was a fine report, in Latin, which the sub-monitor of Torchi brought piteously to Dom Claude, with this dolorous marginal note—*Rixa; prima causa vinum optimum potatum* (quarrels, primary cause, most excellent wine drunk). And, in fact, it was said—a thing quite horrible in a lad of sixteen—that his excesses oftentimes led him as far as the Rue de Glatigny (then famous for its gambling-houses).

Owing to all this, Claude, saddened and discouraged in his human affections, had thrown himself the more eagerly into the arms of Science—that sister who, at all events, does not laugh in your face, but always repays you, though sometimes in rather hollow coin, for the attentions bestowed upon her. He became more and more learned—and, at the same time, by a natural consequence, more and more rigid as a priest, more and more gloomy as a man. There are in each individual of us certain parallelisms between our intelligence, our habits and our character, which develop without interruption, and are broken off only by the greater disturbances of life.

As Claude Frollo had, from his youth, gone through almost the entire circle of human knowledge, positive, external and lawful, he was under the absolute necessity, unless he was to stop *ubi defuit orbis* (at the end of the world), of going farther, and seeking other food for the insatiable activity of his intellect. The ancient symbol of the serpent biting its own tail is especially appropriate to science; and it would appear that Claude Frollo had experienced this. Many grave persons affirmed that after exhausting the *fas* (lawful) of human knowledge he had dared to penetrate into the *nefas* (unlawful). He had, they said, successively tasted every apple upon the tree of knowledge; and, whether from hunger or disgust, he had ended by tasting the forbidden fruit. He had taken his place by turns, as our readers have seen, at the conferences of the theologians at the Sorbonne; at the meetings of the faculty of arts at the image of Saint Hilaire; at the disputations of the decretists at the image of Saint Martin; at the congregations of the physicians by the holy water font of Notre-Dame, *ad cupam nostrae dominae* (to the font of Notre-Dame). All the viands, permitted and approved, which those four great kitchens called the four faculties could prepare and serve up to the understanding, he had devoured; and satiety had come before his hunger was appeased. Then he had delved deeper—underneath all that finite, material, limited science; he had perhaps risked his soul, and seated himself in the cavern, at that mysterious table of the alchemists, the astrologers, the hermetics, headed by Averroës, Guillaume de Paris and Nicolas Flamel, in the Middle Ages, and which extended in the East, under the light of the seven-branched candlestick, up to Solomon, Pythagoras and Zoroaster.

This is, at least, what was supposed, whether rightly or not.

It is certain that the archdeacon often visited the cemetery of the Holy Innocents, where, it is true, his father and mother had been buried, with the other victims of the plague of 1466; but he seemed far less interested in the cross at the head of their grave than in the strange figures upon the tomb of Nicolas Flamel and his wife Claude Pernelle, which stood close by it.

It is certain that he had been seen often walking along the Rue des Lombards, and furtively entering a small house at the corner of the Rue des Ecrivains and the Rue Marivault. It was the house built by Nicolas Flamel, in which he had died about 1417, and which, uninhabited ever since, was beginning to fall into ruins, so greatly had the hermetics and alchemists of all countries worn away its walls merely by scratching their names upon them. Some of the neighbours even affirmed that they had once seen, through an air-hole, the archdeacon Claude digging and turning over the earth in the two cellars, whose supports had been scrawled over with innumerable couplets and hieroglyphics by Nicolas Flamel himself. It was supposed that Flamel had buried the philosopher's stone in these cellars; and for two centuries, the alchemists, from Magistri to Father Pacifique, never ceased to worry the soil, until the house, so mercilessly ransacked and turned inside out, ended by crumbling into dust under their feet.

Again, it is certain that the archdeacon had been seized with a singular passion for the symbolical doorway of Notre-Dame, that page of conjuration written in stone by Bishop William of Paris, who has undoubtedly been damned for attaching so infernal a frontispiece to the sacred poem eternally chanted by the rest of the structure. Archdeacon Claude also passed for having sounded the mysteries of the colossal Saint Christopher, and of that long enigmatical statue which then stood at the entrance to the Square in front of the cathedral, and which the people had nicknamed Monsieur Legris. But what everyone might have noticed was the interminable hours which he would often spend, seated upon the parapet of this same Square, in contemplating the carvings on the portal—now examining the foolish virgins with their lamps reversed, now the wise virgins with their lamps upright—at other times calculating the angle of vision of that raven clinging to the left side of the doorway, looking at some mysterious spot in the church—where the philosopher's stone is certainly concealed if it be not in Nicolas Flamel's cellar. It was a singular destiny (we may remark in passing) for the church of Notre-Dame, at that period, to be thus beloved in different degrees, and with such devotion, by two beings so dissimilar as Claude and Quasimodo —loved by the one, a sort of instinctive and savage half-man, for its beauty, for its stature, for the harmonies which emanated from its magnificent whole—loved by the other, a being of cultivated and ardent imagination, for its signification, for its myth, for its hidden meaning, for the symbol lurking under the sculptures on its front, like the first text under the second in a palimpsest—in short, for the enigma which it eternally propounds to the understanding.

Furthermore, it is certain that the archdeacon had established himself, in that one of the two towers which looks upon the Grève, close to the belfry, in a small and secret cell, into which no one entered—not even the bishop, it was said—without his leave. This cell, contrived of old, almost at the top of the tower, among the crows' nests, by Bishop Hugo de Besançon ('Hugo II de Bisuncio,' 1326-1332), who had practised sorcery there in his day. What this cell contained no one knew. But from the strand of the Terrain there was often seen, at night, to appear, disappear and reappear, at short and regular intervals, at a small dormer window at the back of the tower, a certain red, intermittent, singular glow, seeming as if it followed the irregular puffing of a bellows, and as if proceeding from a flame rather than a light. In the darkness, at that height, it had a very weird appearance; and the housewives would say: 'There is the archdeacon blowing! Hell is making sparks up there!'

There were not, after all, any great proofs of sorcery; but still there was quite enough smoke to make the good people suppose a flame; and the archdeacon had a somewhat formidable reputation. We are bound to declare, however, that the sciences of Egypt—that necromancy—that magic—even the clearest and most innocent—had no more violent enemy, no more merciless denouncer before the officials of Notre-Dame, than himself. Whether it was sincere abhorrence, or merely the trick of the robber who cries Stop, thief! this did not prevent the archdeacon from being considered by the wise heads of the chapter as one who risked his soul upon the threshold of hell—one lost in the caverns of the cabala—groping his way among the shadows of the occult sciences. Neither were the people deceived thereby; to the mind of any one possessed of the least sagacity, Quasimodo passed for the demon, and Claude Frollo the sorcerer; it was evident that the bell-ringer was to serve the archdeacon for a given time, at the expiration of which he was to carry off the latter's soul by way of payment. Thus the archdeacon, despite the excessive austerity of his life, was in bad odour with all pious souls; and there was no devout nose, however inexperienced, but could smell him out for a magician.

And if, as he grew older, he had formed to himself abysses in science, others had likewise opened themselves in his heart. So at least they were led to believe who narrowly observed that face, in which his soul shone forth as through a sombre cloud. Whence that large bald brow—that head constantly bowed—that breast forever heaved with sighs? What secret thought wreathed that bitter smile about his lips, at the same instant when his lowering brows approached each other fierce as two encountering bulls? Why were his remaining hairs already gray? What internal fire was that which shone forth occasionally in his glance, to such a degree that his eye resembled a hole pierced in the wall of a furnace?

These symptoms of a violent moral preoccupation had acquired an especially high degree of intensity at the period to which our narrative refers. More than once had a choir-boy fled affrighted at finding him alone in the church, so strange and fiery was his look. More than once, in the choir, during divine service, his neighbour in the stalls had heard him mingle, in the full song *ad omnem tonum* (note for note), unintelligible parentheses. More than once had the laundress of the Terrain, who was employed 'to wash the chapter,' observed, not without dread, marks of nails and clenched fingers in the surplice of Monsieur the Archdeacon of Josas.

However, he became doubly rigid, and had never been more exemplary. By character, as well as by calling, he had always held himself aloof from women; and he seemed to hate them more than ever. The mere crackling of a silken corsage brought his hood down over his eyes. On this point so jealous were his austerity and reserve that when the king's daughter, the Lady of Beaujeu, came in December, 1481, to visit the cloister of Notre-Dame, he gravely opposed her entrance, reminding the bishop of the statute in the Livre Noir or Black Book, dating from the vigil Saint Bartholomew, 1344, forbidding access to the cloister to every woman 'whatsoever, old or young, mistress or maid.' Whereupon the bishop having been constrained to cite to him the ordinance of the legate, Odo, which makes exception in favour of certain ladies of high rank— *aliquae magnates mulieres, quae sine scandalo evitari non possunt* (certain great ladies who cannot be excluded without scandal)—the archdeacon still protested; objecting that the legate's ordinance, being dated as far back as the year 1207, was a hundred and twenty-seven years anterior to the Livre Noir, and was consequently abrogated by it. And he refused to make his appearance before the princess.

It was also remarked that, for some time past, his abhorrence of gypsy women and zingari had been redoubled. He had solicited from the bishop an edict expressly forbidding the gypsies from coming to dance and play upon the tambourine in the *Place du Parvis ;* and for the same length of time he had been rummaging among the mouldy archives of the official in order to collect together all the cases of wizards and witches condemned to the flames or the halter for having been accomplices in sorcery with he-goats, she-goats or sows.

6

Unpopularity

THE archdeacon and the bell-ringer, as we have already said, were but little esteemed among the small and great folks of the environs of the cathedral. When Claude and Quasimodo went forth together, as frequently happened, and they were observed in company traversing the clean, but narrow and dusky, streets of the neighbourhood of Notre-Dame, the servant following his master, more than one malicious word, more than one ironical couplet, more than one insulting jest, stung them on their way; unless Claude Frollo—though this happened rarely—walked with head erect, exhibiting his stern and almost august brow to the gaze of the abashed scoffers.

The pair were in that quarter like the 'poets' of whom Régnier speaks:

All sorts of folk do after poets hie,
As after owls the tomtits shriek and fly.

Occasionally an ill-natured body would risk his skin and bones for the ineffable pleasure of running a pin into Quasimodo's hump. Again, a pretty girl, more full of frolic and boldness than became her, would rustle the priest's black gown, singing in his face the sardonic ditty: 'Nestle, nestle, the Devil is caught.' Sometimes a squalid group of old women, crouching in line down the shady side of the steps of a porch, grumbled aloud as the archdeacon and the bell-ringer passed, or called after them with curses this encouraging greeting: 'Ho! here comes one with a soul as crooked as the other's body.' Or a band of school-boys and street urchins playing at hopscotch would jump up together and salute them classically with some cry in Latin, as '*Eia! eia! Claudius cum claudo!*' ('Ah! ah! Claude with the cripple.')

Generally, the insult passed unperceived by the priest and the bell-ringer. Quasimodo was too deaf and Claude too deeply absorbed in his thoughts to hear these gracious salutations.

BOOK FIVE

I

Abbas Beati Martini *

DOM CLAUDE's fame had spread far and wide. It procured for him, about the period he refused to see Madame de Beaujeu, a visit which he long remembered.

It was on a certain evening. He had just withdrawn, after divine service, to his canon's cell in the cloister of Notre-Dame. This cell, with the exception perhaps of some glass phials, relegated to a corner, and filled with a certain equivocal powder which strongly resembled gunpowder, offered nothing extraordinary or mysterious. There were, indeed, here and there, several inscriptions upon the walls; but they were merely sentences relative to science or religion, and extracted from good authors. The archdeacon had just seated himself by the light of a three-beaked copper lamp, before a large cabinet loaded with manuscripts. He leaned his elbow upon the open volume of Honorius d'Autun, *De Prædestinatione et libero arbitrio* (on predestination and free will,) and he was turning over in profound meditation the leaves of a folio which he had brought in with him, the only product of the printing-press which his cell contained. In the midst of his reverie a knock was heard at the door. 'Who is there?' cried the sage, in the gracious tone of a hungry dog who is disturbed at his bone.

A voice replied from without: 'Your friend, Jacques Coictier.' He went to open the door.

It was, in fact, the king's physician, a person of some fifty years of age, whose harsh physiognomy was only corrected by his crafty eye. Another man accompanied him. Both wore long slate-coloured robes, furred with minever, belted and buttoned, with bonnets of the same stuff and colour. Their hands disappeared in their long sleeves, their feet under their robes and their eyes beneath their caps.

'God help me, gentlemen!' said the archdeacon, showing them in, 'I was not expecting so honourable a visit at such an hour'—and while speaking in this courteous manner he cast an anxious and scrutinizing glance from the physician to his companion.

'It is never too late to visit so distinguished a scholar as Dom Claude Frollo de Tirechappe,' replied the Doctor Coictier, whose

* Abbé of the Blessed Saint Martin.

Franche-Comté accent caused all his phrases to drag with the majesty of a court-train.

Then began between the physician and the archdeacon one of those congratulatory prologues which preceded, according to the custom of the time, all conversation between men of learning, and which did not prevent them detesting each other in the most cordial manner in the world. However, it is the same to-day; the lips of each wise man who compliments another sage are like a cup of honeyed gall.

Claude Frollo's congratulations to Jacques Coictier referred principally to the numerous temporal advantages which the worthy physician, in the course of his much envied career, had succeeded in extracting from each malady of the king, the operation of an alchemy better and more certain than the pursuit of the philosopher's stone.

'In truth, Monsieur le Docteur Coictier, I had great joy in learning of the bishopric granted to your nephew, my reverend seigneur Pierre Versé. Is he not Bishop of Amiens?'

'Yes, Monsieur Archdeacon, it is a favour and mercy from God.'

'Do you know that you made a very fine figure on Christmas day at the head of your company from the Chamber of Accounts, Monsieur President?'

'Vice-President, Dom Claude. Alas! nothing more.'

'At what point is the work on your superb house in the Rue Saint André des Arcs? It is another Louvre. I like exceedingly the apricot-tree which is carved over the door with the pleasant play upon the words à L'ABRI COTIER.'

'Alas! Master Claude, all that masonry is costing me heavily. In proportion as the house rises I am ruined.'

'Ho! Have you not your revenues from the jail and the bailiwick of the Palace, and the rents of all the houses, butchers' stalls and booths of the enclosure? 'Tis a fine cow to milk.'

'My Poissy castellany has brought me nothing this year.'

'But your tolls of Triel, of Saint James and of Saint Germain en Laye are always good.'

'Six score livres, and not even Paris livres.'

'You have your place as king's counsellor, that is fixed.'

'Yes, Brother Claude, but that accursed manor of Poligny, about which they make so much noise, is not worth to me sixty gold crowns to the year, good or bad.'

There was, in the compliments which Dom Claude addressed to Jacques Coictier, that satirical, biting and mocking accent combined with that cruel, sad smile of a superior but unhappy man, who for a moment's distraction plays with the fat prosperity of a vulgarian. The other did not perceive it.

'Upon my soul,' exclaimed Claude, finally, pressing his hand, 'I am glad to see you in such good health.'

'Thanks, Master Claude.'

'By the way,' said Dom Claude, 'how is your royal patient?'

'He does not pay sufficiently his physician,' replied the doctor, glancing at his companion.

'Think you so, friend Coictier?' said his comrade.

These words, uttered in a tone of surprise and reproach, drew the attention of the archdeacon upon the unknown personage, which, to tell the truth, had not been diverted from him a single moment since the stranger had crossed his threshold. It had even required all the thousand reasons which he had for conciliating Doctor Jacques Coictier, the all-powerful physician of King Louis XI, to induce him to receive the latter thus accompanied. Hence, his mien was but little cordial when Jacques Coictier said to him: 'By the way, Dom Claude, I bring you a colleague who has desired to see you on account of your renown.'

'Does the gentleman belong to science?' asked the archdeacon, fixing his piercing eye upon Coictier's companion. He found beneath the brows of the stranger a glance no less piercing or less defiant than his own. He was, so far as the feeble light of the lamp permitted one to judge, an old man about sixty years of age, of medium stature, who appeared somewhat sickly and broken down. His profile, though commonplace in outline, was still strong and severe; his eye flashed from beneath an overhanging brow like a light from the depths of a cave; and under the cap that was well drawn down and fell upon his nose, one recognized the broad expanse of a brow of genius.

He took it upon himself to reply to the archdeacon's question:

'Reverend master,' he said, in a grave tone, 'your renown has reached my ears, and I wish to consult you. I am but a poor provincial gentleman, who removeth his shoes before entering the presence of learned men. You must know my name. I am called Friend Tourangeau.'

'Strange name for a gentleman!' thought the archdeacon. Nevertheless he felt himself in the presence of a character both strong and serious. The instinct of his own lofty intelligence enabled him to recognize a no less able mind under the furred bonnet of Friend Tourangeau; and as he contemplated that grave countenance, the ironical smile, which the presence of Jacques Coictier had called to his gloomy face, faded slowly away as twilight upon the evening horizon. He had reseated himself, stern and silent, in his great arm-chair, his elbow in its accustomed place upon the table and his forehead in his hand. After a few moments of meditation, he beckoned to his visitors to be seated, and addressed Friend Tourangeau.

'You come to consult me, master, and upon what science?'

'Your reverence,' replied Friend Tourangeau, 'I am ill, very ill. You are said to be a great Æsculapius, and I am come to ask your advice in medicine.'

'Medicine!' said the archdeacon, tossing his head. He appeared to meditate for a moment, then resumed. 'Friend Tourangeau, since that is your name, turn your head and you will find my reply already written upon the wall.'

The Friend Tourangeau obeyed, and read, engraved upon the wall over his head, the following inscription: '*Medicine is the daughter of dreams.*'—JAMBLIQUE.

Meanwhile, Doctor Jacques Coictier had heard his companion's question with a displeasure which Dom Claude's reply had only redoubled. He leaned down to the ear of Friend Tourangeau and said to him, softly enough to escape the hearing of the archdeacon: 'I warned you that he was mad. You insisted on seeing him.'

'But it is quite possible that he is right, this madman, Doctor Jacques,' replied the Friend, in the same tone and with a bitter smile.

'As you please,' answered Coictier, dryly. Then, addressing the archdeacon: 'You are a quick workman, Dom Claude, and you have as little trouble with Hippocrates as a monkey does with a nut. Medicine a dream! I doubt me the pharmacopolists and the master physicians would feel it their duty to stone you, if they were here. So you deny the influence of philters upon the blood, of unguents upon the flesh! You deny that eternal pharmacy of the flowers and the metals, which we call the world, and which was expressly made for that eternal invalid we call man!'

'I deny,' said Dom Claude, coldly, 'neither pharmacy nor the invalid. I deny the physician.'

'Then it is not true,' continued Coictier, with warmth, 'that the gout is an internal ringworm; that a bullet wound can be cured by the application of a roasted mouse, and that young blood, properly infused, restores youth to aged veins; it is not true that two and two make four, and that emprostathonos follows opistathonos?'

The archdeacon replied calmly: 'There are certain things upon which I think in a certain manner.'

Coictier became red with anger.

'There, there, my good Coictier, let us not get angry,' said the Friend Tourangeau. 'Monsieur the archdeacon is our friend.'

Coictier calmed down, muttering in a low tone, 'After all, he is mad!'

'*Pasquedieu*, Master Claude,' resumed Friend Tourangeau, after a silence, 'you embarrass me greatly. I had two subjects for consultation with you; one touching my health, the other touching my star.'

'Sir!' responded the archdeacon, 'if that be your object you would have done as well not to have wasted your breath in climbing my stairs. I do not believe in medicine; I do not believe in astrology.'

'Indeed!' replied the stranger, with surprise.

Coictier gave a forced laugh.

'You see obviously that he is mad,' said he in a low tone to Friend Tourangeau. 'He does not believe in astrology.'

'What reason to imagine,' pursued Dom Claude, 'that each ray from a star is a thread that touches the head of a man!'

'And what, then, do you believe?' cried Friend Tourangeau.

The archdeacon rested a moment uncertain, then upon his lips appeared a sombre smile which seemed to give the lie to his response: '*Credo in Deum.*'

'*Dominum nostrum*,' added Friend Tourangeau, making the sign of the cross.

'*Amen*,' said Coictier.

'Reverend master,' resumed Tourangeau, 'in my soul am I rejoiced to find you of such religious mind. But have you reached a point, great savant that you are, of no longer believing in science?'

'No,' said the archdeacon, seizing Father Tourangeau by the arm, and a light of enthusiasm illumined his dull eye, 'no, I do not deny science; I have not crawled so long upon my belly with my nails in the earth amid the countless mazes of the cavern without perceiving, far away beyond me at the end of the obscure gallery, a light, a flame, something, a reflection, doubtless of the dazzling central laboratory, where the patient and the wise have taken God by surprise.'

'But, after all,' interrupted Tourangeau, 'what do you hold to be true and certain?'

'Alchemy.'

'*Pardieu*,' exclaimed Coictier, 'alchemy has its good without doubt, Dom Claude, but why blaspheme medicine and astrology?'

'Naught is your science of man, naught is your science of the stars,' said the archdeacon, imperiously.

'That is making short work of Epidaurus and Chaldea,' replied the doctor, sneeringly.

'Listen, Messire Jacques. This is said in good faith. I am not the king's physician, and his Majesty has not given me the garden of Dædalus in which to observe the constellations . . . —do not get angry, but listen to me. What truth have you derived—I will not say from medicine, which is too foolish a thing, but from astrology?'

'Do you deny,' said Coictier, 'the sympathetic force of the collar-bone and the cabalistics which are derived therefrom?'

'Error, Messire Jacques. None of your formulas end in reality while alchemy has its discoveries. Do you dispute such results as these? Ice imprisoned under ground for a thousand years becomes rock crystal. Lead is the father of all metals. For gold is not a metal; gold is light. Lead requires four periods of two hundred years each to change successively from the state of lead to that of red arsenic, from red arsenic to tin, from tin to silver. Are not these facts? But to believe in the collar-bone, in the great circle and in the stars is as ridiculous as to believe with the inhabitants of Grand Cathay that the golden oriole turns into a mole, and that grains of wheat turn into fish of the carp species.'

'I have studied hermetics,' cried Coictier, 'and I insist—'

The fiery archdeacon did not allow him to finish: 'And I have studied medicine, astrology and hermetics. Here alone is the truth' (and as he spoke thus he took from the cabinet a phial full of the powder of which we spoke above), 'here alone is light! Hippocrates is a dream; Urania is a dream; Hermes is but a thought. Gold is the sun; to make gold is to become God. Behold the unique science. I have sounded the depths of medicine and astrology, I tell you! They are naught, naught! The human body, shadows! the planets, shadows!'

And he fell back into his arm-chair in commanding and inspired attitude. Friend Tourangeau observed him in silence. Coictier forced a sneer, and imperceptibly shrugging his shoulders, said in a low voice: 'A madman!'

'And,' said suddenly Tourangeau, 'the splendid goal, have you attained it—have you made gold?'

'Had I made it,' replied the archdeacon, slowly articulating, like a man who is reflecting, 'the king of France would be called Claude and not Louis.'

The stranger frowned.

'What do I say?' continued Claude, with a smile of disdain. 'What would the throne of France be to me, when I could rebuild the empire of the Orient?'

'Very good,' said the stranger.

'Oh, the poor fool,' murmured Coictier.

The archdeacon continued, appearing to reply only to his thoughts.

'But no, I am still crawling. I bruise my face and my knees upon the stones of the subterranean way; I see dimly, I do not contemplate the full glory, I do not read, I spell!'

'And when you can read!' demanded the stranger, 'will you make gold?'

'Who doubts it?' said the archdeacon.

'In that case, Our Lady knows that I am in sore need of money, and I would gladly learn to read in your books. Tell me, reverend master, is your science hostile or displeasing to Our Lady?'

To this question of Tourangeau, Dom Claude merely replied with calm dignity:

'To whom am I archdeacon?'

"Tis true, my master. Will it, then, please you to initiate me? Teach me to spell with you.'

Claude took the majestic and pontifical attitude of a Samuel.

'Old man, it takes longer years than rest to you to undertake the voyage through mysterious things. Your head is very gray! One leaves not the cavern but with whitened hair, and their locks must be dark who enter it. Science alone knows well how to hollow, wither and wrinkle human faces; she needs not that old age should bring her features already furrowed. If, however, the desire possesses you to submit yourself to discipline at your age, and of deciphering the formidable alphabet of the sages, come to me; it is well—I will make the effort. I will not tell you, poor old man, go visit the sepulchral chambers of the Pyramids, of which the ancient Herodotus speaks, nor the brick tower of Babylon, nor the great white marble sanctuary of the Indian temple of Eklinga. I, no more than you, have seen the Chaldean masonry constructed in the sacred form of Sikra, nor the temple of Solomon, which is destroyed, nor the stone doors of the sepulchre of the kings of Israel, which are broken. We will content ourselves with the fragments of the book of Hermes, which we have here. I will explain to you the statue of Saint Christopher, the symbol of the Sower, and that of the two angels which are at the door of the Sainte Chapelle, one of whom has his hand in a vase and the other in a cloud—'

Here, Jacques Coictier, who had been nonplussed by the archdeacon's impetuous replies, regained confidence and interrupted him with the triumphant tone of a savant who corrects another: '*Erras amice, Claudi* (thou errest, friend Claude). The symbol is not the number. You take Orpheus for Hermes.'

'It is you who are in error,' replied gravely the archdeacon. 'Dædalus is the basement; Orpheus is the wall; Hermes is the edifice,— the whole. Come when you will,' continued he, turning toward Tourangeau, 'I will show you the particles of gold which remained at the bottom of Nicolas Flamel's crucible, and you may compare it with the gold of Guillaume de Paris. I will teach you the secret virtues of the Greek word, '*peristera.*' But before all, I will make you read, one after the other, the marble letters of the alphabet, the granite pages of the book. We shall go from the portal of the Bishop Guillaume and of Saint Jean le Rond to La Sainte Chapelle, then to the house of Nicolas Flamel, Rue Marivault, to his tomb which is at the Holy Innocents, to his two hospitals, Rue de Montmorency. I shall make you read the hieroglyphs which cover the four great iron dogs at the door of the hospital of Saint Gervais and of the Rue de la Ferronnerie. We will spell out together the façade of Saint Côme, of Sainte Geneviève des Ardents, of Saint Martin, of Saint Jacques de la Boucherie—'

For some time, Friend Tourangeau, intelligent though his glance was, had obviously failed to follow Dom Claude. He interrupted.

'*Pasquedieu!* What sort of books are these, then?'

'Here is one,' said the archdeacon.

And opening the window of his cell, he pointed to the vast church of Notre-Dame, which outlining darkly its two towers against the starry sky, with its stone flanks and its enormous back, appeared a gigantic two-headed sphinx crouching in the midst of the city.

For some time the archdeacon considered the enormous edifice in silence, then with a sigh, extending his right hand towards the printed book which lay open upon his table, and with his left hand extended towards Notre-Dame, his eyes sadly wandered from the book to the church. 'Alas!' he said, 'this will kill that.'

Coictier, who had eagerly approached the book, could not repress an exclamation: 'Why! But what is there so terrible in this: GLOSSA IN EPISTOLAS D. PAULI. *Norimbergæ, Antonius Koburger*, 1474. This is not new. It is a book of Pierre Lombard, the master of Maxims. Is it because it is printed?'

'You have said it,' responded Claude, who appeared absorbed in a profound meditation, and stood with his forefinger resting upon the folio which had come from the famous press of Nuremberg. Then he added these mysterious words: 'Alas! Alas! Small things overcome great ones; the Nile rat kills the crocodile, the swordfish kills the whale, the book will kill the edifice.'

The curfew of the cloister sounded the same moment that Doctor Jacques repeated to his companion in low tones his eternal refrain: '*He is mad!*' To which his companion this time replied: 'I believe that he is.'

It was the hour when no stranger could remain within the cloister. The two visitors withdrew.

'Master,' said Friend Tourangeau, in taking leave of the arch-deacon, 'I love wise men and great minds, and I hold you in singular esteem. Come to-morrow to the Palace des Tournelles and ask for the Abbot of Saint Martin de Tours.'

The archdeacon returned to his chamber dumbfounded, under-standing at last who this Friend Tourangeau was, and recalling that passage from the cartulary of Saint Martin de Tours : *Abbas beati Martini*, SCILICET REX FRANCIÆ, *est canonicus de consuetudine et habet parvam præbendam quam habet sanctus Venantius et debet sedere in sede thesaurarii.* *

It is affirmed that since that time the archdeacon had frequent conferences with Louis XI when his Majesty came to Paris, and that the influence of Dom Claude quite overshadowed that of Oliver Le Daim and Jacques Coictier, the latter of whom, as was his wont, roundly took the king to task on this account.

2

One Shall Destroy the Other

OUR fair readers will pardon us if we pause a moment to search for the hidden meaning of those enigmatic words of the arch-deacon : 'The one shall destroy the other. The book will kill the edifice.'

In our opinion this idea might present two aspects. In the first place, it was the thought of a priest. It was the alarm of the priest in the presence of a new agent, printing. It was the horror and astonishment of the man of the sanctuary before the dazzling results of Guttenberg's press. It was the pulpit and the manuscript, the spoken word and the written word taking fright at the printed word : something similar to the stupor of the sparrow who should see the angel Legion unfold its six million wings. It was the cry of the prophet who already hears the roar of emancipated humanity, who beholds in the future intelligence undermining faith, opinion dethroning belief, the world at large shaking Rome. It was the prognostic of the philosopher, who sees human thought volatilized by the press, evaporating from the theocratic recipient. It was the terror of the soldier who examines the brazen battering-ram and says the town will fall. It signified that one power was succeeded by another. It meant, 'The press shall kill the Church.' But under this thought, without doubt the first and the most simple, there was in our belief another, more new, a corollary of the first less easy to perceive but more easy to contest, a view equally philosophic and not confined alone to the priest, but shared by the savant and the artist. It was the presentiment that human thought in changing

---

* The abbot of Saint Martin, namely, the King of France, is canon according to custom and holds the office of prebendary which Saint Venantius holds and should sit in the seat of the Treasurer.

its form would also change its mode of expression; that the dominant idea of each generation would no longer be written with the same material and in the same manner; that the book of stone, so solid and so enduring, was about to make way for the book of paper, more solid and still more enduring. In this relation the archdeacon's vague formula had another meaning, it signified that one art would dethrone another art. 'Printing would kill architecture.'

Indeed, from the origin of things down to and including the fifteenth century of the Christian era, architecture is the great book of humanity, the principal expression of man in his various stages of development, both as regards force and intellect.

When the memory of the first races felt itself surcharged, when the load of recollections which mankind had to bear became so heavy and confused that language, naked and simple, risked its loss by the way, men wrote them upon the ground in a manner most visible and most natural. They sealed each tradition beneath a monument.

The first monuments were mere fragments of stone, 'which iron had not touched,' says Moses. Architecture began like all writing. It was at first the alphabet. A stone was placed upright; it was a letter, and each letter was a hieroglyph and upon each hieroglyph reposed a group of ideas, like the capital upon the column. Thus did the first races everywhere simultaneously over the entire surface of the world. We find the 'standing stones' of the Celts in Asiatic Siberia: in the pampas of America.

Later on they made words; they placed stone upon stone, they coupled these syllables of granite; the verb essayed a few combinations. The Celtic dolmen and cromlech, the Etruscan tumulus, the Hebrew galgal, are words. Some of them, particularly the tumulus, are proper names. Sometimes even, where there was plenty of stone and vast coast, they wrote a phrase. The immense pile of Karnac is a complete sentence.

Finally men made books. Traditions had created symbols, which hid them as the leaves hide the trunk of a tree. All these symbols in which humanity had faith, continued to grow, to multiply, to intersect, to become more and more complicated: the first monuments were not sufficient to contain them, they overflowed them on every side; scarcely did these monuments still explain their original tradition, like themselves simple, naked and prone upon the earth. The symbol must needs expand into the edifice. Architecture then developed with the human thought, it became a giant with a thousand heads and a thousand arms, and fixed all that floating symbolism in an eternal, visible, palpable form. While Dædalus, who is force, measured; while Orpheus, who is intelligence, sang: the pillar, which is a letter; the arcade, which is a syllable; the pyramid, which is a word, set in motion alike by a geometric and poetic law, grouped themselves, combined, amalgamated, descended, arose, were juxtaposed upon the ground, ranged themselves in stories in the sky, until they had written under the general dictation of an epoch, those marvellous books which were likewise marvellous edifices: the Pagoda of Eklinga, the Rhamseion of Egypt, the Temple of Solomon.

The generating idea, the word, was not alone at the foundation of all these structures, but also to be traced in their form. The temple of Solomon, for example, was not only the binding of the holy book, but was the holy book itself. Upon each one of its concentric walls, the priest could read the Word, interpreted and manifested to the eye; and thus they followed its transformations from sanctuary to sanctuary until they seized it in the inner tabernacle, in its most concrete form, which was still architectural, the Ark itself. Thus the Word was concealed within the edifice, but its image was upon its envelope, like the human form upon the sarcophagus of a mummy.

And not only the forms of these buildings, but the sites that were chosen for them, arouse the thought they represented. According as the symbol they expressed was graceful or grave, Greece crowned her mountains with a temple harmonious to the eye; India disembowelled hers to chisel therein those deformed and subterranean pagodas supported by colossal ranks of granite elephants.

Thus during the first six thousand years of the world, from the most immemorial pagoda of Hindustan to the cathedral of Cologne, architecture has been the great handwriting of humankind. And this is so far true that not only all religious symbol, but also all human thought, has its page and its monument in this immense book.

All civilization begins with a theocracy and ends with a democracy. This law of liberty succeeding unity is written in architecture. For, and let us insist upon this point, masonry must not be thought powerful alone to erect the temple, to express the myth and sacerdotal symbolism, to transcribe in hieroglyphs upon its pages of stone the mysterious tables of the law. If it were thus,— as there comes in every human society a moment when the sacred symbol is worn and becomes obliterated under the influence of free thought, when man escapes from the priest, and when the excrescences born of philosophies and systems devour the fair features of religion—architecture could not reproduce this new state of the human mind; its leaves so crowded upon the face would be blank on the back; its work would be mutilated; its book incomplete. But no. Let us take for example the Middle Ages, which period we can regard with clearer insight, being nearer to us. During the first half, while theocracy was organizing Europe, while the Vatican rallied and reclassified around it the elements of a Rome made with the Rome that lay in ruins about the Capitol, while Christianity was seeking among the rubbish of former civilizations all the various stages of society, and rebuilding with its fragments a new hierarchic universe with priesthood as the keystone of the arch, a solution is arising out of this chaos, one sees —appearing little by little, under the breath of Christianity, out of barbarian hands, from among the litter of dead architectures, Greek and Roman, we see arising that mysterious Roman architecture, sister of the theocratic masonries of Egypt and India, the unchanging emblem of pure Catholicism, the immutable hieroglyph of Papal unity. All the thought of the time is written in that sombre Roman style. There is felt everywhere, authority, unity, the impenetrable, the absolute, Gregory VII: everywhere the priest, never the man; everywhere caste, nowhere the people. But the Crusades arrive. It is a great popular movement, and every great popular movement, whatever be its cause or its end, releases the spirit of liberty from its final precipitate. New ideas come to light. Here begin the stormy days of the Jacqueries, the Pragueries and the Leagues. Authority is shaken. Unity is divided. Feudalism insists upon sharing with theocracy, in awaiting until the people shall inevitably rise and, as usual, seize the lion's share: *Quia nominor leo* (because I am called lion). The nobles force their way through the ranks of the priesthood, the people those of the nobles. The face of Europe is changed. Well! the face of architecture is also changed. Like civilization she has turned her page, and the new spirit of the time finds her ready to write as it dictates. Architecture has come back from the Crusades with the pointed arch as the nations returned bringing liberty. Then while Rome is gradually dismembered Roman architecture dies. The hieroglyph deserts the cathedral and goes forth to emblazon the donjon and give prestige to feudalism. The cathedral, that edifice before time so dogmatic, is henceforth invaded by the commoners, by the masses, by liberty, escapes from the priest and falls into the power of the artist. The artist builds to his fancy. Farewell to mystery, myth and the law. Welcome fantasy and caprice. Provided the priest has his basilica and his altar, he has nothing to say. The four walls belong to the artist. The architectural book belongs no longer to the priesthood, to religion, to Rome; it is the property of imagination, of poetry, of the people. Hence the rapid and innumerable transformations of this architecture which endures only three centuries, and which is so striking after the stagnant immobility of the Roman period covering six or seven. Art, however, marches with giant strides. Genius and the originality of the people do the task formerly performed by the bishops. Each race as it passes leaves its line upon the great book; it erases the old Roman hieroglyphs from the frontispiece of the cathedral, and only here and there can be perceived the dogma penetrating through the stratum of new symbolism which covers it. The popular covering leaves scarcely visible the religious framework. It is impossible to form an idea of the liberties which the architects then took even towards the church.

We find capitals of columns interlaced with monks and nuns shamefully paired, as in the Hall of the Fireplaces, in the Palace of Justice, Paris, the adventures of Noah, sculptured with all detail, as under the great door of Bourges; or some bacchic monk with ass's ears, glass in hand, laughing in the face of an entire community, as in the lavatory of the abbey of Bocherville. There existed at that epoch, for thoughts transcribed in stone, a liberty, comparable only to the present freedom of the press. It was the liberty of architecture. This freedom goes to great lengths. Occasionally a portal, a façade, an entire church, is presented in a symbolical sense entirely foreign to its creed, and even hostile to the church. In the thirteenth century, Guillaume de Paris, in the fifteenth Nicolas Flamel, both are guilty of these seditious pages. Saint Jacques de la Boucherie was a church of opposition throughout.

This was the only freedom of expression at that period; it could inscribe itself within those books which we call edifices; freedom of thought would have been burned in the public place by the hand of the executioner in the form of manuscript, had it been so imprudent as to choose that form of expression; thoughts engraved over the door of a church would have witnessed their own execution when printed upon the pages of a book. Thus having alone in masonry a channel of expression, it left no opportunity neglected. Hence the immense number of cathedrals which covered Europe —a number so prodigious as to seem almost incredible, even after it had been verified. All the material forces, all the intellectual forces, converged towards the same point, architecture. In this manner, under the pretext of building churches to God, art developed in magnificent proportions.

Then, whosoever was born poet became architect. Genius, scattered through the masses, compressed on all sides by feudalism, as under a *testudo*, of brazen bucklers, found its only issue through the medium of architecture, burst forth through this art, and its Iliad took the form of cathedrals. All other arts obeyed and placed themselves under the discipline of architecture. They were the workmen of the great work. The architect, the poet, the master, embodied in its person the sculpture, which chiselled its façades, the painting which illumined its windows, the music which set its bells in motion and breathed into its organs. As for poetry, properly so called, there was none that obstinately refused to vegetate in manuscript form, but was compelled, in order to be of value, to find its place in the church as a 'hymn' or a 'prose;' the same rôle, after all, which the tragedies of Æschylus had played in the sacerdotal festivals of Greece, Genesis in the temple of Solomon.

Thus, down to the days of Guttenberg, architecture is the principal, the universal writing. This book of granite, begun by the Orient, was continued by Greek and Roman antiquity; the Middle Ages wrote the last page. Moreover, this phenomenon of an architecture of the people succeeding an architecture of caste, which we have just observed in the Middle Ages, repeats itself with every analogous movement in the human intelligence in the other great epochs of history. Thus, in order to enunciate here only summarily a law which it would require volumes to develop: in the upper Orient, the cradle of the primitive races, after the Hindu architecture came the Phœnician, that opulent mother of the Arabic style: in antiquity, after the Egyptian architecture, of which the Etruscan form and the Cyclopean monuments are but one variety, came the Greek architecture, of which the Roman style is only a prolongation, surcharged with the Carthaginian dome: in modern times, after the Roman architecture, the Gothic. And by separating these three series we find again in these three elder sisters, Hindu architecture, Egyptian architecture, Roman architecture, the same symbol; that is to say, theocracy, caste, unity, dogmatism, the myth, God: and for the three younger sisters, Phœnician architecture, the Greek and the Gothic and whatever may be the diversity of form inherent in their nature, the same signification in each, that is to say, liberty, the people, man.

In all the masonry of the Hindu, Egyptian or Roman, one feels always the priest, nothing but the priest, whether he be called Brahmin, Magian or Pope. It is not the same in the architectures of the people. They are more rich and less devotional. In Phœnician one recognizes the merchant; in the Greek, the republican; in the Gothic, the citizen. The general characteristics of all theocratic architecture are immutability, horror of progress, the conservation of traditional lines, of primitive types, a constant bending of all the forms of nature and mankind to the incomprehensible caprices of symbolism. They are books of darkness which only the initiated can decipher. Furthermore, every form and even every deformity has here a sense which renders it inevitable. Do not ask the Hindu, Egyptian or Roman structures to change their design or improve their statues. Any attempt at perfecting would be impious. In these architectures it would appear that the severity of the dogma seems to overlie the stone like a second petrifaction. On the contrary, the general characteristics of the masonries of the people are truth, progress, originality, opulence, perpetual movement. They are sufficiently removed from their religion to give thought to beauty and to cherish it; to correct and improve continually their ornamentation of statues and arabesques. They are of the century. They have a human sentiment mingled with the divine symbolism under whose inspiration they are still produced. Hence these edifices, open to every soul, to every intelligence, to every imagination: symbolical still, but easy of comprehension as the face of nature. Between theocratic architecture and this one there is the difference that exists between a sacred language and a vulgar one, between hieroglyphs and art, between Solomon and Phidias. If the reader will review what we have hitherto briefly, very briefly, indicated, omitting countless proofs and also a thousand objections, we are led to this conclusion: that architecture up to the fifteenth century was the principal register of humanity; that during this period, not a single thought of a complicated nature appeared in the world but was transformed into masonry; that all popular ideas as well as all religious law had its monuments; and finally, that mankind possessed no important thought which has not been written in stone. And why? It is because every thought, be it religious, be it philosophical, seeks to perpetuate itself; it is that the ideas which have moved one generation desire to move other generations likewise, and to leave their trace. Indeed, what immortality is more precarious than that of a manuscript? How much more durable, solid and lasting is a book of stone! To destroy the written word, the torch and the Turk have proved sufficient. To demolish the builded word, a social revolution, a terrestrial revolution is necessary. The barbarians have passed over the Coliseum; the deluge, perhaps, over the Pyramids.

In the fifteenth century all changes.

Human thought discovers a medicine by which to perpetuate itself, not alone more durable and more resisting than architecture, but still more simple and easier. Architecture is dethroned. To the letters of stone of Orpheus are about to succeed the letters of lead of Gutenberg.

'Alas! Alas! small things overcome great ones; the Nile rat kills the crocodile, the swordfish kills the whale, the book will kill the edifice.'

The invention of printing is the greatest event in history. It is the mother of revolution. It is a total renewal of the means of human expression: it is human thought which divests itself of one form and takes on another; it is the complete and definite changing of the skin of that symbolical serpent which since Adam has represented Intelligence.

In its printed form thought is more imperishable than ever; it is more volatile, more intangible, more indestructible. It is mingled with the very air. In the time of architecture it made itself a mountain and took powerful possession of a century, of a place. Now, thought is transformed into a flock of birds which scatter themselves to the four winds and occupy at once every point of air and space.

We repeat it, who does not perceive that in this manner it is far more indelible? From a state of solidity it has become animated. It passes from duration to immortality. A mass can be demolished; how extirpate ubiquity? A deluge comes; the mountain would have disappeared beneath its waves long before the birds ceased to fly above it, and if a single ark should float upon the surface of the cataclysm, they will alight thereon, will float with it, watch with it the going down of the waters, and the new world that shall emerge from this chaos will see soaring above it the thought of the submerged world, winged and alive.

And when one observes that this mode of expression is not only the most conservative, but also the most simple, the most convenient, the most practicable of all; when one considers that it does not drag after it a bulky baggage, and requires no cumbersome apparatus; when we compare the thought requiring for its interpretation in a building, to put in motion four or five other arts and tons of gold, a mountain of stone and a forest of timber as well as a whole population of workmen; when one compares to it the thought becoming a book, needing only a little paper, a little ink and a pen, why be surprised that human intelligence should have quitted architecture for printing? Cut abruptly the original bed of a river by a canal dug below its level, the stream will forsake its channel.

Behold how, beginning with the discovery of printing, architecture gradually declines, withers and becomes denuded. How one feels the water sinking, the sap departing, that the thought of the time and the people is departing from it. The indifference is almost imperceptible in the fifteenth century; the press is yet too weak and can only draw off somewhat of the superabundant life of mighty architecture. But beginning with the sixteenth century the malady of architecture becomes visible: it no longer is the essential expression of society; it transforms itself into a miserable classic art; from being Gallic, European, indigenous, it becomes Greek and Roman, from the true and the modern, it becomes pseudo-antique. It is this decadence which is called Renaissance. Magnificent decadence, however; for the ancient Gothic genius, whose sun sets behind the gigantic press of Mayence, for some time longer penetrates with its last rays that range of hybrid Latin arcade and Corinthian columns.

It is the setting sun which we mistake for an aurora.

However, from the moment when architecture is an art like any other, when it is no longer art in totality, the sovereign, the tyrant, architecture has no longer the force to retain the other arts. They emancipate themselves, break the yoke of the architect, and go each its own way. Each of them gains by this divorce. Isolation enlarges all. Sculpture becomes statuary. Imagery becomes painting. The pipe becomes music. One might compare it to a dismembered empire at the death of its Alexander, whose provinces become kingdoms.

Hence Raphael, Michel Angelo, Jean Goujon, Palestrina, those splendours of the dazzling sixteenth century. At the same time as the arts, thought emancipates itself in all directions. The heresiarchs of the Middle Ages had already made large breaches into Catholicism. The sixteenth century shatters religious unity. Before printing reform had been merely a schism, printing converted it into a revolution. Take away the press; heresy becomes unnerved. Be it fatality or the work of Providence, Gutenberg is the precursor of Luther.

Be this as it may, when the sun of the Middle Ages is completely set, when the genius of the Gothic is forever extinct upon the horizon, architecture gradually becomes dim, loses its colour and little by little fades away. The printed book, the gnawing worm of the edifice, sucks and devours it. Architecture decays, crumbles and becomes emaciated before the eye. It is poor, it is cheap, it is null. It expresses nought, not even the souvenir of the art of the past. Reduced to itself, abandoned by the other arts because it is abandoned by human thought, it summons journeymen instead of artists. Window-glass replaces the coloured panes. The stonecutter succeeds to the place of the sculptor. Farewell all sap, all originality, all intelligence. It debases itself like a lamentable workshop mendicant from copy to copy. Michel Angelo, who, no doubt, even at the beginning of the sixteenth century had felt that it was dying, had a last idea, an idea of despair. That Titan of art piled the Pantheon upon the Parthenon, and made Saint Peter's at Rome. Great work which is deservedly unique, the last originality of architecture, signature of a giant artist at the bottom of the colossal register of stone which was closing forever. Michel Angelo dead, what becomes of that miserable architecture which outlives itself in a shadowy, ghostly state? It takes Saint Peter's at Rome, copies it, parodies it. It is a mania. It is pitiable. Each century has its Saint Peter's of Rome. In the seventeenth the Val de Grace; in the eighteenth Sainte Geneviève. Each country has its Saint Peter's of Rome. London, St. Petersburg, Paris has two or three. Trifling inheritance, last dotage of a great art which becomes decrepit and falls into infancy before it dies.

If, instead of the characteristic monuments we have just described, we examine the general aspect of the art of the sixteenth and seventeenth centuries, we shall see the same phenomena of decay and phthisis. From the time of Francis II the architectural form diminishes more and more in the construction, leaving visible the geometrical character, like the bony framework of the emaciated invalid. The fine lines of art make way for the cold, inexorable forms of geometry. An edifice is no longer an edifice; it is a polyhedron. Architecture, however, still struggles to conceal this nudity. Look at the Greek pediment inscribed within the Roman, and vice versa. It is always the Pantheon within the Parthenon, Saint Peter's of Rome. Here are the brick houses with stone corners dating from Henry IV in the Place Royal, in the Place Dauphine. Here are the churches of Louis III, heavy, squat, thick-set, crowded, loaded with a dome as with a hump. We have the Mazarin architecture, the bad pasticcio Italian of the Quatre-Nations. Witness the palaces of Louis XIV, long barracks for courtiers, stiff, cold, tiresome. Finally we come to the style of Louis XV, with its chiccory and vermicelli ornament, the warts and fungi which disfigure that decrepit, toothless, coquettish old architecture. From Francis II to Louis XV the evil has increased in geometrical progression. Art has nothing but skin and bones left. It perishes miserably.

Meanwhile, what becomes of printing? All the life which abandons architecture is absorbed by it. In proportion as architecture dies, printing swells and grows in power. The capital of energy which human thought once expended upon buildings is expended henceforth upon books. Indeed, from the sixteenth century the press, lifted to the level of diminished architecture, contends with it and conquers it. In the seventeenth century the press has gained such an ascendancy, such a triumph, such a victory over its rival as to give to the world the feast of a great literary age. In the eighteenth, having reposed for a long time at the court of Louis XIV, it again seizes the old sword of Luther, places it in the hands of Voltaire and rushes forth tumultuously to the attack of ancient Europe, whose architectural expression it has already destroyed. At the close of the eighteenth century, it has destroyed everything. In the nineteenth it begins to reconstruct.

Now, we ask, which of the two arts has really represented human thought during the past three centuries? which translated it? not expressing alone its literary and artistic vagaries, but its vast, profound, universal movement? Which superposes itself, constantly, without rupture or gap, upon the human race, ever progressing like a monster with a thousand feet? Architecture or printing? It is printing. Let one here make no mistake; architecture is dead, irrevocably dead, killed by the printed book, killed because less lasting, killed because of greater cost. Each cathedral represents millions. Let the reader now imagine the capital necessary to rewrite the architectural book, to raise again the myriad edifices; to return once more to the time when the throng of monuments was such, in the words of an eye-witness, 'that one would have said that the world had shaken off its old habiliments in order to clothe itself in a white garment of churches.' *Erat enim atsi mundus, ipse excutiendo semet, rejecta vetustate, candidam ecclesiarum vestem indueret.* (For it was as if the world shaking itself had cast aside its old garments to clothe itself with a shining white vestment of churches)—*Glaber Radulphus.*

A book is soon made, costs but little and can go so far! Why should there be surprise that all human thought glides through this channel? This does not imply that architecture shall not yet here and there produce a fine monument, an isolated masterpiece. It is yet possible, from time to time, even under the reign of printing, I suppose, for an army to make a column of melted cannon, as we had during the reign of architecture. Iliads and Romanceros, Mahâbhâratas and Nibelungenlieds, made by a whole people out of combined and collected rhapsodies. The great accident of an architect of genius may occur in the twentieth century, as that of Dante in the thirteenth. But architecture will not again be the social art, the collective, the dominant art. The great poem, the great edifice, the great work of humanity will no longer be constructed; it will be printed.

And if, henceforth, architecture should again rise by accident, it will never be mistress. It will be subservient to the law of literature, formerly subject to it. The respective positions of the two arts will be reversed. It is certain that during the domination of architecture such rare poems as appeared, resembled the monuments. In India, Vyasa is as complex, strange and impenetrable as a pagoda. In Egypt poetry has, like its buildings, both vastness and repose of line; in ancient Greece beauty, serenity and calm; in Christian Europe, the majesty of the Catholic faith, the simplicity of popular taste; the rich and luxuriant vegetation of an epoch of renewal. The Bible resembles the Pyramids, the Iliad the Parthenon, Homer, Phidias. Dante in the thirteenth century is the last Roman church; Shakespeare in the sixteenth, the last Gothic cathedral.

Thus, to sum up what we have thus far stated in a manner

necessarily incomplete and mutilated, humanity has two books, two registers, two testaments; masonry and printing, the Word in stone and the Word in paper. Without doubt when one contemplates these two testaments, laying so broadly before us the history of the centuries, it is permissible to regret the visible majesty of that granite record, those gigantic alphabets of colonnades, of pylons, of obelisks, this species of human mountains which cover the world and the past, from the Pyramid to the steeple, from Cheops to Strasburg. The past as recorded upon these marble pages should be read again and again. This great book of architecture should have our incessant perusal and admiration; but we must not refuse to acknowledge the grandeur of the edifice which has in turn been raised by printing.

This edifice is colossal. I do not know what statistician has made the calculation that, were all the volumes which have issued from the press since Gutenberg's day piled one upon another, they would fill the space from the earth to the moon; but this is not the sort of greatness of which we desire to speak. However, when one tries to collect a comprehensive image in one's mind, of the total product of printing down to our days, does this image not take the form of an immense construction based upon the entire world, and upon which humanity labours without ceasing and whose monstrous crest is lost in the mists of the future? It is the anthill of human intelligence. It is the hive where all the creations of imagination, those golden bees, arrive with their honey. The edifice has a thousand stories. Here and there upon its landings we see the openings to the gloomy caverns of science which cross each other in the profound depths. Everywhere upon its surface the eye is gratified by an artistic luxury of arabesques, rose-windows and delicate lace carving. There each individual work, however capricious and isolated it may seem, has its place and its importance. Harmony results from the whole. From the cathedral of Shakespeare to the mosque of Byron, a thousand belfries crowd each other pell-mell above this metropolis of universal thought. At its base have been written again some ancient titles of humanity which architecture had failed to preserve. At the left of the entrance, fixed in the wall, is the antique bas-relief in white marble of Homer; at the right the Bible of all languages rears its seven heads. The hydra of the Romancero, with the Vedas and Nibelungen, mingled with other hybrid forms, can be descried farther on. But the immense building is never completed. The printing-press, that giant machine which pumps unceasingly all the intellectual sap of society, perpetually vomits forth fresh materials for its work.

The whole human race is upon the scaffolding. Every mind is a mason. The most humble may stop a hole or place a stone. Rétif de la Bretonne brings his hod of plaster. Each day a new course rises. Independently of the original and individual product of each writer, there are collective contingents. The eighteenth century gives the *Encyclopædia*, the revolution gives the *Moniteur*. Assuredly, it is a construction which grows and piles up in spirals without end; there also are confusion of tongues, unceasing activity, indefatigable labour, the heated rivalry of all humanity; a refuge promised to intelligence from another Deluge, against an overflow of barbarians. It is the second tower of Babel of the human race.

BOOK SIX

I

An Impartial Glance at the Ancient Magistracy

A right enviable personage, in the year of grace 1482, was the noble gentleman Robert d'Estouteville, knight, Sieur of Beyne, Baron of Ivry and Saint Andry in Marche, councillor and chamberlain to the king and keeper of the provostry of Paris. Already it was nearly seventeen years since he had received from the king, on the 7th of November, 1465, the year of the comet *, that fine place of Provost of Paris, which was considered rather as a dignity than an office—*Dignitas*, says Joannes Lœmnœus, *quæ cum non exigua potestate politiam concernente, atque prærogativis multis et juribus conjuncta est* (a dignity, to which is joined no small influence in affairs of state and many prerogatives and rights). It was an extraordinary thing in 1482 for a gentleman to hold a commission from the king, whose letters of institution dated as far back as the time of the marriage of the natural daughter of Louis XI with monsieur the bastard of Bourbon. On the same day that Robert d'Estouteville had taken the place of Jacques de Villiers in the provostry of Paris, Maître Jean Dauvet succeeded Messire Hélye de Thorrettes in the first presidency of the court of parliament, Jean Jouvénel des Ursins supplanted Pierre de Morvilliers in the office of Chancellor of France, and Regnault des Dormans relieved Pierre Puy of the post of master of requests in ordinary to the king's household. Over how many heads had the presidency, the chancellorship and the mastership travelled since Robert d'Estouteville had held the provostry of Paris! It had been 'granted into his keeping,' said the letters-patent; and well had he kept it forsooth. So closely had he clung to it, so completely had he incorporated himself, identified himself with it, that he had escaped that mania for change which possessed Louis XI, a suspicious, tormenting and toiling sovereign, bent upon maintaining, by frequent appointments and dismissals, the elasticity of his power. Nay, more—the worthy knight had procured the reversion of his office for his son; and for two years past the name of the noble gentleman Jacques d'Estouteville, Esquire, figured beside his own at the head of the register of the ordinary of the provostry of Paris. Rare, indeed, and signal favour! True it is that Robert d'Estouteville was a good soldier; that he

---

* This comet, against which Pope Calixtus, uncle of Borgia, ordered public prayers, is the same which reappeared in 1835.

had loyally raised the banner against 'the league of the public weal;' and that he had presented the queen, on the day of her entry into Paris in the year 14—, a most wonderful stag, all made of sweetmeats. He had, moreover, a good friend in Messire Tristan l'Hermite, provost-marshal of the king's household. Thus Messire Robert enjoyed a very smooth and pleasant existence. First of all, he had a very good salary; to which were attached and from which hung extra bunches of grapes from his vine, the revenues of the registries, civil and criminal, of the provostry; plus the revenues, civil and criminal, of the Auditoires d'Embas, or inferior courts, of the Châtelet; to say nothing of some little toll at the bridge of Mante and Corbeil, the tax on all the onions, leeks and garlic brought into Paris, and on the corders of firewood and the measurers of salt. Add to all this the pleasure of displaying, in his official rides through the town, in contrast with the gowns, half red and half tawny, of the sheriffs and police, his fine military dress, which you may still admire sculptured upon his tomb at the abbey of Valmont in Normandy, and his richly embossed morion at Montlhéry. Besides, was it nothing to have entire supremacy over the sergeants of the police, the porter and the watch of the Châtelet—*auditores Castelleti* (auditors of the Châtelet)—the sixteen commissaries of the sixteen quarters, the jailor of the Châtelet, the the four enfeoffed sergeants, the hundred and twenty mounted sergeants, the hundred and twenty sergeants of the wand, and the knight of the watch, with his watch, the under-watch, the counter-watch and the rear-watch? Was it nothing to exercise high and low justice, to exercise the right of interrogating, hanging and drawing, besides the jurisdiction over minor offences in the first resort—*in prima instantia* (in the first instance), as the charters have it—over that viscounty of Paris, to which were so gloriously appended seven noble bailiwicks? Can anything more gratifying be conceived than to issue orders and pass judgment, as Messire Robert d'Estouteville daily did in the Grand Châtelet, beneath the wide elliptic arches of Philip Augustus; and to go, as was his wont, every evening to that charming house situate in the Rue Galilee, in the purlieus of the Palais Royal, which he held in right of his wife, Madame Ambroise de Loré, to rest from the fatigue of having sent some poor devil to pass the night in 'that little lodge in the Rue de l'Escorcherie, which the provosts and échevins of Paris were wont to make their prison; the same being (according to the accounts of the estate, 1383) eleven feet in length, seven feet four inches in width and eleven feet in height?'

And not only had Messire Robert d'Estouteville his particular court as provost and viscount of Paris, but also he had a share, both by presence and action, in the grand justice of the king. There was not a head of any distinction but passed through his hands before it fell into those of the executioner. It was he who had gone to the Bastille Saint Antoine to fetch Monsieur de Nemours from thence to the Halles; and to conduct to the Grève Monsieur de Saint Pol, who clamoured and resisted, to the great joy of monsieur the provost, who did not love monsieur the constable.

Here, assuredly, was more than enough to make a life happy and illustrious, and to deserve some day a notable page in that interesting history of the provosts of Paris, where we learn that Oudard de Villeneuve had a house in the Rue des Boucheries; that Guillaume de Hangest bought the great and the little Savoie; that Guillaume Thiboust gave his houses in the Rue Clopin to the nuns of Sainte Geneviève; that Hugues Aubriot lived in the Hôtel du Porc Epic; and other domestic incidents.

And yet, with all these reasons for taking life patiently and cheerfully, Messire Robert d'Estouteville had waked on the morning of the 7th of January, 1482, in a very surly and peevish mood. Whence came this ill-temper? He could not have told himself. Was it because the sky was gray? or because the buckle of his old Montlhéry sword-belt was badly fastened, and girded too militarily his provostal portliness? or had he beheld ribald fellows marching through the street, four by four, under his window, jeering at him as they passed by, in doublets without shirts, hats without crowns, and wallet and bottle at their side? Was it a vague presentiment of the three hundred and seventy livres sixteen sols eight deniers which the future king, Charles VIII, was to deduct the following year from the revenues of the provostry? The reader can take his choice; we, for our part, are much inclined to believe that he was in an ill-humour simply because he was in an ill-humour.

Moreover, it was the day after a holiday—a tiresome day for everyone, and above all for the magistrate whose business it was to sweep away all the filth, whether literally or figuratively, that a holiday accumulated in Paris. And then he was to hold a sitting in the Grand Châtelet. Now we have noticed, that judges in general contrive matters so, that their day of sitting shall also be their day of ill-humour, in order that they may always have some one upon whom to vent it conveniently, in the name of the king and the law.

However, the audience had begun without him. His deputies, civil, criminal and private, were acting for him, according to custom; and since the hour of eight in the morning, some scores of citizens, men and women, crowded and crammed into a dark corner of the lower court-room of the Châtelet, between the wall and a strong barrier of oak, were blissfully looking on at the varied and exhilarating spectacle of the administration of civil and criminal justice by Maître Florian Barbedienne, auditor at the Châtelet, deputy of monsieur the provost, in a somewhat confused and utterly haphazard manner.

The room was small, low and vaulted. A table, studded with fleurs-de-lis, stood at one end, with a large arm-chair of carved oak for the provost, which was empty, and, on the left hand of it, a stool for the auditor, Maître Florian. Below sat the registrar, scribbling. Opposite were the populace; and in front of the door, and in front of the table, were a number of sergeants of the provostry in their sleeveless jackets of violet camlet with white crosses. Two sergeants of the Parloir aux Bourgeois, or Common-hall, in jackets of Toussaint half red and half blue, stood sentry before a low closed door, which was visible at the other end, behind the table. A single arched window, deep set in the massive wall, cast a ray of pale January sun upon two grotesque figures : the fantastic demon carved upon the keystone of the vaulted ceiling, and the judge, seated at the extremity of the chamber, upon the fleurs-de-lis.

Picture to yourself, in fact, at the provostal table, between two bundles of papers—leaning on his elbows, with his foot on the train of his gown of plain brown cloth, and his face in its framing of white lamb's wool, from which his eyebrows seemed to stand out —red—harsh-looking—winking, bearing majestically the load of his fat cheeks, which met under his chin—Maître Florian Barbedienne, auditor at the Châtelet.

Now, the auditor was deaf. A slight defect for an auditor. Maître Florian delivered judgment, none the less, without appeal and quite competently. It is certainly quite sufficient that a judge should appear to listen ; and the venerable auditor the better fulfilled this condition, the only one essential to strict justice, as his attention could not possibly be distracted by any noise.

Moreover, there was among the audience a merciless censor of his deeds and gestures, in the person of our friend Jehan Frollo du Moulin, the little student of the previous day—that 'stroller' who was sure to be met with everywhere in Paris, except before the professor's chair.

'Look you,' said he in a low tone to his companion Robin Poussepain, who was tittering beside him, while he commented on the scenes that were passing before them ; 'yonder is Jehanneton du Buisson. The beautiful daughter of the lazy dog at the Marché Neuf !—On my soul, he condemns her too, the old brute ! He must have no more eyes than ears ! Fifteen sous four deniers parisis for having worn two rosaries—'tis rather dear. *Lex duri carminis* (harsh law of invocation)—Who's that ?—Robin Chief de Ville, hauberk-maker. For having been passed and admitted a master of the said trade. That is his entrance-money. So, ho! two gentlemen among these rascals—Aiglet de Soins, Hutin de Mailly. Two esquires!—*Corpus Christi!*—Ha! they've been dicing. When shall we see our rector here? A hundred livres parisis (fine) to the king! Barbedienne hits like a deaf man—as he is!—May I be my brother the archdeacon, if that shall hinder me from gaming; gaming by day, gaming by night, gaming while I live, gaming till I die, and staking my soul after my shirt! Holy Virgin! what a lot of girls! —one after another, my lambs! Ambroise Lécuyère! Isabeau la Paynette! Bérarde Gironin! I know them all, by my fay! Fine 'em! fine 'em! That will teach you to wear gilt belts! Ten sols parisis, you coquettes!—Oh, the old snout of a judge! deaf and imbecile! Oh, Florian the blockhead! Oh, Barbedienne the dolt! There he is at the table—he dines off the pleader—he dines off the case—he eats—he chews—he crams—he fills himself! Fines—estrays—dues—expenses—costs—wages—damages—and interest—torture—prison and jail, and stocks with expenses—are to him Christmas spice-cake and marchpanes of Saint John. Look at him, the hog! Now then! Good!—another amorous wench! Thibaude la Thibaude, neither more nor less!—For going out of the Rue Glatigny!—What's this youth? Gieffroy Mabonne, gendarme bearing the cross-bow—he's been cursing the name of the Father. A fine for La Thibaude! a fine for Gieffroy! a fine for them both! The deaf old fool! he must have mixed up the two cases! Ten to one but he makes the girl pay for the oath, and the gendarme for the amour! Attention, Robin Poussepain! What are they bringing in now? Here are plenty of sergeants, by Jupiter! all the hounds of the pack. This must be the grand piece of game of all—a wild boar, at least! 'Tis one, Robin—'tis one! and a fine one, too!—Hercle! 'tis our prince of yesterday—our fools' pope—our ringer—our one-eyed—our hunchback—our grin of grins! 'Tis Quasimodo!'

It was he indeed.

It was Quasimodo, bound, girded, roped, pinioned and well guarded. The detachment of sergeants that surrounded him were accompanied by the knight of the watch, in person, bearing the arms of France embroidered on his breast, and those of the Town on his back. There was nothing, however, about Quasimodo, excepting his deformity, to justify all this display of halberts and arquebusses. He was gloomy, silent and tranquil; only now and then did his single eye cast a sly and wrathful glance upon the bonds which confined him.

He cast the same glance about him; but it was so dull and sleepy that the women only pointed him out with their fingers in derision.

Meanwhile, Maître Florian, the auditor, turned over attentively the document in the complaint entered against Quasimodo, which the clerk handed him, and having glanced at it, appeared to reflect for a moment. Thanks to this precaution, which he was always careful to take at the moment of proceeding to an interrogatory, he knew beforehand the name, titles and misdeeds of the accused, made premeditated replies to answers foreseen; and so contrived to extricate himself from all the sinuosities of the interrogatory without too much exposing his deafness. The written charge was to him as the dog to the blind man. If it so happened that his infirmity betrayed itself here and there, by some incoherent apostrophe or unintelligible question, it passed with some for profundity, with others for imbecility. In either case the honour of the magistracy did not suffer; for it is better that a judge should be reputed imbecile or profound than deaf. So he took great care to disguise his deafness from the observation of all; and he commonly succeeded so well that he had come at last even to deceive himself. This, indeed, is easier than one would imagine. Every hunchback walks with head erect; every stammerer harangues; every deaf person speaks low. As for him, he believed, at the most, that his ear was a little refractory. It was the sole concession in this respect that he made to public opinion, in his moments of frankness and self-examination.

Having, then, well ruminated on the affair of Quasimodo, he threw back his head and half closed his eyes, by way of greater majesty and impartiality; so that, at that moment, he was blind as well as deaf—a double condition, without which no judge is perfect. It was in this magisterial attitude that he commenced the interrogatory:

'Your name?'

Now here was a case which had not been 'foreseen by the law,' that of one deaf man interrogated by another.

Quasimodo, receiving no intimation of the question thus addressed to him, continued to look fixedly at the judge, and made no reply. The deaf judge, receiving no intimation of the deafness of the accused, thought that he had answered, as accused persons generally did; and continued, with his mechanical and stupid self-confidence:

'Very well—your age?'

Again Quasimodo made no answer to this question. The judge, thinking it replied to, went on:

'Now—your calling?'

Still the same silence. The bystanders, however, were beginning to whisper and to exchange glances.

'Enough!' added the imperturbable auditor, when he supposed that the accused had finished his third reply. 'You are accused before us—firstly, with nocturnal disturbance; secondly, with dishonest violence upon the person of a foolish woman—*in prejudicium meretricis* (as an example of a prostitute); thirdly, of rebellion and disloyalty toward the archers of the guard of our lord the king. Explain yourself on all these points. Clerk, have you taken down what the prisoner has said thus far?'

At this unlucky question a burst of laughter rose from both clerk and audience—so violent, so uncontrollable, so contagious, so universal, that neither of the deaf men could help perceiving it. Quasimodo turned round, shrugging his hump with disdain; while Maître Florian, equally astonished, and supposing that the laughter of the spectators had been excited by some irreverent reply from the accused, rendered visible to him by that shrug, apostrophized him indignantly.

'For that answer, fellow, you deserve the halter. Know you to whom you speak?'

This sally was not likely to check the explosion of the general mirth. It seemed to all present so incongruous and whimsical, that the wild laughter spread to the very sergeants of the Parloir aux Bourgeois, a sort of pikemen, whose stupidity was part of their uniform. Quasimodo alone preserved his gravity; for the very good reason that he understood nothing of what was going on around him. The judge, more and more irritated, felt obliged to proceed in the same strain, hoping thereby to strike the accused with a terror that would react upon the bystanders, and bring them back to a proper sense of respect:

'So, this is as much as to say, perverse and thieving knave that you are, that you presume to be lacking in respect to the auditor of the Châtelet; to the magistrate in charge of the chief police courts of Paris; appointed to inquire into all crimes, offences and misdemeanours; to control all trades and prevent monopoly; to repair the pavements; to put down hucksters of poultry, fowl and wild game; to superintend the measuring of firewood and other sorts of wood; to cleanse the town of mud and the air of contagious distempers; in a word, with attending continually to public affairs, without wages, or hope of salary. Know you that I am called Florian Barbedienne, monsieur the provost's own proper deputy, and, moreover, commissary, inquisitor, comptroller and examiner, with equal power in provostry, bailiwick, conservatorship and presidial court?'

There is no reason why a deaf man talking to a deaf man should ever stop. Heaven knows where and when Maître Florian would have landed, thus launched at full speed in lofty eloquence, if the low door behind him had not suddenly opened and given entrance to monsieur the provost in person.

Maître Florian did not stop short at his entrance, but, turning half round upon his heel, and abruptly directing to the provost the harangue with which, a moment before, he was overwhelming Quasimodo:

'Monsieur,' said he, 'I demand such penalty as it shall please you upon the accused here present, for flagrant and aggravated contempt of court.'

And he seated himself, utterly breathless, wiping away the great drops of sweat that fell from his brow and moistened, like tears, the parchments spread out before him. Messire Robert d'Estoute-ville frowned, and made a gesture to Quasimodo to attend, in a manner so imperious and significant that the deaf one in some degree understood it.

The provost addressed him sternly: 'What hast thou done to be brought hither, varlet?'

The poor devil, supposing that the provost was asking his name, broke the silence which he habitually kept, and in a harsh and guttural voice, replied:—'Quasimodo.'

The answer matched the question so little that the loud laugh began to circulate once more; and Messire Robert cried out, red with wrath: 'Dost mock me too, thou arrant knave?'

'Bell-ringer of Notre-Dame,' answered Quasimodo, thinking himself called upon to explain to the judge who he was.

'Bell-ringer!' returned the provost, who, as we have already said, had got up that morning in so bad a humour that his fury needed not to be kindled by such unaccountable answers—'Bell-ringer, indeed! I'll make them ring a peal of rods on thy back through every street in Paris—dost thou hear, rascal?'

'If you want to know my age,' said Quasimodo, 'I believe I shall be twenty next Martinmas.'

This was too much. The provost could endure it no longer.

'Ha! so you jeer at the provostry, you wretch! Messieurs the sergeants of the wand, you will take me this knave to the pillory in the Grève, and there flog him and turn him for an hour. He shall pay for his impudence, 'Sdeath! And I order that this present sentence be proclaimed by four sworn trumpeters, in the seven castellanies of the viscounty of Paris.'

The clerk instantly fell to work to record the sentence.

'Zounds! but that's a good sentence,' cried the little schoolboy, Jehan Frollo du Moulin, from his corner.

The provost turned and fixed his flashing eyes once more on Quasimodo. 'I believe the fellow said Zounds! Clerks, add a fine of twelve deniers parisis for swearing; and let one-half of it go to the vestry of Saint Eustache—I have a particular devotion for Saint Eustache.'

In a few minutes the sentence was drawn up. The tenor of it was simple and brief. The common law of the provostry and vis-county of Paris had not yet been elaborated by the president, Thibaut Baillet, and Roger Barmue, king's advocate; it was not yet obscured by that lofty hedge of quibbles and procedure which the two jurisconsults planted in it at the beginning of the sixteenth century. All was clear, expeditive, explicit; one went straight to the point—and at the end of every path was immediately visible, without thickets and without turnings, the wheel, the gibbet, or the pillory. One at least knew whither one was going.

The registrar presented the sentence to the provost, who affixed his seal to it, and departed, to pursue his round at the several audi-tories, in a frame of mind which seemed destined to fill every jail in Paris that day. Jehan Frollo and Robin Poussepain were laugh-ing in their sleeves; Quasimodo gazed on the whole with an indifferent and astonished air.

However, at the moment when Maître Florian Barbedienne was in his turn reading over the judgment before signing it, the registrar felt himself moved with pity for the poor condemned wretch; and, in the hope of obtaining some mitigation of the penalty, he ap-proached the auditor's ear as close as he could, and said, pointing to Quasimodo: 'That man is deaf.'

He hoped that a sense of their common infirmity would awaken Maître Florian's interest in behalf of the condemned. But, in the first place, as we have already observed, Maître Florian did not care to have his deafness remarked; in the next place, he was so hard of hearing that he did not catch a single word of what the clerk said to him; nevertheless, he wished to appear to have heard, and replied: 'Ah! ah! that is different—I did not know that. An hour more of the pillory, in that case.'

And he signed the sentence thus modified.

''Tis well done!' said Robin Poussepain, who cherished a grudge against Quasimodo, 'that will teach him to handle people roughly.'

2

The Rat Hole

WITH the reader's permission we shall conduct him back to the Place de Grève, which we quitted yesterday with Gringoire, to follow La Esmeralda.

It is the hour of ten in the morning. The appearance of every-thing indicates the morrow of a festival. The pavement is strewn with rubbish, ribbons, rags, feathers from tufts of plumes, drops of wax from the torches and fragments from the public banquet. A good many of the townspeople loiter about—turning over with their feet the extinct brands of the bonfire—going into raptures before the Maison aux Piliers at the recollection of the fine hangings of the preceding day, and now contemplating the nails that fastened them, the only remnant of the ravishing spectacle. The venders of beer and cider are trundling their barrels among the groups. Some busy passers-by come and go. The shopkeepers chatter and call to one another from their thresholds. The holiday, the ambassadors, Coppenole, the Fools' Pope, are in every one's mouth; each striving to crack the best jokes and laugh the loudest. And yet, four sergeants on horseback, who have just posted themselves at the four sides of the pillory, have already gathered around them a good part of the populace scattered on the Place, which condemns itself to immobility and fatigue in the hope of a small execution.

Now, if the reader will, after surveying this lively and noisy scene which is being enacted in all parts of the square, turn his eyes toward that ancient half-Gothic, half-Roman building, the Tour Roland, which stands at the western corner next the quay, he will observe, at the angle of its façade, a large public breviary richly illuminated, protected from the rain by a small penthouse, and from thieves by a grating, which, however, permits of the leaves being turned. Close by this breviary is a narrow, arched window-hole, guarded by two iron bars placed crosswise, and looking toward the square—the only opening through which a little air and light are admitted into a small cell without a door, built on the ground-floor, in the thickness of the wall of the old house—and filled with a stillness the more profound, a silence the more dead, inasmuch as a public square, the most populous and the noisiest in Paris, is swarming and clamouring around it.

This cell had been celebrated in Paris for nearly three centuries, since Madame Rolande, of Roland's Tower, in mourning for her father who died in the Crusades, had caused it to be hollowed out of the wall of her own house, to shut herself up in it forever, keeping of all her palace only this wretched nook, the door of which was walled up, and the window open to the elements, in winter as in summer—giving all the rest to God and to the poor. The disconsolate damsel had, in fact, awaited death for twenty years in this premature tomb, praying day and night for the soul of her father, sleeping in ashes, without even a stone for her pillow, clad in black sackcloth, and living only upon such bread and water as the pity of the passers-by deposited upon the edge of her window-place—thus receiving charity after she had given it. At her death —at the moment of her passing into the other sepulchre—she had bequeathed this one in perpetuity to women in affliction, mothers, widows or maidens, who should have occasion to pray much for others or for themselves, and should choose to bury themselves alive in the greatness of their grief or their penitence. The poor of her day paid her the best of funeral rites in their tears and blessings; but, to their great regret, the pious maiden had not been canonized, for lack of patronage. Such of them as were a little inclined to impiety, had hoped that the thing would be done more easily in heaven than at Rome, and had frankly besought God, instead of the Pope, in behalf of the deceased. Most of them, however, had contented themselves with holding the memory of Rolande sacred and converting her rags into relics. The City, on its side, had founded, in honour of the lady, a public breviary, which was fastened near the window of the cell, in order that the passersby might halt there from time to time, were it only to pray; that prayer might remind them of alms; and that the poor recluses, inheriting the stony cave of Madame Rolande, might not absolutely die of famine and neglect.

Moreover, this sort of tomb was not so very rare a thing in the cities of the Middle Ages. There might often be found, in the most frequented street, in the most crowded and noisy market-place—in the very midst—under the horses' feet and the wagon-wheels, as it were—a cave—a well—a walled and grated cabin—within which a human being prayed day and night, voluntarily devoted to some everlasting lamentation or some great expiation. And all the reflections which that strange spectacle would awaken in us to-day—that horrible cell, a sort of intermediary link between the house and the tomb, the city and the cemetery—that living being cut off from human community, and thenceforth reckoned among the dead—that lamp consuming its last drop of oil in the darkness—that remnant of life flickering in the grave—that breath, that voice, that everlasting prayer, encased in stone—that face forever turned toward the other world—that eye already illumined by another sun—that ear glued to the wall of the sepulchre—that soul a prisoner in that body—that body a prisoner in that dungeon and under that double envelope of flesh and granite, the murmur of that soul in pain—nothing of all this was noted by the crowd.

The piety of that age, unreasoning and far from subtle, did not see so many sides in an act of religion. It took things in the gross; honouring, venerating and hallowing, at need, the sacrifice; but not analyzing the sufferings, nor feeling any depth of pity for them. It brought some pittance, from time to time, to the miserable penitent; looked through the hole, to see if he were yet living; knew not his name; hardly knew how many years ago he had begun to die; and to the stranger, who questioned them about the living skeleton rotting in that cellar, the neighbours replied simply, 'It is the recluse.'

Everything was then viewed without metaphysics, without exaggeration, without magnifying-glass, with the naked eye. The microscope had not yet been invented, either for material or for spiritual things.

However, the instances of this sort of seclusion in the heart of cities, though they raised but little wonder, were, as we have already observed, in reality frequent. There were in Paris a considerable number of those cells of penitence and prayer; and nearly all of them were occupied. It is true that the clergy did not care to leave them empty, as that implied lukewarmness among the faithful; and that lepers were put into them when penitents were not to be had. Besides the cell on the Grève, there was one at Montfaucon, one at the charnel-house of the Holy Innocents, another we hardly recollect where—at the Clichon House, we believe—and others still at many spots, where traces of them are found in traditions, in default of memorials. The University had also its own. On the Montagne Sainte Geneviève, a sort of Job of the Middle Ages sang for thirty years the seven penitential psalms, upon a dung-heap at the bottom of a cistern, beginning anew when he had come to the end—singing louder in the night time, *magna voce per umbras* (a loud voice through the shadows); and the antiquary still fancies that he hears his voice, as he enters the Rue du Puits-qui-parle, or street of the talking well.

To confine ourselves here to the cell in Roland's Tower—we are bound to declare that it had scarcely ever lacked for recluses. Since Madame Rolande's death, it had rarely been vacant even for a year or two. Many a woman had come thither and mourned until death over the memory of her parent, her lover, or her failings. Parisian malice, which meddles with everything, even with those things which concern it least, affirmed that it had beheld but few widows there.

According to the manner of that period, a Latin inscription on the wall, indicated to the lettered passer-by the pious purpose of this cell. The custom was retained until the middle of the sixteenth century, of placing a brief explanatory motto above the entrance of a building. Thus in France one still reads over the wicket of the prison belonging to the seigniorial mansion of Tourville, *Sileto et spera* (Be silent and hope); in Ireland, under the escutcheon placed above the great gate-way of Fortescue Castle, *Forte scutum, salus ducum* (Strong shield, the safety of lords); and in England, over the principal entrance of the hospitable mansion of the Earls Cowper, *Tuum est* (It is thine). In those days every edifice embodied a thought.

As there was no door to the walled-up cell of the Tour Roland, there had been carved, in large Roman capitals, over the window, these two words:

TU, ORA*

Hence the people, whose common-sense sees not so many subtleties in things, but readily translates *Ludovico Magno* into *Porte Saint Denis*, gave to this dark, damp, dismal cavity the name of *Trou aux Rats* (signifying rat-hole)—an explanation possibly less sublime than the other, but more picturesque.

3

The Story of a Wheaten Cake

At the time of which this story treats the cell in the Tour Roland was occupied. If the reader wishes to know by whom, he has but to listen to the conversation of three fair gossips, who, at the moment that we have called his attention to the Rat-Hole, were proceeding toward the same spot, going up the river-side from the Châtelet toward the Grève.

Two of these women were dressed like good *bourgeoises* of Paris. Their fine white ruffs; their petticoats of linsey-woolsey, with red and blue stripes; their white knitted stockings, with clocks embroidered in colours, pulled well up over the leg; the square-toed shoes, of tawny leather with black soles; and above all, their head-gear, that sort of tinsel horn, loaded with ribbons and lace, still worn by the women of Champagne, in common with the grenadiers of the Russian imperial guard, announced that they belonged to that class of rich tradeswomen which holds the middle-ground between what the lackeys call *a woman* and what they term *a lady*. They wore neither rings nor gold crosses; but it was easy to see that this was not from poverty, but simply from fear of a fine. Their companion was decked out nearly in the same manner; but there was that indescribable something in her dress and bearing which suggested the wife of a country notary. It was evident, from the shortness of her waist, that she had not been long in Paris; add to this a plaited tucker—knots of ribbon upon her shoes—her skirt striped across instead of downward—and various other enormities which shocked good taste.

The first two walked with the step peculiar to Parisian women showing Paris to their country friends. The provincial one held by the hand a big, chubby boy, who held in his a large, flat cake. We

* Pray, thou.

regret to be obliged to add that, owing to the rigour of the season, his tongue was performing the office of his pocket-handkerchief.

The boy was being dragged along, *non passibus æquis* (unequal steps), as Virgil says, stumbling every moment, with many exclamations from his mother. It is true that he was looking more at the cake than upon the ground. Some serious reason, no doubt. prevented him from biting it (the cake), for he contented himself with looking at it affectionately. But the mother ought surely to have taken charge of the cake herself; it was cruel thus to make a Tantalus of the chubby-cheeked boy.

Meanwhile the three damoiselles (for the epithet of dame or lady was then reserved for noble women) were all talking at once.

'Let us make haste, Damoiselle Mahiette,' said the youngest, who was also the lustiest of the three, to her country friend. 'I am much afraid we shall be too late; we were told at the Châtelet that they were to put him in the pillory forthwith.'

'Ah, bah! what are you talking about, Damoiselle Oudarde Musnier?' interrupted the other Parisian. 'He will stay two hours on the pillory. We shall have time enough. Have you ever seen any one in the pillory, my dear Mahiette?'

'Yes,' said the provincial; 'at Rheims.'

'Ah, bah! what's that, your pillory at Rheims? A paltry cage, where they turn nothing but peasants. A fine sight, truly!'

'Nothing but peasants?' said Mahiette. 'In the cloth-market! at Rheims! We've seen some very fine criminals there—people who had killed both father and mother! Peasants, indeed! What do you take us for, Gervaise?'

It is certain that the country dame was on the point of taking offence for the honour of her pillory. Luckily, the discreet Damoiselle Oudarde Musnier gave a seasonable turn to the conversation.

'By-the-by, Damoiselle Mahiette, what say you to our Flemish ambassadors? Have you any so fine at Rheims?'

'I confess,' replied Mahiette, 'that it's only at Paris one can see Flemings such as they.'

'Did you see, among the embassy, that great ambassador who is a hosier?' asked Oudarde.

'Yes,' said Mahiette; 'he looks like a very Saturn.'

'And that fat one, with a face like a round paunch? And that little fellow with small eyes and red lids, as ragged and hairy as a head of thistle?'

'Their horses are the finest sight,' said Oudarde; 'dressed out as they are in the fashion of their country.'

'Ah! my dear,' interrupted the rustic Mahiette, assuming in her turn an air of superiority, 'what would you say, then, if you had seen, in '61, at the coronation at Rheims, eighteen years ago, the

horses of the princes and of the king's retinue! Housings and
trappings of all sorts; some of Damascus cloth, fine cloth of gold,
garnished with sables—others of velvet, furred with ermine—
others all loaded with goldwork and great gold and silver fringe.
And the money that it all cost—and the beautiful boy-pages that
were upon them!'

'That does not alter the fact,' dryly responded Damoiselle
Oudarde, 'that the Flemings have very fine horses—and that
yesterday they had a splendid supper given them by monsieur
the provost-merchant, at the Hôtel de Ville; where they served up
sweetmeats, hippocrass, spices, and such like singularities.'

'What are you talking about, neighbour?' cried Gervaise—'it
was with the lord cardinal, at the Petit Bourbon, that the Flemings
supped.'

'No, no—it was at the Hôtel de Ville.'

'Yes, yes, I tell you—it was at the Petit Bourbon.'

'So surely was it at the Hôtel de Ville,' returned Oudarde
sharply, 'that Doctor Scourable made them a speech in Latin,
with which they seemed mightily pleased. It was my husband, who
is one of the licensed booksellers, who told me so.'

'So surely was it at the Petit Bourbon,' returned Gervaise no
less warmly, 'that I'll just tell you what my lord cardinal's attorney
made them a present of—twelve double quarts of hippocrass,
white, claret and vermilion; four-and-twenty cases of gilt double
Lyons marchpane; as many wax-torches of two pounds each; and
six half-casks of Beaune wine, white and red, the best that could
be found. I hope that's decisive. I have it from my husband, who
is captain of fifty men in the Commonalty Hall, and who was
making a comparison this morning between the Flemish ambassadors and those of Prester John and the Emperor of Trebizond,
who came to Paris from Mesopotamia, in the last king's time, and
who had rings in their ears.'

'So true is it that they supped at the Hôtel de Ville,' replied
Oudarde, not a whit moved by all this display of eloquence, 'that
never was there seen so fine a show of meats and sugar-plums.'

'But I tell you that they were waited on by Le Sec, one of the
city guard, at the Hôtel du Petit Bourbon—and 'tis that has
misled you.'

'At the Hôtel de Ville, I tell you.'

'At the Petit Bourbon, my dear!—for they illuminated the
word *Hope* which is written over the great doorway, with magical
glasses.'

'At the Hôtel de Ville! at the Hôtel de Ville!—for Hussen le
Voir was playing the flute to them.'

'I tell you, no.'

'I tell you, yes.'

'I tell you, no.'

The good plump Oudarde was making ready to reply; and the quarrel might perhaps have gone on to the pulling of caps, if Mahiette had not suddenly exclaimed, 'See those people, crowding together at the end of the bridge! There's something in the midst of them that they are looking at.'

'Surely I hear the sound of a tambourine,' said Gervaise. 'I think it's little Smeralda, doing her mummeries with her goat. Quick, Mahiette—make haste, and pull your boy along. You are come here to see the curiosities of Paris. Yesterday you saw the Flemings—to-day you must see the little gypsy.'

'The gypsy?' exclaimed Mahiette, turning sharply round and grasping tightly the arm of her son. 'God forbid! She would steal my child—Come, Eustache!'

And she set off running along the quay toward the Grève, until she had left the bridge far behind her. But the boy, whom she dragged after her, stumbled and fell upon his knees; she stopped out of breath. Oudarde and Gervaise now came up with her.

'That gypsy steal your child!' said Gervaise; 'that's an odd notion of yours!'

Mahiette shook her head thoughtfully.

''Tis singular,' observed Oudarde, 'that the Sachette has the same notion about gypsy women.'

'What's the Sachette?' inquired Mahiette.

'Hey!' said Oudarde, 'Sister Gudule.'

'And what is Sister Gudule?' returned Mahiette.

'You are indeed from your Rheims—not to know that!' answered Oudarde. 'She is the recluse of the Rat-Hole.'

'What?' asked Mahiette; 'the poor woman to whom we are carrying the cake?'

Oudarde nodded affirmatively.

'Just so. You will see her presently, at her window on the Grève. She looks as you do upon those vagabonds of Egypt who go about tambourining and fortune-telling. Nobody knows what has given her this horror of zingari and Egyptians. But you, Mahiette, wherefore should you take to your heels thus at the mere sight of them?'

'Oh!' said Mahiette, clasping with both hands the chubby head of her boy; 'I would not have that happen to me which happened to Pâquette la Chantefleurie!'

'Ah! you must tell us that story, good Mahiette,' said Gervaise, taking her arm.

'I will gladly,' answered Mahiette; 'but you must, indeed, be from Paris—not to know that! You must know, then (but we need not stop while I tell you the story), that Pâquette la Chantefleurie was a pretty girl of eighteen when I was one too, that is to say eighteen years ago; and that it's her own fault if she is not at this day, as I am, a good, hearty, fresh-looking mother of six-and-thirty, with a husband and a boy—but alack! from the time that she was fourteen years old, it was too late. She was the daughter of Guybertaut, a boat-minstrel at Rheims—the same that played before King Charles VII at his coronation; when he went down our river Vesle from Sillery to Muison, and, more by token, the Maid of Orleans was in the barge with him. The old father died while Pâquette was quite a child, so she had only her mother, who was sister to Monsieur Matthieu Pradon, a master-brazier and coppersmith at Paris, Rue Parin Garlin, who died last year. You see she came of good family. The mother was unluckily a simple woman, and taught Pâquette little but to make finery and playthings, which did not hinder the little girl from growing very tall and remaining very poor. The two lived at Rheims, by the riverside, Rue de Follo Peine—mark that! for, I believe 'tis that which brought ill-luck to Pâquette. In '61, the year of the coronation of our King Louis XI, whom God preserve! Pâquette was so gay and so pretty, that everywhere they called her La Chantefleurie (the song blossom). Poor girl! What beautiful teeth she had! and she would laugh that she might show them. Now a girl who likes to laugh is on the high-road to weep—fine teeth are the ruin of fine eyes. Such was La Chantefleurie. She and her mother had hard work to earn their bread—they were fallen very low since the minstrel's death—their needle-work brought them scarce more than six deniers a week, which is not quite two eagle farthings. Where was the time when father Guybertaut used to get twelve Paris pence, at a coronation, for a single song! One winter (it was in that same year '61), when the two women had neither logs nor fagots, the weather was very cold, and gave such a beautiful colour to La Chantefleurie, that the men called her "Pâquette"—some called her "Pâquerette" (a daisy)—and then she was ruined— Eustache, let me see you bite the cake, if you dare!—We saw directly that she was ruined, one Sunday when she came to church with a gold cross on her neck.—At fourteen years of age! think of that! First it was the young Viscount de Cormontreuil, whose castle is about three-quarters of a league from Rheims; then, Messire Henri de Triancourt, the king's equerry; then, something lower, Chiart de Beaulion, sergeant-at-arms; then lower still, Guery Aubergeon, the king's carver; then Macé de Frépus, monsieur the dauphin's barber; then Thévenin le Moine, the king's first cook; then, still descending, to men older and less noble, she fell to Guillaume Racine, viol-player—and to Thierry de Mer, lamp-maker. Then, poor Chantefleurie, she became common property—she was come to the last sou of her gold-piece. What think you, my damoiselles? At the coronation, in the same year '61, it was she that made the bed for the king of the ribalds! —That self-same year!—'

Mahiette sighed, and wiped away a tear that had started to her eyes.

'Here's a story,' said Gervaise, 'that's not very uncommon; and I do not see that it has anything to do with either gypsies or children.'

'Patience!' resumed Mahiette—'As for a child, we shall soon come to it. In '66, sixteen years ago this month, on Saint Paul's day, Pâquette was brought to bed of a little girl. Poor creature; she was in great joy at it—she had long wished for a child. Her mother, poor simple woman, who'd never known how to do anything but shut her eyes; her mother was dead. Pâquette had nothing in the world to love and none to love her. For five years past, since she had gone astray, poor Chantefleurie had been a wretched creature. She was alone, alone in the world; pointed at, shouted after, through the streets; beaten by the sergeants; mocked by little ragged boys. And then she had seen her twentieth year —and twenty is old age for light women. Her wantonness was beginning to bring her in scarcely more than her needle-work had formerly. Every fresh wrinkle made a crown less in her pocket; winter became again a hard season; again wood was scarce on her hearth, and bread in her cupboard. She could no longer work; for in giving way to pleasure she had become idle, and she suffered much more than formerly, because when she became idle she longed for pleasure. At least, it is thus that monsieur the curé of Saint Remy explains how it is that such women feel cold and hunger more than other poor creatures do, when they are old—'

'Yes,' interrupted Gervaise; 'but the gypsies?'

'Wait a moment, Gervaise!' said Oudarde, whose attention was less impatient; 'what should we have at the end, if everything was at the beginning? Continue, Mahiette, I beg. That poor Chantefleurie!—'

Mahiette continued:

'Well, then—she was very sorrowful, very wretched, and her tears wore deep furrows in her cheeks. But in the midst of her shame, her folly and her debauchery, she thought she would be less shameful, less wild and less dissipated, if there were something or some one in the world that she could love, and that could love her. It must be a child, for only a child could be innocent enough for that. She was aware of this after trying to love a thief, the only man that would have anything to say to her—but in a little time she had found out that the thief despised her. Those women of love require either a lover or a child to fill their hearts. Otherwise they are very unhappy. Not being able to find a lover, all her wishes turned toward having a child; and, as she had all along been pious, she prayed to God continually to send her one. So the good God took pity on her and gave her a little girl. I can not describe to you her joy—it was a fury of tears, kisses and caresses. She suckled the child herself; she made it swaddling-clothes out of her coverlet, the only one she had upon her bed; and no longer felt cold or hungry. She became beautiful once more in consequence of it. An old maid makes a young mother. Gallantry claimed her once more; men came again to see La Chantefleurie; she found customers for her wares; and out of all those horrors she made baby-clothes, capes and bibs, lace robes and little satin caps—without so much as thinking of buying herself another coverlet—Master Eustache, I've already told you not to eat that cake—It is certain that little Agnès—that was the child's name: its Christian name—for, as to a surname, it was long since La Chantefleurie had ceased to have one!—certain it is that the little thing was more swathed with ribbons and embroideries than a dauphiness of Dauphiny. Among other things, she had a pair of little shoes, the like of which King Louis XI certainly never had. Her mother had stitched and embroidered them herself; she had lavished on them all her skill as an embroideress, and all the embellishments of a robe for the Holy Virgin. They were the two sweetest little pink shoes that ever were seen. They were no longer than my thumb; and unless one saw the child's tiny feet slip out of them, one would never have believed they could have gone in. To be sure, the little feet were so small, so pretty, so rosy—rosier than the satin of the shoes! When you have children, Oudarde, you will know that there is nothing prettier than those little feet and those little hands.'

'I wish for nothing better,' said Oudarde, sighing; 'but I must wait the good pleasure of Monsieur Andry Musnier.'

'Besides,' resumed Mahiette, 'Pâquette's child had not pretty feet only. I saw her when she was but four months old; she was a little love. Her eyes were larger than her mouth, and she had the most beautiful, fine, dark hair, which already curled. She would have made a superb brunette at sixteen! Her mother became more and more crazy about her every day. She hugged her—kissed her—tickled her—washed her—dressed her out—devoured her! She lost her head over her; she thanked God for her. Its pretty little rosy feet above all were an endless source of wonderment; they were a delirium of joy! She was always pressing her lips to them, and could not recover from amazement at their smallness. She put them into the little shoes, took them out, admired them—wondered at them—held them up to the light—would pity them while she was trying to make them walk upon her bed—and would gladly have passed her life on her knees, putting the shoes on and off those little feet, as if they had been those of an infant Jesus.'

'The tale is fair and very good,' said Gervaise, in an undertone, 'but what is there about gypsies in all that?'

'Why, here,' replied Mahiette. 'One day there came to Rheims a very odd sort of gentry. They were beggars and vagabonds, who were roving about the country, headed by their duke and their counts. They were swarthy, their hair all curly, and rings of silver in their ears. The women were still uglier than the men. Their faces were darker, and always uncovered; they wore a sorry kirtle about their body; an old cloth woven with cords, bound upon their shoulder; and their hair hanging like a horse's tail. The children wallowing under their feet would have frightened an ape. An excommunicated gang! They were all come in a straight line from lower Egypt to Rheims, through Poland. The Pope had confessed them, it was said, and had ordered them by way of penance to wander for seven years together without sleeping in a bed; and so they called themselves penancers, and stank. It seems that they were once Saracens; so they must have believed in Jupiter, and demanded ten Tours pounds from all archbishops, bishops and abbots that carried crosier and mitre. It was a papal bull gave them this right. They came to Rheims to tell fortunes in the name of the King of Algiers and the Emperor of Germany. You can readily imagine that no more was needed for them to be forbidden entrance to the town. Then the whole band encamped of their own accord near the gate of Braine, upon that mound where there's a windmill, close by the old chalk-pits. And all Rheims went to see them. They looked into your hand, and told you marvellous prophecies—they were equal to predicting to Judas that he would become Pope. Nevertheless, there were ugly rumours about their child-stealing, purse-cutting and eating of human flesh. The wise folks said to the foolish ones, "Don't go there!" and then went themselves by stealth. It was an infatuation. The fact is, that they said things fit to astonish a cardinal. Mothers boasted loudly of their children after the gypsy-women had read all sorts of miracles in their hands, written in Turkish and Pagan. One of them had got an emperor—another a pope—another a captain. Poor Chantefleurie was seized with curiosity—she had a mind to know what she had got, and whether her pretty little Agnès would not some day be Empress of Armenia, or of elsewhere. So she carried her to the gypsies; and the gypsy-women admired the child, fondled it, kissed it with their black mouths and wondered

over its little hand—alas! to the great joy of its mother. They were
particularly delighted with the pretty feet and the pretty shoes.
The child was not yet a year old. She had begun to lisp a word or
two—laughed at her mother like a little madcap—was plump and
quite round—and had a thousand little gestures of the angels in
paradise. But she was frightened at the gypsy-women, and fell
a-crying. Her mother kissed her the harder, and went away over-
joyed at the good fortune which the sooth-sayers had told her
Agnès. She was to be beautiful, virtuous and a queen. So she
returned to her garret in the Rue Folle Peine, quite proud to
carry with her a queen. The next day she took advantage of a
moment when the child was asleep on her bed (for she always had
it to sleep with herself), gently left the door ajar, and ran to tell a
neighbour, in the Rue de la Séchesserie, that the day was to come
when her daughter Agnès was to be waited on at table by the
King of England and the Archduke of Ethiopia—and a hundred
other marvels. On her return, hearing no sound as she went up
the stairs, she said to herself, "Good, the child is still asleep." She
found her door wider open than she had left it—the poor mother,
however, went in and ran to the bed. The child was no longer
there—the place was empty. Nothing remained of the child but
one of its pretty shoes. She rushed out of the room, flew down the
stairs, and began to beat her head against the wall, crying, "My
child! who has my child? who has taken my child?" The street
was deserted—the house stood alone—no one could tell her anything about it; she went about the town—searched all the streets
—ran hither and thither the whole day, wild, mad, terrible,
peeping at the doors and windows like a wild beast that has lost
its little ones. She was panting, dishevelled, frightful to look upon
—and in her eyes there was a fire that dried her tears. She
stopped the passers-by, and cried, "My daughter! my daughter!
my pretty little daughter!—he that will restore me my daughter,
I will be his servant—the servant of his dog, and he shall eat my
heart if he likes." She met monsieur the curé of Saint Remy, and
said to him, "Monsieur le curé, I will till the earth with my finger-
nails—but give me back my child!" It was heartrending, Oudarde
—and I saw a very hardhearted man, Maître Ponce Lacabre, the
attorney, that wept. Ah! the poor mother! When night came she
went home. During her absence, a neighbour had seen two gypsy-
women steal slyly up stairs with a bundle in their arms; then come
down again, after shutting the door, and hurry off. After they were
gone, something like the cries of a child were heard in Pâquette's
room—the mother laughed wildly—ran up the stairs as if on
wings—burst in her door like a cannon going off, and entered
the room. A frightful thing to tell, Oudarde!—instead of her sweet

little Agnès, so fresh and rosy, who was a gift from the good God, there was a sort of little monster, hideous, shapeless, one-eyed, with its limbs all awry, crawling and squalling upon the floor. She hid her eyes in horror. "Oh!" said she, "can it be that the witches have changed my child into that frightful animal!" They carried the little club-footed creature away as quick as possible. He would have driven her mad. He was the monstrous offspring of some gypsy-woman given over to the devil. He seemed to be about four years old, and spoke a language which was not a human tongue—there were words that were impossible. La Chantefleurie flung herself upon the little shoe, all that was left her of all that she had loved. There she remained so long motionless, speechless, breathless, that they thought she was dead. Suddenly she trembled all over—covered her relic with frantic kisses, and burst out sobbing, as if her heart were broken. I assure you we all wept with her. She said, "Oh, my little girl! my pretty little girl! where art thou?"—and it wrung your very heart. I weep still when I think of it. Our children, I can tell you, are the very marrow of our bones. My poor Eustache! thou art so handsome! If you did but know how clever he is! Yesterday he said to me, "I want to be a gendarme, I do." Oh, my Eustache, if I were to lose thee!— All at once Chantefleurie sprang up and ran through the streets of Rheims, shouting: "To the gypsies' camp! to the gypsies' camp! Bring guards to burn the witches!" The gypsies were gone—it was pitch dark. No one could follow them. On the morrow, two leagues from Rheims, on a heath between Gueux and Tilloy, the remains of a large fire were found, some ribbons which had belonged to Pâquette's child, drops of blood and some goat's dung. The night just passed happened to be a Saturday night. There could be no further doubt that the Egyptians had held their Witches' Sabbath on that heath, and had devoured the child in company with Beelzebub, as the Mahometans do. When La Chantefleurie learnt these horrible things, she did not weep—she moved her lips as if to speak, but could not. On the morrow her hair was gray. On the second day she had disappeared.'

''Tis in truth a frightful tale!' said Oudarde; 'enough to draw tears from a Burgundian!'

'I am no longer surprised,' added Gervaise, 'that the fear of gypsies should haunt you so.'

'And you had all the reason,' resumed Oudarde, 'to flee with your Eustache just now, since these, too, are gypsies from Poland.'

'Not so,' said Gervaise; ''tis said that they come from Spain and Catalonia.'

'Catalonia!—well, that may be,' answered Oudarde; 'Polonia,

Catalonia, Valonia—those places are all one to me. There's one thing sure, they are gypsies.'

'Who certainly,' added Gervaise, 'have teeth long enough to eat little children. And I should not be surprised if La Smeralda ate a little, too, for all her dainty airs. That white goat of hers has got too many mischievous tricks for there not to be some wickedness behind.'

Mahiette walked on in silence. She was absorbed in that reverie which is a sort of prolongation of a doleful story, and which ends only after having communicated the emotion, from vibration to vibration, to the very last fibres of the heart. Gervaise, however, addressed her: 'And so it was never known what became of La Chantefleurie?' Mahiette made no answer—Gervaise repeated her question, shaking her arm and calling her by her name. Mahiette seemed to awake from her reverie:

'What became of La Chantefleurie?' said she, mechanically repeating the words whose impression was still fresh in her ear. Then, making an effort to recall her attention to the meaning of the words—'Ah,' she said sharply, 'it was never known.'

After a pause she added:

'Some said she had been seen to quit Rheims at nightfall by the Fléchembault gate; others, at daybreak, by the old Basée gate. A poor man found her gold cross hanging on the stone cross in the field where the fair is held. It was that trinket that had ruined her in '61. It was a gift from the handsome Viscount de Cormontreuil, her first lover. Pâquette would never part with it, even in her greatest wretchedness—she clung to it as to life. So when we saw this cross abandoned, we all thought she was dead. However, there were people, at the Cabaret les Vautes, who said they'd seen her go by on the Paris road, walking barefoot over the stones. But then she must have gone out through the Porte de Vesle, and all that did not agree. Or rather, I believe, that she did actually go out by the gate of Vesle, but she went out of this world.'

'I do not understand you,' said Gervaise.

'The Vesle,' answered Mahiette, with a melancholy smile, 'is the river.'

'Poor Chantefleurie!' said Oudarde, with a shiver; 'drowned!'

'Drowned,' replied Mahiette. 'And who could have foretold to the good father Guybertaut, when he floated down the stream under the Tinqueux bridge, singing in his boat, that his dear little Pâquette should one day pass under that same bridge, but with neither song nor boat!'

'And the little shoe?' inquired Gervaise.

'Disappeared with the mother,' answered Mahiette.

'Poor little shoe!' said Oudarde.

Oudarde, a fat and tender-hearted woman, would have been quite content to sigh in company with Mahiette. But Gervaise, more curious, had not yet come to the end of her questions.

'And the monster?' said she all at once to Mahiette.

'What monster?' asked the other.

'The little gypsy monster left by the witches at La Chantefleurie's in exchange for her child. What was done with it? I hope you drowned it, too.'

'Not so,' answered Mahiette.

'What? burned it then? I' faith, that was a better way of disposing of a witch's child.'

'Neither the one nor the other, Gervaise. Monsieur the archbishop took an interest in the child of Egypt; he exorcised it, blessed it, carefully took the devil out of its body, and sent it to Paris to be exposed upon the wooden bed at Notre-Dame as a foundling.'

'Those bishops!' muttered Gervaise; 'because they're learned, forsooth, they can never do anything like other folks. I just put it to you, Oudarde—the idea of placing the devil among the foundlings—for that little monster was assuredly the devil. Well, Mahiette, and what did they do with him in Paris? I suppose no charitable person wanted him.'

'I don't know, indeed,' answered the native of Rheims. 'It was just at that time that my husband bought the place of notary at Beru, two leagues from the town; and we thought no more of all that story—particularly as right by Beru there are the two hills of Cernay, which quite hide the spires of Rheims cathedral.'

While talking thus, the three worthy bourgeoises had arrived at the Place de Grève. In their preoccupation they had passed the public breviary of the Tour Roland without stopping, and were proceeding mechanically toward the pillory, around which the crowd increased momentarily. Probably the sight, which at this instant attracted every eye, would have made them completely forget the Rat-Hole and the halt which they intended to make there, if the sturdy six-years-old Eustache, whom Mahiette led by the hand, had not suddenly reminded them of it. 'Mother,' said he, as though some instinct warned him that the Rat-Hole was behind them, 'now may I eat the cake?'

Had Eustache been more adroit, that is to say, less greedy, he would have waited a little longer; and not until they had reached home, in the University, at Maître Andry Musnier's, in the Rue Madame la Valence, when the two channels of the Seine and the five bridges of the City would have been between the cake and the Rat-Hole, would he have hazarded that simple question—'Mother, now may I eat the cake?'

This same question, an imprudent one at the moment when it was put by Eustache, roused Mahiette's attention.

'By the way,' she exclaimed, 'we are forgetting the recluse! Show me your Rat-Hole, that I may carry her the cake.'

'At once,' said Oudarde, 'for 'tis charity.'

This was not at all to Eustache's liking.

'Oh, my cake!' said he, rubbing both ears alternately with his shoulders, which in such cases betokens supreme discontent.

The three women retraced their steps; and as they approached the house of the Tour Roland, Oudarde said to the other two:

'We must not all three look into the hole at once, lest we should frighten the Sachette. You two pretend to read the Dominus in the breviary, while I take a peep at the window-hole. The Sachette knows me a little. I'll tell you when you may come.

She went to the window alone. The moment that she looked in, profound pity took possession of every feature, and her frank, gay visage altered its expression and colour as suddenly as if it had passed from a ray of sunshine to a ray of moonlight; her eyes grew moist, and her mouth quivered as if she were about to weep. A moment later, she put her finger to her lips and beckoned to Mahiette to come and look.

Mahiette, much moved, joined her silently and on tip-toe, like one approaching a deathbed.

It was in truth a melancholy sight that presented itself to the eyes of the two women, as they gazed through the grated window of the Rat-Hole, neither stirring nor breathing.

The cell was small, broader than it was long, with an arched ceiling, and, seen from within, looked like the inside of a huge bishop's mitre. On the bare flag-stones that formed its floor, in one corner, a woman was sitting, or rather crouching. Her chin rested on her knees, which her crossed arms pressed closely against her breast. Doubled up in this manner, clad in brown sackcloth which covered her loosely from head to foot, her long, gray hair pulled over in front and hanging over her face, down her legs to her feet—she seemed at first only a strange form outlined against the dark background of the cell—a sort of dusky triangle, which the ray of light entering at the window divided distinctly into two tones, one dark, the other illuminated. It was one of those spectres, half light, half shade, such as are seen in dreams, and in the extraordinary work of Goya—pale—motionless—sinister—crouching over a tomb, or leaning against the grating of a dungeon. It was neither woman nor man, nor living being nor definite form; it was a figure, a sort of vision, in which the real and the fanciful intermingled like twilight and daylight. Beneath her hair, which fell to the ground, the outlines of a stern and emaciated profile were barely visible; scarcely did her garment permit the extremity of a bare foot to escape, which contracted in the hard, cold pavement. The little of human form that was discernible under that mourning envelope caused a shudder.

This figure, which looked as if riveted to the flag-stones, seemed to have neither motion, thought, nor breath. In that thin sackcloth, in January, lying on a stone floor, without fire, in the darkness of a dungeon, whose oblique loophole admitted only the chill blast, and never the sun—she appeared not to suffer, not even to feel. She seemed to have been turned to stone like her dungeon, to ice like the season. Her hands were clasped; her eyes were fixed. At the first glance she seemed a spectre; at the second, a statue.

At intervals, however, her blue lips were parted by a breath, and trembled, but as dead and mechanical as the leaves which the wind sweeps aside.

Meanwhile those haggard eyes cast a look, an ineffable look, a profound, lugubrious, imperturbable look, incessantly fixed on one corner of the cell, which could not be seen from without; a gaze which seemed to concentrate all the gloomy thoughts of that suffering spirit upon some mysterious object.

Such was the creature who was called from her habitation the *recluse*, and from her coarse garment the Sachette.

The three women (for Gervaise had come up to Mahiette and Oudarde) peered through the aperture. Their heads intercepted the feeble light in the cell, without the wretched being whom they thus deprived of it seeming to pay any attention to them. 'Let us not disturb her,' whispered Oudarde; 'she is in her ecstasy; she is praying.'

But Mahiette was gazing with an ever increasing anxiety at that wan, withered, dishevelled head, and her eyes filled with tears.

'That would indeed be singular!' muttered she.

Passing her head through the bars of the window, she contrived to get a glimpse of the corner upon which the unfortunate woman's eyes were invariably riveted.

When she withdrew her head from the window her cheeks were bathed with tears.

'What do you call that woman?' said she to Oudarde.

Oudarde answered, 'We call her Sister Gudule.'

'And I,' returned Mahiette, 'call her Pâquette la Chantefleurie.'

Then, laying her finger on her lips, she motioned to the amazed Oudarde to put her head through the aperture, and look.

Oudarde looked and saw, in the corner upon which the eye of the recluse was fixed in that gloomy absorption, a tiny shoe of pink satin, embroidered with countless gold and silver spangles.

Gervaise looked after Oudarde; and then the three women, gazing upon the unhappy mother, began to weep.

But neither their looks nor their tears disturbed the recluse. Her hands remained clasped; her lips mute; her eyes fixed; and to any one who knew her story, that gaze of hers upon that little shoe was heartrending.

The three women had not yet breathed a word; they dared not speak, even in a whisper. This profound silence, this great grief, this entire oblivion of all but one thing, had upon them the effect of the high altar at Easter or Christmas. They were silent, absorbed, ready to fall upon their knees. It seemed to them as if they had just entered a church on the Saturday in Passion-week.

At length Gervaise, the most curious of the three, and therefore the least sensitive, tried to make the recluse speak: 'Sister! Sister Gudule!'

Thrice did she repeat this call, raising her voice every time. The recluse stirred not—there was no word, no look, no sigh, no sign of life.

Oudarde in her turn, in a sweeter and more caressing voice, said to her, 'Sister—holy Sister Gudule!'

The same silence, the same immobility.

'A strange woman!' exclaimed Gervaise, 'and one who would not start at a bombard.'

'She is perchance deaf,' said Oudarde, with a sigh.

'Perchance blind,' said Gervaise.

'Perchance dead,' observed Mahiette.

It is certain that if the spirit had not already quitted that inert, torpid, lethargic body, it had at least retired within it, and hidden itself in depths whither the perceptions of the external organs no longer penetrated.

'We shall have to leave the cake on the window-sill,' said Oudarde; 'and some lad will take it. What can we do to rouse her?'

Eustache, whose attention had until that moment been diverted by a little cart drawn by a great dog, which had just passed, noticed all at once that his three conductresses were looking at something through the hole in the wall; and curiosity taking possession of him in turn he climbed upon a stone post, raised himself on tip-toe, and thrusting his red, chubby face through the opening, cried out, 'Mother, let me see, too.'

At the sound of this childish voice, clear, fresh and ringing, the recluse started. She turned her head with the sharp, abrupt movement of a steel spring; her two long, thin hands brushed back the hair from her forehead; and she fixed upon the child a look of astonishment, bitterness and despair. That look was but a flash.

'Oh, my God!' she exclaimed suddenly, hiding her head upon her knees—and it seemed as if her hoarse voice tore her breast in passing—'at least do not show me those of others!'

'Good-day, madame,' said the boy, gravely.

But the shock, however, had, as it were, awakened the recluse. A long shiver ran through her entire frame, from head to foot; her teeth chattered; she half raised her head, and said, pressing her elbows to her sides, and clasping her feet in her hands, as if to warm them:

'Oh, how cold it is!'

'Poor creature,' said Oudarde, with deep pity, 'would you like a little fire?'

She shook her head in token of refusal.

'Well,' resumed Oudarde, offering her a flask, 'here is some hippocrass, that will warm you. Drink.'

Again she shook her head, looked at Oudarde fixedly, and replied: 'Water!'

Oudarde insisted: 'No, sister; that is no January beverage. You must drink a little hippocrass, and eat this leavened cake of maize, which we have baked for you.'

She put aside the cake, which Mahiette offered her, and said, 'Some black bread!'

'Come,' said Gervaise, seized with a charitable impulse in her turn, and unfastening her woollen mantle—'here is a cloak something warmer than yours—put this over your shoulders.'

She refused the cloak as she had the flask and the cake, and answered, 'Sacking!'

'But surely,' resumed the kind-hearted Oudarde, 'you must have perceived, I should think, that yesterday was a holiday.'

'I am aware of it,' said the recluse. ''Tis two days now since I have had any water in my crock.'

She added, after a pause, ''Tis a holiday, and they forget me —they do well. Why should the world think of me, who think not of it? When the fire goes out the ashes are soon cold.'

And as though fatigued with having said so much, she dropped her head on her knees again. The simple and charitable Oudarde, who fancied that she understood from her last words that she was still complaining of the cold, replied innocently, 'Then will you have a little fire?'

'Fire?' said the Sachette with a strange accent—'and will you make a little, also, for the poor little one who has been beneath the sod for these fifteen years?'

Her limbs shook, her voice trembled, her eyes flashed. She raised herself upon her knees; suddenly she stretched her thin white hand towards the child, who was looking at her in surprise.

'Take away that child!' she cried, 'the Egyptian woman is about to pass by.'

Then she fell with her face to the ground, and her forehead struck the floor with the sound of one stone upon another. The three women thought her dead. But a moment later she stirred, and they saw her crawl upon her hands and knees to the corner where the little shoe was. Then they dared not look; they no longer saw her, but they heard a thousand kisses and sighs, mingled with heartrending cries and dull blows, like those of a head striking against a wall; then, after one of these blows, so violent that they all three started, they heard nothing more.

'Has she killed herself?' said Gervaise, venturing to put her head in at the aperture. 'Sister! Sister Gudule!'

'Sister Gudule!' repeated Oudarde.

'Ah, good heavens! she no longer stirs!' exclaimed Gervaise—'Is she dead, think you?—Gudule! Gudule!'

Mahiette, whose utterance had been choked until then, now made an effort. 'Wait,' said she; and then, bending down to the window, 'Pâquette!' she cried, 'Pâquette la Chantefleurie!'

A child who thoughtlessly blows upon the ill-lighted fuse of a petard, and makes it explode in his face, is no more terrified than was Mahiette at the effect of this name thus suddenly flung into the cell of Sister Gudule.

The recluse shook all over; sprang upon her feet, and bounded to the window with eyes so flaming that Mahiette and Oudarde and the other woman and the child retreated to the parapet of the quay.

But still the forbidding face of the recluse appeared pressed against the bars of the window. 'Oh, oh!' she cried, with a frightful laugh, ''tis the Egyptian who calls me!'

At this instant the scene which was passing at the pillory caught her wild eye. Her forehead wrinkled with horror—she stretched out of her den her two skeleton arms, and cried out, in a voice that resembled a death-rattle:—'So, 'tis thou once more, daughter of Egypt—'Tis thou who callest me, stealer of children! Well, be thou accursed! accursed! accursed!—'

4

A Tear for a Drop of Water

THESE words were, so to speak, the connecting link between two scenes which, until that moment, had been simultaneously developing themselves, each upon its particular stage—the one, that which has just been related, at the Trou aux Rats; the other, now to be described, at the pillory. The former was witnessed only by the three women whose acquaintance the reader has just made; the latter had for spectators the whole crowd which we saw some time since collect upon the Place de Grève, around the pillory and the gibbet.

This crowd, which the four sergeants posted from nine o'clock in the morning at the four corners of the pillory had inspired with the hope of some sort of an execution—not a hanging, probably —but a whipping, a cutting off of ears, something in short—this crowd had increased so rapidly that the four sergeants, too closely besieged, had been obliged more than once to 'press it,' as they expressed it, by sound blows of their whitleather whips and the haunches of their horses.

The populace, well accustomed to wait for public executions, did not manifest great impatience. It amused itself looking at the pillory—a very simple sort of structure, consisting of a cubical mass of stonework, some ten feet high, and hollow within. A very steep flight of steps, of unhewn stone, called by distinction the 'ladder,' led to the upper platform, upon which was seen a horizontal wheel of solid oak. The victim was bound upon this wheel, on his knees, and his arms pinioned. An upright shaft of timber, set in motion by a capstan concealed inside the little structure, gave a rotary motion to the wheel, which always maintained its horizontal position, thus presenting the face of the culprit successively to each side of the Square in turn. This was called 'turning' a criminal.

It is evident that the pillory of the Grève was far from possessing all the attractions of the pillory of the Markets. There was nothing architectural, nothing monumental. There was no iron-cross roof —no octagonal lantern—there were no slender columns, spreading out at the edge of the roof into capitals composed of foliage and flowers—no fantastic and monster-headed gutter-spouts—no carved woodwork—no delicate sculpture cut deep into the stone.

They were forced to be content with those four rough stone walls, with two buttresses of sandstone, with a sorry stone gibbet, meagre and bare, on one side.

The treat would have been indeed a poor one for lovers of Gothic architecture. It is true, however, that none were ever less interested in architecture than the good cockneys of the Middle Ages, who cared very little for the beauty of a pillory.

At last the culprit arrived, tied to the tail of a cart, and as soon as he was hoisted upon the platform, so that he could be seen from all parts of the Square, bound with cords and straps to the wheel of the pillory, a prodigious hooting, mingled with laughter and acclamations, burst from the assemblage in the Square. They had recognized Quasimodo.

It was he, in fact. It was a strange reverse. Pilloried on the very place where the day before he had been saluted, acclaimed and proclaimed Pope and Prince of Fools, escorted by the Duke of Egypt, the King of Tunis and the Emperor of Galilee. One thing is certain, and that is that there was not a soul in the crowd—not even himself, in turn triumphant and a victim, who could clearly make out in his own mind the connection between the two situations. Gringoire and his philosophy were lacking from this spectacle.

Presently, Michel Noiret, sworn trumpeter to the king, imposed silence on the louts and proclaimed the sentence, pursuant to the ordinance and command of monsieur the provost. He then fell back behind the cart, with his men in livery surcoats.

Quasimodo, impassive, did not wince. All resistance on his part was rendered impossible by what was then called, in the language of criminal law, 'the vehemence and firmness of the bonds'—that is to say, that the small straps and chains probably entered his flesh. This, by-the-by, is a tradition of the jail and the galleys which is not yet lost, and which the handcuffs still preserve with care among us, a civilized, mild, and humane people (the guillotine between parentheses).

He had allowed himself to be led, thrust, carried, hoisted, bound and bound again. Nothing was to be seen upon his countenance but the astonishment of a savage or an idiot. He was known to be deaf; he seemed to be blind.

They placed him on his knees on the circular plank; he made no resistance. He was stripped of shirt and doublet to the waist; he submitted. They bound him down under a fresh system of straps and buckles; he let them buckle and strap him. Only from time to time he breathed heavily, like a calf, whose head hangs dangling over the side of the butcher's cart.

'The dolt!' said Jehan Frollo du Moulin to his friend Robin Poussepain (for the two students had followed the sufferer, as in duty bound), 'he understands no more about it than a cockchafer shut up in a box.'

There was a wild laugh among the crowd when they saw, stripped naked to their view, Quasimodo's hump, his camel breast, his callous and hairy shoulders. Amidst all this mirth, a man of short stature and robust frame, in the livery of the city, ascended the platform, and placed himself by the culprit. His name speedily circulated among the spectators—it was Maître Pierrat Torterue, official torturer at the Châtelet.

He began by depositing on one corner of the pillory a black

hour-glass, the upper cup of which was filled with red sand, which was filtering through into the lower receptacle. Then he took off his parti-coloured doublet; and there was seen hanging from his right hand a slender whip with long, white thongs, shining, knotted, braided and armed with points of metal. With his left hand he carelessly rolled his right shirt-sleeve up to his armpit.

Meanwhile Jehan Frollo shouted, lifting his curly, blond head above the crowd (he had mounted for that purpose on the shoulders of Robin Poussepain), 'Come and see—messieurs! mesdames!— they're going to peremptorily flagellate Master Quasimodo, the bell-ringer of my brother monsieur the Archdeacon of Josas—a knave of oriental architecture, who has a back like a dome, and legs like twisted columns!'

And the people laughed, especially the boys and young girls.

At length the executioner stamped with his foot. The wheel began to turn; Quasimodo staggered under his bonds. The amazement suddenly depicted upon his deformed visage redoubled the bursts of laughter all around him.

All at once, at the moment when the wheel in its rotation presented to Maître Pierrat Quasimodo's humped back, Maître Pierrat raised his arm, the thin lashes hissed sharply in the air like a handful of vipers, and fell with fury upon the poor wretch's shoulders.

Quasimodo made a spring as if starting from his sleep. He now began to understand. He writhed in his bonds. A violent contraction of surprise and pain distorted the muscles of his face; but he heaved not a sigh. Only he turned his head backward to the right, then to the left, balancing it as a bull does when stung in the flank by a gadfly.

A second stroke followed the first—then a third—then another —and another—and so on and on. The wheel did not cease to turn, nor the blows to rain down.

Soon the blood spurted; it streamed in countless rivulets over the swarthy shoulders of the hunchback; and the slender thongs in their rotary motion which rent the air sprinkled drops of it upon the crowd.

Quasimodo had relapsed, in appearance at least, into his former apathy. At first he had striven, silently and without any great external effort, to burst his bonds. His eye had been seen to kindle, his muscles to stiffen, his limbs to gather all their force and the straps and chains stretched. The effort was powerful, prodigious, desperate—but the old shackles of the provostry resisted. They cracked; and that was all. Quasimodo sank down exhausted. Amazement gave place in his countenance to an expression of bitter and deep discouragement. He closed his only eye, dropped his head upon his breast, and seemed as if he were dead.

Thenceforward he stirred no more. Nothing could wring any motion from him—neither his blood, which continued to flow; nor the blows which fell with redoubled fury; nor the rage of the executioner, who worked himself up and became intoxicated with the execution; nor the noise of the horrid lashes, keener and sharper than the stings of a wasp.

At length an usher of the Châtelet, clothed in black, mounted on a black horse, and stationed by the side of the steps from the commencement of the punishment, extended his ebony wand toward the hour-glass. The executioner stopped. The wheel stopped. Quasimodo's eye slowly reopened.

The flagellation was finished. Two assistants of the official torturer bathed the bleeding shoulders of the sufferer, anointed them with some kind of unguent, which immediately closed all the wounds, and threw over his back a sort of yellow cloth cut in the form of a chasuble. Meanwhile Pierrat Torterue let the blood that soaked the lashes of his scourge drain from them in drops upon the ground.

But all was not yet over for Quasimodo. He had still to undergo that hour on the pillory which Maître Florian Barbedienne had so judiciously added to the sentence of Messire Robert d'Estouteville—all to the greater glory of the old physiological and psychological play upon words of Jean de Cumène—*Surdus absurdus* (a deaf man is absurd).

The hour-glass was therefore turned, and the hunchback was left bound to the plank, that justice might be fully satisfied.

The populace, particularly in the Middle Ages, is in society what the child is in a family. So long as they remain in that state of primitive ignorance, of moral and intellectual minority, it may be said of them as of a child,

'That age is a stranger to pity.'

We have already shown that Quasimodo was generally hated —for more than one good reason, it is true. There was hardly a spectator among that crowd but either had or thought he had some cause of complaint against the malevolent hunchback of Notre-Dame. The joy at seeing him appear thus in the pillory had been universal; and the harsh punishment he had just undergone, and the piteous plight in which it had left him, far from softening the hearts of the populace, had but rendered their hatred more malicious by arming it with the sting of mirth.

Accordingly, 'public vengeance,' as the legal jargon still styles it, once satisfied, a thousand private spites had now their turn. Here, as in the Great Hall, the women were most vehement. All bore him some grudge—some for his mischievousness, others for his ugliness. The latter were the more furious.

'Oh! thou phiz of Antichrist!' exclaimed one.

'Thou broomstick-rider!' cried another.

'What a fine tragical grin!' bawled a third, 'and one that would have made him Fools' Pope if to-day had been yesterday.'

''Tis well!' chimed in an old woman. 'This is the pillory grin; when is he to give us the gallows grin?'

'When art thou to have thy big bell clapped upon thy head a hundred feet under ground, thou cursed ringer?' shouted one.

'And to think 'tis this devil rings the Angelus!'

'Oh! thou deaf man! thou one-eyed creature! thou hunchback! thou monster!'

'A face to make a woman miscarry, better than all the drugs and medicines.'

And the two students, Jehan du Moulin and Robin Poussepain, sang at the top of their lungs, the old popular refrain—

A halter for the gallows rogue!
A fagot for the witch!

Countless other insults rained upon him, and hootings, and imprecations, and laughter, and now and then a stone.

Quasimodo was deaf, but his sight was good; and the public fury was not less forcibly expressed on their faces than by their words. Besides, the stones that struck him explained the bursts of laughter.

He bore it for a time. But, by degrees, that patience which had resisted the lash of the torturer relaxed and gave way under these insect stings. The Asturian bull that has borne unmoved the attacks of the picador is irritated by the dogs and the banderillas.

At first he slowly rolled around a look of menace at the crowd. But, shackled as he was, his look was powerless to chase away those flies which galled his wound. He then struggled in his bonds; and his furious contortions made the old wheel of the pillory creak upon its timbers. All which but increased the derision and the hooting.

Then the poor wretch, unable to break the collar which chained him like a wild beast, once more became quiet; only, at intervals, a sigh of rage heaved the hollows of his breast. On his face there was not a blush nor a trace of shame. He was too far from the social state, and too near the state of nature, to know what shame was. Moreover, with such a degree of deformity, is infamy a thing that can be felt? But resentment, hatred, despair, slowly spread over that hideous visage a cloud which grew darker and darker, more and more charged with electricity which burst forth in a thousand flashes from the eye of the cyclops.

However, that cloud was lightened for a moment as a mule passed through the crowd, bearing a priest on his back. As far away as he could see that mule and that priest, the poor sufferer's countenance softened. The fury which convulsed it gave way to a strange smile, full of ineffable sweetness, gentleness, tenderness. As the priest approached this smile became more pronounced, more distinct, more radiant. It was as if the unfortunate creature hailed the arrival of a deliverer. But the moment the mule was near enough to the pillory for its rider to recognize the sufferer, the priest cast down his eyes, wheeled about, clapped spurs to his beast, as if in haste to escape a humiliating appeal, and by no means desirous of being known and addressed by a poor devil in such a situation.

This priest was the Archdeacon Dom Claude Frollo.

Quasimodo's brow was overcast by a darker cloud than ever. The smile was still mingled with it for a time; but bitter, disheartened and profoundly sad.

Time passed. He had been there at least an hour and a half; lacerated, abused, mocked, and almost stoned to death.

All at once he again struggled in his chains, with redoubled desperation, that shook the whole framework that held him; and, breaking the silence which he had hitherto obstinately kept, he cried in a hoarse and furious voice, which was more like a bark than a human cry, and which drowned the noise of the hooting, 'Water!'

This exclamation of distress, far from exciting compassion, heightened the mirth of the good people of Paris who surrounded the pillory, and who, it must be admitted, taken as a whole and as a multitude, were at this time scarcely less cruel and brutal than that horrible tribe of Truands, to whom we have already introduced the reader, and who were simply the lowest stratum of the people. Not a voice was raised around the unhappy victim, except to jeer at his thirst. Certainly he was at this moment more grotesque and repulsive than he was pitiable—with his face purple and dripping, his wild eye, his mouth foaming with rage and suffering, and his tongue lolling half out. It must also be stated that had there even been any good, charitable soul of a townsman or townswoman among the rabble, who might have been tempted to carry a glass of water to that miserable creature in pain, so strong an idea of shame and ignominy was attached to the infamous steps of the pillory as would have sufficed to repel the good Samaritan.

In a few minutes, Quasimodo cast a despairing look upon the crowd, and repeated in a still more heart-rending voice, 'Water!'

Everyone laughed.

'Drink this!' cried Robin Poussepain, flinging in his face a sponge which had been dragged in the gutter. 'There, deaf scoundrel, I am thy debtor!'

A woman threw a stone at his head, saying: 'That will teach thee to waken us at night with thy cursed ringing!'

'Well, my lad!' bawled a cripple, striving to reach him with his crutch, 'wilt thou cast spells on us again from the top of the towers of Notre-Dame?'

'Here's a porringer to drink out of,' said one man, hurling a broken pitcher at his breast. ''Tis thou that, with only passing before her, made my wife be brought to bed of a child with two heads!'

'And my cat of a kitten with six paws!' yelped an old crone as she flung a tile at him.

'Water!' repeated Quasimodo for the third time, panting.

At that moment, he saw the populace make way. A young girl, fantastically dressed, emerged from the throng. She was followed by a little white goat with gilded horns, and carried a tambourine in her hand.

Quasimodo's eye sparkled. It was the gypsy-girl whom he had attempted to carry off the night before, for which piece of presumption he had some confused notion that they were punishing him at that very moment—which, in point of fact, was not in the least the case, since he was punished only for the misfortune of being deaf and of being tried by a deaf judge. He doubted not that she, too, was come to take her revenge, and to deal her blow like all the rest.

Thus, he beheld her rapidly ascend the steps. He was choking with rage and vexation. He would have liked to crumble the pillory to atoms; and could the flash of his eye have dealt death, the gypsy would have been reduced to ashes before she could have reached the platform.

Without a word, she approached the sufferer, who writhed in a vain effort to escape her; and detaching a gourd from her girdle, she raised it gently to the poor wretch's parched lips.

Then in that eye, hitherto so dry and burning, a big tear was seen to start, which fell slowly down that misshapen face so long convulsed by despair. It was possibly the first that the unfortunate creature had ever shed.

Meanwhile, he forgot to drink. The gypsy-girl made her little pout with impatience; and smiling, pressed the neck of the gourd to the tusked mouth of Quasimodo.

He drank deep draughts. His thirst was burning.

When he had done, the poor wretch put out his black lips, undoubtedly to kiss the fair hand which had just succoured him; but the young girl, who, remembering the violent attempt of the preceding night, was perhaps not without some mistrust, drew back her hand with the frightened gesture of a child afraid of being bitten by some animal.

Then the poor deaf creature fixed upon her a look of reproach and unutterable sorrow.

It would have been a touching sight anywhere—this beautiful, fresh, pure, charming girl, who was at the same time so weak, thus piously hastening to the relief of so much wretchedness, deformity and malevolence. On a pillory the spectacle was sublime.

The very populace were moved by it, and clapped their hands, shouting, 'Noël, Noël!'

It was at that moment that the recluse caught sight from the loophole of her cell of the gypsy-girl on the pillory, and hurled at her her sinister imprecation, 'Accursed be thou, daughter of Egypt! accursed! accursed!'

5

End of the Story of the Cake

ESMERALDA turned pale, and with faltering step descended from the pillory; the voice of the recluse pursued her still. 'Get thee down! get thee down! Egyptian thief! thou shalt go up there again!'

'The Sachette is in one of her humours,' said the people, grumbling—and that was the end of it. For that sort of woman was feared, which rendered them sacred. Nobody in those days was willing to attack any one that prayed day and night.

The hour had come to release Quasimodo. He was unbound, and the crowd dispersed.

Near the Grand Pont, Mahiette, who was going away with her companions, suddenly halted.

'By-the-by, Eustache,' said she, 'what hast thou done with the cake?'

'Mother,' said the boy, 'while you were talking to that lady in the hole, there was a great dog came and bit of my cake—and then I bit of it too.'

'What, sir!' cried she, 'have you eaten it all?'

'Mother, it was the dog. I told him so; but he would not listen to me. Then I bit a piece too—that's all.'

''Tis a terrible child,' said the mother, smiling and scolding at the same time. 'Look you, Oudarde—he already eats by himself all the fruit from the cherry-tree in our croft at Charlerange. So his grandfather says he'll be a captain. Just let me catch you at it again, Master Eustache. Get along, you fat, little pig!'

BOOK SEVEN

I

On the Danger of Confiding One's Secret to a Goat

SEVERAL weeks had passed. It was now the beginning of March. The sun, which Dubartas, that classic ancestor of periphrasis, had not yet named 'the grand duke of the candles,' was none the less cheerful and radiant. It was one of those days of the early spring which are so mild and beautiful that all Paris turns out into the squares and promenades, and celebrates them as if they were Sundays. On days so brilliant, so warm, and so serene, there is one hour in particular, at which one should go and admire the portal of Notre-Dame. It is the moment when the sun, already sinking in the west, almost exactly faces the cathedral. Its rays, becoming more and more horizontal, withdraw slowly from the pavement of the Place, and climb along the pinnacled façade, causing its thousands of figures in relief to stand out from their shadows, while the great central rose-window glares like a cyclops' eye lighted by reflections from his forge.

It was just that hour.

Opposite the lofty cathedral, reddened by the setting sun, upon a stone balcony, over the porch of a handsome Gothic house, at the corner of the Place and the Rue du Parvis, some lovely young girls were laughing and chatting gracefully and playfully. By the length of the veil which hung from the peak of their pointed coif, twined with pearls, down to their heels—by the fineness of the worked chemisette which covered their shoulders, revealing, according to the engaging fashion of that time, the swell of their fair virgin bosoms—by the richness of their under petticoats, still more costly than the upper skirt (admirable refinement!)—by the gauze, the silk and the velvet, with which the whole was loaded—and above all, by the whiteness of their hands, which proved that they led a life of idle ease—it was easy to divine that they were noble and wealthy heiresses. They were, in fact, Damoiselle Fleur-de-Lys de Gondelaurier, and her companions, Diane de Christeuil, Amelotte de Montmichel, Colombe de Gaillefontaine, and the little De Champchevrier, all damsels of good birth, assembled at that moment at the house of the widowed lady of De Gondelaurier, on account of Monseigneur de Beaujeu and madame his wife, who were to come to Paris in the month of

April, there to choose maids of honour for the Dauphiness Marguerite, on the occasion of her reception in Picardy, at the hands of the Flemings. Now, all the gentry for thirty leagues around were seeking this honour for their daughters, and a goodly number had already brought or sent them to Paris. The damsels in question had been entrusted by their parents to the care of the discreet and venerable Madame Aloïse de Gondelaurier, widow of a former master of the king's cross-bowmen, now living in retirement with her only daughter, at her house in the Place du Parvis-Notre-Dame, at Paris.

The balcony on which these young girls were opened into an apartment richly hung with fawn-coloured Flanders leather stamped with golden foliage. The beams that ran across the ceiling, diverting the eye with a thousand fantastic carvings, were painted and gilded. Splendid enamels gleamed here and there upon carved chests; and a boar's head made of pottery crowned a magnificent sideboard, the two steps of which showed that the mistress of the house was the wife or widow of a knight banneret. At the farther end, by a high fireplace, covered with armorial bearings and escutcheons from top to bottom, sat in a rich crimson velvet armchair, the lady of Gondelaurier, whose fifty-five years were as plainly written in her dress as on her face.

By her side stood a young man of imposing though somewhat vain and swaggering mien, one of those handsome fellows about whom all women agree, though the grave and discerning men shake their heads at them. This young cavalier wore the brilliant uniform of a captain of the archers of the household troops—which too closely resembled the costume of Jupiter, which the reader has already been enabled to admire in the first book of this history, for us to inflict upon him a second description.

The damsels were seated, partly in the room, partly on the balcony; some on cushions of Utrecht velvet with gold corner-plates; others on oaken stools carved with flowers and figures. Each of them held on her lap a portion of a large piece of tapestry, on which they were all working together, while a good part of it lay on the matting which covered the floor.

They talked together in that whispering tone, and with those half-stifled laughs, peculiar in an assembly of young girls in whose midst there is a young man. The young man, whose presence served to set in play all these feminine wiles, appeared, himself, to care very little about it; and, while these lovely girls were vieing with each other to attract his attention, he seemed to be chiefly absorbed in polishing the buckle of his sword-belt with his doeskin glove.

From time to time, the old lady addressed him in a low voice, and he replied as best he could, with awkward and forced courtesy. From the smiles and significant gestures of Madame Aloïse, from the glances she threw toward her daughter Fleur-de-Lys as she spoke low to the captain, it was evident that there was here a question of some betrothal concluded, some marriage near at hand, no doubt, between the young man and Fleur-de Lys. And from the cold embarrassed air of the officer, it was easy to see that on his side at least there was no question of love. His whole manner expressed constraint and weariness, which a modern French subaltern on garrison duty would admirably render by the exclamation, 'What a beastly bore!'

The good lady, infatuated, as any silly mother might be, with her daughter's charms, did not perceive the officer's want of enthusiasm, but exerted herself in a low voice to attract his attention to the infinite grace with which Fleur-de-Lys plied her needle or wound a skein of silk.

'Do look now, cousin,' said she, pulling him by the sleeve that she might speak in his ear. 'Look at her! see, now she stoops.'

'Yes, indeed,' answered the young man, and he relapsed into his cold abstracted silence.

Shortly after, he had to lean again, on Dame Aloïse saying:

'Did you ever see a more charming lightsome face than that of your betrothed? Can anyone be more fair or more lovely? Are not those hands perfect? and that neck, does it not assume every graceful curve of the swan's?—How I envy you at times! and how happy you are, in being a man, wicked rogue that you are! Is not my Fleur-de-Lys adorably beautiful? and are you not passionately in love with her?'

'Assuredly,' answered he, while his thoughts were occupied elsewhere.

'Speak to her, then,' said Madame Aloïse, pushing him by the shoulder; 'say something to her; you're grown quite timid.'

We can assure the reader that timidity was neither a virtue nor a defect of the captain. He endeavoured, however, to do as he was bid.

'Fair cousin,' said he, approaching Fleur-de-Lys, 'what is the subject of this tapestry which keeps you so busy?'

'Gentle cousin,' answered Fleur-de-Lys, in a pettish tone, 'I have already told you three times; it is the grotto of Neptunus.'

It was evident that Fleur-de-Lys saw more clearly than her mother through the cold, absent manner of the captain. He felt that he must needs make conversation.

'And for whom is all this fine Neptune-work intended?' asked he.

'For the abbey of Saint-Antoine des Champs,' said Fleur-de-Lys, without raising her eyes.

The captain took up a corner of the tapestry: 'And pray, my

fair cousin, who is that big gendarme blowing his trumpet till his
cheeks are bursting?'

'That is Triton,' answered she.

There was still an offended tone perceptible in the few words
uttered by Fleur-de-Lys. The young man understood that it was
indispensable he should whisper in her ear some pretty nothing,
some gallant compliment—no matter what. He accordingly leaned
over, but his imagination could furnish nothing more tender or
familiar than this: 'Why does your mother always wear that
petticoat embroidered with her arms, like our grandmothers of
Charles VII's time? Pray tell her, fair cousin, that it's not the
fashion of the present day, and that her hinge (*gond*) and laurel
(*laurier*) embroidered upon her dress make her look like a walking
mantelpiece. 'Pon honour, no one sits under their banner in that
way now, I do swear.'

Fleur-de-Lys raised her fine eyes toward his reproachfully:

'Is that all you have to swear to me?' said she in a low tone.

Meanwhile the good Dame Aloïse, delighted to see them thus
leaning over and whispering to each other, exclaimed, playing all
the while with the clasps of her prayer-book: 'Touching picture
of love!'

The captain, more and more embarrassed, returned to the subject of the tapestry. 'It is really a beautiful piece of work!' he cried.

At this juncture, Colombe de Gaillefontaine, another beautiful,
white-skinned blonde, in a high-necked gown of blue damask,
ventured timidly to put in a word, addressed to Fleur-de-Lys, but
in the hope that the handsome captain would answer her: 'My dear
Gondelaurier, did you ever see the tapestries at the Hôtel de la
Roche-Guyon?'

'Is that not the hotel where the garden is attached to the linen-
maker of the Louvre?' asked Diane de Christeuil, laughing; for,
having fine teeth, she laughed on all occasions.

'And near that great old tower of the ancient wall of Paris?'
added Amelotte de Montmichel, a pretty, curly-haired, rosy-
cheeked brunette, who had a habit of sighing, as the other of
laughing, without knowing why.

'My dear Colombe,' said Dame Aloïse, 'are you speaking of the
hotel which belonged to Monsieur de Bacqueville in the reign of
Charles VI? There is indeed magnificent tapestry there, of the
high warp.'

'Charles VI! King Charles VI!' muttered the young captain
curling his mustache. 'Mon Dieu! what a memory the good lady
has for by-gone things!'

Madame de Gondelaurier continued: 'Superb tapestry indeed!
So superior that it is considered unique!'

At this moment, Bérangère de Champchevrier, a little sylph of seven years of age, who was gazing into the square through the trefoils of the balcony railing, cried out, 'Oh! do look, dear godmamma Fleur-de-Lys, at that pretty dancing-girl who is dancing on the pavement, and playing the tambourine among the people yonder!'

The sonorous vibration of a tambourine was, in fact, heard by the party.

'Some gypsy-girl from Bohemia,' replied Fleur-de-Lys, turning nonchalantly toward the square.

'Let us see! let us see!' cried her lively companions, running to the front of the balcony, while Fleur-de-Lys, musing over the coldness of her affianced lover, followed slowly; and the latter, released by this incident, which cut short an embarrassing conversation, returned to the farther end of the room with the satisfied air of a soldier relieved from duty. And yet no unpleasing service was that of the lovely Fleur-de Lys; and such it had once appeared to him; but the captain had by degrees become weary of it, and the prospect of an approaching marriage grew less attractive to him each day. Besides, he was of a fickle disposition; and, if the truth must be told, rather vulgar in his tastes. Although of noble birth, he had contracted, under his officer's accoutrements, more than one of the habits of the common soldier. He delighted in the tavern and its accompaniments, and was never at his ease save amidst coarse witticisms, military gallantries, easy beauties, and as easy conquests. He had notwithstanding received from his family some education and polish; but he began his career too young, had too early kept garrison, and each day the varnish of the gentleman became more and more worn away under the friction of the gendarme's baldric. Though still continuing to visit her occasionally, prompted by some small remnant of common respect, he felt doubly constrained with Fleur-de-Lys. In the first place, because he distributed his love so promiscuously that he had but little left for her; and in the second, because, surrounded by a number of stately, starched and modest ladies, he was constantly in fear lest his tongue, accustomed to the language of oaths, should inadvertently break through its bounds and let slip some unfortunate tavern-slang. The effect may be imagined!

And yet, with all this were mingled great pretensions to elegance in dress and noble bearing. Let these things be reconciled as they may—I am but the historian.

He had been for some minutes thinking, or not thinking, but leaning in silence against the carved mantelpiece, when Fleur-de-Lys turning suddenly, addressed him—for after all, the poor girl only pouted in self-defence:

'Gentle cousin, did you not tell us of a little gypsy-girl you saved from a parcel of thieves a month or more ago, as you were on the night patrol?'

'I believe I did, fair cousin,' said the captain.

'Well,' rejoined she, 'perhaps it is that very gypsy-girl who is now dancing in the Parvis. Come and see if you recognize her, cousin Phœbus.'

A secret desire of reconciliation was perceptible in the gentle invitation she gave him to draw near her, and in the care she took to call him by his name. Captain Phœbus de Châteaupers (for it is he whom the reader has had before him from the beginning of this chapter) with tardy steps approached the balcony. 'There,' said Fleur-de-Lys tenderly, placing her hand on his arm, 'look at that little girl, dancing there in the ring!—Is that your gypsy?'

Phœbus looked, and said:

'Yes—I know her by her goat.'

'Ah!—so there is!—a pretty little goat, indeed!' said Amelotte, clasping her hands with delight.

'Are its horns really gold?' asked little Bérangère.

Without moving from her fauteuil, Dame Aloïse inquired:

'Is it one of those gypsy-girls that arrived last year by the Porte Gibard?'

'Mother,' said Fleur-de-Lys gently, 'that gate is now called Porte d'Enfer.'

Mademoiselle de Gondelaurier knew how much the captain's notions were shocked by her mother's antiquated modes of speech. Indeed he was already beginning to sneer and muttering between his teeth: 'Porte Gibard! Porte Gibard! That's to make way for King Charles VI.'

'Godmamma,' exclaimed Bérangère, whose eyes, incessantly in motion, were suddenly raised toward the top of the towers of Notre-Dame, 'who is that black man up there?'

All the girls raised their eyes. A man was indeed leaning with his elbows upon the topmost balustrade of the northern tower, overlooking the Grève. It was the figure of a priest; and they could clearly discern both his costume and his face resting on both his hands. He was motionless as a statue. His steady gaze was riveted on the Place.

There was in it something of the immobility of the kite when it has just discovered a nest of sparrows and is looking down upon it.

'It is monsieur the Archdeacon of Josas,' said Fleur-de-Lys.

'You have good eyes if you know him at this distance,' observed La Gaillefontaine.

'How he looks at the little dancing-girl,' remarked Diane de Christeuil.

'Let the Egyptian girl beware,' said Fleur-de-Lys; 'for he loves not Egypt.'

''Tis a great shame that man stares at her so,' added Amelotte de Montmichel; 'for she dances delightfully.'

'Fair cousin Phœbus,' said Fleur-de-Lys, suddenly, 'since you know this little gypsy-girl beckon to her to come up. It will amuse us.'

'Oh, yes!' exclaimed all the young girls, clapping their hands.

'Why! 'tis not worth while,' replied Phœbus. 'She has no doubt forgotten me; and I know not even her name. However, since you wish it, ladies, I will try.' And leaning over the balustrade of the balcony, he began to call out—'Little one!'

The dancing-girl was not at that moment playing her tambourine. She turned her head toward the point whence this call proceeded; her brilliant eyes rested on Phœbus, and she stopped short suddenly.

'Little one,' repeated the captain, and he beckoned to her to come in.

The young girl looked at him again; then blushed as if a flame had risen to her cheeks; and, taking her tambourine under her arm, she made her way through the midst of the gaping spectators, toward the door of the house where Phœbus was, with slow, faltering steps, and with the agitated look of a bird yielding to the fascination of a serpent.

A moment or two after, the tapestry door hanging was raised, and the gypsy appeared on the threshold of the room, blushing, confused, breathless, her large eyes cast down, and not daring to advance a step farther.

Bérangère clapped her hands.

Meanwhile, the dancer stood motionless at the entrance of the apartment. Her appearance had produced a singular effect upon this group of young girls. It is certain that all of them were more or less influenced by a vague and indefined desire of pleasing the handsome officer; that the splendid uniform was the object at which all their coquetry was aimed; and that, ever since his entrance, there had been a certain secret suppressed rivalry among them, which they scarcely acknowledged even to themselves, but which broke forth none the less in their gestures and remarks. Nevertheless, as they all possessed nearly the same degree of beauty, they contended with equal arms, and each might reasonably hope for victory. The arrival of the gypsy-girl suddenly destroyed this equilibrium. Her beauty was so rare that, the moment she appeared at the entrance of the apartment, it seemed as though she diffused a sort of light peculiar to herself. Within this enclosed chamber, surrounded by its dusky hangings and wainscotings, she was incomparably more beautiful and radiant than in the public square. She was as the torch suddenly brought from the midday light into the shade. The noble damsels were dazzled by it in spite of themselves. Each felt that her beauty had in some degree suffered. Hence their battle-front (if we may be allowed the expression) was changed immediately, though not a single word passed between them. But they understood each other perfectly. The instincts of women comprehend and respond to each other more quickly than the understandings of men. An enemy had arrived in their midst; all felt it—all rallied. One drop of wine is sufficient to redden a whole glass of water: to tinge a whole company of pretty women with a certain degree of ill humour, it is only necessary for one still prettier to make her appearance—especially when there is but one man in the party.

Thus the gypsy-girl's reception proved mightily freezing. They eyed her from head to foot; then exchanged glances; and all was said—they understood each other. Meanwhile the young girl was waiting to be spoken to, in such emotion that she dared not raise her eyelids.

The captain was the first to break silence.

'Upon my word,' said he, with his tone of brainless assurance, 'here is a charming creature! What think you of her, fair cousin?'

This remark, which a more delicate admirer would at least have made in an undertone, did not tend to dissipate the feminine jealousies which were on the alert in the presence of the gypsy-girl.

Fleur-de-Lys answered the captain with a simpering affectation of disdain—'Not bad.'

The others whispered together.

At length, Madame Aloïse, who was not the less jealous because she was so for her daughter, addressed the dancer:

'Come hither, little one,' said she.

'Come hither, little one!' repeated, with comical dignity, little Bérangère, who would have stood about as high as her hip.

The gypsy advanced toward the noble dame.

'My pretty girl,' said Phœbus, with emphasis, taking several steps towards her, 'I do not know whether I have the supreme felicity of being recognized by you.'

She interrupted him with a look and smile of infinite sweetness.

'Oh! yes,' said she.

'She has a good memory,' observed Fleur-de-Lys.

'Well, now,' resumed Phœbus, 'you escaped nimbly the other evening. Did I frighten you?'

'Oh! no,' said the gypsy.

There was, in the intonation of that 'Oh! no,' uttered after that 'Oh! yes,' an ineffable something which wounded Fleur-de-Lys.

'You left me in your stead, my beauty,' continued the captain, whose tongue became unloosed while speaking to a girl from the streets, 'a rare grim-faced fellow, humpbacked and one-eyed, the ringer of the bishop's bells, I believe. They tell me he's an archdeacon's bastard and a devil by birth. He has a droll name too; they call him Quatre-Temps (Ember week), Pâques-Fleuries (Palm Sunday), Mardi-Gras (Shrove Tuesday), I don't know what!—the name of some bell-ringing festival, in short. And so he thought fit to carry you off, as if you were made for such fellows as beadles! That is going a little too far. What the deuce could that screechowl want with you? Hey, tell me!'

'I do not know,' she replied.

'What insolence! a bell-ringer to carry off a girl, like a viscount! a lout poaching on the game of gentlemen! a rare piece of assurance, truly! But he paid pretty dear for it. Maître Pierrat Torterue is as rough a groom as ever curried a rascal; and your ringer's hide—if that will please you—got a thorough dressing at his hands, I warrant you.'

'Poor man!' said the gypsy-girl—the scene of the pillory brought back to her remembrance by these words.

The captain burst out laughing. 'By the bull's horns! here's pity about as well placed as a feather in a pig's tail. May I have a belly like a pope, if . . . .'

He stopped suddenly short. 'Pardon me, ladies—I fear I was about to let slip some nonsense or other.'

'Fie, monsieur!' said La Gaillefontaine.

'He speaks to this creature in her own language,' added Fleur-de-Lys in an undertone, her irritation increasing every moment. This irritation was not diminished by seeing the captain, delighted with the gypsy, and most of all with himself, turn round on his heel and repeat with coarse, naïve and soldierlike gallantry: 'A lovely girl, upon my soul!'

'Very barbarously dressed!' said Diane de Christeuil, with the smile which showed her fine teeth.

This remark was a flash of light to the others. It showed them the gypsy's assailable point; as they could not carp at her beauty, they fell foul of her dress.

'Very true,' said La Montmichel. 'Pray, little girl, where did you learn to run about the streets in that way, without either neckerchief or tucker?'

'That petticoat is so short that it makes one tremble!' added La Gaillefontaine.

'My dear, you will get yourself taken up by the sumptuary police for your gilded girdle,' continued Fleur-de-Lys, with decided sharpness.

'Little girl, little girl,' resumed Christeuil, with an implacable smile, 'if you had the decency to wear sleeves on your arms they would not get so sun-burned.'

It was a sight worthy a more intelligent spectator than Phœbus, to watch how these fair damsels, with their envenomed and angry tongues, twisted, glided and writhed, as it were, around the street dancer; they were at once cruel and graceful; they searched and pried maliciously into her poor silly toilet of spangles and tinsel. Then followed the laugh, the ironical jest, humiliations without end. Sarcasms, haughty condescensions, and evil looks rained down upon the gypsy-girl. One might have fancied them some of those young Roman ladies that used to amuse themselves with thrusting golden pins into the bosom of some beautiful slave; or have likened them to elegant greyhounds, turning, wheeling with distended nostrils and eager eyes, around some poor hind of the forest which their master's eye prevents them from devouring.

After all, what was a poor dancing-girl of the public square to those high-born maidens? They seemed to take no heed of her presence; but spoke of her, before her, and to herself, aloud, as of something unclean, abject, and yet at the same time passably pretty.

The gypsy-girl was not insensible to these pin-pricks. From time to time, a glow of shame, or a flash of anger inflamed her eyes or her cheeks—a disdainful exclamation seemed to hover on her lips—she made contemptuously the little grimace with which the reader is already familiar—but remained motionless; she fixed on Phœbus a sad, sweet, resigned look. There was also happiness and tenderness in that gaze. It seemed as if she restrained herself for fear of being driven away.

Phœbus laughed and took the gypsy's part, with a mixture of pity and impertinence.

'Let them talk, little one,' repeated he, jingling his gold spurs; 'doubtless, your dress is a little wild and extravagant; but in a charming girl like you, what does that signify?'

'Dear me!' exclaimed the blonde Gaillefontaine, drawing up her swan-like throat with a bitter smile, 'I see that messieurs the king's archers take fire easily at bright gypsy eyes.'

'And why not?' said Phœbus.

At this rejoinder, uttered carelessly by the captain, like a stray stone whose fall one does not even watch, Colombe began to laugh, as well as Amelotte, Diane, and Fleur-de-Lys, into whose eyes a tear started at the same time.

The gypsy, who had dropped her eyes on the floor as Colombe and Gaillefontaine spoke, raised them beaming with joy and pride, and fixed them once more on Phœbus. She was very beautiful at that moment.

The old dame, who was watching this scene, felt offended without understanding why.

'Holy Virgin!' cried she suddenly, 'what's that about my legs? Ah! the villainous beast!'

It was the goat which had just arrived in search of its mistress, and which, in hurrying toward her, had entangled its horns in the load of drapery which the noble dame's garments heaped around her when she was seated.

This made a diversion. The gypsy disentangled its horns without saying a word.

'Oh! here's the little goat with golden hoofs,' cried Bérangère, jumping with joy.

The gypsy crouched upon her knees, and pressed her cheek against the caressing head of the goat. It seemed as if she were asking its pardon for having left it behind.

Meanwhile, Diane bent over and whispered in Colombe's ear:

'Ah! good heavens! how is it I did not think of it before? 'Tis the gypsy with the goat. They say she's a sorceress, and that her goat performs very marvellous tricks.'

'Well,' said Colombe, 'let the goat amuse us now in its turn, and perform us a miracle.'

Diane and Colombe eagerly addressed the gypsy: 'Little one, make your goat perform a miracle.'

'I do not know what you mean,' said the dancing-girl.

'Why, a miracle—a conjuring trick—a feat of witchcraft.'

'I do not understand.' And she turned to caressing the pretty animal again, repeating, 'Djali! Djali!'

At that moment Fleur-de-Lys noticed a little bag of embroidered leather hung round the goat's neck.

'What is that?' she asked of the gypsy.

The girl raised her large eyes toward her, and replied gravely, 'That is my secret.'

'I should like to know your secret,' thought Fleur-de-Lys.

Meanwhile, the good dame had risen angrily. 'Come, come, gypsy, if neither you nor your goat have anything to dance to us, what are you doing here?'

The gypsy directed her steps slowly toward the door without making any reply. But the nearer she approached it, the slower were her steps. An irresistible magnet seemed to retard her. Suddenly, she turned her eyes moistened with tears toward Phœbus, and stood still.

'Zounds!' cried the captain, 'you shall not go away thus. Come back and dance for us something. By-the-by, my beauty, what's your name?'

'Esmeralda,' said the dancer, without taking her eyes off him.

At this strange name the young women burst into an extravagant laugh.

'A formidable name indeed, for a girl,' said Diane.

'You see,' remarked Amelotte, 'that she's an enchantress.'

'My dear,' exclaimed Dame Aloïse, solemnly, 'your parents never fished that name for you out of the baptismal font.'

Meanwhile, Bérangère, without attracting attention, had, a few minutes before, enticed the goat into a corner of the room with a piece of nut-cake. In an instant they had become good friends; and the curious child had untied the little bag which hung at the goat's neck, had opened it, and spread the contents on the matting; it was an alphabet, each letter being inscribed separately on a small tablet of wood. No sooner were these toys displayed upon the matting, than the child saw, with surprise, the goat (one of whose miracles, doubtless, it was) select with her gilded hoof certain letters, and arrange them in a particular order by gently pushing them together. In a moment they formed a word which the goat seemed practised in composing, so slight was her hesitation; and Bérangère suddenly cried out, clasping her hands with admiration:

'Godmamma Fleur-de-Lys—do see what the goat has been doing!'

Fleur-de-Lys hastened to look, and suddenly started. The letters arranged on the floor formed this word,

PHOEBUS

'Did the goat write that?' she asked, with a faltering voice.

'Yes, godmamma,' answered Bérangère.

It was impossible to doubt her; the child could not spell.

'Here's the secret!' thought Fleur-de-Lys.

Meanwhile, at the child's exclamation they had all hurried forward to look; the mother, the young ladies, the gypsy, and the officer.

The gypsy saw the blunder the goat had committed. She turned red—then pale—and began to tremble like a culprit before the captain, who regarded her with a smile of satisfaction and astonishment.

'*Phœbus!*' whispered the girls, in amazement, 'that's the captain's name!'

'You have a wonderful memory!' said Fleur-de-Lys to the stupefied gypsy. Then bursting into sobs: 'Oh!' stammered she tearfully, hiding her face between her two fair hands, 'she is a sorceress!' while she heard a voice yet more bitter whisper from her inmost heart, 'she is a rival!'

She fell fainting to the floor.

'My child! my child!' cried the terrified mother. 'Begone, you fiendish gypsy!'

Esmeralda gathered together the unlucky letters in the twinkling of an eye, made a sign to Djali, and quitted the room at one door as Fleur-de-Lys was being carried out through the other.

Captain Phœbus, left alone, hesitated a moment between the two doors; then followed the gypsy.

2

*Showing that a Priest and a Philosopher
Are Different Persons*

THE priest whom the young ladies had observed on the top of the northern tower, leaning over toward the Square, and so attentive to the gypsy-girl's dancing, was, in fact, the Archdeacon Claude Frollo.

Our readers have not forgotten the mysterious cell which the archdeacon had appropriated to himself in this tower. (I do not know, let me observe by the way, whether it is the same cell, the interior of which may be seen to this day through a small square window, opening toward the east, at about the height of a man from the floor, upon the platform from which the towers spring; a mere hole, now naked, empty, and falling to decay; the ill-plastered walls of which are to-day *decorated* here and there with a parcel of sorry yellow engravings representing cathedral fronts. I presume that this hole is jointly inhabited by bats and spiders, and, consequently, a double war of extermination is carried on against the flies).

Every day, an hour before sunset, the archdeacon ascended the staircase of the tower and shut himself up in this cell, where he sometimes passed whole nights. On this day, just as he had reached the low door of his retreat, and was putting into the lock the complicated little key, which he always carried with him in the purse suspended at his side, the sound of a tambourine and castanets reached his ear. This sound proceeded from the Square in front of the cathedral. The cell, as we have already said, had but one window, looking upon the back of the church. Claude Frollo had hastily withdrawn the key, and in an instant was on the summit of the tower, in that gloomy, thoughtful attitude in which the young ladies had first seen him.

There he stood, grave, motionless, absorbed in one sight, one thought. All Paris lay at his feet; with her thousand spires and her circular horizon of gently rolling hills; with her river winding under her bridges, and her people flowing to and fro through her streets; with the cloud of her smoke; with the mountainous chain of roofs pressing about Notre-Dame range upon range. But, in all that city, the archdeacon saw but one spot on its pavement, the Place du Parvis; in all that crowd, but one figure, that of the gypsy.

It would have been difficult to say what was the nature of that glance, or whence arose the flame that issued from it. It was a fixed gaze, but full of tumult and perturbation. And yet from the profound quiescence of his whole body, scarcely shaken now and then by an involuntary shiver, as a tree by the wind; from the rigidity of his arms, more marble-like than the balustrade on which they leaned; from the petrified smile which contracted his countenance, one might have said that no part of Claude Frollo was alive but his eyes.

The gypsy-girl was dancing, twirling her tambourine on the tip of her finger, and tossing it in the air as she danced Provençal sarabands; agile, light, joyous and unconscious of the formidable gaze which fell directly on her head.

The crowd swarmed around her; from time to time, a man, tricked out in a red and yellow coat, went round to make them keep the ring; then returned, seated himself in a chair a few paces from the dancer, and took the goat's head on his knees. This man appeared to be the companion of the gypsy. Claude Frollo, from his elevated post, could not distinguish his features.

From the moment that the archdeacon perceived this stranger his attention seemed divided between the dancer and him, and his countenance became more and more sombre. All at once he started up, and a thrill shook his whole frame. 'Who can that man be?' he muttered between his teeth. 'Until now I have always seen her alone.'

He then plunged down under the winding vault of the spiral staircase, and once more descended. In passing the door of the belfry, which was ajar, he saw something which struck him; he beheld Quasimodo, who, leaning out of one of the apertures in those great slate eaves which resemble enormous blinds, was likewise gazing into the Square. He was so absorbed in profound contemplation that he was not aware of his adoptive father passing by. His wild eye had a singular expression; it was a charmed, tender look. 'Strange!' murmured Claude; 'can it be the Egyptian at whom he is thus looking?' He continued his descent. In a few minutes the moody archdeacon sallied forth into the Square by the door at the base of the tower.

'What has become of the gypsy?' said he, mingling with the group of spectators which the sound of the tambourine had collected.

'I know not,' answered one of those nearest him; 'she has but just disappeared. I think she is gone to dance some of her fandangos in the house opposite, whither they called her.'

In the place of the gipsy-girl, upon the same carpet whose arabesques but a moment before had seemed to vanish beneath the fantastic figures of her dance, the archdeacon saw no one but the red and yellow man, who, in order to earn a few testers in his turn, was parading around the circle, his elbows on his hips, his head thrown back, his face red, his neck outstretched, with a chair between his teeth. On this chair he had tied a cat, which a woman of the neighbourhood had lent him, and which was spitting in great affright.

'By Our Lady!' cried the archdeacon, just as the mountebank, perspiring heavily, passed in front of him with his pyramid of chair and cat; 'what does Maître Pierre Gringoire there?'

The harsh voice of the archdeacon threw the poor devil into such commotion that he lost his equilibrium, and down fell the whole edifice, chair and cat and all, pell-mell upon the heads of the bystanders in the midst of inextinguishable hootings.

It is probable that Maître Pierre Gringoire (for he indeed it was) would have had a sorry account to settle with the neighbour who owned the cat, and all the bruised and scratched faces around him, if he had not hastened to profit by the tumult to take refuge in the church, whither Claude Frollo had motioned to him to follow.

The cathedral was already dark and deserted; the transepts were full of shadows, and the lamps of the chapels twinkled like stars, so black had the arched roofs become. Only the great rose-window of the façade, whose thousand tints were steeped in a ray of horizontal sunlight, glistened in the dark like a cluster of diamonds, and threw its dazzling reflection to the other end of the nave.

When they had proceeded a few steps, Dom Claude leaned his back against a pillar and looked steadfastly at Gringoire. This look was not the one which Gringoire had dreaded, ashamed as he was at being surprised by so grave and learned a personage in that merry-andrew garb. There was nothing mocking or ironical in the priest's glance; it was serious, calm and searching. The archdeacon was the first to break silence.

'Come, now, Maître Pierre,' said he, 'you are to explain many things to me. And first of all, how comes it that you have not been seen these two months, and that now one finds you in the public squares, in rare guise, i' faith, half red, half yellow, like a Caudebec apple?'

'Messire,' said Gringoire, piteously, 'it is in sooth a monstrous garb, and behold me about as comfortable in it as a cat with a calabash clapped on her head. 'Tis wrong, I admit, to expose messieurs, the sergeants of the watch, to the liability of cudgelling, under this cassock, the shoulders of a Pythagorean philosopher. But what could I do, reverend master? 'Tis the fault of my ancient jerkin, which basely forsook me at the beginning of the winter, under the pretext that it was falling into tatters, and that it required repose in the basket of rag-picker. What was to be done? Civilization has not yet arrived at the point where one may go stark naked, as ancient Diogenes wished. Add to this, that the wind blew very cold, and the month of January is not the time that one can successfully attempt to make humanity take this new step. This garment offered itself—I took it, and left off my old black frock, which, for a hermetic like myself, was far from being hermetically closed. Behold me, then, in my buffoon's habit, like Saint Genest. What would you have? It's an eclipse. Apollo, you know, tended the swine of Admetus.'

'' Tis a fine trade you've taken up,' replied the priest.

'I confess, my master, that it's better to philosophize and poetize —to blow the flame in the furnace, or receive it from heaven— than to wear cats as a coat-of-arms. So, when you addressed me, I felt as foolish as an ass before a roasting-jack. But what was to be done, messire?—one must eat every day; and the finest Alexandrine verses are not so toothsome as a piece of Brie cheese. Now, I composed for the Lady Margaret of Flanders, that famous epithalamium, as you know; and the town has not paid me for it, saying that it was not of the best—as though one could give a tragedy of Sophocles for four crowns. Hence, I was near dying of hunger. Happily, I found that I was rather strong in the jaw; so I said to this jaw: "Perform some feats of strength and equilibrium—find food for thyself—*Ale te ipsam.*" A pack of vagabonds, who are become my good friends, taught me twenty different kinds of Herculean tricks; and now I give to my teeth every night the bread they have earned during the day by the sweat of my brow. After all, *concedo*, I grant that it is but a sorry employ of my intellectual faculties, and that man is not made to pass his life in playing the tambourine and biting chairs. But, reverend master, one must not only live, but also gain a livelihood.'

Dom Claude listened in silence. All at once his hollow eyes assumed an expression so sagacious and penetrating that Gringoire felt himself, so to speak, searched to the bottom of the soul by that look.

'Very good, Maître Pierre; but how comes it that you are now in company with that gypsy-dancer?'

'I'faith,' said Gringoire, ''tis because she is my wife and I am her husband.'

The dark eye of the priest flashed fire.

'And hast thou done that, miserable man?' he cried, seizing Gringoire's arm with fury; 'and hast thou been so abandoned by God as to lay thy hand upon that girl?'

'By my hope of Paradise, monseigneur,' answered Gringoire, trembling in every limb, 'I swear to you that I have never touched her—if that be what disturbs you.'

'But what speakest thou, then, of husband and wife?' said the priest.

Gringoire eagerly related to him, as succinctly as possible, what the reader already knows—his adventure of the Cour des Miracles, and his marriage by the broken jug. It appeared, moreover, that this marriage had led to no results whatever, and that each evening the gypsy-girl contrived to cheat him of his nuptials as she had done on the first night. ''Tis a mortification,' he said in conclusion; 'but that comes of my having had the misfortune to wed a virgin.'

'What mean you?' asked the archdeacon, whose agitation had gradually subsided.

''Tis rather difficult to explain,' answered the poet. ''Tis a superstition. My wife is, according to what an old thief, who is called among us the Duke of Egypt, has told me, a foundling—or a lostling, which is the same thing. She wears on her neck an amulet, which it is affirmed will some day cause her to find her parents again, but which would lose its virtue if the young maid were to lose hers. Hence it follows that both of us remain quite virtuous.'

'So,' resumed Claude, whose brow cleared more and more, 'you believe, Maître Pierre, that this creature has not been approached by any man?'

'What chance, Dom Claude, can a man have against a superstition? She has got that into her head. I assuredly esteem as a rarity this nun-like prudery which is preserved untamed amid those gypsy-girls, who are so easily brought into subjection. But she has three things to protect her: the Duke of Egypt, who has taken her under his safeguard, reckoning, perchance, that he shall sell her to some gay abbé; her whole tribe, who hold her in singular veneration, like an Our Lady; and a certain tiny poniard, which the sly minx always wears about her in spite of the provost's ordinances, and which darts forth in her hand when you but clasp her waist. 'Tis a fierce wasp, I can tell you.'

The archdeacon pressed Gringoire with questions.

La Esmeralda was, in Gringoire's opinion, an inoffensive, charming, pretty creature, with the exception of the pout peculiar to herself—an artless and warm-hearted girl, ignorant of everything, and enthusiastic about everything, not yet aware of the difference between a man and a woman, even in her dreams; just simple like that; fond, above all things, of dancing, of bustle, of the open air—a sort of a woman bee, with invisible wings on her feet, and living in a perpetual whirl. She owed this disposition to the wandering life she had always led. Gringoire had contrived to ascertain that, while quite a child, she had traversed Spain and Catalonia to Sicily; he believed that she had even been taken by the caravan of Zingari, to which she belonged, to the kingdom of Algiers—a country situated in Achaia—which country adjoins on one side Lesser Albania and Greece, and on the other the Sicilian sea, which is the road to Constantinople. The gypsies, said Gringoire, were vassals to the King of Algiers, in his capacity of chief of the nation of the white Moors. Certain it was that La Esmeralda had come into France while yet very young, by way of Hungary. From all those countries the girl had brought with her fragments of fantastic jargons, foreign songs and ideas, which made her language as motley as her costume, half Parisian, half African. For the rest, the people of the quarters which she frequented loved her for her gaiety, her gracefulness, her lively ways, her dances and her songs. In all the town, she believed herself to be hated by two persons only, of whom she often spoke with dread: the Sachette of the Tour-Roland, a miserable recluse, who bore a secret grudge against gypsy-women, and who cursed the poor dancing-girl every time she passed before her loophole; and a priest who never met her without casting upon her looks and words that affrighted her. The mention of this latter circumstance disturbed the archdeacon greatly, though Gringoire scarcely noticed his perturbation; the two months that had elapsed having been quite sufficient to make the heedless poet forget the singular details of that night when he had first met with the gypsy-girl, and the presence of the archdeacon on that occasion. Otherwise the little dancer feared nothing. She did not tell fortunes, and so was secure from those prosecutions for magic that were so frequently instituted against the gypsy-women. And then, Gringoire was as a brother to her, if not as a husband. After all, the philosopher very patiently endured this kind of Platonic marriage. At any rate he was sure of food and lodging. Every morning he set out from the headquarters of the Truands, generally with the gypsy-girl; he assisted her in the crossways to gather her harvest of targes (an ancient Burgundian coin) and petits-blancs (an ancient French coin). Every evening he returned with her under the same roof, let her bolt herself in her own little chamber, and slept the sleep of the just—a very agreeable existence on the whole, said he, and very favourable to reverie. And then, in his heart and conscience, the philosopher was not very sure that he was madly in love with the gypsy. He loved her goat almost as much. It was a charming, gentle, intelligent, clever animal; a learned goat. Nothing was more common in the Middle Ages than those learned animals, which excited general wonder, and which frequently brought their instructors to the stake. However, the witchcraft of the goat with the gilded hoofs were very harmless tricks indeed. Gringoire explained them to the archdeacon, whom these particulars seemed to interest deeply. In most cases it was sufficient to present the tambourine to the goat in such or such a manner, in order to obtain from it the trick desired. It had been trained to that by the gypsy, who possessed, in these delicate arts, so rare a talent that two months had sufficed to teach the goat to write with movable letters the word 'Phœbus.'

'Phœbus!' said the priest. 'Why Phœbus?'

'I know not,' replied Gringoire; 'perhaps it is a word which she believes endowed with some magical and secret virtue. She often repeats it in an undertone when she thinks she is alone.'

'Are you sure,' rejoined Claude, with his penetrating look, 'that it is only a word and not a name?'

'Name of whom?' said the poet.

'How should I know?' said the priest.

'That is what I am thinking, messire; these gypsies are a sort of Guebres, and worship the sun—hence Phœbus.'

'That does not seem so clear to me as to you, Maître Pierre.'

'After all, that does not concern me. Let her mumble her Phœbus to her heart's content. One thing is certain. Djali loves me almost as much as she does her.'

'Who is this Djali?'

'The goat.'

The archdeacon dropped his chin into his hand and appeared to reflect for a moment. Then suddenly turning to Gringoire:

'And thou wilt swear that thou hast never touched her?'

'Who?' said Gringoire. 'The goat?'

'No—that woman.'

'My wife? I swear to you I have not.'

'And you are often alone with her?'

'Every evening for a good hour.'

Dom Claude knit his brows.

'Oh, ho! *Solus cum sola non cogitabuntur orare Pater Noster.*' (He alone with her [alone] will not think of saying paternosters.)

'Upon my soul, I might say the *Pater*, and the *Ave Maria*, and the *Credo in Deum patrem omnipotentem* (I believe in God the Father Almighty), without her taking any more notice of me than a hen does of a church.'

'Swear to me by thy mother's womb,' repeated the archdeacon violently, 'that thou hast not so much as touched that creature with the tip of thy finger.'

'I could also swear it by my father's head, for the two things have more than one affinity. But, my reverend master, permit me a question in my turn.'

'Speak, sir.'

'What concern is it of yours?'

The pale face of the archdeacon crimsoned like the cheek of a girl. He kept silence for a moment, then answered with visible embarrassment:

'Hearken, Maître Pierre Gringoire. You are not yet damned, so far as I know. I take an interest in you, and wish you well. Now, the least contact with this Egyptian child of the devil would make you a vassal of Satan. 'Tis the body, you know, which ruins the soul. Woe to you, if you approach that woman. That is all.'

'I tried once,' said Gringoire, scratching his ear; 'it was the first day, but I got stung.'

'You had that effrontery, Maître Pierre?'

And the priest's brow darkened again.

'Another time,' continued the poet, smiling, 'before I went to bed, I peeped through the keyhole, and I beheld the most delicious damsel in her shift that ever made a bed creak under her bare foot.'

'Get thee gone to the devil!' cried the priest, with a terrible look; and pushing the amazed Gringoire by the shoulders, he plunged with long strides beneath the darkest arches of the cathedral.

3

The Bells

SINCE his morning on the pillory, the inhabitants in the neighbourhood of Notre-Dame thought they noticed that Quasimodo's bell-ringing ardour had grown cool. Formerly the bells were going on all occasions—long matin chimes which lasted from primes to complines; peals from the belfry for high mass; rich scales running up and down the small bells for a wedding or a christening, and mingling in the air like a rich embroidery of all sorts of delightful sounds. The old church, vibrating and sonorous, was in a perpetual joyous whirl of bells. Some spirit of noise and caprice seemed to sing continuously through those mouths of brass. Now that spirit seemed to have departed. The cathedral seemed gloomy and wilfully silent. Festivals and funerals had the simple peal, bare and unadorned—what the ritual demanded, nothing more; of the double sound proceeding from a church, that of the organ within, and of the bells without, the organ alone remained. It seemed as if there was no longer any musician in the steeples. Quasimodo, nevertheless, was still there; what had happened to him, then? was it that the shame and despair of the pillory still rankled in his heart, that the lashes of his tormentor's whip reverberated unceasingly in his soul, and that his grief at such treatment had wholly extinguished in him even his passion for the bells? Or was it rather that Marie had a rival in the heart of the ringer of Notre-Dame, and that the big bell and her fourteen sisters were neglected for something more beautiful and pleasing?

It happened that in the year of Our Lord 1482, the Annunciation fell on Tuesday, the 25th of March. On that day the air was so pure and light that Quasimodo felt some returning affection for his bells. He therefore went up into the northern tower, while the beadle below threw wide open the doors of the church, which were then enormous panels of strong wood, covered with leather, bordered with nails of iron gilt, and framed in carvings 'most cunningly wrought.'

Having reached the high loft of the belfry, Quasimodo gazed for some time, with a sorrowful shake of the head, on his six song-stresses, as if lamenting that some other object had intruded into his heart between them and him. But when he had set them in motion—when he felt that cluster of bells moving under his hand —when he saw, for he did not hear it, the palpitating octave ascend and descend that sonorous scale like a bird hopping from branch to branch—when the demon of music, that demon who shakes a glittering quiver of stretti, trills and arpeggios, had taken possession of the poor deaf creature, then he became happy once more; he forgot everything, and his heart expanding made his countenance radiant.

He went and came, he clapped his hands; he ran from rope to rope, he encouraged the six chimes with voice and gesture, as a leader of the orchestra spurs on intelligent musicians.

'Go on, Gabrielle,' said he, 'go on, pour forth all thy sound into the Square; 'tis a festival to-day. No laziness, Thibauld. What! thou'rt lagging! Get on with thee. Art grown rusty, lazybones? That is well!—quick!—quick!—let not thy clapper be seen. Make them all deaf like me. Bravo! Thibauld. Guillaume! Guillaume, thou art the biggest, and Pasquier is the smallest, and Pasquier does best. I'll lay anything that those that can hear, hear him better than thee. Good! good! my Gabrielle—harder! harder! Hey! you there, The Sparrows, what are you both about? I don't see you make the least noise. What's the meaning of those brazen beaks of yours, that seem to be gaping when they ought to be singing? Come—work away! 'tis the Annunciation. The sun is fine, the chime must be fine also. Poor Guillaume—thou art quite out of breath, my big fellow!'

He was wholly absorbed in goading on his bells, which were all six leaping, each better than the other, and shaking their shining haunches like a noisy team of Spanish mules urged forward by the apostrophizings of the muleteer.

All at once, letting his glance fall between the large slate scales which cover, at a certain height, the perpendicular wall of the belfry, he descried on the Square a young girl fantastically dressed, who stopped, spread out on the ground a carpet on which a little goat came and placed itself, and around whom a group of spectators made a circle. This view suddenly changed the course of his ideas, and congealed his musical enthusiasm as a breath of air congeals melted rosin. He stopped, turned his back to the bells, and crouched behind the slate eaves, fixing on the dancer that thoughtful, tender and softened look which had already astonished the archdeacon on one occasion. Meanwhile, the forgotten bells died away abruptly and all together, to the great disappointment of the lovers of chimes who were listening to the peal in good earnest from off the Pont-au-Change, and who went away dumbfounded, like a dog who has been offered a bone and given a stone.

4

'Ανάγκη [*]

IT chanced that upon one fine morning in this same month of March—I think it was on Saturday, the 29th, St. Eustache's day —our young college friend, Jehan Frollo du Moulin, perceived, as he was dressing himself, that his breeches, which contained his purse, emitted no metallic sound. 'Poor purse!' said he, drawing it forth from his pocket. 'What! not one little parisis! How cruelly have dice, beer-pots and Venus depleted thee! Behold thee empty, wrinkled and limp! Thou art like the throat of a fury! I ask you, Messire Cicero and Messire Seneca, whose dog's-eared tomes I see scattered upon the floor, what profits it me to know better than a governor of the mint, or a Jew of the Pont-aux-Changeurs, that a gold écu stamped with the crown is worth thirty-five unzains at twenty-five sous eight deniers parisis each;

*   Doom.

and that an écu stamped with the crescent is worth thirty-six unzains at twenty-six sous six deniers tournois apiece, if I have not one miserable black liard to risk upon the double-six? Oh! Consul Cicero! this is not a calamity from which one extricates one's self with periphrases—by *quem-ad-modums* ('after-the-manner-in-whiches') and by *verum-enim-veros* ('but-indeeds').

He dressed himself sadly. A thought struck him as he was lacing his boots, but he at first rejected it; nevertheless, it returned, and he put on his waistcoat wrong side out, an evident sign of a violent internal struggle. At last he dashed his cap vehemently on the ground, and exclaimed: 'Be it so! come what may, I'll go to my brother. I shall catch a sermon, but I shall also catch a crown.'

He then hastily donned his fur-trimmed jacket, picked up his cap, and rushed out like a madman.

He turned down the Rue de la Harpe, in the direction of the City. Passing the Rue de la Huchette, the odour from those admirable spits, which were incessantly going, tickled his olfactories, and he cast an affectionate glance toward that cyclopean cookshop which one day drew from Calatagirone, the Franciscan, the pathetic exclamation: *Veramente, queste rotisserie sono cosa stupenda!* (Verily, these cook-shops be stupendous places!) But Jehan had not the wherewithal to buy a breakfast; and he plunged, with a profound sigh, under the gateway of the Petit-Châtelet, that huge, double trefoil of massive towers which guarded the entrance to the City.

He did not even take the time to throw a stone in passing, as it was then customary, at the wretched statue of that Perinet Leclerc who had given up the Paris of Charles VI to the English, a crime which his effigy, the face battered with stones and soiled with mud, expiated during three centuries, at the corner of the streets de la Harpe and de Bussy, as in a perpetual pillory.

Crossing the Petit-Pont, and striding down the Rue Neuve-Sainte-Geneviève, Jehan de Molendino found himself in front of Notre-Dame. Then all his indecision returned, and he walked about for some moments around the statue of M. Le Gris, repeating to himself with anguish, 'The sermon is sure, the crown piece is doubtful.'

He stopped a beadle who was coming from the cloisters— 'Where is monsieur the Archdeacon of Josas?'

'I believe he is in his cell in the tower,' said the beadle; 'and I would not advise you to disturb him there unless you come from some one like the pope or the king himself.'

Jehan clapped his hands.

'By Satan! here is a splendid opportunity for seeing the famous sorcery-box!'

Being brought to a decision by this reflection, he boldly entered through the little, dark doorway, and began to ascend the winding staircase of Saint Gilles, which leads to the upper stories of the tower. 'I shall see!' he said, as he proceeded. 'By the ravens of the Holy Virgin! it must needs be a curious thing, that cell which my reverend brother hides so secretly! 'Tis said that he lights up the kitchens of hell there, and cooks the philosopher's stone over the blaze. Egad! I care as little for the philosopher's stone as for a pebble; and I'd rather find an omelet of Easter eggs fried in lard on his oven than the biggest philosopher's stone in the world!'

Reaching the gallery of little columns, he stopped to breathe a moment, swearing against the interminable staircase by we know not how many million cart-loads of devils; he then continued his ascent by the narrow door of the northern tower, which is now closed to the public. Just after he had passed the cage of the bells, he came upon a little landing-place, built in a lateral recess, and, under the arch, a low pointed door; while a loophole opposite, in the circular wall of the staircase, enabled him to discern its enormous lock and strong iron bars. Persons desirous of visiting this door at the present time may recognize it by this inscription, in white letters, on the black wall: J'ADORE CORALIE. 1829. *Signé*, *Ugène*. (I adore Coralie. 1829. Signed, Ugène.) *'Signé'* is in the original.

'Whew!' said the scholar. ''Tis here, no doubt.'

The key was in the lock. The door was close to him; he pushed it gently, and put his head through the opening.

The reader has without doubt seen some of those admirable sketches by Rembrandt—that Shakespeare of painting. Among many marvellous engravings there is one especial etching which is supposed to represent Doctor Faustus, and at which it is impossible to look without being dazzled. It represents a gloomy cell; in the middle is a table, loaded with hideous objects—death's heads, spheres, alembics, compasses, hieroglyphic parchments. The doctor is at this table, clad in his coarse great-coat, and covered to the very eyebrows with his fur cap. Only half of his body is seen. He has half risen from his immense armchair, his clenched fists rest on the table, and he is gazing with curiosity and terror at a luminous circle, formed of magic letters, which gleams from the wall in the background like the solar spectrum in the camera obscura. This cabalistic sun seems to tremble before the eye, and fills the wan cell with its mysterious radiance. It is horrible and it is beautiful.

Something very similar to Faust's cell appeared to Jehan when he ventured to put his head in at the half-open door. It was a similar, gloomy, dimly-lighted retreat. There also was a large

armchair and a large table; compasses; alembics; skeletons of
animals suspended from the ceiling; a globe rolling on the floor;
hippocephali pell-mell with glass jars in which quivered leaf gold;
skulls placed on parchments scrawled over with figures and
letters; thick manuscripts piled up, all open, without any pity
for the cracking corners of the parchment; in short, all the rubbish
of science; dust and cobwebs covering the whole heap; but there
was no circle of luminous letters, no doctor in ecstasy, contemplating the flaming vision as the eagle gazes at the sun.

And yet the cell was not deserted. A man sat in the armchair,
bending over the table. Jehan, to whom his back was turned,
could only see his shoulders and the back of his head; but he had
no difficulty in recognizing that bald head, which Nature had
provided with an everlasting tonsure, as if wishing to mark, by
this outward symbol, the archdeacon's irresistible clerical
vocation.

Jehan accordingly recognized his brother; but the door had
been opened so gently that Dom Claude was not aware of his
presence. The inquisitive student availed himself of the opportunity to examine the cell for a few moments at his leisure. A large
furnace, which he had not at first observed, was to the left of the
armchair, beneath the dormer-window. The ray of light which
penetrated through this aperture made its way through the
circular web of a spider, which tastefully inscribed its delicate
rose in the arch of the window, and in whose centre the insect
architect hung motionless, like the nave of this lace wheel. On the
furnace were heaped in disorder all sorts of vessels—earthenware
flasks, glass retorts, coal mattresses. Jehan noticed with a sigh
that there was not a single saucepan. 'The kitchen utensils are
cold!' thought he.

In fact, there was no fire in the furnace, nor did it appear to
have been lighted for a considerable time. A glass mask, which
Jehan noted among the alchemist's tools, and doubtless used to
protect the archdeacon's face when handling any dangerous substance, lay in a corner, covered with dust, and apparently forgotten. Beside it lay a pair of bellows, equally dusty, the upper
side of which bore this motto encrusted in letters of copper—
Spira, spera! (Blow, and hope!)

Other mottoes were, according to the custom of the hermetic
philosophers, written on the walls in great number; some traced
in ink, others engraved with a metallic point. There were, moreover, Gothic, Hebrew, Greek and Roman characters, pell-mell
together; inscriptions overflowing at random, one upon the other,
the newest effacing the oldest, and all entangled together like the
branches in a thicket, or pikes in an affray. It was, in fact, a

confused medley of all human philosophy, thought and knowledge.
Here and there one shone out above the rest like a banner amid
the spear-heads. Generally, it was some brief Latin or Greek
device, such as the Middle Ages knew so well how to formulate:
Unde? Inde? (Whence? Thence?) *Homo homini monstrum!* (Man a
marvel to man.) *Astra, castra, nomen, numen.* (Thy stars, my camp;
thy name, my power.) Μέγα βιβλίον μέγα κακόν. (A great book, a
great evil.) *Sapere aude.* (Dare to know.) *Fiat ubi vult.* (It bloweth
whither it listeth.) Etc. Sometimes a word apparently devoid of all
meaning, as 'Ανάγκοφαγία (Hard fare)—which perhaps concealed
some bitter allusion to the monastic system; sometimes a simple
maxim of clerical discipline, set forth in a regular hexameter:

> *Cælestem dominum, terrestrem dicito domnum.*

There were also Hebrew hieroglyphics, of which Jehan, who
as yet knew even little Greek, understood nothing; and the whole
was crossed in all directions with stars, figures of men or animals,
and triangles intersecting each other; which contributed in no
small degree to liken the daubed wall of the cell to a sheet of paper
over which a monkey has been dragging about a penful of ink.

The general appearance of the cell, in short, was one of neglect
and ruin; and the sorry condition of the utensils led to the conjecture that their owner had for some time been distracted from
his labours by other cares.

This master, however, bending over a vast manuscript, adorned
with singular paintings, seemed tormented with a thought which
mingled constantly with his meditations. At least, so Jehan judged
from hearing him exclaim, with the pensive pauses of a dreamer,
who thinks aloud:

'Yes; so Manou asserted and Zoroaster taught! the sun is born
of fire; the moon of the sun. Fire is the soul of the universe; its
elementary atoms are diffused and in constant flow throughout
the world, by an infinite number of channels. At the points where
these currents cross each other in the heavens they produce light;
at their points of intersection in the earth they produce gold.
Light—gold; the same thing. From fire to the concrete state. The
difference between the visible and the palpable, the fluid and the
solid, in the same substance—between steam and ice—nothing
more. These are not mere dreams; it is the general law of Nature.
But how are we to wrest from science the secret of this general
law? Why! this light which bathes my hand is gold! these same
atoms expanded in harmony with a certain law only require to be
condensed in accordance with a certain other law! And how?
Some have thought it was by burying a sunbeam. Averroës—yes,
it was Averroës—Averroës interred one under the first column to

the left in the sanctuary of the Koran, in the great mosque of Cordova; but the vault may not be opened, to see if the operation be successful, until eight thousand years have passed.'

'The devil!' said Jehan to himself, 'here's a long while to wait for a crown.'

'Others have thought,' continued the archdeacon, musing, 'that it would be better to operate upon a ray of Sirius. But it is difficult to obtain one of his rays pure, because of the simultaneous presence of other stars, whose rays mingle with it. Flamel esteemed it more simple to operate upon terrestrial fire. Flamel! there's predestination in the name! *Flamma!*—Yes, fire. That is all. The diamond is in charcoal; gold is in fire. But how to extract it? Magistri affirms that there are certain feminine names which possess a charm so sweet and mysterious that it suffices to pronounce them during the operation. Let us read what Manou says on the matter: "Where women are honoured, the divinities rejoice; where they are despised, it is useless to pray to God. A woman's mouth is ever pure; it is like running water, like a sunbeam. A woman's name should be pleasing, soft and fanciful, should end with a long vowel, and resemble words of benediction." Yes, the sage is right; in truth, Maria—Sophia—Esmeral . . . . Damnation! Again that thought.'

And he closed the book with violence.

He passed his hand across his brow, as if to drive away the idea which possessed him; then he took from the table a nail and a small hammer, the handle of which was curiously painted in cabalistic characters.

'For some time,' said he, with a bitter smile, 'I have failed in all my experiments; one idea possesses me, and sears my brain like a red-hot iron. I have not even been able to discover the secret of Cassiodoros, whose lamp burned without wick or oil—and yet a simple matter.'

'A plague upon it!' said Jehan through his teeth.

'A single wretched thought, then,' continued the priest, 'is enough to make a man weak or mad! Oh! how Claude Pernelle would laugh at me—she who could not for a moment turn aside Nicolas Flamel from his pursuit of the great work! What! I hold in my hand the magic hammer of Ezekiel! At every blow which the formidable rabbi, from the depths of his cell, struck upon this nail with this hammer, that one of his enemies whom he had condemned, were he two thousand leagues off, sank a cubit's depth into the earth, which swallowed him up. The king of France himself, in consequence of having one evening inconsiderately knocked at the door of the thaumaturgus, sank up to the knees in the pavement of his own city of Paris. This happened three centuries ago. Well! I have the hammer and the nail, and yet these implements are no more formidable in my hands than a club in the hands of a maker of edged tools. And yet it is only necessary to discover the magic word which Ezekiel pronounced as he struck upon the nail.'

'Nonsense!' thought Jehan.

'Come, let us try,' resumed the archdeacon, eagerly. 'If I succeed, I shall behold a blue spark flash from the head of the nail. *Emen-hetan! Emen-hetan!* That's not it. *Sigeani! Sigeani!* May this nail open the grave for whosoever bears the name of Phœbus! .... A curse upon it! still, again, eternally the same idea!'

And he flung the hammer from him angrily. Then he sank so deep into his armchair and over the table that Jehan lost sight of him behind the high back of the chair. For some moments he saw nothing but his fist convulsively clenched upon a book. All at once, Dom Claude arose, took a pair of compasses, and silently engraved upon the wall, in capital letters, this Greek word:

ΑΝΑΓΚΗ

'My brother is mad,' said Jehan to himself; 'it would have been much simpler to have written *Fatum*—every one is not obliged to know Greek.'

The archdeacon resumed his seat in his armchair, and leaned his head on both his hands, like a sick man whose brow is heavy and burning.

The student watched his brother in surprise. He, who carried his heart in his hand, who observed no other law in the world but the good old law of Nature, who allowed his passions to flow according to their natural tendency, and in whom the lake of powerful emotions was always dry, so assiduous was he every morning in making new channels to drain it—he knew not how furiously the sea of the human passions ferments and boils when all egress is denied to it, how it accumulates, how it swells, how it overflows, how it hollows out the heart, how it breaks forth in repressed sobs and stifled convulsions, until it has rent its dykes and burst its bed. The austere and icy exterior of Claude Frollo, that cold surface of rugged and inaccessible virtue, had always misled Jehan. The jovial student had never dreamt of the lava, deep and furious, which boils beneath the snowy crest of Ætna.

We know not whether any sudden perception of this kind crossed his mind; but, feather-brain though he was, he understood that he had seen what he ought not to have seen, that he had surprised the soul of his elder brother in one of its most secret attitudes—and that he must not let Claude perceive it. Seeing that the archdeacon had relapsed into his former immobility, he withdrew his head very softly, and made some noise with his feet outside the door, like some one just arriving and giving notice of his approach.

'Come in,' cried the archdeacon from the interior of his cell. 'I was expecting you; I left the key in the door purposely; come in, Maître Jacques.'

The student entered boldly. The archdeacon, much annoyed by such a visit in such a place, started in his chair. 'What! is it you, Jehan?'

''Tis a J, at any rate,' said the student, with his ruddy, merry and impudent face.

The countenance of Dom Claude resumed its usual, severe expression.

'What brings you hither?'

'Brother,' replied the student, endeavouring to assume a decent, serious and modest demeanour, twirling his cap in his hands with an air of innocence, 'I am come to ask of you—'

'What?'

'A little moral lecture, of which I have great need.' Jehan dared not add aloud, 'and a little money, of which I have still greater need.' This last part of his sentence remained unuttered.

'Sir,' said the archdeacon in a cold tone, 'I am greatly displeased with you.'

'Alas!' sighed the student.

Dom Claude turned half around in his chair and looked steadily at Jehan: 'I am very glad to see you.'

This was a formidable exordium. Jehan prepared for a rough encounter.

'Jehan, I hear complaints of you every day. What affray was that in which you beat with a cudgel a certain little viscount, Albert de Ramonchamp?'

'Oh!' said Jehan; 'a vast thing that! a scurvy page amused himself with splashing the students by making his horse gallop through the mire.'

'How about that Mahiet Fargel, whose gown you tore? *Tunicam dechiraverunt*, (They have torn the robe,) saith the complaint.'

'Pshaw! a sorry Montaigu hood! that's all.'

'The accusation says *tunicam*—not *cappettam*. Do you know Latin?'

Jehan made no answer.

'Yes,' continued the priest, shaking his head, 'this is what study and letters are come to now! The Latin tongue is scarcely understood; the Syriac unknown; the Greek so odious that it is not considered ignorance in the most learned to skip a Greek word without reading it, and to say: *Græcum est, non legitur.*'(It is Greek, it is not read.)

The student raised his eyes boldly. 'Monsieur my brother, doth it please you that I shall explain in good French vernacular that Greek word which is written yonder on the wall?'

'What word?'

''Ανάγκη.'

A slight flush spread over the high cheekbones of the archdeacon, like the puff of smoke announcing externally the secret commotions of a volcano. The student hardly noticed it.

'Well, Jehan,' stammered the elder brother, with an effort, 'what is the meaning of yonder word?'

'FATE.'

Dom Claude turned pale again, and the student pursued carelessly:

'And that word below it, graven by the same hand, 'Ανάγνεία, signifies impurity. You see I know my Greek.'

The archdeacon remained silent. This Greek lesson had set him musing.

Master Jehan, who had all the cunning of a spoiled child, judged the moment a favourable one to venture his request. Assuming, therefore, a particularly soft tone, he began:

'My dear brother, do you hate me so, then, as to look grim at me on account of a few paltry cuffs and blows dealt, in fair fight, amongst a pack of boys and marmosets, *quibusdam marmosetis?* You see I know my Latin, brother Claude.'

But all this fawning hypocrisy had not its accustomed effect on the severe elder brother. Cerberus did not bite at the honey-cake. The archdeacon's brow did not lose a single wrinkle.

'What are you driving at?' said he, dryly.

'Well, in point of fact, this,' answered Jehan, bravely, 'I need money.'

At this bold declaration the archdeacon's face assumed quite a pedagogic and paternal expression:

'You know, Master Jehan, that our fief of Tirechappe only brings in, including both the quit-rents and the rents of the twenty-one houses, thirty-nine pounds eleven pence six Paris farthings. It's half as much again as in the time of the brothers Paclet; but it is not much.'

'I need money,' said Jehan, stoically.

'You know that the official decided that our twenty-one houses were held in full fee of the bishopric, and that we could only redeem this homage by paying to his reverence the bishop two marks of silver gilt, at six Paris pounds each. Now these two marks I have not yet been able to get together. You know it.'

'I know that I need money,' repeated Jehan, for the third time.

'And what would you do with it?'

This question caused a flash of hope to gleam before Jehan's eyes. He resumed his demure, caressing manner.

'Hark you, dear brother Claude—I would not come to you with any evil intention. It is not to cut a dash in the taverns with your money, or to parade the streets of Paris in gold brocade trappings, with my lackeys—*cum meo laquasio*. No, brother; 'tis for a good work.'

'What good work?' asked Claude, somewhat surprised.

'Two of my friends wish to purchase an outfit for the infant of a poor Haudriette widow—it is a charity—it will cost three florins, and I should like to contribute my share.'

'What are the names of your two friends?'

'Pierre l'Assommeur and Baptiste Croque-Oison.' (Peter the Slaughterer and Baptist Crack-Gosling.)

'Humph!' said the archdeacon; 'those are names as fit for a good work as a catapult for the high altar.'

It is certain that Jehan had chosen very badly the names of his two friends. He realized it too late.

'And then,' continued the shrewd Claude, 'what sort of an infant's outfit is it that is to cost three florins, and that for the child of a Haudriette? Since when have the Haudriette widows taken to having brats in swaddling-clothes?'

Jehan broke the ice once more.—'Well, then, I want some money to go and see Isabeau la Thierrye, to-night, at the Val d'Amour.'

'Impure wretch!' exclaimed the priest.

'Ἀναγνεία!' (Impurity!) said Jehan.

This quotation, which the student borrowed, perhaps mischievously, from the wall of the cell, had a singular effect upon the priest. He bit his lip, and his wrath was extinguished in a crimson flush.

'Begone!' said he to Jehan; 'I am expecting some one.'

The scholar made one more effort.

'Brother Claude, give me, at least, one little farthing for something to eat.'

'How far have you got in the decretals of Gratian?' asked Dom Claude.

'I've lost my copy-books.'

'Where are you in the Latin humanities?'

'Somebody has stolen my copy of Horatius.'

'Where are you in Aristotle?'

'I' faith, brother, what father of the Church is it who says the

errors of heretics have ever found shelter amid the thickets of
Aristotle's metaphysics? A fig for Aristotle! I'll never mangle my
religion with his metaphysics.'

'Young man,' continued the archdeacon, 'at the king's last
entry there was a gentleman, named Philippe de Comines, who
wore embroidered on the housings of his horse this device, upon
which I counsel you to meditate: *Qui non laborat non manducet.*' (He
who labours not eats not.)

The student remained silent a moment, his finger in his ear, his
eyes bent on the ground, and an angry countenance.

All at once he turned toward Claude with the brisk motion of
a water-wagtail.

'So, good brother, you refuse to give me a penny to buy me a
crust at the baker's?'

'*Qui non laborat non manducet.*'

At this answer of the inflexible archdeacon, Jehan hid his head
between his hands, like a woman sobbing, and exclaimed, with an
expression of despair, ''Ο τοτοτοτοτοι!' (An exclamation indica-
tive of despair.)

'What does all this mean, sir?' asked Claude, amazed at this
outburst.

'What, indeed?' said the student, and he looked up at Claude
with impudent eyes, into which he had been rubbing his fists, to
make them look as if they were red with tears; 'it is Greek—'tis an
anapest of Æschylus which expresses grief perfectly.'

And here he burst into a laugh, so droll and so ungovernable
that the archdeacon could not help smiling. It was in fact Claude's
fault: why had he so spoiled this boy?

'Oh, good brother Claude,' continued Jehan, emboldened by
this smile, 'see now my broken buskins. Can any tragedy in the
world be more pathetic than boots whose soles are hanging out
their tongues?'

The archdeacon had quickly resumed his former sternness. 'I
will send you new boots, but no money.'

'Only one poor little penny, brother,' persisted the suppliant
Jehan. 'I'll learn Gratian by heart—I'll believe well in God—
I'll be a perfect Pythagoras of science and virtue! Only one little
penny, for pity's sake! Would you have me devoured by famine,
whose jaws are gaping before me, blacker, deeper and more
noisome than Tartarus or than a monk's nose?'

Dom Claude shook his wrinkled head— '*Qui non laborat . . . .*'
Jehan did not let him finish.

'Well, then,' cried he, 'to the devil! Now for a joyous time! I'll
go to the tavern—I'll fight—I'll break pots, and go and see the
wenches!'

Thereupon he hurled his cap at the wall, and snapped his fingers like castanets.

The archdeacon eyed him with gloomy look.

'Jehan, you have no soul.'

'In that case, according to Epicurus, I lack a something, made of another something, which has no name.'

'Jehan, you must think seriously of reform.'

'Oh, come now,' cried the student, looking alternately at his brother and at the alembics on the furnace, 'everything's atwist here; I see—ideas as well as bottles.'

'Jehan, you are on a very slippery, downward path; know you whither you are going?'

'To the tavern,' said Jehan.

'The tavern leads to the pillory.'

''Tis a lantern like any other, and 'twas perhaps the one with which Diogenes found his man.'

'The pillory leads to the gallows.'

'The gallows is a balance which has a man at one end and the whole world at the other. 'Tis fine to be the man.'

'The gallows leads to hell.'

'That's a rousing fire.'

'Jehan, Jehan! The end will be bad.'

''Twill have had a good beginning.'

At this moment the sound of a footfall was heard on the stairs.

'Silence!' said the archdeacon, putting his finger to his lip; 'here is Maître Jacques. Hark you, Jehan,' added he, in a low tone, 'beware of ever speaking of what you have seen and heard here. Hide yourself quickly under this furnace, and do not breathe.'

The student crept under the furnace, and there a happy thought struck him.

'By the way, brother Claude—a florin for not breathing!'

'Silence! I promise it.'

'You must give it to me.'

'Take it, then!' said the archdeacon, throwing him his pouch angrily. Jehan crept under the furnace again, and the door opened.

5

The Two Men in Black

THE personage who entered wore a black gown and a gloomy
mien. What, at the first glance, struck our friend Jehan (who, as
may well be supposed, so placed himself in his corner as to be
able to see and hear everything at his good pleasure) was the
perfect sadness of the garb and the countenance of this new-
comer. A certain meekness at the same time overspread that face;
but it was the meekness of a cat, or of a judge—a sort of affected
gentleness. He was very gray and wrinkled, bordering on sixty; his
eyes blinked, his eyebrows were white, his lip pendulous and his
hands large. When Jehan saw that it was nobody—that is, probably, only a physician or a magistrate—and that this man's nose was
at a great distance from his mouth, a sign of stupidity, he ensconced
himself in his hole, in despair at having to pass an indefinite length of
time in such an uncomfortable position, and in such poor company.

The archdeacon, meanwhile, had not even risen to receive this
person. He motioned to him to be seated on a stool near the door;
and after a few moments' silence, during which he seemed to be
pursuing a previous meditation, he said, to him in a somewhat
patronizing tone, 'Good-day, Maître Jacques.'

'Greeting, maître,' replied the man in black.

In the two ways of pronouncing, on the one hand, this *Maître
Jacques*, and, on the other, this *maître* by itself, the difference
being my lord and sir, between *domine* (sir) and *domne* (sire). It
clearly bespoke the teacher and the disciple.

'Well,' resumed the archdeacon, after another silence, which
Maître Jacques took good care not to break, 'are you succeeding?'

'Alas! maître,' said the other with a sorrowful smile; 'I keep
on blowing. Plenty of ashes, but not a spark of gold.'

Dom Claude made a gesture of impatience.

'I was not talking of that, Maître Jacques Charmolue, but of
the trial of your magician—is it not Marc Cenaine that you call
him?—the butler of the Court of Accounts? Does he confess his
sorcery? Have you been successful with the torture?'

'Alas, no!' replied Maître Jacques, still with his sad smile, 'we
have not that consolation. That man is a stone; we might boil
him at the Pig-market before he would say anything. However, we
spare no pains to get at the truth. He has already every joint
dislocated. We are trying everything we can think of, as saith the
old comic writer Plautus:

Adversum stimulos, laminas, crucesque, compedesque,
Nervos, catenas, carceres, numellas, pedicas, boias. *

But all to no purpose—that man is terrible; I lose my labour with him.'

'You have found nothing further in his house?'

'I' faith, yes,' said Maître Jacques, fumbling in his pouch; 'this parchment. There are words in it which we do not understand. Monsieur the criminal advocate, Philippe Lheuiler, knows, however, a little Hebrew, which he learned in that affair of the Jews of the Kantersten Street, at Brussels.'

So saying, Maître Jacques unrolled a parchment.

'Give it here,' said the archdeacon. And casting his eyes over the scroll, 'Pure magic, Maître Jacques!' cried he. '*Emenhetan!* that is the cry of the witches as they appear at their Sabbath. *Per ipsum, et cum ipso, et in ipso!* (Through Him, and with Him, and in Him!) that is the command which chains the devil down in hell again. *Hax, pax, max!* that has to do with medicine. A spell against the bite of mad dogs. Maître Jacques! you are king's attorney in the ecclesiastical court—this parchment is abominable.'

'We will put the man to the torture again. Here again,' added Maître Jacques rummaging again in his bag, 'is something we found at Marc Cenaine's.'

It was a vessel belonging to the same family as those which covered the furnace of Dom Claude. 'Ah!' said the archdeacon, 'a crucible for alchemy!'

'I confess to you,' replied Maître Jacques, with his timid and constrained smile, 'that I have tried it over the furnace; but I have succeeded no better with it than with my own.'

The archdeacon set about examining the vessel. 'What has he engraved on his crucible?—*Och! och!*—the word to drive away fleas! This Marc Cenaine is an ignoramus. I can easily believe you will not make gold with this! it will do to put in your alcove in the summer, and that is all.'

'Since we are talking of errors,' said the king's attorney, 'I have just been studying the figures on the portal below, before ascending hither. Is your reverence quite sure that the opening of the work of physics is there portrayed on the side toward the Hôtel-Dieu, and that, among the seven nude figures at the feet of Our Lady, that which has wings on his heels is Mercurius?'

'Yes,' replied the priest; ''tis Augustin Nypho who writes it, that Italian doctor who had a bearded demon that acquainted

---

* Against the whips, the searing-irons, and the crosses and the fetters,
  The cords, the chains, the prisons, the stocks, the shackles, the collars.

him with all things. But we will go down, and I will explain to you from the text.'

'Thanks, my maître,' said Charmolue, bowing to the ground. 'By-the-way, I was on the point of forgetting! When doth it please you that I shall apprehend the little sorceress?'

'What sorceress?'

'That gypsy-girl, you know, who comes and dances every day on the Parvis, in spite of the official's prohibition. She has a goat with devil's horns, which is possessed; it reads and writes, understands mathematics like Picatrix, and would suffice to hang all Bohemia. The prosecution is all ready; 'twill soon be got through with. A pretty creature, I warrant on my soul, that dancer—the handsomest black eyes!—two Egyptian carbuncles! When shall we begin?'

The archdeacon was excessively pale.

'I will let you know,' he stammered, in a voice scarcely articulate; then he resumed with an effort, 'Look you to Marc Cenaine.'

'Never fear,' said Charmolue, smiling; 'when I get back I'll have him buckled on the bed of leather again. But he's a devil of a man—he wearies Pierrat Torterue himself, who hath hands larger than my own. As the excellent Plautus saith—

> *Nudus vinctus, centum pondo, es quando pennes perpedes.'* *

'The torture of the wheel! That is the best we have; he shall take a turn at that.'

Dom Claude seemed absorbed in gloomy reverie. He turned toward Charmolue.

'Maître Pierrat . . . . Maître Jacques, I mean—look to Marc Cenaine.'

'Yes, yes, Dom Claude. Poor man! he will have suffered like Mummol. But what an idea! a butler of the Court of Accounts, who must know the text of Charlemagne, *Stryga vel masca*, (Witch or vampire,) to attend the witches' sabbath. As for the girl—'Smeralda, as they call her—I will await your orders. Ah! as we go through the portal, you will explain to me the gardener painted in fresco, that one sees on entering the church—the Sower, is it not? Eh, maître, what are you thinking about?'

Dom Claude, plunged in his own thoughts, heard him no longer. Charmolue, following the direction of his eye, saw that it was fixed mechanically on the large spider's web stretched across the small window. At this moment, a giddy fly, attracted by the March sun, flew into this net and became entangled in it. Upon the vibration of the web, the enormous spider made a sudden rush from his central cell; then at one bound sprang upon the fly, which he bent double with his fore-antennæ, while with his

---

* Bound naked, thou art a hundred weight when thou hangest by the feet.

hideous proboscis he scooped out its head. 'Poor fly!' said the king's attorney of the ecclesiastical court; and he raised his hand to save it. The archdeacon, as if starting out of sleep, held back his arm with convulsive violence.

'Maître Jacques,' cried he, 'meddle not with fate!'

The king's procurator turned in alarm. It seemed as if his arm were held by iron pincers. The eye of the priest was fixed, haggard, wild, and remained glaring on the horrible little group of the spider and the fly.

'Oh! yes,' continued the priest, in a voice which seemed to issue from his very bowels; 'there is the universal symbol! She flies—she is joyous—she emerges into life—she courts the spring, the open air, liberty! Oh! yes, but she strikes against the fatal network—the spider issues from it, the hideous spider! Poor dancer! poor predestined fly! Maître Jacques, I do not interfere! 'tis fate! Alas! Claude, thou art the spider! Claude, thou art also the fly! Thou didst hasten on in search of knowledge, of light, of the sun. Thy only thought was to reach the pure air, the broad day of eternal truth; but, in rushing toward the dazzling loophole which opens upon another world—a world of brightness, of intellect, of science—infatuated fly! insensate sage! thou didst not see the subtle web suspended by destiny between the light and thee. Thou didst madly dash thyself against it, wretched maniac— and now thou dost struggle, with crushed head and mangled wings, between the iron antennæ of fate! Maître Jacques, Maître Jacques, let the spider do its work!'

'I assure you,' said Charmolue, who looked at him without comprehending, 'that I will not touch it. But let go my arm, maître, for mercy's sake! you have a hand like a vice.'

The archdeacon heard him not. 'Oh! fool!' continued he, without taking his eyes off the window. 'And even couldst thou have broken through that formidable web, with thy frail wings, thoughtest thou to have attained the light? Alas! that glass beyond—that transparent obstacle—that wall of crystal harder than brass, which separates all philosophy from the truth—how couldst thou have passed beyond it? Oh! vanity of science! how many sages have come fluttering from afar, to dash their heads against it! How many systems come buzzing to rush pell-mell against this eternal window!'

He was silent. These last ideas, which had insensibly brought back his thoughts from himself to science, appeared to have calmed him. Jacques Charmolue brought him back completely to a sense of reality by addressing to him this question: 'Come now, my maître, when will you come and help me to make gold? I long to succeed.'

The archdeacon shook his head with a bitter smile. 'Maître Jacques, read Michael Psellus, *Dialogus de energiâ et operatione dæmonum.* (Dialogue—philosophical—on the power and agency of evil spirits). What we are doing is not altogether innocent.'

'Speak lower, maître! I fear you are right,' said Charmolue. 'But one must practise a little hermetic philosophy when one is but a poor king's attorney of the ecclesiastical court, at thirty crowns tournois a year. Only, let us speak low.'

At that moment the noise of jaws in the act of mastication, proceeding from under the furnace, struck upon the anxious ear of Charmolue.

'What is that?' he asked.

It was the student, who, very cramped and uneasy in his hiding-place, had managed to discover a stale crust and a corner of mouldy cheese, and had begun to eat, without further ceremony, by way of consolation and breakfast. As he was very hungry, he made a great noise, laying strong emphasis on each mouthful, and this it was that had startled and alarmed the king's attorney.

''Tis a cat of mine,' said the archdeacon, quickly, 'regaling herself under there with a mouse.'

This explanation satisfied Charmolue.

'Why, indeed, maître,' answered he, with a respectful smile, 'every great philosopher has his familiar animal. You know what Servius says—*Nullus enim locus sine genio est.*' (For there is no place without its genius.)

Meanwhile Dom Claude, fearing some new prank of Jehan, reminded his worthy disciple that they had some figures on the portal to study together; and they both quitted the cell, with an exclamation from the student who began seriously to fear that his knees would bear the mark of his chin.

6

*The Effect which Seven Oaths
Produce in the Open Air*

'*Te Deum laudamus!*' (We praise thee, O God!) exclaimed Master Jehan, issuing from his hole, 'the two screech-owls are gone at last. *Och! och!—Hax! pax! max!*—fleas! mad dogs! the devil! I've had enough of their conversation! My head rings like a belfry. Mouldy cheese into the bargain! Whew! let me get down and take the big brother's purse to convert all these coins into bottles.'

He cast a glance of tenderness and admiration into the precious pouch; adjusted his dress; rubbed up his boots; dusted his poor furred sleeves, all gray with ashes; whistled an air; cut a caper; looked around to see if there was anything else in the cell that he could take; scraped up here and there from the furnace some amulet of glassware by way of trinket to give to Isabeau la Thierrye; finally pushed open the door which his brother had left unfastened as a last indulgence, and which he in turn left open as a last piece of mischief; and descended the winding stairs, skipping like a bird.

In the midst of the darkness of the spiral way he elbowed something, which drew aside with a growl. He presumed that it was Quasimodo; and it struck him as so droll that he descended the rest of the stairs holding his sides with laughter, and was still laughing when he got out into the Square.

He stamped his foot when he found himself again on the ground. 'Oh!' said he, 'good and honourable pavement of Paris! Cursed stairs, fit to put the angels of Jacob's ladder out of breath! What was I thinking of to thrust myself into that stone gimlet which pierces the sky, and all to eat bearded cheese and to look at the steeples of Paris through a hole in the wall!'

He advanced a few steps, and caught sight of the two screech-owls, that is to say, Dom Claude and Maître Jacques Charmolue, contemplating one of the carvings on the portal. He approached them on tiptoe, and heard the archdeacon say in a whisper to Charmolue: 'It was William of Paris who had a Job engraven on that stone of the hue of lapis-lazuli, gilded on the edges. Job represents the philosopher's stone, which must be tried and tortured in order to become perfect, as saith Raymon Lulle— *Sub conservatione formæ specificæ salva anima.*'(Under the preservation of a specific form save your souls.)

'That is all one to me,' said Jehan; ''tis I who have the purse.'

At that moment he heard a powerful and sonorous voice behind him pour forth a formidable volley of oaths:—'*Sang-Dieu! Ventre-Dieu! Bé-Dieu! Corps de Dieu! Nombril de Belzébuth! Nom d'un pape! Corne et tonnère!*' (By the blood of God! by the belly of God! by God! by the body of God! by the belly of Beelzebub! by the name of the pope! horns and thunder!)

'My life for it,' exclaimed Jehan; 'that can be none other than my friend Captain Phœbus.'

This name of Phœbus reached the ears of the archdeacon just as he was explaining to the king's attorney the dragon hiding his tail in a bath from whence issued smoke and a king's head. Dom Claude started, stopped short, to the great astonishment of Charmolue, turned round, and saw his brother Jehan accosting a tall officer at the door of the Condelaurier mansion.

It was, in fact, Captain Phœbus de Chateaupers. He was leaning against the corner of the house of his betrothed, and swearing like a Turk.

'By my faith, Captain Phœbus,' said Jehan, grasping his hand, 'you swear with a rare fancy.'

'Blood and thunder!' replied the captain.

'Blood and thunder yourself!' rejoined the student. 'How now, gentle captain? Whence comes this overflow of fine phrases?'

'Pardon me, good comrade Jehan,' cried Phœbus, shaking him by the hand: 'a galloping horse cannot stop short. Now, I was swearing at full gallop. I've just left those silly women, and when I come away I always find my throat full of curses; I must spit them out or strangle—blood and thunder!'

'Will you come and drink?' asked the student.

This proposal calmed the captain.

'I fain would, but I have no money.'

'But I have.'

'Nonsense! let's see it.'

Jehan displayed the pouch before the captain's eyes with dignity and simplicity. Meanwhile, the archdeacon, having left Charmolue quite astounded, had approached them, and halted a few paces distant, watching them both without their noticing him, so absorbed were they in looking at the pouch.

Phœbus exclaimed: 'A purse in your pocket, Jehan! 'tis the moon in a bucket of water; one sees it, but 'tis not there; there is nothing but the reflection. Egad! I will wager they are but pebbles.'

Jehan replied coldly, 'Here are the pebbles wherewith I pave my fob.'

And without another word he emptied the pouch upon a neighbouring post with the air of a Roman saving his country.

'True gold!' growled Phœbus—'Targes! big and little silver pieces! coppers, every two worth one of Tournay! Paris farthings! and real eagle liards. 'Tis dazzling.'

Jehan remained dignified and unmoved. A few liards rolled into the mud; the captain, in his enthusiasm, stooped to pick them up. Jehan withheld him—'Fie, Captain Phœbus de Chateaupers!'

Phœbus counted the coins; and, turning with solemn look toward Jehan, 'Know you, Jehan,' said he, 'that here are three and twenty Paris pence? Whom did you rifle last night in Rue Coupe-Gueule (cut-gullet)?'

Jehan flung back his blonde, curly head, and said, half closing his eyes disdainfully, 'One may have a brother who is an archdeacon and a simpleton!'

'Horns of the devil!' cried Phœbus, 'the worthy man!'

'Let's go and drink,' said Jehan.

'Where shall we go?' said Phœbus; 'to La Pomme d'Eve?'

'No, captain; let us go to the Vieille-Science—An old woman (*vieille*) who saws (*scie*) a basket-handle (*anse*). 'Tis a rebus, and I like that.'

'A plague on rebuses, Jehan; the wine is better at the Pomme d'Eve; and then, by the side of the door there's a vine in the sun which cheers me while I'm drinking.'

'Very well, then; here goes for Eve and her apple,' said the student, taking Phœbus by the arm. 'By the way, my dear captain, you said just now, Rue Coupe-Gueule (cut-gullet). That is a very bad form of speech; we are no longer so barbarous—we say Rue Coupe Gorge (cut-throat).'

The two friends set out toward Pomme d'Eve. It is needless to say that they first gathered up the money, and that the archdeacon followed them.

The archdeacon followed them haggard and gloomy. Was this the Phœbus whose accursed name, ever since his interview with Gringoire, had been mingled with all his thoughts? He knew not; but it was at least a Phœbus; and that magic name was sufficient inducement for the archdeacon to follow the two heedless comrades with stealthy step, listening to their words and observing their slightest gestures with anxious attention. Indeed, nothing was easier than to hear everything they said, so loud they talked, not in the least concerned that the passers-by were taken into their confidence. They talked of duels, wenches, flagons and frolics.

At the turn of a street, the sound of a tambourine reached them from a neighbouring crossway. Dom Claude heard the officer say to the student, 'Thunder! let us hasten our steps.'

'Why, Phœbus?'

'I am afraid lest the gypsy will see me.'

'What gypsy?'

'The little one with a goat.'

'La 'Smeralda?'

'The same, Jehan. I always forget her devil of a name. Let us make haste: she will recognize me, and I would not wish that girl to accost me in the streets.'

'Are you then acquainted with her, Phœbus?'

Here the archdeacon saw Phœbus chuckle, stoop to Jehan's ear, and whisper a few words in it; Phœbus then burst into a laugh, and tossed his head with a triumphant air.

'For a truth?' said Jehan.

'On my soul!' said Phœbus.

'This evening?'

'This evening!'

'Are you sure she will come?'

'Are you a fool, Jehan? Can there ever be any doubt in such matters?'

'Captain Phœbus, you are a lucky soldier.'

The archdeacon overheard all this conversation. His teeth chattered; a visible shiver ran through his whole body. He stopped a moment, leaned against a post like a drunken man, then followed in the track of the two jolly scamps.

When he came up with them again they had changed the subject; and he heard them singing, at the top of their lungs, the refrain:

> *'The lads the dice who merrily throw,*
> *Merrily to the gallows go.'*

7

The Spectre Monk

The celebrated wine-shop of La Pomme d'Eve was situated in the University, at the corner of the Rue de la Rondelle and the Rue du Bâtonnier. It was a very spacious but very low room on the ground floor, with an arched roof, the central spring of which rested on a huge wooden pillar, painted yellow; tables everywhere; shining pewter jugs hung on the wall; always a large number of drinkers; a plenty of wenches; a window on the street; a vine at the door, and over the door a creaking square of sheet-iron, with an apple and a woman painted upon it, rusted by the rain, and swinging in the wind on an iron rod. This kind of weathercock, which looked towards the pavement, was the signboard.

Night was falling; the street was dark; the wine-shop, full of candles, flamed from afar like a forge in the darkness; the noise of glasses and feasting, of oaths and quarrels, could be heard through the broken panes. Through the mist which the heat of the room spread over the front casement, a multitude of swarming figures could be seen confusedly; and from time to time a burst of noisy laughter broke forth from it. The passers-by whose business called them that way hastened by this noisy window without casting their eyes on it. Only, now and then, some little ragged urchin would raise himself on tiptoe as far as the window-sill, and shout into the wine-shop the old bantering cry with which it was then the custom to greet drunkards:

> *'Back to your glasses,*
> *You drunken, drunken asses.'*

One man, however, paced imperturbably back and forth in front of the noisy tavern, looking at it incessantly, and going no farther from it than a pikeman from his sentry-box. He was cloaked up to the nose. This cloak he had just bought of the old clothes man near La Pomme d'Eve, doubtless to protect himself from the cold of a March night—perhaps also to conceal his costume. From time to time he paused before the dim lattice-leaded casement, listened, looked and stamped his foot.

At length the tavern-door opened. It was for this that he seemed to have been waiting. Two tipplers came out. The ray of light which escaped from the door cast a glow for a moment on their jovial faces. The man in the cloak stationed himself under a porch on the other side of the street.

'Thunder and guns!' said one of the two drinkers, ''tis on the stroke of seven—the hour of my appointed meeting!'

'I tell you,' repeated his companion, with a thick utterance, 'that I don't live in the Rue des Mauvaises Paroles (bad words)—*Indignus qui inter mala verba habitat*. (Unworthy he who lives among bad words). I lodge in the Rue Jean Pain Mollet—*in vico Joannis Pain Mollet*—and you are more horned than a unicorn if you say the contrary. Everybody knows that he that gets once upon a bear's back is never afraid—but you've a nose for smelling out a dainty bit, like Saint James-of-the-Hospital.'

'Jehan, my friend, you are drunk,' said the other.

The other replied, staggering: 'It pleases you to say so, Phœbus; but it hath been proved that Plato had the profile of a hound.'

The reader has no doubt already recognized our two worthy friends, the captain and the student. The man who was watching them in the dark appeared also to have recognized them; for he followed with slow steps all the zigzags which the reeling student forced the captain to describe, who, being a more seasoned drinker, had retained all his self-possession. By listening attentively, the man in the cloak was enabled to catch the whole of the following interesting conversation:

'*Corbacque!* (Body o' Bacchus!) try to walk straight, master bachelor; you know that I must leave you. There is seven o'clock. I have to meet a woman.'

'Leave me, then! I can see stars and darts of fire. You are like Dampmartin Castle, that's bursting with laughter.'

'By the warts of my grandmother, Jehan, but this is talking nonsense a little too hard. By the way, Jehan, have you no money left?'

'Monsieur the rector, there is no mistake. The little shambles—*parva boucheria—*'

'Jehan—friend Jehan—you know I have promised to meet that

little girl at the end of the Pont Saint Michel; that I can take her no-where but to La Falourdel's, the old crone of the bridge, and that I must pay for the room. The white-whiskered old jade will give me no credit. Jehan, for pity's sake, have we drunk up the whole of the priest's pouch? Haven't you a penny left?'

'The consciousness of having spent the other hours well is a just and savoury sauce for the table.'

'Belly and guts! a truce to your gibberish. Tell me—you devil of a Jehan—have you any coin left? Give it me, by heaven! or I'll search you all over, were you as leprous as Job, and as mangy as Cæsar.'

'Sir, the Rue Galiache is a street with the Rue de la Verrerie at one end of it, and the Rue de la Tixeranderie at the other.'

'Well—yes—my good friend Jehan—my poor comrade—the Rue Galiache—good—very good. But, in the name of heaven, come to your senses. I want but a few pence, and seven o'clock is the hour.'

'Silence to the song and attention to the chorus:

> '"When mice have every case devour'd,
>   The King of Arras shall be lord;
>   When the sea, so deep and wide,
>   Is frozen o'er at Saint John's tide,
>   Across the ice we then shall see
>   The Arras men their city flee."'

'Well, scholar of Antichrist, mayst thou be strangled with the guts of thy mother!' exclaimed Phœbus; and he gave the tipsy student a rough push, which sent him reeling against the wall, whence he fell gently upon the pavement of Philip Augustus. With a remnant of fraternal pity which never quite forsakes the heart of a drinker, Phœbus rolled Jehan with his foot upon one of those pillows of the poor man which Providence keeps ready at the corner of every street-post in Paris, and which the rich scornfully stigmatize with the name of dung-heaps. The captain placed Jehan's head on an inclined plane of cabbage-stalks, and forth-with the student fell to snoring in a most magnificent bass. Yet the heart of the captain was not wholly free from animosity. 'So much the worse for thee, if the devil's cart picks thee up as it goes by,' said he to the poor, sleeping clerk; and he went his way.

The man in the cloak ceased following him and stopped for a moment beside the prostrate student, as if agitated by indecision; then heaving a deep sigh, he continued to follow the captain.

Like them, we will leave Jehan sleeping under the friendly watch of the bright stars, and speed after them, if it so please the reader.

On turning into the Rue Saint André des Arcs, Captain Phœbus perceived that some one was following him. As he accidentally glanced behind him, he saw a sort of shadow creeping behind him along the walls. He stopped—it stopped; he went on—the shadow went on again also. This, however, gave him very little concern. 'Ah! bah!' said he to himself, 'I have not a penny about me.'

In front of the Collège d'Autun he came to a halt. It was at that college that he shuffled through what he was pleased to call his studies; and from a certain mischievous schoolboy habit which still clung to him, he never passed the front of that college without inflicting on the statue of Cardinal Pierre Bertrand, carved on the right hand of the gateway, the affront of which Priapus complains so bitterly in the satire of Horace, *Olim truncus eram ficulnus.* (I was once a fig-tree). He had done this with so much unrelenting animosity that the inscription, *Eduensis Episcopus* (Bishop of Autun), had become almost effaced. Therefore, he halted before the statue according to his wont. The street was utterly deserted. As he was retagging nonchalantly his doublet with his head thrown back, he saw the shadow approaching him slowly—so slowly that he had full time to observe that this shadow had a cloak and a hat. When it had come up to him, it stopped, and remained as motionless as the statue of Cardinal Bertrand. But it riveted upon Phœbus two intent eyes, glaring with that vague light which issues at night from those of a cat.

The captain was brave, and would have cared little for a robber with a rapier in his hand. But this walking statue, this petrified man, made his blood run cold. At that time there were certain strange rumours afloat about a spectre monk, a nocturnal prowler about the streets of Paris in the night-time, and they now came confusedly to his mind. He stood stupefied for a few moments, then finally broke silence with a laugh.

'Sir,' said he, 'if you be a thief, as I hope is the case, you're just now for all the world like a heron attacking a walnut-shell. My dear fellow, I am the son of a ruined family. Try your hand hard by here. In the chapel of this college there's some wood of the true cross, set in silver.'

The hand of the shadow came forth from under its cloak, and descended upon the arm of Phœbus with the force of an eagle's grip; at the same time the shadow spoke:

'Captain Phœbus de Chateaupers!'

'What, the devil!' said Phœbus; 'you know my name?'

'I know not your name alone,' returned the man in the cloak, with his sepulchral voice; 'but I know that you have an appointment this evening.'

'Yes,' answered Phœbus, in amazement.

'At seven o'clock.'

'In a quarter of an hour.'

'At the Falourdel's.'

'Exactly so.'

'The old hag of the Pont Saint Michel.'

'Of Saint Michel, the archangel, as the Paternoster saith.'

'Impious man!' muttered the spectre. 'With a woman?'

'*Confiteor.*' (I confess).

'Whose name is . . . .'

'La 'Smeralda,' said Phœbus gaily, all his heedlessness having gradually returned to him.

At this name the shadow's grasp shook Phœbus's arm furiously.

'Captain Phœbus de Chateaupers, thou liest!'

Any one who could have seen, at that moment, the captain's inflamed countenance—his leap backwards, so violent that it disengaged him from the clutch which held him—the haughty mien with which he clapped his hand on his sword-hilt—and, in the presence of this wrath, the sullen stillness of the man in the cloak; any one who could have beheld this would have been frightened. There was in it somewhat of the combat of Don Juan and the statue.

'Christ and Satan!' cried the captain; 'that's a word that seldom assails the ear of a Chateaupers! Thou durst not repeat it.'

'Thou liest!' said the shadow coldly.

The captain ground his teeth. Spectre monk—phantom—superstitions—all were forgotten at that moment. He now saw nothing but a man and an insult. 'Ha, it is well!' spluttered he in a voice choking with rage. He drew his sword; then, stuttering, for anger as well as fear makes a man tremble—'Here!' said he, 'on the spot! Come on! Swords! swords! Blood upon these stones!'

But the other did not stir. When he saw his adversary on guard, and ready to lunge, 'Captain Phœbus,' said he, and his voice quivered with bitterness, 'you forgot your assignation.'

The fits of rage of such men as Phœbus are like boiling milk, whose ebullition is calmed by a drop of cold water. These few words brought down the point of the sword which glittered in the captain's hand.

'Captain,' continued the man, 'to-morrow—the day after to-morrow—a month hence—ten years hence—you will find me quite ready to cut your throat. But first go to your assignation.'

'In sooth,' said Phœbus, as if seeking to capitulate with himself, 'a sword and a girl are two delightful things to encounter at a trysting-place; but I cannot see why I should miss one of them for the sake of the other, when I may have both.'

He replaced his sword in his scabbard.

'Go to your assignation,' resumed the unknown.

'Sir,' answered Phœbus, with some embarrassment, 'gramercy for your courtesy. It will, in truth, be time enough to-morrow to chop up father Adam's doublet into slashes and buttonholes. I am beholden to you for allowing me to pass one more agreeable quarter of an hour. I did indeed hope to have laid you quietly in the gutter, and yet be in time for the fair one—the more so as it is genteel to make women wait a little in such cases. But you appear to be a mettlesome chap, and it is safer to put off our game until to-morrow. I will, therefore, betake myself to my appointment. It is for the hour of seven, as you know.' Here Phœbus scratched his ear. 'Ah! by my halidom! I forgot! I have not a penny to pay the price of the garret, and the old hag will want to be paid beforehand; she distrusts me.'

'Here is the wherewithal to pay.'

Phœbus felt the stranger's cold hand slip into his a large coin. He could not help taking the money, and grasping the hand. 'God's truth!' he exclaimed, 'but you're a good fellow!'

'One condition,' said the man. 'Prove to me that I was wrong, and that you spoke truth. Hide me in some corner whence I may see whether this woman be really she whose name you uttered.'

'Oh,' replied Phœbus, ''tis all one to me. We will take the Saint Martha chamber. You can see at your ease from the kennel hard by.'

'Come, then,' rejoined the shadow.

'At your service,' said the captain. 'I know not indeed whether you be not Messer Diabolus *in propria persona* (in person). But let us be good friends to-night; to-morrow I'll pay you all debts, of purse and of sword.'

They set out again at a rapid pace. In a few minutes the sound of the river below apprised them that they were upon the bridge of Saint Michel, then covered with houses.

'I will first let you in,' said Phœbus to his companion; 'then I will go fetch the wench who was to wait for me near the Petit-Châtelet.'

That companion made no reply; since they had been walking side by side, he had not uttered a word. Phœbus stopped before a low door and knocked loudly. A light appeared through the cracks of the door. 'Who's there?' cried a mumbling voice.

'By the body! by the belly! by the head of God!' answered the captain.

The door opened instantly, and revealed to the new-comers an old woman and an old lamp, both of which trembled. The old woman was bent double—dressed in rags—with a shaking head, pierced by two small eyes, and coiffed with a dish clout—wrinkled everywhere, on hands and face and neck—her lips receding under her gums—and all round her mouth she had tufts of white hair, which gave her the whiskered and demure look of a cat.

The interior of the hovel was no less dilapidated than herself; the walls were of plaster; black rafters ran across the ceiling; a dismantled fireplace; cobwebs in every corner; in the middle of the room a tottering company of maimed stools and tables; a dirty child played in the ash-heap; and at the farther end a stair-case, or rather a wooden ladder, led to a trap-door in the ceiling.

As he entered this den, Phœbus's mysterious companion drew his cloak up to his eyes. Meanwhile, the captain, swearing like a Turk, hastened 'to make the sun flash from a crown-piece,' as saith our admirable Régnier.

'The Saint Martha room,' said he.

The old woman addressed him as monseigneur, and deposited the crown in a drawer. It was the coin which the man in the black cloak had given Phœbus. While her back was turned, the ragged, dishevelled little boy, who was playing in the ashes, went slyly to the drawer, abstracted the crown-piece, and put in its place a dry leaf which he had plucked from a fagot.

The hag beckoned to the two gentlemen, as she called them, to follow her, and ascended the ladder before them. On reaching the upper story, she placed her lamp upon a chest; and Phœbus, like a frequenter of the house, opened the door of a dark closet. 'Go in there, my dear fellow,' said he to his companion. The man in the cloak complied without uttering a word; the door closed upon him; he heard Phœbus bolt it, and, a moment afterward, go down-stairs again with the old woman. The light had disappeared.

8

The Advantage of Windows Overlooking the River

CLAUDE FROLLO (for we presume that the reader, more clever than Phœbus, has seen in this whole adventure no other spectre monk than the archdeacon himself) Claude Frollo groped about for some moments in the dark hole into which the captain had bolted him. It was one of those nooks such as architects sometimes leave at the junction of the roof and the outer wall. The vertical section of this kennel, as Phœbus had so aptly termed it, would have made a triangle. There was neither window nor skylight, and the pitch of the roof prevented one from standing upright. Claude, therefore, crouched down in the dust and plaster which crum-

bled beneath him. His head was burning. Feeling about him with
his hands, he found on the floor a bit of broken glass, which he
pressed to his brow, its coolness affording him some relief.

What was passing at that moment in the dark soul of the archdeacon? God and himself alone could tell.

In what fatal order did he arrange in imagination La Esmeralda,
Phœbus, Jacques Charmolue, his younger brother, so beloved, yet
abandoned by him in the mire, his archdeacon's cassock, his
reputation, perhaps at stake at the Falourdel's—all these images,
all these adventures? It is impossible to say; but it is certain that
these ideas formed a horrible group in his mind.

He had been waiting a quarter of an hour; it seemed to him
that he had grown a century older. All at once he heard the wooden
staircase creak; some one was coming up. The trap-door opened
once more; light reappeared. In the worm-eaten door of his nook
there was a crack of considerable width; to this he glued his face.
Thus he could see all that went on in the adjoining chamber.
The cat-faced old woman appeared first through the trap-door
with lamp in hand; then Phœbus, twirling his moustache; then a
third person, that lovely, graceful creature, La Esmeralda. The
priest beheld her rise from below like a dazzling apparition.
Claude trembled; a cloud spread over his eyes; his pulse beat
violently; everything swam before him; he no longer saw or
heard anything.

When he came to himself again, Phœbus and Esmeralda were
alone, seated on the wooden chest, beside the lamp, whose light
revealed to the archdeacon's eyes their two youthful figures, and
a miserable pallet at the farther end of the garret.

Beside the pallet was a window, broken, through the panes of
which, like a cobweb upon which rain has fallen, could be seen a
small patch of sky, with the moon in the distance resting on a
pillow of soft clouds.

The young girl was blushing, confused, palpitating. Her long
drooping lashes shaded her glowing cheeks. The face of the officer,
to which she dared not lift her eyes, was radiant. Mechanically,
and with a charming air of embarrassment, she traced with the
tip of her finger meaningless lines upon the bench, and watched
her finger. Her feet were not visible, for the little goat was nestling
upon them.

The captain was very gallantly arrayed. At his neck and wrists
he had tufts of embroidery, the great elegance of the day.

Dom Claude could only hear with great difficulty what they
said to each other, through the humming of the blood that was
boiling in his temples.

An amorous chitchat is a very commonplace sort of thing. It is a perpetual 'I love you,'—a very monotonous and very insipid musical strain to indifferent ears, unless set off with a few flourishes and grace-notes. But Claude was no indifferent listener.

'Oh!' said the young girl, without lifting her eyes, 'despise me not, Monseigneur Phœbus; I feel that what I am doing is wrong.'

'Despise you, my pretty dear,' replied the officer with a consequential and modish air of gallantry; 'despise you, good lack! and why should I?'

'For having accompanied you.'

'On that score, my charmer, we don't at all agree. I ought not only to despise you, but to hate you.'

The young girl looked at him in affright: 'Hate me! What, then, have I done?'

'For requiring so much solicitation.'

'Alas!' said she, ''tis because I am breaking a vow—I shall never find my parents—the amulet will lose its virtue; but what then? What need have I for father and mother now?'

As she thus spoke she fixed upon the captain her large, dark eyes, moist with joy and tenderness.

'Deuce take me, if I understand you,' exclaimed Phœbus.

Esmeralda remained silent for a moment; then a tear fell from her eye, a sigh from her lips, and she said, 'Oh, monseigneur, I love you.'

Such a perfume of chastity, such a charm of virtue, surrounded the young girl that Phœbus did not feel quite at his ease with her. These words, however, emboldened him. 'You love me!' said he with rapture, and he threw his arm round the gypsy's waist. He had only been waiting for this opportunity.

The priest saw him, and tested with the tip of his finger the point of a dagger concealed in his breast.

'Phœbus,' continued the Bohemian, gently disengaging her waist from the tenacious hands of the captain, 'you are good—you are generous—you are handsome—you have saved me—me, who am but a poor gypsy foundling. I have long dreamed of an officer who should save my life. It was of you that I dreamed, before I knew you, my Phœbus. The officer of my dream had a beautiful uniform like yours, a grand air, a sword. Your name is Phœbus—'tis a beautiful name. I love your name, I love your sword. Draw your sword, Phœbus, that I may see it.'

'Child!' said the captain; and he unsheathed his rapier with a smile.

The gypsy-girl looked at the hilt, then at the blade; examined with adorable curiosity the cypher upon the guard, and kissed the weapon, saying, 'You are the sword of a brave man. I love my captain.'

Phœbus again took advantage of the situation to imprint on her lovely bent neck a kiss which made the girl start up as red as a cherry. It made the priest grind his teeth in the darkness.

'Phœbus,' resumed the gypsy, 'let me talk to you. Just walk about a little, that I may see you at your full height, and hear the sound of your spurs. How handsome you are!'

The captain rose to comply, chiding her at the same time with a smile of satisfaction.

'What a child you are! By the way, my charmer, have you ever seen me in my state uniform?'

'Alas, no!'

'Ha, that is really fine!'

Phœbus returned and seated himself beside her, but much closer than before.

'Hark you, my dear . . . .'

The gypsy gave him a few little taps on the lips with her pretty hand with a childish playfulness, full of gaiety and grace.

'No, no, I will not listen. Do you love me? I want you to tell me if you love me.'

'Do I love thee, angel of my life?' cried the captain, half kneeling before her. 'My body, my blood, my soul—all are thine —all are for thee. I love thee, and have never loved any but thee.'

The captain had repeated this phrase so many times, on many similar occasions, that he delivered it all in a breath, and without making a single mistake. At this impassioned declaration, the gypsy raised to the dingy ceiling a look full of angelic happiness. 'Oh!' murmured she, 'this is the moment when one should die!'

Phœbus thought 'the moment' a good one to steal another kiss, which tortured the wretched archdeacon in his lair.

'Die!' cried the amorous captain; 'what are you talking of, my lovely angel? 'Tis the time to live—or Jupiter is but a scamp. Die at the beginning of so sweet a thing! By the horns of the bull! what a jest! That would not do. Listen, my dear Similar— Esmenarda—Your pardon! but you have so prodigiously Saracen a name that I never can get it straight; I get entangled in it like a brier.'

'Good heavens!' said the poor girl, 'and I thought my name pretty because of its singularity! But, since it displeases you, I would that I were called Goton.'

'Ah! do not weep for such a trifle, my graceful maid; 'tis a name to which one must get used, that is all. When once I know it by heart, 'twill come ready enough. So hark ye, my dear Similar. I adore you passionately; I love you so that 'tis really marvellous. I know a little girl that's bursting with rage about it.'

The jealous girl interrupted him. 'Who?'

'What matters that to us?' said Phœbus; 'do you love me?'

'Oh!' said she.

'Well, that is all. You will see how I love you, too. May the great devil Neptunus spear me if I don't make you the happiest creature alive. We'll have a pretty little lodging somewhere. I'll make my archers parade under your windows; they're all on horseback, and don't care a fig for Captain Mignon's men. There are spear-men, crossbow-men and culverin-men. I'll take you to the great musters of the Parisians at the Grange de Rully. It is very magnificent. Eighty thousand armed men; thirty thousand white harnesses, short coats or coats of mail; the sixty-seven banners of the trades; the standards of the Parliament, of the Chamber of Accounts, of the treasury of the generals, of the assistants of the mint—the devil's own turnout, in short. I will conduct you to see the lions of the king's palace—which are wild beasts. All the women like that.'

For some moments the young girl, absorbed in her pleasing reflections, had been dreaming to the sound of his voice, without heeding the meaning of his words.

'Oh, how happy you will be!' continued the captain, and at the same time he gently unbuckled the gypsy's girdle.

'What are you doing?' she said quickly. This 'act of violence' had roused her from her reverie.

'Nothing,' answered Phœbus. 'I was only saying that you must abandon all this garb of folly and street-running when you are with me.'

'When I am with thee, my Phœbus!' said the young girl tenderly. She again became pensive and silent.

The captain, emboldened by her gentleness, clasped her waist without her making any resistance; then began softly to unlace the poor child's bodice, and so greatly disarranged her neckerchief that the panting priest beheld the gypsy's lovely shoulder emerge from the gauze, round and dusky like the moon rising through the mists of the horizon.

The young girl let Phœbus have his way. She seemed unconscious of what he was doing. The bold captain's eyes sparkled.

All at once she turned towards him.

'Phœbus,' said she, with an expression of infinite love, 'instruct me in thy religion.'

'My religion!' cried the captain, bursting into a laugh. 'I instruct you in my religion. Blood and thunder! what do you want with my religion?

'That we may be married,' she replied.

The captain's face assumed a mingled expression of surprise, disdain, carelessness and licentious passion.

'Bah,' said he, 'why should one marry?'

The gypsy turned pale, and her head drooped sadly on her breast.

'My sweet love,' resumed Phœbus, tenderly, 'what are all these foolish ideas? Marriage is a grand affair, to be sure. Is any one less loving for not having spouted Latin in a priest's shop?'

While speaking thus in his softest tone, he approached extremely near the gypsy-girl; his caressing hands resumed their place around the lithe, slender waist. His eye kindled more and more, and everything showed that Master Phœbus was on the verge of one of those moments in which Jupiter himself commits so many follies that the good Homer is obliged to summon a cloud to his rescue.

Dom Claude meanwhile saw all from his hiding-place. Its door was made of decayed puncheon staves, leaving between them ample passage for his look of a bird of prey. This brown-skinned, broad-shouldered priest, hitherto condemned to the austere virginity of the cloister, was quivering and boiling in the presence of this night-scene of love and voluptuousness. The young and lovely girl, her garments in disorder, abandoning herself to the ardent young man, seemed to infuse molten lead into his veins. An extraordinary agitation shook him; his eye sought with lustful desire to penetrate beneath all those unfastened pins. Any one who could then have seen the wretched man's countenance close against the worm-eaten bars might have thought they saw a tiger's face glaring from the depths of a cage at some jackal devouring a gazelle.

Suddenly, with a rapid motion, Phœbus snatched off the gypsy's neckerchief. The poor girl, who had remained pale and dreamy, started up as if suddenly awakened; she hastily drew back from the enterprising officer; and casting a glance at her bare neck and shoulders, blushing, confused, and mute with shame, she crossed her two lovely arms upon her bosom to hide it. But for the flush that crimsoned her cheeks, to see her thus silent and motionless, one might have thought her a statue of Modesty. Her eyes were bent upon the ground.

But the captain's action had exposed the mysterious amulet which she wore about her neck.

'What is that?' said he, seizing this pretext to approach once more the beautiful creature whom he had just alarmed.

'Touch it not,' she replied quickly; ''tis my protector. It will help me to find my family again, if I remain worthy to do so. Oh, leave me, sir! My mother! my poor mother! my mother! where art thou? Come to my rescue! Have pity, Captain Phœbus; give me back my neckerchief.'

Phœbus drew back, and said coldly:

'Oh, young lady, I see plainly that you do not love me.'

'Not love him!' exclaimed the unhappy child, and at the same time clinging to the captain and drawing him to a seat by her side. 'Not love thee, my Phœbus? What art thou saying, wicked man, to rend my heart? Oh, come—take me—take all—do with me as thou wilt—I am thine. What matters the amulet to me now? What matters my mother to me now? Thou art my mother, since I love thee. Phœbus, my beloved Phœbus, dost thou see me? 'Tis I. Look at me. 'Tis that little girl whom thou wilt surely not repulse—who comes, who comes herself to seek thee. My soul, my life, my body, my person, all is one thing—which is thine, my captain. Well, no! let us not marry, since it bothers thee; and then, what am I? A wretched girl of the gutters—while thou, Phœbus, art a gentleman. A fine thing, truly! a dancer wed an officer! I was mad! No, Phœbus, no; I will be thy mistress—thy amusement—thy pleasure—when thou wilt—a girl who will be only thine. I was only made for that, soiled, despised, dishonoured; but what then—loved! I shall be the proudest and the happiest of women. And when I grow old and ugly, Phœbus—when I am no longer fit to love thee, my lord, thou wilt still suffer me to serve thee. Others will embroider scarfs for thee; I, thy servant, will take care of them. Thou wilt let me polish thy spurs, brush thy doublet, and dust thy riding-boots. Thou wilt have this much pity; wilt thou not, my Phœbus? Meantime, take me. Here, Phœbus, all this belongs to thee. Only love me. We gypsy-girls need nothing more —air and love.'

So saying, she threw her arms around the officer's neck; she looked up at him imploringly and smiled through her tears. Her delicate neck rubbed against his cloth doublet with its rough embroidery. She twisted her beautiful, half-naked limbs around his knees. The intoxicated captain pressed his burning lips to those lovely African shoulders. The young girl, her eyes cast upward to the ceiling, her head thrown back, quivered, all palpitating beneath this kiss.

All at once, above the head of Phœbus, she beheld another head —a green, livid, convulsed face, with the look of a lost soul; beside this face there was a hand which held a dagger. It was the face and hand of the priest; he had broken open the door, and he was there. Phœbus could not see him. The young girl was motionless, frozen mute at the frightful apparition—like a dove which chances to raise its head at the instant when the hawk is glaring into her nest with his round eyes.

She could not even utter a cry. She saw the poniard descend upon Phœbus, and rise again reeking.

'Malediction!' said the captain, and he fell.

She fainted.

As her eyes closed, as all consciousness left her, she thought she felt a fiery touch upon her lips, a kiss more burning than the executioner's branding-iron.

When she recovered her senses, she was surrounded by soldiers of the watch; they were carrying off the captain weltering in his blood; the priest had disappeared; the window at the back of the room, looking upon the river, was wide open; they picked up a cloak which they supposed to belong to the officer, and she heard them saying around her:

''Tis a sorceress who has stabbed a captain.'

BOOK EIGHT

I

The Crown Changed into a Withered Leaf

GRINGOIRE and the whole Court of Miracles were in a state of terrible anxiety. For a whole month no one knew what had become of La Esmeralda, which sorely grieved the Duke of Egypt and his friends the vagrants; nor what had become of her goat, which redoubled Gringoire's sorrow. One night the gypsy had disappeared; and since that time had given no signs of life. All search had proved fruitless. Some malicious 'street tumblers' told Gringoire they had met her that same evening in the neighbourhood of the Pont Saint Michel, walking off with an officer; but this husband after the fashion of Bohemia was an incredulous philosopher, and besides, he, better than any one else, knew to what a point his wife was chaste. He had been able to judge what invincible modesty resulted from the two combined virtues of the amulet and the gypsy, and he had mathematically calculated the resistance of that chastity multiplied into itself. On that score, at least, his mind was at ease.

Thus he could not explain her disappearance. It was a great grief to him. He would have grown thinner upon it, had that been possible. He had forgotten everything else, even to his literary pursuits, even his great work, *De figuris regularibus et irregularibus* (concerning regular and irregular figures), which he intended to have printed with the first money he should procure. (For he raved about printing ever since he had seen the *Didascolon* of Hugues de Saint Victor printed with the celebrated types of Vindelin of Spires).

One day, as he was passing sadly before the Criminal Tournelle, he perceived a crowd at one of the doors of the Palace of Justice.

'What is there?' he inquired of a young man who was coming out.

'I know not, sir,' replied the young man. ''Tis said a woman is being tried for the murder of a man-at-arms. As there seems to be something of sorcery in the business, the bishop and the judge of the Bishop's Court have interposed in the cause; and my brother, the archdeacon of Josas, can think of nothing else. Now, I wished to speak to him; but could not get at him for the crowd —which vexes me mightily, for I am in need of money.'

'Alas! sir,' said Gringoire, 'I would I could lend you some; but, though my breeches are in holes, it's not from the weight of crown-pieces.'

He dared not tell the young man that he knew his brother, the archdeacon, to whom he had not returned since the scene in the church—a negligence which embarrassed him.

The student went his way, and Gringoire followed the crowd going up the staircase of the Great Hall. To his mind there was nothing equal to the sight of a criminal trial for dispelling melancholy; the judges are generally so delightfully stupid. The people with whom he had mingled were moving on and elbowing each other in silence. After a slow and tiresome shuffling along a long gloomy passage, which wound through the Palace like the intestinal canal of the old edifice, he arrived at a low door opening into a hall, which his tall stature permitted him to overlook above the undulating heads of the crowd.

The hall was huge and ill-lighted, which latter circumstance made it seem still larger. The day was declining; the high, pointed windows admitted but a faint ray of light, which faded before it reached the vaulted ceiling, an enormous trellis-work of carved wood, whose countless figures seemed to move confusedly in the shadows. There were already several candles lighted here and there upon tables, and glimmering over the heads of the clerks bending over musty documents. The front of the hall was occupied by the crowd; to the right and left were lawyers in their robes seated at tables; at the farther end, upon a raised platform, were a number of judges, the last rows of whom were lost in the darkness—with immovable and sinister-looking faces. The walls were dotted with innumerable fleurs-de-lis. A large crucifix might be vaguely descried above the judges, and everywhere there were pikes and halberds, which the light of the candles seemed to tip with fire.

'Sir,' said Gringoire to one of his neighbours, 'who are all those persons yonder, ranged like prelates in council?'

'Sir,' answered the neighbour, 'those are the councillors of the High Chamber on the right; and the councillors of inquiry on the left; the masters in black gowns, and the honourables in scarlet ones.'

'Yonder, above them,' continued Gringoire, 'who is that big red-faced fellow who is perspiring so?'

'That is monsieur the president.'

'And those sheep behind him?' proceeded Gringoire, who, as we have already said, loved not the magistracy—which arose, possibly, from the ill-will he bore the Palace of Justice since his dramatic misadventure.

'They are messieurs, the masters of requests of the king's household.'

'And that wild boar in front of him?'

'That is the clerk to the court of parliament.'

'And that crocodile on the right?'

'Maître Philippe Lheulier, advocate extraordinary to the king.'

'And that great black cat to the left?'

'Maître Jacques Charmolue, king's attorney in the ecclesiastical court, with the gentlemen of the officiality.'

'And now, sir,' said Gringoire, 'what are all those good folk about?'

'They are trying some one.'

'Trying whom? I see no prisoner.'

''Tis a woman, sir. You can not see her. Her back is toward us, and she is concealed by the crowd. Stay, yonder she is, where you see that group of halberds.'

'Who is the woman?' asked Gringoire. 'Do you know her name?'

'No, sir; I am but just come. I suppose, however, that there is sorcery in the matter, since the judge of the Bishop's Court is present at the trial.'

'Well,' said our philosopher, 'we will see all these men of the gown devour human flesh. It is as good a sight as any other.'

'Think you not, sir,' observed his neighbour, 'that Maître Jacques Charmolue looks very mild?'

'Hum!' answered Gringoire, 'I distrust a mildness which hath pinched nostrils and thin lips.'

Here the bystanders imposed silence on the two talkers. An important deposition was being heard.

'My lords,' an old woman in the middle of the hall was saying, whose face was so concealed beneath her garments that she might have been taken for a walking bundle of rags—'my lords, the thing is as true as it is true that my name is Falourdel, and that for forty years I have lived on the Pont Saint Michel, and paid regularly my rent, dues and quit-rent. The door is opposite the house of Tassin Caillart, the dyer, who lives on the side looking up the river. An old woman now! a pretty girl once, my gentlemen! Some one said to me but lately, "Mother Falourdel, spin not too much of an evening; the devil is fond of combing the distaffs of old women with his horns. 'Tis certain that the spectre monk that roamed last year about the Temple now wanders in the City. Take care, La Falourdel, that he doesn't knock at your door." One evening I was spinning at my wheel, when there comes a knock at my door. I ask who is there. Some one swears. I open the door. Two men enter—one in black, with a handsome officer. Of the one in black nothing could be seen but his eyes—two coals of fire. All the rest was cloak and hat. And so they say to me, "The Saint Martha room." 'Tis my upper chamber, my lords—my best. They give me a crown. I lock the crown in my drawer, and I say, "This shall go to buy tripe to-morrow at the Gloriette shambles." We go up-stairs. On reaching the upper room, and while my back was turned, the black man disappears. This startled me a bit. The officer, who was as handsome as a great lord, goes down-stairs with me. He leaves the house. In about time enough to spin a quarter of a bobbin, he comes back again with a beautiful young girl—a doll who would have shone like the sun had her hair been dressed. She had with her a goat, a great he-goat, whether black or white I no longer remember. That set me to thinking. The girl —that was no concern of mine;—but the goat! I don't like those animals; they have a beard and horns—it is like a man; and then they smack of the witches' sabbath. However, I said nothing. I had the crown-piece. That was only fair; was it not, my lord judge? I show the captain and the girl into the up-stairs room, and leave them alone—that is to say, with the goat. I go down and get to my spinning again. I must tell you that my house has a ground-floor and a floor above; the back of it looks upon the river, like the other houses on the bridge, and the windows, both of the ground-floor and of the chamber, open upon the water. Well, as I was saying, I had got to my spinning. I know not why I fell to thinking of the spectre monk whom the goat had put into my head again—and then the beautiful girl was rather strangely tricked out. All at once I hear a cry overhead, and something falls on the floor, and the window opens. I run to mine, which is beneath it, and I see a dark mass drop past my eyes into the water. It was a phantom clad like a priest. The moon was shining; I saw it quite plainly. It was swimming toward the City. Then, all of a tremble, I call the watch. The gentlemen of the police come in; and being merry, not know-ing at first what was the matter, they fell to beating me. I explained to them. We go up-stairs, and what do we find? My poor chamber all blood—the captain stretched out at full length with a dagger in his neck—the girl pretending to be dead—and the goat all in a fright. "Pretty work!" say I. "It will take more than fifteen days to wash that floor. It must be scraped. It will be a terrible job." They carry off the officer—poor young man, and the girl, all in disorder. But wait. The worst is, that on the next day, when I went to get the crown to buy tripe, I found a withered leaf in its place.'

The old woman ceased. A murmur of horror ran through the audience.

'That phantom, that goat, all that smacks of sorcery,' said one of Gringoire's neigbours.

'And that withered leaf!' added another.

'No doubt,' continued a third, ''tis some witch who has dealings

with the spectre monk to plunder officers.' Gringoire himself was
not far from considering this combination as alarming and
probable.

'Woman Falourdel,' said the president majestically, 'have you
nothing further to communicate to the court?'

'No, my lord,' replied the crone, 'unless it is that in the report
my house has been called a crazy, filthy hovel—which is an outrageous way of talking. The houses on the bridge are not so goodly
as some, because there are so many people there; but the butchers
dwell there, for all that, and they are rich men, married to fine,
proper sort of women.'

The magistrate whom Gringoire had likened to a crocodile
now rose.

'Silence,' said he; 'I beg you, gentlemen, to bear in mind that
a poniard was found on the accused. Woman Falourdel, have
you brought the leaf into which the crown was changed that the
demon gave you?'

'Yes, monseigneur,' answered she; 'I found it. Here it is.'

An usher of the court handed the withered leaf to the crocodile,
who, with a doleful shake of the head, passed it on to the president,
who gave it to the king's attorney in the ecclesiastical court; and
thus it made the circuit of the hall.

'It is a birch-leaf,' said Maître Jacques Charmolue; 'an additional proof of magic.'

A counsellor then began:

'Witness, two men went up-stairs together in your house—the
black man whom you first saw disappear, then swim the Seine in
priest's clothes, and the officer. Which of the two gave you the
crown?'

The old woman considered for a moment, and then said 'It was
the officer.' A murmur ran through the crowd.

'Ha,' thought Gringoire, 'that shakes my conviction.'

But Maître Philippe Lheulier, king's advocate extraordinary,
again interposed.

'I will recall to these gentlemen that in the deposition taken at
his bedside, the murdered officer, while admitting that he had a
confused idea, at the moment when the black man accosted him,
that it might be the spectre monk, added that the phantom had
eagerly pressed him to keep his appointment with the prisoner;
and on his, the captain's, observing that he was without money,
he had given him the crown which the said officer had paid La
Falourdel. Hence, the crown is a coin from hell.'

This conclusive observation appeared to dispel all the doubts
of Gringoire and the other sceptics in the audience.

'Gentlemen, you are in possession of the documents,' added the king's advocate, seating himself; 'you can consult the deposition of Phœbus de Chateaupers.'

At that name the accused sprang up; her head rose above the throng. Gringoire, aghast, recognized Esmeralda.

She was pale; her hair, once so gracefully plaited and spangled with sequins, hung in disorder; her lips were livid; her hollow eyes were terrible. Alas!

'Phœbus!' said she, wildly; 'where is he? Oh, messeigneurs! before you kill me, tell me, for pity's sake, whether he yet lives!'

'Be silent, woman,' answered the president; 'that is no concern of ours.'

'Oh, have mercy! tell me if he is alive,' continued she, clasping her beautiful, emaciated hands; and her chains were heard as they brushed along her dress.

'Well,' said the king's advocate roughly, 'he is dying. Does that content you?'

The wretched girl fell back on her seat, speechless, tearless, white as a wax figure.

The president leaned over to a man at his feet, who wore a gilt cap and black gown, a chain round his neck and a wand in his hand:

'Usher, bring in the second accused.'

All eyes were now turned toward a small door, which opened, and, to the great agitation of Gringoire, made way for a pretty goat with gilded hoofs and horns. The dainty creature paused for a moment on the threshold, stretching out its neck as though, perched, on the summit of a rock, it had before its eyes a vast horizon. All at once it caught sight of the gypsy-girl; and leaping over the table and a registrar's head in two bounds it was at her knees. It then rolled gracefully on its mistress's feet, begging for a word or a caress; but the prisoner remained motionless, and poor Djali itself obtained not a glance.

'Eh, why—'tis my villainous beast,' said the old Falourdel; 'I recognize the pair of them well enough.'

Jacques Charmolue interposed.

'If it please you, gentlemen, we will proceed to the examination of the goat.'

Such was, in fact, the second prisoner. Nothing was more common in those times than to indict animals for sorcery. Among others, in the accounts of the provost's office for 1466, may be seen a curious detail concerning the expenses of the trial of Gillet-Soulart and his sow, executed 'for their demerits' at Corbeil. Everything is there: the cost of the pen in which the sow was put; the five hundred bundles of short fagots from the wharf of Morsant; the three pints of wine and the bread, the last repast of the victim, shared in a brotherly manner by the executioner; down to the eleven days' custody and feed of the sow, at eight Paris pence each. Sometimes they even went beyond animals. The capitularies of Charlemagne and Louis le Débonnaire impose severe penalties on fiery phantoms which may presume to appear in the air.

Meanwhile, the king's attorney in the ecclesiastical court cried out: 'If the demon which possesses this goat, and which has resisted all exorcisms, persist in its deeds of witchcraft—if he alarm the court with them—we warn him that we shall be obliged to put in requisition against it the gibbet or the stake.'

Gringoire broke out into a cold perspiration. Charmolue took from a table the gypsy's tambourine, and, presenting it in a certain manner to the goat, he asked the latter:

'What o'clock is it?'

The goat looked at him with an intelligent eye, raised her gilt foot, and struck seven blows. It was indeed seven o'clock. A movement of terror ran through the crowd.

Gringoire could no longer contain himself.

'She'll be her own ruin,' cried he aloud; 'you see that she knows not what she is doing!'

'Silence among the louts at the end of the hall!' said the bailiff, sharply.

Jacques Charmolue, by means of the same manœuvres with the tambourine, made the goat perform several other tricks connected with the day of the month, the month of the year, etc., which the reader has already witnessed. And, by an optical illusion peculiar to judicial proceedings, these same spectators who had probably more than once applauded in the public squares Djali's innocent magic, were terrified at it beneath the roof of the Palace of Justice. The goat was indisputably the devil.

It was still worse when, the king's attorney having emptied on the floor a certain leathern bag full of detached letters which Djali wore about her neck, they beheld the goat sort out with its foot from among the scattered alphabet the fatal name: *Phœbus*. The sorcery of which the captain had been the victim seemed unanswerably proved; and, in the eyes of all, the gypsy-girl, that enchanting dancer, who had so often dazzled the passers-by with her grace, was no longer anything but a frightful vampire.

However, she gave no sign of life; neither the graceful evolutions of Djali, nor the threats of the magistrates, nor the muttered imprecations of the audience—nothing seemed to reach her ear.

In order to arouse her, a sergeant was obliged to shake her unmercifully, while the president solemnly raised his voice:

'Girl, you are of Bohemian race, addicted to deeds of witchcraft. You, in complicity with the bewitched goat, implicated in the charge, did, on the night of the 29th of March last, wound and poniard, in concert with the powers of darkness, by the aid of charms and spells, a captain of the king's archers, Phœbus de Chateaupers by name. Do you persist in denying it?'

'Horrible!' exclaimed the young girl, hiding her face with her hands. 'My Phœbus! Oh, this is indeed hell!'

'Do you persist in your denial?' demanded the president, coldly.

'Do I deny it!' said she, in terrible accents; and she rose with flashing eyes.

The president continued bluntly:

'Then how do you explain the facts laid to your charge?'

She answered in a broken voice:

'I have already told you I know not. It is a priest—a priest whom I do not know—an infernal priest, who pursues me!'

'Just so,' replied the judge; 'the spectre monk!'

'Oh, gentlemen, have pity! I am only a poor girl . . . .'

'Of Egypt,' said the judge.

Maître Jacques Charmolue interposed sweetly—'In view of the sad obstinacy of the accused, I demand the application of the torture.'

'Granted,' said the president.

A shudder ran through the whole frame of the wretched girl. She rose, however, at the order of the halberdiers, and walked with a tolerably firm step, preceded by Charmolue and the priests of the officiality, between two rows of halberds, toward a false door, which suddenly opened and closed again behind her, which produced upon the unhappy Gringoire the effect of a horrible mouth which had just devoured her.

When she disappeared, a plaintive bleating was heard. It was the little goat wailing.

The sitting of the court was suspended. A counsellor having remarked that the gentlemen were fatigued, and that it would be a long time for them to wait before the torture was over, the president answered that a magistrate must be ready to sacrifice himself to his duty.

'What a troublesome, vexatious jade!' said an old judge, 'to get herself put to the question when one has not supped!'

2

Continuation of the
Crown Changed into a Withered Leaf

AFTER ascending and descending some steps in passages so dark
that they were lighted in broad day by lamps, Esmeralda, still
surrounded by her lugubrious attendants, was pushed forward by
the sergeants of the Palace, into a room of sinister aspect. This
chamber, circular in shape, occupied the ground floor of one of
those great towers which still in our day rise above through the
layer of modern structures with which modern Paris has covered
the old city. There are no windows to this cellar; no other opening
than the entrance, which was low and closed by an enormous
iron door. Nevertheless, light was not lacking. A furnace had been
constructed in the thickness of the wall; a large fire was lighted in
it, which filled the vault with its crimson reflection, and stripped
of every ray a miserable tallow-dip placed in a corner. The iron
grating which served to close the furnace being raised at that
moment only showed at the mouth of the flaming chasm against
the dark wall the lower edge of its bars, like a row of sharp, black
teeth set at regular intervals, which made the furnace look like
the mouth of one of those legendary dragons that spit forth fire.
By the light which it cast, the prisoner saw all about the room
frightful instruments whose use she did not understand. In the
middle was a leathern mattress laid almost flat upon the ground,
over which hung a thong with a buckle fastened to a copper ring
which a flat-nosed monster carved in the keystone of the vault
held between his teeth. Tongs, pincers, large plowshares, were
heaped inside the furnace, and were heating red-hot, promiscuously upon the burning coals. The blood-red glow of the furnace
illuminated in the chamber only a confused mass of horrible things.

This Tartarus was called simply the question chamber.

Upon the bed was seated carelessly Pierrat Torterue, the
official torturer. His underlings, two square-faced gnomes, with
leathern aprons and tarpaulin coats, were turning about the irons
on the coals.

In vain the poor girl called up all her courage; on entering this
room she was seized with horror.

The sergeants of the bailiff of the Palace ranged themselves on
one side; the priests of the Bishop's Court on the other. A clerk
and a table with writing materials were in one corner.

Maître Jacques Charmolue approached the gypsy with a very
sweet smile.

'My dear child,' said he, 'do you still persist in your denial?'

'Yes,' she replied in a faint voice.

'In that case,' resumed Charmolue, 'it will be our painful duty to question you more urgently than we should otherwise wish. Have the goodness to sit down on this bed. Maître Pierrat, give place to mademoiselle, and shut the door.'

Pierrat rose with a growl.

'If I shut the door,' muttered he, 'my fire will go out.'

'Well, then, my good fellow,' replied Charmolue, 'leave it open.'

Meanwhile, La Esmeralda remained standing. That leathern bed, on which so many poor wretches had writhed, frightened her. Terror froze her very marrow; there she stood bewildered and stupefied. At a sign from Charmolue, the two assistants laid hold of her and seated her on the bed. They did her no harm; but when those men touched her—when that leather touched her—she felt all her blood flow back to her heart. She looked wildly around the room. She fancied she saw moving and walking from all directions towards her, to crawl upon her body and pinch and bite her, all those hideous implements of torture, which, as compared to the instruments of all sorts she had hitherto seen, were like what bats, centipedes and spiders are to birds and insects.

'Where is the doctor?' asked Charmolue.

'Here,' answered a black gown that she had not observed before. She shuddered.

'Mademoiselle,' resumed the fawning voice of the attorney of the ecclesiastical court, 'for the third time, do you persist in denying the facts of which you are accused?'

This time she could only make a sign with her head; her voice failed her.

'You persist?' said Jacques Charmolue. 'Then it grieves me deeply, but I must fulfil the duty of my office.'

'Monsieur, the king's procurator,' said Pierrat gruffly, 'with what shall we begin?'

Charmolue hesitated a moment, with the doubtful grimace of a poet seeking rhyme.

'With the boot,' said he at last.

The unfortunate creature felt herself so utterly abandoned by God and man that her head fell upon her breast like a thing inert, destitute of all strength.

The torturer and the doctor approached her both at once. The two assistants began rummaging in their hideous arsenal.

At the sound of those frightful irons the unfortunate girl quivered like a dead frog which is being galvanized. 'Oh,' murmured she, so low that no one heard her, 'Oh, my Phœbus!' She then relapsed into her former immobility and petrified silence.

This spectacle would have rent any heart but the hearts of judges. She resembled a poor sinful soul tormented by Satan beneath the scarlet wicket of hell. The miserable body upon which that frightful array of saws, wheels and racks was to fasten—the being whom the rough hands of executioners and pincers were to handle,— was, then, this gentle, fair and fragile creature; a poor grain of millet which human justice was handing over to the terrible mills of torture to grind.

Meanwhile, the horny hands of Pierrat Torterue's assistants had brutally bared that beautiful leg, that little foot, which had so often delighted the by-standers with their grace and loveliness in the streets of Paris.

''Tis a pity,' growled out the torturer as he remarked the grace and delicacy of their form.

Had the archdeacon been present he would assuredly have bethought him at that moment of his symbol of the spider and the fly. Presently the poor girl saw through the mist which spread before her eyes the 'boot' approach; soon she saw her foot, encased between the iron-bound boards, disappear in the frightful apparatus. Then terror restored her strength.

'Take off that,' she cried frantically; and starting up all dishevelled, 'Mercy!'

She sprang from the bed to fling herself at the feet of the king's attorney; but her leg was held fast in the heavy block of oak and iron-work, and she sank upon the boot more helpless than a bee with a leaden weight upon its wings.

At a sign from Charmolue she was replaced on the bed and two coarse hands fastened round her small waist the leathern strap which hung from the ceiling.

'For the last time, do you confess the facts of the charge?' asked Charmolue, with his imperturbable benignity.

'I am innocent.'

'Then, mademoiselle, how do you explain the circumstances brought against you?'

'Alas, sir, I know not.'

'You deny, then?'

'All!'

'Proceed,' said Charmolue to Pierrat.

Pierrat turned the handle of the screwjack; the boot tightened, and the wretched victim uttered one of those horrible shrieks which have no orthography in any human language.

'Stop,' said Charmolue to Pierrat.

'Do you confess?' said he to the gypsy.

'Everything!' cried the wretched girl. 'I confess! I confess! Mercy!'

She had not calculated her strength when she faced the torture. Poor child! whose life hitherto had been so joyous, so pleasant, so sweet; the first pang vanquished her.

'Humanity forces me to tell you,' observed the king's attorney, 'that, in confessing, you have only to look for death.'

'I hope so,' said she; and she sank back upon the leathern bed lifeless, bent double, suspended by the thong buckled round her waist.

'So, my beauty, hold up a bit,' said Maître Pierrat, raising her. 'You look like the golden sheep that hangs about Monsieur of Burgundy's neck.'

Jacques Charmolue raised his voice:

'Clerk, write. Bohemian girl, you confess your participation in the love-feasts, witches' sabbaths and practices of hell, with wicked spirits, witches and hobgoblins? Answer.'

'Yes,' said she, so low that it was lost in a whisper.

'You confess to having seen the ram which Beelzebub causes to appear in the clouds to call together the witches' sabbath, and which is only seen by sorcerers?'

'Yes.'

'You confess to having adored the heads of Bophomet, those abominable idols of the Templars?'

'Yes.'

'To having had habitual dealings with the devil in the shape of a tame goat, included in the prosecution?'

'Yes.'

'Lastly, you avow and confess having, with the assistance of the demon and of the phantom commonly called the spectre monk, on the night of the twenty-ninth of March last, murdered and assassinated a captain named Phœbus de Chateaupers?'

She raised her large staring eyes to the magistrate and replied, as if mechanically, without effort or emotion:

'Yes.'

It was evident that she was utterly broken.

'Write down, registrar,' said Charmolue; and addressing the torturers: 'Let the prisoner be unbound and taken back into court.'

When the prisoner had been 'unbooted' the attorney of the ecclesiastical court examined her foot, still paralyzed with pain. 'Come,' said he, 'there's no great harm done. You cried out in time. You could dance yet, my beauty!'

He then turned to his acolytes of the officiality.

'At length justice is enlightened! that is a consolation, gentlemen! Mademoiselle will at least bear this testimony, that we have acted with all possible gentleness.'

The End of the
Crown Changed into a Withered Leaf

WHEN, pale and limping, she re-entered the court, a general hum of pleasure greeted her. On the part of the audience, it was that feeling of gratified impatience which one experiences at the theatre, at the conclusion of the last interlude of a play, when the curtain rises and the last act is about to begin. On the part of the judges, it was the hope of supping ere long. The little goat, too, bleated with joy. She tried to run to her mistress, but they had tied her to the bench.

Night had quite set in. The candles, whose number had not been increased, gave so little light that the walls of the hall could not be seen. Darkness enveloped every object in a sort of mist. A few apathetic judges' faces were just visible. Opposite to them, at the extremity of the long hall, they could distinguish a vague white patch against the dark background. It was the accused.

She had dragged herself to her place. When Charmolue had magisterially installed himself in his, he sat down; then rose and said, without exhibiting too much of the self-complacency of success, 'The accused has confessed all.'

'Bohemian girl,' continued the president, 'you have confessed all your acts of sorcery, prostitution and assassination upon Phœbus de Chateaupers?'

Her heart was wrung. She was heard sobbing amid the darkness.

'Whatever you will,' answered she feebly; 'but kill me quickly.'

'Monsieur, the king's attorney in the ecclesiastical court,' said the president, 'the chamber is ready to hear your requisitions.'

Maître Charmolue produced a tremendous roll of paper, from which he began to read, with much gesticulation and the exaggerated emphasis of the bar, a Latin oration, wherein all the proofs of the suit were drawn up in Ciceronian periphrases, flanked with quotations from Plautus, his favourite comic author. We regret that we can not present our readers with this extraordinary composition. The orator delivered it with wonderful action. Before he had finished the exordium the perspiration was starting from his brow, and his eyes from his head.

All at once, in the middle of a finely turned period, he broke off, and his countenance, usually mild enough, and indeed stupid, became black as a thunder-cloud.

'Gentlemen,' cried he (this time in French, for it was not in the scroll), 'Satan plays so large a part in this affair that here he is present at our councils, and making mock of their majesty. Behold him!'

So saying, he pointed to the little goat, which, seeing Charmolue gesticulate, thought it was but right she should do the same, and had seated herself on her haunches, mimicking as well as she could, with her fore-feet and bearded head, the pathetic pantomime of the king's attorney in the ecclesiastical court. This was, it may be remembered, one of her prettiest tricks. This incident, this final proof, produced a great effect. The goat's feet were bound together, and the king's attorney resumed the thread of his eloquence.

It was very long, but the peroration was admirable. The last sentence ran thus—the reader may imagine the hoarse voice and breathless gestures of Maître Charmolue:

'*Ideo, domini, coram stryga demonstrata, crimine patente, intentione criminis existente, in nomine sanctæ ecclesiæ Nostræ Dominæ Parisiensis, quæ est in saisina habendi omnimodam altam et bassam justitiam in illa hac intemerata Civitatis insula, tenore præsentium declaramus nos requirere, primo, aliquandam pecuniariam indemnitatem; secundo, amendationem honorabilem ante portalium maximum Nostræ Dominæ ecclesiæ cathedralis; tertio, sententiam in virtute cujus ista stryga cum sua capella, seu in trivio vulgariter dicto* la Grève, *seu in insula exeunte in fluvio Sequanæ, juxta pointam jardini regalis, executatæ sint!*' *

He put on his cap and sat down.

'Alas!' sighed Gringoire, heart-broken; '*bassa tatinitas!*' (low latinity!)

Another man in a black gown near the prisoner then rose; it was her advocate. The fasting judges began to murmur.

'Mr. Advocate, be brief,' said the president.

'Monsieur, the president,' replied the advocate, 'since the defendant has confessed the crime, I have only one word to say to these gentlemen. Here is a clause in the Salic law: "If a witch hath eaten a man, and if she be convicted of it, she shall pay a fine of eight thousand deniers, which make two hundred pence in gold." May it please the chamber to condemn my client to the fine?'

---

* Therefore, gentlemen, the witchcraft being proved, and the crime made manifest, as likewise the criminal intention—in the name of the holy church of our Lady of Paris, which is seised of the right of all manner of justice, high and low, within this inviolate island of the City—we declare, by the tenor of these presents, that we require, firstly, some pecuniary compensation; secondly, penance before the great portal of the cathedral church of Our Lady; thirdly, a sentence, by virtue of which this witch, together with her she-goat, shall, either in the public square, commonly called *La Grève*, or in the island standing forth in the river Seine, adjacent to the point of the royal gardens, be executed.

'A clause that has become obsolete,' said the advocate extraordinary to the king.

'I deny it,' replied the prisoner's advocate.

'Put it to the vote,' said a councillor; 'the crime is manifest—and it is late.'

The question was put to the vote without leaving the hall. The judges nodded assent; they were in haste. Their capped heads were seen uncovered one after another in the dusk at the lugubrious question addressed to them in a low voice by the president. The poor accused seemed to be looking at them, but her bewildered eye no longer saw anything.

The clerk of the court began to write; then he handed the president a long scroll of parchment.

The unhappy girl then heard a stir among the people, the pikes clash and a chilling voice say:

'Bohemian girl, on such day as it shall please our lord the king, at the hour of noon, you shall be taken in a tumbrel, in your shift, barefoot, with a rope around your neck, before the great portal of Notre-Dame; and there you shall do penance with a wax torch of two pounds weight in your hand; and from thence you shall be taken to the Place de Grève, where you shall be hanged and strangled on the Town gibbet, and likewise this, your goat; and you will pay to the Bishop's Court three lions of gold, in reparation of the crimes, by you committed and confessed, of sorcery, magic, debauchery and murder, upon the person of the sieur Phœbus de Chateaupers. So God have mercy on your soul!'

'Oh! 'tis a dream!' murmured she; and she felt rough hands bearing her away.

4

'Leave All Hope Behind'

In the Middle Ages, when an edifice was complete, there was almost as much of it under the ground as above it. Unless built upon piles, like Notre-Dame, a palace, a fortress or a church had always a double bottom. In cathedrals it was, as it were, another subterranean cathedral, low, dark, mysterious, blind, mute, under the upper nave which was overflowing with light and resounding night and day with the music of bells and organs. Sometimes it was a sepulchre. In palaces and fortresses it was a prison; sometimes a sepulchre also, sometimes both together. Those mighty masses of masonry, whose mode of formation and slow growth we have explained elsewhere, had not foundations merely; they might be said to have roots branching out under ground in chambers, galleries and staircases, like the structure above. Thus, churches, palaces and fortresses were buried midway in the earth. The vaults of a building were another building into which one descended instead of ascended, and whose subterranean stories extended downward beneath the pile of exterior stories of the edifice, like those forests and mountains which are reversed in the mirror-like waters of a lake beneath the forests and mountains of the banks.

At the fortress of Saint Antoine, at the Palace of Justice of Paris, at the Louvre, these subterranean edifices were prisons. The stories of these prisons, as they went deeper into the ground, grew narrower and darker. They formed so many zones, presenting various degrees of horror. Dante could never have imagined anything better for his hell. These tunnel-like dungeons usually ended in a deep hole, shaped like the bottom of a tub, where Dante placed his Satan, and where society placed those condemned to death. When once a miserable human existence was there interred, then farewell light, air, life, *ogni speranza* (all hope behind); it only came forth to the gibbet or to the stake. Sometimes it rotted there; human justice called that *forgetting*. Between mankind and himself the condemned one felt an accumulation of stones and jailers weighing down upon his head, and the entire prison, the massive fortress, was but one enormous complicated lock that barred him out of the living world.

It was in a dungeon hole of this kind, in the *oubliettes* excavated by Saint Louis in the *in pace* (prison in which monks were shut up for life) of the Tournelle, that—for fear of her escaping, no doubt —Esmeralda had been placed when condemned to the gibbet, with the colossal Palace of Justice over her head. Poor fly, that could not have stirred the smallest of its stones!

Assuredly, Providence and mankind had been equally unjust; such an excess of misfortune and torture was not necessary to crush so frail a creature.

She was there, lost in the darkness, buried, entombed. Any one who could have beheld her in this state, after having seen her laugh and dance in the sun, would have shuddered. Cold as night, cold as death, not a breath of air in her tresses, not a human sound in her ear, no longer a ray of light in her eyes, bent double, loaded with chains, crouching beside a jug and a loaf of bread upon a little straw in the pool of water formed beneath her by the damp oozing of her cell, without motion, almost without breath, she was now scarcely sensible even to suffering. Phœbus, the sunshine, noonday, the open air, the streets of Paris, the dances with the applauses of the spectators, the sweet prattlings of love with the officer; then the priest, the old crone, the poniard, blood, the torture, the gibbet—all this did indeed float before her mind, now as a harmonious and golden vision, again as a hideous nightmare. But it was now no more than a horrible and indistinct struggle veiled in darkness, or than distant music played above on the earth, and which was no longer audible at the depth to which the unfortunate creature had fallen.

Since she had been there she neither waked nor slept. In that misery, in that dungeon, she could no more distinguish waking from sleeping, dreams from reality, than she could the day from the night. All was mingled, broken, floating, confusedly scattered in her mind. She felt nothing, knew nothing, thought nothing; at best she only dreamed. Never did living creature plunge so far into the realm of nothingness.

Thus benumbed, frozen, petrified, had she scarcely noticed the sound of a trap-door which was twice or thrice opened somewhere above her, without even admitting a ray of light, and through which a hand had thrown a crust of black bread. Yet this was her only remaining communication with mankind—the periodical visit of the jailer. One thing alone still mechanically occupied her ear; over her head the dampness filtered through the mouldy stones of the vault, and a drop of water dropped from them at regular intervals. She listened stupidly to the noise made by this drop of water as it fell into the pool beside her.

This drop of water falling into the pool was the only movement still stirring around her, the only clock to mark the time, the only sound that reached her of all the noises made upon the surface of the earth.

Although, indeed, she also felt, from time to time, in that sink of mire and darkness, something cold passing here and there over her foot or her arm, and she shuddered.

How long had she been there? She knew not. She had a recollection of a sentence of death pronounced somewhere against some one; then she was borne away, and she awaked icy cold in the midst of night and silence. She had crawled along upon her hands, then iron rings cut her ankles and chains clanked. She discovered that all around her was wall, that underneath her were flag-stones covered with water, and a bundle of straw; but there was neither lamp nor air-hole. Then she seated herself upon the straw, and occasionally, for a change of position, on the lowest of some stone steps in her dungeon.

At one time she had tried to count the dark moments measured for her by the drop of water; but soon that mournful employment of her sick brain had ceased of its own accord and left her in stupor.

At length, one day, or one night (for midnight and noon had the same hue in this sepulchre), she heard above her a louder noise than that usually made by the turnkey when he brought her bread and jug of water. She raised her head and saw a reddish light through the crevices of the sort of trap-door made in the arch of the *in pace*.

At the same time the heavy lock creaked, the trap-door grated on its rusty hinges, turned, and she beheld a lantern, a hand, and the lower part of the bodies of two men, the door being too low for her to see their heads. The light pained her so acutely that she shut her eyes.

When she reopened them the door was closed, the lantern was placed on a step of the staircase, one man alone was standing before her. A black gown fell to his feet, a cowl of the same hue concealed his face. Nothing was visible of his person, neither his face nor his hands. It looked like a long black winding-sheet standing upright, beneath which something seemed to move. She gazed fixedly for some moments at this sort of spectre. Still neither she nor he spoke. They were like two statues confronting each other. Two things only seemed to have life in the vault : the wick of the lantern, which sputtered from the dampness of the atmosphere, and the drop of water from the roof, which interrupted this irregular crepitation by its monotonous plash, and made the reflection of the lantern quiver in concentric waves upon the oily water of the pool.

At length the prisoner broke silence.

'Who are you?'

'A priest.'

The word, the accent, the sound of the voice made her start. The priest continued in a hollow tone :

'Are you prepared?'

'For what?'

'To die.'

'Oh!' said she, 'will it be soon?'

'To-morrow.'

Her head, which she had raised with a look of joy, again sank upon her bosom.

'That is very long yet,' murmured she; 'what difference would a day make to them?'

'Are you then very unhappy?' asked the priest after a short silence.

'I am very cold,' replied she.

She took her feet in her hands, a habitual gesture with unfortunate creatures who are cold, and which we have already observed in the recluse of the Tour-Roland, and her teeth chattered.

The priest's eyes appeared to be wandering from under his hood around the dungeon.

'Without light! without fire! in the water! It is horrible!'

'Yes,' answered she with the bewildered air which misery had given her. 'The day belongs to every one; why do they give me only night?'

'Do you know,' resumed the priest, after another silence, 'why you are here?'

'I think I knew once,' said she, passing her thin fingers across her brow, as if to assist her memory, 'but I know no longer.'

All at once she began to weep like a child.

'I want to go away from here, monsieur. I am cold—I am afraid —and there are creatures that crawl over my body.'

'Well, follow me.'

So saying, the priest took her arm. The poor girl was chilled to her very vitals, yet that hand felt cold to her.

Oh!' murmured she, ''tis the icy hand of death. Who are you?'

The priest threw back his hood; she looked: it was that sinister visage which had so long pursued her—that demon's head which had appeared to her at La Falourdel's over the adored head of her Phœbus—that eye which she last saw glaring beside a dagger.

This apparition, always so fatal to her, and which had thus driven her on from misfortune to misfortune, even to an ignominious death, roused her from her stupor. It seemed to her that the veil which had clouded her memory was rent asunder. All the details of her mournful adventure, from the nocturnal scene at La Falourdel's to her condemnation at the Tournelle, rushed upon her mind at once, not vague and confused as heretofore, but clear, distinct, vivid, living, terrible. These recollections, almost obliterated by excess of suffering, were revived at the sight of the sombre figure before her, as the heat of fire brings out afresh upon white paper invisible letters traced upon it with sympathetic ink. All the wounds of her heart seemed to be torn open afresh and bleed simultaneously.

'Ha!' she cried, pressing her hands to her eyes, with a convulsive shudder, 'it is the priest!'

Then she let fall her unnerved arm and remained sitting, with bent head, eyes fixed on the ground, mute, and still trembling.

The priest gazed at her with the eye of a hawk which has long hovered high in the heavens above a poor meadow-lark cowering in the wheat, gradually and silently descending in ever lessening circles, and suddenly swooping upon his prey like a flash of lightning, and holds it panting between his talons.

She began to murmur in a low tone:

'Finish! finish! the last blow!' And her head sank between her shoulders in terror, like a sheep awaiting the blow of the butcher's axe.

'You look upon me with horror, then,' he asked at length.

She made no answer.

'Do you look on me with horror?' he repeated.

Her lips contracted as if she were smiling.

'Yes,' said she; 'the executioner taunts the condemned! For months he pursues me, threatens me, terrifies me. But for him, my God, how happy I would be! It is he who has cast me into this abyss! Oh, heavens! it was he who killed—it was he who killed him—my Phœbus!'

Here she burst into sobs, and raising her eyes toward the priest:

'Oh! wretch! who are you? what have I done to you? do you then hate me so? Alas! what have you against me?'

'I love thee!' cried the priest.

Her tears suddenly ceased; she eyed him with the vacant stare of an idiot. He had fallen on his knees and was devouring her with eyes of flame.

'Dost thou hear? I love thee!' cried he again.

'What love!' ejaculated the unhappy creature.

He continued:

'The love of a damned soul!'

Both remained silent for several minutes, crushed under the weight of their emotions—he maddened, she stupefied.

'Listen,' said the priest at last, and a strange calm came over him; 'thou shalt know all. I am about to tell thee what hitherto I have scarcely dared tell myself, when I secretly questioned my conscience, in those dead hours of the night when it is so dark that it seems as though God no longer sees us. Listen. Before I saw thee, young girl, I was happy . . .'

'And I too!' sighed she feebly.

'Interrupt me not! Yes, I was happy; or, at least, I thought so. I was pure; my soul was filled with limpid light. No head was raised more proudly or more radiantly than mine. Priests consulted me on chastity, doctors on doctrines. Yes, science was all in all to me; it was a sister—and a sister sufficed me. Not but that, growing older, other ideas came across my mind. More than once my flesh was thrilled as a woman's form passed by. That force of sex and passion which, foolish youth, I had thought stifled forever, had more than once shaken convulsively the chain of the iron vows which bind me, miserable wretch, to the cold stones of the altar. But fasting, prayer, study, the macerations of the cloister again made the spirit ruler of the body. And then I shunned women. Morever, I had but to open a book, for all the impure vapours of the brain to evaporate before the splendour of science. In a few minutes I saw the gross things of earth flee far away, and I was once more calm and serene, bathed in the tranquil light of eternal truth. So long as the Demon sent only vague shadows of women to attack me, passing casually before my eyes, in the church, in the streets, in the fields, and scarcely recurring in my dreams, I vanquished him easily. Alas! if the victory has not remained with me, it is the fault of God, who made not man and the Demon of equal strength. Listen. One day . . .'

Here the priest paused, and the prisoner heard deep sighs burst from his bosom, each one seeming like the last breath of agony.

He resumed:

'One day, I was leaning on the window of my cell. What book was I reading? Oh! all that is whirling now in my brain. I was reading. The window opened upon a square. I heard the sound of a tambourine and music. Vexed at being thus disturbed in my reverie, I glanced into the square. What I saw, others saw beside myself—and yet it was not a spectacle for mortal eye. There, in the middle of the pavement—it was noon, brilliant sunshine—a creature was dancing, a creature so beautiful that God would have preferred her to the Virgin—would have chosen her for His mother—would have been born of her, had she existed when He was made man. Her eyes were black and lustrous; amidst her raven hair, certain locks, through which the sunbeams shone, were glistening like threads of gold. Her feet moved so swiftly that they appeared indistinct, like the spokes of a wheel revolving rapidly. Around her head, amongst her ebon tresses, were plates of metal, which sparkled in the sun, and formed about her temples a diadem of stars. Her dress, thickest with spangles, twinkled, blue and with a thousand sparks, like a summer night. Her brown and pliant arms twined and untwined about her waist like two silken scarfs. Her figure was of surpassing beauty. Oh! how resplendent that form, which stood out like something luminous even in the very light of the sun itself! Alas! young girl, it was thou! Surprised, intoxicated, charmed, I allowed myself to gaze upon thee. I looked at thee so long that suddenly I shuddered with affright. I felt that the hand of Fate was upon me.'

The priest, oppressed by emotion, again paused for a moment; then continued:

'Already half fascinated, I strove to cling to something and to stay myself from falling. I recalled the snares which Satan had already set for me. The creature before me was of that preternatural beauty which can only be of heaven or hell. That was no mere girl moulded of our common clay, and faintly lighted within by the flickering ray of a woman's spirit. It was an angel, but of darkness—of flame, not of light. At the moment that I was thinking thus, I saw beside thee a goat, a beast of the witches, which looked at me laughingly. The midday sun gilded its horns with fire. Then

I perceived the snare of the Demon, and I no longer doubted that thou camest from hell, and that thou camest for my perdition. I believed it.'

Here the priest looked the prisoner in the face, and added coldly:

'I believe it still. However, the charm operated little by little. Thy dancing whirled in my brain; I felt the mysterious spell at work within me. All that should have waked in my soul was lulled to sleep; and, like those who perish in the snow, I took pleasure in yielding to that slumber. All at once thou didst begin to sing. What could I do, wretch that I was? Thy song was still more bewitching than thy dance. I tried to flee—impossible. I was nailed, rooted to the ground. It seemed as if the marble flags had risen to my knees. I was forced to remain until the end. My feet were ice, my brain was boiling. At length thou didst, perhaps, take pity on me: thou didst cease to sing; thou didst disappear. The reflection of the dazzling vision, the reverberation of the enchanting music, gradually faded from my eyes and ears. Then I sank into the corner of the window, more stiff and helpless than a fallen statue. The vesper bell roused me. I rose, I fled; but, alas! something within me had fallen to rise no more; something came upon me from which I could not flee!'

He made another pause and proceeded:

'Yes; from that day forth there was within me a man I knew not. I had recourse to all my remedies—the cloister, the altar, work, books—follies! Oh! how empty science sounds when we beat against it in despair a head filled with frantic passion! Knowest thou, young girl, what I saw ever after between the book and me? Thee, thy shadow, the image of the luminous apparition which had one day passed before me. But that image was no longer of the same hue; it was gloomy, funereal, darksome—like the black circle that long hangs about the vision of the imprudent one who has been gazing steadfastly at the sun.

'Unable to rid myself of it—hearing thy song ever humming in my head—constantly seeing thy feet dancing on my breviary—constantly feeling at night, in my dreams, thy form against my own—I wished to see thee again—to touch thee—to know who thou wast—to see whether I should find thee indeed equal to the ideal image that had remained of thee—to dispel, perhaps, my dream with the reality. At all events, I hoped a new impression would efface the first, and the first had become insupportable. I sought thee. I saw thee again. Misery! When I had seen thee twice, I wished to see thee a thousand times, I wished to see thee always! Then—how stop short on that steep descent to hell? Then I was no longer my own master. The other end of the thread which the Demon had tied about my wings was fastened to his foot. I became vagrant and wandering like thyself, I waited for thee under porches, I spied thee out at the corners of streets, I watched thee from the top of my tower. Each night I found myself more charmed, more despairing, more fascinated, more lost!

'I had learned who thou wast—a gypsy, a Bohemian, a gitana, a zingara. How could I doubt the witchcraft? Listen. I hoped that a trial would rid me of the charm. A sorceress had bewitched Bruno of Asti; he had her burned, and was cured. I knew it; I wished to try the remedy. First, I tried to have thee forbidden the square in front of Notre-Dame, hoping to forget thee if thou camest no more. Thou didst not heed. Thou camest again. Then came the idea of carrying thee off. One night I attempted it. There were two of us. Already we had laid hold on thee, when that wretched officer came upon us. He delivered thee. Thus was he the beginning of thy misfortunes, of mine, and of his own. At length, not knowing what to do or what was to become of me, I denounced thee to the official.

'I thought I should be cured like Bruno of Asti. I, also, had a confused idea that a trial would deliver thee into my hands; that in a prison I should hold thee, I should have thee; that there thou couldst not escape me; that thou hadst possessed me a sufficiently long time to give me the right to possess thee in my turn. When one does evil, one should do it thoroughly. 'Tis madness to stop midway in the monstrous! The extremity of crime has its delirium of joy. A priest and a witch may mingle in ecstasy upon the straw of a dungeon floor!

'So I denounced thee. 'Twas then that I used to terrify thee whenever I met thee. The plot which I was weaving against thee, the storm which I was brewing over thy head, burst from me in muttered threats and lightning glances. Still I hesitated. My project had its appalling sides, which made me shrink back.

'Perhaps I might have renounced it, perhaps might my hideous thought have withered in my brain without bearing fruit. I thought it would always depend upon me to follow up or set aside this prosecution. But every evil thought is inexorable, and insists on becoming a deed; where I supposed myself all-powerful, Fate was mightier than I. Alas! alas! 'tis she who has laid hold on thee, and cast thee amid the terrible machinery of the engine I had secretly constructed! Listen; I am nearing the end.

'One day—again the sun was shining brightly—I beheld a man pass me who pronounced thy name and laughed, and who carried profligacy in his eyes. Damnation! I followed him. Thou knowest the rest.'

He ceased.

The young girl could find but one word:

'Oh, my Phœbus!'

'Not that name!' said the priest, seizing her arm with violence. 'Pronounce not that name! Oh! unhappy wretches that we are; 'tis that name which has ruined us! or rather, we have ruined each other by the inexplicable play of fate! Thou art suffering, art thou not? Thou art cold; darkness blinds thee; the dungeon wraps thee round; but, perhaps, thou hast still some light shining within thee—were it only thy childish love for that empty being who was trifling with thy heart? while I—I bear the dungeon within me; within me is winter, ice, despair; I have the darkness in my soul.

'Knowest thou all that I have suffered? I was present at thy trial. I was seated on the bench with the officials. Yes, under one of those priestly hoods were the contortions of a damned spirit. When thou wast brought in, I was there; when thou wast interrogated, I was there. The den of wolves! 'Twas my own crime; 'twas my own gibbet they were slowly constructing over thy head! At each deposition, at each proof, at each pleading, I was there; I could count each of thy steps on the road of agony. I was there, again, when that wild beast . . . Oh! I had not foreseen the torture! Listen. I followed thee to the chamber of anguish. I saw thee stripped and handled by the vile hands of the torturer. I saw thy foot—that foot, upon which I would have given an empire to press a single kiss and die; that foot, beneath which I would with rapture have been crushed—that foot I beheld encased in the horrible boot, that boot which converts the limb of a living being into bleeding pulp! Oh! wretched me! while I looked on at that I grasped beneath my sackcloth a dagger with which I lacerated my breast. At the shriek which thou utteredst, I plunged it in my flesh; at a second cry, it would have entered my heart. Look; I think it still bleeds.'

He opened his cassock. His breast was indeed torn as if by a tiger's claws, and in his side was a large, ill-closed wound.

The prisoner shrank back with horror.

'Oh!' said the priest, 'girl, have pity on me! Thou thinkest thyself unhappy. Alas! alas! thou knowest not what misery is. Oh! to love a woman—to be a priest—to be hated—to love her with all the fury of your soul—to feel that you would give for the least of her smiles your blood, your vitals, your reputation, your salvation, immortality and eternity, this life and the other—to regret you are not a king, a genius, an emperor, an archangel, God, that you might place a greater slave beneath her feet—to clasp her day and night in your dreams, in your thoughts; and to see her in love with the trappings of a soldier, and have nothing to offer her but a priest's dirty cassock, which will terrify and disgust her. To be present with your jealousy and your rage while she lavishes on a miserable, blustering imbecile treasures of love and beauty! To behold that body whose form inflames you, that bosom which has so much sweetness, that flesh tremble and blush under the kisses of another! Oh heavens! to love her foot, her arm, her shoulder! to think of her blue veins, of her brown skin, until one writhes for nights together on the pavement of one's cell; and to see all those caresses one has dreamed of end in torture! to have succeeded only on laying her on the bed of leather! Oh, these are the true pincers heated at the fires of hell! Oh happy is he that is sawed asunder between two planks, or torn to pieces by four horses! Knowest thou what torture he feels through long nights? whose arteries boil, whose heart seems bursting, whose head seems splitting, whose teeth tear his hands—fell tormentors which turn him incessantly, as on a fiery gridiron, over a thought of love, jealousy and despair? Mercy, girl! A truce for a moment! A few ashes on this living coal! Wipe away, I beseech thee, the big drops of sweat that trickle from my brow! Child! torture me with one hand, but caress me with the other! Have pity, maiden! have pity on me.'

The priest writhed on the wet pavement and beat his head against the edges of the stone steps. The young girl listened to him, looked at him.

When he ceased speaking, panting and exhausted, she repeated in an undertone:

'Oh, my Phœbus!'

The priest dragged himself towards her on his knees.

'I implore thee,' cried he, 'if thou hast any bowels of compassion, repulse me not! Oh! I love thee! I am a miserable wretch! When thou utterest that name, unhappy girl, it is as if thou wert grinding between thy teeth every fibre of my heart! Mercy! If thou comest from hell, I go thither with thee. I have done everything to that end. The hell where thou art will be my paradise; the sight of thee is more entrancing than that of God. Oh! say! wilt thou none of me, then? I should have thought the mountains would have been shaken on their foundations the day a woman would repulse such a love. Oh! if thou wouldst . . . Oh! how happy could we be! We would flee; I would help thee to flee; we would go somewhere; we would seek that spot on the earth where the sun is brightest, the trees most luxuriant, the sky the bluest. We would love each other; we would pour our two souls one into the other and we would each have an inextinguishable thirst for the other which we would quench incessantly and together at the inexhaustible fountain of love!'

She interrupted him with a loud and terrible laugh.

'Look, father! you have blood upon your fingers!'

The priest remained for some moments petrified, his eyes fixed on his hand.

'Yes, 'tis well,' he resumed at length with strange gentleness; 'insult me, taunt me, overwhelm me with scorn! but come, come away. Let us hasten. It is to be to-morrow, I tell thee. The gibbet on the Grève, thou knowest! It is ever ready. 'Tis horrible! to see thee borne in that tumbrel! Oh! mercy! Never did I feel as at this moment how dearly I love thee. Oh! follow me. Thou shalt hate me as long as thou wilt. Only come. To-morrow! to-morrow! the gibbet! thy execution! Oh! save thyself! spare me!'

He seized her arm; he was frantic; he strove to drag her away. She fixed her eye intently on him.

'What has become of my Phœbus?'

'Ah!' said the priest, letting go her arm, 'you have no pity!'

'What has become of Phœbus?' she repeated coldly.

'He is dead!' cried the priest.

'Dead!' said she, still cold and passionless; 'then why do you talk to me of living?'

He heard her not.

'Oh, yes!' said he, as if talking to himself, 'he must indeed be dead. The blade entered deep. I believe I touched his heart with the point. Oh! my very soul was in that dagger's point!'

The young girl rushed upon him like an enraged tigress, and thrust him against the flight of steps with supernatural strength.

'Begone, monster! begone, murderer! leave me to die! May the blood of us both mark thy brow with an everlasting stain . . . Be thine! priest? Never! never! nothing shall unite us! not hell itself! Begone, accursed! Never!'

The priest had stumbled to the steps. He silently disengaged his feet from the folds of his cassock, took up his lantern, and began slowly to ascend the steps leading to the door; he reopened the door and went out.

All at once the young girl beheld his head re-appear; his face wore a frightful expression, and he cried to her, hoarse with rage and despair:

'I tell thee, he is dead!'

She fell face downwards on the ground, and no sound was heard in the dungeon save the sob of the drop of water which made the pool palpitate amid the darkness.

5

The Mother

I do not think there is anything in the world more gladsome than
the ideas which awake in a mother's heart at the sight of her child's
little shoe; above all, when it is the holiday, the Sunday, the
christening shoe—the shoe embroidered to the very sole, a shoe
in which the child has not yet taken one step. That shoe has so
much daintiness and grace, it is so impossible for it to walk, that
it seems to the mother as though she saw her child. She smiles at
it, she kisses it, she talks to it, she asks herself whether there can
actually be a foot so tiny; and, if the child be absent, the pretty
shoe suffices to bring the soft and fragile creature before her eyes.
She fancies she sees it—she does see it—full of life and laughter,
with its delicate hands, its round head, its pure lips, its serene eyes,
whose white is blue. If it be winter, there it is, crawling on the
carpet, climbing laboriously upon a stool; and the mother trembles
lest it go too near the fire. If it be summer, it creeps about the
yard, the garden, plucks up the grass from between the stones,
gazes with artless wonder, and fearlessly, at the big dogs, the great
horses, plays with the shell-work, the flowers, and makes the
gardener scold when he finds the gravel on the beds and the
mould upon the walks. Everything smiles, everything is bright,
everything is playful, like itself, even to the zephyr and the sunbeam, which sport in rivalry amidst its wanton curls. The shoe
recalls all this to the mother, and her heart melts before it as wax
before the fire.

But when the child is lost, those thousand images of joy, of
delight, of tenderness, which swarmed around the little shoe,
become so many sources of horror. The pretty little embroidered
shoe is now only an instrument of torture, incessantly racking the
heart of the mother. It is still the same chord which vibrates, the
fibre the most sensitive, the most profound; but instead of its
being touched by an angel, it is now wrenched by a demon.

One morning, as the May sun was rising in one of those deep
blue skies in which Garofolo loves to picture the descent from the
cross, the recluse of the Tour-Roland heard the sound of wheels,
the tramp of horses and the clanking of irons in the Place de Grève.
She was but little roused by it, fastened her hair over her ears to
deaden the sound, and on her knees resumed her contemplation
of the inanimate object which she had been thus adoring for fifteen years. That little shoe, we have already said, was to her the

universe. Her thoughts were locked up in it, never to be parted from it but by death. What bitter imprecations she had breathed to heaven, what heart-rending complaints, what prayers and sobs about this charming, rosy, satin toy, the gloomy cave of the Tour-Roland only knew. Never was keener anguish lavished upon a thing more charming or more delicate.

That morning it seemed as if her grief was venting itself more violently than usual, and she was heard from without lamenting in a loud and monotonous voice that wrung to the heart.

'Oh! my child,' said she, 'my child! my poor, dear, little babe, I shall see thee then no more! Is it then over? It always seems to me as if it happened but yesterday! My God! my God! to take her from me so soon; it would have been better not to have given her to me! You do not know, then, that our children are of our own bowels, and a mother that has lost her child believes no longer in God? Ah! wretched that I am, to have gone out that day! Lord! Lord! to take her from me thus! You never saw me with her, then, when I warmed her all joyous at my fire, when she laughed at me as I gave her suck, when I made her little feet creep up my bosom to my lips? Oh! if you had but seen that, my God! you would have had pity on my joy; you would not have taken from me the only love that was yet left in my heart! Was I such a wretched creature, then, Lord, that you could not look at me before you condemned me? Alas! alas! there is the shoe; but the foot, where is it? where is the child? My babe! my babe, what have they done with thee? Lord, give her back to me! For fifteen years have I torn my knees in praying to thee, my God! Is that not enough? Give her back to me for one day, one hour, one minute, but for one minute, Lord, and then cast me to the evil one forever! Oh! if I only knew where lay but the hem of your garment, I would cling to it with both my hands, and you would be obliged to give me back my child! Her pretty little shoe, have you no pity on it, Lord? Can you condemn a poor mother to these fifteen years of torture? Good Virgin! good Virgin of Heaven! my infant Jesus has been taken from me; they have stolen it, they have eaten it on the wild heath, they have drunk its blood, they have crushed its bones! Good Virgin! have pity on me! My daughter! I must have my daughter! What care I that she should be in heaven! I'll none of your angel, I want my child! I am the lioness, I want my whelp! Oh, I'll writhe upon the ground, I'll dash my forehead against the stones, I'll damn myself and curse you, Lord, if you keep from me my child! You see how my arms are bitten, Lord! Has the good God no pity? Oh, give me but black bread and salt, only let me have my child to warm me like a sun! Alas! Lord God, I am only a vile sinner, but my child made me pious. I was full of religion for love of her, and I saw you through her smile as through an opening of heaven. Oh, let me only once, once again, but a single time, put this shoe on her pretty, little, rosy foot, and I will die, good Virgin, blessing you! Ah! fifteen years! she would be grown up now. Unhappy child! What! is it true, then, I shall never see her more, not even in heaven? for I shall never go there. Oh, what misery to say, "There is her shoe, and that is all!"

The wretched woman had thrown herself on this shoe, for so many years her consolation and despair, and her heart was rent with sobs as on the first day—for to a mother that has lost her child, it is always the first day. That grief never grows old. The mourning garments may wear out and lose their dye, the heart remains dark. At that moment, fresh and joyous children's voices passed before the cell. Whenever any children met her eye or ear, the poor mother used to rush in the darkest corner of her sepulchre, and seemed as if she would plunge her head into the stone that she might not hear them. This time, on the contrary, she started up and listened eagerly. One of the little boys had just said:

'They're going to hang a gypsy-woman to-day.'

With a sudden bound, like that of the spider which we have seen rush upon a fly at the trembling of her web, she ran to her loophole, which looked out, as the reader is aware, upon the Place de Grève. There, indeed, was a ladder reared against the permanent gibbet, and the hangman's assistant was busy adjusting the chains rusted by the rain. Some people were standing around.

The smiling group of children was already far away. The recluse sought with her eyes some passer-by whom she might interrogate. Close to her cell she perceived a priest, who pretended to be reading in the public breviary, but whose mind was much less occupied with the lattice-guarded volume than with the gibbet, toward which he cast from time to time a stern and gloomy look. She recognized Monsieur the archdeacon of Josas, a holy man.

'Father,' asked she, 'whom are they about to hang yonder?'

The priest looked at her without answering; she repeated the question, and then he said, 'I don't know.'

'There were some children that said it was a gypsy-woman,' continued the recluse.

'I believe it is,' said the priest.

Then Paquette la Chantefleurie burst into a hyena-like laughter.

'Sister,' said the archdeacon, 'you greatly hate the gypsy-women then?'

'Hate them!' cried the recluse; 'they are witches, child stealers! They devoured my little girl, my child, my only child! I have no heart left; they have devoured it!'

She was frightful. The priest looked at her coldly.

'There is one of them whom I hate above all, and whom I have cursed,' resumed she; 'a young one, who is the age my girl would be if her mother had not eaten my girl. Every time that young viper passes before my cell she makes my blood boil.'

'Well, sister, be joyful,' said the priest, icy as a sepulchral statue; 'that is the one you are about to see die.'

His head fell upon his breast and he moved slowly away.

The recluse writhed her arms with joy.

'I had foretold it to her that she would go up there again. Thank you, priest,' cried she.

And then she began to pace with rapid steps before the bars of her window, her hair dishevelled, her eyes glaring, striking her shoulder against the wall, with the wild air of a caged she-wolf that has long been hungry and feels that the hour of her repast is approaching.

6

Three Human Hearts Differently Constituted

PHŒBUS, however, was not dead. Men of that stamp are hard to kill. When Maître Philippe Lheulier, king's advocate extraordinary, had said to poor Esmeralda, 'he is dying,' it was an error or in jest. When the archdeacon had repeated to the condemned girl, 'he is dead,' the fact was that he knew nothing about the matter, but he believed it, he made sure of it and he had no doubt of it. It would have been too hard for him to give favourable news of his rival to the woman whom he loved. Any man would have done the same in his place.

Not that Phœbus's wound was not severe, but it was less so than the archdeacon flattered himself. The surgeon, to whose house the soldiers of the watch had at once carried him, had, for a week, feared for his life, and had even told him so in Latin. However, youth triumphed; and as often happens, notwithstanding prognostics and diagnostics, Nature amused herself by saving the patient, in spite of the physician. It was while he was still lying upon the leech's pallet that he underwent the first interrogatories of Philippe Lheulier and the official inquisitors, which he had found especially wearisome. Accordingly, one fine morning, feeling himself better, he had left his golden spurs in payment to the man of medicine, and taken himself off. This, however, had not in the least affected the judicial proceedings. Justice in those days cared little about clearness and precision in the proceedings against a criminal. Provided only that the accused was hung, that was all that was necessary. Now the judges had ample proof against La Esmeralda. They believed Phœbus to be dead—and that was the end of the matter.

Phœbus, for his part, had fled to no great distance. He had simply rejoined his company in garrison at Queue-en-Brie, in the Isle of France, a few stages from Paris.

After all, it did not please him in the least to appear in this suit. He had a vague impression that he would play a ridiculous part in it. In fact, he did not very well know what to think of the whole affair. Irreligious and superstitious, like every soldier who is nothing but a soldier, when he came to question himself about this adventure, he was not altogether without his suspicions of the little goat, of the singular fashion in which he had first met La Esmeralda, of the no less strange manner in which she had betrayed her love, of her being a gypsy, and lastly of the spectre monk. He perceived in all these incidents much more magic than love; probably a sorceress; perhaps a devil; a sort of drama, in short; or, to speak the language of that day, a mystery—very disagreeable indeed—in which he played a very awkward part, that of the personage beaten and laughed at. The captain felt abashed at this; he experienced that sort of shame which Lafontaine has so admirably defined:

Ashamed as a fox caught by a hen

Moreover, he hoped that the affair would not be noised abroad; that, himself being absent, his name would hardly be pronounced in connection with it, and that in any case it would not go beyond the court room of the Tournelle. In this he was not mistaken. There was then no *Gazette des Tribunaux;* and as hardly a week passed in which there was not some counterfeiter to boil, some witch to hang, or some heretic to burn, at some of the numberless *justices* of Paris, people were so much accustomed to see at every crossway the ancient feudal Themis, bare-armed, with sleeves turned up, doing her work at the gibbets, the whipping posts and pillories, that they hardly paid any heed to it. The aristocracy of that day scarcely knew the name of the victim who passed by at the corner of the street; and, at most, it was only the populace that regaled itself with this coarse fare. An execution was a common incident in the public highways, like the baker's braising pan or the butcher's slaughter house. The executioner was but a sort of butcher of a little deeper dye than the rest.

Phœbus, therefore, soon set his mind at rest in regard to the enchantress Esmeralda or Similar, as he called her, to the dagger thrust which he had received from the gypsy-girl, or from the spectre monk (it mattered little to him which), and to the issue of the trial. But no sooner was his heart vacant on that score, than the image of Fleur-de-Lys returned thither; for the heart of Captain Phœbus, like the natural philosophy of the day, abhorred a vacuum.

Moreover, he found it very dull staying at Queue-en-Brie, a village of farriers and cow-girls with chapped hands; a long string of poor huts and thatched cottages, bordering the highway on both sides for half a league; a tail *(queue)* in short, as its name imports.

Fleur-de-Lys was his last flame but one—a pretty girl, a delightful dowry. Accordingly, one fine morning, quite cured, and fairly presuming that after two months had elapsed, the affair of the gypsy-girl must be over and forgotten, the amorous cavalier arrived on a prancing horse at the door of the Gondelaurier mansion.

He paid no heed to a somewhat numerous rabble which had gathered in the Place du Parvis, before the portal of Notre-Dame. He recollected that it was the month of May; he supposed it to be some procession, some Whitsuntide or holiday; fastened his horse's bridle to the ring at the gate, and gaily ascended the stairs in search of his fair betrothed.

She was alone with her mother.

Fleur-de-Lys had still weighing upon her heart the scene of the sorceress with her goat and its accursed alphabet, and the lengthened absence of Phœbus. Nevertheless, when she beheld her captain enter, she thought him so handsome, his doublet so new, his baldric so shining, and his air so impassioned, that she blushed with pleasure. The noble damoiselle herself was more charming than ever. Her magnificent fair locks were braided to perfection; she was clad in all that heavenly blue which so well becomes fair people (a bit of coquetry she had learned from Colombe), and her eyes swam in that languor of love which becomes them still better.

Phœbus, who had seen nothing in the line of beauty since he quitted the country wenches of Queue-en-Brie, was intoxicated with the sight of Fleur-de-Lys—which imparted to our officer so eager and gallant an air that his peace was made immediately. Madame de Gondelaurier herself, still maternally seated in her big arm-chair, had not the courage to scold him. As for Fleur-de-Lys's reproaches, they died away in tender cooings.

The young lady was seated near the window, still embroidering her grotto of Neptunus. The captain was leaning over the back of her chair, while she murmured to him her gentle upbraidings.

'What have you been doing with yourself for these two months past, you naughty man?'

'I swear,' replied Phœbus, a little embarrassed by the question, 'that you are beautiful enough to set an archbishop to dreaming.'

She could not help smiling.

'Good, good, sir. Let my beauty alone and answer me. Fine beauty, indeed!'

'Well, my dear cousin, I was recalled to the garrison.'

'And where was that, if you please? and why did you not come to bid me farewell?'

'At Queue-en-Brie.'

Phœbus was delighted that the first question had helped him to elude the second.

'But that is quite close by, sir. How happened it that you came not once to see me?'

Here Phœbus was very seriously perplexed. 'Because—the service—and then, charming cousin, I have been ill.'

'Ill!' she repeated in alarm.

'Yes—wounded.'

'Wounded!'

The poor girl was quite overcome.

'Oh, do not be frightened at that,' said Phœbus, carelessly; 'it was nothing. A quarrel—a sword cut—what is that to you?'

'What is that to me!' exclaimed Fleur-de-Lys, lifting her beautiful eyes filled with tears. 'Oh! you do not say what you think when you speak thus. What sword cut was that? I wish to know all.'

'Well, my dear fair one, I had a quarrel with Mahé Fédy, you know, the lieutenant of Saint Germain-en-Laye; and we have ripped open a few inches of skin for each other—that is all.'

The mendacious captain was well aware that an affair of honour always set a man off to advantage in the eyes of a woman. In fact, Fleur-de-Lys looked him in the face with mingled sensations of fear, pleasure and admiration. Still, she was not completely reassured.

'Provided that you are wholly cured, my Phœbus!' said she. 'I do not know your Mahé Fédy, but he is a villainous man. And whence arose this quarrel?'

Here Phœbus, whose imagination was only tolerably active, began to be rather at a loss how to find a means of extricating himself for his prowess.

'Oh, I know not; a mere nothing; a horse; a remark! Fair cousin,' he exclaimed, by way of turning the conversation, 'what noise is that in the square?' He went to the window.

'Oh, heavens! fair cousin, what a great crowd in the Place.'

'I do not know,' said Fleur-de-Lys; 'it appears that a witch is to do penance this morning before the church, and thereafter to be hanged.'

So absolutely did the captain believe the affair of La Esmeralda to be terminated, that he was little affected by these words of Fleur-de-Lys. Nevertheless, he asked her one or two questions.

'What is the name of this witch?'

'I do not know,' she replied.

'And what is she said to have done?'

She again shrugged her white shoulders.

'I know not.'

'Oh, my sweet Saviour!' said the mother, 'there are so many sorcerers nowadays that they burn them, I verily believe, without knowing their names. One might as well seek the name of every cloud in the sky. After all, one may be tranquil. The good God keeps his register.' Here the venerable dame rose and went to the window. 'Good Lord!' she cried, 'you are right, Phœbus—there is indeed a great crowd of the populace. There they are, blessed be God! even on the house-tops! Do you know, Phœbus, this reminds me of my young days—the entry of King Charles VII, when there was also such a crowd. I no longer remember what year it was. When I speak of this to you it produces upon you the effect —does it not?—of something very old, and upon me of something very young. Oh! the crowd was far finer than now. There were some even upon the battlements of the Porte Saint Antoine. The king had the queen on a pillion; and after their highnesses came all the ladies mounted behind all the lords. I remember there was much laughing; for by the side of Amanyon de Garlande, who was very short of stature, there was the Sire Matefelon, a knight of gigantic stature, who had killed heaps of English. It was very fine. A procession of all the gentlemen of France, with their red banners waving in the air. There were some with pennons, and some with banners. Let me see—there was the Sire of Calan, with his pennon; Jean de Chateaumorant, with his banner; the Sire of Coucy, with his banner, and a richer one, too, than any of the others, except the Duke of Bourbon's. Alas! 'tis a sad thing to think all that has existed, and exists no longer.'

The two lovers were not listening to the worthy dowager. Phœbus had returned to lean over the back of the chair of his betrothed; a charming situation, whence his libertine gaze could invade every opening in Fleur-de-Lys's collarette. This collarette gaped so opportunely, and revealed to him so many exquisite things, and led him to divine so many others, that Phœbus, dazzled by this skin with its gleams of satin, said to himself, 'How can one love any but a fair skin?'

Both were silent. The young girl raised sweet, enraptured eyes to him, from time to time, and their hair mingled in a ray of spring sunshine.

'Phœbus,' said Fleur-de-Lys suddenly, in a low tone, 'we are to be married in three months—swear to me that you have never loved any woman but myself.'

'I swear it, fair angel!' replied Phœbus; and his passionate gaze combined with the truthful tone of his voice to convince Fleur-de-Lys. Perhaps, indeed, at that moment, he himself believed what he was saying.

Meanwhile, the good mother, delighted to see the betrothed pair on such excellent terms, had left the apartment to attend to some household matter. Phœbus observed it; and this so much emboldened the adventurous captain, that some very strange ideas entered his brain. Fleur-de-Lys loved him; he was her betrothed; she was alone with him; his former inclination for her had revived, not with all its freshness, but with all its ardour; after all, there was no great harm in tasting one's fruit before it is harvested. I do not know whether these ideas actually crossed his mind, but so much is certain, that Fleur-de-Lys was suddenly alarmed at the expression of his glance. She looked around and saw that her mother was no longer there.

'Good heavens!' said she, flushed and uneasy, 'I am very warm!'

'I think, indeed,' returned Phœbus, 'it must be almost noon. The sun is troublesome; we need only draw the curtains.'

'No, no!' cried the trembling damsel; 'on the contrary, I need air.'

And, like a fawn that scents the breath of the approaching pack, she rose, hurried to the window, opened it, and rushed upon the balcony.

Phœbus, considerably vexed, followed her.

The Place du Parvis Notre-Dame, upon which, as we know, the balcony looked, presented, at that moment, a singular and sinister spectacle, which suddenly altered the nature of the timid Fleur-de-Lys's alarm.

An immense crowd, which overflowed into all the neighbouring streets, blocked up the square itself. The low wall, breast high, inclosing the Parvis, would not have sufficed to keep it clear, had it not been lined by dense ranks of the sergeants of the Onze-vingts, and of hack-buteers, culverin in hand. Owing, however, to this grove of pikes and arque-busses, the Parvis was empty. Its entrance was guarded by a body of the bishop's own halberdiers. The great doors of the church were shut, in contrast to the countless windows overlooking the square, which, open up to the very gables, revealed thousands of heads heaped one upon another, something like the balls in a park of artillery.

The surface of this mob was gray, dirty and squalid. The spectacle which it was awaiting was evidently one of those which have the privilege of extracting and collecting all that is most unclean in the population. Nothing could be more hideous than the noise which arose from that swarm of soiled caps and unkempt heads. In this crowd there was more laughter than shouting, more women than men.

Ever and anon some sharp, shrill voice pierced the general uproar.

'Hi! Mahiet Baliffre! Is she to be hanged yonder?'

'Simpleton! 'tis here she is to do penance in her shift. The priest will spit a little Latin in her face. That is always done here at midday. If 'tis the gallows you want, you must e'en go to the Grève.'

'I'll go there afterwards.'

'Tell me, Boucanbry, is it true that she has refused a confessor?'

'So it seems, La Bechaigne.'

'Look at that, the heathen!'

'Sir, it is the custom. The Palace bailiff is bound to deliver the malefactor, ready sentenced, for execution; if 'tis a layman, to the provost of Paris; if 'tis a clerk, to the official of the bishopric.'

'Thank you, sir.'

'Oh, heavens!' said Fleur-de-Lys, 'the poor creature!'

This thought filled with sadness the glance which she cast upon the crowd. The captain, much more occupied with her than with that pack of rabble, was amorously fingering her girdle behind. She turned around with smiling entreaty.

'For pity's sake, let me alone, Phœbus! if my mother were to return she would see your hand.'

At that moment, the clock of Notre-Dame slowly struck twelve. A murmur of satisfaction burst from the crowd. The last vibration of the twelfth stroke had hardly died away, when all the heads surged like the waves before a sudden gale, and an immense shout went up from the pavement, from the windows, and from the roofs, 'There she is!'

Fleur-de-Lys covered her eyes with her hands, that she might not see.

'My charmer,' said Phœbus, 'will you go in?'

'No,' replied she; and those eyes which she had just closed through fear, she opened again through curiosity.

A tumbrel drawn by a strong Norman dray horse, and quite surrounded by horsemen in violet livery with white crosses, had just entered the square from the Rue Saint-Pierre-aux-Bœufs. The sergeants of the watch cleared a passage for it through the crowd by a vigorous use of their whit-leather whips. Beside the tumbrel rode some officers of justice and police, recognizable by their black costume and their awkwardness in the saddle. Maître Jacques Charmolue paraded at their head.

In the fatal cart sat a young girl, her hands tied behind her, and with no priest at her side. She was in her shift; her long black hair (the custom then was to cut it only at the foot of the gibbet) fell in disorder upon her half-bared throat and shoulders.

Athwart that waving hair, more glossy than a raven's plumage, a rough, gray cord was seen, twisted and knotted, chafing her delicate skin and winding about the poor girl's graceful neck like an earthworm around a flower. Beneath that rope glittered a small amulet, ornamented with bits of green glass, which had been left to her, no doubt, because nothing is refused to those about to die. The spectators at the windows could see in the bottom of the tumbrel her naked legs, which she strove to conceal under her as by a final feminine instinct. At her feet lay a little goat, bound. The prisoner was holding together with her teeth her ill-tied chemise. It seemed as if even in her misery she still suffered from being thus exposed almost naked before all eyes. Alas! it was not for such shocks that modesty was made.

'Jesus!' said Fleur-de-Lys hastily to the captain, 'look there, fair cousin—it is that horrid gypsy-girl with the goat.'

So saying, she turned to Phœbus. His eyes were fixed on the tumbrel. He was very pale.

'What gypsy-girl with the goat?' he stammered.

'Why,' rejoined Fleur-de-Lys, 'do you not remember?'

Phœbus interrupted her:

'I do not know what you mean.'

He stepped back to re-enter the room, but Fleur-de-Lys, whose jealousy, already so deeply stirred by this same gypsy-girl, was now re-awakened, cast at him a glance full of penetration and mistrust. She now vaguely recollected having heard a captain mentioned who had been implicated in the trial of this sorceress.

'What ails you?' said she to Phœbus; 'one would think that this woman disturbed you.'

Phœbus forced a sneering smile.

'Me! not the least in the world! Me, indeed!'

'Remain, then,' returned she imperiously, 'and let us see the end.'

The unlucky captain was obliged to remain. He was somewhat reassured by the fact that the condemned girl kept her eyes fixed upon the bottom of the tumbrel. It was but too truly La Esmeralda. In this last stage of ignominy and misfortune she was still beautiful; her great, dark eyes looked larger on account of the hollowness of her cheeks; her pale profile was pure and sublime. She resembled what she had been, as a virgin of Masaccio resembles a Virgin of Raphael's, weaker, thinner, more delicate.

Moreover, her whole being was tossed hither and thither, and, save for her sense of modesty, she had abandoned everything, so utterly was she crushed by stupor and despair. Her body rebounded at every jolt of the cart, like some shattered, lifeless thing; her gaze was fixed and unconscious; a tear still lingered in her eye, but motionless, and as it were frozen.

Meanwhile, the dismal cavalcade had traversed the crowd, amid shouts of joy and stare of the curious. Nevertheless, historical fidelity calls upon us to state that on seeing her so beautiful and so forlorn, many were moved to pity, even among the most hardhearted. The tumbrel entered the Parvis.

Before the central doorway of the church it stopped. The escort drew up in line on either side. The mob was silenced; and amid this silence so solemn and anxious the two halves of the great door turned, as if of themselves, upon their hinges, which creaked like the sound of a fife. Then the deep interior of the church was seen in its whole extent, gloomy, hung with black, faintly lighted by a few wax tapers twinkling afar off upon the high altar, yawning like the mouth of a cavern upon the square resplendent with sunshine. At the farthest extremity in the dusk of the chancel, was dimly seen a colossal silver cross, standing out in relief against a black cloth, which hung from the roof to the pavement. The whole nave was deserted; but heads of priests were seen moving confusedly in the distant choir stalls; and at the moment when the great door opened there burst from the church a loud, solemn and monotonous chant, hurling as it were in gusts, fragments of doleful psalms at the head of the condemned one:—

' . . . *Non timebo millia populi circumdantis me; exsurge, Domine: salvum me fac, Deus!*' (. . . I will not fear the thousands of the people gathered about me; arise, O Lord! save me, O my God.)

' . . . *Salvum me fac, Deus, quoniam intraverunt aquæ usque ad animam meam!*' (. . . Save me, O God; albeit the waters have entered, even unto my soul.)

' . . . *Infixus sum in limo profundi; et non est substantia.*' (. . . Behold, I am set fast in the slime of the great deep and there is no ground under my feet.)

At the same time another voice, separate from the choir, intoned from the steps of the high altar, this mournful offertory:

' . . . *Qui verbum meum audit, et credit ei qui misit me, habet vitam æternam, et in judicium non venit; sed transit a morte in vitam.*' (. . . Whoso heareth my word, and believeth in him that sent me, hath life everlasting; he cometh not into judgment, but from death he passeth unto life.)

This chant, which a few old men, buried in their own gloom, sang from afar over this beautiful creature full of youth and life, wooed by the warm air of spring, and bathed in sunshine, was the mass for the dead.

The people listened devoutly.

The unfortunate girl, bewildered, seemed to lose her sight and her consciousness in the dark interior of the church. Her pale lips moved as if in prayer; and when the hangman's assistant approached to help her down from the cart, he heard her repeating in a whisper, this word: 'Phœbus.'

They untied her hands, made her alight, accompanied by her goat, which was also unbound, and which bleated with joy at finding itself free. She was then led barefoot over the hard pavement to the foot of the steps leading to the portal. The cord about her neck trailed behind her like a serpent pursuing her.

Then the chanting in the church ceased. A great golden cross and a row of wax candles began to move through the gloom. The halberds of the motley dressed beadles clanked, and a few moments later a long procession of priests in chasubles and deacons in dalmatics marched solemnly towards the prisoner, singing psalms as they came into view. But her eyes were riveted upon him who walked at their head, immediately after the cross-bearer.

'Oh!' she said in a low tone with a shudder, ''tis he again! the priest!'

It was in fact the archdeacon. On his left walked the subchanter; and on his right, the precentor, carrying his staff of office. He advanced with head thrown back, eyes fixed and opened wide, chanting in a loud voice:

'*De ventre inferi clamavi, et exaudisti vocem meam.*' (Out of the bowels of the earth I have called unto thee, and thou hast heard my voice.)

'*Et projecisti me in profundum in corde maris, et flumen circumdedit me.*' (And thou hast cast me into the depths of the sea, and the waters have gone about me.)

When he appeared in the broad daylight, beneath the lofty arched portal, covered with an ample cope of silver, barred with a black cross, he was so pale that more than one amongst the crowd thought that one of the marble bishops kneeling upon the monuments in the choir had risen and had come forth to receive on the threshold of the tomb her who was about to die.

She, equally pale and rigid, hardly noticed that they had placed in her hand a heavy lighted taper of yellow wax. She had not heard the shrill voice of the clerk, reading the fatal lines of the penance; only, when told to answer amen, she said 'Amen!' It was only the sight of the priest making a sign to her guards to retire, and himself advancing toward her, that brought back to her any sense of life and strength.

Then the blood boiled in her veins, and a lingering spark of indignation was re-kindled in that already numb, cold soul.

The archdeacon approached her slowly. Even in this extremity she saw him gaze upon her nakedness with eyes glittering with passion, jealousy and desire. Then he said to her in a loud voice, 'Young woman, have you asked pardon of God for your sins and your offences?' He bent to her ear, and added (the spectators supposed that he was receiving her last confession), 'Wilt thou be mine? I can even yet save thee!'

She looked steadily at him: 'Begone, demon! or I denounce thee!'

He smiled—a horrible smile. 'They will not believe thee. Thou wilt but add scandal to guilt. Answer quickly! wilt thou be mine?'

'What hast thou done with my Phœbus?'

'He is dead,' said the priest.

At this moment the miserable archdeacon raised his head mechanically, and saw, at the opposite side of the square, on the balcony of the Gondelaurier house, the captain standing by Fleur-de-Lys. He staggered, passed his hand over his eyes, looked again, muttered a malediction, and all his features were violently contorted.

'Well, then, die, thou!' said he, between his teeth; 'no one shall have thee!'

Then raising his hand over the gypsy, he exclaimed, in a sepulchral voice, '*I nunc anima anceps, et sit tibi Deus misericors.*' (Go thy way now, lingering soul, and may God have mercy upon thee!)

This was the awful formula with which it was the custom to close that gloomy ceremonial. It was the signal given by the priest to the executioner.

The people knelt.

'*Kyrie Eleison!*' (Lord, have mercy upon us!) said the priests, who remained beneath the arch of the portal.

'*Kyrie Eleison!*' repeated the throng, with that murmur which runs over a sea of heads, like the waves of a troubled sea.

'Amen!' said the archdeacon.

He turned his back upon the prisoner; his head again fell upon his breast; his hands were crossed; he rejoined his train of priests, and a moment later he disappeared with cross, candles and copes beneath the dim arches of the cathedral, and his sonorous voice gradually died away down the choir while chanting these words of despair:—

'*Omnes gurgites tui et fluctus tui super me transierunt!*' (All thy whirlpools, O Lord, and all thy waves, have gone over me!)

At the same time, the intermittent clang of the iron butts of the beadles' halberds dying away by degrees among the columns of the nave, sounded like a clock hammer striking the last hour of the condemned.

The doors of Notre-Dame remained open, showing the interior of the church, empty, deserted, draped in mourning, torchless and voiceless.

The condemned girl remained motionless in her place, awaiting her doom. One of the vergers was obliged to notify Maître Charmolue of the fact, who, during all this scene, had set himself to study that bas-relief of the great portal, representing, according to some, Abraham's sacrifice, according to others the great Alchemical Operation, the sun being typified by the angel, the fire by the fagot and the operator by Abraham.

He was with some difficulty withdrawn from this contemplation; but at length he turned, and at a sign from him, two men in yellow, the executioner's assistants, approached the gypsy-girl to bind her hands once more.

The unhappy creature at the moment of re-mounting the fatal cart, and setting out on her last stage, was perhaps seized with some poignant clinging to life. She raised her dry, red eyes to heaven, to the sun, to the silvery clouds, intermingled with patches of brilliant blue; then she cast them around her upon the ground, the people, the houses. All at once, while the man in yellow was pinioning her arms, she uttered a terrible cry, a cry of joy. Yonder, on that balcony, at the corner of the Place, she had just caught sight of him, her friend, her lord, Phœbus, the other apparition of her life!

The judge had lied! the priest had lied! it was he indeed, she could not doubt it. He was there, handsome, alive, dressed in his brilliant uniform, his plume on his head, his sword by his side!

'Phœbus!' she cried, 'my Phœbus!'

And she tried to stretch towards him arms trembling with love and rapture, but they were bound.

Then she saw the captain knit his brows; a fine young woman, leaning upon his arm, looked at him with scornful lip and angry eye; then Phœbus uttered some words which did not reach her; and then he and the lady both disappeared precipitately through the window of the balcony, which closed after them.

'Phœbus!' she cried, wildly; 'dost thou too believe it?'

A monstrous thought had dawned upon her. She recollected that she had been condemned for the murder of Phœbus de Chateaupers.

She had borne up until now, but this last blow was too severe. She fell senseless upon the ground.

'Come,' said Charmolue, 'carry her to the cart, and make an end of it.'

No one had observed in the gallery of statues of the kings, carved just above the arches of the portal, a strange-looking spectator, who, until now, watched all that passed with such impassiveness, a neck so outstretched, a visage so deformed, that, but for his parti-coloured red and violet garb, he might have been taken for one of the stone monsters through whose jaws the long gutters of the cathedral have disgorged themselves for six centuries past. This spectator had missed nothing that had taken place since midday in front of the portal of Notre-Dame. And at the very beginning, without any one noticing him, he had securely fastened to one of the small columns of the gallery a strong knotted rope, the other end of which trailed on the top of the steps below. This done, he began to look on tranquilly, whistling from time to time when a blackbird flitted past

Suddenly, at the moment when the executioner's assistants were preparing to execute Charmolue's phlegmatic order, he threw his leg over the balustrade of the gallery, gripped the rope with his feet, his knees and his hands; then he was seen to slide down the façade, as a drop of rain slips down a windowpane, run up to the two sub-executioners with the speed of a cat just dropped from a house-top, knock them down with two enormous fists, pick up the gypsy with one hand, as a child might a doll, and leap, at one bound, into the church, lifting the girl above his head, and shouting in a tremendous voice, 'Sanctuary!'

This was done with such rapidity that, had it been night, the whole might have been seen by the glare of a single flash of lightning.

'Sanctuary! Sanctuary!' repeated the crowd; and the clapping of ten thousand hands made Quasimodo's only eye sparkle with joy and pride.

This shock restored the prisoner to her senses. She raised her eyelids, looked at Quasimodo, then closed them again suddenly, as if terrified at her deliverer.

Charmolue, the executioners and the whole escort were confounded. In fact, within the precincts of Notre-Dame the condemned was inviolable. The cathedral was a recognized place of refuge; all temporal jurisdiction expired upon its threshold.

Quasimodo had stopped under the great portal. His broad feet seemed to rest as solidly upon the floor of the church as the heavy Roman pillars themselves. His big bushy head was buried between his shoulders like the head of a lion, which also has a mane, but no neck. He held the trembling girl, suspended in his horny hands, like a piece of white drapery, but he carried her with as much care as if he feared he should break or injure her. He seemed to feel that a thing so delicate, exquisite and precious was not made for such hands as his. At times he looked as if he dared not touch her, even with his breath. Then, all at once, he would press her close in his arms to his angular breast, as his own, his treasure, as her mother might have done. His gnome-like eye, resting upon her, flooded her with tenderness, grief and pity, and was suddenly lifted, flashing fire. Then the women laughed and wept, the crowd stamped their feet with enthusiasm, for at that moment Quasimodo had a beauty of his own. He was fine; he, that orphan, that foundling, that outcast; he felt himself august and strong; he looked full in the face that society from which he was banished, and into which he had so powerfully intervened; that human justice from which he had snatched its prey; all those tigers whose jaws perforce remained empty; those myrmidons, those judges, those executioners; all that royal power which he, poor, insignificant being, had foiled with the power of God.

Then, too, there was something touching in the protection afforded by a being so deformed to a being so unfortunate; in the circumstance of a poor girl condemned to death being saved by Quasimodo. They were the two extremes, natural and social wretchedness, coming into contact and aiding each other.

However, after a few moments of triumph, Quasimodo plunged abruptly into the church with his burden. The people, fond of any display of prowess, sought him with their eyes under the gloomy nave, regretting that he had so quickly withdrawn from their acclamations. All at once he was seen to reappear at one extremity of the gallery of the kings of France. He ran along it like a madman, holding his conquest aloft, and shouting: 'Sanctuary!' Fresh plaudits burst from the multitude. Having traversed the gallery, he plunged again into the interior of the church. A moment later he reappeared upon the upper platform, with the gypsy still in his arms, still running wildly along, still shouting 'Sanctuary!' and the throng applauded. Finally he made a third appearance on the top of the tower of the great bell: from thence he seemed to show exultingly to the whole city her whom he had saved; and his thundering voice, that voice so rarely heard by any one, and never by himself, thrice repeated with frenzy that pierced the very clouds: 'Sanctuary! Sanctuary! Sanctuary!'

'Noël! Noël!' cried the people in their turn; and that prodigious shout resounded upon the opposite shore of the Seine, to the astonishment of the crowd assembled in the Place de Grève, and of the recluse who was still waiting with her eyes fixed on the gibbet.

BOOK NINE

I

Delirium

CLAUDE FROLLO was no longer in Notre-Dame when his adopted son thus abruptly cut the fatal knot in which the unhappy archdeacon had bound the gypsy-girl and caught himself. On returning into the sacristy, he had torn off the albe, cope and stole; flung them all into the hands of the amazed verger; fled through the private door of the cloister; ordered a boatman of the Terrain to carry him over to the left bank of the Seine, and plunged in among the hilly streets of the University, going he knew not whither; meeting, at every step, parties of men and women hastening gaily towards the Pont Saint Michel, in the hope that they might still 'arrive in time' to see the witch hanged—pale, wild, more troubled, more blind and more fierce than a night bird let loose and pursued by a troop of children in broad daylight. He knew not where he was, what he did, whether he dreamed. He went forward, walking, running, taking any street at random, making no choice, only urged ever by the Grève, that horrible Grève, which he confusedly felt to be behind him.

In this manner he skirted Mount Sainte Geneviève, and finally emerged from the town by the Porte Saint Victor. He continued his flight so long as he could see, on turning, the towered enclosure of the University, and the scattered houses of the faubourg; but when at last a ridge completely hid that odious Paris—when he could imagine himself a hundred leagues from it—in the country —in a desert—he paused, and it seemed to him as if he breathed more freely.

Then frightful ideas rushed upon his mind. He saw once more clear into his soul, and shuddered. He thought of that unfortunate girl who had destroyed him, and whom he had destroyed. He cast a haggard eye over the two winding paths, along which fate had driven their separate destinies, to that point of intersection at which she had pitilessly dashed them against each other. He thought of the folly of eternal vows, the emptiness of chastity, science, religion, virtue, the uselessness of God. He indulged in evil thoughts to his heart's content, and, while plunging deeper into them, he felt as if the fiend were laughing within him.

And, as he thus sifted his soul to the bottom, when he perceived how large a space Nature had prepared there for the passions, he sneered more bitterly still. He stirred up in the depths of his heart all his hatred, all his malevolence; and he discovered with the cool eye of a physician examining a patient, that this hatred, this malevolence, were but vitiated love, that love, the source of every virtue in man, turned to horrible things in the heart of a priest, and that a man constituted as he was, by making himself a priest, made himself a demon. Then he laughed frightfully, and suddenly became pale again, in contemplating the worst side of his fatal passion, of that corroding, venomous, malignant, implacable love, which had driven one of them to the gibbet, the other to hell-fire; her to condemnation, him to damnation.

And then he laughed anew, as he reflected that Phœbus was alive; that, after all, the captain lived, was light-hearted and happy, had finer doublets than ever, and a new mistress, whom he brought to see the old one hanged. And he sneered at himself with redoubled bitterness, when he reflected that, of all the living beings whose death he had desired, the only creature he did not hate, was the only one who had not escaped him.

Then his thoughts wandered from the captain to the populace, and he was overcome with jealousy of an unheard of kind. He reflected that the people, also, the entire mob, had had before their eyes the woman he loved, in her shift, almost naked. He wrung his hands in agony at the thought that the woman, whose form half seen by him alone in darkness, would have afforded him supreme delight, had been exposed, in broad daylight, at noontide, to the gaze of a whole multitude, clad as for a bridal night. He wept with rage over all those mysteries of love profaned, sullied, exposed, withered forever. He wept with rage, picturing to himself the foul eyes that had been gratified by that scanty covering, that this lovely girl, this virgin lily, this cup of purity and delight, to which he dared not place his lips without trembling, had been converted, as it were, into a public trough, at which the vilest rabble of Paris, thieves, beggars, lackeys, had come to quaff together a shameless, impure and depraved pleasure.

And when he strove to picture to himself the felicity which he might have found upon earth, had she not been a gypsy and he not a priest, had Phœbus never existed, and had she but loved him; when he imagined the life of serenity and love which might have been possible for him too; when he thought that there were at that very instant happy couples here and there upon the earth, engaged in sweet converse, in orange groves, on the banks of murmuring streams, in the light of the setting sun, or under a starry sky, and that, had it been God's will, he might have formed with her one of those blessed couples—his heart melted in tenderness and despair.

Oh, she—still she! It was this fixed idea that haunted him incessantly, that tortured him, that turned his brain and gnawed his vitals. He regretted nothing, repented nothing; all that he had done, he was ready to do again; he liked better to see her in the hands of the executioner than in the arms of the captain. But he suffered; suffered so intensely, that at moments he tore out his hair by handfuls to see if it were not turning white.

There was one moment, among the rest, when it occurred to him that, perhaps at that very minute, the hideous chain which he had seen that morning, was drawing its iron noose closer and closer around that slender, graceful neck; this idea made the perspiration start from every pore.

There was another moment when, laughing diabolically at himself, he pictured to his imagination, at one and the same time, La Esmeralda as on the first day he had seen her—lively, careless, joyous, gaily attired, dancing, winged, harmonious—and La Esmeralda of the last day, in her scanty shift, with the rope about her neck, slowly ascending with her naked feet the rough ladder to the gibbet. This double picture was so vivid that he uttered a terrific cry.

While this whirlwind of despair overturned, broke, tore up, bent to the earth, uprooted all within him, he gazed upon nature around him. At his feet some fowls were pecking and scratching about among the bushes, enamelled beetles crawled in the sunshine. Over his head groups of dappled gray clouds sailed over a blue sky. In the horizon, the spire of the abbey of Saint Victor shot up its obelisk of slate above the intervening ridge of ground. And the miller of the Butte Copeaux whistled light-heartedly as he watched the steady-turning sails of his mill. All this active, industrious, tranquil life recurring around him in a thousand forms hurt him. He resumed his flight.

Thus he sped through the country until nightfall. This flight from Nature, life, himself, man, God, everything, lasted the whole day. Sometimes he threw himself face downward upon the earth, and tore up the young corn with his nails. Sometimes he paused in some deserted village street, and his thoughts were so unendurable that he would seize his head in both hands, as if to tear it from his shoulders and dash it on the stones.

Toward the hour of sunset he examined himself again, and found himself almost mad. The storm which had been raging within him from the moment when he had lost all hope and wish to save the gypsy, had left him unconscious of a single sound idea, a single rational thought. His reason lay prostrate, almost utterly destroyed. His mind retained but two distinct images, La Esmeralda and the gibbet, all the rest was black. These two images together formed a horrible group; and the more he fixed upon them such power of attention and thought as he was yet master of, the more they seemed to increase according to a fantastic progression—the one in grace, in charm, in beauty, in light, the other in horror—until, at last, La Esmeralda appeared like a star, the gibbet as an enormous fleshless arm.

It is remarkable that, during all this torture, he never seriously thought of putting an end to himself. The wretch was made thus; he clung to life—perhaps, indeed, he really saw hell in prospect.

Meanwhile, daylight was declining. The living being still existing within him began vaguely to think of returning. He believed himself to be far from Paris; but, on looking around, he discovered that he had only made the circuit of the University. The spire of Saint Sulpice and the three lofty pinnacles of Saint Germain-des-Prés, shot up above the horizon on his right. He bent his steps in that direction. When he heard the challenge of the abbot's men-at-arms around the battlemented walls of Saint Germain, he turned aside, took a path that lay before him, between the abbey mill and the lazaretto of the suburb, and in a few minutes found himself upon the border of the Pré-aux-Clercs. This meadow was celebrated by reason of the brawls which went on there night and day; it was the *hydra* of the poor monks of Saint Germain. *Quod monachis Sancti Germani Pratensis hydra fuit, clericis nova semper dissidiorum capita suscitantibus.* (Which was the *hydra* of the monks of Saint Germain-des-Prés, the laymen constantly raising some new heads of dissension.) The archdeacon was afraid of meeting some one there; he dreaded any human face; he had avoided the University and the hamlet of Saint Germain; he wished to go through the streets again as late as possible. He passed along the side of the Pré-aux-Clercs, took the deserted path which separated it from the Dieu-Neuf, and at length reached the waterside. There Dom Claude found a boatman, who, for a few farthings, took him up the Seine to the extremity of the island of the city, and landed him upon that uninhabited tongue of land where the reader has already beheld Gringoire musing, and which extended beyond the king's gardens, parallel to the islet of the Passeur-aux-Vaches.

The monotonous rocking of the boat, and the murmur of the water, had somewhat stupefied the unhappy Claude. When the boatman had left him, he remained standing stupidly upon the bank, staring straight before him, and seeing everything in a sort of tremulous mist, which made all seem like a phantasmagoria. It is no uncommon thing for the exhaustion of violent grief to produce this effect upon the mind.

The sun had set behind the lofty Tour de Nesle. It was now the twilight hour. The sky was white; the water of the river was white. Between these two white expanses the left bank of the Seine, on which his eyes were fixed, extended its sombre length, which, gradually diminishing in the perspective, plunged into the gray horizon like a black spire. It was covered with houses, of which nothing was distinguishable but the dark outline standing out in strong relief in the dark from the clear light of the sky and the water. Lights began to glimmer here and there in the windows. The immense black obelisk, thus isolated between the two white masses of sky and river, the latter very broad just here, produced a singular effect on Dom Claude, such as might be felt by a man lying flat on his back at the foot of the Strasburg Cathedral and gazing up at the enormous spire piercing the twilight shadows above his head; only in this case it was Claude who was erect, and the obelisk which was horizontal. But as the river, reflecting the sky, deepened indefinitely the abyss beneath him, the vast promontory seemed to shoot into space as boldly as any cathedral spire, and the impression produced was the same. The impression was made even stronger and more profound; that, although it was indeed the steeple of Strasburg, it was the steeple of Strasburg two leagues high; something unheard of, gigantic, immeasurable; a structure such as no human eye ever beheld; a Tower of Babel. The chimneys of the houses, the battlements of the walls, the fantastically-cut gables of the roofs, the spire of the Augustines, the Tour de Nesle—all these projections which indented the profile of the colossal obelisk—added to the illusion by their odd resemblance to the outline of a florid and fanciful sculpture.

Claude, in the state of hallucination in which he then was, believed that he saw—saw with his bodily eyes—the pinnacles of hell. The innumerable lights gleaming from one end to the other of the fearful tower, seemed to him to be so many openings of the vast furnace within; the voices and the sounds which arose from it like so many shrieks and groans. Then he was terrified; he clapped his hands to his ears that he might not hear, turned his back that he might not see, and fled from the frightful vision with hasty strides.

But the vision was within him.

When he once more entered the streets, the people passing to and fro in the light of the shop-windows appeared to him like an everlasting coming and going of spectres about him. There were strange noises in his ears; extraordinary fancies disturbed his brain. He saw neither houses, nor pavement, nor vehicles, nor men and women, but a chaos of undefined objects blending one into another. At the corner of the Rue de la Barillerie, there was a chandler's shop, which had its sloping roof above the window, according to immemorial custom, hung with tin hoops, from each of which was suspended a circle of wooden candles, which shook in the wind and rattled like castanets. He fancied he heard the heap of skeletons at Montfaucon knocking their bones against one another.

'Oh!' muttered he, 'the night wind dashes them one against another, and mingles the clanking of their chains with the rattling of their bones. Perhaps she too is there among them!'

Distracted, he knew not whither he went. Presently he found himself upon the Pont Saint Michel. There was a light in the window of a ground-floor room—he went up to it. Through a cracked pane he saw a dirty room, which awakened confused recollections in his mind. In this room, ill-lighted by a small lamp, there was a young man, fair and fresh-looking, with a merry face, throwing his arms, with boisterous laughter, about a girl very immodestly attired; and near the lamp there was an old woman spinning and singing in a quavering voice. As the young man did not laugh constantly, the old woman's song made its way in fragments to the ear of the priest; it was something unintelligible yet frightful:

> 'Growl, Grève! bark, Grève!
> Spin away, my distaff brave!
>   Let the hangman have his cord,
>   That whistles in the prison-yard.
> Growl, Grève! bark, Grève!

> 'Hemp, that makes the pretty rope—
> Sow it widely, give it scope—
>   Better hemp, than wheaten sheaves;
>   Thief there's none that ever thieves
> The pretty rope, the hempen rope.

> 'Bark, Grève! growl, Grève!
> To see the girl of pleasure brave
>   Dangling on the gibbet high,
>   Every window is an eye—
> Bark, Grève! growl Grève!'

Thereupon the young man laughed and caressed the wench. The old woman was La Falourdel; the girl was a courtesan; the young man was his brother Jehan.

He continued to gaze; as well this sight as another.

He saw Jehan go to a window at the back of the room, open it, cast a glance at the quay, where countless lighted windows gleamed in the distance, and heard him say, as he shut the window again:

'By my soul, 'tis night already! The townsfolk are lighting their candles, and God Almighty his stars.'

Then Jehan came back to the wench, and smashing a bottle that stood on a table, exclaimed:

'Empty already, by Jove! and I have no more money. Isabeau, my dear, I shall not be satisfied with Jupiter until he has changed your two white nipples into two black bottles, that I may suck Beaune wine from them day and night.'

This fine piece of wit made the courtesan laugh, and Jehan took his departure.

Dom Claude had barely time to fling himself on the ground, in order to escape being met, looked in the face, and recognized by his brother. Luckily the street was dark, and the student drunk. Nevertheless, he noticed the archdeacon lying on the pavement in the mud.

'Oh! oh!' said he, 'here's a fellow who has been leading a jolly life to-day.'

He pushed Dom Claude with his foot, and the archdeacon held his breath.

'Dead drunk!' resumed Jehan. 'Come! he's full! a very leech loosed from a cask. He's bald,' added he, stooping over him; ''tis an old man—*Fortunate old man!*'

Then Dom Claude heard him move off, saying:

'All the same! reason is a fine thing, and my brother, the arch-deacon, is a lucky fellow to be wise and have money!'

Then the archdeacon rose, and ran without halting to Notre-Dame, whose enormous towers he could see rising in the dark above the houses.

When he arrived, panting, at the Place du Parvis, he shrunk back, and dared not lift his eyes toward the fatal edifice.

'Oh,' he murmured to himself, 'is it possible that such a thing took place here to-day, this very morning!'

However, he ventured to glance at the church. The front was dark, the sky beyond it glittered with stars, the crescent moon, in her flight upward from the horizon, at that moment reached the summit of the right hand tower, and seemed to have perched upon it, like a luminous bird, on the edge of the black trifoliated balus-trade.

The cloister door was closed; but the archdeacon always carried about him the key of the tower, in which was his laboratory; availing himself of it he entered the church.

He found within it the gloom and silence of a cave. By the heavy shadows falling on all sides in broad masses, he knew that the hangings put up for the morning's ceremony had not been removed. The great silver cross shone from the depths of the gloom, dotted with glittering points, like the milky way of that sepulchral night. The long windows of the choir showed the tops of their pointed arches above the black drapery, their stained glass panes admitting a faint ray of moonlight, had only the doubtful colours of the night, a sort of violet, white and blue, of a tint to be found nowhere else but on the faces of the dead. The archdeacon, seeing these wan spots all round the choir, thought he beheld the mitres of bishops gone to perdition. He closed his eyes; and when he opened them again, he thought they were a circle of pale visages gazing at him.

He fled across the church. Then it seemed to him as if the church itself took life and motion—that each of the great columns was turning into an enormous paw that beat the ground with its big stone spatula, and that the gigantic cathedral was a sort of prodigious elephant, breathing and marching, with its pillars for legs, its two towers for tusks, and the immense black cloth for its housings.

This fever, or madness, had reached such a pitch of intensity, that the external world was no longer anything to the unhappy man but a species of Apocalypse, visible, palpable, terrible.

He had one moment of relief. As he plunged into the side aisles, he perceived a reddish light behind a group of pillars. He rushed towards it as to a star. It was the feeble lamp which burned day and night above the public breviary of Notre-Dame beneath its iron grating. He cast his eye eagerly upon the sacred book, in the hope of finding there some sentence of consolation or encouragement. The volume was open at this passage of Job, over which he ran his burning eye:

'And a spirit passed before my face; and I heard a small voice; and the hair of my flesh stood up.'

On reading this dismal sentence, he felt as a blind man would whose fingers are pricked by the staff which he has picked up. His knees failed him, and he sank upon the pavement, thinking of her who had that day suffered death. Such awful fumes rose up and penetrated his brain, that it seemed to him as if his head had become one of the mouths of hell.

He must have remained long in this posture—neither thinking, nor feeling, helpless and passive, in the hands of the demon. At length some strength returned to him; it occurred to him to take refuge in the tower, near his faithful Quasimodo. He rose; and, as fear was upon him, he took the lamp of the breviary to light him. This was a sacrilege; but he had ceased to heed such trifles.

He slowly climbed the stairs of the towers, filled with a secret dread, which must have been shared by the few passers-by in the square, who saw the mysterious light of his lamp moving at that late hour from loophole to loophole, to the top of the tower.

All at once he felt a breath of cool air on his face, and found himself under the doorway of the upper gallery. The night was cold; the sky was streaked with hurrying clouds, whose large, white masses drifted one upon another like river ice breaking up after a frost. The crescent moon, stranded in the midst of them, looked like a celestial vessel caught among those icebergs of the air.

He lowered his gaze and contemplated for a moment through the railing of slender columns which unites the towers, afar off, through a light veil of mist and smoke, the silent throng of the roofs of Paris, steep, innumerable, crowded and small as the ripples of a calm sea on a summer night.

The moon gave but a feeble light, which imparted to earth and sky an ashy hue.

At this moment the Cathedral clock raised its shrill, cracked voice. Midnight rang out. The priest thought of mid-day. Twelve o'clock had come again.

'Oh,' he whispered to himself, 'she must be cold by this time.'

Suddenly a puff of wind extinguished his lamp, and almost at the same instant there appeared, at the opposite corner of the tower, a shade, a something white, a shape, a female form. He started. By the side of this female form was that of a little goat, that mingled its bleat with the last sound of the bell.

He had strength enough to look—it was she!

She was pale, she was sad. Her hair fell over her shoulders as in the morning, but there was no rope about her neck, her hands were no longer bound; she was free, she was dead.

She was clad in white, and over her head was thrown a white veil.

She came toward him slowly, looking up to heaven. The unearthly goat followed her. He felt as if turned to stone, and too heavy to escape. At each step that she advanced he took one backwards, and that was all. In this way he retreated beneath the dark arch of the stairway. He froze at the thought that she might perhaps enter there too; had she done so, he would have died of terror.

She did, in fact, approach the staircase door, paused there for some moments, looked steadily into the darkness, without appearing to perceive the priest, and passed on. He thought she looked taller than when she was alive. He saw the moon through her white robes; he heard her breathe.

When she had passed on, he began to descend the stairs as slowly as he had seen the spectre move, imagining himself a spectre also—haggard, his hair erect, his extinguished lamp still in his hand—and, as he descended the spiral stairs, he distinctly heard in his ear a mocking voice repeating: 'And a spirit passed before my face; and I heard a small voice; and the hair of my flesh stood up.'

Hunch-backed, One-eyed, Lame

EVERY town in the Middle Ages, and up to the time of Louis XII, every town in France had its places of refuge, or sanctuaries. These sanctuaries, amid the deluge of penal laws and barbarous jurisdictions that inundated the state, were like so many islands rising above the level of human justice. Any criminal that landed upon them was saved. In each district there were almost as many of these places of refuge as there were of execution. The abuse of a privilege went side by side with the abuse of punishment—two bad things endeavouring to correct each other. The royal palaces, the mansions of princes, and especially the churches, had right of sanctuary. Sometimes an entire town which stood in need of re-population was made temporarily a place of refuge for criminals; thus Louis XI made all Paris a sanctuary in 1467.

When once he had set foot within the asylum, the criminal was sacred; but he must beware of leaving it; one step outside the sanctuary, and he fell back into the flood. The wheel, the gibbet, the strappado, kept close guard around the place of refuge, watching incessantly for their prey like sharks around a vessel. Condemned persons thus rescued have been known to grow gray in a cloister, on the staircase of a palace, in the garden of an abbey, in the porch of a church; in this way the sanctuary itself was but a prison under another name. It sometimes happened that a solemn ordinance of the Parliament violated the sanctuary and gave up the condemned to the hands of the executioner, but this was a rare occurrence. The parliaments stood in fear of the bishops; for when there was friction between these two robes, the gown had but a poor chance against the cassock. Occasionally, however, as in the case of the assassins of Petit-Jean, the headsman of Paris, and in that of Emery Rousseau, the murderer of Jean Valleret, justice overleaped the Church and passed on to the execution of its sentences. But, except by virtue of a decree of Parliament, woe to him who violated a place of sanctuary! Everone knows the fate of Robert de Clermont, marshal of France, and Jean de Châlons, marshal of Champagne; and yet the case in question was merely that of one Perrin Marc, a money-changer's man, a miserable assassin; but the two marshals had forced the doors of Saint Méry; therein lay the crime.

Such was the respect with which sanctuaries were invested, that, according to tradition, it occasionally extended even to animals.

Aymoin relates that a stag, chased by Dagobert, having taken refuge at the tomb of Saint Denis, the hounds stopped short, barking.

Churches had usually a small retreat prepared for the reception of the suppliants. In 1407 Nicolas Flamel had built for them upon the arches of Saint Jacques-de-la-Boucherie, a chamber which cost him four pounds sixpence, sixteen Paris farthings.

At Notre-Dame it was a tiny chamber, situated on the roof of the side aisle beneath the flying buttresses, precisely at the spot where the wife of the present keeper of the towers has made a garden, which compares with the hanging gardens of Babylon, as a lettuce with a palm tree, or as a porter's wife with a Semiramis.

Here it was that, after his wild and triumphal race along the towers and galleries, Quasimodo deposited La Esmeralda. So long as that race lasted, the damsel had not recovered her senses, half stupefied, half awake, having only a vague perception that she was ascending in the air, that she was floating, flying there, that something was carrying her upward from the earth. From time to time she heard the loud laugh and the harsh voice of Quasimodo at her ear. She half-opened her eyes; then beneath her she saw, confusedly, Paris all checkered with its countless roofs of tile and slate, like a red and blue mosaic, and above her head Quasimodo's frightful but joy-illumined face. Her eyelids fell; she believed that all was over, that she had been executed during her swoon, and that the misshapen spirit which had presided over her destiny had laid hold of her and was bearing her away. She dared not look at him, but surrendered herself to fate.

But when the breathless and dishevelled bell-ringer laid her down in the cell of refuge; when she felt his clumsy hands gently untying the cord that had cut into her arms, she experienced that kind of shock which startles out of their sleep those on board a ship that runs aground in the middle of a dark night. Her ideas awoke also, and returned to her one by one. She saw that she was in Notre-Dame; she remembered having been snatched from the hands of the executioner; that Phœbus was living; that Phœbus loved her no longer; and these two ideas, one of which imparted so much bitterness to the other, presenting themselves at once to the poor girl, she turned to Quasimodo, who remained standing before her, and whose aspect frightened her, and said to him: 'Why did you save me?'

He looked anxiously at her, as if striving to guess what she said. She repeated her question. He then gave her another look of profound sadness, and fled.

She was amazed.

A few moments later he returned, bringing a bundle, which he laid at her feet. It contained apparel which certain charitable women had left for her at the threshold of the church.

Then she looked down at herself, saw that she was almost naked, and blushed. Life had returned.

Quasimodo seemed to participate in this feeling of modesty. Covering his eye with his broad hand, he again departed, but with lingering steps.

She hastily dressed herself. It was a white robe with a white veil, the habit of a novice of the Hôtel-Dieu.

She had scarcely finished before Quasimodo returned. He carried a basket under one arm and a mattress under the other. This basket contained a bottle, bread and some other provisions. He set the basket on the ground, and said, 'Eat.' He spread out the mattress on the flag-stones, and said, 'Sleep.'

It was his own meal, his own bed, that the bell-ringer had brought her.

The Egyptian lifted her eyes to his face to thank him, but could not utter a word. The poor fellow was absolutely hideous. She drooped her head with a thrill of horror.

Then he said to her:

'I frighten you. I am very ugly, am I not? Do not look at me, only listen to me. In the daytime you will stay here; at night you can walk about all over the church. But stir not a step out of it, either by night or by day. You would be lost. They would kill you, and I should die.'

Moved by his words, she raised her head to reply, but he was gone. Alone once more, she pondered on the singular words of this almost monstrous being, and struck by the tone of his voice, so hoarse and yet so gentle.

She then began to examine her cell. It was a little room, some six feet square, with a small window and a door upon the slightly sloping roof of flat stones. A number of gutter-spouts, terminating in figures of animals, seemed bending over her, and stretching their necks to look at her through the window. Beyond the roof she discerned many chimney-tops, from which issued the smoke of all the fires of Paris, a sad spectacle for the poor gypsy-girl, a foundling, condemned to death—an unfortunate creature, with neither country, family nor home.

Just as the thought of her forlorn situation wrung her heart more keenly than ever, she felt a hairy, shaggy head push between her hands upon her lap. She started (everything alarmed her now), and looked down. It was the poor goat, the nimble Djali, who had escaped with her when Quasimodo scattered Charmolue's men, and who had been lavishing caresses on her feet for nearly an hour without obtaining a single glance. The gypsy covered it with kisses.

'Oh, Djali,' said she, 'how I have forgotten thee! And yet thou thinkest of me. Oh, thou art not ungrateful!'

At the same time, as if an invisible hand had lifted the weight which had so long held back her tears, she began to weep; and as her tears flowed, she felt the sharpest and bitterest of her grief depart with them.

When evening came she thought the night so beautiful, the moonlight so soft, that she made the circuit of the gallery which surrounds the church. It afforded her some relief, so calm did the earth appear when viewed from that height.

3

Deaf

ON the following morning she perceived, on awaking, that she had slept. This strange fact amazed her; she had been so long unaccustomed to sleep! A bright beam from the rising sun came in at her window, and shone in on her face. But with the sun, she saw at the window an object that frightened her—the unfortunate face of Quasimodo. She involuntarily closed her eyes again, but in vain; she fancied that she still saw, through her rosy lids, that gnome's mask, one-eyed and gap-toothed. Then, still keeping her eyes shut, she heard a rough voice saying, very gently:

'Do not be afraid. I am your friend. I came to watch you sleep. It does not hurt you, does it, that I should come and see you sleep? What does it matter to you if I am here when you have your eyes shut? Now I am going. Stay, I have placed myself behind the wall; now you may open your eyes again.'

There was something still more plaintive than these words; it was the tone in which they were uttered. The gypsy, touched by it, opened her eyes. He was no longer at the window. She went to it and saw the poor hunch-back crouching in a corner of the wall, in a sad and resigned attitude. She made an effort to overcome the repugnance with which he inspired her. 'Come hither,' she said to him, gently. From the motion of her lips Quasimodo thought she was bidding him to go away; then he rose up and retreated, limping, slowly, with drooping head, not venturing to raise to the young girl his face full of despair. 'Come hither, I say,' cried she; but he continued to move off. Then she darted out of the cell, ran to him, and took hold of his arm. On feeling her touch, Quasimodo trembled in every limb. He lifted a beseeching eye; and finding that she was trying to draw him with her, his whole face beamed with joy and tenderness. She tried to make him enter her cell; but he persisted in remaining on the threshold. 'No, no,' said he, 'the owl enters not the nest of the lark.'

Then she threw herself gracefully upon her couch, with her goat fast asleep at her feet. Both were motionless for several minutes, contemplating in silence—he, so much grace—she, so much ugliness. Every moment she discovered in Quasimodo some additional deformity. Her eye wandered from his crooked legs to the hump on his back, from the hump on his back to his one eye. She could not understand how a being so awkwardly fashioned could be in existence. But withal there was so much sadness and gentleness about him that she began to be reconciled to it.

He was the first to break silence. 'So you were telling me to return.'

She nodded affirmatively, and said, 'Yes.'

He understood the motion of her head. 'Alas!' said he, as though hesitating whether to finish, 'I am—I am deaf.'

'Poor man!' exclaimed the gypsy-girl, with an expression of kindly pity.

He smiled sorrowfully.

'You think that was all I lacked, do you not? Yes, I am deaf. That is the way I am made. It is horrible, is it not? And you—you are beautiful.'

There was so deep a sense of his wretchedness in the poor creature's tone, that she had not the courage to say a word. Besides, he would not have heard it. He continued:

'Never did I see my ugliness as now. When I compare myself with you, I do indeed pity myself, poor unhappy monster that I am. I must look to you like a beast, eh? You—you are a sunbeam, a dewdrop, a bird's song. As for me—I am something frightful, neither man nor beast—something harder, and more trodden under foot, and more unshapely than a flint-stone.'

Then he began to laugh, and that laugh was the most heartbreaking thing in the world. He went on:

'Yes, I am deaf, but you will speak to me by gestures, by signs. I have a master who talks to me that way. And then, I shall, very soon, know your wish from the movement of your lips, and from your look.'

'Well then,' replied she, smiling, 'tell me why you saved me.'

He watched her attentively as she spoke.

'I understand,' he answered, 'you ask me why I saved you. You have forgotten a poor wretch that tried to carry you off one night —a poor wretch to whom you brought relief, the very next day, on their infamous pillory; a drop of water and a little pity. That is more than I can repay with my life. You have forgotten that poor wretch, but he remembers.'

She listened to him with deep emotion. A tear started in the bell-ringer's eye, but it did not fall; he seemed to make it a point of honour to repress it.

'Listen,' he resumed, when he no longer feared that this tear would fall. 'We have here very high towers; a man who should fall from one would be dead before he touched the pavement; when it shall please you to have me to fall, you will not have to even utter a word; a glance will suffice.'

Then he rose. This odd being, unhappy as the gypsy was, still aroused some compassion in her breast. She motioned to him to remain.

'No, no,' said he, 'I must not stay too long, I am not at my ease. It is out of pity that you do not turn away your eyes. I will go where I can see you without your seeing me; it will be better so.'

He drew from his pocket a small metal whistle. 'There,' said he; 'when you want me, when you wish me to come, when you do not feel too much horror at the sight of me, use this whistle. I can hear this sound.'

He laid the whistle on the ground and fled.

4

Earthenware and Crystal

TIME went on. Calm gradually returned to the soul of La Esmeralda. Excessive grief, like excessive joy, is a violent thing, which is of short duration. The human heart cannot long remain in either extremity. The gypsy had suffered so much that surprise was now the o. emotion of which she was capable.

With the feeling of security, hope had returned to her. She was out of the pale of society, out of the pale of life; but she vaguely felt that it might not perhaps be impossible to return to them. She was like one dead, keeping in reserve a key to her tomb.

She felt the terrible images which had so long beset her gradually fading away. All the hideous phantoms, Pierrat Torterue, Jacques Charmolue, vanished from her mind—all, even the priest himself.

And then, Phœbus was alive; she was sure of it; she had seen him. To her the life of Phœbus was everything. After the series of fatal shocks which had laid waste all within her, she found but one thing intact in her soul, one sentiment—her love for the captain. Love is like a tree; it shoots of itself; it sends its deep roots through all our being, and often continues to flourish over a heart in ruins.

And the inexplicable part of it is that the blinder this passion the more it is tenacious. It is never stronger than when it is most unreasonable.

No doubt La Esmeralda could not think of the captain without a tinge of bitterness. No doubt it was frightful that he too should have been deceived; that he too should have deemed such a thing possible; that he too should have conceived of a dagger's thrust coming from her who would have given a thousand lives to save him. But, after all, she must not blame him too severely; for had she not acknowledged her crime? had she not yielded, weak woman as she was, to the torture? The fault was all her own; she ought rather to have let them tear the nails from her feet than such an avowal from her lips. But then, could she but see Phœbus once more, for a single minute, a word, a look, would suffice to undeceive him, to bring him back. She had no doubt of it. She also strove to account to herself for many singular things; for the accident of Phœbus's presence on the day of her penance, and for his being with a young lady. It was his sister, no doubt—an explanation by no means plausible, but with which she contented herself, because she must needs believe that Phœbus still loved her, and her alone. Had he not sworn it to her? And what stronger assurance did she require, simple and credulous as she was? And, furthermore, in the sequel of the affair, were not appearances much more strongly against herself than against him? Therefore she waited and hoped.

We may add that the church itself, the vast edifice which enveloped her upon every side, protecting her, guarding her, was a sovereign tranquilizer. The solemn lines of its architecture, the religious attitude of all the objects by which the girl was surrounded, the pious and serene thoughts escaping, as it were, from every pore of those venerable stones, acted upon her unconsciously. The structure had sounds, too, of blessedness and such majesty, that they soothed that suffering spirit. The monotonous chant of the performers of the service, the services of the people to the priests, now inarticulate, now in thundering loudness; the organs bursting forth like the voice of a hundred trumpets; the three bell-towers humming like hives of enormous bees—all that orchestra, with its gigantic gamut, incessantly ascending and descending from the voice of the multitude to that of the tower, overruled her memory, her imagination and her sorrow. The bells especially soothed her. It was like powerful magnetism which those vast machines poured in large waves over her.

Thus each sunrise found her less pale, calmer, and breathing more freely. In proportion as her internal wounds healed, grace and beauty bloomed again on her countenance, but more retiring and composed. Her former character also returned—something even of her gaiety, her pretty pout, the fondness for her goat, her love of singing, her feminine bashfulness. She was careful to dress each morning in the corner of her little chamber, lest some inhabitant of the neighbouring garrets should see her through her window.

When her thoughts of Phœbus allowed her leisure, the gypsy-girl sometimes thought of Quasimodo. He was the only link, the only means of communication with mankind, with the living, that remained to her. Poor child! She was even more out of the world than Quasimodo himself. She knew not what to make of the strange friend whom chance had given her. Often she reproached herself for not having a gratitude sufficient to shut her eyes; but, positively, she could not reconcile herself to the sight of the ringer; he was too ugly.

She had left the whistle he had given her lying upon the ground. This, however, did not prevent Quasimodo from reappearing, from time to time, during the first days. She strove hard to restrain herself from turning away with too strong an appearance of repugnance when he came to bring her the basket of provisions or the pitcher of water; but he always perceived the slightest motion of the kind, and went away sorrowful.

One day he came at the moment she was caressing Djali. For a while he stood, full of thought, before the graceful group of the goat and the gypsy; at length he said, shaking his heavy and misshapen head:

'My misfortune is, that I am still too much like a man—would that I were wholly a beast, like that goat.'

She raised her eyes towards him with a look of astonishment.

To this look he answered, 'Oh, I well know why!' and went his way.

Another time he came to the door of the cell (which he never entered) at that moment when La Esmeralda was singing an old Spanish ballad, the words of which she did not understand, but which had lingered in her ear because the gypsy-woman had lulled her to sleep with it when quite a child. At the sight of that ugly face, which made its appearance so abruptly in the middle of her song, the girl broke it off with an involuntary gesture of alarm. The unhappy bell-ringer fell upon his knees on the threshold, and with a beseeching look clasped his clumsy, shapeless hands. 'Oh!' said he, sorrowfully, 'go on, I pray you, and send me not away.' She was unwilling to pain him; and so, trembling all over, she resumed her song. By degrees her alarm subsided, and she abandoned herself wholly to the expression of the plaintive air she was singing. He, the while, remained upon his knees, with his hands joined as in prayer, attentive, hardly breathing, his gaze riveted upon the gypsy's brilliant eyes. It seemed as if he was reading her song from her eyes.

On another occasion he came to her with an awkward and timid air. 'Listen,' said he, with an effort; 'I have something to say to you.' She made him a sign that she was listening. Then he began to sigh, half opened his lips, seemed for a moment to be on the point of speaking, then looked at her again, shook his head, and slowly withdrew, his hand pressed to his brow, leaving the gypsy stupefied.

Among the grotesque figures carved upon the wall, there was one for which he had a particular affection, and with which he often seemed to exchange fraternal glances. Once the gypsy heard him say to it: 'Oh! why am I not of stone like thee!'

At last, one morning, La Esmeralda had advanced to the verge of the roof, and was looking into the Place over the pointed roof of Saint-Jean-le-Rond. Quasimodo was there behind her. He used to so place himself of his own accord, in order to spare the young girl as much as possible the unpleasantness of seeing him. Suddenly the gypsy started; a tear and a flash of joy sparkled simultaneously in her eyes; she knelt down on the edge of the roof, and stretched out her arms in anguish toward the Place, crying out 'Phœbus! oh! come! come hither! One word! but one word, in heaven's name! Phœbus! Phœbus!' Her voice, her face, her gesture, her whole person had the heart-rending aspect of a shipwrecked mariner making the signal of distress to some gay vessel passing in the distant horizon in a gleam of sunshine.

Quasimodo leaned over and saw that the object of this tender and agonizing prayer was a young man, a captain, a handsome cavalier, glistening with arms and accoutrements, prancing across the end of the square, and saluting with his plume a beautiful young lady smiling at her balcony. The officer, however, did not hear the unhappy girl calling him, for he was too far off.

But the poor deaf man heard it. A deep sigh heaved his breast. He turned round. His heart was swollen with the tears which he repressed; his convulsively clenched fists struck against his head, and when he withdrew them there was in each of them a handful of red hair.

The gypsy was paying no attention to him. He said, in an undertone, grinding his teeth:

'Damnation! That is how one ought to look then! One need but have a handsome outside!'

Meanwhile she remained kneeling, crying with extraordinary agitation:

'Oh, there! he alights from his horse. He is going into that house. Phœbus! He does not hear me. Phœbus! Oh! that wicked woman, to talk to him at the same time that I do! Phœbus! Phœbus!'

The deaf man was watching her. He understood this pantomime. The poor ringer's eye filled with tears, but he let none fall. All at once he pulled her gently by the border of her sleeve. She turned round. He had assumed a look of composure, and said to her: 'Shall I go and fetch him?'

She uttered a cry of joy.

'Oh, go! go! Run! quick!—that captain, that captain! bring him to me! I will love thee!'

She clasped his knees. He could not help shaking his head sorrowfully.

'I will bring him to you,' said he, in a faint voice. Then he turned his head, and plunged hastily down the staircase, his heart bursting with sobs.

When he reached the Place, he found only the handsome horse fastened at the door of the Gondelaurier mansion; the captain had just gone in.

He looked up at the roof of the church. La Esmeralda was still there, on the same spot, in the same posture. He made her a melancholy sign of the head; then set his back against one of the posts of the porch of the mansion, determined to wait until the captain should come forth.

In the Gondelaurier house it was one of those gala days which precede a marriage. Quasimodo saw many people enter, and no one come out. From time to time he looked up at the roof of the church; the gypsy did not stir any more than he. A groom came and untied the horse, and led him to the stable of the household.

The entire day passed thus—Quasimodo against the post, La Esmeralda upon the roof, Phœbus, no doubt, at the feet of Fleur-de-Lys.

At length night came; a dark, moonless night. In vain did Quasimodo fix his gaze upon La Esmeralda; she was but a white spot in the twilight, then nothing was to be seen. All had vanished, all was black.

Quasimodo saw the front windows from top to bottom of the Gondelaurier mansion illuminated. He saw the other casements in the Place lighted one by one; he also saw them extinguished to the very last, for he remained the whole evening at his post. The officer did not come forth. When the last passers-by had returned home, when the windows of all the other houses were in darkness, Quasimodo remained entirely alone, entirely in the dark. There were at that time no lamps in the square of Notre-Dame.

But the windows of the Gondelaurier mansion continued lighted, even after midnight. Quasimodo, motionless and attentive, beheld a throng of lively dancing shadows pass athwart the many coloured painted panes. Had he not been deaf, in proportion as the murmur of slumbering Paris died away, he would have heard more and more distinctly, from within the Logis Gondelaurier, a sound of feasting, laughter and music.

Towards one o'clock in the morning the guests began to take their leave. Quasimodo, wrapped in darkness, watched them all pass out through the porch; none of them was the captain.

He was full of melancholy thoughts; at times he looked up into the air, like one weary of waiting. Great black clouds, heavy, torn, split, hung like ragged festoons of crape beneath the starry arch of night.

In one of those moments he suddenly saw the long folding window that opened upon the balcony, whose stone balustrade projected above his head, mysteriously open. The frail glass door gave passage to two persons, then closed noiselessly behind them. It was not without difficulty that Quasimodo, in the dark, recognized in the man the handsome captain, in the woman, the young lady whom he had seen in the morning welcoming the officer from that very balcony. The square was quite dark, and a double crimson curtain, which had fallen behind the glass door the moment it closed, allowed no light to reach the balcony from the apartment.

The young man and the young girl, as far as our deaf man could judge without hearing a word they said, appeared to abandon themselves to a very tender tête-à-tête. The young lady seemed to have permitted the officer to make a girdle for her waist of his arm, and was gently resisting a kiss.

Quasimodo looked on from below this scene, all the more interesting to witness, as it was not intended to be seen. He contemplated, with bitterness, that happiness, that beauty. After all, nature was not silent in the poor fellow, and his vertebral column, wretchedly distorted as it was, quivered no less than another's. He thought of the miserable portion which Providence had allotted to him; that woman, love and its pleasures, would pass forever before his eyes without his ever doing anything but witness the felicity of others. But what pained him most of all in this spectacle, what mingled indignation with his chagrin, was the thought of what the gypsy would suffer could she behold it. True it was that the night was very dark, that La Esmeralda, if she had remained at the same place, as he doubted not she had, was at a considerable distance, and that it was all that he himself could do to distinguish the lovers on the balcony; this consoled him.

Meanwhile their conversation grew more and more animated. The young lady seemed to be entreating the officer to ask nothing more from her. Quasimodo could only distinguish the fair clasped hands, the mingled smiles and tears, the young girl's glances directed to the stars, and the eyes of the captain lowered ardently upon her.

Fortunately, for the young girl was beginning to resist but feebly, the door of the balcony suddenly reopened, and an old lady made her appearance; the young beauty looked confused, the officer annoyed, and all three went in.

A moment later a horse was prancing under the porch, and the brilliant officer, enveloped in his night cloak, passed rapidly before Quasimodo.

The bell-ringer allowed him to turn the corner of the street, then ran after him, with his ape-like agility, shouting: 'Hi! captain!'

The captain halted.

'What does the rascal want with me?' said he, espying in the dark that uncouth figure running toward him limping.

Quasimodo, however, had come up to him, and boldly taken his horse by the bridle: 'Follow me, captain; there is one here who desires to speak with you.'

'By Mahound's horns,' grumbled Phœbus, 'here's a villainous ragged bird that I fancy I've seen somewhere. Hello! sirrah! leave hold of my horse's bridle!'

'Captain,' answered the deaf man, 'do you not ask me who it is?'

'I tell thee to let go my horse,' returned Phœbus, impatiently. 'What means the rogue hanging thus from my bridle rein? Dost thou take my horse for a gallows?'

Quasimodo, far from releasing the bridle, was preparing to make him turn round. Unable to comprehend the captain's resistance, he hastened to say to him:

'Come, captain; 'tis a woman who is waiting for you.' He added, with an effort, 'a woman who loves you.'

'A rare varlet!' said the captain, 'who thinks me obliged to go after every woman that loves me, or says she does—and if perchance she resembles thee with thy face of a screech-owl? Tell her that sent thee that I am going to be married, and that she may go to the devil.'

'Hark ye!' cried Quasimodo, thinking to overcome his hesitation with a word; 'come, monseigneur; 'tis the gypsy-girl that you know of.'

This word did, in fact, make a great impression on Phœbus, but not that which the deaf man expected. It will be remembered that our gallant officer had retired with Fleur-de-Lys several moments before Quasimodo had rescued the condemned girl from the hands of Charmolue. Since then, in all his visits at the Logis Gondelaurier, he had taken care not to mention that woman, the recollection of whom was besides painful to him; and Fleur-de-Lys, on her part, had not deemed it politic to tell him that the gypsy was alive. Hence, Phœbus believed poor *Similar* dead a month or two ago. Add to this, for some moments the captain had been thinking of the extreme darkness of the night, the super-natural ugliness and sepulchral voice of the strange messenger; that it was past midnight; that the street was as solitary as the night that the spectre monk had accosted him, and that his horse panted as it looked at Quasimodo.

'The gypsy!' he exclaimed, almost frightened. 'How now! Art thou come from the other world?' And he laid his hand on the hilt of his dagger.

'Quick! quick!' said the deaf man, endeavouring to drag the horse along; 'this way!'

Phœbus dealt him a vigorous kick in the breast.

Quasimodo's eye flashed. He made a movement as if to fling himself upon the captain. Then, checking himself, he said:

'Oh, how happy you are to have some one who loves you!'

He emphasized the words 'some one,' and leaving hold of the horse's bridle, said:

'Begone!'

Phœbus spurred on in all haste, swearing. Quasimodo watched him disappear in the misty darkness of the street.

'Oh!' said the poor deaf creature to himself, 'to refuse that!'

He returned to Notre-Dame, lighted his lamp, and climbed up the tower again. As he expected, the gypsy-girl was still at the same spot.

The moment she perceived he was coming she ran to meet him.

'Alone!' she cried, clasping her pretty hands in anguish.

'I could not find him again,' said Quasimodo coldly.

'You should have waited for him all night,' returned she passionately.

He saw her angry gesture, and understood the reproof.

'I'll watch him better another time,' said he, hanging his head.

'Get you gone,' said she.

He left her. She was dissatisfied with him. He would have preferred being chided by her than to cause her pain. He had kept all the grief for himself.

From that day forward the gypsy saw him no more; he ceased coming to her cell. Now and then, indeed, she caught a distant glimpse of the ringer's countenance looking mournfully upon her from the top of some tower; but as soon as she perceived him, he would disappear.

We must admit that she was but little troubled by the voluntary absence of the poor hunch-back. At the bottom of her heart she felt grateful to him for it. Nor was Quasimodo himself under any delusion upon this point.

She saw him no more, but she felt the presence of a good genius about her. Her provisions were renewed by an invisible hand while she slept. One morning she found upon her window-sill a cage of birds. Over her cell there was a piece of sculpture that frightened her. She had repeatedly evinced this feeling in Quasimodo's presence. One morning (for all these things were done in the night) she saw it no longer; it had been broken off. He who had climbed to that piece of carving must have risked his life.

Sometimes, in the evening, she heard the voice of one concealed behind the great blind of the belfry, singing, as if to lull her to sleep, a melancholy and fantastic song, verses without rhyme or rhythm, such as a deaf man might make:

> Oh, look not on the face,
> Young maid, look on the heart:
> The heart of a fine young man is oft deformed;
> There are some hearts will hold no love for long.
> Young maid, the pine's not fair to see,
> Not fair to the eye as the poplar,
> Yet it keeps its leaves in winter-time.
> Alas! it's vain to talk of this;
> What is not fair ought not to be—
> Beauty will only beauty love—
> April looks not on January.

> Beauty is perfect,
> Beauty wins all,
> Beauty alone exists not by half.

> The crow flies but by day;
> The owl flies but by night;
> The swan flies night and day.

On waking one morning, she saw in her window two jars full of flowers; one of them a glass vessel, very beautiful and brilliant, but cracked; it had let all the water escape, and the flowers it contained were faded. The other vessel was of earthenware, rude and common, but it had kept the water, so that its flowers were fresh and blooming.

I do not know whether she did it intentionally, but La Esmeralda took the faded nosegay and wore it all day in her bosom.

That day she did not hear the voice from the tower singing.

She felt little concern about it. She passed her days in caressing Djali, watching the door of the Logis Gondelaurier, in talking low to herself about Phœbus, and crumbling her bread to the swallows.

She had altogether ceased to see or to hear Quasimodo. The poor ringer seemed to have departed from the church. One night, however, as she lay wakeful, thinking of her handsome captain, she heard a sigh, near to her cell. She rose up affrighted, and saw, by the moonlight, a shapeless mass lying before her door. It was Quasimodo sleeping there upon the stones.

5

The Key of the Red Door

MEANWHILE public rumour had acquainted the archdeacon with the miraculous manner in which the gypsy-girl had been saved. When he learned this, he felt he knew not what. He had reconciled his mind to the thought of La Esmeralda's death, and thus he had become calm; he had touched the depths of possible grief. The human heart (and Dom Claude had meditated upon these matters) cannot contain more than a certain quantity of despair. When the sponge is thoroughly soaked, the sea may pass over it without its imbibing one tear more.

Now, Esmeralda being dead, the sponge was filled to its utmost; all was over for Dom Claude upon this earth. But to feel that she was alive, and Phœbus also—that was the recommencement of torture, of pangs, of vicissitudes, of life—and Dom Claude was weary of all that.

When this piece of intelligence reached him, he shut himself in his cloister cell. He appeared neither at the conferences of the chapter, nor at the services in the church. He closed his door against every one, even the bishop. He kept himself thus immured for several weeks. He was thought to be ill, and so indeed he was.

What was he doing, shut up thus? With what thoughts was the unfortunate man contending? Was he making a final struggle against his formidable passion? Was he combining some final plan of death for her and perdition for himself?

His Jehan, his cherished brother, his spoiled child, came once to his door, knocked, swore, entreated, announced himself ten times over. Claude would not open.

He passed whole days with his face pressed against the casement of his window. From that window, situated in the cloister, he could see the cell of Esmeralda; he often saw herself, with her goat—sometimes with Quasimodo. He remarked the assiduities of the ugly deaf man, his obedience, his delicate and submissive behaviour to the gypsy-girl. He recollected—for he had a good memory, and memory is the tormentor of the jealous—he recollected the singular look which the ringer had cast upon the dancing-girl on a certain evening. He asked himself what motive could have urged Quasimodo to save her. He was an eye-witness to a thousand little scenes which passed between the gypsy and the ringer; where, in their gestures, as seen at that distance and commented on by his passion, appeared to him most tender. He distrusted woman's capriciousness. Then he felt confusedly arising within him a jealousy such as he had never imagined; a jealousy which made him redden with shame and indignation. 'As for the captain,' thought he, 'that might pass—but this one!' And the idea overpowered him.

His nights were frightful. Since he knew the gypsy-girl to be alive, those cold images of spectres and the grave, which had beset him for a whole day, had vanished from his spirit, and the flesh began again to torment him. He writhed upon his bed at the thought that the dark-skinned damsel was so near him.

Each night his delirious imagination represented to him La Esmeralda in all the attitudes that had most strongly excited his passion. He beheld her stretched across the body of the poniarded captain, her eyes closed, her fair neck crimsoned with the blood of Phœbus; at that moment of wild delight when the archdeacon had imprinted on her pale lips that kiss of which the unfortunate girl, half dying as she was, had felt the burning pressure. Again he beheld her undressed by the savage hands of the torturers, letting them thrust her little foot naked into the horrid iron-screwed buskin, her round and delicate leg, her white and supple knee; and then he saw that ivory knee alone appearing, all below it being enveloped in Torterue's horrible apparatus. He figured to himself the young girl, in her slight chemise, with the rope about her neck, with bare feet and uncovered shoulders, almost naked, as he had seen her upon the last day. These voluptuous images made him clench his hands, and sent a shiver through his frame.

One night in particular, they so cruelly inflamed his priestly virgin blood, that he tore his pillow with his teeth, leaped from bed, threw a surplice over his night-robe, and went out of his cell with his lamp in hand, half naked, wild, with flaming eyes.

He knew where to find the key of the red door, opening from the cloister into the church; and, as the reader is aware, he always carried about him a key of the tower staircase.

6

Sequel to the Key of the Red Door

THAT night La Esmeralda had fallen asleep in her little chamber, full of forgetfulness, of hope and of happy thoughts. She had been sleeping some time, dreaming, as usual, of Phœbus, when she thought she heard some noise about her. Her sleep was light and restless—the sleep of a bird; the slightest thing awakened her. She opened her eyes. The night was very dark. Yet she discerned at the little window a face regarding her; there was a lamp which cast its light upon this apparition. The moment that it perceived itself to be observed by La Esmeralda, it blew out the lamp. Nevertheless, the young girl had caught a glimpse of its features; her eyelids dropped with terror. 'Oh!' said she in a faint voice, 'the priest!'

All her past misfortune flashed upon her mind, and she fell back frozen upon her bed with horror.

A moment after, she felt a contact the whole length of her body, which made her shudder so violently that she started up in bed wide awake and furious. The priest had glided to her side and clasped her in his arms.

She strove to cry out, but could not.

'Begone, monster! begone, assassin!' said she, in a voice low and faltering with anger and horror.

'Mercy! mercy!' murmured the priest, pressing his lips to her shoulders.

She seized his bald head with both her hands by the remaining hairs, and strove to repel his kisses, as if he had been biting her.

'Mercy!' repeated the wretched man. 'Didst thou but know what is my love for thee! 'Tis fire! 'tis molten lead! 'tis a thousand daggers in my heart!'

And he held back both her arms with super-human strength. Quite desperate, 'Let me go,' she cried, 'or I spit in thy face!'

He released her. 'Vilify me, strike me, be cruel, do what thou wilt, but have mercy! love me!'

Then she struck him with the fury of a child. She drew up her beautiful hands to tear his face. 'Begone, demon!'

'Love me! love me! have pity!' cried the poor priest, rolling upon her and answering her blows with caresses.

All at once she felt that he was overpowering her. 'There must be an end of this,' said he, grinding his teeth.

She was conquered, crushed and quivering in his arms. She felt

340

a lascivious hand wandering over her. She made a last effort, and shrieked: 'Help! help me! A vampire! a vampire!'

But nothing came. Only Djali was awake and bleated piteously. 'Silence!' said the panting priest.

Suddenly, in the midst of her struggles, as the gypsy retreated upon the floor, her hand came in contact with something cold and metallic. It was Quasimodo's whistle. She seized it with a convulsion of hope, put it to her lips, and blew with all her remaining strength. The whistle sounded clear, shrill, piercing.

'What is that?' said the priest.

Almost at the same instant he felt himself lifted by a vigorous arm. The cell was dark; he could not clearly distinguish who it was that held him thus; but he heard teeth clenching with rage, and there was just light enough mingled with the darkness for him to see shining over his head a large cutlass.

The priest thought he could discern the form of Quasimodo. He supposed it could be no other. He recollected having stumbled, in entering, over a bundle that was lying across the doorway outside. Yet, as the new-comer uttered no word, he knew not what to think. He threw himself upon the arm that held the cutlass, crying, 'Quasimodo!' forgetting, in that moment of distress, that Quasimodo was deaf.

In the twinkling of an eye the priest was thrown upon the floor, and felt a knee of lead weighing upon his breast. By the angular imprint of that knee he recognized Quasimodo. But what was he to do? how was he to make himself known to the other? Night made the deaf man blind.

He was lost. The young girl, devoid of pity, as an enraged tigress, did not interfere to save him. The cutlass approached his head; the moment was critical. Suddenly his adversary appeared to hesitate. 'No blood upon her!' said he, in an undertone.

It was, in fact, the voice of Quasimodo.

Then the priest felt the great hand dragging him by the foot out of the cell; it was there he was to die. Luckily for him, the moon had been risen for a few moments.

When they had cleared the door of the chamber, its pale rays fell upon the features of the priest. Quasimodo looked in his face; a tremor came over him; he relaxed his hold of the priest and shrank back.

The gypsy having come forward to the threshold of her cell, was surprised to see them suddenly change parts; for now it was the priest who threatened, and Quasimodo who implored.

The priest, heaping gestures of anger and reproof upon the deaf man, violently motioned to him to withdraw.

The deaf man bowed his head, then came and knelt before the

gypsy's door. 'Monseigneur,' said he, in a tone of gravity and resignation,'afterwards you will do what you please but kill me first.'

So saying, he presented his cutlass to the priest; and the priest, beside himself, rushed forward to grasp it; but the girl was quicker than he. She snatched the cutlass from Quasimodo's hand, and burst into a frantic laugh. 'Approach!' said she to the priest.

She held the blade aloft. The priest hesitated. She would certainly have struck. 'Thou durst not approach now, coward!' she exclaimed. Then she added, in a pitiless accent, and well knowing that it would be plunging a red-hot iron into the heart of the priest: 'Ha! I know that Phœbus is not dead!'

The priest overthrew Quasimodo with a kick, and plunged, trembling with rage, under the vault of the staircase.

When he had gone, Quasimodo picked up the whistle that had just saved the gypsy. 'It was growing rusty,' said he, as he gave it to her, and then he left her alone.

The young girl, overpowered by this violent scene, fell exhausted upon her couch, and burst into a flood of tears. Again her horizon was growing overcast.

As for the priest, he had groped his way back into his cell.

'Twas done. Dom Claude was jealous of Quasimodo. He repeated pensively to himself his fatal sentence: 'No one shall have her!'

BOOK TEN

I

Gringoire has a Succession of Bright Ideas in the Rue des Bernardins

FROM the time that Pierre Gringoire had seen the turn that this affair was taking, and that torture, hanging and various other disagreeables were decidedly in store for the principal personages in this comedy, he no longer felt any desire to take part in it. The Truands, amongst whom he had remained, considering that, after all, they were the best company in Paris—the Truands had continued to feel interested in the gypsy. This he found very natural in people who, like herself, had nothing but Charmolue and Torterue in prospect, and who did not, like himself, soar into the regions of imagination between the two wings of Pegasus. He had learned from their discourse that his bride of the broken pitcher had found refuge in Notre-Dame, and he was glad of it. But he did not even feel tempted to go and see her there. He sometimes thought of the little goat, and that was all. For the rest, by day he exerted his wits to get his bread; and by night he lucubrated a memorial against the Bishop of Paris, for he remembered being drenched by his mill-wheels, and he bore him malice therefor. He occupied himself also with a commentary upon the fine work of Baudry-le-Rouge, Bishop of Noyon and of Tournay, de *Cupa Petrarum*, which had given him a violent inclination for architecture, an inclination which had supplanted in his breast his passion for hermetics, of which, too, it was but a natural consequence, seeing that there is an intimate connection between the hermetic philosophy and masonry. Gringoire had passed from the love of an idea to the love of the form of that idea.

One day he had stopped near the church of Saint-Germain-l'Auxerrois, at the corner of a building called *le For-l'Evêque*, which was opposite another called *le For-le-Roi*. There was at this For-l'Evêque a beautiful chapel of the Fourteenth century, whose apsis was on the street. Gringoire was examining devoutly its external sculptures. It was one of those moments of selfish, exclusive and supreme enjoyment in which the artist sees nothing in the world but his art, and the world itself in that art. All at once, he felt a hand fall heavily on his shoulder; he turned round—it was his old friend, his old master, monsieur, the archdeacon.

He was quite confounded. It was long since he had seen the

archdeacon; and Dom Claude was one of those grave and ardent beings, a meeting with whom always disturbs the equilibrium of a sceptical philosopher.

The archdeacon maintained silence for some moments, during which Gringoire had leisure to observe him. He found Dom Claude much altered, pale as a winter morning, with hollow eyes and hair almost white. The priest was the first to break this silence, by saying in a calm but freezing tone: 'How do you do, Maître Pierre?'

'As to my health,' answered Gringoire, 'eh! eh! one can say both one thing and another on that score. Still it is good, on the whole. I do not take too much of anything. You know, master, the secret of keeping well, according to Hippocrates: *Id est: cibi, potus, somni venus, omnia moderata sint.*' (That is: love of food, drink, slumber, let all things be in moderation.)

'You have no care, then, Maître Pierre?' resumed the archdeacon, looking steadily at Gringoire.

'Faith, not I!'

'And what are you doing now?'

'As you see, master. I am examining the cutting of these stones, and the style in which this bas-relief is executed.'

The priest began to smile with that bitter smile which raises only one corner of the mouth. 'And that amuses you?'

''Tis paradise!' exclaimed Gringoire. And, leaning over the sculptures with the fascinated air of a demonstrator of living phenomena: 'Now, for example, do you not think that that metamorphosis, in bas-relief, is executed with a great deal of skill, delicacy and patience? Look at that small column; was ever capital entwined with leaves more graceful or more exquisitely touched by the chisel? Here are three alto-relievos by Jean Maillevin. They are not the finest specimens of that great genius. Nevertheless, the simplicity, the sweetness of those faces, the sportiveness of the attitudes and the draperies, and that undefinable charm which is mingled with all the imperfections, render the small figures very light and delicate—perchance even too much so. You do not find it interesting?'

'Oh, yes!' said the priest.

'And if you were to see the interior of the chapel!' continued the poet, with his loquacious enthusiasm. 'Carvings everywhere! 'Tis as thickly clustered as the heart of the cabbage! The apsis is of a very devout fashion, and so peculiar that I have never seen anything like it anywhere else!'

Dom Claude interrupted him: 'You are happy, then?'

Gringoire replied with conviction: 'On my honour, yes! First, I loved women, then animals; now I love stones. They are quite as amusing as animals or women, and less treacherous.'

The priest passed his hand across his brow. It was his habitual gesture.

'Indeed!'

'Hark you,' said Gringoire; 'one has one's enjoyments.' He took the arm of the priest, who yielded to his guidance, and led him under the staircase turret of the For-l'Evêque. 'There's a staircase!' he exclaimed. 'Whenever I see it I am happy. That flight of steps is the most simple and the most uncommon in Paris. Every step is chamfered underneath. Its beauty and simplicity consist in the circumstance of the steps, which are a foot broad, or thereabout, being interlaced, mortised, jointed, enchained, enchased, set one in the other, and biting into each other, in a way that is truly firm and admirable.'

'And you desire nothing?' said the priest.

'No!'

'And you regret nothing?'

'Neither regret nor desire. I have arranged my mode of life.'

'What man arranges,' said Claude, 'circumstances disarrange.'

'I am a Pyrrhonian philosopher,' answered Gringoire, 'and hold everything in equilibrium.'

'And how do you earn your living?'

'I still write, now and then, epics and tragedies; but that which brings me in the most is that certain industry of mine, of which you are aware, master—carrying pyramids of chairs on my teeth.'

'A scurvy trade for a philosopher!'

'It is still equilibrium,' said Gringoire. 'When one has an idea, one finds it in everything.'

'I know that,' replied the archdeacon.

After a short silence, the priest resumed:

'You are, nevertheless, poor enough?'

'Poor? Yes, but not unhappy.'

At that moment the sound of horses was heard; and our two interlocutors saw filing off at the end of the street a company of the king's archers, with their lances raised, and an officer at their head. The cavalcade was brilliant, and its march resounded on the pavement.

'How you look at that officer!' said Gringoire to the archdeacon.

'I think I know him!' was the reply.

'How do you call him?'

'I believe,' said Claude, 'his name is Phœbus de Châteaupers.'

'Phœbus! a curious sort of a name! There's Phœbus, too, Count of Foix. I recollect I knew a girl once who never swore but by Phœbus.'

'Come hither,' said the priest; 'I have something to say to you.'

Since the passing of the troop, some agitation was perceptible under the frozen exterior of the archdeacon. He walked on. Gringoire followed him, being wont to obey him, like all who had once approached that commanding personality. They reached in silence the Rue des Bernardins, which was almost deserted. Dom Claude stopped.

'What have you to say to me, master?' asked Gringoire.

'Do you not think,' answered the archdeacon, with an air of profound reflection, 'that the dress of those cavaliers, whom we have just seen, is handsomer than yours and mine?'

Gringoire shook his head.

'I' faith, I like better my red and yellow jerkin than those scales of iron and steel. A fine sort of thing, to make a noise in going along like an iron quay in an earthquake!'

'Then, Gringoire, you have never envied those fine fellows in their warlike hacquetons?'

'Envied what, monsieur the archdeacon? their strength, their armour, their discipline? Give me rather philosophy and independence in rags. I would rather be the head of a fly than the tail of a lion.'

'That is singular,' said the musing priest. 'A fine uniform is a fine thing, nevertheless.'

Gringoire, seeing him absorbed in thought, quitted him to go and admire the porch of a neighbouring house. He returned, clapping his hands.

'If you were less occupied with the fine clothes of men of war, monsieur the archdeacon, I would beg you to go and see that doorway. I have always said it; the Sieur Aubry's house has the most superb entrance in the world.'

'Pierre Gringoire,' said the archdeacon, 'what have you done with that little gypsy dancer?'

'Esmeralda? You change the conversation very abruptly.'

'Was she not your wife?'

'Yes, by virtue of a broken pitcher. We were in for it for four years. By-the-by,' added Gringoire, looking at the archdeacon with a half-bantering air, 'you think of her still, then?'

'And you—do you no longer think of her?'

'Very little. I have so many things! Good heavens! how pretty the little goat was!'

'Did not that Bohemian girl save your life?'

''Tis true, pardieu.'

'Well, what became of her? what have you done with her?'

'I cannot tell you. I believe they have hanged her.'

'You believe?'

'I am not sure. When I saw there was hanging in the case, I kept out of the business.'

'And that is all you know of it?'

'Stay. I was told she had taken refuge in Notre-Dame, and that she was there in safety; and I am delighted at it; and I have not been able to discover whether the goat escaped with her, and that is all I know about the matter.'

'I will tell you more,' cried Dom Claude; and his voice, till then low, deliberate and hollow, became like thunder. 'She has, indeed, taken refuge in Notre-Dame. But in three days justice will drag her again from thence, and she will be hanged at the Grève. There is a decree of the Parliament for it!'

'Now, that is a shame,' said Gringoire.

The priest in a moment had become cool and calm again.

'And who the devil,' continued the poet, 'has taken the trouble to solicit a decree of reintegration? Could they not leave the Parliament alone? Of what consequence can it be that a poor girl takes shelter under the buttresses of Notre-Dame, among the swallows' nests?'

'There are Satans in the world,' answered the archdeacon.

'That's a devilish bad piece of work,' observed Gringoire.

The archdeacon resumed, after a short silence:

'So then, she saved your life?'

'Yes, among my good friends the Truands. I was within an inch of being hanged. They would have been sorry for it now.'

'Will you not do something for her, then?'

'I should rejoice to be of service, Dom Claude; but if I were to bring a bad piece of business about my ears!'

'What can it signify?'

'The deuce! what can it signify! You are very kind, master! I have two great works begun.'

The priest struck his forehead. In spite of the composure which he affected, a violent gesture betrayed from time to time his inward struggles.

'How is she to be saved?'

'Master,' said Gringoire, 'I will answer you—*Il padelt*—which means, in the Turkish, "God is our hope."'

'How is she to be saved?' repeated Claude, dreamily.

Gringoire, in his turn, struck his forehead.

'Hark you, master; I have some imagination. I will find expedients for you. What if we were to entreat the king's mercy?'

'Mercy! of Louis XI!'

'Why not?'

'Go take from the tiger his bone!'

Gringoire began to seek fresh expedients.

'Well, stay. Shall I address a memorial to the midwives, declaring that the girl is with child?'

At this the priest's sunken eyeballs glared.

'With child! Fellow! do you know anything about it?'

Gringoire was terrified at his manner. He hastened to say:

'Oh, not I. Our marriage was a regular *forismaritagium*. I'm altogether out of it. But, at any rate, one would obtain a reprieve.'

'Madness! infamy! hold thy peace!'

'You are wrong to be angry,' muttered Gringoire. 'One gets a respite; that does no harm to anybody, and it puts forty deniers parisis into the pockets of the midwives, who are poor women.'

The priest heard him not.

'She must leave there, nevertheless,' murmured he. 'The decree is to be put in force within three days. Otherwise, it would not be valid. That Quasimodo! Women have very depraved tastes!' He raised his voice: 'Maître Pierre, I have well considered the matter. There is but one means of saving her.'

'And what is it? For my part, I see none.'

'Hark ye, Maître Pierre; remember that you owe your life to her. I will tell you candidly my idea. The church is watched day and night; no one is allowed to come out but those who have been seen to go in. Thus you can go in. You shall come, and I will take you to her. You will change clothes with her. She will take your doublet, and you will take her petticoat.'

'So far, so good,' observed the philosopher; 'and what then?'

'What then? Why, she will go out in your clothes, and you will remain in hers. You may get hanged, perhaps, but she will be saved.'

Gringoire scratched his ear with a very serious air.

'Well!' said he, 'there is an idea that would never have come into my head of itself.'

At Dom Claude's unexpected proposal, the open and benign countenance of the poet had abruptly clouded over, like a smiling Italian landscape when an unlucky gust of wind throws a cloud across the sun.

'Well, Gringoire, what say you to the plan?'

'I say, master, that I shall not be hanged perhaps, but that I shall be hanged indubitably.'

'That concerns us not.'

'The deuce!' said Gringoire.

'She saved your life. 'Tis a debt you are discharging.'

'There are many others which I do not discharge.'

'Maître Pierre, it must absolutely be so.'

The archdeacon spoke imperiously.

'Hark you, Dom Claude,' answered the poet, in great consternation. 'You hold to that idea, and you are wrong. I don't see why I should get myself hanged instead of another.'

'What have you, then, which attaches you so strongly to life?'

'Ah! a thousand reasons.'

'What are they, pray?'

'What are they? The air, the sky, the morning, the evening, the moonlight, my good friends the Truands, our jeers with the old hags, the fine architecture of Paris to study, three great books to write, one of them against the bishop and his mills; more than I can tell. Anaxagoras used to say he had come into the world to admire the sun. And then, I have the felicity of passing the whole of my days, from morning till night, with a man of genius—who is myself—which is very agreeable.'

'A head fit for a mule bell!' muttered the archdeacon. 'Speak, then; this life that thou findst so charming, who preserved it for thee? To whom art thou indebted for the privilege of breathing that air, of seeing that sky, of being still able to amuse thy linnet-head with humbugs and follies? Had it not been for her, where wouldst thou be? Thou wilt have her die then, she through whom thou livest; thou wilt have her die, that creature so lovely, so sweet, so adorable—a creature necessary to the light of the world, more divine than divinity itself; whilst thou, half sage, half fool, a mere sketch of something, a sort of vegetable which fancies it walks and thinks, thou wouldst continue to live with the life thou hast stolen from her, as useless as a taper at noonday! Come, Gringoire, a little pity! be generous in thy turn; she has set the example.'

The priest was vehement. Gringoire listened to him, at first with an air of indecision, then became moved, and concluded with making a tragical grimace which made his wan countenance resemble that of a new-born child in a fit of the colic.

'You are pathetic!' said he, wiping away a tear. 'Well! I will think about it. 'Tis an odd idea of yours.' . . . 'After all,' pursued he, after a moment's silence, 'who knows? perhaps they'll not hang me; there's many a slip between the cup and the lip. When they find me in that box, so grotesquely muffled in cap and petticoat, perhaps they'll burst out laughing. . . And if they do hang me, what then? The rope—'tis a death like another. Or, rather, 'tis not a death like another. 'Tis a death worthy of the sage who has wavered all his life; a death which is neither fish nor flesh, like the mind of the true sceptic; a death fully marked with Pyrrhonism and hesitation, which holds the medium between heaven and earth, which leaves you in suspense. 'Tis a philosopher's death, and I was predestined thereto, perchance. It is magnificent to die as one has lived—'

The priest interrupted him: 'Is it agreed?'

'What is death, after all?' pursued Gringoire, with exaltation. 'A disagreeable moment, a turnpike-gate, the passage from little-

ness to nothingness. Some one having asked Cercidas of Mega-
lopolis whether he could die willingly: "Why should I not?"
answered he; "for after my death, I shall see those great men,
Pythagoras among the philosophers, Hecatæus among the historians, Homer among the poets, Olympus among the musicians."'

The archdeacon held out his hand to him. 'It is settled, then?
you will come to-morrow?'

The gesture brought Gringoire back to reality.

"Faith, no!' said he, with the tone of a man just awaking. 'To
get hanged! 'tis too absurd. I will not.'

'Farewell, then;' and the archdeacon added between his teeth,
'I will find thee again.'

'I do not want that devil of a man to find me again,' thought
Gringoire; and he ran after Dom Claude. 'Stay, monsieur the
archdeacon,' said he; 'old friends should not fall out. You take
an interest in that girl—my wife, I mean. 'Tis well. You have
devised a scheme for getting her out of Notre-Dame; but your
plan is extremely unpleasant for me, Gringoire. Now, if I could
suggest another, myself!—I beg to say, a most luminous inspiration
has just occurred to me. If I had an expedient for extracting her
from her sorry plight, without compromising my neck in the
smallest degree with a slip-knot, what would you say? would not
that suffice you? Must I absolutely be hanged before you are
content?'

The priest was tearing the buttons from his cassock with impatience. 'Stream of words! What is thy plan?'

'Yes,' resumed Gringoire, talking to himself, and clapping his
forefinger to his nose in sign of deep cogitation; 'that is it! The
Truands are fine fellows! The tribe of Egypt love her! They will
rise at the first word! Nothing easier! A bold stroke! Under cover
of the disorder, they will easily carry her off! To-morrow evening.
Nothing would please them better,'

'The plan!—speak!' said the priest, shaking him.

Gringoire turned majestically toward him: 'Let me alone! you
see that I am composing!' He reflected a few moments more, then
began to clap his hands at his thought, exclaiming: 'Admirable!
success is sure!'

'The plan!' repeated Claude, angrily.

Gringoire was radiant.

'Come hither,' said he; 'let me tell you this in your ear. 'Tis
truly a gallant counterplot, which will get us all out of the scrape.
Egad! you must admit that I am no fool!'

He stopped short.

'Ah! by the way, is the little goat with the girl?'

'Yes—the devil take thee!'

'They would have hanged it also, would they not?'

'What is that to me?'

'Yes, they would have hanged it. They hanged a sow last month. The executioner likes that; he eats the animal after. Hang my pretty Djali! poor little lamb!'

'A curse upon thee!' cried Dom Claude. 'The hangman is thyself. What means of safety hast thou found, fellow! Wilt thou never be delivered of thy scheme?'

'Softly, master! You shall hear.'

Gringoire bent towards the archdeacon, and spoke very low in his ear, casting an anxious look from one end of the street to the other, though no one was near. When he had done, Dom Claude took his hand, and said, coolly: ''Tis well. To-morrow.'

'To-morrow,' repeated Gringoire; and while the archdeacon withdrew one way, he went off the other, saying low to himself: 'This is a grand affair, Monsieur Pierre Gringoire. Never mind —it's not to be said that because one is of little account one is to be frightened at a great undertaking. Biton carried a great bull on his shoulders; wagtails, linnets and buntings traverse the ocean.'

2

Turn Vagabond!

On re-entering the cloister, the archdeacon found at the door of his cell his brother, Jehan du Moulin, who was waiting for him, and who had beguiled the tedium of waiting by drawing on the wall, with a piece of charcoal, a profile of his elder brother, embellished with a nose of immoderate dimensions.

Dom Claude scarcely looked at his brother; his thoughts were elsewhere. That merry scamp's face, whose radiance had so often cleared away the gloom from the physiognomy of the priest, was now powerless to dissipate the cloud which each day gathered thicker and thicker over that corrupt, mephitic and stagnant soul.

'Brother,' said Jehan, timidly, 'I am come to see you.'

The archdeacon did not so much as raise his eyes toward him. 'Well?'

'Brother,' continued the hypocrite, 'you are so good to me, and give me such wise counsel, that I always return to you.'

'What next?'

'Alas! brother, you were very right when you used to say to me: "Jehan! Jehan, *cessat doctorum doctrina, discipulorum disciplina*. (Cease the doctrine of the doctors, the discipline of the disciples.) Jehan, be prudent. Jehan, be studious. Jehan, pass not the night outside of the college without lawful occasion and leave of the master. Cudgel not the Picards. *Noli, Joannes, verberrare Picardos.* (Beat not the Picards.) Rot not like an unlettered ass, *quasi asinus illiteratus,* upon the straw seats of the schools. Jehan, allow yourself to be punished at the discretion of the master. Jehan, go every evening to chapel, and sing an anthem with verse and orison to our lady, the glorious Virgin Mary." Alas! how excellent was that advice!'

'And then?'

'Brother, you see before you a culprit, a criminal, a miscreant, a libertine, a reprobate! My dear brother, Jehan hath made of your counsels straw and dung to trample under foot. Well am I chastised for it—and God Almighty is exceeding just. So long as I had money, I feasted and led a joyous, foolish life. Oh! how grim-faced and vile behind is debauchery which is so charming in front! Now I have not a coin left; I have sold my table-cloth, my shirt and my towel. A merry life no longer! the bright taper is extinguished, and nothing is left me but noisome tallow dip, which stinks under my nostrils. The girls mock at me. I drink water. I am tormented with remorse and creditors.'

'The rest?' said the archdeacon.

'Alas! my very dear brother, I would fain lead a better life. I come to you full of contrition. I am penitent. I confess my faults. I beat my breast with heavy blows. You are very right to wish I should one day become a licentiate and sub-monitor of the Torchi College. At the present moment I feel a remarkable vocation for that office. But I have no more ink—I must buy some; I have no more pens—I must buy some; I have no more paper, no more books—I must buy some. For these purposes I am greatly in need of a little money, and I come to you, brother, with my heart full of contrition.'

'Is that all?'

'Yes,' said the student. 'A little money.'

'I have none.'

The student then said, with an air at once grave and decided: 'Well, brother, I am sorry to be obliged to tell you that I have received from other quarters very advantageous offers and proposals. You will not give me any money? No? In that case I will turn Truand.'

On pronouncing this monstrous word, he assumed the mien of an Ajax expecting to see the thunderbolt fall on his head.

The archdeacon said coldly to him: 'Turn Truand then.'

Jehan made him a low bow, and descended the cloister stairs whistling.

As he was passing through the court-yard of the cloister, beneath the window of his brother's cell, he heard that window open, raised his head, and saw the archdeacon's stern face looking through the opening. 'Get thee to the devil!' said Dom Claude; 'here is the last money thou shalt have of me.'

So saying the priest flung Jehan a purse, which made a great bump on the student's forehead, and with which Jehan set off, both vexed and content, like a dog that is pelted with marrow-bones.

3

Long Live Mirth!

THE reader has probably not forgotten that a part of the Court of Miracles was enclosed within the ancient walls of the Town, a goodly number of whose towers were beginning, even at that epoch, to fall into decay. One of these towers had been converted into a pleasure resort by the Truands. There was a dram-shop on the lowest floor, and the rest was carried on in the upper stories. This tower was the point the most alive, and consequently the most hideous of the whole outcast den. It was a sort of monstrous hive, which was humming day and night. At night, when the remainder of the rabble were asleep, when not a lighted window was to be seen in the dingy fronts of the houses bordering the square, when not a sound was heard to issue from its innumerable families, from those ant-hills of thieves, loose women, and stolen or bastard children, the joyous tower might always be distinguished by the noise which proceeded from it, by the crimson light which, gleaming at once from the air-holes, the windows, the crevices in the gaping walls, escaped, as it were, from every pore.

The cellar, then, formed the public-house. One entered it through a low door and down a staircase as steep as a classic Alexandrine. Over the door, by way of a sign, was a marvellous daub representing new-coined sols and dead chickens, with this punning inscription underneath: *Aux sonneurs pour les trépassés.* ('The ringers for the dead.')

One evening, at the moment when the curfew was ringing from all the belfries in Paris, the sergeants of the watch might have remarked, had they been permitted to enter the formidable Court of Miracles, that more tumult than usual was going on in the Truands' tavern; that they were drinking deeper and swearing louder. Without, in the square, were numerous groups, conversing in low tones, as if some great plot was hatching; while here and there a knave squatted down, whetting some wicked-looking blade upon the pavement.

Meanwhile, within the tavern, wine and gaming so powerfully diverted the minds of the Truandry from the ideas which occupied them that evening, that it would have been difficult to have divined from the conversation of the drinkers what was the affair in hand. Only they had a gayer air than usual, and between the legs of each some weapon was seen glittering, a pruning-hook, a hatchet, a large bludgeon, or the crook of an old hackbut.

The apartment, of a circular form, was very spacious; but the tables were so close together and the tipplers so numerous, that the whole contents of the tavern, men, women, benches, beer-jugs, the drinkers, the sleepers, the gamblers, the able-bodied, the crippled, seemed thrown pell-mell together with about as much order and arrangement as a heap of oyster shells. A few tallow dips were burning upon the tables; but the real light of the tavern, that which sustained in the pot-house the character of the chandelier in an opera house, was the fire. That cellar was so damp that the fire was never allowed to go out, even in the height of summer; an immense chimney, with a carved mantel, and thick-set with heavy iron dogs and kitchen utensils, had in it, then, one of those large fires composed of wood and peat, which, at night, in a village street, bring out in red relief the windows of some forge upon the opposite wall. A large dog, gravely seated in the ashes, was turning before the glowing fire a spit loaded with meat.

In spite of the confusion, after the first glance, one might distinguish amid this multitude, three principal groups, pressing around three several personages with whom the reader is already acquainted. One of these personages, fantastically bedizened with many an Oriental trinket, was Mathias Hungadi Spicali, Duke of Egypt and Bohemia. The old rogue was seated on the table, with his legs crossed and his finger in the air, while in a loud voice he explained his skill in white and black magic to the many gaping faces which surrounded him. Another crowd was gathered thick around our old friend, the valiant King of Tunis, armed to the teeth; Clopin Trouillefou, with a very serious air and in a low voice, was superintending the pillage of an enormous cask of arms, staved wide before him, from which were issuing in profusion axes, swords, bassinets, coats of mail, lance and pike heads, crossbow bolts and arrows, like apples and grapes out of a cornucopia. Each one was taking something from the heap; one a head-piece, another a long rapier, and a third, the crosshandled *misericorde* or small dagger. The very children were arming; and even the cripples in bowls were barbed and cuirassed, and moved between the legs of the drinkers, like large beetles.

And lastly, a third audience, the most noisy, the most jovial, and the most numerous of all, was crowding the benches and the tables, from the midst of which a flute-like voice, haranguing and swearing, escaped from under a heavy suit of mail, complete from casque to spurs. The individual who had thus screwed himself up in full panoply, was so hidden by his warlike trappings that nothing was seen of his person but a red, impudent, turned-up nose, a lock of fair hair, a red mouth and two daring eyes. His belt was full of daggers and poniards; a large sword hung by his hip; a rusty cross-bow was on his left, and an immense wine-pot before him, without counting a strapping, dishevelled wench who was seated on his right. All the mouths around him were laughing, swearing and drinking.

Add to these twenty secondary groups; the waiters, male and female, running backward and forward with pitchers on their heads; the gamesters stooping over taws, *merèlles*, dice, *vachettes*, the exciting game of the tringlet (a kind of backgammon); quarrels in one corner—kisses in another; and some idea may then be formed of the whole collective scene; over which wavered the light of a great flaming fire, making a thousand grotesque and enormous shadows dance upon the wall.

As for the noise, it might be likened to the interior of a bell in full peal.

The dripping-pan, in which a shower of grease was crackling from the spit, filled up, with its continuous snapping, the intervals of those thousand dialogues which crossed each other in all directions from one side to another of the great circular room.

Amidst all this uproar there was, on one side of the tavern, upon the bench within the great open fireplace, a philosopher meditating, with his feet in the ashes, and his eyes upon the burning brands. It was Pierre Gringoire.

'Be quick! make haste! get under arms! we must march in an hour,' said Clopin Trouillefou to his Argotiers.

A wench was humming an air:

> *'Father and mother, good-night;*
> *The latest up rake the fire.'*

Two card players were disputing. 'Knave,' cried the reddest-faced of the two, shaking his fist at the other, 'I'll mark thee with a club. Thou might go and take Mistigri's place in messeigneur the king's own card party.'

'Ugh!' roared a Norman, easily known by his nasal accent, 'we're all heaped together here like the saints of Pebbletown!'

'My children,' said the Duke of Egypt to his auditory, speaking in a falsetto voice, 'the witches of France go to the sabbath without ointment, broomstick, or anything to ride on, with only a few magic words. The witches of Italy have always a he-goat that waits for them at their door. All of them are bound to go out up the chimney.'

The voice of the young scamp armed from head to foot was heard above the general hum.

'Noël! Noël!' cried he. 'My first day in armour! A Truand! I'm a Truand, ventre de Christ! Fill my glass. Friends, my name is Jehan Frollo du Moulin, and I'm a gentleman. 'Tis my opinion that if God were a guardsman he'd turn robber. Brethren, we go upon a noble expedition. We are valiant fellows. Besiege the church, force the doors, bring away the pretty girl, save her from the judges, save her from the priests; dismantle the cloister, burn the bishop in his house; we will do all that in less time than a burgomaster takes to eat a spoonful of soup. Our cause is just; we'll plunder Notre-Dame, and that's all about it. We'll hang Quasimodo. Do you know Quasimodo, mesdemoiselles? Have you seen him puffing upon the great bell on a Pentecost festival? By Beelzebub's horns, it is very fine. You'd take him for a devil astride of a ghoul. Hark ye, my friends, I'm a Truand from the bottom of my heart; I'm a vagabond in my soul, a cadger born. I was very rich, and I have spent my all. My mother wanted to make me an officer; my father, a sub-deacon; my aunt, a councillor of the inquests; my grandmother, king's prothonotary; my great aunt, treasurer of the short robe; but I would make myself a Truand. I told my father so, and he spit his malediction in my face. I told my mother so, and she, poor old lady, began to cry and chatter like yonder fagot on the iron dogs there. Let's be merry! I'm a real Bicêtre. Barmaid, my dear, more wine! I've still some money left. But mind, I'll have no more of that Surène wine—it hurts my throat. I'd as lief gargle myself, cor-bœuf, with a basket!'

Meanwhile the rabble applauded with boisterous laughter; and, finding that the tumult was redoubling around him, the scholar exclaimed:

'Oh, what a glorious noise! *Populi debacchantis populosa debacchatio!*' (The ravings of the people, popular fury.) Then he began to sing out, with an eye as if swimming in ecstasy, and the tone of a canon leading the vesper chant: '*Quæ cantica! quæ organa! quæ cantilenæ! quæ melodiæ hic sine fine decantantur! Sonant melliflua hymnorum organa, suavissima angelorum melodia, cantica canticorum mira!*' (What songs, what instruments, what chants here without end are sung! Here sound sweet-toned instruments of hymns, most sweet melodies of angels, wonderful song of songs!) He broke off. 'Hey, you there, the devil's own barmaid! give me some supper!'

There followed a moment of comparative silence, during which the shrill voice of the Duke of Egypt was heard in its turn, instructing his Bohemians.

'The weasel,' said he, 'goes by the name of Aduine; a fox is called Blue-foot or the Woodranger; a wolf, Gray-foot or Gilt-foot; a bear, the Old one or the Grandfather. A gnome's cap makes one invisible, and makes one see invisible things. Whenever a toad is to be christened, it ought to be dressed in velvet, red or black, with a little bell at its neck and one at its feet. The godfather holds it by the head, and the godmother by the hinder parts. 'Tis the demon Sidragasum who hath the power to make wenches dance naked.'

'By the mass,' interrupted Jehan, 'I should like to be the demon Sidragasum!'

Meanwhile, the Truands continued to arm themselves and whisper at the other end of the tavern.

'That poor Esmeralda!' exclaimed one of the gypsy-men; 'she is our sister; we must release her.'

'Is she still at Notre-Dame?' asked a Jew-looking peddler.

'Yes, pardieu!' was the reply.

'Well, then, comrades,' cried the peddler, 'to Notre-Dame! All the more because there in the chapel of Saints Féréol and Ferrution there are two statues, the one of Saint John the Baptist, the other of Saint Anthony, of solid gold, weighing together seventeen gold marks and fifteen esterlins; and the pedestals, of silver gilt, weigh seventeen marks five ounces. I know that; I am a goldsmith.'

Here they set Jehan's supper before him. He exclaimed, as he threw himself upon the bosom of the girl that sat by him:

'By Saint-Voult-de-Lucques, called by the people Saint Gogulu, I am perfectly happy! I see a blockhead there, straight before me, that's looking at me with a face as smooth as an archduke. Here's another, at my left hand, with teeth so long that one can't see his chin. And then, I'm like the Maréchal de Gié at the siege of Pontoise; I've my right resting upon a hillock. Ventre-Mahom! comrade! you look like a tennis-ball merchant! and you come and sit down by me! I am noble, my friend. Trade is incompatible with nobility. Get thee away. Hello! you there! don't fight! What! Baptiste Croque-Oison! with a fine nose like thine! wilt thou go and risk it against that blockhead's great fists? You simpleton! *Non cuiquam datum est habere nasum.* (Not to everyone is it given to have a nose.) Truly, thou'rt divine, Jacqueline-of-the-Red-Ear! it's a pity thou hast no hair on thy head! Hello! My name is Jehan Frollo, and my brother's an archdeacon! the devil fly away with him! All that I tell you's the truth. By turning Truand I've given up one-half of a house, situate in Paradise, which my brother had promised me—*dimidiam domum in paradiso* (half a dwelling in Paradise)—those are the very words. I've a fief in the Rue Tirechappe, and all the women are in love with me, as true as it is that Saint Eloi was an excellent goldsmith, and that the five trades of the good city of Paris are the tanners, the leather dressers, the baldric-makers, the purse-makers and the cordwainers; and that Saint Laurence was broiled over egg-shells. I swear to you, comrades,

> *For full twelve months I'll drink no wine,*
> *If this be any lie of mine!*

'My charmer, 'tis moonlight. See yonder, through the air-hole, how the wind rumples those clouds, just as I do thy gorgerette! Girls, snuff the candles and the children. Christ and Mahom, what am I eating now, in the name of Jupiter? Hey, there, old jade! the hairs that are not to be found on thy wenches' heads we find in the omelets. Do you hear, old woman? I like my omelets bald. The devil flatten thy nose! A fine tavern of Beelzebub is this, where the wenches comb themselves with the forks?' And thereupon he broke his plate upon the floor and began to sing with all his might:

> '*And for this self of mine,*
> *By the Blood Divine!*
> *No creed I crave,*
> *Nor law to save:*
> *I have no fire,*
> *I have no hut,*
> *Nor faith to put*
> *In sovereign high*
> *Or Deity!*'

Meanwhile, Clopin Trouillefou had finished his distribution of weapons. He approached Gringoire, who seemed absorbed in profound reverie, with his feet on an andiron.

'Friend Pierre,' said the King of Tunis, 'what the devil art thou thinking about?'

Gringoire turned to him with a melancholy smile:

'I love the fire, my dear lord. Not for the trivial reason that fire warms the feet or cooks the soup, but because it throws out sparks. Sometimes I pass whole hours in watching the sparks. I discover a thousand things in those stars that sprinkle the dark background of the chimney-place. Those stars are also worlds.'

'Thunder, if I understand thee,' said the Truand. 'Dost know what o'clock it is?'

'I do not know,' answered Gringoire.

Clopin then went up to the Duke of Egypt.

'Comrade Mathias,' said he, 'this is not a good time we've hit upon. King Louis XI is said to be in Paris.'

'The more need to get our sister out of his clutches,' answered the old gypsy.

'You speak like a man, Mathias,' said the King of Tunis. 'Moreover, we will act promptly. No resistance is to be feared in the church. The canons are like so many hares, and we are in force. The Parliament's men will be finely balked to-morrow when they come to seek her. Guts of the Pope! I would not have them hang the pretty girl!'

Clopin went out of the tavern.

Meantime, Jehan was shouting in a hoarse voice: 'I drink! I eat! I'm drunk! I'm Jupiter! Hey! you there, Pierre the Slaughterer! look at me like that again and I'll fillip the dust off your nose.'

Gringoire, on the other hand, roused from his meditations, had begun to contemplate the wild and noisy scene around him, and muttered between his teeth: '*Luxuriosa res vinum et tumultuosa ebrietas.* (Wine is a thing of luxury, drunkenness of tumult.) Alas! what good reason I have to abstain from drinking! and how excellent is the saying of Saint Benedict: *Vinum apostatare facit etiam sapientes!*' (To abjure wine also makes wise men.)

At that moment Clopin re-entered, and shouted in a voice of thunder, 'Midnight!'

At this word, which produced the effect of a call to boot and saddle on a regiment at halt, all the Truands—men, women and children—rushed in a mass from the tavern with great noise of arms and iron implements.

The moon was now obscured.

The Court of Miracles was entirely dark. Not a light was to be seen; but it was far from being deserted. A crowd of men and women talking in low tones could be distinguished. They could be heard buzzing, and all sorts of weapons were glittering in the darkness. Clopin mounted upon a large stone.

'To your ranks, Argot!' cried he. 'Fall into line, Egypt! To your ranks, Galilee!'

A movement began in the darkness. The immense multitude seemed to be forming in column. In a few minutes the King of Tunis again raised his voice:

'Now, silence! to march through Paris. The password is, *Petite flambe en bagnenaud.* (Little light in a bladder-nut.) The torches must not be lighted till we reach Notre-Dame. March!'

Ten minutes later the horsemen of the watch fled in terror before a long procession of men descending in darkness and silence toward the Pont-au-Change, through the winding streets that intersect in every direction the close-built neighbourhood of the Halles.

4

An Awkward Friend

THAT same night Quasimodo slept not. He had just gone his last round through the church. He had not noticed, at the moment when he was closing the doors, that the archdeacon had passed near him and had displayed some degree of ill-humour at seeing him bolt and padlock with care the enormous iron bars which gave to these closed portals the solidity of a wall. Dom Claude appeared even more preoccupied than usual. Moreover, since the nocturnal adventure of the cell, he was constantly ill-treating Quasimodo; but in vain he used him harshly, even striking him sometimes; nothing could shake the submission, the patience, the devoted resignation of the faithful ringer. From the archdeacon he could endure anything—insults, threats, blows—without murmuring a reproach, without uttering a complaint. At most he would follow Dom Claude anxiously with his eye, as he ascended the staircase of the towers; but the archdeacon had of himself abstained from again appearing before the gypsy-girl.

On that night, accordingly, Quasimodo, after casting one look toward his poor forsaken bells, Jacqueline, Marie, and Thibault, mounted to the top of the northern tower, and there, placing his well-closed dark-lantern on the leads, took a survey of Paris. The night, as we have already said, was very dark. Paris, which, comparatively speaking, was not lighted at that period, presented to the eye a confused heap of black masses, intersected here and there by the whitish curve of the Seine. Not a light could Quasimodo see except from the window of a distant edifice, the vague and gloomy profile of which was distinguishable, rising above the roofs in the direction of the Porte Saint Antoine. There, too, was some one wakeful.

While his only eye was thus hovering over that horizon of mist and darkness, the ringer felt within him an inexpressible uneasiness. For several days he had been upon the watch. He had seen constantly wandering around the church men of sinister aspect, who never took their eyes from the young girl's asylum. He feared lest some plot might be hatching against the unfortunate refugee. He fancied that she was an object of popular hatred as well as himself, and that something sinister might probably happen soon. Thus he remained on his tower, on the lookout, 'dreaming in his dreamplace,' as Rabelais says, his eye alternately directed on the cell and on Paris, keeping faithful watch like a trusty dog, with a thousand suspicions in his mind.

All at once, while he was reconnoitring the great city with that eye which nature, as if by way of compensation, had made so piercing that it almost supplied the deficiency of other organs in Quasimodo, it struck him that there was something unusual in the appearance of the outline of the quay of the Vielle-Pelleterie, that there was some movement at that point, that the line of the parapet which stood out black against the whiteness of the water was not so straight and tranquil as that of the other quays, but that it undulated before the eye like waves of a river, or the heads of a crowd in motion.

This appeared strange to him. He redoubled his attention. The movement appeared to be towards the city. No light was to be seen. It remained some time on the quay, then flowed off it by degrees, as if whatever was passing along was entering the interior of the island; then it ceased entirely, and the line of the quay became straight and motionless again.

Just as Quasimodo was exhausting himself in conjectures, it seemed to him that the movement was reappearing in the Rue du Parvis, which runs into the city perpendicularly to the front of Notre-Dame. In fact, notwithstanding the great darkness, he could see the head of a column issuing from that street, and in an instant a crowd spreading over the square, of which he could distinguish nothing further than that it was a crowd.

This spectacle was not without its terror. It is probable that that singular procession, which seemed so anxious to conceal itself in profound darkness, observed a silence no less profound. Still some sound must have escaped from it, were it only the tramping of the feet. But even this noise could not reach the deaf watcher; and this great multitude, of which he could see scarcely anything, and of which he could hear nothing, though it was marching and moving so near him, produced on him the effect of an assemblage of dead men, mute, impalpable, lost in vapour. He seemed to see advancing toward him a mist peopled with men, to see shades moving in the shade.

Then his fears returned; the idea of an attempt against the Egyptian presented itself again to his mind. He had a vague feeling that he was about to find himself in a critical situation. In this crisis he held counsel with himself, and his reasoning was more just and prompt than might have been expected from a brain so ill-organized. Should he awaken the Egyptian? assist her to escape? Which way? The streets were beset; behind the church was the river; there was no boat, no egress! There was but one measure to be taken: to meet death on the threshold of Notre-Dame; to resist at least until some assistance came, if any were to come, and not to disturb the sleep of Esmeralda. The unhappy girl would be awakened soon enough to die. This resolution once taken, he proceeded to reconnoitre the *enemy* more calmly.

The crowd seemed to be increasing every moment in the Parvis. He concluded, however, that very little noise was made, since the windows of the streets and the square remained closed. All at once a light flashed up, and in an instant seven or eight lighted torches were waving above the heads, shaking in the darkness their tufts of flame. Quasimodo then saw distinctly surging, in the Parvis, a frightful troop of men and women in rags, armed with scythes, pikes, pruning-hooks, partisans, the thousand points of which all glittered. Here and there black pitchforks formed horns to those hideous visages. He had a confused recollection of that populace, and thought he recognized all the heads which, a few months before, had saluted him Pope of the Fools. A man holding a torch in one hand and a club in the other mounted a stone post and appeared to be haranguing them. At the same time the strange army performed some evolutions, as if taking post around the church. Quasimodo picked up his lantern and descended to the platform between the towers, to obtain a nearer view and to arrange his means of defence.

Clopin Trouillefou, having arrived before the principal door of Notre-Dame, had, in fact, ranged his troops in order of battle. Although he did not anticipate any resistance, yet, like a prudent general, he wished to preserve such a degree of order as would, in case of need, enable him to face a sudden attack of the watch or of the guardsmen. He had accordingly stationed his brigade in such a manner that, seen from on high and at a distance, it might have been taken for the Roman triangle of the battle of Ecnoma, the pig's head of Alexander, or the famous wedge of Gustavus Adolphus. The base of this triangle was formed along the back of the square, so as to bar the entrance to the Rue du Parvis; one of the sides looked toward the Hôtel-Dieu, the other toward the Rue Saint-Pierre-aux-Bœufs. Clopin Trouillefou had placed himself at the point, with the Duke of Egypt, our friend Jehan, and the boldest of the scavengers.

An enterprise such as the Truands were now attempting against Notre-Dame was no uncommon occurrence in the cities of the Middle Ages. What we in our day call police did not then exist. In populous towns, in capitals especially, there was no central power, sole and commanding all the rest. Feudality had constructed those great municipalities after a strange fashion. A city was an assemblage of innumerable seigneuries, which divided it into compartments of all forms and sizes. From thence arose a thousand contradictory establishments of police, or, rather, no police at all. In Paris, for example, independently of the hundred and forty-one lords claiming censive or manorial dues, there were twenty-five claiming administration of justice and quitrent from the Bishop of Paris, who had five hundred streets, to the Prior of Notre-Dame-des-Champs, who had only four. All these feudal justiciaries recognized only nominally the authority of their suzerain, the king. All had right of superintendence of highways. All were their own masters. Louis XI, that indefatigable workman, who had commenced so effectively the demolition of the feudal edifice, carried on by Richelieu and Louis XIV to the advantage of the royalty, and completed by Mirabeau to the advantage of the people—Louis XI had indeed striven to burst this network of seigneuries which covered Paris, by throwing violently athwart it two or three ordinances of general police. Thus, in 1465, the inhabitants were ordered to light candles in their windows at nightfall, and to shut up their dogs, under pain of the halter; in the same year they were ordered to close the streets in the evening with iron chains, and forbidden to carry daggers or other offensive weapons in the streets at night. But in a short time all these attempts at municipal legislation fell into disuse. The townspeople allowed the candles at the windows to be extinguished by the wind, and their dogs to stray; the iron chains were only stretched in time of public disturbance; and the prohibition against carrying daggers brought about no other change than that of the name of the Rue Coupe-gueule into Rue Coupe-gorge [Cut-jaws into Cut-throat?], which, to be sure, was a manifest improvement. The old framework of the feudal jurisdictions remained standing—an immense accumulation of bailiwicks and seigneuries, crossing one another in all directions throughout the city, straitening and entangling each other, interwoven with each other, and projecting one into another—a useless thicket of watches, under-watches, counter-watches, through the midst of which the armed hand of brigandage, rapine and sedition was constantly passing. Hence, in this state of disorder, deeds of violence on the part of the populace directed against a palace, a hôtel, or an ordinary mansion, in the most thickly populated quarters, were not unheard of occurrences. In most cases, the neighbours did not interfere in the affair unless the pillage reached themselves. They stopped their ears against the report of the musketry, closed their shutters, barricaded their doors, and let the struggle exhaust itself with or without the watch; and the next day it was in Paris, 'Last night, Etienne Barbette was broken open;' or, 'The Maréchal de Clermont was seized, etc.' Hence, not only the royal residences—the Louvre, the Palais, the Bastille, the Tournelles—but such as were simply seigneurial, the Petit-Bourbon, the Hôtel-de-Sens, the Hôtel d'Angoulême, etc., had their battlemented walls and their machicolated gates. The churches were protected by their sanctity. Some of them, nevertheless, among which was Notre-Dame, were fortified. The Abbé of Saint-Germain-des-Prés was fortified like a baron, and there was more weight of metal to be found in his house in bombards than in bells. His fortress was still to be seen in 1630. To-day barely the church remains.

To return to Notre-Dame.

When the first arrangements were completed—and we must say, to the honour of Truand discipline, that Clopin's orders were executed in silence and with admirable precision—the worthy leader mounted the parapet of the Parvis, and raised his hoarse and surly voice, his face turned toward Notre-Dame, and brandishing his torch, whose flame, tossed by the wind and veiled at intervals by its own smoke, made the glowing front of the church by turns appear and disappear before the eye:

'Unto thee, Louis de Beaumont, Bishop of Paris, councillor in the court of parliament: thus say I, Clopin Trouillefou, King of Tunis, Grand-Coësre, Prince of Argot, Bishop of the Fools: Our sister, falsely condemned for magic, has taken refuge in thy church. Thou owest to her shelter and safe-guard. But now, the court of parliament is to take her thence, and thou consentest to it; so that to-morrow she would be hanged at the Grève, if God and the Truands were not on hand. Therefore, we are come to thee, bishop. If thy church is sacred, so is our sister; if our sister is not sacred, neither is thy church. Wherefore we summon thee to give up the girl, if thou wilt save thy church; or we will take the girl and plunder the church. Which will be good. In witness whereof, I here plant my banner, and God have thee in his keeping, Bishop of Paris.'

Quasimodo, unfortunately, could not hear these words, which were uttered with a sort of sullen, savage majesty. A Truand presented the standard to Clopin, who gravely planted it between two of the paving-stones. It was a pitchfork, from the prongs of which hung a bleeding quarter of carrion.

This done, the King of Tunis turned about, and cast his eyes over his army, a ferocious multitude whose eyes flashed almost like the pikes. After a moment's pause:

'Forward, my sons!' cried he. 'To your work, locksmiths.'

Thirty stout men, fellows with brawny limbs and the faces of blacksmiths, sprang from the ranks, with hammers, pincers and iron crows on their shoulders. They advanced toward the principal door of the church; ascended the steps; and directly they were to be seen stooping down under the pointed arches of the portal, heaving at the door with pincers and levers. A crowd of Truands followed them, to assist or look on; so that the whole eleven steps were covered with them.

The door, however, stood firm. 'Diable! but she's hard and headstrong,' said one. 'She's old, and her gristles are tough,' said another. 'Courage, my friends!' cried Clopin. 'I'll wager my head against a slipper that you'll have burst the door, taken the girl, and undressed the great altar, before there is one beadle awake. Stay! I think the lock is giving way.'

Clopin was interrupted by a frightful noise which at that moment resounded behind him. He turned round; an enormous beam had just fallen from on high, crushing a dozen of the Truands upon the church steps, and rebounding upon the pavement with the sound of a piece of artillery; breaking legs here and there in the crowd of vagabonds who sprang aside with cries of terror. In a twinkling the narrow precincts of the Parvis were cleared. The locksmiths, though protected by the deep arches of the portal, abandoned the door, and Clopin himself fell back to a respectful distance from the church.

'I have escaped fine!' cried Jehan; 'I felt the wind of it, by the head of the bull! but Pierre the Slaughterer is slaughtered!'

It is impossible to describe the astonishment mixed with dread which fell upon the bandits with this beam. They remained for some minutes gazing fixedly upward, in greater consternation at this piece of wood than they would have been at twenty thousand king's archers.

'Satan!' growled the Duke of Egypt, 'but this smells of magic!'

''Tis the moon that throws this log at us,' said Andry-le-Rouge.

'Why,' remarked François Chanteprune, 'they say the moon's a friend of the Virgin.'

'A thousand Popes!' exclaimed Clopin, 'you are all imbeciles!' Yet he knew not how to account for the fall of the beam.

All this while nothing was distinguishable upon the grand front of the building, to the top of which the light from the torches did not reach. The ponderous piece of timber lay in the middle of the Parvis; and groans were heard from the miserable wretches who had received its first shock, and been almost cut in two upon the angles of the stone steps.

At last the King of Tunis, his first astonishment over, hit upon an explanation which his comrades thought plausible.

'God's throat!' said he, 'are the canons making a defence? To the sack, then! to the sack!'

'To the sack!' repeated the mob with a furious hurrah. And they made a general discharge of cross-bows and hackbuts against the front of the church.

This report awoke the peaceable inhabitants of the neighbouring houses; several window-shutters were seen to open, and nightcaps and hands holding candles appeared at the casements.

'Fire at the windows!' cried Clopin. The windows were immediately shut again, and the poor citizens, who scarcely had time to cast a bewildered look upon that scene of glare and tumult, went back shaking with fear to their wives, asking themselves whether the witches' Sabbath was now held in the Parvis Notre-Dame, or whether there was an assault by the Burgundians, as in the year '64. Then the husbands dreamt of robbery, the wives of violence, and all trembled.

'To the sack!' repeated the Argotiers; but they dared not approach. They looked first at the church and then at the marvellous beam. The beam lay perfectly still; the edifice kept its calm and solitary look; but something froze the courage of the Truands.

'To your work, locksmiths!' cried Trouillefou. 'Come! force the door!'

Nobody advanced a step.

'Beard and belly!' said Clopin; 'here are men afraid of a rafter!'

An old lock-picker now addressed him:

'Captain, it is not the rafter that we care about; 'tis the door, that's all sewed up with iron bars. The pincers can do nothing with it.'

'What should you have, then, to burst it open with?' asked Clopin.

'Why, we should have a battering ram.'

The King of Tunis ran bravely up to the formidable piece of timber, and set his foot upon it. 'Here's one!' cried he; 'the canons have sent it to you.' And he made a mock reverence to the cathedral. 'Thank you, canons,' he added.

This bravado had great effect; the spell of the wonderful beam was broken. The Truands recovered courage; and soon the heavy timber, picked up like a feather by two hundred vigorous arms, was driven with fury against the great door which had before been attacked. Seen thus, by the sort of half light which the few scattered torches of the Truands cast over the Place, the long beam, borne along by that multitude of men rushing on with its extremity pointed against the church, looked like some monstrous animal, with innumerable legs, running, head foremost, to attack a stone giantess.

At the shock given by the beam, the half metal door sounded like an immense drum. It was not burst in, but the whole cathedral shook, and in its deepest recesses could be heard rumblings. At the same moment, a shower of great stones began to fall from the upper part of the façade upon the assailants.

'The devil!' cried Jehan, 'are the towers shaking down their balustrades upon our heads?'

But the impulse was given. The King of Tunis stuck to his text.

It was decidedly the bishop making a defence. And so they only battered the door the more furiously, in spite of the stones that were fracturing their skulls right and left.

It must be remarked that these stones all fell one by one; but they followed one another closely. The Argotiers always felt two of them at one and the same time, one against their legs, the other upon their heads. Nearly all of them took effect; and already the dead and wounded were thickly strewn, bleeding and panting under the feet of the assailants, who, now grown furious, filled up instantly and without intermission the places of the disabled. The long beam continued battering the door with periodical strokes, like the clapper of a bell, the stones to shower down, the door to groan.

The reader has undoubtedly not waited till this time to divine that this unexpected resistance which had exasperated the Truands proceeded from Quasimodo.

Accident had unfortunately favoured but too well the brave deaf mute.

When he had descended upon the platform between the towers, his ideas were all in confusion. He ran to and fro along the gallery for some minutes, like one insane, beholding from above the compact mass of the Truands ready to throw themselves against the church, demanding of the devil or of God to save the gypsy. He once thought of mounting the southern steeple, and sounding the tocsin; but before he could have set the bell in motion, before Marie's voice could have uttered a single sound, was there not time for the door of the church to be forced ten times over? It was precisely the time when the lock-pickers were advancing toward it with their tools. What was to be done?

All at once he recollected that some masons had been at work all day, repairing the wall, the timber-work and the roofing of the southern tower. This was a flash of light. The wall was of stone; the roof was of lead; the timber-work of wood. (That prodigious timber-work was so dense that it went by the name of 'the forest.')

Quasimodo ran to this tower. The lower chambers were, in fact, full of materials. There were piles of rough blocks of stone, sheets of lead rolled up, bundles of laths, heavy beams already notched with the saw, heaps of rubbish; in short, an arsenal complete.

Time pressed. The pikes and hammers were at work below. With a strength multiplied tenfold by the sense of danger, he seized one of the beams, the heaviest and longest. He managed to push it through one of the loopholes; then, grasping it again outside the tower, he shoved it over the outer angle of the balustrade surrounding the platform, and launched it into the abyss.

The enormous beam, in this fall of a hundred and sixty feet, grazing the wall, breaking the carvings, turned several times on its centre, like the arm of a windmill, flying off alone through space. At last it reached the ground; the horrible cry arose; and the black beam, as it rebounded from the pavement, was like a serpent making a leap.

Quasimodo saw the Truands scattered by the fall of the beam, like ashes at the breath of a child. He took advantage of their fright, and while they fixed their superstitious gaze upon the immense log fallen from heaven, and while they peppered the stone saints of the portal with a discharge of bolts and bullets, Quasimodo was silently piling up rubbish, rough blocks of stone, and even the masons' bags of tools, on the edge of that balustrade from which the beam had already been hurled.

Thus, as soon as they began to batter the great door, the shower of blocks of stone began to fall, and it seemed to them that the church was demolishing itself over their heads.

Any one who could have seen Quasimodo at that moment would have been frightened. Independently of the missiles which he had piled up on the balustrade, he had collected a heap of stones on the platform itself. As fast as the blocks heaped on the outer edge were exhausted, he had recourse to this latter heap. Then he stooped, rose, stooped and rose again, with incredible agility. He thrust his great gnome's head over the balustrade; then there dropped an enormous stone, then another, then another. Now and then he followed some big stone with his eye; and when it did good execution, he ejaculated: 'Hum!'

The beggars, meanwhile, did not lose courage. The massive door which they were so furiously assailing had already trembled more than twenty times beneath the weight of their oaken battering-ram, multiplied by the strength of a hundred men. The panels cracked, the carvings flew in splinters; the hinges, at each shock, leaped from their hooks; the planks were forced out of their places, the wood was falling in dust, ground between the sheathings of iron. Fortunately for Quasimodo, there was more iron than wood.

Nevertheless he felt that the great door was yielding. Although he did not hear it, each stroke of the battering-ram reverberated in the caverns of the church, and within him. From above he beheld the Truands, full of exultation and rage, shaking their fists at the dark front of the edifice; and he coveted, for the gypsy-girl and himself, the wings of the owls that were flocking away affrighted over his head.

His shower of stone blocks was not sufficient to repel the assailants.

At this moment of anguish he noticed a little below the balustrade from which he had been crushing the Argotiers, two long stone gutters which disgorged immediately over the great door. The inner orifice of these gutters was on a level with the platform. An idea struck him. He ran to his bell-ringer's lodge for a fagot; laid over the fagot many bundles of laths and rolls of lead—ammunition of which he had not yet made any use; and having placed this pile in front of the hole of the two gutters, he set fire to it with his lantern.

While he was thus employed, since the stones no longer fell, the Truands ceased to gaze into the air. The brigands, panting like a pack of hounds baying the wild boar in his lair, pressed tumultuously round the great door, all disfigured and shapeless from the blows of the ram, but still erect. They awaited with a thrill of impatience the last grand blow, the blow which was to burst it in. Each was striving to get nearest, in order to be the first, when it should open, to rush into that well-stored cathedral, a vast repository in which had been successively accumulating the riches of three centuries. They reminded one another, with roars of exultation and greedy desire, of the fine silver crosses, the fine brocade copes, the fine silver gilt monuments, of all the magnificence of the choir, the dazzling holiday displays, the Christmas illuminations with torches, the Easter suns, all those splendid solemnities, in which shrines, candlesticks, pyxes, tabernacles, and reliquaries, embossed the altars as it were with a covering of gold and jewels. Assuredly, at that hopeful moment, thieves and pseudo-sufferers, doctors in stealing and vagabonds, were thinking much less of delivering the gypsy-girl than of pillaging Notre-Dame. Nay, we could even believe that, for a goodly number among them, La Esmeralda was only a pretext—if thieves needed a pretext.

All at once, at the moment that they were crowding about the battering-ram for a final effort, each one holding in his breath and stiffening his muscles, so as to give full force to the decisive stroke, a howl more frightful still than that which had burst forth and expired beneath the beam, arose from the midst of them. Those who did not cry out, those who were still alive, looked. Two jets of melted lead were falling from the top of the edifice into the thickest of the rabble. That sea of men had gone down under the boiling metal, which, at the two points where it fell, had made two black and smoking holes in the crowd, like hot water thrown on snow. There were to be seen dying wretches burned half to a cinder, and moaning with agony. Around the two principal jets there were drops of that horrible rain which scattered upon the assailants, and entered their skulls like fiery gimlet points. It was a ponderous fire which riddled the crowd with a thousand hail-stones.

The outcry was heart-rending. They fled in disorder, hurling the beam upon the dead bodies—the boldest as well as the most timid—and the Parvis was left empty a second time.

All eyes were raised to the top of the church. They beheld there an extraordinary sight. On the crest of the highest gallery, higher than the central rose window, was a great flame ascending between the two towers, with whirlwinds of sparks; a great flame, irregular and furious, a tongue of which, by the action of the wind, was at times borne into the smoke. Underneath that flame, underneath the trifoliated balustrade showing darkly against its glare, two monster-headed gutters were vomiting incessantly that burning shower, whose silver stream shone out against the darkness of the lower façade. As they approached the earth, these two jets of liquid lead spread out into myriads of drops like water sprinkled from the many holes of a watering-pot. Above the flame the huge towers, two sides of each of which were visible in sharp outline, the one wholly black, the other wholly red, seemed still more vast by all the immensity of shadow which they cast even into the sky. Their innumerable sculptured demons and dragons assumed a formidable aspect. The restless, flickering light from the unaccountable flame, made them seem as if they were moving. There were griffins which seemed to be laughing, gargoyles to be heard yelping; salamanders puffing fire, tarasques sneezing in the smoke.* And among the monsters, thus awakened from their stony slumber by this unearthly flame, by this clamour, there was one who walked about and who was seen from time to time passing across the glowing front of the pile like a bat before a torch.

Assuredly, this strange beacon-light must have awakened the wood-cutter far away on the Bicêtre hills, terrified to behold the gigantic shadows of the towers of Notre-Dame quivering over his heaths.

A terrified silence ensued among the Truands; during which nothing was heard but the cries of alarm from the canons, shut up in their cloisters and more uneasy than horses in a burning stable, the furtive sound of windows hastily opened, and still more hastily closed, the stir in the interior of the houses and of the Hôtel-Dieu, the wind agitating the flame, the last groans of the dying, and the continued crackling of the shower of boiling lead upon the pavement.

Meanwhile the principal Truands had retired beneath the porch of the Logis Gondelaurier, and were holding a council of war. The

* A fictitious animal solemnly drawn in processions in Tarascon and a few other French towns.—J. C. B.

Duke of Egypt, seated on a stone post, was contemplating with religious awe the phantasmagoric pile blazing two hundred feet aloft in the air. Clopin Trouillefou was gnawing his huge fists with rage.

'Impossible to get in!' muttered he between his teeth.

'An old church enchanted!' growled the old Bohemian, Mathias Hungadi Spicali.

'By the Pope's whiskers!' added a gray-headed scamp of a soldier, who had once been in service, 'here are two church gutters that spit molten lead at you better than the fortifications at Lectoure!'

'Do you see that demon, going back and forth before the fire?' cried the Duke of Egypt.

'Par-Dieu!' said Clopin, ''tis the damned ringer—'tis Quasimodo.'

The Bohemian shook his head. 'I tell you, no; 'tis the spirit Sabnac, the great marquis, the demon of fortifications. He has the form of an armed soldier, with a lion's head. Sometimes he rides a hideous horse. He turns men into stones, and builds towers of them. He commands fifty legions. 'Tis he, indeed. I recognize him. Sometimes he is clad in a fine robe of gold, figured after the Turkish fashion.'

'Where is Bellevigne-de-l'Etoile?' demanded Clopin.

'He is dead,' answered a Truandess.

Andry-le-Rouge laughed idiotically.

'Notre-Dame makes work for the hospital.'

'Is there then no way of forcing this door?' said the King of Tunis, stamping his foot.

The Duke of Egypt pointed sadly to the two streams of boiling lead, which continued to streak the black front of the building like two long phosphoric distaffs.

'Churches have been known to defend themselves so,' observed he with a sigh. 'St. Sophia's, at Constantinople, forty years ago, hurled to the ground, three times in succession, the crescent of Mahound, by shaking her domes, which are her heads. William of Paris, who built this one, was a magician.'

'Must we then slink away pitifully, like so many running footmen?' said Clopin. 'What! leave our sister there, for those hooded wolves to hang to-morrow!'

'And the sacristy—where there are cart-loads of gold!' added a rascal, whose name we regret that we do not know.

'Beard of Mahound!' exclaimed Trouillefou.

'Let us try once more,' rejoined the Truand.

Mathias Hungadi shook his head.

'We shall never get in by the door. We must find the defect in the old elf's armour, a hole, a false postern, some joint or other.

'Who's for it?' said Clopin. 'I'll go at it again. By-the-by, where's the little student, Jehan, who was so incased in iron?'

'He's dead, no doubt,' answered some one, 'for no one hears him laugh.'

The King of Tunis knit his brows. 'So much the worse!' said he. 'There was a stout heart under that ironmongery. And Maître Pierre Gringoire?'

'Captain Clopin,' said Andry-le-Rouge, 'he slipped away before we had got as far as the Pont-aux-Changeurs.'

Clopin stamped his foot. '*Gueule-Dieu!* 'Tis he who pushed us on hither, and then leaves us here just in the thick of the job. Cowardly chatterer, with a slipper for a helmet!'

'Captain Clopin,' cried Andry-le-Rouge, looking up the Rue de Parvis, 'yonder comes the little student!'

'Praise be to Pluto!' said Clopin. 'But what the devil is he dragging after him?'

It was in fact Jehan, coming as quick as he found practicable under his ponderous knightly accoutrements, with a long ladder, which he was dragging stoutly over the pavement, more breathless than an ant harnessed to a blade of grass twenty times its own length.

'Victory! *Te Deum!*' shouted the student. 'Here's the ladder belonging to the unladers of Saint Landry's wharf.'

Clopin went up to him.

'Child, what are you going to do, *corne-Dieu!* with this ladder?'

'I have it,' replied Jehan, panting. 'I knew where it was. Under the shed of the lieutenant's house. There's a girl there, whom I know, who thinks me a Cupid for beauty. I made use of her to get the ladder, and now I have the ladder, *Pasque-Mahom!* The poor girl came out in her shift to let me in.'

'Yes, yes,' said Clopin; 'but what are you going to do with this ladder?'

Jehan gave him a roguish, knowing look, and snapped his fingers like castanets. At that moment he was sublime. He had upon his head one of those overloaded helmets of the fifteenth century which daunted the enemy by their monstrous-looking peaks. His was jagged with no less than ten beaks of steel, so that Jehan might have disputed the formidable epithet of ten beaks with the Homeric ship of Nestor.

'What am I going to do with it, august King of Tunis?' said he. 'Do you see that row of statues there, that look like blockheads, over the three portals?'

'Yes. Well?'

''Tis the gallery of the Kings of France.'

'What is that to me?' said Clopin.

'Wait a bit. At the end of that gallery there's a door that's always on the latch. With this ladder I reach it, and I am in the church.'

'Boy, let me go first.'

'No, comrade; the ladder is mine. Come, you shall be the second.'

'Beelzebub strangle thee!' said surly Clopin. 'I'll be second to no one.'

'Then, Clopin, find a ladder.'

Jehan set off on a run across the Place, dragging his ladder, and shouting: 'Follow me, boys!'

In an instant the ladder was raised and placed against the balustrade of the lower gallery, over one of the side doorways. The crowd of Truands, uttering loud acclamations, pressed to the foot of it for the purpose of ascending. But Jehan maintained his right, and was the first to set foot on the steps of the ladder. The way was somewhat long. The gallery of the Kings of France is, at this day, about sixty feet from the ground; to which elevation was, at that period, added the height of the eleven steps of entrance. Jehan mounted slowly, much encumbered with his heavy armour, with one hand upon the ladder and the other grasping his cross-bow. When he reached the middle of the ladder he cast a melancholy glance upon the poor dead Truands strewn upon the steps of the grand portal. 'Alas!' said he, 'here is a heap of dead worthy of the fifth book of the Iliad!' Then he continued his ascent. The Truands followed him. There was one upon each step of the ladder. To see that line of cuirassed backs thus rise, undulating, in the darkness, one might have imagined it a serpent with steely scales, rearing itself up to assail the church. Jehan formed the head, and whistled shrilly; this completed the illusion.

The student at length reached the parapet of the gallery, and sprang lightly over it, amid the applause of the whole Truandry. Thus master of the citadel, he uttered a joyful shout, but stopped short, suddenly petrified. He had just discovered, concealed behind one of the royal statues, Quasimodo, his eye glittering in the shadow.

Before another of the besiegers had time to gain foothold on the gallery, the formidable hunch-back sprang to the head of the ladder, seized, without saying a word, the ends of the two uprights with his powerful hands; heaved them away from the edge of the balustrade; balanced for a moment, amid cries of anguish, the long bending ladder, crowded with Truands from top to bottom; then suddenly, with superhuman strength, he threw back that clustering mass of men into the square. For a moment or two the most resolute trembled. The ladder thus hurled backward, with all that living burden, remained perpendicular for an instant;

then it wavered; then, suddenly describing a frightful arc of eighty feet radius, it came down upon the pavement, with its load of brigands, more swiftly than a drawbridge when its chains give way. There arose one vast imprecation; then all was still, and a few mutilated creatures were seen crawling from under the heap of dead.

A mingled murmur of pain and resentment among the besiegers succeeded their first shouts of triumph. Quasimodo, unmoved, his elbows resting upon the balustrade, was quietly looking on, with the mien of some old long-haired king looking out at his window.

Jehan Frollo, on the other hand, was in a critical situation. He found himself in the gallery with the redoubtable ringer—alone, separated from his companions by eighty feet of perpendicular wall. While Quasimodo was dealing with the ladder, the student had run to the postern, which he expected to find on the latch. Not so. The ringer, upon entering the gallery, had fastened it behind him. Jehan had then hidden himself behind one of the stone kings, not daring to draw breath, but fixing upon the monstrous hunch-back a look of wild apprehension, like the man who, making love to the wife of a menagerie-keeper, and going one evening to meet her by appointment, scaled the wrong wall, and suddenly found himself tête-a-tête with a white bear.

For the first few moments the hunch-back took no notice of him; but at length he turned his head and started, for the scholar had just caught his eye.

Jehan prepared for a rude encounter, but his deaf antagonist remained motionless; he had only turned toward the scholar, at whom he continued looking.

'Ho, ho!' said Jehan, 'why dost thou look at me with that one melancholy eye of thine?'

And so saying, the young rogue was stealthily adjusting his cross-bow.

'Quasimodo,' he cried, 'I'm going to change thy surname. They shall call thee the blind.'

The arrow parted and whistled through the air, burying its point into the left arm of the hunch-back. This no more disturbed Quasimodo than a scratch would have done his stone neighbour, King Pharamond. He laid his hand to the dart, drew it out of his arm, and quietly broke it over his big knee. Then he dropped, rather than threw, the two pieces on the ground. But he did not give Jehan time to discharge a second shaft. The arrow broken, Quasimodo, breathing heavily, bounded like a grasshopper upon the scholar, whose armour was flattened against the wall by the shock.

Then, through that atmosphere in which wavered the light of torches, was dimly seen a terrible sight.

Quasimodo had grasped in his left hand both the arms of Jehan, who made no struggle, so completely did he give himself up for lost. With his right hand the hunch-back took off, one after another, with ominous deliberation, the several pieces of his armour —the sword, the daggers, the helmet, the breastplate, the arm-pieces—as if it had been a monkey peeling a walnut. Quasimodo dropped at his feet, piece after piece, the scholar's iron shell.

When the scholar had found himself disarmed and undressed, feeble and naked, in those terrible hands, he did not offer to speak to his deaf enemy; but he fell to laughing audaciously in his face, and singing, with the careless assurance of a boy of sixteen, a popular air of the time:

> 'She is clad in bright array,
> The city of Cambray;
> Marafin plundered her one day . . . .'

He did not finish. Quasimodo was seen standing upon the parapet of the gallery, holding the scholar by the feet with one hand only, and swinging him round like a sling over the abyss. Then a noise was heard like a box made of bone dashing against a wall; and something was seen falling, which stopped a third part of the way down, being arrested in its descent by one of the architectural projections. It was a dead body which hung there, bent double, the loins broken, and the skull empty.

A cry of horror arose from the Truands.

'Vengeance!' cried Clopin. 'Sack!' answered the multitude. 'Assault! assault!'

Then there was a prodigious howling, mixed with all languages, all dialects and all tones of voice. The poor student's death inspired the crowd with a frantic ardour. They were seized with shame and resentment at having been so long kept in check, before a church, by a hunch-back. Their rage found them ladders, multiplied their torches, and in a few minutes Quasimodo, in confusion and despair, saw a frightful swarm ascending from all sides to the assault of Notre-Dame. Those who had not ladders had knotted ropes; and those who had not ropes climbed up by means of the projections of the sculpture. They clung to one another's rags. No means of resisting this rising tide of frightful visages. Fury seemed to writhe in those ferocious countenances; their dirty foreheads streamed with perspiration; their eyes flashed; all these varieties of grimace and ugliness beset Quasimodo. It seemed as if some other church had sent her gorgons, her dogs, her mediæval creatures, her demons, all her most fantastic carvings, to assail Notre-Dame. It was a coat of living monsters covering the stone monsters of the façade.

Meanwhile, a thousand torches had kindled in the square. This scene of disorder, buried until then in thick obscurity, was wrapped in a sudden blaze of light. The Parvis shone resplendent, and cast a radiance on the sky, while the beacon that had been lighted on the high platform of the church still burned and illumined the city far around. The vast outline of the two towers, projected afar upon the roofs of Paris, cast amid that light a deep shadow. The whole town seemed to be roused. Distant tocsins were mournfully sounding; the Truands were howling, panting, swearing, climbing; and Quasimodo, powerless against so many enemies, trembling for the gypsy, watched those furious faces approach nearer and nearer to his gallery, and implored a miracle from heaven, as he wrung his arms in despair.

5

The Retreat in which Monsieur Louis of France says his Prayers

THE reader has probably not forgotten that Quasimodo, a moment before he perceived the nocturnal band of the Truands in motion, while looking over Paris from the height of his belfry, saw but one remaining light, twinkling at a window in the topmost story of a lofty and gloomy building close by the Porte Saint Antoine. That building was the Bastille, and that twinkling light was the candle of Louis XI.

Louis XI had, in fact, been two days in Paris. He was to set out again the next day but one for his citadel of Montilz-les-Tours. His visits to his good city of Paris were rare and short, as he did not there feel himself surrounded by a sufficient number of trapdoors, gibbets and Scottish archers.

He had come that day to sleep at the Bastille. His great chamber at the Louvre, five toises * square, with its huge chimney-piece loaded with twelve great beasts and thirteen great prophets, and his grand bed, eleven feet by twelve, were little to his taste. He felt himself lost amidst all those grandeurs. This burgher king preferred the Bastille with a chamber and a bed of humbler dimensions. Besides, the Bastille was stronger than the Louvre.

This little chamber which the king reserved for himself in that famous state prison was also tolerably spacious, occupying the

---

* An ancient long measure in France, containing six feet and nearly five inches English measure.—J. C. B.

topmost floor of a turret in the keep. This retreat was circular in shape, carpeted with mats of shining straw; ceiled with wooden beams decorated with raised fleurs-de-lys of gilt metal, with coloured spaces between them; wainscoted with rich carvings interspersed with rosettes of white metal, and painted of a fine light green made of orpiment and fine indigo.

There was but one window, a long pointed casement, latticed with iron bars and brass wire, still further darkened with fine glass painted with the arms of the king and queen, each pane of which had cost two-and-twenty sols.

There was but one entrance, a modern door with an overhanging arch, covered inside with a piece of tapestry, and outside with one of those porches of Irish wood, frail structures of curious cabinet-work, which were still to be seen abounding in old French mansions a hundred and fifty years ago. 'Although they disfigure and encumber the places,' says Sauval in despair, 'yet our old gentlemen will not get rid of them, but keep them in spite of everybody.'

In this chamber was to be seen none of the furniture of ordinary apartments; neither benches, nor trestles, nor forms, nor common box stools, nor fine stools supported by pillars and counter pillars, at four sols a-piece. There was only one folding arm-chair, very magnificent; the wood was painted with roses on a red ground; the seat was of scarlet Spanish leather, garnished with long silken fringe and studded with abundance of gold-headed nails. This solitary chair testified that one person only was entitled to be seated in that apartment. By the chair, and near the window, there was a table, the cover of which was figured with birds. On this table stood an ink-horn, spotted with ink, some scrolls of parchment, some pens and a large goblet of chased silver. A little further on were a brazier, and, for the purpose of prayer, a praying-stool of crimson velvet embossed with studs of gold. Finally, at the extreme end, a simple bed of yellow and pink damask, with neither tinsel nor lace, having only an ordinary fringe. This bed, famous for having borne the sleep or the sleeplessness of Louis XI, was still to be seen two hundred years ago, at the house of a councillor of state, where it was seen by the aged Madame Pilou, celebrated in the great romance of 'Cyrus' under the name *Arricidie* and of *La Morale Vivante*.

Such was the chamber which was called 'the retreat where Louis of France says his prayers.'

At the moment when we have introduced the reader, this retreat was very dark. The curfew had sounded an hour before; night was come, and there was but one flickering wax candle set on the table to light five persons variously grouped in the chamber.

The first upon whom the light fell was a seigneur splendidly attired in a doublet and hose of scarlet striped with silver, and a loose coat with half sleeves of cloth of gold with black figures. This splendid costume, as the light played upon it, glittered flamingly at every fold. The man who wore it had upon his breast his arms embroidered in brilliant colours—a chevron accompanied by a deer passant. The escutcheon was flanked on the right by an olive branch, on the left by a stag's horn. This man wore in his girdle a rich dagger, whose hilt, of silver gilt, was chased in the form of a helmet, and surrounded by a count's coronet. He had a forbidding air, a haughty mien and a head held high. At the first glance one read arrogance in his face; at the second, craftiness.

He was standing bareheaded, a long written scroll in his hand, behind the arm-chair, in which was seated, his body ungracefully doubled up, his knees thrown one across the other, and his elbow resting on the table, a person in shabby habiliments. Imagine, in fact, on the rich seat of Cordova leather, a pair of crooked joints, a pair of lean thighs poorly clad in knitted black worsted, a body enveloped in a cloak of fustian with fur trimming, of which more leather than hair was visible, and, to crown all, an old greasy hat of the meanest cloth, bordered with a circular string of small leaden figures. This, together with a dirty skull-cap, which allowed scarcely a hair to straggle from beneath it, was all that could be seen of the sitting personage. He held his head so bent upon his breast that nothing could be seen of his face thus thrown into shadow, excepting the tip of his nose, on which a ray of light fell, and which was evidently long. The thinness of his wrinkled hand showed it to be an old man. It was Louis XI.

At some distance behind them were conversing in low tones two men habited after the Flemish fashion, who were not so completely lost in the darkness but that any one who had attended the performance of Gringoire's mystery could recognize in them two of the principal Flemish envoys, Guillaume Rym, the sagacious pensionary of Ghent, and Jacques Coppenole, the popular hosier. It will be recollected that these two men were concerned in the secret politics of Louis XI.

And quite behind all the rest, near the door, in the dark, there stood motionless as a statue, a stout, brawny, thick-set man, in military accoutrements, with an emblazoned surcoat, whose square face, with prominent eyes, slit with an immense mouth, his ears concealed each under a great mat of hair, and with scarcely any forehead, partook at once of the dog and the tiger.

All were uncovered except the king.

The nobleman standing near the king was reading over to him

a sort of long memorial, to which his majesty seemed to listen attentively. The two Flemings were whispering.

'By the rood!' muttered Coppenole, 'I am tired of standing. Is there never a chair here?'

Rym answered by a negative gesture, accompanied by a discreet smile.

'By the mass!' resumed Coppenole, quite wretched at being obliged thus to lower his voice, 'I feel a mighty itching to sit myself down on the floor, with my legs across, hosier-like, as I do in my own shop.'

'Beware of doing so, Maître Jacques!'

'Hey-day! Maître Guillaume—must one only remain here on one's feet?'

'Or on his knees,' said Rym.

At that moment the king's voice was raised. They were silent.

'Fifty sols for the gowns of our valets, and twelve pounds for the cloaks of the clerks of our crown! That's it! Pour out gold by the ton! Are you mad, Olivier?'

So saying the old man raised his head. The golden shells of the collar of Saint Michel could be seen to glitter about his neck. The candle shone full upon his gaunt and morose profile. He snatched the paper from the other's hands.

'You are ruining us,' cried he, casting his hollow eyes over the scroll. 'What is all this? What need have we of so prodigious a household? Two chaplains at the rate of ten pounds a month each, and a chapel clerk at a hundred sols! A valet-de-chambre at ninety pounds a year! Four head cooks at six score pounds a year each! A spit-cook, an herb-cook, a sauce-cook, a butler, an armoury-keeper, two sumpter-men, at ten pounds a month each! Two turnspits at eight pounds! A groom and his two helpers at four-and-twenty pounds a month! A porter, pastry-cook, a baker, two carters, each sixty pounds a year! And the farrier six score pounds! And the master of our exchequer chamber twelve hundred pounds! And the comptroller five hundred! And how do I know what else! 'Tis monstrous! The wages of our domestics are laying France under pillage! All the treasure in the Louvre will melt away in such a blaze of expense! We shall have to sell our plate! And next year, if God and Our Lady' (here he raised his hat from his head) 'grant us life, we shall drink our potions from a pewter pot!'

So saying, he cast his eye upon the silver goblet that was glittering on the table. He coughed, and continued:

'Maître Olivier! princes who reign over great estates, as kings and emperors, should not let sumptuousness be engendered in their households, for 'tis a fire that will spread from thence into their provinces. Therefore, Maître Olivier, consider this said once for all. Our expenditure increases every year. The thing displeases us. Why? Pasque-Dieu! until the year '79, it never exceeded thirty-six thousand pounds; in '80, it rose to forty-three thousand six hundred and nineteen pounds; I have the figures in my head. In '81, it came to sixty-six thousand six hundred and eighty; and this year, by the faith of my body, it will reach eighty thousand pounds! Doubled in four years! Monstrous!'

He paused, breathless, then resumed vehemently:

'I behold around me only people who fatten upon my leanness. You suck crowns from me at every pore!'

All kept silence. It was one of those fits of passion which must have its run. He continued:

'''Tis like that Latin memorial from the gentlemen of France, requesting that we re-establish what they call the great offices of the crown. Charges, indeed! charges that crush! Ha! messieurs, you tell us that we are no king to reign *dapifero nullo, buticulario nullo*. (With no steward, no butter.) We will let you see, Pasque-Dieu! whether we are not a king.'

Here he smiled in the consciousness of his power; his ill-humour was allayed by it, and he turned to the Flemings:

'Look you, Compère Guillaume, the grand baker, the grand butler, the grand chamberlain, the grand seneschal, are not worth the meanest valet. Bear this in mind, Compère Coppenole; they are of no service whatever. Standing thus useless around the king, they put me in mind of the four evangelists that surround the face of the big clock of the Palace, and that Philippe Brille has just been renovating. They are gilt, but they do not mark the hour, and the hands can get on without them.'

He remained thoughtful for a moment, and then added, shaking his aged head:

'Ho, ho! by Our Lady, but I am not Philippe Brille, and I will not regild the great vassals. Proceed, Olivier.'

The person whom he designated by this name again took the scroll in his hands, and began again reading aloud:

'To Adam Tenon, keeper of the seals of the provostry of Paris, for the silver, workmanship and engraving of the said seals, which have been made new, because the former ones, by reason of their being old and worn out, could no longer be used, twelve pounds parisis.

'To Guillaume, his brother, the sum of four pounds four sols parisis, for his trouble and cost in having fed and nourished the pigeons in the two pigeon-houses at the Hôtel des Tournelles, during the months of January, February and March of this year, for the which he has furnished seven sextiers of barley.

'To a gray friar, for confessing a criminal, four sols parisis.'

The king listened in silence. From time to time he coughed; then lifted the goblet to his lips, and swallowed a draught, making a wry face.

'In this year have been made,' continued the reader, 'by judicial order, and to sound of trumpet, through the squares of Paris, fifty-six proclamations. Account to be paid.

'For search made in divers places, in Paris and elsewhere, after treasure said to have been concealed in the said places, but nothing has been found, forty-five pounds parisis—'

'Burying a crown to dig up a sou!' said the king.

'For setting in the Hôtel des Tournelles six panes of white glass, at the place where the iron cage is, thirteen sols. For making and delivering, by the king's command, on the day of the musters, four escutcheons, bearing the arms of our said lord, and wreathed all round with chaplets of roses, six pounds. For two new sleeves to the king's old doublet, twenty sols. For a box of grease to grease the king's boots, fifteen deniers. A new sty for keeping the king's black swine, thirty pounds parisis. Divers partitions, planks and trap-doors, for the safe keeping of the lions at the Hôtel Saint Pol, twenty-two pounds.'

'Costly beasts, those!' said Louis XI. 'But no matter; 'tis a seemly piece of royal magnificence. There's a great red lion that I love for his pretty ways. Have you seen him, Maître Guillaume? Princes must have those wondrous animals. For dogs we kings should have lions, and for cats, tigers. What is great befits a crown. In the time of the pagans of Jupiter, when the people offered up at the churches a hundred oxen and a hundred sheep, the emperors gave a hundred lions and a hundred eagles. That was very wild and very fine. The kings of France have always had those roarings about their throne. Nevertheless, this justice must be done me, that I spend less money in that way than my predecessors, and that I have a more moderate stock of lions, bears, elephants and leopards. Go on, Maître Olivier. We had a mind to say thus much to our Flemish friends.'

Guillaume Rym made a low bow, while Coppenole, with his gruff countenance, looked much like one of the bears of whom his majesty spoke. The king did not observe it; he had just then put the goblet to his lips, and was spitting out what remained in his mouth of the unsavoury beverage, saying, 'Foh! the nauseous herb-tea!' He who read continued:

'For the food of a rogue and vagabond, locked up for these six months in the lodge of the slaughter-house till it is settled what to do with him, six pounds four sols.'

'What's that?' interrupted the king. 'Feeding what ought to

be hanged? Pasque-Dieu! I'll not give a single sol toward such feeding. Olivier, arrange that matter with Monsieur d'Estouteville, and this very night you'll make preparations for uniting this gentleman in holy matrimony to a gallows.—Go on.'

Olivier made a mark with his thumb-nail at the rogue and vagabond article, and went on:

'To Henriet Cousin, executioner-in-chief at the justice of Paris, the sum of sixty sols parisis, to him adjudged by monseigneur the provost of Paris, for having bought, by order of the said lord the provost, a large broad-bladed sword, to be used in executing and beheading persons judicially condemned for their delinquencies, and had it furnished with a scabbard and all other appurtenances, as also for repairing and putting in order the old sword which had been splintered and jagged by executing justice upon Messire Louis of Luxemburg, as will more fully appear—'

Here the king interrupted him. 'Enough,' said he; 'I allow the sum with great good will. Those are expenses which I do not begrudge. I have never regretted that money. Proceed.'

'For having made over a great cage—'

'Ha!' said the king, grasping the arms of his chair with both hands, 'I knew well I came hither to this Bastille for some purpose. Stop, Maître Olivier, I will see that cage myself. You shall read me the cost while I examine it. Messieurs the Flemings, you must come and see that; 'tis curious.'

He then rose, leaned on the arm of his interlocutor, made a sign to the sort of mute who stood before the door to precede, to the two Flemings to follow, and left the chamber.

The royal train was recruited at the door by men-at-arms ponderous with steel, and slender pages bearing torches. It proceeded for some time through the interior of the gloomy donjon, intersected by staircases and corridors even in the very thickness of the walls. The captain of the Bastille went first, and directed the opening of the wickets before the bent and aged king, who coughed as he walked.

At each wicket all heads were obliged to stoop, except that of the old man bent with age.

'Hum!' said he, between his gums, for he had no teeth left. 'We are already quite prepared for the door of the sepulchre. A low door needs a bent passer.'

At length, after making their way through the last door of all, so loaded with locks that a quarter of an hour was required to open it, they entered a vast and lofty chamber, of Gothic vaulting, in the centre of which was discernible, by the light of the torches, a huge cubic mass of masonry, iron and wood-work. The interior was hollow. It was one of those famous cages for state prisoners which were called familiarly *les fillettes du roi*. (Little daughters of the king.) In its walls there were two or three small windows, so closely trellised with massive iron bars as to leave no glass visible. The door consisted of a large flat stone slab like those on tombs—one of those doors that serve for entrance only. Only here the occupant was alive.

The king began to walk slowly round the small edifice, examining it carefully, while Maître Olivier, following him, read aloud the memoranda :

'For making anew a great cage of wood of heavy beams, joists and rafters, measuring inside nine feet long by eight feet broad, and seven feet high between the planks ; mortised and bolted with great iron bolts ; which has been fixed in a certain chamber of one of the towers of the Bastille of Saint Antoine; in which said cage is placed and detained, by command of our lord the king, a prisoner, who formerly inhabited an old, decayed and worn-out cage. Used, in making the said new cage, ninety-six horizontal beams and fifty-two perpendicular ; ten joists, each three toises long. Employed, in squaring, planing and fitting all the said wood-work, in the yard of the Bastille, nineteen carpenters for twenty days—'

'Very fine heart of oak,' said the king, striking the wood-work with his fist.

'There were used for this cage,' continued the other, 'two hundred and twenty great iron bolts, nine feet and a half long, the rest of a medium length, together with the plates and nuts for fastening the said bolts, the said irons weighing altogether three thousand seven hundred and thirty-five pounds ; besides eight heavy squares of iron, serving to attach the said cage in its place, with clamps and nails, weighing altogether two hundred and eighteen pounds ; without reckoning the iron for the trellis-work of the windows of the chamber in which the said cage has been placed, the iron bar of the door of the chamber, and other articles—'

'A great deal of iron,' observed the king, 'to restrain levity of spirit.'

'The whole amounts to three hundred and seventeen pounds, five sols, seven farthings.'

'Pasque-Dieu !' cried the king.

At this oath, which was the favourite one of Louis XI, some one appeared to rouse up in the interior of the cage. The sound of chains was heard grating on the floor, and a feeble voice was heard, which seemed to issue from the tomb, exclaiming : 'Sire, sire ! mercy, mercy !' The one who spoke thus could not be seen.

'Three hundred and seventeen pounds, five sols, seven farthings !' repeated Louis XI.

The voice of lamentation which had issued from the cage chilled the blood of all present, even that of Maître Olivier. The king alone looked as if he had not heard it. At his command, Maître Olivier resumed his reading, and his majesty coolly continued his inspection of the cage.

'Besides the above, there has been paid to a mason for making the holes to fix the window-grates and the floor of the chamber containing the cage, because the other floor would not have been strong enough to support such cage by reason of its weight, twenty-seven pounds fourteen Paris pence—'

The voice began to moan again:

'Mercy, sire! I swear to you that it was Monsieur the Cardinal of Angers who committed the treason, and not I!'

'The mason is high,' said the king. 'Proceed, Olivier.'

Olivier continued:

'To a joiner for window-frames, bedstead, close-stool and other matters, twenty pounds two Paris pence—'

The voice also continued:

'Alas, sire! will you not listen to me? I protest it was not I who wrote that matter to Monseigneur of Guyenne; it was monsieur the Cardinal Balue.'

'The joiner is dear,' quoth the king. 'Is that all?'

'No, sire. To a glazier for the window-glass of the said chamber, forty-six pence eight Paris farthings.'

'Have mercy, sire! Is it not enough that all my property has been given to my judges, my plate to Monsieur de Torcy, my library to Maître Pierre Doriolle, and my tapestry to the Governor of Roussillon? I am innocent. For fourteen years I have shivered in an iron cage! Have mercy, sire! and you will find it in heaven!'

'Maître Olivier,' said the king, 'what is the sum total?'

'Three hundred and sixty-seven pounds, eight pence, three Paris farthings.'

'Our Lady!' exclaimed the king. 'Here's a cage out of all reason.'

He snatched the account from the hands of Maître Olivier, and began to reckon it up himself upon his fingers, examining, by turns, the paper and the cage. But the prisoner could be heard sobbing. It was lugubrious in the darkness. The faces of the by-standers turned pale as they looked at one another.

'Fourteen years, sire! Fourteen years now! since the month of April, 1469. In the name of the Holy Mother of God, sire, hearken to me. During all this time you have enjoyed the warmth of the sun; shall I, poor wretch, never again see the light? Mercy, sire! be merciful! Clemency is a noble virtue in a king, that turns aside the stream of wrath. Does your majesty believe that at the hour of death it will be a great satisfaction to a king to have left no offence unpunished? Besides, sire, it was not I that betrayed your majesty; it was Monsieur of Angers. And I have a very heavy chain to my foot, and a great ball of iron at the end of it, much heavier than is needful. Eh, sire, have pity on me!'

'Olivier,' said the king, shaking his head, 'I perceive that they put me down the bushel of plaster at twenty sols, though it's only worth twelve. You will make out this account afresh.'

He turned his back on the cage, and began to move toward the door of the chamber. The wretched prisoner judged from the receding torches and noise that the king was taking his departure.

'Sire! sire!' cried he in despair. The door closed. He no longer saw anything, and heard only the hoarse voice of the turnkey singing in his ears a popular song of the day:

> *Maître Jehan Balue*
> *Has lost out of view*
> *His good bishoprics all:*
> *Monsieur de Verdun*
> *Cannot now boast of one;*
> *They are gone, one and all.*

The king reascended in silence to his retreat, and his suit followed him, terrified by the last groans of the condemned man. All at once his majesty turned to the Governor of the Bastille.

'By-the-way,' said he, 'was there not some one in that cage?'

'Par-Dieu, yes, sire!' answered the governor, astounded at the question.

'And who, pray?'

'Monsieur the Bishop of Verdun.'

The king knew this better than any one else. But it was a mania of his.

'Ah!' said he, with an air of simplicity, as if he thought of it for the first time, 'Guillaume de Harancourt, the friend of Monsieur the Cardinal Balue. A good fellow of a bishop.'

A few moments later, the door of the retreat had opened again, then closed upon the five personages whom the reader found there at the beginning of this chapter, and who resumed their places, their attitudes and their whispered conversations.

During the king's absence, several dispatches had been laid upon the table. He himself broke their seals. Then he began to read them over diligently one after another; motioned to Maître Olivier, who seemed to act as his minister, to take up a pen; and, without communicating to him the contents of the dispatches, he began, in a low voice, to dictate to him the answers, which the latter wrote, in an uncomfortable position, on his knees before the table.

Guillaume Rym was on the watch.

The king spoke so low that the Flemings heard nothing of what he was dictating, except here and there a few isolated and scarcely intelligible fragments, as thus:

'To maintain the fertile places by commerce, the sterile ones by manufactures. To show the English lords our four bombards, the Londres, the Brabant, the Bourg-en-Bresse, the Saint Omer—It is owing to artillery that war is now more judiciously carried on —To our friend Monsieur de Bressuire—Armies cannot be maintained without tribute, etc.'

Once he spoke aloud:

'Pasque-Dieu! Monsieur the King of Sicily seals his letters with yellow wax like a King of France! Perhaps we do wrong to permit him so to do. My fair cousin of Burgundy granted no armorial bearings with field gules. The greatness of a house is secured by maintaining the integrity of its prerogatives. Note this, friend Olivier.'

Another time:

'Oh, oh,' said he, 'the long message! What doth our friend the emperor claim?' Then running his eye over the missive, and breaking his perusal with interjections: 'Certes! Germany is so large and powerful that it's hardly credible!—But we forget not the old proverb: "The finest country is Flanders; the finest duchy, Milan; the finest kingdom, France!" Is it not so, messieurs the Flemings?'

This time Coppenole bowed in company with Guillaume Rym. The hosier's patriotism was tickled.

The last dispatch made Louis XI frown.

'What's this?' he exclaimed. 'Complaints and grievances against our garrisons in Picardy! Olivier, write with all speed to Monsieur the Marshal de Rouault. That discipline is relaxed. That the men-at-arms, the feudal nobles, the free archers, the Swiss, do infinite mischief to the rustics. That the military, not content with what they find in the houses of the farmers, compel them, with heavy blows of cudgel or lash, to go and fetch from the town, wine, fish, spices and other unreasonable articles. That their lord the king knows all this. That we mean to protect our people from annoyance, theft and pillage. That such is our will, by Our Lady! That furthermore, it does not please us that any musician, barber or servant-at-arms should go clad like a prince, in velvet, silk and gold rings. That such vanities are hateful to God! That we, who are a gentleman, content ourselves with a doublet made of cloth at sixteen sols the Paris ell. That messieurs the serving-men of the army may very well come down to that price likewise. Order and command. To our friend, Monsieur de Rouault. Good.'

He dictated this letter aloud, in a firm tone, and in short abrupt sentences. At the moment when he had finished, the door opened, and gave passage to a new personage, who rushed all aghast into the chamber, crying:

'Sire! sire! there's a sedition of the populace in Paris!'

The grave countenance of Louis XI was contracted; but all visible sign of his emotion passed away like a flash. He contained himself, and said with quiet severity:

'Friend Jacques, you enter very abruptly.'

'Sire, sire, there's a revolt!' repeated Friend Jacques, quite out of breath.

The king, who had risen, seized him roughly by the arm, and said in his ear, so as to be heard by him alone, with an expression of concentrated anger, and a side-long glance at the Flemings:

'Hold thy tongue—or speak low!'

The new-comer comprehended and began in a low tone to give a very terrified narration, to which the king listened calmly, while Guillaume Rym was calling Coppenole's attention to the face and dress of the new arrival—his furred hood (*caputia furrata*)—his short cape (*epitogia curta*) and his black velvet gown, which bespoke a President of the Court of Accompts.

No sooner had this person given the king some explanations, than Louis XI exclaimed with a burst of laughter:

'Nay, in sooth, speak aloud, Gossip Coictier. What occasion have you to whisper so? Our Lady knows we have no secrets with our good Flemish friends.'

'But, sire—'

'Speak up!' said the king.

Gossip Coictier was struck dumb with surprise.

'So, then,' resumed the king, 'speak out, sir. There is a commotion among the louts in our good city of Paris?'

'Yes, sire.'

'And which is directed, you say, against Monsieur the Bailiff of the Palais de Justice?'

'So it appears,' said the *gossip*, who still stammered, utterly astounded at the sudden and inexplicable change which had taken place in the mind of the king.

Louis XI resumed: 'Where did the watch meet with the rabble?'

'Coming along from the great Truandry toward the Pont-aux-Changeurs, sire. I met it myself as I was coming hither in obedience to your majesty's orders. I heard some of them shouting: "Down with the Bailiff of the Palais!"'

'And what grievances have they against the bailiff?'

'Ah,' said Gossip Jacques, 'that he is their lord.'

'Really?'

'Yes, sire. They are rascals from the Court of Miracles. They have long been complaining of the bailiff, whose vassals they are. They will not acknowledge him either as justiciary or as keeper of the highways.'

'So, so,' said the king, with a smile of satisfaction, which he strove in vain to disguise.

'In all their petitions to the Parliament,' continued Gossip Jacques, 'they pretend that they have only two masters—your majesty and their god, whom I believe to be the devil.'

'Eh! eh!' said the king.

He rubbed his hands, laughed with that internal exultation which makes the countenance beam, and was quite unable to dissemble his joy, though he endeavoured at moments to compose himself. No one understood it in the least, not even Maître Olivier. At length his majesty remained silent for a moment, with a thoughtful but satisfied air.

'Are they in force?' he suddenly inquired.

'Yes, assuredly, sire,' answered Gossip Jacques.

'How many?'

'At least six thousand.'

The king could not help saying, 'Good!' He went on:
'Are they armed?'

'Yes, sire, with scythes, pikes, hackbuts, pickaxes. All sorts of very dangerous weapons.'

The king did not appear in the least disturbed by this list. Gossip Jacques deemed it his duty to add: 'Unless your majesty sends speedy succour to the bailiff, he is lost!'

'We will send,' said the king, with affected seriousness. ''Tis well! certainly we will send. Monsieur the bailiff is our friend. Six thousand! They're determined rogues! Their boldness is marvellous, and deeply are we wroth at it. But we have few men about us to-night. It will be time enough to-morrow morning.'

Gossip Jacques exclaimed: 'At once, sire! They'll have time to sack the bailiff's house twenty times over, violate the seigneury, to hang the bailiff. For God's sake, sire, send before to-morrow morning.'

The king looked him full in the face. 'I have told you to-morrow morning.'

It was one of those looks to which there is no reply.

After a pause, Louis XI again raised his voice. 'My Friend Jacques, you should know that. What was . . .' (he corrected himself). 'What is the bailiff's feudal jurisdiction?'

'Sire, the Bailiff of the Palais has the Rue de la Calandre, as far as the Rue de l'Herberie; the Place St. Michel, and the localities commonly called Les Mureaux, situated near the Church of

Notre-Dame-des-Champs' (here the king lifted the brim of his hat), 'which mansions amount to thirteen; also the Court of Miracles, and the lazaretto called the Banlieue; also the entire highway beginning at the lazaretto and ending at the Porte Saint Jacques. Of these divers places he is keeper of the ways—chief, mean and inferior justiciary—full and entire lord.'

'So ho!' said the king, scratching his left ear with his right hand, 'that makes a goodly bit of my city! Ah! monsieur the bailiff was king of all that!'

This time he did not correct himself. He continued ruminating and as if talking to himself:

'Very fine, monsieur the bailiff, you had there between your teeth a very pretty slice of our Paris.'

All at once he burst forth: 'Pasque-Dieu! what are all these people that pretend to be highway-keepers, justiciaries, lords and masters along with us, that have their toll-gate at the corner of every field, their gallows and their hangman at every cross-road among our people? so that, as the Greek believed he had as many gods as there were fountains, and the Persian as many as he saw stars, the Frenchman counts as many kings as he sees gibbets. Par-Dieu! this is an evil state of things. I like not the confusion. I should like to be told, now, if it be God's pleasure, that there should be at Paris any other lord than the king—any justiciary but our Parliament—any emperor but ourself in this empire. By the faith of my soul! the day must come when there shall be in France but one king, but one lord, one judge, one headsman, as there is but one God in heaven.'

Here he lifted his cap again, and continued, still ruminating, and with the look and accent of a huntsman cheering on his pack: 'Good, my people! bravely done! Down with these false lords! At them! have at them! Pillage, hang, sack them! . . . Ah, you want to be kings, messeigneurs? On, my people, on!'

Here he stopped short, bit his lips as if to catch the thought which had half escaped him, fixed his piercing eye in turn upon each of the five persons around him, and then, suddenly seizing his hat with both hands, and looking steadfastly at it, he said: 'Oh, I would burn thee, if thou didst know what I have in my head!'

Then again casting around him the cautious, uneasy look of a fox stealing back to his hole:

'No matter,' said he; 'we will send succour to monsieur the bailiff. Unfortunately, we have but few troops here at the present moment against such a number of the populace. We must wait till to-morrow. Order then shall be restored in the city; and all who are taken shall be hanged forthwith.'

'Apropos, sire,' said Gossip Coictier, 'I had forgotten this in my first alarm. The watch have seized two stragglers belonging to the band. If it be your majesty's pleasure to see the men, they are here.'

'If it be my pleasure!' exclaimed the king. 'What, Pasque-Dieu! Thou forgettest a thing like that? Run! quick! Olivier, go and fetch them in.'

Maître Olivier left the room, and presently returned with the two prisoners surrounded by archers of the guard. The first of the two had a great, idiotic, drunken and astonished face. He was clothed in tatters, and walked with one knee bent and the foot dragging along. The other had a pallid, smiling countenance, with which the reader is already acquainted.

The king scrutinized them a moment without saying a word; then addressing the first one abruptly:

'What is thy name?'

'Geoffroy Pincebourde.'

'Thy trade?'

'A Truand.'

'What wert thou going to do in this damnable sedition?'

The Truand stared at the king, swinging his arms with a besotted look. His was one of those misshapen heads where intelligence is about as much at its ease as a light beneath an extinguisher.

'I know not,' said he. 'They were going, so I went.'

'Were you not going to outrageously attack and pillage your lord the Bailiff of the Palais?'

'I know they were going to take something at somebody's, that's all.'

A soldier brought to the king a pruning-hook, which had been found upon the Truand.

'Dost thou know this weapon?' asked the king.

'Yes; it is my hook. I'm a vine-dresser.'

'And dost thou know that man for thy comrade?' asked Louis XI, pointing to the other prisoner.

'No, I know him not.'

'Enough,' said the king. And making a sign with his finger to the silent person, who stood motionless beside the door, to whom we have already called the reader's attention: 'Friend Tristan.' said he, 'there's a man for you.'

Tristan l'Hermite bowed. He gave an order in a low voice to a couple of archers, who led away the poor vagabond.

The king, meanwhile, turned to the second prisoner, who was perspiring profusely. 'Thy name?'

'Sire, it is Pierre Gringoire.'

'Thy trade?'

'A philosopher, sire.'

'How durst thou, knave, to go and beset our friend monsieur the Bailiff of the Palais? and what hast thou to say concerning this agitation of the populace?'

'Sire, I was not of it.'

'How now, varlet! hast thou not been apprehended by the watch in this bad company?'

'No, sire, there is a mistake. 'Tis a fatality. I write tragedies, sire. I implore your majesty to hear me. I am a poet. 'Tis the hard lot of men of my profession to roam the streets at night. I was passing that way this evening. 'Twas the merest chance. They apprehended me wrongfully. I am innocent of this commotion. Your majesty saw that the Truand did not recognize me. I entreat your majesty—'

'Hold thy tongue,' said the king, between two draughts of his potion; 'you split our head!'

Tristan l'Hermite stepped forward, and, pointing to Gringoire:

'Sire, may we hang that one, too?' This was the first word he had uttered.

'Bah!' answered the king, carelessly, 'I see no objection.'

'But I see many,' said Gringoire.

At this moment, our philosopher's countenance was more green than an olive. He saw, by the cool and indifferent manner of the king, that he had no resource but in something extremely pathetic; and he threw himself at the feet of Louis XI with a gesture of despair:

'Sire, your majesty will vouchsafe to hear me. Sire, let not your thunder fall upon so poor a thing as I. God's great thunderbolts strike not the lowly plant. Sire, you are an august and most powerful monarch—have pity on a poor honest man, as incapable of fanning the flame of revolt as an icicle of striking a spark. Most gracious sire, mildness is the virtue of a lion and of a king. Alas! severity does but exasperate; the fierce blasts of the north wind make not the traveller lay aside his cloak; but the sun granting its rays little by little, warms him so that at length he strips himself to his shirt. Sire, you are the sun. I protest to you, my sovereign lord and master, that I am not a companion of Truands, thievish and disorderly. Rebellion and pillage go not in the train of Apollo. I am not the man to rush into those clouds which burst in seditious clamour. I am a faithful vassal of your majesty. The same jealousy which the husband has for the honour of his wife, the affection with which the son should requite his father's love, a good vassal should feel for the glory of his king. He should burn with zeal for the upholding of his house and the promoting of his service. Any other passion that should possess him would be madness. Such, sire, are my maxims of state; do not, then, judge me to be seditious and plundering because my garment is out at elbows. If you show me mercy, sire, I will wear it out at the knees praying for you morning and night. Alas! I am not exceeding rich, it is true; indeed, I am rather poor; but I am not wicked for all that. It is no fault of mine. Every one knows that great wealth is not to be acquired by literature, and that the most accomplished writers have not always a good fire in winter. The gentlemen of the law take all the wheat and leave but the chaff for the other learned professions. There are forty most excellent proverbs upon the philosopher's threadbare cloak. Oh, sire, clemency is the only light that can illumine the interior of a great soul. Clemency carries the torch before all other virtues. Without her they are but blind, and seek God in the dark. Mercy, which is the same thing as clemency, produces loving subjects, who are the most potent body-guard of the prince. What can it signify to your majesty, by whom all faces are dazzled, that there should be one poor man more upon the earth? a poor, innocent philosopher, feeling his way in the darkness of calamity, with his empty purse lying echoing upon his empty stomach. Besides, sire, I am a man of letters. Great kings add a jewel to their crown by protecting letters. Hercules did not disdain the title of Musagetes. Matthias Corvinus showed favour to Jean de Monroyal, the ornament of mathematics. Now, 'tis an ill way of protecting letters, to hang the lettered. What a stain upon Alexander if he had hanged Aristoteles! The act would not have been a patch upon the face of his reputation to embellish it, but a virulent ulcer to disfigure it. Sire, I wrote a very appropriate epithalamium for Mademoiselle of Flanders and Monseigneur the most august Dauphin. That was not like a firebrand of rebellion. Your majesty sees that I am no dunce, that I have studied excellently and that I have much natural eloquence. Grant me mercy, sire. So doing, you will do an act of gallantry to Our Lady, and I swear to you that I am very much frightened at the idea of being hanged!'

So saying, the desolate Gringoire kissed the king's slippers, while Guillaume Rym whispered to Coppenole: 'He does well to crawl upon the floor; kings are like the Jupiter of Crete—they hear only through their feet.' And, quite inattentive to the Cretan Jupiter, the hosier answered, with a heavy smile, his eyes fixed upon Gringoire: 'Ah, 'tis well done! I fancy I heard the Chancellor Hugonet asking me for mercy.'

When Gringoire stopped at length out of breath, he raised his eyes, trembling, toward the king, who was scratching with his fingernail a spot upon his breeches' knee, after which his majesty took another draught from the goblet of ptisan. But he uttered not a syllable, and this silence kept Gringoire in torture. At last the king looked at him. 'Here's a terrible brawler,' said he. Then, turning to Tristan l'Hermite: 'Pshaw! let him go.'

Gringoire fell backward, sitting upon the ground, quite thunderstruck with joy.

'Let him go!' grumbled Tristan. 'Is it not your majesty's pleasure that he should be caged for a little while?'

'Friend,' returned Louis XI, 'dost thou think it is for birds like this that we have cages made at three hundred and sixty-seven pounds, eight pence, three farthings apiece? Let him go directly, the wanton [Louis XI affected this word 'wanton,' *paillard*, which together with *Pasque-Dieu* was his favourite jest], and send him forth with a drubbing.'

'Oh,' exclaimed Gringoire, in ecstasy, 'this in indeed a great king.'

Then, for fear of a countermand, he made haste toward the door, which Tristan opened for him with a very ill grace. The soldiers went out with him, driving him before them with sturdy blows of their fists, which Gringoire endured like a true stoic philosopher.

The good humour of the king, since the revolt against the bailiff had been announced to him, manifested itself in everything. This unusual clemency of his was no mean proof of it. Tristan l'Hermite, in his corner, was looking as surly as a mastiff balked of his meal.

Meanwhile the king gaily drummed the Pont-Audemer march with his fingers upon the chair arm. Though a dissembling prince, he was much better able to conceal his sorrow than his rejoicing. These external manifestations of joy on the receipt of any good news sometimes carried him to great lengths; as, for instance, at the death of Charles the Bold of Burgundy, when he vowed balustrades of silver to Saint Martin of Tours, and on his accession to the throne, to that of forgetting to give orders for his father's obsequies.

'Eh, sire!' suddenly exclaimed Jacques Coictier, 'what is become of the sharp pains for which your majesty summoned me?'

'Oh!' said the king, 'truly, my gossip, I suffer greatly. I have a ringing in my ears, and rakes of fire are harrowing my breast.'

Coictier took the hand of the king and felt his pulse with a learned air.

'Look, Coppenole,' said Rym in a low tone. 'There you have him between Coictier and Tristan. That's his whole court—a physician for himself and a hangman for others.'

While feeling the king's pulse Coictier assumed a look of greater and greater alarm. Louis XI watched him with some anxiety. Coictier grew visibly more gloomy. The king's bad health was the worthy man's only farm. He made the most of it.

'Oh! oh!' muttered he at length, 'this is serious, indeed!'

'Is it not?' said the king, uneasily.

'*Pulsus creber, anhelans, crepitans, irregularis*' (quick, short, rattling, irregular), continued the physician.

'Pasque-Dieu!'

'This might carry a man off in less than three days!'

'Our Lady!' cried the king. 'And the remedy, gossip?'

'I am considering it, sire.'

He made Louis XI put out his tongue; shook his head; made a wry face; and in the midst of this grimacing:

'Par-Dieu, sire,' said he, all on a sudden, 'I must tell you that there is a receivership of episcopal revenues vacant, and that I have a nephew.'

'Thy nephew shall have my receivership, Gossip Jacques,' answered the king; 'but take this fire out of my breast!'

'Since your majesty is so gracious,' resumed the physician, 'you will not refuse to assist me a little in the building of my house in the Rue Saint André-des-Arcs.'

'Heugh!' said the king.

'I am at the end of my finances,' pursued the doctor; 'and it would really be a pity that the house should be left without a roof—not for the sake of the house itself, which is quite plain and homely; but for the sake of the paintings by Jehan Fourbault, that adorn its wainscoting. There is a Diana flying in the air, so excellently done, so tender, so delicate, with action so natural, the head so well coiffed and crowned with a crescent, the flesh so white, that she leads into temptation those who examine her too curiously. There is also a Ceres. She, too, is a very beautiful divinity. She is seated upon corn sheaves, and crowned with a gay wreath of ears of corn intertwined with purple goat's-beard and other flowers. Never were seen more amorous eyes, rounder limbs, a nobler air, or a more gracefully flowing skirt. She is one of the most innocent and most perfect beauties ever produced by the brush.'

'Tormentor!' grumbled Louis XI, 'what art thou driving at?'

'I must have a roof over these paintings, sire; and, although it is but a trifle, I have no more money.'

'What will thy roof cost?'

'Well . . . a roof of copper, embellished and gilt . . . not above two thousand pounds.'

'Ha! the assassin!' cried the king. 'He never draws me a tooth but he makes a diamond of it.'

'Shall I have my roof?' said Coictier.

'Yes, the devil take you! but cure me.'

Jacques Coictier made a low bow, and said:

'Sire, it is a repellent that will save you. We will apply to your loins the great defensive, composed of cerate, Armenian bole, white of eggs, oil and vinegar. You will continue your potion, and we will answer for your majesty.

A lighted candle never attracts one gnat only. Maître Olivier, perceiving the king to be in a liberal mood, and deeming the moment propitious, approached in his turn: 'Sire!'

'What next?' said Louis XI.

'Sire, your majesty knows that Maître Simon Radin is dead.'

'Well?'

'He was king's councillor for the jurisdiction of the treasury.'

'Well?'

'Sire, his place is vacant.'

While thus speaking, Maître Olivier's haughty countenance had exchanged the arrogant for the fawning expression. It is the only change which ever takes place in the countenance of a courtier. The king looked him full in the face and said, in a dry tone: 'I understand.'

He resumed:

'Maître Olivier, Marshal de Boucicault used to say, "There's no good gift but from a king; there's no good fishing but in the sea." I see that you are of the marshal's opinion. Now, hear this. We have a good memory. In the year '68, we made you groom of our chamber; in '69 castellan of the bridge of Saint Cloud, with a salary of a hundred pounds tournois—you wanted them parisis. In November, '73, by letters given at Gergeaule, we appointed you keeper of the Bois de Vincennes, in lieu of Gilbert Acle, esquire; in '75, warden of the forest of Rouvray-les-Saint-Cloud, in the place of Jacques Le Maire; in '78, we graciously settled upon you, by letters-patent sealed on extra label with green wax, an annuity of ten pounds parisis, to you and your wife, upon the Place-aux-Marchands, situated at the Ecole Saint Germain. In '79, we made you warden of the forest of Senart, in room of that poor Jehan Daiz; then captain of the castle of Loches; then governor of Saint Quentin; then captain of the bridge of Meulan, of which you call yourself count. Out of the fine of five sols paid by every barber that shaves on a holiday, you get three, and we get what you leave. We were pleased to change your name of "Le Mauvais" ("the bad"), which was too much like your countenance. In '74, we granted you, to the great displeasure of our nobility, armorial bearings of a thousand colours, which give you a breast like a peacock. Pasque-Dieu! are you not surfeited? Is not the draught of fishes fine and miraculous enough? And are you not afraid lest a single salmon more may sink your boat? Pride will ruin you, my gossip. Pride is ever pressed close by ruin and shame. Consider this and be silent.'

These words, uttered in a tone of severity, caused Maître

Olivier's countenance to resume its former insolent expression.

'Good!' muttered he, almost aloud. ''Tis plain enough that the king is ill to-day; he giveth all to the leech.'

Louis XI, far from being irritated at this piece of presumption, resumed, with some mildness: 'Stay—I forgot to add that I made you ambassador to Madame Marie at Ghent. Yes, gentlemen,' added the king, turning to the Flemings, 'this one hath been an ambassador. There, my gossip,' continued he, again addressing Maître Olivier, 'let us not fall out, we are old friends. 'Tis now very late. We have finished our labours. Shave me.'

Our readers have doubtless already recognized in Maître Olivier that terrible Figaro, whom Providence, the great dramatist of all, so artfully mixed up in the long and bloody comedy of Louis XI's reign. We shall not here undertake to portray at length that singular character. This royal barber had three names. At court he was called politely Olivier-le-Daim (from the daim, or stag, upon his escutcheon), among the people, Olivier the Devil. His real name was Olivier-le-Mauvais, or the Bad.

Olivier-le-Mauvais then stood motionless, looking sulkily at the king, and askance at Jacques Coictier. 'Yes, yes—the physician!' he said between his teeth.

'Well, yes—the physician!' retorted Louis XI with singular good humour; 'the physician has more credit than thou. 'Tis very simple. He has got our whole body in his hands; and thou dost but hold us by the chin. Come, come, my poor barber, there's nothing amiss. What wouldst thou say, and what would become of thy office, if I were a king like King Chilperic, whose gesture consisted in holding his beard with one hand. Come, my gossip, fulfil thine office; shave me. Go fetch thine implements.'

Olivier, seeing that the king was in a laughing humour, and that there was no means even of provoking him, went out, grumbling, to execute his commands.

The king rose, went to the window, and suddenly opening it in extraordinary agitation:

'Oh, yes!' exclaimed he, clapping his hands; 'there's a glare in the sky over the city. It's the bailiff burning; it cannot be anything else. Ha! my good people, so you help me, then, at last, to pull down the seigneuries!'

Then turning to the Flemings: 'Gentlemen,' said he, 'come and see. Is it not a fire which glows yonder?'

The two men from Ghent came forward to look.

'It is a great fire,' said Guillaume Rym.

'Oh,' added Coppenole, whose eyes suddenly sparkled, 'that reminds me of the burning of the house of the Seigneur d'Hymbercourt. There must be a stout revolt there.'

'You think so, Maître Coppenole?' said the king; and he looked almost as much pleased as the hosier himself. 'Don't you think it will be difficult to resist?' he added.

'By the Holy Rood! sire, it may cost your majesty many a company of good soldiers.'

'Ha! cost me! that's quite another thing,' returned the king. 'If I chose—'

The hosier rejoined boldly: 'If that revolt be what I suppose, you would choose in vain, sire.'

'Friend,' said Louis XI, 'two companies of my ordnance, and the discharge of a serpentine, are quite sufficient to rout a mob of the common people.'

The hosier, in spite of the signs that Guillaume Rym was making to him, seemed determined to hold his own against the king.

'Sire,' said he, 'the Swiss were common people, too. Monsieur the Duke of Burgundy was a great gentleman, and made no account of the rabble. At the battle of Grandson, sire, he called out, "Cannoneers, fire upon those villains!" and he swore by Saint George. But the advoyer, Scharnactal, rushed upon the fine duke with his mace and his people; and at the shock of the peasants, with their bull-hides, the shining Burgundian army was shattered like a pane of glass by a pebble. Many a knight was killed there by those base churls; and Monsieur de Château-Guyon, the greatest lord in Burgundy, was found dead, with his great gray horse hard by in a marshy meadow.'

'Friend,' returned the king, 'you're talking of a battle; but here's only a riot, and I can put an end to it with a frown, when I please.'

The other replied, unconcernedly:

'That may be, sire. In that case the people's hour is not yet come.'

Guillaume Rym thought it time to interfere. 'Maître Coppenole,' said he, 'You are talking to a mighty king.'

'I know it,' answered the hosier, gravely.

'Let him speak, Monsieur Rym, my friend,' said the king; 'I like this plain speaking. My father, Charles VII, used to say that truth was sick! For my part I thought she was dead, and had found no confessor; but Maître Coppenole undeceives me.'

Then laying his hand familiarly upon Coppenole's shoulder: 'You were saying, then, Maître Jacques—'

'I say, sire, that perhaps you are right; that the people's hour is not yet come with you.'

Louis XI looked at him with his penetrating eye: 'And when will that hour come, Maître?'

'You will hear it strike.'

'By what clock, pray?'

Coppenole, with his quiet and homely self-possession, motioned to the king to approach the window.

'Hark you, sire,' said he; 'here there are a donjon, an alarm-bell, cannon, towns-people, soldiers. When the alarm-bell shall sound; when the cannon shall roar; when, with great clamour, the donjon walls shall crumble; when the townspeople and soldiers shall shout and kill each other—then the hour will strike.'

The countenance of Louis XI became gloomy and thoughtful. He remained silent for a moment; then tapping gently with his hand against the massive wall of the donjon, as if patting the haunches of a war-horse: 'Ah, no, no!' said he, 'thou wilt not so easily be shattered, wilt thou, my good Bastille?'

Then, turning with an abrupt gesture to the bold Fleming: 'Have you ever seen a revolt, Maître Jacques?'

'I have made one,' said the hosier.

'And how do you set about it,' said the king, 'to make a revolt?'

'Oh!' answered Coppenole, ''tis not very difficult. There are a hundred ways. First of all, there must be discontentment in the town. That is not uncommon. And then, the character of the inhabitants. Those of Ghent are easy to stir into revolt. They always love the son of the prince, the prince, never. Well! one morning, we will suppose, some one enters my shop, and says, Father Coppenole, there is this and that; as that the Lady of Flanders wishes to save her ministers; that the high bailiff is doubling the toll on vegetables, or what not—anything you like. Then I throw by my work, go out into the street, and cry: *To the sack!* There is always some empty cask at hand. I mount it, and say in loud tones the first words that come into my head, what's uppermost in my heart, and when one belongs to the people, sire, one has always something upon one's heart. Then a crowd assembles; they shout, they ring the tocsin; the people get arms by disarming the soldiers; the market people join in, and they fall to. And it will always be thus so long as there are lords in the manors, burghers in the towns and peasants in the country.'

'And against whom do ye thus rebel?' inquired the king. 'Against your bailiffs, against your lords?'

'Sometimes. That's as it may happen. Against the duke, too, sometimes.'

Louis XI returned to his seat, and said, with a smile: 'Ah! here they have as yet only got as far as the bailiffs.'

At that instant Olivier-le-Daim re-entered. He was followed by two pages who bore the king's toilet articles; but what struck Louis XI was that he was also accompanied by the provost of Paris and the knight of the watch, who seemed to be in great consternation.

The rancorous barber also wore an air of consternation; but satisfaction lurked beneath it. It was he who spoke first.

'Sire, I ask your majesty's pardon for the calamitous news I bring.'

The king, turning sharply round, scraped the mat on the floor with the feet of his chair.

'What does this mean?' said he.

'Sire,' returned Olivier-le-Daim, with the malicious air of a man rejoicing that he is about to deal a violent blow, 'it is not against the Bailiff of the Palais that this popular sedition is directed.'

'Against whom, then?'

'Against you, sire.'

The aged king rose, erect and straight, like a young man:

'Explain thyself, Olivier, and look well to thy head, my gossip, for I swear to thee, by the cross of Saint Lô, that if thou liest to us at this hour, the sword that cut the throat of Monsieur of Luxemburg is not so notched but it shall saw thine as well.'

The oath was formidable. Louis XI had never but twice in his life sworn by the cross of Saint Lô.

Olivier opened his mouth to reply. 'Sire—'

'On thy knees!' interrupted the king, violently. 'Tristan, look to this man.'

Olivier knelt, and said composedly: 'Sire, a witch has been condemned to death by your court of parliament. She has taken refuge in Notre-Dame. The people wish to take her thence by main force. Monsieur the provost and monsieur the knight of the watch who are come straight from the spot, are here to contradict me if I speak not the truth. It is Notre-Dame that the people are besieging.'

'Ah, ah,' said the king, in a low tone, pale and trembling with wrath; 'Notre-Dame! They are besieging Our Lady, my good mistress, in her own cathedral! Rise, Olivier. Thou art right; I give thee Simon Radin's office. Thou art right; 'tis I whom they are attacking. The witch is under the safeguard of the church; the church is under my safeguard. And I, who thought it was all about the bailiff! 'Tis against myself!'

Then, invigorated by passion, he began to stride up and down. He laughed no longer; he was terrible; he went to and fro. The fox was changed into a hyena. He seemed to be choking with rage; his lips moved, and his fleshless fists were clenched. All at once he raised his head; his hollow eye seemed full of light, and his voice burst forth like a clarion: 'Upon them, Tristan! Fall upon the knaves! Go, Tristan, my friend! Kill! kill!'

This explosion over, he returned to his seat and said, with cold, concentrated rage:

'Here, Tristan! There are here with us in this Bastille the fifty lances of the Viscount de Gié, making three hundred horse; you'll take them. There is also Monsieur de Chateaupers's company of the archers of our ordonnance; you will take it. You are provost-marshal, and have the men of your provostry; you will take them. At the Hôtel Saint Pol, you will find forty archers of Monsieur the Dauphin's new guard; you will take them. And, with the whole, you will make all speed to Notre-Dame. Ha! messieurs the clowns of Paris—so you presume to fly in the face of the crown of France, the sanctity of Our Lady, and the peace of this commonwealth? Exterminate, Tristan! exterminate! and let not one escape except for Montfaucon!'

Tristan bowed. ''Tis well, sire.'

He added after a pause: 'And what shall I do with the sorceress?'

This question set the king musing.

'Ah,' said he, 'the sorceress! Monsieur d'Estouteville, what would the people with her?'

'Sire,' replied the provost of Paris, 'I fancy that, since the populace is come to drag her away from her asylum in Notre-Dame, 'tis because her impunity offends them, and they desire to hang her.'

The king appeared to reflect deeply; then, addressing himself to Tristan l'Hermite: 'Well, my gossip, exterminate the people and hang the sorceress.'

'Just so,' whispered Rym to Coppenole. 'Punish the people for wishing, and do what they wish.'

'Enough, sire,' answered Tristan. 'If the witch be still in Notre-Dame, is she to be taken despite the sanctuary?'

'Pasque-Dieu! the sanctuary!' said the king, scratching his ear; 'and yet this woman must be hanged.'

Here, as though seized with a sudden idea, he flung himself on his knees before his chair, took off his hat, placed it on the seat, and devoutly fixing his eyes on one of the leaden amulets with which it was loaded: 'Oh,' said he, with clasped hands, 'Our Lady of Paris, my gracious patroness, pardon me. I will only do it this once. This criminal must be punished. I assure you, O Lady Virgin, my good mistress, that she is a sorceress, unworthy your gentle protection. You know, Lady, that many very pious princes have trespassed upon the privileges of churches, for the glory of God and the necessity of the state. Saint Hugh, Bishop of England, permitted King Edward to hang a magician in his church. My master, Saint Louis of France, transgressed for the like purpose in the church of Monsieur Saint Paul, as did also Monsieur Alphonse, King of Jerusalem, in the church of the Holy Sepulchre itself. Pardon me, then, for this once, Our Lady of Paris. I will never again do so, and I will give you a fine statue of silver like the one which I gave last year to Our Lady of Ecouys. Amen.'

He made the sign of the cross, rose, donned his hat once more, and said to Tristan: 'Make all speed, my gossip. Take Monsieur de Chateaupers with you. Sound the tocsin. Crush the populace. Hang the sorceress. That's settled. You yourself will defray the costs of the execution. Report to me upon it. Come, Olivier, I shall not get to bed this night. Shave me.'

Tristan l'Hermite bowed and departed. Then the king, dismissing Rym and Coppenole with a gesture: 'God keep you, messieurs, my good Flemish friends!' said he. 'Go take a little rest. The night is far spent, and we are nearer to morning than evening.'

Both withdrew, and on reaching their apartments, to which they were conducted by the captain of the Bastille, Coppenole said to Guillaume Rym: 'Humph! I've had enough of this coughing king! I have seen Charles of Burgundy drunk; he was less mischievous than Louis XI ailing.'

'Maître Jacques,' replied Rym, ''tis because wine renders kings less cruel than does barley-water.'

6

The Password

ON quitting the Bastille, Gringoire ran down the Rue Saint Antoine with the speed of a runaway horse. When he had reached the Porte Baudoyer, he walked straight to the stone cross which rose in the middle of the open space there, as though he were able to discern in the dark the figure of a man clad and hooded in black, sitting upon the steps of the cross.

'Is it you, master?' said Gringoire.

The black figure started up.

'Death and passion! you make me boil, Gringoire. The man upon the tower of Saint Gervais has just cried half-past one in the morning!'

'Oh,' returned Gringoire, ''tis no fault of mine, but of the watch and the king. I have just had a narrow escape. I always just miss being hung. 'Tis my predestination.'

'You miss everything,' said the other. 'But come quickly. Have you the pass-word?'

'Only fancy, master. I have seen the king. I have just come from him. He wears fustian breeches. 'Tis a real adventure.'

'Oh, thou word-spinner! What care I for thy adventure? Hast thou the password of the vagabonds?'

'I have it. Make yourself easy. *Petite flambe en baguenaud.*'

"Tis well. Otherwise we should not be able to reach the church. The rabble block up the streets. Fortunately, they seem to have met with resistance. We may, perhaps, still be there in time.'

'Yes, master; but how are we to get into Notre-Dame?'

'I have the key to the towers.'

'And how are we to get out again?'

'There is a small door behind the cloister, which leads to the Terrain, and so to the water-side. I have taken the key to it, and I moored a boat there this morning.'

'I have had a pretty escape from being hung,' repeated Gringoire.

'Eh—quick! come!' said the other.

Both then proceeded at a rapid pace towards the city.

7

Chateaupers to the Rescue

THE reader will, perhaps, recall the critical situation in which we left Quasimodo. The brave deaf man, assailed on all sides, had lost, if not all courage, at least all hope of saving, not himself—he thought not of himself—but the gypsy-girl. He ran distractedly along the gallery. Notre-Dame was on the point of being carried by the Truands. All at once a great galloping of horses filled the neighbouring streets, and, with a long file of torches, and a dense column of horsemen, lances and bridles lowered, these furious sounds came rushing into the Place like a hurricane:

'France! France! Cut down the knaves! Chateaupers to the rescue! Provostry! provostry!'

The Truands in terror faced about.

Quasimodo, who heard nothing, saw the drawn swords, the flambeaux, the spear-heads, all that cavalry, at the head of which he recognized Captain Phœbus; he saw the confusion of the vagabonds, the terror of some of them, the perturbation of the stoutest-hearted among them, and this unexpected succour so much revived his own energies that he hurled back from the church the first assailants, who were already climbing into the gallery.

It was, in fact, the king's troops who had arrived.

The Truands bore themselves bravely. They defended themselves desperately. Attacked in flank from the Rue Saint-Pierre-aux-Bœufs, and in rear from the Rue du Parvis, driven to bay against Notre-Dame, which they still assailed and Quasimodo defended, at once besieging and besieged, they were in the singular situation in which, subsequently, at the famous siege of Turin, in 1640, Count Henri d'Harcourt found himself between Prince Thomas of Savoy, whom he was besieging, and the Marquis of Leganez, who was blockading him—*Taurinum obsessor idem et obsessus* (besieger of Turin and besieged), as his epitaph expresses it.

The conflict was frightful. Wolves' flesh calls for dogs' teeth, as Father Matthieu phrases it. The king's horsemen, amid whom Phœbus de Chateaupers bore himself valiantly, gave no quarter, and they who escaped the thrust of the lance fell by the edge of the sword. The Truands, ill-armed, foamed and bit with rage and despair. Men, women and children threw themselves upon the cruppers and chests of the horses, and clung to them like cats with tooth and nail. Others struck the archers in the face with their torches; others thrust their iron hooks into the necks of the horsemen and dragged them down. They slashed in pieces those who fell.

One of them was seen with a large glittering scythe, with which, for a long time, he mowed the legs of the horses. He was frightful. He was singing a song with a nasal intonation, taking long and sweeping strokes with his scythe. At each stroke he described round him a great circle of severed limbs. He advanced in this manner into the thickest of the cavalry, with the quiet slowness, the regular motion of the head and drawing of the breath of a harvester mowing a field of corn. This was Clopin Trouillefou. He fell by the shot of an arquebus.

Meantime the windows had opened again. The neighbours, hearing the shouts of the king's men, had taken part in the affair, and from every story bullets rained upon the Truands. The Parvis was filled with a thick smoke, which the musketry streaked with fire. Through it could be indistinctly seen the front of Notre-Dame, and the decrepit Hôtel-Dieu, with a few pale-faced invalids looking from the top of its roof, studded with dormer windows.

At length the vagabonds gave way. Exhaustion, want of good weapons, the fright of this surprise, the discharges of musketry from the windows, and the spirited charge of the king's troops all combined to overpower them. They broke through the line of their assailants and fled in all directions, leaving the Parvis strewn with dead.

When Quasimodo, who had not for a moment ceased fighting, beheld this rout, he fell on his knees, and raised his hands to heaven. Then, intoxicated with joy, he ran, and ascended with the swiftness of a bird to that cell, the approaches to which he had so gallantly defended. He had now but one thought—it was to kneel before her whom he had just saved for the second time.

When he entered the cell he found it empty.

BOOK ELEVEN

I

The Little Shoe

AT the moment when the Truands had attacked the church Esmeralda was asleep.

Soon the ever-increasing uproar around the edifice, and the plaintive bleating of her goat, which awoke before her, roused her from her slumbers. She sat up, listened, and looked about her; then, frightened at the light and the noise, she had hurried from her cell to see what it was. The aspect of the square, the strange vision moving in it, the disorder of that nocturnal assault, that hideous crowd leaping like a cloud of frogs, half seen in the darkness; the croaking of that hoarse multitude, the few red torches dancing to and fro in the obscurity, like those meteors of the night that play over the misty surface of a marsh; all together seemed to her like some mysterious battle commenced between the phantoms of a witches' Sabbath and the stone monsters of the church. Imbued from infancy with the superstitions of the Bohemian tribe, her first thought was that she had surprised in their magic revels the strange creatures peculiar to the night. Then she ran in terror to cower in her cell, and ask of her humble couch some less horrible vision.

By degrees, however, the first vapours of terror gradually dispersed; from the constantly increasing din, and from other signs of reality, she discovered that she was beset, not by spectres, but by human beings. Then her fear, though it did not increase, changed its nature. She had dreamed of the possibility of a popular rising to drag her from her asylum. The idea of once more losing life, hope, Phœbus, who still was ever present to her hopes; her extreme helplessness; all flight cut off, no support; her abandonment, her isolation; these thoughts and a thousand others had overwhelmed her. She had fallen upon her knees, with her head upon her couch, and her hands clasped upon her head, apprehensive and trembling; and gypsy, idolatress and heathen as she was, she began with sobs to implore mercy of the God of the Christians, and to pray to Our Lady her protectress. For, even if one believes in nothing, there are moments in life when one is always of the religion of the temple nearest at hand.

She remained thus prostrate for a very long time, trembling, in truth, more than she prayed, her blood running cold at the nearer and nearer approach of the breath of that furious multitude, ignorant of the nature of this outburst, of what was being plotted, of what they were doing, of what they wanted, but feeling a presentiment of some dreadful result.

In the midst of this anguish she heard a footstep close to her. She looked up. Two men, one of whom carried a lantern, had just entered her cell. She uttered a feeble cry.

'Fear nothing,' said a voice which was not unknown to her; ''tis I.'

'Who are you?' asked she.

'Pierre Gringoire.'

This name reassured her. She raised her eyes again and saw that it was indeed the poet. But there stood beside him a black figure, veiled from head to foot, the sight of which struck her dumb.

'Ah!' continued Gringoire, in a reproachful tone, 'Djali recognized me before you.'

The little goat, in fact, had not waited for Gringoire to announce himself. No sooner had he entered than it rubbed itself gently against his knees, covering the poet with caresses and white hairs, for it was shedding its coat. Gringoire returned the caresses.

'Who is that with you?' said the Egyptian, in a low tone.

'Do not be disturbed,' answered Gringoire; 'it is a friend of mine.'

Then the philosopher, setting his lantern on the floor, squatted down upon the stones, and exclaimed with enthusiasm, clasping Djali in his arms:

'Oh! the charming creature! more remarkable, no doubt, for neatness than for size; but clever, cunning and lettered as a grammarian! Let us see, my Djali, hast thou forgotten any of thy pretty tricks. How does Maître Jacques Charmolue do—'

The man in black did not let him finish. He came up to Gringoire and pushed him roughly by the shoulder. Gringoire rose.

'True,' said he; 'I forgot that we were in haste. But that is no reason, my master, for using folks so roughly. My dear, sweet child, your life is in danger, and Djali also. They want to hang you again. We are your friends and have come to save you. Follow us.'

'Is it true?' exclaimed she, quite overcome.

'Yes, quite true. Come quickly!'

'I am willing,' faltered she; 'but why does not your friend speak?'

'Ah!' said Gringoire; 'because his father and mother were whimsical people, who made him of a taciturn disposition.'

She was obliged to content herself with this explanation. Gringoire took her by the hand. His companion picked up the lantern and walked on in front. Fear stunned the young girl. She allowed herself to be led away. The goat skipped after them, so delighted to see Gringoire again that it made him stumble every moment by thrusting its horns between his legs.

'Such is life,' said the philosopher, every time that he came near falling; 'it is often our best friends who throw us down.'

They rapidly descended the staircase of the towers, crossed the interior of the church, which was all dark and solitary, but reverberated from the uproar without, thus offering a frightful contrast; and went out by the red door into the court-yard of the cloister. The cloister was deserted, the canons having taken refuge in the bishop's house, there to offer up their prayers in common; the court-yard was empty, only some terrified serving-men were crouching in the darkest corners. They directed their steps towards the small door leading from this court-yard to the Terrain. The man in black opened it with a key which he had about him. Our readers are aware that the Terrain was a tongue of land enclosed by walls on the side next the city, and belonging to the chapter of Notre-Dame, which terminated the island eastward, behind the church. They found this enclosure entirely deserted. Here, too, they found the tumult in the air sensibly diminished. The noise of the assault by the Truands reached their ears more confusedly and less clamorously. The cool breeze which follows the current of the river, stirred the leaves of the only tree planted at the point of the Terrain, with a sound that was now perceptible to them. Nevertheless, they were still very near the danger. The buildings nearest to them were the bishop's palace and the church. There was evidently great confusion within the residence of the bishop. Its shadowy mass was flashing in all directions with lights hurrying from one window to another; as, after burning a piece of paper, there remains a dark edifice of ashes, over which bright sparks run in a thousand fantastic courses. Close by, the huge towers of Notre-Dame, seen thus from behind, with the long nave over which they rise, standing out in black relief from the red glare which filled the Parvis, looked like the gigantic uprights of some Cyclopean fire-grate.

What was visible of Paris seemed wavering on all sides in a sort of shadow mingled with light. Rembrandt has such backgrounds to his pictures.

The man with the lantern walked straight to the point of the Terrain. At the very brink of the water, there stood the worm-eaten remains of a fence of stakes with laths nailed across, upon which a low vine spread out its few meagre branches like the fingers of an open hand. Behind this sort of latticework, in the shadow which it cast, a small boat lay hidden. The man motioned to Gringoire and his companion to get in. The goat followed them. The man himself stepped in last of all. Then he cut the rope; pushed off from the shore with a long boat-hook, and laying hold of a pair of oars, seated himself in the bow, and rowed with all his might towards mid-stream. The Seine is very rapid at that point, and he found considerable difficulty in clearing the point of the island.

Gringoire's first care, on entering the boat was to place the goat on his knees. He took his seat in the stern; and the young girl, whom the stranger inspired with an indefinable uneasiness, seated herself as closely as possible to the poet. When our philosopher felt the boat in motion, he clapped his hands, and kissed Djali between the horns.

'Oh!' cried he, 'now we are all four saved!'

He added, with the air of a profound thinker: 'We are indebted sometimes to fortune, sometimes to stratagem, for the happy issue of a great undertaking.'

The boat made its way slowly toward the right bank. The young girl watched the unknown with secret terror. He had carefully turned off the light of his dark lantern; he was now faintly seen, in the forepart of the skiff, like a spectre. His hood, still down, formed a sort of mask; and every time that, in rowing, he spread his arms, from which hung wide black sleeves, they looked like a pair of enormous bat's wings. Moreover, he had not yet uttered a word, a syllable. No other sound was heard in the boat but the working of the oars, and the rippling of the water against the side of the skiff.

'Upon my soul!' suddenly exclaimed Gringoire, 'we are as gay and merry as owlets! Mute as Pythagoreans or fish. Pasque-Dieu! my friends, I wish some one would talk to me. The human voice is music to the human ear. That is not a saying of mine, but of Didymus of Alexandria, and a great one it is. Of a certainty, Didymus of Alexandria is no mean philosopher. One word, my pretty child, say but a word to me, I entreat. By the way, you used to have a droll, odd little pout; do you still make it? Do you know, sweetheart, that the Parliament has full jurisdiction over all places of sanctuary, and that you were in great peril in that little box of yours at Notre-Dame? Alas! the little bird, trochylus, maketh its nest in the jaws of the crocodile. Master, here comes the moon again. 'Tis to be hoped that they will not discover us! We are doing a laudable act in saving mademoiselle. And yet they would hang us up in the king's name if they were to catch us. Alas! every human action has two handles. One man gets praised for what another gets blamed for. He admires Cæsar who blames Catiline. Is it not so, master? What say you to this philosophy?

I possess philosophy by instinct, by nature, *ut apes geometriam* (as the bees do geometry). Come! no one answers me. What a plague of a humour ye are both in! I talk to myself. 'Tis what we call, in tragedy, a monologue. Pasque-Dieu! I'd have you to know that I have just seen King Louis XI, and that 'tis from him I have caught this oath. Pasque-Dieu! They are still making a glorious howl in the city. 'Tis an ugly, villainous old king. He is all swathed in furs. He still owes me the money for my epithalamium; and he all but hanged me to-night, which would have been most awkward for me. He is niggardly to men of merit. He should e'en read Salvian of Cologne's four books *adversus Avaritiam* (against avarice). In sooth, 'tis a close-fisted king in his dealings with men of letters, and commits very barbarous cruelties. He is a very sponge in sucking up the money drained from the people. His savings are as the spleen, that grows big upon the pining of the other members. And so the complaints of the hardness of the times turn to murmurs against the prince. Under this mild and pious lord gibbets crack with carcasses, blocks stream with gore, the prisons burst like overfull bellies. This king strips with one hand and hangs with the other. He's grand caterer to Dame Gabelle and Monseigneur Gibet. The great are despoiled of their dignities, and the humble incessantly loaded with fresh burdens. 'Tis an exorbitant prince. I love not this monarch. And you, master?'

The man in black let the loquacious poet run on. He was still struggling against the violent and narrow current that separates the prow of the city from the stern of the Island of Notre-Dame, which we call now-a-days the Island of Saint Louis.

'By-the-by, master,' resumed Gringoire, suddenly, 'just as we reached the Parvis through the raging Truands, did your reverence observe that poor little devil, whose brains your deaf man was dashing out against the balustrade of the gallery of the kings? I am short-sighted, and could not distinguish his features. Who might it be, think you?'

The unknown answered not a word. But he suddenly ceased rowing; his arms dropped as though broken, his head fell upon his breast, and Esmeralda heard him sigh convulsively. She started; she had heard sighs like those before.

The skiff, left to itself, drifted some moments with the stream. But the man in black finally roused himself, seized the oars again, and again set himself to row against the current. He doubled the point of the Island of Notre-Dame, and made for the landing place of the Hay-wharf.

'Ah!' said Gringoire, 'yonder is the Barbeau mansion. There, master, look, that group of black roofs, that make such odd angles, there, below that mass of low, streaky, ragged-looking clouds, in which the moon appears smashed and spread about like the yolk of a broken egg. 'Tis a goodly mansion. There's a chapel with a little arched roof, embellished with ornaments excellently cut. Above you can see the belfry with its delicate tracery. There's also a pleasant garden, consisting of a pond, an aviary, an echo, a mall, a labyrinth, a wild-beast house and plenty of thick-shaded walks very agreeable to Venus. And then there's a rogue of a tree which they call "the lewd," because it once favoured the pleasures of a certain princess and a certain constable of France, a gallant and a wit. Alas! we poor philosophers are to a constable of France what a cabbage-plot or a radish-bed is to a grove of laurels. After all, what does it signify? Human life for the great as well as for us is a mixture of good and evil. Sorrow ever waits on joy, the spondee on the dactyl. Master, I must relate to you the history of the Barbeau mansion. It ends tragically. It was in 1319, in the reign of Philip V, who reigned longer than any of the French kings. The moral of the story is that the temptations of the flesh are pernicious and malign. Let us not gaze too long upon our neighbour's wife, however much our senses may be taken with her beauty. Fornication is a very libertine thought. Adultery is a prying into another man's pleasure. Oh! the noise yonder grows louder!'

The tumult was, in fact, increasing around Notre-Dame. They listened. Shouts of victory could very distinctly be heard. Suddenly a hundred flambeaux, that glittered on the helmets of men-at-arms, spread over the church at all heights; on the towers, on the galleries, on the flying buttresses. These torches seemed to be carried in search of something; and soon distant clamours reached distinctly the ears of the fugitives: 'The Egyptian! the sorceress! death to the Egyptian!'

The unhappy creature dropped her head upon her hands, and the unknown began to row furiously towards the bank. Meanwhile, our philosopher reflected. He clasped the goat in his arms, and sidled gently away from the gypsy-girl, who pressed closer and closer to him, as the only protection left her.

It is certain that Gringoire was in a cruel dilemma. He reflected that, as the law then stood, the goat would be hanged too, if she were retaken; that it would be a great pity, poor Djali! that two condemned ones thus clinging to him were too much for him; that, finally, his companion asked nothing better than to take charge of the gypsy. Yet a violent struggle was taking place in his mind; wherein, like the Jupiter of the Iliad, he placed in the balance alternately the gypsy and the goat; and he looked first at one, then at the other, his eyes moist with tears, and saying between his teeth: 'And yet I cannot save you both!'

A shock apprised them that the skiff had reached the shore. The appalling uproar still rang through the city. The unknown rose, came to the gypsy, and offered to take her arm to assist her to land. She repulsed him, and clung to Gringoire's sleeve, who in turn, absorbed in the goat, almost repulsed her. Then she sprang without help from the boat. She was so disturbed that she knew not what she was doing nor whither she was going. She stood thus for a moment stupefied, watching the water as it flowed. When she recovered herself a little, she found herself alone on the landing-place with the unknown. It appears that Gringoire had taken advantage of the moment of their going ashore to slip away with the goat among the mass of houses of the Rue Grenier-sur-l'Eau.

The poor gypsy shuddered on finding herself alone with that man. She strove to speak, to cry out, to call Gringoire; but her tongue refused its office, and not a sound issued from her lips. All at once she felt the hand of the unknown upon hers. It was a cold, strong hand. Her teeth chattered. She turned paler than the moon-beam that shone upon her. The man spoke not a word. He began to move towards the Place de Grève with hasty steps, holding her by the hand. At that moment she had a vague feeling that Fate is an irresistible power. No resistance was left in her; she let him drag her along, running while he walked. The quay, at that spot, ascended somewhat before them. Yet it seemed to her as if she were descending a declivity.

She looked on all sides. Not a passer-by was to be seen. The quay was absolutely deserted. She heard no sound, she perceived no one stirring, except in the glaring and tumultuous city, from which she was separated only by an arm of the Seine, and whence her name reached her ear mingled with shouts of 'Death!' The rest of Paris lay spread around her in vast masses of shadow.

Meanwhile the unknown continued to drag her along in the same silence and with the same rapidity. She had no recollection of any of the places that she was passing. As she went by a lighted window, she made an effort, suddenly drew back, and cried out: 'Help!'

The burgher who owned the window opened it, appeared at it in his shirt with his lamp in his hand, looked out with drowsy eyes on the quay, uttered some words which she could not hear and closed his shutter again. It was her last ray of hope extinguished.

The man in black uttered not a syllable. He held her fast, and walked quicker than before. She ceased to resist, and followed him helplessly.

From time to time she mustered a little strength, and said, in a voice broken by the unevenness of the pavement and the breathless-ness of their flight: 'Who are you? who are you?' He made no reply.

They arrived thus, keeping still along the quay, at a square of tolerable size. There was then a little moonlight. It was the Grève. In the middle a sort of black cross was visible. It was the gibbet. She recognized all this, and she knew where she was.

The man stopped, turned towards her, and lifted his hood. 'Oh!' faltered she, petrified; 'I knew well that it was he again!'

It was the priest. He looked like the ghost of himself. It was an effect of the moonlight. It seems as if by that light one beholds only the spectres of objects.

'Listen,' said he; and she shuddered at the sound of that fatal voice, which she had not heard for so long. He continued. He spoke with short and panting jerks, which betoken deep internal convulsions. 'Listen. We are here. I have to talk with thee. This is the Grève. This is an extreme point. Fate delivers us up into the hands of each other. I am going to dispose of thy life—thou, of my soul. Beyond this place and this night nothing is to be foretold. Listen to me, then. I shall tell thee. . . . First, talk to me not of thy Phœbus.' (As he spoke he paced backward and forward like a man incapable of standing still, dragging her after him.) 'Talk not of him. Mark me, if thou utterest his name, I know not what I shall do, but it will be something terrible!'

Then, like a body which recovers its centre of gravity, he became motionless once more; but his words betrayed no less agitation. His voice grew lower and lower.

'Turn not thy head aside so. Hearken to me. 'Tis a serious matter. First, I will tell thee what has happened. There will be no laughing about this, I assure thee. What was I saying? remind me. Ah! it is that there is a decree of the Parliament, delivering thee over to execution again. I have just now taken thee out of their hands. But there they are pursuing thee. Look.'

He stretched out his arm towards the city. The search, in fact, seemed to continue. The uproar drew nearer. The tower of the lieutenant's house, situated opposite to the Grève, was full of noise and lights; and soldiers were running on the opposite quay with torches, shouting: 'The Egyptian! where is the Egyptian? Death! Death!'

'Thou seest plainly,' resumed the priest, 'they are pursuing thee, and that I am not deceiving thee. I love thee. Open not thy lips. Speak not a word, if it be to tell me that thou hatest me. I am determined not to hear that again. I have just now saved thee. First, let me finish. I can save thee absolutely. Everything is prepared. Thou hast only to make it thy wish. As thou wilt, I can do.'

He broke off violently. 'No, that is not what I had to say.'

Then running, and drawing her after him, for he still kept hold of her, he went straight to the gibbet, and pointing to it:

'Choose between us,' said he, coolly.

She tore herself from his grasp, and fell at the foot of the gibbet, grasping that funereal support; then she half turned her beautiful head, and looked at the priest over her shoulder. She might have been a Holy Virgin at the foot of the cross. The priest stood motionless, his finger still raised towards the gibbet, his attitude unchanged, like a statue.

At length the gypsy said to him:

'It is less horrible to me than you are.'

Then he let his arm drop slowly, and cast his eyes upon the ground in deep dejection. 'Could these stones speak,' he murmured, 'yes, they would say, that here stands, indeed, an unhappy man!'

He resumed. The young girl, kneeling before the gibbet, veiled by her long flowing hair, let him speak without interrupting him. His accent was now mild and plaintive, contrasting mournfully with the haughty harshness of his features:

'I love you! Oh, that is still very true! And is nothing, then, perceivable without, of that fire which consumes my heart? Alas! young girl—night and day—yes, night and day! does that deserve no pity? 'Tis a love of the night and the day, I tell you—'tis torture! Oh, I suffer too much, my poor child, 'tis a thing worthy of compassion, I do assure you. You see that I speak gently to you. I would fain have you cease to abhor me. After all, when a man loves a woman, 'tis not his fault. Oh, my God! What? will you then never pardon me? will you hate me always? and is it all over? 'Tis this that makes me cruel—ay, hateful to myself. You do not even look at me. You are thinking of something else, perchance while I talk to you as I stand shuddering on the brink of eternity to both of us! Above all, speak not to me of the officer! What! were I to throw myself at your knees! What! I might kiss—not your feet—you would not suffer me, but the ground under your feet. What! I might sob like a child, I might tear from my breast —not words—but my heart and my entrails, to tell you how I love you! all would be in vain—all! And yet naught in your soul but what is kind and tender. You are radiant with the loveliest gentleness; you are wholly sweet, good, merciful, charming! Alas! you have no malevolence but for me alone. Oh, what a fatality!'

He hid his face in his hands. The young girl heard him weeping. It was the first time. Standing thus, erect and convulsed by sobbing, he looked even more wretched and suppliant than on his knees. He wept thus for some time.

'But come,' he continued, these first tears over, 'I have no more words. And yet I had well pondered what I had to say to you. Now I tremble and shiver, I stagger at the decisive moment, I feel that something transcendent wraps us round, and my voice falters.

Oh, I shall fall to the ground if you do not take pity on me, pity on yourself. Condemn not both of us. If you could but know how much I love you! What a heart is mine! Oh, what desertion of all virtue! what desperate abandonment of myself! A doctor, I mock at science; a gentleman, I tarnish my name; a priest, I make my missal a pillow of desire, I spit in the face of my God! All this for thee, enchantress! to be more worthy of thy hell! and thou rejectest the damned one! Oh, let me tell thee all! more still! something more horrible! oh, yet more horrible!'

As he uttered these last words, his look became quite wild. He was silent for a moment; then began again, as if talking to himself, and in a strong voice, 'Cain, what hast thou done with thy brother?'

There was another silence, and he went on:

'What have I done with him, Lord? I received him, nourished him, brought him up, loved him, idolized him and killed him! Yes, Lord, just now, before my eyes, have they dashed his head upon the stones of thine house, and it was because of me, because of this woman, because of her . . .'

His eye was haggard, his voice sinking; he repeated several times, mechanically, at considerable intervals, like a bell prolonging its last vibration: 'Because of her, because of her.'

Then his tongue no longer articulated any perceptible sound, though his lips continued to move. All at once he sank down, like something crumbling to pieces, and remained motionless on the ground with his head between his knees.

A slight movement of the young girl, drawing away her foot from under him, brought him to himself. He passed his hand slowly over his hollow cheeks, and gazed for some moments, in vacant astonishment at his fingers, which were wet. 'What?' murmured he, 'have I wept?'

And turning suddenly to the gypsy, with inexpressible anguish:

'Alas! you have beheld me weep, unmoved! Child, dost thou know that those tears are tears of fire? And is it, then, so true, that from the man we hate nothing can move us? Wert thou to see me die, thou wouldst laugh. But I—I wish not thy death! One word, one single word of forgiveness! Tell me not that thou lovest me, say only that thou wilt, that will suffice, and I will save thee. If not— Oh, the time flies! I entreat thee, by all that is sacred, wait not until I am become of stone again, like this gibbet which claims thee too. Think that I hold both our destinies in my hand, that I am mad, 'tis terrible, that I may let all go, and that there yawns beneath us, unhappy girl, a bottomless abyss, wherein my fall will pursue thine for all eternity! One word of kindness, say one word, but one word!'

She opened her lips to answer him. He threw himself on his

knees before her, to receive with adoration the words, perhaps relenting, which were about to fall from her. She said to him: 'You are an assassin!'

The priest seized her furiously in his arms, and burst into hideous laughter.

'Well, yes, an assassin,' said he, 'and I will have thee. Thou wilt not take me for thy slave; thou shalt have me for thy master. You shall be mine! I have a den, whither I will drag thee. Thou shalt follow me, thou must follow me, or I deliver thee over! Thou must die, my fair one, or be mine—the priest's, the apostate's, the assassin's—this very night; dost thou hear? Come, joy! Come! kiss me, silly girl! The grave! or my couch!'

His eyes were sparkling with rage and licentiousness, and his lascivious lips reddened the neck of the young girl. She struggled in his arms. He covered her with furious kisses.

'Do not bite me, monster!' she cried. 'Oh, the hateful, poisonous monk! Let me go! I'll pull out thy vile gray hair, and throw it by handfuls in thy face!'

He turned red, then pale, then left hold of her, and gazed upon her gloomily. She thought herself victorious, and continued: 'I tell thee, I belong to my Phœbus, that it is Phœbus I love, that 'tis Phœbus who is handsome! Thou, priest, art old! thou art ugly! Get thee gone!'

He uttered a violent cry, like the wretch to whom a red-hot iron is applied. 'Die, then!' said he, grinding his teeth. She saw his frightful look, and strove to fly. But he seized her again, shook her, threw her upon the ground, and walked rapidly toward the angle of the Tour-Roland, dragging her after him over the pavement by her fair hands.

When he had reached it he turned to her:

'Once for all, wilt thou be mine?'

She answered him with emphasis:

'No!'

Then he called in a loud voice:

'Gudule! Gudule! here's the gypsy-woman! take thy revenge!'

The young girl felt herself seized suddenly by the elbow. She looked; it was a fleshless arm extended through a loop-hole in the wall, and held her with a hand of iron.

'Hold fast!' said the priest; 'it's the gypsy-woman escaped. Do not let her go. I'm going to fetch the sergeants. Thou shalt see her hanged.'

A guttural laugh from the interior of the wall made answer to these deadly words: 'Ha! ha! ha!' The gypsy-girl saw the priest hurry away toward the Pont Notre-Dame. Trampling of horses was heard in that direction.

The young girl had recognized the malicious recluse. Panting with terror, she strove to disengage herself. She writhed. She made several bounds in agony and despair, but the other held her with superhuman strength. The lean, bony fingers that pressed her were clenched and met round her flesh; it seemed as if that hand was riveted to her arm. It was more than a chain, more than an iron ring; it was a pair of pincers, endowed with life and understanding, issuing from a wall.

Exhausted, she fell back against the wall, and then the fear of death came over her. She thought of all the charms of life—of youth, of the sight of the heavens, of the aspect of nature, of love, of Phœbus, of all that was flying from her; and then of all that was approaching, of the priest who would denounce her, of the executioner who was coming, of the gibbet that was there. Then she felt terror mounting even to the roots of her hair, and she heard the dismal laugh of the recluse, saying in low tones: 'Ha! ha! thou'rt going to be hanged!'

She turned with a dying look toward the window of her cell, and she saw the savage face of the Sachette through the bars.

'What have I done to you?' said she, almost inarticulately.

The recluse made no answer, but began to mutter, in a singing, irritated and mocking tone: 'Daughter of Egypt! daughter of Egypt! daughter of Egypt!'

The unfortunate Esmeralda let her head drop under her long flowing hair, understanding that it was no human being she had here to deal with.

All at once the recluse exclaimed, as if the gypsy's question had taken all that time to reach her apprehension:

'What hast thou done to me, dost thou say? Ha! what hast thou done to me, gypsy-woman? Well, hark thee! I had a child—dost thou see? I had a child; a child, I tell thee; a pretty little girl, my Agnès!' she continued wildly, kissing something in the gloom. 'Well, dost thou see, daughter of Egypt, they took my child from me, they stole my child, they ate my child! That is what thou hast done to me!'

The young girl answered, like the lamb in the fable: 'Alas! perhaps I was not then born!'

'Oh, yes,' rejoined the recluse; 'thou must have been born then. Thou wast one of them; she would have been thy age. For fifteen years have I been here, fifteen years have I suffered, fifteen years have I prayed, fifteen years have I been knocking my head against these four walls. I tell thee, they were gypsy-women that stole her from me—dost thou hear that? and who ate her with their teeth. Hast thou a heart? Only think what it is; a child playing, suckling, sleeping; it is so innocent! Well, that is what they took from me, what they killed. God Almighty knows it well. To-day it is my turn. I'm going to eat some gypsy-woman's flesh. Oh, how I would bite thee, if the bars did not hinder me; my head is too big. Poor little thing, while she slept! And if they woke her while taking her away, in vain might she cry. I was not there! Ha! ye Egyptian mothers, ye devoured my child; come now and see your own!'

Then she began to laugh or gnash her teeth. The two things resembled each other in that frantic countenance. Day began to dawn. An ashy gleam dimly lighted this scene, and the gibbet grew more and more distinct in the Place. On the other side, towards the bridge of Notre-Dame, the poor victim thought she heard the sound of the horsemen approaching.

'Madame!' she cried, clasping her hands and falling upon her knees, dishevelled, distracted, wild with fright, 'madame, have pity! They are coming. I have done nothing to you. Would you have me die that horrible death before your eyes? You are compassionate, I am sure. 'Tis too frightful. Let me fly, let me go. Have mercy! I wish not to die thus!'

'Give me back my child!' said the recluse.

'Mercy! mercy!'

'Give me back my child!'

'Let me go, in heaven's name!'

'Give me back my child!'

Again the young girl sank down, exhausted, powerless, with the glassy stare of one already in the grave.

'Alas!' faltered she, 'you seek your child; I seek my parents!'

'Give me back my little Agnès!' pursued Gudule. 'Thou knowest not where she is? Then, die! I will tell thee! I was once a girl of pleasure; I had a child; they took my child; it was the Egyptian women. Thou seest plainly that thou must die. When thy mother, the Egyptian, comes to ask for thee, I will say to her: "Mother, look at that gibbet! or give back my child!" Dost thou know where she is, my little girl? Stay, let me show thee; here is her shoe, all that is left of her. Dost thou know where its fellow is? If thou dost, tell me; and if it is at the other end of the earth, I'll go thither on my knees to fetch it!'

So saying, with her other arm extended through the aperture, she showed the gypsy the little embroidered shoe. There was already daylight enough to distinguish its shape and colour.

The gypsy-girl, starting, said: 'Let me see that shoe. Oh, God! God! God!'

And at the same time, with the hand she had at liberty, she eagerly opened the little bag with green glass ornaments which she wore about her neck.

'Go on! go on!' grumbled Gudule, 'fumble in thy amulet of the foul fiend—'

She suddenly stopped short, trembled in every limb, and cried in a voice that came from the very depths of her heart: 'My daughter!'

The gypsy had taken out of the bag a little shoe precisely like the other. To this little shoe was attached a slip of parchment, upon which was inscribed this *charm*:

> '*When thou the like to this shalt see,*
> *Thy mother'll stretch her arms to thee.*'

Quicker than a flash of lightning the recluse had compared the two shoes, read the inscription on the parchment, and thrust close to the window bars her face, beaming with heavenly joy, crying:

'My daughter! my daughter!'

'My mother!' answered the gypsy-girl.

Here all description fails us.

The wall and the iron bars were between them. 'Oh, the wall!' cried the recluse. 'To see her and not embrace her! Thy hand! thy hand!'

The young girl passed her arm through the opening. The recluse threw herself upon that hand, pressed her lips to it, and there remained, absorbed in that kiss, giving no sign of animation but a sob which heaved her bosom from time to time. Meanwhile, she wept in torrents, in the silence, in the darkness, like rain at night. The poor mother poured forth in floods upon that adored hand the deep, dark well of tears, into which her grief had filtered, drop by drop, for fifteen years.

Suddenly she rose, threw back the long gray hair from her face, and without saying a word, strove with both hands, and with the fury of a lioness, to shake the bars of her window hole. The bars were firm. She then went and fetched from one corner of her cell a large paving-stone, which served her for a pillow, and hurled it against them with such violence that one of the bars broke, casting numberless sparks. A second stroke drove out the old iron cross that barricaded the window. Then, with both hands, she managed to loosen and remove the rusty stumps of the bars. There are moments when the hands of a woman possess superhuman strength.

The passage cleared—and it was all done in less than a minute —she seized her daughter by the middle of her body and drew her into the cell. 'Come,' murmured she, 'let me drag thee out of the abyss!'

When her daughter was within the cell, she set her gently on the ground; then took her up again, and carrying her in her arms as if she were still only her little Agnès, she went to and fro in her narrow cell intoxicated, frantic with joy, shouting, singing, kissing her daughter, talking to her, laughing aloud, melting into tears—all at the same time and vehemently.

'My daughter! my daughter!' she said; 'I have my daughter! Here she is! The good God has given her back to me! Ha! you —come all of you—is there anybody there to see that I've got my daughter? Lord Jesus, how beautiful she is! You have made me wait for her fifteen years, my good God, but it was that you might give her back to me beautiful. So the Egyptians did not eat her! Who said that? My little girl! my little girl! kiss me! Those good Egyptians! I love the Egyptians! Is it really thou? 'Twas then that which made my heart leap every time that thou didst go by. And I took that for hatred! Forgive me, my Agnès, forgive me! Thou didst think me very malicious, didst thou not? I love thee. Hast thou still that little mark on thy neck? Let me see. She has it yet. Oh, thou art beautiful! It was I who gave thee those big eyes, mademoiselle. Kiss me. I love thee. What matters it to me that other mothers have children? I can laugh at them now! They have only to come and look. Here is mine. Look at her neck, her eyes, her hair, her hand. Find me anything as beautiful as that? Oh, I promise you she will have lovers. I have wept for fifteen years. All my beauty has departed, and is come again in her. Kiss me.'

She said a thousand other extravagant things to her, the accent in which they were uttered making them beautiful; disordered the poor girl's apparel, even to making her blush; smoothed out her silken tresses with her hand; kissed her foot, her knee, her forehead, her eyelids; was enraptured with everything. The young girl let her do as she pleased, only repeating at intervals, very low and with infinite sweetness, 'My mother!'

'Look you, my little girl,' resumed the recluse, constantly interrupting her words with kisses, 'look you; I shall love thee dearly. We will go away from here. We are going to be so happy. I have inherited something in Reims, in our country. Thou knowest Reims? Ah, no; how couldst thou know that? thou wert too small. If thou didst but know how pretty thou wert at four months old! Tiny feet, which people came to see all the way from Epernay, five leagues away. We shall have a field and a house. Thou shalt sleep in my bed. Oh, my God! who would believe it? I have my daughter again!'

'Oh, my mother!' said the young girl, gathering strength at last to speak in her emotion; 'the gypsy-woman told me so. There was a good gypsy among our people who died last year, and she had always taken care of me like a foster-mother. It was she that had put this little bag on my neck. She used always say to me: "Little one, guard this trinket well; 'tis a treasure; it will enable thee to find thy mother again. Thou wearest thy mother about thy neck." She foretold it—the gypsy-woman.'

Again the Sachette clasped her daughter in her arms.

'Come,' said she, 'let me kiss thee. Thou sayest that so prettily! When we are in the country, we'll put the little shoes on the feet of an infant Jesus in a church. We certainly owe that to the good, Holy Virgin. Heavens! what a pretty voice thou hast. When thou wast talking to me just now, it was like music. Ah, my Lord God! I have found my child again! But is it credible now—all this story? Surely nothing will kill one, or I should have died of joy.'

And then she clapped her hands again, laughing and exclaiming: 'We shall be so happy.'

At that moment the cell resounded with a clattering of arms and galloping of horses, which seemed to be advancing from the bridge of Notre-Dame, and approaching nearer and nearer along the quay. The gypsy threw herself in agony into the arms of the Sachette: 'Save me! save me! my mother! they are coming!'

The recluse turned pale again.

'Oh, heaven! what dost thou say? I had forgotten. They are pursuing thee. What hast thou done, then?'

'I know not,' replied the unfortunate child, 'but I am condemned to die.'

'To die!' exclaimed Gudule, reeling as if struck by a thunderbolt. 'To die!' she repeated slowly, gazing at her daughter with a fixed stare.

'Yes, my mother,' repeated the young girl, with wild despair, 'they want to kill me. They are coming to hang me. That gallows is for me. Save me! save me! They are coming. Save me!'

The recluse remained for a few seconds in petrified silence, then shook her head doubtingly, and, suddenly bursting into laughter, the old frightful laughter which had come back to her:

'Oh, oh, no! 'tis a dream thou art telling me. Ah! well! I lost her; that lasted fifteen years; and then I find her again, and that is to last but a minute! And they would take her from me again! now that she is handsome, that she is grown up, that she talks to me, that she loves me; it is now they would come and devour her before my very eyes, who am her mother. Oh, no! such things cannot be. God Almighty permits not such things as that.'

Here the cavalcade appeared to halt, and a distant voice was heard saying:

'This way, Messire Tristan. The priest says we shall find her at the Rat-hole.' The tramp of the horses began again.

The recluse started up with a shriek of despair:

'Fly, fly, my child! It all comes back to me. Thou art right. 'Tis thy death! horror! malediction! fly!'

She put her head to the loop-hole, and drew it back again hastily.

'Stay,' said she, in an accent low, brief and doleful, pressing convulsively the hand of the gypsy, who was more dead than alive. 'Stay where you are. Do not breathe. There are soldiers everywhere. Thou canst not get away. It is too light.'

Her eyes were dry and burning. For a moment she said nothing, only paced the cell hurriedly, stopping now and then to pluck out handfuls of gray hair, which she afterwards tore with her teeth.

All at once she said: 'They are coming. I will speak to them. Hide thyself in that corner. They will not see thee. I will tell them thou hast escaped; that I let thee go, i' faith.'

She set down her daughter (for she was still carrying her) in one corner of the cell which was not visible from without. She made her crouch down; arranged her carefully, so that neither foot nor hand should project from the shadow; unbound her black hair, and spread it over her white robe, to conceal it; and placed before her the water-jug and paving-stone—the only articles of furniture she had—imagining that this jug and stone would hide her. And when this was done, she became more calm and knelt down and prayed. The day was only dawning; it still left many shadows in the Rat-hole.

At that moment, the voice of the priest—that infernal voice—passed very near the cell, crying:

'This way, Captain Phœbus de Chateaupers.'

At that name, at that voice, Esmeralda, crouching in her corner made a movement.

'Stir not,' said Gudule.

Scarcely had she said this before a tumultuous crowd of men, swords and horses, stopped around the cell. The mother rose quickly, and went and posted herself at the loop-hole, to cover the aperture. She beheld a large troop of armed men, horse and foot, drawn up on the Grève. The commander dismounted and came toward her.

'Old woman,' said this man, who had an atrocious face, 'we are in search of a witch, to hang her. We were told that thou hadst her.'

The poor mother, assuming as indifferent a look as she could, replied:

'I don't quite know what you mean.'

The other resumed: 'Tête-Dieu! Then what sort of a tale was that crazy archdeacon telling us? Where is he?'

'Monseigneur,' said a soldier, 'he has disappeared.'

'Come, now, old mad woman,' resumed the commander, 'tell me no lies. A sorceress was given you to keep. What have you done with her?'

The recluse, not wishing to deny all, for fear of awakening suspicion, replied, in a sincere and surly tone:

'If you mean a tall young girl that was given me to hold just now, I can tell you that she bit me, and I let her go. There! Leave me in peace.'

The commander made a grimace of disappointment.

'Let me have no lying, old spectre,' he said. 'My name is Tristan l'Hermite, and I am the king's companion. Tristan l'Hermite! Dost thou hear?' he added, casting his eyes around the Place de Grève. ''Tis a name that has echoes here.'

'If you were Satan l'Hermite,' rejoined Gudule, gaining hope, 'I should have nothing else to tell you; nor should I be afraid of you.'

'Tête-Dieu,' said Tristan, 'here's a gossip. Ha! so the witch-girl has got away. And which way did she take?'

Gudule answered carelessly: 'By the Rue du Mouton, I believe.'

Tristan turned his head, and motioned to his men to prepare to march. The recluse breathed again.

'Monseigneur,' said an archer all at once, 'just ask the old elf how it is that her window-bars are broken out so?'

This question brought anguish again to the heart of the miserable mother. Still she did not lose all presence of mind. 'They were always so,' stammered she.

'Pshaw!' returned the archer; 'they formed but yesterday a fine black cross that made a man feel devout.'

Tristan cast an oblique glance at the recluse.

'I think the old crone is confused,' said he.

The unfortunate woman felt that all depended on her self-possession; and so, with death in her soul, she began to jeer. Mothers possess such strength.

'Bah!' said she, 'the man is drunk. 'Tis more than a year since the back of a cart laden with stones backed against my window and broke the grating. And how I cursed the driver!'

''Tis true,' said another archer. 'I was there.'

There are always to be found, in all places, people who have seen everything. This unlooked-for testimony from the archer revived the spirits of the recluse, to whom this interrogatory was like crossing an abyss on the edge of a knife.

But she was doomed to a perpetual alternation of hope and alarm.

'If a cart had done that,' resumed the first soldier, 'the stumps of the bars would be driven inward, whereas they have been forced outward.'

'Ha! ha!' said Tristan to the soldier, 'thou hast the nose of an inquisitor at the Châtelet. Answer what he says, old woman.'

'Good heavens!' exclaimed she, driven to bay, and with tears in her voice in spite of herself, 'I swear to you, monseigneur, that it was a cart which broke those bars. You hear, that man saw it. And besides, what has that to do with your sorceress?'

'Hum!' growled Tristan.

'The devil!' continued the soldier, flattered by the provost's commendation, 'these breaks in the iron are quite fresh!'

Tristan shook his head. She turned pale.

'How long is it, say you, since the cart affair?' he asked.

'A month, perhaps a fortnight, monseigneur. I cannot recollect exactly.'

'She said at first above a year,' observed the soldier.

'That looks queer!' said the provost.

'Monseigneur,' cried she, still standing close to the opening, and trembling lest suspicion should prompt them to thrust in their heads and look into the cell—'monseigneur, I swear to you that 'twas a cart which broke this grating; I swear it to you by all the angels in paradise. If it was not done by a cart, I wish I may go to everlasting perdition, and I deny my God!'

'Thou art very hot in that oath of thine,' said Tristan with his inquisitorial glance.

The poor woman felt her assurance forsaking her more and more. She was already making blunders, and she perceived with terror that she was not saying what she should have said.

Another soldier now came up, crying:

'Monseigneur, the old elf lies. The sorceress has not gotten away by the Rue du Mouton. The chain of that street has been stretched across all night, and the chain-keeper has seen nobody go by.'

Tristan, whose countenance became every moment more sinister, addressed the recluse:

'What hast thou to say to that?'

She still strove to make headway against this fresh incident. 'That I know not, monseigneur, that I may have been mistaken. In fact, I think she crossed the water.'

'That is in the opposite direction,' said the provost. 'And it is not very likely that she would wish to re-enter the city, where they were making search for her. You lie, old woman.'

'And then,' added the first soldier, 'there is no boat either on this side of the stream or on the other.'

'She must have swum across,' replied the recluse, defending her ground inch by inch.

'Do women swim?' said the soldier.

'Tête-Dieu! old woman! thou liest! thou liest!' exclaimed Tristan, angrily; 'I've a good mind to leave the witch and hang thee. A quarter of an hour's torture will perhaps bring the truth out of thy throat. Come, thou shalt go along with us.'

She caught eagerly at these words:

'As you please, monseigneur. Do it! do it! Torture! I am willing. Take me with you. Quick, quick! let us go directly.' In the meantime, thought she, my daughter will make her escape.

"Sdeath!' said the provost, 'what an appetite for the rack. This mad creature is past my comprehension.'

An old gray-headed sergeant of the guard now stepped out of the ranks, and, addressing the provost:

'Mad, in sooth, monseigneur! If she has let loose the Egyptian, 'tis not her fault, for she has no liking for Egyptians. For these fifteen years I have belonged to the watch, and every night I hear her cursing against those Bohemian dames with execrations without end. If the one we are seeking be, as I believe, the little dancing-girl with the goat, she hates that one above all the rest.'

Gudule made an effort, and said:

'That one above all the rest.'

The unanimous testimony of the men of the watch confirmed the old sergeant's words to the provost. Tristan l'Hermite, despairing of getting anything out of the recluse, turned his back upon her, and she, with inexpressible anxiety, watched him go slowly towards his horse.

'Come,' said he, between his teeth, 'forward! we must continue the search. I will not sleep till the Egyptian be hanged.'

Still he hesitated for a while before mounting his horse. Gudule was palpitating between life and death as she saw him cast round the Place that restless look of a hound that feels himself to be near the lair of the game and is reluctant to go away. At last he shook his head and sprang into his saddle.

Gudule's heart, which had been so horribly oppressed, expanded now, and she said in a whisper, casting a glance upon her daughter, whom she had not ventured to look at while they were there, 'Saved!'

The poor child had been all this time in her corner, without breathing or stirring; with the image of death staring her in the face. No particular of the scene between Gudule and Tristan had escaped her; she had shared all the agonies endured by her mother. She had heard, as it were, each successive cracking of the thread which had held her suspended over the abyss; twenty times she thought she saw it breaking asunder, and only now began to take breath and to feel the ground steady under her feet. At this moment she heard a voice saying to the provost:

'Cor-bœuf! monsieur the provost, 'tis no business of mine, who am a guardsman, to hang sorceresses. The rabble of the populace is put down. I leave you to do your own work by yourself. You will permit me to rejoin my company, since it is without a captain.'

The voice was that of Phœbus de Chateaupers. What took place within her was indescribable. He was there, her friend, her protector, her support, her shelter, her Phœbus! She started up; and before her mother could prevent her, she had sprung to the window, crying:

'Phœbus! hither! my Phœbus!'

Phœbus was no longer there. He had just galloped round the corner of the Rue de la Coutellerie. But Tristan was not yet gone.

The recluse rushed upon her daughter with the roar of a wild beast; she dragged her violently back, her nails entering the flesh of the poor girl's neck. A tigress mother does not stand on trifles. But it was too late. Tristan had seen.

'Ha, ha,' he cried, with a grin which showed all his teeth, and made his face resemble that of a wolf, 'two mice in the trap.'

'I suspected as much,' said the soldier.

Tristan slapped him on the shoulder:

'Thou art a good cat! Come,' he added, 'where is Henriet Cousin?'

A man who had neither the garb nor the mien of a soldier, stepped forth from the ranks. He wore a dress half gray, half brown, had lank hair, leathern sleeves and a coil of rope in his huge fist. This man always accompanied Tristan, who always accompanied Louis XI.

'Friend,' said Tristan l'Hermite, 'I presume that yonder is the sorceress whom we are seeking. Thou wilt hang me this one. Hast thou thy ladder?'

'There is one under the shed of the Maison-aux-Piliers,' replied the man. 'Is it on this *justice* that the thing is to be done?' continued he, pointing to the stone gibbet.

'Yes.'

'So, ho!' said the man, with a loud laugh, more brutal still than that of the provost, 'we shall not have far to go!'

'Make haste,' said Tristan, 'and do thy laughing after.'

Meanwhile, since Tristan had seen her daughter, and all hope was lost, the recluse had not uttered a word. She had flung the poor gypsy, half dead, into the corner of the cell, and had posted herself again at the loop-hole, both hands resting upon the edge of the stone sill, like two claws. In this attitude her eyes, which had again become wild and fierce, were seen to wander fearlessly over the surrounding soldiers. When Henriet Cousin approached her place, her look was so ferocious that he started back.

'Monseigneur,' said he, turning back to the provost, 'which are we to take?'

'The young one.'

'So much the better, for the old one seemeth difficult.'

'Poor little dancing-girl with the goat!' said the old sergeant of the watch.

Henriet Cousin again approached the window-hole. The mother's eye made his own droop. He said with some timidity:

'Madame—'

She interrupted him in a very low but furious voice: 'What wouldst thou?'

'Not you,' said he, 'but the other.'

'What other?'

'The young one.'

She began to shake her head, crying:

'There is no one! no one! no one!'

'There is,' replied the executioner, 'and well you know it. Let me take the young one; I will not harm you.'

She said, with a strange sneer: 'Ah! thou wilt not harm me!'

'Let me have the other, madame. 'Tis the will of monsieur the provost.'

She repeated with an expression of frenzy, 'There's nobody!'

'I tell you there is,' rejoined the hang-man. 'We've all seen that there are two of you.'

'You look, then,' said the recluse, with her strange sneer. 'Thrust your head through the window.'

The hangman eyed the mother's nails, and durst not venture.

'Make haste!' cried Tristan, who had been drawing up his men in a semi-circle round the Rat-hole, and posted himself on horseback near the gibbet.

Henriet once more went back to the provost, quite discountenanced. He had laid his ropes upon the ground, and, with a sheepish look, was turning his hat in his hands.

'Monseigneur,' he asked, 'how must I get in?'

'Through the door.'

'There is none.'

'Through the window, then.'

'It's not wide enough.'

'Widen it then,' said Tristan, angrily. 'Hast thou no picks?'

The mother, from the interior of the cave, was still fixedly watching them. She had ceased to hope; she no longer knew what she wanted, except that they should not have her daughter.

Henriet Cousin went to fetch the box of tools from under the shed of the Pillar House. He also brought from the same place the double ladder, which he immediately set up against the gibbet. Five or six of the provost's men provided themselves with picks and crowbars, and Tristan went with them to the window of the cell.

'Old woman,' said the provost, in a tone of severity, 'give up the girl quietly.'

She looked at him as one who does not understand.

'God's head!' added Tristan; 'what good can it do thee to hinder that witch from being hanged as it pleases the king?'

The wretched woman burst into her wild laugh.

'What good can it do me? She is my daughter!'

The tone in which this word was uttered produced a shudder even in Henriet Cousin.

'I'm sorry for it,' returned the provost; 'but it's the king's pleasure.'

She shrieked, redoubling her terrible laughter, 'What's thy king to me? I tell thee she is my daughter!'

'Make a way through the wall,' said Tristan.

To make an opening sufficiently large, it was only necessary to remove one course of stone underneath the window. When the mother heard the picks and the levers undermining her fortress, she uttered a dreadful cry. Then she began to circle with frightful quickness round and round her cell—a habit of a wild beast, which her long residence in the cage had given her. She said nothing more, but her eyes were flaming. The soldiers felt their blood chilled to the very heart.

All at once she took up her paving-stone, laughed and threw it with both hands at the workmen. The stone, ill-aimed (for her hands were trembling), touched no one, but fell harmless at the feet of Tristan's horse. She gnashed her teeth.

Meanwhile, although the sun was not yet risen, it had become broad daylight, and a fine roseate tint beautified the decaying chimneys of the Pillar House. It was the hour when the windows of the earliest risers in the great city open joyfully upon the roofs. A few labouring people, a few fruit-sellers, going to the Halles upon their asses, were beginning to cross the Grève; they stopped for a moment before the group of soldiers gathered about the Rat-hole, gazed at them with looks of astonishment, and passed on.

The recluse had seated herself close to her daughter, covering her with her own body, her eyes fixed, listening to the poor girl, who stirred not, but was murmuring low the one word—'Phœbus! Phœbus!' In proportion as the work of the demolishers advanced the mother mechanically shrunk away, pressing the young girl closer and closer against the wall. All at once the recluse saw the stones (for she was on the watch, and never removed her eye from them) beginning to give way, and she heard the voice of Tristan encouraging the workmen. Then starting out of the prostration into which her spirit had sunk for some minutes, she cried out— and, as she spoke, her voice now pierced the ear like a saw, then stammered as if every species of malediction had crowded to her lips to burst forth at one and the same time:

'Ho, ho, ho! but this is horrible! You are robbers! Are you really going to take my daughter from me? I tell you she is my daughter! Oh, the cowards! oh, the hangman lackeys! the miserable murdering sutlers! Help! help! fire! And will they take my child from me thus? Who is he, then, whom they call the good God?'

Then, addressing herself to Tristan, with foaming mouth and haggard eyes, on all fours, and bristling like a panther:

'Come, then, and take my daughter. Dost thou not understand that this woman tells thee it's her daughter? Dost thou know what it is to have a child, eh? thou hewolf! Hast thou never laid with thy mate? Hast thou never had a cub by her? And if thou hast little ones, when they howl hast thou no bowels to feel?'

'Down with the stones!' said Tristan; 'they are loose now.'

The crowbars now raised the heavy course of stone. It was, as we have said, the mother's last bulwark. She threw herself upon it, she would fain have held it in its place, she scratched the stones with her nails, but the heavy mass, put in motion by six men, escaped her grasp, and fell gently to the ground along the iron levers.

The mother, seeing the breach effected, threw herself on the floor across the opening, barricading it with her body, writhing her arms, beating her head against the flag-stones and crying in a voice, hoarse and nearly inarticulate from exhaustion : 'Help, help! fire, fire!'

'Now, take the girl,' said Tristan, still imperturbable.

The mother looked at the soldiers in so formidable a manner, that they had more disposition to retreat than to advance.

'Now for it!' responded the provost. 'You, Henriet Cousin.'

No one stirred a step.

The provost swore. '*Tête-Christ!* my fighting men! Afraid of a woman!'

'Monseigneur,' said Henriet, 'do you call that a woman?'

'She has a lion's mane,' said another.

'Come!' continued the provost; 'the gap is large enough. Go in three abreast, as at the breach of Pontoise. Let's get done with it, by the dead Mahomet! The first man who turns I'll cleave him in two.'

Placed thus between the provost and the mother, the soldiers hesitated a moment; then, making their choice, advanced upon the Rat-hole.

When the recluse saw this, she suddenly reared herself upon her knees, threw aside her hair from her face, then dropped her lean, grazed hands upon her thighs. Great tears started one by one from her eyes, coursing down her furrowed cheeks, like a torrent down the bed that it has worn itself. At the same time she began to speak, but in a voice so suppliant, so gentle, so submissive, so heartrending, that more than one old hardened galley sergeant among those who surrounded Tristan wiped his eyes.

'Gentlemen,' said she, 'sergeants! one word! There's a thing I must tell you. She is my daughter, do you see—my darling little daughter, whom I had lost. Listen; it is quite a story. You must know that I am very well acquainted with messieurs the sergeants. They were always good to me in those times when the little boys used to throw stones at me because I was a girl of pleasure. So you see, you will leave me my child when you know all! I was a poor woman of the town. It was the gypsy-women who stole her away from me. I have kept her shoe these fifteen years. See! here it is. She'd a foot like that. At Reims, La Chantefleurie, Rue Folle-Peine. Perhaps you know all that. It was I. In your youth, in those days, it was a merry time, and there were merry doings. You will have pity on me, won't you, sirs? The gypsy-women stole her from me. They hid her from me for fifteen years. I thought she was dead! Only think, my good friends; I thought she was dead! I've passed fifteen years here, in this cave, without fire in the winter. 'Tis hard, that! The poor dear little shoe! I cried so much that at last God Almighty heard me. This night he has given me back my daughter. It is a miracle of God Almighty's. She was not dead. You will not take her from me, I am sure you will not. If it were myself, now, I would not say no; but to take her, a child of sixteen! Let her have time to see the sun. What has she done to you? Nothing at all. Nor no more have I. If you did but know that I have but her, that I am old, that she is a blessing sent down to me by the Holy Virgin! And then, you are all so kind! You did not know it was my daughter, but you know now. Oh, I love her. Monsieur the great provost, I would rather have a hole in my side than a scratch upon her finger! You look like a good, kind gentleman. What I tell you now explains the thing to you, doesn't it? Oh, if you have had a mother, sir! You are the captain, leave me my child. Only consider that I am praying to you on my knees, as they pray to Christ Jesus! I ask nothing of anybody. I am from Reims, gentlemen; I've a little field there, left me by my uncle, Mahiet Pradon. I am not a beggar. I want nothing, but I must have my child. Oh, I wish to keep my child. God Almighty, who is master of all, has not given her back to me for nothing. The king—you say, the king. It can't be any great pleasure to him that they should kill my little girl. And then, the king is good. It is my daughter, it is my daughter; mine; she's not the king's, she's not yours! I want to go away from here, we both want to go; and when two women are going, mother and daughter, you let them go quietly. Let us go quietly. We belong to Reims. Oh, you are kind sergeants. I love you all. You'll not take my dear little one from me; it is impossible. Is it not, now, quite impossible? My child! my child!'

We shall not attempt to give an idea of her gesture, her accent, the tears which she drank while speaking, the clasping and the wringing of her hands, the heartrending smiles, the appealing looks, the sighs, the moans, the agonizing and piercing cries which she mingled with these wild, incoherent and rambling words. When she ceased, Tristan l'Hermite knit his brows, but it was to conceal a tear that was dimmed in his tigerish eye. However, he overcame his weakness, and said, with brief utterance: 'It is the king's will.'

Then he whispered in the ear of Henriet Cousin: 'Get done quickly.' It might be that the redoubtable provost felt his own heart failing him—even his.

The executioner and the sergeants entered the cell. The mother made no resistance; she only dragged up to her daughter and clasped her madly. When the gypsy-girl saw the soldiers approaching, the horror of death revived.

'My mother!' cried she, in a tone of indescribable distress; 'oh, my mother! they are coming; defend me!'

'Yes, my love, I am defending thee!' answered the mother, in a faint voice; and clasping her close to her arms, she covered her with kisses. To see them both thus upon the ground, the mother guarding the daughter, was truly piteous.

Henriet Cousin took the gypsy-girl by the body, just below her beautiful shoulders. When she felt his hands touching her, she cried out and fainted. The executioner, from whose eye big tears were falling upon her drop by drop, offered to carry her away in his arms. He strove to unclasp the embrace of the mother, who had, as it were, knotted her hands about her daughter's waist; but the grasp which thus bound her to her child was so powerful that he found it impossible to part them. Henriet Cousin therefore dragged the young girl out of the cell, and her mother after her. The eyes of the mother were also closed.

The sun was rising at that moment; and already there was a considerable collection of people in the square, looking from a distance to see what they were thus dragging over the pavement toward the gibbet. For this was a way of the Provost Tristan's at executions; he had a mania for preventing the curious from coming near.

There was nobody at the windows. Only far away, on the top of that one of the towers of Notre-Dame which looks upon the

Grève, two men could be seen who stood darkly out against the clear morning sky, and who seemed to be looking on.

Henriet Cousin paused with the object he was dragging, at the foot of the fatal ladder; and, with troubled breath (so strongly was he moved to pity), he passed the rope round the young girl's lovely neck. The unfortunate girl felt the horrible contact of the hempen cord. She raised her eyelids, and beheld the skeleton arm of the stone gibbet extended over her head. Then she shook off her torpor, and cried, in a loud and agonizing voice: 'No! no! I will not!' The mother, whose head was buried by her daughter's garments, said not a word; but her entire body was convulsed, and she was heard redoubling her kisses upon the form of her child. The executioner seized that moment to unclasp, by a strong and sudden effort, the arms with which she held fast the prisoner, and, whether from exhaustion or despair, they yielded. He then took the young girl upon his shoulder, from whence her charming figure fell gracefully bending over his large head, and set his foot upon the ladder in order to ascend.

At this instant, the mother, who had sunk upon the ground, opened wide her eyes. Without uttering a cry, she started up with a terrific expression upon her face; then, like a beast rushing upon its prey, she threw herself upon the executioner's hand, and set her teeth in it. It was like a flash of lightning. The executioner howled with pain. They ran to his relief, and with difficulty liberated his bleeding hand from the teeth of the mother. She kept a profound silence. They pushed her away with brutal violence, and it was remarked that her head fell back heavily upon the ground. They raised her; she fell back again. She was dead.

The hangman, who had not loosed his hold of the young girl, kept on up the ladder.

2

The Beautiful Creature Clad in White

WHEN Quasimodo saw that the cell was empty; that the gypsy-girl was no longer there; that, while he had been defending her, she had been abducted, he took his head between his hands and stamped with rage and astonishment. Then he began to run over all the church, seeking his Bohemian, howling strange cries at every corner, strewing his red hair on the pavement. It was just at the moment when the king's archers were making their victorious entry into Notre-Dame, likewise in search of the gypsy-girl. Quasimodo assisted them, having no suspicion, poor deaf creature, of their fatal intentions; he thought that the enemies of the Egyptian were the Truands. He himself took Tristan l'Hermite to every possible hiding-place; opened for him all the secret doors, the double backs to the altars, the inner sacristies. Had the unfortunate girl still been there, he himself would have delivered her up to them.

When the irksomeness of seeking in vain had discouraged Tristan, who was not easily discouraged, Quasimodo continued the search alone. Twenty times, a hundred times over, did he make the circuit of the church, from one end to the other, from top to bottom—ascending, descending, running, calling, shouting, peeping, rummaging, ferreting, putting his head into every hole, thrusting a torch under every arch, desperate, mad, haggard and moaning like a beast that has lost its mate.

At length, when he was sure, perfectly sure, that she was gone, that all was over, that she had been stolen from him, he slowly went up the steps of the towers, those steps that he had mounted so nimbly and triumphantly on the day he saved her. He now passed those same places with drooping head, voiceless, tearless and hardly drawing breath. The church was again deserted and silent as before. The archers had quitted it to track the sorceress in the city. Quasimodo, left alone in that vast Notre-Dame, but a moment before besieged and full of tumult, betook himself once more to the cell where the gypsy had slept for so many weeks under his protection.

As he approached it, he could not help fancying that he might, perhaps, find her there. When, at the turn of the gallery which opens on the roof of the side aisle, he could see the narrow little lodging, with its small window and tiny door, sheltered under one of the great buttresses, like a bird's nest under a bough, the poor fellow's heart failed him, and he leaned against a pillar to keep from falling. He imagined that she might have returned thither; that some good genius had no doubt brought her back; that that little chamber was too quiet, too safe, too charming for her not to be there, and he dared not advance a step farther, for fear of dispelling his illusion. 'Yes,' said he to himself, 'she is sleeping, perhaps, or praying; I must not disturb her.'

At last he summoned up courage, approached on tip-toe, looked, entered. Empty! the cell was still empty! The unhappy man paced slowly round it, lifted up her couch, and looked underneath it, as if she could have been hidden between the mattress and the stones; he then shook his head and stood stupefied. All at once he furiously trampled upon his torch, and without word or sigh, he rushed at full speed head-foremost against the wall, and fell senseless upon the floor.

When he recovered his senses he threw himself on the bed, rolled upon it and frantically kissed the place, still warm, where the damsel had lain; he remained thus for some minutes, as motionless as if life had fled; he then rose, bathed in perspiration, panting, beside himself, and fell to beating his head against the wall with the frightful regularity of a pendulum, and the resolution of a man determined to dash out his brains. At length he sank exhausted a second time. Presently he crawled on his knees out of the cell, and crouched down opposite the door in an attitude of astonishment.

He remained thus for more than an hour, his eye fixed upon the deserted cell, more gloomy and thoughtful than a mother seated between an empty cradle and a full coffin. He uttered not a word; only at long intervals a sob shook violently his whole body; but it was a sobbing without tears, like summer lightning, which makes no noise.

It appears to have been then that, seeking amid his desolate thoughts to discover who could have been the unexpected abductor of the gypsy-girl, he bethought himself of the archdeacon. He recollected that Dom Claude alone possessed a key to the staircase leading to the cell; he remembered his nocturnal attempts upon La Esmeralda, the first of which he, Quasimodo, had assisted, the second of which he had prevented. He called to mind a thousand details, and soon no longer doubted that the archdeacon had taken the gypsy-girl from him. Yet such was his reverence for the priest, gratitude, devotion and love for that man were so deeply rooted in his heart, that they resisted, even at this dire moment, the fangs of jealousy and despair.

He reflected that the archdeacon had done this thing, and that sanguinary, deadly resentment which he would have felt against any other individual, was turned in the poor deaf man's breast, the moment when Claude Frollo was in question, into simply an increase of sorrow.

At the moment that his thoughts were thus fixed on the priest, while the buttresses were beginning to whiten in the dawn, he descried, on the upper gallery of Notre-Dame, at the angle formed by the external balustrade which runs round the apsis, a figure walking. The figure was coming towards him. He recognized it. It was the archdeacon. Claude walked with a slow, grave step. He did not look before him as he went; he was going toward the northern tower, but his face was turned to the right bank of the Seine; and he carried his head erect, as if striving to obtain a view of something over the roofs. The owl has often that oblique attitude. It flies in one direction and gazes in another. In this manner the priest passed above Quasimodo without seeing him.

The deaf man, who was confounded by this sudden apparition,

saw him disappear through the door of the staircase of the northern tower. The reader is aware that it is that one which commands a view of the Hôtel-de-Ville. Quasimodo rose and followed the archdeacon.

Quasimodo went up the steps of the tower, to ascend it and to ascertain why the priest went up. The poor ringer knew not what he was going to do (he, Quasimodo), what he was going to say, what he wanted. He was full of rage and full of dread. The archdeacon and the Egyptian came into conflict in his heart.

When he reached the top of the tower, before he issued from the darkness of the stairs upon the open platform, he cautiously observed the whereabouts of the priest. The priest had his back toward him. An open-work balustrade surrounds the platform of the spire. The priest, whose eyes were bent upon the town, was leaning his breast upon the one of the four sides of the balustrade which looks upon the bridge of Notre-Dame.

Quasimodo stole with the stealthy tread of a wolf behind him to see at what he was thus gazing.

The priest's attention was so completely absorbed elsewhere that he heard not the step of the hunch-back near him.

Paris is a magnificent and captivating spectacle, and at that day it was even more so, viewed from the summit of the towers of Notre-Dame, in the fresh light of a summer dawn. The day in question might have been in July. The sky was perfectly serene. A few lingering stars were fading away in different directions, and eastward there was a very brilliant one in the lightest part of the heavens. The sun was on the point of rising. Paris began to be astir. A very white, pure light brought out vividly to the eye all the outlines which its countless buildings present to the east. The gigantic shadows of the spires extended from roof to roof from one end of the great city to the other. Already voices and noises were to be heard from several quarters of the town. Here was heard the stroke of a bell, there that of a hammer, and there again the complicated clatter of a dray in motion. Already smoke was escaping from some of the chimneys scattered over all the surface of roofs, as through the fissures of an immense sulphurous crater. The river, whose waters are rippled by the piers of so many bridges and the points of so many islands, was wavering in folds of silver. Around the town, outside the ramparts, the view was lost in a great circle of fleecy vapours, through which were indistinctly discernible the dim line of the plains and the graceful swell of the heights. All sorts of floating sounds were dispersed over this half-awakened city. And eastward, the morning breeze was chasing across the sky a few white tufts torn from the misty fleece of the hills.

In the Parvis some good women, with their milk-jugs in their hands, were pointing out to one another, in astonishment, the singularly shattered state of the great door of Notre-Dame, and the two congealed streams of lead in the crevices of the stone. This was all that remained of the tempest of the night before. The pile kindled by Quasimodo between the towers was extinct. Tristan had already cleared the square, and had the dead thrown into the Seine. Kings like Louis XI are careful to clean the pavement speedily after a massacre.

Outside the balustrade of the tower, directly under the point where the priest had paused was one of those fantastically carved stone gutters with which Gothic edifices bristle; and in a crevice of this gutter, two pretty wall-flowers in full bloom, shaken and vivified as it were by the breath of the morning, made sportive salutation to each other. Above the towers on high, far above in the sky, were heard the voices of little birds.

But the priest neither saw nor heard any of these things. He was one of the men for whom there are neither mornings, nor birds, nor flowers. In all that immense horizon, spread round him with such diversity of aspect, his contemplation was concentrated on a single point.

Quasimodo burned to ask him what he had done with the gypsy-girl, but the archdeacon seemed at that moment to be out of the world. He was visibly in one of those critical moments of life when one would not feel the earth crumble.

With his eyes steadily fixed on a certain spot, he remained motionless and silent; and in that silence and immobility there was something so formidable that the untamed bell-ringer shuddered at it, and dared not intrude upon it. Only (and this was one way of interrogating the archdeacon) he followed the direction of his eye; and, thus guided, that of the unhappy hunch-back fell upon the Place de Grève.

He thus discovered what the priest was looking at. The ladder was set up against the permanent gibbet. There were a few people in the Place, and a number of soldiers. A man was dragging along the ground something white, to which something black was clinging. This man stopped at the foot of the gibbet. Here something took place which Quasimodo could not clearly see, not because his only eye had not preserved its long range, but a group of soldiers prevented his seeing everything. Moreover, at that instant the sun appeared, and such a flood of light burst over the horizon, that it seemed as if every point in Paris, spires, chimneys, gables, took fire all at once.

Meantime, the man began to mount the ladder. Quasimodo now saw him distinctly again. He was carrying a woman on his shoulder—a young girl clad in white. That young girl had a noose about her neck. Quasimodo recognized her.

It was she!

The man reached the top of the ladder. There he arranged the noose. Here the priest, in order to see better, knelt upon the balustrade.

Suddenly the man pushed away the ladder with his heel, and Quasimodo, who had not breathed for some moments, beheld the unfortunate child dangling at the end of the rope, about two fathoms above the ground, with the man squatted upon her shoulders. The rope made several gyrations on itself, and Quasimodo beheld horrible convulsions run along the gypsy's body. The priest, on his part, with outstretched neck and starting eyeballs, contemplated that frightful group of the man and the girl—the spider and the fly!

At the most awful moment, a demoniacal laugh, a laugh such as can come only from one who is no longer human, burst from the livid visage of the priest. Quasimodo did not hear that laugh, but he saw it.

The ringer retreated a few steps behind the archdeacon, and then, suddenly rushing furiously upon him with his huge hands, he pushed him by the back into the abyss over which Dom Claude was leaning.

The priest shrieked, 'Damnation!' and fell.

The spout, above which he stood, arrested his fall. He clung to it with desperate gripe; but, at the moment when he opened his mouth to give a second cry, he beheld the formidable and avenging face of Quasimodo thrust over the edge of the balustrade above his head. Then he was silent.

The abyss was beneath him, a fall of full two hundred feet—and the pavement.

In this dreadful situation the archdeacon said not a word, breathed not a groan. Only he writhed upon the gutter, making incredible efforts to re-ascend; but his hands had no hold on the granite, his feet slid along the blackened wall without catching hold. People who have ascended the towers of Notre-Dame know that the stone-work swells out just beneath the balustrade. It was on this retreating angle that the miserable archdeacon exhausted himself in fruitless efforts. It was not with a wall merely perpendicular that he was dealing, but with a wall that sloped away from under him.

Quasimodo had but to stretch out his hand to draw him from the gulf, but he did not so much as look at him. He was looking at the Grève, he was looking at the gibbet, he was looking at the gypsy.

The deaf man was leaning with his elbows on the balustrade, at the very spot where the archdeacon had been a moment before, and there, never turning his eye from the only object which existed for him at that moment, he was mute and motionless, like one struck by lightning, and a long stream of tears flowed in silence from that eye which until then had never shed but one.

Meanwhile the archdeacon was panting; his bald brow was dripping with perspiration; his nails were bleeding against the stones; the skin was rubbed from his knees against the wall.

He heard his cassock, which was caught on the spout, crack and rip with each jerk that he gave it. To complete his misfortune, this spout ended in a leaden pipe, which he could feel slowly bending under the weight of his body. The wretched man said to himself, that when his hands should be worn out with fatigue, when his cassock should tear asunder, when the leaden pipe should yield, he must of necessity fall, and horror thrilled his very vitals. Now and then he glanced wildly at a sort of narrow ledge formed, some ten feet lower, by projections in the sculpture; and he implored heaven from the bottom of his agonized soul, that he might be permitted to spend the remainder of his life upon that narrow space of two feet square, though it were to last a hundred years. Once, he glanced below him into the Place, into the abyss; the head which he raised again had its eyes closed and its hair erect.

There was something frightful in the silence of these two men. While the archdeacon struggled with death in this horrible manner, but a few feet from him, Quasimodo looked at the Grève and wept.

The archdeacon, finding that all his exertions served but to shake the only frail support left to him, at length remained quite still. There he hung, clasping the gutter, scarcely breathing, no longer stirring, without any other motion than that mechanical convulsion of the stomach, which one experiences in a dream when one fancies himself falling. His fixed eyes were wide open with a stare of pain and astonishment. Little by little, however, he lost ground; his fingers slipped along the spout; he felt more and more the weakness of his arms and the weight of his body; the leaden pipe which supported him bent more and more every moment towards the abyss. He saw beneath him, frightful sight, the sharp roof of the church of Saint-Jean-de-Rond, as small as a card bent double. He looked, one after another, at the imperturbable sculptures of the tower, like him suspended over the precipice, but without fear for themselves or pity for him. All about him was stone; before his eyes, the gaping monsters; below, quite at the bottom, in the Place, the pavement; above his head, Quasimodo weeping.

In the Parvis there were several groups of curious good people who were tranquilly striving to divine what madman it could be who was amusing himself in so strange a fashion. The priest could hear them saying, for their voices reached him clear and shrill: 'Why, he'll surely break his neck.'

Quasimodo wept.

At length the archdeacon, foaming with rage and horror, became sensible that all was in vain. Nevertheless, he gathered what strength remained to him for one last effort. He straightened himself on the gutter, set both his knees against the wall, clung with his hands to a cleft in the stone-work and succeeded in climbing up, perhaps, one foot; but his struggle caused the leaden beak which supported him to give way suddenly. The same effort rent his cassock asunder. Then, finding everything under him giving way, having only his stiffened and crippled hands to hold by, the unhappy wretch closed his eyes and let go of the spout. He fell.

Quasimodo watched him falling.

A fall from such a height is seldom perpendicular. The archdeacon, launched into space, fell at first with his head downward and his arms extended, then he turned over several times. The wind blew him upon the roof a house, where the miserable man broke some of his bones. Nevertheless, he was not dead when he reached it. The ringer could perceive him still make an effort to cling to the gable with his hands, but the slope was too steep, and he had no strength left. He glided rapidly down the roof like a loosened tile, then rebounded on the pavement; there he stirred no more.

Quasimodo then lifted his eye to the gypsy, whose body, suspended from the gibbet, he beheld afar, quivering under its white robe, in the last agonies of death; then he looked at the archdeacon, stretched a shapeless mass at the foot of the tower, and he said, with a sob that heaved his deep breast: 'Oh! all that I have ever loved!'

3

The Marriage of Phœbus

Toward the evening of that day, when the judicial officers of the bishop came to remove the mangled body of the archdeacon, Quasimodo had disappeared from Notre-Dame.

Many rumours were circulated concerning this accident. It was considered unquestionable that the day had at length arrived when, according to compact, Quasimodo—that is to say, the devil —was to carry off Claude Frollo—that is to say, the sorcerer. It was presumed that he had shattered the body in taking the soul, as a monkey cracks the shell to get at the nut.

It was for this reason that the archdeacon was not interred in consecrated ground.

Louis XI died the following year, in August, 1483.

As for Pierre Gringoire, he succeeded in saving the goat, and obtained considerable success as a writer of tragedy. It appears that after dipping into astrology, philosophy, architecture, hermetics—in short, in every vanity—he came back to tragedy, which is the vainest of all. This he called coming to a tragical end. On the subject of his dramatic triumphs, we read in the 'Ordinary's Accounts for 1483' the following:

'To Jehan Marchand and Pierre Gringoire, carpenter and composer, for making and composing the mystery performed at the Châtelet of Paris on the day of the entry of Monsieur the Legate; for duly ordering the characters, with properties and habiliments proper for the said mystery, and likewise for making the wooden stages necessary for the same, one hundred pounds.'

Phœbus de Chateaupers also came to a tragical end; he married.

4

The Marriage of Quasimodo

WE have already said that Quasimodo disappeared from Notre-Dame on the day of the death of the gypsy and the archdeacon. Indeed, he was never seen again, nor was it known what became of him.

In the night following the execution of Esmeralda, the executioner's men had taken down her body from the gibbet, and, according to custom, had carried it to the vault of Montfaucon.

Montfaucon, to use the words of Sauval, 'was the most ancient and the most superb gibbet in the kingdom.' Between the suburbs of the Temple and Saint Martin, at the distance of about one hundred and sixty yards from the walls of Paris, and a few bowshots from the village of La Courtille, was to be seen on the summit of a gentle, almost imperceptibly sloping hill, but on a spot sufficiently elevated to be visible for several leagues round, an edifice of strange form, much resembling a Druidical cromlech, and having, like the cromlech, its human sacrifices.

Let the reader imagine at the top of a chalk hill a great oblong mass of stone-work, fifteen feet high, thirty feet wide and forty long, and having a door, an external railing and a platform. Upon this platform sixteen enormous pillars of unhewn stone, thirty feet high, ranged in a colonnade around three of the four sides of the square supporting them, and connected at the top by heavy beams, from which chains are hanging at short intervals. At each of those chains swing skeletons; not far off, in the plain, are a stone cross and two secondary gibbets, rising like shoots from the central tree, and in the sky, hovering over the whole, a perpetual flock of carrion crows. Such was Montfaucon.

At the end of the fifteenth century this formidable gibbet, which had stood since 1328, was already much dilapidated; the beams were decayed, the chains were corroded with rust, the pillars green with mould, the courses of hewn stone were gaping at their joints, and the grass was growing upon that platform to which no foot reached. The structure made a horrible outline against the sky—especially at night, when the moonlight gleamed upon those whitened skulls, or when the evening breeze stirred the chains and skeletons, making them rattle in the darkness. The presence of this gibbet sufficed to make all the surrounding places gloomy.

The mass of stone-work that formed the base of the repulsive edifice was hollow. An immense cavern had been constructed within it, the entrance of which was closed by an old battered iron grating, and into which were thrown not only the human relics taken down from the chains of Montfaucon, but also the carcasses of the victims of all the other permanent gibbets of Paris. In that vast charnel-house, wherein so many human remains and so many crimes have festered together, many of the great ones of the world, and many of the innocent, have from time to time contributed their bones—from Enguerrand de Marigni, the first victim, and who was one of the just, down to the Admiral De Coligni, who was the last and was of the just also.

As for the mysterious disappearance of Quasimodo, all that we have been able to ascertain respecting it is this:

About a year and a half or two years after the events with which this history concludes, when search was made in the vault of Montfaucon for the body of Olivier le Daim, who had been hanged two days before, and to whom Charles VIII granted the favour of being buried in Saint Laurent in better company, there were found, among all those hideous carcasses, two skeletons, one of which held the other in a singular embrace. One of these skeletons, which was that of a woman, had still about it some tattered fragments of a garment, that had once been white; and about the neck was a string of adrezarach beads, with a little silken bag, ornamented with green glass, which was open and empty. These objects were of so little value that the executioner had probably not cared to take them. The other, which held this one in a close embrace, was the skeleton of a man. It was noticed that the spine was crooked, the head depressed between the shoulders, and that one leg was shorter than the other. Moreover, there was no rupture of the vertebræ at the nape of the neck, whence it was evident that he had not been hanged. Hence the man to whom it belonged must have come thither and have died there. When they strove to detach this skeleton from the one it was embracing it crumbled to dust.

BIBLIOGRAPHY

Poetical Works:—

1822   *Odes et Poésies Diverses.*
1824   *Nouvelles Odes.*
1826   *Odes et Ballades.*
1829   *Les Orientales.*
1831   *Les Feuilles d'Automne.*
1835   *Les Chants du Crépuscule.*
1837   *Les Voix Intérieures.*
1840   *Les Rayons et les Ombres.*
1852   *Napoléon le Petit.*
1853   *Les Châtiments.*
1856   *Les Contemplations.*
1859–83   *La Légende des Siècles.*
1865   *Les Chansons des Rues et des Bois.*
1872   *L'Année Terrible.*
1877   *L'Art d'être Grand-père.*
1878   *Le Pape.*
1879   *La Pitié Suprême.*
1880   *Religions et Religion.*
        L'Âne.
1881   *Les Quatre Vents de l'Esprit.*

Prose Works:—

1823   *Han d'Islande.*
1826   *Bug-Jargal.*
1829   *Le Dernier Jour d'un Condamné.*
1831   *Notre-Dame de Paris.*
1834   *Littérature et Philosophie Mêlées.*
        Glaude Gueux.
1842   *Le Rhin.*
1862   *Les Misérables.*
1864   *William Shakespeare.*
1866   *Les Travailleurs de la Mer.*
1869   *L'Homme Qui Rit.*
1874   *Quatre-Vingt-Treize.*
        Mes Fils.
1875–6   *Actes et Paroles.*
1877   *L'Histoire d'un Crime.*

1883   *L'Archipel de la Manche.*
1887   *Choses Vues.*

Dramatic Works :–

1827   *Cromwell.*
1830   *Hernani.*
1831   *Marion de Lorme.*
1832   *Le Roi s'Amuse.*
1833   *Lucrèce Borgia.*
         Marie Tudor.
1835   *Angelo.*
1838   *Ruy Blas.*
1843   *Les Burgraves.*
1882   *Torquemada.*
1886   *Théâtre en Liberté.*

Collected Editions:–

The most comprehensive edition of Hugo's works is that sometimes known as the *Ollendorff Edition.* It first came out in 1903 edited by Paul Meurice and Gustave Simon and was distributed up to 1933 by the Librairie Ollendorff and subsequently by the Librairie Albin Michel.

The following works contain information on his life and works :–

Choses Vues   ⎱
Actes et Paroles ⎰   Autobiographical works.
Victor Hugo : Raconté par un Témoin de sa Vie by A. Vaquerie. 1863.
Victor Hugo : his Life and Works by A.F. Davidson. 1912.
Victor Hugo by Mary Duclaux (From the French) 1921.
Victor Hugo : the Man and the Poet by W.F. Giese. New York. 1926.
Victor Hugo by Matthew Josephson. New York. 1942.
The Career of Victor Hugo by Elliott M. Grant, Cambridge, Mass. 1945.
Victor Hugo by André Maurois. 1956.
Victor Hugo and His World by André Maurois. 1966.